www.morningstar.com
Morningstar "rates" mutual funds and provides excellent general information. Register for free.

biz.yahoo.com/funds
Yahoo Finance has an excellent mutual fund information site. See *Fund Screener*.

www.bloomberg.com
Look for the *Mutual Funds* link in the left margin.

*The following links have information on Exchange-Traded Funds:*

www.indexfunds.com
See the *ETFzone* link. See *How To Use Our Data* for fund screening and comparison of index funds and ETFs.

www.amex.com
The American Stock Exchange. See the *ETF* link in the left margin.

www.cboe.com
Touch the *Products* tab at the top of the page for ETF information at the Chicago Board Options Exchange.

www.nyse.com
See the *Indexes and ETFs* link at the New York Stock Exchange.

www.amfi.com/cgi-bin/web.cgi?KEY=AMG000001
This is the website for the Association of Mutual Funds Investors.

*The following are specific mutual fund organization websites:*

flagship.vanguard.com

www.fidelity.com

## CHAPTER 5
### HISTORY OF INTEREST RATES AND RISK PREMIUMS

www.bloomberg.com/markets/index.html
Visit this site to review the world's largest stock indices.

www.cbs.marketwatch.com/news/default.asp?siteID=mktw
Review the recent performance of major U.S. stock indices under the *Markets* link. Find major international indices (left margin) under the *Global Markets* link at the top of the home page.

www.finance.lycos.com
Review a full list of domestic indices via the *More Indices Activity* under the NYSE graphic on the upper left of the page.

www.bloomberg.com
Go to the *Markets* link, then *Rates and Bonds* for current interest rates and graphics on U.S. and international government bonds and other key interest rates.

*These sites provide bond information, indices, current market rates, and yield curves.*

www.bondsonline.com

www.investinginbonds.com

www.stls.frb.org
This site contains current and historical data on a variety of interest rates. Download historical economic data and interest rates at the FRED (Federal Reserve Economic Data) database. There are excellent graphics at FRED II. Link to *Economic Research* at the home page. Link to *Publications and U.S. Financial Data* (pull-down tab) for graphic presentation of monetary data and selected interest rates.

## CHAPTER 6
### RISK AND RISK AVERSION

www.rce.rutgers.edu/money/investmentrisk.asp
This site offers a quick look at the risk-return trade-off provided by capital market investments.

www.mutualofomaha.com/rpd/investment_concepts.html
A financial service provider discussed the risk-return trade-off with its potential clients.

www.datalife.com/mall/pages/glossary/GLOSS_R.HTM
Visit this site for a discussion of risks that generate re___

w___ investment.shtml
T___

w___
Th___ ve calculators, provid___ some of the concepts appearing in this chapter.

## CHAPTER 7
### PORTFOLIO THEORY

www.aegisfund.com/english/portfolio/portfolio.asp
This site provides Aegis Fund's recent portfolio allocation recommendations.

www.fool.com/workshop/1999/workshop991109.htm
Review the Motley Fool's recommendation for pre-asset allocation action.

www.401k-advice-center.com/empl6.html
This site explores portfolio allocation as a part of the overall financial planning process.

moneycentral.msn.com/investor/home.asp
Take the MSN quiz, "How much can you handle?"

moneycentral.msn.com/content/investing/simplestrategies/p38655.asp
Use this site to assess risk tolerance.

www.womeninvesting.net/risk_tolerance.html
Review the risk tolerance discussion from Women Investing 101.

www.evansonasset.com/index.cfm/page/2.htm
Consider the discussion of active vs. passive investment strategies.

www.fundsupermart.com/main/research/viewHTML.tpl?articleNo=388
Examine index fund strategies.

www.indexfunds.com
Visit this site to learn about index funds.

## CHAPTER 8
### OPTIMAL RISKY PORTFOLIOS

finance.yahoo.com
This site provides historical price information that is useful in estimating returns, standard deviation of returns, and covariance of returns for individual securities. The information is available within the chart function for individual securities.

www.financialengines.com
Do you recognize the person behind this website? This site contains risk measures that can be used to compare individual stocks to an average hypothetical portfolio. Start the *First Time User's* demo for real applications of concepts in this chapter.

www.efficientfrontier.com/ef/402/siegel.htm
Visit this site for an interesting discussion and analysis of the risk-return trade-off.

www.moneychimp.com/articles/volatility/standard_deviation.htm
This site offers an interactive calculator related to the effects of varying stock and cash investment proportions.

www.moneychimp.com/articles/risk/efficient_frontier.htm
Review the discussion of the efficient frontier.

(continued on next page)

## CHAPTER 9
### THE CAPITAL ASSET PRICING MODEL

www.efficientfrontier.com
This site contains practical information related to modern portfolio theory and portfolio allocation.

www.moneychimp.com/articles/valuation/capm.htm
Try the CAPM calculator at Moneychimp.com

*The sites listed below contain estimates of beta coefficients for individual securities and mutual funds.*

finance.yahoo.com
Enter the ticker symbol, then link to the *Profile* report.

moneycentral.msn.com/investor/home.asp
Enter the ticker symbol, then link to the *Company Report* from the *Research* menu on the left.

www.wallpost.com
See *Profiles*

www.411stocks.com

## CHAPTER 10
### INDEX MODELS
*All of the following sites provide estimated beta coefficients based on the single index model:*

www.dailystocks.com

finance.yahoo.com
Enter ticker symbol of company, then link to *Profile* report.

www.wallpost.com

www.quicken.com
Enter ticker symbol, then see the *Fundamentals* report for beta a growth rates of the company.

## CHAPTER 11
### ARBITRAGE PRICING THEORY AND MULTIFACTOR MODELS OF RISK AND RETURN

www.onelook.com/?w=arbitrage+pricing+theory
APT is defined here.

www.aimr.com/pdf/apgapt.pdf
This site serves as a practitioner's guide to APT.

www.bus.ed.ac.uk/cfm/cfmr021.htm
This site offers an application of CAPM and APT to the Italian stock market.

www.datalife.com/mall/pages/glossary/GLOSS_R.HTM
Visit this site for a discussion of several risks that generate return volatility.

## CHAPTER 12
### MARKET EFFICIENCY AND BEHAVIORAL FINANCE

www.efficientfrontier.com/ef/index.shtml
This website contains an online journal entitled *Efficient Frontier: An Online Journal of Practical Asset Allocation.* It contains short articles related to assessment of investment strategies that can be downloaded in *Adobe Acrobat.*

*These sites provide extended analysis of behavioral finance:*

econpapers.hhs.se/paper/cwlcwldpp/1385.htm

www.investorhome.com./psych.htm

www.investopedia.com/terms/b/behavioralfinance.asp

*The following sites contain information on market efficiency, individual stocks, and mutual funds. Enter the stock ticker symbol for easy access.*

www.wsrn.com

www.marketguide.com/home.asp

www.corporateinformation.com
Free but requires registration.

www.businessweek.com

## CHAPTER 13
### EMPIRICAL EVIDENCE ON SECURITY RETURNS

www.efficientfrontier.com
This website listed gives you access to the *Efficient Frontier: An Online Journal of Practical Asset Allocation*, which contains articles related to performance and efficiency.

www.morningstar.com
Morningstar reports longer-term performance of mutual funds. Rankings for all types of mutual funds and performance measures are also available. Link to *Funds*, and then *Mutual Fund Performance*.

www.anderson.ucla.edu/acad_unit/finance/wp/2001/10-01.pdf
This site provides an example using the Fama-French three-factor model.

cepa.newschool.edu/het/schools/finance.htm
Visit this site to review a short history of the development of portfolio theory.

## CHAPTER 14
### BOND PRICES AND YIELDS

*General bond yield data may be found at these sites:*

www.bloomberg.com

www.money.cnn.com/markets/bondcenter

www.smartmoney.com/bondmarketup

*Detailed information on bonds may be found at these comprehensive sites:*

www.investinginbonds.com

www.bondsonline.com

bonds.yahoo.com

www.fool.com/school/basics/investingbasics005.htm

www.fintools.com

*Bond rating services are available at the following sites:*

www.standardandpoors.com

www.moodys.com

www.fitchratings.com

## CHAPTER 15
### THE TERM STRUCTURE OF INTEREST RATES

www.smartmoney.com/bonds/
This is a good source for current rates and current and past yield curves. (Be sure to check out *The Living Yield Curve*.) Review the current factors influencing bond prices and yields under *Bond Market Updates*.

www.research.stlouisfed.org/fred/data/irates.html
Access historic bond yields from the FRED database (of the Federal Reserve Bank of St. Louis).

www.investinginbonds.com
This site contains current and historical price and yield information.

(continued on inside back cover)

# INVESTMENTS

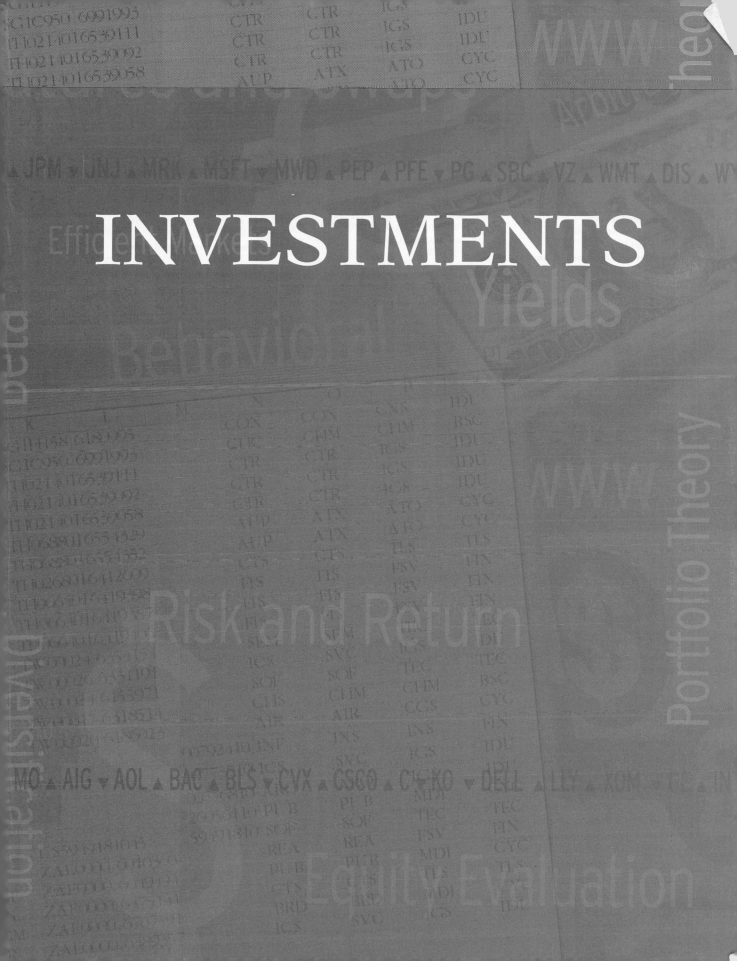

# The McGraw-Hill/Irwin Series in Finance, Insurance and Real Estate

Stephen A. Ross
Franco Modigliani Professor of Finance and Economics
*Sloan School of Management*
*Massachusetts Institute of Technology*
Consulting Editor

## FINANCIAL MANAGEMENT

Adair
**Excel Applications for Corporate Finance**

Benninga and Sarig
**Corporate Finance:**
**A Valuation Approach**

Block and Hirt
**Foundations of Financial Management**
*Eleventh Edition*

Brealey and Myers
**Principles of Corporate Finance**
*Seventh Edition*

Brealey, Myers, and Marcus
**Fundamentals of Corporate Finance**
*Fourth Edition*

Brooks
**FinGame Online 4.0**

Bruner
**Case Studies in Finance:**
**Managing for Corporate Value Creation**
*Fourth Edition*

Chew
**The New Corporate Finance:**
**Where Theory Meets Practice**
*Third Edition*

Chew and Gillan
**Corporate Governance at the Crossroads:**
**A Book of Readings**
*First Edition*

DeMello
**Cases in Finance**

Grinblatt and Titman
**Financial Markets and**
**Corporate Strategy**
*Second Edition*

Helfert
**Techniques of Financial Analysis:**
**A Guide to Value Creation**
*Eleventh Edition*

Higgins
**Analysis for Financial Management**
*Seventh Edition*

Kester, Fruhan, Piper, and Ruback
**Case Problems in Finance**
*Twelfth Edition*

Ross, Westerfield, and Jaffe
**Corporate Finance**
*Seventh Edition*

Ross, Westerfield, and Jordan
**Essentials of Corporate Finance**
*Fourth Edition*

Ross, Westerfield, and Jordan
**Fundamentals of Corporate Finance**
*Sixth Edition*

Smith
**The Modern Theory**
**of Corporate Finance**
*Second Edition*

White
**Financial Analysis with**
**an Electronic Calculator**
*Fifth Edition*

## INVESTMENTS

Bodie, Kane, and Marcus
**Essentials of Investments**
*Fifth Edition*

Bodie, Kane, and Marcus
**Investments**
*Sixth Edition*

Cohen, Zinbarg, and Zeikel
**Investment Analysis and Portfolio**
**Management**
*Fifth Edition*

Corrado and Jordan
**Fundamentals of Investments:**
**Valuation and Management**
*Third Edition*

Farrell
**Portfolio Management:**
**Theory and Applications**
*Second Edition*

Hirt and Block
**Fundamentals of**
**Investment Management**
*Seventh Edition*

## FINANCIAL INSTITUTIONS
## AND MARKETS

Cornett and Saunders
**Fundamentals of Financial**
**Institutions Management**

Rose and Hudgins
**Bank Management and Financial Services**
*Sixth Edition*

Rose
**Money and Capital Markets:**
**Financial Institutions and Instruments**
**in a Global Marketplace**
*Eighth Edition*

Santomero and Babbel
**Financial Markets, Instruments,**
**and Institutions**
*Second Edition*

Saunders and Cornett
**Financial Institutions Management:**
**A Risk Management Approach**
*Fourth Edition*

Saunders and Cornett
**Financial Markets and Institutions:**
**A Modern Perspective**
*Second Edition*

## INTERNATIONAL FINANCE

Beim and Calomiris
**Emerging Financial Markets**

Eun and Resnick
**International Financial Management**
*Third Edition*

Levich
**International Financial Markets:**
**Prices and Policies**
*Second Edition*

## REAL ESTATE

Brueggeman and Fisher
**Real Estate Finance and Investments**
*Twelfth Edition*

Corgel, Ling, and Smith
**Real Estate Perspectives:**
**An Introduction to Real Estate**
*Fourth Edition*

Ling and Archer
**Real Estate Principles: A Value Approach**
*First Edition*

## FINANCIAL PLANNING
## AND INSURANCE

Allen, Melone, Rosenbloom, and Mahoney
**Pension Planning:**
**Pension, Profit-Sharing, and**
**Other Deferred Compensation Plans**
*Ninth Edition*

Crawford
**Life and Health Insurance Law**
*Eighth Edition (LOMA)*

Harrington and Niehaus
**Risk Management and Insurance**
*Second Edition*

Hirsch
**Casualty Claim Practice**
*Sixth Edition*

Kapoor, Dlabay, and Hughes
**Personal Finance**
*Seventh Edition*

Skipper
**International Risk and Insurance:**
**An Environmental-Managerial Approach**

Williams, Smith, and Young
**Risk Management and Insurance**
*Eighth Edition*

SIXTH EDITION

# INVESTMENTS

**ZVI BODIE**
BOSTON UNIVERSITY

**ALEX KANE**
UNIVERSITY OF CALIFORNIA, SAN DIEGO

**ALAN J. MARCUS**
BOSTON COLLEGE

Boston   Burr Ridge, IL   Dubuque, IA   Madison, WI   New York   San Francisco   St. Louis
Bangkok   Bogotá   Caracas   Kuala Lumpur   Lisbon   London   Madrid   Mexico City
Milan   Montreal   New Delhi   Santiago   Seoul   Singapore   Sydney   Taipei   Toronto

*To our families with love and gratitude.*

**INVESTMENTS**
**Sixth Edition**
International Edition 2005

Exclusive rights by McGraw-Hill Education (Asia), for manufacture and export. This book cannot be re-exported from the country to which it is sold by McGraw-Hill. The International Edition is not available in North America.

10  09  08  07  06  05  04  03
20  09  08  07  06  05
CTF    SLP

**Library of Congress Cataloging-in-Publication Data**

Bodie, Zvi.
    Investments / Zvi Bodie, Alex Kane, Alan J. Marcus. — 6th ed.
        p.  cm.—(The McGraw-Hill/Irwin series in finance, insurance, and real estate)
    Includes bibliographical references and indexes.
    ISBN 0-07-286178-9
        1. Investments.  2. Portfolio management.  I. Kane, Alex.  II. Marcus, Alan J.
    III. Title.  IV. Series
HG4521.B564  2005
332.6—dc22                                                                      2003061512


007-123935-9 (Premium card)

**When ordering this title, use ISBN 007-123820-4 (Premium and S&P card)**


Printed in Singapore


www.mhhe.com

## Zvi Bodie
### BOSTON UNIVERSITY

Zvi Bodie is professor of finance and economics at Boston University School of Management. He holds a Ph.D. from the Massachusetts Institute of Technology and has served on the finance faculty at Harvard Business School and MIT's Sloan School of Management. Professor Bodie has published widely on pension finance and investment strategy in leading professional journals. His books include *Worry-Free Investing: A Safe Approach to Achieving Your Lifetime Financial Goals* and *Foundations of Pension Finance.* Professor Bodie is a managing director of Integrated Finance Limited, a specialized investment bank and financial engineering company. He is also a member of the Advisory Board of the Pension Research Council.

## Alex Kane
### UNIVERSITY OF CALIFORNIA, SAN DIEGO

Alex Kane is professor of finance and economics at the Graduate School of International Relations and Pacific Studies at the University of California, San Diego. He has been visiting professor at the Faculty of Economics, University of Tokyo; Graduate School of Business, Harvard; Kennedy School of Government, Harvard; and research associate, National Bureau of Economic Research. An author of many articles in finance and management journals, Professor Kane's research is mainly in corporate finance, portfolio management, and capital markets, most recently in the measurement of market volatility and pricing of options.

## Alan J. Marcus
### BOSTON COLLEGE

Alan Marcus is professor of finance in the Wallace E. Carroll School of Management at Boston College. He received his Ph.D. in economics from MIT. Professor Marcus has been a visiting professor at the Athens Laboratory of Business Administration and at MIT's Sloan School of Management and has served as a research associate at the National Bureau of Economic Research. Professor Marcus has published widely in the fields of capital markets and portfolio management. His consulting work has ranged from new product development to provision of expert testimony in utility rate proceedings. He also spent 2 years at the Federal Home Loan Mortgage Corporation (Freddie Mac), where he developed models of mortgage pricing and credit risk. He currently serves on the Research Foundation Advisory Board of the Association for Investment Management and Research (AIMR).

# CONTENTS IN BRIEF

# CONTENTS

We wrote the first edition of this textbook more than 15 years ago. The intervening years have been a period of rapid and profound change in the investments industry. This is due in part to an abundance of newly designed securities, in part to the creation of new trading strategies that would have been impossible without concurrent advances in computer technology, and in part to rapid advances in the theory of investments that have come out of the academic community. In no other field, perhaps, is the transmission of theory to real-world practice as rapid as is now commonplace in the financial industry. These developments place new burdens on practitioners and teachers of investments far beyond what was required only a short while ago.

*Investments,* Sixth Edition, is intended primarily as a textbook for courses in investment analysis. Our guiding principle has been to present the material in a framework that is organized by a central core of consistent fundamental principles. We make every attempt to strip away unnecessary mathematical and technical detail, and we have concentrated on providing the intuition that may guide students and practitioners as they confront new ideas and challenges in their professional lives.

This text will introduce you to major issues currently of concern to all investors. It can give you the skills to conduct a sophisticated assessment of current issues and debates covered by both the popular media as well as more-specialized finance journals. Whether you plan to become an investment professional, or simply a sophisticated individual investor, you will find these skills essential.

Our primary goal is to present material of practical value, but all three of us are active researchers in the science of financial economics and find virtually all of the material in this book to be of great intellectual interest. Fortunately, we think, there is no contradiction in the field of investments between the pursuit of truth and the pursuit of money. Quite the opposite. The capital asset pricing model, the arbitrage pricing model, the efficient markets hypothesis, the option-pricing model, and the other centerpieces of modern financial research are as much intellectually satisfying subjects of scientific inquiry as they are of immense practical importance for the sophisticated investor.

In our effort to link theory to practice, we also have attempted to make our approach consistent with that of the Institute of Chartered Financial Analysts (ICFA), a subsidiary of the Association of Investment Management and Research (AIMR). In addition to fostering research in finance, the AIMR and ICFA administer an education and certification program to candidates seeking the title of Chartered Financial Analyst (CFA). The CFA curriculum represents the consensus of a committee of distinguished scholars and practitioners regarding the core of knowledge required by the investment professional. This text also is used by the CAIA Association, a nonprofit association that provides education concerning nontraditional investment vehicles and sponsors the Chartered Alternative Investment Analyst designation.

There are many features of this text that make it consistent with and relevant to the CFA curriculum. The end-of-chapter problem sets contain questions from past CFA exams, and, for students who will be taking the exam, Appendix B is a useful tool that lists each CFA question in the text and the exam from which it has been taken. Chapter 3 includes excerpts from the "Code of Ethics and Standards of Professional Conduct" of the ICFA. Chapter 26, which discusses investors and the investment process, is modeled after the ICFA outline.

In the Sixth Edition, we have further extended our systematic collection of Excel spreadsheets that give tools to explore concepts more deeply than was previously possible.

These spreadsheets are available on the website for this text (**www.mhhe.com/bkm**), and provide a taste of the sophisticated analytic tools available to professional investors.

# UNDERLYING PHILOSOPHY

Of necessity, our text has evolved along with the financial markets. In the Sixth Edition, we address many of the changes in the investment environment.

At the same time, many basic *principles* remain important. We believe that attention to these few important principles can simplify the study of otherwise difficult material and that fundamental principles should organize and motivate all study. These principles are crucial to understanding the securities already traded in financial markets and in understanding new securities that will be introduced in the future. For this reason, we have made this book thematic, meaning we never offer rules of thumb without reference to the central tenets of the modern approach to finance.

The common theme unifying this book is that *security markets are nearly efficient,* meaning most securities are usually priced appropriately given their risk and return attributes. There are few free lunches found in markets as competitive as the financial market. This simple observation is, nevertheless, remarkably powerful in its implications for the design of investment strategies; as a result, our discussions of strategy are always guided by the implications of the efficient markets hypothesis. While the degree of market efficiency is, and always will be, a matter of debate, we hope our discussions throughout the book convey a good dose of healthy criticism concerning much conventional wisdom.

**Distinctive Themes**     *Investments* is organized around several important themes:

1. The central theme is the near-informational-efficiency of well-developed security markets, such as those in the United States, and the general awareness that competitive markets do not offer "free lunches" to participants.

   A second theme is the risk–return trade-off. This too is a no-free-lunch notion, holding that in competitive security markets, higher expected returns come only at a price: the need to bear greater investment risk. However, this notion leaves several questions unanswered. How should one measure the risk of an asset? What should be the quantitative trade-off between risk (properly measured) and expected return? The approach we present to these issues is known as *modern portfolio theory,* which is another organizing principle of this book. Modern portfolio theory focuses on the techniques and implications of *efficient diversification,* and we devote considerable attention to the effect of diversification on portfolio risk as well as the implications of efficient diversification for the proper measurement of risk and the risk–return relationship.

2. This text places greater emphasis on asset allocation than most of its competitors. We prefer this emphasis for two important reasons. First, it corresponds to the procedure that most individuals actually follow. Typically, you start with all of your money in a bank account, only then considering how much to invest in something riskier that might offer a higher expected return. The logical step at this point is to consider other risky asset classes, such as stock, bonds, or real estate. This is an asset allocation decision. Second, in most cases, the asset allocation choice is far more important in determining overall investment performance than is the set of security selection decisions. Asset allocation is the primary determinant of the risk-return profile of the investment portfolio, and so it deserves primary attention in a study of investment policy.

3. This text offers a much broader and deeper treatment of futures, options, and other derivative security markets than most investments texts. These markets have become both crucial and integral to the financial universe and are the major sources of innovation in that universe. Your only choice is to become conversant in these markets—whether you are to be a finance professional or simply a sophisticated individual investor.

# NEW IN THE SIXTH EDITION

Following is a summary of the content changes in the Sixth Edition:

**The Investment Environment (Chapter 1)**
Chapter 1 contains extensive new material on failures in corporate governance in the boom years of the 1990s and the conflicts of interest that gave rise to the many scandals of those years.

**How Securities Are Traded (Chapter 3)**
We have added new material on securities trading including initial public offerings, electronic trading, and regulatory reforms in the wake of recent corporate scandals to Chapter 3.

**History of Interest Rates and Risk Premiums (Chapter 5)**
We have extended the historical evidence on security returns to include international comparisons as well as new approaches to estimating the mean market return. We also have added an introduction to value at risk using historic returns as a guideline.

**Arbitrage Pricing Theory and Multifactor Models of Risk and Return (Chapter 11)**
We have largely rewritten this chapter. There is now greater focus on the use of factor models as a means to understand and measure various risk exposures. The intuition for the multifactor risk–return relation has been enhanced, and the comparison between the multifactor APT and CAPM has been further developed.

**Market Efficiency and Behavioral Finance (Chapter 12)**
We have fully reworked our treatment of behavioral finance by adding more careful development of behavioral hypotheses, their implications for security pricing, and their relation to the empirical evidence on security pricing.

**Empirical Evidence on Security Returns (Chapter 13)**
We have updated our discussion of the value and size effects, with an emphasis on competing interpretations of these premiums.

**Bond Prices and Yields (Chapter 14)**
We have added new spreadsheet material helpful in analyzing bond prices and yields. This new material enables students to price bonds between coupon dates.

**Equity Valuation Models (Chapter 18)**
We have added new material on quality of earnings, earnings management, and the use of accounting data in valuation analysis to this chapter.

**Financial Statement Analysis (Chapter 19)** We have added new material related to the accounting scandals of the last few years to this chapter. It discusses ways in which accounting rules were skirted in the 1990s and ongoing reforms in accounting standards.

**Option Valuation (Chapter 21)** We have extended the binomial option pricing model to a multiperiod example to illustrate how the model may be used to obtain realistic prices.

**International Diversification (Chapter 25)** We have fully rewritten this chapter, which now contains considerably more evidence on global financial markets and security returns.

In addition to these changes, we have updated and edited our treatment of topics wherever it was possible to improve exposition or coverage.

**The Process of Portfolio Management (Chapter 26)** We have added to this chapter an appendix containing an extensive spreadsheet model for sophisticated financial planning. The spreadsheets (available as well at the course website) allow students to study the interaction of taxes and inflation on long-term financial strategies.

## ORGANIZATION AND CONTENT

The text is composed of seven sections that are fairly independent and may be studied in a variety of sequences. Since there is enough material in the book for a two-semester course, clearly a one-semester course will require the instructor to decide which parts to include.

**Part I** is introductory and contains important institutional material focusing on the financial environment. We discuss the major players in the financial markets, provide an overview of the types of securities traded in those markets, and explain how and where securities are traded. We also discuss in depth mutual funds and other investment companies, which have become an increasingly important means of investing for individual investors.

The material presented in Part I should make it possible for instructors to assign term projects early in the course. These projects might require the student to analyze in detail a particular group of securities. Many instructors like to involve their students in some sort of investment game and the material in these chapters will facilitate this process.

**Parts II and III** contain the core of modern portfolio theory. Chapter 5 is a general discussion of risk and return, making the general point that historical returns on broad asset classes are consistent with a risk–return trade-off. We focus more closely in Chapter 6 on how to describe investors' risk preferences. In Chapter 7 we progress to asset allocation and then in Chapter 8 to portfolio optimization.

After our treatment of modern portfolio theory in Part II, we investigate in Part III the implications of that theory for the equilibrium structure of expected rates of return on risky assets. Chapters 9 and 10 treat the capital asset pricing model and its implementation using index models, and Chapter 11 covers multifactor descriptions of risk and the arbitrage pricing theory. We complete Part II with a chapter on the efficient markets hypothesis, including its rationale as well as the behavioral critique of the hypothesis, the evidence for and against it, and a chapter on empirical evidence concerning security returns. The empirical evidence chapter in this edition follows the efficient markets chapter so that the student can use the perspective of efficient market theory to put other studies on returns in context.

**Part IV** is the first of three parts on security valuation. This Part treats fixed-income securities—bond pricing (Chapter 14), term structure relationships (Chapter 15), and interest-rate risk management (Chapter 16). The next two Parts deal with equity securities and derivative securities. For a course emphasizing security analysis and excluding portfolio theory, one may proceed directly from Part I to Part III with no loss in continuity.

# Walkthrough

This book contains several features designed to make it easy for the student to understand, absorb, and apply the concepts and techniques presented.

## Concept Check

A unique feature of this book is the inclusion of Concept Checks in the body of the text. These self-test questions and problems enable the student to determine whether he or she has understood the preceding material. Detailed solutions are provided at the end of each chapter.

**CONCEPT CHECK☞ QUESTION 1**

*a.* Suppose the real interest rate is 3% per year and the expected inflation rate is 8%. What is the nominal interest rate?

*b.* Suppose the expected inflation rate rises to 10%, but the real rate is unchanged. What happens to the nominal interest rate?

### Bills and Inflation, 1963–2002

The Fisher equation predicts a close connection between inflation and the rate of return on T-bills. This is apparent in Figure 5.2, which plots both time series on the same set of axes. Both series tend to move together, which is consistent with our previous statement that expected inflation is a significant force determining the nominal rate of interest.

For a holding period of 30 days, the difference between actual and expected inflation is not large. The 30-day bill rate will adjust rapidly to changes in expected inflation induced by observed changes in actual inflation. It is not surprising that we see nominal rates on bills move roughly in tandem with inflation over time.

**SOLUTIONS TO CONCEPT CHECKS**

1. $\text{NAV} = \dfrac{\$2,885.9 - \$2.3}{370.4} = \$7.79$

2. The net investment in the Class A shares after the 4% commission is \$9,600. If the fund earns a 10% return, the investment will grow after $n$ years to $\$9,600 \times (1.10)^n$. The Class B shares have no front-end load. However, the net return to the investor after 12b-1 fees will be only 9.5%. In addition, there is a back-end load that reduces

Current Event Boxes

Short articles from business periodicals are included in boxes throughout the text. The articles are chosen for relevance, clarity of presentation, and consistency with good sense.

## SPUN GOLD

## DID WALL STREET FIRMS BRIBE BOSSES WITH SHARES?

Back in 1997, reports that Robertson Stephens, a Silicon Valley investment bank, was "spinning" IPO shares to executives who rewarded them with banking mandates prompted an SEC probe into the practice. The probe was soon abandoned. The practice boomed, becoming one of the more lucrative ways in which executives combined with Wall Street to abuse ordinary shareholders.

On August 30th Citigroup told congressional investigators that in 1997–2000 it had allocated IPO shares to Bernie Ebbers that had generated profits of $11m for the former boss of WorldCom, a telecoms firm which was a big Citigroup client, and is now bust thanks to fraud. Other World-Com executives had also benefited. Citi claims that these investment-banking business in return. Its "host of benign" explanations for why some shares were allocated retrospectively, giving executives a risk-free gain, seems thin. So does its claim that Jack Grubman, until last month the bank's top telecoms analyst, played no part in allocating shares to executives. Among the documents that Citigroup sent to Congress was a memo copied to Mr. Grubman that listed executives at several telecoms firms who had expressed interest in shares in IPOs.

Regulators and the courts will have to decide whether allocations of shares to executives were, in effect, bribes. If so, the punishment could be severe. Nor is Citi the only firm at risk. Credit Suisse First Boston gave shares in IPOs

Excel Applications

The Sixth Edition has expanded the boxes featuring Excel Spreadsheet Applications. A sample spreadsheet is presented in the text with an interactive version and related questions available on the book website at **www.mhhe.com/bkm**.

## EXCEL APPLICATIONS

### SHORT SALE

This Excel spreadsheet model was built using the text example for DotBomb. The model allows you to analyze the effects of returns, margin calls, and different levels of initial and maintenance margins. The model also includes a sensitivity analysis for ending stock price and return on investment.

You can learn more about this spreadsheet model using the interactive version available at our Online Learning Center at **www.mhhe.com/bkm**.

| | A | B | C | D | E |
|---|---|---|---|---|---|
| 1 | | | | | |
| 2 | | | Action or Formula | Ending | Return on |
| 3 | | | for Column B | St Price | Investment |
| 4 | Initial Investment | $50,000.00 | Enter data | | 58.33% |
| 5 | Initial Stock Price | $100.00 | Enter data | $170.00 | -133.33% |
| 6 | Number of Shares Sold Short | 1,000 | (B4/B9)/B5 | 160.00 | -116.67% |
| 7 | Ending Stock Price | $70.00 | Enter data | 150.00 | -100.00% |
| 8 | Cash Dividends Per Share | $0.00 | Enter data | 140.00 | -83.33% |
| 9 | Initial Margin Percentage | 50.00% | Enter data | 130.00 | -66.67% |
| 10 | Maintenance Margin Percentage | 30.00% | Enter data | 120.00 | -50.00% |

Summary and End-of-Chapter Problems

At the end of each chapter, a detailed Summary outlines the most important concepts presented. The problems that follow the Summary progress from simple to challenging and many are taken from CFA examinations. These represent the kinds of questions that professionals in the field believe are relevant to the "real world" and are indicated by an icon in the text margin.

**SUMMARY**

1. Speculation is the undertaking of a risky investment for its risk premium. The risk premium has to be large enough to compensate a risk-averse investor for the risk of the investment.

2. A fair game is a risky prospect that has a zero-risk premium. It will not be undertaken by a risk-averse investor.

3. Investors' preferences toward the expected return and volatility of a portfolio may be expressed by a utility function that is higher for higher expected returns and lower for higher portfolio variances. More risk-averse investors will apply greater penalties for risk. We can describe these preferences graphically using indifference curves.

**PROBLEMS**

1. Suppose you discover a treasure chest of $10 billion in cash.
   a. Is this a real or financial asset?
   b. Is society any richer for the discovery?
   c. Are you wealthier?
   d. Can you reconcile your answers to *(b)* and *(c)*? Is anyone worse off as a result of the discovery?

2. Lanni Products is a start-up computer software development firm. It currently owns computer equipment worth $30,000 and has cash on hand of $20,000 contributed by Lanni's owners. For each of the following transactions, identify the real and/or fnancial assets that trade hands. Are any financial assets created or destroyed in the transaction?

**CFA®** PROBLEMS

2. A municipal bond carries a coupon of 6¾% and is trading at par; to a taxpayer in a 34% tax bracket, this bond would provide a taxable equivalent yield of:
   a. 4.5%
   b. 10.2%
   c. 13.4%
   d. 19.9%

**CFA®** PROBLEMS

3. Which is the *most risky* transaction to undertake in the stock index option markets if the stock market is expected to increase substantially after the transaction is completed?
   a. Write a call option.
   b. Write a put option

## Websites

Another feature in this edition is the inclusion of website addresses. The sites have been chosen for relevance to the chapter and for accuracy so students can easily research and retrieve financial data and information.

---

**WEBSITES**

www.executivelibrary.com
This site gives access to instant financial and market news from around the world.

ceoexpress.com/default.asp
This site provides a comprehensive list of links for business and financial managers.

---

## Internet Exercises: *E-Investments*

These exercises provide students with a structured set of steps to finding financial data on the Internet. Easy-to-follow instructions and questions are presented so students can utilize what they've learned in class in today's Web-driven world.

---

**E-INVESTMENTS**
**Choosing a Mutual Fund**

Here are the websites for three of the largest mutual fund companies:

Fidelity Investments: **www.fidelity.com**

Putnam Investments: **www.putnaminv.com**

Vanguard Group: **www.vanguard.com**

Pick three or four funds from one of these sites. What are the investment objectives of each fund? Find the expense ratio of each fund. Which fund has had the best recent performance? What are the major holdings of each fund?

---

## Internet Exercises: Standard & Poor's Problems

New to this edition! Relevant chapters contain problems directly incorporating the Educational Version of Market Insight, a service based on Standard & Poor's renowned COMPUSTAT® database. Problems are based on real market data to gain a better understanding of practical business situations.

---

**STANDARD & POOR'S**

Go to **www.mhhe.com/business/finance/edumarketinsight**. Select a company from the *Population* and from the Company Research Page, link to the *EDGAR* materials from the menu at the left of the page. What SEC reports are required of public companies? (Check the Archives for prior reports filed by your company.) Briefly explain the role of each in achieving the mission of the SEC.

**Part V** is devoted to equity securities. We proceed in a "top down" manner, starting with the broad macroeconomic environment (Chapter 17), next moving on to equity valuation (Chapter 18), and then using this analytical framework, we treat fundamental analysis including financial statement analysis (Chapter 19).

**Part VI** covers derivative assets such as options, futures, swaps, and callable and convertible securities. It contains two chapters on options and two on futures. This material covers both pricing and risk management applications of derivatives.

Finally, **Part VII** presents extensions of previous material. Topics covered in this Part include evaluation of portfolio performance (Chapter 24), portfolio management in an international setting (Chapter 25), a general framework for the implementation of investment strategy in a nontechnical manner modeled after the approach presented in CFA study materials (Chapter 26), and an overview of active portfolio management (Chapter 27).

## SUPPLEMENTS

**For the Instructor**    **Instructor's Resource CD 0072861819** This comprehensive CD contains all the following instructor supplements. We have compiled them in electronic format for easier access and convenience. Print copies are available through your publisher's representative.

- **Instructor's Manual** The Instructor's Manual, prepared by Richard D. Johnson, Colorado State University, has been revised and improved in this edition. Each chapter includes a chapter overview, a review of learning objectives, an annotated chapter outline (organized to include the Transparency Masters/PowerPoint package), and teaching tips and insights. Transparency Masters are located at the end of each chapter.

- **PowerPoint Presentation Software** These presentation slides, also developed by Richard D. Johnson, provide the instructor with an electronic format of the Transparency Masters. These slides, revised for this edition, follow the order of the chapters, but if you have PowerPoint software, you may choose to customize the presentations to fit your own lectures.

- **Test Bank** The Test Bank, prepared by Larry Prather, East Tennessee State University, has been revised to increase the quantity and variety of questions. Short-answer essay questions are also provided for each chapter to further test student comprehension and critical thinking abilities. The Test Bank is also available in computerized format for Windows.

**The Wall Street Journal Edition** Your students can subscribe to *The Wall Street Journal* for 15 weeks (which includes access to the Dow Jones Interactive Online Asset) at a specially priced rate of $20.00 in addition to the price of the text. Students will receive a "How to Use the WSJ" handbook plus a pass code card shrink-wrapped with the text.

**Videos    0072861835** There are seven video segments covering careers, financial markets, bonds, going public, derivatives, portfolio management, and foreign exchange.

# For the Student

**Solutions Manual 007286186X** The Solutions Manual, prepared by Bruce Swensen, Adelphi University, provides detailed solutions to the end-of-chapter problems. This manual is available for packing with the text. Please contact your local McGraw-Hill/Irwin representative for further details on how to order the Solutions Manual/Textbook package.

**Student Problem Manual 0072861843** New to this edition! To give students a better resource for working through problems, we have created a comprehensive problem manual. This useful supplement, also developed by Larry Prather, contains problems created to specifically relate to the concepts discussed in each chapter. Solutions are provided at the end of each chapter.

**Online Learning Center** Find a wealth of information online! At **www.mhhe.com/bkm**, instructors will have access to teaching support such as electronic files for the ancillary material and students will have access to study materials created specifically for this text. The Excel Applications spreadsheets, also prepared by Bruce Swensen, are located at this site. Additional information on the text and authors and links to our powerful support materials are also available.

**Standard & Poor's Educational Version of Market Insight** McGraw-Hill/Irwin and the Institutional Market Services division of Standard & Poor's are pleased to announce an exclusive partnership that offers instructors and students access to the educational version of Standard & Poor's Market Insight. The Educational Version of Market Insight is a rich online resource that provides 6 years of fundamental financial data for over 500 companies in the renowned COMPUSTAT® database. Standard and Poor's and McGraw-Hill/Irwin have selected the best, most-often researched companies in the database. S&P-specific problems can be found at the end of relevant chapters in this text.

**PowerWeb** With PowerWeb, getting information online has never been easier. This McGraw-Hill/Irwin website is a reservoir of course-specific articles and current events. Simply type in a discipline-specific topic for instant access to articles, essays, and news for your class.

All of the articles have been recommended to PowerWeb by professors, which means you will not get all the clutter that seems to pop up with typical search engines. However, PowerWeb is much more than a search engine. Students can visit PowerWeb to take a self-grading quiz, work through interactive exercises, click through an interactive glossary, and even check the daily news. In fact, an expert for each discipline analyzes the day's news to show students how it is relevant to their field of study.

**Investments Online** Introducing Investments Online! For each of the 18 different topics, the student completes challenging exercises and discussion questions that draw on recent articles, company reports, government data, and other Web-based resources. The "Finance Tutor Series" provides questions and problems that not only assess and improve students' understanding of the subject but also help students to apply it in real-world contexts.

# ACKNOWLEDGMENTS

Throughout the development of this text, experienced instructors have provided critical feedback and suggestions for improvement. These individuals deserve a special thanks for their valuable insights and contributions. The following instructors played a vital role in the development of this and previous editions of *Investments*:

Scott Besley
*University of Florida*

John Binder
*University of Illinois at Chicago*

Paul Bolster
*Northeastern University*

Phillip Braun
*Northwestern University*

L. Michael Couvillion
*Plymouth State University*

Anna Craig
*Emory University*

David C. Distad
*University of California at Berkeley*

Craig Dunbar
*University of Western Ontario*

Michael C. Ehrhardt
*University of Tennessee at Knoxville*

David Ellis
*Babson College*

Greg Filbeck
*University of Toledo*

Jeremy Goh
*Washington University*

Richard Grayson
*Loyola College*

John M. Griffin
*Arizona State University*

Mahmoud Haddad
*Wayne State University*

Robert G. Hansen
*Dartmouth College*

Joel Hasbrouck
*New York University*

Andrea Heuson
*University of Miami*

Eric Higgins
*Drexel University*

Shalom J. Hochman
*University of Houston*

Eric Hughson
*University of Colorado*

A. James Ifflander
*A. James Ifflander and Associates*

Robert Jennings
*Indiana University*

Richard D. Johnson
*Colorado State University*

Susan D. Jordan
*University of Kentucky*

G. Andrew Karolyi
*Ohio State University*

Josef Lakonishok
*University of Illinois at Champaign/Urbana*

Malek Lashgari
*University of Hartford*

Dennis Lasser
*Binghamton University*

Larry Lockwood
*Texas Christian University*

Christopher K. Ma
*Texas Tech University*

Anil K. Makhija
*University of Pittsburgh*

Steven Mann
*University of South Carolina*

Deryl W. Martin
*Tennessee Technical University*

Jean Masson
*University of Ottawa*

Ronald May
*St. John's University*

Rick Meyer
*University of South Florida*

Mbodja Mougoue
*Wayne State University*

Gurupdesh Pandner
*DePaul University*

Don B. Panton
*University of Texas at Arlington*

Dilip Patro
*Rutgers University*

Robert Pavlik
*Southwest Texas State*

Herbert Quigley
*University of D.C.*

Speima Rao
*University of Southwestern Louisiana*

Leonard Rosenthal
*Bentley College*

Eileen St. Pierre
*University of Northern Colorado*

Anthony Sanders
*Ohio State University*

Don Seeley
*University of Arizona*

John Settle
*Portland State University*

Edward C. Sims
*Western Illinois University*

Robert Skena
*Carnegie Mellon University*

Steve L. Slezak
*University of North Carolina at Chapel Hill*

Keith V. Smith
*Purdue University*

Patricia B. Smith
*University of New Hampshire*

Laura T. Starks
*University of Texas*

Manuel Tarrazo
*University of San Francisco*

Steve Thorley
*Brigham Young University*

Jack Treynor
*Treynor Capital Management*

Charles A. Trzincka
*SUNY Buffalo*

Yiuman Tse
*Suny Binghampton*

Gopala Vasuderan
*Suffolk University*

Joseph Vu
*De Paul University*

Simon Wheatley
*University of Chicago*

Marilyn K. Wiley
*Florida Atlantic University*

James Williams
*California State University at Northridge*

Tony R. Wingler
*University of North Carolina at Greensboro*

Guojun Wu
*University of Michigan*

Hsiu-Kwang Wu
*University of Alabama*

Thomas J. Zwirlein
*University of Colorado at Colorado Springs*

For granting us permission to include many of their examination questions in the text, we are grateful to the Institute of Chartered Financial Analysts.

Much credit is due also to the development and production team: our special thanks go to Steve Patterson, Executive Editor/Publisher; Rhonda Seelinger, Senior Marketing Manager; Meg Beamer, Marketing Specialist; Christina Kouvelis and Denise McGuinness, Developmental Editors; Jean Lou Hess, Senior Project Manager; Keith McPherson, Director of Design; Michael McCormick, Production Supervisor; Cathy Tepper, Supplements Coordinator; and Kai Chiang, Media Technology Lead Producer.

Finally, we thank Judy, Hava, and Sheryl, who contributed to the book with their support and understanding.

**Zvi Bodie**
**Alex Kane**
**Alan J. Marcus**

# INTRODUCTION

www.mhhe.com/bkm

# THE INVESTMENT ENVIRONMENT

Even a cursory glance at *The Wall Street Journal* reveals a bewildering collection of securities, markets, and financial institutions. Although it may appear so, the financial environment is not chaotic: There is rhyme and reason behind the array of instruments and markets. The central message we want to convey in this chapter is that financial markets and institutions evolve in response to the desires, technologies, and regulatory constraints of the investors in the economy.

In fact, we could *predict* the general shape of the investment environment (if not the design of particular securities) if we knew nothing more than these desires, technologies, and constraints. This chapter provides a broad overview of the investment environment. We begin by examining the differences between financial assets and real assets. We proceed to a discussion of the many roles of financial markets in the economy, and digress to consider the crisis in corporate governance of the late 1990s. We then turn to the three broad sectors of the financial environment: households, businesses, and government. We see how many features of the investment environment are natural responses of profit-seeking firms and individuals to opportunities created by the demands of these sectors, and we examine the driving forces behind financial innovation. Finally, we conclude with a discussion of recent trends in financial markets.

## 1.1   REAL ASSETS VERSUS FINANCIAL ASSETS

The material wealth of a society is determined ultimately by the productive capacity of its economy—the goods and services that can be provided to its members. This productive capacity is a function of the **real assets** of the economy: the land, buildings, knowledge, and machines that are used to produce goods and the workers whose skills are necessary to use those resources. Together, physical and "human" assets generate the entire spectrum of output produced and consumed by the society.

In contrast to such real assets are **financial assets** such as stocks or bonds. These assets, per se, do not represent a society's wealth. Shares of stock are no more than sheets of paper or, more likely, computer entries and do not directly contribute to the productive capacity of the economy. Instead, financial assets contribute to the productive capacity of the economy *indirectly*, because they allow for separation of the ownership and management of the firm and facilitate the transfer of funds to enterprises with attractive investment opportunities. Financial assets certainly contribute to the wealth of the individuals or firms holding them. This is because financial assets are *claims* to the income generated by real assets or claims on income from the government.

When the real assets used by a firm ultimately generate income, the income is allocated to investors according to their ownership of the financial assets, or securities, issued by the firm. Bondholders, for example, are entitled to a flow of income based on the interest rate and par value of the bond. Equityholders or stockholders are entitled to any residual income after bondholders and other creditors are paid. In this way the values of financial assets derive from and depend on the values of the underlying real assets of the firm.

Real assets produce goods and services, whereas financial assets define the allocation of income or wealth among investors. Individuals can choose between consuming their current endowments of wealth today and investing for the future. When they invest for the future, they may choose to hold financial assets. The money a firm receives when it issues securities (sells them to investors) is used to purchase real assets. Ultimately, then, the returns on a financial asset come from the income produced by the real assets that are financed by the issuance of the security. In this way, it is useful to view financial assets as the means by which individuals hold their claims on real assets in well-developed economies. Most of us cannot personally own auto plants (a real asset), but we can hold *shares* of General Motors or Ford (financial assets), which provide us with income derived from the production of automobiles.

Real and financial assets are distinguished operationally by the balance sheets of individuals and firms in the economy. Whereas real assets appear only on the asset side of the balance sheet, financial assets always appear on both sides of balance sheets. Your financial claim on a firm is an asset, but the firm's issuance of that claim is the firm's liability. When we aggregate over all balance sheets, financial assets will cancel out, leaving only the sum of real assets as the net wealth of the aggregate economy.

Another way of distinguishing between financial and real assets is to note that financial assets are created *and destroyed* in the ordinary course of doing business. For example, when a loan is paid off, both the creditor's claim (a financial asset) and the debtor's obligation (a financial liability) cease to exist. In contrast, real assets are destroyed only by accident or by wearing out over time.

The distinction between real and financial assets is apparent when we compare the composition of national wealth in the United States, presented in Table 1.1, with the financial assets and liabilities of U.S. households shown in Table 1.2. National wealth consists of structures, equipment, inventories of goods, and land. (A major omission in Table 1.1 is

## Table 1.1   Domestic Net Worth

| Assets | $ Billion |
|---|---|
| Real estate | $19,111 |
| Equipment and software | 3,142 |
| Inventories | 1,264 |
| Consumer durables | 2,914 |
| TOTAL | $26,431 |

Note: Column sums may differ from total because of rounding error.
Source: *Flow of Funds Accounts of the United States,* Board of Governors of the Federal Reserve System, September 2002.

the value of "human capital"—the value of the earnings potential of the work force.) In contrast, Table 1.2 includes financial assets such as bank accounts, corporate equity, bonds, and mortgages.

Persons in the United States tend to hold their financial claims in an indirect form. In fact, only about 40% of the adult U.S. population holds shares directly. The claims of most individuals on firms are mediated through institutions that hold shares on their behalf: institutional investors such as pension funds, insurance companies, mutual funds, and endowment funds. Table 1.3 shows that today approximately half of all U.S. equity is held by institutional investors.

## Table 1.2   Balance Sheet of U.S. Households

| Assets | $ Billion | % Total | Liabilities and Net Worth | $ Billion | % Total |
|---|---|---|---|---|---|
| **Real assets** | | | **Liabilities** | | |
| Real estate | $14,351 | 29.7% | Mortgages | $ 5,798 | 12.0% |
| Consumer durables | 2,914 | 6.0 | Consumer credit | 1,706 | 3.5 |
| Other | 122 | 0.3 | Bank and other loans | 321 | 0.7 |
| Total real assets | $17,387 | 35.9% | Other | 493 | 1.0 |
| | | | Total liabilities | $ 8,319 | 17.2% |
| **Financial assets** | | | | | |
| Deposits | $ 4,895 | 10.1% | | | |
| Life insurance reserves | 915 | 1.9 | | | |
| Pension reserves | 8,349 | 17.3 | | | |
| Corporate equity | 5,035 | 10.4 | | | |
| Equity in noncorp. business | 4,972 | 10.3 | | | |
| Mutual fund shares | 2,840 | 5.9 | | | |
| Personal trusts | 842 | 1.7 | | | |
| Debt securities | 2,402 | 5.0 | | | |
| Other | 761 | 1.6 | | | |
| Total financial assets | 31,009 | 64.1 | Net worth | 40,078 | 82.8 |
| TOTAL | $48,396 | 100.0% | | $48,396 | 100.0% |

Note: Column sums may differ from total because of rounding error.
Source: *Flow of Funds Accounts of the United States,* Board of Governors of the Federal Reserve System, September 2002.

**Table 1.3    Holdings of Corporate Equities in the United States**

| Sector | Share Ownership, $ Billions | % Total |
|---|---|---|
| Private pension funds | $ 1,591.3 | 11.7% |
| State and local pension funds | 1,100.3 | 8.1 |
| Insurance companies | 990.4 | 7.3 |
| Mutual and closed-end funds | 2,470.4 | 18.1 |
| Bank personal trusts | 206.2 | 1.5 |
| Foreign investors | 1,524.4 | 11.2 |
| Households and nonprofit organizations | 5,471.8 | 40.2 |
| Other | 270.4 | 2.0 |
| *TOTAL* | $13,625.2 | 100.0% |

Source: *New York Stock Exchange Fact Book*, NYSE, 2001.

---

**CONCEPT CHECK☞ QUESTION 1**

Are the following assets real or financial?

a. Patents

b. Lease obligations

c. Customer goodwill

d. A college education

e. A $5 bill

---

## 1.2    FINANCIAL MARKETS AND THE ECONOMY

We stated earlier that real assets determine the wealth of an economy, whereas financial assets merely represent claims on real assets. Nevertheless, financial assets and the markets in which they trade play several crucial roles in developed economies. Financial assets allow us to make the most of the economy's real assets.

**Consumption Timing**    Some individuals in an economy are earning more than they currently wish to spend. Others—for example, retirees—spend more than they currently earn. How can you shift your purchasing power from high-earnings periods to low-earnings periods of life? One way is to "store" your wealth in financial assets. In high-earnings periods, you can invest your savings in financial assets such as stocks and bonds. In low-earnings periods, you can sell these assets to provide funds for your consumption needs. By so doing, you can shift your consumption over the course of your lifetime, thereby allocating your consumption to periods that provide the greatest satisfaction. Thus financial markets allow individuals to separate decisions concerning current consumption from constraints that otherwise would be imposed by current earnings.

**Allocation of Risk**    Virtually all real assets involve some risk. When GM builds its auto plants, for example, its management cannot know for sure what cash flows those plants will generate. Financial markets and the diverse financial instruments traded in those markets allow investors with the greatest taste for risk to bear that risk, while other less-risk-tolerant individuals can, to a greater extent, stay on the sidelines. For example, if GM raises the funds to build its auto plant by selling both stocks and bonds to the public, the more optimistic, or risk-tolerant, investors buy shares of stock in GM. The more conservative individuals can buy GM bonds, which promise to provide a fixed payment. The stockholders bear most of the business risk, but reap potentially higher rewards. Thus capital markets allow the risk that is inherent to all investments to be borne by the investors most willing to bear that risk.

This allocation of risk also benefits the firms that need to raise capital to finance their investments. When investors can self-select into security types with risk–return characteristics that best suit their preferences, each security can be sold for the best possible price. This facilitates the process of building the economy's stock of real assets.

## Separation of Ownership and Management

Many businesses are owned and managed by the same individual. This simple organization, well-suited to small businesses, in fact was the most common form of business organization before the Industrial Revolution. Today, however, with global markets and large-scale production, the size and capital requirements of firms have skyrocketed. For example, General Electric lists on its balance sheet about $44 billion of property, plant, and equipment. Corporations of such size simply could not exist as owner-operated firms. General Electric actually has more than one-half million stockholders, whose ownership stake in the firm is proportional to their holdings of shares.

Such a large group of individuals obviously cannot actively participate in the day-to-day management of the firm. Instead, they elect a board of directors, which in turn hires and supervises the management of the firm. This structure means that the owners and managers of the firm are different. This gives the firm a stability that the owner-managed firm cannot achieve. For example, if some stockholders decide they no longer wish to hold shares in the firm, they can sell their shares to other investors, with no impact on the management of the firm. Thus financial assets and the ability to buy and sell those assets in financial markets allow for easy separation of ownership and management.

How can all of the disparate owners of the firm, ranging from large pension funds holding thousands of shares to small investors who may hold only a single share, agree on the objectives of the firm? Again, the financial markets provide some guidance. All may agree that the firm's management should pursue strategies that enhance the value of their shares. Such policies will make all shareholders wealthier and allow them all to better pursue their personal goals, whatever those goals might be.

Do managers really attempt to maximize firm value? It is easy to see how they might be tempted to engage in activities not in the best interest of the shareholders. For example, they might engage in empire building or avoid risky projects to protect their own jobs or overconsume luxuries such as corporate jets, reasoning that the cost of such perquisites is largely borne by the shareholders. These potential conflicts of interest are called **agency problems** because managers, who are hired as agents of the shareholders, may pursue their own interests instead.

Several mechanisms have evolved to mitigate potential agency problems. First, compensation plans tie the income of managers to the success of the firm. A major part of the total compensation of top executives is typically in the form of stock options, which means that the managers will not do well unless the stock price increases, benefiting shareholders. (Of course, we've learned more recently that overuse of options can create its own agency problem. Options can create an incentive for managers to manipulate information to prop up a stock price temporarily, giving them a chance to cash out before the price returns to a level reflective of the firm's true prospects. More on this shortly.) Second, while boards of directors are sometimes portrayed as defenders of top management, they can, and in recent years increasingly do, force out management teams that are underperforming. Third, outsiders such as security analysts and large institutional investors such as pension funds monitor firms closely and make the life of poor performers at the least uncomfortable.

Finally, bad performers are subject to the threat of takeover. If the board of directors is lax in monitoring management, unhappy shareholders in principle can elect a different board. They do this by launching a *proxy contest* in which they seek to obtain enough proxies (i.e., rights to vote the shares of other shareholders) to take control of the firm and vote in another board. However, this threat is usually minimal. Shareholders who attempt such a fight have to use their own funds, while management can defend itself using corporate coffers. Most proxy fights fail.

**EXAMPLE 1.1**

## The Hewlett-Packard/Compaq Proxy Fight

When Carly Fiorini, the CEO of Hewlett-Packard, proposed a merger with Compaq Computer, Walter Hewlett, son of the company's founder and member of the HP board of directors, dissented. The merger had to be approved by shareholders, and Hewlett engaged in a proxy fight to block the deal. One estimate is that HP spent $150 million to lobby shareholders to support the merger; even small shareholders of HP reported receiving 20 or more phone calls from the company in support of the deal.[1] The merger ultimately was approved in an uncharacteristically close vote. No surprise that less than 1% of public companies face proxy contests in any particular year.

The real takeover threat is from other firms. If one firm observes another underperforming, it can acquire the underperforming business and replace management with its own team. The stock price should rise to reflect the prospects of improved performance, which provides incentive for firms to engage in such takeover activity.

**A Crisis in Corporate Governance**    Nevertheless, neither monitoring nor market discipline is perfect, and most observers agree that boards have not been sufficiently diligent in monitoring management. Despite these mechanisms to align incentives of shareholders and managers, the 3 years between 2000 and 2002 were filled with a seemingly unending series of scandals that collectively point to a crisis in corporate governance. The nearby box provides a scorecard for many of the most prominent scandals, but it is far from exhaustive. These episodes suggest that agency and incentive problems are far from solved.

Most (but not all) of the scandals fell into three broad categories: manipulation of financial data to misrepresent the actual condition of the firm; systematically misleading and overly optimistic research reports put out by stock market analysts; and allocations of initial public offerings to corporate executives as a quid pro quo for personal favors or the promise to direct future business back to the manager of the IPO. Perhaps the underlying theme that ties these scandals together is distorted incentives that tilted decisions toward short-term payoffs rather than long-term value.

**Accounting Scandals.**  The spate of accounting scandals is symbolized by Enron and its auditor Arthur Andersen. Enron used so-called special purpose entities to hide massive amounts of debt, inflate reported profits, and funnel massive profits to corporate insiders. Arthur Andersen was convicted for obstructing justice by shredding documents. Enron proved to be only the tip of the iceberg, however. It soon emerged that other firms such as telecom companies Global Crossing, Qwest Communications, and WorldCom also had

---

[1] See *The Economist,* "Designed by Committee," June 13, 2002.

# SCANDAL SCORECARD

| Firm | Allegations | Outcome |
|---|---|---|
| Adelphia Communication (cable company) | • That company's founding family members looted firm and spent company funds on personal expenses, including a $12 million golf course. | Three members of Rigas family indicted on fraud charges. Government is seeking $2.5 billion in allegedly illegal proceeds from the Rigases. |
| Arthur Andersen (accounting firm) | • That firm obstructed SEC investigation of Enron by shredding tons of documents. | Andersen convicted of obstruction, fined $500,000, sentenced to 5 years probation, and barred from auditing public companies. |
| CSFB (Credit Suisse First Boston, investment banking) | • That firm allocated shares in initial public offerings to officers of other firms in exchange for the investment banking business of those firms.<br>• That firm allocated IPO shares in return for brokerage business at inflated prices.<br>• That firm produced biased research to support its investment banking business.<br>• That investment banking star Frank Quattrone encouraged employees to destroy documents after being advised that the CSFB was the subject of civil and criminal inquiries. | CSFB pays $100 million to settle investigation into the alleged kickback scheme associated with its IPO allocations and $200 million in connection with its flawed research reports. Quattrone leaves CSFB and faces obstruction of justice and witness tempering charges as well as possible ban from securities business. |
| Citigroup/Salomon Smith Barney (investment banking) | • That the securities group (in particular, Jack Grubman, its telecom analyst) provided overly optimistic assessment of firms in return for their investment banking business.<br>• That shares in IPOs were directed to officers of other firms in exchange for the investment banking business of those firms. | Mr. Grubman resigned, paid a $15 million fine, and was barred from the securities industry for life. Citigroup announced charge of $1.3 billion for settling investigation into its stock-research and IPO practices, as well as to establish reserve for anticipated litigation involving shareholder claims. |
| Enron (energy and trading) | • That Enron used off-book partnerships and questionable accounting practices to hide massive debt and inflate earnings.<br>• That company insiders improperly profited from these special purpose vehicles. | Andrew Fastow, CFO, indicted for fraud and money laundering. Possibility of future indictment of former CEOs Kenneth Lay and Jeffrey Skilling. Enron declared bankruptcy in late 2001. |
| Global Crossing/Qwest Communications (telecom) | • That these firms swapped network capacity to artificially inflate reported profits. | Global Crossing filed for bankruptcy in 2002. Qwest will restate up to $1.5 billion in earnings. |
| Imclone Systems (drug maker) | • That CEO Samuel Waksal gave inside information about pending regulatory rejection of a cancer drug to family and friends, including Martha Stewart. | Waksal sentenced to 7-year prison term and $4 million in fines for insider trading, securities fraud, and other charges. Martha Stewart is indicted for obstruction of justice and securities fraud. |
| Merrill Lynch (brokerage) | • That its analysts, notably Henry Blodget, gave investors overly rosy research reports about the stocks of its investment-banking clients | Merrill to pay $100 million to settle the case against it. Faces huge potential fraud claims by investors who bought stock based on Merrill recommendations. |
| Tyco (conglomerate) | • That CEO, L. Dennis Kozlowski, and CFO, Mark Swartz, took more than $170 million in unauthorized compensation, used company funds for personal purposes, and illegally reaped an additional $430 million through stock sales. | Kozlowski and Swartz indicted on charges that they stole company funds. Kozlowski also indicted on charges of evading N.Y. sales tax on $13 million in art. |
| WorldCom (telecom) | • That top executives participated in accounting fraud to inflate profits by more than $11 billion over 4 years. | Firm pays $750 million settlement and declares bankrupty, reemerging from Chapter 11 as MCI. CEO, Bernard Ebbers, was ousted in April 2002 and has been indicted for accounting fraud. CFO, Scott Sullivan, was fired and indicted on fraud and other charges. Further indictments are expected. |

Source: *The Wall Street Journal Online,* http://online.wsj.com/documents.info-scanscore02-frameset.html, downloaded January 16, 2003; original information updated by authors.

**Table 1.4    Largest Option Exercises by Heads of Major U.S. Companies, 1997–2001**

| Executive | Company | Year of Exercise | Payout ($ millions) |
|---|---|---|---|
| Lawrence Ellison | Oracle | 2001 | $706 |
| Michael Eisner | Walt Disney | 1998 | 570 |
| Michael Dell | Dell Computer | 2000 | 233 |
| Sanford Weill | Citigroup | 1997 | 220 |
| Thomas Siebel | Siebel Systems | 2001 | 175 |
| Stephen Case | AOL Time Warner | 1997 | 158 |
| John Chambers | Cisco Systems | 2000 | 156 |
| Gerald Levin | AOL Time Warner | 2000 | 153 |

Source: *The Wall Street Journal,* December 17, 2002.

manipulated and misstated their accounts to the tune of billions of dollars. Sunbeam, Xerox, and other firms used questionable sales assumptions to inflate profits.[2]

One reason this sort of manipulation paid is that executives commonly were compensated with potentially massive stock options. Even if the stock price could be propped up by misleading information only for a short period, this could give option holders enough time to cash out before the firm's true prospects were revealed. Table 1.4 lists some of the largest stock option payoffs in history; not all were of questionable propriety, but they do illustrate the temptation to manage information about the company even if the market can be fooled only temporarily.

What about the auditors who were supposed to be the watchdogs of the firms? Here too, incentives were skewed. Recent changes in business practice made the consulting arm of these firms more lucrative than the auditing function. For example, Andersen earned more money in 2000 by consulting for Enron than by auditing it; it would not be surprising to see that Andersen, and other auditors, might be lenient in their auditing work to protect their consulting contracts.

**Analyst Scandals.**  Wall Street stock analysts regularly publish research reports on a wide range of firms along with buy or sell recommendations. Yet only the smallest fraction of firms (less than 2%) were assigned sell recommendations and, as it turns out, many firms given buy recommendations were privately called dogs (or worse) by these market analysts. Rather than provide unbiased reports, analysts were pressed into the service of the investment bankers. In effect, favorable analysis was traded for the promise of future investment banking business. The most notorious of these episodes involved Jack Grubman of Salomon Smith Barney (part of Citigroup) who allegedly upgraded his rating of AT&T to win Salomon a role as co-manager of AT&T's massive stock sale. But he was hardly alone. Ten Wall Street firms paid $1.4 billion (including $475 million to fund independent stock research) to settle claims of improper behavior.

Again, conflicts of interest and distorted incentives—in short, agency problems—played a role in these scandals. Analysts were commonly compensated not for the accuracy or insightfulness of their analysis, but for their role in garnering investment banking business for their firms. And the payoffs could be huge. In the year after Merrill Lynch analyst Henry Blodget participated in 52 investment banking deals, his compensation reportedly increased from $3 million to $12 million.

---

[2] We review some of these practices in Chapter 18.

**Initial Public Offerings.**  As we will see in Chapter 3, firms that wish to raise funds by selling stock to the public for the first time hire investment banking firms to manage their initial public offering, or IPO. The investment banker assesses demand for the offering and allocates shares to interested investors. Because IPOs typically provide excellent initial returns, these allocations are highly coveted. Some investment banking firms that managed IPOs made a practice of awarding allocations to favored clients in what resembled kickback schemes. For example, CSFB allocated shares with the expectation that recipients would direct stock trading business to its brokerage arm. Other allocations were apparently granted to corporate executives in return for their promise of investment banking business.

These episodes indicate that many investment bankers were more focused on short-term profits than long-term reputations. In the boom years, there was considerable temptation to focus on the short term; investment bankers earned about $10 billion in fees by issuing $245 billion in new securities in just the 1½ years ending in the first quarter of 2000.[3] We will discuss in Chapter 3 some of the specific regulatory responses to these scandals. For the most part, however, they are focused on re-aligning incentives, for example by severing the link between stock market analyst compensation and investment banking business, by making corporate executives and board members personally responsible for the accuracy of financial reports, by mandating a greater role for disinterested outsiders on the board of directors, by creating a new oversight board to oversee the auditing of public companies, by prohibiting auditors from providing various other services to clients, and by beefing up the budget of the SEC.

One proposal that has not been yet endorsed by regulators is for firms to move from option-based to stock-based compensation, with added restrictions that executives hold shares for longer periods. The goal would be to align their incentives with the long-term success of the firm and to eliminate the incentive to curry short-term advantage at the cost of long-term performance. In fact, while this has not yet been required, grants of such restricted stock to top executives jumped between 2002 and 2003 and the median value of these grants has increased by about 65%, even as the use of stock options has declined.[4] Microsoft, historically one of the largest users of employee stock options, announced in July 2003 that it would replace option grants with restricted stock.

Wall Street and its regulators are seeking ways to restore credibility. There is (admittedly belated) recognition that markets require trust to function. In the wake of the scandals, the value of reputation and straightforward incentive structures has increased. For example, Lazard, Blackstone, and Greenhill, a "boutique" investment banker that provides advice but doesn't have its own capital market operation with conflicting interests, has picked up considerable business, As one Wall Street insider put it, "This is an industry of trust; it's one of its key assets . . . [Wall Street] is going to have to invest in getting [that trust] back . . . without that trust, there's nothing."[5]

# 1.3   CLIENTS OF THE FINANCIAL SYSTEM

We start our analysis with a broad view of the major clients that place demands on the financial system. By considering the needs of these clients, we can gain considerable insight into why organizations and institutions have evolved as they have.

---

[3] *Business Week,* "How Corrupt is Wall Street?" May 13, 2002.
[4] Joann Lublin, "With Options Tainted, Companies Award Restricted Stock," *The Wall Street Journal,* March 3, 2003, p. B1.
[5] *Business Week,* "How Corrupt Is Wall Street?" May 13, 2002.

We can classify the clientele of the investment environment into three groups: the household sector, the corporate sector, and the government sector. This scheme is not perfect; it excludes some organizations such as not-for-profit agencies and has difficulty with some hybrids such as unincorporated or family-run businesses. Nevertheless, from the standpoint of capital markets, the three-group classification is useful.

## The Household Sector

Households constantly make economic decisions concerning activities such as work, job training, retirement planning, and savings versus consumption. We will take most of these decisions as being already made and focus on financial decisions specifically. Essentially, we concern ourselves only with what financial assets households desire to hold.

Even this limited focus, however, leaves a broad range of issues to consider. Most households are potentially interested in a wide array of assets, and the assets that are attractive can vary considerably depending on the household's economic situation. Even a limited consideration of taxes and risk preferences can lead to widely varying asset demands, and this demand for variety is, as we shall see, a driving force behind financial innovation.

Taxes lead to varying asset demands because people in different tax brackets "transform" before-tax income to after-tax income at different rates. For example, high-tax-bracket investors naturally will seek securities that are exempt from state and local taxes. This, in turn, creates demand for portfolios that specialize in tax-exempt bonds of one particular state. In other words, differential tax status creates "tax clienteles" that in turn give rise to demand for a range of assets with a variety of tax implications. The demand of investors encourages entrepreneurs to offer such portfolios (for a fee, of course!).

Risk considerations also create demand for a diverse set of investment alternatives. At an obvious level, differences in risk tolerance create demand for assets with a variety of risk–return combinations. Individuals also have particular hedging requirements that contribute to diverse investment demands.

Consider, for example, a resident of New York City who plans to sell her house and retire to Miami, Florida, in 15 years. Such a plan seems feasible if real estate prices in the two cities do not diverge before her retirement. How can one hedge Miami real estate prices now, short of purchasing a home there immediately rather than at retirement? One way to hedge the risk is to purchase securities that will increase in value if Florida real estate becomes more expensive. This creates a hedging demand for an asset with a particular risk characteristic. Such demands lead profit-seeking financial corporations to supply the desired goods: observe Florida real estate investment trusts (REITs) that allow individuals to invest in securities whose performance is tied to Florida real estate prices. If Florida real estate becomes more expensive, the REIT will increase in value. The individual's loss as a potential purchaser of Florida real estate is offset by her gain as an investor in that real estate. This is only one example of how a myriad of risk-specific assets are demanded *and created* by agents in the financial environment.

Risk motives also lead to demand for ways that investors can easily diversify their portfolios and even out their risk exposure. We will see that these diversification motives inevitably give rise to mutual funds that offer small individual investors the ability to invest in a wide range of stocks, bonds, precious metals, and virtually all other financial instruments.

## The Business Sector

Whereas household financial decisions are concerned with how to invest money, businesses typically need to raise money to finance their investments in real assets: plant, equipment, technological know-how, and so forth. Table 1.5 presents balance sheets of U.S. corporations as a whole. The heavy concentration in real assets is obvious. Broadly speaking, there are two ways for businesses to raise money—they can borrow it, either from banks or directly from households by issuing bonds, or they can "take in new partners" by issuing stocks, which are ownership shares in the firm.

Businesses issuing securities to the public have several objectives. First, they want to get the best price possible for their securities. Second, they want to market the issues to the public at the lowest possible cost. This has two implications. First, businesses might want to farm out the marketing of their securities to firms that specialize in such security issuance, because it is unlikely that any single firm is in the market often enough to justify a full-time security issuance division. Issue of securities requires immense effort. The security issue must be brought to the attention of the public. Buyers then must subscribe to the issue, and records of subscriptions and deposits must be kept. The allocation of the security to each buyer must be determined, and subscribers finally must exchange money for securities. These activities clearly call for specialists. The complexities of security issuance have been the catalyst for creation of an investment banking industry to cater to business demands. We will return to this industry shortly.

The second implication of the desire for low-cost security issuance is that most businesses will prefer to issue fairly simple securities that require the least extensive incremental analysis and, correspondingly, are the least expensive to arrange. Such a demand for simplicity or uniformity by business-sector security issuers is likely to be at odds with the household sector's demand for a wide variety of risk-specific securities. This mismatch of objectives gives rise to an industry of middlemen who act as intermediaries between the two sectors, specializing in transforming simple securities into complex issues that suit particular market niches.

**The Government Sector**  Like businesses, governments often need to finance their expenditures by borrowing. Unlike businesses, governments cannot sell equity shares; they are restricted to borrowing to raise funds when tax revenues are not sufficient to cover

### Table 1.5   Balance Sheet of Nonfinancial U.S. Business

| Assets | $ Billion | % Total | Liabilities and Net Worth | $ Billion | % Total |
|---|---|---|---|---|---|
| **Real assets** | | | **Liabilities** | | |
| Equipment and software | $ 3,142 | 17.2% | Bonds and mortgages | $ 3,447 | 18.9% |
| Real estate | 4,760 | 26.1 | Bank loans | 772 | 4.2 |
| Inventories | 1,264 | 6.9 | Other loans | 675 | 3.7 |
| Total real assets | $ 9,166 | 50.2% | Trade debt | 1,289 | 7.1 |
| | | | Other | 3,515 | 19.2 |
| **Financial assets** | | | Total liabilities | $ 9,698 | 53.1% |
| Deposits and cash | $ 556 | 3.0% | | | |
| Marketable securities | 503 | 2.8 | | | |
| Consumer credit | 53 | 0.3 | | | |
| Trade credit | 1,729 | 9.5 | | | |
| Other | 6,264 | 34.3 | | | |
| Total financial assets | 9,106 | 49.8 | Net worth | 8,573 | 46.9 |
| TOTAL | $18,271 | 100.0% | | $18,271 | 100.0% |

Note: Column sums may differ from total because of rounding error.
Source: *Flow of Funds Accounts of the United States,* Board of Governors of the Federal Reserve System, September 2002.

expenditures. They also can print money, of course, but this source of funds is limited by its inflationary implications, and so most governments usually try to avoid excessive use of the printing press.

Governments have a special advantage in borrowing money because their taxing power makes them very creditworthy and, therefore, able to borrow at the lowest rates. The financial component of the federal government's balance sheet is presented in Table 1.6. Notice that the major liabilities are government securities, such as Treasury bonds or Treasury bills.

A second, special role of the government is in regulating the financial environment. Some government regulations are relatively innocuous. For example, the Securities and Exchange Commission is responsible for disclosure laws that are designed to enforce truthfulness in various financial transactions. Other regulations have been much more controversial.

One example is Regulation Q, which for decades put a ceiling on the interest rates that banks were allowed to pay to depositors, until it was repealed by the Depository Institutions Deregulation and Monetary Control Act of 1980. The result was predictable: Bank competitors stepped in to fill the void created by Regulation Q. The great success of money market funds in the 1970s came in large part from depositors leaving banks that were prohibited from paying competitive rates. Indeed, much financial innovation may be viewed as responses to government tax and regulatory rules.

# 1.4   THE ENVIRONMENT RESPONDS TO CLIENTELE DEMANDS

When enough clients demand and are willing to pay for a service, it is likely in a capitalistic economy that a profit-seeking supplier will find a way to provide and charge for that service. This is the mechanism that leads to the diversity of financial markets. Let us consider the market responses to the disparate demands of the three sectors.

**Financial Intermediation**   Recall that the financial problem facing households is how best to invest their funds. The relative smallness of most households makes direct investment intrinsically difficult. A small investor obviously cannot advertise in the local newspaper his or her willingness to lend money to businesses that need to finance investments. Instead, **financial intermediaries** such as banks, investment companies, insurance companies, or credit unions naturally evolve to bring the two sectors together. Financial intermediaries sell their own liabilities to raise funds that are used to purchase liabilities of other corporations.

## Table 1.6   Financial Assets and Liabilities of the U.S. Government

| Assets | $ Billion | % Total | Liabilities | $ Billion | % Total |
|---|---|---|---|---|---|
| Deposits, currency, gold | $111 | 19.3% | Currency | $   25 | 0.6% |
| Mortgages | 76 | 13.1 | Government securities | 3,433 | 79.4 |
| Loans | 199 | 34.7 | Insurance and pension reserves | 801 | 18.5 |
| Other | 189 | 32.9 | Other | 62 | 1.4 |
| TOTAL | $575 | 100.0% | TOTAL | $4,321 | 100.0% |

Note: Column sums may differ from total because of rounding error.
Source: *Flow of Funds Accounts: Flows & Outstandings,* Board of Governors of the Federal Reserve System, September 2002.

For example, a bank raises funds by borrowing (taking in deposits) and lending that money to (purchasing the loans of) other borrowers. The spread between the interest rates paid to depositors and the rates charged to borrowers is the source of the bank's profit. In this way, lenders and borrowers do not need to contact each other directly. Instead, each goes to the bank, which acts as an intermediary between the two. The problem of matching lenders with borrowers is solved when each comes independently to the common intermediary. The convenience and cost savings the bank offers the borrowers and lenders allow it to profit from the spread between the rates on its loans and the rates on its deposits. In other words, the problem of coordination creates a market niche for the bank as intermediary. Profit opportunities alone dictate that banks will emerge in a trading economy.

Financial intermediaries are distinguished from other businesses in that both their assets and their liabilities are overwhelmingly financial. Table 1.7 shows that the balance sheets of financial institutions include very small amounts of real assets. Compare Table 1.7 with Table 1.5, the balance sheet of the nonfinancial corporate sector. The contrast arises precisely because intermediaries are middlemen, simply moving funds from one sector to another. In fact, from a bird's-eye view, this is the primary social function of such intermediaries, to channel household savings to the business sector.

Other examples of financial intermediaries are investment companies, insurance companies, and credit unions. All these firms offer similar advantages, in addition to playing a middleman role. First, by pooling the resources of many small investors, they are able to lend considerable sums to large borrowers. Second, by lending to many borrowers, intermediaries achieve significant diversification, meaning they can accept loans that individually might be risky. Third, intermediaries build expertise through the volume of business

### Table 1.7   Balance Sheet of Financial Institutions

| Assets | $ Billion | % Total | Liabilities and Net Worth | $ Billion | % Total |
|---|---|---|---|---|---|
| **Real assets** | | | **Liabilities** | | |
| Equipment and structures | $ 528 | 3.1% | Deposits | $ 3,462 | 20.1% |
| Land | 99 | 0.6 | Mutual fund shares | 1,564 | 0.1 |
| Total tangibles | $ 628 | 3.6% | Life insurance reserves | 478 | 2.8 |
| | | | Pension reserves | 4,651 | 27.0 |
| | | | Money market securities | 1,150 | 6.7 |
| | | | Bonds and mortgages | 1,589 | 9.2 |
| **Financial assets** | | | Other | 3,078 | 17.8 |
| Deposits and cash | $ 364 | 2.1% | Total liabilities | $15,971 | 92.6% |
| Government securities | 3,548 | 20.6 | | | |
| Corporate bonds | 1,924 | 11.2 | | | |
| Mortgages | 2,311 | 13.4 | | | |
| Consumer credit | 894 | 5.2 | | | |
| Other loans | 1,803 | 10.4 | | | |
| Corporate equity | 3,310 | 19.2 | | | |
| Other | 2,471 | 14.3 | | | |
| Total financial assets | 16,625 | 96.4 | Net worth | 1,281 | 7.4 |
| TOTAL | $17,252 | 100.0% | TOTAL | $17,252 | 100.0% |

Note: Column sums may differ from total because of rounding error.
Source: Balance Sheets for the U.S. Economy, 1945–94, Board of Governors of the Federal Reserve System, June 1995..

they do. One individual trying to borrow or lend directly would have much less specialized knowledge of how to structure and execute the transaction with another party.

**Investment companies,** which pool together and manage the money of many investors, also arise out of the "smallness problem." Here, the problem is that most household portfolios are not large enough to be spread across a wide variety of securities. It is very expensive in terms of brokerage and trading costs to purchase one or two shares of many different firms, and it clearly is more economical for stocks and bonds to be purchased and sold in large blocks. This observation reveals a profit opportunity that has been filled by *mutual funds* offered by many investment companies.

Mutual funds pool the limited funds of small investors into large amounts, thereby gaining the advantages of large-scale trading; investors are assigned a prorated share of the total funds according to the size of their investment. This system gives small investors advantages that they are willing to pay for in the form of a management fee to the mutual fund operator. Mutual funds are logical extensions of an investment club or cooperative, in which individuals themselves team up and pool funds. The fund sets up shop as a firm that accepts the assets of many investors, acting as an investment agent on their behalf. Again, the advantages of specialization are sufficiently large that the fund can provide a valuable service and still charge enough for it to clear a handsome profit.

Economies of scale also explain the proliferation of analytic services available to investors. Newsletters, databases, and brokerage house research services all exploit the fact that the expense of collecting information is best borne by having a few agents engage in research to be sold to a large client base. This setup arises naturally. Investors clearly want information, but, with only small portfolios to manage, they do not find it economical to incur the expense of collecting it. Hence a profit opportunity emerges: A firm can perform this service for many clients and charge for it.

## Investment Banking

Just as economies of scale and specialization create profit opportunities for financial intermediaries, so too do these economies create niches for firms that perform specialized services for businesses. We said before that firms raise much of their capital by selling securities such as stocks and bonds to the public. Because these firms do not do so frequently, however, investment banking firms that specialize in such activities are able to offer their services at a cost below that of running an in-house security issuance division.

**Investment bankers** such as Merrill Lynch, Citigroup, or Goldman, Sachs advise the issuing firm on the prices it can charge for the securities issued, market conditions, appropriate interest rates, and so forth. Ultimately, the investment banking firm handles the marketing of the security issue to the public.

Investment bankers can provide more than just expertise to security issuers. Because investment bankers are constantly in the market, assisting one firm or another to issue securities, it is in the banker's interest to protect and maintain its reputation for honesty. The investment banker will suffer along with investors if it turns out that securities it has underwritten have been marketed to the public with overly optimistic or exaggerated claims, for the public will not be so trusting the next time that investment banker participates in a security sale. As we have seen, this lesson was re-learned with considerable pain in the boom years of the late 1990s and the subsequent high-tech crash of 2000–2002. Too many investment bankers seemed to get caught up in the flood of money that could be made by pushing stock issues to an overly eager public. The failure of many of these offerings soured the public on both the stock market and the firms managing the IPOs. At least some on Wall Street belatedly recognize that they squandered a valuable asset—reputational capital—and there are signs that they recognize as well that the conflicts of interest that engendered these deals are not only wrong but are bad for business as well.

The investment banker's effectiveness and ability to command future business thus depends on the reputation it has established over time. The economic incentives to maintain a trustworthy reputation are not nearly as strong for firms that plan to go to the securities markets only once or very infrequently. Therefore, investment bankers (whose reputations are intact) can provide a certification role—a "seal of approval"—to security issuers. Their investment in reputation is another type of scale economy that arises from frequent participation in the capital markets.

## Financial Innovation and Derivatives

The investment diversity desired by households is far greater than most businesses have a desire to satisfy. Most firms find it simpler to issue "plain vanilla" securities, leaving exotic variants to others who specialize in financial markets. This, of course, creates a profit opportunity for innovative security design and repackaging that investment bankers are only too happy to fill.

Consider for example the astonishing changes in the mortgage markets since 1970, when mortgage pass-through securities were first introduced by the Government National Mortgage Association (GNMA, or Ginnie Mae). These pass-throughs aggregate individual home mortgages into relatively homogenous pools. Each pool acts as backing for a GNMA **pass-through security.** GNMA security holders receive the principal and interest payments made on the underlying mortgage pool. For example, the pool might total $100 million of 10 percent, 30-year conventional mortgages. The purchaser of the pool receives all monthly interest and principal payments made on the pool. The banks that originated the mortgages continue to service them but no longer own the mortgage investments; these have been passed through to the GNMA security holders.

Pass-through securities were a tremendous innovation in mortgage markets. The *securitization* of mortgages meant that mortgages could be traded just like other securities in national financial markets. Availability of funds no longer depended on local credit conditions; with mortgage pass-throughs trading in national markets, mortgage funds could flow from any region to wherever demand was greatest.

Although some aspects of these securities are relatively complex, the lesson is that security demand elicited a market response. The waves of product development in the last two decades are responses to perceived profit opportunities created by as-yet unsatisfied demands for securities with particular risk, return, tax, and timing attributes. As the investment banking industry becomes ever more sophisticated, security creation and customization become more routine. A Wall Street joke asks how many investment bankers it takes to sell a lightbulb. The answer is 100—one to break the bulb and 99 to sell off the individual fragments.

This discussion leads to the notion of primitive versus derivative securities. A **primitive security** offers returns based only on the status of the issuer. For example, bonds make stipulated interest payments depending only on the solvency of the issuing firm. Dividends paid to stockholders depend as well on the board of directors' assessment of the firm's financial position. In contrast, **derivative securities** yield returns that depend on additional factors pertaining to the prices of other assets. For example, the payoff to stock options depends on the price of the underlying stock. Much of the innovation in security design may be viewed as the continual creation of new types of derivative securities from the available set of primitive securities.

Derivatives have become an integral part of the investment environment. One use of derivatives, perhaps the primary use, is to hedge risks. However, derivatives also can be used to take highly speculative positions. Moreover, when complex derivatives are misunderstood, firms that believe they are hedging might in fact be increasing their exposure to various sources of risk.

While occasional large losses attract considerable attention, they are in fact the exception to the more common use of derivatives as risk-management tools. Derivatives will continue to play an important role in portfolio management and the financial system. We will return to this topic later in the text. For the time being, however, we direct you to the primer on derivatives in the nearby box.

CONCEPT CHECK ☞ QUESTIONS 2 & 3

If you take out a car loan, is the loan a primitive security or a derivative security?

Explain how a car loan from a bank creates both financial assets and financial liabilities.

## Response to Taxation and Regulation

We have seen that much financial innovation and security creation may be viewed as a natural market response to unfulfilled investor needs. Another driving force behind innovation is the ongoing game played between governments and investors on taxation and regulation. Many financial innovations are direct responses to government attempts either to regulate or to tax investments of various sorts. We can illustrate with several examples.

We have already noted how Regulation Q, which limited bank deposit interest rates, spurred the growth of the money market industry. It also was one reason for the birth of the Eurodollar market. Eurodollars are dollar-denominated time deposits in foreign accounts. Because Regulation Q did not apply to these accounts, many U.S. banks and foreign competitors established branches in London and other cities outside the United States, where they could offer competitive rates outside the jurisdiction of U.S. regulators. The growth of the Eurodollar market was also the result of another U.S. regulation: reserve requirements. Foreign branches were exempt from such requirements and were thus better able to compete for deposits. Ironically, despite the fact that Regulation Q no longer exists, the Eurodollar market continues to thrive, thus complicating the lives of U.S. monetary policymakers.

Another innovation attributable largely to tax avoidance motives is the long-term deep discount, or zero-coupon, bond. These bonds, often called *zeros*, make no annual interest payments, instead providing returns to investors through a redemption price that is higher than the initial sales price. Corporations were allowed for tax purposes to impute an implied interest expense based on this built-in price appreciation. The government's technique for imputing tax-deductible interest expenses, however, proved to be too generous in the early years of the bonds' lives, so corporations issued these bonds widely to exploit the resulting tax benefit. Ultimately, the Treasury caught on and amended its interest imputation procedure, and the flow of new zeros dried up.

Meanwhile, however, the financial markets had discovered that zeros were useful ways to lock in a long-term investment return. When the supply of primitive zero-coupon bonds ended, financial innovators created derivative zeros by purchasing U.S. Treasury bonds, "stripping" off the coupons, and selling them separately as zeros.

There are plenty of other examples. The Eurobond market came into existence as a response to changes in U.S. tax law. Financial futures markets were stimulated by abandonment in the early 1970s of the system of fixed exchange rates and by new federal regulations that overrode state laws treating some financial futures as gambling arrangements.

The general tendency is clear: Tax and regulatory pressures on the financial system very often lead to unanticipated financial innovations when profit-seeking investors make an

What are derivatives anyway, and why are people saying such terrible things about them?

Some critics see the derivatives market as a multi-trillion-dollar house of cards composed of interlocking, highly leveraged transactions. They fear that the default of a single large player could stun the world financial system.

But others, including Federal Reserve Chairman Alan Greenspan, say the risk of such a meltdown is negligible. Proponents stress that the market's hazards are more than outweighed by the benefits derivatives provide in helping banks, corporations and investors manage their risks.

Because the science of derivatives is relatively new, there's no easy way to gauge the ultimate impact these instruments will have. There are now more than 1,200 different kinds of derivatives on the market, most of which require a computer program to figure out. Surveying this complex subject, dozens of derivatives experts offered these insights:

**Q: What is the broadest definition of derivatives?**

A: Derivatives are financial arrangements between two parties whose payments are based on, or "derived" from, the performance of some agreed-upon benchmark. Derivatives can be issued based on currencies, commodities, government or corporate debt, home mortgages, stocks, interest rates, or any combination.

Company stock options, for instance, allow employees and executives to profit from changes in a company's stock price without actually owning shares. Without knowing it, homeowners frequently use a type of privately traded "forward" contract when they apply for a mortgage and lock in a borrowing rate for their house closing, typically for as many as 60 days in the future.

**Q: What are the most common forms of derivatives?**

A: Derivatives come in two basic categories, option-type contracts and forward-type contracts. These may be exchange-listed, such as futures and stock options, or they may be privately traded.

Options give buyers the right, but not the obligation, to buy or sell an asset at a preset price over a specific period. The option's price is usually a small percentage of the underlying asset's value.

Forward-type contracts, which include forwards, futures and swaps, commit the buyer and the seller to trade a given asset at a set price on a future date. These are "price fixing" agreements that saddle the buyer with the same price risks as actually owning the asset. But normally, no money changes hands until the delivery date, when the contract is often settled in cash rather than by exchanging the asset.

**Q: In business, what are they used for?**

A: While derivatives can be powerful speculative instruments, businesses most often use them to hedge. For instance, companies often use forwards and exchange-listed futures to protect against fluctuations in currency or commodity prices, thereby helping to manage import and raw-materials costs. Options can serve a similar purpose; interest-rate options such as caps and floors help companies control financing costs in much the same way that caps on adjustable-rate mortgages do for homeowners.

**Q: How do over-the-counter derivatives generally originate?**

A: A derivatives dealer, generally a bank or securities firm, enters into a private contract with a corporation, investor or another dealer. The contract commits the dealer to provide a return linked to a desired interest rate, currency or other asset. For example, in an interest-rate swap, the dealer might receive a floating rate in return for paying a fixed rate.

**Q: Why are derivatives potentially dangerous?**

A: Because these contracts expose the two parties to market moves with little or no money actually changing hands, they involve leverage. And that leverage may be vastly increased by the terms of a particular contract.

When things go well, that leverage provides a big return, compared with the amount of capital at risk. But it also causes equally big losses when markets move the wrong way. Even companies that use derivatives to hedge, rather than speculate, may be at risk, since their operation would rarely produce perfectly offsetting gains.

**Q: If they are so dangerous, why are so many businesses using derivatives?**

A: They are among the cheapest and most readily available means at companies' disposal to buffer themselves against shocks in currency values, commodity prices and interest rates. Donald Nicoliasen, a Price Waterhouse expert on derivatives, says derivatives "are a new tool in everybody's bag to better manage business returns and risks."

end run around the government's restrictions. The constant game of regulatory catch-up sets off another flow of new innovations.

## 1.5   MARKETS AND MARKET STRUCTURE

Just as securities and financial institutions come into existence as natural responses to investor demands, so too do markets evolve to meet needs. Consider what would happen if organized markets did not exist. Households that wanted to borrow would need to find others that wanted to lend. Inevitably, a meeting place for borrowers and lenders would be settled on, and that meeting place would evolve into a financial market. In old London a pub called Lloyd's launched the maritime insurance industry. A Manhattan curb on Wall Street became synonymous with the financial world.

We can differentiate four types of markets: direct search markets, brokered markets, dealer markets, and auction markets.

A **direct search market** is the least organized market. Here, buyers and sellers must seek each other out directly. One example of a transaction taking place in such a market would be the sale of a used refrigerator in which the seller advertises for buyers in a local newspaper. Such markets are characterized by sporadic participation and low-priced and nonstandard goods. It does not pay most people or firms to seek profits by specializing in such an environment.

The next level of organization is a **brokered market.** In markets where trading in a good is sufficiently active, brokers can find it profitable to offer search services to buyers and sellers. A good example is the real estate market, where economies of scale in searches for available homes and for prospective buyers make it worthwhile for participants to pay brokers to conduct the searches for them. Brokers in given markets develop specialized knowledge on valuing assets traded in that given market.

An important brokered investment market is the *primary market*, where new issues of securities are offered to the public. In the primary market investment bankers act as brokers; they seek out investors to purchase securities directly from the issuing corporation.

Another brokered market is that for large *block transactions*, in which very large blocks of stock are bought or sold. These blocks are so large (technically more than 10,000 shares but usually much larger) that brokers or "block houses" often are engaged to search directly for other large traders, rather than bringing the trade directly to the stock exchange where relatively smaller investors trade.

When trading activity in a particular type of asset increases, **dealer markets** arise. Here, dealers specialize in various assets, purchasing them for their own inventory and selling them for a profit from their inventory. Dealers, unlike brokers, trade assets for their own accounts. The dealer's profit margin is the "bid–asked" spread—the difference between the price at which the dealer buys for and sells from inventory. Dealer markets save traders on search costs because market participants can easily look up prices at which they can buy from or sell to dealers. Obviously, a fair amount of market activity is required before dealing in a market is an attractive source of income. The over-the-counter securities market is one example of a dealer market.

Trading among investors of already issued securities is said to take place in *secondary markets*. Therefore, the over-the-counter market is one example of a secondary market. Trading in secondary markets does not affect the outstanding amount of securities; ownership is simply transferred from one investor to another.

The most integrated market is an **auction market,** in which all transactors in a good converge at one place to bid on or offer a good. The New York Stock Exchange (NYSE) is an example of an auction market. An advantage of auction markets over dealer markets is that one need not search to find the best price for a good. If all participants converge, they can arrive at mutually agreeable prices and thus save the bid–asked spread.

Continuous auction markets (as opposed to periodic auctions such as in the art world) require very heavy and frequent trading to cover the expense of maintaining the market. For this reason, the NYSE and other exchanges set up listing requirements, which limit the shares traded on the exchange to those of firms in which sufficient trading interest is likely to exist.

The organized stock exchanges are also secondary markets. They are organized for investors to trade existing securities among themselves.

**CONCEPT CHECK QUESTION 4**

**Many assets trade in more than one type of market. In what types of markets do the following trade?**

*a.* **Used cars**

*b.* **Paintings**

*c.* **Rare coins**

## 1.6   ONGOING TRENDS

Several important trends have changed the contemporary investment environment:

1. Globalization.
2. Securitization.
3. Financial engineering.
4. Revolution in information and communication networks.

**Globalization**   If a wider range of investment choices can benefit investors, why should we limit ourselves to purely domestic assets? **Globalization** requires efficient communication technology and the dismantling of regulatory constraints. These tendencies in worldwide investment environments have encouraged international investing in recent years.

U.S. investors commonly participate in foreign investment opportunities in several ways: (1) purchase foreign securities using American Depository Receipts (ADRs), which are domestically traded securities that represent claims to shares of foreign stocks; (2) purchase foreign securities that are offered in dollars; (3) buy mutual funds that invest internationally; and (4) buy derivative securities with payoffs that depend on prices in foreign security markets.

U.S. investors who wish to purchase foreign shares can often do so using American Depository Receipts. Brokers who act as intermediaries for such transactions purchase an inventory of stock of some foreign issuer. The broker then issues an ADR that represents a claim to some number of those foreign shares held in inventory. The ADR is denominated in dollars and can be traded on U.S. stock exchanges but is in essence no more than a claim on a foreign stock. Thus, from the investor's point of view, there is no more difference between buying a French versus a U.S. stock than there is in holding a Massachusetts-based stock compared with a California-based stock. Of course, the investment implications may differ.

A variation on ADRs are WEBS (World Equity Benchmark Shares), which use the same depository structure to allow investors to trade *portfolios* of foreign stocks in a selected country. Each WEBS security tracks the performance of an index of share returns for a particular country. WEBS can be traded by investors just like any other security (they trade

**Figure 1.1
Globalization
and American
Depositary
Receipts**

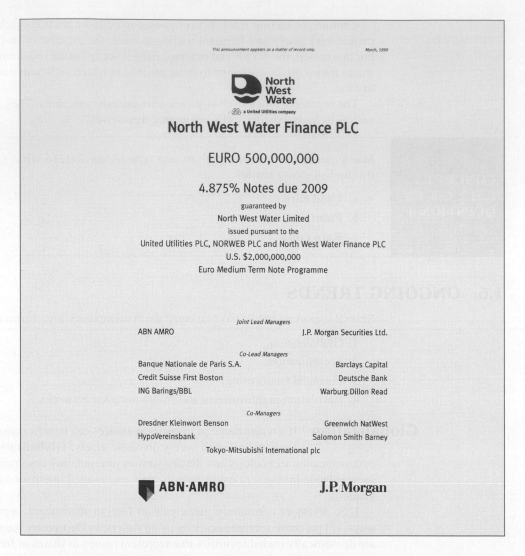

This announcement appears as a matter of record only.          March, 1999

**North West Water**
a United Utilities company

# North West Water Finance PLC

## EURO 500,000,000

### 4.875% Notes due 2009

guaranteed by
North West Water Limited
issued pursuant to the
United Utilities PLC, NORWEB PLC and North West Water Finance PLC
U.S. $2,000,000,000
Euro Medium Term Note Programme

*Joint Lead Managers*

ABN AMRO                                        J.P. Morgan Securities Ltd.

*Co-Lead Managers*

Banque Nationale de Paris S.A.                  Barclays Capital
Credit Suisse First Boston                      Deutsche Bank
ING Barings/BBL                                 Warburg Dillon Read

*Co-Managers*

Dresdner Kleinwort Benson                       Greenwich NatWest
HypoVereinsbank                                 Salomon Smith Barney
Tokyo-Mitsubishi International plc

**ABN·AMRO**                                    **J.P. Morgan**

on the American Stock Exchange), and thus enable U.S. investors to obtain diversified portfolios of foreign stocks in one fell swoop.

A giant step toward globalization took place in 1999, when 11 European countries established a new currency called the *euro*.[6] The idea behind the euro is that a common currency will facilitate trade and encourage integration of markets across national boundaries. Figure 1.1 is an announcement of a loan in the amount of 500 million euros. (Each euro is currently worth about $1; the symbol for the euro is €.)

**Securitization**   Until recently, financial intermediaries were the only means to channel funds from national capital markets to smaller local ones. **Securitization,** however, now allows borrowers to enter capital markets directly. In this procedure pools of loans typically are aggregated into pass-through securities, such as mortgage pool pass-throughs. Then, investors can invest in securities backed by those pools. The transformation of these pools into standardized securities enables issuers to deal in a volume

---

[6] The 11 countries are: Belgium, Germany, Spain, France, Ireland, Italy, Luxembourg, The Netherlands, Austria, Portugal, and Finland. Greece became the twelfth country to participate in the common currency in 2001.

**Figure 1.2
Asset-backed
securities
outstanding
by major types
of credit**

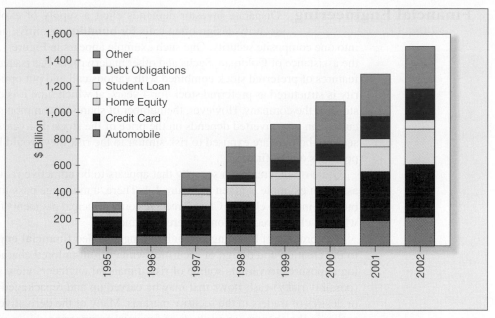

Source: Bond Market Association.

large enough that they can bypass intermediaries. We have already discussed this phenomenon in the context of the securitization of the mortgage market. Today, most conventional
mortgages are securitized by government-sponsored mortgage agencies.

Another example of securitization is the collateralized automobile receivable (CAR), a
pass-through arrangement for car loans. The loan originator passes the loan payments
through to the holder of the CAR. Aside from mortgages, the biggest asset-backed securities are for credit card debt, car loans, home equity loans, student loans, and debt of firms.
Figure 1.2 documents the composition and growth of the asset-backed securities market in
the United States.

Securitization also has been used to allow U.S. banks to unload their portfolios of shaky
loans to developing nations. So-called Brady bonds (named after Nicholas Brady, former
secretary of the Treasury) were formed by securitizing bank loans to several countries in
shaky fiscal condition. The U.S. banks exchange their loans to developing nations for
bonds backed by those loans. The payments that the borrowing nation would otherwise
make to the lending bank are directed instead to the holder of the bond. These bonds are
traded in capital markets. Therefore, if they choose, banks can remove these loans from
their portfolios simply by selling the bonds. In addition, the United States in many cases
has enhanced the credit quality of these bonds by designating a quantity of Treasury bonds
to serve as partial collateral for the loans. In the event of a foreign default, the holders of
the Brady bonds would have claim to the collateral.

**CONCEPT
CHECK☞
QUESTION 5**

When mortgages are pooled into securities, the pass-through agencies (Freddie Mac and Fannie Mae) typically guarantee the underlying mortgage loans.
If the homeowner defaults on the loan, the pass-through agency makes good
on the loan; the investor in the mortgage-backed security does not bear the
credit risk.

*a.* **Why does the allocation of default risk to the pass-through agency
rather than the security holder make economic sense?**

*b.* **Why is the allocation of default risk less of an issue for Brady bonds?**

**Financial Engineering**    Disparate investor demands elicit a supply of exotic securities. Creative security design often calls for **bundling** primitive and derivative securities into one composite security. One such example appears in Figure 1.3. Boise Cascade, with the assistance of Goldman, Sachs and other underwriters, has issued a hybrid security with features of preferred stock combined with various call and put option contracts. The security is structured as preferred stock for 4 years, at which time it is converted into common stock of the company. However, the number of shares of common stock into which the security can be converted depends on the price of the stock in 4 years, which means that the security holders are exposed to risk similar to the risk they would bear if they held option positions on the firm.

Quite often, creating a security that appears to be attractive requires **unbundling** of an asset. An example is given in Figure 1.4. There, a mortgage pass-through certificate is unbundled into two classes. Class 1 receives only principal payments from the mortgage pool, whereas class 2 receives only interest payments.

The process of bundling and unbundling is called **financial engineering,** which refers to the creation and design of securities with custom-tailored characteristics, often regarding exposures to various source of risk. Financial engineers view securities as bundles of (possibly risky) cash flows that may be carved up and repackaged according to the needs or desires of traders in the security markets. Many of the derivative securities we spoke of earlier in the chapter are products of financial engineering.

**Figure 1.3    Bundling creates a complex security**

**Figure 1.4    Unbundling of mortgages into principal- and interest-only securities**

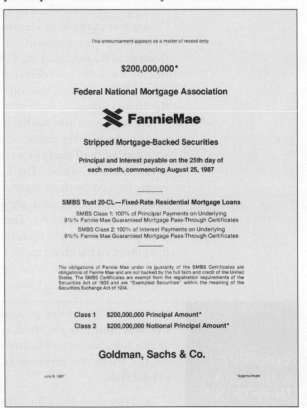

Source: *The Wall Street Journal,* December 19, 2001.

**CONCEPT CHECK☞ QUESTION 6**

How can tax motives contribute to the desire for unbundling?

**Computer Networks**  The Internet and other advances in computer networking have transformed many sectors of the economy, and few more so than the financial sector. These advances will be treated in greater detail in Chapter 3, but for now we can mention a few important innovations: online trading, online information dissemination, automated trade crossing, and the tentative beginnings of Internet investment banking.

Online trading connects a customer directly to a brokerage firm. Online brokerage firms can process trades more cheaply and therefore can charge lower commissions. The average commission for an online trade is now below $20, compared to trades at full-service brokers that commonly run more than $100.

The Internet has also allowed vast amounts of information to be made cheaply and widely available to the public. Individual investors today can obtain data, investment tools, and even analyst reports that only a decade ago would have been available only to professionals.

Electronic communication networks that allow direct trading among investors have exploded in recent years. These networks allow members to post buy or sell orders and to have those orders automatically matched up or "crossed" with orders of other traders in the system without benefit of an intermediary such as a securities dealer.

Firms that wish to sell new securities to the public almost always use the services of an investment banker. In 1995, Spring Street Brewing Company was the firm to sidestep this mechanism by using the Internet to sell shares directly to the public. It posted a page on the World Wide Web to let investors know of its stock offering and successfully sold and distributed shares through its Internet site. Based on its success, it established its own Internet investment banking operation. To date, such Internet investment banks have barely made an impact on the market, but they may augur changes in the future.

## SUMMARY

1. Real assets are used to produce the goods and services created by an economy. Financial assets are claims to the income generated by real assets. Securities are financial assets. Financial assets are part of an investor's wealth, but not part of national wealth. Instead, financial assets determine how the "national pie" is split up among investors.

2. The three sectors of the financial environment are households, businesses, and government. Households decide on investing their funds. Businesses and government, in contrast, typically need to raise funds.

3. The diverse tax and risk preferences of households create a demand for a wide variety of securities. In contrast, businesses typically find it more efficient to offer relatively uniform types of securities. This conflict gives rise to an industry that creates complex derivative securities from primitive ones.

4. The smallness of households creates a market niche for financial intermediaries, mutual funds, and investment companies. Economies of scale and specialization are factors supporting the investment banking industry.

5. Four types of markets may be distinguished: direct search, brokered, dealer, and auction markets. Securities are sold in all but direct search markets.

6. Four recent trends in the financial environment are globalization, securitization, financial engineering, and advances in computer networks and communication.

## KEY TERMS

| | | |
|---|---|---|
| real assets | pass-through security | auction market |
| financial assets | primitive security | globalization |
| agency problem | derivative security | securitization |
| financial intermediaries | direct search market | bundling |
| investment companies | brokered market | unbundling |
| investment bankers | dealer markets | financial engineering |

## WEBSITES

www.executivelibrary.com
This site gives access to instant financial and market news from around the world.

ceoexpress.com/default.asp
This site provides a comprehensive list of links for business and financial managers.

www.wallpost.com
This site provides a comprehensive list of links to financial, economic, and market information.

www.aaii.com
The American Association of Individual Investors site provides excellent basic investment information on current issues.

www.finpipe.com
Check out the *Markets* link.

www.financewise.com
This is an excellent finance search engine.

www.federalreserve.gov/otherfrb.htm
Check out the Federal Reserve Bank in your region of the country and its Web page. See the FRED I and II economic and financial databases at the Federal Reserve Bank of St. Louis.

fisher.osu.edu/fin/osudata.htm
*The Financial Data Finder* provides a comprehensive list of links.

finance.yahoo.com
This site offers extensive financial market information and excellent company research links.

moneycentral.msn.com/home.asp
Similar to Yahoo Finance, this site offers excellent investment links.

**PROBLEMS**

1. Suppose you discover a treasure chest of $10 billion in cash.

   a. Is this a real or financial asset?

   b. Is society any richer for the discovery?

   c. Are you wealthier?

   d. Can you reconcile your answers to *(b)* and *(c)*? Is anyone worse off as a result of the discovery?

2. Lanni Products is a start-up computer software development firm. It currently owns computer equipment worth $30,000 and has cash on hand of $20,000 contributed by Lanni's owners. For each of the following transactions, identify the real and/or fnancial assets that trade hands. Are any financial assets created or destroyed in the transaction?

   a. Lanni takes out a bank loan. It receives $50,000 in cash and signs a note promising to pay back the loan over 3 years.

   b. Lanni uses the cash from the bank plus $20,000 of its own funds to finance the development of new financial planning software.

   c. Lanni sells the software product to Microsoft, which will market it to the public under the Microsoft name. Lanni accepts payment in the form of 1,500 shares of Microsoft stock.

   d. Lanni sells the shares of stock for $80 per share and uses part of the proceeds to pay off the bank loan.

3. Reconsider Lanni Products from Problem 2.

   a. Prepare its balance sheet just after it gets the bank loan. What is the ratio of real assets to total assets?

   b. Prepare the balance sheet after Lanni spends the $70,000 to develop the product. What is the ratio of real assets to total assets?

   c. Prepare the balance sheet after it accepts payment of shares from Microsoft. What is the ratio of real assets to total assets?

4. Examine the balance sheet of the financial sector (Table 1.7). What is the ratio of real assets to total assets? What is the ratio for nonfinancial firms (Table 1.5)? Why should this difference be expected?

5. In the 1960s, the U.S. government instituted a 30% withholding tax on interest payments on bonds sold in the United States to overseas investors. (It has since been repealed.) What connection does this have to the contemporaneous growth of the huge Eurobond market, where U.S. firms issue dollar-denominated bonds overseas?

6. Discuss the advantages and disadvantages of the following forms of managerial compensation in terms of mitigating agency problems, that is, potential conflicts of interest between managers and shareholders.

   a. A fixed salary.

   b. Stock in the firm.

   c. Call options on shares of the firm.

7. We noted that oversight by large institutional investors or creditors is one mechanism to reduce agency problems. Why don't individual investors in the firm have the same incentive to keep an eye on management?

8. Consider Figure 1.5 below, which describes an issue of American gold certificates.

   a. Is this issue a primary or secondary market transaction?

   b. Are the certificates primitive or derivative assets?

   c. What market niche is filled by this offering?

9. Why would you expect securitization to take place only in highly developed capital markets?

10. Suppose that you are an executive of General Motors and that a large share of your potential income is derived from year-end bonuses that depend on GM's annual profits.

    a. Would purchase of GM stock be an effective hedging strategy for the executive who is worried about the uncertainty surrounding her bonus?

    b. Would purchase of Toyota stock be an effective hedge strategy?

11. Consider again the GM executive in Problem 10. In light of the fact that the design of the annual bonus exposes the executive to risk that she would like to shed, why doesn't GM instead pay her a fixed salary that doesn't entail this uncertainty?

12. What is the relationship between securitization and the role of financial intermediaries in the economy? What happens to financial intermediaries as securitization progresses?

13. Many investors would like to invest part of their portfolios in real estate but obviously cannot on their own purchase office buildings or strip malls. Explain how this situation creates a profit incentive for investment firms that can sponsor REITs (real estate investment trusts).

14. Financial engineering has been disparaged as nothing more than paper shuffling. Critics argue that resources that go to *rearranging wealth* (i.e., bundling and unbundling financial assets) might better be spent on *creating* wealth (i.e., creating real assets). Evaluate this criticism. Are there any benefits realized by creating an array of derivative securities from various primary securities?

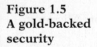
**Figure 1.5
A gold-backed security**

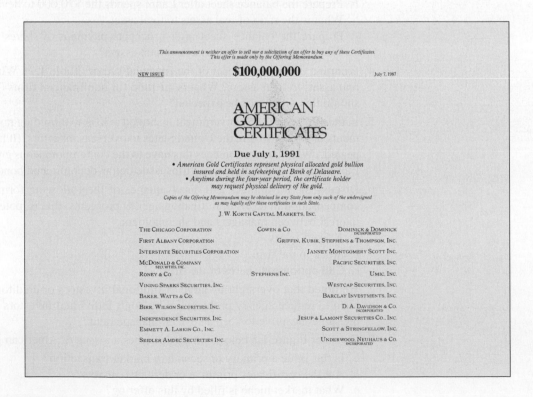

15. Although we stated that real assets comprise the true productive capacity of an economy, it is hard to conceive of a modern economy without well-developed financial markets and security types. How would the productive capacity of the U.S. economy be affected if there were no markets in which one could trade financial assets?

16. Why does it make sense that the first futures markets introduced in 19th-century America were for trades in agricultural products? For example, why did we not see instead futures for goods such as paper or pencils?

---

**STANDARD & POOR'S**

The purchase of this text provides you with access to a very powerful database of company and industry information, called *Standard & Poor's Market Insight.* You have access via **www.mhhe.com/business/finance/edumarketinsight** (use the password provided in your book cover) to 6 years of data for almost 500 companies. (Bookmark the site!) The site provides 14 different Excel Analytics Reports including financial statements, ratios (6 years of ratios, actual and charted, with variances from industry average), stock performance reports, and many more. Industry information (companies and profile) and company business activity are also reported. (*Note: If you have purchased this text used, the site ID may be expired. You may purchase a password at the website address above. Also, some of you may have to update your Windows to access the Excel pages in the database.*)

Enter the above link and review the introductions page. Proceed by clicking on the *Continue* icon, then enter your ID number and you are in. Carefully review the *News and Notes* table of contents to the right and the profile (*Learn More*) presented for each area. Take a look at almost 500 companies in the database by clicking the *Company* icon at the top of the page, then *Population.* Click on a particular firm to review the contents available from Market Insight. Look over the reports via the table of contents on the left.

The *Company Profile* contains recent market valuation information and a link to the company's website. *Financial Highlights* provides current quarter information on sales, market data, ratios, etc. Click the linked terms, for example, *Employees,* and you will be provided a definition of the term, very useful when getting started. Get familiar with Market Insight in preparation for later assignments.

---

**E-INVESTMENTS**
**Track Your Portfolio**

Here's $1,000,000! Why not invest it and let Yahoo! Finance's Portfolio Manager keep track of your performance this term? Go to **finance.yahoo.com** and select *Create Portfolio.* You will have to register (free) and be able to set up a My Yahoo page, including a portfolio of stocks. Select five to eight companies of interest to you, allocate the $1,000,000 among the stocks . . . and off you go. Check the performance on a regular basis throughout the term . . . and later, after you have learned something about performance evaluation, assess your stock selecting ability.

*Visit us at www.mhhe.com/bkm*

1. The real assets are patents, customer relations, and the college education. These assets enable individuals or firms to produce goods or services that yield profits or income. Lease obligations are simply claims to pay or receive income and do not in themselves create new wealth. Similarly, the $5 bill is only a paper claim on the government and does not produce wealth.

2. The car loan is a primitive security. Payments on the loan depend only on the solvency of the borrower.

3. The borrower has a financial liability, the loan owed to the bank. The bank treats the loan as a financial asset.

4. *a.* Used cars trade in direct search markets when individuals advertise in local newspapers, and in dealer markets at used-car lots or automobile dealers.

   *b.* Paintings trade in broker markets when clients commission brokers to buy or sell art for them, in dealer markets at art galleries, and in auction markets.

   *c.* Rare coins trade mostly in dealer markets in coin shops, but they also trade in auctions (e.g., eBay or Sotheby's) and in direct search markets when individuals advertise they want to buy or sell coins.

5. *a.* The pass-through agencies are far better equipped to evaluate the credit risk associated with the pool of mortgages. They are constantly in the market, have ongoing relationships with the originators of the loans, and find it economical to set up "quality control" departments to monitor the credit risk of the mortgage pools. Therefore, the pass-through agencies are better able to incur the risk; they charge for this "service" via a "guarantee fee."

   *b.* Investors might not find it worthwhile to purchase these securities if they had to assess the credit risk of these loans for themselves. It is far cheaper for them to allow the agencies to collect the guarantee fee. In contrast to mortgage-backed securities, which are backed by pools of large numbers of mortgages, the Brady bonds are backed by large government loans. It is more feasible for the investor to evaluate the credit quality of a few governments than dozens or hundreds of individual mortgages.

6. Creative unbundling can separate interest or dividend from capital gains income. Dual funds do just this. In tax regimes where capital gains are taxed at lower rates than other income, or where gains can be deferred, such unbundling may be a way to attract different tax clienteles to a security.

# FINANCIAL INSTRUMENTS

This chapter covers a range of financial securities and the markets in which they trade. Our goal is to introduce you to the features of various security types. This foundation will be necessary to understand the more analytic material that follows in later chapters. Financial markets are traditionally segmented into **money markets** and **capital markets.** Money market instruments include short-term, marketable, liquid, low-risk debt securities. Money market instruments sometimes are called *cash equivalents*, or just *cash* for short. Capital markets, in contrast, include longer-term and riskier securities. Securities in the capital market are much more diverse than those found within the money market. For this reason, we will subdivide the capital market into four segments: longer-term bond markets, equity markets, and the derivative markets for options and futures. We first describe money market instruments. We then move on to debt and equity securities. We explain the structure of various stock market indexes in this chapter because market benchmark portfolios play an important role in portfolio construction and evaluation. Finally, we survey the derivative security markets for options and futures contracts.

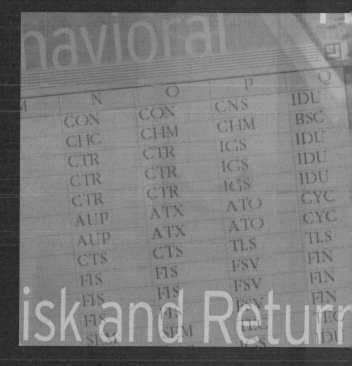

**Figure 2.1
Rates on money
market securities**

## Money Rates

Friday, January 3, 2003

The key U. S. and foreign annual interest rates below are a guide to general levels but don't always represent actual transactions.

**Prime Rate:** 4.25% (effective 11/07/02).

**Discount Rate:** 0.75% (effective 11/06/02).

**Federal Funds:** 1.250% high, 0.500% low, 0.875% near closing bid, 1.000% offered. Effective rate: 1.15%. Source: Prebon Yamane (USA) Inc. Federal-funds target rate: 1.250% (effective 11/06/02).

**Call Money:** 3.00% (effective 11/07/02).

**Commercial Paper:** Placed directly by General Electric Capital Corp.: 1.27% 30 to 83 days; 1.25% 84 to 89 days; 1.28% 90 to 174 days; 1.25% 175 to 179 days; 1.29% 180 to 239 days; 1.30% 240 to 270 days.

**Euro Commercial Paper:** Placed directly by General Electric Capital Corp.: 2.86% 30 days; 2.85% two months; 2.83% three months; 2.80% four months; 2.78% five months; 2.78% six months.

**Dealer Commercial Paper:** High-grade unsecured notes sold through dealers by major corporations: 1.31% 30 days; 1.31% 60 days; 1.31% 90 days.

**Certificates of Deposit:** 1.32% one month; 1.32% three months; 1.34% six months.

**Bankers Acceptances:** 1.31% 30 days; 1.30% 60 days; 1.31% 90 days; 1.31% 120 days; 1.31% 150 days; 1.32% 180 days. Source: Prebon Yamane (USA) Inc.

**Eurodollars:** 1.30% - 1.33% one month; 1.30% - 1.33% two months; 1.30% - 1.33% three months; 1.30% - 1.33% four months; 1.30% - 1.33% five months; 1.34% - 1.37% six months. Source: Prebon Yamane (USA) Inc.

**London Interbank Offered Rates (Libor):** 1.3800% one month; 1.3900% three months; 1.40375% six months; 1.5400% one year. Effective rate for contracts entered into two days from date appearing at top of this column.

**Euro Libor:** 2.89413% one month; 2.86163% three months; 2.80675% six months; 2.78775% one year. Effective rate for contracts entered into two days from date appearing at top of this column.

**Euro Interbank Offered Rates (Euribor):** 2.898% one month; 2.863% three months; 2.814% six months; 2.797% one year. Source: Reuters.

**Foreign Prime Rates:** Canada 4.50%; European Central Bank 2.75%; Japan 1.375%; Switzerland 2.63%; Britain 4.00%.

**Treasury Bills:** Results of the Monday, December 30, 2002, auction of short-term U.S. government bills, sold at a discount from face value in units of $1,000 to $1 million: 1.185% 13 weeks; 1.220% 26 weeks. Tuesday, December 31, 2002 auction: 1.175% 4 weeks.

**Overnight Repurchase Rate:** 1.26%. Source: Garban Intercapital.

**Freddie Mac:** Posted yields on 30-year mortgage commitments. Delivery within 30 days 5.53%, 60 days 5.61%, standard conventional fixed-rate mortgages: 4.125%, 2% rate capped one-year adjustable rate mortgages.

**Fannie Mae:** Posted yields on 30 year mortgage commitments (priced at par) for delivery within 30 days 5.60%, 60 days 5.69%, standard conventional fixed-rate mortgages; 3.30%, 6/2 rate capped one-year adjustable rate mortgages. Constant Maturity Debt Index: 1.272% three months; 1.297% six months; 1.470% one year.

**Merrill Lynch Ready Assets Trust:** 0.97%.

**Consumer Price Index:** November, 181.3, up 2.2% from a year ago. Bureau of Labor Statistics.

Source: *The Wall Street Journal*, January 6, 2003. Reprinted by permission of *The Wall Street Journal*, © 2003 Dow Jones & Company, Inc. All Rights Reserved Worldwide.

## 2.1  THE MONEY MARKET

The money market is a subsector of the fixed-income market. It consists of very short-term debt securities that usually are highly marketable. Many of these securities trade in large denominations, and so are out of the reach of individual investors. Money market funds, however, are easily accessible to small investors. These mutual funds pool the resources of many investors and purchase a wide variety of money market securities on their behalf.

Figure 2.1 is a reprint of a money rates listing from *The Wall Street Journal*. It includes the various instruments of the money market that we will describe in detail. Table 2.1 lists outstanding volume in 2002 of the major instruments of the money market.

**Treasury Bills**    U.S. *Treasury bills* (T-bills, or just bills, for short) are the most marketable of all money market instruments. T-bills represent the simplest form of borrowing: The government raises money by selling bills to the public. Investors buy the bills at a discount from the stated maturity value. At the bill's maturity, the holder receives from the government a payment equal to the face value of the bill. The difference between the purchase price and ultimate maturity value constitutes the investor's earnings.

T-bills are issued with initial maturities of 28, 91, or 182 days. Individuals can purchase T-bills directly, at auction, or on the secondary market from a government securities dealer. T-bills are highly liquid; that is, they are easily converted to cash and sold at low transaction cost and with not much price risk. Unlike most other money market instruments,

| Table 2.1 | Major Components of the Money Market (December 2002) |
|---|---|

|  | $ Billion |
|---|---|
| Repurchase agreements | $ 376.6 |
| Small-denomination time deposits* | 970.1 |
| Large-denomination time deposits | 793.3 |
| Eurodollars | 225.2 |
| Treasury bills | 811.2 |
| Commercial paper | 1,320.6 |
| Savings deposits | 2,304.5 |
| Money market mutual funds | 2,179.3 |

*Small denominations are less than $100,000.
Sources: *Economic Report of the President*, U.S. Government Printing Office, 2002; *Flow of Funds Accounts: Flows & Outstandings*, Board of Governors of the Federal Reserve System, September 2002.

which sell in minimum denominations of $100,000, T-bills sell in minimum denominations of only $10,000. The income earned on T-bills is exempt from all state and local taxes, another characteristic distinguishing bills from other money market instruments.

## Certificates of Deposit

A **certificate of deposit,** or CD, is a time deposit with a bank. Time deposits may not be withdrawn on demand. The bank pays interest and principal to the depositor only at the end of the fixed term of the CD. CDs issued in denominations greater than $100,000 are usually negotiable, however; that is, they can be sold to another investor if the owner needs to cash in the certificate before its maturity date. Short-term CDs are highly marketable, although the market significantly thins out for maturities of 3 months or more. CDs are treated as bank deposits by the Federal Deposit Insurance Corporation, so they are insured for up to $100,000 in the event of a bank insolvency.

## Commercial Paper

Large, well-known companies often issue their own short-term unsecured debt notes rather than borrow directly from banks. These notes are called **commercial paper.** Very often, commercial paper is backed by a bank line of credit, which gives the borrower access to cash that can be used (if needed) to pay off the paper at maturity.

Commercial paper maturities range up to 270 days; longer maturities would require registration with the Securities and Exchange Commission and so are almost never issued. Most often, commercial paper is issued with maturities of less than 1 or 2 months. Usually, it is issued in multiples of $100,000. Therefore, small investors can invest in commercial paper only indirectly, via money market mutual funds.

Commercial paper is considered to be a fairly safe asset, because a firm's condition presumably can be monitored and predicted over a term as short as 1 month. Many firms issue commercial paper intending to roll it over at maturity, that is, issue new paper to obtain the funds necessary to retire the old paper.

## Bankers' Acceptances

A **banker's acceptance** starts as an order to a bank by a bank's customer to pay a sum of money at a future date, typically within 6 months. At this stage, it is similar to a postdated check. When the bank endorses the order for payment as "accepted," it assumes responsibility for ultimate payment to the holder of the acceptance. At this point, the acceptance may be traded in secondary markets like any other claim on the bank. Bankers' acceptances are considered very safe assets because traders can substitute the bank's credit standing for their own. They are used widely in foreign trade where the creditworthiness of one trader is unknown to the trading partner. Acceptances sell at a discount from the face value of the payment order, just as T-bills sell at a discount from par value.

## Eurodollars

**Eurodollars** are dollar-denominated deposits at foreign banks or foreign branches of American banks. By locating outside the United States, these banks escape regulation by the Federal Reserve Board. Despite the tag "Euro," these accounts need not be in European banks, although that is where the practice of accepting dollar-denominated deposits outside the United States began.

Most Eurodollar deposits are for large sums, and most are time deposits of less than 6 months' maturity. A variation on the Eurodollar time deposit is the Eurodollar certificate of deposit. A Eurodollar CD resembles a domestic bank CD except that it is the liability of a non-U.S. branch of a bank, typically a London branch. The advantage of Eurodollar CDs over Eurodollar time deposits is that the holder can sell the asset to realize its cash value before maturity. Eurodollar CDs are considered less liquid and riskier than domestic CDs, however, and thus offer higher yields. Firms also issue Eurodollar bonds, which are dollar-denominated bonds outside the U.S., although bonds are not a money market investment because of their long maturities.

## Repos and Reverses

Dealers in government securities use **repurchase agreements,** also called "repos" or "RPs," as a form of short-term, usually overnight, borrowing. The dealer sells government securities to an investor on an overnight basis, with an agreement to buy back those securities the next day at a slightly higher price. The increase in the price is the overnight interest. The dealer thus takes out a 1-day loan from the investor, and the securities serve as collateral.

A *term repo* is essentially an identical transaction, except that the term of the implicit loan can be 30 days or more. Repos are considered very safe in terms of credit risk because the loans are backed by the government securities. A *reverse repo* is the mirror image of a repo. Here, the dealer finds an investor holding government securities and buys them, agreeing to sell them back at a specified higher price on a future date.

## Federal Funds

Just as most of us maintain deposits at banks, banks maintain deposits of their own at a Federal Reserve bank. Each member bank of the Federal Reserve System, or "the Fed," is required to maintain a minimum balance in a reserve account with the Fed. The required balance depends on the total deposits of the bank's customers. Funds in the bank's reserve account are called **federal funds,** or *fed funds*. At any time, some banks have more funds than required at the Fed. Other banks, primarily big banks in New York and other financial centers, tend to have a shortage of federal funds. In the federal funds market, banks with excess funds lend to those with a shortage. These loans, which are usually overnight transactions, are arranged at a rate of interest called the federal funds rate.

Although the fed funds market arose primarily as a way for banks to transfer balances to meet reserve requirements, today the market has evolved to the point that many large banks use federal funds in a straightforward way as one component of their total sources of funding. Therefore, the fed funds rate is simply the rate of interest on very short-term loans among financial institutions.

**Brokers' Calls**   Individuals who buy stocks on margin borrow part of the funds to pay for the stocks from their broker. The broker in turn may borrow the funds from a bank, agreeing to repay the bank immediately (on call) if the bank requests it. The rate paid on such loans is usually about 1% higher than the rate on short-term T-bills.

**The LIBOR Market**   The **London Interbank Offered Rate** (LIBOR) is the rate at which large banks in London are willing to lend money among themselves. This rate, which is quoted on dollar-denominated loans, has become the premier short-term interest rate quoted in the European money market, and it serves as a reference rate for a wide range of transactions. For example, a corporation might borrow at a floating rate equal to LIBOR plus 2%.

**Yields on Money Market Instruments**   Although most money market securities are of low risk, they are not risk-free. For example, the commercial paper market was rocked in 1970 by the Penn Central bankruptcy, which precipitated a default on $82 million of commercial paper. Money market investors became more sensitive to creditworthiness after this episode, and the yield spread between low- and high-quality paper widened.

   The securities of the money market do promise yields greater than those on default-free T-bills, at least in part because of greater relative riskiness. In addition, many investors require more liquidity; thus they will accept lower yields on securities such as T-bills that can be quickly and cheaply sold for cash. Figure 2.2 shows that bank CDs, for example, consistently have paid a risk premium over T-bills. Moreover, that risk premium increased with economic crises such as the energy price shocks associated with the two OPEC disturbances, the failure of Penn Square bank, the stock market crash in 1987, or the collapse of Long Term Capital Management in 1998.

## 2.2  THE BOND MARKET

The bond market is composed of longer-term borrowing or debt instruments than those that trade in the money market. This market includes Treasury notes and bonds, corporate bonds, municipal bonds, mortgage securities, and federal agency debt.

   These instruments are sometimes said to comprise the *fixed-income capital market*, because most of them promise either a fixed stream of income or a stream of income that is

**Figure 2.2   The spread between 3-month CD and Treasury bill rates**

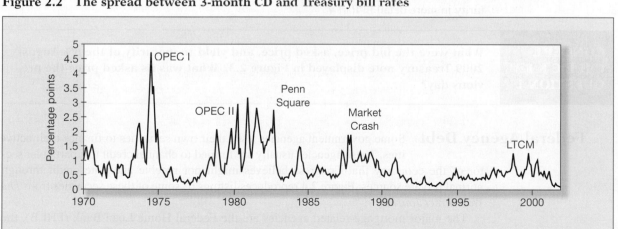

determined according to a specific formula. In practice, these formulas can result in a flow of income that is far from fixed. Therefore, the term "fixed income" is probably not fully appropriate. It is simpler and more straightforward to call these securities either debt instruments or bonds.

**Treasury Notes and Bonds**    The U.S. government borrows funds in large part by selling **Treasury notes** and **Treasury bonds.** T-note maturities range up to 10 years, whereas bonds are issued with maturities ranging from 10 to 30 years. Both are issued in denominations of $1,000 or more. The Treasury announced in late 2001 that it would no longer issue bonds with maturities beyond 10 years. So, all the bonds it now issues would more properly be called notes. Nevertheless, investors still commonly call them Treasury or T-bonds. Both notes and bonds make semiannual interest payments called *coupon payments*, a name derived from precomputer days, when investors would literally clip coupons attached to the bond and present a coupon to receive the interest payment. Aside from their differing maturities at issuance, the only major distinction between T-notes and T-bonds is that T-bonds may be callable during a given period, usually the last 5 years of the bond's life. The call provision gives the Treasury the right to repurchase the bond at par value. However, the Treasury hasn't issued callable bonds since 1984.

Figure 2.3 is an excerpt from a listing of Treasury issues in *The Wall Street Journal*. Notice the highlighted note that matures in November 2008. The coupon income, or interest, paid by the note is 4¾% of par value, meaning that a $1,000 face-value note pays $47.50 in annual interest in two semiannual installments of $23.75 each. The numbers to the right of the colon in the bid and asked prices represent units of ⅟₃₂ of a point.

The bid price of the note is 107²⁵⁄₃₂, or 107.7813. The asked price is 107²⁶⁄₃₂, or 107.8125. Although notes and bonds are sold in denominations of $1,000 par value, the prices are quoted as a percentage of par value. Thus the bid price of 107.7813 should be interpreted as 107.7813% of par, or $1,077.813, for the $1,000 par value security. Similarly, the note could be bought from a dealer for $1,078.125. The +1 change means the closing price on this day rose ⅟₃₂ (as a percentage of par value) from the previous day's closing price. Finally, the yield to maturity on the note based on the asked price is 3.27%.

The **yield to maturity** reported in the financial pages is calculated by determining the semiannual yield and then doubling it, rather than compounding it for two half-year periods. This use of a simple interest technique to annualize means that the yield is quoted on an annual percentage rate (APR) basis rather than as an effective annual yield. The APR method in this context is also called the *bond equivalent yield*. We discuss the yield to maturity in more detail in Part 4.

| CONCEPT CHECK☞ QUESTION 1 | What were the bid price, asked price, and yield to maturity of the 6% August 2009 Treasury note displayed in Figure 2.3? What was its asked price the previous day? |
| --- | --- |

**Federal Agency Debt**    Some government agencies issue their own securities to finance their activities. These agencies usually are formed to channel credit to a particular sector of the economy that Congress believes might not receive adequate credit through normal private sources. Figure 2.4 reproduces listings of some of these securities from *The Wall Street Journal*.

The major mortgage-related agencies are the Federal Home Loan Bank (FHLB), the Federal National Mortgage Association (FNMA, or Fannie Mae), the Government National Mortgage Association (GNMA, or Ginnie Mae), and the Federal Home Loan Mortgage

**Figure 2.3**
**Treasury bonds and notes**

## Treasury Bonds, Notes and Bills

### Explanatory Notes

Representative Over-the-Counter quotation based on transactions of $1 million or more. Treasury bond, note and bill quotes are as of mid-afternoon. Colons in bid-and-asked quotes represent 32nds; 101:01 means 101 1/32. Net changes in 32nds. n-Treasury note. i-Inflation-Indexed issue. Treasury bill quotes in hundredths, quoted on terms of a rate of discount. Days to maturity calculated from settlement date. All yields are to maturity and based on the asked quote. Latest 13-week and 26-week bills are boldfaced. For bonds callable prior to maturity, yields are computed to the earliest call date for issues quoted above par and to the maturity date for issues below par. *When issued.
Source: eSpeed/Cantor Fitzgerald

U.S. Treasury strips as of 3 p.m. Eastern time, also based on transactions of $1 million or more. Colons in bid and asked quotes represent 32nds; 99:01 means 99 1/32. Net changes in 32nds. Yields calculated on the asked quotation. ci-stripped coupon interest. bp-Treasury bond, stripped principal. np-Treasury note, stripped principal. For bonds callable prior to maturity, yields are computed to the earliest call date for issues quoted above par and to the maturity date for issues below par.
Source: Bear, Stearns & Co. via Street Software Technology Inc.

| RATE | MATURITY MO/YR | BID | ASKED | CHG | ASK YLD | RATE | MATURITY MO/YR | BID | ASKED | CHG | ASK YLD |
|---|---|---|---|---|---|---|---|---|---|---|---|
| **Government Bonds & Notes** | | | | | | 5.500 | Feb 08n | 111:16 | 111:17 | 1 | 3.04 |
| 4.750 | Jan 03n | 100:07 | 100:08 | -1 | 0.82 | 5.625 | May 08n | 112:04 | 112:05 | 1 | 3.14 |
| 5.500 | Jan 03n | 100:09 | 100:10 | -1 | 0.88 | 8.375 | Aug 08 | 104:08 | 104:09 | -1 | 1.29 |
| 6.250 | Feb 03n | 100:16 | 100:17 | -2 | 1.18 | 4.750 | Nov 08n | 107:25 | 107:26 | 1 | 3.27 |
| 10.750 | Feb 03 | 101:00 | 101:01 | -3 | 1.20 | 8.750 | Nov 08 | 106:06 | 106:07 | -2 | 1.40 |
| 4.625 | Feb 03n | 100:15 | 100:16 | -1 | 1.08 | 3.875 | Jan 09i | 110:21 | 110:22 | 2 | 1.98 |
| 5.500 | Feb 03n | 100:20 | 100:21 | ... | 0.99 | 5.500 | May 09n | 112:00 | 112:00 | 4 | 3.38 |
| 4.250 | Mar 03n | 100:22 | 100:23 | -1 | 1.05 | 9.125 | May 09 | 109:27 | 109:28 | -8 | 1.71 |
| 7.875 | Nov 04n | 111:08 | 111:09 | -1 | 1.67 | 6.000 | Aug 09n | 114:23 | 114:24 | 4 | 3.48 |
| 11.625 | Nov 04 | 118:03 | 118:04 | -1 | 1.66 | 10.375 | Nov 09 | 115:13 | 115:14 | -2 | 1.87 |
| 2.000 | Nov 04n | 100:16 | 100:17 | 1 | 1.71 | 4.250 | Jan 10i | 112:30 | 112:31 | -1 | 2.24 |
| **1.750** | **Dec 04n** | **99:29** | **99:30** | **1** | **1.77** | 6.500 | Feb 10n | 117:29 | 117:30 | 5 | 3.62 |
| 7.500 | Feb 05n | 111:23 | 111:24 | ... | 1.80 | 11.750 | Feb 10 | 119:30 | 119:31 | -2 | 2.02 |
| 6.500 | May 05n | 110:16 | 110:17 | ... | 1.90 | 10.000 | May 10 | 117:29 | 117:30 | 1 | 2.15 |
| 6.750 | May 05n | 111:00 | 111:00 | ... | 1.94 | 5.750 | Aug 10n | 113:11 | 113:12 | 5 | 3.71 |
| 12.000 | May 05 | 123:05 | 123:06 | ... | 1.89 | 12.750 | Nov 10 | 128:20 | 128:21 | ... | 2.32 |
| 6.500 | Aug 05n | 111:09 | 111:10 | -1 | 2.02 | 3.500 | Jan 11i | 108:14 | 108:15 | -3 | 2.33 |
| 10.750 | Aug 05 | 122:00 | 122:00 | -1 | 2.04 | 5.000 | Feb 11n | 108:08 | 108:09 | 5 | 3.80 |
| 5.750 | Nov 05n | 109:29 | 109:30 | ... | 2.14 | 13.875 | May 11 | 136:13 | 136:14 | 1 | 2.48 |
| 5.875 | Nov 05n | 110:09 | 110:10 | 1 | 2.13 | 5.000 | Aug 11n | 108:02 | 108:03 | 5 | 3.88 |
| 5.625 | Feb 06n | 110:01 | 110:02 | 2 | 2.25 | 14.000 | Nov 11 | 141:04 | 141:05 | -1 | 2.69 |
| 9.375 | Feb 06 | 121:06 | 121:07 | 1 | 2.27 | 3.375 | Jan 12i | 108:01 | 108:02 | 1 | 2.38 |
| 4.625 | May 06n | 107:03 | 107:04 | 1 | 2.40 | 4.875 | Feb 12n | 106:30 | 106:31 | 6 | 3.96 |
| 6.875 | May 06n | 114:08 | 114:09 | 2 | 2.41 | 3.000 | Jul 12i | 105:01 | 105:02 | 2 | 2.40 |
| 7.000 | Jul 06n | 115:03 | 115:04 | 1 | 2.49 | 4.375 | Aug 12n | 102:27 | 102:28 | 6 | 4.01 |
| 6.500 | Oct 06n | 113:30 | 113:31 | 2 | 2.59 | 4.000 | Nov 12n | 99:24 | 99:25 | 7 | 4.03 |
| 3.500 | Nov 06n | 103:05 | 103:06 | 2 | 2.62 | 10.375 | Nov 12 | 132:13 | 132:14 | ... | 3.12 |
| 3.375 | Jan 07i | 107:17 | 107:18 | -1 | 1.43 | 12.000 | Aug 13 | 144:04 | 144:05 | 3 | 3.31 |
| 6.250 | Feb 07n | 113:22 | 113:23 | 2 | 2.70 | 13.250 | May 14 | 155:06 | 155:07 | 1 | 3.49 |
| 6.625 | May 07n | 115:19 | 115:20 | 2 | 2.79 | 3.875 | Apr 29i | 120:17 | 120:18 | 2 | 2.77 |
| 4.375 | May 07n | 106:10 | 106:11 | 2 | 2.82 | 6.125 | Aug 29 | 114:19 | 114:20 | 13 | 5.11 |
| 3.250 | Aug 07n | 101:12 | 101:13 | 1 | 2.92 | 6.250 | May 30 | 116:27 | 116:28 | 12 | 5.10 |
| 6.125 | Aug 07n | 113:26 | 113:27 | 2 | 2.89 | 5.375 | Feb 31 | 106:12 | 106:13 | 11 | 4.95 |
| **3.000** | **Nov 07n** | **100:01** | **100:02** | **1** | **2.98** | 3.375 | Apr 32i | 113:18 | 113:19 | 3 | 2.70 |
| 3.625 | Jan 08i | 109:00 | 109:00 | 2 | 1.74 | | | | | | |

Corporation (FHLMC, or Freddie Mac). The FHLB borrows money by issuing securities and lends this money to savings and loan institutions to be lent in turn to individuals borrowing for home mortgages.

Freddie Mac and Ginnie Mae were organized to provide liquidity to the mortgage market. Until the pass-through securities sponsored by these agencies were established (see the discussion of mortgages and mortgage-backed securities later in this section), the lack of a secondary market in mortgages hampered the flow of investment funds into mortgages and made mortgage markets dependent on local, rather than national, credit availability.

Some of these agencies are government owned, and therefore can be viewed as branches of the U.S. government. Thus their debt is fully free of default risk. Ginnie Mae is an example of a government-owned agency. Other agencies, such as the farm credit agencies, the Federal Home Loan Bank, Fannie Mae, and Freddie Mac, are merely federally *sponsored*.

Although the debt of federally sponsored agencies is not explicitly insured by the federal government, it is widely assumed that the government would step in with assistance if

**Figure 2.4
Government
agency issues**

## Government Agency & Similar Issues

Over-the-Counter mid-afternoon quotations based on large transactions, usually $1 million or more. Colons in bid and asked quotes represent 32nds; 101:01 means 101 1/32.

All yields are calculated to maturity, and based on the asked quote.

*Callable issue, maturity date shown. For issues callable prior to maturity, yields are computed to the earliest call date for issues quoted above par, or 100, and to the maturity date for issues below par.

Source: Bear, Steams & Co. via Street Software Technology Inc.

### Fannie Mae Issues

| RATE | MAT | BID | ASKED | YLD |
|---|---|---|---|---|
| 5.13 | 2-04 | 103:30 | 104:00 | 1.43 |
| 4.75 | 3-04 | 103:25 | 103:27 | 1.47 |
| 3.63 | 4-04 | 102:18 | 102:20 | 1.54 |
| 5.63 | 5-04 | 105:10 | 105:12 | 1.59 |
| 3.00 | 6-04 | 101:28 | 101:30 | 1.63 |
| 6.50 | 8-04 | 107:15 | 107:17 | 1.72 |
| 3.50 | 9-04 | 102:26 | 102:28 | 1.77 |
| 7.13 | 2-05 | 110:15 | 110:17 | 2.00 |
| 3.88 | 3-05 | 103:31 | 104:01 | 1.99 |
| 5.75 | 6-05 | 108:18 | 108:20 | 2.11 |
| 7.00 | 7-05 | 111:19 | 111:21 | 2.22 |
| 3.13 | 8-05* | 100:19 | 100:21 | 2.01 |
| 2.88 | 10-05 | 101:14 | 101:16 | 2.31 |
| 2.75 | 11-05* | 100:02 | 100:04 | 2.41 |
| 6.00 | 12-05 | 110:02 | 110:04 | 2.41 |
| 2.75 | 12-05* | 100:02 | 100:04 | 2.63 |
| 5.50 | 2-06 | 108:27 | 108:29 | 2.50 |
| 5.50 | 5-06 | 107:24 | 107:26 | 3.01 |
| 5.25 | 6-06 | 108:09 | 108:11 | 2.69 |
| 5.50 | 7-06* | 102:04 | 102:06 | 1.30 |
| 5.25 | 8-06* | 102:06 | 102:08 | 1.45 |
| 4.38 | 10-06 | 105:12 | 105:14 | 2.84 |
| 4.50 | 10-06* | 101:29 | 101:31 | 1.92 |
| 4.00 | 11-06* | 101:08 | 101:10 | 2.45 |
| 4.75 | 12-06* | 102:18 | 102:20 | 1.95 |
| 4.75 | 1-07 | 105:07 | 105:09 | 3.32 |
| 5.00 | 1-07* | 107:17 | 107:19 | 2.98 |
| 5.00 | 1-07* | 102:30 | 103:00 | 2.05 |
| 7.13 | 3-07 | 116:03 | 116:05 | 2.99 |
| 5.25 | 3-07* | 103:23 | 103:25 | 2.07 |
| 5.25 | 4-07 | 108:17 | 108:19 | 3.09 |
| 5.00 | 5-07* | 103:15 | 103:17 | 2.33 |

| RATE | MAT | BID | ASKED | YLD |
|---|---|---|---|---|
| 4.25 | 7-07 | 104:14 | 104:16 | 3.17 |
| 6.63 | 10-07 | 114:19 | 114:21 | 3.28 |
| 3.50 | 10-07* | 99:13 | 99:15 | 3.62 |
| 3.25 | 11-07 | 99:23 | 99:25 | 3.30 |
| 5.75 | 2-08 | 110:29 | 110:31 | 3.39 |
| 6.00 | 5-08 | 112:03 | 112:05 | 3.49 |
| 5.25 | 1-09 | 108:03 | 108:05 | 3.72 |
| 6.38 | 6-09 | 114:07 | 114:09 | 3.85 |
| 6.63 | 9-09 | 115:21 | 115:23 | 3.93 |
| 7.25 | 1-10 | 119:17 | 119:19 | 4.02 |
| 7.13 | 6-10 | 119:00 | 119:02 | 4.12 |
| 6.63 | 11-10 | 115:27 | 115:29 | 4.22 |
| 6.25 | 2-11 | 110:10 | 110:12 | 4.69 |
| 5.50 | 3-11 | 108:06 | 108:08 | 4.30 |
| 6.00 | 5-11 | 111:15 | 111:17 | 4.34 |
| 6.25 | 7-11* | 105:03 | 105:05 | 2.79 |
| 5.50 | 10-11* | 103:07 | 103:09 | 3.58 |
| 5.38 | 11-11 | 106:30 | 107:00 | 4.41 |
| 5.00 | 11-11* | 101:06 | 101:08 | 4.28 |
| 6.00 | 12-11* | 104:18 | 104:20 | 3.52 |
| 6.00 | 1-12* | 105:01 | 105:03 | 3.38 |
| 6.13 | 3-12 | 112:12 | 112:14 | 4.46 |
| 6.25 | 3-12* | 106:07 | 106:09 | 1.00 |
| 5.50 | 7-12* | 103:06 | 103:08 | 4.14 |
| 5.25 | 8-12 | 102:29 | 102:31 | 4.86 |
| 4.38 | 9-12 | 98:23 | 98:25 | 4.53 |
| 6.25 | 5-29 | 108:25 | 108:29 | 5.60 |
| 7.13 | 1-30 | 120:30 | 121:02 | 5.60 |
| 7.25 | 5-30 | 122:24 | 122:28 | 5.60 |
| 6.63 | 11-30 | 114:18 | 114:22 | 5.58 |

### Freddie Mac

| RATE | MAT | BID | ASKED | YLD |
|---|---|---|---|---|
| 3.25 | 12-03 | 101:21 | 101:23 | 1.38 |
| 5.00 | 1-04 | 103:19 | 103:21 | 1.39 |
| 3.25 | 1-04 | 101:26 | 101:28 | 1.39 |

| RATE | MAT | BID | ASKED | YLD |
|---|---|---|---|---|
| 5.25 | 2-04 | 104:03 | 104:05 | 1.44 |
| 3.75 | 4-04 | 102:22 | 102:24 | 1.55 |
| 5.00 | 5-04 | 104:16 | 104:18 | 1.59 |
| 6.25 | 7-04 | 106:25 | 106:27 | 1.68 |
| 3.00 | 7-04 | 101:29 | 101:31 | 1.69 |
| 4.50 | 8-04 | 104:10 | 104:12 | 1.72 |
| 3.25 | 11-04 | 102:15 | 102:17 | 1.85 |
| 6.88 | 1-05 | 109:22 | 109:24 | 1.93 |
| 4.13 | 2-05* | 100:07 | 100:09 | 0.38 |
| 3.88 | 2-05 | 103:27 | 103:29 | 1.97 |
| 4.50 | 4-05* | 100:28 | 100:30 | 1.02 |
| 4.25 | 6-05 | 104:28 | 104:30 | 2.16 |
| 3.88 | 6-05* | 101:06 | 101:08 | 1.21 |
| 7.00 | 7-05 | 111:19 | 111:21 | 2.22 |
| 2.88 | 9-05* | 101:14 | 101:16 | 2.29 |
| 2.88 | 9-05* | 100:10 | 100:12 | 2.33 |
| 5.25 | 1-06 | 108:01 | 108:03 | 2.46 |
| 5.50 | 7-06* | 109:04 | 109:06 | 2.74 |
| 5.50 | 3-07 | 107:04 | 107:06 | 3.03 |
| 4.50 | 7-07* | 102:11 | 102:13 | 2.89 |
| 3.50 | 9-07 | 101:01 | 101:03 | 3.25 |
| 5.75 | 11-01 | 111:01 | 111:03 | 3.43 |
| 5.13 | 10-08 | 107:28 | 107:30 | 3.59 |
| 5.75 | 3-09 | 110:29 | 110:31 | 3.75 |
| 5.75 | 4-09* | 104:05 | 104:07 | 2.46 |
| 4.75 | 8-09* | 101:20 | 101:22 | 3.65 |
| 6.63 | 9-09 | 115:25 | 115:27 | 3.91 |
| 7.00 | 3-10 | 118:10 | 118:12 | 4.03 |
| 6.88 | 9-10 | 117:18 | 117:20 | 4.17 |
| 5.63 | 3-11 | 109:06 | 109:08 | 4.28 |
| 5.88 | 3-11 | 108:02 | 108:04 | 4.67 |
| 6.00 | 6-11 | 111:19 | 111:21 | 4.34 |
| 6.38 | 8-11* | 106:30 | 107:00 | 4.24 |
| 5.50 | 9-11 | 107:30 | 108:00 | 4.38 |
| 5.75 | 1-12 | 109:21 | 109:23 | 4.43 |
| 6.25 | 3-12* | 106:27 | 106:29 | 4.41 |
| 6.00 | 5-12* | 104:19 | 104:21 | 2.55 |
| 5.13 | 7-12 | 104:22 | 104:24 | 4.51 |
| 5.13 | 8-12* | 100:12 | 100:14 | 4.84 |
| 4.75 | 10-12* | 98:26 | 98:28 | 4.90 |
| 5.25 | 11-12* | 101:06 | 101:08 | 4.95 |
| 6.75 | 9-29 | 115:30 | 116:02 | 5.58 |
| 6.75 | 3-31 | 116:28 | 117:00 | 5.55 |
| 6.25 | 7-32 | 109:30 | 110:02 | 5.55 |

### Federal Farm Credit Bank

| RATE | MAT | BID | ASKED | YLD |
|---|---|---|---|---|
| 3.88 | 12-04 | 103:22 | 103:24 | 1.90 |
| 3.88 | 2-05 | 103:23 | 103:25 | 1.99 |
| 4.88 | 4-05 | 105:02 | 105:04 | 2.53 |
| 2.50 | 11-05 | 100:11 | 100:13 | 2.35 |

### Federal Home Loan Bank

| RATE | MAT | BID | ASKED | YLD |
|---|---|---|---|---|
| 5.38 | 1-04 | 103:28 | 103:30 | 1.37 |
| 4.88 | 4-04 | 104:02 | 104:04 | 1.58 |
| 3.63 | 10-04 | 103:03 | 103:05 | 1.80 |
| 4.13 | 11-04 | 104:00 | 104:02 | 1.88 |
| 4.00 | 2-05 | 104:00 | 104:02 | 2.01 |
| 4.38 | 2-05 | 104:27 | 104:29 | 1.99 |
| 6.88 | 8-05 | 111:14 | 111:16 | 2.30 |
| 5.13 | 3-06 | 108:01 | 108:03 | 2.45 |
| 5.38 | 5-06 | 108:14 | 108:15 | 2.71 |
| 4.88 | 11-06 | 106:30 | 107:00 | 2.94 |
| 4.88 | 2-07 | 106:28 | 106:30 | 3.06 |
| 5.38 | 2-07 | 108:16 | 108:18 | 3.13 |
| 5.80 | 9-08 | 111:04 | 111:06 | 3.59 |
| 6.00 | 5-11 | 108:27 | 108:29 | 4.70 |
| 5.63 | 11-11 | 108:06 | 108:08 | 4.49 |
| 5.75 | 5-12 | 109:26 | 109:28 | 4.45 |

### GNMA Mtge. Issues

| RATE | MAT | BID | ASKED | YLD |
|---|---|---|---|---|
| 4.50 | 30Yr | 95:31 | 96:01 | 5.14 |
| 5.00 | 30Yr | 99:05 | 99:07 | 5.17 |
| 5.50 | 30Yr | 101:25 | 101:27 | 5.15 |
| 6.00 | 30Yr | 103:24 | 103:26 | 4.76 |
| 6.50 | 30Yr | 104:24 | 104:26 | 3.73 |
| 7.00 | 30Yr | 105:25 | 105:27 | 2.51 |
| 7.50 | 30Yr | 106:16 | 106:18 | 2.35 |
| 8.00 | 30Yr | 107:26 | 107:28 | 2.72 |
| 8.50 | 30Yr | 108:10 | 108:12 | 3.35 |

### Tennessee Valley Authority

| RATE | MAT | BID | ASKED | YLD |
|---|---|---|---|---|
| 4.75 | 7-04 | 104:15 | 104:17 | 1.72 |
| 6.38 | 6-05 | 109:26 | 109:28 | 2.20 |
| 5.38 | 11-08 | 109:00 | 109:02 | 3.64 |
| 5.63 | 1-11 | 108:22 | 108:24 | 4.32 |
| 6.75 | 11-25 | 114:29 | 115:00 | 5.58 |
| 7.13 | 5-30 | 121:13 | 121:17 | 5.58 |

Source: *The Wall Street Journal*, January 6, 2003. Reprinted by permission of *The Wall Street Journal*, 2003 Dow Jones & Company, Inc. All Rights Reserved Worldwide.

an agency neared default. Thus these securities are considered extremely safe assets, and their yield spread above Treasury securities is usually small.

**CONCEPT CHECK QUESTION 2**

Using Figure 2.3 and 2.4, compare the yields to maturity of some agency bonds with that of a Treasury bond of the same maturity date.

## International Bonds

Many firms borrow abroad and many investors buy bonds from foreign issuers. In addition to national capital markets, there is a thriving international capital market, largely centered in London.

A *Eurobond* is a bond denominated in a currency other than that of the country in which it is issued. For example, a dollar-denominated bond sold in Britain would be called a Eurodollar bond. Similarly, investors might speak of Euroyen bonds, yen-denominated bonds sold outside Japan. Since the new European currency is called the euro, the term Eurobond may be confusing. It is best to think of them simply as international bonds.

In contrast to bonds that are issued in foreign currencies, many firms issue bonds in foreign countries but in the currency of the investor. For example, a Yankee bond is a dollar-denominated bond sold in the United States by a non-U.S. issuer. Similarly, Samurai bonds are yen-denominated bonds sold in Japan by non-Japanese issuers.

## Municipal Bonds

**Municipal bonds** are issued by state and local governments. They are similar to Treasury and corporate bonds except that their interest income is exempt from federal income taxation. The interest income also is exempt from state and local taxation in the issuing state. Capital gains taxes, however, must be paid on "munis" when the bonds mature or if they are sold for more than the investor's purchase price.

There are basically two types of municipal bonds. These are *general obligation* bonds, which are backed by the "full faith and credit" (i.e., the taxing power) of the issuer, and *revenue bonds*, which are issued to finance particular projects and are backed either by the revenues from that project or by the particular municipal agency operating the project. Typical issuers of revenue bonds are airports, hospitals, and turnpike or port authorities. Obviously, revenue bonds are riskier in terms of default than general obligation bonds.

An *industrial development bond* is a revenue bond that is issued to finance commercial enterprises, such as the construction of a factory that can be operated by a private firm. In effect, these private-purpose bonds give the firm access to the municipality's ability to borrow at tax-exempt rates.

Like Treasury bonds, municipal bonds vary widely in maturity. A good deal of the debt issued is in the form of short-term *tax anticipation notes*, which raise funds to pay for expenses before actual collection of taxes. Other municipal debt is long term and used to fund large capital investments. Maturities range up to 30 years.

The key feature of municipal bonds is their tax-exempt status. Because investors pay neither federal nor state taxes on the interest proceeds, they are willing to accept lower yields on these securities. These lower yields represent a huge savings to state and local governments. Correspondingly, they constitute a huge drain of potential tax revenue from the federal government, and the government has shown some dismay over the explosive increase in use of industrial development bonds.

By the mid-1980s, Congress became concerned that these bonds were being used to take advantage of the tax-exempt feature of municipal bonds rather than as a source of funds for publicly desirable investments. The Tax Reform Act of 1986 placed new restrictions on the issuance of tax-exempt bonds. Since 1988, each state is allowed to issue mortgage revenue and private-purpose tax-exempt bonds only up to a limit of $50 per capita or $150 million, whichever is larger. In fact, the outstanding amount of industrial revenue bonds stopped growing after 1986, as evidenced in Figure 2.5.

An investor choosing between taxable and tax-exempt bonds must compare after-tax returns on each bond. An exact comparison requires a computation of after-tax rates of return that explicitly accounts for taxes on income and realized capital gains. In practice, there is a simpler rule of thumb. If we let $t$ denote the investor's marginal tax bracket and $r$ denote the total before-tax rate of return available on taxable bonds, then $r(1 - t)$ is the after-tax rate available on those securities. If this value exceeds the rate on municipal bonds, $r_m$, the investor does better holding the taxable bonds. Otherwise, the tax-exempt municipals provide higher after-tax returns.

One way to compare bonds is to determine the interest rate on taxable bonds that would be necessary to provide an after-tax return equal to that of municipals. To derive this value, we set after-tax yields equal, and solve for the **equivalent taxable yield** of the tax-exempt bond. This is the rate a taxable bond must offer to match the after-tax yield on the tax-free municipal.

$$r(1 - t) = r_m \tag{2.1}$$

or

$$r = r_m/(1 - t) \tag{2.2}$$

**Figure 2.5    Tax-exempt debt outstanding**

Source: *Flow of Funds Accounts: Flows and Outstandings*, Washington, D.C.: Board of Governors of the Federal Reserve System, September 2002.

**Table 2.2    Equivalent Taxable Yields Corresponding to Various Tax-Exempt Yields**

| | Tax-Exempt Yield | | | | |
|---|---|---|---|---|---|
| Marginal Tax Rate | 1% | 2% | 3% | 4% | 5% |
| 20% | 1.25% | 2.50% | 3.75% | 5.00% | 6.25% |
| 30 | 1.43 | 2.86 | 4.29 | 5.71 | 7.14 |
| 40 | 1.67 | 3.33 | 5.00 | 6.67 | 8.33 |
| 50 | 2.00 | 4.00 | 6.00 | 8.00 | 10.00 |

Thus the equivalent taxable yield is simply the tax-free rate divided by $1 - t$. Table 2.2 presents equivalent taxable yields for several municipal yields and tax rates.

This table frequently appears in the marketing literature for tax-exempt mutual bond funds because it demonstrates to high-tax-bracket investors that municipal bonds offer highly attractive equivalent taxable yields. Each entry is calculated from equation 2.2. If the equivalent taxable yield exceeds the actual yields offered on taxable bonds, the investor is better off after taxes holding municipal bonds. Notice that the equivalent taxable interest rate increases with the investor's tax bracket; the higher the bracket, the more valuable the tax-exempt feature of municipals. Thus high-tax-bracket investors tend to hold municipals.

We also can use equation 2.1 or 2.2 to find the tax bracket at which investors are indifferent between taxable and tax-exempt bonds. The cutoff tax bracket is given by solving equation 2.2 for the tax bracket at which after-tax yields are equal. Doing so, we find that

$$t = 1 - \frac{r_m}{r} \qquad (2.3)$$

Thus the yield ratio $r_m/r$ is a key determinant of the attractiveness of municipal bonds. The higher the yield ratio, the lower the cutoff tax bracket, and the more individuals will prefer to hold municipal debt. Figure 2.6 graphs the yield ratio since 1955.

**Figure 2.6   Ratio of yields on tax-exempt to taxable bonds**

Source: Data from Moody's Investors Service.

| EXAMPLE 2.1 | **Taxable versus Tax-Exempt Yields** |
| --- | --- |

Figure 2.6 shows that in recent years, the ratio of tax-exempt to taxable yields has fluctuated around .75. What does this imply about the cutoff tax bracket above which tax-exempt bonds provide higher after-tax yields? Equation 2.3 shows that an investor whose tax bracket (federal plus local) exceeds $1 - .75 = .25$, or 25%, will derive a greater after-tax yield from municipals. Note, however, that it is difficult to control precisely for differences in the risks of these bonds, so the cutoff tax bracket must be taken as approximate.

| **CONCEPT CHECK☞ QUESTION 3** | **Suppose your tax bracket is 30%. Would you prefer to earn a 6% taxable return or a 4% tax-free return? What is the equivalent taxable yield of the 4% tax-free yield?** |
| --- | --- |

**Corporate Bonds**   Corporate bonds are the means by which private firms borrow money directly from the public. These bonds are similar in structure to Treasury issues—they typically pay semiannual coupons over their lives and return the face value to the bondholder at maturity. They differ most importantly from Treasury bonds in degree of risk. Default risk is a real consideration in the purchase of corporate bonds, and Chapter 14 discusses this issue in considerable detail. For now, we distinguish only among *secured bonds*, which have specific collateral backing them in the event of firm bankruptcy; unsecured bonds, called *debentures*, which have no collateral; and *subordinated debentures,* which have a lower-priority claim to the firm's assets in the event of bankruptcy.

Corporate bonds often come with options attached. *Callable bonds* give the firm the option to repurchase the bond from the holder at a stipulated call price. *Convertible bonds* give the bondholder the option to convert each bond into a stipulated number of shares of stock. These options are treated in more detail in Chapter 14.

Figure 2.7 is a partial listing of corporate bond prices from *The Wall Street Journal.* The listings are similar to those for Treasury bonds. The highlighted AT&T bond listed has a coupon rate of 7¾% and a maturity date of 2007. Only 54 bonds traded on this particular day. The closing price of the bond was 106% of par, or $1,060, which was lower than the previous day's close by .50% of par value.

The **current yield** on a bond is annual coupon income per dollar invested in the bond. For this AT&T bond, the current yield is thus

$$\text{Current yield} = \frac{\text{Annual coupon income}}{\text{Price}} = \frac{77.50}{1,060} = .073, \text{ or } 7.3\%$$

Note that current yield ignores the difference between the price of a bond and its eventual value at maturity and is a different measure than yield to maturity. The differences are explored in Part 4.

## Mortgages and Mortgage-Backed Securities

An investments text of 30 years ago probably would not include a section on mortgage loans, because investors could not invest in these loans. Now, because of the explosion in mortgage-backed securities, almost anyone can invest in a portfolio of mortgage loans, and these securities have become a major component of the fixed-income market.

**Figure 2.7
Corporate bond
listings**

### U.S. Exchange Bonds

4 p.m. ET Friday, January 3, 2003

**Explanatory Notes**

For New York and American Bonds
Yield is Current yield.
**cv**-Convertible bond. **cf**-Certificates. **cld**-Called. **dc**-Deep discount. **ec**-European currency units. **f**-Dealt in flat. **li**-Italian lire. **kd**-Danish kroner. **m**-Matured bonds, negotiability impaired by maturity. **na**-No accrual. **r**-Registered. **rp**-Reduced principal. **st, sd**-Stamped. **t**-Floating rate. **wd**-When distributed. **ww**-With warrants. **x**-Ex interest. **xw**-Without warrants. **zr**-Zero coupon.
**vj**-In bankruptcy or receivership or being reorganized under the Bankruptcy Act, or securities assumed by such companies.

### NEW YORK BONDS
**Corporation Bonds**

| BONDS | CUR YLD | VOL | CLOSE | NET CHG |
|---|---|---|---|---|
| AES Cp 4½05 | cv | 20 | 48 | 0.25 |
| AES Cp 8s8 | 14.0 | 160 | 57 | ... |
| AT&T 5½04 | 5.5 | 8 | 101.50 | ... |
| AT&T 6½04 | 6.3 | 384 | 102 | ... |
| AT&T 7½04 | 7.3 | 45 | 103.38 | -0.88 |
| AT&T 7s05 | 6.8 | 163 | 102.50 | -0.88 |
| AT&T 7½06 | 7.2 | 70 | 104.50 | -1.00 |
| ATT 7¾07 | 7.3 | 54 | 106 | 0.50 |
| AT&T 6s09 | 6.1 | 190 | 97.75 | -1.00 |
| AT&T 6½13 | 6.7 | 190 | 97.50 | ... |
| AT&T 8½22 | 8.3 | 220 | 97.88 | -0.13 |
| AT&T 8½24 | 8.3 | 5 | 97.63 | -0.38 |
| ATT 8.35s25 | 8.4 | 128 | 99.75 | 1.13 |
| AT&T 6½29 | 7.5 | 309 | 86.13 | ... |
| AT&T 8½31 | 8.6 | 205 | 99.75 | ... |
| ATTBdb 8½13 | 7.5 | 81 | 111.38 | -0.63 |
| ATTBdb 9.45s22 | 8.0 | 435 | 117.38 | 1.38 |
| AllmerF 7s25 | - | 5 | 66 | ... |
| BellsoT 6¾04 | 6.1 | 20 | 104.63 | ... |

| BONDS | CUR YLD | VOL | CLOSE | NET CHG |
|---|---|---|---|---|
| Hilton 5s06 | cv | 1 | 96 | -0.50 |
| Honywll zr05 | ... | 10 | 88.25 | -0.38 |
| KCS En 8⅞06 | 11.8 | 75 | 75.50 | ... |
| K&B Hm 7¾04 | 7.5 | 5 | 103 | -0.75 |
| Leucadia 7¾13 | 7.6 | 25 | 101.75 | -0.13 |
| Loews 3½07 | cv | 45 | 92.88 | 2.88 |
| LgIsLt 8.2s23 | 7.9 | 10 | 104 | 0.38 |
| Lucent 7½06 | 12.3 | 644 | 59 | 1.63 |
| Lucent 5½08 | 11.0 | 379 | 50.25 | 1.75 |
| Lucent 6½28 | 14.6 | 127 | 44.38 | -0.50 |
| Lucent 6.45s29 | 14.1 | 133 | 45.75 | 1.25 |
| MBNA 8.28s26 | 8.4 | 72 | 98.38 | -0.50 |
| Malan 9½04 | cv | 15 | 96.88 | -1.13 |
| McDnl 7⅜33 | 7.2 | 3 | 102 | 0.75 |
| MPac 4¾20f | ... | 2 | 73 | -1.00 |
| MPac 4¾30f | ... | 2 | 69 | -2.75 |
| MPac 5s45f | ... | 81 | 65.50 | 0.25 |
| Monon 6s07f | ... | 110 | 103.75 | 3.75 |
| NETelTel 7⅞22 | 7.6 | 20 | 104 | 0.38 |
| NYTel 7¼24 | 7.1 | 10 | 101.63 | -1.63 |
| NYTel 6½05 | 6.1 | 5 | 106.13 | -0.25 |
| NYTel 4⅞06 | 4.8 | 176 | 100.75 | -0.38 |
| NYTel 6.70s23 | 6.8 | 5 | 98.13 | -0.13 |
| NYTel 7s33 | 6.9 | 8 | 101.50 | -0.25 |
| Noram 6s12 | cv | 6 | 72 | -0.25 |
| ParkerD 5½04 | cv | 100 | 93.75 | 1.25 |
| PhilPt 6.65s03 | 6.6 | 12 | 100.03 | -0.38 |
| PhilPt 7.92s23 | 7.6 | 5 | 103.75 | 0.13 |
| PhilPt 7.2s23 | 7.0 | 5 | 103.50 | -0.50 |
| PhilIP 7⅛28 | 6.6 | 67 | 107.75 | 3.00 |
| PSvEG 7s24 | 6.9 | 10 | 101.75 | -0.88 |
| ReynTob 7⅝03 | 7.6 | 26 | 100.78 | 0.25 |
| ReynTob 8¾07 | 8.4 | 5 | 104.50 | 0.63 |
| ReynTob 9¼13 | 8.7 | 15 | 106.50 | 0.50 |
| RoyCarib zr2-21 | ... | 18 | 38.63 | 1.63 |
| Ryder 9s16 | 8.3 | 2 | 108.88 | 3.63 |
| Safwy 9.65s04 | 9.0 | 50 | 106.75 | 0.75 |
| SearsAc 6¾05 | 6.5 | 24 | 103.25 | 0.25 |
| SilicnGr 5¼04 | cv | 5 | 61 | 1.00 |
| Solectrn zrM20 | ... | 1 | 60.25 | 0.13 |
| Sprint 6⅞28 | 8.5 | 10 | 80.50 | 0.38 |
| TVA 7¼30 | 7.2 | 20 | 107 | -1.30 |
| TVA 8¼42 | 6.9 | 5 | 119.88 | 0.88 |
| Tenet 5⅜06 | 5.7 | 197 | 94.13 | 0.38 |

Until the 1970s, almost all home mortgages were written for a long term (15- to 30-year maturity), with a fixed interest rate over the life of the loan, and with equal fixed monthly payments. These so-called conventional mortgages are still the most popular, but a diverse set of alternative mortgage designs has developed.

Fixed-rate mortgages have posed difficulties to lenders in years of increasing interest rates. Because banks and thrift institutions traditionally issued short-term liabilities (the deposits of their customers) and held long-term assets such as fixed-rate mortgages, they suffered losses when interest rates increased and the rates paid on deposits increased while mortgage income remained fixed.

The *adjustable-rate mortgage* was a response to this interest rate risk. These mortgages require the borrower to pay an interest rate that varies with some measure of the current market interest rate. For example, the interest rate might be set at 2 percentage points above the current rate on 1-year Treasury bills and might be adjusted once a year. Usually, the contract sets a limit, or cap, on the maximum size of an interest rate change within a year and over the life of the contract. The adjustable-rate contract shifts much of the risk of fluctuations in interest rates from the lender to the borrower.

Because of the shifting of interest rate risk to their customers, lenders are willing to offer lower rates on adjustable-rate mortgages than on conventional fixed-rate mortgages. This can be a great inducement to borrowers during a period of high interest rates. As interest rates fall, however, conventional mortgages typically regain popularity.

A *mortgage-backed security* is either an ownership claim in a pool of mortgages or an obligation that is secured by such a pool. These claims represent securitization of mortgage loans. Mortgage lenders originate loans and then sell packages of these loans in the secondary market. Specifically, they sell their claim to the cash inflows from the mortgages as those loans are paid off. The mortgage originator continues to service the loan, collecting principal and interest payments, and passes these payments along to the purchaser of the mortgage. For this reason, these mortgage-backed securities are called *pass-throughs*.

For example, suppose that ten 30-year mortgages, each with a principal value of $100,000, are grouped together into a million-dollar pool. If the mortgage rate is 10%, then the first month's payment for each loan would be $877.57, of which $833.33 would be interest and $44.24 would be principal repayment. The holder of the mortgage pool would receive a payment in the first month of $8,775.70, the total payments of all 10 of the mortgages in the pool.[1] In addition, if one of the mortgages happens to be paid off in any month, the holder of the pass-through security also receives that payment of principal. In future months, of course, the pool will comprise fewer loans, and the interest and principal payments will be lower. The prepaid mortgage in effect represents a partial retirement of the pass-through holder's investment.

---

[1] Actually, the institution that services the loan and the pass-through agency that guarantees the loan each retain a portion of the monthly payment as a charge for their services. Thus the interest rate received by the pass-through investor is a bit less than the interest rate paid by the borrower. For example, although the 10 homeowners together make total monthly payments of $8,775.70, the holder of the pass-through security may receive a total payment of only $8,340.

Mortgage-backed pass-through securities were first introduced by the Government National Mortgage Association (GNMA, or Ginnie Mae) in 1970. GNMA pass-throughs carry a guarantee from the U.S. government that ensures timely payment of principal and interest, even if the borrower defaults on the mortgage. This guarantee increases the marketability of the pass-through. Thus investors can buy or sell GNMA securities like any other bond.

Other mortgage pass-throughs have since become popular. These are sponsored by FNMA (Federal National Mortgage Association, or Fannie Mae) and FHLMC (Federal Home Loan Mortgage Corporation, or Freddie Mac). As of late 2002, roughly $3.0 trillion of mortgages were securitized into mortgage-backed securities. This makes the mortgage-backed securities market bigger than the $2.7 trillion corporate bond market and almost the size of the $3.2 trillion market in Treasury securities. Figure 2.8 illustrates the explosive growth of mortgage-backed securities since 1979.

The success of mortgage-backed pass-throughs has encouraged introduction of pass-through securities backed by other assets. For example, the Student Loan Marketing Association (SLMA, or Sallie Mae) sponsors pass-throughs backed by loans originated under the Guaranteed Student Loan Program and by other loans granted under various federal programs for higher education.

Although pass-through securities often guarantee payment of interest and principal, they do not guarantee the rate of return. Holders of mortgage pass-throughs therefore can be severely disappointed in their returns in years when interest rates drop significantly. This is because homeowners usually have an option to prepay, or pay ahead of schedule, the remaining principal outstanding on their mortgages.

**Figure 2.8    Mortgage-backed securities outstanding, 1979–2002**

Source: *Flow of Funds Accounts of the United States,* Washington D.C.: Board of Governors of the Federal Reserve System, September 2002.

## 2.3   EQUITY SECURITIES

**Common Stock as Ownership Shares**

*Common stocks*, also known as *equity securities* or **equities,** represent ownership shares in a corporation. Each share of common stock entitles its owner to one vote on any matters of corporate governance that are put to a vote at the corporation's annual meeting and to a share in the financial benefits of ownership.[2]

The corporation is controlled by a board of directors elected by the shareholders. The board, which meets only a few times each year, selects managers who actually run the corporation on a day-to-day basis. Managers have the authority to make most business decisions without the board's specific approval. The board's mandate is to oversee the management to ensure that it acts in the best interests of shareholders.

The members of the board are elected at the annual meeting. Shareholders who do not attend the annual meeting can vote by *proxy,* empowering another party to vote in their name. Management usually solicits the proxies of shareholders and normally gets a vast majority of these proxy votes. Thus, management usually has considerable discretion to run the firm as it sees fit—without daily oversight from the equityholders who actually own the firm.

We noted in Chapter 1 that such separation of ownership and control can give rise to "agency problems," in which managers pursue goals not in the best interests of shareholders. However, there are several mechanisms designed to alleviate these agency problems. Among these are: compensation schemes that link the success of the manager to that of the firm; oversight by the board of directors as well as outsiders such as security analysts, creditors, or large institutional investors; the threat of a proxy contest in which unhappy shareholders attempt to replace the current management team; or the threat of a takeover by another firm.

The common stock of most large corporations can be bought or sold freely on one or more stock exchanges. A corporation whose stock is not publicly traded is said to be closely held. In most closely held corporations, the owners of the firm also take an active role in its management. Therefore, takeovers are generally not an issue.

**Characteristics of Common Stock**

The two most important characteristics of common stock as an investment are its **residual claim** and **limited liability** features.

Residual claim means that stockholders are the last in line of all those who have a claim on the assets and income of the corporation. In a liquidation of the firm's assets the shareholders have a claim to what is left after all other claimants such as the tax authorities, employees, suppliers, bondholders, and other creditors have been paid. For a firm not in liquidation, shareholders have claim to the part of operating income left over after interest and taxes have been paid. Management can either pay this residual as cash dividends to shareholders or reinvest it in the business to increase the value of the shares.

Limited liability means that the most shareholders can lose in the event of failure of the corporation is their original investment. Unlike owners of unincorporated businesses, whose creditors can lay claim to the personal assets of the owner (house, car, furniture), corporate shareholders may at worst have worthless stock. They are not personally liable for the firm's obligations.

---

[2] A corporation sometimes issues two classes of common stock, one bearing the right to vote, the other not. Because of its restricted rights, the nonvoting stock might sell for a lower price.

CONCEPT
CHECK☞
QUESTION 4

*a.* If you buy 100 shares of IBM stock, to what are you entitled?

*b.* What is the most money you can make on this investment over the next year?

*c.* If you pay $50 per share, what is the most money you could lose over the year?

**Stock Market Listings**  Figure 2.9 is a partial listing from *The Wall Street Journal* of stocks traded on the New York Stock Exchange. The NYSE is one of several markets in which investors may buy or sell shares of stock. We will examine these markets in detail in Chapter 3.

To interpret the information provided for each stock, consider the highlighted listing for General Electric. The first column indicates that GE shares have so far increased by 4.3% this year. The next two columns give the highest and lowest prices at which the stock has traded over the last 52 weeks, $41.84 and $21.40, respectively. The .76 figure means that the last quarter's dividend was $.19 a share, which is consistent with annual dividend payments of $.19 × 4 = $.76. This corresponds to a dividend yield of 3.0%: since GE is selling at $25.40 (the last recorded or "close" price in the next-to-last column), the dividend yield is .76/25.40 = .030, or 3.0%.

The dividend yield on the stock is like the current yield on a bond. Both look at the current income as a percentage of the price. Both ignore prospective **capital gains** (i.e., price increases) or losses and therefore do not correspond to total rates of return. Low-dividend firms presumably offer greater prospects for capital gains, or investors would not be willing to hold these firms in their portfolios. If you scan Figure 2.9, you will see that dividend yields vary widely across companies.

**Figure 2.9   Stock market listings**

## NEW YORK STOCK EXCHANGE COMPOSITE TRANSACTIONS

| YTD %CHG | 52-WEEK HI | LO | STOCK (SYM) | DIV | YLD % | PE | VOL 100s | CLOSE | NET CHG | YTD %CHG | 52-WEEK HI | LO | STOCK (SYM) | DIV | YLD % | PE | VOL 100s | CLOSE | NET CHG |
|---|---|---|---|---|---|---|---|---|---|---|---|---|---|---|---|---|---|---|---|
| 0.2 | 29.99 | 21.65♦ | Energen EGN | .72 | 2.5 | 17 | 1220 | 29.15 | -0.05 | 2.3 | 38.80 | 27.10 | GenuinePart GPC | 1.16 | 3.7 | 18 | 2802 | 31.50 | -0.11 |
| 1.3 | 31.92 | 18.50 | EnrgzrHldg ENR | ... | ... | 14 | 3557 | 28.25 | -0.34 | 0.7 | 27.20 | 17.20 | GA Gulf GGC | .32 | 1.4 | 46 | 920 | 23.31 | -0.49 |
| 5.5 | 14.85 | 2.10 | GenICbI BGC | ... | ... | dd | 2022 | 4.01 | -0.04 | 4.0 | 33.88 | 6.51 | ICN Pharm ICN | .31 | 2.7 | 30 | 3505 | 11.35 | -0.14 |
| 2.3 | 111.18 | 73.25 | GenDynam GD | 1.20 | 1.5 | 16 | 7208 | 81.20 | 0.30 | 0.1 | 40.99 | 20.87 | IDACORP IDA | 1.86 | 7.5 | 11 | 1451 | 24.85 | 0.05 |
| -0.5 | 26.90 | 24.25 | GEC PINES 6.625 n | 1.66 | 6.3 | ... | 596 | 26.52 | -0.28 | -2.3 | 23.32 | 15.05♦ | IDT Cp IDT | ... | ... | dd | 2246 | 16.90 | -0.30 |
| 4.3 | 41.84 | 21.40 | GenElec GE | .76f | 3.0 | 16 | 148191 | 25.40 | -0.08 | -2.3 | 20.35 | 13.09♦ | IDT B IDTB | ... | ... | ... | 962 | 15.15 | 0.20 |
| -0.7 | 52.29 | 38.72 | GenGrthProp GGP | 2.88 | 5.6 | ... | 2448 | 51.62 | 0.22 | 0.4 | 36.46 | 21.08♦ | IHOP Cp IHP | ... | ... | 13 | 543 | 24.09 | -0.42 |
| -0.7 | 14.20 | 4.78 | GenMaritime GMR | ... | ... | cc | 439 | 7.40 | -0.09 | 4.2 | 14.25 | 6.38 | IKON IKN | .16 | 2.1 | 8 | 3530 | 7.45 | 0.20 |
| 1.2 | 51.10 | 37.38 | GenMills GIS | 1.10 | 2.3 | 30 | 11457 | 47.50 | -0.15 | -0.2 | 15.55 | 8.52 | IMC GlbI IGL | .08 | .8 | dd | 5156 | 10.65 | -0.13 |
| 4.6 | 68.17 | 30.80 | GenMotor GM | 2.00 | 5.2 | 18 | 59475 | 38.54 | -0.41 | 0.1 | 11.55 | 4.95♦ | IMCO Recyc IMR | ... | ... | 58 | 327 | 8.14 | -0.39 |
| 5.1 | 17.55 | 8 | GenMotor H GMH | ... | ... | ... | 15895 | 11.25 | 0.12 | 4.0 | 22.59 | 12.90 | IMS Hlth RX | .08 | .5 | 28 | 15355 | 16.64 | 0.04 |
| 1.6 | 29 | 21.35 | GM DebA GXM n | .55p | ... | ... | 452 | 24.65 | -0.02 | 3.3 | 27.75 | 12.76 | ING Grp ADS ING | .90e | 5.2 | ... | 3414 | 17.40 | -0.30 |
| 3.0 | 30.20 | 19.51 | GM DebB GBM n | .64p | ... | ... | 12353 | 23.79 | 0.17 | 0.4 | 25.38 | 25 | ING Groep INZ n | ... | ... | ... | 2613 | 25.37 | 0.07 |
| -1.8 | 28.30 | 10.65 | Genesco GCO | ... | ... | 12 | 1644 | 18.29 | -0.70 | 0.1 | 25.70 | 24.05 | INGGroep IND n | .72e | 2.9 | ... | 254 | 25.14 | -0.01 |
| 1.3 | 26.30 | 15.70 | GeneseWY A GWR s | ... | ... | 15 | 177 | 20.61 | 0.06 | 6.9 | 6.50 | 3.50 | IRSA GDR IRS | b | ... | ... | 120 | 5.45 | 0.20 |

The P/E ratio, or **price-earnings ratio,** is the ratio of the current stock price to last year's earnings per share. The P/E ratio tells us how much stock purchasers must pay per dollar of earnings that the firm generates. For GE, the ratio of price to earnings is 16. The P/E ratio also varies widely across firms. Where the dividend yield and P/E ratio are not reported in Figure 2.9 the firms have zero dividends, or zero or negative earnings. We shall have much to say about P/E ratios in Chapter 18.

The sales column shows that 148,191 hundred shares of the stock were traded. Shares commonly are traded in round lots of 100 shares each. Investors who wish to trade in smaller "odd lots" generally must pay higher commissions to their stockbrokers. The last, or closing, price of $25.40 was down $.08 from the closing price of the previous day.

## Preferred Stock

**Preferred stock** has features similar to both equity and debt. Like a bond, it promises to pay to its holder a fixed amount of income each year. In this sense preferred stock is similar to an infinite-maturity bond, that is, a perpetuity. It also resembles a bond in that it does not convey voting power regarding the management of the firm. Preferred stock is an equity investment, however. The firm retains discretion to make the dividend payments to the preferred stockholders; it has no contractual obligation to pay those dividends. Instead, preferred dividends are usually *cumulative;* that is, unpaid dividends cumulate and must be paid in full before any dividends may be paid to holders of common stock. In contrast, the firm does have a contractual obligation to make the interest payments on the debt. Failure to make these payments sets off corporate bankruptcy proceedings.

Preferred stock also differs from bonds in terms of its tax treatment for the firm. Because preferred stock payments are treated as dividends rather than interest, they are not tax-deductible expenses for the firm. This disadvantage is somewhat offset by the fact that corporations may exclude 70% of dividends received from domestic corporations in the computation of their taxable income. Preferred stocks therefore make desirable fixed-income investments for some corporations.

Even though preferred stock ranks after bonds in terms of the priority of its claims to the assets of the firm in the event of corporate bankruptcy, preferred stock often sells at lower yields than do corporate bonds. Presumably, this reflects the value of the dividend exclusion, because the higher risk of preferred would tend to result in higher yields than those offered by bonds. Individual investors, who cannot use the 70% exclusion, generally will find preferred stock yields unattractive relative to those on other available assets.

Preferred stock is issued in variations similar to those of corporate bonds. It may be callable by the issuing firm, in which case it is said to be *redeemable*. It also may be convertible into common stock at some specified conversion ratio. A relatively recent innovation is adjustable-rate preferred stock, which, similar to adjustable-rate bonds, ties the dividend to current market interest rates.

## 2.4  STOCK AND BOND MARKET INDEXES

### Stock Market Indexes

The daily performance of the Dow Jones Industrial Average is a staple portion of the evening news report. Although the Dow is the best-known measure of the performance of the stock market, it is only one of several indicators. Other more broadly based indexes are computed and published daily. In addition, several indexes of bond market performance are widely available.

The ever-increasing role of international trade and investments has made indexes of foreign financial markets part of the general news. Thus foreign stock exchange indexes such as the Nikkei Average of Tokyo and the Financial Times index of London are fast becoming household names.

**Dow Jones Averages**    The Dow Jones Industrial Average (DJIA) of 30 large, "blue-chip" corporations has been computed since 1896. Its long history probably accounts for its preeminence in the public mind. (The average covered only 20 stocks until 1928.)

Originally, the DJIA was calculated as the simple average of the stocks included in the index. Thus, if there were 30 stocks in the index, one would add up the prices of the 30 stocks and divide by 30. The percentage change in the DJIA would then be the percentage change in the average price of the 30 shares.

This procedure means that the percentage change in the DJIA measures the return (excluding dividends) on a portfolio that invests one share in each of the 30 stocks in the index. The value of such a portfolio (holding one share of each stock in the index) is the sum of the 30 prices. Because the percentage change in the *average* of the 30 prices is the same as the percentage change in the *sum* of the 30 prices, the index and the portfolio have the same percentage change each day.

Because the Dow measures the return (excluding dividends) on a portfolio that holds one share of each stock, it is called a **price-weighted average.** The amount of money invested in each company represented in the portfolio is proportional to that company's share price.

## EXAMPLE 2.2    Price-Weighted Average

Consider the data in Table 2.3 for a hypothetical two-stock version of the Dow Jones Average. Stock ABC sells initially at $25 a share, while XYZ sells for $100. Therefore, the initial value of the index would be $(25 + 100)/2 = 62.5$. The final share prices are $30 for stock ABC and $90 for XYZ, so the average falls by 2.5 to $(30 + 90)/2 = 60$. The 2.5 point drop in the index is a 4% decrease: $2.5/62.5 = .04$. Similarly, a portfolio holding one share of each stock would have an initial value of $25 + $100 = $125 and a final value of $30 + $90 = $120, for an identical 4% decrease.

Notice that price-weighted averages give higher-priced shares more weight in determining performance of the index. For example, although ABC increased by 20%, while XYZ fell by only 10%, the index dropped in value. This is because the 20% increase in ABC represented a smaller price gain ($5 per share) than the 10% decrease in XYZ ($10 per share). The "Dow portfolio" has four times as much invested in XYZ as in ABC because XYZ's price is four times that of ABC. Therefore, XYZ dominates the average.

You might wonder why the DJIA is now (in mid 2003) at a level of about 9,000 if it is supposed to be the average price of the 30 stocks in the index. The DJIA no longer equals the average price of the 30 stocks because the averaging procedure is adjusted whenever a stock splits or pays a stock dividend of more than 10%, or when one company in the group of 30 industrial firms is replaced by another. When these events occur, the divisor used to compute the "average price" is adjusted so as to leave the index unaffected by the event.

**Table 2.3   Data to Construct Stock Price Indexes**

| Stock | Initial Price | Final Price | Shares (million) | Initial Value of Outstanding Stock ($ million) | Final Value of Outstanding Stock ($ million) |
|-------|---------------|-------------|------------------|-----------------------------------------------|----------------------------------------------|
| ABC   | $ 25          | $30         | 20               | $500                                          | $600                                         |
| XYZ   | 100           | 90          | 1                | 100                                           | 90                                           |
| TOTAL |               |             |                  | $600                                          | $690                                         |

**Table 2.4   Data to Construct Stock Price Indexes after a Stock Split**

| Stock | Initial Price | Final Price | Shares (million) | Initial Value of Outstanding Stock ($ million) | Final Value of Outstanding Stock ($ million) |
|-------|---------------|-------------|------------------|-----------------------------------------------|----------------------------------------------|
| ABC   | $25           | $30         | 20               | $500                                          | $600                                         |
| XYZ   | 50            | 45          | 2                | 100                                           | 90                                           |
| TOTAL |               |             |                  | $600                                          | $690                                         |

## EXAMPLE 2.3   Splits and Price-Weighted Averages

Suppose XYZ were to split two for one so that its share price fell to $50. We would not want the average to fall, as that would incorrectly indicate a fall in the general level of market prices. Following a split, the divisor must be reduced to a value that leaves the average unaffected. Table 2.4 illustrates this point. The initial share price of XYZ, which was $100 in Table 2.3, falls to $50 if the stock splits at the beginning of the period. Notice that the number of shares outstanding doubles, leaving the market value of the total shares unaffected. The divisor, $d$, which originally was 2.0 when the two-stock average was initiated, must be reset to a value that leaves the "average" unchanged. Because the sum of the post-split stock prices is 75, while the presplit average price was 62.5, we calculate the new value of $d$ by solving $75/d = 62.5$. The value of $d$, therefore, falls from its original value of 2.0 to $75/62.5 = 1.20$, and the initial value of the average is unaffected by the split: $75/1.20 = 62.5$.

At period-end, ABC will sell for $30, while XYZ will sell for $45, representing the same negative 10% return it was assumed to earn in Table 2.3. The new value of the price-weighted average is $(30 + 45)/1.20 = 62.5$. The index is unchanged, so the rate of return is zero, rather than the $-4\%$ return that would be calculated in the absence of a split.

This return is greater than that calculated in the absence of a split. The relative weight of XYZ, which is the poorer-performing stock, is reduced by a split because its initial price is lower; hence the performance of the average is higher. This example illustrates that the implicit weighting scheme of a price-weighted average is somewhat arbitrary, being determined by the prices rather than by the outstanding market values (price per share times number of shares) of the shares in the average.

# DOW JONES INDUSTRIAL AVERAGE: CHANGES SINCE OCTOBER 1, 1928

| Oct. 1, 1928 | 1929 | 1930s | 1940s | 1950s | 1960s | 1970s | 1980s | 1990s | Nov. 1, 1999 |
|---|---|---|---|---|---|---|---|---|---|
| Wright Aeronautical | Curtiss-Wright ('29) | Hudson Motor ('30)<br>Coca-Cola ('32)<br>National Steel ('35) | | Aluminum Co. of America ('59) | | | | | Alcoa* ('99) |
| Allied Chemical & Dye | | | | | | | Allied Signal* ('85) | | Honeywell |
| North American | | Johns-Manville ('30) | | | | | Amer. Express ('82) | | American Express |
| Victor Talking Machine | Natl Cash Register ('29) | IBM ('32)<br>AT&T ('39) | | | | | | | AT&T |
| International Nickel | | | | | | Inco Ltd.* ('76) | Boeing ('87) | | Boeing |
| International Harvester | | | | | | | Navistar* ('86) | Caterpillar ('91) | Caterpillar |
| Westinghouse Electric | | | | | | | | Travelers Group ('97) | Citigroup* ('98) |
| Texas Gulf Sulphur | | Intl. Shoe ('32)<br>United Aircraft ('33)<br>National Distillers ('34) | | Owens-Illinois ('59) | | | Coca-Cola ('87) | | Coca-Cola |
| American Sugar | | Borden ('30)<br>DuPont ('35) | | | | | | | DuPont |
| American Tobacco (B) | | Eastman Kodak ('30) | | | | | | | Eastman Kodak |
| Standard Oil (N.J.) | | | | | | Exxon* ('72) | | | ExxonMobil |
| General Electric | | | | | | | | | General Electric |
| General Motors | | | | | | | | | General Motors |
| Texas Corp. | | | | Texaco* ('59) | | | | Hewlett-Packard ('97) | Hewlett-Packard |
| Sears Roebuck | | | | | | | | | Home Depot |
| Chrysler | | | | | | IBM ('79) | | | IBM |
| Atlantic Refining | | Goodyear ('30) | | | | | | | Intel† |
| Paramount Publix | | Loew's ('32) | | Intl. Paper ('56) | | | | | International Paper |
| Bethlehem Steel | | | | | | | | Johnson & Johnson ('97) | Johnson & Johnson |
| General Railway Signal | | Liggett & Myers ('30)<br>Amer. Tobacco ('32) | | | | | McDonald's ('85) | | McDonald's |
| Mack Trucks | | Drug Inc. ('32)<br>Corn Products ('33) | | Swift & Co. ('59) | | Esmark* ('73)<br>Merck ('79) | | | Merck |
| Union Carbide | | | | | | | | | Microsoft |
| American Smelting | | | | Anaconda ('59) | | Minn. Mining ('76) | | | Minn. Mining (3M) |
| American Can | | | | | | | Primerica* ('87) | J.P. Morgan ('91) | J.P. Morgan |
| Postum Inc. | General Foods* ('29) | | | | | | Philip Morris ('85) | | Philip Morris |
| Nash Motors | | United Air Trans. ('30)<br>Procter & Gamble ('32) | | | | | | | Procter & Gamble |
| Goodrich | | Standard Oil (Calif) ('30) | | | | | Chevron* ('84) | | SBC Communications |
| Radio Corp. | | Nash Motors ('32)<br>United Aircraft ('39) | | | | United Tech.* ('75) | | | United Technologies |
| Woolworth | | | | | | | | Wal-Mart Stores ('97) | Wal-Mart Stores |
| U.S. Steel | | | | | | | USX Corp.* ('86) | Walt Disney ('91) | Walt Disney |

Note: Year of change shown in ( ); * denotes name change, in some cases following a takeover or merger. To track changes in the components, begin in the column for 1928 and work across. For instance, American Sugar was replaced by Borden in 1930, which in turn was replaced by Du Pont in 1935. Unlike past changes, each of the last four new stocks added doesn't specifically replace any of the departing stocks; it's simply a four-for-four switch. Home Depot has been grouped as replacing Sears because of their shared industry, but the other three incoming stocks are designated alphabetically next to a departing stock.

Source: From *The Wall Street Journal,* October 27, 1999. Reprinted by permission of Dow Jones & Company, Inc. via Copyright Clearance Center, Inc. © 1999. Dow Jones & Company, Inc. All Rights Reserved Worldwide.

Because the Dow Jones Averages are based on small numbers of firms, care must be taken to ensure that they are representative of the broad market. As a result, the composition of the average is changed every so often to reflect changes in the economy. The last change took place on November 1, 1999, when Microsoft, Intel, Home Depot, and SBC Communications were added to the index and Chevron, Goodyear Tire & Rubber, Sears Roebuck, and Union Carbide were dropped. The nearby box presents the history of the firms in the index since 1928. The fate of many companies once considered "the bluest of the blue chips" is striking evidence of the changes in the U.S. economy in the last 70 years.

In the same way that the divisor is updated for stock splits, if one firm is dropped from the average and another firm with a different price is added, the divisor has to be updated to leave the average unchanged by the substitution. By 2003, the divisor for the Dow Jones Industrial Average had fallen to a value of about .146.

| CONCEPT CHECK☞ QUESTION 5 | Suppose XYZ in Table 2.3 increases in price to $110, while ABC falls to $20. Find the percentage change in the price-weighted average of these two stocks. Compare that to the percentage return of a portfolio that holds one share in each company. |
|---|---|

Dow Jones & Company also computes a Transportation Average of 20 airline, trucking, and railroad stocks; a Public Utility Average of 15 electric and natural gas utilities; and a Composite Average combining the 65 firms of the three separate averages. Each is a price-weighted average, and thus overweights the performance of high-priced stocks.

**Standard & Poor's Indexes**    The Standard & Poor's Composite 500 (S&P 500) stock index represents an improvement over the Dow Jones Averages in two ways. First, it is a more broadly based index of 500 firms. Second, it is a **market-value-weighted index.** In the case of the firms XYZ and ABC in Example 2.2, the S&P 500 would give ABC five times the weight given to XYZ because the market value of its outstanding equity is five times larger, $500 million versus $100 million.

The S&P 500 is computed by calculating the total market value of the 500 firms in the index and the total market value of those firms on the previous day of trading. The percentage increase in the total market value from one day to the next represents the increase in the index. The rate of return of the index equals the rate of return that would be earned by an investor holding a portfolio of all 500 firms in the index in proportion to their market values, except that the index does not reflect cash dividends paid by those firms.

**EXAMPLE 2.4    Value-Weighted Indexes**

To illustrate how value-weighted indexes are computed, look again at Table 2.3. The final value of all outstanding stock in our two-stock universe is $690 million. The initial value was $600 million. Therefore, if the initial level of a market-value-weighted index of stocks ABC and XYZ were set equal to an arbitrarily chosen starting value such as 100, the index value at year-end would be $100 \times (690/600) = 115$. The increase in the index reflects the 15% return earned on a portfolio consisting of those two stocks held in proportion to outstanding market values.

Unlike the price-weighted index, the value-weighted index gives more weight to ABC. Whereas the price-weighted index fell because it was dominated by higher-price XYZ, the value-weighted index rises because it gives more weight to ABC, the stock with the higher total market value.

Note also from Tables 2.3 and 2.4 that market-value-weighted indexes are unaffected by stock splits. The total market value of the outstanding XYZ stock increases from $100 million to $110 million regardless of the stock split, thereby rendering the split irrelevant to the performance of the index.

A nice feature of both market-value-weighted and price-weighted indexes is that they reflect the returns to straightforward portfolio strategies. If one were to buy each share in the index in proportion to its outstanding market value, the value-weighted index would perfectly track capital gains on the underlying portfolio. Similarly, a price-weighted index tracks the returns on a portfolio comprised of equal shares of each firm.

Investors today can purchase shares in mutual funds that hold shares in proportion to their representation in the S&P 500 or another index. These **index funds** yield a return equal to that of the index and so provide a low-cost passive investment strategy for equity investors.

Standard & Poor's also publishes a 400-stock Industrial Index, a 20-stock Transportation Index, a 40-stock Utility Index, and a 40-stock Financial Index.

| CONCEPT CHECK☞ QUESTION 6 | Reconsider companies XYZ and ABC from Concept Check 5. Calculate the percentage change in the market-value-weighted index. Compare that to the rate of return of a portfolio that holds $500 of ABC stock for every $100 of XYZ stock (i.e., an index portfolio). |
|---|---|

### Other U.S. Market-Value Indexes

The New York Stock Exchange publishes a market-value-weighted composite index of all NYSE-listed stocks, in addition to subindexes for industrial, utility, transportation, and financial stocks. These indexes are even more broadly based than the S&P 500. The National Association of Securities Dealers publishes an index of 4,000 over-the-counter (OTC) firms traded on the Nasdaq market.

The ultimate U.S. equity index so far computed is the Wilshire 5000 index of the market value of all NYSE and American Stock Exchange (Amex) stocks plus actively traded Nasdaq stocks. Despite its name, the index actually includes about 7,000 stocks. Figure 2.10 reproduces a *Wall Street Journal* listing of stock index performance. Vanguard offers an index mutual fund, the Total Stock Market Portfolio, that enables investors to match the performance of the Wilshire 5000 index, and a small stock portfolio that matches the MSCI U.S. small-capitalization 1750 index.

### Equally Weighted Indexes

Market performance is sometimes measured by an equally weighted average of the returns of each stock in an index. Such an averaging technique, by placing equal weight on each return, corresponds to an implicit portfolio strategy that places equal dollar values on each stock. This is in contrast to both price weighting (which requires equal numbers of shares of each stock) and market value weighting (which requires investments in proportion to outstanding value).

Unlike price- or market-value-weighted indexes, equally weighted indexes do not correspond to buy-and-hold portfolio strategies. Suppose that you start with equal dollar

**Figure 2.10
Performance of
stock indexes**

## Major Stock Indexes

| Dow Jones Averages | DAILY HIGH | DAILY LOW | DAILY CLOSE | DAILY NET CHG | DAILY % CHG | 52-WEEK HIGH | 52-WEEK LOW | 52-WEEK % CHG | YTD % CHG |
|---|---|---|---|---|---|---|---|---|---|
| 30 Industrials | 8635.49 | 8552.87 | 8601.69 | − 5.83 | −0.07 | 10635.25 | 7286.27 | −16.16 | +3.12 |
| 20 Transportations | 2375.50 | 2358.11 | 2364.94 | − 7.81 | −0.33 | 3049.96 | 2013.02 | −16.44 | +2.38 |
| 15 Utilities | 222.15 | 219.50 | 221.20 | + 1.42 | +0.65 | 310.75 | 167.57 | −24.81 | +2.80 |
| 65 Composite | 2451.51 | 2431.02 | 2443.26 | − 0.26 | −0.01 | 3093.84 | 2033.44 | −17.95 | +2.88 |
| **Nasdaq Stock Market** | | | | | | | | | |
| Composite | 1389.44 | 1374.61 | 1387.08 | + 2.23 | +0.16 | 2059.38 | 1114.11 | −32.65 | +3.86 |
| Nasdaq 100 | 1033.37 | 1018.16 | 1031.63 | + 3.77 | +0.37 | 1675.03 | 804.64 | −38.41 | +4.80 |
| Biotech | 511.44 | 504.96 | 506.44 | − 3.39 | −0.66 | 884.53 | 403.98 | −42.74 | +1.93 |
| Computer | 654.32 | 645.53 | 654.14 | + 3.62 | +0.56 | 1070.28 | 503.26 | −38.76 | +5.07 |
| Telecommunications | 113.56 | 112.03 | 113.19 | − 0.61 | −0.54 | 245.54 | 81.43 | −53.90 | +4.04 |
| **Standard & Poor's Indexes** | | | | | | | | | |
| 500 Index | 910.99 | 903.23 | 908.59 | − 0.44 | −0.05 | 1172.51 | 776.76 | −22.51 | +3.27 |
| MidCap 400 | 441.54 | 438.03 | 439.34 | − 2.20 | −0.50 | 550.38 | 372.88 | −15.19 | +2.22 |
| SmallCap 600 | 201.78 | 200.11 | 200.11 | − 1.67 | −0.83 | 257.81 | 170.73 | −15.71 | +1.77 |
| SuperComp 1500 | 200.89 | 199.15 | 200.26 | − 0.22 | −0.11 | 256.74 | 171.10 | −21.76 | +3.14 |
| **New York Stock Exchange** | | | | | | | | | |
| Composite | 487.74 | 483.97 | 486.16 | − 0.57 | −0.12 | 609.53 | 421.09 | −18.51 | +2.81 |
| Industrials | 601.55 | 596.71 | 599.29 | − 1.39 | −0.23 | 763.43 | 532.91 | −19.21 | +2.63 |
| Finance | 527.03 | 523.14 | 525.63 | + 0.21 | +0.04 | 622.09 | 437.72 | −12.72 | +2.97 |
| **Others** | | | | | | | | | |
| Russell 2000 | 392.58 | 389.75 | 390.31 | − 2.27 | −0.58 | 522.95 | 327.04 | −21.83 | +1.88 |
| Wilshire 5000 | 8618.41 | 8548.73 | 8593.22 | − 8.02 | −0.09 | 10953.64 | 7342.84 | −21.40 | +3.00 |
| Value Line | 271.94 | 270.14 | 270.70 | − 1.14 | −0.42 | 382.26 | 219.50 | −28.46 | +2.55 |
| Amex Composite | 838.32 | 833.56 | 837.63 | + 4.02 | +0.48 | 962.69 | 771.87 | − 0.45 | +1.61 |

Source: *The Wall Street Journal*, January 6, 2003. Reprinted by permission of *The Wall Street Journal*, © 2003 Dow Jones & Company, Inc. All Rights Reserved Worldwide.

investments in the two stocks of Table 2.3, ABC and XYZ. Because ABC increases in value by 20% over the year while XYZ decreases by 10%, your portfolio no longer is equally weighted. It is now more heavily invested in ABC. To reset the portfolio to equal weights, you would need to rebalance: sell off some ABC stock and/or purchase more XYZ stock. Such rebalancing would be necessary to align the return on your portfolio with that on the equally weighted index.

**Foreign and International Stock Market Indexes**   Development in financial markets worldwide includes the construction of indexes for these markets. Among these are the Nikkei (Japan), FTSE (U.K.; pronounced "footsie"), DAX (Germany), Hang Seng (Hong Kong), and TSX (Canada).

A leader in the construction of international indexes has been MSCI (Morgan Stanley Capital International), which computes over 50 country indexes and several regional indexes. Table 2.5 presents many of the indexes computed by MSCI.

**Bond Market Indicators**   Just as stock market indexes provide guidance concerning the performance of the overall stock market, several bond market indicators measure the performance of various categories of bonds. The three most well-known groups of indexes are those of Merrill Lynch, Lehman Brothers, and Salomon Smith Barney (now Citigroup). Table 2.6, Panel A, lists the components of the bond market at the end of 2002. Panel B presents a profile of the characteristics of the three major bond indexes.

## Table 2.5    Sample of MSCI Stock Indexes

| Regional Indexes | | Countries | |
|---|---|---|---|
| **Developed Markets** | **Emerging Markets** | **Developed Markets** | **Emerging Markets** |
| EAFE (Europe, Australia, Far East) | Emerging Markets (EM) | Australia | Argentina |
| EASEA (EAFE ex Japan) | EM Asia | Austria | Brazil |
| Europe | EM Far East | Belgium | Chile |
| European Monetary Union (EMU) | EM Latin America | Canada | China |
| Far East | Emerging Markets Free (EMF) | Denmark | Colombia |
| Kokusai (World ex Japan) | EMF Asia | Finland | Czech Republic |
| Nordic Countries | EMF Eastern Europe | France | Egypt |
| North America | EMF Europe | Germany | Greece |
| Pacific | EMF Europe & Middle East | Hong Kong | Hungary |
| The World Index | EMF Far East | Ireland | India |
| G7 countries | EMF Latin America | Italy | Indonesia |
| World ex U.S. | | Japan | Israel |
| | | Netherlands | Jordan |
| | | New Zealand | Korea |
| | | Norway | Malaysia |
| | | Portugal | Mexico |
| | | Singapore | Morocco |
| | | Spain | Pakistan |
| | | Sweden | Peru |
| | | Switzerland | Philippines |
| | | U.K. | Poland |
| | | U.S. | Russia |
| | | | South Africa |
| | | | Sri Lanka |
| | | | Taiwan |
| | | | Thailand |
| | | | Turkey |
| | | | Venezuela |

Source: www.msci.com

The major problem with these indexes is that true rates of return on many bonds are difficult to compute because the infrequency with which the bonds trade make reliable up-to-date prices difficult to obtain. In practice, some prices must be estimated from bond valuation models. These "matrix" prices may differ from true market values.

## 2.5    DERIVATIVE MARKETS

One of the most significant developments in financial markets in recent years has been the growth of futures, options, and related derivatives markets. These instruments provide pay-offs that depend on the values of other assets such as commodity prices, bond and stock prices, or market index values. For this reason these instruments sometimes are called **derivative assets,** or **contingent claims.** Their values derive from or are contingent on the values of other assets.

**Options**    A **call option** gives its holder the right to purchase an asset for a specified price, called the **exercise** or **strike price,** on or before a specified expiration

## Table 2.6    The U.S. Fixed-Income Market and Its Indexes

**A. The fixed-income market**

| Sector | Size ($ billion) | % of Market |
|---|---|---|
| Treasury | $ 3,213.3 | 22.9% |
| Government-sponsored enterprise | 2,199.6 | 15.6 |
| Corporate | 2,673.4 | 19.0 |
| Tax-exempt* | 1,441.8 | 10.3 |
| Mortgage-backed | 3,041.8 | 21.6 |
| Asset-backed | 1,489.9 | 10.6 |
| *TOTAL* | $14,059.8 | 100.0% |

**B. Profile of bond indexes**

| | Lehman Brothers | Merrill Lynch | Salomon Smith Barney |
|---|---|---|---|
| Number of issues | Over 6,500 | Over 5,000 | Over 5,000 |
| Maturity of included bonds | $\geq 1$ year | $\geq 1$ year | $\geq 1$ year |
| Excluded issues | Junk bonds | Junk bonds | Junk bonds |
| | Convertibles | Convertibles | Convertibles |
| | Floating rate | | Floating rate |
| Weighting | Market value | Market value | Market value |
| Reinvestment of intramonth cash flows | No | Yes (in specific bond) | Yes (at one-month T-bill rate) |
| Daily availability | Yes | Yes | Yes |

*Includes private purpose tax-exempt debt.

Source: *Panel A: Flow of Funds Accounts, Flows and Outstandings,* Board of Governors of the Federal Reserve System, September 2002. *Panel B:* Frank K. Reilly, G. Wenchi Kao, and David J. Wright, "Alternative Bond Market Indexes," *Financial Analysts Journal* (May–June 1992), pp. 44–58.

date. For example, a January call option on IBM stock with an exercise price of $80 entitles its owner to purchase IBM stock for a price of $80 at any time up to and including the expiration date in January. Each option contract is for the purchase of 100 shares. However, quotations are made on a per-share basis. The holder of the call need not exercise the option; it will be profitable to exercise only if the market value of the asset that may be purchased exceeds the exercise price.

When the market price exceeds the exercise price, the option holder may "call away" the asset for the exercise price and reap a payoff equal to the difference between the stock price and the exercise price. Otherwise, the option will be left unexercised. If not exercised before the expiration date of the contract, the option simply expires and no longer has value. Calls therefore provide greater profits when stock prices increase and thus represent bullish investment vehicles.

In contrast, a **put option** gives its holder the right to sell an asset for a specified exercise price on or before a specified expiration date. A January put on IBM with an exercise price of $80 thus entitles its owner to sell IBM stock to the put writer at a price of $80 at any time before expiration in January, even if the market price of IBM is lower than $80. Whereas profits on call options increase when the asset increases in value, profits on put options increase when the asset value falls. The put is exercised only if its holder can deliver an asset worth less than the exercise price in return for the exercise price.

Figure 2.11 presents stock option quotations from *The Wall Street Journal*. The highlighted options are for IBM. The repeated number under the name of the firm is the current price of IBM shares, $81.65. The two columns to the right of IBM give the exercise price

Figure 2.11
Options market
listings

# LISTED OPTIONS QUOTATIONS

| OPTION/STRIKE | | EXP | -CALL- VOL | LAST | -PUT- VOL | LAST | OPTION/STRIKE | | EXP | -CALL- VOL | LAST | -PUT- VOL | LAST | OPTION/STRIKE | | EXP | -CALL- VOL | LAST | -PUT- VOL | LAST |
|---|---|---|---|---|---|---|---|---|---|---|---|---|---|---|---|---|---|---|---|---|
| Bk of Am | 65 | Jan | 11 | 5.30 | 680 | 0.30 | 28.63 | 22.50 | Apr | ... | ... | 1083 | 0.90 | Qualcom | 35 | Jan | 889 | 1.80 | 2040 | 1.20 |
| 70.24 | 70 | Jan | 1417 | 1.55 | 567 | 1.45 | 28.63 | 25 | Jan | ... | ... | 2314 | 0.20 | 35.70 | 37.50 | Jan | 1837 | 0.65 | 605 | 2.60 |
| 70.24 | 70 | May | 1776 | 4.90 | 1755 | 5.20 | 28.63 | 25 | Feb | ... | ... | 1100 | 0.60 | 35.70 | 40 | Jan | 1038 | 0.20 | 355 | 4.40 |
| Bemis | 45 | Feb | ... | ... | 943 | 0.50 | 28.63 | 30 | Jan | 2620 | 0.20 | 8 | 1.65 | QstDiag | 60 | Jan | 666 | 1.50 | 500 | 2.30 |
| BestBuy | 20 | Jan | 3 | 4.40 | 1175 | 0.15 | iShSm600 | 100 | Jan | 988 | 1.70 | ... | ... | QwestCom | 5 | Jan | 255 | 0.55 | 1112 | 0.20 |
| 23.86 | 22.50 | Jan | 97 | 1.85 | 911 | 0.55 | IntgDv | 10 | May | 1200 | 0.80 | ... | ... | RF MicD | 7.50 | Jan | 1425 | 0.90 | 108 | 0.30 |
| 23.86 | 22.50 | Feb | 27 | 2.80 | 927 | 1.50 | Intel | 15 | Jan | 1342 | 1.75 | 598 | 0.30 | RJReyn | 42.50 | Jan | 38 | 0.90 | 2686 | 1.90 |
| 23.86 | 25 | Jan | 1786 | 0.60 | 482 | 1.75 | 16.52 | 17.50 | Jan | 18573 | 0.40 | 1228 | 1.40 | RetailHT | 70 | Jan | 855 | 1.30 | 511 | 1.90 |
| 23.86 | 25 | Feb | 233 | 1.55 | 1205 | 2.70 | 16.52 | 17.50 | Feb | 2120 | 0.90 | 107 | 2 | RockwlAut | 22.50 | Jul | 4700 | 1.50 | ... | ... |
| Biovail | 25 | Feb | 20 | 5.40 | 1032 | 1.20 | 16.52 | 17.50 | Apr | 686 | 1.55 | 269 | 2.60 | SBC Cm | 30 | Jan | 1513 | 0.25 | 78 | 1.75 |
| 29.00 | 30 | Jan | 836 | 0.90 | ... | ... | InterMune | 22.50 | Jan | 10 | 3.70 | 660 | 0.85 | Schering | 22.50 | Jan | 612 | 1 | 734 | 0.40 |
| Boeing | 35 | Jan | 652 | 0.50 | 10 | 1.35 | I B M | 60 | Apr | 1 | 22 | 1385 | 1.10 | 23.12 | 25 | Jan | 778 | 0.15 | 1 | 2 |
| BostSc | 17.50 | Feb | 957 | 1 | 10 | 4.50 | 81.65 | 70 | Jan | 139 | 11.80 | 825 | 0.35 | Schlmb | 50 | Jan | 1650 | 0.10 | 150 | 7 |
| 43.80 | 45 | Jan | 683 | 0.70 | 360 | 1.95 | 81.65 | 75 | Jan | 208 | 7.60 | 1044 | 0.90 | Schwab | 12.50 | Jan | 1189 | 0.15 | 12 | 1.10 |
| 43.80 | 45 | Jan | 2578 | 1.90 | 19 | 2.95 | 81.65 | 80 | Jan | 4457 | 3.60 | 1637 | 2.05 | Sears | 15 | Apr | 1880 | 9.30 | 360 | 0.55 |
| BrMySq | 22.50 | Jan | 220 | 2.30 | 1184 | 0.20 | 81.65 | 80 | Feb | 257 | 5.30 | 1157 | 3.70 | SemiHTr | 20 | Jan | 521 | 3.80 | 1808 | 0.15 |
| 24.75 | 25 | Jan | 3072 | 0.60 | 658 | 0.90 | 81.65 | 85 | Jan | 3484 | 1.20 | 381 | 4.70 | 24.05 | 22.50 | Jan | 751 | 2.05 | 557 | 0.50 |
| 24.75 | 25 | Feb | 838 | 1.25 | 165 | 1.60 | 81.65 | 90 | Jan | 1475 | 0.25 | 24 | 9 | 24.05 | 25 | Jan | 3055 | 0.60 | 552 | 1.55 |
| Brocade | 5 | Jan | 1202 | 0.15 | 213 | 0.60 | Intersil | 15 | Jan | 683 | 0.65 | 15 | 1.25 | SiebelSys | 7.50 | Jan | 1956 | 0.65 | 215 | 0.25 |
| Cadence | 10 | Feb | 7519 | 0.50 | 8218 | 1.25 | Intuit | 45 | Jan | 1507 | 2.90 | 55 | 0.95 | SP Fncl | 20 | Mar | ... | ... | 1000 | 0.40 |
| CardnlHl | 50 | Mar | ... | ... | 1418 | 1.20 | Invitrogn | 32.50 | May | 1650 | 2.55 | ... | ... | Starbcks | 22.50 | Feb | 1547 | 0.45 | 10 | 1.55 |
| CarMax | 17.50 | Jan | ... | ... | 698 | 0.90 | JDS Uni | 2.50 | Jan | 681 | 0.35 | 21 | 0.10 | 21.12 | 22.50 | Apr | 1102 | 1 | ... | ... |
| Celgene | 25 | Apr | 953 | 1.75 | ... | ... | JPMorgCh | 17.50 | Jan | 14 | 8.10 | 971 | 0.05 | SunMicro | 5 | Apr | 801 | 0.25 | 17 | 1.70 |
| Cendant | 10 | Feb | 43 | 1.75 | 3336 | 0.60 | 25.94 | 22.50 | Jan | 857 | 3.50 | 706 | 0.15 | Synops | 45 | Jan | 776 | 0.55 | 761 | 3.20 |

Source: *The Wall Street Journal*, January 6, 2003. Reprinted by permission of *The Wall Street Journal*, © 2003 Dow Jones & Company, Inc. All Rights Reserved Worldwide.

and expiration month of each option. Thus we see that the paper reports data on call and put options on IBM with exercise prices ranging from $60 to $90 per share and with expiration dates in January, February, and April. These exercise prices bracket the current price of IBM shares.

The next four columns provided trading volume and closing prices of each option. For example, 4,457 contracts traded on the January expiration call with an exercise price of $80. The last trade price was $3.60, meaning that an option to purchase one share of IBM at an exercise price of $80 sold for $3.60. Each option *contract*, therefore, cost $360.

Notice that the prices of call options decrease as the exercise price increases. For example, the January maturity call with exercise price $85 costs only $1.20. This makes sense, because the right to purchase a share at a higher exercise price is less valuable. Conversely, put prices increase with the exercise price. The right to sell a share of IBM at a price of $80 in January cost $2.05 while the right to sell at $85 cost $4.70.

Option prices also increase with time until expiration. Clearly, one would rather have the right to buy IBM for $80 at any time until February rather than at any time until January. Not surprisingly, this shows up in a higher price for the February expiration options. For example, the call with exercise price $80 expiring in February sells for $5.30, compared to only $3.60 for the January call.

**CONCEPT CHECK ☞ QUESTION 7**

What would be the profit or loss per share of stock to an investor who bought the January maturity IBM call option with exercise price $80 if the stock price at the expiration of the option is $84? What about a purchaser of the put option with the same exercise price and maturity?

**Futures Contracts**   A **futures contract** calls for delivery of an asset (or in some cases, its cash value) at a specified delivery or maturity date for an agreed-upon price, called the futures price, to be paid at contract maturity. The *long position* is held by the trader who commits to purchasing the asset on the delivery date. The trader who takes the *short position* commits to delivering the asset at contract maturity.

Figure 2.12 illustrates the listing of several stock index futures contracts as they appear in *The Wall Street Journal*. The top line in boldface type gives the contract name, the exchange on which the futures contract is traded in parentheses, and the contract size. Thus the third contract listed is for the S&P 500 index, traded on the Chicago Mercantile Exchange (CME). Each contract calls for delivery of $250 times the value of the S&P 500 stock price index.

The next several rows detail price data for contracts expiring on various dates. The March 2003 maturity contract opened during the day at a futures price of 907.50 per unit of the index. (Decimal points are left out to save space.) The last line of the entry shows that the S&P 500 index was at 908.59 at close of trading on the day of the listing. The highest futures price during the day was 910.70, the lowest was 901.70, and the settlement price (a representative trading price during the last few minutes of trading) was 909.90. The settlement price increased by 2.50 from the previous trading day. The highest and lowest

**Figure 2.12**
**Financial futures listings**

**Index Futures**

| | OPEN | HIGH | LOW | SETTLE | CHG | LIFETIME HIGH | LIFETIME LOW | OPEN INT |
|---|---|---|---|---|---|---|---|---|
| **DJ Industrial Average** (CBT)-$10 x index | | | | | | | | |
| Mar | 8591 | 8620 | 8535 | 86(4 | 13 | 10400 | 7170 | 25,758 |
| Est vol 9,673; vol Thu 22,927; open int 76,094, +1,991. | | | | | | | | |
| Idx prl: Hi 8635.49; Lo 8552.87; Close 8501.69, -5.83. | | | | | | | | |
| **Mini DJ Industrial Average** (CBT)-$5 x index | | | | | | | | |
| Mar | 8586 | 8621 | 8535 | 8618 | 23 | 9019 | 7268 | 582 |
| Vol Thu 19,570; open int 9,807, +354. | | | | | | | | |
| **S&P 500 Index** (CME)-$250 x index | | | | | | | | |
| Mar | 90750 | 91070 | 90170 | 90990 | 250 | 140160 | 76750 | 572,944 |
| June | 90400 | 91000 | 90200 | 90940 | 250 | 113200 | 77060 | 14,668 |
| Est vol 53,375; vol Thu 58,934; open int 590,793, +6,467. | | | | | | | | |
| Idx prl: Hi 911.25; Lo 903.07; Close 908.59, -.44. | | | | | | | | |
| **Mini S&P 500** (CME)-$50 x index | | | | | | | | |
| Mar | 90750 | 91075 | 90175 | 91000 | 250 | 95350 | 76900 | 210,665 |
| Vol Thu 469,692; open int 210,957, +27,382. | | | | | | | | |
| **S&P Midcap 400** (CME)-$500 x index | | | | | | | | |
| Mar | 441.50 | 442.00 | 437.80 | 441.50 | ... | 563.50 | 372.75 | 13,802 |
| Est vol 756; vol Thu 978; open int 13,802, -19. | | | | | | | | |
| Idx prl: Hi 441.54; Lo 438.02; Close 439.34, -2.20. | | | | | | | | |
| **Nasdaq 100** (CME)-$100 x index | | | | | | | | |
| Mar | 102700 | 103700 | 102000 | 103600 | 1100 | 116200 | 81300 | 62,199 |
| Est vol 9,526; vol Thu 12,944; open int 62,244, +1,124. | | | | | | | | |
| Idx prl: Hi 1033.37; Lo 1018.16; Close 1031.63, +3.77. | | | | | | | | |
| **Mini Nasdaq 100** (CME)-$20 x index | | | | | | | | |
| Mar | 1026.5 | 1037.5 | 1020.0 | 1036.0 | 11.0 | 1159.0 | 807.0 | 125,234 |
| Vol Thu 214,633; open int 125,240, +7,036. | | | | | | | | |
| **GSCI** (CME)-$250 x nearby index | | | | | | | | |
| Jan | 242.30 | 247.20 | 242.00 | 246.50 | 5.70 | 247.20 | 202.50 | 15,585 |
| Est vol 134; vol Thu 169; open int 15,640, +9. | | | | | | | | |
| Idx prl: Hi 247.34; Lo 242.27; Close 246.88, +6.03. | | | | | | | | |
| **Russell 2000** (CME)-$500 x index | | | | | | | | |
| Mar | 392.00 | 392.50 | 388.50 | 392.25 | .75 | 529.50 | 326.85 | 25,391 |
| Est vol 2,106; vol Thu 3,212; open int 25,391, +87. | | | | | | | | |
| Idx prl: Hi 392.58; Lo 389.75; Close 390.31, -2.27. | | | | | | | | |
| **Russell 1000** (NYFE)-$500 x index | | | | | | | | |
| Mar | 480.00 | 482.00 | 478.00 | 481.50 | 1.00 | 492.50 | 460.25 | 58,785 |
| Est vol 1,411; vol Thu 680; open int 60,841, -109. | | | | | | | | |
| Idx prl: Hi 482.46; Lo 478.43; Close 481.15, -.22. | | | | | | | | |

Source: *The Wall Street Journal*, January 6, 2003. Reprinted by permission of *The Wall Street Journal*, © 2003 Dow Jones & Company, Inc. All Rights Reserved Worldwide.

futures prices over the contract's life to date have been 1,401.60 and 767.50, respectively. Finally, open interest, or the number of outstanding contracts, was 572,944. Corresponding information is given for each maturity date.

The trader holding the long position profits from price increases. Suppose that at expiration the S&P 500 index is at 912.90. Because each contract calls for delivery of $250 times the index, ignoring brokerage fees, the profit to the long position who entered the contract at a futures price of 909.90 would equal $250 \times (912.90 - 909.90) = $750. Conversely, the short position must deliver $250 times the value of the index for the previously agreed-upon futures price. The short position's loss equals the long position's profit.

The right to purchase the asset at an agreed-upon price, as opposed to the obligation, distinguishes call options from long positions in futures contracts. A futures contract *obliges* the long position to purchase the asset at the futures price; the call option, in contrast, *conveys the right* to purchase the asset at the exercise price. The purchase will be made only if it yields a profit.

Clearly, a holder of a call has a better position than does the holder of a long position on a futures contract with a futures price equal to the option's exercise price. This advantage, of course, comes only at a price. Call options must be purchased; futures contracts may be entered into without cost. The purchase price of an option is called the *premium*. It represents the compensation the holder of the call must pay for the ability to exercise the option only when it is profitable to do so. Similarly, the difference between a put option and a short futures position is the right, as opposed to the obligation, to sell an asset at an agreed-upon price.

## SUMMARY

1. Money market securities are very short-term debt obligations. They are usually highly marketable and have relatively low credit risk. Their low maturities and low credit risk ensure minimal capital gains or losses. These securities trade in large denominations, but they may be purchased indirectly through money market funds.

2. Much of U.S. government borrowing is in the form of Treasury bonds and notes. These are coupon-paying bonds usually issued at or near par value. Treasury notes and bonds are similar in design to coupon-paying corporate bonds.

3. Municipal bonds are distinguished largely by their tax-exempt status. Interest payments (but not capital gains) on these securities are exempt from federal income taxes. The equivalent taxable yield offered by a municipal bond equals $r_m/(1 - t)$, where $r_m$ is the municipal yield and $t$ is the investor's tax bracket.

4. Mortgage pass-through securities are pools of mortgages sold in one package. Owners of pass-throughs receive the principal and interest payments made by the borrowers. The originator that issued the mortgage merely services the mortgage, simply "passing through" the payments to the purchasers of the mortgage. A federal agency may guarantee the payment of interest and principal on mortgages pooled into these pass-through securities.

5. Common stock is an ownership share in a corporation. Each share entitles its owner to one vote on matters of corporate governance and to a prorated share of the dividends paid to shareholders. Stock, or equity, owners are the residual claimants on the income earned by the firm.

6. Preferred stock usually pays fixed dividends for the life of the firm; it is a perpetuity. A firm's failure to pay the dividend due on preferred stock, however, does not precipitate corporate bankruptcy. Instead, unpaid dividends simply cumulate. Newer varieties of preferred stock include convertible and adjustable-rate issues.

Visit us at www.mhhe.com/bkm

7. Many stock market indexes measure the performance of the overall market. The Dow Jones Averages, the oldest and best-known indicators, are price-weighted indexes. Today, many broad-based, market-value-weighted indexes are computed daily. These include the Standard & Poor's 500 Stock Index, the NYSE index, the Nasdaq index, the Wilshire 5000 Index, and indexes of many non-U.S. stock markets.

8. A call option is a right to purchase an asset at a stipulated exercise price on or before a maturity date. A put option is the right to sell an asset at some exercise price. Calls increase in value while puts decrease in value as the price of the underlying asset increases.

9. A futures contract is an obligation to buy or sell an asset at a stipulated futures price on a maturity date. The long position, which commits to purchasing, gains if the asset value increases while the short position, which commits to purchasing, loses.

## KEY TERMS

| | | |
|---|---|---|
| money market | Treasury bonds | price-weighted average |
| capital markets | yield to maturity | market-value-weighted |
| certificate of deposit | municipal bonds | index |
| commercial paper | equivalent taxable yield | index funds |
| banker's acceptance | current yield | derivative assets |
| Eurodollars | equities | contingent claims |
| repurchase agreements | residual claim | call option |
| federal funds | limited liability | exercise (strike) price |
| London Interbank Offered | capital gains | put option |
| Rate | price-earnings ratio | futures contract |
| Treasury notes | preferred stock | |

## WEBSITES

www.wallpost.com
Look at the variety of *Market Data* links.

www.finpipe.com
Check out the *Markets* links.

www.nyse.com
You can link to introductory information under the *Getting Started* link at the bottom of the page.

www.bloomberg.com
Markets rely on new information from sources like Bloomberg

finance.yahoo.com
This site offers extensive financial market information and excellent company research links.

www.investorwords.com
This site boasts an extensive glossary of investment terms.

*(continued)*

Visit us at www.mhhe.com/bkm

## WEBSITES

www.investinginbonds.com
All about bond markets. See *Bond Glossary* to find any bond-related term.

www.theminingweb.com
Follow the gold and metals market.

The following sites have considerable information about derivatives securities:

www.amex.com
The American Stock Exchange trades a number of derivative securities.

www.cboe.com/LearnCenter
The Chicago Board Options Exchange site has an excellent glossary of terms.

www.commoditytrader.net
Review the information provided to Commodity Trader.com's customers under *Search for Products*.

www.fiafii.org
The Futures Industry Trade Association's *Site Map* provides an orientation to the role of specific industry trade associations.

www.isda.org/index.html
The International Swap and Derivative Association website provides current information, education, and other valuable services to members. Trade associations are useful sources of industry information.

## PROBLEMS

1. A firm's preferred stock often sells at yields below its bonds because:
   a. Preferred stock generally carries a higher agency rating.
   b. Owners of preferred stock have a prior claim on the firm's earnings.
   c. Owners of preferred stock have a prior claim on a firm's assets in the event of liquidation.
   d. Corporations owning stock may exclude from income taxes most of the dividend income they receive.

2. A municipal bond carries a coupon of 6¾% and is trading at par; to a taxpayer in a 34% tax bracket, this bond would provide a taxable equivalent yield of:
   a. 4.5%
   b. 10.2%
   c. 13.4%
   d. 19.9%

CFA®
PROBLEMS

3. Which is the *most risky* transaction to undertake in the stock index option markets if the stock market is expected to increase substantially after the transaction is completed?

    *a.* Write a call option.

    *b.* Write a put option

    *c.* Buy a call option.

    *d.* Buy a put option.

4. Turn back to Figure 2.3 and look at the Treasury note maturing in May 2008.

    *a.* How much would you have to pay to purchase one of these notes?

    *b.* What is its coupon rate?

    *c.* What is the current yield of the note?

5. In what ways is preferred stock like long-term debt? In what ways is it like equity?

6. Why are money market securities sometimes referred to as "cash equivalents"?

7. Suppose investors can earn a return of 2% per 6 months on a Treasury note with 6-months remaining until maturity. What price would you expect a 6-month maturity Treasury bill to sell for?

8. Find the after-tax return to a corporation that buys a share of preferred stock at $40, sells it at year-end at $40, and receives a $4 year-end dividend. The firm is in the 30% tax bracket.

9. Turn to Figure 2.9 and look at the listing for General Mills.

    *a.* What was the firm's closing price *yesterday?*

    *b.* How many shares could you buy for $5,000?

    *c.* What would be your annual dividend income from those shares?

    *d.* What must be its earnings per share?

10. Consider the three stocks in the following table. $P_t$ represents price at time $t$, and $Q_t$ represents shares outstanding at time $t$. Stock C splits two for one in the last period.

| | $P_0$ | $Q_0$ | $P_1$ | $Q_1$ | $P_2$ | $Q_2$ |
|---|---|---|---|---|---|---|
| A | 90 | 100 | 95 | 100 | 95 | 100 |
| B | 50 | 200 | 45 | 200 | 45 | 200 |
| C | 100 | 200 | 110 | 200 | 55 | 400 |

    *a.* Calculate the rate of return on a price-weighted index of the three stocks for the first period ($t = 0$ to $t = 1$).

    *b.* What must happen to the divisor for the price-weighted index in year 2?

    *c.* Calculate the rate of return for the second period ($t = 1$ to $t = 2$).

11. Using the data in Problem 10, calculate the first-period rates of return on the following indexes of the three stocks:

    *a.* A market-value-weighted index.

    *b.* An equally weighted index.

12. An investor is in a 30% tax bracket. If corporate bonds offer 9% yields, what must municipals offer for the investor to prefer them to corporate bonds?

13. Short-term municipal bonds currently offer yields of 4%, while comparable taxable bonds pay 5%. Which gives you the higher after-tax yield if your tax bracket is:

    a. Zero

    b. 10%

    c. 20%

    d. 30%

14. Find the equivalent taxable yield of the municipal bond in the previous problem for tax brackets of zero, 10%, 20%, and 30%.

15. The coupon rate on a tax-exempt bond is 5.6%, and the rate on a taxable bond is 8%. Both bonds sell at par. The tax bracket (marginal tax rate) at which an investor would be indifferent between the two bonds is:

    a. 30.0%

    b. 39.6%

    c. 41.7%

    d. 42.9%

16. Which security should sell at a greater price?

    a. A 10-year Treasury bond with a 9% coupon rate versus a 10-year T-bond with a 10% coupon.

    b. A 3-month maturity call option with an exercise price of $40 versus a 3-month call on the same stock with an exercise price of $35.

    c. A put option on a stock selling at $50, or a put option on another stock selling at $60 (all other relevant features of the stocks and options may be assumed to be identical).

17. Look at the futures listings for the Russell 2000 index in Figure 2.12.

    a. Suppose you buy one contract for March delivery. If the contract closes in March at a level of 430, what will your profit be?

    b. How many March maturity contracts are outstanding?

18. Turn back to Figure 2.11 and look at the Best Buy options. Suppose you buy a January maturity call option with exercise price $22.50.

    a. Suppose the stock price in January is $24.50. Will you exercise your call? What are the profit and rate of return on your position?

    b. What if you had bought the January call with exercise price $25?

    c. What if you had bought a January put with exercise price $22.50?

19. Why do call options with exercise prices greater than the price of the underlying stock sell for positive prices?

20. Both a call and a put currently are traded on stock XYZ; both have strike prices of $50 and maturities of 6 months. What will be the profit to an investor who buys the call for $4 in the following scenarios for stock prices in 6 months? What will be the profit in each scenario to an investor who buys the put for $6?

    a. $40

    b. $45

    c. $50

    d. $55

    e. $60

21. Explain the difference between a put option and a short position in a futures contract.

22. Explain the difference between a call option and a long position in a futures contract.

23. What would you expect to happen to the spread between yields on commercial paper and Treasury bills if the economy were to enter a steep recession?

24. Examine the first 25 stocks listed in the stock market listings for NYSE stocks in your local newspaper. For how many of these stocks is the 52-week high price at least 50% greater than the 52-week low price? What do you conclude about the volatility of prices on individual stocks?

---

Enter the Market Insight database at **www.mhhe.com/business/finance/edumarket insight/** and link to *Company,* then *Population.* Select a company of interest to you and link to the *Company Research* page with a menu of company information reports on the left. Link to the *Company Profile* report and review the information provided. In what market is your company's stock traded? What is the stock ticker symbol? (Remember the ticker to access company information quickly on financial websites.) Finally, what is the industry classification of your company and its major competitors?

---

**E-INVESTMENTS**
**Security Prices and Returns**

Go to **finance.yahoo.com**. What was the return on the S&P 500 today? Chart its value over the last day and the last year. What is the current yield on 10-year maturity Treasury bonds? At what price is IBM stock selling? Find the price of the nearest-to-maturity IBM call option with exercise price equal to IBM's stock price rounded down to the nearest $5. What was the return on the following indexes: Nikkei 225, FTSE 100, DAX?

---

**SOLUTIONS TO CONCEPT CHECKS**

1. The bond sells for 114:23 bid which is a price of 114²³⁄₃₂% of par, or $1,147.1875, and 114:24 asked or $1,147.50. This asked price corresponds to a yield of 3.48%. The asked price rose ⁴⁄₃₂ from its level yesterday, so the asked price then must have been 114:20, or $1,146.25.

2. Compare the August 2012 Treasury note, selling at a yield to maturity of 4.01%, to the August 2012 Fannie Mae bonds, selling at a yield to maturity of 4.86%, the August 2012 Freddie Mac bonds, selling at a yield to maturity of 4.84%, or the May 2012 Federal Home Loan Bank bonds, selling at a yield to maturity of 4.45%. The agency bonds offer a yield premium over the safer Treasury bonds.

3. A 6% taxable return is equivalent to an after-tax return of 6(1 − .30) = 4.2%. Therefore, you would be better off in the taxable bond. The equivalent taxable yield of the tax-free bond is 4/(1 − .30) = 5.71%. So a taxable bond would have to pay a 5.71% yield to provide the same after-tax return as a tax-free bond offering a 4% yield.

4. *a.* You are entitled to a prorated share of IBM's dividend payments and to vote in any of IBM's stockholder meetings.

**SOLUTIONS
TO CONCEPT
CHECKS**
*(Concluded)*

b. Your potential gain is unlimited because IBM's stock price has no upper bound.

c. Your outlay was $50 × 100 = $5,000. Because of limited liability, this is the most you can lose.

5. The price-weighted index increases from 62.5 [i.e., (100 + 25)/2] to 65 [i.e., (110 + 20)/2], a gain of 4%. An investment of one share in each company requires an outlay of $125 that would increase in value to $130, for a return of 4% (i.e., 5/125), which equals the return to the price-weighted index.

6. The market-value-weighted index return is calculated by computing the increase in the value of the stock portfolio. The portfolio of the two stocks starts with an initial value of $100 million + $500 million = $600 million and falls in value to $110 million + $400 million = $510 million, a loss of 90/600 = .15, or 15%. The index portfolio return is a weighted average of the returns on each stock with weights of ⅙ on XYZ and ⅚ on ABC (weights proportional to relative investments). Because the return on XYZ is 10%, while that on ABC is −20%, the index portfolio return is ⅙ × 10% + ⅚ × (−20%) = −15%, equal to the return on the market-value-weighted index.

7. The payoff to the call option is $4 per share at maturity. The option cost is $3.60 per share. The dollar profit is therefore $.40. The put option expires worthless. Therefore, the investor's loss is the cost of the put, or $2.05.

# HOW SECURITIES ARE TRADED

The first time a security trades is when it is issued. Therefore, we begin our examination of trading with a look at how securities are first marketed to the public by investment bankers, the midwives of securities. Then we turn to the various exchanges where already-issued securities can be traded among investors. We examine the competition among the New York Stock Exchange, regional and non-U.S. exchanges, and the Nasdaq market for the patronage of security traders. Next we turn to the mechanics of trading in these various markets. We describe the role of the specialist in exchange markets and the dealer in over-the-counter markets. We also touch briefly on block trading and the SuperDot system of the NYSE for electronically routing orders to the floor of the exchange. We discuss the costs of trading and consider the ongoing debate between the NYSE and its competitors over which market provides the lowest-cost trading arena. Finally, we describe the essentials of specific transactions such as buying on margin and selling stock short

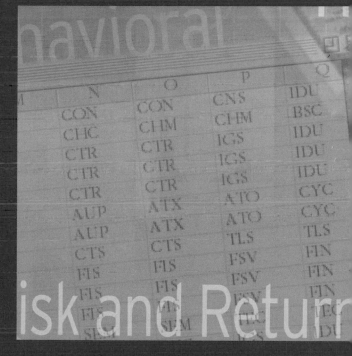

and discuss relevant regulations governing security trading. We will see that some regulations, such as those governing insider trading, can be difficult to interpret in practice.

# 3.1    HOW FIRMS ISSUE SECURITIES

When firms need to raise capital they may choose to sell (or *float*) new securities. These new issues of stocks, bonds, or other securities typically are marketed to the public by investment bankers in what is called the **primary market.** Trading of already-issued securities among private investors takes place in the **secondary market.**

There are two types of primary market issues of common stock. **Initial public offerings,** or *IPOs,* are stocks issued by a formerly privately owned company selling stock to the public for the first time. *Seasoned new issues* are offered by companies that already have floated equity. A sale by IBM of new shares of stock, for example, would constitute a seasoned new issue.

We also distinguish between two types of primary market issues: a *public offering*, which is an issue of stock or bonds sold to the general investing public that can then be traded on the secondary market; and a *private placement,* which is an issue that is sold to a few wealthy or institutional investors at most, and, in the case of bonds, is generally held to maturity.

**Investment Bankers and Underwriting**    Public offerings of both stocks and bonds typically are marketed by investment bankers, who in this role are called **underwriters.** More than one investment banker usually markets the securities. A lead firm forms an *underwriting syndicate* of other investment bankers to share the responsibility for the stock issue.

The bankers advise the firm regarding the terms on which it should attempt to sell the securities. A preliminary registration statement must be filed with the Securities and Exchange Commission (SEC) describing the issue and the prospects of the company. This *preliminary prospectus* is known as a *red herring* because of a statement printed in red that the company is not attempting to sell the security before the registration is approved. When the statement is finalized and approved by the SEC, it is called the **prospectus.** At this time the price at which the securities will be offered to the public is announced.

In a typical underwriting arrangement the investment bankers purchase the securities from the issuing company and then resell them to the public. The issuing firm sells the securities to the underwriting syndicate for the public offering price less a spread that serves as compensation to the underwriters. This procedure is called a *firm commitment.* The underwriters receive the issue and assume the full risk that the shares cannot in fact be sold to the public at the stipulated offering price. Besides being compensated by the spread between the purchase price and the public offering price, the investment banker may receive shares of common stock or other securities of the firm. Figure 3.1 depicts the relationship among the firm issuing the security, the underwriting syndicate, and the public.

An alternative to firm commitment is the *best-efforts* agreement. In this arrangement, which is far less common than the firm commitment, the investment banker agrees to help the firm sell the issue to the public but does not actually purchase the securities. The banker simply acts as an intermediary between the public and the firm and thus does not bear the risk of being unable to resell purchased securities at the offering price.

As part of their marketing of the firm's securities, the underwriting syndicate typically takes out advertisements in the financial press announcing the prospective sale. An example of these so-called *tombstone* advertisements is given in Figure 3.2. The underwriters plan to sell 115 million shares of stock at a price of $18.50, to raise $2,127.5 million for the Principal Financial Group. The lead underwriter is Goldman, Sachs. The co-lead underwriters are presented in larger type diagonally below Goldman; the participating underwriters, which take a smaller role in marketing the securities, are presented further below in smaller type. Most of the shares will be sold in the United States, but 15% of the issue

**Figure 3.1
Relationship
among a firm
issuing securities,
the underwriters,
and the public**

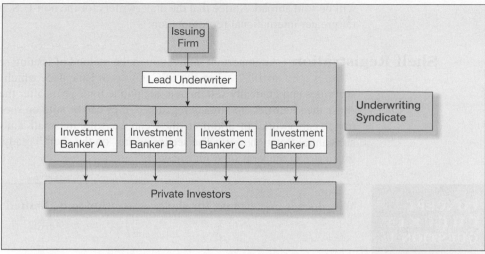

**Figure 3.2
A tombstone
advertisement**

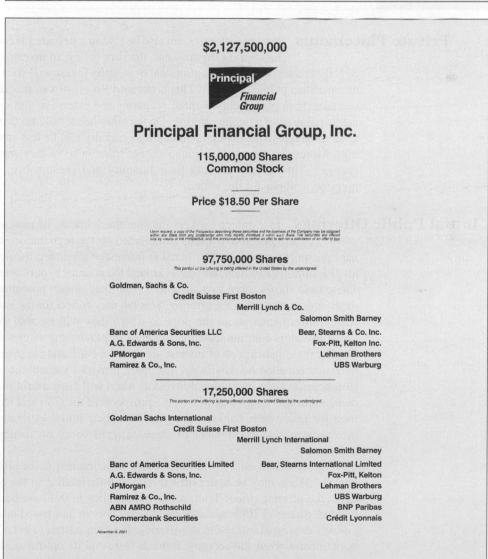

will be sold abroad. Notice that the underwriters for the non-U.S. portion of the issue have far greater international representation.

**Shelf Registration**  An important innovation in the method of issuing securities was introduced in 1982, when the SEC approved Rule 415, which allows firms to register securities and gradually sell them to the public for 2 years after the initial registration. Because the securities are already registered, they can be sold on short notice with little additional paperwork. In addition, they can be sold in small amounts without incurring substantial flotation costs. The securities are "on the shelf," ready to be issued, which has given rise to the term *shelf registration*.

| | |
|---|---|
| **CONCEPT CHECK☞ QUESTION 1** | **Why does it make sense for shelf registration to be limited in time?** |

**Private Placements**  Primary offerings can also be sold in a **private placement** rather than a public offering. In this case, the firm (using an investment banker) sells shares directly to a small group of institutional or wealthy investors. Private placements can be far cheaper than public offerings. This is because Rule 144A of the SEC allows corporations to make these placements without preparing the extensive and costly registration statements required of a public offering. On the other hand, because private placements are not made available to the general public, they generally will be less suited for very large offerings. Moreover, private placements do not trade in secondary markets such as stock exchanges. This greatly reduces their liquidity and presumably reduces the prices that investors will pay for the issue.

**Initial Public Offerings**  Investment bankers manage the issuance of new securities to the public. Once the SEC has commented on the registration statement and a preliminary prospectus has been distributed to interested investors, the investment bankers organize *road shows* in which they travel around the country to publicize the imminent offering. These road shows serve two purposes. First, they attract potential investors and provide them information about the offering. Second, they collect for the issuing firm and its underwriters information about the price at which they will be able to market the securities. Large investors communicate their interest in purchasing shares of the IPO to the underwriters; these indications of interest are called a *book* and the process of polling potential investors is called *bookbuilding*. The book provides valuable information to the issuing firm because large institutional investors often will have useful insights about the market demand for the security as well as the prospects of the firm and its competitors. It is common for investment bankers to revise both their initial estimates of the offering price of a security and the number of shares offered based on feedback from the investing community.

Why would investors truthfully reveal their interest in an offering to the investment banker? Might they be better off expressing little interest in the hope that this will drive down the offering price? Truth is the better policy in this case because truth-telling is rewarded. Shares of IPOs are allocated to investors in part based on the strength of each investor's expressed interest in the offering. If a firm wishes to get a large allocation when it is optimistic about the security, it needs to reveal its optimism. In turn, the underwriter needs to offer the security at a bargain price to these investors to induce them to participate

**Figure 3.3   Average initial returns for IPOs in various countries**

Provided by Professor J. Ritter of the University of Florida, 2001. This is an updated version of the information contained in T. Loughran, J. Ritter, and K. Rydquist, "Initial Public Offerings," *Pacific-Basin Finance Journal* 2 (1994), pp. 165–99.

in bookbuilding and share their information. Thus IPOs commonly are underpriced compared to the price at which they could be marketed. Such underpricing is reflected in price jumps on the date when the shares are first traded in public security markets. The most dramatic case of underpricing occurred in December 1999 when shares in VA Linux were sold in an IPO at $30 a share and closed on the first day of trading at $239.25, a 698% 1-day return.

While the explicit costs of an IPO tend to be around 7% of the funds raised, such underpricing should be viewed as another cost of the issue. For example, if VA Linux had sold its shares for the $239.25 that investors obviously were willing to pay for them, its IPO would have raised eight times as much as it actually did. The money "left on the table" in this case far exceeded the explicit costs of the stock issue.

Figure 3.3 presents average first-day returns on IPOs of stocks across the world. The results consistently indicate that the IPOs are marketed to the investors at attractive prices. Underpricing of IPOs makes them appealing to all investors, yet institutional investors are allocated the bulk of a typical new issue. Some view this as unfair discrimination against small investors. However, our discussion suggests that the apparent discounts on IPOs may be no more than fair payments for a valuable service, specifically, the information contributed by the institutional investors. The right to allocate shares in this way may contribute to efficiency by promoting the collection and dissemination of such information.[1]

Both views of IPO allocations probably contain some truth. IPO allocations to institutions do serve a valid economic purpose as an information-gathering tool. Nevertheless, the

---

[1] An elaboration of this point and a more complete discussion of the bookbuilding process is provided in Lawrence Benveniste and William Wilhelm, "Initial Public Offerings: Going by the Book," *Journal of Applied Corporate Finance* 9 (Spring 1997).

# DID WALL STREET FIRMS BRIBE BOSSES WITH SHARES?

Back in 1997, reports that Robertson Stephens, a Silicon Valley investment bank, was "spinning" IPO shares to executives who rewarded them with banking mandates prompted an SEC probe into the practice. The probe was soon abandoned. The practice boomed, becoming one of the more lucrative ways in which executives combined with Wall Street to abuse ordinary shareholders.

On August 30th Citigroup told congressional investigators that in 1997–2000 it had allocated IPO shares to Bernie Ebbers that had generated profits of $11m for the former boss of WorldCom, a telecoms firm which was a big Citigroup client, and is now bust thanks to fraud. Other WorldCom executives had also benefited. Citi claims that these allocations were not in return for investment-banking work; rather, they were a reward to the best customers of its private-banking arm. Underwriters and issuing firms are free to allocate shares however they wish, Citi notes—while in the same breath promising to change its allocation procedures.

Citigroup has yet to show that it was as generous to other private-banking clients who could not offer potential investment-banking business in return. Its "host of benign" explanations for why some shares were allocated retrospectively, giving executives a risk-free gain, seems thin. So does its claim that Jack Grubman, until last month the bank's top telecoms analyst, played no part in allocating shares to executives. Among the documents that Citigroup sent to Congress was a memo copied to Mr. Grubman that listed executives at several telecoms firms who had expressed interest in shares in IPOs.

Regulators and the courts will have to decide whether allocations of shares to executives were, in effect, bribes. If so, the punishment could be severe. Nor is Citi the only firm at risk. Credit Suisse First Boston gave shares in IPOs to executives minded to award it investment-banking business, via so-called "Friends of Frank" accounts, named after Frank Quattrone, its top technology investment banker.

CSFB and Goldman, Sachs now form part of the congressional investigation. And Morgan Stanley may soon face scrutiny over the role of Mary Meeker, formerly its top Internet analyst.

Source: Abridged from "Spun Gold . . . ," *The Economist,* September 7, 2002.

---

system can be—and has been—abused. Part of the Wall Street scandals of 2000–2002 centered on the allocation of shares in IPOs. Some investment bankers used IPO allocations to corporate insiders to curry favors, in effect as implicit kickback schemes. Underwriters apparently would award generous IPO allocations to executives of particular firms in return for the firm's future investment banking business. In other cases, most notably at Credit Suisse First Boston, IPO allocations were awarded in return for a promise to direct excessive and expensive securities trading to the brokerage arm of the investment banking firm. The nearby box discusses some of these practices.

Pricing of IPOs is not trivial, and not all IPOs turn out to be underpriced. Some stocks do poorly after the initial issue and others cannot even be fully sold to the market. Underwriters left with unmarketable securities are forced to sell them at a loss on the secondary market. Therefore, the investment banker bears the price risk of an underwritten issue.

Interestingly, despite their dramatic initial investment performance, IPOs have been poor long-term investments. Figure 3.4 compares the stock price performance of IPOs with shares of other firms of the same size for each of the 5 years after issue of the IPO. The year-by-year underperformance of the IPOs is dramatic, suggesting that on average, the investing public may be too optimistic about the prospects of these firms.[2]

---

[2] It is worth noting in this regard that by December 2000 shares in VA Linux (now renamed VA Software) were selling for less than $9 a share, and by mid-2003, less than $2 a share. This example is extreme but consistent with the generally poor long-term investment performance of IPOs.

**Figure 3.4
Long-term relative
performance of
initial public
offerings**

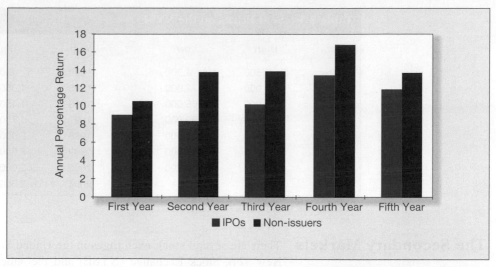

Professor J. Ritter, University of Florida, 2001.

IPOs can be expensive, especially for small firms. The landscape seemed to change in 1995 when Spring Street Brewing Company, which produces Wit beer, came out with an Internet IPO. It posted a page on the World Wide Web to let investors know of the stock offering and distributed the prospectus along with a subscription agreement as word-processing documents over the Web. By the end of the year, the firm had sold 860,000 shares to 3,500 investors, and had raised $1.6 million, all without an investment banker. This was admittedly a small IPO, but a low-cost one that was well-suited to such a small firm. Based on this success, a new company named Wit Capital was formed, with the goal of arranging low-cost Web-based IPOs for other firms. Wit also participates in the under-writing syndicates of more conventional IPOs; unlike conventional investment bankers, it allocates shares on a first-come, first-served basis.

Another relatively new entry to the underwriting field is W. R. Hambrecht & Co., which also conducts IPOs on the Internet geared toward smaller, retail investors. Unlike typical investment bankers, which tend to favor institutional investors in the allocation of shares, and which determine an offer price through the bookbuilding process, Hambrecht conducts a "Dutch auction." In this procedure, which Hambrecht has dubbed OpenIPO, investors submit a price for a given number of shares. The bids are ranked in order of bid price, and shares are allocated to the highest bidders until the entire issue is absorbed. All shares are sold at an offer price equal to the highest price at which all the issued shares will be ab-sorbed by investors. Those investors who bid below that cut-off price get no shares. By al-locating shares based on bids, this procedure minimizes underpricing.

To date, however, upstarts like Wit Capital and Hambrecht have captured only a tiny share of the underwriting market. Their long-term prospects are still unclear.

## 3.2   WHERE SECURITIES ARE TRADED

Once securities are issued to the public, investors may trade them among themselves. Purchase and sale of already-issued securities take place in the secondary markets, which consist of (1) national and local securities exchanges, (2) the over-the-counter market, and (3) direct trading between two parties.

### Table 3.1  Seat Prices on the NYSE

| Year | High | Low | Year | High | Low |
|------|------|-----|------|------|-----|
| 1875 | $ 6,800 | $ 4,300 | 1990 | $ 430,000 | $ 250,000 |
| 1905 | 85,000 | 72,000 | 1995 | 1,050,000 | 785,000 |
| 1935 | 140,000 | 65,000 | 1996 | 1,450,000 | 1,225,000 |
| 1965 | 250,000 | 190,000 | 1997 | 1,750,000 | 1,175,000 |
| 1975 | 138,000 | 55,000 | 1998 | 2,000,000 | 1,225,000 |
| 1980 | 275,000 | 175,000 | 1999 | 2,650,000 | 2,000,000 |
| 1985 | 480,000 | 310,000 | 2000 | 2,000,000 | 1,650,000 |
|      |        |         | 2001 | 2,300,000 | 2,000,000 |

Source: New York Stock Exchange *Fact Book*, 2001.

## The Secondary Markets

There are several **stock exchanges** in the United States. Two of these, the New York Stock Exchange (NYSE) and the American Stock Exchange (Amex), are national in scope. The others, such as the Boston and Pacific exchanges, are regional exchanges, which primarily list firms located in a particular geographic area. There are also several exchanges for trading of options and futures contracts, which we'll discuss in the options and futures chapters.

An exchange provides a facility for its members to trade securities, and only members of the exchange may trade there. Therefore memberships, or *seats*, on the exchange are valuable assets. The majority of seats are *commission broker* seats, most of which are owned by the large full-service brokerage firms. The seat entitles the firm to place one of its brokers on the floor of the exchange where he or she can execute trades. The exchange member charges investors for executing trades on their behalf. The commissions that members can earn through this activity determine the market value of a seat. A seat on the NYSE has sold over the years for as little as $4,000 in 1878, and as much as $2.65 million in 1999. See Table 3.1 for a history of seat prices.

The NYSE is by far the largest single exchange. The shares of approximately 2,800 firms trade there, and about 3,000 stock issues (common and preferred stock) are listed. Daily trading volume on the NYSE averaged 1.24 billion shares in 2001. The NYSE accounts for about 85–90% of the trading that takes place on U.S. stock exchanges.

The American Stock Exchange, or Amex,[3] focuses on listing smaller and younger firms than does the NYSE. It also has been a leader in the development and trading of exchange-traded funds, which are securities that represent claims to entire portfolios of stock and which today account for a large share of total trading on the exchange. These products are described in greater detail in the following chapter.

Table 3.2 gives some initial listing requirements for the NYSE. These requirements ensure that a firm is of significant trading interest before the NYSE will allocate facilities for it to be traded on the floor of the exchange. If a listed company suffers a decline and fails to meet the criteria in Table 3.2, it may be delisted from the exchange.

Regional exchanges also sponsor trading of some firms that are traded on national exchanges. This dual listing enables local brokerage firms to trade in shares of large firms without needing to purchase a membership on the NYSE. However, the NYSE is still by far the preferred exchange for large traders, and its market share of exchange-listed companies when measured in share volume rather than number of trades has been stable in the last decade, between 82% and 84%.

---

[3] Amex merged with Nasdaq in 1998 but still operates as an independent exchange. In June 2003, GTCR Golder Rauner, an investment firm, agreed to buy the Amex from the National Association of Security Dealers, which owns the Nasdaq market.

| Table 3.2 | Some Initial Listing Requirements for the NYSE | |
|---|---|---:|
| | Pretax income in last year | $    2,500,000 |
| | Average annual pretax income in previous 2 years | $    2,000,000 |
| | Revenue | $100,000,000 |
| | Market value of publicly held stock | $  60,000,000 |
| | Shares publicly held | 1,100,000 |
| | Number of holders of 100 shares or more | 2,000 |

Source: Data from the New York Stock Exchange *Fact Book*, 2001.

| Table 3.3 | Average Daily Trading Volume in National Stock Markets, 2001 | |
|---|---|---|
| **Market** | **Shares Traded (millions)** | **Dollar Volume ($ billion)** |
| NYSE | 1,240.0 | $42.3 |
| Nasdaq | 1,873.1 | 44.1 |
| Amex | 65.3 | 3.3 |

Source: NYSE *Fact Book*, 2001, and www.nasdaq.com.

The over-the-counter Nasdaq market (described in detail shortly) has posed a bigger competitive challenge to the NYSE. Its share of trading volume in NYSE-listed firms increased from 2.2% in 1988 to about 8.6% in 2001. Moreover, many large firms that would be eligible to list their shares on the NYSE now choose to list on Nasdaq. Some of the well-known firms currently trading on Nasdaq are Microsoft, Intel, Apple Computer, and Sun Microsystems. Total trading volume in over-the-counter stocks on the computerized Nasdaq system has increased dramatically in the last decade, rising from about 50 million shares per day in 1984 to nearly 2 billion shares in 2002. Table 3.3 shows trading activity in securities listed in national markets in 2001.

While most common stocks are traded on the exchanges, most bonds and other fixed-income securities are not. Corporate bonds are traded both on the exchanges and over the counter, but most federal and municipal government bonds are traded over the counter.

## The Over-the-Counter Market

Roughly 35,000 issues are traded on the **over-the-counter** (OTC) **market** and any security may be traded there, but the OTC market is not a formal exchange. There are no membership requirements for trading, nor are there listing requirements for securities (although there are requirements to be listed on Nasdaq, the computer-linked network for trading of OTC securities). In the OTC market thousands of brokers register with the SEC as dealers in OTC securities. Security dealers quote prices at which they are willing to buy or sell securities. A broker can execute a trade by contacting a dealer listing an attractive quote.

Before 1971, all OTC quotations of stock were recorded manually and published daily. The so-called *pink sheets* were the means by which dealers communicated their interest in trading at various prices. This was a cumbersome and inefficient technique, and published quotes were a full day out of date. In 1971 the National Association of Securities Dealers Automated Quotation system, or **Nasdaq,** began to offer immediate information on a computer-linked system of bid and asked prices for stocks offered by various dealers. The **bid price** is that at which a dealer is willing to purchase a security; the **asked price** is that at which the dealer will sell a security. A dealer who receives a buy or sell order from an investor can examine all current quotes, contact the dealer with the best quote, and execute a trade.

**Table 3.4    Partial Requirements for Initial Listing on the Nasdaq Markets**

|  | Nasdaq National Market | Nasdaq SmallCap Market |
|---|---|---|
| Shareholders' equity | $15 million | $5 million |
| Shares in public hands | 1.1 million | 1 million |
| Market value of shares | $8 million | $5 million |
| Minimum price of stock | $5 | $4 |
| Pretax income | $1 million | $750,000 |
| Shareholders | 400 | 300 |

Source: www.nasdaq.com January 2003.

This system, now called the Nasdaq stock market, is divided into two sectors, the Nasdaq National Market System (comprising about 3,000 companies) and the Nasdaq SmallCap Market (comprised of about 850 smaller companies). The National Market securities must meet more stringent listing requirements and trade in a more liquid market. Some of the more important initial listing requirements for each of these markets are presented in Table 3.4. For even smaller firms, Nasdaq maintains an electronic "OTC Bulletin Board," which is not part of the Nasdaq market but is simply a means for brokers and dealers to get and post current price quotes over a computer network. Finally, the smallest stocks continue to be listed on the pink sheets distributed through the National Association of Securities Dealers.

Nasdaq has three levels of subscribers. The highest, Level 3, is for firms dealing, or "making markets," in OTC securities. These market makers maintain inventories of a security and continually stand ready to buy these shares from or sell them to the public at the quoted bid and asked price. They earn profits from the spread between the bid price and the asked price. Level 3 subscribers may enter the bid and asked prices at which they are willing to buy or sell stocks into the computer network and update these quotes as desired.

Level 2 subscribers receive all bid and asked quotes but cannot enter their own quotes. These subscribers tend to be brokerage firms that execute trades for clients but do not actively deal in the stocks for their own accounts. Brokers attempting to buy or sell shares call the market maker who has the best quote to execute a trade.

Level 1 subscribers receive only the median, or "representative," bid and asked prices on each stock. Level 1 subscribers are investors who are not actively buying and selling securities, yet the service provides them with general information.

**E-INVESTMENTS**
**Listing**
**Requirements**

Go to **www.nasdaq.com**. Click "Inside Nasdaq" and look for *Listing Information.* Identify the following items in Initial Listing Requirements for the National Market System, Standards 1, 2, and 3, and the Nasdaq Small Cap Market for domestic companies:

Public Float in millions of shares

Market Value of Public Float

Shareholders of round lots

Go to **www.nyse.com** and select the listed companies item or information bullet. Under the bullet select the *Listing Standards* tab. Identify the same items for NYSE (U.S. Standards) initial listing requirements.

In what two categories are the listing requirements most significantly different?

**Table 3.5   Electronic Communication Networks (ECNs)**

| ECN Name | Ticker Symbol |
|---|---|
| Archipelago | ARCA |
| Attain | ATTN |
| Bloomberg Tradebook | BTRD |
| Brass Utility | BRUT |
| GlobeNet ECN | GNET |
| Instinet Corporation | INCA |
| Island ECN | ISLD |
| MarketXT | MKXT |
| NexTrade | NTRD |
| RediBook | REDI |

## The Third and Fourth Markets

The **third market** refers to trading of exchange-listed securities on the OTC market. Until the 1970s, members of the NYSE were required to execute all their trades of NYSE-listed securities on the exchange and to charge commissions according to a fixed schedule. This schedule was disadvantageous to large traders, who were prevented from realizing economies of scale on large trades. The restriction led brokerage firms that were not members of the NYSE, and so not bound by its rules, to establish trading in the OTC market on large NYSE-listed firms. These trades took place at lower commissions than would have been charged on the NYSE, and the third market grew dramatically until 1972 when the NYSE allowed negotiated commissions on orders exceeding $300,000. On May 1, 1975, frequently referred to as "May Day," commissions on all orders became negotiable.

> **CONCEPT CHECK ☞ QUESTION 2**
>
> Look again at Table 3.1, which gives the history of seat prices on the NYSE. Interpret the data for 1975 in light of the changes instituted on May Day.

The **fourth market** refers to direct trading between investors in exchange-listed securities without benefit of a broker. The direct trading among investors that characterizes the fourth market has exploded in recent years due to the advent of the **electronic communication network,** or **ECN.** The ECN is an alternative to either formal stock exchanges like the NYSE or dealer markets like Nasdaq for trading securities. These networks allow members to post buy or sell orders and to have those orders matched up or "crossed" with orders of other traders in the system. Both sides of the trade benefit because direct crossing eliminates the bid–ask spread that otherwise would be incurred. (Traders pay a small price per trade or per share rather than incurring a bid–ask spread, which tends to be far more expensive.) In addition to speed and cost savings, these systems provide traders greater anonymity than they could otherwise achieve. This is important since big traders do not want to publicly signal their desire to buy or sell large quantities of shares for fear of moving prices in advance of their trades.

ECNs have been highly successful and have captured about 40% of the trading volume in Nasdaq-listed stocks. They must be certified by the SEC and registered with the National Association of Security Dealers to participate in the Nasdaq market. Table 3.5 is a list of registered ECNs at the start of 2003. The two biggest ECNs are Island/Instinet (formed by a merger of the two firms) and Archipelago. Instinet is the oldest ECN with the highest share of trading volume. Island ranked second and makes its order book available for no fee over the Internet.

By teaming up with the Pacific Exchange, Archipelago is classified as a stock exchange and can list stocks over the National Market System, which ties it to other exchanges (see below for a discussion of the National Market System). Archipelago also links to other ECNs if there are no matches for a trade on its own system.

The success of ECNs is putting increasing pressure on both the NYSE and Nasdaq to respond. In particular, big brokerage firms have called for the NYSE to beef up its capabilities to automate orders without human intervention. Moreover, as they push the NYSE to change, these firms are hedging their bets by investing in ECNs on their own. In fact, several financial firms (Goldman, Sachs; Merrill Lynch; Salomon Smith Barney; Morgan Stanley; and Bernard Madoff) have combined to build an electronic trading network called Primex, which is open to NASD broker/dealers, who in turn have the ability to offer public access to the market. As we will see below, Nasdaq has introduced its SuperMontage system to match some of the capabilities of ECNs.

## The National Market System

The Securities Act Amendments of 1975 directed the Securities and Exchange Commission to implement a national competitive securities market. Such a market would entail centralized reporting of transactions and a centralized quotation system, and would result in enhanced competition among market makers. In 1975 a "Consolidated Tape" began reporting trades on the NYSE, the Amex, and the major regional exchanges, as well as on Nasdaq-listed stocks. In 1977 the Consolidated Quotations Service began providing online bid and asked quotes for NYSE securities also traded on various other exchanges. This enhances competition by allowing market participants such as brokers or dealers who are at different locations to interact, and it allows orders to be directed to the market in which the best price can be obtained.

In 1978 the Intermarket Trading System was implemented. It currently links 9 exchanges by computer (NYSE, Amex, Boston, Cincinnati, Pacific, Philadelphia, Chicago, Nasdaq, and Chicago Board Options Exchange). About 4,500 issues are eligible for trading on the ITS; these account for most of the securities that are traded on more than one exchange. The system allows brokers and market makers to display and view quotes for all markets and to execute cross-market trades when the Consolidated Quotations Service shows better prices in other markets. For example, suppose a specialist firm on the Boston Exchange is currently offering to buy a security for $20, but a broker in Boston who is attempting to sell shares for a client observes a superior bid price on the NYSE, say $20.12. The broker should route the order to the specialist's post on the NYSE where it can be executed at the higher price. The transaction is then reported on the Consolidated Tape. Moreover, a specialist who observes a better price on another exchange is also expected either to match that price or route the trade to that market.

While the ITS does much to unify markets, it has some important shortcomings. First, it does not provide for automatic execution in the market with the best price. The trade must be directed there by a market participant, who might find it inconvenient (or unprofitable) to do so. Moreover, some feel that the ITS is too slow to integrate prices off the NYSE.

A logical extension of the ITS as a means to integrate securities markets would be the establishment of a central limit order book. Such an electronic "book" would contain all orders conditional on both prices and dates. All markets would be linked and all traders could compete for all orders.

While market integration seems like an desirable goal, the recent growth of ECNs has led to some concern that markets are in fact becoming more fragmented. This is because participants in one ECN do not necessarily know what prices are being quoted on other networks. ECNs do display their best-priced offers on the Nasdaq system, but other limit orders are not available. Only stock exchanges may participate in the Intermarket Trading System, which means that most ECNs are excluded. Moreover, during the after-hours trading enabled by ECNs, trades take place on these private networks while other, larger markets are closed and current prices for securities are harder to assess. In the wake of growing concern about market fragmentation, some big Wall Street brokerage houses have called for an electronically driven central limit order book but full market integration has proven elusive.

**Bond Trading**   The New York Stock Exchange also operates a bond exchange where U.S. government, corporate, municipal, and foreign bonds may be traded. The centerpiece of the NYSE bond market is the Automated Bond System (ABS), which is an automated trading system that allows trading firms to obtain market information, to enter and execute trades over a computer network, and to receive immediate confirmations of trade execution.

However, the vast majority of bond trading occurs in the over-the-counter market among bond dealers, even for bonds that are actually listed on the NYSE. This market is a network of bond dealers such as Merrill Lynch, Citigroup, or Goldman, Sachs that is linked by a computer quotation system. However, because these dealers do not carry extensive inventories of the wide range of bonds that have been issued to the public, they cannot necessarily offer to sell bonds from their inventory or even buy bonds for their inventory. They may instead work to locate an investor who wishes to take the opposite side of a trade. In practice, therefore, the corporate bond market often is quite "thin," in that it may be difficult to find investors interested in trading a specific bond at any particular time. As a result, the bond market is subject to a type of liquidity risk, for it can be difficult to sell one's holdings quickly if the need arises.

# 3.3   TRADING ON EXCHANGES

Most of the material in this section applies to all securities traded on exchanges. Some of it, however, applies just to stocks, and in such cases we use the term *stocks* or *shares*.

**The Participants**   When an investor instructs a broker to buy or sell securities, a number of players must act to consummate the trade. We start our discussion of the mechanics of exchange trading with a brief description of the potential parties to a trade.

The investor places an order with a broker. The brokerage firm owning a seat on the exchange contacts its *commission broker,* who is on the floor of the exchange, to execute the order. *Floor brokers* are independent members of the exchange who own their own seats and handle work for commission brokers when those brokers have too many orders to handle.

The **specialist** is central to the trading process. Specialists maintain a market in one or more listed securities. All trading in a given stock takes place at one location on the floor of the exchange called the *specialist's post*. At the specialist's post is a computer monitor, called the Display Book, that presents all the current offers from interested traders to buy or sell shares at various prices as well as the number of shares these quotes are good for. The specialist manages the trading in the stock. The market-making responsibility for each stock is assigned by the NYSE to one specialist firm. There is only one specialist per stock, but most firms will have responsibility for trading in several stocks. The specialist firm also may act as a dealer in the stock, trading for its own account. We will examine the role of the specialist in more detail shortly.

## Types of Orders

**Market Orders.** Market orders are simply buy or sell orders that are to be executed immediately at current market prices. For example, an investor might call his broker and ask for the market price of General Electric. The retail broker will relay this request to the commission broker on the floor of the exchange, who will approach the specialist's post and ask the specialist for best current quotes. Finding that the current quotes are $28 per share bid and $28.15 asked, the investor might direct the broker to buy 100 shares "at market," meaning that he is willing to pay $28.15 per share for an immediate transaction. Similarly, an order to "sell at market" will result in stock sales at $28 per share. When a trade is executed, the specialist's clerk will fill out an order card that reports the time, price, and quantity of shares traded, and the transaction is reported on the exchange's ticker tape.

There are two potential complications to this simple scenario, however. First, as noted earlier, the posted quotes of $28 and $28.15 actually represent commitments to trade up to a specified number of shares. If the market order is for more than this number of shares, the order may be filled at multiple prices. For example, if the asked price is good for orders of up to 600 shares, and the investor wishes to purchase 1,000 shares, it may be necessary to pay a slightly higher price for the last 400 shares than the quoted asked price.

The second complication arises from the possibility of trading "inside the quoted spread." If the broker who has received a market buy order for GE meets another broker who has received a market sell order for GE, they can agree to trade with each other at a price of $28.10 per share. By meeting inside the quoted spread, both the buyer and the seller obtain "price improvement," that is, transaction prices better than the best quoted prices. Such "meetings" of brokers are more than accidental. Because all trading takes place at the specialist's post, floor brokers know where to look for counterparties to take the other side of a trade.

**Limit Orders.** Investors may also place limit orders, whereby they specify prices at which they are willing to buy or sell a security. If the stock falls below the limit on a *limit-buy order* then the trade is to be executed. If GE is selling at $28 bid, $28.15 asked, for example, a limit-buy order may instruct the broker to buy the stock if and when the share price falls below $25. Correspondingly, a *limit-sell order* instructs the broker to sell as soon as the stock price goes above the specified limit.

Figure 3.5 is a portion of the limit-order book for shares in Intel on the Island exchange on one particular day. Notice that the best orders are at the top of the list: the offers to buy at the highest price and to sell at the lowest price. The buy and sell orders at the top of the list—$27.88 and $27.93—are called the *inside quotes*; they are the buy and sell orders with the closest prices. For Intel, the inside spread is only 5 cents per share.

What happens if a limit order is placed between the quoted bid and ask prices? For example, suppose you have instructed your broker to buy GE at a price of $28.10 or better. The order may not be executed immediately, since the quoted asked price for the shares is $28.15, which is more than you are willing to pay. However, your willingness to buy at $28.10 is better than the quoted bid price of $28 per share. Therefore, you may find that there are traders who were unwilling to sell their shares at the $28 bid price but are happy to sell shares to you at your higher bid price of $28.10.

Until 2001, when U.S. markets adopted decimal pricing, the minimum possible bid–asked spread was "one tick," which on the NYSE was $⅛ until 1997 and $¹⁄₁₆ thereafter.

**Figure 3.5**
**The limit-order book for Intel on the Island exchange, November 9, 2001**

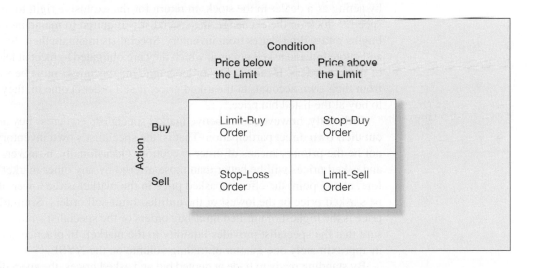

refresh | island home | disclamer | help

**₿INTC**

GET STOCK
INTC | go

| LAST MATCH | | TODAY'S ACTIVITY | |
|---|---|---|---|
| Price | 27.8900 | Orders | 16,774 |
| Time | 14:24:45 | Volume | 4,631,778 |

| BUY ORDERS | | SELL ORDERS | |
|---|---|---|---|
| Shares | Price | Shares | Price |
| 100 | 27.8800 | 1,000 | 27.9300 |
| 500 | 27.8500 | 1,000 | 27.9690 |
| 200 | 27.8500 | 1,000 | 27.9800 |
| 1,000 | 27.8200 | 1,000 | 27.9900 |
| 3,300 | 27.8100 | 1,000 | 28.0000 |
| 300 | 27.8000 | 1,800 | 28.0600 |
| 75 | 27.7500 | 1,000 | 28.0800 |
| 101 | 27.7300 | 1,000 | 28.1000 |
| 5,000 | 27.7200 | 2,000 | 28.1100 |
| 1,000 | 27.72 | 1,000 | 28.1800 |
| (416 more) | | (395 more) | |

**Figure 3.6**
**Limit orders**

Condition

| | Price below the Limit | Price above the Limit |
|---|---|---|
| Buy | Limit-Buy Order | Stop-Buy Order |
| Sell | Stop-Loss Order | Limit-Sell Order |

Action

With decimal pricing, the spread can be far lower. In 2002, the average quoted bid–asked spread on the NYSE was about 8 cents.

*Stop-loss orders* are similar to limit orders in that the trade is not to be executed unless the stock hits a price limit. In this case, however, the stock is to be sold if its price falls *below* a stipulated level. As the name suggests, the order lets the stock be sold to stop further losses from accumulating. Symmetrically, *stop-buy orders* specify that the stock should be bought when its price rises above a given limit. These trades often accompany short sales, and they are used to limit potential losses from the short position. Short sales are discussed in greater detail in Section 3.7. Figure 3.6 organizes these four types of trades in a simple matrix.

Orders also can be limited by a time period. Day orders, for example, expire at the close of the trading day. If it is not executed on that day, the order is canceled. *Open or good-till-canceled orders*, in contrast, remain in force for up to 6 months unless canceled by the customer. At the other extreme, *fill or kill orders* expire if the broker cannot fill them immediately.

## Specialists and the Execution of Trades

A **specialist** "makes a market" in the shares of one or more firms. This task may require the specialist to act as either a broker or dealer. The specialist's role as a broker is simply to execute the orders of other brokers. Specialists may also buy or sell shares of stock for their own portfolios. When no other broker can be found to take the other side of a trade, specialists will do so even if it means they must buy for or sell from their own accounts. The NYSE commissions these companies to perform this service and monitors their performance. In this role, specialists act as dealers in the stock.

Part of the specialist's job as a broker is simply clerical. The specialist maintains a "book" listing all outstanding unexecuted limit orders entered by brokers on behalf of clients. (Actually, the book is now a computer console.) When limit orders can be executed at market prices, the specialist executes, or "crosses," the trade.

The specialist is required to use the highest outstanding offered purchase price and lowest outstanding offered selling price when matching trades. Therefore, the specialist system results in an auction market, meaning all buy and all sell orders come to one location, and the best orders "win" the trades. In this role, the specialist acts merely as a facilitator.

The more interesting function of the specialist is to maintain a "fair and orderly market" by acting as a dealer in the stock. In return for the exclusive right to make the market in a specific stock on the exchange, the specialist is required to maintain an orderly market by buying and selling shares from inventory. Specialists maintain their own portfolios of stock and quote bid and asked prices at which they are obligated to meet at least a limited amount of market orders. If market buy orders come in, specialists must be willing to sell shares from their own accounts at the asked price; if sell orders come in, they must stand willing to buy at the listed bid price.[4]

Ordinarily, however, in an active market specialists can cross buy and sell orders without their own direct participation. That is, the specialist's own inventory of securities need not be the primary means of order execution. Occasionally, however, the specialist's bid and asked prices will be better than those offered by any other market participant. Therefore, at any point the effective asked price in the market is the lower of either the specialist's asked price or the lowest of the unfilled limit-sell orders. Similarly, the effective bid price is the highest of unfilled limit-buy orders or the specialist's bid. These procedures ensure that the specialist provides liquidity to the market. In practice, specialists participate in approximately one-quarter of trading volume on the NYSE.

By standing ready to trade at quoted bid and asked prices, the specialist is potentially exposed to exploitation by other traders. Large traders with ready access to late-breaking news will initiate trades with specialists if the specialists' quoted prices are temporarily out of line with assessments of value based on that information. Specialists who cannot match the information resources of large traders will be at a disadvantage when their quoted prices offer profit opportunities to more-informed traders.

You might wonder why specialists do not protect their interests by setting a low bid price and a high asked price. A specialist using that strategy would not suffer losses by maintaining a too-low asked price or a too-high bid price in a period of dramatic

---

[4] Actually, the specialist's published price quotes are valid only for a given number of shares. If a buy or sell order is placed for more shares than the quotation size, the specialist has the right to revise the quote.

movements in the stock price. Specialists who offer a narrow spread between the bid and the asked prices have little leeway for error and must constantly monitor market conditions to avoid offering other investors advantageous terms.

Large bid–asked spreads are not viable options for the specialist for two reasons. First, one source of the specialist's income is derived from frequent trading at the bid and asked prices, with the spread as the trading profit. A too-large spread would make the specialist's quotes noncompetitive with the limit orders placed by other traders. If the specialist's bid and asked quotes are consistently worse than those of public traders, it will not participate in any trades and will lose the ability to profit from the bid–asked spread.

An equally important reason that specialists cannot use large bid–ask spreads to protect their interests is that they are obligated to provide *price continuity* to the market. To illustrate the principle of price continuity, suppose that the highest limit-buy order for a stock is $30 while the lower limit-sell order is at $32. When a market buy order comes in, it is matched to the best limit-sell at $32. A market sell order would be matched to the best limit-buy at $30. As market buys and sells come to the floor randomly, the stock price would fluctuate between $30 and $32. The exchange would consider this excessive volatility, and the specialist would be expected to step in with bid and/or asked prices between these values to reduce the bid–asked spread to an acceptable level, typically less than $.15 for large firms. When a firm is newly listed on an exchange, specialist firms vigorously compete to be awarded the rights by the exchange to maintain the market in those shares. A major criterion on which they are evaluated is their past performance in maintaining price continuity. Specialists, therefore, have considerable incentive to maintain tight spreads.

Specialists earn income both from commissions for acting as brokers for orders and from the spread between the bid and asked prices at which they buy and sell securities. Some believe that specialists' access to their book of limit orders gives them unique knowledge about the probable direction of price movement over short periods of time. For example, suppose the specialist sees that a stock now selling for $45 has limit-buy orders for more than 100,000 shares at prices ranging from $44.50 to $44.75. This latent buying demand provides a cushion of support, because it is unlikely that enough sell pressure could come in during the next few hours to cause the price to drop below $44.50. If there are very few limit-sell orders above $45, some transient buying demand could raise the price substantially. The specialist in such circumstances realizes that a position in the stock offers little downside risk and substantial upside potential. Such immediate access to the trading intentions of other market participants seems to allow a specialist to earn substantial profits on personal transactions. One can easily overestimate such advantages, however, because ever more of the large orders are negotiated "upstairs," that is, as fourth-market deals.

**Block Sales**   Institutional investors frequently trade blocks of several thousand shares of stock. Table 3.6 shows that **block transactions** of over 10,000 shares now account for about half of all trading on the NYSE. Although a 10,000-share trade is considered commonplace today, large blocks often cannot be handled comfortably by specialists who do not wish to hold very large amounts of stock in their inventory. For example, one huge block transaction in 2001 was for $485.6 million worth of shares in John Hancock Financial Services.

In response to this problem, "block houses" have evolved to aid in the placement of block trades. Block houses are brokerage firms that help to find potential buyers or sellers of large block trades. Once a trader has been located, the block is sent to the exchange floor, where the trade is executed by the specialist. If such traders cannot be identified, the block house might purchase all or part of a block sale for its own account. The broker then can resell the shares to the public.

**Table 3.6    Block Transactions on the New York Stock Exchange**

| Year | Shares (millions) | Percentage of Reported Volume | Average Number of Block Transactions per Day |
|---|---|---|---|
| 1965 | 48 | 3.1% | 9 |
| 1970 | 451 | 15.4 | 68 |
| 1975 | 779 | 16.6 | 136 |
| 1980 | 3,311 | 29.2 | 528 |
| 1985 | 14,222 | 51.7 | 2,139 |
| 1990 | 19,682 | 49.6 | 3,333 |
| 1995 | 49,737 | 57.0 | 7,793 |
| 2000 | 135,772 | 51.7 | 21,941 |
| 2001 | 148,056 | 48.1 | 23,758 |

Source: Data from the New York Stock Exchange *Fact Book*, 2001.

**The SuperDOT System**    SuperDOT enables exchange members to send orders directly to the specialist over computer lines. In 2001, SuperDOT processed an average of 2.7 million orders per day, with an average execution time for market orders of 18 seconds.

SuperDOT is especially useful to program traders. A **program trade** is a coordinated purchase or sale of an entire portfolio of stocks. Many trading strategies (such as index arbitrage, a topic we will study in Chapter 23) require that an entire portfolio of stocks be purchased or sold simultaneously in a coordinated program. SuperDOT is the tool that enables the many trading orders to be sent out at once and executed almost simultaneously.

The vast majority of all orders are submitted through SuperDOT. However, these tend to be smaller orders, and in 2001 they accounted for about two-thirds of total trading volume.

**Settlement**    Since June 1995, an order executed on the exchange must be settled within 3 working days. This requirement is often called T + 3, for trade date plus 3 days. The purchaser must deliver the cash, and the seller must deliver the stock to his or her broker, who in turn delivers it to the buyer's broker. Transfer of the shares is made easier when the firm's clients keep their securities in *street name*, meaning that the broker holds the shares registered in the firm's own name on behalf of the client. This arrangement can speed security transfer. T + 3 settlement has made such arrangements more important: It can be quite difficult for a seller of a security to complete delivery to the purchaser within the 3-day period if the stock is kept in a safe deposit box.

Settlement is simplified further by a clearinghouse. The trades of all exchange members are recorded each day, with members' transactions netted out, so that each member need only transfer or receive the net number of shares sold or bought that day. Each member settles only with the clearinghouse, instead of with each firm with whom trades were executed.

## 3.4   TRADING ON THE OTC MARKET

On the exchanges all trading takes place through a specialist. Trades on the OTC market, however, are negotiated directly through dealers. Each dealer maintains an inventory of selected securities. Dealers sell from their inventories at asked prices and buy for them at bid prices. Because the Nasdaq system does not require a specialist, OTC trades do not require a centralized trading floor as do exchange-listed stocks. Dealers can be located anywhere, as long as they can communicate effectively with other buyers and sellers.

An investor who wishes to purchase or sell shares engages a broker, who tries to locate the dealer offering the best deal on the security. This contrasts with exchange trading, where all buy or sell orders are negotiated through the specialist, who arranges for the best bids to get the trade. In the OTC market brokers must search the offers of dealers directly to find the best trading opportunity. In this sense, Nasdaq is largely a price quotation, not a trading system. While bid and asked prices can be obtained from the Nasdaq computer network, the actual trade still requires direct negotiation between the broker and the dealer in the security.

One disadvantage of the decentralized dealer market is that the investing public is vulnerable to *trading through,* which refers to the practice of dealers to trade with the public at their quoted bid or asked prices even if other customers have offered to trade at better prices. For example, a dealer who posts a $20 bid and $20.30 asked price for a stock may continue to fill market buy orders at this asked price and market sell orders at this bid price, even if there are limit orders by public customers "inside the spread," for example, limit orders to buy at $20.10, or limit orders to sell at $20.20. This practice harms the investor whose limit order is not filled (is "traded through"), as well as the investor whose market buy or sell order is not filled at the best available price.

Trading through on Nasdaq sometimes results from imperfect coordination among dealers. A limit order placed with one broker may not be seen by brokers for other traders because computer systems are not linked and only the broker's own bid and asked prices are posted on the Nasdaq system. In contrast, trading through is strictly forbidden on the NYSE or Amex, where "price priority" requires that the specialist fill the best-priced order first. Moreover, because all traders in an exchange market must trade through the specialist, the exchange provides true *price discovery*, meaning that market prices reflect prices at which *all* participants at that moment are willing to trade. This is the advantage of a centralized auction market.

However, in the wake of the stock market crash of 1987, Nasdaq instituted a Small-Order Execution System (SOES), which is in effect a trading system. Under SOES, market makers in a security who post bid or asked prices on Nasdaq may be contacted over the network by other traders and are required to trade at the prices they currently quote. Dealers must accept SOES orders at their posted prices up to some limit, which may be 1,000 shares, but usually is smaller, depending on factors such as trading volume in the stock.

In 2002, Nasdaq introduced a successor to SOES called SuperMontage. This is an integrated order display and execution system that is touted as providing a more liquid and transparent market. SuperMontage allows market makers to enter multiple quotes and orders at different prices. It can aggregate limit orders at all price levels and make available total trading interest at the best prices as well as the next-best four prices. Investors therefore can look at the top five layers of the order book. By aggregating orders from participating market makers at all price points, SuperMontage can serve as a central limit-order book for all Nasdaq-listed securities. However, its viability in this role depends on the participation of other traders. As of early 2003, Instinet/Island, which has a share of almost 30% of the trading volume of shares listed on SuperMontage, had not yet chosen to participate and Archipelago seemed likely to drop out of the system.

SuperMontage is Nasdaq's competitive response to the growing popularity of ECNs, which have captured a growing share of order flow. By enabling automatic trade execution, SuperMontage allows Nasdaq to function much like an ECN. One issue not yet resolved is whether only market makers will be allowed to enter limit orders into SuperMontage or whether order-entry firms also will be allowed to enter limit orders, as they can in ECNs.

## Market Structure in Other Countries

The structure of security markets varies considerably from one country to another. A full cross-country comparison is far beyond the scope of this text. Therefore, we instead briefly review three of the biggest non-U.S. stock markets: the London, Euronext, and Tokyo exchanges. Figure 3.7 shows the volume of trading in major world markets.

**London.** Until 1997, trading arrangements in London were similar to those on Nasdaq. Competing dealers who wished to make a market in a stock would enter bid and asked prices into the Stock Exchange Automated Quotations (SEAQ) system. As in the United States, London security firms acted as both dealers and as brokerage firms, that is, both making a market in securities and executing trades for their clients.

In 1997, the London Stock Exchange introduced an electronic trading system dubbed SETS (Stock Exchange Electronic Trading Service). This is an electronic clearing system similar to ECNs in which buy and sell orders are submitted via computer networks and any buy and sell orders that can be crossed are executed automatically.

Most trading in London equities is now conducted using SETS, particularly for shares in larger firms. However, SEAQ continues to operate and may be more likely to be used for the "upstairs market" in large-block transactions or other less-liquid transactions.

**Euronext.** Euronext was formed in 2000 by a merger of the Paris, Amsterdam, and Brussels exchanges. Euronext, like most European exchanges, uses an electronic trading system. Its system, called NSC (for Nouveau Système de Cotation, or New Quotation System), has fully automated order routing and execution. In fact, investors can enter their orders directly without contacting their brokers. An order submitted to the system is

**Figure 3.7**
**Annual dollar volume of trading on major world exchanges, 2001**

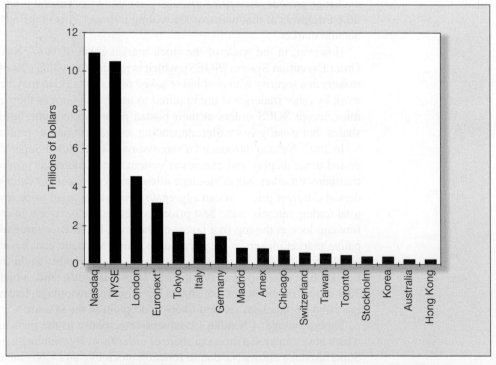

Source: International Federation of Stock Exchanges, www.fibv.com; e-mail: secretariat@fibv.com; Tel: (33 1) 44 01 05 45 Fax (33 1) 47 54 94 22; 22 Blvd de Courcelles Paris 75017.

*The Euronext exchange was formed by a merger of the Paris, Amsterdam, and Brussels exchanges.

executed immediately if it can be crossed against an order in the public limit-order book; if it cannot be executed, it is entered into the limit-order book.

Euronext is in the process of establishing cross-trading agreements with several other European exchanges such as Helsinki or Luxembourg. In 2001, it also purchased LIFFE, the London International Financial Futures and Options Exchange.

**Tokyo.** The Tokyo Stock Exchange (TSE) is the largest stock exchange in Japan, accounting for about 80% of total trading. There is no specialist system on the TSE. Instead, a *saitori* maintains a public limit-order book, matches market and limit orders, and is obliged to follow certain actions to slow down price movements when simple matching of orders would result in price changes greater than exchange-prescribed limits. In their clerical role of matching orders saitoris are somewhat similar to specialists on the NYSE. However, saitoris do not trade for their own accounts and therefore are quite different from either dealers or specialists in the United States.

Because the saitoris perform an essentially clerical role, there are no market-making services or liquidity provided to the market by dealers or specialists. The limit-order book is the primary provider of liquidity. In this regard, the TSE bears some resemblance to the fourth market in the United States in which buyers and sellers trade directly via ECNs. On the TSE, however, if order imbalances would result in price movements across sequential trades that are considered too extreme by the exchange, the saitori may temporarily halt trading and advertise the imbalance in the hope of attracting additional trading interest to the "weak" side of the market.

The TSE organizes stocks into two categories. The First Section consists of about 1,200 of the most actively traded stocks. The Second Section is for less actively traded stocks. Trading in the larger First Section stocks occurs on the floor of the exchange. The remaining securities in the First Section and the Second Section trade electronically.

## Globalization of Stock Markets

All stock markets have come under increasing pressure in recent years to make international alliances or mergers. Much of this pressure is due to the impact of electronic trading. To a growing extent, traders view the stock market as a computer network that links them to other traders, and there are increasingly fewer limits on the securities around the world in which they can trade. Against this background, it becomes more important for exchanges to provide the cheapest mechanism by which trades can be executed and cleared. This argues for global alliances that can facilitate the nuts and bolts of cross-border trading, and can benefit from economies of scale. Moreover, in the face of competition from electronic networks, established exchanges feel that they eventually need to offer 24-hour global markets. Finally, companies want to be able to go beyond national borders when they wish to raise capital.

Merger talks and international strategic alliances blossomed in the late 1990s. We have noted the Euronext merger as well as its alliance with other European exchanges. The Stockholm, Copenhagen, and Oslo exchanges formed a "Nordic Country Alliance" in 1999. Nasdaq began a pilot program to co-list shares on the Stock Exchange of Hong Kong and launched Nasdaq Europe, Nasdaq Japan, and Nasdaq Canada markets. The NYSE and TSE initiated discussions about the possibility of common listing standards. However, in the wake of the stock market decline of 2000–2002, globalization initiatives have faltered. With less investor interest in markets, and a dearth of initial public offerings, the international Nasdaq markets have not attracted substantial trading volume. Nasdaq abandoned its Japanese venture in 2002, and there is some doubt about the future of its European market.

Nevertheless, many markets continue to increase their international focus. For example, Nasdaq and the NYSE each list over 400 non-U.S. firms, and foreign firms account for about 10% of trading volume on the NYSE.

## 3.5    TRADING COSTS

Part of the cost of trading a security is obvious and explicit. Your broker must be paid a commission. Individuals may choose from two kinds of brokers: full-service or discount. Full-service brokers, who provide a variety of services, often are referred to as account executives or financial consultants. Besides carrying out the basic services of executing orders, holding securities for safekeeping, extending margin loans, and facilitating short sales, normally they provide information and advice relating to investment alternatives. Full-service brokers usually are supported by a research staff that issues analyses and forecasts of general economic, industry, and company conditions and often makes specific buy or sell recommendations.

Some customers take the ultimate leap of faith and allow a full-service broker to make buy and sell decisions for them by establishing a *discretionary account*. This step requires an unusual degree of trust on the part of the customer, because an unscrupulous broker can "churn" an account, that is, trade securities excessively, to generate commissions.

Discount brokers, on the other hand, provide "no-frills" services. They buy and sell securities, hold them for safekeeping, offer margin loans, and facilitate short sales, and that is all. The only information they provide about the securities they handle consists of price quotations. Increasingly, the line between full-service and discount brokers can be blurred. Some brokers are purely no-frill, some offer limited services, and others charge for specific services.

In recent years, discount brokerage services have become increasingly available. Today, many banks, thrift institutions, and mutual fund management companies offer such services to the investing public as part of a general trend toward the creation of one-stop financial "supermarkets."

The commission schedule for trades in common stocks for one prominent discount broker is as follows:

| Transaction Method | Commission |
| --- | --- |
| Online trading | $25 or $0.025 per share, whichever is greater |
| Automated telephone trading | $40 or $0.025 per share, whichever is greater |
| Orders desk (through an associate) | $45 + $0.05 per share |

Notice that there is a minimum charge regardless of trade size and that cost as a fraction of the value of traded shares falls as trade size increases. Note also that these prices (and most advertised prices) are for the cheapest market orders. Limit orders are more expensive.

In addition to the explicit part of trading costs—the broker's commission—there is an implicit part—the dealer's **bid–asked spread**. Sometimes the broker is a dealer in the security being traded and will charge no commission but will collect the fee entirely in the form of the bid–asked spread.

Another implicit cost of trading that some observers would distinguish is the price concession an investor may be forced to make for trading in any quantity that exceeds the quantity the dealer is willing to trade at the posted bid or asked price.

One continuing trend is toward online trading either through the Internet or through software that connects a customer directly to a brokerage firm. In 1994, there were no online brokerage accounts; only 5 years later, there were around 7 million such accounts at "e-brokers" such as Ameritrade, Charles Schwab, Fidelity, and E*Trade, and roughly one in five trades were initiated over the Internet.

While there is little conceptual difference between placing your order using a phone call versus through a computer link, online brokerage firms can process trades more cheaply since they do not have to pay as many brokers. The average commission for an online trade is now approximately $25, compared to more than $100 at full-service brokers.

Moreover, these e-brokers are beginning to offer some of the services provided by full-service brokers such as online company research and, to a lesser extent, the opportunity to participate in IPOs. The traditional full-service brokerage firms have responded to this competitive challenge by introducing online trading for their own customers. Some of these firms charge by the trade; others charge through fee-based accounts, in which the customer pays a percentage of assets in the account for the right to trade online.

An ongoing controversy between the NYSE and its competitors is the extent to which better execution on the NYSE offsets the generally lower explicit costs of trading in other markets. Execution refers to the size of the effective bid–asked spread and the amount of price impact in a market. The NYSE believes that many investors focus too intently on the costs they can see, despite the fact that quality of execution can be a far more important determinant of total costs. Many trades on the NYSE are executed at a price inside the quoted spread. This can happen because floor brokers at the specialist's post can bid above or sell below the specialist's quote. In this way, two public orders cross without incurring the specialist's spread.

In contrast, in a dealer market such as Nasdaq, all trades go through the dealer, and all trades, therefore, are subject to a bid–asked spread. The client never sees the spread as an explicit cost, however. The price at which the trade is executed incorporates the dealer's spread, but this part of the trading cost is never reported to the investor. Similarly, regional markets are disadvantaged in terms of execution because their lower trading volume means that fewer brokers congregate at a specialist's post, resulting in a lower probability of two public orders crossing.

A controversial practice related to the bid–asked spread and the quality of trade execution is "paying for order flow." This entails paying a broker a rebate for directing the trade to a particular dealer rather than to the NYSE. By bringing the trade to a dealer instead of to the exchange, however, the broker eliminates the possibility that the trade could have been executed without incurring a spread. Moreover, a broker that is paid for order flow might direct a trade to a dealer that does not even offer the most competitive price. (Indeed, the fact that dealers can afford to pay for order flow suggests that they are able to lay off the trade at better prices elsewhere and, therefore, that the broker also could have found a better price with some additional effort.) Many of the online brokerage firms rely heavily on payment for order flow, since their explicit commissions are so minimal. They typically do not actually execute orders, instead sending an order either to a market maker or to a stock exchange for some listed stocks.

Such practices raise serious ethical questions, because the broker's primary obligation is to obtain the best deal for the client. Payment for order flow might be justified if the rebate were passed along to the client either directly or through lower commissions, but it is not clear that such rebates are passed through.

Online trading and electronic communications networks have already changed the landscape of the financial markets, and this trend can only be expected to continue. The accompanying box considers some of the implications of these new technologies for the future structure of financial markets.

What should our securities markets look like to serve to-day's investor best? Congress addressed this very question a generation ago, when markets were threatened with fragmentation from an increasing number of competing dealers and exchanges. This led the SEC to establish the national market system, which enabled investors to obtain the best quotes on stocks from any of the major exchanges.

Today it is the proliferation of electronic exchanges and after-hours trading venues that threatens to fragment the market. But the solution is simple, and would take the inter-market trading system devised by the SEC a quarter century ago to its next logical step. The highest bid and the lowest offer for every stock, no matter where they originate, should be displayed on a screen that would be available to all investors, 24 hours a day, seven days a week.

If the SEC mandated this centralization of order flow, competition would significantly enhance investor choice and the quality of the trading environment.

Would brokerage houses or even exchanges exist, as we now know them? I believe so, but electronic communication networks would provide the crucial links between buyers and sellers. ECNs would compete by providing far more sophisticated services to the investor than are currently available—not only the entering and execution of standard limit and market orders, but the execution of contingent orders, buys and sells dependent on the levels of other stocks, bonds, commodities, even indexes.

The services of brokerage houses would still be in much demand, but their transformation from commission-based to flat-fee or asset-based pricing would be accelerated. Although ECNs will offer almost costless processing of the basic investor transactions, brokerages would aid investors in placing more-sophisticated orders. More importantly, brokers would provide investment advice. Although today's investor has access to more and more information, this does not mean that he has more understanding of the forces that rule the market or the principles of constructing the best portfolio.

As the spread between the best bid and offer price has collapsed, some traditional concerns of regulators are less pressing than they once were. Whether to allow dealers to step in front of customers to buy or sell, or allow brokerages to cross their orders internally at the best price, regardless of other orders at the price on the book, have traditionally been burning regulatory issues. But with spreads so small and getting smaller, these issues are of virtually no consequence to the average investor as long as the integrity of the order flow information is maintained.

None of this means that the SEC can disappear once it establishes the central order-flow system. A regulatory authority is needed to monitor the functioning of the new systems and ensure that participants live up to their promises. By making clear that the commission's role is to encourage competition to best serve investors, not to impose or dictate the ultimate structure of the markets, the SEC would be poised to take stock trading into the new millennium.

Source: Jeremy J. Siegel, "The SEC Prepares for a New World of Stock Trading," *The Wall Street Journal,* September 27, 1999. Reprinted by permission of Dow Jones & Company, Inc. via Copyright Clearance Center, Inc. © 1999 Dow Jones & Company, Inc. All Rights Reserved Worldwide.

## 3.6 BUYING ON MARGIN

When purchasing securities, investors have easy access to a source of debt financing called *brokers' call loans*. The act of taking advantage of brokers' call loans is called *buying on margin*.

Purchasing stocks on margin means the investor borrows part of the purchase price of the stock from a broker. The **margin** in the account is the portion of the purchase price contributed by the investor; the remainder is borrowed from the broker. The broker, in turn, borrows money from banks at the call money rate to finance these purchases, and charges its clients that rate plus a service charge for the loan. All securities purchased on margin must be left with the brokerage firm in street name, because the securities are used as collateral for the loan.

The Board of Governors of the Federal Reserve System sets limits on the extent to which stock purchases may be financed via margin loans. Currently, the initial margin requirement is 50%, meaning that at least 50% of the purchase price must be paid for in cash, with the rest borrowed.

# BUYING ON MARGIN

The *Excel* spreadsheet model below makes it easy to analyze the impacts of different margin levels and the volatility of stock prices. It also allows you to compare return on investment for a margin trade with a trade using no borrowed funds.

You can learn more about this spreadsheet model using the interactive version available at the Online Learning Center at **www.mhhe.com/bkm**.

| | A | B | C | D | E | F | G | H |
|---|---|---|---|---|---|---|---|---|
| 1 | | | | | | | | |
| 2 | | | Action or Formula | Ending | Return on | | Ending | Return with |
| 3 | | | for Column B | St Price | Investment | | St Price | No Margin |
| 4 | Initial Equity Investment | $10,000.00 | Enter data | | -42.00% | | | -19.00% |
| 5 | Amount Borrowed | $10,000.00 | (B4/B10)-B4 | $20.00 | -122.00% | | $20.00 | -59.00% |
| 6 | Initial Stock Price | $50.00 | Enter data | 25.00 | -102.00% | | 25.00 | -49.00% |
| 7 | Shares Purchased | 400 | (B4/B10)/B6 | 30.00 | -82.00% | | 30.00 | -39.00% |
| 8 | Ending Stock Price | $40.00 | Enter data | 35.00 | -62.00% | | 35.00 | -29.00% |
| 9 | Cash Dividends During Hold Per. | $0.50 | Enter data | 40.00 | -42.00% | | 40.00 | -19.00% |
| 10 | Initial Margin Percentage | 50.00% | Enter data | 45.00 | -22.00% | | 45.00 | -9.00% |
| 11 | Maintenance Margin Percentage | 30.00% | Enter data | 50.00 | -2.00% | | 50.00 | 1.00% |
| 12 | | | | 55.00 | 18.00% | | 55.00 | 11.00% |
| 13 | Rate on Margin Loan | 8.00% | Enter data | 60.00 | 38.00% | | 60.00 | 21.00% |
| 14 | Holding Period in Months | 6 | Enter data | 65.00 | 58.00% | | 65.00 | 31.00% |
| 15 | | | | 70.00 | 78.00% | | 70.00 | 41.00% |
| 16 | **Return on Investment** | | | 75.00 | 98.00% | | 75.00 | 51.00% |
| 17 | Capital Gain on Stock | -$4,000.00 | B7*(B8-B6) | 80.00 | 118.00% | | 80.00 | 61.00% |
| 18 | Dividends | $200.00 | B7*B9 | | | | | |
| 19 | Interest on Margin Loan | $400.00 | B5*(B14/12)*B13 | | | | | |
| 20 | Net Income | -$4,200.00 | B17+B18-B19 | | | LEGEND: | | |
| 21 | Initial Investment | $10,000.00 | B4 | | | Enter data | | |
| 22 | Return on Investment | -42.00% | B20/B21 | | | Value calculated | | |

## EXAMPLE 3.1    Margin

The *percentage margin* is defined as the ratio of the net worth, or "equity value," of the account to the market value of the securities. To demonstrate, suppose that the investor initially pays $6,000 toward the purchase of $10,000 worth of stock (100 shares at $100 per share), borrowing the remaining $4,000 from the broker. The initial balance sheet looks like this:

| Assets | | Liabilities and Owner's Equity | |
|---|---|---|---|
| Value of stock | $10,000 | Loan from broker | $4,000 |
| | | Equity | $6,000 |

The initial percentage margin is

$$\text{Margin} = \frac{\text{Equity in account}}{\text{Value of stock}} = \frac{\$6,000}{\$10,000} = .60$$

If the stock's price declines to $70 per share, the account balance becomes:

| Assets | | Liabilities and Owner's Equity | |
|---|---|---|---|
| Value of stock | $7,000 | Loan from broker | $4,000 |
| | | Equity | $3,000 |

The equity in the account falls by the full decrease in the stock value, and the percentage margin is now

$$\text{Margin} = \frac{\text{Equity in account}}{\text{Value of stock}} = \frac{\$3,000}{\$7,000} = .43, \text{ or } 43\%$$

If the stock value in Example 3.1 were to fall below $4,000, equity would become negative, meaning that the value of the stock is no longer sufficient collateral to cover the loan from the broker. To guard against this possibility, the broker sets a *maintenance margin*. If the percentage margin falls below the maintenance level, the broker will issue a *margin call* requiring the investor to add new cash or securities to the margin account. If the investor does not act, the broker may sell the securities from the account to pay off enough of the loan to restore the percentage margin to an acceptable level.

Margin calls can occur with little warning. For example, on April 14, 2000, when the Nasdaq index fell by a record 355 points, or 9.7%, the accounts of many investors who had purchased stock with borrowed funds ran afoul of their maintenance margin requirements. Some brokerage houses, concerned about the incredible volatility in the market and the possibility that stock prices would fall below the point that remaining shares could cover the amount of the loan, gave their customers only a few hours or less to meet a margin call rather than the more typical notice of a few days. If customers could not come up with the cash, or were not at a phone to receive the notification of the margin call until later in the day, their accounts were sold out. In other cases, brokerage houses sold out accounts without notifying their customers.

## EXAMPLE 3.2    Maintenance Margin

Suppose the maintenance margin is 30%. How far could the stock price fall before the investor would get a margin call?

Let $P$ be the price of the stock. The value of the investor's 100 shares is then $100P$, and the equity in his or her account is $100P - \$4,000$. The percentage margin is therefore $(100P - \$4,000)/100P$. The price at which the percentage margin equals the maintenance margin of .3 is found by solving for $P$ in the equation

$$\frac{100P - \$4,000}{100P} = .3$$

which implies that $P = \$57.14$. If the price of the stock were to fall below $57.14 per share, the investor would get a margin call.

| CONCEPT CHECK ☞ QUESTION 3 | **If the maintenance margin in Example 3.2 were 40%, how far could the stock price fall before the investor would get a margin call?** |
|---|---|

Why do investors buy stocks (or bonds) on margin? They do so when they wish to invest an amount greater than their own money alone would allow. Thus they can achieve greater upside potential, but they also expose themselves to greater downside risk.

To see how, let us suppose that an investor is bullish (optimistic) on IBM stock, which is currently selling at $100 per share. The investor has $10,000 to invest and expects IBM stock to increase in price by 30% during the next year. Ignoring any dividends, the expected rate of return would thus be 30% if the investor spent $10,000 to buy 100 shares.

But now let us assume that the investor also borrows another $10,000 from the broker and invests it in IBM also. The total investment in IBM would thus be $20,000 (for 200 shares). If the interest rate on the margin loan is 9% per year, what will be the investor's rate of return (again ignoring dividends) if IBM stock does go up 30% by year's end?

The 200 shares will be worth $26,000. Paying off $10,900 of principal and interest on the margin loan leaves $26,000 − $10,900 = $15,100. The rate of return on the investor's funds, therefore, will be

$$\frac{\$15,100 - \$10,000}{\$10,000} = 51\%$$

The investor has parlayed a 30% rise in the stock's price into a 51% rate of return on the $10,000 investment.

Doing so, however, magnifies the downside risk. Suppose that instead of going up by 30% the price of IBM stock goes down by 30% to $70 per share. In that case the 200 shares will be worth $14,000, and the investor is left with $3,100 after paying off the $10,900 of principal and interest on the loan. The result is a disastrous rate of return:

$$\frac{\$3,100 - \$10,000}{\$10,000} = -69\%$$

Table 3.7 summarizes the possible results of these hypothetical transactions. Note that if there is no change in IBM's stock price, the investor loses 9%, the cost of the loan.

**CONCEPT CHECK☞ QUESTION 4** — Suppose that the investor borrows only $5,000 at the same interest rate of 9% per year. What will be the rate of return if the price of IBM stock goes up by 30%? If it goes down by 30%? If it remains unchanged?

## 3.7  SHORT SALES

A **short sale** allows investors to profit from a decline in a security's price. An investor borrows a share of stock from a broker and sells it. Later, the short-seller must purchase a share of the same stock in the market to replace the share that was borrowed. This is called *covering the short position*. Table 3.8 compares stock purchases to short sales.

The short-seller anticipates the stock price will fall, so that the share can be purchased at a lower price than it initially sold for; the short-seller will then reap a profit. Short-sellers

**Table 3.7   Illustration of Buying Stock on Margin**

| Change in Stock Price | End of Year Value of Shares | Repayment of Principal and Interest | Investor's Rate of Return* |
|---|---|---|---|
| 30% increase | $26,000 | $10,900 | 51% |
| No change | 20,000 | 10,900 | −9 |
| 30% decrease | 14,000 | 10,900 | −69 |

*Assuming the investor buys $20,000 worth of stock by borrowing $10,000 at an interest rate of 9% per year.

## Table 3.8   Cash Flows from Purchasing versus Short Selling Shares of Stock

| Time | Action | Cash Flow |
|------|--------|-----------|
| **Purchase of Stock** | | |
| 0 | Buy share | − Initial price |
| 1 | Receive dividend, sell share | Ending price + dividend |
| Profit = (Ending price + dividend) − Initial price | | |
| **Short Sale of Stock** | | |
| 0 | Borrow share; sell it | + Initial price |
| 1 | Repay dividend and buy share to replace the share originally borrowed | − (Ending price + dividend) |
| Profit = Initial price − (Ending price + dividend) | | |

Note: A negative cash flow implies a cash outflow.

must not only replace the shares but also pay the lender of the security any dividends paid during the short sale.

In practice, the shares loaned out for a short sale are typically provided by the short-seller's brokerage firm, which holds a wide variety of securities in street name. The owner of the shares will not even know that the shares have been lent to the short-seller. If the owner wishes to sell the shares, the brokerage firm will simply borrow shares from another investor. Therefore, the short sale may have an indefinite term. However, if the brokerage firm cannot locate new shares to replace the ones sold, the short-seller will need to repay the loan immediately by purchasing shares in the market and turning them over to the brokerage firm to close out the loan.

Exchange rules permit short sales only when the last recorded change in the stock price is positive. This rule apparently is meant to prevent waves of speculation against the stock. In other words, the votes of "no confidence" in the stock that short sales represent may be entered only after a price increase.

Finally, exchange rules require that proceeds from a short sale must be kept on account with the broker. The short-seller, therefore, cannot invest these funds to generate income. However, large or institutional investors typically will receive some income from the proceeds of a short sale being held with the broker. In addition, short-sellers are required to post margin (which is essentially collateral) with the broker to ensure that the trader can cover any losses sustained should the stock price rise during the period of the short sale.[5]

**EXAMPLE 3.3**

## Short Sales

To illustrate the mechanics of short selling, suppose that you are bearish (pessimistic) on DotBomb stock and that its current market price is $100 per share. You tell your broker to sell short 1,000 shares. The broker borrows 1,000 shares either from another customer's account or from another broker.

The $100,000 cash proceeds from the short sale are credited to your account. Suppose the broker has a 50% margin requirement on short sales. This means that you must have other cash or securities in your account worth at least $50,000 that can serve as margin (that is, collateral) on the short sale. Let us suppose that you have $50,000 in Treasury bills. Your account with the broker after the short sale will then be:

---

[5] We should note that although we have been describing a short sale of a stock, bonds also may be sold short.

| Assets | | Liabilities and Owner's Equity | |
| --- | --- | --- | --- |
| Cash | $100,000 | Short position in DotBomb stock | $100,000 |
| T-bills | $50,000 | (1,000 shares owed) | |
| | | Equity | $50,000 |

Your initial percentage margin is the ratio of the equity in the account, $50,000, to the current value of the shares you have borrowed and eventually must return, $100,000:

$$\text{Percentage margin} = \frac{\text{Equity}}{\text{Value of stock owed}} = \frac{\$50,000}{\$100,000} = .50$$

Suppose you are right, and DotBomb stock falls to $70 per share. You can now close out your position at a profit. To cover the short sale, you buy 1,000 shares to replace the ones you borrowed. Because the shares now sell for $70, the purchase costs only $70,000. Because your account was credited for $100,000 when the shares were borrowed and sold, your profit is $30,000: The profit equals the decline in the share price times the number of shares sold short. On the other hand, if the price of DotBomb stock goes up while you are short, you lose money and may get a margin call from your broker.

Like investors who purchase stock on margin, a short-seller must be concerned about margin calls. If the stock price rises, the margin in the account will fall; if margin falls to the maintenance level, the short-seller will receive a margin call.[6]

## EXAMPLE 3.4   Margin Calls on Short Positions

Suppose that the broker has a maintenance margin of 30% on short sales. This means that the equity in your account must be at least 30% of the value of your short position at all times. How far can the price of DotBomb stock go up before you get a margin call?

Let $P$ be the price of DotBomb stock. Then the value of the shares you must return is $1,000P$, and the equity in your account is $\$150,000 - 1,000P$. Your short position margin ratio is therefore $(\$150,000 - 1,000P)/1,000P$. The critical value of $P$ is thus

$$\frac{\text{Equity}}{\text{Value of shares owed}} = \frac{\$150,000 - 1,000P}{1,000P} = .3$$

which implies that $P = \$115.38$ per share. If DotBomb stock should rise above $115.38 per share, you will get a margin call, and you will either have to put up additional cash or cover your short position.

You can see now why stop-buy orders often accompany short sales. Imagine that you short sell DotBomb when it is selling at $100 per share. If the share price falls, you will profit from the short sale. On the other hand, if the share price rises, let's say to $130, you will lose $30 per share. But suppose that when you initiate the short sale, you also enter a stop-buy order at $120. The stop-buy will be executed if the share price surpasses $120, thereby limiting your losses to $20 per share. (If the stock price drops, the stop-buy will

---

[6] Notice that when buying on margin, you borrow a given number of dollars from your broker, so the amount of the loan is independent of the share price. In contrast, when short selling you borrow a given number of *shares*, which must be returned. Therefore, when the price of the shares changes, the value of the loan also changes.

## SHORT SALE

This Excel spreadsheet model was built using the text example for DotBomb. The model allows you to analyze the effects of returns, margin calls, and different levels of initial and maintenance margins. The model also includes a sensitivity analysis for ending stock price and return on investment.

You can learn more about this spreadsheet model using the interactive version available at our Online Learning Center at **www.mhhe.com/bkm**.

| | A | B | C | D | E |
|---|---|---|---|---|---|
| 1 | | | | | |
| 2 | | | Action or Formula | Ending | Return on |
| 3 | | | for Column B | St Price | Investment |
| 4 | Initial Investment | $50,000.00 | Enter data | | 58.33% |
| 5 | Initial Stock Price | $100.00 | Enter data | $170.00 | -133.33% |
| 6 | Number of Shares Sold Short | 1,000 | (B4/B9)/B5 | 160.00 | -116.67% |
| 7 | Ending Stock Price | $70.00 | Enter data | 150.00 | -100.00% |
| 8 | Cash Dividends Per Share | $0.00 | Enter data | 140.00 | -83.33% |
| 9 | Initial Margin Percentage | 50.00% | Enter data | 130.00 | -66.67% |
| 10 | Maintenance Margin Percentage | 30.00% | Enter data | 120.00 | -50.00% |
| 11 | | | | 110.00 | -33.33% |
| 12 | **Return on Short Sale** | | | 100.00 | -16.67% |
| 13 | Capital Gain on Stock | $30,000.00 | B6*(B5-B7) | 90.00 | 0.00% |
| 14 | Dividends Paid | $0.00 | B8*B6 | 80.00 | 16.67% |
| 15 | Net Income | $30,000.00 | B13-B14 | 70.00 | 33.33% |
| 16 | Initial Investment | $50,000.00 | B4 | 60.00 | 50.00% |
| 17 | Return on Investment | 60.00% | B15/B16 | 50.00 | 66.67% |
| 18 | | | | 40.00 | 83.33% |
| 19 | **Margin Positions** | | | 30.00 | 100.00% |
| 20 | Margin Based on Ending Price | 114.29% | (B4+(B5*B6)-B14-(B6*B7))/(B6*B7) | 20.00 | 116.67% |
| 21 | | | | 10.00 | |
| 22 | Price for Margin Call | $115.38 | (B4+(B5*B6)-B14)/(B6*(1+B10)) | | |
| 23 | | | | | LEGEND: |
| 24 | | | | | Enter data |
| 25 | | | | | Value calculated |

never be executed.) The stop-buy order thus provides protection to the short-seller if the share price moves up.

**CONCEPT CHECK ☞ QUESTION 5**

**If the short position maintenance margin in Example 3.4 were 40%, how far could the stock price rise before the investor would get a margin call?**

## 3.8  REGULATION OF SECURITIES MARKETS

**Government Regulation** Trading in securities markets in the United States is regulated under a myriad of laws. The two major laws are the Securities Act of 1933 and the Securities Exchange Act of 1934. The 1933 act requires full disclosure of relevant information relating to the issue of new securities. This is the act that requires registration of new securities and the issuance of a prospectus that details the financial prospects of the firm. SEC approval of a prospectus or financial report does not mean that it views the security as a good investment. The SEC cares only that the relevant facts are disclosed; investors make their own evaluations of the security's value.

The 1934 act established the Securities and Exchange Commission to administer the provisions of the 1933 act. It also extended the disclosure principle of the 1933 act by requiring firms with issued securities on secondary exchanges to periodically disclose relevant financial information.

The 1934 act also empowered the SEC to register and regulate securities exchanges, OTC trading, brokers, and dealers. The act thus established the SEC as the administrative agency responsible for broad oversight of the securities markets. The SEC, however, shares oversight with other regulatory agencies. For example, the Commodity Futures Trading Commission (CFTC) regulates trading in futures markets, whereas the Federal Reserve has broad responsibility for the health of the U.S. financial system. In this role the Fed sets margin requirements on stocks and stock options and regulates bank lending to securities markets participants.

The Securities Investor Protection Act of 1970 established the Securities Investor Protection Corporation (SIPC) to protect investors from losses if their brokerage firms fail. Just as the Federal Deposit Insurance Corporation provides federal protection to depositors against bank failure, the SIPC ensures that investors will receive securities held for their account in street name by the failed brokerage firm up to a limit of $500,000 per customer. The SIPC is financed by levying an "insurance premium" on its participating, or member, brokerage firms. It also may borrow money from the SEC if its own funds are insufficient to meet its obligations.

In addition to federal regulations, security trading is subject to state laws. The laws providing for state regulation of securities are known generally as *blue sky laws*, because they attempt to prevent the false promotion and sale of securities representing nothing more than blue sky. State laws to outlaw fraud in security sales were instituted before the Securities Act of 1933. Varying state laws were somewhat unified when many states adopted portions of the Uniform Securities Act, which was proposed in 1956.

## Regulatory Responses to Recent Scandals

The scandals of 2000–2002 centered largely on three broad practices: allocations of shares in IPOs, tainted securities research and recommendations put out to the public, and, probably most important, misleading financial statements and accounting practices. The regulatory response to these issues is still nascent, but some initiatives have been put in place. Many of these are contained in the Sarbanes-Oxley Act passed by Congress in 2001. Among the key provisions of the act are:

- Creation of a Public Company Accounting Oversight Board to oversee the auditing of public companies.
- Rules requiring independent financial experts to serve on audit committees of a firm's board of directors. Currently, however, the precise definitions of "independent" and "financial expert" for the purposes of the act are unclear. For example, is a large shareholder independent? Would Warren Buffett—who is not an accountant—be considered a financial expert? The SEC will be charged with working out these fine points.
- CEOs and CFOs must now personally certify that their firms' financial reports, "fairly represent, in all material respects, the operations and financial condition of the company" and are subject to personal penalties if those reports turn out to be misleading. Following the letter of GAAP rules may still be necessary, but it is no longer sufficient accounting practice.

- Auditors may no longer provide several other services to their clients. This is intended to prevent potential profits on consulting work from influencing the quality of their audit.

The NYSE and Nasdaq also have weighed in with proposals to improve corporate governance and reduce incentives for false dealing. They have called for all listed companies to:

- Require that the board of directors comprise independent directors. (Again, however, defining "independent" may be problematic.)
- Hold regular meetings of directors in which company management is not present (and therefore cannot impede or influence the discussion).
- Require that all members of the compensation, nominating, and audit committees be independent directors and that the head of the audit committee have financial expertise. Stock-option plans for executive compensation must be approved by shareholders.

The SEC's Regulation FD (for Fair Disclosure), introduced in 2000, prohibits firms from divulging material information to one outside group (e.g., stock analysts) before making it available to the entire market. In addition, to settle charges brought by New York Attorney General Eliot Spitzer concerning their publication of biased stock research as a quid pro quo for IPO allocations and investment banking contracts, major investment banks (Citigroup; CSFB; Morgan Stanley; Goldman, Sachs; and Merrill Lynch) agreed in late 2002 to pay $900 million in penalties, contribute over $450 million to finance independent stock research, and provide $85 million to fund investor education programs. The agreement also lays out guidelines designed to fence off stock research from the investment banking side of the firm. For example, the firms have agreed to remove the link between analyst compensation and the amount of investment banking business they bring into the firm and to bar analysts from participating in IPO road shows. The accord also limits "spinning," the practice of awarding IPO allocations to corporate executives who can reward underwriters with future investment banking business.

To date, there has been little talk of new legislation governing initial public offerings.

| **E-INVESTMENTS** **The Securities and Exchange Commission** | The Securities and Exchange Commission (**www.sec.gov**) serves several important functions for U.S. equity markets. At the home page, link to *About the SEC* and *What We Do*. What is the mission of the SEC and what activities are undertaken to achieve this mission? What laws does the SEC enforce? |
| --- | --- |

## Self-Regulation and Circuit Breakers

Much of the securities industry relies on self-regulation. The SEC delegates to secondary exchanges much of the responsibility for day-to-day oversight of trading. Similarly, the National Association of Securities Dealers oversees trading of OTC securities. The Association for Investment Management and Research's Code of Ethics and Professional Conduct sets out principles that govern the behavior of members with the Chartered Financial Analyst designation, commonly referred to as CFAs. The nearby box presents a brief outline of those principles.

The market collapse of 1987 prompted several suggestions for regulatory change. Among these was a call for "circuit breakers" to slow or stop trading during periods of extreme volatility. Some of the current circuit breakers are as follows:

## Standard I: Fundamental Responsibilities

Members shall maintain knowledge of and comply with all applicable laws, rules, and regulations including AIMR's Code of Ethics and Standards of Professional Conduct.

## Standard II: Responsibilities to the Profession

- Professional Misconduct. Members shall not engage in any professional conduct involving dishonesty, fraud, deceit, or misrepresentation.
- Prohibition against Plagiarism.

## Standard III: Responsibilities to the Employer

- Obligation to Inform Employer of Code and Standards. Members shall inform their employer that they are obligated to comply with these Code and Standards.
- Disclosure of Additional Compensation Arrangements. Members shall disclose to their employer all benefits that they receive in addition to compensation from that employer.

## Standard IV:
## Responsibilities to Clients and Prospects

- Investment Process and Research Reports. Members shall exercise diligence and thoroughness in making investment recommendations . . . distinguish between facts and opinions in research reports . . . and use reasonable care to maintain objectivity.
- Interactions with Clients and Prospects. Members must place their clients' interests before their own.
- Portfolio Investment Recommendations. Members shall make a reasonable inquiry into a client's financial situation, investment experience, and investment objectives prior to making appropriate investment recommendations. . . .
- Priority of Transactions. Transactions for clients and employers shall have priority over transactions for the benefit of a member.
- Disclosure of Conflicts to Clients and Prospects. Members shall disclose to their clients and prospects all matters, including ownership of securities or other investments, that reasonably could be expected to impair the members' ability to make objective recommendations.

## Standard V: Responsibilities to the Public

- Prohibition against Use of Material Nonpublic [Inside] Information. Members who possess material nonpublic information related to the value of a security shall not trade in that security.
- Performance Presentation. Members shall not make any statements that misrepresent the investment performance that they have accomplished or can reasonably be expected to achieve.

Source: Abridged from *The Standards of Professional Conduct* of the Association for Investment Management and Research.

---

- *Trading halts.* If the Dow Jones Industrial Average falls by 10%, trading will be halted for 1 hour if the drop occurs before 2:00 P.M. (Eastern Standard Time), for ½ hour if the drop occurs between 2:00 and 2:30, but not at all if the drop occurs after 2:30. If the Dow falls by 20%, trading will be halted for 2 hours if the drop occurs before 1:00 P.M., for 1 hour if the drop occurs between 1:00 and 2:00, and for the rest of the day if the drop occurs after 2:00. A 30% drop in the Dow would close the market for the rest of the day, regardless of the time.

- *Collars.* When the Dow moves about 2 percentage points[7] in either direction from the previous day's close, Rule 80A of the NYSE requires that index arbitrage orders pass a "tick test." In a falling market, sell orders may be executed only at a plus tick or zero-plus tick, meaning that the trade may be done at a higher price than the last trade (a plus tick) or at the last price if the last recorded change in the stock price is positive (a zero-plus tick). The rule remains in effect for the rest of the day unless the Dow returns to within 1% of the previous day's close.

---

[7] The exact threshold is computed as 2% of the average closing value of the Dow Jones Industrial Average for the last month of the previous quarter, rounded down to the nearest 10 points.

The idea behind circuit breakers is that a temporary halt in trading during periods of very high volatility can help mitigate informational problems that might contribute to excessive price swings. For example, even if a trader is unaware of any specific adverse economic news, if she sees the market plummeting, she will suspect that there might be a good reason for the price drop and will become unwilling to buy shares. In fact, the trader might decide to sell shares to avoid losses. Thus feedback from price swings to trading behavior can exacerbate market movements. Circuit breakers give participants a chance to assess market fundamentals while prices are temporarily frozen. In this way, they have a chance to decide whether price movements are warranted while the market is closed.

Of course, circuit breakers have no bearing on trading in non-U.S. markets. It is quite possible that they simply have induced those who engage in program trading to move their operations into foreign exchanges.

## Insider Trading

One of the important restrictions on trading involves *insider trading*. It is illegal for anyone to transact in securities to profit from **inside information,** that is, private information held by officers, directors, or major stockholders that has not yet been divulged to the public. The difficulty is that the definition of *insiders* can be ambiguous. Although it is obvious that the chief financial officer of a firm is an insider, it is less clear whether the firm's biggest supplier can be considered an insider. However, the supplier may deduce the firm's near-term prospects from significant changes in orders. This gives the supplier a unique form of private information, yet the supplier does not necessarily qualify as an insider. These ambiguities plague security analysts, whose job is to uncover as much information as possible concerning the firm's expected prospects. The distinction between legal private information and illegal inside information can be fuzzy.

An important Supreme Court decision in 1997, however, came down on the side of an expansive view of what constitutes illegal insider trading. The decision upheld the so-called misappropriation theory of insider trading, which holds that traders may not trade on nonpublic information even if they are not company insiders.

The SEC requires officers, directors, and major stockholders of all publicly held firms to report all of their transactions in their firm's stock. A compendium of insider trades is published monthly in the SEC's *Official Summary of Securities Transactions and Holdings*. The idea is to inform the public of any implicit votes of confidence or no confidence made by insiders.

Do insiders exploit their knowledge? The answer seems to be, to a limited degree, yes. Two forms of evidence support this conclusion. First, there is abundant evidence of "leakage" of useful information to some traders before any public announcement of that information. For example, share prices of firms announcing dividend increases (which the market interprets as good news concerning the firm's prospects) commonly increase in value a few days *before* the public announcement of the increase.[8] Clearly, some investors are acting on the good news before it is released to the public. Similarly, share prices tend to increase a few days before the public announcement of above-trend earnings growth.[9] At the same time, share prices still rise substantially on the day of the public release of good news, indicating that insiders, or their associates, have not fully bid up the price of the stock to the level commensurate with that news.

---

[8] See, for example, J. Aharony and I. Swary, "Quarterly Dividend and Earnings Announcement and Stockholders' Return: An Empirical Analysis," *Journal of Finance* 35 (March 1980).

[9] See, for example, George Foster, Chris Olsen, and Terry Shevlin, "Earnings Releases, Anomalies, and the Behavior of Security Returns," *The Accounting Review*, October 1984.

The second sort of evidence on insider trading is based on returns earned on trades by insiders. Researchers have examined the SEC's summary of insider trading to measure the performance of insiders. In one of the best known of these studies, Jaffe[10] examined the abnormal return on stock over the months following purchases or sales by insiders. For months in which insider purchasers of a stock exceeded insider sellers of the stock by three or more, the stocks had an abnormal return in the following 8 months of about 5%. When insider sellers exceeded inside buyers, however, the stock tended to perform poorly.

**SUMMARY**

1. Firms issue securities to raise the capital necessary to finance their investments. Investment bankers market these securities to the public on the primary market. Investment bankers generally act as underwriters who purchase the securities from the firm and resell them to the public at a markup. Before the securities may be sold to the public, the firm must publish an SEC-approved prospectus that provides information on the firm's prospects.

2. Issued securities are traded on the secondary market, that is, on organized stock exchanges, the over-the-counter market, or, for large traders, through direct negotiation. Only members of exchanges may trade on the exchange. Brokerage firms holding seats on the exchange sell their services to individuals, charging commissions for executing trades on their behalf. The NYSE has fairly strict listing requirements. Regional exchanges provide listing opportunities for local firms that do not meet the requirements of the national exchanges.

3. Trading of common stocks in exchanges takes place through specialists. Specialists act to maintain an orderly market in the shares of one or more firms, maintaining "books" of limit-buy and limit-sell orders and matching trades at mutually acceptable prices. Specialists also will accept market orders by selling from or buying for their own inventory of stocks.

4. The over-the-counter market is not a formal exchange but an informal network of brokers and dealers who negotiate sales of securities. The Nasdaq system provides online computer quotes offered by dealers in the stock. When an individual wishes to purchase or sell a share, the broker can search the listing of offered bid and asked prices, contact the dealer who has the best quote, and execute the trade.

5. Block transactions account for about half of trading volume. These trades often are too large to be handled readily by specialists, and thus block houses have developed that specialize in these transactions, identifying potential trading partners for their clients.

6. Buying on margin means borrowing money from a broker to buy more securities. By buying securities on margin, an investor magnifies both the upside potential and the downside risk. If the equity in a margin account falls below the required maintenance level, the investor will get a margin call from the broker.

7. Short selling is the practice of selling securities that the seller does not own. The short-seller borrows the securities sold through a broker and may be required to cover the short position at any time on demand. The cash proceeds of a short sale are kept in escrow by the broker, and the broker usually requires that the short-seller deposit additional cash or securities to serve as margin (collateral) for the short sale.

8. Securities trading is regulated by the Securities and Exchange Commission, as well as by self-regulation of the exchanges. Many of the important regulations have to do with

---

[10] Jeffrey F. Jaffe, "Special Information and Insider Trading," *Journal of Business* 47 (July 1974).

full disclosure of relevant information concerning the securities in question. Insider trading rules also prohibit traders from attempting to profit from inside information.

9. In addition to providing the basic services of executing buy and sell orders, holding securities for safekeeping, making margin loans, and facilitating short sales, full-service brokers offer investors information, advice, and even investment decisions. Discount brokers offer only the basic brokerage services but usually charge less.

10. Total trading costs consist of commissions, the dealer's bid–asked spread, and price concessions.

## KEY TERMS

| | | |
|---|---|---|
| primary market | Nasdaq | block transactions |
| secondary market | bid price | program trades |
| initial public offerings | asked price | bid–asked spread |
| underwriters | third market | margin |
| prospectus | fourth market | short sale |
| private placement | electronic communication | inside information |
| stock exchanges | network (ECN) | |
| over-the-counter market | specialist | |

## WEBSITES

www2.standardandpoors.com
This site provides information about Standard & Poor's Global Indexes.

www.investorlinks.com
Under the *Exchanges* links, look at the number and variety of market exchanges.

Review the "listing" requirements at each of these major markets:

www.nyse.com
The New York Stock Exchange

www.nasdaq.com
Nasdaq

www.amex.com
American Stock Exchange

The following sites contain information about initial public offerings:

www.ipo.com
IPO.com provides information on IPOs, secondary offerings, and venture capital market current events.

*(continued)*

| **WEBSITES** | www.unlockdates.com<br>Unlockdates.com provides information about when "insiders" can first trade shares after a public offering. |
|---|---|

www.unlockdates.com
Unlockdates.com provides information about when "insiders" can first trade shares after a public offering.

moneycentral.msn.com/investor/market/ipomain.asp
Money Central has an excellent IPO site.

www.123jump.com
See the 123jump.com *IPO Center.*

The following are financial market regulators:

www.sec.gov
The Securities and Exchange Commission

www.cftc.gov/cftc/cftchome.htm
The Commodity Futures Trading Commission

www.federalreserve.gov
The Federal Reserve Board of Governors

www.sipc.org
The Securities Investor Protection Corporation

www.nasdr.com/state_regulators.asp
State securities regulators

**PROBLEMS**

1. FBN, Inc., has just sold 100,000 shares in an initial public offering. The underwriter's explicit fees were $70,000. The offering price for the shares was $50, but immediately upon issue the share price jumped to $53.

   a. What is your best guess as to the total cost to FBN of the equity issue?

   b. Is the entire cost of the underwriting a source of profit to the underwriters?

2. Suppose that you sell short 100 shares of IBX, now selling at $70 per share.

   a. What is your maximum possible loss?

   b. What happens to the maximum loss if you simultaneously place a stop-buy order at $78?

3. Dée Trader opens a brokerage account and purchases 300 shares of Internet Dreams at $40 per share. She borrows $4,000 from her broker to help pay for the purchase. The interest rate on the loan is 8%.

   *a.* What is the margin in Dée's account when she first purchases the stock?

   *b.* If the price falls to $30 per share by the end of the year, what is the remaining margin in her account? If the maintenance margin requirement is 30%, will she receive a margin call?

   *c.* What is the rate of return on her investment?

4. Old Economy Traders opened an account to short sell 1,000 shares of Internet Dreams from the previous problem. The initial margin requirement was 50%. (The margin account pays no interest.) A year later, the price of Internet Dreams has risen from $40 to $50, and the stock has paid a dividend of $2 per share.

   *a.* What is the remaining margin in the account?

   *b.* If the maintenance margin requirement is 30%, will Old Economy receive a margin call?

   *c.* What is the rate of return on the investment?

5. An expiring put will be exercised and the stock will be sold if the stock price is below the exercise price. A stop-loss order causes a stock sale when the stock price falls below some limit. Compare and contrast the two strategies of purchasing put options versus issuing a stop-loss order.

6. Compare call options and stop-buy orders.

7. Here is some price information on Marriott:

| | Bid | Asked |
|---|---|---|
| Marriott | $37.80 | $38.10 |

   You have placed a stop-loss order to sell at $38. What are you telling your broker? Given market prices, will your order be executed?

8. Do you think it is possible to replace market-making specialists by a fully automated computerized trade-matching system?

9. Consider the following limit-order book of a specialist. The last trade in the stock took place at a price of $50.

| Limit-Buy Orders | | Limit-Sell Orders | |
|---|---|---|---|
| Price ($) | Shares | Price ($) | Shares |
| $49.75 | 500 | $50.25 | 100 |
| 49.50 | 800 | 51.50 | 100 |
| 49.25 | 500 | 54.75 | 300 |
| 49.00 | 200 | 58.25 | 100 |
| 48.50 | 600 | | |

   *a.* If a market-buy order for 100 shares comes in, at what price will it be filled?

   *b.* At what price would the next market-buy order be filled?

   *c.* If you were the specialist, would you desire to increase or decrease your inventory of this stock?

10. What purpose does the Designated Order Turnaround system (SuperDot) serve on the New York Stock Exchange?

11. Who sets the bid and asked price for a stock traded over the counter? Would you expect the spread to be higher on actively or inactively traded stocks?

12. Consider the following data concerning the NYSE:

| Year | Average Daily Trading Volume (Thousands of Shares) | Annual High Price of an Exchange Membership |
|------|------|------|
| 1991 | 178,917 | $  440,000 |
| 1992 | 202,266 | 600,000 |
| 1993 | 264,519 | 775,000 |
| 1994 | 291,351 | 830,000 |
| 1995 | 346,101 | 1,050,000 |
| 1996 | 411,953 | 1,450,000 |

What do you conclude about the short-run relationship between trading activity and the value of a seat?

13. Suppose that Intel currently is selling at $40 per share. You buy 500 shares, using $15,000 of your own money and borrowing the remainder of the purchase price from your broker. The rate on the margin loan is 8%.

 a. What is the percentage increase in the net worth of your brokerage account if the price of Intel *immediately* changes to (i) $44; (ii) $40; (iii) $36? What is the relationship between your percentage gain or loss and the percentage change in the price of Intel?

 b. If the maintenance margin is 25%, how low can Intel's price fall before you get a margin call?

 c. How would your answer to (b) change if you had financed the initial purchase with only $10,000 of your own money?

 d. What is the rate of return on your margined position (assuming again that you invest $15,000 of your own money) if Intel is selling *after 1 year* at (i) $44; (ii) $40; (iii) $36? What is the relationship between your percentage return and the percentage change in the price of Intel? Assume that Intel pays no dividends.

 e. Continue to assume that a year has passed. How low can Intel's price fall before you get a margin call?

14. Suppose that you sell short 500 shares of Intel, currently selling for $40 per share, and give your broker $15,000 to establish your margin account.

 a. If you earn no interest on the funds in your margin account, what will be your rate of return after 1 year if Intel stock is selling at (i) $44; (ii) $40; (iii) $36? Assume that Intel pays no dividends.

 b. If the maintenance margin is 25%, how high can Intel's price rise before you get a margin call?

 c. Redo parts (a) and (b), now assuming that Intel's dividend (paid at year end) is $1 per share. Prices in (a) should be interpreted as ex dividend, that is, prices just after the dividend is paid.

15. Here is some price information on Fincorp stock. Suppose first that Fincorp trades in a dealer market.

| Bid | Asked |
|------|------|
| $55.25 | $55.50 |

 a. Suppose you have submitted an order to your broker to buy at market. At what price will your trade be executed?

  b. Suppose you have submitted an order to sell at market. At what price will your trade be executed?

  c. Suppose an investor has submitted a limit order to sell at $55.38. What will happen?

  d. Suppose another investor has submitted a limit order to buy at $55.38. What will happen?

16. Now reconsider the previous problem assuming that Fincorp sells in an exchange market like the NYSE.

  a. Is there any chance for price improvement in the market orders considered in parts (a) and (b)?

  b. Is there any chance of an immediate trade at $55.38 for the limit-buy order in part (d)?

17. You are bullish on Telecom stock. The current market price is $25 per share, and you have $5,000 of your own to invest. You borrow an additional $5,000 from your broker at an interest rate of 8% per year and invest $10,000 in the stock.

  a. What will be your rate of return if the price of Telecom stock goes up by 10% during the next year? (Ignore any expected dividend.)

  b. How far does the price of Telecom stock have to fall for you to get a margin call if the maintenance margin is 30%?

18. You've borrowed $20,000 on margin to buy shares in Disney, which is now selling at $40 per share. Your account starts at the initial margin requirement of 50%. The maintenance margin is 35%. Two days later, the stock price falls to $35 per share.

  a. Will you receive a margin call?

  b. How low can the price of Disney shares fall before you receive a margin call?

19. You are bearish on Telecom stock and decide to sell short 100 shares at the current market price of $25 per share.

  a. How much in cash or securities must you put into your brokerage account if the broker's initial margin requirement is 50% of the value of the short position?

  b. How high can the price of the stock go before you get a margin call if the maintenance margin is 30% of the value of the short position?

20. On January 1, you sold short one round lot (i.e., 100 shares) of Zenith stock at $14 per share. On March 1, a dividend of $2 per share was paid. On April 1, you covered the short sale by buying the stock at a price of $9 per share. You paid 50 cents per share in commissions for each transaction. What is the value of your account on April 1?

21. Call one full-service broker and one discount broker and find out the transaction costs of implementing the following strategies:

  a. Buying 100 shares of IBM now and selling them 6 months from now.

  b. Investing an equivalent amount of 6-month at-the-money call options (calls with strike price equal to the stock price) on IBM stock now and selling them 6 months from now.

The following questions are from past CFA examinations:

22. If you place a stop-loss order to sell 100 shares of stock at $55 when the current price is $62, how much will you receive for each share if the price drops to $50?

  a. $50.

  b. $55.

  c. $54.90.

  d. Cannot tell from the information given.

23. You wish to sell short 100 shares of XYZ Corporation stock. If the last two transactions were at $34.10 followed by $34.15, you only can sell short on the next transaction at a price of

   a. $34.10 or higher.
   b. $34.15 or higher.
   c. $34.15 or lower.
   d. $34.10 or lower.

24. Specialists on the New York Stock Exchange do all of the following except

   a. Act as dealers for their own accounts.
   b. Execute limit orders.
   c. Help provide liquidity to the marketplace.
   d. Act as odd-lot dealers.

---

**STANDARD &POOR'S**

Go to **www.mhhe.com/business/finance/edumarketinsight**. Select a company from the *Population* and from the Company Research Page, link to the *EDGAR* materials from the menu at the left of the page. What SEC reports are required of public companies? (Check the Archives for prior reports filed by your company.) Briefly explain the role of each in achieving the mission of the SEC.

---

**E-INVESTMENTS
Short Sales**

Go to the website for Nasdaq at **www.nasdaq.com**. When you enter the site, a dialog box appears that allows you to get quotes for up to 10 stocks. Request quotes for the following companies as identified by their ticker: Noble Drilling (NE), Diamond Offshore (DO), and Haliburton (HAL). Once you have entered the tickers for each company, click the item called *Info Quotes* that appears directly below the dialog box for quotes.

On which market or exchange do these stocks trade? Identify the high and low based on the current day's trading.

Below each of the info quotes another dialog box is present. Click the item labeled *Fundamentals* for the first stock. Some basic information on the company will appear along with an additional submenu. One of the items is labeled *Short Interest*. When you select that item a 12-month history of short interest will appear. You will need to complete the above process for each of the stocks.

Describe the trend, if any exists, for short sales over the last year. What is meant by the term "Days to Cover" that appears on the history for each company? Which of the companies has the largest relative number of shares that have been sold short?

---

**SOLUTIONS TO CONCEPT CHECKS**

1. Limited-time shelf registration was introduced because of its favorable trade-off of saving issue costs against mandated disclosure. Allowing unlimited-time shelf registration would circumvent blue sky laws that ensure proper disclosure.

2. The advent of negotiated commissions reduced the prices that brokers charged to execute trades on the NYSE. This reduced the profitability of a seat on the exchange, which in turn resulted in the lower seat prices in 1975 that is evident in Table 3.1. Eventually, however, trading volume increased dramatically, which more than made up for lower commissions per trade, and the value of a seat on the exchange rapidly increased after 1975.

**SOLUTIONS
TO CONCEPT
CHECKS**
*(Concluded)*

3. $\dfrac{100P - \$4,000}{100P} = .4$

$100P - \$4,000 = 40P$

$60P = \$4,000$

$P = \$66.67$ per share

4. The investor will purchase 150 shares, with a rate of return as follows:

| Year-End Change in Price | Year-End Value of Shares | Repayment of Principal and Interest | Investor's Rate of Return |
|---|---|---|---|
| 30% | 19,500 | $5,450 | 40.5% |
| No change | 15,000 | 5,450 | −4.5 |
| −30 | 10,500 | 5,450 | −49.5 |

5. $\dfrac{\$150,000 - 1,000P}{1,000P} = .4$

$\$150,000 - 1,000P = 400P$

$1,400P = \$150,000$

$P = \$107.14$ per share

## CHAPTER FOUR

# MUTUAL FUNDS AND OTHER INVESTMENT COMPANIES

The previous chapter introduced you to the mechanics of trading securities and the structure of the markets in which securities trade. Commonly, however, individual investors do not trade securities directly for their own accounts. Instead, they direct their funds to investment companies that purchase securities on their behalf. The most important of these financial intermediaries are open-end investment companies, more commonly known as mutual funds, to which we devote most of this chapter. We also touch briefly on other types of investment companies such as unit investment trusts and closed-end funds. We begin the chapter by describing and comparing the various types of investment companies available to investors. We then examine the functions of mutual funds, their investment styles and policies, and the costs of investing in these funds. Next we take a first look at the investment performance  of these funds. We consider the impact of expenses and turnover on net performance and examine the extent to which performance is consistent from one period to the next. In other words, will the mutual funds that were the best *past* performers be the best *future* performers? Finally, we discuss sources of information on mutual funds, and we consider in detail the information provided in the most comprehensive guide, Morningstar's *Mutual Fund Sourcebook*.

# 4.1   INVESTMENT COMPANIES

**Investment companies** are financial intermediaries that collect funds from individual investors and invest those funds in a potentially wide range of securities or other assets. Pooling of assets is the key idea behind investment companies. Each investor has a claim to the portfolio established by the investment company in proportion to the amount invested. These companies thus provide a mechanism for small investors to "team up" to obtain the benefits of large-scale investing.

Investment companies perform several important functions for their investors:

1. *Record keeping and administration.* Investment companies issue periodic status reports, keeping track of capital gains distributions, dividends, investments, and redemptions, and they may reinvest dividend and interest income for shareholders.

2. *Diversification and divisibility.* By pooling their money, investment companies enable investors to hold fractional shares of many different securities. They can act as large investors even if any individual shareholder cannot.

3. *Professional management.* Many, but not all, investment companies have full-time staffs of security analysts and portfolio managers who attempt to achieve superior investment results for their investors.

4. *Lower transaction costs.* Because they trade large blocks of securities, investment companies can achieve substantial savings on brokerage fees and commissions.

While all investment companies pool assets of individual investors, they also need to divide claims to those assets among those investors. Investors buy shares in investment companies, and ownership is proportional to the number of shares purchased. The value of each share is called the **net asset value,** or **NAV.** Net asset value equals assets minus liabilities expressed on a per-share basis:

$$\text{Net asset value} = \frac{\text{Market value of assets minus liabilities}}{\text{Shares outstanding}}$$

## EXAMPLE 4.1   Net Asset Value

Consider a mutual fund that manages a portfolio of securities worth $120 million. Suppose the fund owes $4 million to its investment advisers and owes another $1 million for rent, wages due, and miscellaneous expenses. The fund has 5 million shareholders. Then

$$\text{Net asset value} = \frac{\$120 \text{ million} - \$5 \text{ million}}{5 \text{ million shares}} = \$23 \text{ per share}$$

**CONCEPT CHECK☞ QUESTION 1**

Consider these data from the October 31, 2002, balance sheet of the Total International Stock Index Fund sponsored by the Vanguard Group. What was the net asset value of the portfolio?

| | |
|---|---|
| **Assets:** | **$2,885.9 million** |
| **Liabilities:** | **2.3 million** |
| **Shares:** | **370.4 million** |

## 4.2   TYPES OF INVESTMENT COMPANIES

In the United States, investment companies are classified by the Investment Company Act of 1940 as either unit investment trusts or managed investment companies. The portfolios of unit investment trusts are essentially fixed and thus are called "unmanaged." In contrast, managed companies are so named because securities in their investment portfolios continually are bought and sold: The portfolios are managed. Managed companies are further classified as either closed-end or open-end. Open-end companies are what we commonly call mutual funds.

### Unit Investment Trusts

**Unit investment trusts** are pools of money invested in a portfolio that is fixed for the life of the fund. To form a unit investment trust, a sponsor, typically a brokerage firm, buys a portfolio of securities which are deposited into a trust. It then sells to the public shares, or "units," in the trust, called *redeemable trust certificates*. All income and payments of principal from the portfolio are paid out by the fund's trustees (a bank or trust company) to the shareholders.

There is little active management of a unit investment trust because once established, the portfolio composition is fixed; hence these trusts are referred to as *unmanaged*. Trusts tend to invest in relatively uniform types of assets; for example, one trust may invest in municipal bonds, another in corporate bonds. The uniformity of the portfolio is consistent with the lack of active management. The trusts provide investors a vehicle to purchase a pool of one particular type of asset, which can be included in an overall portfolio as desired. The lack of active management of the portfolio implies that management fees can be lower than those of managed funds.

Sponsors of unit investment trusts earn their profit by selling shares in the trust at a premium to the cost of acquiring the underlying assets. For example, a trust that has purchased $5 million of assets may sell 5,000 shares to the public at a price of $1,030 per share, which (assuming the trust has no liabilities) represents a 3% premium over the net asset value of the securities held by the trust. The 3% premium is the trustee's fee for establishing the trust.

Investors who wish to liquidate their holdings of a unit investment trust may sell the shares back to the trustee for net asset value. The trustees can either sell enough securities from the asset portfolio to obtain the cash necessary to pay the investor, or they may instead sell the shares to a new investor (again at a slight premium to net asset value).

### Managed Investment Companies

There are two types of managed companies: closed-end and open-end. In both cases, the fund's board of directors, which is elected by shareholders, hires a management company to manage the portfolio for an annual fee that typically ranges from .2% to 1.5% of assets. In many cases the management company is the firm that organized the fund. For example, Fidelity Management and Research Corporation sponsors many Fidelity mutual funds and is responsible for managing the portfolios. It assesses a management fee on each Fidelity fund. In other cases, a mutual fund will hire an outside portfolio manager. For example, Vanguard has hired Wellington Management as the investment adviser for its Wellington Fund. Most management companies have contracts to manage several funds.

**Open-end funds** stand ready to redeem or issue shares at their net asset value (although both purchases and redemptions may involve sales charges). When investors in open-end funds wish to "cash out" their shares, they sell them back to the fund at NAV. In contrast, **closed-end funds** do not redeem or issue shares. Investors in closed-end funds who wish to cash out must sell their shares to other investors. Shares of closed-end funds are traded on organized exchanges and can be purchased through brokers just like other common stock; their prices therefore can differ from NAV.

Figure 4.1 is a listing of closed-end funds from *The Wall Street Journal*. The first column after the name of the fund indicates the exchange on which the shares trade (A: Amex; C: Chicago; N: NYSE; O: Nasdaq; T: Toronto; z: does not trade on an exchange). The next four columns give the fund's most recent net asset value, the closing share price, the change in the closing price from the previous day, and trading volume in round lots of 100 shares. The premium or discount is the percentage difference between price and NAV: (Price − NAV)/NAV. Notice that there are more funds selling at discounts to NAV (indicated by negative differences) than premiums. Finally, the annual dividend and 52-week return based on the percentage change in share price plus dividend income is presented in the last column.

The common divergence of price from net asset value, often by wide margins, is a puzzle that has yet to be fully explained. To see why this is a puzzle, consider a closed-end fund that is selling at a discount from net asset value. If the fund were to sell all the assets in the portfolio, it would realize proceeds equal to net asset value. The difference between the market price of the fund and the fund's NAV would represent the per-share increase in the wealth of the fund's investors. Despite this apparent profit opportunity, sizable discounts seem to persist for long periods of time.

Interestingly, while many closed-end funds sell at a discount from net asset value, the prices of these funds when originally issued are often above NAV. This is a further puzzle, as it is hard to explain why investors would purchase these newly issued funds at a premium to NAV when the shares tend to fall to a discount shortly after issue.

Many investors consider closed-end funds selling at a discount to NAV to be a bargain. Even if the market price never rises to the level of NAV, the dividend yield on an investment in the fund at this price would exceed the dividend yield on the same securities held outside the fund. To see this, imagine a fund with an NAV of $10 per share holding a

**Figure 4.1 Closed-end mutual funds**

## CLOSED-END FUNDS

Closed-end funds sell a limited number of shares and invest the proceeds in securities. Unlike open-end funds, closed-ends generally do not buy their shares back from investors who wish to cash in their holdings. Instead, fund shares trade on a stock exchange.

### Friday, November 16, 2001

| STOCK (SYM) | EXCH NAV | CLOSE | NET CHG | VOL 100s | PREM /DISC | DIV | 52 WK MKT RET |
|---|---|---|---|---|---|---|---|
| **General Equity Funds** | | | | | | | |
| AdamsExp ADX a | N 16.18 | 14.39 | − 0.08 | 869 | − 11.1 | 1.65e | − 28.3 |
| AllncAll AMO | N 22.13 | 21.94 | 0.14 | 85 | − 0.9 | 7.12e | − 24.3 |
| Avalon Capital MIST | O 15.80 | 15.00 | NA | NA | − 5.1 | NA | 15.4 |
| BergstrmCap BEM | A 165.14 | 149.00 | − 2.00 | 10 | − 9.8 | 11.25e | − 29.6 |
| BlueChipVal BLU | N 6.97 | 7.56 | 0.02 | 333 | 8.5 | .81e | 8.3 |
| BouldrTotR BTF | N 17.02 | 15.21 | − 0.28 | 31 | − 10.6 | .20 | 30.6 |
| BrntlyCap BBDC | O NA | 8.75 | − 0.30 | 78 | NA | .62 | 6.8 |
| CntlSec CET a | A 27.52 | 23.75 | 1.45 | 124 | − 13.7 | 1.80e | − 14.0 |
| **Specialized Equity Funds** | | | | | | | |
| ASA ASA c | N 22.87 | 18.80 | 0.05 | 786 | − 17.8 | .60a | 33.2 |
| CntlFdCan g CEF cl | A 3.33 | 3.32 | 0.02 | 132 | − 0.3 | .01g | 13.2 |
| CohnStrsAdvtg RLF a | N 13.60 | 14.56 | 0.21 | 375 | 7.1 | 1.26 | NS |
| CohenStrsTR RFI a | N 13.17 | 13.65 | 0.11 | 117 | 3.6 | .96a | 30.7 |
| Dundee Prec Mtls DPM.A cy | T 13.10 | 9.30 | NA | NA | − 29.0 | NA | 26.1 |
| FstFnlFd FF | N 14.36 | 12.15 | 0.05 | 349 | − 15.4 | e | 30.0 |
| GabelliMlti GGT | N 10.16 | 8.60 | 0.05 | 103 | − 15.4 | 1.56e | − 18.0 |
| GabelliUt GUT | N 7.34 | 9.04 | − 0.05 | 73 | 23.2 | .72 | 26.4 |

| STOCK (SYM) | EXCH NAV | CLOSE | NET CHG | VOL 100s | PREM /DISC | DIV | 12 MO YIELD |
|---|---|---|---|---|---|---|---|
| **U.S. Govt. Bond Funds** | | | | | | | |
| ACM OppFd AOF | N 8.05 | 8.89 | 0.01 | 50 | 10.4 | .72a | 8.7 |
| ACM IncFd ACG | N 8.38 | 8.13 | − 0.13 | 7100 | − 3.0 | .84 | 10.2 |
| EIS Fund EIS c | N 18.41 | 16.70 | − 0.02 | 1 | − 9.3 | 1.05e | 6.2 |
| MFS GvMkTr MGF a | N 7.27 | 6.67 | 0.05 | 526 | − 8.3 | .38 | 6.5 |
| MSDW Gvtln GVT | N 9.65 | 8.96 | − 0.07 | 785 | − 7.2 | .54 | 5.9 |
| ScudderGvt KGT a | N 7.39 | 7.07 | − 0.01 | 641 | − 4.3 | .48 | 6.9 |
| **Convertible Sec's. Funds** | | | | | | | |
| BancroftFd BCV | A 21.03 | 19.35 | 0.05 | 78 | − 8.0 | .69e | 1.2 |
| CastleFd CVF | A 26.10 | 24.41 | − 0.19 | 17 | − 6.5 | 1.32a | 18.3 |
| ElsworthFd ECF | A 8.80 | 8.62 | − 0.18 | 279 | − 2.0 | .48e | 11.2 |
| GabelliConv GCV | N 9.95 | 10.75 | 0.04 | 34 | 8.0 | .80a | 24.5 |
| LncInNtlSec LNV c | N 16.08 | 14.14 | − 0.06 | 57 | − 12.1 | .72m | − 12.4 |
| PutnmCvOpp PCV a | N 17.82 | 17.20 | 0.15 | 34 | − 3.5 | 1.22 | 1.8 |
| PutnmHilnco PCF a | N 7.03 | 7.00 | 0.00 | 48 | − 0.4 | .65 | 6.4 |
| RensncCap RENN | O 12.11 | 10.78 | 0.07 | 4 | − 11.0 | .54e | 8.0 |
| TCW Fd CVT | N 6.80 | 8.75 | 0.08 | 643 | 28.7 | .84a | 4.6 |
| **World Equity Funds** | | | | | | | |
| AbrdnAusEq IAF | A 6.41 | 5.52 | − 0.03 | 103 | − 13.9 | .68e | 5.7 |
| ArgntnaFd AF | N 8.41 | 8.16 | 0.01 | 135 | − 3.0 | .50 | − 18.8 |
| AsiaPacFd APB | N 9.53 | 7.70 | 0.08 | 649 | − 19.2 | e | − 12.3 |
| AsiaTigers GRR | N 7.67 | 6.51 | − 0.06 | 173 | − 15.1 | .29e | − 6.4 |
| AustriaFd OST | N 6.63 | 6.30 | 0.05 | 172 | − 5.0 | .16e | − 16.2 |
| BrazilFd BZF | N 17.46 | 14.30 | − 0.05 | 6 | − 18.1 | .92 | − 1.2 |
| BrazilEqty BZL | N 4.95 | 4.00 | − 0.10 | 31 | − 19.2 | .42 | − 20.9 |

portfolio that pays an annual dividend of $1 per share; that is, the dividend yield to investors that hold this portfolio directly is 10%. Now suppose that the market price of a share of this closed-end fund is $9. If management pays out dividends received from the shares as they come in, then the dividend yield to those that hold the same portfolio through the closed-end fund will be $1/$9, or 11.1%.

Variations on closed-end funds are *interval closed-end funds* and *discretionary closed-end funds*. Interval closed-end funds may purchase from 5% to 25% of outstanding shares from investors at intervals of 3, 6, or 12 months. Discretionary closed-end funds may purchase any or all outstanding shares from investors, but no more frequently than once every 2 years. The repurchase of shares for either of these funds takes place at net asset value plus a repurchase fee that may not exceed 2%.

In contrast to closed-end funds, the price of open-end funds cannot fall below NAV, because these funds stand ready to redeem shares at NAV. The offering price will exceed NAV, however, if the fund carries a **load.** A load is, in effect, a sales charge, which is paid to the seller. Load funds are sold by securities brokers and directly by mutual fund groups.

Unlike closed-end funds, open-end mutual funds do not trade on organized exchanges. Instead, investors simply buy shares from and liquidate through the investment company at net asset value. Thus the number of outstanding shares of these funds changes daily.

## Other Investment Organizations

There are intermediaries not formally organized or regulated as investment companies that nevertheless serve functions similar to investment companies. Three of the more important are commingled funds, real estate investment trusts, and hedge funds.

**Commingled Funds.**  Commingled funds are partnerships of investors that pool their funds. The management firm that organizes the partnership, for example, a bank or insurance company, manages the funds for a fee. Typical partners in a commingled fund might be trust or retirement accounts which have portfolios that are much larger than those of most individual investors but are still too small to warrant managing on a separate basis.

Commingled funds are similar in form to open-end mutual funds. Instead of shares, though, the fund offers units, which are bought and sold at net asset value. A bank or insurance company may offer an array of different commingled funds from which trust or retirement accounts can choose. Examples are a money market fund, a bond fund, and a common stock fund.

**Real Estate Investment Trusts (REITs).**  A REIT is similar to a closed-end fund. REITs invest in real estate or loans secured by real estate. Besides issuing shares, they raise capital by borrowing from banks and issuing bonds or mortgages. Most of them are highly leveraged, with a typical debt ratio of 70%.

There are two principal kinds of REITs. *Equity trusts* invest in real estate directly, whereas *mortgage trusts* invest primarily in mortgage and construction loans. REITs generally are established by banks, insurance companies, or mortgage companies, which then serve as investment managers to earn a fee.

REITs are exempt from taxes as long as at least 95% of their taxable income is distributed to shareholders. For shareholders, however, the dividends are taxable as personal income.

**Hedge Funds.**  Like mutual funds, **hedge funds** are vehicles that allow private investors to pool assets to be invested by a fund manager. However, hedge funds are not registered as mutual funds and are not subject to SEC regulation. They typically are open only to wealthy or institutional investors. As hedge funds are only lightly regulated, their managers can pursue investment strategies that are not open to mutual fund managers, including for example, heavy use of derivatives, short sales, and leverage.

Hedge funds typically attempt to exploit temporary misalignments in security valuations. For example, if the yield on mortgage-backed securities seems abnormally high compared to that on Treasury bonds, the hedge fund would buy mortgage-backed and short sell Treasury securities. Notice that the fund is *not* betting on broad movement in the entire bond market; it buys one type of bond and sells another. By taking a long mortgage/short Treasury position, the fund "hedges" its interest rate exposure, while making a bet on the *relative* valuation across the two sectors. The idea is that when yield spreads converge back to their "normal" relationship, the fund will profit from the re-alignment regardless of the general trend in the level of interest rates. In this respect, it strives to be "market neutral," which gives rise to the term "hedge fund."

Of course even if the fund's position is market neutral, this does not mean that it is low risk. The fund still is speculating on valuation differences across the two sectors, often taking a very large position, and this decision can turn out to be right or wrong. Because the funds often operate with considerable leverage, returns can be quite volatile.

# 4.3    MUTUAL FUNDS

Mutual funds are the common name for open-end investment companies. This is the dominant investment company today, accounting for roughly 90% of investment company assets. Assets under management in the mutual fund industry were approximately $6.4 trillion at the end of 2002.

**Investment Policies**    Each mutual fund has a specified investment policy, which is described in the fund's prospectus. For example, money market mutual funds hold the short-term, low-risk instruments of the money market (see Chapter 2 for a review of these securities), while bond funds hold fixed-income securities. Some funds have even more narrowly defined mandates. For example, some bond funds will hold primarily Treasury bonds, others primarily mortgage-backed securities.

Management companies manage a family, or "complex," of mutual funds. They organize an entire collection of funds and then collect a management fee for operating them. By managing a collection of funds under one umbrella, these companies make it easy for investors to allocate assets across market sectors and to switch assets across funds while still benefiting from centralized record keeping. Some of the most well-known management companies are Fidelity, Vanguard, Putnam, and Dreyfus. Each offers an array of open-end mutual funds with different investment policies. There were more than 8,000 mutual funds at the end of 2001, which were offered by fewer than 500 fund complexes.

Some of the more important fund types, classified by investment policy, are discussed next.

**Money Market Funds.**    These funds invest in money market securities. They usually offer check-writing features, and net asset value is fixed at $1 per share, so that there are no tax implications such as capital gains or losses associated with redemption of shares.

**Equity Funds.**    Equity funds invest primarily in stock, although they may, at the portfolio manager's discretion, also hold fixed-income or other types of securities. Funds commonly will hold between 4% and 5% of total assets in money market securities to provide liquidity necessary to meet potential redemption of shares.

It is traditional to classify stock funds according to their emphasis on capital appreciation versus current income. Thus, *income funds* tend to hold shares of firms with consistently high dividend yields. *Growth funds* are willing to forgo current income, focusing instead on prospects for capital gains. While the classification of these funds is couched in terms of income versus capital gains, it is worth noting that in practice the more relevant distinction concerns the level of risk these funds assume. Growth stocks and therefore growth funds are typically riskier and respond far more dramatically to changes in economic conditions than do income funds.

Some equity funds, called *sector* funds, concentrate on a particular industry. For example, Fidelity markets dozens of "select funds," each of which invests in a specific industry such as biotechnology, utilities, precious metals, or telecommunications. Other funds specialize in securities of particular countries.

**Bond Funds.**  As the name suggests, these funds specialize in the fixed-income sector. Within that sector, however, there is considerable room for specialization. For example, various funds will concentrate on corporate bonds, Treasury bonds, mortgage-backed securities, or municipal (tax-free) bonds. Indeed, some of the municipal bond funds will invest only in bonds of a particular state (or even city!) to satisfy the investment desires of residents of that state who wish to avoid local as well as federal taxes on the interest paid on the bonds. Many funds will also specialize by the maturity of the securities, ranging from short-term to intermediate to long-term, or by the credit risk of the issuer, ranging from very safe to high-yield or "junk" bonds.

**International Funds.**  Many funds have international focus. *Global funds* invest in securities worldwide, including the United States. In contrast, *international funds* invest in securities of firms located outside the United States. *Regional funds* concentrate on a particular part of the world, and *emerging market funds* invest in companies of developing nations.

**Balanced and Income Funds.**  Some funds are designed to be candidates for an individual's entire investment portfolio. Therefore, they hold both equities and fixed-income securities in relatively stable proportions. According to Wiesenberger, such funds are classified as income or balanced funds. *Income funds* strive to maintain safety of principal consistent with "as liberal a current income from investments as possible," while *balanced funds* "minimize investment risks so far as this is possible without unduly sacrificing possibilities for long-term growth and current income."

**Asset Allocation and Flexible Funds.**  These funds are similar to balanced funds in that they hold both stocks and bonds. However, asset allocation funds may dramatically vary the proportions allocated to each market in accord with the portfolio manager's forecast of the relative performance of each sector. Hence these funds are engaged in market timing and are not designed to be low-risk investment vehicles.

**Index Funds.**  An index fund tries to match the performance of a broad market index. The fund buys shares in securities included in a particular index in proportion to each security's representation in that index. For example, the Vanguard 500 Index Fund is a mutual fund that replicates the composition of the Standard & Poor's 500 stock price index. Because the S&P 500 is a value-weighted index, the fund buys shares in each S&P 500 company in proportion to the market value of that company's outstanding equity. Investment in an index fund is a low-cost way for small investors to pursue a passive investment strategy—that is, to invest without engaging in security analysis. Of course, index funds

**Table 4.1    Classification of mutual funds, December 2001**

|  | Assets ($ billion) | % of Total |
|---|---|---|
| **Common stock** | | |
| Aggressive growth | $   576.2 | 8.3% |
| Growth | 1,047.5 | 15.0 |
| Growth & income | 1,066.6 | 15.3 |
| Equity income | 125.4 | 1.8 |
| International | 415.1 | 6.0 |
| Emerging markets | 13.7 | 0.2 |
| Sector funds | 173.6 | 2.5 |
| *Total equity funds* | $3,418.1 | 49.0% |
| **Bond funds** | | |
| Corporate, investment grade | $   161.0 | 2.3% |
| Corporate, high yield | 94.3 | 1.4 |
| Government & agency | 90.9 | 1.3 |
| Mortgage-backed | 73.4 | 1.1 |
| Global bond funds | 19.0 | 0.3 |
| Strategic income | 191.6 | 2.7 |
| Municipal single state | 141.0 | 2.0 |
| Municipal general | 154.0 | 2.2 |
| *Total bond funds* | $   925.2 | 13.3% |
| **Mixed (hybrid) asset classes** | | |
| Balanced | $   231.1 | 3.3% |
| Asset allocation & flexible | 115.3 | 1.7 |
| *Total hybrid funds* | $   346.3 | 5.0% |
| **Money market** | | |
| Taxable | $2,012.9 | 28.9% |
| Tax-free | 272.4 | 3.9 |
| *Total money market funds* | $2,285.3 | 32.8% |
| *TOTAL* | $6,974.9 | 100.0% |

Note: Column sums subject to rounding error.
Source: *Mutual Fund Fact Book,* Investment Company Institute, 2002.

can be tied to nonequity indexes as well. For example, Vanguard offers a bond index fund and a real estate index fund.

Table 4.1 breaks down the number of mutual funds by investment orientation as of the end of 2001. Figure 4.2 is part of the listings for mutual funds from *The Wall Street Journal*. Notice that the funds are organized by the fund family. Focus on the listings for the Vanguard Group funds. The first two columns after the name of each fund present the net asset value of the fund and the change in NAV from the previous day. The last two columns are the year-to-date return and 3-year return on the fund.

Often the fund name describes its investment policy. For example, Vanguard's GNMA fund invests in mortgage-backed securities, the municipal intermediate fund (MuInt) invests in intermediate-term municipal bonds, and the high-yield corporate bond fund (HY-Cor) invests in large part in speculative grade, or "junk," bonds with high yields. You can see (third column) that Vanguard offers about 20 index funds, including portfolios indexed

**Figure 4.2
Listing of
mutual fund
quotations**

| FUND | NAV | NET CHG | YTD %RET | 3-YR %RET | FUND | NAV | NET CHG | YTD %RET | 3-YR %RET | FUND | NAV | NET CHG | YTD %RET | 3-YR %RET |
|---|---|---|---|---|---|---|---|---|---|---|---|---|---|---|
| **Smith Barney B & P** | | | | | **VANGUARD FDS** | | | | | PrecMtls r | 11.44 | -0.19 | 5.1 | 24.9 |
| AgGrB t | 72.43 | 0.66 | 25.5 | -9.6 | AssetA | 20.74 | 0.08 | 15.4 | -2.9 | Primcp r | 46.66 | 0.35 | 20.7 | -11.8 |
| ApprB t | 12.23 | ... | 11.7 | -4.6 | CAIT | 11.50 | -0.01 | 2.4 | 7.1 | REIT r | 13.62 | 0.01 | 17.7 | 13.4 |
| CaMuB t | 16.72 | ... | 1.1 | 6.0 | CALT | 12.06 | -0.01 | 2.9 | 7.8 | SelValu r | 13.11 | 0.10 | 14.4 | 10.3 |
| CapPresB p | 11.54 | -0.01 | 2.3 | NS | CapOp r | 21.47 | 0.31 | 26.3 | -10.3 | STAR | 15.98 | 0.04 | 12.4 | 2.3 |
| CpPresBll t | 11.68 | -0.02 | 2.2 | NS | CapValue | 8.92 | 0.09 | 22.0 | NS | STCor | 10.89 | -0.01 | 3.2 | 7.2 |
| DvsInB t | 6.76 | ... | 7.3 | 4.3 | Convrt | 11.93 | 0.07 | 16.3 | -2.0 | STFed | 10.69 | -0.01 | 1.6 | 7.8 |
| FdValB t | 11.66 | 0.06 | 20.5 | -5.9 | DivdGro | 9.93 | 0.01 | 14.0 | -7.6 | StratgcEq | 16.26 | 0.22 | 24.1 | 5.5 |
| GvScB t | 10.10 | -0.01 | 1.8 | 7.7 | Energy r | 25.90 | -0.09 | 11.6 | 8.2 | STTsry | 10.79 | -0.01 | 1.8 | 7.7 |
| HilncB t | 6.81 | 0.02 | 17.8 | -0.5 | EqInc | 20.54 | 0.02 | 11.2 | 0.9 | TxMBal r | 16.91 | 0.03 | 10.1 | -2.0 |
| InvGdB t | 13.26 | -0.01 | 5.2 | 11.0 | Explr | 56.57 | 0.85 | 24.4 | -4.0 | TxMCap r | 22.96 | 0.14 | 17.8 | -13.1 |
| LgCapGB p | 18.47 | 0.12 | 29.3 | -11.1 | FLLT | 12.09 | -0.01 | 3.6 | 8.8 | TxMGI r | 21.98 | 0.08 | 15.6 | -10.6 |
| LgCpCoB p | 14.72 | 0.06 | 13.1 | -15.5 | GlbEq | 12.76 | -0.03 | 17.8 | 2.0 | TxMIn r | 7.25 | -0.06 | 12.8 | -13.0 |
| MdCpCoB p | 17.36 | 0.18 | 14.3 | -7.2 | GNMA | 10.67 | -0.01 | 1.9 | 8.6 | TxMSC r | 15.06 | 0.28 | 18.9 | 3.3 |
| MgMuB t | 15.62 | 0.01 | 1.5 | 6.5 | GroInc | 24.97 | 0.10 | 15.6 | -10.0 | USGro | 13.90 | 0.08 | 15.3 | -27.6 |
| MuNYB | 13.68 | ... | 1.6 | 6.6 | GrowthEq | 8.23 | 0.08 | 23.9 | -24.5 | USValue | 10.97 | 0.07 | 14.7 | 3.8 |
| SBCapIncB t | 13.88 | 0.06 | 19.4 | -0.9 | HlthCare r | 110.17 | -0.17 | 14.7 | 3.3 | Wellsl | 20.72 | -0.02 | 6.2 | 10.2 |
| SmCpValB p | 17.40 | 0.17 | 16.3 | 11.5 | HYCor r | 6.23 | ... | 10.3 | 4.4 | Welltn | 26.66 | 0.02 | 10.1 | 5.5 |
| TotRtnB t | 11.60 | ... | 4.4 | 10.2 | InflaPro | 12.08 | -0.01 | 4.3 | 11.3 | Wndsr | 14.17 | 0.11 | 18.8 | 3.6 |
| **Smith Barney L,O&I** | | | | | IntlGr | 13.74 | -0.09 | 13.0 | -12.9 | WndsrII | 23.89 | 0.07 | 16.1 | 2.3 |
| AdjIncL p | 9.70 | ... | 0.4 | 4.1 | IntlVal | 21.57 | -0.09 | 14.6 | -7.8 | **VANGUARD INDEX FDS** | | | | |
| AgGrL t | 72.78 | 0.65 | 25.5 | -9.6 | ITCorp | 10.35 | -0.01 | 5.4 | 10.9 | 500 | 93.14 | 0.34 | 15.6 | -10.7 |
| ApprL t | 12.24 | -0.01 | 11.7 | -4.6 | ITTsry | 11.77 | -0.02 | 2.8 | 11.0 | Balanced | 17.23 | 0.05 | 11.5 | -2.2 |
| CapPresL t | 11.54 | -0.01 | 2.3 | NS | LifeCon | 13.88 | 0.02 | 9.7 | 1.1 | CalSoc | 6.90 | 0.05 | 18.6 | -13.2 |
| CpPresL II | 11.69 | -0.01 | 2.3 | NS | LifeGro | 16.38 | 0.04 | 14.8 | -6.6 | DevMkt | 6.48 | -0.05 | 12.9 | NA |
| DsipL | 6.74 | ... | 7.4 | 4.2 | LifeInc | 12.99 | 0.01 | 7.1 | 4.9 | EmerMkt r | 9.32 | -0.01 | 22.1 | -5.0 |
| FdValL | 11.66 | 0.06 | 20.6 | -5.9 | LifeMod | 15.42 | 0.03 | 12.3 | -2.5 | Europe | 18.17 | -0.09 | 12.1 | -12.1 |
| GpSpcFdL t | 8.04 | 0.04 | 9.2 | NS | LTCorp | 9.57 | -0.01 | 6.7 | 12.5 | Extnd | 23.02 | 0.26 | 22.9 | -8.9 |
| HilncL t | 6.82 | 0.02 | 17.8 | -0.4 | LTTsry | 11.95 | -0.02 | 4.7 | 11.8 | Growth | 22.92 | 0.15 | 15.5 | -16.6 |
| LgCapGl t | 18.47 | 0.12 | 29.3 | -11.1 | MATxEx | 10.33 | ... | 3.3 | 8.2 | ITBond | 11.05 | -0.02 | 5.4 | 11.4 |
| MdCpCoL t | 17.36 | 0.18 | 14.3 | -7.2 | Morg | 13.41 | 0.11 | 20.3 | -12.9 | LTBond | 13.03 | 0.05 | 6.1 | 12.7 |
| MgMuL | 15.61 | 0.01 | 1.5 | 6.4 | MuHY | 10.80 | ... | 3.8 | 7.6 | MidCp | 11.44 | 0.11 | 15.8 | 1.0 |
| MuLtdL p | 6.64 | ... | 2.7 | NS | MuInlg | 13.07 | ... | 3.6 | 8.4 | Pacific | 6.74 | -0.10 | 14.6 | -15.1 |
| PsAllCpGr t | 7.03 | 0.08 | 18.8 | -15.4 | MuInt | 13.74 | -0.01 | 2.7 | 7.0 | SmCap | 19.30 | 0.28 | 23.2 | -2.1 |
| **Smith Barney Y** | | | | | MuLong | 11.58 | -0.01 | 3.3 | 8.5 | SmGth | 11.20 | 0.21 | 22.1 | -2.3 |
| AggGrowY t | 81.65 | 0.74 | 26.2 | -8.5 | MuLtd | 11.12 | -0.01 | 1.8 | 5.8 | SmVal | 9.79 | 0.10 | 14.9 | 8.1 |
| GrowIncY | 13.00 | 0.03 | 18.4 | NS | MuSht | 15.79 | ... | 1.0 | 4.0 | STBond | 10.42 | -0.01 | 2.7 | 7.7 |
| HansBgrY | 9.93 | 0.01 | 15.6 | -8.7 | NJLT | 12.39 | ... | 3.4 | 8.3 | TotBd | 10.45 | -0.01 | 3.3 | 9.0 |
| HilncY | 6.82 | 0.02 | 18.3 | 0.4 | NYLT | 11.61 | -0.01 | 3.1 | 8.4 | TotIntl | 8.78 | -0.06 | 13.7 | -12.4 |
| InvGdY | 13.27 | -0.01 | 5.7 | 11.9 | OHLTte | 12.54 | ... | 3.3 | 8.6 | TotSt | 23.33 | 0.12 | 17.0 | -10.0 |
| LgCapGrY | 19.71 | 0.13 | 30.0 | -10.1 | PALT | 11.81 | ... | 3.5 | 8.4 | Value | 16.90 | 0.02 | 16.3 | -4.6 |

Source: *The Wall Street Journal,* January 23, 2002. Reprinted by permission of Dow Jones & Company, Inc., via Copyright Clearance Center, Inc. © 2002 Dow Jones & Company, Inc. All Rights Reserved Worldwide.

to the bond market (TotBd), the Wilshire 5000 index (TotSt), the MSCI U.S. Small Cap Index (SmCap), as well as European- and Pacific Basin–indexed portfolios (Europe and Pacific). However, names of common stock funds frequently reflect little or nothing about their investment policies. Examples are Vanguard's Windsor and Wellington funds.

## How Funds Are Sold

Most mutual funds have an underwriter that has exclusive rights to distribute shares to investors. Mutual funds are generally marketed to the public either directly by the fund underwriter or indirectly through brokers acting on behalf of the underwriter. Direct-marketed funds are sold through the mail, various offices of the fund, over the phone, and, increasingly, over the Internet. Investors contact the fund directly to purchase shares. For example, if you look at the financial pages of your local newspaper, you will see several advertisements for funds, along with toll-free phone numbers that you can call to receive a fund's prospectus and an application to open an account with the fund.

A bit less than half of fund sales today are distributed through a sales force. Brokers or financial advisers receive a commission for selling shares to investors. (Ultimately, the commission is paid by the investor. More on this shortly.) In some cases, funds use a "captive" sales force that sells only shares in funds of the mutual fund group they represent.

The trend today, however, is toward "financial supermarkets," which sell shares in funds of many complexes. This approach was made popular by the OneSource program of Charles Schwab & Co. Schwab allows customers of the OneSource program to buy funds from many different fund groups. Instead of charging customers a sales commission,

Schwab splits management fees with the mutual fund company. Another advantage is unified record-keeping for all funds purchased from the supermarket, even if the funds are offered by different complexes. On the other hand, many contend that these supermarkets result in higher expense ratios because mutual funds pass along the costs of participating in these supermarkets in the form of higher management fees.

## 4.4    COSTS OF INVESTING IN MUTUAL FUNDS

**Fee Structure**    An individual investor choosing a mutual fund should consider not only the fund's stated investment policy and past performance but also its management fees and other expenses. Comparative data on virtually all important aspects of mutual funds are available in the annual reports prepared by Wiesenberger Investment Companies Services or in Morningstar's *Mutual Fund Sourcebook*, which can be found in many academic and public libraries. You should be aware of four general classes of fees.

**Front-End Load.**  A front-end load is a commission or sales charge paid when you purchase the shares. These charges, which are used primarily to pay the brokers who sell the funds, may not exceed 8.5%, but in practice they are rarely higher than 6%. *Low-load funds* have loads that range up to 3% of invested funds. *No-load funds* have no front-end sales charges. Loads effectively reduce the amount of money invested. For example, each $1,000 paid for a fund with an 8.5% load results in a sales charge of $85 and fund investment of only $915. You need cumulative returns of 9.3% of your net investment (85/915 = .093) just to break even.

**Back-End Load.**  A back-end load is a redemption, or "exit," fee incurred when you sell your shares. Typically, funds that impose back-end loads start them at 5% or 6% and reduce them by 1 percentage point for every year the funds are left invested. Thus an exit fee that starts at 6% would fall to 4% by the start of your third year. These charges are known more formally as "contingent deferred sales charges."

**Operating Expenses.**  Operating expenses are the costs incurred by the mutual fund in operating the portfolio, including administrative expenses and advisory fees paid to the investment manager. These expenses, usually expressed as a percentage of total assets under management, may range from 0.2% to 2%. Shareholders do not receive an explicit bill for these operating expenses; however, the expenses periodically are deducted from the assets of the fund. Shareholders pay for these expenses through the reduced value of the portfolio.

**12b-1 Charges.**  The Securities and Exchange Commission allows the managers of so-called 12b-1 funds to use fund assets to pay for distribution costs such as advertising, promotional literature including annual reports and prospectuses, and, most important, commissions paid to brokers who sell the fund to investors. These **12b-1 fees** are named after the SEC rule that permits use of these plans. Funds may use 12b-1 charges instead of, or in addition to, front-end loads to generate the fees with which to pay brokers. As with operating expenses, investors are not explicitly billed for 12b-1 charges. Instead, the fees are deducted from the assets of the fund. Therefore, 12b-1 fees (if any) must be added to operating expenses to obtain the true annual expense ratio of the fund. The SEC now requires that all funds include in the prospectus a consolidated expense table that summarizes all relevant fees. The 12b-1 fees are limited to 1% of a fund's average net assets per year.[1]

Some funds offer "classes" that represent ownership in the same portfolio of securities, but with different combinations of fees. For example Class A shares might have front-end loads while Class B shares rely on 12b-1 fees.

**EXAMPLE 4.2**   **Fees for Various Classes (Dreyfus Premier Growth Fund)**

Here are fees for different classes of the Dreyfus Premier Growth Fund as of early 2003. Notice the trade-off between the front-end loads versus 12b-1 charges.

|                      | Class A       | Class B  | Class C  | Class T       |
|----------------------|---------------|----------|----------|---------------|
| Front-end load       | 0–5.75%[a]    | 0        | 0        | 0–4.50%[a]    |
| Back-end load        | 0             | 0–4%[b]  | 0–1%[b]  | 0             |
| 12b-1 fees[c]        | .25%          | 1.0%     | 1.0%     | .50%          |
| Expense ratio        | 1.25%         | 1.25%    | 1.25%    | 1.25%         |

[a]Depending on size of investment.
[b]Depending on years until holdings are sold.
[c]Including service fee of .25%.

Each investor must choose the best combination of fees. Obviously, pure no-load no-fee funds distributed directly by the mutual fund group are the cheapest alternative, and these will often make most sense for knowledgeable investors. However, many investors are willing to pay for financial advice, and the commissions paid to advisers who sell these funds are the most common form of payment. Alternatively, investors may choose to hire a fee-only financial manager who charges directly for services and does not accept commissions. These advisers can help investors select portfolios of low- or no-load funds (as well as provide other financial advice). Independent financial planners have become increasingly important distribution channels for funds in recent years.

If you do buy a fund through a broker, the choice between paying a load and paying 12b-1 fees will depend primarily on your expected time horizon. Loads are paid only once for each purchase, whereas 12b-1 fees are paid annually. Thus if you plan to hold your fund for a long time, a one-time load may be preferable to recurring 12b-1 charges.

You can identify funds with various charges by the following letters placed after the fund name in the listing of mutual funds in the financial pages: *r* denotes redemption or exit fees; *p* denotes 12b-1 fees; *t* denotes both redemption and 12b-1 fees. The listings do not allow you to identify funds that involve front-end loads, however; while NAV for each fund is presented, the offering price at which the fund can be purchased, which may include a load, is not.

**Fees and Mutual Fund Returns**   The rate of return on an investment in a mutual fund is measured as the increase or decrease in net asset value plus income distributions such as dividends or distributions of capital gains expressed as a fraction of net asset

---

[1] The maximum 12b-1 charge for the sale of the fund is .75%. However, an additional service fee of .25% of the fund's assets also is allowed for personal service and/or maintenance of shareholder accounts.

value at the beginning of the investment period. If we denote the net asset value at the start and end of the period as $NAV_0$ and $NAV_1$, respectively, then

$$\text{Rate of return} = \frac{NAV_1 - NAV_0 + \text{Income and capital gain distributions}}{NAV_0}$$

For example, if a fund has an initial NAV of $20 at the start of the month, makes income distributions of $.15 and capital gain distributions of $.05, and ends the month with NAV of $20.10, the monthly rate of return is computed as

$$\text{Rate of return} = \frac{\$20.10 - \$20.00 + \$.15 + \$.05}{\$20.00} = .015, \text{ or } 1.5\%$$

Notice that this measure of the rate of return ignores any commissions such as front-end loads paid to purchase the fund.

On the other hand, the rate of return is affected by the fund's expenses and 12b-1 fees. This is because such charges are periodically deducted from the portfolio, which reduces net asset value. Thus the rate of return on the fund equals the gross return on the underlying portfolio minus the total expense ratio.

## EXAMPLE 4.3    Fees and Net Returns

To see how expenses can affect rate of return, consider a fund with $100 million in assets at the start of the year and with 10 million shares outstanding. The fund invests in a portfolio of stocks that provides no income but increases in value by 10%. The expense ratio, including 12b-1 fees, is 1%. What is the rate of return for an investor in the fund?

The initial NAV equals $100 million/10 million shares = $10 per share. In the absence of expenses, fund assets would grow to $110 million and NAV would grow to $11 per share, for a 10% rate of return. However, the expense ratio of the fund is 1%. Therefore, $1 million will be deducted from the fund to pay these fees, leaving the portfolio worth only $109 million, and NAV equal to $10.90. The rate of return on the fund is only 9%, which equals the gross return on the underlying portfolio minus the total expense ratio.

Fees can have a big effect on performance. Table 4.2 considers an investor who starts with $10,000 and can choose between three funds that all earn an annual 12% return on investment before fees but have different fee structures. The table shows the cumulative amount in each fund after several investment horizons. Fund A has total operating expenses of .5%, no load, and no 12b-1 charges. This might represent a low-cost producer like Vanguard. Fund B has no load but has 1% in management expenses and .5% in 12b-1 fees. This level of charges is fairly typical of actively managed equity funds. Finally, Fund C has 1% in management expenses, no 12b-1 charges, but assesses an 8% front-end load on purchases.

Note the substantial return advantage of low-cost Fund A. Moreover, that differential is greater for longer investment horizons.

Although expenses can have a big impact on net investment performance, it is sometimes difficult for the investor in a mutual fund to measure true expenses accurately. This is because of the common practice of paying for some expenses in **soft dollars.** A portfolio manager earns soft-dollar credits with a stockbroker by directing the fund's trades to that broker. Based on those credits, the broker will pay for some of the mutual fund's expenses, such as databases, computer hardware, or stock-quotation systems. The soft-dollar arrangement means that the stockbroker effectively returns part of the trading commission to the

**Table 4.2   Impact of Costs on Investment Performance**

| | Cumulative Proceeds (All Dividends Reinvested) | | |
| --- | --- | --- | --- |
| | Fund A | Fund B | Fund C |
| Initial investment* | $10,000 | $10,000 | $ 9,200 |
| 5 years | 17,234 | 16,474 | 15,502 |
| 10 years | 29,699 | 27,141 | 26,123 |
| 15 years | 51,183 | 44,713 | 44,018 |
| 20 years | 88,206 | 73,662 | 74,173 |

*After front-end load, if any.
Notes:
1. Fund A is no-load with .5% expense ratio.
2. Fund B is no-load with 1.5% expense ratio.
3. Fund C has an 8% load on purchases and a 1% expense ratio.
4. Gross return on all funds is 12% per year before expenses.

fund. The advantage to the mutual fund is that purchases made with soft dollars are not included in the fund's expenses, so the fund can advertise an unrealistically low expense ratio to the public. Although the fund may have paid the broker needlessly high commissions to obtain the soft-dollar "rebate," trading costs are not included in the fund's expenses. The impact of the higher trading commission shows up instead in net investment performance. Soft-dollar arrangements make it difficult for investors to compare fund expenses, and periodically these arrangements come under attack.

---

**CONCEPT CHECK ☞ QUESTION 2**

The Equity Fund sells Class A shares with a front-end load of 4% and Class B shares with 12b-1 fees of .5% annually as well as back-end load fees that start at 5% and fall by 1% for each full year the investor holds the portfolio (until the fifth year). Assume the rate of return on the fund portfolio net of operating expenses is 10% annually. What will be the value of a $10,000 investment in Class A and Class B shares if the shares are sold after (*a*) 1 year, (*b*) 4 years, (*c*) 10 years? Which fee structure provides higher net proceeds at the end of the investment horizon?

---

## 4.5   TAXATION OF MUTUAL FUND INCOME

Investment returns of mutual funds are granted "pass-through status" under the U.S. tax code, meaning that taxes are paid only by the investor in the mutual fund, not by the fund itself. The income is treated as passed through to the investor as long as the fund meets several requirements, most notably that virtually all income is distributed to shareholders. A fund's short-term capital gains, long-term capital gains, and dividends are passed through to investors as though the investor earned the income directly.[2]

---

[2] An interesting problem that an investor needs to be aware of derives from the fact that capital gains and dividends on mutual funds are typically paid out to shareholders once or twice a year. This means that an investor who has just purchased shares in a mutual fund can receive a capital gain distribution (and be taxed on that distribution) on transactions that occurred long before he or she purchased shares in the fund. This is particularly a concern late in the year when such distributions typically are made.

The pass through of investment income has one important disadvantage for individual investors. If you manage your own portfolio, you decide when to realize capital gains and losses on any security; therefore, you can time those realizations to efficiently manage your tax liabilities. When you invest through a mutual fund, however, the timing of the sale of securities from the portfolio is out of your control, which reduces your ability to engage in tax management. Of course, if the mutual fund is held in a tax-deferred retirement account such as an IRA or 401(k) account, these tax management issues are irrelevant.

A fund with a high portfolio turnover rate can be particularly "tax inefficient." **Turnover** is the ratio of the trading activity of a portfolio to the assets of the portfolio. It measures the fraction of the portfolio that is "replaced" each year. For example, a $100 million portfolio with $50 million in sales of some securities with purchases of other securities would have a turnover rate of 50%. High turnover means that capital gains or losses are being realized constantly, and therefore that the investor cannot time the realizations to manage his or her overall tax obligation.

In 2000, the SEC instituted rules requiring funds to disclose the tax impact of portfolio turnover. Funds must include in their prospectus after-tax returns for the past 1-, 5-, and 10-year periods. Marketing literature that includes performance data also must include after-tax results. The after-tax returns are computed accounting for the impact of the taxable distributions of income and capital gains passed through to the investor, assuming the investor is in the maximum federal tax bracket.

---

**CONCEPT CHECK☞ QUESTION 3**

An investor's portfolio currently is worth $1 million. During the year, the investor sells 1,000 shares of Microsoft at a price of $80 per share and 2,000 shares of Ford at a price of $40 per share. The proceeds are used to buy 1,600 shares of IBM at $100 per share.

a. What was the portfolio turnover rate?

b. If the shares in Microsoft originally were purchased for $70 each and those in Ford were purchased for $35, and the investor's tax rate on capital gains income is 20%, how much extra will the investor owe on this year's taxes as a result of these transactions?

---

## 4.6    EXCHANGE-TRADED FUNDS

**Exchange-traded funds** (ETFs) are offshoots of mutual funds that allow investors to trade index portfolios just as they do shares of stock. The first ETF was the "spider," a nickname for SPDR, or Standard & Poor's Depositary Receipt, which is a unit investment trust holding a portfolio matching the S&P 500 index. Unlike mutual funds, which can be bought or sold only at the end of the day when NAV is calculated, investors can trade spiders throughout the day, just like any other share of stock. Spiders gave rise to many similar products such as "diamonds" (based on the Dow Jones Industrial Average, ticker DIA), "qubes" (based on the Nasdaq 100 Index, ticker QQQ), and "WEBS" (World Equity Benchmark Shares, which are shares in portfolios of foreign stock market indexes). There are now dozens of ETFs on broad market indexes as well as narrow industry portfolios. Some of the sponsors of ETFs and their brand names are given in Table 4.3.

ETFs offer several advantages over conventional mutual funds. First, as we just noted, a mutual fund's net asset value is quoted—and therefore, investors can buy or sell their

**Table 4.3   ETF Sponsors and Products**

**A. ETF Sponsors**

| Sponsor | Product Name |
|---|---|
| Barclays Global Investors | i-Shares |
| Merrill Lynch | HOLDRS (Holding Company Depository Receipts: "Holders") |
| StateStreet/Merrill Lynch | Select Sector SPDRs (S&P Depository Receipts: "Spiders") |
| Vanguard | VIPER (Vanguard Index Participation Equity Receipts: "Vipers") |

**B. Sample of ETF Products**

| Name | Ticker | Index Tracked |
|---|---|---|
| **Broad U.S. indexes** | | |
| Spiders | SPY | S&P 500 |
| Diamonds | DIA | Dow Jones Industrials |
| Qubes | QQQ | Nasdaq 100 |
| iShares Russell 2000 | IWM | Russell 2000 |
| VIPERS | VTI | Wilshire 5000 |
| **Industry indexes** | | |
| Energy Select Spider | XLE | S&P 500 energy companies |
| iShares Energy Sector | IYE | Dow Jones energy companies |
| Financial Sector Spider | XLF | S&P 500 financial companies |
| iShares Financial Sector | IYF | Dow Jones financial companies |
| **International indexes** | | |
| WEBS United Kingdom | EWU | MCSI U.K. Index |
| WEBS France | EWQ | MCSI France Index |
| WEBS Japan | EWJ | MCSI Japan Index |

shares in the fund—only once a day. In contrast, ETFs trade continuously. (ETFs account for a high fraction of total trading on the Amex.) Moreover, like other shares, but unlike mutual funds, ETFs can be sold short or purchased on margin.

ETFs also offer a potential tax advantage over mutual funds. When large numbers of mutual fund investors redeem their shares, the fund must sell securities to meet the redemptions. This can trigger large capital gains taxes, which are passed through to and must be paid by the remaining shareholders. In contrast, when small investors wish to redeem their position in an ETF, they simply sell their shares to other traders, with no need for the fund to sell any of the underlying portfolio. Again, a redemption does not trigger a stock sale by the fund sponsor.

The ability of large investors to redeem ETFs for a portfolio of stocks comprising the index, or to exchange a portfolio of stocks for shares in the corresponding ETF, ensures that the price of an ETF cannot depart significantly from the net asset value of that portfolio. Any meaningful discrepancy would offer arbitrage trading opportunities for these large traders, which would quickly eliminate the disparity.

ETFs are also cheaper than mutual funds. Investors who buy ETFs do so through brokers rather than buying directly from the fund. Therefore, the fund saves the cost of marketing itself directly to small investors. This reduction in expenses translates into lower management fees.

There are some disadvantages to ETFs, however. Because they trade as securities, there is the possibility that their prices can depart by small amounts from net asset value. As noted, this discrepancy cannot be too large without giving rise to arbitrage opportunities for large traders, but even small discrepancies can easily swamp the cost advantage of ETFs over mutual funds. Second, while mutual funds can be bought at no expense from no-load funds, ETFs must be purchased from brokers for a fee.

## 4.7    MUTUAL FUND INVESTMENT PERFORMANCE: A FIRST LOOK

We noted earlier that one of the benefits of mutual funds for the individual investor is the ability to delegate management of the portfolio to investment professionals. The investor retains control over the broad features of the overall portfolio through the asset allocation decision: Each individual chooses the percentages of the portfolio to invest in bond funds versus equity funds versus money market funds, and so forth, but can leave the specific security selection decisions within each investment class to the managers of each fund. Shareholders hope that these portfolio managers can achieve better investment performance than they could obtain on their own.

What is the investment record of the mutual fund industry? This seemingly straightforward question is deceptively difficult to answer because we need a standard against which to evaluate performance. For example, we clearly would not want to compare the investment performance of an equity fund to the rate of return available in the money market. The vast differences in the risk of these two markets dictate that year-by-year as well as average performance will differ considerably. We would expect to find that equity funds outperform money market funds (on average) as compensation to investors for the extra risk incurred in equity markets. How then can we determine whether mutual fund portfolio managers are performing up to par *given* the level of risk they incur? In other words, what is the proper benchmark against which investment performance ought to be evaluated?

Measuring portfolio risk properly and using such measures to choose an appropriate benchmark is an extremely difficult task. We devote all of Parts II and III of the text to issues surrounding the proper measurement of portfolio risk and the trade-off between risk and return. In this chapter, therefore, we will satisfy ourselves with a first look at the question of fund performance by using only very simple performance benchmarks and ignoring the more subtle issues of risk differences across funds. However, we will return to this topic in Chapter 12, where we take a closer look at mutual fund performance after adjusting for differences in the exposure of portfolios to various sources of risk.

Here we use as a benchmark for the performance of equity fund managers the rate of return on the Wilshire 5000 Index. Recall from Chapter 2 that this is a value-weighted index of about 7,000 stocks that trade on the NYSE, Nasdaq, and Amex stock markets. It is the most inclusive index of the performance of U.S. equities. The performance of the Wilshire 5000 is a useful benchmark with which to evaluate professional managers because it corresponds to a simple passive investment strategy: Buy all the shares in the index in proportion to their outstanding market value. Moreover, this is a feasible strategy for even small investors, because the Vanguard Group offers an index fund (its Total Stock Market Portfolio) designed to replicate the performance of the Wilshire 5000 index. Using the Wilshire 5000 Index as a benchmark, we may pose the problem of evaluating the performance of mutual fund portfolio managers this way: How does the typical performance of actively managed equity mutual funds compare to the performance of a passively managed portfolio that simply replicates the composition of a broad index of the stock market?

**Figure 4.3**
**Percent of equity**
**mutual funds**
**outperformed by**
**Wilshire 5000**
**Index, 1972–2001**

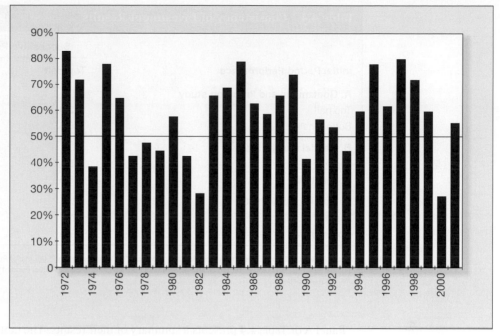

Source: The Vanguard Group.

Casual comparisons of the performance of the Wilshire 5000 index versus that of professionally managed mutual fund portfolios show disappointing results for most fund managers. Figure 4.3 shows the percentage of mutual fund managers whose performance was inferior in each year to the Wilshire 5000. In more years than not, the Index has outperformed the median manager.[3] In fact, since 1971, the compound return of the Wilshire 5000 was 12.20% versus 11.11% for the average fund. The 1.09% margin is substantial.

This result may seem surprising. After all, it would not seem unreasonable to expect that professional money managers should be able to outperform a very simple rule such as "hold an indexed portfolio." As it turns out, however, there may be good reasons to expect such a result. We explore them in detail in Chapter 12, where we discuss the efficient market hypothesis.

Of course, one might argue that there are good managers and bad managers, and that good managers can, in fact, consistently outperform the index. To test this notion, we examine whether managers with good performance in one year are likely to repeat that performance in a following year. Is superior performance in any particular year due to luck, and therefore random, or due to skill, and therefore consistent from year to year?

To answer this question, Goetzmann and Ibbotson[4] examined the performance of a large sample of equity mutual fund portfolios over the 1976–1985 period. Dividing the funds into two groups based on total investment return for different subperiods, they posed the question: "Do funds with investment returns in the top half of the sample in one two-year period continue to perform well in the subsequent two-year period?"

---

[3] Of course, actual funds incur trading costs while the Wilshire index does not. Vanguard's Wilshire 5000 fund charges an expense ratio of .20%, and, because it engages in little trading, it incurs low trading costs. To facilitate the comparison in Figure 4.3, the returns on the Wilshire 5000 Index were reduced by .30%.

[4] William N. Goetzmann and Roger G. Ibbotson, "Do Winners Repeat?" *Journal of Portfolio Management* (Winter 1994), pp. 9–18.

### Table 4.4    Consistency of Investment Results

| Initial Period Performance | Successive Period Performance | |
| --- | --- | --- |
| | Top Half | Bottom Half |
| **A. Goetzmann and Ibbotson study** | | |
| Top half | 62.0% | 38.0% |
| Bottom half | 36.6 | 63.4 |
| **B. Malkiel study, 1970s** | | |
| Top half | 65.1 | 34.9 |
| Bottom half | 35.5 | 64.5 |
| **C. Malkiel study, 1980s** | | |
| Top half | 51.7 | 48.3 |
| Bottom half | 47.5 | 52.5 |

Sources: *Panel A:* William N. Goetzmann and Roger G. Ibbotson, "Do Winners Repeat?" *Journal of Portfolio Management* (Winter 1994), pp. 9–18; *Panels B and C:* Burton G. Malkiel, "Returns from Investing in Equity Mutual Funds 1971–1991," *Journal of Finance* 50 (June 1995), pp. 549–72.

Panel A of Table 4.4 presents a summary of their results. The table shows the fraction of "winners" (i.e., top-half performers) in the initial period that turn out to be winners or losers in the following 2-year period. If performance were purely random from one period to the next, there would be entries of 50% in each cell of the table, as top- or bottom-half performers would be equally likely to perform in either the top or bottom half of the sample in the following period. On the other hand, if performance were due entirely to skill, with no randomness, we would expect to see entries of 100% on the diagonals and entries of 0% on the off-diagonals: Top-half performers would all remain in the top half while bottom-half performers similarly would all remain in the bottom half. In fact, the table shows that 62.0% of initial top-half performers fall in the top half of the sample in the following period, while 63.4% of initial bottom-half performers fall in the bottom half in the following period. This evidence is consistent with the notion that at least part of a fund's performance is a function of skill as opposed to luck, so that relative performance tends to persist from one period to the next.[5]

On the other hand, this relationship does not seem stable across different sample periods. Malkiel[6] uses a larger sample, but a similar methodology (except that he uses 1-year instead of 2-year investment returns) to examine performance consistency. He finds that while initial-year performance predicts subsequent-year performance in the 1970s (see Table 4.4, Panel B), the pattern of persistence in performance virtually disappears in the 1980s (Panel C).

To summarize, the evidence that performance is consistent from one period to the next is suggestive, but it is inconclusive. In the 1970s, top-half funds in one year were twice as likely in the following year to be in the top half as the bottom half of funds. In the 1980s, the odds that a top-half fund would fall in the top half in the following year were essentially equivalent to those of a coin flip.

---

[5] Another possibility is that performance consistency is due to variation in fee structure across funds. We return to this possibility in Chapter 12.

[6] Burton G. Malkiel, "Returns from Investing in Equity Mutual Funds 1971–1991," *Journal of Finance* 50 (June 1995), pp. 549–72.

Other studies suggest that bad performance is more likely to persist than good performance. This makes some sense: It is easy to identify fund characteristics that will predictably lead to consistently poor investment performance, notably high expense ratios, and high turnover ratios with associated trading costs. It is far harder to identify the secrets of successful stock picking. (If it were easy, we would all be rich!) Thus the consistency we do observe in fund performance may be due in large part to the poor performers. This suggests that the real value of past performance data is to avoid truly poor funds, even if identifying the future top performers is still a daunting task.

**CONCEPT CHECK ☞ QUESTION 4**

**Suppose you observe the investment performance of 400 portfolio managers and rank them by investment returns during the year. Twenty percent of all managers are truly skilled, and therefore always fall in the top half, but the others fall in the top half purely because of good luck. What fraction of this year's top-half managers would you expect to be top-half performers next year?**

## 4.8   INFORMATION ON MUTUAL FUNDS

The first place to find information on a mutual fund is in its prospectus. The Securities and Exchange Commission requires that the prospectus describe the fund's investment objectives and policies in a concise "Statement of Investment Objectives" as well as in lengthy discussions of investment policies and risks. The fund's investment adviser and its portfolio manager are also described. The prospectus also presents the costs associated with purchasing shares in the fund in a fee table. Sales charges such as front-end and back-end loads as well as annual operating expenses such as management fees and 12b-1 fees are detailed in the fee table.

Funds provide information about themselves in two other sources. The Statement of Additional Information, also known as Part B of the prospectus, includes a list of the securities in the portfolio at the end of the fiscal year, audited financial statements, and a list of the directors and officers of the fund. The fund's annual report, which is generally issued semiannually, also includes portfolio composition and financial statements, as well as a discussion of the factors that influenced fund performance over the last reporting period.

With more than 8,000 mutual funds to choose from, it can be difficult to find and select the fund that is best suited for a particular need. Several publications now offer "encyclopedias" of mutual fund information to help in the search process. Two prominent sources are Wiesenberger's *Investment Companies* and Morningstar's *Mutual Fund Sourcebook*. The Investment Company Institute (www.ici.org), the national association of mutual funds, closed-end funds, and unit investment trusts, publishes an annual *Directory of Mutual Funds* that includes information on fees as well as phone numbers to contact funds. To illustrate the range of information available about funds, we consider Morningstar's report on Fidelity's Magellan Fund, reproduced in Figure 4.4.

Some of Morningstar's analysis is qualitative. The top box on the left-hand side of the page provides a short description of the fund, in particular the types of securities in which the fund tends to invest, and a short biography of the current portfolio manager. The bottom box on the left ("Analysis") is a more detailed discussion of the fund's income strategy. The short statement of the fund's investment policy is in the top right-hand corner: Magellan is a "large blend" fund, meaning that it tends to invest in large firms and tends not to specialize in either value versus growth stocks—it holds a blend of these.

## Figure 4.4　Morningstar report

### Fidelity Magellan

| | Ticker | Load | NAV | Yield | Total Assets | Mstar Category |
|---|---|---|---|---|---|---|
| | FMAGX | Closed | $102.55 | 0.4% | $75,376.1 mil | Large Blend |

**Manager Strategy**

Stansky likes to move into growth areas when they are temporarily depressed. Because the fund is so large, he cannot trade in and out of positions easily. Thus, he looks for stocks he can hold for several years. Because of the fund's size, it owns stocks across varied industries.

**Historical Profile**

| | |
|---|---|
| Return | Average |
| Risk | Average |
| Rating | ★★★ |
| | Neutral |

Equity percentages: 89% 96% 94% 92% 96% 94% 94%

**Investment Style**
Equity
Stock %

▼ Manager Change
▽ Partial Manager Change

**Fund Performance vs. Category Average.**
Quarterly Fund Return
+/- Category Average
— Category Baseline

**Performance Quartile** (within Category)

**Portfolio Manager(s)**

Robert E. Stansky, CFA. Since 06-96. BA '78 Nichols C.; MBA '83 New York U.

| | 1991 | 1992 | 1993 | 1994 | 1995 | 1996 | 1997 | 1998 | 1999 | 2000 | 2001 | 03-02 | History |
|---|---|---|---|---|---|---|---|---|---|---|---|---|---|
| | 68.61 | 63.01 | 70.85 | 66.80 | 85.98 | 80.65 | 95.27 | 120.82 | 136.63 | 119.30 | 104.22 | 102.55 | NAV |
| | 41.03 | 7.01 | 24.66 | -1.81 | 36.82 | 11.69 | 26.59 | 33.63 | 24.05 | -9.29 | -11.65 | -1.60 | Total Return % |
| | 10.55 | -0.61 | 14.60 | -3.12 | -0.72 | 11.25 | -6.76 | 5.05 | 3.01 | -0.19 | 0.23 | -1.87 | +/-S&P 500 |
| | 8.59 | -0.64 | 14.82 | -2.26 | -0.78 | -10.47 | -6.43 | 5.00 | 2.22 | 1.67 | 1.12 | -2.30 | +/-Wilshire top 750 |
| | 2.46 | 1.93 | 1.22 | 0.18 | 0.88 | 1.41 | 1.57 | 0.72 | 0.63 | 0.20 | 0.39 | 0.00 | Income Return % |
| | 38.57 | 5.08 | 23.44 | -1.99 | 35.94 | 10.28 | 25.02 | 32.91 | 23.42 | 9.49 | -12.04 | 1.60 | Capital Return % |
| | 14 | 57 | 5 | 68 | 21 | 97 | 62 | 5 | 29 | 58 | 30 | 76 | Total Rtn % Rank Cat |
| | 1.30 | 1.25 | 0.75 | 0.13 | 0.59 | 1.10 | 1.25 | 0.67 | 0.73 | 0.27 | 0.46 | 0.00 | Income $ |
| | 5.43 | 8.82 | 6.50 | 2.64 | 4.69 | 12.85 | 5.21 | 5.15 | 11.39 | 4.69 | 0.80 | 0.00 | Capital Gains $ |
| | 1.06 | 1.05 | 1.00 | 0.99 | 0.96 | 0.92 | 0.64 | 0.61 | 0.60 | 0.74 | 0.88 | — | Expense Ratio % |
| | 2.47 | 1.57 | 2.11 | 1.07 | 0.39 | 0.95 | 1.75 | 0.77 | 0.66 | 0.46 | 0.29 | — | Income Ratio % |
| | 135 | 172 | 155 | 132 | 120 | 155 | 67 | 34 | 37 | 28 | 24 | — | Turnover Rate % |
| | 19,257 | 22,269 | 31,705 | 36,442 | 53,702 | 53,989 | 63,766 | 83,552 | 105,939 | 93,067 | 79,515 | 75,376 | Net Assets $mil |

**Performance** 03-31-02

| | 1st Qtr | 2nd Qtr | 3rd Qtr | 4th Qtr | Total |
|---|---|---|---|---|---|
| 1998 | 14.22 | 3.37 | -11.05 | 27.22 | 33.63 |
| 1999 | 7.39 | 5.93 | -5.97 | 15.97 | 24.05 |
| 2000 | 4.85 | -3.96 | -0.58 | -9.40 | -9.29 |
| 2001 | -12.41 | 7.18 | -15.36 | 11.18 | -11.65 |
| 2002 | -1.60 | — | — | — | — |

| Trailing | Total Return% | +/- S&P 500 | +/-Wilshire top 750 | %Rank All Cat | Growth of $10,000 |
|---|---|---|---|---|---|
| 3 Mo | -1.60 | -1.87 | -2.30 | 79 76 | 9,840 |
| 6 Mo | 9.40 | -1.59 | -2.70 | 48 70 | 10,940 |
| 1 Yr | -0.76 | -1.00 | -1.60 | 67 50 | 9,924 |
| 3 Yr Avg | -3.07 | -0.54 | 0.01 | 81 59 | 9,107 |
| 5 Yr Avg | 10.72 | 0.55 | 0.82 | 17 20 | 16,639 |
| 10 Yr Avg | 12.80 | -0.45 | -0.02 | 15 26 | — |
| 15 Yr Avg | 12.76 | 0.46 | 0.76 | 10 13 | 60,580 |

| Tax Analysis | Tax-Adj Ret% | %Rank Cat | %Pretax Ret | %Rank Cat |
|---|---|---|---|---|
| 3 Yr Avg | -4.17 | 61 | — | — |
| 5 Yr Avg | 9.27 | 19 | 86.0 | 30 |
| 10 Yr Avg | 10.26 | 44 | 80.0 | 54 |

Potential Capital Gain Exposure: 28% of assets

**Risk Analysis**

| Time Period | Load-Adj Return % | Risk %Rank All Cat | Morningstar Return Risk | Morningstar Risk-Adj Rating |
|---|---|---|---|---|
| 1 Yr | -3.73 | | | |
| 3 Yr | -4.04 | 70 61 | -1.79 0.98 | ★★ |
| 5 Yr | 10.05 | 68 57 | 1.18 0.93 | ★★★ |
| 10 Yr | 12.46 | 73 64 | 1.19 0.94 | ★★★ |

Average Historical Rating(196 months): 4.6★s

1=low, 100=high　2 T-Bill return substituted for category avg.

| Category Rating (3 Yr) | | |
|---|---|---|
| ①②③④⑤ | | |
| Worst　　Best | | |
| Return | Below Avg | |
| Risk | Average | |

| Other Measures | Standard Index S&P 500 | Best Fit Index S&P 500 |
|---|---|---|
| Alpha | -0.3 | -0.3 |
| Beta | 1.02 | 1.02 |
| R-Squared | 97 | 97 |
| Standard Deviation | 17.00 | |
| Mean | -3.07 | |
| Sharpe Ratio | -0.53 | |

**Portfolio Analysis** 09-30-01

Share change since 03-01 Total Stocks:257

| Sector | PE | YTD Ret% | % Assets |
|---|---|---|---|
| ⊖ General Elec | Industrials | 27.3 | 7.01 | 4.76 |
| ⊖ Citigroup | Financials | 18.2 | -3.26 | 3.95 |
| ⊕ American Intl Grp | Financials | 35.7 | -6.50 | 2.99 |
| ⊕ ExxonMobil | Energy | 19.8 | 9.12 | 2.83 |
| ⊖ Tyco Intl | Industrials | 11.9 | -46.01 | 2.69 |
| ⊕ Pfizer | Health | 32.6 | -4.34 | 2.64 |
| ⊕ Microsoft | Technology | 55.3 | -15.69 | 2.64 |
| ⊕ Viacom Cl B | Services | — | — | 2.18 |
| ⊕ Wal-Mart Stores | Retail | 41.1 | 2.88 | 1.99 |
| ⊖ Fannie Mae | Financials | 14.0 | 4.81 | 1.87 |
| ⊕ AOL Time Warner | Technology | — | -30.16 | 1.77 |
| ⊖ Philip Morris | Staples | 13.6 | 18.13 | 1.77 |
| ⊕ Bristol-Myers Squibb | Health | 15.2 | -35.31 | 1.65 |
| ⊖ IBM | Technology | 23.9 | 19.50 | 1.57 |
| ⊖ Home Depot | Retail | 37.7 | -4.29 | 1.55 |
| ⊕ Wells Fargo | Financials | 25.1 | 13.34 | 1.55 |
| ⊕ Cardinal Health | Health | 36.0 | 5.60 | 1.38 |
| ⊕ SBC Comms | Services | 17.6 | -4.06 | 1.36 |
| ⊕ Verizon Comms | Services | NMF | -4.03 | 1.33 |
| | Bank of America | Financials | 13.7 | 10.52 | 1.29 |
| | Freddie Mac | Financials | 11.2 | 2.64 | 1.21 |
| | Coca-Cola | Staples | 32.7 | 11.13 | 1.21 |
| ⊕ Intel | Technology | NMF | -4.39 | 1.14 |
| ⊖ Morgan Stanley/Dean Witter | Financials | 18.4 | 0.75 | 1.09 |
| ⊖ Eli Lilly | Health | 29.9 | -3.67 | 1.08 |

**Current Investment Style**

| | Stock Port Avg | Relative S&P 500 Current Hist | Rel Cat |
|---|---|---|---|
| Price/Earnings Ratio | 29.9 | 0.94 1.10 | 0.94 |
| Price/Book Ratio | 5.5 | 0.99 1.12 | 1.00 |
| Price/Cash Flow | 18.2 | 1.02 1.10 | 0.99 |
| 3 Yr Earnings Growth | 14.1 | 1.24 1.34 | 1.01 |
| Med Mkt Cap $mil | 82,802 | 1.42 1.90 | 1.71 |

**Analysis** by Scott Cooley 03-22-02

Fidelity Magellan is still solid, if less than spectacular.

To be sure, the fund hasn't turned any heads so far in 2002. For the year to date through March 21, the fund had dropped 0.8%, trailing three fourths of its large-blend rivals. Although manager Bob Stansky may sometimes seem to hug the S&P 500, he had a significant wager on Tyco International, the fund's fourth-largest position at year-end. Unfortunately, Tyco has fallen 42% so far this year, as investors have raised questions about its aggressive accounting practices. Although the fund's cyclical holdings, including media giant Viacom, have rallied in recent weeks, as more good news about the economy has emerged, that hasn't been enough to offset Tyco's drag on the portfolio.

Earlier this year, anyway, Stansky showed no signs of radically revising the portfolio. As of Jan. 31, when Fidelity last released portfolio information, he still had a below-average tech weight. Stansky has long been concerned about the sector's rich valuations. And as a way to play an economic rebound, he had an above-S&P 500 weight in retail and media issues. Stocks like Viacom have posted sharp gains this year, offsetting

losses elsewhere in the portfolio.

Although the recent news here hasn't been great, it's worth noting that Stansky has delivered the goods over the long haul. Thanks in part to some excellent picks in the tech sector, especially in 1998 and 1999, the fund's five-year return still tops the S&P 500's and more than 80% of its rivals'. Stansky has generated those returns without taking huge positions in individual stocks or making large asset-allocation bets, as his predecessor did.

Therefore, despite the fund's recent hiccup, we think it's still a solid, dependable core holding

**Special Securities** % assets 09-30-01

| | |
|---|---|
| Restricted/Illiquid Secs | Trace |
| Emerging Markets Secs | 0 |
| Options/Futures/Warrants | No |

| Composition % assets 09-30-01 | | Market Cap | |
|---|---|---|---|
| | | Giant | 65.8 |
| Cash | 5.6 | Large | 26.8 |
| Stocks | 94.4 | Medium | 7.0 |
| Bonds | 0.0 | Small | 0.1 |
| Other | 0.0 | Micro | 0.4 |
| Foreign (% assets) | 2.9 | | |

| Sector Weightings | % of Stocks | Rel S&P | 3-Year High Low |
|---|---|---|---|
| Utilities | 0.2 | 0.1 | 0 0 |
| Energy | 7.6 | 1.1 | 8 6 |
| Financials | 22.3 | 1.2 | 22 14 |
| Industrials | 12.8 | 1.1 | 13 11 |
| Durables | 1.1 | 0.6 | 2 1 |
| Staples | 6.1 | 0.8 | 6 3 |
| Services | 13.7 | 1.2 | 16 13 |
| Retail | 7.5 | 1.0 | 11 7 |
| Health | 14.8 | 1.0 | 15 10 |
| Technology | 13.8 | 0.8 | 29 14 |

| Address: | 82 Devonshire Street Boston, MA 02109 800-544-8888 | Minimum Purchase: | Closed | Add: $250 | IRA: $500 |
|---|---|---|---|---|---|
| | | Min Auto Inv Plan: | Closed | Add: $100 | |
| Web Address: | www.fidelity.com | Sales Fees: | 3.00%L | | |
| Inception: | 05-02-63 | Management Fee: | 0.57%, 0.20%P | | |
| Advisor: | Fidelity Management & Research | Actual Fees: | Mgt:0.57% | Dist: — | |
| Subadvisor: | FMR (Far East), FMR (U.K.) | Expense Projections: | 3Yr:$532 | 5Yr:$704 | 10Yr:$1202 |
| NTF Plans: | Fidelity Instl-NTF | Income Distrib: | Semi-Annually | | |

**Total Cost** (relative to category): Below Avg

**MORNINGSTAR® Mutual Funds**

The table on the left labeled "Performance" reports on the fund's returns over the last few years and over longer periods up to 15 years. Comparisons of returns to relevant indexes, in this case, the S&P 500 and the Wilshire top 750 indexes, are provided to serve as benchmarks in evaluating the performance of the fund. The values under these columns give the performance of the fund relative to the index. The returns reported for the fund are calculated net of expenses, 12b-1 fees, and any other fees automatically deducted from fund assets, but they do not account for any sales charges such as front-end loads or back-end charges. Next appear the percentile ranks of the fund compared to all other funds (see column headed by "All") and to all funds with the same investment objective (see column headed by "Cat"). A rank of 1 means the fund is a top performer. A rank of 80 would mean that it was beaten by 80% of funds in the comparison group. Finally, growth of $10,000 invested in the fund over various periods ranging from the past 3 months to the past 15 years is given in the last column.

More data on the performance of the fund are provided in the graph at the top right of the figure. The bar charts give the fund's rate of return for each quarter of the last 10 years. Below the graph is a box for each year that depicts the relative performance of the fund for that year. The shaded area on the box shows the quartile in which the fund's performance falls relative to other funds with the same objective. If the shaded band is at the top of the box, the firm was a top quartile performer in that period, and so on. The table below the bar charts presents historical data on characteristics of the fund such as return data and expense ratios.

The table on the right entitled "Portfolio Analysis" presents the 25 largest holdings of the portfolio, including the price-earning ratio and year-to-date return of each of those securities. Investors can thus get a quick look at the manager's biggest bets.

Below the portfolio analysis is a box labeled "Current Investment Style." In this box, Morningstar evaluates style along two dimensions: One dimension is the size of the firms held in the portfolio as measured by the market value of outstanding equity; the other dimension is a value/growth measure. Morningstar defines *value stocks* as those with low ratios of market price per share to various measures of value. It puts stocks on a growth-value continuum based on the ratios of stock price to the firm's earnings, book value, sales, cash flow, and dividends. These are called value stocks because they have a low price relative to these two measures of value. In contrast, *growth stocks* have high ratios, suggesting that investors in these firms must believe that the firm will experience rapid growth to justify the prices at which the stocks sell. The shaded box for Magellan shows that the portfolio tends to hold larger firms (top row) and blend stocks (middle column). A year-by-year history of Magellan's investment style is presented in the sequence of such boxes at the top of the figure.

The center of the figure, labeled "Risk Analysis," is one of the more complicated but interesting facets of Morningstar's analysis. The column labeled "Load-Adj Return" rates a fund's return compared to other funds with the same investment policy. Returns for periods ranging from 1 to 10 years are calculated with all loads and back-end fees applicable to that investment period subtracted from total income. The return is then divided by the average return for the comparison group of funds to obtain the "Morningstar Return"; therefore, a value of 1.0 in the Return column would indicate average performance while a value of 1.10 would indicate returns 10% above the average for the comparison group (e.g., 11% return for the fund versus 10% for the comparison group).

Morningstar's risk measure is based in part on the overall volatility of returns, but it focuses more intently on episodes of underperformance relative to Treasury bills. This measure also is scaled by dividing by the average downside risk measure for all firms with the same investment objective. Therefore, the average value in the Risk column is 1.0.

# THOSE FIVE-STAR FUNDS DON'T NECESSARILY OUTPERFORM THEIR LOWER-RANKING PEERS

Two methods for rating mutual funds, including the widely used Morningstar system, have come under fire.

A new study concludes that mutual funds given high ratings by Morningstar and Value Line—both used by investors to choose among funds—don't necessarily perform better than those with middling ratings.

The ratings are widely trumpeted in mutual funds' advertisements, and many people rely on them to make key investment decisions, such as where to put their retirement savings. Last year, for example, stock funds with coveted four- and five-star ratings from Morningstar took in nearly $80 billion, compared with the more than $108 billion that was withdrawn from lower-rated funds, according to Nov. 30 data from Financial Research Corp.

"Mutual-fund ratings services can't really predict winners," says the study's author, finance professor Matthew R. Morey of New York's Pace University.

To test ratings' predictive abilities, Prof. Morey sifted the fund market for diversified stock funds that had at least three years of history at the end of 1994. He then tracked the performance of these funds over the next six years to see how funds with high ratings from Morningstar and Value Line compared with those with lower ratings.

Prof. Morey found that, from 1995 through 2000, lower-rated funds kept slumping to some extent. But highly rated funds, which draw heavy promotion and sales, didn't tend to perform any better than funds with middle-of-the-pack ratings.

Morningstar previously compared funds in four categories: U.S. stock, foreign stock, taxable bond and municipal bond. But this past summer the firm began comparing funds in 48 narrower stock- and bond-fund categories. The narrower categories keep one group from ending up with a disproportionate percentage of the top ratings, such as when 90% of rated tech funds had five stars at the end of 1999.

So, how should investors use fund ratings? Cautiously.

The best approach is to research how a rating is derived and, if you're comfortable with its criteria, only use it as a first cut to winnow the vast field of options. A ratings screen will leave you with a more manageable pack of funds to study closely and shoe-horn into a well-diversified portfolio.

Source: Abridged from Ian McDonald, "Mutual-Fund Ratings Come under Fire." *The Wall Street Journal,* January 15, 2003.

---

The two columns to the left of Morningstar risk and return are the percentile scores of risk and return for each fund. The risk-adjusted rating, ranging from one to five stars, is based on the Morningstar return score minus the risk score. The stars each fund earns are based on risk-adjusted performance relative to other funds in the same style group. To allow funds to be compared to other funds with similar investment styles, Morningstar recently increased the number of categories; there are now 48 separate stock and bond fund categories. Of course, we are accustomed to the notice that "past performance is not a reliable measure of future results," and this is true as well of the coveted Morningstar five-star rating. The nearby box discusses the predictive value of Morningstar's ranking.

The tax analysis box on the left provides some evidence on the tax efficiency of the fund by comparing pretax and after-tax returns. The after-tax return, given in the first column, is computed based on the dividends paid to the portfolio as well as realized capital gains, assuming the investor is in the maximum tax bracket at the time of the distribution. State and local taxes are ignored. The "tax efficiency" of the fund is defined as the ratio of after-tax to pretax returns; it is presented in the second column, labeled "% Pretax Return." Tax efficiency will be lower when turnover is higher because capital gains are taxed as they are realized.

| E-INVESTMENTS<br>**Morningstar<br>Reviews** | Review, update, and summarize the performance of Fidelity Magellan (FMAGX) at Morningstar.com (**www.morningstar.com**). Enter FMAGX in the box at the left of the home page screen. What are the current NAV, Morningstar rating, front load, expense ratio, and top five company investments? What have been the major changes since the Figure 4.4 report in your chapter? What is the basis for the Morningstar ratings? |
| --- | --- |

## SUMMARY

1. Unit investment trusts, closed-end management companies, and open-end management companies are all classified and regulated as investment companies. Unit investment trusts are essentially unmanaged in the sense that the portfolio, once established, is fixed. Managed investment companies, in contrast, may change the composition of the portfolio as deemed fit by the portfolio manager. Closed-end funds are traded like other securities; they do not redeem shares for their investors. Open-end funds will redeem shares for net asset value at the request of the investor.

2. Net asset value equals the market value of assets held by a fund minus the liabilities of the fund divided by the shares outstanding.

3. Mutual funds free the individual from many of the administrative burdens of owning individual securities and offer professional management of the portfolio. They also offer advantages that are available only to large-scale investors, such as discounted trading costs. On the other hand, funds are assessed management fees and incur other expenses, which reduce the investor's rate of return. Funds also eliminate some of the individual's control over the timing of capital gains realizations.

4. Mutual funds are often categorized by investment policy. Major policy groups include money market funds; equity funds, which are further grouped according to emphasis on income versus growth; fixed-income funds; balanced and income funds; asset allocation funds; index funds; and specialized sector funds.

5. Costs of investing in mutual funds include front-end loads, which are sales charges; back-end loads, which are redemption fees or, more formally, contingent-deferred sales charges; fund operating expenses; and 12b-1 charges, which are recurring fees used to pay for the expenses of marketing the fund to the public.

6. Income earned on mutual fund portfolios is not taxed at the level of the fund. Instead, as long as the fund meets certain requirements for pass-through status, the income is treated as being earned by the investors in the fund.

7. The average rate of return of the average equity mutual fund in the last 25 years has been below that of a passive index fund holding a portfolio to replicate a broad-based index like the S&P 500 or Wilshire 5000. Some of the reasons for this disappointing record are the costs incurred by actively managed funds, such as the expense of conducting the research to guide stock-picking activities, and trading costs due to higher portfolio turnover. The record on the consistency of fund performance is mixed. In some sample periods, the better-performing funds continue to perform well in the following periods; in other sample periods they do not.

## KEY TERMS

| | | |
| --- | --- | --- |
| investment company | closed-end fund | soft dollars |
| net asset value (NAV) | hedge fund | turnover |
| unit investment trust | load | exchange-traded funds |
| open-end fund | 12b-1 fees | |

Visit us at www.mhhe.com/bkm

## WEBSITES

The following sites have considerable information about mutual funds:

www.ici.org
www.brill.com
See Brill's *Funds 101* link for interesting reading and a look at the related areas of mutual fund investing.

www.mfea.com
The Mutual Fund Education Alliance. Yes, there is more to know than could be placed in this long chapter! See *Getting Started*.

www.morningstar.com
Morningstar "rates" mutual funds and provides excellent general information. Register for free.

biz.yahoo.com/funds
Yahoo! Finance has an excellent mutual fund information site. See *Fund Screener*.

www.bloomberg.com
Look for the *Mutual Funds* link in the left margin.

The following links have information on Exchange-Traded Funds:

www.indexfunds.com
See the *ETFzone* link. See *How To Use Our Data* for fund screening and comparison of index funds and ETFs.

www.amex.com
The American Stock Exchange. See the *ETF* link at the left margin.

www.cboe.com
Touch the *Products* tab at the top of the page for ETF information at the Chicago Board Options Exchange.

www.nyse.com
See the *Indexes and ETFs* link at the New York Stock Exchange.

www.amfi.com/cgi-bin/web.cgi?KEY=AMG000001
This is the website for the Association of Mutual Funds Investors.

The following are specific mutual fund organization websites:

flagship.vanguard.com
Vanguard Group

www.fidelity.com
Fidelity

**PROBLEMS**

1. Would you expect a typical open-end fixed-income mutual fund to have higher or lower operating expenses than a fixed-income unit investment trust? Why?

2. An open-end fund has a net asset value of $10.70 per share. It is sold with a front-end load of 6%. What is the offering price?

3. If the offering price of an open-end fund is $12.30 per share and the fund is sold with a front-end load of 5%, what is its net asset value?

4. The composition of the Fingroup Fund portfolio is as follows:

| Stock | Shares | Price |
|-------|--------|-------|
| A | 200,000 | $35 |
| B | 300,000 | 40 |
| C | 400,000 | 20 |
| D | 600,000 | 25 |

The fund has not borrowed any funds, but its accrued management fee with the portfolio manager currently totals $30,000. There are 4 million shares outstanding. What is the net asset value of the fund?

5. Reconsider the Fingroup Fund in the previous problem. If during the year the portfolio manager sells all of the holdings of stock D and replaces it with 200,000 shares of stock E at $50 per share and 200,000 shares of stock F at $25 per share, what is the portfolio turnover rate?

6. The Closed Fund is a closed-end investment company with a portfolio currently worth $200 million. It has liabilities of $3 million and 5 million shares outstanding.
   a. What is the NAV of the fund?
   b. If the fund sells for $36 per share, what is its premium or discount as a percent of net asset value?

7. Corporate Fund started the year with a net asset value of $12.50. By year end, its NAV equaled $12.10. The fund paid year-end distributions of income and capital gains of $1.50. What was the (pretax) rate of return to an investor in the fund?

8. A closed-end fund starts the year with a net asset value of $12.00. By year end, NAV equals $12.10. At the beginning of the year, the fund was selling at a 2% premium to NAV. By the end of the year, the fund is selling at a 7% discount to NAV. The fund paid year-end distributions of income and capital gains of $1.50.
   a. What is the rate of return to an investor in the fund during the year?
   b. What would have been the rate of return to an investor who held the same securities as the fund manager during the year?

9. What are some comparative advantages of investing in the following:
   a. Unit investment trusts.
   b. Open-end mutual funds.
   c. Individual stocks and bonds that you choose for yourself.

10. Open-end equity mutual funds find it necessary to keep a significant percentage of total investments, typically around 5% of the portfolio, in very liquid money market assets. Closed-end funds do not have to maintain such a position in "cash-equivalent" securities. What difference between open-end and closed-end funds might account for their differing policies?

Visit us at www.mhhe.com/bkm

11. Balanced funds and asset allocation funds invest in both the stock and bond markets. What is the difference between these types of funds?

12. *a.* Impressive Fund had excellent investment performance last year, with portfolio returns that placed it in the top 10% of all funds with the same investment policy. Do you expect it to be a top performer next year? Why or why not?

    *b.* Suppose instead that the fund was among the poorest performers in its comparison group. Would you be more or less likely to believe its relative performance will persist into the following year? Why?

13. Consider a mutual fund with $200 million in assets at the start of the year and with 10 million shares outstanding. The fund invests in a portfolio of stocks that provides dividend income at the end of the year of $2 million. The stocks included in the fund's portfolio increase in price by 8%, but no securities are sold, and there are no capital gains distributions. The fund charges 12b-1 fees of 1%, which are deducted from portfolio assets at year-end. What is net asset value at the start and end of the year? What is the rate of return for an investor in the fund?

14. The New Fund had average daily assets of $2.2 billion last year. The fund sold $400 million worth of stock and purchased $500 million during the year. What was its turnover ratio?

15. If New Fund's expense ratio (see Problem 14) was 1.1% and the management fee was .7%, what were the total fees paid to the fund's investment managers during the year? What were other administrative expenses?

16. You purchased 1,000 shares of the New Fund at a price of $20 per share at the beginning of the year. You paid a front-end load of 4%. The securities in which the fund invests increase in value by 12% during the year. The fund's expense ratio is 1.2%. What is your rate of return on the fund if you sell your shares at the end of the year?

17. The Investments Fund sells Class A shares with a front-end load of 6% and Class B shares with 12b-1 fees of .5% annually as well as back-end load fees that start at 5% and fall by 1% for each full year the investor holds the portfolio (until the fifth year). Assume the portfolio rate of return net of operating expenses is 10% annually. If you plan to sell the fund after 4 years, are Class A or Class B shares the better choice for you? What if you plan to sell after 15 years?

18. Suppose you observe the investment performance of 350 portfolio managers for 5 years, and rank them by investment returns during each year. After 5 years, you find that 11 of the funds have investment returns that place the fund in the top half of the sample in each and every year of your sample. Such consistency of performance indicates to you that these must be the funds whose managers are in fact skilled, and you invest your money in these funds. Is your conclusion warranted?

19. You are considering an investment in a mutual fund with a 4% load and expense ratio of .5%. You can invest instead in a bank CD paying 6% interest.

    *a.* If you plan to invest for 2 years, what annual rate of return must the fund portfolio earn for you to be better off in the fund than in the CD? Assume annual compounding of returns.

    *b.* How does your answer change if you plan to invest for 6 years? Why does your answer change?

    *c.* Now suppose that instead of a front-end load the fund assesses a 12b-1 fee of .75% per year. What annual rate of return must the fund portfolio earn for you to be better off in the fund than in the CD? Does your answer in this case depend on your time horizon?

20. Suppose that every time a fund manager trades stock, transaction costs such as commissions and bid–asked spreads amount to .4% of the value of the trade. If the portfolio turnover rate is 50%, by how much is the total return of the portfolio reduced by trading costs?

21. You expect a tax-free municipal bond portfolio to provide a rate of return of 4%. Management fees of the fund are .6%. What fraction of portfolio income is given up to fees? If the management fees for an equity fund also are .6%, but you expect a portfolio return of 12%, what fraction of portfolio income is given up to fees? Why might management fees be a bigger factor in your investment decision for bond funds than for stock funds? Can your conclusion help explain why unmanaged unit investment trusts tend to focus on the fixed-income market?

---

**STANDARD & POOR'S**

1. Go to **www.mhhe.com/business/finance/edumarketinsight** and link to *Company*, then *Population*. Select a company of interest to you and link to the *Company Research* page with a menu of company information reports on the left. Link to the *S&P Stock Reports*. What information is presented in the *S&P stock report*? What is the S&P stock rating for the company? What are the fair value ($) and the risk rating? How does the fair value compare with the recent stock price, listed at the top of the report?

---

**E-INVESTMENTS**
**Choosing a Mutual Fund**

Here are the websites for three of the largest mutual fund companies:

    Fidelity Investments: **www.fidelity.com**

    Putnam Investments: **www.putnaminv.com**

    Vanguard Group: **www.vanguard.com**

Pick three or four funds from one of these sites. What are the investment objectives of each fund? Find the expense ratio of each fund. Which fund has had the best recent performance? What are the major holdings of each fund?

---

**SOLUTIONS TO CONCEPT CHECKS**

1. $\text{NAV} = \dfrac{\$2,885.9 - \$2.3}{370.4} = \$7.79$

2. The net investment in the Class A shares after the 4% commission is $9,600. If the fund earns a 10% return, the investment will grow after $n$ years to $\$9,600 \times (1.10)^n$. The Class B shares have no front-end load. However, the net return to the investor after 12b-1 fees will be only 9.5%. In addition, there is a back-end load that reduces

the sales proceeds by a percentage equal to (5 – years until sale) until the fifth year, when the back-end load expires.

| Horizon | Class A Shares $9,600 \times (1.10)^n$ | Class B Shares $10,000 \times (1.095)^n \times (1 - \text{percentage exit fee})$ |
|---|---|---|
| 1 year | $10,560 | $10,000 \times (1.095) \times (1 - .04)$ = $10,512 |
| 4 years | $14,055 | $10,000 \times (1.095)^4 \times (1 - .01)$ = $14,233 |
| 10 years | $24,900 | $10,000 \times (1.095)^{10}$ = $24,782 |

**SOLUTIONS TO CONCEPT CHECKS** *(Concluded)*

For a very short horizon such as one year, the Class A shares are the better choice. The front-end and back-end loads are equal, but the Class A shares don't have to pay the 12b-1 fees. For moderate horizons such as four years, the Class B shares dominate because the front-end load of the Class A shares is more costly than the 12b-1 fees and the now-smaller exit fee. For long horizons of 10 years or more, Class A again dominates. In this case, the one-time front-end load is less expensive than the continuing 12b-1 fees.

3. *a.* Turnover = $160,000 in trades per $1 million of portfolio value = 16%.

   *b.* Realized capital gains are $10 \times 1,000 = $10,000 on Microsoft and $5 \times 2,000 = $10,000 on Ford. The tax owed on the capital gains is therefore .20 \times $20,000 = $4,000.

4. Twenty percent of the managers are skilled, which accounts for .2 \times 400 = 80 of those managers who appear in the top half. There are 120 slots left in the top half, and 320 other managers, so the probability of an unskilled manager "lucking into" the top half in any year is 120/320, or .375. Therefore, of the 120 lucky managers in the first year, we would expect .375 \times 120 = 45 to repeat as top-half performers next year. Thus, we should expect a total of 80 + 45 = 125, or 62.5%, of the better initial performers to repeat their top-half performance.

# PORTFOLIO THEORY

## CHAPTER FIVE

# HISTORY OF INTEREST RATES AND RISK PREMIUMS

Individuals must be concerned with both the expected return and the risk of the assets that might be included in their portfolios. To help us form reasonable expectations for the performance of a wide array of potential investments, this chapter surveys the historical performance of the major asset classes. It uses a risk-free portfolio of Treasury bills as a benchmark to evaluate that performance. Therefore, we start the chapter with a review of the determinants of the risk-free interest rate, the rate available on Treasury bills, paying attention to the distinction between real and nominal returns. We then turn to the measurement of the expected returns and volatilities of risky assets, and show how historical data can be used to construct estimates of such statistics for several broadly diversified portfolios. Finally, we review the historical record of several portfolios of interest to provide a sense of the range of performance in the past several decades.

We compare the performance of stock portfolios in the United States and other developed countries, and discuss whether historical returns on U.S. stocks can serve as a guide to future investment performance.

# 5.1   DETERMINANTS OF THE LEVEL OF INTEREST RATES

Interest rates and forecasts of their future values are among the most important inputs into an investment decision. For example, suppose you have $10,000 in a savings account. The bank pays you a variable interest rate tied to some short-term reference rate such as the 30-day Treasury bill rate. You have the option of moving some or all of your money into a longer-term certificate of deposit that offers a fixed rate over the term of the deposit.

Your decision depends critically on your outlook for interest rates. If you think rates will fall, you will want to lock in the current higher rates by investing in a relatively long-term CD. If you expect rates to rise, you will want to postpone committing any funds to long-term CDs.

Forecasting interest rates is one of the most notoriously difficult parts of applied macroeconomics. Nonetheless, we do have a good understanding of the fundamental factors that determine the level of interest rates:

1. The supply of funds from savers, primarily households.
2. The demand for funds from businesses to be used to finance investments in plant, equipment, and inventories (real assets or capital formation).
3. The government's net supply of or demand for funds as modified by actions of the Federal Reserve Bank.

Before we elaborate on these forces and resultant interest rates, we need to distinguish real from nominal interest rates.

## Real and Nominal Rates of Interest

Suppose exactly 1 year ago you deposited $1,000 in a 1-year time deposit guaranteeing a rate of interest of 10%. You are about to collect $1,100 in cash.

Is your $100 return for real? That depends on what money can buy these days, relative to what you *could* buy a year ago. The consumer price index (CPI) measures purchasing power by averaging the prices of goods and services in the consumption basket of an average urban family of four. Although this basket may not represent your particular consumption plan, suppose for now that it does.

Suppose the rate of inflation (the percent change in the CPI, denoted by $i$) for the last year amounted to $i = 6\%$. This tells you that the purchasing power of money is reduced by 6% a year. The value of each dollar depreciates by 6% a year in terms of the goods it can buy. Therefore, part of your interest earnings are offset by the reduction in the purchasing power of the dollars you will receive at the end of the year. With a 10% interest rate, after you net out the 6% reduction in the purchasing power of money, you are left with a net increase in purchasing power of about 4%. Thus we need to distinguish between a **nominal interest rate**—the growth rate of your money—and a **real interest rate**—the growth rate of your purchasing power. If we call $R$ the nominal rate, $r$ the real rate, and $i$ the inflation rate, then we conclude

$$r \approx R - i$$

In words, the real rate of interest is the nominal rate reduced by the loss of purchasing power resulting from inflation.

In fact, the exact relationship between the real and nominal interest rate is given by

$$1 + r = \frac{1 + R}{1 + i}$$

This is because the growth factor of your purchasing power, $1 + r$, equals the growth factor of your money, $1 + R$, divided by the new price level, that is, $1 + i$ times its value in the previous period. The exact relationship can be rearranged to

$$r = \frac{R - i}{1 + i}$$

which shows that the approximation rule overstates the real rate by the factor $1 + i$.

## EXAMPLE 5.1   Approximating the Real Rate

If the nominal interest rate on a 1-year CD is 8%, and you expect inflation to be 5% over the coming year, then using the approximation formula, you expect the real rate of interest to be $r = 8\% - 5\% = 3\%$. Using the exact formula, the real rate is $r = \dfrac{.08 - .05}{1 + .05} = .0286$, or 2.86%. Therefore, the approximation rule overstates the expected real rate by only .14% (14 basis points). The approximation rule is more exact for small inflation rates and is perfectly exact for continuously compounded rates. We discuss further details in the appendix to this chapter.

Before the decision to invest, you should realize that conventional certificates of deposit offer a guaranteed *nominal* rate of interest. Thus you can only infer the expected real rate on these investments by subtracting your expectation of the rate of inflation.

It is always possible to calculate the real rate after the fact. The inflation rate is published by the Bureau of Labor Statistics (BLS). The future real rate, however, is unknown, and one has to rely on expectations. In other words, because future inflation is risky, the real rate of return is risky even when the nominal rate is risk-free.

**The Equilibrium Real Rate of Interest**   Three basic factors—supply, demand, and government actions—determine the *real* interest rate. The nominal interest rate, which is the rate we actually observe, is the real rate plus the expected rate of inflation. So a fourth factor affecting the interest rate is the expected rate of inflation.

Although there are many different interest rates economywide (as many as there are types of securities), these rates tend to move together, so economists frequently talk as if there were a single representative rate. We can use this abstraction to gain some insights into the real rate of interest if we consider the supply and demand curves for funds.

Figure 5.1 shows a downward-sloping demand curve and an upward-sloping supply curve. On the horizontal axis, we measure the quantity of funds, and on the vertical axis, we measure the real rate of interest.

The supply curve slopes up from left to right because the higher the real interest rate, the greater the supply of household savings. The assumption is that at higher real interest rates households will choose to postpone some current consumption and set aside or invest more of their disposable income for future use.[1]

The demand curve slopes down from left to right because the lower the real interest rate, the more businesses will want to invest in physical capital. Assuming that businesses rank

---

[1] There is considerable disagreement among experts on the issue of whether household saving does go up in response to an increase in the real interest rate.

**Figure 5.1
Determination of
the equilibrium
real rate of
interest**

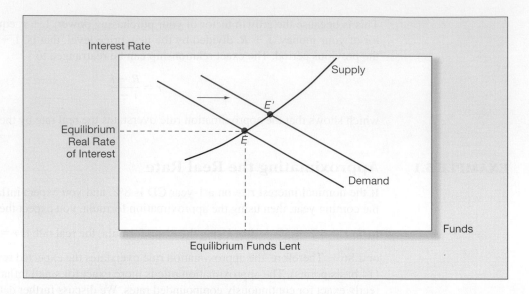

projects by the expected real return on invested capital, firms will undertake more projects the lower the real interest rate on the funds needed to finance those projects.

Equilibrium is at the point of intersection of the supply and demand curves, point $E$ in Figure 5.1.

The government and the central bank (the Federal Reserve) can shift these supply and demand curves either to the right or to the left through fiscal and monetary policies. For example, consider an increase in the government's budget deficit. This increases the government's borrowing demand and shifts the demand curve to the right, which causes the equilibrium real interest rate to rise to point $E'$. That is, a forecast that indicates higher than previously expected government borrowing increases expected future interest rates. The Fed can offset such a rise through an expansionary monetary policy, which will shift the supply curve to the right.

Thus, although the fundamental determinants of the real interest rate are the propensity of households to save and the expected productivity (or we could say profitability) of investment in physical capital, the real rate can be affected as well by government fiscal and monetary policies.

**The Equilibrium
Nominal Rate
of Interest**

We've seen that the real rate of return on an asset is approximately equal to the nominal rate minus the inflation rate. Because investors should be concerned with their real returns—the increase in their purchasing power—we would expect that as the inflation rate increases, investors will demand higher nominal rates of return on their investments. This higher rate is necessary to maintain the expected real return offered by an investment.

Irving Fisher (1930) argued that the nominal rate ought to increase one for one with increases in the expected inflation rate. If we use the notation $E(i)$ to denote the current expectation of the inflation rate that will prevail over the coming period, then we can state the so-called Fisher equation formally as

$$R = r + E(i)$$

The equation implies that if real rates are reasonably stable, then increases in nominal rates ought to predict higher inflation rates. This relationship has been debated and empirically

**Figure 5.2    Interest and inflation rates, 1963–2002**

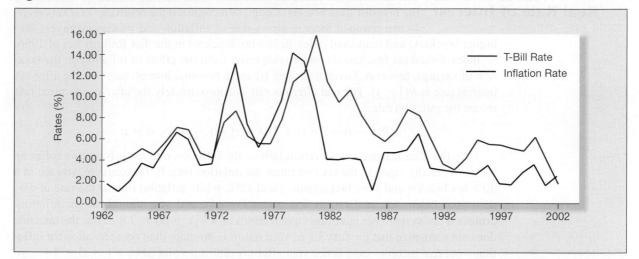

investigated. The results are mixed; although the data do not strongly support this relationship, nominal interest rates seem to predict inflation as well as alternative methods, in part because we are unable to forecast inflation well with any method.

One reason it is difficult to determine the empirical validity of the Fisher hypothesis that changes in nominal rates predict changes in future inflation rates is that the real rate also changes unpredictably over time. Nominal interest rates can be viewed as the sum of the required real rate on nominally risk-free assets, plus a "noisy" forecast of inflation.

In Part 4 we discuss the relationship between short- and long-term interest rates. Longer rates incorporate forecasts for long-term inflation. For this reason alone, interest rates on bonds of different maturity may diverge. In addition, we will see that prices of longer-term bonds are more volatile than those of short-term bonds. This implies that expected returns on longer-term bonds may include a risk premium, so that the expected real rate offered by bonds of varying maturity also may vary.

**CONCEPT CHECK☞ QUESTION 1**

*a.* **Suppose the real interest rate is 3% per year and the expected inflation rate is 8%. What is the nominal interest rate?**

*b.* **Suppose the expected inflation rate rises to 10%, but the real rate is unchanged. What happens to the nominal interest rate?**

### Bills and Inflation, 1963–2002

The Fisher equation predicts a close connection between inflation and the rate of return on T-bills. This is apparent in Figure 5.2, which plots both time series on the same set of axes. Both series tend to move together, which is consistent with our previous statement that expected inflation is a significant force determining the nominal rate of interest.

For a holding period of 30 days, the difference between actual and expected inflation is not large. The 30-day bill rate will adjust rapidly to changes in expected inflation induced by observed changes in actual inflation. It is not surprising that we see nominal rates on bills move roughly in tandem with inflation over time.

**Taxes and the Real Rate of Interest**    Tax liabilities are based on *nominal* income and the tax rate determined by the investor's tax bracket. Congress recognized the resultant "bracket creep" (when nominal income grows due to inflation and pushes taxpayers into higher brackets) and mandated index-linked tax brackets in the Tax Reform Act of 1986.

Index-linked tax brackets do not provide relief from the effect of inflation on the taxation of savings, however. Given a tax rate ($t$) and a nominal interest rate ($R$), the after-tax interest rate is $R(1 - t)$. The real after-tax rate is approximately the after-tax nominal rate minus the inflation rate:

$$R(1 - t) - i = (r + i)(1 - t) - i = r(1 - t) - it$$

Thus the after-tax real rate of return falls as the inflation rate rises. Investors suffer an inflation penalty equal to the tax rate times the inflation rate. If, for example, you are in a 30% tax bracket and your investments yield 12%, while inflation runs at the rate of 8%, then your before-tax real rate is approximately 4%, and you *should*, in an inflation-protected tax system, net after taxes a real return of 4%(1 − .3) = 2.8%. But the tax code does not recognize that the first 8% of your return is no more than compensation for inflation—not real income—and hence your after-tax return is reduced by 8% × .3 = 2.4%, so that your after-tax real interest rate, at .4%, is almost wiped out.

---

**E-INVESTMENTS**
**Inflation and Rates**

The Federal Reserve Bank of St. Louis has several sources of information available on interest rates and economic conditions. One publication called *Monetary Trends* contains graphs and tabular information relevant to assess conditions in the capital markets. Go to the most recent edition of *Monetary Trends* at the following site (look for the "Publications" tab, and then "Economic Research," where you will find *Monetary Trends*) and answer the following questions.

**http://www.stls.frb.org/**

1. What is the most current level of 3-month and 30-year Treasury yields?
2. Have nominal interest rates increased, decreased, or remained the same over the last 3 months?
3. Have real interest rates increased, decreased, or remained the same over the last 2 years?
4. Examine the information comparing recent U.S. inflation and long-term interest rates with the inflation and long-term interest rate experience of Japan. Are the results consistent with theory?

---

## 5.2    RISK AND RISK PREMIUMS

Suppose you are considering investing in a stock market index fund. The price of a share in the fund is currently $100, and your investment horizon is 1 year. You expect the cash dividend during the year to be $4, so your expected *dividend yield* (dividends earned per dollar invested) is 4%.

Your total holding-period return (HPR) will depend on the price that will prevail 1 year from now. Suppose your best guess is that it will be $110 per share. Then your *capital gain* will be $10 and your HPR will be 14%. The definition of the holding-period return is capital gain income plus dividend income per dollar invested in the stock:

$$\text{HPR} = \frac{\text{Ending price of a share} - \text{Beginning price} + \text{Cash dividend}}{\text{Beginning price}}$$

In our case we have

$$\text{HPR} = \frac{\$110 - \$100 + \$4}{\$100} = .14, \text{ or } 14\%$$

This definition of the HPR assumes the dividend is paid at the end of the holding period. To the extent that dividends are received earlier, the HPR ignores reinvestment income between the receipt of the payment and the end of the holding period. Recall also that the percent return from dividends is called the dividend yield, and so the dividend yield plus the capital gains yield equals the HPR.

There is considerable uncertainty about the price of a share a year from now, however, so you cannot be sure about your eventual HPR. We can try to quantify our beliefs about the state of the economy and the stock market in terms of three possible scenarios with probabilities as presented in Table 5.1.

How can we evaluate this probability distribution? Throughout this book we will characterize probability distributions of rates of return in terms of their expected or mean return, $E(r)$, and their standard deviation, $\sigma$. The expected rate of return is a probability-weighted average of the rates of return in each scenario. Calling $p(s)$ the probability of each scenario and $r(s)$ the HPR in each scenario, where scenarios are labeled or "indexed" by the variable $s$, we may write the expected return as

$$E(r) = \sum_s p(s)r(s) \tag{5.1}$$

Applying this formula to the data in Table 5.1, we find that the expected rate of return on the index fund is

$$E(r) = (.25 \times 44\%) + (.5 \times 14\%) + [.25 \times (-16\%)] = 14\%$$

The standard deviation of the rate of return ($\sigma$) is a measure of risk. It is defined as the square root of the variance, which in turn is the expected value of the squared deviations from the expected return. The higher the volatility in outcomes, the higher will be the average value of these squared deviations. Therefore, variance and standard deviation measure the uncertainty of outcomes. Symbolically,

$$\sigma^2 = \sum_s p(s)\,[r(s) - E(r)]^2 \tag{5.2}$$

Therefore, in our example,

$$\sigma^2 = .25(44 - 14)^2 + .5(14 - 14)^2 + .25(-16 - 14)^2 = 450$$

and

$$\sigma = \sqrt{450} = 21.21\%$$

Clearly, what would trouble potential investors in the index fund is the downside risk of a $-16\%$ rate of return, not the upside potential of a 44% rate of return. The standard deviation of the rate of return does not distinguish between these two; it treats both simply

| Table 5.1 | Probability Distribution of HPR on the Stock Market | | |
|---|---|---|---|
| State of the Economy | Probability | Ending Price | HPR |
| Boom | .25 | $140 | 44% |
| Normal growth | .50 | 110 | 14 |
| Recession | .25 | 80 | -16 |

as deviations from the mean. As long as the probability distribution is more or less symmetric about the mean, σ is an adequate measure of risk. In the special case where we can assume that the probability distribution is normal—represented by the well-known bell-shaped curve—$E(r)$ and σ are perfectly adequate to characterize the distribution.

Getting back to the example, how much, if anything, should you invest in the index fund? First, you must ask how much of an expected reward is offered for the risk involved in investing money in stocks.

We measure the reward as the difference between the *expected* HPR on the index stock fund and the **risk-free rate,** that is, the rate you can earn by leaving money in risk-free assets such as T-bills, money market funds, or the bank. We call this difference the **risk premium** on common stocks. If the risk-free rate in the example is 6% per year, and the expected index fund return is 14%, then the risk premium on stocks is 8% per year. The difference in any particular period between the *actual* rate of return on a risky asset and the risk-free rate is called **excess return.** Therefore, the risk premium is the expected excess return.

The degree to which investors are willing to commit funds to stocks depends on **risk aversion.** Financial analysts generally assume investors are risk averse in the sense that, if the risk premium were zero, people would not be willing to invest any money in stocks. In theory, then, there must always be a positive risk premium on stocks in order to induce risk-averse investors to hold the existing supply of stocks instead of placing all their money in risk-free assets.

Although this sample scenario analysis illustrates the concepts behind the quantification of risk and return, you may still wonder how to get a more realistic estimate of $E(r)$ and σ for common stocks and other types of securities. Here history has insights to offer.

## 5.3   THE HISTORICAL RECORD

**Bills, Bonds, and Stocks, 1926–2002**

The record of past rates of return is one possible source of information about risk premiums and standard deviations. We can estimate the historical risk premium by taking an average of the past differences between the returns on an asset class and the risk-free rate. Table 5.2 on pages 146 and 147 presents the annual rates of return on five asset classes for the period 1926–2002.

"Large Stocks" in Table 5.2 refers to Standard & Poor's market-value-weighted portfolio of 500 U.S. common stocks with large market capitalization. "Small Stocks" represents the value-weighted portfolio of the lowest-capitalization quintile (that is, the firms in the bottom 20% of all companies traded on the NYSE when ranked by market capitalization). Since 1982, this portfolio has included smaller stocks listed on the Amex and Nasdaq markets as well.

"Long-Term T-Bonds" are represented by a government bond with about a 20-year maturity and approximately current-level coupon rate.[2] "Intermediate-Term T-Bonds" have around a 7-year maturity with a current-level coupon rate.

"T-Bills" in Table 5.2 are of approximately 30-day maturity, and the 1-year HPR represents a policy of "rolling over" the bills as they mature. Because T-bill rates can change from month to month, the total rate of return on these T-bills is riskless only for 30-day holding periods.[3] The last column of Table 5.2 gives the annual inflation rate as measured by the rate of change in the Consumer Price Index.

---

[2] The importance of the coupon rate when comparing returns is discussed in Part 3.

[3] The few negative returns in this column, all dating from before World War II, reflect periods where, in the absence of T-bills, returns on government securities with about 30-day maturity have been used. However, these securities included options to be exchanged for other securities, thus increasing their price and lowering their yield relative to what a simple T-bill would have offered.

**Figure 5.3    Rates of return on stocks, bonds, and T-bills, 1926–2002**

Source: Prepared from data in Table 5.2.

At the bottom of each column are four descriptive statistics. The first is the arithmetic mean or average holding-period return. For bills, it is 3.82%; for long-term government bonds, 5.68%; and for large stocks, 12.04%. The numbers in that row imply a positive average excess return suggesting a risk premium of, for example, 8.22% on large stocks (the average excess return is the average HPR less the average risk-free rate of 3.82%).

The second statistic at the bottom of Table 5.2 is the standard deviation. The higher the standard deviation, the higher the variability of the HPR. This standard deviation is based on historical data rather than forecasts of *future* scenarios as in equation 5.2. The formula for historical variance, however, is similar to equation 5.2:

$$\sigma^2 = \frac{n}{n-1} \sum_{t=1}^{n} \frac{(r_t - \bar{r})^2}{n}$$

Here, each year's outcome ($r_t$) is taken as a possible scenario. Deviations are taken from the historical average, $\bar{r}$, instead of the expected value, $E(r)$. Each historical outcome is taken as equally likely and given a "probability" of $1/n$. [We multiply by $n/(n-1)$ to eliminate statistical bias for a "lost degree of freedom" in the estimate of variance.]

Figure 5.3 gives a graphic representation of the relative variabilities of the annual HPR for three different asset classes. We have plotted the three time series on the same set of axes, each in a different color. The graph shows very clearly that the annual HPR on stocks is the most variable series. The standard deviation of large-stock returns has been 20.55% (and that of small stocks larger still) compared to 8.24% for long-term government bonds and 3.18% for bills. Here is evidence of the risk–return trade-off that characterizes security markets: The markets with the highest average returns also are the most volatile.

The other summary measures at the end of Table 5.2 show the highest and lowest annual HPR (the range) for each asset over the 77-year period. The extent of this range is another measure of the relative riskiness of each asset class. It, too, confirms the ranking of stocks as the riskiest and bills as the least risky of the three asset classes.

An all-stock portfolio with a standard deviation of 20.55% would represent a very volatile investment. For example, if stock returns are normally distributed with a standard deviation of 20.55% and an expected rate of return of 12.04% (the historical average), in roughly one year out of three, returns will be less than −8.51% (12.04 − 20.55) or greater than 32.59% (12.04 + 20.55).

## Table 5.2*    Rates of Return, 1926–2002

| Year | Small Stocks | Large Stocks | Long-Term T-Bonds | Intermediate-Term T-Bonds | T-Bills | Inflation |
|------|------|------|------|------|------|------|
| 1926 | −8.91 | 12.21 | 4.54 | 4.96 | 3.19 | −1.12 |
| 1927 | 32.23 | 35.99 | 8.11 | 3.34 | 3.12 | −2.26 |
| 1928 | 45.02 | 39.29 | −0.93 | 0.96 | 3.82 | −1.16 |
| 1929 | −50.81 | −7.66 | 4.41 | 5.89 | 4.74 | 0.58 |
| 1930 | −45.69 | −25.90 | 6.22 | 5.51 | 2.35 | −6.40 |
| 1931 | −49.17 | −45.56 | −5.31 | −5.81 | 1.02 | −9.32 |
| 1932 | 10.95 | −9.14 | 11.89 | 8.44 | 0.81 | −10.27 |
| 1933 | 187.82 | 54.56 | 1.03 | 0.35 | 0.29 | 0.76 |
| 1934 | 25.13 | −2.32 | 10.15 | 9.00 | 0.15 | 1.52 |
| 1935 | 68.44 | 45.67 | 4.98 | 7.01 | 0.17 | 2.99 |
| 1936 | 84.47 | 33.55 | 6.52 | 3.77 | 0.17 | 1.45 |
| 1937 | −52.71 | −36.03 | 0.43 | 1.56 | 0.32 | 2.86 |
| 1938 | 24.69 | 29.42 | 5.25 | 5.64 | 0.04 | −2.78 |
| 1939 | −0.10 | −1.06 | 5.90 | 4.52 | 0.01 | 0.00 |
| 1940 | −11.81 | −9.65 | 6.54 | 2.03 | −0.06 | 0.71 |
| 1941 | −13.08 | −11.20 | 0.99 | −0.59 | 0.04 | 9.93 |
| 1942 | 51.01 | 20.80 | 5.39 | 1.81 | 0.26 | 9.03 |
| 1943 | 99.79 | 26.54 | 4.87 | 2.78 | 0.34 | 2.96 |
| 1944 | 60.53 | 20.96 | 3.59 | 1.98 | 0.32 | 2.30 |
| 1945 | 82.24 | 36.11 | 6.84 | 3.60 | 0.32 | 2.25 |
| 1946 | −12.80 | −9.26 | 0.15 | 0.69 | 0.35 | 18.13 |
| 1947 | −3.09 | 4.88 | −1.19 | 0.32 | 0.46 | 8.84 |
| 1948 | −6.15 | 5.29 | 3.07 | 2.21 | 0.98 | 2.99 |
| 1949 | 21.56 | 18.24 | 6.03 | 2.22 | 1.11 | −2.07 |
| 1950 | 45.48 | 32.68 | −0.96 | 0.25 | 1.21 | 5.93 |
| 1951 | 9.41 | 23.47 | −1.95 | 0.36 | 1.48 | 6.00 |
| 1952 | 6.36 | 18.91 | 1.93 | 1.63 | 1.64 | 0.75 |
| 1953 | −5.68 | −1.74 | 3.83 | 3.63 | 1.78 | 0.75 |
| 1954 | 65.13 | 52.55 | 4.88 | 1.73 | 0.86 | −0.74 |
| 1955 | 21.84 | 31.44 | −1.34 | −0.52 | 1.56 | 0.37 |
| 1956 | 3.82 | 6.45 | −5.12 | −0.90 | 2.42 | 2.99 |
| 1957 | −15.03 | −11.14 | 9.46 | 7.84 | 3.13 | 2.90 |
| 1958 | 70.63 | 43.78 | −3.71 | −1.29 | 1.42 | 1.76 |
| 1959 | 17.82 | 12.95 | −3.55 | −1.26 | 2.82 | 1.73 |
| 1960 | −5.16 | 0.19 | 13.78 | 11.98 | 2.58 | 1.36 |
| 1961 | 30.48 | 27.63 | 0.19 | 2.23 | 2.16 | 0.67 |
| 1962 | −16.41 | −8.79 | 6.81 | 7.38 | 2.72 | 1.33 |
| 1963 | 12.20 | 22.63 | −0.49 | 1.79 | 3.15 | 1.64 |
| 1964 | 18.75 | 16.67 | 4.51 | 4.45 | 3.52 | 0.97 |
| 1965 | 37.67 | 12.50 | −0.27 | 1.27 | 3.97 | 1.92 |
| 1966 | −8.08 | −10.25 | 3.70 | 5.14 | 4.71 | 3.46 |
| 1967 | 103.39 | 24.11 | −7.41 | 0.16 | 4.15 | 3.04 |

| | | | | | | |
|---|---|---|---|---|---|---|
| **Table 5.2** *(Concluded)* | | | | | | |
| Year | Small Stocks | Large Stocks | Long-Term T-Bonds | Intermediate-Term T-Bonds | T-Bills | Inflation |
| 1968 | 50.61 | 11.00 | −1.20 | 2.48 | 5.29 | 4.72 |
| 1969 | −32.27 | −8.33 | −6.52 | −2.10 | 6.59 | 6.20 |
| 1970 | −16.54 | 4.10 | 12.69 | 13.93 | 6.38 | 5.57 |
| 1971 | 18.44 | 14.17 | 17.47 | 8.71 | 4.32 | 3.27 |
| 1972 | −0.62 | 19.14 | 5.55 | 3.80 | 3.89 | 3.41 |
| 1973 | −40.54 | −14.75 | 1.40 | 2.90 | 7.06 | 8.71 |
| 1974 | −29.74 | −26.40 | 5.53 | 6.03 | 8.08 | 12.34 |
| 1975 | 69.54 | 37.26 | 8.50 | 6.79 | 5.82 | 6.94 |
| 1976 | 54.81 | 23.98 | 11.07 | 14.20 | 5.16 | 4.86 |
| 1977 | 22.02 | −7.26 | 0.90 | 1.12 | 5.15 | 6.70 |
| 1978 | 22.29 | 6.50 | −4.16 | 0.32 | 7.31 | 9.02 |
| 1979 | 43.99 | 18.77 | 9.02 | 4.29 | 10.69 | 13.29 |
| 1980 | 35.34 | 32.48 | 13.17 | 0.83 | 11.52 | 12.52 |
| 1981 | 7.79 | −4.98 | 3.61 | 6.09 | 14.86 | 8.92 |
| 1982 | 27.44 | 22.09 | 6.52 | 33.39 | 10.66 | 3.83 |
| 1983 | 34.49 | 22.37 | −0.53 | 5.44 | 8.85 | 3.79 |
| 1984 | −14.02 | 6.46 | 15.29 | 14.46 | 9.96 | 3.95 |
| 1985 | 28.21 | 32.00 | 32.68 | 23.65 | 7.68 | 3.80 |
| 1986 | 3.40 | 18.40 | 23.96 | 17.22 | 6.06 | 1.10 |
| 1987 | −13.95 | 5.34 | −2.65 | 1.68 | 5.38 | 4.43 |
| 1988 | 21.72 | 16.86 | 8.40 | 6.63 | 6.32 | 4.42 |
| 1989 | 8.37 | 31.34 | 19.49 | 14.82 | 8.22 | 4.65 |
| 1990 | −27.08 | −3.20 | 7.13 | 9.05 | 7.08 | 6.11 |
| 1991 | 50.24 | 30.66 | 18.39 | 16.67 | 5.51 | 3.06 |
| 1992 | 27.84 | 7.71 | 7.79 | 7.25 | 3.40 | 2.90 |
| 1993 | 20.30 | 9.87 | 15.48 | 12.02 | 2.90 | 2.75 |
| 1994 | −3.34 | 1.29 | −7.18 | −4.42 | 3.88 | 2.67 |
| 1995 | 33.21 | 37.71 | 31.67 | 18.07 | 5.53 | 2.54 |
| 1996 | 16.50 | 23.07 | −0.81 | 3.99 | 5.14 | 3.32 |
| 1997 | 22.36 | 33.17 | 15.08 | 7.69 | 5.08 | 1.70 |
| 1998 | −2.55 | 28.58 | 13.52 | 8.62 | 4.78 | 1.61 |
| 1999 | 21.26 | 21.04 | −8.74 | 0.41 | 4.56 | 2.68 |
| 2000 | −3.02 | −9.10 | 20.27 | 10.26 | 5.79 | 3.39 |
| 2001 | −1.03 | −11.90 | 4.21 | 8.16 | 3.72 | 1.55 |
| 2002 | −21.58 | −22.10 | 16.79 | 9.28 | 1.66 | 2.38 |
| Average | 17.74 | 12.04 | 5.68 | 5.35 | 3.82 | 3.14 |
| Standard deviation | 39.30 | 20.55 | 8.24 | 6.30 | 3.18 | 4.37 |
| Minimum | −52.71 | −45.56 | −8.74 | −5.81 | −0.06 | −10.27 |
| Maximum | 187.82 | 54.56 | 32.68 | 33.39 | 14.86 | 18.13 |

\*You can find this spreadsheet on the Website for the text at **www.mhhe.com/bkm**. Look for the link to Chapter 5 spreadsheets.

Sources: Inflation data—Bureau of Labor Statistics; Returns on T-bills, large and small stocks—Center for Research in Security Prices; Treasury bonds—Center for Research in Security Prices for 1926–1995 returns and Lehman Brothers long-term and intermediate Treasury indexes for 1996 and later returns.

**Figure 5.4
The normal
distribution**

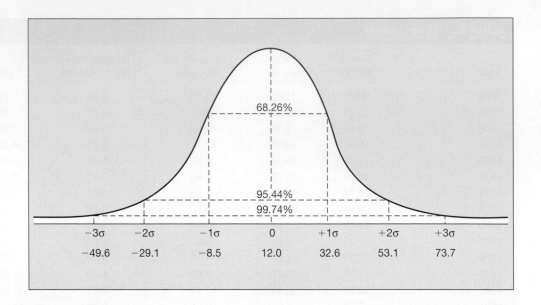

Figure 5.4 is a graph of the normal curve with mean 12.04% and standard deviation 20.55%. The graph shows the theoretical probability of rates of return within various ranges given these parameters.

Figure 5.5 presents another view of the historical data, the actual frequency distribution of returns on various asset classes over the period 1926–2002. Again, the greater range of stock returns relative to bill or bond returns is obvious. The first column of the figure gives the geometric averages of the historical rates of return on each asset class; this figure thus represents the compound rate of growth in the value of an investment in these assets. The second column shows the arithmetic averages that, absent additional information, might serve as forecasts of the future HPRs for these assets. The last column is the variability of asset returns, as measured by standard deviation. The historical results are consistent with the risk–return trade-off: Riskier assets have provided higher expected returns, and historical risk premiums are considerable.

Figure 5.6 presents graphs of wealth indexes for investments in various asset classes over the period of 1926–2002. The plot for each asset class assumes you invest $1 at year-end 1925 and traces the value of your investment in following years. The inflation plot demonstrates that to achieve the purchasing power represented by $1 in year-end 1925, one would require $10.11 at year-end 2002. One dollar continually invested in T-bills starting at year-end 1925 would have grown to $17.38 by year-end 2002, but provided only 1.72 times the original purchasing power (17.38/10.11 = 1.72). That same dollar invested in large stocks would have grown to $1,548.32, providing 153 times the original purchasing power of the dollar invested—despite the great risk evident from sharp downturns during the period. Hence, the lesson of the past is that risk premiums can translate into vast increases in purchasing power over the long haul.

We should stress that variability of HPR in the past can be an unreliable guide to risk, at least in the case of the risk-free asset. For an investor with a holding period of 1 year, for example, a 1-year T-bill is a riskless investment, at least in terms of its nominal return, which is known with certainty. However, the standard deviation of the 1-year T-bill rate estimated from historical data is not zero: This reflects variation over time in expected returns rather than fluctuations of actual returns around prior expectations.

**Figure 5.5
Frequency
distribution of
annual HPRs,
1926–2002
(figures in
percent)**

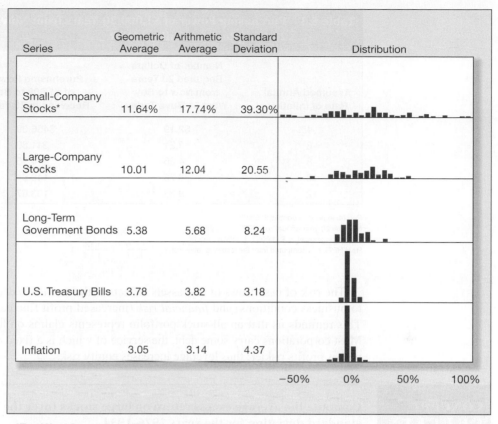

| Series | Geometric Average | Arithmetic Average | Standard Deviation | Distribution |
|---|---|---|---|---|
| Small-Company Stocks* | 11.64% | 17.74% | 39.30% | |
| Large-Company Stocks | 10.01 | 12.04 | 20.55 | |
| Long-Term Government Bonds | 5.38 | 5.68 | 8.24 | |
| U.S. Treasury Bills | 3.78 | 3.82 | 3.18 | |
| Inflation | 3.05 | 3.14 | 4.37 | |

*The 1933 small-company stock total return was 187.82% (not in diagram)
Source: Prepared from data in Table 5.2.

**Figure 5.6
Wealth indexes
of investments
in the U.S.
capital markets,
1925–2002 (year-
end 1925 = $1;
logarithmic scale)**

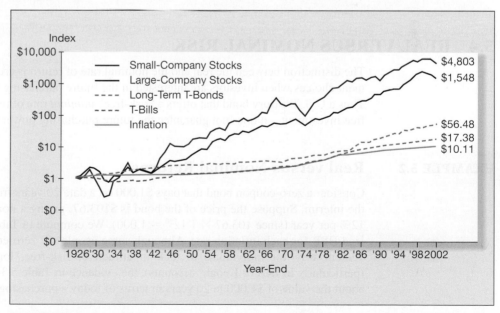

Source: Table 5.2.

| Table 5.3 | Purchasing Power of $1,000 20 Years from Now and 20-Year Real Annualized HPR | | |
| --- | --- | --- | --- |
| Assumed Annual Rate of Inflation | Number of Dollars Required 20 Years from Now to Buy What $1 Buys Today | Purchasing Power of $1,000 to Be Received in 20 Years | Annualized Real HPR |
| 4% | $2.19 | $456.39 | 7.69% |
| 6 | 3.21 | 311.80 | 5.66 |
| 8 | 4.66 | 214.55 | 3.70 |
| 10 | 6.73 | 148.64 | 1.82 |
| 12 | 9.65 | 103.67 | 0.00 |

Purchase price of bond is $103.67.
Nominal 20-year annualized HPR is 12% per year.
Purchasing power = $1,000/(1 + inflation rate)$^{20}$.
Real HPR, $r$, is computed from the following relationship: $r = \dfrac{1+R}{1+i} - 1 = \dfrac{1.12}{1+i} - 1$

The risk of cash flows of real assets reflects both *business risk* (profit fluctuations due to business conditions) and *financial risk* (increased profit fluctuations due to leverage). This reminds us that an all-stock portfolio represents claims on leveraged corporations. Most corporations carry some debt, the service of which is a fixed cost. Greater fixed cost makes profits riskier; thus leverage increases equity risk.

| CONCEPT CHECK ☞ QUESTION 2 | Compute the average excess return on large stocks (over the T-bill rate) and its standard deviation for the years 1926–1934. |
| --- | --- |

## 5.4    REAL VERSUS NOMINAL RISK

The distinction between the real and the nominal rate of return is crucial in making investment choices when investors are interested in the future purchasing power of their wealth. Thus a U.S. Treasury bond that offers a "risk-free" *nominal* rate of return is not truly a risk-free investment—it does not guarantee the future purchasing power of its cash flow.

**EXAMPLE 5.2**    ### Real versus Nominal Returns

Consider a zero-coupon bond that pays $1,000 on a date 20 years from now but nothing in the interim. Suppose the price of the bond is $103.67, giving a nominal rate of return of 12% per year (since $103.67 \times 1.12^{20} = 1,000$). We compute in Table 5.3 the real annualized HPR for each inflation rate. Although some people see zero-coupon bonds as a convenient way for individuals to lock in attractive, risk-free, long-term interest rates (particularly in IRA or Keogh[4] accounts), the evidence in Table 5.3 is rather discouraging about the value of $1,000 in 20 years in terms of today's purchasing power.

---

[4] A tax shelter for self-employed individuals.

A revealing comparison is at a 12% rate of inflation. At that rate, Table 5.3 shows that the purchasing power of the $1,000 to be received in 20 years would be $103.67, the amount initially paid for the bond. The real HPR in these circumstances is zero. When the rate of inflation equals the nominal rate of interest, the price of goods increases just as fast as the money accumulated from the investment, and there is no growth in purchasing power.

At an inflation rate of only 4% per year, however, the purchasing power of $1,000 will be $456.39 in terms of today's prices; that is, the investment of $103.67 grows to a real value of $456.39, for a real 20-year annualized HPR of 7.69% per year.

Again looking at Table 5.3, you can see that an investor expecting an inflation rate of 8% per year anticipates a real annualized HPR of 3.70%. If the actual rate of inflation turns out to be 10% per year, the resulting real HPR is only 1.82% per year. These differences show the important distinction between expected and actual inflation rates.

Even professional economic forecasters acknowledge that their inflation forecasts are hardly certain even for the next year, not to mention the next 20. When you look at an asset from the perspective of its future purchasing power, you can see that an asset that is risk-less in nominal terms can be very risky in real terms.[5]

| CONCEPT CHECK ☞ QUESTION 3 | **Suppose the rate of inflation turns out to be 13% per year. What will be the real annualized 20-year HPR on the nominally risk-free bond?** |

## 5.5   RETURN DISTRIBUTIONS AND VALUE AT RISK

What does history teach us about the risk of a representative portfolio of stocks? The distribution of stock returns over the last 77 years may be a rough guide as to potential losses from future investments in the market. Let's take a brief look at that distribution, focusing particularly on its "left tail," representing investment losses.

The valuation of a stock is based on its (discounted) expected future cash flows, and the equilibrium price is set so as to yield a fair expected return, commensurate with its risk. Deviations of the actual return from its expectation result from forecasting errors concerning the various economic factors that affect future cash flows. It is natural to expect that the net effect of these many potential forecasting errors, and hence rates of return on stocks, will be at least approximately normally distributed.[6]

The **normal distribution** has at least two attractive properties. First, it is symmetric and completely described by two parameters, its mean and standard deviation. This property implies that the risk of a normally distributed investment return is fully described by its standard deviation. Second, a weighted average of variables that are normally distributed

---

[5] In 1997 the Treasury began issuing inflation-indexed bonds called TIPS (for Treasury Inflation Protected Securities) which offer protection against inflation uncertainty. We discuss these bonds in more detail in Chapter 14. However, the vast majority of bonds make payments that are fixed in dollar terms; the real returns on these bonds are subject to inflation risk.

[6] The Cental Limit Theorem tells us that in many circumstances the combined effect of many random variables will be approximately normally distributed. Since new information about economic factors flows practically continuously, it is more reasonable to describe continuously compounded returns, rather than holding-period returns, using a normal distribution. See the appendix for a refresher on continuous compounding.

also will be normally distributed. Therefore, when individual stock returns are normally distributed, the return on any portfolio combining any set of stocks will also be normally distributed and its standard deviation will fully convey its risk. For these reasons, it is useful to know whether the assumption of normality is warranted. Figure 5.5 is derived from raw annual returns and is too crude to make this determination.

Figure 5.7 compares the cumulative probability distributions of continuously compounded monthly returns on large and small stocks with those of normal distributions with matching means and standard deviations. While the cumulative distributions of both large and small stocks roughly match the normal distribution, we can see that extreme values are more frequent than suggested by the normal. Moreover, these extreme values appear to be more frequent at the negative end of the distribution.

**Figure 5.7
Actual versus normal cumulative frequencies of monthly returns for (*a*) large stocks and (*b*) small stocks, 1926–2002 (returns are annualized and expressed as continuously compounded percentage rates)**

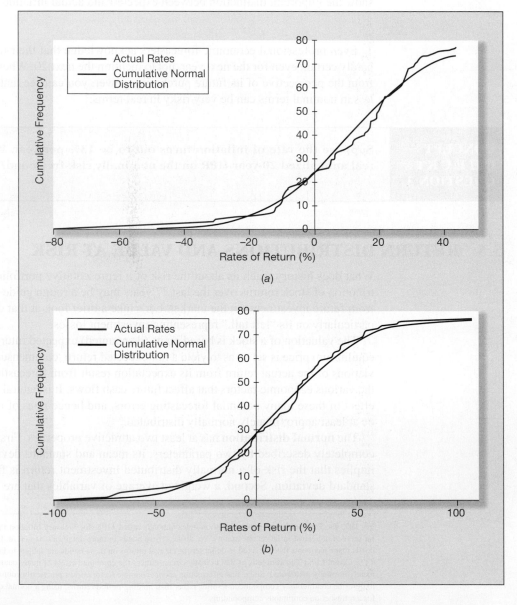

We would like a measure that reveals whether extreme negative values are too large and frequent to be adequately characterized by the normal distribution. One approach is to compute the standard deviation separately for the negative deviations. This statistic is called *lower partial standard deviation* (LPSD). If the LPSD is large relative to the overall standard deviation, it should replace the standard deviation as a measure of risk, since investors presumably think about risk as the possibility of large *negative* outcomes.

Another way to describe the negative extreme values is to quantify the asymmetry of the distribution. This we do by averaging the cubed (instead of squared) deviations from the mean. Just as the variance is called the second moment around the mean, the average cubed deviation is called the *third moment* of the distribution. The cubed deviations preserve sign, which allows us to distinguish good from bad outcomes. Moreover, since cubing exaggerates larger deviations, the sign and magnitude of the average cubed deviation reveal the direction and extent of the asymmetry. To scale the third moment (its unit is percent cubed), we divide it by the cubed standard deviation. The resulting statistic is called the skew of the distribution, and *skewness* is a measure of asymmetry. Table 5.4 compares the lower partial standard deviations of large and small stocks to the overall standard deviations. Indeed, the LPSD is much larger than the overall standard deviation. The next line indicates that both distributions are negatively skewed.

Professional investors extensively use a risk measure that highlights the potential loss from extreme negative returns, called **value at risk**, denoted by VaR (to distinguish it from VAR or Var, commonly used to denote variance). The VaR is another name for the *quantile* of a distribution. The quantile ($q$) of a distribution is the value below which lie $q\%$ of the values. Thus the median of the distribution is the 50% quantile. Practitioners commonly call the 5% quantile the VaR of the distribution. It tells us that, with a probability of 5%, we can expect a loss equal to or greater than the VaR. For a normal distribution, which is completely described by its mean and standard deviation, the VaR always lies 1.65 standard deviations below the mean, and thus, while it may be a convenient benchmark, it adds no information about risk. But if the distribution is not adequately described by the normal, the VaR does give useful information about the magnitude of loss we can expect in a "bad" (i.e., 5% quantile) scenario.

Table 5.4 shows the 5% VaR based on normal distributions with the same means and standard deviations as large and small stocks. Actual VaR based on historic returns show significantly greater losses for large stocks ($-30\%$ vs. $-23\%$) and for small stocks ($-62\%$ vs. $-44\%$). One can compute the VaR corresponding to other quantiles, for example a 1% VaR. The VaR has become widely used by portfolio managers and regulators as a measure of potential losses.

| Table 5.4 | Deviations from Normality and VaR (Continuously Compounded Monthly Returns, 1926–2002) | |
|---|---|---|
| | **Large Stocks** | **Small Stocks** |
| Mean | 9.54% | 11.01% |
| Standard deviation | 19.83% | 33.25% |
| LPSD | 28.36% | 39.90% |
| Skew | −0.98 | −0.66 |
| VaR Normal | −23.18% | −43.85% |
| VaR Actual | −30.07% | −62.04% |

## 5.6   A GLOBAL VIEW OF THE HISTORICAL RECORD

As financial markets around the world grow and become more regulated and transparent, U.S. investors look to improve diversification by investing internationally. Foreign investors that traditionally used U.S. financial markets as a safe haven to supplement home-country investments also seek international diversification to reduce risk. The question arises as to how historical U.S. experience compares with that of stock markets around the world.

Figure 5.8 shows a century-long history (1900–2000) of average nominal and real returns in stock markets of 16 developed countries. We find the United States in fourth place in terms of real, average returns, behind Sweden, Australia, and South Africa. Figure 5.9 shows the standard deviations of real stock and bond returns for these same countries. We find the United States tied with four other countries for third place in terms of lowest standard deviation of real stock returns. So the United States has done well, but not abnormally so, compared with these countries.

One interesting feature of these figures is that the countries with the worst results, measured by the ratio of average real returns to standard deviation, are Italy, Belgium, Germany, and Japan—the countries most devastated by World War II. The top-performing countries are Australia, Canada, and the United States, the countries least devastated by the wars of the twentieth century. Another, perhaps more telling feature, is the insignificant difference between the real returns in the different countries. The difference between the highest average real rate (Sweden, at 7.6%) from the average return across the 16 countries (5.1%) is 2.5%. Similarly, the difference between the average and the lowest country return (Belgium, at 2.5%) is 2.6%. Using the average standard deviation of 23%, the $t$-statistic for a difference of 2.6% with 100 observations is

$$t\text{-Statistic} = \frac{\text{Difference in mean}}{\text{Standard deviation}/\sqrt{n}} = \frac{2.6}{23/\sqrt{100}} = 1.3$$

which is far below conventional levels of statistical significance. We conclude that the U.S. experience cannot be dismissed as an outlier case. Hence, using the U.S. stock market as a yardstick for return characteristics may be reasonable.

## 5.7   FORECASTS FOR THE LONG HAUL

While portfolio managers struggle daily to adjust their portfolios to changing expectations, individual investors are more concerned with long-term expectations. A middle-aged investor at the age of 40 is typically saving largely for retirement with a horizon of some 25 years. With a $100,000 investment, a 1% increase in the average real rate, from 6% to 7%, would increase the real retirement fund in 25 years from $100,000 \times 1.06^{25} = \$429,187$ to $542,743, a difference of $113,556 in real-consumption dollars. You can see why a reliable long-term return forecast is crucial to the determination of how much to save and how much of the savings to invest in risky assets for the risk premium they offer.

The Japanese experience in the 1990s provides another idea of the stakes involved. In 1990, the Nikkei 225 (an index of Japanese stocks akin to the S&P 500 in the United States) stood at just about 40,000. By 2003, that index stood at about 8,000, a nominal loss of 80% over 13 years and an even greater loss in real terms. A Japanese investor who invested in stocks at the age 50 in 1990 would have found himself in 2003, only a few years before retirement, with less than 20% of his 1990 savings. For such investors, the rosy long-term history of stock market investments is cold comfort.

**Figure 5.8   Nominal and real equity returns around the world, 1900–2000**

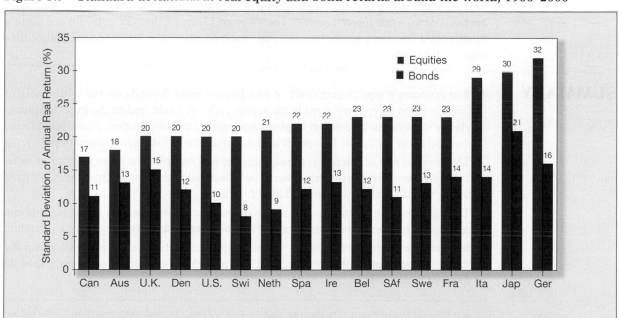

Source: Elroy Dimson, Paul Marsh, and Mike Staunton, *Triumph of the Optimists: 101 Years of Global Investment Returns,* Princeton University Press, 2002.

**Figure 5.9   Standard deviations of real equity and bond returns around the world, 1900–2000**

Source: Elroy Dimson, Paul Marsh, and Mike Staunton, *Triumph of the Optimists: 101 Years of Global Investment Returns,* Princeton University Press, 2002.

These days, practitioners and scholars are debating whether the historical U.S. average risk-premium of large stocks over T-bills of 8.22% (12.04% − 3.82%; see Table 5.2), is a reasonable forecast for the long term. This debate centers around two questions: First, do economic factors that prevailed over that historic period (1926–2002) adequately represent those that may prevail over the forecasting horizon? Second, is the arithmetic average from the available history a good yardstick for long-term forecasts?

Fama and French[7] note that the risk premium on equities over the period 1872–1949 was 4.62%, much lower than the 8.41% premium realized over the period 1950–1999. They argue that returns over the later half of the twentieth century were largely driven by unexpected capital gains that cannot be expected to prevail in the next century.

Figure 5.5 shows that the large-stock risk premium as measured by geometric averages over the period 1926–2002 is much lower, at 6.23% (i.e., 10.01% − 3.78%), than the 8.22% premium based on the arithmetic average. This difference alone would take away about half of the range of the debate. So which average should we use?

The use of the arithmetic average to forecast future rates of return derives from the statistical property that it is unbiased. This desirable property has made arithmetic averages the norm for estimating expected holding-period rates of return. However, for forecasts of *cumulative returns* over long horizons, the arithmetic average is inadequate. Jacquier, Kane, and Marcus[8] show that the correct forecast of total returns over long horizons requires compounding at a weighted average of the arithmetic and geometric historical averages. The proper weight applied to the geometric average equals the ratio of the length of the forecast horizon to the length of the estimation period. For example, if we wish to forecast the cumulative return for a 25-year horizon from a 77-year history, an unbiased estimate would be to compound at a rate of

$$\text{Geometric average} \times \frac{25}{77} + \text{Arithmetic average} \times \frac{(77 - 25)}{77}$$

This correction would take about 0.7% off the historical arithmetic average risk premium on large stocks and about 2% off the arithmetic average of small stocks. A forecast for the next 77 years would require compounding at only the geometric average, and for longer horizons at an even lower number. The forecast horizons that are relevant for current middle-aged investors must, however, be resolved primarily on economic rather than statistical grounds.

## SUMMARY

1. The economy's equilibrium level of real interest rates depends on the willingness of households to save, as reflected in the supply curve of funds, and on the expected profitability of business investment in plant, equipment, and inventories, as reflected in the demand curve for funds. It depends also on government fiscal and monetary policy.

2. The nominal rate of interest is the equilibrium real rate plus the expected rate of inflation. In general, we can directly observe only nominal interest rates; from them, we must infer expected real rates, using inflation forecasts.

3. The equilibrium expected rate of return on any security is the sum of the equilibrium real rate of interest, the expected rate of inflation, and a security-specific risk premium.

4. Investors face a trade-off between risk and expected return. Historical data confirm our intuition that assets with low degrees of risk provide lower returns on average than do those of higher risk.

---

[7] Eugene Fama and Kenneth French, "The Equity Premium," *Journal of Finance* 57 (April 2000), pp. 637–60. Similar evidence appears in Ravi Jagannathan, Ellen R. McGrattan, and Anna Scherbina, "The Declining U.S. Equity Premium," *Federal Reserve Bank of Minneapolis Quarterly Review* 24 (Fall 2000), pp. 3–19.

[8] Eric Jacqier, Alex Kane and Alan J. Marcus, "Geometric or Arithmetic Means: A Reconsideration," *Financial Analysts Journal* (November/December 2003).

5. Assets with guaranteed nominal interest rates are risky in real terms because the future inflation rate is uncertain.

6. Historical returns on stocks exhibit more frequent large negative deviations from the mean than would be predicted from a normal distribution. The lower partial standard deviation (LPSD) and the skewness of the actual distribution quantify the deviation from normality. The LPSD, instead of the standard deviation, is sometimes used by practitioners as a measure of risk.

7. A widely used measure of risk is value at risk (VaR). VaR measures the loss that will be exceeded with a specified probability such as 5%. The VaR does not add new information when returns are normally distributed. When negative deviations from the average are larger and more frequent than the normal distribution, the 5% VaR will be more than 1.65 standard deviations below the average return.

8. Historical rates of return over the twentieth century in developed capital markets suggest the U.S. history of stock returns is not an outlier compared to other countries.

9. The arithmetic average of the risk premium on stocks over the period 1926–2002 is arguably too optimistic as a forecast for long-term investments. Some evidence suggests returns over the later half of the twentieth century were unexpectedly high, and hence the full-century average is upward biased. In addition, the arithmetic average return may give upward biased estimates of long-term cumulative return. Long-term forecasts require compounding at an average of the geometric and arithmetic historical means, which reduces the forecast.

## KEY TERMS

| | | |
|---|---|---|
| nominal interest rate | risk premium | normal distribution |
| real interest rate | excess return | value at risk |
| risk-free rate | risk aversion | |

## WEBSITES

www.bloomberg.com/markets/wei.html
Visit this site to review the world's largest stock indices.

www.quote.bloomberg.com/cgi-bin/regionalind.cgi
Check out the U.S. regional economies indices, including the recent performance in your region of the United States.

cbs.marketwatch.com/news/default.asp?siteID=mktw
Review the recent performance of major U.S. stock indices under the *Markets* link. Find major international indices (left margin) under the *Global Markets* link at the top of the home page.

finance.lycos.com
Review a full list of domestic indices via the *More Indices Activity* under the NYSE graphic on the upper left of the page.

*(continued)*

Visit us at www.mhhe.com/bkm

## WEBSITES

www.bloomberg.com
Go to the *Markets* link, then *Rates and Bonds* for current interest rates and graphics on U.S. and international government bonds and other key interest rates.

www.bondsonline.com
www.investinginbonds.com
These sites provide bond information, indices, current market rates, and yield curves.

www.stls.frb.org
This site contains current and historical data on a variety of interest rates. Download historical economic data and interest rates at the *FRED* (Federal Reserve Economic Data) database. There are excellent graphics at *FRED II*. Link to *Economic Research* at the home page. Link to *Publications* and *U.S. Financial Data* (pull-down tab) for graphic presentation of monetary data and selected interest rates.

## PROBLEMS

1. You have $5,000 to invest for the next year and are considering three alternatives:
   a. A money market fund with an average maturity of 30 days offering a current yield of 6% per year.
   b. A 1-year savings deposit at a bank offering an interest rate of 7.5%.
   c. A 20-year U.S. Treasury bond offering a yield to maturity of 9% per year.
   What role does your forecast of future interest rates play in your decisions?

2. Use Figure 5.1 in the text to analyze the effect of the following on the level of real interest rates:
   a. Businesses become more pessimistic about future demand for their products and decide to reduce their capital spending.
   b. Households are induced to save more because of increased uncertainty about their future social security benefits.
   c. The Federal Reserve Board undertakes open-market purchases of U.S. Treasury securities in order to increase the supply of money.

3. You are considering the choice between investing $50,000 in a conventional 1-year bank CD offering an interest rate of 7% and a 1-year "Inflation-Plus" CD offering 3.5% per year plus the rate of inflation.
   a. Which is the safer investment?
   b. Which offers the higher expected return?
   c. If you expect the rate of inflation to be 3% over the next year, which is the better investment? Why?
   d. If we observe a risk-free nominal interest rate of 7% per year and a risk-free real rate of 3.5% on inflation-indexed bonds, can we infer that the market's expected rate of inflation is 3.5% per year?

4. Look at Table 5.1 in the text. Suppose you now revise your expectations regarding the stock market as follows:

| State of the Economy | Probability | Ending Price | HPR |
|---|---|---|---|
| Boom | .35 | $140 | 44% |
| Normal growth | .30 | 110 | 14 |
| Recession | .35 | 80 | −16 |

Use equations 5.1 and 5.2 to compute the mean and standard deviation of the HPR on stocks. Compare your revised parameters with the ones in the text.

5. Derive the probability distribution of the 1-year HPR on a 30-year U.S. Treasury bond with an 8% coupon if it is currently selling at par and the probability distribution of its yield to maturity a year from now is as follows:

| State of the Economy | Probability | YTM |
|---|---|---|
| Boom | .20 | 11.0% |
| Normal growth | .50 | 8.0 |
| Recession | .30 | 7.0 |

For simplicity, assume the entire 8% coupon is paid at the end of the year rather than every 6 months.

6. Using the historical risk premiums as your guide, what would be your estimate of the expected annual HPR on the S&P 500 stock portfolio if the current risk-free interest rate is 6%?

7. Compute the means and standard deviations of the annual HPR of large stocks and long-term Treasury bonds using only the last 30 years of data in Table 5.2, 1973–2002. How do these statistics compare with those computed from the data for the period 1926–1941? Which do you think are the most relevant statistics to use for projecting into the future?

8. During a period of severe inflation, a bond offered a nominal HPR of 80% per year. The inflation rate was 70% per year.

   a. What was the real HPR on the bond over the year?
   b. Compare this real HPR to the approximation $r \approx R - i$.

9. Suppose that the inflation rate is expected to be 3% in the near future. Using the historical data provided in this chapter, what would be your predictions for:

   a. The T-bill rate?
   b. The expected rate of return on large stocks?
   c. The risk premium on the stock market?

10. An economy is making a rapid recovery from steep recession, and businesses foresee a need for large amounts of capital investment. Why would this development affect real interest rates?

11. Given $100,000 to invest, what is the expected risk premium in dollars of investing in equities versus risk-free T-bills (U.S. Treasury bills) based on the following table?

| Action | Probability | Expected Return |
|---|---|---|
| Invest in equities | .6 | $50,000 |
|  | .4 | −$30,000 |
| Invest in risk-free T-bill | 1.0 | $ 5,000 |

a. $13,000.
b. $15,000.
c. $18,000.
d. $20,000.

**CFA PROBLEMS**

12. Based on the scenarios below, what is the expected return for a portfolio with the following return profile?

| | Market Condition | | |
|---|---|---|---|
| | Bear | Normal | Bull |
| Probability | .2 | .3 | .5 |
| Rate of return | −25% | 10% | 24% |

a. 4%.
b. 10%.
c. 20%.
d. 25%.

Use the following expectations on Stocks X and Y to answer questions 13 through 15 (round to the nearest percent).

| | Bear Market | Normal Market | Bull Market |
|---|---|---|---|
| Probability | 0.2 | 0.5 | 0.3 |
| Stock X | −20% | 18% | 50% |
| Stock Y | −15% | 20% | 10% |

**CFA PROBLEMS**

13. What are the expected rates of return for Stocks X and Y?

| | Stock X | Stock Y |
|---|---|---|
| a. | 18% | 5% |
| b. | 18% | 12% |
| c. | 20% | 11% |
| d. | 20% | 10% |

**CFA PROBLEMS**

14. What are the standard deviations of returns on Stocks X and Y?

| | Stock X | Stock Y |
|---|---|---|
| a. | 15% | 26% |
| b. | 20% | 4% |
| c. | 24% | 13% |
| d. | 28% | 8% |

**CFA PROBLEMS**

15. Assume that of your $10,000 portfolio, you invest $9,000 in Stock X and $1,000 in Stock Y. What is the expected return on your portfolio?

a. 18%.
b. 19%.
c. 20%.
d. 23%.

16. Probabilities for three states of the economy, and probabilities for the returns on a particular stock in each state are shown in the table below.

| State of Economy | Probability of Economic State | Stock Performance | Probability of Stock Performance in Given Economic State |
|---|---|---|---|
| Good | .3 | Good | .6 |
| | | Neutral | .3 |
| | | Poor | .1 |
| Neutral | .5 | Good | .4 |
| | | Neutral | .3 |
| | | Poor | .3 |
| Poor | .2 | Good | .2 |
| | | Neutral | .3 |
| | | Poor | .5 |

The probability that the economy will be neutral *and* the stock will experience poor performance is

a. .06.

b. .15.

c. .50.

d. .80.

17. An analyst estimates that a stock has the following probabilities of return depending on the state of the economy:

| State of Economy | Probability | Return |
|---|---|---|
| Good | .1 | 15% |
| Normal | .6 | 13 |
| Poor | .3 | 7 |

The expected return of the stock is:

a. 7.8%.

b. 11.4%.

c. 11.7%.

d. 13.0%.

Problems 18–19 represent a greater challenge. You may need to review the definitions of call and put options in Chapter 2.

18. You are faced with the probability distribution of the HPR on the stock market index fund given in Table 5.1 of the text. Suppose the price of a put option on a share of the index fund with exercise price of $110 and maturity of 1 year is $12.

a. What is the probability distribution of the HPR on the put option?

b. What is the probability distribution of the HPR on a portfolio consisting of one share of the index fund and a put option?

c. In what sense does buying the put option constitute a purchase of insurance in this case?

19. Take as given the conditions described in the previous question, and suppose the risk-free interest rate is 6% per year. You are contemplating investing $107.55 in a 1-year CD and simultaneously buying a call option on the stock market index fund with an exercise price of $110 and a maturity of 1 year. What is the probability distribution of your dollar return at the end of the year?

---

**STANDARD &POOR'S**

Go to **http://www.mhhe.com/business/finance/edumarketinsight** (Bookmark this page!) and link to *Company,* then *Population.* Select a company of interest to you and link to the *Company Research* page with a menu of company information reports on the left. Link to the *Excel Analytics* reports and open the *annual income statement* for your company. The report will open using the Excel viewer software. You will note that the Excel Analytic reports provide 6 years of data, in this case, income statements. To work with the file, for example, to recalculate the income statement as a percent of total sales (percentage composition of sales), save the file to a folder, open Excel, and make any changes desired. The *Excel Analytics* output now is your page to work with as you like. (More on this later in the text.) If you cannot access the *Excel Analytics* pages, you may have to update your Windows and/or MS Office package. Review the various reports for later reference.

---

**E-INVESTMENTS
Analytics
Tutorial**

Go to **http://gozips.uakron.edu/~drd/downloadtutorial.html**. Review the step-by-step tutorial providing instructions for downloading economic and financial data in a variety of file formats into Excel. Work through the example provided at the end of the tutorial. Later assignments in this text will ask you to use the data that you have downloaded, so learning how to access it is a first step for later assignments.

---

**SOLUTIONS
TO CONCEPT
CHECKS**

1. *a.*  $1 + R = (1 + r)(1 + i) = (1.03)(1.08) = 1.1124$
       $R = 11.24\%$
   *b.*  $1 + R = (1.03)(1.10) = 1.133$
       $R = 13.3\%$

2. The mean excess return for the period 1926–1934 is 3.55% (below the historical average), and the standard deviation (dividing by $n - 1$) is 32.55 (above the historical average). These results reflect the severe downturn of the great crash and the unusually high volatility of stock returns in this period.

3. $r = (.12 - .13)/1.13 = -.00885$, or $-.885\%$. When the inflation rate exceeds the nominal interest rate, the real rate of return is negative.

---

## APPENDIX: CONTINUOUS COMPOUNDING

Suppose that your money earns interest at an annual nominal percentage rate (APR) of 6% per year compounded semiannually. What is your *effective* annual rate of return, accounting for compound interest?

We find the answer by first computing the per (compounding) period rate, 3% per half-year, and then computing the future value (FV) at the end of the year per dollar invested at the beginning of the year. In this example, we get

$$FV = (1.03)^2 = 1.0609$$

The effective annual rate ($R_{EFF}$), that is, the annual rate at which your funds have grown, is just this number minus 1.0.

$$R_{EFF} = 1.0609 - 1 = .0609 = 6.09\% \text{ per year}$$

The general formula for the effective annual rate is

$$R_{EFF} = \left(1 + \frac{APR}{n}\right)^n - 1$$

where APR is the annual percentage rate and $n$ is the number of compounding periods per year. Table 5A.1 presents the effective annual rates corresponding to an annual percentage rate of 6% per year for different compounding frequencies.

As the compounding frequency increases, $(1 + APR/n)^n$ gets closer and closer to $e^{APR}$, where $e$ is the number 2.71828 (rounded off to the fifth decimal place). In our example, $e^{.06} = 1.0618365$. Therefore, if interest is continuously compounded, $R_{EFF} = .0618365$, or 6.18365% per year.

Continuously compounded rates are extensively used for two reasons. First, as noted in section 5.5, since information flows into capital markets continuously, rates of return are best modeled as evolving and compounding continuously. Second, pricing models for derivative assets such as call and put options on stocks often are based on continuously rebalanced portfolios. The need to model stock prices as trading continuously calls for continuously compounded rates of return.

With continuous compounding the effective rate is given by

$$1 + R_{EFF} = e^{APR}$$

We also can compute the continuously compounded rate from the observed effective holding-period returns as

$$\text{Continuously compounded rate} = \ln(1 + R_{EFF})$$

For short-term (e.g., daily) holding-period returns, the difference between the effective and continuously compounded rate is quite small. But for longer-term rates such as quarterly or annual, the difference is greater.

Using continuously compounded rates simplifies the algebraic relationship between real and nominal rates of return. To see how, let us compute the real rate of return first using

| Table 5A.1   Effective Annual Rates for APR of 6% | | |
|---|---|---|
| Compounding Frequency | $n$ | $R_{EFF}$ (%) |
| Annually | 1 | 6.00000 |
| Semiannually | 2 | 6.09000 |
| Quarterly | 4 | 6.13636 |
| Monthly | 12 | 6.16778 |
| Weekly | 52 | 6.17998 |
| Daily | 365 | 6.18313 |

annual compounding and then using continuous compounding. Assume the nominal interest rate is 6% per year compounded annually and the rate of inflation is 4% per year compounded annually. Using the relationship

$$\text{Real rate} = \frac{1 + \text{Nominal rate}}{1 + \text{Inflation rate}} - 1$$

$$r = \frac{(1 + R)}{(1 + i)} - 1 = \frac{R - i}{1 + i}$$

we find that the effective annual real rate is

$$r = 1.06/1.04 - 1 = .01923 = 1.923\% \text{ per year}$$

With continuous compounding, the relationship becomes

$$e^r = e^R/e^i = e^{R - i}$$

Taking natural logarithms, we get

$$r = R - i$$

$$\text{Real rate} = \text{Nominal rate} - \text{Inflation rate}$$

all expressed as annual, continuously compounded percentage rates.

Thus if we assume a nominal interest rate of 6% per year compounded continuously and an inflation rate of 4% per year compounded continuously, the real rate is 2% per year compounded continuously.

To pay a fair interest rate to a depositor, the compounding frequency must be at least equal to the frequency of deposits and withdrawals. Only when you compound at least as frequently as transactions in an account can you assure that each dollar will earn the full interest due for the exact time it has been in the account. These days, online computing for deposits is common, so the use of continuous or at least daily compounding is the norm.

# RISK AND RISK AVERSION

The investment process consists of two broad tasks. One task is security and market analysis, by which we assess the risk and expected-return attributes of the entire set of possible investment vehicles. The second task is the formation of an optimal portfolio of assets. This task involves the determination of the best risk-return opportunities available from feasible investment portfolios and the choice of the best portfolio from the feasible set. We start our formal analysis of investments with this latter task, called *portfolio theory.* We return to the security analysis task in later chapters.

This chapter introduces three themes in portfolio theory, all centering on risk. The first is the basic tenet that investors avoid risk and demand a reward for engaging in risky investments. The reward is taken as a risk premium, the difference between the expected rate of return and that available on alternative risk-free investments. The second theme allows us to quantify investors' personal trade-offs between portfolio risk and expected 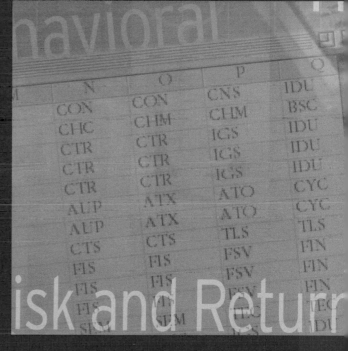 return. To do this we introduce the *utility function,* which assumes that investors can assign a welfare or "utility" score to any investment portfolio depending on its risk and return. Finally, the third fundamental principle is that we cannot evaluate the risk of an asset separate from the portfolio of which it is a part; that is, the proper way to measure the risk of an individual asset is to assess its impact on the volatility of the entire portfolio of investments. Taking this approach, we find that seemingly risky securities may be portfolio stabilizers and actually low-risk assets.

Appendix A to this chapter describes the theory and practice of measuring portfolio risk by the variance or standard deviation of returns. We discuss other potentially relevant characteristics of the probability distribution of portfolio returns, as well as the circumstances in which variance is sufficient to measure risk. Appendix B discusses the classical theory of risk aversion.

## 6.1   RISK AND RISK AVERSION

**Risk with Simple Prospects**   The presence of risk means that more than one outcome is possible. A *simple prospect* is an investment opportunity in which a certain initial wealth is placed at risk, and there are only two possible outcomes. For the sake of simplicity, it is useful to elucidate some basic concepts using simple prospects.[1]

Take as an example initial wealth, $W$, of $100,000, and assume two possible results. With a probability $p = .6$, the favorable outcome will occur, leading to final wealth $W_1 = \$150,000$. Otherwise, with probability $1 - p = .4$, a less favorable outcome, $W_2 = \$80,000$, will occur. We can represent the simple prospect using an event tree:

Suppose an investor is offered an investment portfolio with a payoff in 1 year described by such a simple prospect. How can you evaluate this portfolio?

First, try to summarize it using descriptive statistics. For instance, the mean or expected end-of-year wealth, denoted $E(W)$, is

$$E(W) = pW_1 + (1 - p)W_2$$
$$= (.6 \times 150,000) + (.4 \times 80,000)$$
$$= \$122,000$$

The expected profit on the $100,000 investment portfolio is $22,000: $122,000 − $100,000. The variance, $\sigma^2$, of the portfolio's payoff is calculated as the expected value of the squared deviation of each possible outcome from the mean:

$$\sigma^2 = p[W_1 - E(W)]^2 + (1 - p)[W_2 - E(W)]^2$$
$$= .6(150,000 - 122,000)^2 + .4(80,000 - 122,000)^2$$
$$= 1,176,000,000$$

The standard deviation, $\sigma$, which is the square root of the variance, is therefore $34,292.86.

Clearly, this is risky business: The standard deviation of the payoff is large, much larger than the expected profit of $22,000. Whether the expected profit is large enough to justify such risk depends on the alternatives to this portfolio.

---

[1] Chapters 6 through 8 rely on some basic results from elementary statistics. For a refresher, see the Quantitative Review in the Appendix at the end of the book.

Let us suppose Treasury bills are one alternative to the risky portfolio. Suppose that at the time of the decision, a 1-year T-bill offers a rate of return of 5%; $100,000 can be invested to yield a sure profit of $5,000. We can now draw the decision tree.

Earlier we showed the expected profit on the prospect to be $22,000. Therefore, the expected marginal, or incremental, profit of the risky portfolio over investing in safe T-bills is

$$\$22,000 - \$5,000 = \$17,000$$

meaning that one can earn a **risk premium** of $17,000 as compensation for the risk of the investment.

The question of whether a given risk premium provides adequate compensation for an investment's risk is age-old. Indeed, one of the central concerns of finance theory (and much of this text) is the measurement of risk and the determination of the risk premiums that investors can expect of risky assets in well-functioning capital markets.

<table>
<tr><td>CONCEPT<br>CHECK ☞<br>QUESTION 1</td><td>What is the risk premium of the risky portfolio in terms of rate of return rather than dollars?</td></tr>
</table>

## Risk, Speculation, and Gambling

One definition of *speculation* is "the assumption of considerable business risk in obtaining commensurate gain." Although this definition is fine linguistically, it is useless without first specifying what is meant by "commensurate gain" and "considerable risk."

By "commensurate gain" we mean a positive risk premium, that is, an expected profit greater than the risk-free alternative. In our example, the dollar risk premium is $17,000, the incremental expected gain from taking on the risk. By "considerable risk" we mean that the risk is sufficient to affect the decision. An individual might reject a prospect that has a positive risk premium because the added gain is insufficient to make up for the risk involved.

To gamble is "to bet or wager on an uncertain outcome." If you compare this definition to that of speculation, you will see that the central difference is the lack of "commensurate gain." Economically speaking, a gamble is the assumption of risk for no purpose but enjoyment of the risk itself, whereas speculation is undertaken *in spite* of the risk involved because one perceives a favorable risk–return trade-off. To turn a gamble into a speculative prospect requires an adequate risk premium to compensate risk-averse investors for the risks they bear. Hence, *risk aversion and speculation are not inconsistent*.

In some cases a gamble may appear to the participants as speculation. Suppose two investors disagree sharply about the future exchange rate of the U.S. dollar against the British pound. They may choose to bet on the outcome. Suppose that Paul will pay Mary $100 if the value of £1 exceeds $1.70 one year from now, whereas Mary will pay Paul if the pound is worth less than $1.70. There are only two relevant outcomes: (1) the pound will exceed $1.70, or (2) it will fall below $1.70. If both Paul and Mary agree on the probabilities of the two possible outcomes, and if neither party anticipates a loss, it must be that they assign $p = .5$ to each outcome. In that case the expected profit to both is zero and each has entered one side of a gambling prospect.

What is more likely, however, is that the bet results from differences in the probabilities that Paul and Mary assign to the outcome. Mary assigns it $p > .5$, whereas Paul's assessment is $p < .5$. They perceive, subjectively, two different prospects. Economists call this case of differing beliefs "heterogeneous expectations." In such cases investors on each side of a financial position see themselves as speculating rather than gambling.

Both Paul and Mary should be asking, Why is the other willing to invest in the side of a risky prospect that I believe offers a negative expected profit? The ideal way to resolve heterogeneous beliefs is for Paul and Mary to "merge their information," that is, for each party to verify that he or she possesses all relevant information and processes the information properly. Of course, the acquisition of information and the extensive communication that is required to eliminate all heterogeneity in expectations is costly, and thus up to a point heterogeneous expectations cannot be taken as irrational. If, however, Paul and Mary enter such contracts frequently, they would recognize the information problem in one of two ways: Either they will realize that they are creating gambles when each wins half of the bets, or the consistent loser will admit that he or she has been betting on the basis of inferior forecasts.

<table>
<tr><td>CONCEPT<br>C H E C K ☞<br>QUESTION 2</td><td>Assume that dollar-denominated T-bills in the United States and pound-denominated bills in the United Kingdom offer equal yields to maturity. Both are short-term assets, and both are free of default risk. Neither offers investors a risk premium. However, a U.S. investor who holds U.K. bills is subject to exchange rate risk, because the pounds earned on the U.K. bills eventually will be exchanged for dollars at the future exchange rate. Is the U.S. investor engaging in speculation or gambling?</td></tr>
</table>

**Risk Aversion and Utility Values**    We have discussed risk with simple prospects and how risk premiums bear on speculation. A prospect that has a zero risk premium is called a *fair game*. Investors who are **risk averse** reject investment portfolios that are fair games or worse. Risk-averse investors are willing to consider only risk-free or speculative prospects with positive risk premia. Loosely speaking, a risk-averse investor "penalizes" the expected rate of return of a risky portfolio by a certain percentage (or penalizes the expected profit by a dollar amount) to account for the risk involved. The greater the risk, the larger the penalty. One might wonder why we assume risk aversion as fundamental. We believe that most investors would accept this view from simple introspection, but we discuss the question more fully in Appendix B of this chapter.

We can formalize the notion of a risk-penalty system. To do so, we will assume that each investor can assign a welfare, or **utility,** score to competing investment portfolios based on the expected return and risk of those portfolios. The utility score may be viewed as a means of ranking portfolios. Higher utility values are assigned to portfolios with more attractive risk-return profiles. Portfolios receive higher utility scores for higher expected returns and lower scores for higher volatility. Many particular "scoring" systems are legitimate. One reasonable function that is commonly employed by financial theorists and the AIMR (Association of Investment Management and Research) assigns a portfolio with expected return $E(r)$ and variance of returns $\sigma^2$ the following utility score:

$$U = E(r) - .005A\sigma^2 \tag{6.1}$$

where $U$ is the utility value and $A$ is an index of the investor's risk aversion. The factor of .005 is a scaling convention that allows us to express the expected return and standard deviation in equation 6.1 as percentages rather than decimals.

Equation 6.1 is consistent with the notion that utility is enhanced by high expected returns and diminished by high risk. Whether variance is an adequate measure of portfolio risk is discussed in Appendix A. The extent to which variance lowers utility depends on $A$, the investor's degree of risk aversion. More risk-averse investors (who have the larger $A$s) penalize risky investments more severely. Investors choosing among competing investment portfolios will select the one providing the highest utility level.

Risk aversion obviously will have a major impact on the investor's appropriate risk–return trade-off. The box on pages 170–171 discusses some techniques that financial advisers use to gauge the risk aversion of their clients.

Notice in equation 6.1 that the utility provided by a risk-free portfolio is simply the rate of return on the portfolio, because there is no penalization for risk. This provides us with a convenient benchmark for evaluating portfolios.

## EXAMPLE 6.1 — Evaluating Investments by Using Utility Scores

Recall the earlier investment problem, choosing between a portfolio with an expected return of 22% and a standard deviation $\sigma = 34\%$ and T-bills providing a risk-free return of 5%. Although the risk premium on the risky portfolio is large, 17%, the risk of the project is so great that an investor would not need to be very risk averse to choose the safe all-bills strategy. Even for $A = 3$, a moderate risk-aversion parameter, equation 6.1 shows the risky portfolio's utility value as $22 - (.005 \times 3 \times 34^2) = 4.66\%$, which is slightly lower than the risk-free rate. In this case, one would reject the portfolio in favor of T-bills.

The downward adjustment of the expected return as a penalty for risk is $.005 \times 3 \times 34^2 = 17.34\%$. If the investor were less risk averse (more risk tolerant), for example, with $A = 2$, she would adjust the expected rate of return downward by only 11.56%. In that case the utility level of the portfolio would be 10.44%, higher than the risk-free rate, leading her to accept the prospect.

---

**CONCEPT CHECK ☞ QUESTION 3**

A portfolio has an expected rate of return of 20% and standard deviation of 20%. Bills offer a sure rate of return of 7%. Which investment alternative will be chosen by an investor whose $A = 4$? What if $A = 8$?

---

Because we can compare utility values to the rate offered on risk-free investments when choosing between a risky portfolio and a safe one, we may interpret a portfolio's utility value as its "certainty equivalent" rate of return to an investor. That is, the **certainty equivalent rate** of a portfolio is the rate that risk-free investments would need to offer with certainty to be considered equally attractive as the risky portfolio.

Now we can say that a portfolio is desirable only if its certainty equivalent return exceeds that of the risk-free alternative. A sufficiently risk-averse investor may assign any risky portfolio, even one with a positive risk premium, a certainty equivalent rate of return that is below the risk-free rate, which will cause the investor to reject the portfolio. At the same time, a less risk-averse (more risk-tolerant) investor may assign the same portfolio a certainty equivalent rate that exceeds the risk-free rate and thus will prefer the portfolio to

What four-letter word should pop into mind when the stock market takes a harrowing nose dive?

No, not those. R-I-S-K.

Risk is the potential for realizing low returns or even losing money, possibly preventing you from meeting important objectives, like sending your kids to the college of their choice or having the retirement lifestyle you crave.

But many financial advisers and other experts say that when times are good, some investors don't take the idea of risk as seriously as they should, and overexpose themselves to stocks. So before the market goes down and stays down, be sure that you understand your tolerance for risk and that your portfolio is designed to match it.

Assessing your risk tolerance, however, can be tricky. You must consider not only how much risk you can *afford* to take but also how much risk you can *stand* to take.

Determining how much risk you can stand—your temperamental tolerance for risk—is more difficult. It isn't easy to quantify.

To that end, many financial advisers, brokerage firms and mutual-fund companies have created risk quizzes to help people determine whether they are conservative, moderate or aggressive investors. Some firms that offer such quizzes include Merrill Lynch, T. Rowe Price Associates Inc., Baltimore, Zurich Group Inc.'s Scudder Kemper Investments Inc., New York, and Vanguard Group in Malvern, Pa.

Typically, risk questionnaires include seven to 10 questions about a person's investing experience, financial security and tendency to make risky or conservative choices.

The benefit of the questionnaires is that they are an objective resource people can use to get at least a rough idea of their risk tolerance. "It's impossible for someone to assess their risk tolerance alone," says Mr. Bernstein. "I may say I don't like risk, yet will take more risk than the average person."

Many experts warn, however, that the questionnaires should be used simply as a first step to assessing risk tolerance. "They are not precise," says Ron Meier, a certified public accountant.

The second step, many experts agree, is to ask yourself some difficult questions, such as: How much you can stand to lose over the long term?

"Most people can stand to lose a heck of a lot temporarily," says Mr. Schatsky, a financial adviser in New York. The real acid test, he says, is how much of your portfolio's value you can stand to lose over months or years.

As it turns out, most people rank as middle-of-the-road risk-takers, say several advisers. "Only about 10% to 15% of my clients are aggressive," says Mr. Roge.

## What's Your Risk Tolerance?
Circle the letter that corresponds to your answer

1. Just 60 days after you put money into an investment, its price falls 20%. Assuming none of the fundamentals have changed, what would you do?
   a. Sell to avoid further worry and try something else
   b. Do nothing and wait for the investment to come back
   c. Buy more. It was a good investment before; now it's a cheap investment, too

2. Now look at the previous question another way. Your investment fell 20%, but it's part of a portfolio being used to meet investment goals with three different time horizons.

2A. What would you do if the goal were five years away?
   a. Sell
   b. Do nothing
   c. Buy more

2B. What would you do if the goal were 15 years away?
   a. Sell
   b. Do nothing
   c. Buy more

the risk-free alternative. If the risk premium is zero or negative to begin with, any downward adjustment to utility only makes the portfolio look worse. Its certainty equivalent rate will be below that of the risk-free alternative for all risk-averse investors.

In contrast to risk-averse investors, **risk-neutral** investors judge risky prospects solely by their expected rates of return. The level of risk is irrelevant to the risk-neutral investor, meaning that there is no penalization for risk. For this investor a portfolio's certainty equivalent rate is simply its expected rate of return.

A **risk lover** is willing to engage in fair games and gambles; this investor adjusts the expected return upward to take into account the "fun" of confronting the prospect's risk. Risk lovers will always take a fair game because their upward adjustment of utility for risk gives the fair game a certainty equivalent that exceeds the alternative of the risk-free investment.

2C. What would you do if the goal were 30 years away?

a. Sell
b. Do nothing
c. Buy more

3. The price of your retirement investment jumps 25% a month after you buy it. Again, the fundamentals haven't changed. After you finish gloating, what do you do?

a. Sell it and lock in your gains
b. Stay put and hope for more gain
c. Buy more; it could go higher

4. You're investing for retirement, which is 15 years away. Which would you rather do?

a. Invest in a money-market fund or guaranteed investment contract, giving up the possibility of major gains, but virtually assuring the safety of your principal
b. Invest in a 50-50 mix of bond funds and stock funds, in hopes of getting some growth, but also giving yourself some protection in the form of steady income
c. Invest in aggressive growth mutual funds whose value will probably fluctuate significantly during the year, but have the potential for impressive gains over five or 10 years

5. You just won a big prize! But which one? It's up to you

a. $2,000 in cash
b. A 50% chance to win $5,000
c. A 20% chance to win $15,000

6. A good investment opportunity just came along. But you have to borrow money to get in. Would you take out a loan?

a. Definitely not
b. Perhaps
c. Yes

7. Your company is selling stock to its employees. In three years, management plans to take the company public. Until then, you won't be able to sell your shares and you will get no dividends. But your investment could multiply as much as 10 times when the company goes public. How much money would you invest?

a. None
b. Two months' salary
c. Four months' salary

**Scoring Your Risk Tolerance**
To score the quiz, add up the number of answers you gave in each category a–c, then multiply as shown to find your score

(a) answers _____ × 1 = _____ points
(b) answers _____ × 2 = _____ points
(c) answers _____ × 3 = _____ points

**YOUR SCORE** _____ points

**If you scored . . .** You may be a:

| | |
|---|---|
| 9–14 points | Conservative investor |
| 15–21 points | Moderate investor |
| 22–27 points | Aggressive investor |

We can depict the individual's trade-off between risk and return by plotting the characteristics of potential investment portfolios that the individual would view as equally attractive on a graph with axes measuring the expected value and standard deviation of portfolio returns. Figure 6.1 plots the characteristics of one portfolio.

Portfolio $P$, which has expected return $E(r_P)$ and standard deviation $\sigma_P$, is preferred by risk-averse investors to any portfolio in quadrant IV because it has an expected return equal to or greater than any portfolio in that quadrant and a standard deviation equal to or smaller than any portfolio in that quadrant. Conversely, any portfolio in quadrant I is preferable to portfolio $P$ because its expected return is equal to or greater than $P$'s and its standard deviation is equal to or smaller than $P$'s.

**Figure 6.1
The trade-off
between risk
and return of
a potential
investment
portfolio**

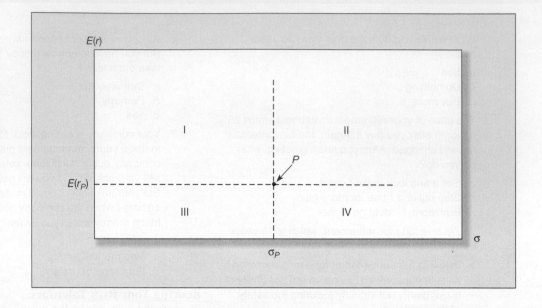

This is the mean-standard deviation, or equivalently, **mean-variance (M-V) criterion.**
It can be stated as: *A* dominates *B* if

$$E(r_A) \geq E(r_B)$$

and

$$\sigma_A \leq \sigma_B$$

and at least one inequality is strict (rules out the equality).

In the expected return–standard deviation plane in Figure 6.1, the preferred direction is northwest, because in this direction we simultaneously increase the expected return *and* decrease the variance of the rate of return. This means that any portfolio that lies northwest of *P* is superior to *P*.

What can be said about portfolios in the quadrants II and III? Their desirability, compared with *P*, depends on the exact nature of the investor's risk aversion. Suppose an investor identifies all portfolios that are equally attractive as portfolio *P*. Starting at *P*, an increase in standard deviation lowers utility; it must be compensated for by an increase in expected return. Thus point *Q* in Figure 6.2 is equally desirable to this investor as *P*. Investors will be equally attracted to portfolios with high risk and high expected returns compared with other portfolios with lower risk but lower expected returns. These equally preferred portfolios will lie in the mean–standard deviation plane on a curve that connects all portfolio points with the same utility value (Figure 6.2), called the **indifference curve.**

To determine some of the points that appear on the indifference curve, examine the utility values of several possible portfolios for an investor with $A = 4$, presented in Table 6.1. Note that each portfolio offers identical utility, because the high-return portfolios also have high risk.

**CONCEPT
C H E C K ☞
QUESTION 4**

*a.* **How will the indifference curve of a less risk-averse investor compare to the indifference curve drawn in Figure 6.2?**

*b.* **Draw both indifference curves passing through point *P*.**

**Figure 6.2**
**The indifference curve**

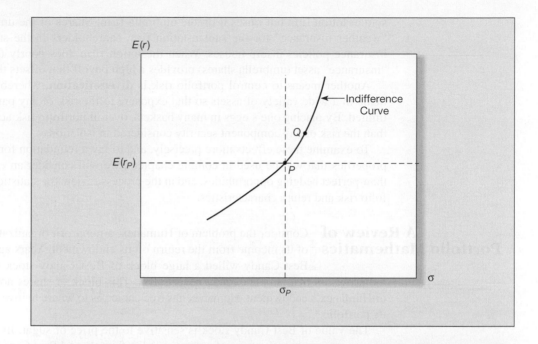

**Table 6.1   Utility Values of Possible Portfolios for Investor with Risk Aversion, $A = 4$**

| Expected Return, $E(r)$ | Standard Deviation, $\sigma$ | Utility $= E(r) - .005A\sigma^2$ |
|---|---|---|
| 10% | 20.0% | $10 - .005 \times 4 \times 400 \quad = 2$ |
| 15 | 25.5 | $15 - .005 \times 4 \times 650 \quad = 2$ |
| 20 | 30.0 | $20 - .005 \times 4 \times 900 \quad = 2$ |
| 25 | 33.9 | $25 - .005 \times 4 \times 1{,}150 = 2$ |

## 6.2   PORTFOLIO RISK

**Asset Risk versus Portfolio Risk**   Investor portfolios are composed of diverse types of assets. In addition to direct investment in financial markets, investors may have stakes in pension funds, life insurance policies with savings components, homes, and not least, the earning power of their skills (human capital).

Investors must take account of the interplay between asset returns when evaluating the risk of a portfolio. At a most basic level, for example, an insurance contract serves to reduce risk by providing a large payoff when another part of the portfolio is faring poorly. A fire insurance policy pays off when another asset in the portfolio—a house or factory, for example—suffers a big loss in value. The offsetting pattern of returns on these two assets (the house and the insurance policy) stabilizes the risk of the overall portfolio. Investing in an asset with a payoff pattern that offsets exposure to a particular source of risk is called **hedging.**

Insurance contracts are obvious hedging vehicles. In many contexts financial markets offer similar, although perhaps less direct, hedging opportunities. For example, consider two firms, one producing suntan lotion, the other producing umbrellas. The shareholders of each firm face weather risk of an opposite nature. A rainy summer lowers the return on the suntan-lotion firm but raises it on the umbrella firm. Shares of the umbrella firm act as "weather insurance" for the suntan-lotion firm shareholders in the same way that fire insurance policies insure houses. When the lotion firm does poorly (bad weather), the "insurance" asset (umbrella shares) provides a high payoff that offsets the loss.

Another means to control portfolio risk is **diversification**, whereby investments are made in a wide variety of assets so that exposure to the risk of any particular security is limited. By placing one's eggs in many baskets, overall portfolio risk actually may be less than the risk of any component security considered in isolation.

To examine these effects more precisely, and to lay a foundation for the mathematical properties that will be used in coming chapters, we will consider an example with less-than-perfect hedging opportunities, and in the process review the statistics underlying portfolio risk and return characteristics.

## A Review of Portfolio Mathematics

Consider the problem of Humanex, a nonprofit organization deriving most of its income from the return on its endowment. Years ago, the founders of Best Candy willed a large block of Best Candy stock to Humanex with the provision that Humanex may never sell it. This block of shares now comprises 50% of Humanex's endowment. Humanex has free choice as to where to invest the remainder of its portfolio.[2]

The value of Best Candy stock is sensitive to the price of sugar. In years when world sugar crops are low, the price of sugar rises significantly and Best Candy suffers considerable losses. We can describe the fortunes of Best Candy stock by using the following scenario analysis:

| | Normal Year for Sugar | | Abnormal Year |
| | Bullish Stock Market | Bearish Stock Market | Sugar Crisis |
|---|---|---|---|
| Probability | .5 | .3 | .2 |
| Rate of return | 25% | 10% | −25% |

To summarize these three possible outcomes using conventional statistics, we review some of the key rules governing the properties of risky assets and portfolios.

**Rule 1.** The mean or **expected return** of an asset is a probability-weighted average of its return in all scenarios. Calling $\Pr(s)$ the probability of scenario $s$ and $r(s)$ the return in scenario $s$, we may write the expected return, $E(r)$, as

$$E(r) = \sum_s \Pr(s) r(s) \tag{6.2}$$

Applying this formula to the case at hand, with three possible scenarios, we find that the expected rate of return of Best Candy's stock is

$$E(r_{\text{Best}}) = (.5 \times 25) + (.3 \times 10) + .2(-25) = 10.5\%$$

**Rule 2.** The **variance** of an asset's returns is the expected value of the squared deviations from the expected return. Symbolically,

$$\sigma^2 = \sum_s \Pr(s)[r(s) - E(r)]^2 \tag{6.3}$$

---

[2] The portfolio is admittedly unusual. We use this example only to illustrate the various strategies that might be used to control risk and to review some useful results from statistics.

Therefore, in our example

$$\sigma_{Best}^2 = .5(25 - 10.5)^2 + .3(10 - 10.5)^2 + .2(-25 - 10.5)^2 = 357.25$$

The **standard deviation** of Best's return, which is the square root of the variance, is $\sqrt{357.25} = 18.9\%$.

Humanex has 50% of its endowment in Best's stock. To reduce the risk of the overall portfolio, it could invest the remainder in T-bills, which yield a sure rate of return of 5%. To derive the return of the overall portfolio, we apply rule 3.

**Rule 3.** The rate of return on a portfolio is a weighted average of the rates of return of each asset comprising the portfolio, with portfolio proportions as weights. This implies that the *expected* rate of return on a portfolio is a weighted average of the *expected* rate of return on each component asset.

Humanex's portfolio proportions in each asset are .5, and the portfolio's expected rate of return is

$$E(r_{Humanex}) = .5E(r_{Best}) + .5r_{Bills}$$
$$= (.5 \times 10.5) + (.5 \times 5) = 7.75\%$$

The standard deviation of the portfolio may be derived from rule 4.

**Rule 4.** When a risky asset is combined with a risk-free asset, the portfolio standard deviation equals the risky asset's standard deviation multiplied by the portfolio proportion invested in the risky asset.

The Humanex portfolio is 50% invested in Best stock and 50% invested in risk-free bills. Therefore,

$$\sigma_{Humanex} = .5\sigma_{Best} = .5 \times 18.9 = 9.45\%$$

By reducing its exposure to the risk of Best by half, Humanex reduces its portfolio standard deviation by half. The cost of this risk reduction, however, is a reduction in expected return. The expected rate of return on Best stock is 10.5%. The expected return on the one-half T-bill portfolio is 7.75%. Thus, while the risk premium for Best stock over the 5% rate on risk-free bills is 5.5%, it is only 2.75% for the half T-bill portfolio. By reducing the share of Best stock in the portfolio by one-half, Humanex reduces its portfolio risk premium by one-half, from 5.5% to 2.75%.

In an effort to improve the contribution of the endowment to the operating budget, Humanex's trustees hire a consultant to perform some security analysis. Researching the sugar and candy industry, the consultant discovers, not surprisingly, that during years of sugar shortage, Sugarcane, a big Hawaiian sugar company, reaps unusual profits and its stock price soars. A scenario analysis of Sugarcane's stock looks like this:

| | Normal Year for Sugar | | Abnormal Year |
| --- | --- | --- | --- |
| | Bullish Stock Market | Bearish Stock Market | Sugar Crisis |
| Probability | .5 | .3 | .2 |
| Rate of return | 1% | −5% | 35% |

The expected rate of return on Sugarcane's stock is 6%, and its standard deviation is 14.73%. Thus Sugarcane is almost as volatile as Best, yet its expected return is only a notch better than the T-bill rate. This cursory analysis makes Sugarcane appear to be an unattractive investment. For Humanex, however, the stock holds great promise.

Sugarcane offers excellent hedging potential for holders of Best stock because its return is highest precisely when Best's return is lowest—during a sugar crisis. Consider Humanex's portfolio when it splits its investment evenly between Best and Sugarcane. The rate of return for each scenario is the simple average of the rates on Best and Sugarcane because the portfolio is split evenly between the two stocks (see rule 3).

| | Normal Year for Sugar | | Abnormal Year |
| | Bullish Stock Market | Bearish Stock Market | Sugar Crisis |
| --- | --- | --- | --- |
| Probability | .5 | .3 | .2 |
| Rate of return | 13.0% | 2.5% | 5.0% |

The expected rate of return on Humanex's hedged portfolio is 8.25% with a standard deviation of 4.83%.

We can now summarize the reward and risk of the three alternatives as follows:

| Portfolio | Expected Return | Standard Deviation |
| --- | --- | --- |
| All in Best Candy | 10.50% | 18.90% |
| Half in T-bills | 7.75 | 9.45 |
| Half in Sugarcane | 8.25 | 4.83 |

The numbers speak for themselves. The hedge portfolio with Sugarcane clearly dominates the simple risk-reduction strategy of investing in safe T-bills. It has higher expected return *and* lower standard deviation than the one-half T-bill portfolio. The point is that, despite Sugarcane's large standard deviation of return, it is a hedge (risk reducer) for investors holding Best stock.

We learn from this example a crucial lesson: The risk of individual assets in a portfolio must be measured in the context of the effect of their return on overall portfolio variability. This example demonstrates that assets with returns that are inversely associated with the initial risky position are powerful hedge assets.

---

**CONCEPT CHECK ☞ QUESTION 5**

Suppose the stock market offers an expected rate of return of 20%, with a standard deviation of 15%. Gold has an expected rate of return of 6%, with a standard deviation of 17%. In view of the market's higher expected return and lower uncertainty, will anyone choose to hold gold in a portfolio?

---

To quantify the hedging or diversification potential of an asset, we use the concepts of covariance and correlation. The **covariance** measures how much the returns on two risky assets move in tandem. A positive covariance means that asset returns move together. A negative covariance means that they vary inversely, as in the case of Best and Sugarcane.

To measure covariance, we look at return "surprises," or deviations from expected value, in each scenario. Consider the product of each stock's deviation from expected return in a particular scenario:

$$[r_{\text{Best}} - E(r_{\text{Best}})][r_{\text{Cane}} - E(r_{\text{Cane}})]$$

This product will be positive if the returns of the two stocks move together, that is, if both returns exceed their expectations or both fall short of those expectations in the scenario in question. On the other hand, if one stock's return exceeds its expected value when the other's falls short, the product will be negative. Thus a good measure of the degree to which the returns move together is the *expected value* of this product across all scenarios, which is defined as the covariance:

$$\text{Cov}(r_{\text{Best}}, r_{\text{Cane}}) = \sum_s \text{Pr}(s)[r_{\text{Best}}(s) - E(r_{\text{Best}})][r_{\text{Cane}}(s) - E(r_{\text{Cane}})] \tag{6.4}$$

**EXAMPLE 6.2**    ## Covariance

With $E(r_{\text{Best}}) = 10.5\%$ and $E(r_{\text{Cane}}) = 6\%$, and with returns in each scenario summarized in the following table, we compute the covariance by applying equation 6.4. The covariance between the two stocks is

$$\begin{aligned} \text{Cov}(r_{\text{Best}}, r_{\text{Cane}}) &= .5(25 - 10.5)(1 - 6) \\ &+ .3(10 - 10.5)(-5 - 6) + .2(-25 - 10.5)(35 - 6) \\ &= -240.5 \end{aligned}$$

The negative covariance confirms the hedging quality of Sugarcane stock relative to Best Candy. Sugarcane's returns move inversely with Best's.

|  | Normal Year for Sugar | | Abnormal Year |
|---|---|---|---|
|  | Bullish Stock Market | Bearish Stock Market | Sugar Crisis |
| Probability | .5 | .3 | .2 |
|  | Rate of Return (%) | | |
| Best Candy | 25 | 10 | −25 |
| Sugarcane | 1 | −5 | 35 |

An easier statistic to interpret than the covariance is the **correlation coefficient,** which scales the covariance to a value between −1 (perfect negative correlation) and +1 (perfect positive correlation). The correlation coefficient between two variables equals their covariance divided by the product of the standard deviations. Denoting the correlation by the Greek letter ρ, we find that

$$\begin{aligned} \rho(\text{Best, Sugarcane}) &= \frac{\text{Cov}[r_{\text{Best}}, r_{\text{Sugarcane}}]}{\sigma_{\text{Best}}\,\sigma_{\text{Sugarcane}}} \\ &= \frac{-240.5}{18.9 \times 14.73} = -.86 \end{aligned} \tag{6.5}$$

This large negative correlation (close to −1) confirms the strong tendency of Best and Sugarcane stocks to move inversely, or "out of phase" with one another.

The impact of the covariance of asset returns on portfolio risk is apparent in the following formula for portfolio variance.

**Rule 5.** When two risky assets with variances $\sigma_1^2$ and $\sigma_2^2$, respectively, are combined into a portfolio with portfolio weights $w_1$ and $w_2$, respectively, the portfolio variance $\sigma_p^2$ is given by

$$\sigma_p^2 = w_1^2 \, \sigma_1^2 + w_2^2 \, \sigma_2^2 + 2w_1 w_2 \text{Cov}(r_1, r_2)$$

## EXAMPLE 6.3    Calculating Portfolio Variance

In our example, we had equal weights in Best and Sugarcane. Therefore, $w_1 = w_2 = .5$. With $\sigma_{\text{Best}} = 18.9\%$, $\sigma_{\text{Cane}} = 14.73\%$, and $\text{Cov}(r_{\text{Best}}, r_{\text{Cane}}) = -240.5$, we find that

$$\sigma_p^2 = (.5^2 \times 18.9^2) + (.5^2 \times 14.73^2) + [2 \times .5 \times .5 \times (-240.5)] = 23.3$$

so that $\sigma_p = \sqrt{23.3} = 4.83\%$, precisely the same answer for the standard deviation of the returns on the hedged portfolio that we derived earlier from the scenario analysis.

Rule 5 for portfolio variance highlights the effect of covariance on portfolio risk. A positive covariance increases portfolio variance, and a negative covariance acts to reduce portfolio variance. This makes sense because returns on negatively correlated assets tend to be offsetting, which stabilizes portfolio returns.

Basically, hedging involves the purchase of a risky asset that is negatively correlated with the existing portfolio. This negative correlation makes the volatility of the hedge asset a risk-reducing feature. A hedge strategy is a powerful alternative to the simple risk-reduction strategy of including a risk-free asset in the portfolio.

In later chapters we will see that, in a rational market, hedge assets will offer relatively low expected rates of return. The perfect hedge, an insurance contract, is by design perfectly negatively correlated with a specified risk. As one would expect in a "no free lunch" world, the insurance premium reduces the portfolio's expected rate of return.

---

**CONCEPT CHECK☞ QUESTION 6**

Suppose that the distribution of Sugarcane stock were as follows:

| | Bullish Stock Market | Bearish Stock Market | Sugar Crisis |
|---|---|---|---|
| | 7% | −5% | 20% |

a. What would be its correlation with Best?

b. Is Sugarcane stock a useful hedge asset now?

c. Calculate the portfolio rate of return in each scenario and the standard deviation of the portfolio from the scenario returns. Then evaluate $\sigma_p$ using rule 5.

d. Are the two methods of computing portfolio standard deviation consistent?

## SUMMARY

1. Speculation is the undertaking of a risky investment for its risk premium. The risk premium has to be large enough to compensate a risk-averse investor for the risk of the investment.

2. A fair game is a risky prospect that has a zero-risk premium. It will not be undertaken by a risk-averse investor.

3. Investors' preferences toward the expected return and volatility of a portfolio may be expressed by a utility function that is higher for higher expected returns and lower for higher portfolio variances. More risk-averse investors will apply greater penalties for risk. We can describe these preferences graphically using indifference curves.

4. The desirability of a risky portfolio to a risk-averse investor may be summarized by the certainty equivalent value of the portfolio. The certainty equivalent rate of return is a value that, if it is received with certainty, would yield the same utility as the risky portfolio.

5. Hedging is the purchase of a risky asset to reduce the risk of a portfolio. The negative correlation between the hedge asset and the initial portfolio turns the volatility of the hedge asset into a risk-*reducing* feature. When a hedge asset is perfectly negatively correlated with the initial portfolio, it serves as a perfect hedge and works like an insurance contract on the portfolio.

## KEY TERMS

| | | |
|---|---|---|
| risk premium | mean-variance (M-V) | variance |
| risk averse | criterion | standard deviation |
| utility | indifference curve | covariance |
| certainty equivalent rate | hedging | correlation coefficient |
| risk neutral | diversification | |
| risk lover | expected return | |

## WEBSITES

www.rce.rutgers.edu/money/investmentrisk.asp
This site offers a quick look at the risk–return trade-off provided by capital market investments.

www.mutualofomaha.com/rpd/investment_concepts.html
A financial service provider discusses the risk–return trade-off with its potential clients.

www.datalife.com/mall/pages/glossary/GLOSS_R.HTM
Visit this site for a discussion of several types of risks that generate return volatility.

www.tradersclub.com/traderstools/calculators/investment.shtml
This site provides investment calculators.

www.moneychimp.com
This site offers an extensive variety of interactive investment calculators, providing visual presentation of some of the concepts appearing in this chapter.

Visit us at www.mhhe.com/bkm

**PROBLEMS**

1. Consider a risky portfolio. The end-of-year cash flow derived from the portfolio will be either $70,000 or $200,000 with equal probabilities of .5. The alternative risk-free investment in T-bills pays 6% per year.

   a. If you require a risk premium of 8%, how much will you be willing to pay for the portfolio?

   b. Suppose that the portfolio can be purchased for the amount you found in (a). What will be the expected rate of return on the portfolio?

   c. Now suppose that you require a risk premium of 12%. What is the price that you will be willing to pay?

   d. Comparing your answers to (a) and (c), what do you conclude about the relationship between the required risk premium on a portfolio and the price at which the portfolio will sell?

2. Consider a portfolio that offers an expected rate of return of 12% and a standard deviation of 18%. T-bills offer a risk-free 7% rate of return. What is the maximum level of risk aversion for which the risky portfolio is still preferred to bills?

3. Draw the indifference curve in the expected return–standard deviation plane corresponding to a utility level of 5% for an investor with a risk aversion coefficient of 3. (Hint: Choose several possible standard deviations, ranging from 5% to 25%, and find the expected rates of return providing a utility level of 5%. Then plot the expected return–standard deviation points so derived.)

4. Now draw the indifference curve corresponding to a utility level of 4% for an investor with risk aversion coefficient $A = 4$. Comparing your answers to problems 3 and 4, what do you conclude?

5. Draw an indifference curve for a risk-neutral investor providing utility level 5%.

6. What must be true about the sign of the risk aversion coefficient, $A$, for a risk lover? Draw the indifference curve for a utility level of 5% for a risk lover.

Use the following data in answering questions 7, 8, and 9.

| Utility Formula Data | | |
| --- | --- | --- |
| Investment | Expected Return $E(r)$ | Standard Deviation $\sigma$ |
| 1 | 12% | 30% |
| 2 | 15 | 50 |
| 3 | 21 | 16 |
| 4 | 24 | 21 |

$$U = E(r) - .005A\sigma^2 \qquad \text{where } A = 4$$

7. Based on the utility formula above, which investment would you select if you were risk averse with $A = 4$?

   a. 1
   b. 2
   c. 3
   d. 4

8. Based on the utility formula above, which investment would you select if you were risk neutral?
   a. 1
   b. 2
   c. 3
   d. 4

9. The variable (A) in the utility formula represents the:
   a. investor's return requirement.
   b. investor's aversion to risk.
   c. certainty equivalent rate of the portfolio.
   d. preference for one unit of return per four units of risk.

Consider historical data showing that the average annual rate of return on the S&P 500 portfolio over the past 70 years has averaged about 8.5% more than the Treasury bill return and that the S&P 500 standard deviation has been about 20% per year. Assume these values are representative of investors' expectations for future performance and that the current T-bill rate is 5%. Use these values to solve problems 10 to 12.

10. Calculate the expected return and variance of portfolios invested in T-bills and the S&P 500 index with weights as follows:

| $W_{bills}$ | $W_{index}$ |
|---|---|
| 0 | 1.0 |
| 0.2 | 0.8 |
| 0.4 | 0.6 |
| 0.6 | 0.4 |
| 0.8 | 0.2 |
| 1.0 | 0 |

11. Calculate the utility levels of each portfolio of problem 10 for an investor with $A = 3$. What do you conclude?

12. Repeat problem 11 for an investor with $A = 5$. What do you conclude?

Reconsider the Best and Sugarcane stock market hedging example in the text, but assume for questions 13 to 15 that the probability distribution of the rate of return on Sugarcane stock is as follows:

| | Bullish Stock Market | Bearish Stock Market | Sugar Crisis |
|---|---|---|---|
| Probability | .5 | .3 | .2 |
| Rate of return | 10% | −5% | 20% |

13. If Humanex's portfolio is half Best stock and half Sugarcane, what are its expected return and standard deviation? Calculate the standard deviation from the portfolio returns in each scenario.

14. What is the covariance between Best and Sugarcane?

15. Calculate the portfolio standard deviation by using rule 5 and show that the result is consistent with your answer to question 13.

---

---

**E-INVESTMENTS**
**Risk and Return**

You will find interactive risk–return software at **http://www.moneychimp.com/articles/risk/ longterm.htm**. Try varying the inputs and observe the impact on the distribution of returns. List two important chapter concepts that are reinforced in this exercise.

---

**SOLUTIONS
TO CONCEPT
CHECKS**

1. The expected rate of return on the risky portfolio is $22,000/$100,000 = .22, or 22%. The T-bill rate is 5%. The risk premium therefore is 22% − 5% = 17%.

2. The investor is taking on exchange rate risk by investing in a pound-denominated asset. If the exchange rate moves in the investor's favor, the investor will benefit and will earn more from the U.K. bill than the U.S. bill. For example, if both the U.S. and U.K. interest rates are 5%, and the current exchange rate is $1.50 per pound, a $1.50 investment today can buy one pound, which can be invested in England at a certain rate of 5%, for a year-end value of 1.05 pounds. If the year-end exchange rate is $1.60 per pound, the 1.05 pounds can be exchanged for 1.05 × $1.60 = $1.68 for a rate of return in dollars of 1 + r = $1.68/$1.50 = 1.12, or 12%, more than is available from U.S. bills. Therefore, if the investor expects favorable exchange rate movements, the U.K. bill is a speculative investment. Otherwise, it is a gamble.

3. For the $A = 4$ investor the utility of the risky portfolio is

$$U = 20 - (.005 \times 4 \times 20^2) = 12$$

while the utility of bills is

$$U = 7 - (.005 \times 4 \times 0) = 7$$

The investor will prefer the risky portfolio to bills. (Of course, a mixture of bills and the portfolio might be even better, but that is not a choice here.)

   For the $A = 8$ investor, the utility of the risky portfolio is

$$U = 20 - (.005 \times 8 \times 20^2) = 4$$

while the utility of bills is again 7. The more risk-averse investor therefore prefers the risk-free alternative.

4. The less risk-averse investor has a shallower indifference curve. An increase in risk requires less increase in expected return to restore utility to the original level.

SOLUTIONS
TO CONCEPT
CHECKS
*(Continued)*

5. Despite the fact that gold investments *in isolation* seem dominated by the stock market, gold still might play a useful role in a diversified portfolio. Because gold and stock market returns have very low correlation, stock investors can reduce their portfolio risk by placing part of their portfolios in gold.

6. *a.* With the given distribution for Sugarcane, the scenario analysis looks as follows:

| | Normal Year for Sugar | | Abnormal Year |
|---|---|---|---|
| | Bullish Stock Market | Bearish Stock Market | Sugar Crisis |
| Probability | .5 | .3 | .2 |
| | | Rate of Return (%) | |
| Best Candy | 25 | 10 | −25 |
| Sugarcane | 7 | −5 | 20 |
| T-bills | 5 | 5 | 5 |

The expected return and standard deviation of Sugarcane is now

$$E(r_{\text{Sugarcane}}) = (.5 \times 7) + .3(-5) + (.2 \times 20) = 6$$

$$\sigma_{\text{Sugarcane}} = [.5(7 - 6)^2 + .3(-5 - 6)^2 + .2(20 - 6)^2]^{1/2} = 8.72$$

The covariance between the returns of Best and Sugarcane is

$$\text{Cov(Sugarcane, Best)} = .5(7 - 6)(25 - 10.5) + .3(-5 - 6)(10 - 10.5)$$
$$+ .2(20 - 6)(-25 - 10.5) = -90.5$$

and the correlation coefficient is

$$\rho_{(\text{Sugarcane, Best})} = \frac{\text{Cov (Sugarcane, Best)}}{\sigma_{\text{Sugarcane}} \, \sigma_{\text{Best}}}$$
$$= \frac{-90.5}{8.72 \times 18.90} = -.55$$

**SOLUTIONS TO CONCEPT CHECKS** *(Concluded)*

The correlation is negative, but less so than before ($-.55$ instead of $-.86$) so we expect that Sugarcane will now be a less powerful hedge than before. Investing 50% in Sugarcane and 50% in Best will result in a portfolio probability distribution of

| Probability | .5 | .3 | .2 |
|---|---|---|---|
| Portfolio return | 16 | 2.5 | −2.5 |

resulting in a mean and standard deviation of

$$E(r_{\text{Hedged portfolio}}) = (.5 \times 16) + (.3 \times 2.5) + .2(-2.5) = 8.25$$

$$\sigma_{\text{Hedged portfolio}} = [.5(16 - 8.25)^2 + .3(2.5 - 8.25)^2 + .2(-2.5 - 8.25)^2]^{1/2} = 7.94$$

b. It is obvious that even under these circumstances the hedging strategy dominates the risk-reducing strategy that uses T-bills (which results in $E(r) = 7.75\%$, $\sigma = 9.45\%$). At the same time, the standard deviation of the hedged position (7.94%) is not as low as it was using the original data.

c, d. Using rule 5 for portfolio variance, we would find that

$$\sigma^2 = (.5^2 \times \sigma^2_{\text{Best}}) + (.5^2 \times \sigma^2_{\text{Sugarcane}}) + [2 \times .5 \times .5 \times \text{Cov(Sugarcane, Best)}]$$

$$= (.5^2 \times 18.9^2) + (.5^2 \times 8.72^2) + [2 \times .5 \times .5 \times (-90.5)] = 63.06$$

which implies that $\sigma = 7.94\%$, precisely the same result that we obtained by analyzing the scenarios directly.

# APPENDIX A: A DEFENSE OF MEAN-VARIANCE ANALYSIS

**Describing Probability Distributions.**  The axiom of risk aversion needs little defense. So far, however, our treatment of risk has been limiting in that it took the variance (or, equivalently, the standard deviation) of portfolio returns as an adequate risk measure. In situations in which variance alone is not adequate to measure risk this assumption is potentially restrictive. Here we provide some justification for mean-variance analysis.

The basic question is how one can best describe the uncertainty of portfolio rates of return. In principle, one could list all possible outcomes for the portfolio over a given period. If each outcome results in a payoff such as a dollar profit or rate of return, then this payoff value is the *random variable* in question. A list assigning a probability to all possible values of a random variable is called the probability distribution of the random variable.

The reward for holding a portfolio is typically measured by the expected rate of return across all possible scenarios, which equals

$$E(r) = \sum_{s=1}^{n} \text{Pr}(s)r(s)$$

where $s = 1, \ldots, n$ are the possible outcomes or scenarios, $r(s)$ is the rate of return for outcome $s$, and $\text{Pr}(s)$ is the probability associated with it.

Actually, the expected value or mean is not the only candidate for the central value of a probability distribution. Other candidates are the median and the mode.

The *median* is defined as the outcome value that exceeds the outcome values for half the population and is exceeded by the other half. Whereas the expected rate of return is a weighted average of the outcomes, the weights being the probabilities, the median is based on the rank order of the outcomes and takes into account only the order of the outcome values.

The median differs significantly from the mean in cases where the expected value is dominated by extreme values. One example is the income (or wealth) distribution in a population. A relatively small number of households command a disproportionate share of total income (and wealth). The mean income is "pulled up" by these extreme values, which makes it nonrepresentative. The median is free of this effect, since it equals the income level that is exceeded by half the population, regardless of by how much.

Finally, a third candidate for the measure of central value is the *mode*, which is the most likely value of the distribution or the outcome with the highest probability. However, the expected value is by far the most widely used measure of central or average tendency.

We now turn to the characterization of the risk implied by the nature of the probability distribution of returns. In general, it is impossible to quantify risk by a single number. The idea is to describe the likelihood and magnitudes of "surprises" (deviations from the mean) with as small a set of statistics as is needed for accuracy. The easiest way to accomplish this is to answer a set of questions in order of their informational value and to stop at the point where additional questions would not affect our notion of the risk–return trade-off.

The first question is, What is a typical deviation from the expected value? A natural answer would be, The expected deviation from the expected value is _____. Unfortunately, this answer is not helpful because it is necessarily zero: Positive deviations from the mean are offset exactly by negative deviations.

There are two ways of getting around this problem. The first is to use the expected *absolute value* of the deviation which turns all deviations into positive values. This is known as MAD (mean absolute deviation), which is given by

$$\sum_{s=1}^{n} \Pr(s) \times \text{Absolute value}[r(s) - E(r)]$$

The second is to use the expected *squared* deviation from the mean, which also must be positive, and which is simply the variance of the probability distribution:

$$\sigma^2 = \sum_{s=1}^{n} \Pr(s)[r(s) - E(r)]^2$$

Note that the unit of measurement of the variance is "percent squared." To return to our original units, we compute the standard deviation as the square root of the variance, which is measured in percentage terms, as is the expected value. The variance is also called the *second central moment* around the mean, with the expected return itself being the first moment.

Although the variance measures the average squared deviation from the expected value, it does not provide a full description of risk. To see why, consider the two probability distributions for rates of return on a portfolio, in Figure 6A.1.

*A* and *B* are probability distributions with identical expected values and variances. The graphs show that the variances are identical because probability distribution *B* is the mirror image of *A*.

What is the principal difference between *A* and *B*? *A* is characterized by more likely but small losses and less likely but extreme gains. This pattern is reversed in *B*. The difference is important. When we talk about risk, we really mean "*bad* surprises." The bad surprises in *A*, although they are more likely, are small (and limited) in magnitude. The bad surprises

**Figure 6A.1    Skewed probability distributions for rates of return on a portfolio**

in $B$ are more likely to be extreme. A risk-averse investor will prefer $A$ to $B$ on these grounds; hence it is worthwhile to quantify this characteristic. The asymmetry of a distribution is called *skewness*, which we measure by the third central moment, given by

$$M_3 = \sum_{s=1}^{n} \Pr(s)[r(s) - E(r)]^3$$

Cubing the deviations from the expected value preserves their signs, which allows us to distinguish good from bad surprises. Because this procedure gives greater weight to larger deviations, it causes the "long tail" of the distribution to dominate the measure of skewness. Thus the skewness of the distribution will be positive for a right-skewed distribution such as $A$ and negative for a left-skewed distribution such as $B$. The asymmetry is a relevant characteristic, although it is not as important as the magnitude of the standard deviation.

To summarize, the first moment (expected value) represents the reward. The second and higher central moments characterize the uncertainty of the reward. All the even moments (variance, $M_4$, etc.) represent the likelihood of extreme values. Larger values for these moments indicate greater uncertainty. The odd moments ($M_3$, $M_5$, etc.) represent measures of asymmetry. Positive numbers are associated with positive skewness and hence are desirable.

We can characterize the risk aversion of any investor by the preference scheme that the investor assigns to the various moments of the distribution. In other words, we can write the utility value derived from the probability distribution as

$$U = E(r) - b_0\sigma^2 + b_1M_3 - b_2M_4 + b_3M_5 - \cdots$$

where the importance of the terms lessens as we proceed to higher moments. Notice that the "good" (odd) moments have positive coefficients, whereas the "bad" (even) moments have minus signs in front of the coefficients.

How many moments are needed to describe the investor's assessment of the probability distribution adequately? Samuelson's "Fundamental Approximation Theorem of Portfolio

Analysis in Terms of Means, Variances, and Higher Moments"[3] proves that in many important circumstances:

1. The importance of all moments beyond the variance is much smaller than that of the expected value and variance. In other words, disregarding moments higher than the variance will not affect portfolio choice.
2. The variance is as important as the mean to investor welfare.

Samuelson's proof is the major theoretical justification for mean-variance analysis. Under the conditions of this proof mean and variance are equally important, and we can overlook all other moments without harm.

The major assumption that Samuelson makes to arrive at this conclusion concerns the "compactness" of the distribution of stock returns. The distribution of the rate of return on a portfolio is said to be compact if the risk can be controlled by the investor. Practically speaking, we test for compactness of the distribution by posing a question: Will the risk of my position in the portfolio decline if I hold it for a shorter period, and will the risk approach zero if I hold the portfolio for only an instant? If the answer is yes, then the distribution is compact.

In general, compactness may be viewed as being equivalent to continuity of stock prices. If stock prices do not take sudden jumps, then the uncertainty of stock returns over smaller and smaller time periods decreases. Under these circumstances investors who can rebalance their portfolios frequently will act so as to make higher moments of the stock return distribution so small as to be unimportant. It is not that skewness, for example, does not matter in principle. It is, instead, that the actions of investors in frequently revising their portfolios will limit higher moments to negligible levels.

Continuity or compactness is not, however, an innocuous assumption. Portfolio revisions entail transaction costs, meaning that rebalancing must of necessity be somewhat limited and that skewness and other higher moments cannot entirely be ignored. Compactness also rules out such phenomena as the major stock price jumps that occur in response to takeover attempts. It also rules out such dramatic events as the 25% 1-day decline of the stock market on October 19, 1987. Except for these relatively unusual events, however, mean-variance analysis is adequate. In most cases, if the portfolio may be revised frequently, we need to worry about the mean and variance only.

Portfolio theory, for the most part, is built on the assumption that the conditions for mean-variance (or mean–standard deviation) analysis are satisfied. Accordingly, we typically ignore higher moments.

| | |
|---|---|
| **CONCEPT CHECK ☞ QUESTION A.1** | **How does the simultaneous popularity of both lotteries and insurance policies confirm the notion that individuals prefer positive to negative skewness of portfolio returns?** |

**Normal and Lognormal Distributions.**   Modern portfolio theory, for the most part, assumes that asset returns are normally distributed. This is a convenient assumption because the normal distribution can be described completely by its mean and variance, consistent with mean-variance analysis. The argument has been that even if individual asset

---

[3] Paul A. Samuelson, "The Fundamental Approximation Theorem of Portfolio Analysis in Terms of Means, Variances, and Higher Moments," *Review of Economic Studies* 37 (1970).

returns are not exactly normal, the distribution of returns of a large portfolio will resemble a normal distribution quite closely.

The data support this argument. Table 6A.1 shows summaries of the results of 1-year investments in many portfolios selected randomly from NYSE stocks. The portfolios are listed in order of increasing degrees of diversification; that is, the numbers of stocks in each portfolio sample are 1, 8, 32, and 128. The percentiles of the distribution of returns for each portfolio are compared to what one would have expected from portfolios identical in mean and variance but drawn from a normal distribution.

Looking first at the single-stock portfolio ($n = 1$), the departure of the return distribution from normality is significant. The mean of the sample is 28.2%, and the standard deviation is 41.0%. In the case of normal distribution with the same mean and standard deviation, we would expect the fifth percentile stock to lose 39.2%, but the fifth percentile stock actually lost 14.4%. In addition, although the normal distribution's mean coincides with its median, the actual sample median of the single stock was 19.6%, far below the sample mean of 28.2%.

In contrast, the returns of the 128-stock portfolio are virtually identical in distribution to the hypothetical normally distributed portfolio. The normal distribution therefore is a pretty good working assumption for well-diversified portfolios. How large a portfolio must be for this result to take hold depends on how far the distribution of the individual stocks is from normality. It appears from the table that a portfolio typically must include at least 32 stocks for the 1-year return to be close to normally distributed.

There remain theoretical objections to the assumption that individual stock returns are normally distributed. Given that a stock price cannot be negative, the normal distribution cannot be truly representative of the behavior of a holding-period rate of return because it allows for any outcome, including the whole range of negative prices. Specifically, rates of return lower than −100% are theoretically impossible because they imply the possibility of negative security prices. The failure of the normal distribution to rule out such outcomes must be viewed as a shortcoming.

**Table 6A.1    Frequency Distribution of Rates of Return from a 1-Year Investment in Randomly Selected Portfolios from NYSE-Listed Stocks**

| Statistic | N = 1 Observed | N = 1 Normal | N = 8 Observed | N = 8 Normal | N = 32 Observed | N = 32 Normal | N = 128 Observed | N = 128 Normal |
|---|---|---|---|---|---|---|---|---|
| Minimum | −71.1 | NA | −12.4 | NA | 6.5 | NA | 16.4 | NA |
| 5th percentile | −14.4 | −39.2 | 8.1 | 4.6 | 17.4 | 16.7 | 22.7 | 22.6 |
| 20th percentile | −.5 | 6.3 | 16.3 | 16.1 | 22.2 | 22.3 | 25.3 | 25.3 |
| 50th percentile | 19.6 | 28.2 | 26.4 | 28.2 | 27.8 | 28.2 | 28.1 | 28.2 |
| 70th percentile | 38.7 | 49.7 | 33.8 | 35.7 | 31.6 | 32.9 | 30.0 | 30.0 |
| 95th percentile | 96.3 | 95.6 | 54.3 | 51.8 | 40.9 | 39.9 | 34.1 | 33.8 |
| Maximum | 442.6 | NA | 136.7 | NA | 73.7 | NA | 43.1 | NA |
| Mean | 28.2 | 28.2 | 28.2 | 28.2 | 28.2 | 28.2 | 28.2 | 28.2 |
| Standard deviation | 41.0 | 41.0 | 14.4 | 14.4 | 7.1 | 7.1 | 3.4 | 3.4 |
| Skewness ($M_3$) | 255.4 | 0.0 | 88.7 | 0.0 | 44.5 | 0.0 | 17.7 | 0.0 |
| Sample size | 1,227 | — | 131,072 | — | 32,768 | — | 16,384 | — |

Source: Lawrence Fisher and James H. Lorie, "Some Studies of Variability of Returns on Investments in Common Stocks," *Journal of Business* 43 (April 1970).

An alternative assumption is that the continuously compounded annual rate of return is normally distributed. If we call this rate $r$ and we call the effective annual rate $r_e'$, then $r_e = e^r - 1$, and because $e^r$ can never be negative, the smallest possible value for $r_e$ is $-1$, or $-100\%$. Thus this assumption nicely rules out the troublesome possibility of negative prices while still conveying the advantages of working with normal distributions. Under this assumption the distribution of $r_e$ will be *lognormal*. This distribution is depicted in Figure 6A.2.

Call $r_e(t)$ the effective rate over an investment period of length $t$. For *short* holding periods, that is, where $t$ is small, the approximation of $r_e(t) = e^{rt} - 1$ by $rt$ is quite accurate and the normal distribution provides a good approximation to the lognormal. With $rt$ normally distributed, the effective annual return over short time periods may be taken as approximately normally distributed.

For short holding periods, therefore, the mean and variance of the effective holding-period returns are proportional to the mean and variance of the annual, continuously compounded rate of return on the stock and to the time interval.

Therefore, if the standard deviation of the annual, continuously compounded rate of return on a stock is 40% ($\sigma = .40$ and $\sigma^2 = .16$), then the variance of the holding-period return for 1 month, for example, is for all practical purposes

$$\sigma^2(\text{monthly}) = \frac{\sigma^2}{12} = \frac{.16}{12} = .0133$$

and the monthly standard deviation is $\sqrt{.0133} = .1155$, or 11.55%.

**Figure 6A.2**
**The lognormal distribution for three values of $\sigma$**

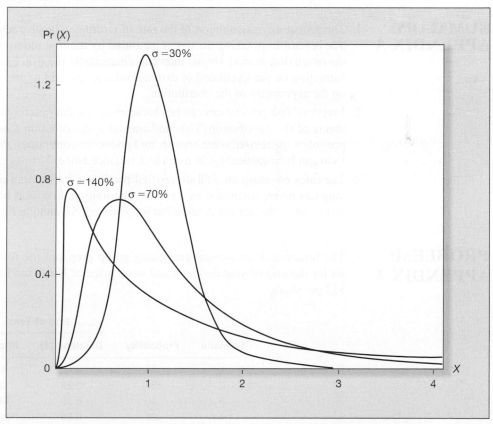

Source: J. Atchison and J. A. C. Brown, *The Lognormal Distribution* (New York: Cambridge University Press, 1976).

To illustrate this principle, suppose that the Dow Jones Industrial Average went up one day by 50 points from 10,000 to 10,050. Is this a "large" move? Looking at annual, continuously compounded rates on the Dow Jones portfolio, we find that the annual standard deviation in postwar years has averaged about 16%. Under the assumption that the return on the Dow Jones portfolio is lognormally distributed and that returns between successive subperiods are uncorrelated, the 1-day distribution has a standard deviation (based on 250 trading days per year) of

$$\sigma(day) = \sigma(year) \sqrt{1/250} = \frac{.16}{\sqrt{250}} = .0101 = 1.01\% \text{ per day}$$

Applying this to the opening level of the Dow Jones on the trading day, 10,000, we find that the daily standard deviation of the Dow Jones index is 10,000 × .0101 = 101 points per day.

If the daily rate on the Dow Jones portfolio is approximately normal, we know that in 1 day out of 3, the Dow Jones will move by more than 1% either way. Thus a move of 50 points would hardly be an unusual event.

**CONCEPT CHECK☞ QUESTION A.2**

Look again at Table 6A.1. Are you surprised that the minimum rates of return are less negative for more diversified portfolios? Is your explanation consistent with the behavior of the sample's maximum rates of return?

## SUMMARY: APPENDIX A

1. The probability distribution of the rate of return can be characterized by its moments. The reward from taking the risk is measured by the first moment, which is the mean of the return distribution. Higher moments characterize the risk. Even moments provide information on the likelihood of extreme values, and odd moments provide information on the asymmetry of the distribution.

2. Investors' risk preferences can be characterized by their preferences for the various moments of the distribution. The fundamental approximation theorem shows that when portfolios are revised often enough, and prices are continuous, the desirability of a portfolio can be measured by its mean and variance alone.

3. The rates of return on well-diversified portfolios for holding periods that are not too long can be approximated by a normal distribution. For short holding periods (e.g., up to 1 month), the normal distribution is a good approximation for the lognormal.

## PROBLEM: APPENDIX A

1. The Smartstock investment consulting group prepared the following scenario analysis for the end-of-year dividend and stock price of Klink Inc., which is selling now at $12 per share:

| Scenario | Probability | End-of-Year Dividend ($) | Price ($) |
|---|---|---|---|
| 1 | .10 | 0 | 0 |
| 2 | .20 | 0.25 | 2.00 |
| 3 | .40 | 0.40 | 14.00 |
| 4 | .25 | 0.60 | 20.00 |
| 5 | .05 | 0.85 | 30.00 |

Compute the rate of return for each scenario and

*a.* The mean, median, and mode.

*b.* The standard deviation and mean absolute deviation.

*c.* The first moment, and the second and third moments around the mean. Is the probability distribution of Klink stock positively skewed?

---

**SOLUTIONS TO CONCEPT CHECKS**

A.1.  Investors appear to be more sensitive to extreme outcomes relative to moderate outcomes than variance and higher *even* moments can explain. Casual evidence suggests that investors are eager to insure against extreme losses and express great enthusiasm for highly positively skewed lotteries. This hypothesis is, however, extremely difficult to prove with properly controlled experiments.

A.2.  The better diversified the portfolio, the smaller is its standard deviation, as the sample standard deviations of Table 6A.1 confirm. When we draw from distributions with smaller standard deviations, the probability of extreme values shrinks. Thus the expected smallest and largest values from a sample get closer to the mean value as the standard deviation gets smaller. This expectation is confirmed by the samples of Table 6A.1 for both the sample maximum and minimum annual rate.

---

## APPENDIX B:   RISK AVERSION, EXPECTED UTILITY, AND THE ST. PETERSBURG PARADOX

We digress in this appendix to examine the rationale behind our contention that investors are risk averse. Recognition of risk aversion as central in investment decisions goes back at least to 1738. Daniel Bernoulli, one of a famous Swiss family of distinguished mathematicians, spent the years 1725 through 1733 in St. Petersburg, where he analyzed the following coin-toss game. To enter the game one pays an entry fee. Thereafter, a coin is tossed until the *first* head appears. The number of tails, denoted by $n$, that appears until the first head is tossed is used to compute the payoff, $\$R$, to the participant, as

$$R(n) = 2^n$$

The probability of no tails before the first head ($n = 0$) is 1/2 and the corresponding payoff is $2^0 = \$1$. The probability of one tail and then heads ($n = 1$) is $1/2 \times 1/2$ with payoff $2^1 = \$2$, the probability of two tails and then heads ($n = 2$) is $1/2 \times 1/2 \times 1/2$ and so forth.

The following table illustrates the probabilities and payoffs for various outcomes:

| Tails | Probability | Payoff = $\$R(n)$ | Probability × Payoff |
|-------|-------------|-------------------|----------------------|
| 0 | 1/2 | $1 | $1/2 |
| 1 | 1/4 | $2 | $1/2 |
| 2 | 1/8 | $4 | $1/2 |
| 3 | 1/16 | $8 | $1/2 |
| ⋮ | ⋮ | ⋮ | ⋮ |
| $n$ | $(1/2)^{n+1}$ | $\$2^n$ | $1/2 |

The expected payoff is therefore

$$E(R) = \sum_{n=0}^{\infty} \Pr(n)R(n) = 1/2 + 1/2 + \cdots = \infty$$

The evaluation of this game is called the "St. Petersburg Paradox." Although the expected payoff is infinite, participants obviously will be willing to purchase tickets to play the game only at a finite, and possibly quite modest, entry fee.

Bernoulli resolved the paradox by noting that investors do not assign the same value per dollar to all payoffs. Specifically, the greater their wealth, the less their "appreciation" for each extra dollar. We can make this insight mathematically precise by assigning a welfare or utility value to any level of investor wealth. Our utility function should increase as wealth is higher, but each extra dollar of wealth should increase utility by progressively smaller amounts.[4] (Modern economists would say that investors exhibit "decreasing marginal utility" from an additional payoff dollar.) One particular function that assigns a subjective value to the investor from a payoff of $R$, which has a smaller value per dollar the greater the payoff, is the function $\ln(R)$ where ln is the natural logarithm function. If this function measures utility values of wealth, the subjective utility value of the game is indeed finite, equal to .693.[5] The certain wealth level necessary to yield this utility value is $2.00, because $\ln(2.00) = .693$. Hence the certainty equivalent value of the risky payoff is $2.00, which is the maximum amount that this investor will pay to play the game.

Von Neumann and Morgenstern adapted this approach to investment theory in a complete axiomatic system in 1946. Avoiding unnecessary technical detail, we restrict ourselves here to an intuitive exposition of the rationale for risk aversion.

Imagine two individuals who are identical twins, except that one of them is less fortunate than the other. Peter has only $1,000 to his name while Paul has a net worth of $200,000. How many hours of work would each twin be willing to offer to earn one extra dollar? It is likely that Peter (the poor twin) has more essential uses for the extra money than does Paul. Therefore, Peter will offer more hours. In other words, Peter derives a greater personal welfare or assigns a greater "utility" value to the 1,001st dollar than Paul does to the 200,001st. Figure 6B.1 depicts graphically the relationship between the wealth and the utility value of wealth that is consistent with this notion of decreasing marginal utility.

Individuals have different rates of decrease in their marginal utility of wealth. What is constant is the *principle* that the per-dollar increment to utility decreases with wealth. Functions that exhibit the property of decreasing per-unit value as the number of units grows are called concave. A simple example is the log function, familiar from high school mathematics. Of course, a log function will not fit all investors, but it is consistent with the risk aversion that we assume for all investors.

---

[4] This utility is similar in spirit to the one that assigns a satisfaction level to portfolios with given risk and return attributes. However, the utility function here refers not to investors' satisfaction with alternative portfolio choices but only to the subjective welfare they derive from different levels of wealth.

[5] If we substitute the "utility" value, $\ln(R)$, for the dollar payoff, $R$, to obtain an expected utility value of the game (rather than expected dollar value), we have, calling $V(R)$ the expected utility,

$$V(R) = \sum_{n=0}^{\infty} \Pr(n) \ln[R(n)] = \sum_{n=0}^{\infty} (1/2)^{n+1} \ln(2^n) = .693$$

**Figure 6B.1
Utility of wealth
with a log utility
function**

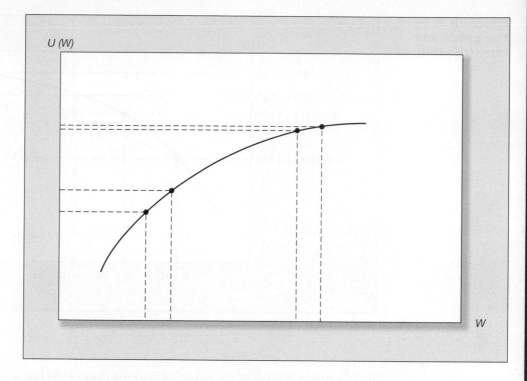

Now consider the following simple prospect:

This is a fair game in that the expected profit is zero. Suppose, however, that the curve in Figure 6B.1 represents the investor's utility value of wealth, assuming a log utility function. Figure 6B.2 shows this curve with numerical values marked.

Figure 6B.2 shows that the loss in utility from losing $50,000 exceeds the gain from winning $50,000. Consider the gain first. With probability $p = .5$, wealth goes from $100,000 to $150,000. Using the log utility function, utility goes from $\ln(100,000) = 11.51$ to $\ln(150,000) = 11.92$, the distance $G$ on the graph. This gain is $G = 11.92 - 11.51 = .41$. In expected utility terms, then, the gain is $pG = .5 \times .41 = .21$.

Now consider the possibility of coming up on the short end of the prospect. In that case, wealth goes from $100,000 to $50,000. The loss in utility, the distance $L$ on the graph, is $L = \ln(100,000) - \ln(50,000) = 11.51 - 10.82 = .69$. Thus the loss in expected utility terms is $(1 - p)L = .5 \times .69 = .35$, which exceeds the gain in expected utility from the possibility of winning the game.

We compute the expected utility from the risky prospect:

$$E[U(W)] = pU(W_1) + (1 - p)U(W_2)$$
$$= \frac{1}{2}\ln(50,000) + \frac{1}{2}\ln(150,000) = 11.37$$

**Figure 6B.2**
**Fair games and**
**expected utility**

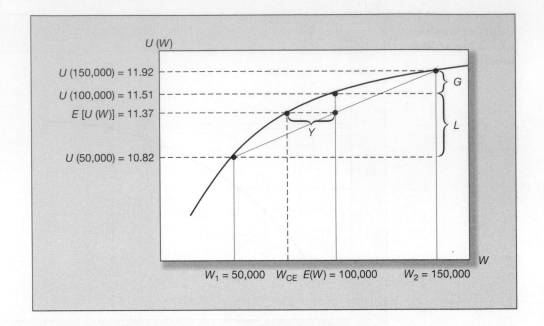

If the prospect is rejected, the utility value of the (sure) $100,000 is ln(100,000) = 11.51, greater than that of the fair game (11.37). Hence the risk-averse investor will reject the fair game.

Using a specific investor utility function (such as the log utility function) allows us to compute the certainty equivalent value of the risky prospect to a given investor. This is the amount that, if received with certainty, she would consider equally attractive as the risky prospect.

If log utility describes the investor's preferences toward wealth outcomes, then Figure 6B.2 can also tell us what is, for her, the dollar value of the prospect. We ask, What sure level of wealth has a utility value of 11.37 (which equals the expected utility from the prospect)? A horizontal line drawn at the level 11.37 intersects the utility curve at the level of wealth $W_{CE}$. This means that

$$\ln(W_{CE}) = 11.37$$

which implies that

$$W_{CE} = e^{11.37} = \$86,681.87$$

$W_{CE}$ is therefore the certainty equivalent of the prospect. The distance $Y$ in Figure 6B.2 is the penalty, or the downward adjustment, to the expected profit that is attributable to the risk of the prospect.

$$Y = E(W) - W_{CE} = \$100,000 - \$86,681.87 = \$13,318.13$$

This investor views $86,681.87 for certain as being equal in utility value as $100,000 at risk. Therefore, she would be indifferent between the two.

**CONCEPT CHECK☞ QUESTION B.1**

Suppose the utility function is $U(W) = \sqrt{W}$.

*a.* What is the utility level at wealth levels $50,000 and $150,000?

*b.* What is expected utility if $p$ still equals .5?

*c.* What is the certainty equivalent of the risky prospect?

*d.* Does this utility function also display risk aversion?

*e.* Does this utility function display more or less risk aversion than the log utility function?

Does revealed behavior of investors demonstrate risk aversion? Looking at prices and past rates of return in financial markets, we can answer with a resounding yes. With remarkable consistency, riskier bonds are sold at lower prices than are safer ones with otherwise similar characteristics. Riskier stocks also have provided higher average rates of return over long periods of time than less risky assets such as T-bills. For example, over the 1926 to 2002 period, the average rate of return on the S&P 500 portfolio exceeded the T-bill return by more than 8% per year.

It is abundantly clear from financial data that the average, or representative, investor exhibits substantial risk aversion. For readers who recognize that financial assets are priced to compensate for risk by providing a risk premium and at the same time feel the urge for some gambling, we have a constructive recommendation: Direct your gambling impulse to investment in financial markets. As Von Neumann once said, "The stock market is a casino with the odds in your favor." A small risk-seeking investment may provide all the excitement you want with a positive expected return to boot!

**PROBLEMS: APPENDIX B**

1. Suppose that your wealth is $250,000. You buy a $200,000 house and invest the remainder in a risk-free asset paying an annual interest rate of 6%. There is a probability of .001 that your house will burn to the ground and its value will be reduced to zero. With a log utility of end-of-year wealth, how much would you be willing to pay for insurance (at the beginning of the year)? (Assume that if the house does not burn down, its end-of-year value still will be $200,000.)

2. If the cost of insuring your house is $1 per $1,000 of value, what will be the certainty equivalent of your end-of-year wealth if you insure your house at:
   *a.* ½ its value.
   *b.* Its full value.
   *c.* 1½ times its value.

**SOLUTIONS TO CONCEPT CHECKS**

**B.1.**  *a.*  $U(W) = \sqrt{W}$
           $U(50,000) = \sqrt{50,000} = 223.61$
           $U(150,000) = 387.30$
      *b.*  $E(U) = (.5 \times 223.61) + (.5 \times 387.30) = 305.45$

Visit us at www.mhhe.com/bkm

**SOLUTIONS
TO CONCEPT
CHECKS**
*(Concluded)*

c. We must find $W_{CE}$ that has utility level 305.45. Therefore

$$\sqrt{W_{CE}} = 305.45$$
$$W_{CE} = 305.45^2 = \$93,301$$

d. Yes. The certainty equivalent of the risky venture is less than the expected outcome of $100,000.

e. The certainty equivalent of the risky venture to this investor is greater than it was for the log utility investor considered in the text. Hence this utility function displays less risk aversion.

# CAPITAL ALLOCATION BETWEEN THE RISKY ASSET AND THE RISK-FREE ASSET

Portfolio managers seek to achieve the best possible trade-off between risk and return. A top-down analysis of their strategies starts with the broadest choices concerning the makeup of the portfolio. For example, the **capital allocation decision** is the choice of the proportion of the overall portfolio to place in safe but low-return money market securities versus risky but higher-return securities like stocks. The choice of the fraction of funds apportioned to risky investments is the first part of the investor's **asset allocation decision,** which describes the distribution of risky investments across broad asset classes—stocks, bonds, real estate, foreign assets, and so on. Finally, the **security selection decision** describes the choice of which particular securities to hold within each asset class. The top-down analysis of portfolio

construction has much to recommend it. Most institutional investors follow a top-down approach. Capital allocation and asset allocation decisions will be made at a high organizational level, with the choice of the specific securities to hold within each asset class delegated to particular portfolio managers. Individual investors typically follow a less-structured approach to money management, but they also typically give priority to broader allocation issues. For example, an individual's first decision is usually how much of his or her wealth must be left in a safe bank or money market account. This chapter treats the broadest part of the asset allocation decision, capital allocation between risk-free assets versus the risky portion of the portfolio. We will take the composition of the risky portfolio as given and refer to it as "the" **risky asset.** In Chapter 8 we will examine how the composition of the risky portfolio may best be determined. For now, however, we start our "top-down journey" by asking how an investor decides how much to invest in the risky versus the risk-free asset. This capital allocation problem may be solved in two stages. First we determine the risk–return trade-off encountered when choosing between the risky and risk-free assets. Then we show how risk aversion determines the optimal mix of the two assets. This analysis leads us to examine so-called passive strategies, which call for allocation of the portfolio between a (risk-free) money market fund and an index fund of common stocks.

# 7.1    CAPITAL ALLOCATION ACROSS RISKY AND RISK-FREE PORTFOLIOS

History shows us that long-term bonds have been riskier investments than investments in Treasury bills and that stock investments have been riskier still. On the other hand, the riskier investments have offered higher average returns. Investors, of course, do not make all-or-nothing choices from these investment classes. They can and do construct their portfolios using securities from all asset classes. Some of the portfolio may be in risk-free Treasury bills, some in high-risk stocks.

The most straightforward way to control the risk of the portfolio is through the fraction of the portfolio invested in Treasury bills and other safe money market securities versus risky assets. This capital allocation decision is an example of an asset allocation choice— a choice among broad investment classes, rather than among the specific securities within each asset class. Most investment professionals consider asset allocation the most important part of portfolio construction. Consider this statement by John Bogle, made when he was chairman of the Vanguard Group of Investment Companies:

> The most fundamental decision of investing is the allocation of your assets: How much should you own in stock? How much should you own in bonds? How much should you own in cash reserves? . . . That decision [has been shown to account] for an astonishing 94% of the differences in total returns achieved by institutionally managed pension funds. . . . There is no reason to believe that the same relationship does not also hold true for individual investors.[1]

Therefore, we start our discussion of the risk–return trade-off available to investors by examining the most basic asset allocation choice: the choice of how much of the portfolio to place in risk-free money market securities versus other risky asset classes.

We will denote the investor's portfolio of risky assets as $P$ and the risk-free asset as $F$. We will assume for the sake of illustration that the risky component of the investor's overall portfolio is comprised of two mutual funds, one invested in stocks and the other invested in long-term bonds. For now, we take the composition of the risky portfolio as given

---

[1] John C. Bogle, *Bogle on Mutual Funds* (Burr Ridge, IL: Irwin Professional Publishing, 1994), p. 235

and focus only on the allocation between it and risk-free securities. In the next chapter, we turn to asset allocation and security selection across risky assets.

When we shift wealth from the risky portfolio to the risk-free asset, we do not change the relative proportions of the various risky assets within the risky portfolio. Rather, we reduce the relative weight of the risky portfolio as a whole in favor of risk-free assets.

For example, assume that the total market value of an initial portfolio is $300,000, of which $90,000 is invested in the Ready Asset money market fund, a risk-free asset for practical purposes. The remaining $210,000 is invested in risky securities—$113,400 in equities ($E$) and $96,600 in long-term bonds ($B$). The equities and long bond holdings comprise "the" risky portfolio, 54% in $E$ and 46% in $B$:

$$E: \quad w_1 = \frac{113,400}{210,000} = .54$$

$$B: \quad w_2 = \frac{96,600}{210,000} = .46$$

The weight of the risky portfolio, $P$, in the **complete portfolio,** including risk-free *and* risky investments, is denoted by $y$:

$$y = \frac{210,000}{300,000} = .7 \text{ (risky assets)}$$

$$1 - y = \frac{90,000}{300,000} = .3 \text{ (risk-free assets)}$$

The weights of each stock in the complete portfolio are as follows:

$$E: \quad \frac{\$113,400}{\$300,000} = .378$$

$$B: \quad \frac{\$96,600}{\$300,000} = .322$$

$$\overline{\text{Risky portfolio}} \qquad\qquad = .700$$

The risky portfolio is 70% of the complete portfolio.

**EXAMPLE 7.1**

## The Risky Portfolio

Suppose that the owner of this portfolio wishes to decrease risk by reducing the allocation to the risky portfolio from $y = .7$ to $y = .56$. The risky portfolio would then total only .56 × $300,000 = $168,000, requiring the sale of $42,000 of the original $210,000 of risky holdings, with the proceeds used to purchase more shares in Ready Asset (the money market fund). Total holdings in the risk-free asset will increase to $300,000 × (1 − .56) = $132,000, or the original holdings plus the new contribution to the money market fund:

$$\$90,000 + \$42,000 = \$132,000$$

The key point, however, is that we leave the proportions of each asset in the risky portfolio unchanged. Because the weights of $E$ and $B$ in the risky portfolio are .54 and .46, respectively, we sell .54 × $42,000 = $22,680 of $E$ and .46 × $42,000 = $19,320 of $B$. After the sale, the proportions of each asset in the risky portfolio are in fact unchanged:

$$E: \quad w_1 = \frac{113,400 - 22,680}{210,000 - 42,000} = .54$$

$$B: \quad w_2 = \frac{96,600 - 19,320}{210,000 - 42,000} = .46$$

Rather than thinking of our risky holdings as $E$ and $B$ stock separately, we may view our holdings as if they were in a single fund that holds equities and bonds in fixed proportions. In this sense we may treat the risky fund as a single risky asset, that asset being a particular bundle of securities. As we shift in and out of safe assets, we simply alter our holdings of that bundle of securities commensurately.

Given this simplification, we can now turn to the desirability of reducing risk by changing the risky/risk-free asset mix, that is, reducing risk by decreasing the proportion $y$. As long as we do not alter the weights of each security within the risky portfolio, the probability distribution of the rate of return on the risky portfolio remains unchanged by the asset reallocation. What will change is the probability distribution of the rate of return on the *complete* portfolio that consists of the risky asset and the risk-free asset.

| CONCEPT CHECK☞ QUESTION 1 | **What will be the dollar value of your position in equities ($E$), and its proportion in your overall portfolio, if you decide to hold 50% of your investment budget in Ready Asset?** |
|---|---|

## 7.2   THE RISK-FREE ASSET

By virtue of its power to tax and control the money supply, only the government can issue default-free bonds. Even the default-free guarantee by itself is not sufficient to make the bonds risk-free in real terms. The only risk-free asset in real terms would be a perfectly price-indexed bond. Moreover, a default-free perfectly indexed bond offers a guaranteed real rate to an investor only if the maturity of the bond is identical to the investor's desired holding period. Even indexed bonds are subject to interest rate risk, because real interest rates change unpredictably through time. When future real rates are uncertain, so is the future price of indexed bonds.

Nevertheless, it is common practice to view Treasury bills as "the" **risk-free asset.** Their short-term nature makes their values insensitive to interest rate fluctuations. Indeed, an investor can lock in a short-term nominal return by buying a bill and holding it to maturity. Moreover, inflation uncertainty over the course of a few weeks, or even months, is negligible compared with the uncertainty of stock market returns.

In practice, most investors use a broader range of money market instruments as a risk-free asset. All the money market instruments are virtually free of interest rate risk because of their short maturities and are fairly safe in terms of default or credit risk.

Most money market funds hold, for the most part, three types of securities—Treasury bills, bank certificates of deposit (CDs), and commercial paper (CP)—differing slightly in their default risk. The yields to maturity on CDs and CP for identical maturity, for example, are always somewhat higher than those of T-bills. The recent history of this yield spread for 90-day CDs is shown in Figure 7.1.

Money market funds have changed their relative holdings of these securities over time but, by and large, T-bills make up only about 15% of their portfolios. Nevertheless, the risk of such blue-chip short-term investments as CDs and CP is minuscule compared with that of most other assets such as long-term corporate bonds, common stocks, or real estate. Hence we treat money market funds as the most easily accessible risk-free asset for most investors.

**Figure 7.1**
**Spread between 3-month CD and T-bill rates**

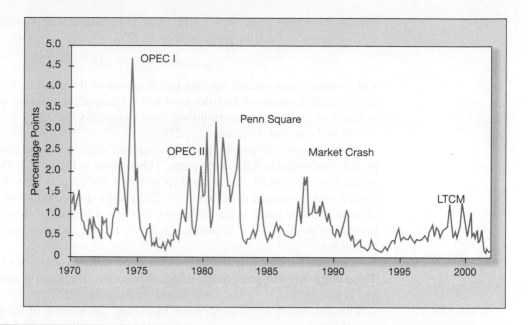

## 7.3    PORTFOLIOS OF ONE RISKY ASSET AND ONE RISK-FREE ASSET

In this section we examine the risk–return combinations available to investors. This is the "technological" part of asset allocation; it deals only with the opportunities available to investors given the features of the broad asset markets in which they can invest. In the next section we address the "personal" part of the problem—the specific individual's choice of the best risk–return combination from the set of feasible combinations.

Suppose the investor has already decided on the composition of the risky portfolio. Now the concern is with the proportion of the investment budget, $y$, to be allocated to the risky portfolio, $P$. The remaining proportion, $1 - y$, is to be invested in the risk-free asset, $F$.

Denote the risky rate of return of $P$ by $r_P$, its expected rate of return by $E(r_P)$, and its standard deviation by $\sigma_P$. The rate of return on the risk-free asset is denoted as $r_f$. In the numerical example we assume that $E(r_P) = 15\%$, $\sigma_P = 22\%$, and that the risk-free rate is $r_f = 7\%$. Thus the risk premium on the risky asset is $E(r_P) - r_f = 8\%$.

With a proportion, $y$, in the risky portfolio, and $1 - y$ in the risk-free asset, the rate of return on the *complete* portfolio, denoted $C$, is $r_C$ where

$$r_C = yr_P + (1 - y)r_f$$

Taking the expectation of this portfolio's rate of return,

$$E(r_C) = yE(r_P) + (1 - y)r_f$$
$$= r_f + y[E(r_P) - r_f] = 7 + y(15 - 7) \tag{7.1}$$

This result is easily interpreted. The base rate of return for any portfolio is the risk-free rate. In addition, the portfolio is *expected* to earn a risk premium that depends on the risk premium of the risky portfolio, $E(r_P) - r_f$, and the investor's position in the risky asset, $y$. Investors are assumed to be risk averse and thus unwilling to take on a risky position without a positive risk premium.

As we noted in Chapter 6, when we combine a risky asset and a risk-free asset in a portfolio, the standard deviation of the resulting complete portfolio is the standard deviation of the risky asset multiplied by the weight of the risky asset in that portfolio. Because the standard deviation of the risky portfolio is $\sigma_P = 22\%$,

$$\sigma_C = y\sigma_P = 22y \tag{7.2}$$

which makes sense because the standard deviation of the portfolio is proportional to both the standard deviation of the risky asset and the proportion invested in it. In sum, the rate of return of the complete portfolio will have expected value $E(r_C) = r_f + y[E(r_P) - r_f] = 7 + 8y$ and standard deviation $\sigma_C = 22y$.

The next step is to plot the portfolio characteristics (given the choice for $y$) in the expected return–standard deviation plane. This is done in Figure 7.2. The risk-free asset, $F$, appears on the vertical axis because its standard deviation is zero. The risky asset, $P$, is plotted with a standard deviation, $\sigma_P = 22\%$, and expected return of 15%. If an investor chooses to invest solely in the risky asset, then $y = 1.0$, and the complete portfolio is $P$. If the chosen position is $y = 0$, then $1 - y = 1.0$, and the complete portfolio is the risk-free portfolio $F$.

What about the more interesting midrange portfolios where $y$ lies between zero and 1? These portfolios will graph on the straight line connecting points $F$ and $P$. The slope of that line is simply $[E(r_P) - r_f]/\sigma_P$ (or rise/run), in this case, 8/22.

The conclusion is straightforward. Increasing the fraction of the overall portfolio invested in the risky asset increases expected return according to equation 7.1 at a rate of 8%. It also increases portfolio standard deviation according to equation 7.2 at the rate of 22%. The extra return per extra risk is thus 8/22 = .36.

To derive the exact equation for the straight line between $F$ and $P$, we rearrange equation 7.2 to find that $y = \sigma_C/\sigma_P$, and we substitute for $y$ in equation 7.1 to describe the expected return–standard deviation trade-off:

$$E(r_C) = r_f + y[E(r_P) - r_f]$$
$$= r_f + \frac{\sigma_C}{\sigma_P}[E(r_P) - r_f] = 7 + \frac{8}{22}\sigma_C \tag{7.3}$$

**Figure 7.2**
**The investment opportunity set with a risky asset and a risk-free asset in the expected return–standard deviation plane**

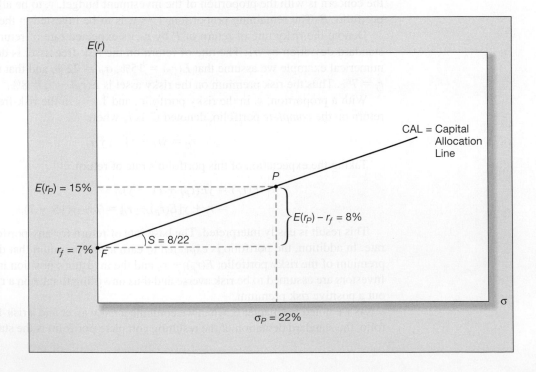

Thus the expected return of the complete portfolio as a function of its standard deviation is a straight line, with intercept $r_f$ and slope as follows:

$$S = \frac{E(r_P) - r_f}{\sigma_P} = \frac{8}{22}$$

Figure 7.2 graphs the *investment opportunity set,* which is the set of feasible expected return and standard deviation pairs of all portfolios resulting from different values of $y$. The graph is a straight line originating at $r_f$ and going through the point labeled $P$.

This straight line is called the **capital allocation line** (CAL). It depicts all the risk–return combinations available to investors. The slope of the CAL, denoted $S$, equals the increase in the expected return of the complete portfolio per unit of additional standard deviation—in other words, incremental return per incremental risk. For this reason, the slope also is called the **reward-to-variability ratio.**

A portfolio equally divided between the risky asset and the risk-free asset, that is, where $y = .5$, will have an expected rate of return of $E(r_C) = 7 + .5 \times 8 = 11\%$, implying a risk premium of 4%, and a standard deviation of $\sigma_C = .5 \times 22 = 11\%$. It will plot on the line $FP$ midway between $F$ and $P$. The reward-to-variability ratio is $S = 4/11 = .36$, precisely the same as that of portfolio $P$, 8/22.

---

**CONCEPT CHECK ☞ QUESTION 2**

Can the reward-to-variability ratio, $S = [E(r_C) - r_f]/\sigma_C$, of any combination of the risky asset and the risk-free asset be different from the ratio for the risky asset taken alone, $[E(r_P) - r_f]/\sigma_P$, which in this case is .36?

---

What about points on the CAL to the right of portfolio $P$? If investors can borrow at the (risk-free) rate of $r_f = 7\%$, they can construct portfolios that may be plotted on the CAL to the right of $P$.

---

**EXAMPLE 7.2**  **Leverage**

Suppose the investment budget is $300,000 and our investor borrows an additional $120,000, investing the total available funds in the risky asset. This is a *leveraged* position in the risky asset; it is financed in part by borrowing. In that case

$$y = \frac{420,000}{300,000} = 1.4$$

and $1 - y = 1 - 1.4 = -.4$, reflecting a short position in the risk-free asset, which is a borrowing position. Rather than lending at a 7% interest rate, the investor borrows at 7%. The distribution of the portfolio rate of return still exhibits the same reward-to-variability ratio:

$$E(r_C) = 7\% + (1.4 \times 8\%) = 18.2\%$$
$$\sigma_C = 1.4 \times 22\% = 30.8\%$$
$$S = \frac{E(r_C) - r_f}{\sigma_C} = \frac{18.2 - 7}{30.8} = .36$$

As one might expect, the leveraged portfolio has a higher standard deviation than does an unleveraged position in the risky asset.

**Figure 7.3
The opportunity
set with
differential
borrowing and
lending rates**

Of course, nongovernment investors cannot borrow at the risk-free rate. The risk of a borrower's default causes lenders to demand higher interest rates on loans. Therefore, the nongovernment investor's borrowing cost will exceed the lending rate of $r_f = 7\%$. Suppose the borrowing rate is $r_f^B = 9\%$. Then in the borrowing range, the reward-to-variability ratio, the slope of the CAL, will be $[E(r_P) - r_f^B]/\sigma_P = 6/22 = .27$. The CAL will therefore be "kinked" at point $P$, as shown in Figure 7.3. To the left of $P$ the investor is lending at 7%, and the slope of the CAL is .36. To the right of $P$, where $y > 1$, the investor is borrowing at 9% to finance extra investments in the risky asset, and the slope is .27.

In practice, borrowing to invest in the risky portfolio is easy and straightforward if you have a margin account with a broker. All you have to do is tell your broker that you want to buy "on margin." Margin purchases may not exceed 50% of the purchase value. Therefore, if your net worth in the account is $300,000, the broker is allowed to lend you up to $300,000 to purchase additional stock.[2] You would then have $600,000 on the asset side of your account and $300,000 on the liability side, resulting in $y = 2.0$.

| CONCEPT CHECK☞ QUESTION 3 | **Suppose that there is a shift upward in the expected rate of return on the risky asset, from 15% to 17%. If all other parameters remain unchanged, what will be the slope of the CAL for $y \leq 1$ and $y > 1$?** |
|---|---|

---

[2] Margin purchases require the investor to maintain the securities in a margin account with the broker. If the value of the securities declines below a "maintenance margin," a "margin call" is sent out, requiring a deposit to bring the net worth of the account up to the appropriate level. If the margin call is not met, regulations mandate that some or all of the securities be sold by the broker and the proceeds used to reestablish the required margin. See Chapter 3, Section 3.6, for further discussion.

| Table 7.1 | Utility Levels for Various Positions in Risky Assets (y) for an Investor with Risk Aversion A = 4 | | | |
|---|---|---|---|---|
| | **(1)** | **(2)** | **(3)** | **(4)** |
| | **y** | **$E(r_C)$** | **$\sigma_C$** | **U** |
| | 0 | 7 | 0 | 7.00 |
| | 0.1 | 7.8 | 2.2 | 7.70 |
| | 0.2 | 8.6 | 4.4 | 8.21 |
| | 0.3 | 9.4 | 6.6 | 8.53 |
| | 0.4 | 10.2 | 8.8 | 8.65 |
| | 0.5 | 11.0 | 11.0 | 8.58 |
| | 0.6 | 11.8 | 13.2 | 8.32 |
| | 0.7 | 12.6 | 15.4 | 7.86 |
| | 0.8 | 13.4 | 17.6 | 7.20 |
| | 0.9 | 14.2 | 19.8 | 6.36 |
| | 1.0 | 15.0 | 22.0 | 5.32 |

## 7.4    RISK TOLERANCE AND ASSET ALLOCATION

We have shown how to develop the CAL, the graph of all feasible risk–return combinations available from different asset allocation choices. The investor confronting the CAL now must choose one optimal portfolio, C, from the set of feasible choices. This choice entails a trade-off between risk and return. Individual investor differences in risk aversion imply that, given an identical opportunity set (that is, a risk-free rate and a reward-to-variability ratio), different investors will choose different positions in the risky asset. In particular, the more risk-averse investors will choose to hold less of the risky asset and more of the risk-free asset.

In Chapter 6 we showed that the utility that an investor derives from a portfolio with a given expected return and standard deviation can be described by the following utility function:

$$U = E(r) - .005A\sigma^2 \tag{7.4}$$

where A is the coefficient of risk aversion and 0.005 is a scale factor. We interpret this expression to say that the utility from a portfolio increases as the expected rate of return increases, and it decreases when the variance increases. The relative magnitude of these changes is governed by the coefficient of risk aversion, A. For risk-neutral investors, A = 0. Higher levels of risk aversion are reflected in larger values for A.

An investor who faces a risk-free rate, $r_f$, and a risky portfolio with expected return $E(r_P)$ and standard deviation $\sigma_P$ will find that, for any choice of y, the expected return of the complete portfolio is given by equation 7.1:

$$E(r_C) = r_f + y[E(r_P) - r_f]$$

From equation 7.2, the variance of the overall portfolio is

$$\sigma_C^2 = y^2\sigma_P^2$$

The investor attempts to maximize utility, U, by choosing the best allocation to the risky asset, y. To illustrate, we use a spreadsheet program to determine the effect of y on the utility of an investor with A = 4. We input y in column (1) and use the spreadsheet in Table 7.1 to compute $E(r_C)$, $\sigma_C$, and U, using equations 7.1–7.4.

**Figure 7.4
Utility as a
function of
allocation to
the risky asset, y**

Figure 7.4 is a plot of the utility function from Table 7.1. The graph shows that utility is highest at $y = .41$. When $y$ is less than .41, investors are willing to assume more risk to increase expected return. But at higher levels of $y$, risk is higher, and additional allocations to the risky asset are undesirable—beyond this point, further increases in risk dominate the increase in expected return and reduce utility.

To solve the utility maximization problem more generally, we write the problem as follows:

$$\underset{y}{\text{Max}}\ U = E(r_C) - .005A\sigma_C^2 = r_f + y[E(r_P) - r_f] - .005Ay^2\sigma_P^2$$

Students of calculus will remember that the maximization problem is solved by setting the derivative of this expression to zero. Doing so and solving for $y$ yields the optimal position for risk-averse investors in the risky asset, $y^*$, as follows:[3]

$$y^* = \frac{E(r_P) - r_f}{.01A\sigma_P^2} \tag{7.5}$$

This solution shows that the optimal position in the risky asset is, as one would expect, *inversely* proportional to the level of risk aversion and the level of risk (as measured by the variance) and directly proportional to the risk premium offered by the risky asset.

**EXAMPLE 7.3**    **Capital Allocation**

Using our numerical example [$r_f = 7\%$, $E(r_P) = 15\%$, and $\sigma_P = 22\%$], the optimal solution for an investor with a coefficient of risk aversion $A = 4$ is

$$y^* = \frac{15 - 7}{.01 \times 4 \times 22^2} = .41$$

In other words, this particular investor will invest 41% of the investment budget in the risky asset and 59% in the risk-free asset. As we saw in Figure 7.4, this is the value of $y$ for which utility is maximized.

---

[3] The derivative with respect to $y$ equals $E(r_P) - r_f - .01yA\ \sigma_P^2$. Setting this expression equal to zero and solving for $y$ yields equation 7.5.

With 41% invested in the risky portfolio, the rate of return of the complete portfolio will have an expected return and standard deviation as follows:

$$E(r_C) = 7 + [.41 \times (15 - 7)] = 10.28\%$$
$$\sigma_C = .41 \times 22 = 9.02\%$$

The risk premium of the complete portfolio is $E(r_C) - r_f = 3.28\%$, which is obtained by taking on a portfolio with a standard deviation of 9.02%. Notice that $3.28/9.02 = .36$, which is the reward-to-variability ratio assumed for this example.

A graphical way of presenting this decision problem is to use indifference curve analysis. Recall from Chapter 6 that the indifference curve is a graph in the expected return–standard deviation plane of all points that result in a given level of utility. The curve displays the investor's required trade-off between expected return and standard deviation.

To illustrate how to build an indifference curve, consider an investor with risk aversion $A = 4$ who currently holds all her wealth in a risk-free portfolio yielding $r_f = 5\%$. Because the variance of such a portfolio is zero, equation 7.4 tells us that its utility value is $U = 5$. Now we find the expected return the investor would require to maintain the *same* level of utility when holding a risky portfolio, say with $\sigma = 1\%$. We use equation 7.4 to find how much $E(r)$ must increase to compensate for the higher value of $\sigma$:

$$U = E(r) - .005 \times A \times \sigma^2$$
$$5 = E(r) - .005 \times 4 \times 1^2$$

This implies that the necessary expected return increases to

$$\text{Required } E(r) = 5 + .005 \times A \times \sigma^2 \qquad (7.6)$$
$$= 5 + .005 \times 4 \times 1^2 = 5.02\%$$

We can repeat this calculation for many other levels of $\sigma$, each time finding the value of $E(r)$ necessary to maintain $U = 5$. This process will yield all combinations of expected return and volatility with utility level of 5; plotting these combinations gives us the indifference curve.

We can readily generate an investor's indifference curves using a spreadsheet. Table 7.2 contains risk–return combinations with utility values of 5% and 9% for two investors, one with $A = 2$ and the other with $A = 4$. For example, column (2) uses equation 7.6 to calculate the expected return that must be paired with the standard deviation in column (1) for an investor with $A = 2$ to derive a utility value of $U = 5$. Column 3 repeats the calculations for a higher utility value, $U = 9$. The plot of these expected return–standard deviation combinations appears in Figure 7.5 as the two curves labeled $A = 2$.

Because the utility value of a risk-free portfolio is simply the expected rate of return of that portfolio, the intercept of each indifference curve in Figure 7.5 (at which $\sigma = 0$) is called the **certainty equivalent** of the portfolios on that curve and in fact is the utility value of that curve. In this context, "utility" and "certainty equivalent" are interchangeable terms. Notice that the intercepts of the indifference curves are at 5% and 9%, exactly the level of utility corresponding to the two curves.

Given the choice, any investor would prefer a portfolio on the higher indifference curve, the one with a higher certainty equivalent (utility). Portfolios on higher indifference curves offer higher expected return for any given level of risk. For example, both indifference curves for the $A = 2$ investor have the same shape, but for any level of volatility, a portfolio on the curve with utility of 9% offers an expected return 4% greater than the corresponding portfolio on the lower curve, for which $U = 5\%$.

Columns (4) and (5) of Table 7.2 repeat this analysis for a more risk-averse investor, one with $A = 4$. The resulting pair of indifference curves in Figure 7.5 demonstrates that the

**Table 7.2   Spreadsheet Calculations of Indifference Curves (Entries in columns 2–4 are expected returns necessary to provide specified utility value.)**

| | A = 2 | | A = 4 | |
| σ | U = 5 | U = 9 | U = 5 | U = 9 |
|---|---|---|---|---|
| 0 | 5.000 | 9.000 | 5.000 | 9.000 |
| 5 | 5.250 | 9.250 | 5.500 | 9.500 |
| 10 | 6.000 | 10.000 | 7.000 | 11.000 |
| 15 | 7.250 | 11.250 | 9.500 | 13.500 |
| 20 | 9.000 | 13.000 | 13.000 | 17.000 |
| 25 | 11.250 | 15.250 | 17.500 | 21.500 |
| 30 | 14.000 | 18.000 | 23.000 | 27.000 |
| 35 | 17.250 | 21.250 | 29.500 | 33.500 |
| 40 | 21.000 | 25.000 | 37.000 | 41.000 |
| 45 | 25.250 | 29.250 | 45.500 | 49.500 |
| 50 | 30.000 | 34.000 | 55.000 | 59.000 |

**Figure 7.5
Indifference
curves for U = 5
and U = 9 with
A = 2 and A = 4**

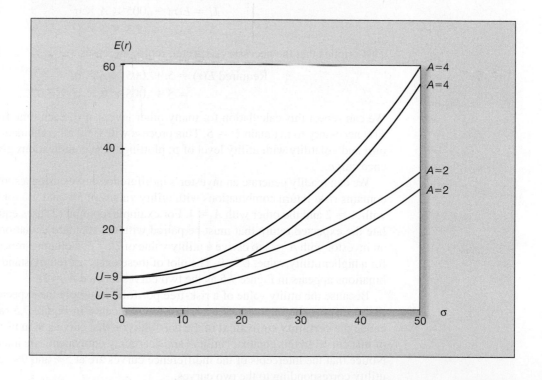

more risk-averse investor has steeper indifference curves than the less risk-averse investor. Steeper curves mean that the investor requires a greater increase in expected return to compensate for an increase in portfolio risk.

Higher indifference curves correspond to higher levels of utility. The investor thus attempts to find the complete portfolio on the highest possible indifference curve. When we

**Figure 7.6
Finding the
optimal complete
portfolio by using
indifference curves**

**Table 7.3   Expected Returns on Four Indifference Curves and the CAL**

| σ | U = 7 | U = 7.8 | U = 8.653 | U = 9.4 | CAL |
|---|---|---|---|---|---|
| 0 | 7.00 | 7.80 | 8.65 | 9.40 | 7.00 |
| 2 | 7.08 | 7.88 | 8.73 | 9.48 | 7.73 |
| 4 | 7.32 | 8.12 | 8.97 | 9.72 | 8.45 |
| 6 | 7.72 | 8.52 | 9.37 | 10.12 | 9.18 |
| 8 | 8.28 | 9.08 | 9.93 | 10.68 | 9.91 |
| 9.02 | 8.63 | 9.43 | 10.28 | 11.03 | 10.28 |
| 10 | 9.00 | 9.80 | 10.65 | 11.40 | 10.64 |
| 12 | 9.88 | 10.68 | 11.53 | 12.28 | 11.36 |
| 14 | 10.92 | 11.72 | 12.57 | 13.32 | 12.09 |
| 18 | 13.48 | 14.28 | 15.13 | 15.88 | 13.55 |
| 22 | 16.68 | 17.48 | 18.33 | 19.08 | 15.00 |
| 26 | 20.52 | 21.32 | 22.17 | 22.92 | 16.45 |
| 30 | 25.00 | 25.80 | 26.65 | 27.40 | 17.91 |

superimpose plots of indifference curves on the investment opportunity set represented by the capital allocation line as in Figure 7.6, we can identify the *highest possible* indifference curve that touches the CAL. That indifference curve is tangent to the CAL, and the tangency point corresponds to the standard deviation and expected return of the optimal complete portfolio.

To illustrate, Table 7.3 provides calculations for four indifference curves (with utility levels of 7, 7.8, 8.653, and 9.4) for an investor with $A = 4$. Columns (2)–(5) use equation

7.6 to calculate the expected return that must be paired with the standard deviation in column (1) to provide the utility value corresponding to each curve. Column (6) uses equation 7.3 to calculate $E(r_C)$ on the CAL for the standard deviation $\sigma_C$ in column (1):

$$E(r_C) = r_f + [E(r_P) - r_f]\frac{\sigma_C}{\sigma_P} = 7 + [15 - 7]\frac{\sigma_C}{22}$$

Figure 7.6 graphs the four indifference curves and the CAL. The graph reveals that the indifference curve with $U = 8.653$ is tangent to the CAL; the tangency point corresponds to the complete portfolio that maximizes utility. The tangency point occurs at $\sigma_C = 9.02\%$ and $E(r_C) = 10.28\%$, the risk–return parameters of the optimal complete portfolio with $y^* = 0.41$. These values match our algebraic solution using equation 7.5.

We conclude that the choice for $y^*$, the fraction of overall investment funds to place in the risky portfolio versus the safer but lower expected-return risk-free asset, is in large part a matter of risk aversion.

---

**CONCEPT CHECK ☞ QUESTION 4**

*a.* **If an investor's coefficient of risk aversion is $A = 3$, how does the optimal asset mix change? What are the new $E(r_C)$ and $\sigma_C$?**

*b.* **Suppose that the borrowing rate, $r_f^B = 9\%$, is greater than the lending rate, $r_f = 7\%$. Show graphically how the optimal portfolio choice of some investors will be affected by the higher borrowing rate. Which investors will *not* be affected by the borrowing rate?**

---

## 7.5    PASSIVE STRATEGIES: THE CAPITAL MARKET LINE

The CAL is derived with the risk-free and "the" risky portfolio, $P$. Determination of the assets to include in risky portfolio $P$ may result from a passive or an active strategy. A **passive strategy** describes a portfolio decision that avoids *any* direct or indirect security analysis.[4] At first blush, a passive strategy would appear to be naive. As will become

---

[4] By "indirect security analysis" we mean the delegation of that responsibility to an intermediary such as a professional money manager.

**Table 7.4   Average Rates of Return and Standard Deviations for Large Stocks, 1-Month Bills, and the Risk Premium over Time**

| | Large Stocks | | 1-Month Bills | | Risk Premium and Sharpe Ratio (Average/SD) | | |
|---|---|---|---|---|---|---|---|
| | Average | SD | Average | SD | Average | SD | Sharpe Ratio |
| 1926–2002 | 12.04 | 20.55 | 3.82 | 3.18 | 8.22 | 20.81 | 0.39 |
| 1983–2002 | 13.98 | 16.90 | 5.60 | 2.08 | 8.37 | 16.26 | 0.52 |
| 1963–1982 | 9.67 | 16.90 | 6.61 | 3.12 | 3.06 | 17.53 | 0.17 |
| 1943–1962 | 16.56 | 18.14 | 1.48 | 0.91 | 15.07 | 18.53 | 0.81 |
| 1926–1942 | 7.23 | 29.58 | 1.20 | 1.58 | 6.03 | 29.56 | 0.20 |

apparent, however, forces of supply and demand in large capital markets may make such a strategy a reasonable choice for many investors.

In Chapter 5, we presented a compilation of the history of rates of return on different asset classes. The data are available at many universities from the University of Chicago's Center for Research in Security Prices (CRSP). This database contains rates of return on several asset classes, including 30-day T-bills, long-term T-bonds, long-term corporate bonds, and common stocks. The CRSP tapes provide a monthly rate of return series for the period 1926 to the present and, for common stocks, a daily rate of return series from 1963 to the present. We can use these data to examine various passive strategies.

A natural candidate for a passively held risky asset would be a well-diversified portfolio of common stocks. Since a passive strategy requires that we devote no resources to acquiring information on any individual stock or group of stocks, we must follow a "neutral" diversification strategy. One way is to select a diversified portfolio of stocks that mirrors the value of the corporate sector of the U.S. economy. This results in a portfolio in which, for example, the proportion invested in GM stock will be the ratio of GM's total market value to the market value of all listed stocks.

The most popular value-weighted index of U.S. stocks is the Standard & Poor's composite index of 500 of the largest capitalization corporations (S&P 500).[5] Table 7.4 summarizes the performance of the S&P 500 portfolio for the period 1926–2002 as well as four subperiods. It is evident that the mean and standard deviation of the distribution of the portfolio return vary considerably over time. The Great Depression years (1926–1942) and the period 1963–1982 are quite different from the post-war years (1943–1962) and technology boom period (1983–2002). The last column of the table shows that the reward-to-variability ratio (the Sharpe ratio) falls in a wide range of .17–.81.

We call the capital allocation line provided by 1-month T-bills and a broad index of common stocks the **capital market line** (CML). A passive strategy generates an investment opportunity set that is represented by the CML.

How reasonable is it for an investor to pursue a passive strategy? Of course, we cannot answer such a question without comparing the strategy to the costs and benefits accruing to an active portfolio strategy. Some thoughts are relevant at this point, however.

First, the alternative active strategy is not free. Whether you choose to invest the time and cost to acquire the information needed to generate an optimal active portfolio of risky assets, or whether you delegate the task to a professional who will charge a fee, constitution

---

[5] Before March 1957 it consisted of 90 of the largest stocks.

of an active portfolio is more expensive than a passive one. The passive portfolio requires only small commissions on purchases of T-bills (or zero commissions if you purchase bills directly from the government) and management fees to a mutual fund company that offers a market index fund to the public. Vanguard, for example, operates the Index 500 Portfolio that mimics the S&P 500 index. It purchases shares of the firms constituting the S&P 500 in proportion to the market values of the outstanding equity of each firm, and therefore essentially replicates the S&P 500 index. The fund thus duplicates the performance of this market index. It has one of the lowest operating expenses (as a percentage of assets) of all mutual stock funds precisely because it requires minimal managerial effort.

A second reason to pursue a passive strategy is the free-rider benefit. If there are many active, knowledgeable investors who quickly bid up prices of undervalued assets and force down prices of overvalued assets (by selling), we have to conclude that at any time most assets will be fairly priced. Therefore, a well-diversified portfolio of common stock will be a reasonably fair buy, and the passive strategy may not be inferior to that of the average active investor. (We will elaborate this argument and provide a more comprehensive analysis of the relative success of passive strategies in later chapters.) The box on the next page points out that passive index funds have actually outperformed actively managed funds in the past decade.

To summarize, a passive strategy involves investment in two passive portfolios: virtually risk-free short-term T-bills (or, alternatively, a money market fund) and a fund of common stocks that mimics a broad market index. The capital allocation line representing such a strategy is called the *capital market line*. Historically, based on 1926 to 2002 data, the passive risky portfolio offered an average risk premium of 8.2% and a standard deviation of 20.8%, resulting in a reward-to-variability ratio of .39.

Passive investors allocate their investment budgets among instruments according to their degree of risk aversion. We can use our analysis to deduce a typical investor's risk-aversion parameter. From Table 1.2 in Chapter 1, we estimate that approximately 74% of net worth is invested in a broad array of risky assets.[6] We assume this portfolio has the same reward-risk characteristics as the S&P 500 has exhibited since 1926, that is, a risk premium of 8.2% and standard deviation of 20.8% as documented in Table 7.4. Substituting these values in equation 7.5, we obtain

$$y^* = \frac{E(r_M) - r_f}{.01 \times A\sigma_M^2}$$

$$= \frac{8.2}{.01 \times A \times 20.8^2} = .74$$

which implies a coefficient of risk aversion of

$$A = \frac{8.2}{.01 \times .74 \times 20.8^2} = 2.6$$

Of course, this calculation is highly speculative. We have assumed without basis that the average investor holds the naive view that historical average rates of return and standard deviations are the best estimates of expected rates of return and risk, looking to the future. To the extent that the average investor takes advantage of contemporary information in addition to simple historical data, our estimate of $A = 2.6$ would be an unjustified inference.

---

[6] We include in the risky portfolio real assets, half of pension reserves, corporate and noncorporate equity, mutual fund shares, and personal trusts and half of "other" assets. This portfolio sums to $35,631 billion, which is 74% of household net worth.

# CRITICISMS OF INDEXING DON'T HOLD UP

Amid the stock market's recent travails, critics are once again taking aim at index funds. But like the firing squad that stands in a circle, they aren't making a whole lot of sense.

Indexing, of course, has never been popular in some quarters. Performance-hungry investors loathe the idea of buying index funds and abandoning all chance of beating the market averages. Meanwhile, most Wall Street firms would love indexing to fall from favor because there isn't much money to be made running index funds.

But the latest barrage of nonsense also reflects today's peculiar stock market. Here is a look at four recent complaints about index funds:

**They're undiversified.** Critics charge that the most popular index funds, those that track the Standard & Poor's 500-stock index, are too focused on a small number of stocks and a single sector, technology.

S&P 500 funds currently have 25.3% of their money in their 10-largest stockholdings and 31.1% of assets in technology companies. This narrow focus made S&P 500 funds especially vulnerable during this year's market swoon.

But the same complaint could be leveled at actively managed funds. According to Chicago researchers Morningstar Inc., diversified U.S. stock funds have an average 36.2% invested in their 10-largest stocks, with 29.1% in technology.

**They're top-heavy.** Critics also charge that S&P 500 funds represent a big bet on big-company stocks. True enough. I have often argued that most folks would be better off indexing the Wilshire 5000, which includes most regularly traded U.S. stocks, including both large and small companies.

But let's not get carried away. The S&P 500 isn't that narrowly focused. After all, it represents some 77.2% of U.S. stock-market value.

Whether you index the S&P 500 or the Wilshire 5000, what you are getting is a fund that pretty much mirrors the U.S. market. If you think index funds are undiversified and top-heavy, there can only be one reason: The market is undiversified and top heavy.

**They're chasing performance.** In the 1990s, the stock market's return was driven by a relatively small number of sizzling performers. As these hot stocks climbed in value, index funds became more heavily invested in these companies, while lightening up on lackluster performers.

That, complain critics, is the equivalent of buying high and selling low. A devastating criticism? Hardly. This is what all investors do. When Home Depot's stock climbs 5%, investors collectively end up with 5% more money riding on Home Depot's shares.

**You can do better.** Sure, there is always a chance you will get lucky and beat the market. But don't count on it

As a group, investors in U.S. stocks can't outperform the market because, collectively, they are the market. In fact, once you figure in investment costs, active investors are destined to lag behind Wilshire 5000-index funds, because these active investors incur far higher investment costs.

But this isn't just a matter of logic. The proof is also in the numbers. Over the past decade, only 28% of U.S. stock funds managed to beat the Wilshire 5000, according to Vanguard.

The problem is, the long-term argument for indexing gets forgotten in the rush to embrace the latest, hottest funds. An indexing strategy will beat most funds in most years. But in any given year, there will always be some funds that do better than the index. These winners garner heaps of publicity, which whets investors' appetites and encourages them to try their luck at beating the market.

Nevertheless, a broad range of studies, taking into account the full range of available assets, places the degree of risk aversion for the representative investor in the range of 2.0 to 4.0.[7]

| CONCEPT CHECK ☞ QUESTION 5 | Suppose that expectations about the S&P 500 index and the T-bill rate are the same as they were in 2003, but you find that today a greater proportion is invested in T-bills than in 2003. What can you conclude about the change in risk tolerance over the years since 2003? |
|---|---|

[7] See, for example, I. Friend and M. Blume, "The Demand for Risky Assets," *American Economic Review* 64 (1974); or S. J. Grossman and R. J. Shiller, "The Determinants of the Variability of Stock Market Prices," *American Economic Review* 71 (1981).

## SUMMARY

1. Shifting funds from the risky portfolio to the risk-free asset is the simplest way to reduce risk. Other methods involve diversification of the risky portfolio and hedging. We take up these methods in later chapters.

2. T-bills provide a perfectly risk-free asset in nominal terms only. Nevertheless, the standard deviation of real rates on short-term T-bills is small compared to that of other assets such as long-term bonds and common stocks, so for the purpose of our analysis we consider T-bills as the risk-free asset. Money market funds hold, in addition to T-bills, short-term relatively safe obligations such as CP and CDs. These entail some default risk, but again, the additional risk is small relative to most other risky assets. For convenience, we often refer to money market funds as risk-free assets.

3. An investor's risky portfolio (the risky asset) can be characterized by its reward-to-variability ratio, $S = [E(r_P) - r_f]/\sigma_P$. This ratio is also the slope of the CAL, the line that, when graphed, goes from the risk-free asset through the risky asset. All combinations of the risky asset and the risk-free asset lie on this line. Other things equal, an investor would prefer a steeper-sloping CAL, because that means higher expected return for any level of risk. If the borrowing rate is greater than the lending rate, the CAL will be "kinked" at the point of the risky asset.

4. The investor's degree of risk aversion is characterized by the slope of his or her indifference curve. Indifference curves show, at any level of expected return and risk, the required risk premium for taking on one additional percentage of standard deviation. More risk-averse investors have steeper indifference curves; that is, they require a greater risk premium for taking on more risk.

5. The optimal position, $y^*$, in the risky asset, is proportional to the risk premium and inversely proportional to the variance and degree of risk aversion:

$$y^* = \frac{E(r_P) - r_f}{.01A\sigma_P^2}$$

   Graphically, this portfolio represents the point at which the indifference curve is tangent to the CAL.

6. A passive investment strategy disregards security analysis, targeting instead the risk-free asset and a broad portfolio of risky assets such as the S&P 500 stock portfolio. If in 2002 investors took the mean historical return and standard deviation of the S&P 500 as proxies for its expected return and standard deviation, then the values of outstanding assets would imply a degree of risk aversion of about $A = 2.6$ for the average investor. This is in line with other studies, which estimate typical risk aversion in the range of 2.0 through 4.0.

## KEY TERMS

| | | |
|---|---|---|
| capital allocation decision | complete portfolio | certainty equivalent |
| asset allocation decision | risk-free asset | passive strategy |
| security selection decision | capital allocation line | capital market line |
| risky asset | reward-to-variability ratio | |

**WEBSITES**

www.aegisfund.com/english/portfolio/portfolio.asp
This site provides Aegis Fund's recent portfolio allocation recommendations.

www.fool.com/workshop/1999/workshop991109.htm
Review the Motley Fool's recommendation for pre-asset allocation action.

swopec.hhs.se/uunewp/abs/uunewp2001_0004.htm
This site examines portfolio allocation over the investor's life cycle.

www.401k-advice-center.com/Empl6.html
This site explores portfolio allocation as a part of the overall financial planning process.

moneycentral.msn.com/investor/calcs/n_riskq/main.asp
Take the MSN quiz, "How much risk can you handle?"

moneycentral.msn.com/content/Investing/Simplestrategies/P38655.asp
Use this site to assess risk tolerance.

www.womeninvesting.net/risk_tolerance.html
Review the risk tolerance discussion from Women Investing 101.

www.evansonassct.com/index.cfm/Page/2.htm
Consider the discussion of active vs. passive investment strategies.

www.fundsupermart.com/main/research/viewHTML.tpl?articleNo=388
Examine index fund strategies.

www.indexfunds.com
Visit this site to learn all about index funds.

**PROBLEMS**   Use these data for Questions 1–10. You manage a risky portfolio with expected rate of return of 18% and standard deviation of 28%. The T-bill rate is 8%.

1. Your client chooses to invest 70% of a portfolio in your fund and 30% in a T-bill money market fund. What is the expected value and standard deviation of the rate of return on his portfolio?

2. Suppose that your risky portfolio includes the following investments in the given proportions:

   | Stock A: | 25% |
   |---|---|
   | Stock B: | 32% |
   | Stock C: | 43% |

Visit us at www.mhhe.com/bkm

What are the investment proportions of your client's overall portfolio, including the position in T-bills?

3. What is the reward-to-variability ratio ($S$) of your risky portfolio? Your client's?

4. Draw the CAL of your portfolio on an expected return–standard deviation diagram. What is the slope of the CAL? Show the position of your client on your fund's CAL.

5. Suppose that your client decides to invest in your portfolio a proportion $y$ of the total investment budget so that the overall portfolio will have an expected rate of return of 16%.

   a. What is the proportion $y$?

   b. What are your client's investment proportions in your three stocks and the T-bill fund?

   c. What is the standard deviation of the rate of return on your client's portfolio?

6. Suppose that your client prefers to invest in your fund a proportion $y$ that maximizes the expected return on the complete portfolio subject to the constraint that the complete portfolio's standard deviation will not exceed 18%.

   a. What is the investment proportion, $y$?

   b. What is the expected rate of return on the complete portfolio?

7. Your client's degree of risk aversion is $A = 3.5$.

   a. What proportion, $y$, of the total investment should be invested in your fund?

   b. What is the expected value and standard deviation of the rate of return on your client's optimized portfolio?

You estimate that a passive portfolio, that is, one invested in a risky portfolio that mimics the S&P 500 stock index, yields an expected rate of return of 13% with a standard deviation of 25%. Continue to assume that $r_f = 8\%$.

8. Draw the CML and your funds' CAL on an expected return–standard deviation diagram.

   a. What is the slope of the CML?

   b. Characterize in one short paragraph the advantage of your fund over the passive fund.

9. Your client ponders whether to switch the 70% that is invested in your fund to the passive portfolio.

   a. Explain to your client the disadvantage of the switch.

   b. Show him the maximum fee you could charge (as a percentage of the investment in your fund, deducted at the end of the year) that would leave him at least as well off investing in your fund as in the passive one. (Hint: The fee will lower the slope of his CAL by reducing the expected return net of the fee.)

10. Consider the client in problem 7 with $A = 3.5$.

    a. If he chose to invest in the passive portfolio, what proportion, $y$, would he select?

    b. Is the fee (percentage of the investment in your fund, deducted at the end of the year) that you can charge to make the client indifferent between your fund and the passive strategy affected by his capital allocation decision (i.e., his choice of $y$)?

11. Look at the data in Table 7.4 on the average risk premium of the S&P 500 over T-bills, and the standard deviation of that risk premium. Suppose that the S&P 500 is your risky portfolio.

    a. If your risk-aversion coefficient is 4 and you believe that the entire 1926–2002 period is representative of future expected performance, what fraction of your portfolio should be allocated to T-bills and what fraction to equity?

   *b.* What if you believe that the 1983–2002 period is representative?

   *c.* What do you conclude upon comparing your answers to (*a*) and (*b*)?

12. What do you think would happen to the expected return on stocks if investors perceived higher volatility in the equity market? Relate your answer to equation 7.5.

13. Consider the following information about a risky portfolio that you manage, and a risk-free asset: $E(r_P) = 11\%$, $\sigma_P = 15\%$, $r_f = 5\%$.

   *a.* Your client wants to invest a proportion of her total investment budget in your risky fund to provide an expected rate of return on her overall or complete portfolio equal to 8%. What proportion should she invest in the risky portfolio, *P*, and what proportion in the risk-free asset?

   *b.* What will be the standard deviation of the rate of return on her portfolio?

   *c.* Another client wants the highest return possible subject to the constraint that you limit his standard deviation to be no more than 12%. Which client is more risk averse?

Suppose that the borrowing rate that your client faces is 9%. Assume that the S&P 500 index has an expected return of 13% and standard deviation of 25%, that $r_f = 5\%$, and that your fund has the parameters given in problem 13.

14. Draw a diagram of your client's CML, accounting for the higher borrowing rate. Superimpose on it two sets of indifference curves, one for a client who will choose to borrow, and one who will invest in both the index fund and a money market fund.

15. What is the range of risk aversion for which a client will neither borrow nor lend, that is, for which $y = 1$?

16. Solve problems 14 and 15 for a client who uses your fund rather than an index fund.

17. What is the largest percentage fee that a client who currently is lending ($y < 1$) will be willing to pay to invest in your fund? What about a client who is borrowing ($y > 1$)?

Use the following graph to answer problems 18 and 19.

18. Which indifference curve represents the greatest level of utility that can be achieved by the investor?

    a. 1
    b. 2
    c. 3
    d. 4

19. Which point designates the optimal portfolio of risky assets?

    a. E
    b. F
    c. G
    d. H

20. Given $100,000 to invest, what is the expected risk premium in dollars of investing in equities versus risk-free T-bills based on the following table?

| Action | Probability | Expected Return |
|---|---|---|
| Invest in equities | .6 | $50,000 |
|  | .4 | −$30,000 |
| Invest in risk-free T-bills | 1.0 | $ 5,000 |

    a. $13,000
    b. $15,000
    c. $18,000
    d. $20,000

21. The change from a straight to a kinked capital allocation line is a result of the:

    a. Reward-to-variability ratio increasing.
    b. Borrowing rate exceeding the lending rate.
    c. Investor's risk tolerance decreasing.
    d. Increase in the portfolio proportion of the risk-free asset.

22. You manage an equity fund with an expected risk premium of 10% and an expected standard deviation of 14%. The rate on Treasury bills is 6%. Your client chooses to invest $60,000 of her portfolio in your equity fund and $40,000 in a T-bill money market fund. What is the expected return and standard deviation of return on your client's portfolio?

| | Expected Return | Standard Deviation of Return |
|---|---|---|
| a. | 8.4% | 8.4% |
| b. | 8.4 | 14.0 |
| c. | 12.0 | 8.4 |
| d. | 12.0 | 14.0 |

23. What is the reward-to-variability ratio for the *equity fund* in problem 22?

    a. .71
    b. 1.00
    c. 1.19
    d. 1.91

Go to **http://www.mhhe.com/business/finance/edumarketinsight** and link to *Industry*. From the pull-down menu, link to an industry of interest to you. From the menu at the left, select the *S&P 500* report under *Industry Financial Highlights*. How has this industry performed relative to the S&P 500 companies over the last year? How many companies from this industry are in the S&P 500? What is their market capitalization relative to the S&P 500 (what is each company's percentage weight of the total S&P 500)?

**E-INVESTMENTS**
**The S&P 500**

The Standard & Poor's 500 index has been the most popular "index" for mutual fund managers to mirror for the last decade. Go to **http://www2.standardandpoors.com**, and link to *Indices, S&P 500*. What sectors of the S&P 500 index have performed best over the last year? What sector dominates the market valuation of the S&P 500 today? What factors might explain the current sector proportions today? What are the pros and cons of a passive S&P 500 index fund investment?

**SOLUTIONS TO CONCEPT CHECKS**

1. Holding 50% of your invested capital in Ready Assets means that your investment proportion in the risky portfolio is reduced from 70% to 50%.

   Your risky portfolio is constructed to invest 54% in E and 46% in B. Thus the proportion of E in your overall portfolio is .5 × 54% = 27%, and the dollar value of your position in E is $300,000 × .27 = $81,000.

2. In the expected return–standard deviation plane all portfolios that are constructed from the same risky and risk-free funds (with various proportions) lie on a line from the risk-free rate through the risky fund. The slope of the CAL (capital allocation line) is the same everywhere; hence the reward-to-variability ratio is the same for all of these portfolios. Formally, if you invest a proportion, $y$, in a risky fund with expected return $E(r_P)$ and standard deviation $\sigma_P$, and the remainder, $1 - y$, in a risk-free asset with a sure rate $r_f$, then the portfolio's expected return and standard deviation are

$$E(r_C) = r_f + y[E(r_P) - r_f]$$
$$\sigma_C = y\sigma_P$$

   and therefore the reward-to-variability ratio of this portfolio is

$$S_C = \frac{E(r_C) - r_f}{\sigma_C} = \frac{y[E(r_P) - r_f]}{y\sigma_P} = \frac{E(r_P) - r_f}{\sigma_P}$$

   which is independent of the proportion $y$.

3. The lending and borrowing rates are unchanged at $r_f = 7\%$, $r_f^B = 9\%$. The standard deviation of the risky portfolio is still 22%, but its expected rate of return shifts from 15% to 17%.

**SOLUTIONS
TO CONCEPT
CHECKS
(Continued)**

The slope of the two-part CAL is

$$\frac{E(r_P) - r_f}{\sigma_P} \text{ for the lending range}$$

$$\frac{E(r_P) - r_f^B}{\sigma_P} \text{ for the borrowing range}$$

Thus in both cases the slope increases: from 8/22 to 10/22 for the lending range, and from 6/22 to 8/22 for the borrowing range.

4. *a.* The parameters are $r_f = 7$, $E(r_P) = 15$, $\sigma_P = 22$. An investor with a degree of risk aversion $A$ will choose a proportion $y$ in the risky portfolio of

$$y = \frac{E(r_P) - r_f}{.01 \times A\sigma_P^2}$$

With the assumed parameters and with $A = 3$ we find that

$$y = \frac{15 - 7}{.01 \times 3 \times 484} = .55$$

When the degree of risk aversion decreases from the original value of 4 to the new value of 3, investment in the risky portfolio increases from 41% to 55%. Accordingly, the expected return and standard deviation of the optimal portfolio increase:

$$E(r_C) = 7 + (.55 \times 8) = 11.4 \text{ (before: 10.28)}$$
$$\sigma_C = .55 \times 22 = 12.1 \text{ (before: 9.02)}$$

*b.* All investors whose degree of risk aversion is such that they would hold the risky portfolio in a proportion equal to 100% or less ($y < 1.00$) are lending rather than borrowing, and so are unaffected by the borrowing rate. The least risk-averse of these investors hold 100% in the risky portfolio ($y = 1$). We can solve for the degree of risk aversion of these "cut off" investors from the parameters of the investment opportunities:

$$y = 1 = \frac{E(r_P) - r_f}{.01 \times A\sigma_P^2} = \frac{8}{4.84A}$$

which implies

$$A = \frac{8}{4.84} = 1.65$$

Any investor who is more risk tolerant (that is, $A < 1.65$) would borrow if the borrowing rate were 7%. For borrowers,

$$y = \frac{E(r_P) - r_f^B}{.01 \times A\sigma_P^2}$$

Suppose, for example, an investor has an $A$ of 1.1. When $r_f = r_f^B = 7\%$, this investor chooses to invest in the risky portfolio:

$$y = \frac{8}{.01 \times 1.1 \times 4.84} = 1.50$$

which means that the investor will borrow an amount equal to 50% of her own investment capital. Raise the borrowing rate, in this case to $r_f^B = 9\%$, and the investor will invest less in the risky asset. In that case:

$$y = \frac{6}{.01 \times 1.1 \times 4.84} = 1.13$$

and "only" 13% of her investment capital will be borrowed. Graphically, the line from $r_f$ to the risky portfolio shows the CAL for lenders. The dashed part *would* be relevant if the borrowing rate equaled the lending rate. When the borrowing rate exceeds the lending rate, the CAL is kinked at the point corresponding to the risky portfolio.

The following figure shows indifference curves of two investors. The steeper indifference curve portrays the more risk-averse investor, who chooses portfolio $C_0$, which involves lending. This investor's choice is unaffected by the borrowing rate. The more risk-tolerant investor is portrayed by the shallower-sloped indifference curves. If the lending rate equaled the borrowing rate, this investor would choose portfolio $C_1$ on the dashed part of the CAL. When the borrowing rate goes up, this investor chooses portfolio $C_2$ (in the borrowing range of the kinked CAL), which involves less borrowing than before. This investor is hurt by the increase in the borrowing rate.

Visit us at www.mhhe.com/bkm

**SOLUTIONS TO CONCEPT CHECKS**
*(Concluded)*

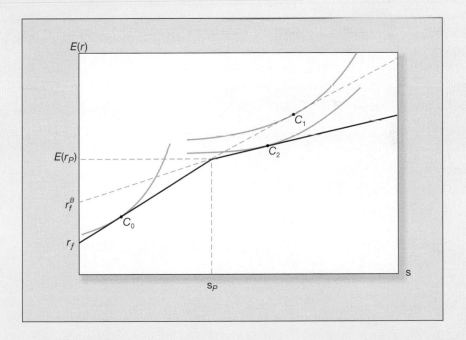

5. If all the investment parameters remain unchanged, the only reason for an investor to decrease the investment proportion in the risky asset is an increase in the degree of risk aversion. If you think that this is unlikely, then you have to reconsider your faith in your assumptions. Perhaps the S&P 500 is not a good proxy for the optimal risky portfolio. Perhaps investors expect a higher real rate on T-bills.

# OPTIMAL RISKY PORTFOLIOS

In Chapter 7 we discussed the capital allocation decision. That decision governs how an investor chooses between risk-free assets and "the" optimal portfolio of risky assets. This chapter explains how to construct that optimal risky portfolio. We begin with a discussion of how diversification can reduce the variability of portfolio returns. After establishing this basic point, we examine efficient diversification strategies at the asset allocation and security selection levels. We start with a simple example of asset allocation that excludes the risk-free asset. To that effect we use two risky mutual funds: a long-term bond fund and a stock fund. With this example we investigate the relationship between investment proportions and the resulting portfolio expected return and standard deviation. We then add a risk-free asset to the menu and determine the optimal asset allocation. We do so by combining the principles of optimal allocation between risky assets and risk-free assets (from Chapter 7) with the risky portfolio construction methodology. Moving from asset allocation to security selection, we first generalize asset allocation to a universe of many risky securities. We show how the best attainable capital allocation line emerges from the efficient portfolio algorithm, so that portfolio optimization can be conducted in two stages, asset allocation and security selection. We examine in two appendixes common fallacies relating the power of diversification to the insurance principle and to investing for the long run.

## 8.1  DIVERSIFICATION AND PORTFOLIO RISK

Suppose your portfolio is composed of only one stock, say, Dell Computer Corporation. What would be the sources of risk to this "portfolio"? You might think of two broad sources of uncertainty. First, there is the risk that comes from conditions in the general economy, such as the business cycle, inflation, interest rates, and exchange rates. None of these macroeconomic factors can be predicted with certainty, and all affect the rate of return on Dell stock. In addition to these macroeconomic factors there are firm-specific influences, such as Dell's success in research and development, and personnel changes. These factors affect Dell without noticeably affecting other firms in the economy.

Now consider a naive **diversification** strategy, in which you include additional securities in your portfolio. For example, place half your funds in ExxonMobil and half in Dell. What should happen to portfolio risk? To the extent that the firm-specific influences on the two stocks differ, diversification should reduce portfolio risk. For example, when oil prices fall, hurting ExxonMobil, computer prices might rise, helping Dell. The two effects are offsetting and stabilize portfolio return.

But why end diversification at only two stocks? If we diversify into many more securities, we continue to spread out our exposure to firm-specific factors, and portfolio volatility should continue to fall. Ultimately, however, even with a large number of stocks we cannot avoid risk altogether, since virtually all securities are affected by the common macroeconomic factors. For example, if all stocks are affected by the business cycle, we cannot avoid exposure to business cycle risk no matter how many stocks we hold.

When all risk is firm-specific, as in Figure 8.1, panel A, diversification can reduce risk to arbitrarily low levels. The reason is that with all risk sources independent, the exposure to any particular source of risk is reduced to a negligible level. The reduction of risk to very low levels in the case of independent risk sources is sometimes called the **insurance principle,** because of the notion that an insurance company depends on the risk reduction achieved through diversification when it writes many policies insuring against many independent sources of risk, each policy being a small part of the company's overall portfolio. (See Appendix B to this chapter for a discussion of the insurance principle.)

When common sources of risk affect all firms, however, even extensive diversification cannot eliminate risk. In Figure 8.1, panel B, portfolio standard deviation falls as the number of securities increases, but it cannot be reduced to zero.[1] The risk that remains even after extensive diversification is called **market risk,** risk that is attributable to marketwide risk sources. Such risk is also called **systematic risk,** or **nondiversifiable risk.** In contrast, the risk that *can* be eliminated by diversification is called **unique risk, firm-specific risk, nonsystematic risk,** or **diversifiable risk.**

This analysis is borne out by empirical studies. Figure 8.2 shows the effect of portfolio diversification, using data on NYSE stocks.[2] The figure shows the average standard deviation of equally weighted portfolios constructed by selecting stocks at random as a function of the number of stocks in the portfolio. On average, portfolio risk does fall with diversification, but the power of diversification to reduce risk is limited by systematic or common sources of risk.

---

[1] The interested reader can find a more rigorous demonstration of these points in Appendix A. That discussion, however, relies on tools developed later in this chapter.

[2] Meir Statman, "How Many Stocks Make a Diversified Portfolio," *Journal of Financial and Quantitative Analysis* 22 (September 1987).

**Figure 8.1
Portfolio risk as
a function of the
number of stocks
in the portfolio**

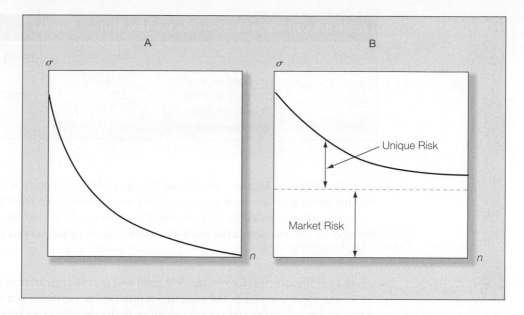

**Figure 8.2    Portfolio diversification. The average standard deviation of returns of portfolios
composed of only one stock was 49.2%. The average portfolio risk fell rapidly as the
number of stocks included in the portfolio increased. In the limit, portfolio risk could be
reduced to only 19.2%.**

Source: Meir Statman, "How Many Stocks Make a Diversified Portfolio," *Journal of Financial and Quantitative Analysis* 22 (September 1987).

# 8.2   PORTFOLIOS OF TWO RISKY ASSETS

In the last section we considered naive diversification using equally weighted portfolios of
several securities. It is time now to study *efficient* diversification, whereby we construct
risky portfolios to provide the lowest possible risk for any given level of expected return.

Portfolios of two risky assets are relatively easy to analyze, and they illustrate the principles and considerations that apply to portfolios of many assets. We will consider a portfolio comprised of two mutual funds, a bond portfolio specializing in long-term debt

| Table 8.1 | Descriptive Statistics for Two Mutual Funds | | |
|---|---|---|---|
| | | **Debt** | **Equity** |
| Expected return, $E(r)$ | | 8% | 13% |
| Standard deviation, $\sigma$ | | 12% | 20% |
| Covariance, $Cov(r_D, r_E)$ | | 72 | |
| Correlation coefficient, $\rho_{DE}$ | | .30 | |

securities, denoted $D$, and a stock fund that specializes in equity securities, $E$. Table 8.1 lists the parameters describing the rate-of-return distribution of these funds.

A proportion denoted by $w_D$ is invested in the bond fund, and the remainder, $1 - w_D$, denoted $w_E$, is invested in the stock fund. The rate of return on this portfolio, $r_p$, will be

$$r_p = w_D r_D + w_E r_E$$

where $r_D$ is the rate of return on the debt fund and $r_E$ is the rate of return on the equity fund.

As shown in Chapter 6, the expected return on the portfolio is a weighted average of expected returns on the component securities with portfolio proportions as weights:

$$E(r_p) = w_D E(r_D) + w_E E(r_E) \tag{8.1}$$

The variance of the two-asset portfolio (rule 5 of Chapter 6) is

$$\sigma_p^2 = w_D^2 \sigma_D^2 + w_E^2 \sigma_E^2 + 2w_D w_E Cov(r_D, r_E) \tag{8.2}$$

Our first observation is that the variance of the portfolio, unlike the expected return, is *not* a weighted average of the individual asset variances. To understand the formula for the portfolio variance more clearly, recall that the covariance of a variable with itself is the variance of that variable; that is

$$Cov(r_D, r_D) = \sum_{\text{scenarios}} \Pr(\text{scenario})[r_D - E(r_D)][r_D - E(r_D)]$$
$$= \sum_{\text{scenarios}} \Pr(\text{scenario})[r_D - E(r_D)]^2 \tag{8.3}$$
$$= \sigma_D^2$$

Therefore, another way to write the variance of the portfolio is as follows:

$$\sigma_p^2 = w_D w_D Cov(r_D, r_D) + w_E w_E Cov(r_E, r_E) + 2w_D w_E Cov(r_D, r_E) \tag{8.4}$$

In words, the variance of the portfolio is a weighted sum of covariances, and each weight is the product of the portfolio proportions of the pair of assets in the covariance term.

Table 8.2 shows how portfolio variance can be calculated from a spreadsheet. Panel A of the table shows the *bordered* covariance matrix of the returns of the two mutual funds. The bordered matrix is the covariance matrix with the portfolio weights for each fund placed on the borders, that is along the first row and column. To find portfolio variance, multiply each element in the covariance matrix by the pair of portfolio weights in its row and column borders. Add up the resultant terms, and you have the formula for portfolio variance given in equation 8.4.

We perform these calculations in panel B, which is the *border-multiplied* covariance matrix: Each covariance has been multiplied by the weights from the row and the column in the borders. The bottom line of panel B confirms that the sum of all the terms in this matrix (which we obtain by adding up the column sums) is indeed the portfolio variance in equation 8.4.

## Table 8.2   Computation of Portfolio Variance from the Covariance Matrix

**A. Bordered Covariance Matrix**

| Portfolio Weights | $w_D$ | $w_E$ |
|---|---|---|
| $w_D$ | $\text{Cov}(r_D, r_D)$ | $\text{Cov}(r_D, r_E)$ |
| $w_E$ | $\text{Cov}(r_E, r_D)$ | $\text{Cov}(r_E, r_E)$ |

**B. Border-multiplied Covariance Matrix**

| Portfolio Weights | $w_D$ | $w_E$ |
|---|---|---|
| $w_D$ | $w_D w_D \text{Cov}(r_D, r_D)$ | $w_D w_E \text{Cov}(r_D, r_E)$ |
| $w_E$ | $w_E w_D \text{Cov}(r_E, r_D)$ | $w_D w_D \text{Cov}(r_E, r_E)$ |
| $w_D + w_E = 1$ | $w_D w_D \text{Cov}(r_D, r_D) + w_E w_D \text{Cov}(r_E, r_D)$ | $w_D w_E \text{Cov}(r_D, r_E) + w_E w_E \text{Cov}(r_E, r_E)$ |
| Portfolio variance | $w_D w_D \text{Cov}(r_D, r_D) + w_E w_D \text{Cov}(r_E, r_D) + w_D w_E \text{Cov}(r_D, r_E) + w_E w_E \text{Cov}(r_E, r_E)$ | |

This procedure works because the covariance matrix is symmetric around the diagonal, that is, $\text{Cov}(r_D, r_E) = \text{Cov}(r_E, r_D)$. Thus each covariance term appears twice.

This technique for computing the variance from the border-multiplied covariance matrix is general; it applies to any number of assets and is easily implemented on a spreadsheet. Concept Check 1 asks you to try the rule for a three-asset portfolio. Use this problem to verify that you are comfortable with this concept.

**CONCEPT CHECK☞ QUESTION 1**

*a.* **First confirm for yourself that this simple rule for computing the variance of a two-asset portfolio from the bordered covariance matrix is consistent with equation 8.2.**

*b.* **Now consider a portfolio of three funds, X, Y, Z, with weights $w_X$, $w_Y$, and $w_Z$. Show that the portfolio variance is**

$$w_X^2 \sigma_X^2 + w_Y^2 \sigma_Y^2 + w_Z^2 \sigma_Z^2 + 2w_X w_Y \text{Cov}(r_X, r_Y) + 2w_X w_Z \text{Cov}(r_X, r_Z) + 2w_Y w_Z \text{Cov}(r_Y, r_Z)$$

Equation 8.2 reveals that variance is reduced if the covariance term is negative. It is important to recognize that even if the covariance term is positive, the portfolio standard deviation *still* is less than the weighted average of the individual security standard deviations, unless the two securities are perfectly positively correlated.

To see this, recall from Chapter 6, equation 6.5, that the covariance can be computed from the correlation coefficient, $\rho_{DE}$, as

$$\text{Cov}(r_D, r_E) = \rho_{DE} \sigma_D \sigma_E$$

Therefore,

$$\sigma_p^2 = w_D^2 \sigma_D^2 + w_E^2 \sigma_E^2 + 2w_D w_E \sigma_D \sigma_E \rho_{DE} \tag{8.5}$$

Because the covariance is higher, portfolio variance is higher when $\rho_{DE}$ is higher. In the case of perfect positive correlation, $\rho_{DE} = 1$, the right-hand side of equation 8.5 is a perfect square and simplifies to

$$\sigma_p^2 = (w_D \sigma_D + w_E \sigma_E)^2$$

or

$$\sigma_p = w_D \sigma_D + w_E \sigma_E$$

# FINDING FUNDS THAT ZIG WHEN THE BLUE CHIPS ZAG

Investors hungry for lower risk are hearing some surprising recommendations from financial advisers:

- mutual funds investing in less-developed nations that many Americans can't immediately locate on a globe.
- funds specializing in small European companies with unfamiliar names.
- funds investing in commodities.

All of these investments are risky by themselves, advisers readily admit. But they also tend to zig when big U.S. stocks zag. And that means that such fare, when added to a portfolio heavy in U.S. blue-chip stocks, actually may damp the portfolio's ups and downs.

Combining types of investments that don't move in lock step "is one of the very few instances in which there is a free lunch—you get something for nothing," says Gary Greenbaum, president of investment counselors Greenbaum & Associates in Oradell, N.J. The right combination of assets can trim the volatility of an investment portfolio, he explains, without reducing the expected return over time.

Getting more variety in one's holdings can be surprisingly tricky. For instance, investors who have shifted dollars into a diversified international-stock fund may not have ventured as far afield as they think, says an article in the most recent issue of *Morningstar Mutual Funds*. Those funds typically load up on European blue-chip stocks that often behave similarly and respond to the same world-wide economic conditions as do U.S. corporate giants.

Many investment professionals use a statistical measure known as a "correlation coefficient" to identify categories of securities that tend to zig when others zag. A figure approaching the maximum 1.0 indicates that two assets have consistently moved in the same direction. A correlation coefficient approaching the minimum, negative 1.0, indicates that the assets have consistently moved in the opposite direction. Assets with a zero correlation have moved independently.

Funds invested in Japan, developing nations, small European companies, and gold stocks have been among those moving opposite to the Vanguard Index 500 over the past several years.

Source: Karen Damato, "Finding Funds That Zig When Blue Chips Zag," *The Wall Street Journal*, June 17, 1997. Excerpted by permission of *The Wall Street Journal*, © 1997 Dow Jones & Company, Inc. All Rights Reserved Worldwide.

---

Therefore, the standard deviation of the portfolio with perfect positive correlation is just the weighted average of the component standard deviations. In all other cases, the correlation coefficient is less than 1, making the portfolio standard deviation *less* than the weighted average of the component standard deviations.

A hedge asset has *negative* correlation with the other assets in the portfolio. Equation 8.5 shows that such assets will be particularly effective in reducing total risk. Moreover, equation 8.1 shows that expected return is unaffected by correlation between returns. Therefore, other things equal, we will always prefer to add to our portfolios assets with low or, even better, negative correlation with our existing position. The above box from *The Wall Street Journal* makes this point when it advises you to find "funds that zig when blue chip [stocks] zag."

Because the portfolio's expected return is the weighted average of its component expected returns, whereas its standard deviation is less than the weighted average of the component standard deviations, *portfolios of less than perfectly correlated assets always offer better risk–return opportunities than the individual component securities on their own*. The lower the correlation between the assets, the greater the gain in efficiency.

How low can portfolio standard deviation be? The lowest possible value of the correlation coefficient is $-1$, representing perfect negative correlation. In this case, equation 8.5 simplifies to

$$\sigma_p^2 = (w_D\sigma_D - w_E\sigma_E)^2$$

and the portfolio standard deviation is

$$\sigma_p = \text{Absolute value } (w_D\sigma_D - w_E\sigma_E)$$

When $\rho = -1$, a perfectly hedged position can be obtained by choosing the portfolio proportions to solve

$$w_D\sigma_D - w_E\sigma_E = 0$$

The solution to this equation is

$$w_D = \frac{\sigma_E}{\sigma_D + \sigma_E}$$

$$w_E = \frac{\sigma_D}{\sigma_D + \sigma_E} = 1 - w_D$$

These weights drive the standard deviation of the portfolio to zero.[3]

**EXAMPLE 8.1**

## Portfolio Risk and Return

Let us apply this analysis to the data of the bond and stock funds as presented in Table 8.1. Using these data, the formulas for the expected return, variance, and standard deviation of the portfolio are

$$E(r_p) = 8w_D + 13w_E$$
$$\sigma_p^2 = 12^2w_D^2 + 20^2w_E^2 + 2 \times 12 \times 20 \times .3 \times w_Dw_E$$
$$= 144w_D^2 + 400w_E^2 + 144w_Dw_E$$
$$\sigma_p = \sqrt{\sigma_p^2}$$

We can experiment with different portfolio proportions to observe the effect on portfolio expected return and variance. Suppose we change the proportion invested in bonds. The effect on expected return is tabulated in Table 8.3 and plotted in Figure 8.3. When the proportion invested in debt varies from zero to 1 (so that the proportion in equity varies from 1 to zero), the portfolio expected return goes from 13% (the stock fund's expected return) to 8% (the expected return on bonds).

What happens when $w_D > 1$ and $w_E < 0$? In this case portfolio strategy would be to sell the equity fund short and invest the proceeds of the short sale in the debt fund. This will decrease the expected return of the portfolio. For example, when $w_D = 2$ and $w_E = -1$, expected portfolio return falls to $2 \times 8 + (-1) \times 13 = 3\%$. At this point the value of the bond fund in the portfolio is twice the net worth of the account. This extreme position is financed in part by short selling stocks equal in value to the portfolio's net worth.

The reverse happens when $w_D < 0$ and $w_E > 1$. This strategy calls for selling the bond fund short and using the proceeds to finance additional purchases of the equity fund.

Of course, varying investment proportions also has an effect on portfolio standard deviation. Table 8.3 presents portfolio standard deviations for different portfolio weights calculated from equation 8.5 using the assumed value of the correlation coefficient, .30, as well as other values of $\rho$. Figure 8.4 shows the relationship between standard deviation and portfolio weights. Look first at the solid curve for $\rho_{DE} = .30$. The graph shows that as the portfolio weight in the equity fund increases from zero to 1, portfolio standard deviation first falls with the initial diversification from bonds into stocks, but then rises again as the

---

[3] It is possible to drive portfolio variance to zero with perfectly positively correlated assets as well, but this would require short sales.

**Table 8.3   Expected Return and Standard Deviation with Various Correlation Coefficients**

| $w_D$ | $w_E$ | $E(r_P)$ | Portfolio Standard Deviation for Given Correlation | | | |
|---|---|---|---|---|---|---|
| | | | $\rho = -1$ | $\rho = 0$ | $\rho = .30$ | $\rho = 1$ |
| 0.00 | 1.00 | 13.00 | 20.00 | 20.00 | 20.00 | 20.00 |
| 0.10 | 0.90 | 12.50 | 16.80 | 18.04 | 18.40 | 19.20 |
| 0.20 | 0.80 | 12.00 | 13.60 | 16.18 | 16.88 | 18.40 |
| 0.30 | 0.70 | 11.50 | 10.40 | 14.46 | 15.47 | 17.60 |
| 0.40 | 0.60 | 11.00 | 7.20 | 12.92 | 14.20 | 16.80 |
| 0.50 | 0.50 | 10.50 | 4.00 | 11.66 | 13.11 | 16.00 |
| 0.60 | 0.40 | 10.00 | 0.80 | 10.76 | 12.26 | 15.20 |
| 0.70 | 0.30 | 9.50 | 2.40 | 10.32 | 11.70 | 14.40 |
| 0.80 | 0.20 | 9.00 | 5.60 | 10.40 | 11.45 | 13.60 |
| 0.90 | 0.10 | 8.50 | 8.80 | 10.98 | 11.56 | 12.80 |
| 1.00 | 0.00 | 8.00 | 12.00 | 12.00 | 12.00 | 12.00 |

| | | | Minimum Variance Portfolio | | | |
|---|---|---|---|---|---|---|
| | $w_D$ | | 0.6250 | 0.7353 | 0.8200 | — |
| | $w_E$ | | 0.3750 | 0.2647 | 0.1800 | — |
| | $E(r_P)$ | | 9.8750 | 9.3235 | 8.9000 | — |
| | $\sigma_P$ | | 0.0000 | 10.2899 | 11.4473 | — |

**Figure 8.3
Portfolio expected
return as a
function of
investment
proportions**

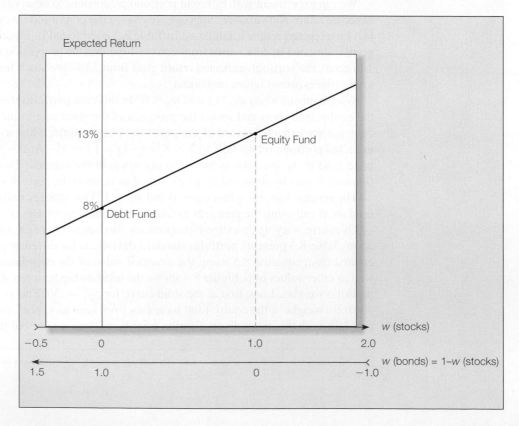

**Figure 8.4
Portfolio standard
deviation as a
function of
investment
proportions**

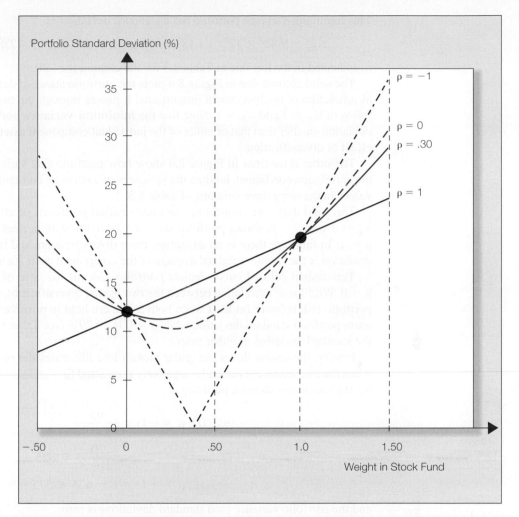

portfolio becomes heavily concentrated in stocks, and again is undiversified. This pattern will generally hold as long as the correlation coefficient between the funds is not too high. For a pair of assets with a large positive correlation of returns, the portfolio standard deviation will increase monotonically from the low-risk asset to the high-risk asset. Even in this case, however, there is a positive (if small) value of diversification.

What is the minimum level to which portfolio standard deviation can be held? For the parameter values stipulated in Table 8.1, the portfolio weights that solve this minimization problem turn out to be:[4]

$$w_{Min}(D) = .82$$
$$w_{Min}(E) = 1 - .82 = .18$$

---

[4] This solution uses the minimization techniques of calculus. Write out the expression for portfolio variance from equation 8.2, substitute $1 - w_D$ for $w_E$, differentiate the result with respect to $w_D$, set the derivative equal to zero, and solve for $w_D$ to obtain

$$w_{Min}(D) = \frac{\sigma_E^2 - Cov(r_D, r_E)}{\sigma_D^2 + \sigma_E^2 - 2Cov(r_D, r_E)}$$

Alternatively, with a computer spreadsheet, you can obtain an accurate solution by generating a fine grid for Table 8.3 and observing the portfolio weights resulting in the lowest standard deviation.

This minimum-variance portfolio has a standard deviation of

$$\sigma_{\text{Min}} = [(.82^2 \times 12^2) + (.18^2 \times 20^2) + (2 \times .82 \times .18 \times 72)]^{1/2} = 11.45\%$$

as indicated in the last line of Table 8.3 for the column $\rho = .30$.

The solid colored line in Figure 8.4 plots the portfolio standard deviation when $\rho = .30$ as a function of the investment proportions. It passes through the two undiversified portfolios of $w_D = 1$ and $w_E = 1$. Note that the **minimum-variance portfolio** has a standard deviation smaller than that of either of the individual component assets. This illustrates the effect of diversification.

The other three lines in Figure 8.4 show how portfolio risk varies for other values of the correlation coefficient, holding the variances of each asset constant. These lines plot the values in the other three columns of Table 8.3.

The solid dark line connecting the undiversified portfolios of all bonds or all stocks, $w_D = 1$ or $w_E = 1$, shows portfolio standard deviation with perfect positive correlation, $\rho = 1$. In this case there is no advantage from diversification, and the portfolio standard deviation is the simple weighted average of the component asset standard deviations.

The dashed colored curve depicts portfolio risk for the case of uncorrelated assets, $\rho = 0$. With lower correlation between the two assets, diversification is more effective and portfolio risk is lower (at least when both assets are held in positive amounts). The minimum portfolio standard deviation when $\rho = 0$ is 10.29% (see Table 8.3), again lower than the standard deviation of either asset.

Finally, the upside-down triangular broken line illustrates the perfect hedge potential when the two assets are perfectly negatively correlated ($\rho = -1$). In this case the solution for the minimum-variance portfolio is

$$w_{\text{Min}}(D; \rho = -1) = \frac{\sigma_E}{\sigma_D + \sigma_E}$$

$$= \frac{20}{12 + 20} = .625 \tag{8.6}$$

$$w_{\text{Min}}(E; \rho = -1) = 1 - .625 = .375$$

and the portfolio variance (and standard deviation) is zero.

We can combine Figures 8.3 and 8.4 to demonstrate the relationship between portfolio risk (standard deviation) and expected return—given the parameters of the available assets. This is done in Figure 8.5. For any pair of investment proportions, $w_D$, $w_E$, we read the expected return from Figure 8.3 and the standard deviation from Figure 8.4. The resulting pairs of expected return and standard deviation are tabulated in Table 8.3 and plotted in Figure 8.5.

The solid colored curve in Figure 8.5 shows the **portfolio opportunity set** for $\rho = .30$. We call it the portfolio opportunity set because it shows all combinations of portfolio expected return and standard deviation that can be constructed from the two available assets. The other lines show the portfolio opportunity set for other values of the correlation coefficient. The solid black line connecting the two funds shows that there is no benefit from diversification when the correlation between the two is positive ($\rho = 1$). The opportunity set is not "pushed" to the northwest. The dashed colored line demonstrates the greater benefit from diversification when the correlation coefficient is lower than .30.

Finally, for $\rho = -1$, the portfolio opportunity set is linear, but now it offers a perfect hedging opportunity and the maximum advantage from diversification.

To summarize, although the expected return of any portfolio is simply the weighted average of the asset expected returns, this is not true of the standard deviation. Potential benefits from diversification arise when correlation is less than perfectly positive. The

**Figure 8.5
Portfolio expected
return as a
function of
standard
deviation**

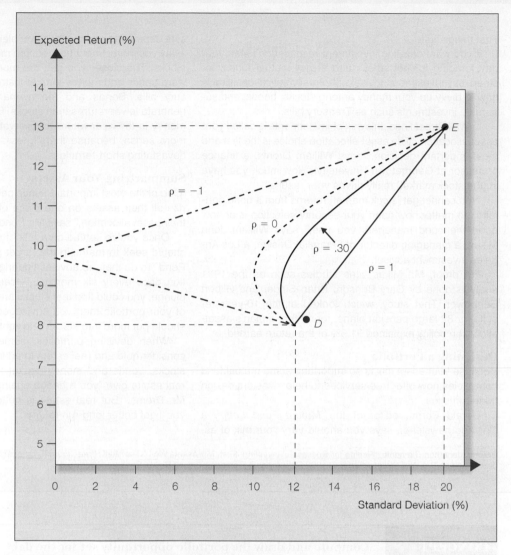

lower the correlation, the greater the potential benefit from diversification. In the extreme case of perfect negative correlation, we have a perfect hedging opportunity and can construct a zero-variance portfolio.

Suppose now an investor wishes to select the optimal portfolio from the opportunity set. The best portfolio will depend on risk aversion. Portfolios to the northeast in Figure 8.5 provide higher rates of return but impose greater risk. The best trade-off among these choices is a matter of personal preference. Investors with greater risk aversion will prefer portfolios to the southwest, with lower expected return but lower risk.[5]

---

[5] Given a level of risk aversion, one can determine the portfolio that provides the highest level of utility. Recall from Chapter 7 that we were able to describe the utility provided by a portfolio as a function of its expected return, $E(r_p)$, and its variance, $\sigma_p^2$, according to the relationship $U = E(r_p) - .005A\sigma_p^2$. The portfolio mean and variance are determined by the portfolio weights in the two funds, $w_E$ and $w_D$, according to equations 8.1 and 8.2. Using those equations and some calculus, we find the optimal investment proportions in the two funds:

$$w_D = \frac{E(r_D) - E(r_E) + .01A(\sigma_E^2 - \sigma_D \sigma_E \rho_{DE})}{.01A(\sigma_D^2 + \sigma_E^2 - 2\sigma_D \sigma_E \rho_{DE})}$$

$$w_E = 1 - w_D$$

First things first.

If you want dazzling investment results, don't start your day foraging for hot stocks and stellar mutual funds. Instead, say investment advisers, the really critical decision is how to divvy up your money among stocks, bonds, and supersafe investments such as Treasury bills.

In Wall Street lingo, this mix of investments is called your asset allocation. "The asset-allocation choice is the first and most important decision," says William Droms, a finance professor at Georgetown University. "How much you have in [the stock market] really drives your results."

"You cannot get [stock market] returns from a bond portfolio, no matter how good your security selection is or how good the bond managers you use," says William John Mikus, a managing director of Financial Design, a Los Angeles investment adviser.

For proof, Mr. Mikus cites studies such as the 1991 analysis done by Gary Brinson, Brian Singer and Gilbert Beebower. That study, which looked at the 10-year results for 82 large pension plans, found that a plan's asset-allocation policy explained 91.5% of the return earned.

### Designing a Portfolio

Because your asset mix is so important, some mutual fund companies now offer free services to help investors design their portfolios.

Gerald Perritt, editor of the *Mutual Fund Letter,* a Chicago newsletter, says you should vary your mix of assets depending on how long you plan to invest. The further away your investment horizon, the more you should have in stocks. The closer you get, the more you should lean toward bonds and money-market instruments, such as Treasury bills. Bonds and money-market instruments may generate lower returns than stocks. But for those who need money in the near future, conservative investments make more sense, because there's less chance of suffering a devastating short-term loss.

### Summarizing Your Assets

"One of the most important things people can do is summarize all their assets on one piece of paper and figure out their asset allocation," says Mr. Pond.

Once you've settled on a mix of stocks and bonds, you should seek to maintain the target percentages, says Mr. Pond. To do that, he advises figuring out your asset allocation once every six months. Because of a stock-market plunge, you could find that stocks are now a far smaller part of your portfolio than you envisaged. At such a time, you should put more into stocks and lighten up on bonds.

When devising portfolios, some investment advisers consider gold and real estate in addition to the usual trio of stocks, bonds and money-market instruments. Gold and real estate give "you a hedge against hyperinflation," says Mr. Droms. "But real estate is better than gold, because you'll get better long-run returns."

| CONCEPT CHECK☞ QUESTION 2 | Compute and draw the portfolio opportunity set for the debt and equity funds when the correlation coefficient between them is $\rho = .25$. |
|---|---|

## 8.3 ASSET ALLOCATION WITH STOCKS, BONDS, AND BILLS

In the previous chapter we examined the simplest asset allocation decision, that involving the choice of how much of the portfolio to leave in risk-free money market securities versus in a risky portfolio. Now we have taken a further step, specifying the risky portfolio as comprised of a stock and bond fund. We still need to show how investors can decide on the proportion of their risky portfolios to allocate to the stock versus the bond market. This, too, is an asset allocation decision. As the box above emphasizes, most investment professionals recognize that "the really critical decision is how to divvy up your money among stocks, bonds and supersafe investments such as Treasury bills."

In the last section, we derived the properties of portfolios formed by mixing two risky assets. Given this background, we now reintroduce the choice of the third, risk-free,

**Figure 8.6**
**The opportunity set of the debt and equity funds and two feasible CALs**

portfolio. This will allow us to complete the basic problem of asset allocation across the three key asset classes: stocks, bonds, and risk-free money market securities. Once you understand this case, it will be easy to see how portfolios of many risky securities might best be constructed.

## The Optimal Risky Portfolio with Two Risky Assets and a Risk-Free Asset

What if our risky assets are still confined to the bond and stock funds, but now we can also invest in risk-free T-bills yielding 5%? We start with a graphical solution. Figure 8.6 shows the opportunity set based on the properties of the bond and stock funds, using the data from Table 8.1.

Two possible capital allocation lines (CALs) are drawn from the risk-free rate ($r_f = 5\%$) to two feasible portfolios. The first possible CAL is drawn through the minimum-variance portfolio $A$, which is invested 82% in bonds and 18% in stocks (Table 8.3, bottom panel). Portfolio $A$'s expected return is 8.90%, and its standard deviation is 11.45%. With a T-bill rate of 5%, the **reward-to-variability ratio**, which is the slope of the CAL combining T-bills and the minimum-variance portfolio, is

$$S_A = \frac{E(r_A) - r_f}{\sigma_A} = \frac{8.9 - 5}{11.45} = .34$$

Now consider the CAL that uses portfolio B instead of A. Portfolio B invests 70% in bonds and 30% in stocks. Its expected return is 9.5% (a risk premium of 4.5%), and its standard deviation is 11.70%. Thus the reward-to-variability ratio on the CAL that is supported by Portfolio B is

$$S_B = \frac{9.5 - 5}{11.7} = .38$$

which is higher than the reward-to-variability ratio of the CAL that we obtained using the minimum-variance portfolio and T-bills. Thus Portfolio B dominates A.

But why stop at Portfolio B? We can continue to ratchet the CAL upward until it ultimately reaches the point of tangency with the investment opportunity set. This must yield the CAL with the highest feasible reward-to-variability ratio. Therefore, the tangency portfolio, labeled P in Figure 8.7, is the optimal risky portfolio to mix with T-bills. We can read the expected return and standard deviation of Portfolio P from the graph in Figure 8.7.

$$E(r_P) = 11\%$$
$$\sigma_P = 14.2\%$$

**Figure 8.7
The opportunity set of the debt and equity funds with the optimal CAL and the optimal risky portfolio**

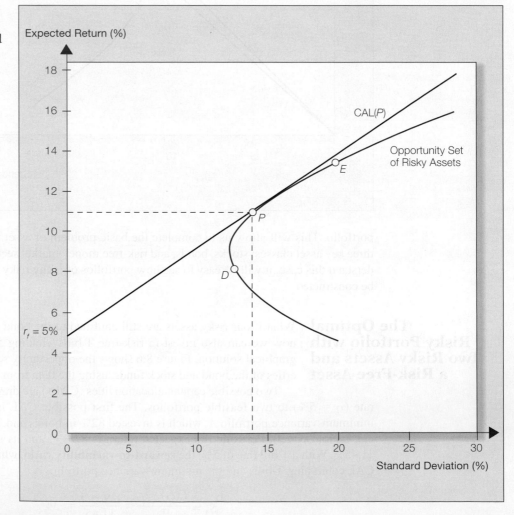

In practice, when we try to construct optimal risky portfolios from more than two risky assets we need to rely on a spreadsheet or another computer program. The spreadsheet we present later in the chapter can be used to construct efficient portfolios of many assets. To start, however, we will demonstrate the solution of the portfolio construction problem with only two risky assets (in our example, long-term debt and equity) and a risk-free asset. In this case, we can derive an explicit formula for the weights of each asset in the optimal portfolio. This will make it easy to illustrate some of the general issues pertaining to portfolio optimization.

The objective is to find the weights $w_D$ and $w_E$ that result in the highest slope of the CAL (i.e., the weights that result in the risky portfolio with the highest reward-to-variability ratio). Therefore, the objective is to maximize the slope of the CAL for any possible portfolio, $p$. Thus our *objective function* is the slope that we have called $S_p$:

$$S_p = \frac{E(r_p) - r_f}{\sigma_p}$$

For the portfolio with two risky assets, the expected return and standard deviation of Portfolio $p$ are

$$E(r_p) = w_D E(r_D) + w_E E(r_E)$$
$$= 8w_D + 13w_E$$
$$\sigma_p = [w_D^2 \sigma_D^2 + w_E^2 \sigma_E^2 + 2w_D w_E \text{Cov}(r_D, r_E)]^{1/2}$$
$$= [144w_D^2 + 400w_E^2 + (2 \times 72w_D w_E)]^{1/2}$$

When we maximize the objective function, $S_p$, we have to satisfy the constraint that the portfolio weights sum to 1.0 (100%), that is, $w_D + w_E = 1$. Therefore, we solve a mathematical problem formally written as

$$\text{Max}_{w_i} S_p = \frac{E(r_p) - r_f}{\sigma_p}$$

subject to $\Sigma w_i = 1$. This is a standard problem in optimization.

In the case of two risky assets, the solution for the weights of the **optimal risky portfolio**, $P$, can be shown to be as follows:[6]

$$w_D = \frac{[E(r_D) - r_f]\sigma_E^2 - [E(r_E) - r_f]\text{Cov}(r_D, r_E)}{[E(r_D) - r_f]\sigma_E^2 + [E(r_E) - r_f]\sigma_D^2 - [E(r_D) - r_f + E(r_E) - r_f]\text{Cov}(r_D, r_E)} \quad (8.7)$$
$$w_E = 1 - w_D$$

---

**EXAMPLE 8.2** **Optimal Risky Portfolio**

Using our data, the solution for the optimal risky portfolio is

$$w_D = \frac{(8 - 5)400 - (13 - 5)72}{(8 - 5)400 + (13 - 5)144 - (8 - 5 + 13 - 5)72} = .40$$
$$w_E = 1 - .40 = .60$$

---

[6] The solution procedure for two risky assets is as follows. Substitute for $E(r_P)$ from equation 8.1 and for $\sigma_P$ from equation 8.5. Substitute $1 - w_D$ for $w_E$. Differentiate the resulting expression for $S_p$ with respect to $w_D$, set the derivative equal to zero, and solve for $w_D$.

The expected return and standard deviation of this optimal risky portfolio are

$$E(r_P) = (.4 \times 8) + (.6 \times 13) = 11\%$$
$$\sigma_P = [(.4^2 \times 144) + (.6^2 \times 400) + (2 \times .4 \times .6 \times 72)]^{1/2} = 14.2\%$$

The CAL of this optimal portfolio has a slope of

$$S_P = \frac{11 - 5}{14.2} = .42$$

which is the reward-to-variability ratio of Portfolio $P$. Notice that this slope exceeds the slope of any of the other feasible portfolios that we have considered, as it must if it is to be the slope of the best feasible CAL.

In Chapter 7 we found the optimal *complete* portfolio given an optimal *risky* portfolio and the CAL generated by a combination of this portfolio and T-bills. Now that we have constructed the optimal risky portfolio, $P$, we can use the individual investor's degree of risk aversion, $A$, to calculate the optimal proportion of the complete portfolio to invest in the risky component.

## EXAMPLE 8.3     Optimal Complete Portfolio

An investor with a coefficient of risk aversion $A = 4$ would take a position in Portfolio $P$ of [7]

$$y = \frac{E(r_P) - r_f}{.01 \times A\sigma_P^2} = \frac{11 - 5}{.01 \times 4 \times 14.2^2} = .7439 \tag{8.8}$$

Thus the investor will invest 74.39% of his or her wealth in Portfolio $P$ and 25.61% in T-bills. Portfolio $P$ consists of 40% in bonds, so the percentage of wealth in bonds will be $yw_D = .4 \times .7439 = .2976$, or 29.76%. Similarly, the investment in stocks will be $yw_E = .6 \times .7439 = .4463$, or 44.63%. The graphical solution of this asset allocation problem is presented in Figures 8.8 and 8.9.

Once we have reached this point, generalizing to the case of many risky assets is straightforward. Before we move on, let us briefly summarize the steps we followed to arrive at the complete portfolio.

1. Specify the return characteristics of all securities (expected returns, variances, covariances).
2. Establish the risky portfolio:
   a. Calculate the optimal risky portfolio, $P$ (equation 8.7).
   b. Calculate the properties of Portfolio $P$ using the weights determined in step ($a$) and equations 8.1 and 8.2.

---

[7] As noted earlier, the .01 that appears in the denominator is a scale factor that arises because we measure returns as percentages rather than decimals. If we were to measure returns as decimals (e.g., .07 rather than 7%), we would not use the .01 in the denominator. Notice that switching to decimals would reduce the scale of the numerator by a multiple of .01 and the denominator by .01$^2$.

**Figure 8.8
Determination
of the optimal
overall portfolio**

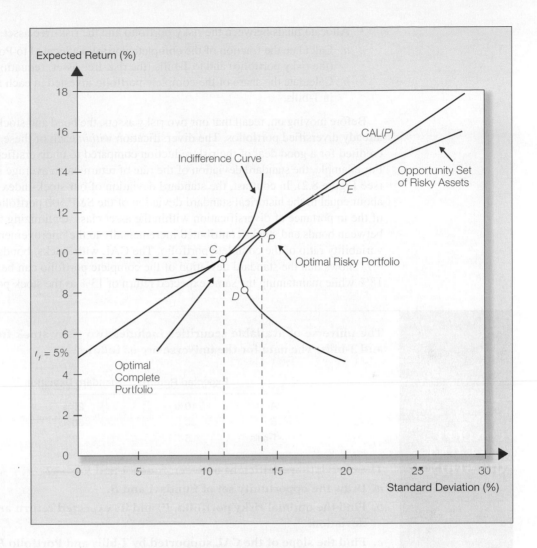

**Figure 8.9
The proportions
of the optimal
overall portfolio**

3. Allocate funds between the risky portfolio and the risk-free asset:
   a. Calculate the fraction of the complete portfolio allocated to Portfolio $P$ (the risky portfolio) and to T-bills (the risk-free asset) (equation 8.8).
   b. Calculate the share of the complete portfolio invested in each asset and in T-bills.

Before moving on, recall that our two risky assets, the bond and stock mutual funds, are already diversified portfolios. The diversification *within* each of these portfolios must be credited for a good deal of the risk reduction compared to undiversified single securities. For example, the standard deviation of the rate of return on an average stock is about 50% (see Figure 8.2). In contrast, the standard deviation of our stock-index fund is only 20%, about equal to the historical standard deviation of the S&P 500 portfolio. This is evidence of the importance of diversification within the asset class. Optimizing the asset allocation between bonds and stocks contributed incrementally to the improvement in the reward-to-variability ratio of the complete portfolio. The CAL with stocks, bonds, and bills (Figure 8.7) shows that the standard deviation of the complete portfolio can be further reduced to 18% while maintaining the same expected return of 13% as the stock portfolio.

---

**CONCEPT CHECK ☞ QUESTION 3**

The universe of available securities includes two risky stock funds, $A$ and $B$, and T-bills. The data for the universe are as follows:

|         | Expected Return | Standard Deviation |
|---------|-----------------|--------------------|
| $A$     | 10%             | 20%                |
| $B$     | 30              | 60                 |
| T-bills | 5               | 0                  |

The correlation coefficient between funds $A$ and $B$ is $-.2$.

a. Draw the opportunity set of Funds $A$ and $B$.

b. Find the optimal risky portfolio, $P$, and its expected return and standard deviation.

c. Find the slope of the CAL supported by T-bills and Portfolio $P$.

d. How much will an investor with $A = 5$ invest in Funds $A$ and $B$ and in T-bills?

---

# 8.4    THE MARKOWITZ PORTFOLIO SELECTION MODEL

**Security Selection**    We can generalize the portfolio construction problem to the case of many risky securities and a risk-free asset. As in the two risky assets example, the problem has three parts. First, we identify the risk–return combinations available from the set of risky assets. Next, we identify the optimal portfolio of risky assets by finding the portfolio weights that result in the steepest CAL. Finally, we choose an appropriate complete portfolio by mixing the risk-free asset with the optimal risky portfolio. Before describing the process in detail, let us first present an overview.

The first step is to determine the risk–return opportunities available to the investor. These are summarized by the **minimum-variance frontier** of risky assets. This frontier is

**Figure 8.10
The minimum-
variance frontier
of risky assets**

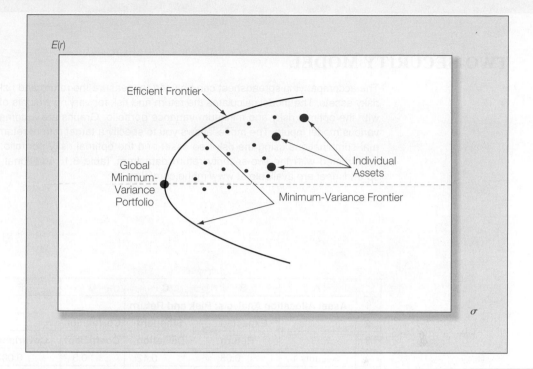

a graph of the lowest possible variance that can be attained for a given portfolio expected return. Given the input data for expected returns, variances, and covariances, we can calculate the minimum-variance portfolio for any targeted expected return. The plot of these expected return–standard deviation pairs is presented in Figure 8.10.

Notice that all the individual assets lie to the right inside the frontier, at least when we allow short sales in the construction of risky portfolios.[8] This tells us that risky portfolios comprising only a single asset are inefficient. Diversifying investments leads to portfolios with higher expected returns and lower standard deviations.

All the portfolios that lie on the minimum-variance frontier from the global minimum-variance portfolio and upward provide the best risk–return combinations and thus are candidates for the optimal portfolio. The part of the frontier that lies above the global minimum-variance portfolio, therefore, is called the **efficient frontier of risky assets**. For any portfolio on the lower portion of the minimum-variance frontier, there is a portfolio with the same standard deviation and a greater expected return positioned directly above it. Hence the bottom part of the minimum-variance frontier is inefficient.

The second part of the optimization plan involves the risk-free asset. As before, we search for the capital allocation line with the highest reward-to-variability ratio (that is, the steepest slope) as shown in Figure 8.11 on page 244.

The CAL that is supported by the optimal portfolio, *P*, is tangent to the efficient frontier. This CAL dominates all alternative feasible lines (the broken lines that are drawn through the frontier). Portfolio *P*, therefore, is the optimal risky portfolio.

---

[8] When short sales are prohibited, single securities may lie on the frontier. For example, the security with the highest expected return must lie on the frontier, as that security represents the *only* way that one can obtain a return that high, and so it must also be the minimum-variance way to obtain that return. When short sales are feasible, however, portfolios can be constructed that offer the same expected return and lower variance. These portfolios typically will have short positions in low-expected-return securities.

# TWO-SECURITY MODEL

The accompanying spreadsheet can be used to measure the return and risk of a portfolio of two risky assets. The model calculates the return and risk for varying weights of each security along with the optimal risky and minimum-variance portfolio. Graphs are automatically generated for various model inputs. The model allows you to specify a target rate of return and solves for optimal combinations using the risk-free asset and the optimal risky portfolio. The spreadsheet is constructed with the two-security return data from Table 8.1. Additional problems using this spreadsheet are available at www.mhhe.com/bkm.

| | A | B | C | D | E | F |
|---|---|---|---|---|---|---|
| 1 | Asset Allocation Analysis: Risk and Return | | | | | |
| 2 | | Expected | Standard | Correlation | | |
| 3 | | Return | Deviation | Coefficient | Covariance | |
| 4 | Security 1 | 0.08 | 0.12 | 0.3 | 0.0072 | |
| 5 | Security 2 | 0.13 | 0.2 | | | |
| 6 | T-Bill | 0.05 | 0 | | | |
| 7 | | | | | | |
| 8 | Weight | Weight | | Expected | Standard | Reward to |
| 9 | Security 1 | Security 2 | | Return | Deviation | Variability |
| 10 | 1 | 0 | | 0.08000 | 0.12000 | 0.25000 |
| 11 | 0.9 | 0.1 | | 0.08500 | 0.11559 | 0.30281 |
| 12 | 0.8 | 0.2 | | 0.09000 | 0.11454 | 0.34922 |
| 13 | 0.7 | 0.3 | | 0.09500 | 0.11696 | 0.38474 |
| 14 | 0.6 | 0.4 | | 0.10000 | 0.12264 | 0.40771 |
| 15 | 0.5 | 0.5 | | 0.10500 | 0.13115 | 0.41937 |
| 16 | 0.4 | 0.6 | | 0.11000 | 0.14199 | 0.42258 |
| 17 | 0.3 | 0.7 | | 0.11500 | 0.15466 | 0.42027 |
| 18 | 0.2 | 0.8 | | 0.12000 | 0.16876 | 0.41479 |
| 19 | 0.1 | 0.9 | | 0.12500 | 0.18396 | 0.40771 |
| 20 | 0 | 1 | | 0.13000 | 0.20000 | 0.40000 |
| 21 | | | | | | |

Finally, in the last part of the problem the individual investor chooses the appropriate mix between the optimal risky portfolio *P* and T-bills, exactly as in Figure 8.8.

Now let us consider each part of the portfolio construction problem in more detail. In the first part of the problem, risk–return analysis, the portfolio manager needs as inputs a set of estimates for the expected returns of each security and a set of estimates for the covariance matrix. (In Part 5 on security analysis we will examine the security valuation techniques

| | A | B | C | D | E | F |
|---|---|---|---|---|---|---|
| 21 | Optimal Risky Portfolio | | | | | |
| 22 | | | | Short Sales | No Short | |
| 23 | | | | Allowed | Sales | |
| 24 | | | Weight 1 | .40 | .40 | |
| 25 | | | Weight 2 | .60 | .60 | |
| 26 | | | Return | .11 | .11 | |
| 27 | | | Std. Dev. | .142 | .142 | |
| 28 | | | | | | |
| 29 | | | | | | |

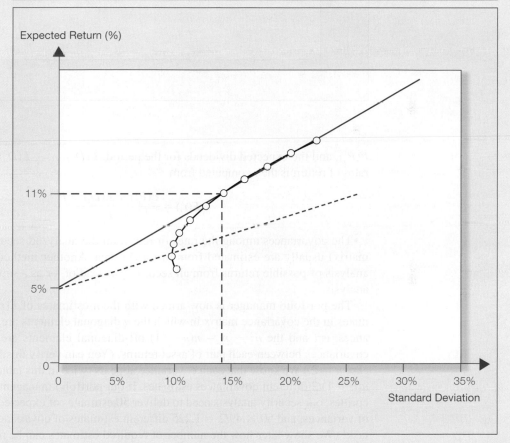

and methods of financial analysis that analysts use. For now, we will assume that analysts already have spent the time and resources to prepare the inputs.).

Suppose that the horizon of the portfolio plan is 1 year. Therefore, all estimates pertain to a 1-year holding-period return. Our security analysts cover $n$ securities. As of now, time 0, we observed these security prices: $P_1^0, \ldots, P_n^0$. The analysts derive estimates for each security's expected rate of return by forecasting end-of-year (time 1) prices: $E(P_1^1), \ldots,$

**Figure 8.11
The efficient
frontier of risky
assets with
the optimal CAL**

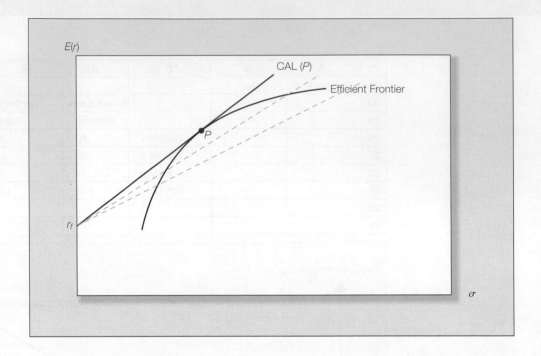

$E(P_n^1)$, and the expected dividends for the period: $E(D_1), \ldots, E(D_n)$. The set of expected rates of return is then computed from

$$E(r_i) = \frac{E(P_i^1) + E(D_i) - P_i^0}{P_i^0}$$

The covariances among the rates of return on the analyzed securities (the covariance matrix) usually are estimated from historical data. Another method is to use a scenario analysis of possible returns from all securities instead of, or as a supplement to, historical analysis.

The portfolio manager is now armed with the $n$ estimates of $E(r_i)$ and the $n \times n$ estimates in the covariance matrix in which the $n$ diagonal elements are estimates of the variances, $\sigma_i^2$, and the $n^2 - n = n(n - 1)$ off-diagonal elements are the estimates of the covariances between each pair of asset returns. (You can verify this from Table 8.2 for the case $n = 2$.) We know that each covariance appears twice in this table, so actually we have $n(n - 1)/2$ different covariances estimates. If our portfolio management unit covers 50 securities, our security analysts need to deliver 50 estimates of expected returns, 50 estimates of variances, and $50 \times 49/2 = 1,225$ different estimates of covariances. This is a daunting task! (We show later how the number of required estimates can be reduced substantially.)

Once these estimates are compiled, the expected return and variance of any risky portfolio with weights in each security, $w_i$, can be calculated from the bordered covariance matrix or, equivalently, from the following formulas:

$$E(r_p) = \sum_{i=1}^{n} w_i E(r_i) \qquad (8.9)$$

$$\sigma_P^2 = \sum_{i=1}^{n} \sum_{j=1}^{n} w_i w_j \text{Cov}(r_i, r_j) \qquad (8.10)$$

**Figure 8.12
The efficient
portfolio set**

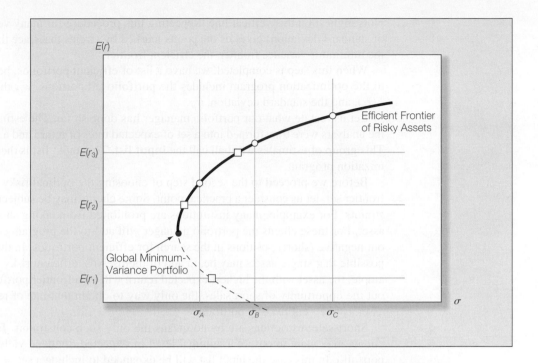

An extended worked example showing you how to do this on a spreadsheet is presented in the next section.

We mentioned earlier that the idea of diversification is age-old. The phrase "don't put all your eggs in one basket" existed long before modern finance theory. It was not until 1952, however, that Harry Markowitz published a formal model of portfolio selection embodying diversification principles, thereby paving the way for his 1990 Nobel Prize for economics.[9] His model is precisely step one of portfolio management: the identification of the efficient set of portfolios, or, as it is often called, the *efficient frontier of risky assets*.

The principal idea behind the frontier set of risky portfolios is that, for any risk level, we are interested only in that portfolio with the highest expected return. Alternatively, the frontier is the set of portfolios that minimize the variance for any target expected return.

Indeed, the two methods of computing the efficient set of risky portfolios are equivalent. To see this, consider the graphical representation of these procedures. Figure 8.12 shows the minimum-variance frontier.

The points marked by squares are the result of a variance-minimization program. We first draw the constraints, that is, horizontal lines at the level of required expected returns. We then look for the portfolio with the lowest standard deviation that plots on each horizontal line—we look for the portfolio that will plot farthest to the left (smallest standard deviation) on that line. When we repeat this for many levels of required expected returns, the shape of the minimum-variance frontier emerges. We then discard the bottom (dashed) half of the frontier, because it is inefficient.

In the alternative approach, we draw a vertical line that represents the standard deviation constraint. We then consider all portfolios that plot on this line (have the same standard deviation) and choose the one with the highest expected return, that is, the portfolio that

[9] Harry Markowitz, "Portfolio Selection," *Journal of Finance*, March 1952.

plots highest on this vertical line. Repeating this procedure for many vertical lines (levels of standard deviation) gives us the points marked by circles that trace the upper portion of the minimum-variance frontier, the efficient frontier.

When this step is completed, we have a list of efficient portfolios, because the solution to the optimization program includes the portfolio proportions, $w_i$, the expected return, $E(r_p)$, and the standard deviation, $\sigma_p$.

Let us restate what our portfolio manager has done so far. The estimates generated by the analysts were transformed into a set of expected rates of return and a covariance matrix. This group of estimates we shall call the **input list**. This input list is then fed into the optimization program.

Before we proceed to the second step of choosing the optimal risky portfolio from the frontier set, let us consider a practical point. Some clients may be subject to additional constraints. For example, many institutions are prohibited from taking short positions in any asset. For these clients the portfolio manager will add to the program constraints that rule out negative (short) positions in the search for efficient portfolios. In this special case it is possible that single assets may be, in and of themselves, efficient risky portfolios. For example, the asset with the highest expected return will be a frontier portfolio because, without the opportunity of short sales, the only way to obtain that rate of return is to hold the asset as one's entire risky portfolio.

Short-sale restrictions are by no means the only such constraints. For example, some clients may want to ensure a minimal level of expected dividend yield from the optimal portfolio. In this case the input list will be expanded to include a set of expected dividend yields $d_1, \ldots, d_n$ and the optimization program will include an additional constraint that ensures that the expected dividend yield of the portfolio will equal or exceed the desired level, $d$.

Portfolio managers can tailor the efficient set to conform to any desire of the client. Of course, any constraint carries a price tag in the sense that an efficient frontier constructed subject to extra constraints will offer a reward-to-variability ratio inferior to that of a less constrained one. The client should be made aware of this cost and should carefully consider constraints that are not mandated by law.

Another type of constraint is aimed at ruling out investments in industries or countries considered ethically or politically undesirable. This is referred to as *socially responsible investing*, which entails a cost in the form of a lower reward-to-variability on the resultant constrained, optimal portfolio. This cost can be justifiably viewed as a contribution to the underlying cause.

## 8.5    A SPREADSHEET MODEL

**Calculation of Expected Return and Variance**    Several software packages can be used to generate the efficient frontier. We will demonstrate the method using Microsoft Excel. Excel is far from the best program for this purpose and is limited in the number of assets it can handle, but working through a simple portfolio optimizer in Excel can illustrate concretely the nature of the calculations used in more sophisticated "black-box" programs. You will find that even in Excel, the computation of the efficient frontier is fairly easy.

We will apply the Markowitz portfolio optimizer to a problem of international diversification. Table 8.4A on pages 248–249 shows average returns, standard deviations, and the correlation matrix for the rates of return on the stock indexes of seven countries over a recent 14-year period. Suppose that the analysts of International Capital Management (ICM) had produced an input list that anticipated these results. As portfolio manager of ICM, what set of efficient portfolios would you have considered as investment candidates?

After we input Table 8.4A into our spreadsheet as shown, we create the covariance matrix in Table 8.4B using the relationship $\text{Cov}(r_i, r_j) = \rho_{ij}\sigma_i\sigma_j$. The table shows both cell formulas (upper panel) and numerical results (lower panel).

Next we prepare the data for the computation of the efficient frontier. To establish a benchmark against which to evaluate our efficient portfolios, we use an equally weighted portfolio, that is, the weights for each of the seven countries is equal to $1/7 = .1429$. To compute the equally weighted portfolio's mean and variance, these weights are entered in the border column A53–A59 and border row B52–H52.[10] We calculate the variance of this portfolio in cell B77 in Table 8.4C. The entry in this cell equals the sum of all elements in the border-multiplied covariance matrix where each element is first multiplied by the portfolio weights given in both the row and column borders.[11] We also include two cells to compute the standard deviation and expected return of the equally weighted portfolio (formulas in cells B62, B63) and find that they yield an expected return of 16.5% with a standard deviation of 17.7% (results in cells B78 and B79).

To compute points along the *efficient frontier* we use the Excel Solver in Table 8.4D (which you can find in the Tools menu).[12] Once you bring up Solver, you are asked to enter the cell of the target (objective) function. In our application, the target is the variance of the portfolio, given in cell B93. Solver will minimize this target. You next must input the cell range of the decision variables (in this case, the portfolio weights, contained in cells A85–A91). Finally, you enter all necessary constraints into the Solver. For an unrestricted efficient frontier that allows short sales, there are two constraints: first, that the sum of the weights equals 1.0 (cell A92 = 1), and second, that the portfolio expected return equals a target mean return. We will choose a target return equal to that of the equally weighted portfolio, 16.5%, so our second constraint is that cell B95 = 16.5. Once you have entered the two constraints you ask the Solver to find the optimal portfolio weights.

The Solver beeps when it has found a solution and automatically alters the portfolio weight cells in row 84 and column A to show the makeup of the efficient portfolio. It adjusts the entries in the border-multiplied covariance matrix to reflect the multiplication by these new weights, and it shows the mean and variance of this optimal portfolio—the minimum variance portfolio with mean return of 16.5%. These results are shown in Table 8.4D, cells B93–B95. The table shows that the standard deviation of the *efficient* portfolio with same mean as the *equally weighted* portfolio is 17.2%, a reduction of risk of about one-half percentage point. Observe that the weights of the efficient portfolio differ radically from equal weights.

To generate the entire efficient frontier, keep changing the required mean in the constraint (cell B95),[13] letting the Solver work for you. If you record a sufficient number of points, you will be able to generate a graph of the quality of Figure 8.13 on page 250.

---

[10] You should not enter the portfolio weights in these rows and columns independently, since if a weight in the row changes, the weight in the corresponding column must change to the same value for consistency. Thus you should *copy* each entry from column A to the corresponding element of row 52.

[11] We need the sum of each element of the covariance matrix, where each term has first been multiplied by the product of the portfolio weights from its row and column. These values appear in panel C of Table 8.4. We will first sum these elements for each column and then add up the column sums. Row 60 contains the appropriate column sums. Therefore, the sum of cells B60–H60, which appears in cell B61, is the variance of the portfolio formed using the weights appearing in the borders of the covariance matrix.

[12] If Solver does not show up under the Tools menu, you should select Add-Ins and then select Analysis. This should add Solver to the list of options in the Tools menu.

[13] Inside Solver, highlight the constraint, click on Change, and enter the new value for the portfolio's mean return.

## Table 8.4   Performance of Stock Indexes of Seven Countries

|  | A | B | C | D | E | F | G | H |
|---|---|---|---|---|---|---|---|---|
| 1 | | | | | | | | |
| 2 | | A. Annualized Standard Deviation, Average Return, | | | | | | |
| 3 | | and Correlation Coefficients of International Stocks, 1980–1993 | | | | | | |
| 4 | | | | | | | | |
| 5 | | Std. Dev. (%) | Average Ret. (%) | | | | | |
| 6 | US | 21.1 | 15.7 | | | | | |
| 7 | Germany | 25.0 | 21.7 | | | | | |
| 8 | UK | 23.5 | 18.3 | | | | | |
| 9 | Japan | 26.6 | 17.3 | | | | | |
| 10 | Australia | 27.6 | 14.8 | | | | | |
| 11 | Canada | 23.4 | 10.5 | | | | | |
| 12 | France | 26.6 | 17.2 | | | | | |
| 13 | | | | | | | | |
| 14 | | Correlation Matrix | | | | | | |
| 15 | | US | Germany | UK | Japan | Australia | Canada | France |
| 16 | US | 1.00 | 0.37 | 0.53 | 0.26 | 0.43 | 0.73 | 0.44 |
| 17 | Germany | 0.37 | 1.00 | 0.47 | 0.36 | 0.29 | 0.36 | 0.63 |
| 18 | UK | 0.53 | 0.47 | 1.00 | 0.43 | 0.50 | 0.54 | 0.51 |
| 19 | Japan | 0.26 | 0.36 | 0.43 | 1.00 | 0.26 | 0.29 | 0.42 |
| 20 | Australia | 0.43 | 0.29 | 0.50 | 0.26 | 1.00 | 0.56 | 0.34 |
| 21 | Canada | 0.73 | 0.36 | 0.54 | 0.29 | 0.56 | 1.00 | 0.39 |
| 22 | France | 0.44 | 0.63 | 0.51 | 0.42 | 0.34 | 0.39 | 1.00 |

|  | A | B | C | D | E | F | G | H |
|---|---|---|---|---|---|---|---|---|
| 27 | | B. Covariance Matrix: Cell Formulas | | | | | | |
| 28 | | | | | | | | |
| 29 | | US | Germany | UK | Japan | Australia | Canada | France |
| 30 | US | b6*b6*b16 | b7*b6*c16 | b8*b6*d16 | b9*b6*e16 | b10*b6*f16 | b11*b6*g16 | b12*b6*h16 |
| 31 | Germany | b6*b7*b17 | b7*b7*c17 | b8*b7*d17 | b9*b7*e17 | b10*b7*f17 | b11*b7*g17 | b12*b7*h17 |
| 32 | UK | b6*b8*b18 | b7*b8*c18 | b8*b8*d18 | b9*b8*e18 | b10*b8*f18 | b11*b8*g18 | b12*b8*h18 |
| 33 | Japan | b6*b9*b19 | b7*b9*c19 | b8*b9*d19 | b9*b9*e19 | b10*b9*f19 | b11*b9*g19 | b12*b9*h19 |
| 34 | Australia | b6*b10*b20 | b7*b10*c20 | b8*b10*d20 | b9*b10*e20 | b10*b10*f20 | b11*b10*g20 | b12*b10*h20 |
| 35 | Canada | b6*b11*b21 | b7*b11*c21 | b8*b11*d21 | b9*b11*e21 | b10*b11*f21 | b11*b11*g21 | b12*b11*h21 |
| 36 | France | b6*b12*b22 | b7*b12*c22 | b8*b12*d22 | b9*b12*e22 | b10*b12*f22 | b11*b12*g22 | b12*b12*h22 |
| 37 | | | | | | | | |
| 38 | | Covariance Matrix: Results | | | | | | |
| 39 | | | | | | | | |
| 40 | | US | Germany | UK | Japan | Australia | Canada | France |
| 41 | US | 445.21 | 195.18 | 262.80 | 145.93 | 250.41 | 360.43 | 246.95 |
| 42 | Germany | 195.18 | 625.00 | 276.13 | 239.40 | 200.10 | 210.60 | 418.95 |
| 43 | UK | 262.80 | 276.13 | 552.25 | 268.79 | 324.30 | 296.95 | 318.80 |
| 44 | Japan | 145.93 | 239.40 | 268.79 | 707.56 | 190.88 | 180.51 | 297.18 |
| 45 | Australia | 250.41 | 200.10 | 324.30 | 190.88 | 761.76 | 361.67 | 249.61 |
| 46 | Canada | 360.43 | 210.60 | 296.95 | 180.51 | 361.67 | 547.56 | 242.75 |
| 47 | France | 246.95 | 418.95 | 318.80 | 297.18 | 249.61 | 242.75 | 707.56 |

|  | A | B | C | D | E | F | G | H |
|---|---|---|---|---|---|---|---|---|
| 49 | | C. Border-Multiplied Covariance Matrix for the Equally Weighted Portfolio and Portfolio Variance: | | | | | | |
| 50 | | Cell Formulas | | | | | | |
| 51 | | US | Germany | UK | Japan | Australia | Canada | France |
| 52 | Weights | a53 | a54 | a55 | a56 | a57 | a58 | a59 |
| 53 | 0.1429 | a53*b52*b41 | a53*c52*c41 | a53*d52*d41 | a53*e52*e41 | a53*f52*f41 | a53*g52*g41 | a53*h52*h41 |
| 54 | 0.1429 | a54*b52*b42 | a54*c52*c42 | a54*d52*d42 | a54*e52*e42 | a54*f52*f42 | a54*g52*g42 | a54*h52*h42 |
| 55 | 0.1429 | a55*b52*b43 | a55*c52*c43 | a55*d52*d43 | a55*e52*e43 | a55*f52*f43 | a55*g52*g43 | a55*h52*h43 |
| 56 | 0.1429 | a56*b52*b44 | a56*c52*c44 | a56*d52*d44 | a56*e52*e44 | a56*f52*f44 | a56*g52*g44 | a56*h52*h44 |
| 57 | 0.1429 | a57*b52*b45 | a57*c52*c45 | a57*d52*d45 | a57*e52*e45 | a57*f52*f45 | a57*g52*g45 | a57*h52*h45 |
| 58 | 0.1429 | a58*b52*b46 | a58*c52*c46 | a58*d52*d46 | a58*e52*e46 | a58*f52*f46 | a58*g52*g46 | a58*h52*h46 |
| 59 | 0.1429 | a59*b52*b47 | a59*c52*c47 | a59*d52*d47 | a59*e52*e47 | a59*f52*f47 | a59*g52*g47 | a59*h52*h47 |
| 60 | Sum(a53:a59) | sum(b53:b59) | sum(c53:c59) | sum(d53:d59) | sum(e53:e59) | sum(f53:f59) | sum(g53:g59) | sum(h53:h59) |
| 61 | Portfolio variance | sum(b60:h60) | | | | | | |
| 62 | Portfolio SD | b61^.5 | | | | | | |
| 63 | Portfolio mean | a53*c6+a54*c7+a55*c8+a56*c9+a57*c10+a58*c11+a59*c12 | | | | | | |

**Table 8.4**   *(Concluded)*

| | A | B | C | D | E | F | G | H |
|---|---|---|---|---|---|---|---|---|
| 64 | | | | | | | | |
| 65 | | C. Border-Multiplied Covariance Matrix for the Equally Weighted Portfolio and Portfolio Variance: | | | | | | |
| 66 | | Results | | | | | | |
| 67 | Portfolio | US | Germany | UK | Japan | Australia | Canada | France |
| 68 | weights | 0.1429 | 0.1429 | 0.1429 | 0.1429 | 0.1429 | 0.1429 | 0.1429 |
| 69 | 0.1429 | 9.09 | 3.98 | 5.36 | 2.98 | 5.11 | 7.36 | 5.04 |
| 70 | 0.1429 | 3.98 | 12.76 | 5.64 | 4.89 | 4.08 | 4.30 | 8.55 |
| 71 | 0.1429 | 5.36 | 5.64 | 11.27 | 5.49 | 6.62 | 6.06 | 6.51 |
| 72 | 0.1429 | 2.98 | 4.89 | 5.49 | 14.44 | 3.90 | 3.68 | 6.06 |
| 73 | 0.1429 | 5.11 | 4.08 | 6.62 | 3.90 | 15.55 | 7.38 | 5.09 |
| 74 | 0.1429 | 7.36 | 4.30 | 6.06 | 3.68 | 7.38 | 11.17 | 4.95 |
| 75 | 0.1429 | 5.04 | 8.55 | 6.51 | 6.06 | 5.09 | 4.95 | 14.44 |
| 76 | 1.0000 | 38.92 | 44.19 | 46.94 | 41.43 | 47.73 | 44.91 | 50.65 |
| 77 | Portfolio variance | 314.77 | | | | | | |
| 78 | Portfolio SD | 17.7 | | | | | | |
| 79 | Portfolio mean | 16.5 | | | | | | |

| | A | B | C | D | E | F | G | H |
|---|---|---|---|---|---|---|---|---|
| 80 | | D. Border-Multiplied Covariance Matrix for the Efficient Frontier Portfolio with Mean of 16.5% | | | | | | |
| 81 | | (after change of weights by solver) | | | | | | |
| 82 | | | | | | | | |
| 83 | Portfolio | US | Germany | UK | Japan | Australia | Canada | France |
| 84 | weights | 0.3467 | 0.1606 | 0.0520 | 0.2083 | 0.1105 | 0.1068 | 0.0150 |
| 85 | 0.3467 | 53.53 | 10.87 | 4.74 | 10.54 | 9.59 | 13.35 | 1.29 |
| 86 | 0.1606 | 10.87 | 16.12 | 2.31 | 8.01 | 3.55 | 3.61 | 1.01 |
| 87 | 0.0520 | 4.74 | 2.31 | 1.49 | 2.91 | 1.86 | 1.65 | 0.25 |
| 88 | 0.2083 | 10.54 | 8.01 | 2.91 | 30.71 | 4.39 | 4.02 | 0.93 |
| 89 | 0.1105 | 9.59 | 3.55 | 1.86 | 4.39 | 9.30 | 4.27 | 0.41 |
| 90 | 0.1068 | 13.35 | 3.61 | 1.65 | 4.02 | 4.27 | 6.25 | 0.39 |
| 91 | 0.0150 | 1.29 | 1.01 | 0.25 | 0.93 | 0.41 | 0.39 | 0.16 |
| 92 | 1.0000 | 103.91 | 45.49 | 15.21 | 61.51 | 33.38 | 33.53 | 4.44 |
| 93 | Portfolio variance | 297.46 | | | | | | |
| 94 | Portfolio SD | 17.2 | | | | | | |
| 95 | Portfolio mean | 16.5 | | | | | | |

| | A | B | C | D | E | F | G | H | I | J |
|---|---|---|---|---|---|---|---|---|---|---|
| 96 | | E. The Unrestricted Efficient Frontier and the Restricted Frontier (with no short sales) | | | | | | | | |
| 97 | | | | | | | | | | |
| 98 | | Standard Deviation | | | Country Weights In Efficient Portfolios | | | | | |
| 99 | Mean | Unrestricted | Restricted | US | Germany | UK | Japan | Australia | Canada | France |
| 100 | 9.0 | 24.239 | not feasible | −0.0057 | −0.2859 | −0.1963 | 0.2205 | 0.0645 | 0.9811 | 0.2216 |
| 101 | 10.5 | 22.129 | | 0.0648 | −0.1966 | −0.1466 | 0.2181 | 0.0737 | 0.8063 | 0.1803 |
| 102 | 10.5 | | 23.388 | 0.0000 | 0.0000 | 0.0000 | 0.0007 | 0.0000 | 0.9993 | 0.0000 |
| 103 | 11.0 | 21.483 | | 0.0883 | −0.1668 | −0.1301 | 0.2173 | 0.0768 | 0.7480 | 0.1665 |
| 104 | 11.0 | | 22.325 | 0.0000 | 0.0000 | 0.0000 | 0.0735 | 0.0000 | 0.9265 | 0.0000 |
| 105 | 12.0 | 20.292 | | 0.1353 | −0.1073 | −0.0970 | 0.2157 | 0.0829 | 0.6314 | 0.1390 |
| 106 | 12.0 | | 20.641 | 0.0000 | 0.0000 | 0.0000 | 0.1572 | 0.0325 | 0.7668 | 0.0435 |
| 107 | 14.0 | 18.408 | | 0.2293 | 0.0118 | −0.0308 | 0.2124 | 0.0952 | 0.3982 | 0.0839 |
| 108 | 14.0 | | 18.416 | 0.2183 | 0.0028 | 0.0000 | 0.2068 | 0.0884 | 0.4020 | 0.0816 |
| 109 | 15.0 | 17.767 | 17.767 | 0.2763 | 0.0713 | 0.0023 | 0.2108 | 0.1013 | 0.2817 | 0.0563 |
| 110 | 16.0 | 17.358 | 17.358 | 0.3233 | 0.1309 | 0.0355 | 0.2091 | 0.1074 | 0.1651 | 0.0288 |
| 111 | 17.0 | 17.200 | 17.200 | 0.3702 | 0.1904 | 0.0686 | 0.2075 | 0.1135 | 0.0485 | 0.0012 |
| 112 | 17.5 | 17.216 | | 0.3937 | 0.2202 | 0.0851 | 0.2067 | 0.1166 | −0.0098 | −0.0125 |
| 113 | 17.5 | | 17.221 | 0.3777 | 0.2248 | 0.0867 | 0.2021 | 0.1086 | 0.0000 | 0.0000 |
| 114 | 18.0 | 17.297 | | 0.4172 | 0.2499 | 0.1017 | 0.2059 | 0.1197 | −0.0681 | −0.0263 |
| 115 | 18.0 | | 17.405 | 0.3285 | 0.2945 | 0.1157 | 0.1869 | 0.0744 | 0.0000 | 0.0000 |
| 116 | 18.5 | 17.441 | | 0.4407 | 0.2797 | 0.1182 | 0.2051 | 0.1227 | −0.1263 | −0.0401 |
| 117 | 18.5 | | 17.790 | 0.2792 | 0.3642 | 0.1447 | 0.1716 | 0.0402 | 0.0000 | 0.0000 |
| 118 | 21.0 | 19.036 | | 0.5582 | 0.4285 | 0.2010 | 0.2010 | 0.1380 | −0.4178 | −0.1090 |
| 119 | 21.0 | | 22.523 | 0.0000 | 0.8014 | 0.1739 | 0.0247 | 0.0000 | 0.0000 | 0.0000 |
| 120 | 22.0 | 20.028 | not feasible | 0.6052 | 0.4880 | 0.2341 | 0.1994 | 0.1442 | −0.5343 | −0.1365 |
| 121 | 26.0 | 25.390 | not feasible | 0.7931 | 0.7262 | 0.3665 | 0.1929 | 0.1687 | −1.0006 | −0.2467 |

**Figure 8.13
Efficient frontier
with seven
countries**

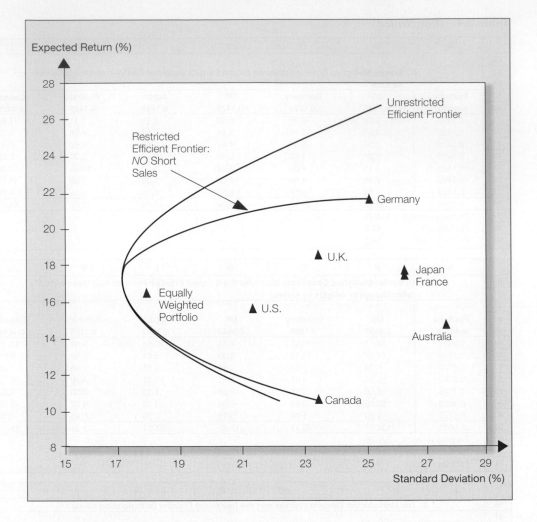

The outer frontier in Figure 8.13 is drawn assuming that the investor may maintain negative portfolio weights. If shortselling is not allowed, we may impose the additional constraints that each weight (the elements in column A and row 84) must be nonnegative; we would then obtain the restricted efficient frontier curve in Figure 8.13, which lies inside the frontier obtained allowing short sales. The superiority of the unrestricted efficient frontier reminds us that restrictions imposed on portfolio choice may be costly.

The Solver allows you to add "no short sales" and other constraints easily. Once they are entered, you repeat the variance-minimization exercise until you generate the entire restricted frontier. By using macros in Excel or—even better—using specialized software, the entire routine can be accomplished with one push of a button.

Table 8.4E presents a number of points on the two frontiers. The first column gives the required mean and the next two columns show the resultant variance of efficient portfolios with and without short sales. Note that the restricted frontier cannot obtain a mean return less than 10.5% (which is the mean in Canada, the country index with the lowest mean return) or more than 21.7% (corresponding to Germany, the country with the highest mean return). The last seven columns show the portfolio weights of the seven country stock indexes in the optimal portfolios. You can see that the weights in restricted portfolios

## OPTIMAL PORTFOLIOS

A spreadsheet model featuring optimal risky portfolios is available on the Online Learning Center at www.mhhe.com/bkm. It contains a template that is similar to the template developed in this section. The model can be used to find optimal mixes of securities for targeted levels of returns for both restricted and unrestricted portfolios. Graphs of the efficient frontier are generated for each set of inputs. The example available at our Web site applies the model to portfolios constructed from equity indexes (called WEBS securities) of several countries. Additional practice problems using this spreadsheet are also available.

|    | A | B | C | D | E | F |
|----|---|---|---|---|---|---|
| 1  | Efficient Frontier for World Equity Benchmark Securities (WEBS) | | | | | |
| 2  | | | | | | |
| 3  | | Mean | Standard | | | |
| 4  | WEBS | Return | Deviation | Country | | |
| 5  | EWD | 15.5393 | 26.4868 | Sweden | | |
| 6  | EWH | 6.3852 | 41.1475 | Hong Kong | | |
| 7  | EWI | 26.5999 | 26.0514 | Italy | | |
| 8  | EWJ | 1.4133 | 26.0709 | Japan | | |
| 9  | EWL | 18.0745 | 21.6916 | Switzerland | | |
| 10 | EWP | 18.6347 | 25.0779 | Spain | | |
| 11 | EWW | 16.2243 | 38.7686 | Mexico | | |
| 12 | S&P 500 | 17.2306 | 17.1944 | | | |

are never negative. For mean returns in the range from about 15%–17%, the two frontiers overlap since the optimal weights in the unrestricted frontier turn out to be positive (see also Figure 8.13).

Notice that despite the fact that German stocks offer the highest mean return and even the highest reward-to-variability ratio, the weight of U.S. stocks is generally higher in both restricted and unrestricted portfolios. This is due to the lower correlation of U.S. stocks with stocks of other countries and illustrates the importance of diversification attributes when forming efficient portfolios. Figure 8.13 presents points corresponding to means and standard deviations of individual country indexes, as well as the equally weighted portfolio. The figure clearly shows the benefits from diversification.

**Capital Allocation and the Separation Property**  Now that we have the efficient frontier, we proceed to step two and introduce the risk-free asset. Figure 8.14 shows the efficient frontier plus three CALs representing various portfolios from the efficient set. As before, we ratchet up the CAL by selecting different portfolios until we reach Portfolio *P*, which is the tangency point of a line from *F* to the efficient frontier. Portfolio *P* maximizes the reward-to-variability ratio, the slope of the line from *F* to portfolios on the efficient frontier. At this point our portfolio manager is done. Portfolio *P* is the optimal risky portfolio for the manager's clients. This is a good time to ponder our results and their implementation.

**Figure 8.14   Capital allocation lines with various portfolios from the efficient set**

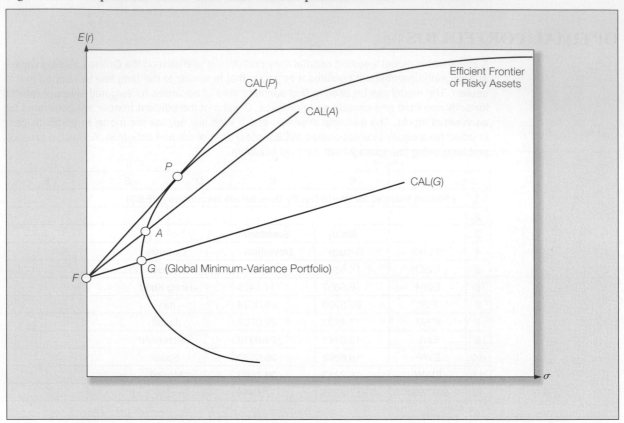

The most striking conclusion is that a portfolio manager will offer the same risky port-folio, *P*, to all clients regardless of their degree of risk aversion.[14] The degree of risk aver-sion of the client comes into play only in the selection of the desired point along the CAL. Thus the only difference between clients' choices is that the more risk-averse client will in-vest more in the risk-free asset and less in the optimal risky portfolio than will a less risk-averse client. However, both will use Portfolio *P* as their optimal risky investment vehicle.

This result is called a **separation property**; it tells us that the portfolio choice problem may be separated into two independent tasks. The first task, determination of the optimal risky portfolio, is purely technical. Given the manager's input list, the best risky portfolio is the same for all clients, regardless of risk aversion. The second task, however, allocation of the complete portfolio to T-bills versus the risky portfolio, depends on personal prefer-ence. Here the client is the decision maker.

The crucial point is that the optimal portfolio *P* that the manager offers is the same for all clients. This result makes professional management more efficient and hence less costly. One management firm can serve any number of clients with relatively small incremental administrative costs.

In practice, however, different managers will estimate different input lists, thus deriving different efficient frontiers, and offer different "optimal" portfolios to their clients. The source of the disparity lies in the security analysis. It is worth mentioning here that the uni-versal rule of GIGO (garbage in–garbage out) also applies to security analysis. If the

---

[14] Clients who impose special restrictions (constraints) on the manager, such as dividend yield, will obtain another optimal port-folio. Any constraint that is added to an optimization problem leads, in general, to a different and less desirable optimum com-pared to an unconstrained program.

quality of the security analysis is poor, a passive portfolio such as a market index fund will result in a better CAL than an active portfolio that uses low-quality security analysis to tilt portfolio weights toward seemingly favorable (mispriced) securities.

As we have seen, optimal risky portfolios for different clients also may vary because of portfolio constraints such as dividend-yield requirements, tax considerations, or other client preferences. Nevertheless, this analysis suggests that a limited number of portfolios may be sufficient to serve the demands of a wide range of investors. This is the theoretical basis of the mutual fund industry.

The (computerized) optimization technique is the easiest part of the portfolio construction problem. The real arena of competition among portfolio managers is in sophisticated security analysis.

**CONCEPT CHECK☞ QUESTION 4**

Suppose that two portfolio managers who work for competing investment management houses each employ a group of security analysts to prepare the input list for the Markowitz algorithm. When all is completed, it turns out that the efficient frontier obtained by portfolio manager *A* dominates that of manager *B*. By dominate, we mean that *A*'s optimal risky portfolio lies northwest of *B*'s. Hence, given a choice, investors will all prefer the risky portfolio that lies on the CAL of *A*.

*a.* **What should be made of this outcome?**

*b.* **Should it be attributed to better security analysis by *A*'s analysts?**

*c.* **Could it be that *A*'s computer program is superior?**

*d.* **If you were advising clients (and had an advance glimpse at the efficient frontiers of various managers), would you tell them to periodically switch their money to the manager with the most northwesterly portfolio?**

## Asset Allocation and Security Selection

As we have seen, the theories of security selection and asset allocation are identical. Both activities call for the construction of an efficient frontier, and the choice of a particular portfolio from along that frontier. The determination of the optimal combination of securities proceeds in the same manner as the analysis of the optimal combination of asset classes. Why, then, do we (and the investment community) distinguish between asset allocation and security selection?

Three factors are at work. First, as a result of greater need and ability to save (for college educations, recreation, longer life in retirement, health care needs, etc.), the demand for sophisticated investment management has increased enormously. Second, the widening spectrum of financial markets and financial instruments has put sophisticated investment beyond the capacity of many amateur investors. Finally, there are strong economies of scale in investment analysis. The end result is that the size of a competitive investment company has grown with the industry, and efficiency in organization has become an important issue.

A large investment company is likely to invest both in domestic and international markets and in a broad set of asset classes, each of which requires specialized expertise. Hence the management of each asset-class portfolio needs to be decentralized, and it becomes impossible to simultaneously optimize the entire organization's risky portfolio in one stage, although this would be prescribed as optimal on *theoretical* grounds.

The practice is therefore to optimize the security selection of each asset-class portfolio independently. At the same time, top management continually updates the asset allocation of the organization, adjusting the investment budget allotted to each asset-class portfolio.

**Figure 8.15
Portfolio selection
without a risk-
free asset**

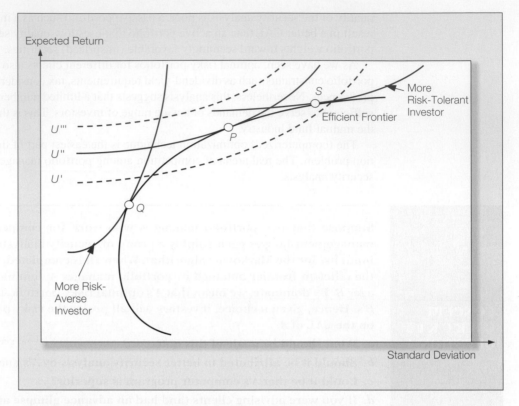

When changed frequently in response to intensive forecasting activity, these reallocations are called *market timing*. The shortcoming of this two-step approach to portfolio construction, versus the theory-based one-step optimization, is the failure to exploit the covariance of the individual securities in one asset-class portfolio with the individual securities in the other asset classes. Only the covariance matrix of the securities within each asset-class portfolio can be used. However, this loss might be small because of the depth of diversification of each portfolio and the extra layer of diversification at the asset allocation level.

## 8.6   OPTIMAL PORTFOLIOS WITH RESTRICTIONS ON THE RISK-FREE ASSET

The availability of a risk-free asset greatly simplifies the portfolio decision. When all investors can borrow and lend at that risk-free rate, we are led to a *unique* optimal risky portfolio that is appropriate for all investors given a common input list. This portfolio maximizes the reward-to-variability ratio. All investors use the same risky portfolio and differ only in the proportion they invest in it versus in the risk-free asset.

What if a risk-free asset is not available? Although T-bills are risk-free assets in nominal terms, their real returns are uncertain. Without a risk-free asset, there is no tangency portfolio that is best for all investors. In this case investors have to choose a portfolio from the efficient frontier of risky assets redrawn in Figure 8.15.

Each investor will now choose an optimal risky portfolio by superimposing a personal set of indifference curves on the efficient frontier as in Figure 8.15. An investor with indifference curves marked $U'$, $U''$, and $U'''$ in Figure 8.15 will choose Portfolio $P$. More risk-averse investors with steeper indifference curves will choose portfolios with lower

**Figure 8.16**
**Portfolio selection**
**with risk-free**
**lending but**
**no borrowing**

means and smaller standard deviations such as Portfolio $Q$, while more risk-tolerant investors will choose portfolios with higher means and greater risk, such as Portfolio $S$. The common feature of all these investors is that each chooses portfolios on the efficient frontier.

Even if virtually risk-free lending opportunities are available, many investors do face borrowing restrictions. They may be unable to borrow altogether, or, more realistically, they may face a borrowing rate that is significantly greater than the lending rate.

## EXAMPLE 8.4    Borrowing Constraints and Portfolio Choice

When a risk-free investment is available, but an investor cannot borrow, a CAL exists but is limited to the line $FP$ as in Figure 8.16. Any investors whose preferences are represented by indifference curves with tangency portfolios on the portion $FP$ of the CAL, such as Portfolio $A$, are unaffected by the borrowing restriction. Such investors are net *lenders* at rate $r_f$.

Aggressive or more risk-tolerant investors, who *would* choose Portfolio $B$ in the absence of the borrowing restriction, are affected, however. Such investors will be driven to portfolios such as Portfolio $Q$, which are on the efficient frontier of risky assets. These investors will not invest in the risk-free asset.

In more realistic scenarios than Example 8.4, individuals who wish to borrow to invest in a risky portfolio will have to pay an interest rate higher than the T-bill rate. For example, the call money rate charged by brokers on margin accounts is higher than the T-bill rate.

**EXAMPLE 8.5**    **Borrowing versus Lending Rate**

Investors who face a borrowing rate greater than the lending rate confront a three-part CAL such as in Figure 8.17. $CAL_1$, which is relevant in the range $FP_1$, represents the efficient portfolio set for defensive (risk-averse) investors. These investors invest part of their funds in T-bills at rate $r_f$. They find that the tangency Portfolio is $P_1$, and they choose a complete portfolio such as Portfolio $A$ in Figure 8.18.

**Figure 8.17**
**The investment opportunity set with differential rates for borrowing and lending**

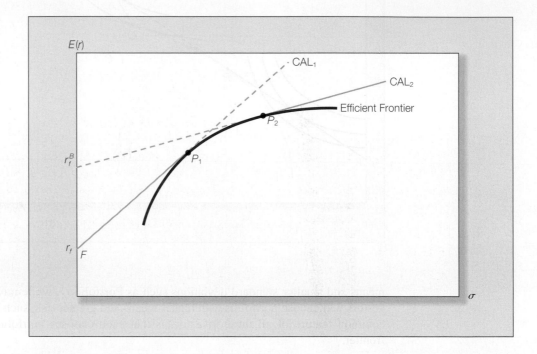

**Figure 8.18**
**The optimal portfolio of defensive investors with differential borrowing and lending rates**

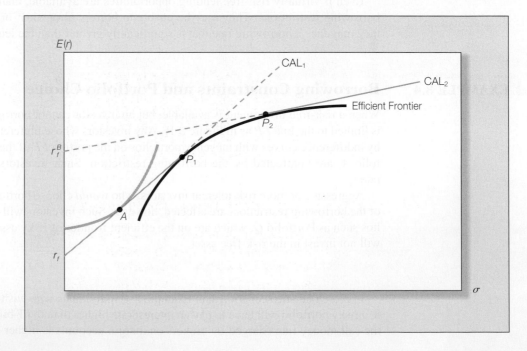

CAL$_2$, which is relevant in a range to the right of Portfolio $P_2$, represents the efficient portfolio set for more aggressive, or risk-tolerant, investors. This line starts at the borrowing rate $r_f^B$, but it is unavailable in the range $r_f^B P_2$, because *lending* (investing in T-bills) is available only at the risk-free rate $r_f$, which is less than $r_f^B$.

Investors who are willing to *borrow* at the higher rate, $r_f^B$, to invest in an optimal risky portfolio will choose Portfolio $P_2$ as the risky investment vehicle. Such a case is depicted in Figure 8.19, which superimposes a relatively risk-tolerant investor's indifference curve on CAL$_2$. The investor with the indifference curve in Figure 8.19 chooses Portfolio $P_2$ as the optimal risky portfolio and borrows to invest in it, arriving at the complete Portfolio $B$.

Investors in the middle range, neither defensive enough to invest in T-bills nor aggressive enough to borrow, choose a risky portfolio from the efficient frontier in the range $P_1 P_2$. This case is depicted in Figure 8.20. The indifference curve representing the investor in Figure 8.20 leads to a tangency portfolio on the efficient frontier, Portfolio $C$.

---

**CONCEPT CHECK ☞ QUESTION 5**

With differential lending and borrowing rates, only investors with about average degrees of risk aversion will choose a portfolio in the range $P_1 P_2$ in Figure 8.18. Other investors will choose a portfolio on CAL$_1$ if they are more risk averse, or on CAL$_2$ if they are more risk tolerant.

*a.* Does this mean that investors with average risk aversion are more dependent on the quality of the forecasts that generate the efficient frontier?

*b.* Describe the trade-off between expected return and standard deviation for portfolios between $P_1$ and $P_2$ in Figure 8.18 compared with portfolios on CAL$_2$ beyond $P_2$.

---

**Figure 8.19
The optimal portfolio of aggressive investors with differential borrowing and lending rates**

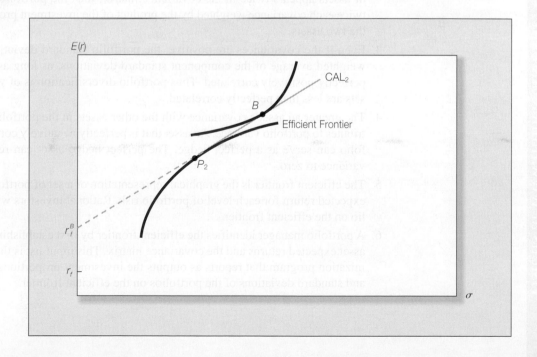

**Figure 8.20
The optimal
portfolio of
moderately risk-
tolerant investors
with differential
borrowing and
lending rates**

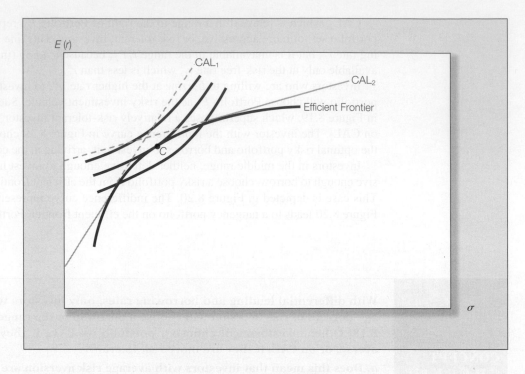

## SUMMARY

1. The expected return of a portfolio is the weighted average of the component security expected returns with the investment proportions as weights.

2. The variance of a portfolio is the weighted sum of the elements of the covariance matrix with the product of the investment proportions as weights. Thus the variance of each asset is weighted by the square of its investment proportion. Each covariance of any pair of assets appears twice in the covariance matrix; thus the portfolio variance includes twice each covariance weighted by the product of the investment proportions in each of the two assets.

3. Even if the covariances are positive, the portfolio standard deviation is less than the weighted average of the component standard deviations, as long as the assets are not perfectly positively correlated. Thus portfolio diversification is of value as long as assets are less than perfectly correlated.

4. The greater an asset's covariance with the other assets in the portfolio, the more it contributes to portfolio variance. An asset that is perfectly negatively correlated with a portfolio can serve as a perfect hedge. The perfect hedge asset can reduce the portfolio variance to zero.

5. The efficient frontier is the graphical representation of a set of portfolios that maximize expected return for each level of portfolio risk. Rational investors will choose a portfolio on the efficient frontier.

6. A portfolio manager identifies the efficient frontier by first establishing estimates for the asset expected returns and the covariance matrix. This input list is then fed into an optimization program that reports as outputs the investment proportions, expected returns, and standard deviations of the portfolios on the efficient frontier.

7. In general, portfolio managers will arrive at different efficient portfolios because of differences in methods and quality of security analysis. Managers compete on the quality of their security analysis relative to their management fees.

8. If a risk-free asset is available and input lists are identical, all investors will choose the same portfolio on the efficient frontier of risky assets: the portfolio tangent to the CAL. All investors with identical input lists will hold an identical risky portfolio, differing only in how much each allocates to this optimal portfolio and to the risk-free asset. This result is characterized as the separation principle of portfolio construction.

9. When a risk-free asset is not available, each investor chooses a risky portfolio on the efficient frontier. If a risk-free asset is available but borrowing is restricted, only aggressive investors will be affected. They will choose portfolios on the efficient frontier according to their degree of risk tolerance.

## KEY TERMS

| | | |
|---|---|---|
| diversification | nonsystematic risk | minimum-variance frontier |
| insurance principle | diversifiable risk | efficient frontier of |
| market risk | minimum-variance | risky assets |
| systematic risk | portfolio | input list |
| nondiversifiable risk | portfolio opportunity set | separation property |
| unique risk | reward-to-variability ratio | |
| firm-specific risk | optimal risky portfolio | |

## WEBSITES

finance.yahoo.com
This site provides historical price information that is useful in estimating returns, standard deviation of returns, and covariance of returns for individuals securities. The information is available within the chart function for individual securities.

www.financialengines.com
Do you recognize the person behind this website? This site contains risk measures that can be used to compare individual stocks to an average hypothetical portfolio. Start the First Time User's demo for real applications of concepts in this chapter.

www.efficientfrontier.com/ef/402/siegel.htm
Visit this site for an interesting discussion and analysis of the risk–return trade-off.

www.moneychimp.com/articles/volatility/standard_deviation.htm
This site offers an interactive calculator related to the effects of varying stock and cash investment proportions.

www.aigvalic.com/agfa/agfaweb.nsf/contents/article_diversity?opendocument&noload
Here's how diversification works.

www.moneychimp.com/articles/risk/efficient_frontier.htm
Review the discussion of the efficient frontier.

Visit us at www.mhhe.com/bkm

**PROBLEMS**    The following data apply to problems 1 through 8:

A pension fund manager is considering three mutual funds. The first is a stock fund, the second is a long-term government and corporate bond fund, and the third is a T-bill money market fund that yields a rate of 8%. The probability distribution of the risky funds is as follows:

|  | Expected Return | Standard Deviation |
| --- | --- | --- |
| Stock fund (S) | 20% | 30% |
| Bond fund (B) | 12 | 15 |

The correlation between the fund returns is .10.

1. What are the investment proportions in the minimum-variance portfolio of the two risky funds, and what is the expected value and standard deviation of its rate of return?

2. Tabulate and draw the investment opportunity set of the two risky funds. Use investment proportions for the stock funds of zero to 100% in increments of 20%.

3. Draw a tangent from the risk-free rate to the opportunity set. What does your graph show for the expected return and standard deviation of the optimal portfolio?

4. Solve numerically for the proportions of each asset and for the expected return and standard deviation of the optimal risky portfolio.

5. What is the reward-to-variability ratio of the best feasible CAL?

6. You require that your portfolio yield an expected return of 14%, and that it be efficient on the best feasible CAL.

   a. What is the standard deviation of your portfolio?

   b. What is the proportion invested in the T-bill fund and each of the two risky funds?

7. If you were to use only the two risky funds, and still require an expected return of 14%, what must be the investment proportions of your portfolio? Compare its standard deviation to that of the optimized portfolio in problem 6. What do you conclude?

8. Suppose that you face the same opportunity set, but you cannot borrow. You wish to construct a portfolio of only stocks and bonds with an expected return of 24%. What are the appropriate portfolio proportions and the resulting standard deviations? What reduction in standard deviation could you attain if you were allowed to borrow at the risk-free rate?

9. Stocks offer an expected rate of return of 18%, with a standard deviation of 22%. Gold offers an expected return of 10% with a standard deviation of 30%.

   a. In light of the apparent inferiority of gold with respect to both mean return and volatility, would anyone hold gold? If so, demonstrate graphically why one would do so.

   b. Given the data above, reanswer (a) with the additional assumption that the correlation coefficient between gold and stocks equals 1. Draw a graph illustrating why one would or would not hold gold in one's portfolio. Could this set of assumptions for expected returns, standard deviations, and correlation represent an equilibrium for the security market?

10. Suppose that there are many stocks in the security market and that the characteristics of Stocks A and B are given as follows:

| Stock | Expected Return | Standard Deviation |
|-------|-----------------|--------------------|
| A | 10% | 5% |
| B | 15 | 10 |
| | Correlation = −1 | |

Suppose that it is possible to borrow at the risk-free rate, $r_f$. What must be the value of the risk-free rate? (Hint: Think about constructing a risk-free portfolio from Stocks $A$ and $B$.)

11. Assume that expected returns and standard deviations for all securities (including the risk-free rate for borrowing and lending) are known. In this case all investors will have the same optimal risky portfolio. (True or false?)

12. The standard deviation of the portfolio is always equal to the weighted average of the standard deviations of the assets in the portfolio. (True or false?)

13. Suppose you have a project that has a .7 chance of doubling your investment in a year and a .3 chance of halving your investment in a year. What is the standard deviation of the rate of return on this investment?

14. Suppose that you have $1 million and the following two opportunities from which to construct a portfolio:

   *a.* Risk-free asset earning 12% per year.

   *b.* Risky asset earning 30% per year with a standard deviation of 40%.

   If you construct a portfolio with a standard deviation of 30%, what will be the rate of return?

The following data apply to problems 15 through 17.

Hennessy & Associates manages a $30 million equity portfolio for the multimanager Wilstead Pension Fund. Jason Jones, financial vice president of Wilstead, noted that Hennessy had rather consistently achieved the best record among the Wilstead's six equity managers. Performance of the Hennessy portfolio had been clearly superior to that of the S&P 500 in 4 of the past 5 years. In the one less-favorable year, the shortfall was trivial.

Hennessy is a "bottom-up" manager. The firm largely avoids any attempt to "time the market." It also focuses on selection of individual stocks, rather than the weighting of favored industries.

There is no apparent conformity of style among the six equity managers. The five managers, other than Hennessy, manage portfolios aggregating $250 million made up of more than 150 individual issues.

Jones is convinced that Hennessy is able to apply superior skill to stock selection, but the favorable returns are limited by the high degree of diversification in the portfolio. Over the years, the portfolio generally held 40–50 stocks, with about 2%–3% of total funds committed to each issue. The reason Hennessy seemed to do well most years was because the firm was able to identify each year 10 or 12 issues which registered particularly large gains.

Based on this overview, Jones outlined the following plan to the Wilstead pension committee:

   Let's tell Hennessy to limit the portfolio to no more than 20 stocks. Hennessy will double the commitments to the stocks that it really favors, and eliminate the remainder. Except for this one new restriction, Hennessy should be free to manage the portfolio exactly as before.

All the members of the pension committee generally supported Jones's proposal because all agreed that Hennessy had seemed to demonstrate superior skill in selecting

Visit us at www.mhhe.com/bkm

stocks. Yet the proposal was a considerable departure from previous practice, and several committee members raised questions. Respond to each of the following questions.

15. *a.* Will the limitations of 20 stocks likely increase or decrease the risk of the portfolio? Explain.

*b.* Is there any way Hennessy could reduce the number of issues from 40 to 20 without significantly affecting risk? Explain.

16. One committee member was particularly enthusiastic concerning Jones's proposal. He suggested that Hennessy's performance might benefit further from reduction in the number of issues to 10. If the reduction to 20 could be expected to be advantageous, explain why reduction to 10 might be less likely to be advantageous. (Assume that Wilstead will evaluate the Hennessy portfolio independently of the other portfolios in the fund.)

17. Another committee member suggested that, rather than evaluate each managed portfolio independently of other portfolios, it might be better to consider the effects of a change in the Hennessy portfolio on the total fund. Explain how this broader point of view could affect the committee decision to limit the holdings in the Hennessy portfolio to either 10 or 20 issues.

The following data are for problems 18 through 20.

The correlation coefficients between pairs of stocks are as follows: Corr($A$,$B$) = .85; Corr($A$,$C$) = .60; Corr($A$,$D$) = .45. Each stock has an expected return of 8% and a standard deviation of 20%.

18. If your entire portfolio is now composed of Stock $A$ and you can add some of only one stock to your portfolio, would you choose (explain your choice):

*a. B.*

*b. C.*

*c. D.*

*d.* Need more data.

19. Would the answer to problem 18 change for more risk-averse or risk-tolerant investors? Explain.

20. Suppose that in addition to investing in one more stock you can invest in T-bills as well. Would you change your answers to problems 18 and 19 if the T-bill rate is 8%?

21. Which one of the following portfolios cannot lie on the efficient frontier as described by Markowitz?

| Portfolio | Expected Return (%) | Standard Deviation (%) |
|---|---|---|
| *a.* | W | 15 | 36 |
| *b.* | X | 12 | 15 |
| *c.* | Z | 5 | 7 |
| *d.* | Y | 9 | 21 |

22. Which statement about portfolio diversification is correct?

*a.* Proper diversification can reduce or eliminate systematic risk.

*b.* Diversification reduces the portfolio's expected return because it reduces a portfolio's total risk.

*c.* As more securities are added to a portfolio, total risk typically would be expected to fall at a decreasing rate.

*d.* The risk-reducing benefits of diversification do not occur meaningfully until at least 30 individual securities are included in the portfolio.

23. The measure of risk for a security held in a diversified portfolio is:
    a. Specific risk.
    b. Standard deviation of returns.
    c. Reinvestment risk.
    d. Covariance.

24. Portfolio theory as described by Markowitz is most concerned with:
    a. The elimination of systematic risk.
    b. The effect of diversification on portfolio risk.
    c. The identification of unsystematic risk.
    d. Active portfolio management to enhance return.

25. Assume that a risk-averse investor owning stock in Miller Corporation decides to add the stock of either Mac or Green Corporation to her portfolio. All three stocks offer the same expected return and total risk. The covariance of return between Miller and Mac is −.05 and between Miller and Green is +.05. Portfolio risk is expected to:
    a. Decline more when the investor buys Mac.
    b. Decline more when the investor buys Green.
    c. Increase when either Mac or Green is bought.
    d. Decline or increase, depending on other factors.

26. Stocks A, B, and C have the same expected return and standard deviation. The following table shows the correlations between the returns on these stocks.

|         | Stock A | Stock B | Stock C |
|---------|---------|---------|---------|
| Stock A | +1.0    |         |         |
| Stock B | +0.9    | +1.0    |         |
| Stock C | +0.1    | −0.4    | +1.0    |

Given these correlations, the portfolio constructed from these stocks having the lowest risk is a portfolio:
    a. Equally invested in stocks A and B.
    b. Equally invested in stocks A and C.
    c. Equally invested in stocks B and C.
    d. Totally invested in stock C.

27. Statistics for three stocks, A, B, and C, are shown in the following tables.

### Standard Deviations of Returns

| Stock:                 | A  | B  | C  |
|------------------------|----|----|----|
| Standard deviation (%): | 40 | 20 | 40 |

### Correlations of Returns

| Stock | A    | B    | C    |
|-------|------|------|------|
| A     | 1.00 | 0.90 | 0.50 |
| B     |      | 1.00 | 0.10 |
| C     |      |      | 1.00 |

Based *only* on the information provided in the tables, and given a choice between a portfolio made up of equal amounts of stocks A and B *or* a portfolio made up of equal amounts of stocks *B* and *C*, state which portfolio you would recommend. Justify your choice.

The following table of compound annual returns by decade applies to problems 28 and 29.

|  | 1920s* | 1930s | 1940s | 1950s | 1960s | 1970s | 1980s | 1990s |
|---|---|---|---|---|---|---|---|---|
| Small-company stocks | −3.72% | 7.28% | 20.63% | 19.01% | 13.72% | 8.75% | 12.46% | 13.84% |
| Large-company stocks | 18.36 | −1.25 | 9.11 | 19.41 | 7.84 | 5.90 | 17.60 | 18.20 |
| Long-term government | 3.98 | 4.60 | 3.59 | 0.25 | 1.14 | 6.63 | 11.50 | 8.60 |
| Intermediate-term government | 3.77 | 3.91 | 1.70 | 1.11 | 3.41 | 6.11 | 12.01 | 7.74 |
| Treasury bills | 3.56 | 0.30 | 0.37 | 1.87 | 3.89 | 6.29 | 9.00 | 5.02 |
| Inflation | −1.00 | −2.04 | 5.36 | 2.22 | 2.52 | 7.36 | 5.10 | 2.93 |

*Based on the period 1926–1929.
Source: Data in Table 5.2.

28. Input the data from the table into a spreadsheet. Compute the serial correlation in decade returns for each asset class and for inflation. Also find the correlation between the returns of various asset classes. What do the data indicate?

29. Convert the asset returns by decade presented in the table into real rates. Repeat the analysis of problem 28 for the real rates of return.

30. George Stephenson's current portfolio of $2.0 million is invested as follows:

**Summary of Stephenson's Current Portfolio**

|  | Value | Percent of Total | Expected Annual Return | Annual Standard Deviation |
|---|---|---|---|---|
| Short-term bonds | $   200,000 | 10% | 4.6% | 1.6% |
| Domestic large-cap equities | 600,000 | 30% | 12.4% | 19.5% |
| Domestic small-cap equities | 1,200,000 | 60% | 16.0% | 29.9% |
| Total portfolio | $2,000,000 | 100% | 13.8% | 23.1% |

Stephenson soon expects to receive an additional $2.0 million and plans to invest the entire amount in an index fund that best complements the current portfolio. Stephanie Coppa, CFA, is evaluating the four index funds shown in the following table for their ability to produce a portfolio that will meet two criteria relative to the current portfolio: (1) maintain or enhance expected return and (2) maintain or reduce volatility.

Each fund is invested in an asset class that is not substantially represented in the current portfolio.

**Index Fund Characteristics**

| Index Fund | Expected Annual Return | Expected Annual Standard Deviation | Correlation of Returns with Current Portfolio |
|---|---|---|---|
| Fund A | 15% | 25% | +0.80 |
| Fund B | 11 | 22 | +0.60 |
| Fund C | 16 | 25 | +0.90 |
| Fund D | 14 | 22 | +0.65 |

State which fund Coppa should recommend to Stephenson. Justify your choice by describing how your chosen fund *best* meets both of Stephenson's criteria. No calculations are required.

31. Abigail Grace has a $900,000 fully diversified portfolio. She subsequently inherits ABC Company common stock worth $100,000. Her financial advisor provided her with the following forecasted information:

### Risk and Return Characteristics

|  | Expected Monthly Returns | Standard Deviation of Monthly Returns |
| --- | --- | --- |
| Original Portfolio | 0.67% | 2.37% |
| ABC Company | 1.25 | 2.95 |

The correlation coefficient of ABC stock returns with the original portfolio returns is 0.40.

a. The inheritance changes Grace's overall portfolio and she is deciding whether to keep the ABC stock. Assuming Grace keeps the ABC stock, calculate the:
   i.   Expected return of her new portfolio which includes the ABC stock.
   ii.  Covariance of ABC stock returns with the original portfolio returns.
   iii. Standard deviation of her new portfolio which includes the ABC stock.

b. If Grace sells the ABC stock, she will invest the proceeds in risk-free government securities yielding 0.42 percent monthly. Assuming Grace sells the ABC stock and replaces it with the government securities, calculate the:
   i.   Expected return of her new portfolio which includes the government securities.
   ii.  Covariance of the government security returns with the original portfolio returns.
   iii. Standard deviation of her new portfolio which includes the government securities.

c. Determine whether the beta of her new portfolio which includes the government securities will be higher or lower than the beta of her original portfolio.

d. Based on conversations with her husband, Grace is considering selling the $100,000 of ABC stock and acquiring $100,000 of XYZ Company common stock instead. XYZ stock has the same expected return and standard deviation as ABC stock. Her husband comments, "It doesn't matter whether you keep all of the ABC stock or replace it with $100,000 of XYZ stock." State whether her husband's comment is correct or incorrect. Justify your response.

e. In a recent discussion with her financial adviser, Grace commented, "If I just don't lose money in my portfolio, I will be satisfied." She went on to say, "I am more afraid of losing money than I am concerned about achieving high returns."
   i.   Describe *one* weakness of using standard deviation of returns as a risk measure for Grace.
   ii.  Identify an alternate risk measure that is more appropriate under the circumstances.

32. Dudley Trudy, CFA, recently met with one of his clients. Trudy typically invests in a master list of 30 equities drawn from several industries. As the meeting concluded, the client made the following statement: "I trust your stock-picking ability and believe that you should invest my funds in your five best ideas. Why invest in 30 companies when you obviously have stronger opinions on a few of them? Trudy plans to respond to his client within the context of Modern Portfolio Theory.

a. Contrast the concepts of systematic risk and firm-specific risk, and give an example of *each* type of risk.

b. Critique the client's suggestion. Discuss how both systematic and firm-specific risk change as the number of securities in a portfolio is increased.

---

**E-INVESTMENTS**
**Risk Comparisons**

Go to **www.morningstar.com** and select the tab entitled *Funds*. In the dialog box for selecting a particular fund, type Fidelity Select and hit the Go button. This will list all of the Fidelity Select funds. Select the Fidelity Select Multimedia Fund. Find the fund's top 25 individual holdings from the displayed information. The top holdings are found in the Style section. Identify the top five holdings by using the ticker symbol.

Once you have obtained this information, go to **www.financialengines.com**. From the Site menu, select the *Forecast and Analysis* tab and then select the fund's *Scorecard* tab. You will find a dialog box that allows you to search for funds or individual stocks. You can enter the name or ticker for each of the individual stocks and the fund. Compare the risk rankings of the individual securities with the risk ranking of the fund. What factors are likely leading to the differences in the individual rankings and the overall fund ranking?

---

**SOLUTIONS TO CONCEPT CHECKS**

1. *a.* The first term will be $w_D \times w_D \times \sigma_D^2$, since this is the element in the top corner of the matrix ($\sigma_D^2$) times the term on the column border ($w_D$) times the term on the row border ($w_D$). Applying this rule to each term of the covariance matrix results in the sum $w_D^2 \sigma_D^2 + w_D w_E \text{Cov}(r_E, r_D) + w_E w_D \text{Cov}(r_D, r_E) + w_E^2 \sigma_E^2$, which is the same as equation 8.2, since $\text{Cov}(r_E, r_D) = \text{Cov}(r_D, r_E)$.

*b.* The bordered covariance matrix is

|       | $w_X$              | $w_Y$              | $w_Z$              |
|-------|--------------------|--------------------|--------------------|
| $w_X$ | $\sigma_X^2$       | $\text{Cov}(r_X, r_Y)$ | $\text{Cov}(r_X, r_Z)$ |
| $w_Y$ | $\text{Cov}(r_Y, r_X)$ | $\sigma_Y^2$       | $\text{Cov}(r_Y, r_Z)$ |
| $w_Z$ | $\text{Cov}(r_Z, r_X)$ | $\text{Cov}(r_Z, r_Y)$ | $\sigma_Z^2$       |

There are nine terms in the covariance matrix. Portfolio variance is calculated from these nine terms:

$$\sigma_P^2 = w_X^2 \sigma_X^2 + w_Y^2 \sigma_Y^2 + w_Z^2 \sigma_Z^2$$
$$+ w_X w_Y \text{Cov}(r_X, r_Y) + w_Y w_X \text{Cov}(r_Y, r_X)$$
$$+ w_X w_Z \text{Cov}(r_X, r_Z) + w_Z w_X \text{Cov}(r_Z, r_X)$$
$$+ w_Y w_Z \text{Cov}(r_Y, r_Z) + w_Z w_Y \text{Cov}(r_Z, r_Y)$$
$$= w_X^2 \sigma_X^2 + w_Y^2 \sigma_Y^2 + w_Z^2 \sigma_Z^2$$
$$+ 2w_X w_Y \text{Cov}(r_X, r_Y) + 2w_X w_Z \text{Cov}(r_X, r_Z) + 2w_Y w_Z \text{Cov}(r_Y, r_Z)$$

2. The parameters of the opportunity set are $E(r_D) = 8\%$, $E(r_E) = 13\%$, $\sigma_D = 12\%$, $\sigma_E = 20\%$, and $\rho(D,E) = .25$. From the standard deviations and the correlation coefficient we generate the covariance matrix:

| Stock | D   | E   |
|-------|-----|-----|
| D     | 144 | 60  |
| E     | 60  | 400 |

The *global minimum-variance* portfolio is constructed so that

$$w_D = \frac{\sigma_E^2 - \text{Cov}(r_D, r_E)}{\sigma_D^2 + \sigma_E^2 - 2\,\text{Cov}(r_D, r_E)}$$

$$= \frac{400 - 60}{(144 + 400) - (2 \times 60)} = .8019$$

$$w_E = 1 - w_D = .1981$$

Its expected return and standard deviation are

$$E(r_P) = (.8019 \times 8) + (.1981 \times 13) = 8.99\%$$

$$\sigma_P = [w_D^2 \sigma_D^2 + w_E^2 \sigma_E^2 + 2 w_D w_E \text{Cov}(r_D, r_E)]^{1/2}$$

$$= [(.8019^2 \times 144) + (.1981^2 \times 400) + (2 \times .8019 \times .1981 \times 60)]^{1/2}$$

$$= 11.29\%$$

For the other points we simply increase $w_D$ from .10 to .90 in increments of .10; accordingly, $w_E$ ranges from .90 to .10 in the same increments. We substitute these portfolio proportions in the formulas for expected return and standard deviation. Note that when $w_E = 1.0$, the portfolio parameters equal those of the stock fund; when $w_D = 1$, the portfolio parameters equal those of the debt fund.

We then generate the following table:

| $w_E$ | $w_D$ | $E(r)$ | $\sigma$ | |
|---|---|---|---|---|
| 0.0 | 1.0 | 8.0 | 12.00 | |
| 0.1 | 0.9 | 8.5 | 11.46 | |
| 0.2 | 0.8 | 9.0 | 11.29 | |
| 0.3 | 0.7 | 9.5 | 11.48 | |
| 0.4 | 0.0 | 10.0 | 12.03 | |
| 0.5 | 0.5 | 10.5 | 12.88 | |
| 0.6 | 0.4 | 11.0 | 13.99 | |
| 0.7 | 0.3 | 11.5 | 15.30 | |
| 0.8 | 0.2 | 12.0 | 16.76 | |
| 0.9 | 0.1 | 12.5 | 18.34 | |
| 1.0 | 0.0 | 13.0 | 20.00 | |
| 0.1981 | 0.8019 | 8.99 | 11.29 | minimum variance portfolio |

SOLUTIONS
TO CONCEPT
CHECKS
*(Continued)*

You can now draw your graph.

3. *a.* The computations of the opportunity set of the stock and risky bond funds are like those of question 2 and will not be shown here. You should perform these computations, however, in order to give a graphical solution to part *a*. Note that the covariance between the funds is

$$\text{Cov}(r_A, r_B) = \rho(A, B) \times \sigma_A \times \sigma_B$$

$$= -.2 \times 20 \times 60 = -240$$

*b.* The proportions in the optimal risky portfolio are given by

$$w_A = \frac{(10 - 5)60^2 - (30 - 5)(-240)}{(10 - 5)60^2 + (30 - 5)20^2 - 30(-240)}$$

$$= .6818$$

$$w_B = 1 - w_A = .3182$$

Visit us at www.mhhe.com/bkm

The expected return and standard deviation of the optimal risky portfolio are

$$E(r_P) = (.6818 \times 10) + (.3128 \times 30) = 16.36\%$$
$$\sigma_P = \{(.6818^2 \times 20^2) + (.3182^2 \times 60^2) + [2 \times .6818 \times .3182(-240)]\}^{1/2}$$
$$= 21.13\%$$

Note that in this case the standard deviation of the optimal risky portfolio is smaller than the standard deviation of stock $A$. Note also that portfolio $P$ is not the global minimum-variance portfolio. The proportions of the latter are given by

$$w_A = \frac{60^2 - (-240)}{60^2 + 20^2 - 2(-240)} = .8571$$
$$w_B = 1 - w_A = .1429$$

With these proportions, the standard deviation of the minimum-variance portfolio is

$$\sigma(\min) = \{(.8571^2 \times 20^2) + (.1429^2 \times 60^2) + [2 \times .8571 \times .1429 \times (-240)]\}^{1/2}$$
$$= 17.57\%$$

which is smaller than that of the optimal risky portfolio.

c. The CAL is the line from the risk-free rate through the optimal risky portfolio. This line represents all efficient portfolios that combine T-bills with the optimal risky portfolio. The slope of the CAL is

$$S = \frac{E(r_P) - r_f}{\sigma_P} = \frac{16.36 - 5}{21.13} = .5376$$

d. Given a degree of risk aversion, $A$, an investor will choose a proportion, $y$, in the optimal risky portfolio of

$$y = \frac{E(r_P) - r_f}{.01 \times A\sigma_P^2} = \frac{16.36 - 5}{.01 \times 5 \times 21.13^2} = .5089$$

This means that the optimal risky portfolio, with the given data, is attractive enough for an investor with $A = 5$ to invest 50.89% of his or her wealth in it. Since stock $A$ makes up 68.18% of the risky portfolio and stock $B$ makes up 31.82%, the investment proportions for this investor are

| | | |
|---|---|---|
| Stock $A$: | $.5089 \times 68.18 =$ | 34.70% |
| Stock $B$: | $.5089 \times 31.82 =$ | 16.19% |
| Total | | 50.89% |

4. Efficient frontiers derived by portfolio managers depend on forecasts of the rates of return on various securities and estimates of risk, that is, the covariance matrix. The forecasts themselves do not control outcomes. Thus preferring managers with rosier forecasts (northwesterly frontiers) is tantamount to rewarding the bearers of good news and punishing the bearers of bad news. What we should do is reward bearers of *accurate* news. Thus if you get a glimpse of the frontiers (forecasts) of portfolio managers on a regular basis, what you want to do is develop the track record of their forecasting accuracy and steer your advisees toward the more accurate forecaster. Their portfolio choices will, in the long run, outperform the field.

5. *a.* Portfolios that lie on the CAL are combinations of the tangency (optimal risky) portfolio and the risk-free asset. Hence they are just as dependent on the accuracy of the efficient frontier as portfolios that are on the frontier itself. If we judge forecasting accuracy by the accuracy of the reward-to-variability ratio, then all portfolios on the CAL will be exactly as accurate as the tangency portfolio.

*b.* All portfolios on $CAL_1$ are combinations of portfolio $P_1$ with lending (buying T-bills). This combination of one risky asset with a risk-free asset leads to a linear relationship between the portfolio expected return and its standard deviation:

$$E(r_P) = r_f + \frac{E(r_{P_1}) - r_f}{\sigma_{P_1}} \sigma_P \qquad (5.b)$$

The same applies to all portfolios on $CAL_2$; just replace $E(r_{P_1})$, $\sigma_{P_1}$ in equation 5.b with $E(r_{P_2})$, $\sigma_{P_2}$.

An investor who wishes to have an expected return between $E(r_{P_1})$ and $E(r_{P_2})$ must find the appropriate portfolio on the efficient frontier of risky assets between $P_1$ and $P_2$ in the correct proportions.

# APPENDIX A: THE POWER OF DIVERSIFICATION

Section 8.1 introduced the concept of diversification and the limits to the benefits of diversification resulting from systematic risk. Given the tools we have developed, we can reconsider this intuition more rigorously and at the same time sharpen our insight regarding the power of diversification.

Recall from equation 8.10 that the general formula for the variance of a portfolio is

$$\sigma_p^2 = \sum_{j=1}^{n} \sum_{i=1}^{n} w_i w_j \text{Cov}(r_i, r_j) \qquad (8A.1)$$

Consider now the naive diversification strategy in which an equally weighted portfolio is constructed, meaning that $w_i = 1/n$ for each security. In this case equation 8A.1 may be rewritten as follows, where we break out the terms for which $i = j$ into a separate sum, noting that $\text{Cov}(r_i, r_i) = \sigma_i^2$.

$$\sigma_p^2 = \frac{1}{n} \sum_{i=1}^{n} \frac{1}{n} \sigma_i^2 + \sum_{\substack{j=1 \\ j \neq i}}^{n} \sum_{i=1}^{n} \frac{1}{n^2} \text{Cov}(r_i, r_j) \qquad (8A.2)$$

Note that there are $n$ variance terms and $n(n-1)$ covariance terms in equation 8A.2.

If we define the average variance and average covariance of the securities as

$$\overline{\sigma}^2 = \frac{1}{n} \sum_{i=1}^{n} \sigma_i^2$$

$$\overline{\text{Cov}} = \frac{1}{n(n-1)} \sum_{\substack{j=1 \\ j \neq i}}^{n} \sum_{i=1}^{n} \text{Cov}(r_i, r_j)$$

we can express portfolio variance as

$$\sigma_p^2 = \frac{1}{n}\,\overline{\sigma}^2 + \frac{n-1}{n}\,\overline{\text{Cov}} \tag{8A.3}$$

Now examine the effect of diversification. When the average covariance among security returns is zero, as it is when all risk is firm-specific, portfolio variance can be driven to zero. We see this from equation 8A.3: The second term on the right-hand side will be zero in this scenario, while the first term approaches zero as $n$ becomes larger. Hence when security returns are uncorrelated, the power of diversification to limit portfolio risk is unlimited.

However, the more important case is the one in which economywide risk factors impart positive correlation among stock returns. In this case, as the portfolio becomes more highly diversified ($n$ increases) portfolio variance remains positive. Although firm-specific risk, represented by the first term in equation 8A.3, is still diversified away, the second term simply approaches $\overline{\text{Cov}}$ as $n$ becomes greater. [Note that $(n-1)/n = 1 - 1/n$, which approaches 1 for large $n$.] Thus the irreducible risk of a diversified portfolio depends on the covariance of the returns of the component securities, which in turn is a function of the importance of systematic factors in the economy.

To see further the fundamental relationship between systematic risk and security correlations, suppose for simplicity that all securities have a common standard deviation, $\sigma$, and all security pairs have a common correlation coefficient, $\rho$. Then the covariance between all pairs of securities is $\rho\sigma^2$, and equation 8A.3 becomes

$$\sigma_p^2 = \frac{1}{n}\sigma^2 + \frac{n-1}{n}\rho\sigma^2 \tag{8A.4}$$

The effect of correlation is now explicit. When $\rho = 0$, we again obtain the insurance principle, where portfolio variance approaches zero as $n$ becomes greater. For $\rho > 0$, however, portfolio variance remains positive. In fact, for $\rho = 1$, portfolio variance equals $\sigma^2$ regardless of $n$, demonstrating that diversification is of no benefit: In the case of perfect correlation, all risk is systematic. More generally, as $n$ becomes greater, equation 8A.4 shows that systematic risk becomes $\rho\sigma^2$.

Table 8A.1 presents portfolio standard deviation as we include ever-greater numbers of securities in the portfolio for two cases, $\rho = 0$ and $\rho = .40$. The table takes $\sigma$ to be 50%. As

**Table 8A.1    Risk Reduction of Equally Weighted Portfolios in Correlated and Uncorrelated Universes**

| Universe Size $n$ | Optimal Portfolio Proportion $1/n$ (%) | $\rho = 0$ | | $\rho = .4$ | |
|---|---|---|---|---|---|
| | | Standard Deviation (%) | Reduction in $\sigma$ | Standard Deviation (%) | Reduction in $\sigma$ |
| 1 | 100 | 50.00 | 14.64 | 50.00 | 8.17 |
| 2 | 50 | 35.36 | | 41.83 | |
| 5 | 20 | 22.36 | 1.95 | 36.06 | 0.70 |
| 6 | 16.67 | 20.41 | | 35.36 | |
| 10 | 10 | 15.81 | 0.73 | 33.91 | 0.20 |
| 11 | 9.09 | 15.08 | | 33.71 | |
| 20 | 5 | 11.18 | 0.27 | 32.79 | 0.06 |
| 21 | 4.76 | 10.91 | | 32.73 | |
| 100 | 1 | 5.00 | 0.02 | 31.86 | 0.00 |
| 101 | 0.99 | 4.98 | | 31.86 | |

one would expect, portfolio risk is greater when $\rho = .40$. More surprising, perhaps, is that portfolio risk diminishes far less rapidly as $n$ increases in the positive correlation case. The correlation among security returns limits the power of diversification.

Note that for a 100-security portfolio, the standard deviation is 5% in the uncorrelated case—still significant compared to the potential of zero standard deviation. For $\rho = .40$, the standard deviation is high, 31.86%, yet it is very close to undiversifiable systematic risk in the infinite-sized security universe, $\sqrt{\rho\sigma^2} = \sqrt{.4 \times 50^2} = 31.62\%$. At this point, further diversification is of little value.

We also gain an important insight from this exercise. When we hold diversified portfolios, the contribution to portfolio risk of a particular security will depend on the *covariance* of that security's return with those of other securities, and *not* on the security's variance. As we shall see in Chapter 9, this implies that fair risk premiums also should depend on covariances rather than total variability of returns.

---

**CONCEPT CHECK☞ QUESTION A.1**

Suppose that the universe of available risky securities consists of a large number of stocks, identically distributed with $E(r) = 15\%$, $\sigma = 60\%$, and a common correlation coefficient of $\rho = .5$.

*a.* What is the expected return and standard deviation of an equally weighted risky portfolio of 25 stocks?

*b.* What is the smallest number of stocks necessary to generate an efficient portfolio with a standard deviation equal to or smaller than 43%?

*c.* What is the systematic risk in this security universe?

*d.* If T-bills are available and yield 10%, what is the slope of the CAL?

---

**SOLUTIONS TO CONCEPT CHECKS**

A.1.  The parameters are $E(r) = 15$, $\sigma = 60$, and the correlation between any pair of stocks is $\rho = .5$.

*a.*  The portfolio expected return is invariant to the size of the portfolio because all stocks have identical expected returns. The standard deviation of a portfolio with $n = 25$ stocks is

$$\sigma_P = [\sigma^2/n + \rho \times \sigma^2(n - 1)/n]^{1/2}$$
$$= [60^2/25 + .5 \times 60^2 \times 24/25]^{1/2} = 43.27$$

*b.*  Because the stocks are identical, efficient portfolios are equally weighted. To obtain a standard deviation of 43%, we need to solve for $n$:

$$43^2 = \frac{60^2}{n} + .5 \times \frac{60^2(n - 1)}{n}$$
$$1,849n = 3,600 + 1,800n - 1,800$$
$$n = \frac{1,800}{49} = 36.73$$

Thus we need 37 stocks and will come in with volatility slightly under the target.

**SOLUTIONS TO CONCEPT CHECKS** *(Concluded)*

    *c.* As *n* gets very large, the variance of an efficient (equally weighted) portfolio diminishes, leaving only the variance that comes from the covariances among stocks, that is

$$\sigma_P = \sqrt{\rho \times \sigma^2} = \sqrt{.5 \times 60^2} = 42.43$$

Note that with 25 stocks we came within .84% of the systematic risk, that is, the nonsystematic risk of a portfolio of 25 stocks is .84%. With 37 stocks the standard deviation is 43%, of which nonsystematic risk is .57%.

    *d.* If the risk-free is 10%, then the risk premium on any size portfolio is $15 - 10 = 5\%$. The standard deviation of a well-diversified portfolio is (practically) 42.43%; hence the slope of the CAL is

$$S = 5/42.43 = .1178$$

## APPENDIX B: THE INSURANCE PRINCIPLE: RISK-SHARING VERSUS RISK-POOLING

Mean-variance analysis has taken a strong hold among investment professionals, and insight into the mechanics of efficient diversification has become quite widespread. Common misconceptions or fallacies about diversification still persist, however. Here we will try to put some to rest.

It is commonly believed that a large portfolio of independent insurance policies is a necessary and sufficient condition for an insurance company to shed its risk. The fact is that a multitude of independent insurance policies is neither necessary nor sufficient for a sound insurance portfolio. Actually, an individual insurer who would not insure a single policy also would be unwilling to insure a large portfolio of independent policies.

Consider Paul Samuelson's (1963) story. He once offered a colleague 2-to-1 odds on a $1,000 bet on the toss of a coin. His colleague refused, saying, "I won't bet because I would feel the $1,000 loss more than the $2,000 gain. But I'll take you on if you promise to let me make a hundred such bets."

Samuelson's colleague, like many others, might have explained his position, not quite correctly, as: "One toss is not enough to make it reasonably sure that the law of averages will turn out in my favor. But with a hundred tosses of a coin, the law of averages will make it a darn good bet."

Another way to rationalize this argument is to think in terms of rates of return. In each bet you put up $1,000 and then get back $3,000 with a probability of one-half, or zero with a probability of one-half. The probability distribution of the rate of return is 200% with $p = \frac{1}{2}$ and $-100\%$ with $p = \frac{1}{2}$.

The bets are all independent and identical and therefore the expected return is $E(r) = \frac{1}{2}(200) + \frac{1}{2}(-100) = 50\%$, regardless of the number of bets. The standard deviation of the rate of return on the portfolio of independent bets is[15]

$$\sigma(n) = \sigma/\sqrt{n}$$

---

[15] This follows from equation 8.10, setting $w_i = 1/n$ and all covariances equal to zero because of the independence of the bets.

where $\sigma$ is the standard deviation of a single bet:

$$\sigma = [\tfrac{1}{2}(200 - 50)^2 + \tfrac{1}{2}(-100 - 50)^2]^{1/2}$$
$$= 150\%$$

The average rate of return on a sequence of bets, in other words, has a smaller standard deviation than that of a single bet. By increasing the number of bets we can reduce the standard deviation of the rate of return to any desired level. It seems at first glance that Samuelson's colleague was correct. But he was not.

The fallacy of the argument lies in the use of a rate of return criterion to choose from portfolios *that are not equal in size*. Although the portfolio is equally weighted across bets, each extra bet increases the scale of the investment by $1,000. Recall from your corporate finance class that when choosing among mutually exclusive projects you cannot use the internal rate of return (IRR) as your decision criterion when the projects are of different sizes. You have to use the net present value (NPV) rule.

Consider the dollar profit (as opposed to rate of return) distribution of a single bet:

$$E(R) = \tfrac{1}{2} \times 2,000 - \tfrac{1}{2} \times (-1,000)$$
$$= \$500$$
$$\sigma_R = [\tfrac{1}{2}(2,000 - 500)^2 + \tfrac{1}{2}(-1,000 - 500)^2]^{1/2}$$
$$= \$1,500$$

These are independent bets where the total profit from $n$ bets is the sum of the profits from the single bets. Therefore, with $n$ bets

$$[R(n)] = \$500n$$

$$\text{Variance}\left(\sum_{i=1}^{n} R_i\right) = n\sigma_R^2$$

$$\sigma_R(n) = \sqrt{n\sigma_R^2} = \sigma_R\sqrt{n}$$

so that the standard deviation of the dollar return *increases* by a factor equal to the square root of the number of bets, $n$, in contrast to the standard deviation of the rate of return, which *decreases* by a factor of the square root of $n$.

As another analogy, consider the standard coin-tossing game. Whether one flips a fair coin 10 times or 1,000 times, the expected percentage of heads flipped is 50%. One expects the actual *proportion* of heads in a typical running of the 1,000-toss experiment to be closer to 50% than in the 10-toss experiment. This is the law of averages.

But the actual *number* of heads will typically depart from its expected value by a greater amount in the 1,000-toss experiment. For example, 504 heads is close to 50% and is 4 more than the expected number. To exceed the expected number of heads by 4 in the 10-toss game would require 9 out of 10 heads, which is a much more extreme departure from the mean. In the many-toss case, there is more volatility of the *number* of heads and less volatility of the *percentage* of heads. This is the same when an insurance company takes on more policies: The *dollar* variance of its portfolio increases while the *rate of return* variance falls.

The lesson is this: Rate of return analysis is appropriate when considering mutually exclusive portfolios of equal size, which is the usual case in portfolio analysis, where we consider a fixed investment budget and investigate only the consequences of varying investment proportions in various assets. But if an insurance company takes on more and more insurance policies, it is increasing the size of the portfolio. The analysis called for in that case must be cast in terms of dollar profits, in much the same way that NPV is called for instead of IRR when we compare different-sized projects. This is why risk-pooling (i.e., accumulating independent risky prospects) does not act to eliminate risk.

Samuelson's colleague should have counteroffered: "Let's make 1,000 bets, each with your $2 against my $1." Then he would be holding a portfolio of fixed size, equal to $1,000, which is diversified into 1,000 identical independent prospects. This would make the insurance principle work.

Another way for Samuelson's colleague to get around the riskiness of this tempting bet is to share the large bets with friends. Consider a firm engaging in 1,000 of Paul Samuelson's bets. In each bet the firm puts up $1,000 and receives $3,000 or nothing, as before. Each bet is too large for you. Yet if you hold a 1/1,000 share of the firm, your position is exactly the same as if you were to make 1,000 small bets of $2 against $1. A 1/1,000 share of a $1,000 bet is equivalent to a $1 bet. Holding a small share of many large bets essentially allows you to replace a stake in one large bet with a diversified portfolio of manageable bets.

How does this apply to insurance companies? Investors can purchase insurance company shares in the stock market, so they can choose to hold as small a position in the overall risk as they please. No matter how great the risk of the policies, a large group of individual small investors will agree to bear the risk if the expected rate of return exceeds the risk-free rate. Thus it is the sharing of risk among many shareholders that makes the insurance industry tick.

# APPENDIX C: THE FALLACY OF TIME DIVERSIFICATION

The insurance story just discussed illustrates a misuse of rate of return analysis, specifically the mistake of comparing portfolios of different sizes. A more insidious version of this error often appears under the guise of "time diversification."

Consider the case of Mr. Frier, who has $100,000. He is trying to figure out the appropriate allocation of this fund between risk-free T-bills that yield 10% and a risky portfolio that yields an annual rate of return with $E(r_P) = 15\%$ and $\sigma_P = 30\%$.

Mr. Frier took a course in finance in his youth. He likes quantitative models, and after careful introspection estimates that his degree of risk aversion, $A$, is 4. Consequently, he calculates that his proper allocation to the risky portfolio is

$$y = \frac{E(r_P) - r_f}{.01 \times A\sigma_P^2} = \frac{15 - 10}{.01 \times 4 \times 30^2} = .14$$

that is, 14% of his wealth ($14,000) in the optimal risky portfolio.

With this strategy, Mr. Frier calculates his complete portfolio expected return and standard deviation as

$$E(r_C) = r_f + y[E(r_P) - r_f] = 10.70\%$$
$$\sigma_C = y\sigma_P = 4.20\%$$

At this point, Mr. Frier gets cold feet because this fund is intended to provide the mainstay of his retirement wealth. He plans to retire in 5 years, and any mistake will be burdensome.

Mr. Frier calls Ms. Mavin, a highly recommended financial adviser. Ms. Mavin explains that indeed the time factor is all-important. She cites academic research showing that asset rates of return over successive holding periods are nearly independent. Therefore, she argues, returns in good years and bad years will tend to cancel out over the 5-year period. Consequently, the average portfolio rate of return over the investment period will be less risky than would appear from the standard deviation of a single-year portfolio return. Because returns in each year are independent, Ms. Mavin argues that a 5-year investment is equivalent to a portfolio of five equally weighted independent assets. With such a portfolio, the (5-year) holding-period return has a mean of

$$E[r_P(5)] = 15\% \text{ per year}$$

and the standard deviation of the average return is[16]

$$\sigma_P(5) = \frac{30}{\sqrt{5}}$$
$$= 13.42\% \text{ per year}$$

Mr. Frier is relieved. He believes that the effective standard deviation is 13.42% rather than 30%, and that the reward-to-variability ratio is much better than his first assessment.

Is Mr. Frier's newfound sense of security warranted? Specifically, is Ms. Mavin's time diversification really a risk-reducer? It is true that the standard deviation of the annualized *rate* of return over 5 years really is only 13.42% as Mavin claims, compared with the 30% 1-year standard deviation. But what about the volatility of Mr. Frier's total retirement fund? With a standard deviation of the 5-year average return of 13.42%, a one-standard-deviation disappointment in Mr. Frier's average return over the 5-year period will affect final wealth by a factor of $(1 - .1342)^5 = .487$, meaning that final wealth will be less than one-half of its expected value. This is a larger impact than the 30% 1-year swing.

Ms. Mavin is wrong: Time diversification does not reduce risk. Although it is true that the *per year* average rate of return has a smaller standard deviation for a longer time horizon, it also is true that the uncertainty compounds over a greater number of years. Unfortunately, this latter effect dominates in the sense that the *total return* becomes more uncertain the longer the investment horizon.

Figures 8C.1 and 8C.2 show the fallacy of time diversification. They represent simulated returns to a stock investment and show the range of possible outcomes. Although the confidence band around the expected *rate* of return on the investment narrows with investment life, the confidence band around the final portfolio value widens.

Again, the coin-toss analogy is helpful. Think of each year's investment return as one flip of the coin. After many years, the average number of heads approaches 50%, but the possible deviation of total heads from one-half the number of flips still will be growing.

The lesson is, once again, that one should not use rate of return analysis to compare portfolios of different size. Investing for more than one holding period means that the amount of risk is growing. This is analogous to an insurer taking on more insurance policies. The fact that these policies are independent does not offset the effect of placing more funds at risk. Focus on the standard deviation of the rate of return should never obscure the more proper emphasis on the possible dollar values of a portfolio strategy.

---

[16] The calculation for standard deviation is only approximate, because it assumes that the 5-year return is the sum of each of the five 1-year returns, and this formulation ignores compounding. The error is small, however, and does not affect the point we want to make.

**Figure 8C.1
Simulated return
distributions
for the period
2000–2019.
Geometric average
annual rates.**

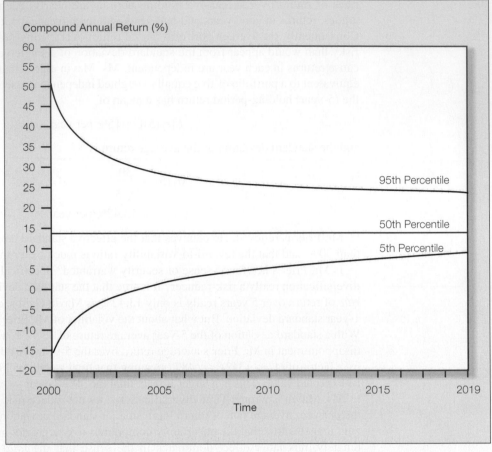

Source: *Stocks, Bonds, Bills, and Inflation: 2000 Yearbook* (Chicago: Ibbotson Associates, Inc., 2000).

As a final comment on this issue, note that one might envision purchasing "rate of return insurance" on some risky asset. The trick to guaranteeing a worst-case return equal to the risk-free rate is to buy a put option on the asset with exercise price equal to the current asset price times $(1 + r)^T$, where $T$ is the investment horizon. Such a put option would provide insurance against a rate of return shortfall on the underlying risky asset. As we discuss in more detail in Chapter 26, the price of such a put necessarily increases as the investment horizon is longer. Therefore, time diversification does not eliminate risk: in fact, the cost of insuring returns *increases* with the investment horizon.

**Figure 8C.2
Dollar returns
on common
stocks. Simulated
distributions of
nominal wealth
index for the
period 2000–2017
(year-end 1999
equals 1.00).**

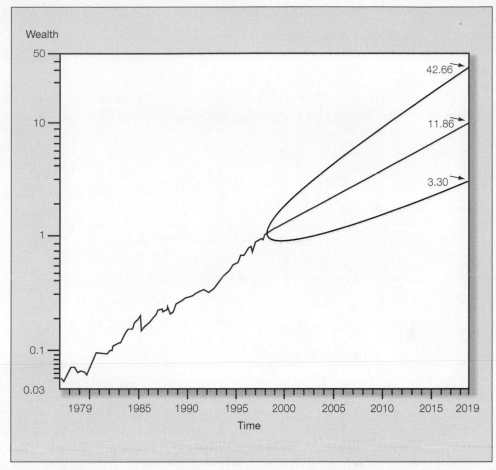

Source: *Stocks, Bonds, Bills, and Inflation: 2000 Yearbook* (Chicago: Ibbotson Associates, Inc., 2000).

# EQUILIBRIUM IN CAPITAL MARKETS

www.mhhe.com/bkm

# THE CAPITAL ASSET PRICING MODEL

The capital asset pricing model, almost always referred to as the CAPM, is a centerpiece of modern financial economics. The model gives us a precise prediction of the relationship that we should observe between the risk of an asset and its expected return. This relationship serves two vital functions. First, it provides a benchmark rate of return for evaluating possible investments. For example, if we are analyzing securities, we might be interested in whether the expected return we forecast for a stock is more or less than its "fair" return given its risk. Second, the model helps us to make an educated guess as to the expected return on assets that have not yet been traded in the marketplace. For example, how do we price an initial public offering of stock? How will a major new investment project affect the return investors require on a company's stock? Although the CAPM does not fully withstand empirical tests, it is widely used because of the insight it offers and because its accuracy suffices for important applications.

# 9.1    THE CAPITAL ASSET PRICING MODEL

The capital asset pricing model is a set of predictions concerning equilibrium expected returns on risky assets. Harry Markowitz laid down the foundation of modern portfolio management in 1952. The CAPM was developed 12 years later in articles by William Sharpe,[1] John Lintner,[2] and Jan Mossin.[3] The time for this gestation indicates that the leap from Markowitz's portfolio selection model to the CAPM is not trivial.

We will approach the CAPM by posing the question "what if," where the "if" part refers to a simplified world. Positing an admittedly unrealistic world allows a relatively easy leap to the "then" part. Once we accomplish this, we can add complexity to the hypothesized environment one step at a time and see how the conclusions must be amended. This process allows us to derive a reasonably realistic and comprehensible model.

We summarize the simplifying assumptions that lead to the basic version of the CAPM in the following list. The thrust of these assumptions is that we try to ensure that individuals are as alike as possible, with the notable exceptions of initial wealth and risk aversion. We will see that conformity of investor behavior vastly simplifies our analysis.

1. There are many investors, each with an endowment (wealth) that is small compared to the total endowment of all investors. Investors are price-takers, in that they act as though security prices are unaffected by their own trades. This is the usual perfect competition assumption of microeconomics.

2. All investors plan for one identical holding period. This behavior is myopic (short-sighted) in that it ignores everything that might happen after the end of the single-period horizon. Myopic behavior is, in general, suboptimal.

3. Investments are limited to a universe of publicly traded financial assets, such as stocks and bonds, and to risk-free borrowing or lending arrangements. This assumption rules out investment in nontraded assets such as education (human capital), private enterprises, and governmentally funded assets such as town halls and international airports. It is assumed also that investors may borrow or lend any amount at a fixed, risk-free rate.

4. Investors pay no taxes on returns and no transaction costs (commissions and service charges) on trades in securities. In reality, of course, we know that investors are in different tax brackets and that this may govern the type of assets in which they invest. For example, tax implications may differ depending on whether the income is from interest, dividends, or capital gains. Furthermore, actual trading is costly, and commissions and fees depend on the size of the trade and the good standing of the individual investor.

5. All investors are rational mean-variance optimizers, meaning that they all use the Markowitz portfolio selection model.

6. All investors analyze securities in the same way and share the same economic view of the world. The result is identical estimates of the probability distribution of future cash flows from investing in the available securities; that is, for any set of security prices, they all derive the same input list to feed into the Markowitz model. Given a set of security prices and the risk-free interest rate, all investors use the same expected returns and covariance matrix of security returns to generate the

---

[1] William Sharpe, "Capital Asset Prices: A Theory of Market Equilibrium," *Journal of Finance,* September 1964.

[2] John Lintner, "The Valuation of Risk Assets and the Selection of Risky Investments in Stock Portfolios and Capital Budgets," *Review of Economics and Statistics,* February 1965.

[3] Jan Mossin, "Equilibrium in a Capital Asset Market," *Econometrica,* October 1966.

efficient frontier and the unique optimal risky portfolio. This assumption is often referred to as **homogeneous expectations** or beliefs.

These assumptions represent the "if" of our "what if" analysis. Obviously, they ignore many real-world complexities. With these assumptions, however, we can gain some powerful insights into the nature of equilibrium in security markets.

We can summarize the equilibrium that will prevail in this hypothetical world of securities and investors briefly. The rest of the chapter explains and elaborates on these implications.

1. All investors will choose to hold a portfolio of risky assets in proportions that duplicate representation of the assets in the **market portfolio** ($M$), which includes all traded assets. For simplicity, we generally refer to all risky assets as *stocks*. The proportion of each stock in the market portfolio equals the market value of the stock (price per share multiplied by the number of shares outstanding) divided by the total market value of all stocks.

2. Not only will the market portfolio be on the efficient frontier, but it also will be the tangency portfolio to the optimal capital allocation line (CAL) derived by each and every investor. As a result, the *capital market line* (CML), the line from the risk-free rate through the market portfolio, $M$, is also the best attainable capital allocation line. All investors hold $M$ as their optimal risky portfolio, differing only in the amount invested in it versus in the risk-free asset.

3. The risk premium on the market portfolio will be proportional to its risk and the degree of risk aversion of the representative investor. Mathematically,

$$E(r_M) - r_f = \bar{A}\sigma_M^2 \times .01$$

where $\sigma_M^2$ is the variance of the market portfolio and $\bar{A}$ is the average degree of risk aversion across investors.[4] Note that because $M$ is the optimal portfolio, which is efficiently diversified across all stocks, $\sigma_M^2$ is the systematic risk of this universe.

4. The risk premium on *individual* assets will be proportional to the risk premium on the market portfolio, $M$, and the *beta coefficient* of the security relative to the market portfolio. Beta measures the extent to which returns on the stock and the market move together. Formally, beta is defined as

$$\beta_i = \frac{\text{Cov}(r_i, r_M)}{\sigma_M^2}$$

and the risk premium on individual securities is

$$E(r_i) - r_f = \frac{\text{Cov}(r_i, r_M)}{\sigma_M^2} [E(r_M) - r_f] = \beta_i[E(r_M) - r_f]$$

We will elaborate on these results and their implications shortly.

**Why Do All Investors Hold the Market Portfolio?** What is the market portfolio? When we sum over, or aggregate, the portfolios of all individual investors, lending and borrowing will cancel out (since each lender has a corresponding borrower), and the value of the aggregate risky portfolio will equal the entire wealth of the economy. This is the market portfolio, $M$. The proportion of each stock in this portfolio equals the market value of

---

[4] As we pointed out in Chapter 8, the scale factor .01 arises because we measure returns as percentages rather than decimals.

**Figure 9.1**
**The efficient**
**frontier and**
**the capital**
**market line**

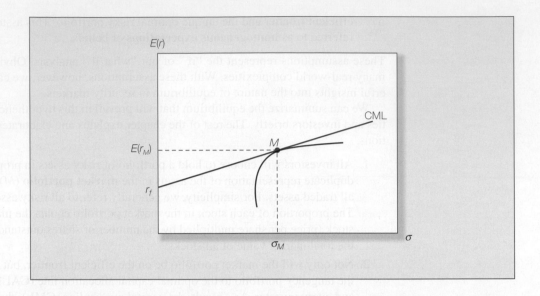

the stock (price per share times number of shares outstanding) divided by the sum of the market values of all stocks.[5] The CAPM implies that as individuals attempt to optimize their personal portfolios, they each arrive at the same portfolio, with weights on each asset equal to those of the market portfolio.

Given the assumptions of the previous section, it is easy to see that all investors will desire to hold identical risky portfolios. If all investors use identical Markowitz analysis (Assumption 5) applied to the same universe of securities (Assumption 3) for the same time horizon (Assumption 2) and use the same input list (Assumption 6), they all must arrive at the same determination of the optimal risky portfolio, the portfolio on the efficient frontier identified by the tangency line from T-bills to that frontier, as in Figure 9.1. This implies that if the weight of GM stock, for example, in each common risky portfolio is 1%, then GM also will comprise 1% of the market portfolio. The same principle applies to the proportion of any stock in each investor's risky portfolio. As a result, the optimal risky portfolio of all investors is simply a share of the market portfolio in Figure 9.1.

Now suppose that the optimal portfolio of our investors does not include the stock of some company, such as Delta Airlines. When all investors avoid Delta stock, the demand is zero, and Delta's price takes a free fall. As Delta stock gets progressively cheaper, it becomes ever more attractive and other stocks look relatively less attractive. Ultimately, Delta reaches a price where it is attractive enough to include in the optimal stock portfolio.

Such a price adjustment process guarantees that all stocks will be included in the optimal portfolio. It shows that *all* assets have to be included in the market portfolio. The only issue is the price at which investors will be willing to include a stock in their optimal risky portfolio.

This may seem a roundabout way to derive a simple result: If all investors hold an identical risky portfolio, this portfolio has to be *M*, the market portfolio. Our intention, however, is to demonstrate a connection between this result and its underpinnings, the equilibrating process that is fundamental to security market operation.

---

[5] As noted previously, we use the term "stock" for convenience; the market portfolio properly includes all assets in the economy.

**The Passive Strategy Is Efficient**  In Chapter 7 we defined the CML (capital market line) as the CAL (capital allocation line) that is constructed from a money market account (or T-bills) and the market portfolio. Perhaps now you can fully appreciate why the CML is an interesting CAL. In the simple world of the CAPM, $M$ is the optimal tangency portfolio on the efficient frontier, as shown in Figure 9.1.

In this scenario the market portfolio that all investors hold is based on the common input list, thereby incorporating all relevant information about the universe of securities. This means that investors can skip the trouble of doing specific analysis and obtain an efficient portfolio simply by holding the market portfolio. (Of course, if everyone were to follow this strategy, no one would perform security analysis and this result would no longer hold. We discuss this issue in greater depth in Chapter 12 on market efficiency.)

Thus the passive strategy of investing in a market index portfolio is efficient. For this reason, we sometimes call this result a **mutual fund theorem**. The mutual fund theorem is another incarnation of the separation property discussed in Chapter 8. Assuming that all investors choose to hold a market index mutual fund, we can separate portfolio selection into two components—a technological problem, creation of mutual funds by professional managers—and a personal problem that depends on an investor's risk aversion, allocation of the *complete* portfolio between the mutual fund and risk-free assets.

In reality, different investment managers do create risky portfolios that differ from the market index. We attribute this in part to the use of different input lists in the formation of the optimal risky portfolio. Nevertheless, the practical significance of the mutual fund theorem is that a passive investor may view the market index as a reasonable first approximation to an efficient risky portfolio.

**CONCEPT CHECK☞ QUESTION 1**  If there are only a few investors who perform security analysis, and all others hold the market portfolio, $M$, would the CML still be the efficient CAL for investors who do not engage in security analysis? Why or why not?

**The Risk Premium of the Market Portfolio**  In Chapter 7 we discussed how individual investors go about deciding how much to invest in the risky portfolio. Returning now to the decision of how much to invest in portfolio $M$ versus in the risk-free asset, what can we deduce about the equilibrium risk premium of portfolio $M$?

We asserted earlier that the equilibrium risk premium on the market portfolio, $E(r_M) - r_f$, will be proportional to the average degree of risk aversion of the investor population and the risk of the market portfolio, $\sigma_M^2$. Now we can explain this result.

Recall that each individual investor chooses a proportion $y$, allocated to the optimal portfolio $M$, such that

$$y = \frac{E(r_M) - r_f}{.01 \times A\sigma_M^2} \qquad (9.1)$$

In the simplified CAPM economy, risk-free investments involve borrowing and lending among investors. Any borrowing position must be offset by the lending position of the creditor. This means that net borrowing and lending across all investors must be zero, and in consequence the average position in the risky portfolio is 100%, or $\bar{y} = 1$. Setting $y = 1$ in equation 9.1 and rearranging, we find that the risk premium on the market portfolio is related to its variance by the average degree of risk aversion:

$$E(r_M) - r_f = .01 \times \bar{A}\sigma_M^2 \qquad (9.2)$$

Data from the period 1926 to 2002 (see Table 5.2) for the S&P 500 index yield
the following statistics: average excess return, 8.2%; standard deviation, 20.6%.

*a.* To the extent that these averages approximated investor expectations for
the period, what must have been the average coefficient of risk aversion?

*b.* If the coefficient of risk aversion were actually 3.5, what risk premium
would have been consistent with the market's historical standard
deviation?

## Expected Returns on Individual Securities

The CAPM is built on the insight that the appropriate risk premium on an
asset will be determined by its contribution to the risk of investors' overall
portfolios. Portfolio risk is what matters to investors and is what governs the
risk premiums they demand.

Remember that all investors use the same input list, that is, the same estimates of expected returns, variances, and covariances. We saw in Chapter 8 that these covariances can
be arranged in a covariance matrix, so that the entry in the fifth row and third column, for
example, would be the covariance between the rates of return on the fifth and third securities. Each diagonal entry of the matrix is the covariance of one security's return with itself,
which is simply the variance of that security. We will consider the construction of the input
list a bit later. For now we take it as given.

Suppose, for example, that we want to gauge the portfolio risk of GM stock. We measure the contribution to the risk of the overall portfolio from holding GM stock by its covariance with the market portfolio. To see why this is so, let us look again at the way the
variance of the market portfolio is calculated. To calculate the variance of the market portfolio, we use the bordered covariance matrix with the market portfolio weights, as discussed in Chapter 8. We highlight GM in this depiction of the $n$ stocks in the market
portfolio.

| Portfolio Weights | $w_1$ | $w_2$ | ... | $w_{GM}$ | ... | $w_n$ |
|---|---|---|---|---|---|---|
| $w_1$ | $Cov(r_1, r_1)$ | $Cov(r_1, r_2)$ | ... | $Cov(r_1, r_{GM})$ | ... | $Cov(r_1, r_n)$ |
| $w_2$ | $Cov(r_2, r_1)$ | $Cov(r_2, r_2)$ | ... | $Cov(r_2, r_{GM})$ | ... | $Cov(r_2, r_n)$ |
| ⋮ | ⋮ | ⋮ | | ⋮ | | ⋮ |
| $w_{GM}$ | $Cov(r_{GM}, r_1)$ | $Cov(r_{GM}, r_2)$ | ... | $Cov(r_{GM}, r_{GM})$ | ... | $Cov(r_{GM}, r_n)$ |
| ⋮ | ⋮ | ⋮ | | ⋮ | | ⋮ |
| $w_n$ | $Cov(r_n, r_1)$ | $Cov(r_n, r_2)$ | ... | $Cov(r_n, r_{GM})$ | ... | $Cov(r_n, r_n)$ |

Recall that we calculate the variance of the portfolio by summing over all the elements of
the covariance matrix, first multiplying each element by the portfolio weights from the row
and the column. The contribution of one stock to portfolio variance therefore can be expressed as the sum of all the covariance terms in the row corresponding to the stock, where
each covariance is first multiplied by both the stock's weight from its row and the weight
from its column.[6]

---

[6] An alternative approach would be to measure GM's contribution to market variance as the sum of the elements in the row *and*
the column corresponding to GM. In this case, GM's contribution would be twice the sum in equation 9.3. The approach that we
take in the text allocates contributions to portfolio risk among securities in a convenient manner in that the sum of the contributions of each stock equals the total portfolio variance, whereas the alternative measure of contribution would sum to twice the portfolio variance. This results from a type of double-counting, because adding both the rows and the columns for each stock would
result in each entry in the matrix being added twice.

For example, the contribution of GM's stock to the variance of the market portfolio is

$$w_{GM}[w_1\text{Cov}(r_1, r_{GM}) + w_2\text{Cov}(r_2, r_{GM}) + \cdots + w_{GM}\text{Cov}(r_{GM}, r_{GM}) + \cdots + w_n\text{Cov}(r_n, r_{GM})] \tag{9.3}$$

Equation 9.3 provides a clue about the respective roles of variance and covariance in determining asset risk. When there are many stocks in the economy, there will be many more covariance terms than variance terms. Consequently, the covariance of a particular stock with all other stocks will dominate that stock's contribution to total portfolio risk. We may summarize the terms in square brackets in equation 9.3 simply as the covariance of GM with the market portfolio. In other words, we can best measure the stock's contribution to the risk of the market portfolio by its covariance with that portfolio:

$$\text{GM's contribution to variance} = w_{GM}\text{Cov}(r_{GM}, r_M)$$

This should not surprise us. For example, if the covariance between GM and the rest of the market is negative, then GM makes a "negative contribution" to portfolio risk: By providing returns that move inversely with the rest of the market, GM stabilizes the return on the overall portfolio. If the covariance is positive, GM makes a positive contribution to overall portfolio risk because its returns amplify swings in the rest of the portfolio.

To demonstrate this more rigorously, note that the rate of return on the market portfolio may be written as

$$r_M = \sum_{k=1}^{n} w_k r_k$$

Therefore, the covariance of the return on GM with the market portfolio is

$$\text{Cov}(r_{GM}, r_M) = \text{Cov}\left(r_{GM}, \sum_{k=1}^{n} w_k r_k\right) = \sum_{k=1}^{n} w_k \text{Cov}(r_{GM}, r_k) \tag{9.4}$$

Notice that the last term of equation 9.4 is precisely the same as the term in brackets in equation 9.3. Therefore, equation 9.3, which is the contribution of GM to the variance of the market portfolio, may be simplified to $w_{GM}\text{Cov}(r_{GM}, r_M)$. We also observe that the contribution of our holding of GM to the risk premium of the market portfolio is $w_{GM}[E(r_M) - r_f]$.

Therefore, the reward-to-risk ratio for investments in GM can be expressed as

$$\frac{\text{GM's contribution to risk premium}}{\text{GM's contribution to variance}} = \frac{w_{GM}[E(r_{GM}) - r_f]}{w_{GM}\text{Cov}(r_{GM}, r_M)} = \frac{E(r_{GM}) - r_f}{\text{Cov}(r_{GM}, r_M)}$$

The market portfolio is the tangency (efficient mean-variance) portfolio. The reward-to-risk ratio for investment in the market portfolio is

$$\frac{\text{Market risk premium}}{\text{Market variance}} = \frac{E(r_M) - r_f}{\sigma_M^2} \tag{9.5}$$

The ratio in equation 9.5 is often called the **market price of risk**[7] because it quantifies the extra return that investors demand to bear portfolio risk. Notice that for *components* of the efficient portfolio, such as shares of GM, we measure risk as the *contribution* to portfolio

---

[7] We open ourselves to ambiguity in using this term, because the market portfolio's reward-to-variability ratio

$$\frac{E(r_M) - r_f}{\sigma_M}$$

sometimes is referred to as the market price of risk. Note that since the appropriate risk measure of GM is its covariance with the market portfolio (its contribution to the variance of the market portfolio), this risk is measured in percent squared. Accordingly, the price of this risk, $[E(r_M) - r_f]/\sigma^2$, is defined as the percentage expected return per percent square of variance.

variance. In contrast, for the efficient portfolio itself, its variance is the appropriate measure of risk.

A basic principle of equilibrium is that all investments should offer the same reward-to-risk ratio. If the ratio were better for one investment than another, investors would rearrange their portfolios, tilting toward the alternative with the better trade-off and shying away from the other. Such activity would impart pressure on security prices until the ratios were equalized. Therefore we conclude that the reward-to-risk ratios of GM and the market portfolio should be equal:

$$\frac{E(r_{GM}) - r_f}{\text{Cov}(r_{GM}, r_M)} = \frac{E(r_M) - r_f}{\sigma_M^2} \tag{9.6}$$

To determine the fair risk premium of GM stock, we rearrange equation (9.6) slightly to obtain

$$E(r_{GM}) - r_f = \frac{\text{Cov}(r_{GM}, r_M)}{\sigma_M^2} [E(r_M) - r_f] \tag{9.7}$$

The ratio $\text{Cov}(r_{GM}, r_M)/\sigma_M^2$ measures the contribution of GM stock to the variance of the market portfolio as a fraction of the total variance of the market portfolio. The ratio is called **beta** and is denoted by $\beta$. Using this measure, we can restate equation 9.7 as

$$E(r_{GM}) = r_f + \beta_{GM}[E(r_M) - r_f] \tag{9.8}$$

This **expected return–beta relationship** is the most familiar expression of the CAPM to practitioners. We will have a lot more to say about the expected return–beta relationship shortly.

We see now why the assumptions that made individuals act similarly are so useful. If everyone holds an identical risky portfolio, then everyone will find that the beta of each asset with the market portfolio equals the asset's beta with his or her own risky portfolio. Hence everyone will agree on the appropriate risk premium for each asset.

Does the fact that few real-life investors actually hold the market portfolio imply that the CAPM is of no practical importance? Not necessarily. Recall from Chapter 8 that reasonably well-diversified portfolios shed firm-specific risk and are left with mostly systematic or market risk. Even if one does not hold the precise market portfolio, a well-diversified portfolio will be so very highly correlated with the market that a stock's beta relative to the market will still be a useful risk measure.

In fact, several authors have shown that modified versions of the CAPM will hold true even if we consider differences among individuals leading them to hold different portfolios. For example, Brennan[8] examined the impact of differences in investors' personal tax rates on market equilibrium, and Mayers[9] looked at the impact of nontraded assets such as human capital (earning power). Both found that although the market portfolio is no longer each investor's optimal risky portfolio, the expected return–beta relationship should still hold in a somewhat modified form.

If the expected return–beta relationship holds for any individual asset, it must hold for any combination of assets. Suppose that some portfolio $P$ has weight $w_k$ for stock $k$, where $k$ takes on values $1, \ldots, n$. Writing out the CAPM equation 9.8 for each stock, and multiplying each equation by the weight of the stock in the portfolio, we obtain these equations, one for each stock:

---

[8] Michael J. Brennan, "Taxes, Market Valuation, and Corporate Finance Policy," *National Tax Journal*, December 1973.
[9] David Mayers, "Nonmarketable Assets and Capital Market Equilibrium under Uncertainty," in *Studies in the Theory of Capital Markets*, ed. M. C. Jensen (New York: Praeger, 1972).

$$w_1 E(r_1) = w_1 r_f + w_1 \beta_1 [E(r_M) - r_f]$$
$$+ w_2 E(r_2) = w_2 r_f + w_2 \beta_2 [E(r_M) - r_f]$$
$$+ \quad \cdots = \cdots$$
$$\underline{+ w_n E(r_n) = w_n r_f + w_n \beta_n [E(r_M) - r_f]}$$
$$E(r_P) = r_f + \beta_P [E(r_M) - r_f]$$

Summing each column shows that the CAPM holds for the overall portfolio because $E(r_P) = \sum_k w_k E(r_k)$ is the expected return on the portfolio, and $\beta_P = \sum_k w_k \beta_k$ is the portfolio beta. Incidentally, this result has to be true for the market portfolio itself,

$$E(r_M) = r_f + \beta_M [E(r_M) - r_f]$$

Indeed, this is a tautology because $\beta_M = 1$, as we can verify by noting that

$$\beta_M = \frac{\text{Cov}(r_M, r_M)}{\sigma_M^2} = \frac{\sigma_M^2}{\sigma_M^2}$$

This also establishes 1 as the weighted-average value of beta across all assets. If the market beta is 1, and the market is a portfolio of all assets in the economy, the weighted-average beta of all assets must be 1. Hence betas greater than 1 are considered aggressive in that investment in high-beta stocks entails above-average sensitivity to market swings. Betas below 1 can be described as defensive.

A word of caution: We are all accustomed to hearing that well-managed firms will provide high rates of return. We agree this is true if one measures the *firm's* return on investments in plant and equipment. The CAPM, however, predicts returns on investments in the *securities* of the firm.

Let us say that everyone knows a firm is well run. Its stock price will therefore be bid up, and consequently returns to stockholders who buy at those high prices will not be excessive. Security prices, in other words, already reflect public information about a firm's prospects; therefore only the risk of the company (as measured by beta in the context of the CAPM) should affect expected returns. In a rational market investors receive high expected returns only if they are willing to bear risk.

Of course, investors do not directly observe or determine expected returns on securities. Rather, they observe security prices and bid those prices up or down. Expected rates of return are determined by the prices investors must pay compared to the cash flows those investments might garner. The connection between security expected returns and the market-price equilibrium process is described in more detail in the Appendix to this chapter.

**CONCEPT CHECK ☞ QUESTION 3**   Suppose that the risk premium on the market portfolio is estimated at 8% with a standard deviation of 22%. What is the risk premium on a portfolio invested 25% in GM and 75% in Ford, if they have betas of 1.10 and 1.25, respectively?

**The Security Market Line**   We can view the expected return–beta relationship as a reward–risk equation. The beta of a security is the appropriate measure of its risk because beta is proportional to the risk that the security contributes to the optimal risky portfolio.

Risk-averse investors measure the risk of the optimal risky portfolio by its variance. In this world we would expect the reward, or the risk premium on individual assets, to depend on the *contribution* of the individual asset to the risk of the portfolio. The beta of a stock measures the stock's contribution to the variance of the market portfolio. Hence we expect, for any asset or portfolio, the required risk premium to be a function of beta. The CAPM confirms this intuition, stating further that the security's risk premium is directly proportional to both the beta and the risk premium of the market portfolio; that is, the risk premium equals $\beta[E(r_M) - r_f]$.

The expected return–beta relationship can be portrayed graphically as the **security market line (SML)** in Figure 9.2. Because the market beta is 1, the slope is the risk premium of the market portfolio. At the point on the horizontal axis where $\beta = 1$ (which is the market portfolio's beta) we can read off the vertical axis the expected return on the market portfolio.

It is useful to compare the security market line to the capital market line. The CML graphs the risk premiums of *efficient* portfolios (i.e., portfolios composed of the market and the risk-free asset) as a function of portfolio standard deviation. This is appropriate because standard deviation is a valid measure of risk for efficiently diversified portfolios that are candidates for an investor's overall portfolio. The SML, in contrast, graphs *individual asset* risk premiums as a function of asset risk. The relevant measure of risk for individual assets held as parts of well-diversified portfolios is not the asset's standard deviation or variance; it is, instead, the contribution of the asset to the portfolio variance, which we measure by the asset's beta. The SML is valid for both efficient portfolios and individual assets.

The security market line provides a benchmark for the evaluation of investment performance. Given the risk of an investment, as measured by its beta, the SML provides the required rate of return necessary to compensate investors for both risk as well as the time value of money.

Because the security market line is the graphic representation of the expected return–beta relationship, "fairly priced" assets plot exactly on the SML; that is, their expected returns are commensurate with their risk. Given the assumptions we made at the start of this section, all securities must lie on the SML in market equilibrium. Nevertheless, we see here how the CAPM may be of use in the money-management industry. Suppose that the SML relation is used as a benchmark to assess the fair expected return on a risky asset. Then security analysis is performed to calculate the return actually expected. (Notice that we

**Figure 9.2**
**The security market line**

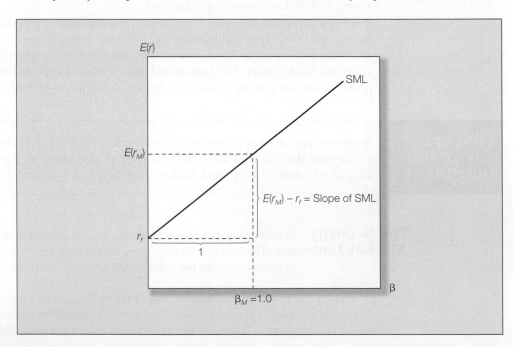

depart here from the simple CAPM world in that some investors now apply their own unique analysis to derive an "input list" that may differ from their competitors'.) If a stock is perceived to be a good buy, or underpriced, it will provide an expected return in excess of the fair return stipulated by the SML. Underpriced stocks therefore plot above the SML: Given their betas, their expected returns are greater than dictated by the CAPM. Overpriced stocks plot below the SML.

The difference between the fair and actually expected rates of return on a stock is called the stock's **alpha**, denoted $\alpha$. For example, if the market return is expected to be 14%, a stock has a beta of 1.2, and the T-bill rate is 6%, the SML would predict an expected return on the stock of $6 + 1.2(14 - 6) = 15.6\%$. If one believed the stock would provide an expected return of 17%, the implied alpha would be 1.4% (see Figure 9.3).

One might say that security analysis (which we treat in Part 5) is about uncovering securities with nonzero alphas. This analysis suggests that the starting point of portfolio management can be a passive market-index portfolio. The portfolio manager will then increase the weights of securities with positive alphas and decrease the weights of securities with negative alphas. We show one strategy for adjusting the portfolio weights in such a manner in Chapter 27.

The CAPM is also useful in capital budgeting decisions. For a firm considering a new project, the CAPM can provide the *required rate of return* that the project needs to yield, based on its beta, to be acceptable to investors. Managers can use the CAPM to obtain this cutoff internal rate of return (IRR), or "hurdle rate" for the project.

The box on page 294 describes how the CAPM can be used in capital budgeting. It also discusses some empirical anomalies concerning the model, which we address in detail in Chapters 12 and 13. The article asks whether the CAPM is useful for capital budgeting in

**Figure 9.3**
**The SML and a positive-alpha stock**

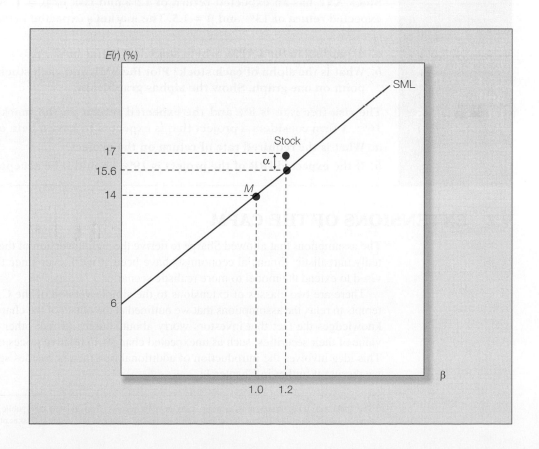

light of these shortcomings; it concludes that even given the anomalies cited, the model still can be useful to managers who wish to increase the fundamental value of their firms.

## EXAMPLE 9.1    Using the CAPM

Yet another use of the CAPM is in utility rate-making cases.[10] In this case the issue is the rate of return that a regulated utility should be allowed to earn on its investment in plant and equipment. Suppose that the equityholders have invested $100 million in the firm and that the beta of the equity is .6. If the T-bill rate is 6% and the market risk premium is 8%, then the fair profits to the firm would be assessed as $6 + .6(8) = 10.8\%$ of the $100 million investment, or $10.8 million. The firm would be allowed to set prices at a level expected to generate these profits.

---

**CONCEPT CHECK ☞ QUESTION 4 and QUESTION 5**

Stock XYZ has an expected return of 12% and risk of $\beta = 1$. Stock ABC has expected return of 13% and $\beta = 1.5$. The market's expected return is 11%, and $r_f = 5\%$.

*a.* According to the CAPM, which stock is a better buy?

*b.* What is the alpha of each stock? Plot the SML and each stock's risk–return point on one graph. Show the alphas graphically.

The risk-free rate is 8% and the expected return on the market portfolio is 16%. A firm considers a project that is expected to have a beta of 1.3.

*a.* What is the required rate of return on the project?

*b.* If the expected IRR of the project is 19%, should it be accepted?

---

## 9.2    EXTENSIONS OF THE CAPM

The assumptions that allowed Sharpe to derive the simple version of the CAPM are admittedly unrealistic. Financial economists have been at work ever since the CAPM was devised to extend the model to more realistic scenarios.

There are two classes of extensions to the simple version of the CAPM. The first attempts to relax the assumptions that we outlined at the outset of the chapter. The second acknowledges the fact that investors worry about sources of risk other than the uncertain value of their securities, such as unexpected changes in relative prices of consumer goods. This idea involves the introduction of additional risk factors besides security returns, and we discuss it further in Chapter 11.

---

[10] This application is fast disappearing, as many states are in the process of deregulating their public utilities and allowing a far greater degree of free market pricing. Nevertheless, a considerable amount of rate setting still takes place.

**The CAPM with Restricted Borrowing: The Zero-Beta Model**

The CAPM is predicated on the assumption that all investors share an identical input list that they feed into the Markowitz algorithm. Thus all investors agree on the location of the efficient (minimum-variance) frontier, where each portfolio has the lowest variance among all feasible portfolios at a target expected rate of return. When all investors can borrow and lend at the safe rate, $r_f$, all agree on the optimal tangency portfolio and choose to hold a share of the market portfolio.

However, when borrowing is restricted, as it is for many financial institutions, or when the borrowing rate is higher than the lending rate because borrowers pay a default premium, the market portfolio is no longer the common optimal portfolio for all investors.

When investors no longer can borrow at a common risk-free rate, they may choose risky portfolios from the entire set of efficient frontier portfolios according to how much risk they choose to bear. The market is no longer the common optimal portfolio. In fact, with investors choosing different portfolios, it is no longer obvious whether the market portfolio, which is the aggregate of all investors' portfolios, will even be on the efficient frontier. If the market portfolio is no longer mean-variance efficient, then the expected return–beta relationship of the CAPM will no longer characterize market equilibrium.

An equilibrium expected return–beta relationship in the case of restrictions on risk-free investments has been developed by Fischer Black.[11] Black's model is fairly difficult and requires a good deal of facility with mathematics. Therefore, we will satisfy ourselves with a sketch of Black's argument and spend more time with its implications.

Black's model of the CAPM in the absence of a risk-free asset rests on the three following properties of mean-variance efficient portfolios:

1. Any portfolio constructed by combining efficient portfolios is itself on the efficient frontier.

2. Every portfolio on the efficient frontier has a "companion" portfolio on the bottom half (the inefficient part) of the minimum-variance frontier with which it is uncorrelated. Because the portfolios are uncorrelated, the companion portfolio is referred to as the **zero-beta portfolio** of the efficient portfolio.

   The expected return of an efficient portfolio's zero-beta companion portfolio can be derived by the following graphical procedure. From any efficient portfolio such as $P$ in Figure 9.4 on page 296 draw a tangency line to the vertical axis. The intercept will be the expected return on portfolio $P$'s zero-beta companion portfolio, denoted $Z(P)$. The horizontal line from the intercept to the minimum-variance frontier identifies the standard deviation of the zero-beta portfolio. Notice in Figure 9.4 that different efficient portfolios such as $P$ and $Q$ have different zero-beta companions.

   These tangency lines are helpful constructs only. They do *not* signify that one can invest in portfolios with expected return–standard deviation pairs along the line. That would be possible only by mixing a risk-free asset with the tangency portfolio. In this case, however, we assume that risk-free assets are not available to investors.

3. The expected return of any asset can be expressed as an exact, linear function of the expected return on any two frontier portfolios. Consider, for example, the minimum-variance frontier portfolios $P$ and $Q$. Black showed that the expected return on any asset $i$ can be expressed as

$$E(r_i) = E(r_Q) + [E(r_P) - E(r_Q)] \frac{\text{Cov}(r_i, r_P) - \text{Cov}(r_P, r_Q)}{\sigma_P^2 - \text{Cov}(r_P, r_Q)} \qquad (9.9)$$

---

[11] Fischer Black, "Capital Market Equilibrium with Restricted Borrowing," *Journal of Business*, July 1972.

**Financial markets' evaluation of risk determines the way firms invest. What if the markets are wrong?**

Investors are rarely praised for their good sense. But for the past two decades a growing number of firms have based their decisions on a model which assumes that people are perfectly rational. If they are irrational, are businesses making the wrong choices?

The model, known as the "capital-asset pricing model," or CAPM, has come to dominate modern finance. Almost any manager who wants to defend a project—be it a brand, a factory or a corporate merger—must justify his decision partly based on the CAPM. The reason is that the model tells a firm how to calculate the return that its investors demand. If shareholders are to benefit, the returns from any project must clear this "hurdle rate."

Although the CAPM is complicated, it can be reduced to five simple ideas:

- Investors can eliminate some risks—such as the risk that workers will strike, or that a firm's boss will quit—by diversifying across many regions and sectors.

- Some risks, such as that of a global recession, cannot be eliminated through diversification. So even a basket of all of the stocks in a stock market will still be risky.

- People must be rewarded for investing in such a risky basket by earning returns above those that they can get on safer assets, such as Treasury bills.

- The rewards on a specific investment depend only on the extent to which it affects the market basket's risk.

- Conveniently, that contribution to the market basket's risk can be captured by a single measure—dubbed "beta"—which expresses the relationship between the investment's risk and the market's.

Beta is what makes the CAPM so powerful. Although an investment may face many risks, diversified investors should care only about those that are related to the market

## Beta Power

basket. Beta not only tells managers how to measure those risks, but it also allows them to translate them directly into a hurdle rate. If the future profits from a project will not exceed that rate, it is not worth shareholders' money.

The diagram shows how the CAPM works. Safe investments, such as Treasury bills, have a beta of zero. Riskier investments should earn a premium over the risk-free rate which increases with beta. Those whose risks roughly match the market's have a beta of one, by definition, and should earn the market return.

So suppose that a firm is considering two projects, A and B. Project A has a beta of ½: when the market rises or falls by 10%, its returns tend to rise or fall by 5%. So its

---

Note that Property 3 has nothing to do with market equilibrium. It is a purely mathematical property relating frontier portfolios and individual securities.

With these three properties, the Black model can be applied to any of several variations: no risk-free asset at all, risk-free lending but no risk-free borrowing, and borrowing at a rate higher than $r_f$. We show here how the model works for the case with risk-free lending but no borrowing.

Imagine an economy with only two investors, one relatively risk averse and one risk tolerant. The risk-averse investor will choose a portfolio on the CAL supported by portfolio $T$ in Figure 9.5, that is, he will mix portfolio $T$ with lending at the risk-free rate. $T$ is the tangency portfolio on the efficient frontier from the risk-free lending rate, $r_f$. The risk-tolerant investor is willing to accept more risk to earn a higher-risk premium; she will risk premium is only half that of the market. Project B's risk premium is twice that of the market, so it must earn a higher return to justify the expenditure.

## Never Knowingly Underpriced

But there is one small problem with the CAPM: Financial economists have found that beta is not much use for explaining rates of return on firms' shares. Worse, there appears to be another measure which explains these returns quite well.

That measure is the ratio of a firm's book value (the value of its assets at the time they entered the balance sheet) to its market value. Several studies have found that, on average, companies that have high book-to-market ratios tend to earn excess returns over long periods, even after adjusting for the risks that are associated with beta.

The discovery of this book-to-market effect has sparked a fierce debate among financial economists. All of them agree that some risks ought to carry greater rewards. But they are now deeply divided over how risk should be measured. Some argue that since investors are rational, the book-to-market effect must be capturing an extra risk factor. They conclude, therefore, that managers should incorporate the book-to-market effect into their hurdle rates. They have labeled this alternative hurdle rate the "new estimator of expected return," or NEER.

Other financial economists, however, dispute this approach. Since there is no obvious extra risk associated with a high book-to-market ratio, they say, investors must be mistaken. Put simply, they are underpricing high book-to-market stocks, causing them to earn abnormally high returns. If managers of such firms try to exceed those inflated hurdle rates, they will forgo many profitable investments. With economists now at odds, what is a conscientious manager to do?

In a new paper,* Jeremy Stein, an economist at the Massachusetts Institute of Technology's business school, offers a paradoxical answer. If investors are rational, then beta cannot be the only measure of risk, so managers should stop using it. Conversely, if investors are irrational, then beta is still the right measure in many cases. Mr. Stein argues that if beta captures an asset's fundamental risk— that is, its contribution to the market basket's risk—then it will often make sense for managers to pay attention to it, even if investors are somehow failing to.

Often, but not always. At the heart of Mr. Stein's argument lies a crucial distinction—that between (a) boosting a firm's long-term value and (b) trying to raise its share price. If investors are rational, these are the same thing: any decision that raises long-term value will instantly increase the share price as well. But if investors are making predictable mistakes, a manager must choose.

For instance, if he wants to increase today's share price—perhaps because he wants to sell his shares, or to fend off a takeover attempt—he must usually stick with the NEER approach, accommodating investors' misperceptions. But if he is interested in long-term value, he should usually continue to use beta. Showing a flair for marketing, Mr. Stein labels this far-sighted alternative to NEER the "fundamental asset risk"—or FAR—approach.

Mr. Stein's conclusions will no doubt irritate many company bosses, who are fond of denouncing their investors' myopia. They have resented the way in which CAPM—with its assumption of investor infallibility—has come to play an important role in boardroom decision-making. But it now appears that if they are right, and their investors are wrong, then those same far-sighted managers ought to be the CAPM's biggest fans.

*Jeremy Stein, "Rational Capital Budgeting in an Irrational World," *The Journal of Business*, October 1996.
Source: "Tales from the FAR Side," *The Economist*, November 16, 1996, p. 8.

choose portfolio $S$. This portfolio lies along the efficient frontier with higher risk and return than portfolio $T$. The aggregate risky portfolio (i.e., the market portfolio, $M$) will be a combination of $T$ and $S$, with weights determined by the relative wealth and degrees of risk aversion of the two investors. Since $T$ and $S$ are each on the efficient frontier, so is $M$ (from Property 1).

From Property 2, $M$ has a companion zero-beta portfolio on the minimum-variance frontier, $Z(M)$, shown in Figure 9.5. Moreover, by Property 3 we can express the return on any security in terms of $M$ and $Z(M)$ as in equation 9.9. But, since by construction $\text{Cov}[r_M, r_{Z(M)}] = 0$, the expression simplifies to

$$E(r_i) = E[r_{Z(M)}] + E[r_M - r_{Z(M)}] \frac{\text{Cov}(r_i, r_M)}{\sigma_M^2} \tag{9.10}$$

**Figure 9.4
Efficient
portfolios
and their
zero-beta
companions**

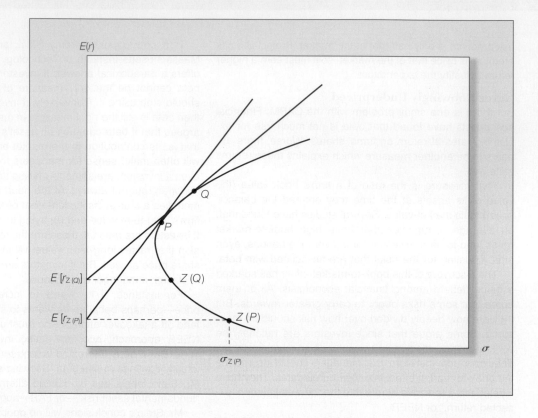

**Figure 9.5
Capital market
equilibrium with
no borrowing**

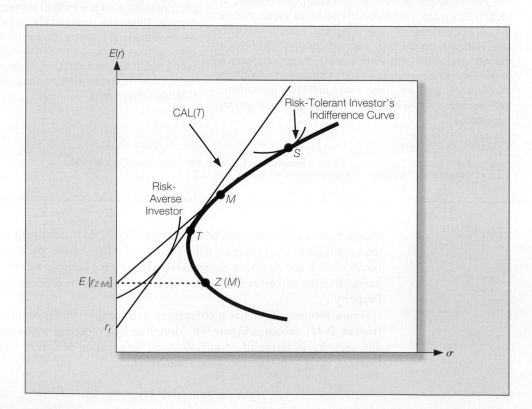

where $P$ from equation 9.9 has been replaced by $M$ and $Q$ has been replaced by $Z(M)$. Equation 9.10 may be interpreted as a variant of the simple CAPM, in which $r_f$ has been replaced with $E[r_{Z(M)}]$.

The more realistic scenario, where investors lend at the risk-free rate and borrow at a higher rate, was considered in Chapter 8. The same arguments that we have just employed can also be used to establish the zero-beta CAPM in this situation. Problem 18 at the end of this chapter asks you to fill in the details of the argument for this situation.

| CONCEPT CHECK☞ QUESTION 6 | Suppose that the zero-beta portfolio exhibits returns that are, on average, greater than the rate on T-bills. Is this fact relevant to the question of the validity of the CAPM? |
| --- | --- |

### Lifetime Consumption and the CAPM

One of the restrictive assumptions for the simple version of the CAPM is that investors are myopic—they plan for one common holding period. Investors actually may be concerned with a lifetime consumption plan and a desire to leave a bequest to children. Consumption plans that are feasible for them depend on current wealth and future rates of return on the investment portfolio. These investors will want to rebalance their portfolios as often as required by changes in wealth.

However, Eugene Fama[12] showed that, even if we extend our analysis to a multiperiod setting, the single-period CAPM still may be appropriate. The key assumptions that Fama used to replace myopic planning horizons are that investor preferences are unchanging over time and the risk-free interest rate and probability distribution of security returns do not change unpredictably over time. Of course, this latter assumption is also unrealistic. A variant of the CAPM that allows for such unpredictability is presented in Chapter 11.

## 9.3   THE CAPM AND LIQUIDITY

**Liquidity** refers to the cost and ease with which an asset can be converted into cash, that is, sold. Traders have long recognized the importance of liquidity, and some evidence suggests that illiquidity can reduce market prices substantially. For example, one study[13] finds that market discounts on closely held (and therefore nontraded) firms can exceed 30%. The nearby box focuses on the relationship between liquidity and stock returns.

A rigorous treatment of the value of liquidity was first developed by Amihud and Mendelson.[14] Several studies show that liquidity plays an important role in explaining rates of return on financial assets.[15] Chordia, Roll, and Subrahmanyam[16] find commonality across stocks in the variable cost of liquidity: quoted spreads, quoted depth, and effective spreads covary with the market and industrywide liquidity. Hence, liquidity risk is systematic and therefore difficult to diversify. We believe that liquidity will become an

---

[12] Eugene F. Fama, "Multiperiod Consumption-Investment Decisions," *American Economic Review* 60 (1970).

[13] Shannon P. Pratt, *Valuing a Business: The Analysis of Closely Held Companies*, 2nd ed. (Homewood, IL.: Dow Jones–Irwin, 1989).

[14] Yakov Amihud and Haim Mendelson, "Asset Pricing and the Bid–Ask Spread," *Journal of Financial Economics* 17 (1986), pp. 223–49.

[15] For example, Venkat Eleswarapu, "Cost of Transacting and Expected Returns in the NASDAQ Market," *Journal of Finance* 2, no. 5 (1993), pp. 2113–27.

[16] Tarun Chordia, Richard Roll, and Avanidhar Subrahmanyam, "Commonality and Liquidity," *Journal of Financial Economics*, April 2000.

Given a choice between liquid and illiquid stocks, most investors, to the extent they think of it at all, opt for issues they know are easy to get in and out of.

But for long-term investors who don't trade often—which includes most individuals—that may be unnecessarily expensive. Recent studies of the performance of listed stocks show that, on average, less-liquid issues generate substantially higher returns—as much as several percentage points a year at the extremes. . . .

## Illiquidity Payoff

Among the academic studies that have attempted to quantify this illiquidity payoff is a recent work by two finance professors, Yakov Amihud of New York University and Tel Aviv University, and Haim Mendelson of the University of Rochester. Their study looks at New York Stock Exchange issues over the 1961–1980 period and defines liquidity in terms of bid–asked spreads as a percentage of overall share price.

Market makers use spreads in quoting stocks to define the difference between the price they'll bid to take stock off an investor's hands and the price they'll offer to sell stock to any willing buyer. The bid price is always somewhat lower because of the risk to the broker of tying up precious capital to hold stock in inventory until it can be resold.

If a stock is relatively illiquid, which means there's not a ready flow of orders from customers clamoring to buy it, there's more of a chance the broker will lose money on the trade. To hedge this risk, market makers demand an even bigger discount to service potential sellers, and the spread will widen further.

The study by Profs. Amihud and Mendelson shows that liquidity spreads—measured as a percentage discount from

the stock's total price—ranged from less than 0.1%, for widely held International Business Machines Corp., to as much as 4% to 5%. The widest-spread group was dominated by smaller, low-priced stocks.

The study found that, overall, the least-liquid stocks averaged an 8.5 percent-a-year higher return than the most-liquid stocks over the 20-year period. On average, a one percentage point increase in the spread was associated with a 2.5% higher annual return for New York Stock Exchange stocks. The relationship held after results were adjusted for size and other risk factors.

An extension of the study of Big Board stocks done at *The Wall Street Journal*'s request produced similar findings. It shows that for the 1980–85 period, a one percentage-point-wider spread was associated with an extra average annual gain of 2.4%. Meanwhile, the least-liquid stocks outperformed the most-liquid stocks by almost six percentage points a year.

## Cost of Trading

Since the cost of the spread is incurred each time the stock is traded, illiquid stocks can quickly become prohibitively expensive for investors who trade frequently. On the other hand, long-term investors needn't worry so much about spreads, since they can amortize them over a longer period.

In terms of investment strategy, this suggests "that the small investor should tailor the types of stocks he or she buys to his expected holding period," Prof. Mendelson says. If the investor expects to sell within three months, he says, it's better to pay up for the liquidity and get the lowest spread. If the investor plans to hold the stock for a year or more, it makes sense to aim at stocks with spreads of 3% or more to capture the extra return.

important part of standard valuation, and therefore present here a simplified version of their model.

Recall Assumption 4 of the CAPM, that all trading is costless. In reality, no security is perfectly liquid, in that all trades involve some transaction cost. Investors prefer more liquid assets with lower transaction costs, so it should not surprise us to find that all else equal, relatively illiquid assets trade at lower prices or, equivalently, that the expected return on illiquid assets must be higher. Therefore, an **illiquidity premium** must be impounded into the price of each asset.

We start with the simplest case, in which we ignore systematic risk. Imagine a world with a large number of uncorrelated securities. Because the securities are uncorrelated, well-diversified portfolios of these securities will have standard deviations near zero and the market portfolio will be virtually as safe as the risk-free asset. In this case, the market risk premium will be zero. Therefore, despite the fact that the beta of each security is 1.0, the expected rate of return on all securities will equal the risk-free rate, which we will take to be the T-bill rate.

Assume that investors know in advance for how long they intend to hold their portfolios, and suppose that there are $n$ types of investors, grouped by investment horizon. Type 1 investors intend to liquidate their portfolios in one period, Type 2 investors in two periods, and so on, until the longest-horizon investors (Type $n$) intend to hold their portfolios for $n$ periods.

We assume that there are only two classes of securities: liquid and illiquid. The liquidation cost of a class L (more liquid) stock to an investor with a horizon of $h$ years (a Type $h$ investor) will reduce the per-period rate of return by $c_L/h\%$. For example, if the combination of commissions and the bid–asked spread on a security resulted in a liquidation cost of 10%, then the per-period rate of return for an investor who holds stock for 5 years would be reduced by approximately 2% per year, whereas the return on a 10-year investment would fall by only 1% per year.[17] Class I (illiquid) assets have higher liquidation costs that reduce the per-period return by $c_I/h\%$, where $c_I$ is greater than $c_L$. Therefore, if you intend to hold a class L security for $h$ periods, your expected rate of return *net* of transaction costs is $E(r_L) - c_L/h$. There is no liquidation cost on T-bills.

The following table presents the expected return investors would realize from the risk-free asset and class L and class I stock portfolios *assuming* that the simple CAPM is correct and all securities have an expected return of $r$:

| Asset: | Risk-Free | Class L | Class I |
|---|---|---|---|
| Gross rate of return: | $r$ | $r$ | $r$ |
| One-period liquidation cost: | 0 | $c_L$ | $c_I$ |

| Investor Type | | Net Rate of Return | |
|---|---|---|---|
| 1 | $r$ | $r - c_L$ | $r - c_I$ |
| 2 | $r$ | $r - c_L/2$ | $r - c_I/2$ |
| ⋮ | ⋮ | ⋮ | ⋮ |
| $n$ | $r$ | $r - c_L/n$ | $r - c_I/n$ |

These net rates of return would be inconsistent with a market in equilibrium, because with equal gross rates of return all investors would prefer to invest in zero-transaction-cost T-bills. As a result, both class L and class I stock prices must fall, causing their expected returns to rise until investors are willing to hold these shares.

Suppose, therefore, that each gross return is higher by some fraction of liquidation cost. Specifically, assume that the gross expected return on class L stocks is $r + xc_L$ and that of class I stocks is $r + yc_I$. The *net* rate of return on class L stocks to an investor with a horizon of $h$ will be $(r + xc_L) - c_L/h = r + c_L(x - 1/h)$. In general, the rates of return to investors will be:

---

[17] This simple structure of liquidation costs allows us to derive a correspondingly simple solution for the effect of liquidity on expected returns. Amihud and Mendelson used a more general formulation, but then needed to rely on complex and more difficult-to-interpret mathematical programming. All that matters for the qualitative results below, however, is that illiquidity costs be less onerous to longer-term investors.

| Asset: | Risk-Free | Class L | Class I |
|---|---|---|---|
| Gross rate of return: | $r$ | $r + xc_L$ | $r + yc_I$ |
| One-period liquidation cost: | 0 | $c_L$ | $c_I$ |

| Investor Type | | Net Rate of Return | |
|---|---|---|---|
| 1 | $r$ | $r + c_L(x - 1)$ | $r + c_I(y - 1)$ |
| 2 | $r$ | $r + c_L(x - 1/2)$ | $r + c_I(y - 1/2)$ |
| $\vdots$ | $\vdots$ | $\vdots$ | $\vdots$ |
| $n$ | $r$ | $r + c_L(x - 1/n)$ | $r + c_I(y - 1/n)$ |

Notice that the liquidation cost has a greater impact on per-period returns for shorter-term investors. This is because the cost is amortized over fewer periods. As the horizon becomes very large, the per-period impact of the transaction cost approaches zero and the net rate of return approaches the gross rate.

Figure 9.6 graphs the net rate of return on the three asset classes for investors of differing horizons. The more illiquid stock has the lowest net rate of return for very short investment horizons because of its large liquidation costs. However, in equilibrium, the stock must be priced at a level that offers a rate of return high enough to induce some investors to hold it, implying that its gross rate of return must be higher than that of the more liquid stock. Therefore, for long enough investment horizons, the net return on class I stocks will exceed that on class L stocks.

**Figure 9.6**
**Net returns as a function of investment horizon**

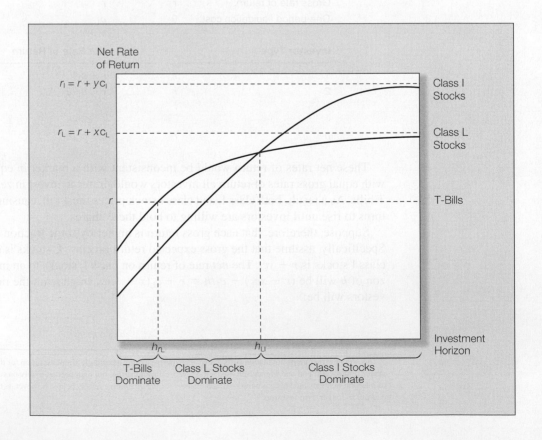

Both stock classes underperform T-bills for very short investment horizons, because the transactions costs then have the largest per-period impact. Ultimately, however, because the *gross* rate of return of stocks exceeds $r$, for a sufficiently long investment horizon, the more liquid stocks in class L will dominate bills. The threshold horizon can be read from Figure 9.6 as $h_{rL}$. Anyone with a horizon that exceeds $h_{rL}$ will prefer class L stocks to T-bills. Those with horizons below $h_{rL}$ will choose bills. For even longer horizons, because $c_I$ exceeds $c_L$, the net rate of return on relatively illiquid class I stocks will exceed that on class L stocks. Therefore, investors with horizons greater than $h_{LI}$ will specialize in the most illiquid stocks with the highest gross rate of return. These investors are harmed least by the effect of trading costs.

Now we can determine equilibrium illiquidity premiums. For the marginal investor with horizon $h_{LI}$, the *net* return from class I and L stocks is the same. Therefore,

$$r + c_L(x - 1/h_{LI}) = r + c_I(y - 1/h_{LI})$$

We can use this equation to solve for the relationship between $x$ and $y$ as follows:

$$y = \frac{1}{h_{LI}} + \frac{c_L}{c_I}\left(x - \frac{1}{h_{LI}}\right)$$

The expected gross return on illiquid stocks is then

$$r_I = r + c_I y = r + \frac{c_I}{h_{LI}} + c_L\left(x - \frac{1}{h_{LI}}\right) = r + c_L x + \frac{1}{h_{LI}}(c_I - c_L) \qquad (9.11)$$

Recalling that the expected gross return on class L stocks is $r_L = r + c_L x$, we conclude that the illiquidity premium of class I versus class L stocks is

$$r_I - r_L = \frac{1}{h_{LI}}(c_I - c_L) \qquad (9.12)$$

Similarly, we can derive the liquidity premium of class L stocks over T-bills. Here, the marginal investor who is indifferent between bills and class L stocks will have investment horizon $h_{rL}$ and a net rate of return just equal to $r$. Therefore, $r + c_L(x - 1/h_{rL}) = r$, implying that $x = 1/h_{rL}$, and the liquidity premium of class L stocks must be $xc_L = c_L/h_{rL}$. Therefore,

$$r_L - r = \frac{1}{h_{rL}} c_L \qquad (9.13)$$

There are two lessons to be learned from this analysis. First, as predicted, equilibrium expected rates of return are bid up to compensate for transaction costs, as demonstrated by equations 9.12 and 9.13. Second, the illiquidity premium is *not* a linear function of transaction costs. In fact, the incremental illiquidity premium steadily declines as transaction costs increase. To see that this is so, suppose that $c_L$ is 1% and $c_I - c_L$ is also 1%. Therefore, the transaction cost increases by 1% as you move out of bills into the more liquid stock class, and by another 1% as you move into the illiquid stock class. Equation 9.13 shows that the illiquidity premium of class L stocks over no-transaction-cost bills is then $1/h_{rL}$, and equation 9.12 shows that the illiquidity premium of class I over class L stocks is $1/h_{LI}$. But $h_{LI}$ exceeds $h_{rL}$ (see Figure 9.5), so we conclude that the incremental effect of illiquidity declines as we move into ever more illiquid assets.

The reason for this last result is simple. Recall that investors will self-select into different asset classes, with longer-term investors holding assets with the highest gross return but that are the most illiquid. For these investors, the effect of illiquidity is less costly because trading costs can be amortized over a longer horizon. Therefore, as these costs increase, the investment horizon associated with the holders of these assets also increases, which mitigates the impact on the required gross rate of return.

**CONCEPT CHECK ☞ QUESTION 7**

Consider a very illiquid asset class of stocks, class V, with $c_V > c_I$. Use a graph like Figure 9.6 to convince yourself that there is an investment horizon, $h_{IV}$, for which an investor would be indifferent between stocks in illiquidity classes I and V. Analogously to equation 9.12, in equilibrium, the differential in gross returns must be

$$r_V - r_I = \frac{1}{h_{IV}} (c_V - c_I)$$

Our analysis so far has focused on the case of uncorrelated assets, allowing us to ignore issues of systematic risk. This special case turns out to be easy to generalize. If we were to allow for correlation among assets due to common systematic risk factors, we would find that the illiquidity premium is simply additive to the risk premium of the usual CAPM.[18] Therefore, we can generalize the CAPM expected return–beta relationship to include a liquidity effect as follows:

$$E(r_i) - r_f = \beta_i[E(r_M) - r_f] + f(c_i)$$

where $f(c_i)$ is a function of trading costs that measures the effect of the illiquidity premium given the trading costs of security $i$. We have seen that $f(c_i)$ is increasing in $c_i$ but at a decreasing rate. The usual CAPM equation is modified because each investor's optimal portfolio is now affected by liquidation cost as well as risk–return considerations.

The model can be generalized in other ways as well. For example, even if investors do not know their investment horizon for certain, as long as investors do not perceive a connection between unexpected needs to liquidate investments and security returns, the implications of the model are essentially unchanged, with expected horizons replacing actual horizons in equations 9.12 and 9.13.

Amihud and Mendelson provided a considerable amount of empirical evidence that liquidity has a substantial impact on gross stock returns. We will defer our discussion of most of that evidence until Chapter 13. However, for a preview of the quantitative significance of the illiquidity effect, examine Figure 9.7, which is derived from their study. It shows that average monthly returns over the 1961–1980 period rose from .35% for the group of stocks with the lowest bid–asked spread (the most liquid stocks) to 1.024% for the highest-spread stocks. This is an annualized differential of about 8%, nearly equal to the historical average risk premium on the S&P 500 index! Moreover, as their model predicts, the effect of the spread on average monthly returns is nonlinear, with a curve that flattens out as spreads increase.

---

[18] The only assumption necessary to obtain this result is that for each level of beta, there are many securities within that risk class, with a variety of transaction costs. (This is essentially the same assumption used by Modigliani and Miller in their famous capital structure irrelevance proposition.) Thus our earlier analysis could be applied within each risk class, resulting in an illiquidity premium that simply adds on to the systematic risk premium.

**Figure 9.7
The relationship
between illiquidity
and average
returns**

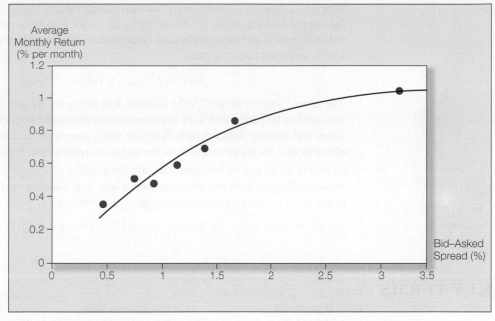

## SUMMARY

1. The CAPM assumes that investors are single-period planners who agree on a common input list from security analysis and seek mean-variance optimal portfolios.

2. The CAPM assumes that security markets are ideal in the sense that:
   a. They are large, and investors are price-takers.
   b. There are no taxes or transaction costs.
   c. All risky assets are publicly traded.
   d. Investors can borrow and lend any amount at a fixed risk-free rate.

3. With these assumptions, all investors hold identical risky portfolios. The CAPM holds that in equilibrium the market portfolio is the unique mean-variance efficient tangency portfolio. Thus a passive strategy is efficient.

4. The CAPM market portfolio is a value-weighted portfolio. Each security is held in a proportion equal to its market value divided by the total market value of all securities.

5. If the market portfolio is efficient and the average investor neither borrows nor lends, then the risk premium on the market portfolio is proportional to its variance, $\sigma_M^2$, and to the average coefficient of risk aversion across investors, $A$:

$$E(r_M) - r_f = .01 \times \bar{A}\sigma_M^2$$

6. The CAPM implies that the risk premium on any individual asset or portfolio is the product of the risk premium on the market portfolio and the beta coefficient:

$$E(r_i) - r_f = \beta_i[E(r_M) - r_f]$$

where the beta coefficient is the covariance of the asset with the market portfolio as a fraction of the variance of the market portfolio

$$\beta_i = \frac{\text{Cov}(r_i, r_M)}{\sigma_M^2}$$

Visit us at www.mhhe.com/bkm

7. When risk-free investments are restricted but all other CAPM assumptions hold, then the simple version of the CAPM is replaced by its zero-beta version. Accordingly, the risk-free rate in the expected return–beta relationship is replaced by the zero-beta portfolio's expected rate of return:

$$E(r_i) = E[r_{Z(M)}] + \beta_i E[r_M - r_{Z(M)}]$$

8. The simple version of the CAPM assumes that investors are myopic. When investors are assumed to be concerned with lifetime consumption and bequest plans, but investors' tastes and security return distributions are stable over time, the market portfolio remains efficient and the simple version of the expected return–beta relationship holds.

9. Liquidity costs can be incorporated into the CAPM relationship. When there is a large number of assets with any combination of beta and liquidity cost $c_i$, the expected return is bid up to reflect this undesired property according to

$$E(r_i) - r_f = \beta_i[E(r_M) - r_f] + f(c_i)$$

## KEY TERMS

| | | |
|---|---|---|
| homogeneous expectations | beta | alpha |
| market portfolio | expected return–beta | zero-beta portfolio |
| mutual fund theorem | relationship | liquidity |
| market price of risk | security market line (SML) | illiquidity premium |

## WEBSITES

finance.yahoo.com (Enter the ticker symbol, then link to the *Profile* report.)
moneycentral.msn.com/investor/home.asp (Enter the ticker symbol, then link to the *Company Report* from the *Research* menu on the left.)
www.wallpost.com (*see Profiles*)
www.411stocks.com
www.thomsoninvest.net (enter ticker symbol)
The sites listed above contain estimates of beta coefficients for individual securities and mutual funds.

www.efficientfrontier.com
This site contains practical information related to modern portfolio theory and portfolio allocation.

www.moneychimp.com/articles/valuation/capm.htm
Try the CAPM calculator at Moneychimp.com.

## PROBLEMS

1. What is the beta of a portfolio with $E(r_P) = 18\%$, if $r_f = 6\%$ and $E(r_M) = 14\%$?

2. The market price of a security is $50. Its expected rate of return is 14%. The risk-free rate is 6% and the market risk premium is 8.5%. What will be the market price

of the security if its correlation coefficient with the market portfolio doubles (and all other variables remain unchanged)? Assume that the stock is expected to pay a constant dividend in perpetuity.

3. You are a consultant to a large manufacturing corporation that is considering a project with the following net after-tax cash flows (in millions of dollars):

| Years from Now | After-Tax Cash Flow |
|----------------|---------------------|
| 0 | −40 |
| 1–10 | 15 |

The project's beta is 1.8. Assuming that $r_f = 8\%$ and $E(r_M) = 16\%$, what is the net present value of the project? What is the highest possible beta estimate for the project before its NPV becomes negative?

4. Are the following true or false? Explain.

   a. Stocks with a beta of zero offer an expected rate of return of zero.
   b. The CAPM implies that investors require a higher return to hold highly volatile securities.
   c. You can construct a portfolio with beta of .75 by investing .75 of the investment budget in T-bills and the remainder in the market portfolio.

5. Consider the following table, which gives a security analyst's expected return on two stocks for two particular market returns:

| Market Return | Aggressive Stock | Defensive Stock |
|---------------|------------------|-----------------|
| 5% | −2% | 6% |
| 25 | 38 | 12 |

   a. What are the betas of the two stocks?
   b. What is the expected rate of return on each stock if the market return is equally likely to be 5% or 25%?
   c. If the T-bill rate is 6% and the market return is equally likely to be 5% or 25%, draw the SML for this economy.
   d. Plot the two securities on the SML graph. What are the alphas of each?
   e. What hurdle rate should be used by the management of the aggressive firm for a project with the risk characteristics of the defensive firm's stock?

If the simple CAPM is valid, which of the following situations in problems 6 to 12 are possible? Explain. Consider each situation independently.

6.

| Portfolio | Expected Return | Beta |
|-----------|-----------------|------|
| A | 20 | 1.4 |
| B | 25 | 1.2 |

7.

| Portfolio | Expected Return | Standard Deviation |
|-----------|-----------------|--------------------|
| A | 30 | 35 |
| B | 40 | 25 |

8.

| Portfolio | Expected Return | Standard Deviation |
|-----------|-----------------|--------------------|
| Risk-free | 10 | 0 |
| Market | 18 | 24 |
| A | 16 | 12 |

9.

| Portfolio | Expected Return | Standard Deviation |
|-----------|-----------------|--------------------|
| Risk-free | 10 | 0 |
| Market | 18 | 24 |
| A | 20 | 22 |

10.

| Portfolio | Expected Return | Beta |
|-----------|-----------------|------|
| Risk-free | 10 | 0 |
| Market | 18 | 1.0 |
| A | 16 | 1.5 |

11.

| Portfolio | Expected Return | Beta |
|-----------|-----------------|------|
| Risk-free | 10 | 0 |
| Market | 18 | 1.0 |
| A | 16 | 0.9 |

12.

| Portfolio | Expected Return | Standard Deviation |
|-----------|-----------------|--------------------|
| Risk-free | 10 | 0 |
| Market | 18 | 24 |
| A | 16 | 22 |

In problems 13 to 15 assume that the risk-free rate of interest is 6% and the expected rate of return on the market is 16%.

13. A share of stock sells for $50 today. It will pay a dividend of $6 per share at the end of the year. Its beta is 1.2. What do investors expect the stock to sell for at the end of the year?

14. I am buying a firm with an expected perpetual cash flow of $1,000 but am unsure of its risk. If I think the beta of the firm is .5, when in fact the beta is really 1, how much *more* will I offer for the firm than it is truly worth?

15. A stock has an expected rate of return of 4%. What is its beta?

16. Two investment advisers are comparing performance. One averaged a 19% rate of return and the other a 16% rate of return. However, the beta of the first investor was 1.5, whereas that of the second was 1.

    *a.* Can you tell which investor was a better selector of individual stocks (aside from the issue of general movements in the market)?

    *b.* If the T-bill rate were 6% and the market return during the period were 14%, which investor would be the superior stock selector?

    *c.* What if the T-bill rate were 3% and the market return were 15%?

17. Suppose the rate of return on short-term government securities (perceived to be risk-free) is about 5%. Suppose also that the expected rate of return required by the market for a portfolio with a beta of 1 is 12%. According to the capital asset pricing model (security market line):

    a. What is the expected rate of return on the market portfolio?
    b. What would be the expected rate of return on a stock with $\beta = 0$?
    c. Suppose you consider buying a share of stock at $40. The stock is expected to pay $3 dividends next year and you expect it to sell then for $41. The stock risk has been evaluated at $\beta = -.5$. Is the stock overpriced or underpriced?

18. Suppose that you can invest risk-free at rate $r_f$ but can borrow only at a higher rate, $r_f^B$. This case was considered in Chapter 8, Section 8.6.

    a. Draw a minimum-variance frontier. Show on the graph the risky portfolio that will be selected by defensive investors. Show the portfolio that will be selected by risk tolerant investors.
    b. What portfolios will be selected by investors who neither borrow nor lend?
    c. Where will the market portfolio lie on the efficient frontier?
    d. Will the zero-beta CAPM be valid in this scenario? Explain. Show graphically the expected return on the zero-beta portfolio.

19. Consider an economy with two classes of investors. Tax-exempt investors can borrow or lend at the safe rate, $r_f$. Taxed investors pay tax rate $t$ on all interest income, so their net-of-tax safe interest rate is $r_f(1 - t)$. Show that the zero-beta CAPM will apply to this economy and that $(1 - t)r_f < E[r_{Z(M)}] < r_f$.

20. Suppose that borrowing is restricted so that the zero-beta version of the CAPM holds. The expected return on the market portfolio is 17%, and on the zero-beta portfolio it is 8%. What is the expected return on a portfolio with a beta of .6?

21. The security market line depicts:

    a. A security's expected return as a function of its systematic risk.
    b. The market portfolio as the optimal portfolio of risky securities.
    c. The relationship between a security's return and the return on an index.
    d. The complete portfolio as a combination of the market portfolio and the risk-free asset.

22. Within the context of the capital asset pricing model (CAPM), assume:

    • Expected return on the market = 15%.
    • Risk-free rate = 8%.
    • Expected rate of return on XYZ security = 17%.
    • Beta of XYZ security = 1.25.

    Which one of the following is correct?

    a. XYZ is overpriced.
    b. XYZ is fairly priced.
    c. XYZ's alpha is −.25%.
    d. XYZ's alpha is .25%.

23. What is the expected return of a zero-beta security?

    a. Market rate of return.
    b. Zero rate of return.
    c. Negative rate of return.
    d. Risk-free rate of return.

Visit us at www.mhhe.com/bkm

24. Capital asset pricing theory asserts that portfolio returns are best explained by:
    a. Economic factors
    b. Specific risk
    c. Systematic risk
    d. Diversification

25. According to CAPM, the expected rate of return of a portfolio with a beta of 1.0 and an alpha of 0 is:
    a. Between $r_M$ and $r_f$.
    b. The risk-free rate, $r_f$.
    c. $\beta(r_M - r_f)$.
    d. The expected return on the market, $r_M$.

The following table shows risk and return measures for two portfolios.

| Portfolio | Average Annual Rate of Return | Standard Deviation | Beta |
|---|---|---|---|
| R | 11% | 10% | 0.5 |
| S&P 500 | 14% | 12% | 1.0 |

26. When plotting portfolio $R$ on the preceding table relative to the SML, portfolio $R$ lies:
    a. On the SML.
    b. Below the SML.
    c. Above the SML.
    d. Insufficient data given.

27. When plotting portfolio $R$ relative to the capital market line, portfolio $R$ lies:
    a. On the CML.
    b. Below the CML.
    c. Above the CML.
    d. Insufficient data given.

28. Briefly explain whether investors should expect a higher return from holding Portfolio A versus Portfolio B under capital asset pricing theory (CAPM). Assume that both portfolios are fully diversified.

| | Portfolio A | Portfolio B |
|---|---|---|
| Systematic risk (beta) | 1.0 | 1.0 |
| Specific risk for each individual security | High | Low |

29. Joan McKay is a portfolio manager for a bank trust department. McKay meets with two clients, Kevin Murray and Lisa York, to review their investment objectives. Each client expresses an interest in changing his or her individual investment objectives. Both clients currently hold well-diversified portfolios of risky assets.
    a. Murray wants to increase the expected return of his portfolio. State what action McKay should take to achieve Murray's objective. Justify your response in the context of the Capital Market Line.
    b. York wants to reduce the risk exposure of her portfolio but does not want to engage in borrowing or lending activities to do so. State what action McKay should

take to achieve York's objective. Justify your response in the context of the Security Market Line.

30. *a.* A mutual fund with beta of .8 has an expected rate of return of 14%. If $r_f = 5\%$, and you expect the rate of return on the market portfolio to be 15%, should you invest in this fund? What is the fund's alpha?

   *b.* What passive portfolio comprised of a market-index portfolio and a money market account would have the same beta as the fund? Show that the difference between the expected rate of return on this passive portfolio and that of the fund equals the alpha from part (*a*).

31. Karen Kay, a portfolio manager at Collins Asset Management, is using the capital asset pricing model for making recommendations to her clients. Her research department has developed the information shown in the following exhibit.

### Forecast Returns, Standard Deviations, and Betas

|                  | Forecast Return | Standard Deviation | Beta |
|------------------|-----------------|--------------------|------|
| Stock X          | 14.0%           | 36%                | 0.8  |
| Stock Y          | 17.0            | 25                 | 1.5  |
| Market index     | 14.0            | 15                 | 1.0  |
| Risk-free rate   | 5.0             |                    |      |

   *a.* Calculate expected return and alpha for each stock.

   *b.* Identify and justify which stock would be more appropriate for an investor who wants to
   i.  add this stock to a well-diversified equity portfolio.
   ii. hold this stock as a single-stock portfolio.

Visit us at www.mhhe.com/bkm

**SOLUTIONS
TO CONCEPT
CHECKS**

1. We can characterize the entire population by two representative investors. One is the "uninformed" investor, who does not engage in security analysis and holds the market portfolio, whereas the other optimizes using the Markowitz algorithm with input from security analysis. The uninformed investor does not know what input the informed investor uses to make portfolio purchases. The uninformed investor knows, however, that if the other investor is informed, the market portfolio proportions will be optimal. Therefore, to depart from these proportions would constitute an uninformed bet, which will, on average, reduce the efficiency of diversification with no compensating improvement in expected returns.

2. *a.* Substituting the historical mean and standard deviation in equation 9.2 yields a coefficient of risk aversion of

$$\bar{A} = \frac{E(r_M) - r_f}{.01 \times \sigma_M^2} = \frac{8.2}{.01 \times 20.6^2} = 1.93$$

   *b.* This relationship also tells us that for the historical standard deviation and a coefficient of risk aversion of 3.5 the risk premium would be

$$E(r_M) - r_f = .01 \times \bar{A}\sigma_M^2 = .01 \times 3.5 \times 20.6^2 = 14.9\%$$

3. For these investment proportions, $w_{Ford}$, $w_{GM}$, the portfolio $\beta$ is

$$\beta_P = w_{Ford}\beta_{Ford} + w_{GM}\beta_{GM}$$
$$= (.75 \times 1.25) + (.25 \times 1.10) = 1.2125$$

   As the market risk premium, $E(r_M) - r_f$, is 8%, the portfolio risk premium will be

$$E(r_P) - r_f = \beta_P[E(r_M) - r_f]$$
$$= 1.2125 \times 8 = 9.7\%$$

4. The alpha of a stock is its expected return in excess of that required by the CAPM.

$$\alpha = E(r) - \{r_f + \beta[E(r_M) - r_f]\}$$
$$\alpha_{XYZ} = 12 - [5 + 1.0(11 - 5)] = 1\%$$
$$\alpha_{ABC} = 13 - [5 + 1.5(11 - 5)] = -1\%$$

*ABC* plots below the SML, while *XYZ* plots above.

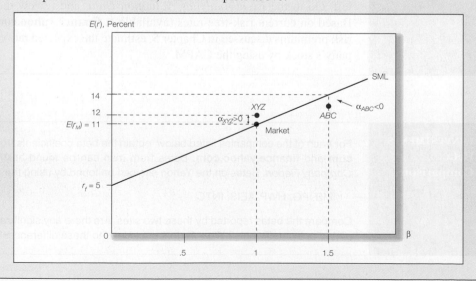

Visit us at www.mhhe.com/bkm

**SOLUTIONS TO CONCEPT CHECKS**
*(Concluded)*

5. The project-specific required return is determined by the project beta coupled with the market risk premium and the risk-free rate. The CAPM tells us that an acceptable expected rate of return for the project is

$$r_f + \beta[E(r_M) - r_f] = 8 + 1.3(16 - 8) = 18.4\%$$

which becomes the project's hurdle rate. If the IRR of the project is 19%, then it is desirable. Any project with an IRR equal to or less than 18.4% should be rejected.

6. If the basic CAPM holds, any zero-beta asset must be expected to earn on average the risk-free rate. Hence the posited performance of the zero-beta portfolio violates the simple CAPM. It does not, however, violate the zero-beta CAPM. Since we know that borrowing restrictions do exist, we expect the zero-beta version of the model is more likely to hold, with the zero-beta rate differing from the virtually risk-free T-bill rate.

7. Consider investors with time horizon $h_{IV}$ who will be indifferent between illiquid (I) and very illiquid (V) classes of stock. Call $z$ the fraction of liquidation cost by which the gross return of class V stocks is increased. For these investors, the indifference condition is

$$[r + y\,c_I] - c_I/h_{LI} = [r + z\,c_V] - c_V/h_{IV}$$

This equation can be rearranged to show that

$$[r + z\,c_V] - [r + y\,c_I] = (c_I - c_V)/h_{IV}$$

## APPENDIX: DEMAND FOR STOCKS AND EQUILIBRIUM PRICES

In this section, we will make more explicit the links between the quest for efficiently diversified portfolios, which drives investor demand for securities, and the process by which equilibrium expected rates of return are established. To understand how market equilibrium is formed we need to connect the determination of optimal portfolios with security analysis and the actual buy/sell transactions of investors. We will show how the quest for efficient diversification leads to a demand schedule for shares. In turn, the supply and demand for shares determine equilibrium prices and expected rates of return.

Imagine a simple world with only two corporations: Bottom Up Inc. (BU) and Top Down Inc. (TD). Stock prices and market values are shown in Table 9A.1. Investors can also invest in a money market fund (MMF) which yields a risk-free interest rate of 5%.

Sigma Fund is a new actively managed mutual fund that has raised $220 million to invest in the stock market. The security analysis staff of Sigma believes that neither BU nor TD will grow in the future and therefore, that each firm will pay level annual dividends for

**Table 9A.1  Share Prices and Market Values of Bottom Up (BU) and Top Down (TD)**

|  | BU | TD |
|---|---|---|
| Price per share ($) | 39.00 | 39.00 |
| Shares outstanding | 5,000,000 | 4,000,000 |
| Market value ($ millions) | 195 | 156 |

**Table 9A.2    Capital Market Expectations of Portfolio Manager**

|  | BU | TD |
|---|---|---|
| Expected annual dividend ($/share) | 6.40 | 3.80 |
| Discount rate = Required return* (%) | 16 | 10 |
| Expected end-of-year price† ($/share) | 40 | 38 |
| Current price | 39 | 39 |
| Expected return (%): Capital gain | 2.56 | −2.56 |
| Dividend yield | 16.41 | 9.74 |
| Total expected return for the year | 18.97 | 7.18 |
| Standard deviation of rate of return | 40% | 20% |
| Correlation coefficient between rates of return on BU and TD | .20 | |

*Based on assessment of risk.
†Obtained by discounting the dividend perpetuity at the required rate of return.

the foreseeable future. This is a useful simplifying assumption because, if a stock is expected to pay a stream of level dividends, the income derived from each share is a perpetuity. Therefore, the present value of each share—often called the *intrinsic value* of the share—equals the dividend divided by the appropriate discount rate. A summary of the report of the security analysts appears in Table 9A.2.

The expected returns in Table 9A.2 are based on the assumption that next year's dividends will conform to Sigma's forecasts, and share prices will be equal to intrinsic values at year-end. The standard deviations and the correlation coefficient between the two stocks were estimated by Sigma's security analysts from past returns and assumed to remain at these levels for the coming year.

Using these data and assumptions Sigma easily generates the efficient frontier shown in Figure 9A.1 and computes the optimal portfolio proportions corresponding to the tangency portfolio. These proportions, combined with the total investment budget, yield the fund's buy orders. With a budget of $220 million, Sigma wants a position in BU of $220,000,000 × .8070 = $177,540,000, or $177,540,000/39 = 4,552,308 shares, and a position in TD of $220,000,000 × .1930 = $42,460,000, which corresponds to 1,088,718 shares.

**Sigma's Demand for Shares**    The expected rates of return that Sigma used to derive its demand for shares of BU and TD were computed from the forecast of year-end stock prices and the current prices. If, say, a share of BU could be purchased at a lower price, Sigma's forecast of the rate of return on BU would be higher. Conversely, if BU shares were selling at a higher price, expected returns would be lower. A new expected return would result in a different optimal portfolio and a different demand for shares.

We can think of Sigma's demand schedule for a stock as the number of shares Sigma would want to hold at different share prices. In our simplified world, producing the demand for BU shares is not difficult. First, we revise Table 9A.2 to recompute the expected return on BU at different current prices given the forecast year-end price. Then, for each price and associated expected return, we construct the optimal portfolio and find the implied position in BU. A few samples of these calculations are shown in Table 9A.3. The first four columns in Table 9A.3 show the expected returns on BU shares given their current price. The optimal proportion (column 5) is calculated using these expected returns. Finally, Sigma's investment budget, the optimal proportion in BU and the current price of a BU share

**Figure 9A.1
Sigma's
efficient frontier
and optimal
portfolio**

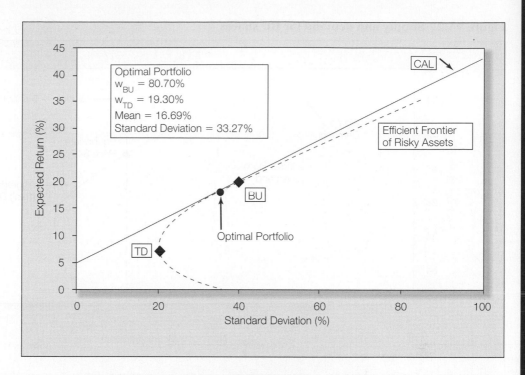

**Table 9A.3   Calculation of Sigma's Demand for BU Shares**

| Current Price ($) | Capital Gain (%) | Dividend Yield (%) | Expected Return (%) | BU Optimal Proportion | Desired BU Shares |
|---|---|---|---|---|---|
| 45.0 | −11.11 | 14.22 | 3.11 | −.4113 | −2,010,582 |
| 42.5 | −5.88 | 15.06 | 9.18 | .3192 | 1,652,482 |
| 40.0 | 0 | 16.00 | 16.00 | .7011 | 3,856,053 |
| 37.5 | 6.67 | 17.07 | 23.73 | .9358 | 5,490,247 |
| 35.0 | 14.29 | 18.29 | 32.57 | 1.0947 | 6,881,225 |

determine the desired number of shares. Note that we compute the demand for BU shares *given* the price and expected return for TD. This means that the entire demand schedule must be revised whenever the price and expected return on TD is changed.

Sigma's demand curve for BU stock is given by the Desired Shares column in Table 9A.3 and is plotted in Figure 9A.2. Notice that the demand curve for the stock slopes downward. When BU's stock price falls, Sigma will desire more shares for two reasons: (1) an income effect—at a lower price Sigma can purchase more shares with the same budget, and (2) a substitution effect—the increased expected return at the lower price will make BU shares more attractive relative to TD shares. Notice that one can desire a negative number of shares, that is, a short position. If the stock price is high enough, its expected return will be so low that the desire to sell will overwhelm diversification motives and investors will want to take a short position. Figure 9A.2 shows that when the price exceeds $44, Sigma wants a short position in BU.

The demand curve for BU shares assumes that the price and therefore expected return of TD remain constant. A similar demand curve can be constructed for TD shares given a

**Figure 9A.2    Supply and demand for BU shares**

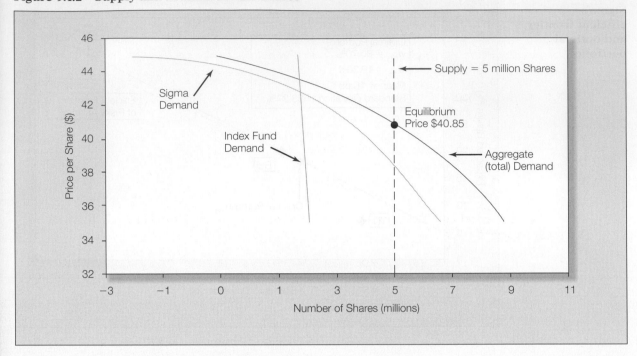

**Figure 9A.3    Supply and demand for TD shares**

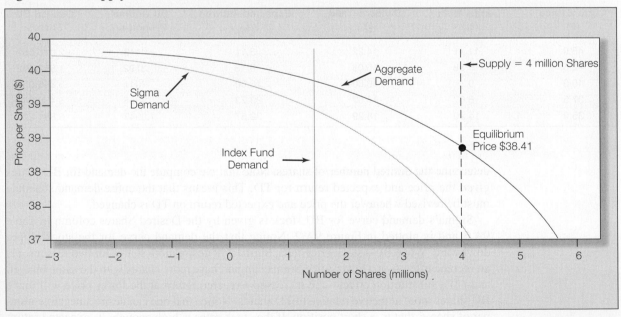

price for BU shares. As before, we would generate the demand for TD shares by revising Table 9A.2 for various current prices of TD, leaving the price of BU unchanged. We use the revised expected returns to calculate the optimal portfolio for each possible price of TD, ultimately obtaining the demand curve shown in Figure 9A.3.

**Table 9A.4   Calculation of Index Demand for BU Shares**

| Current Price | BU Market-Value Proportion | Dollar Investment* ($ million) | Shares Desired |
|---|---|---|---|
| $45.00 | .5906 | 76.772 | 1,706,037 |
| 42.50 | .5767 | 74.966 | 1,763,908 |
| 40.00 | .5618 | 73.034 | 1,825,843 |
| **39.00** | **.5556** | **72.222** | **1,851,852** |
| 37.50 | .5459 | 70.961 | 1,892,285 |
| 35.00 | .5287 | 68.731 | 1,963,746 |

*Dollar investment = BU proportion × $130 million.

**Index Funds' Demands for Stock**   We have seen that index funds play an important role in portfolio selection, so let's see how an index fund would derive its demand for shares. Suppose that $130 million of investor funds in our hypothesized economy are given to an index fund—named Index—to manage. What will it do?

Index is looking for a portfolio that will mimic the market. Suppose current prices and market values are as in Table 9A.1. Then the required proportions to mimic the market portfolio are:

$$w_{BU} = 195/(195 + 156) = .5556 \ (55.56\%); \ w_{TD} = 1 - .5556 = .4444 \ (44.44\%)$$

With $130 million to invest, Index will place .5556 × $130 million = $72.22 million in BU shares. Table 9A.4 shows a few other points on Index's demand curve for BU shares. The second column of the table shows the proportion of BU in total stock market value at each assumed price. In our two-stock example, this is BU's value as a fraction of the combined value of BU and TD. The third column is Index's desired dollar investment in BU and the last column shows shares demanded. The bold row corresponds to the case we analyzed in Table 9A.1, for which BU is selling at $39.

Index's demand curve for BU shares is plotted in Figure 9A.2 next to Sigma's demand, and in Figure 9A.3 for TD shares. Index's demand is smaller than Sigma's because its budget is smaller. Moreover, the demand curve of the index fund is very steep, or "inelastic," that is, demand hardly responds to price changes. This is because an index fund's demand for shares does not respond to expected returns. Index funds seek only to replicate market proportions. As the stock price goes up, so does its proportion in the market. This leads the index fund to invest more in the stock. Nevertheless, because each share costs more, the fund will desire fewer shares.

**Equilibrium Prices and the Capital Asset Pricing Model**   Market prices are determined by supply and demand. At any one time, the supply of shares of a stock is fixed, so supply is vertical at 5,000,000 shares of BU in Figure 9A.2 and 4,000,000 shares of TD in Figure 9A.3. Market demand is obtained by "horizontal aggregation," that is, for each price we add up the quantity demanded by all investors. You can examine the horizontal aggregation of the demand curves of Sigma and Index in Figures 9A.2 and 9A.3. The equilibrium prices are at the intersection of supply and demand.

However, the prices shown in Figures 9A.2 and 9A.3 will likely not persist for more than an instant. The reason is that the equilibrium price of BU ($40.85) was generated by demand curves derived by assuming that the price of TD was $39. Similarly, the equilibrium price of TD ($38.41) is an equilibrium price only when BU is at $39, which also is not

Visit us at www.mhhe.com/bkm

the case. A full equilibrium would require that the demand curves derived for each stock be consistent with the actual prices of all other stocks. Thus, our model is only a beginning. But it does illustrate the important link between security analysis and the process by which portfolio demands, market prices, and expected returns are jointly determined. The CAPM treats the problem of finding a set of mutually consistent equilibrium prices and expected rates of return across all stocks. The model here illustrates the process that underlies the adjustment of market expected returns to demand pressures.

One might wonder why we originally posited that Sigma expects BU's share price to increase only by year-end when we have just argued that the adjustment to the new equilibrium price ought to be instantaneous. The reason is that when Sigma observes a market price of $39, it must assume that this *is* an equilibrium price based on investor beliefs *at the time*. Sigma believes that the market will catch up to its (presumably) superior estimate of intrinsic value of the firm by year-end, when its better assessment about the firm becomes widely adopted. In our simple example, Sigma is the only active manager, so its demand for "low-priced" BU stock would move the price immediately. But more realistically, since Sigma would be a small player compared to the entire stock market, the stock price would barely move in response to Sigma's demand, and the price would remain around $39 until Sigma's assessment was adopted by the average investor.

# INDEX MODELS

Chapter 8 introduced the Markowitz portfolio selection model, which shows
how to obtain the maximum return possible for any level of portfolio risk.
Implementation of the Markowitz portfolio selection model, however,
requires a huge number of estimates of covariances between all pairs
of available securities. Moreover, these estimates have to be fed into a
mathematical optimization program that requires vast computer capacity
to perform the necessary calculations for large portfolios. Because the data
requirements and computer capacity called for in the full-blown Markowitz

procedure are overwhelming,
we must search for a strategy
that reduces the necessary
compilation and processing
of data. We introduce in
this chapter a simplifying
assumption that at once eases
our computational burden and
offers significant new insights
into the nature of systematic
risk versus firm-specific risk.
This abstraction is the notion
of an "index model," specifying
the process by which security
returns are generated.

# 10.1   A SINGLE-INDEX SECURITY MARKET

**Systematic Risk versus Firm-Specific Risk**     The success of a portfolio selection rule depends on the quality of the input list, that is, the estimates of expected security returns and the covariance matrix. In the long run, efficient portfolios will beat portfolios with less reliable input lists and consequently inferior reward-to-risk trade-offs.

Suppose your security analysts can thoroughly analyze 50 stocks. This means that your input list will include the following:

$$n = 50 \text{ estimates of expected returns}$$
$$n = 50 \text{ estimates of variances}$$
$$(n^2 - n)/2 = \underline{1{,}225} \text{ estimates of covariances}$$
$$1{,}325 \text{ estimates}$$

This is a formidable task, particularly in light of the fact that a 50-security portfolio is relatively small. Doubling $n$ to 100 will nearly quadruple the number of estimates to 5,150. If $n = 3{,}000$, roughly the number of NYSE stocks, we need more than 4.5 *million* estimates.

Another difficulty in applying the Markowitz model to portfolio optimization is that errors in the assessment or estimation of correlation coefficients can lead to nonsensical results. This can happen because some sets of correlation coefficients are mutually inconsistent, as the following example demonstrates:[1]

| Asset | Standard Deviation (%) | Correlation Matrix | | |
|:-----:|:----------------------:|:----:|:----:|:----:|
|       |                        | A    | B    | C    |
| A     | 20                     | 1.00 | 0.90 | 0.90 |
| B     | 20                     | 0.90 | 1.00 | 0.00 |
| C     | 20                     | 0.90 | 0.00 | 1.00 |

Suppose that you construct a portfolio with weights: $-1.00$; $1.00$; $1.00$, for assets A; B; C, respectively, and calculate the portfolio variance. You will find that the portfolio variance appears to be negative ($-200$). This of course is not possible because portfolio variances cannot be negative: we conclude that the inputs in the estimated correlation matrix must be mutually inconsistent. Of course, *true* correlation coefficients are always consistent.[2] But we do not know these true correlations and can only estimate them with some imprecision. Unfortunately, it is difficult to determine whether a correlation matrix is inconsistent, providing another motivation to seek a model that is easier to implement.

Covariances between security returns tend to be positive because the same economic forces affect the fortunes of many firms. Some examples of common economic factors are business cycles, interest rates, technological changes, and cost of labor and raw materials. All these (interrelated) factors affect almost all firms. Thus unexpected changes in these variables cause, simultaneously, unexpected changes in the rates of return on the entire stock market.

---

[1] We are grateful to Andrew Kaplin and Ravi Jagannathan, Kellogg Graduate School of Management, Northwestern University, for this example.

[2] The mathematical term for a correlation matrix that cannot generate negative portfolio variance is "positive definite."

Suppose that we summarize all relevant economic factors by one macroeconomic indicator and assume that it moves the security market as a whole. We further assume that, beyond this common effect, all remaining uncertainty in stock returns is firm specific; that is, there is no other source of correlation between securities. Firm-specific events would include new inventions, deaths of key employees, and other factors that affect the fortune of the individual firm without affecting the broad economy in a measurable way.

We can summarize the distinction between macroeconomic and firm-specific factors by writing the holding-period return on security $i$ as

$$r_i = E(r_i) + m_i + e_i \qquad (10.1)$$

where $E(r_i)$ is the expected return on the security as of the beginning of the holding period, $m_i$ is the impact of unanticipated macro events on the security's return during the period, and $e_i$ is the impact of unanticipated firm-specific events. Both $m_i$ and $e_i$ have zero expected values because each represents the impact of unanticipated events, which by definition must average out to zero.

We can gain further insight by recognizing that different firms have different sensitivities to macroeconomic events. Thus if we denote the unanticipated components of the macro factor by $F$, and denote the responsiveness of security $i$ to macroevents by beta, $\beta_i$, then the macro component of security $i$ is $m_i = \beta_i F$, and then equation 10.1 becomes[3]

$$r_i = E(r_i) + \beta_i F + e_i \qquad (10.2)$$

Equation 10.2 is known as a **single-factor model** for stock returns. It is easy to imagine that a more realistic decomposition of security returns would require more than one factor in equation 10.2. We treat this issue later in the chapter. For now, let us examine the simple case with only one macro factor.

Of course, a factor model is of little use without specifying a way to measure the factor that is posited to affect security returns. One reasonable approach is to assert that the rate of return on a broad index of securities such as the S&P 500 is a valid proxy for the common macro factor. This approach leads to an equation similar to the factor model, which is called a **single-index model** because it uses the market index to proxy for the common or systematic factor.

According to the index model, we can separate the actual or realized rate of return on a security into macro (systematic) and micro (firm-specific) components in a manner similar to that in equation 10.2. We write the rate of return on each security as a sum of three components:

|  | Symbol |
|---|---|
| 1. The stock's expected return if the market is neutral, that is, if the market's excess return, $r_M - r_f$, is zero | $\alpha_i$ |
| 2. The component of return due to movements in the overall market; $\beta_i$ is the security's responsiveness to market movements | $\beta_i(r_M - r_f)$ |
| 3. The unexpected component due to unexpected events that are relevant only to this security (firm specific) | $e_i$ |

The holding-period excess return on the stock can be stated as

$$r_i - r_f = \alpha_i + \beta_i(r_M - r_f) + e_i$$

---

[3] You may wonder why we choose the notation $\beta$ for the responsiveness coefficient because $\beta$ already has been defined in Chapter 9 in the context of the CAPM. The choice is deliberate, however. Our reasoning will be obvious shortly.

Let us denote excess returns over the risk-free rate by capital $R$ and rewrite this equation as

$$R_i = \alpha_i + \beta_i R_M + e_i \tag{10.3}$$

We write the index model in terms of excess returns over $r_f$ rather than in terms of total returns because the level of the stock market return represents the state of the macro economy only to the extent that it exceeds or falls short of the rate of return on risk-free T-bills. For example, in 2003, when T-bills were yielding only 1% or 2%, a return of 8% or 9% on the stock market would be considered good news. In contrast, in the early 1980s, when bills were yielding over 10%, that same 8% or 9% would signal disappointing macroeconomic news.[4]

Equation 10.3 says that each security has two sources of risk: *market or systematic risk*, attributable to its sensitivity to macroeconomic factors as reflected in $R_M$, and *firm-specific risk*, as reflected in $e$. If we denote the variance of the excess return on the market, $R_M$, as $\sigma_M^2$, then we can break the variance of the rate of return on each stock into two components:

| | Symbol |
|---|---|
| 1. The variance attributable to the uncertainty of the common macroeconomic factor | $\beta_i^2 \sigma_M^2$ |
| 2. The variance attributable to firm-specific uncertainty | $\sigma^2(e_i)$ |

The covariance between $R_M$ and $e_i$ is zero because $e_i$ is defined as firm specific, that is, independent of movements in the market. Hence the variance of the rate of return on security $i$ equals the sum of the variances due to the common and the firm-specific components:

$$\sigma_i^2 = \beta_i^2 \sigma_M^2 + \sigma^2(e_i)$$

What about the covariance between the rates of return on two stocks? This may be written:

$$\text{Cov}(R_i, R_j) = \text{Cov}(\alpha_i + \beta_i R_M + e_i, \alpha_j + \beta_j R_M + e_j)$$

But since $\alpha_i$ and $\alpha_j$ are constants, their covariance with any variable is zero. Further, the firm-specific terms $(e_i, e_j)$ are assumed uncorrelated with the market and with each other. Therefore, the only source of covariance in the returns between the two stocks derives from their common dependence on the common factor, $R_M$. In other words, the covariance between stocks is due to the fact that the returns on each depend in part on economywide conditions. Thus,

$$\text{Cov}(R_i, R_j) = \text{Cov}(\beta_i R_M, \beta_j R_M) = \beta_i \beta_j \sigma_M^2 \tag{10.4}$$

These calculations show that if we have

$n$ estimates of the expected excess returns, $E(R_i)$
$n$ estimates of the sensitivity coefficients, $\beta_i$
$n$ estimates of the firm-specific variances, $\sigma^2(e_i)$
1 estimate for the variance of the (common) macroeconomic factor, $\sigma_M^2$,

then these $(3n + 1)$ estimates will enable us to prepare the input list for this single-index security universe. Thus for a 50-security portfolio we will need 151 estimates rather than

---

[4] Practitioners often use a "modified" index model that is similar to equation 10.3 but that uses total rather than excess returns. This practice is most common when daily data are used. In this case the rate of return on bills is on the order of only about .01% per day, so total and excess returns are almost indistinguishable.

1,325; for the entire New York Stock Exchange, about 3,000 securities, we will need 9,001 estimates rather than approximately 4.5 million!

It is easy to see why the index model is such a useful abstraction. For large universes of securities, the number of estimates required for the Markowitz procedure using the index model is only a small fraction of what otherwise would be needed.

Another advantage is less obvious but equally important. The index model abstraction is crucial for specialization of effort in security analysis. If a covariance term had to be calculated directly for each security pair, then security analysts could not specialize by industry. For example, if one group were to specialize in the computer industry and another in the auto industry, who would have the common background to estimate the covariance *between* IBM and GM? Neither group would have the deep understanding of other industries necessary to make an informed judgment of co-movements among industries. In contrast, the index model suggests a simple way to compute covariances. Covariances among securities are due to the influence of the single common factor, represented by the market index return, and can be easily estimated using equation 10.4.

The simplification derived from the index model assumption is, however, not without cost. The "cost" of the model lies in the restrictions it places on the structure of asset return uncertainty. The classification of uncertainty into a simple dichotomy—macro versus micro risk—oversimplifies sources of real-world uncertainty and misses some important sources of dependence in stock returns. For example, this dichotomy rules out industry events, events that may affect many firms within an industry without substantially affecting the broad macroeconomy.

Statistical analysis shows that relative to a single index, the firm-specific components of some firms are correlated. Examples are the nonmarket components of stocks in a single industry, such as computer stocks or auto stocks. At the same time, statistical significance does not always correspond to economic significance. Economically speaking, the question that is more relevant to the assumption of a single-index model is whether portfolios constructed using covariances that are estimated on the basis of the single-factor or single-index assumption are significantly different from, and less efficient than, portfolios constructed using covariances that are estimated directly for each pair of stocks. We explore this issue further in Chapter 28 on active portfolio management.

---

**CONCEPT CHECK☞ QUESTION 1**

**Suppose that the index model for the excess returns of stocks $A$ and $B$ is estimated with the following results:**

$$R_A = 1.0\% + .9R_M + e_A$$
$$R_B = -2.0\% + 1.1R_M + e_B$$
$$\sigma_M = 20\%$$
$$\sigma(e_A) = 30\%$$
$$\sigma(e_B) = 10\%$$

**Find the standard deviation of each stock and the covariance between them.**

---

**Estimating the Index Model**   Equation 10.3 also suggests how we might go about actually measuring market and firm-specific risk. Suppose that we observe the excess return on the market index and a specific asset over a number of holding periods. We use as an example monthly excess returns on the S&P 500 index and GM stock for a 1-year period. We can summarize the results for a sample period in a **scatter diagram**, as illustrated in Figure 10.1.

**Figure 10.1
Security
characteristic
line (SCL)
for GM**

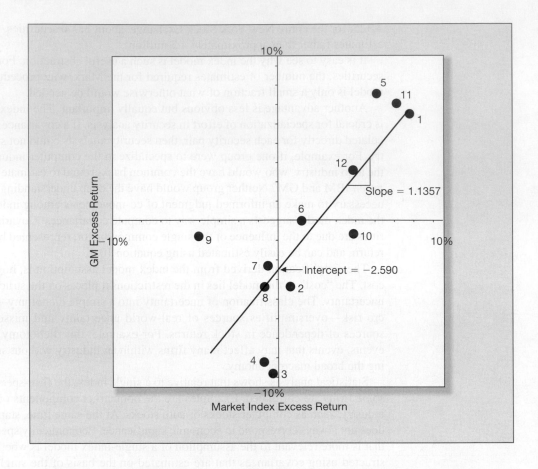

The horizontal axis in Figure 10.1 measures the excess return (over the risk-free rate) on the market index, whereas the vertical axis measures the excess return on the asset in question (GM stock in our example). A pair of excess returns (one for the market index, one for GM stock) constitutes one point on this scatter diagram. The points are numbered 1 through 12, representing excess returns for the S&P 500 and GM for each month from January through December. The single-index model states that the relationship between the excess returns on GM and the S&P 500 is given by

$$R_{GMt} = \alpha_{GM} + \beta_{GM}R_{Mt} + e_{GMt}$$

Note the resemblance of this relationship to a **regression equation.**

In a single-variable regression equation, the dependent variable plots around a straight line with an intercept $\alpha$ and a slope $\beta$. The deviations from the line, $e$, are assumed to be mutually uncorrelated as well as uncorrelated with the independent variable. Because these assumptions are identical to those of the index model we can look at the index model as a regression model. The sensitivity of GM to the market, measured by $\beta_{GM}$, is the slope of the regression line. The intercept of the regression line is $\alpha_{GM}$, representing the average firm-specific excess return when the market's excess return is zero. Deviations of particular observations from the regression line in any period are denoted $e_{GMt}$ and called **residuals.** Each of these residuals is the difference between the actual stock return and the return that would be predicted from the regression equation describing the usual relationship between the stock and the market; therefore, residuals measure the impact of firm-specific events during the particular month. The parameters of interest, $\alpha$, $\beta$, and Var($e$), can be estimated using standard regression techniques.

## Table 10.1  Characteristic Line for GM Stock

| Month | GM Return | Market Return | Monthly T-Bill Rate | Excess GM Return | Excess Market Return |
|---|---|---|---|---|---|
| January | 6.06 | 7.89 | 0.65 | 5.41 | 7.24 |
| February | −2.86 | 1.51 | 0.58 | −3.44 | 0.93 |
| March | −8.18 | 0.23 | 0.62 | −8.79 | −0.38 |
| April | −7.36 | −0.29 | 0.72 | −8.08 | −1.01 |
| May | 7.76 | 5.58 | 0.66 | 7.10 | 4.92 |
| June | 0.52 | 1.73 | 0.55 | −0.03 | 1.18 |
| July | −1.74 | −0.21 | 0.62 | −2.36 | −0.83 |
| August | −3.00 | −0.36 | 0.55 | −3.55 | −0.91 |
| September | −0.56 | −3.58 | 0.60 | −1.16 | −4.18 |
| October | −0.37 | 4.62 | 0.65 | −1.02 | 3.97 |
| November | 6.93 | 6.85 | 0.61 | 6.32 | 6.25 |
| December | 3.08 | 4.55 | 0.65 | 2.43 | 3.90 |
| Mean | 0.02 | 2.38 | 0.62 | −0.60 | 1.75 |
| Standard deviation | 4.97 | 3.33 | 0.05 | 4.97 | 3.32 |
| Regression results | $r_{GM} - r_f = \alpha + \beta(r_M - r_f)$ | | | | |
| | $\alpha$ | | $\beta$ | | |
| Estimated coefficient | −2.590 | | 1.1357 | | |
| Standard error of estimate | (1.547) | | (0.309) | | |

Variance of residuals = 12.601
Standard deviation of residuals = 3.550
$R^2$ = .575

Estimating the regression equation of the single-index model gives us the **security characteristic line** (SCL), which is plotted in Figure 10.1. (The regression results and raw data appear in Table 10.1.) The SCL is a plot of the typical excess return on a security as a function of the excess return on the market.

This sample of holding-period returns is, of course, too small to yield reliable statistics. We use it only for demonstration. For this sample period we find that the beta coefficient of GM stock, as estimated by the slope of the regression line, is 1.1357, and that the intercept for this SCL is −2.59% per month.

For each month, $t$, our estimate of the residual, $e_t$, which is the deviation of GM's excess return from the prediction of the SCL, equals

$$\text{Deviation} = \text{Actual} - \text{Predicted return}$$
$$e_{GMt} = R_{GMt} - (\beta_{GM}R_{Mt} + \alpha_{GM})$$

These residuals are estimates of the monthly unexpected *firm-specific* component of the rate of return on GM stock. Hence we can estimate the firm-specific variance by[5]

$$\sigma^2(e_{GM}) = \frac{1}{10}\sum_{t=1}^{12} e_t^2 = 12.60$$

---

[5] Because the mean of $e_t$ is zero, $e_t^2$ is the squared deviation from its mean. The average value of $e_t^2$ is therefore the estimate of the variance of the firm-specific component. We divide the sum of squared residuals by the degrees of freedom of the regression, $n - 2 = 12 - 2 = 10$, to obtain an unbiased estimate of $\sigma^2(e)$.

The standard deviation of the firm-specific component of GM's return, $\sigma(e_{GM})$, is $\sqrt{12.60} = 3.55\%$ per month, equal to the standard deviation of the regression residual.

**The Index Model and Diversification**   The index model, first suggested by Sharpe,[6] also offers insight into portfolio diversification. Suppose that we choose an equally weighted portfolio of $n$ securities. The excess rate of return on each security is given by

$$R_i = \alpha_i + \beta_i R_M + e_i$$

Similarly, we can write the excess return on the portfolio of stocks as

$$R_P = \alpha_P + \beta_P R_M + e_P \tag{10.5}$$

We now show that, as the number of stocks included in this portfolio increases, the part of the portfolio risk attributable to nonmarket factors becomes ever smaller. This part of the risk is diversified away. In contrast, the market risk remains, regardless of the number of firms combined into the portfolio.

To understand these results, note that the excess rate of return on this equally weighted portfolio, for which each portfolio weight $w_i = 1/n$, is

$$
\begin{aligned}
R_P = \sum_{i=1}^{n} w_i R_i &= \frac{1}{n} \sum_{i=1}^{n} R_i = \frac{1}{n} \sum_{i=1}^{n} (\alpha_i + \beta_i R_M + e_i) \\
&= \frac{1}{n} \sum_{i=1}^{n} \alpha_i + \left( \frac{1}{n} \sum_{i=1}^{n} \beta_i \right) R_M + \frac{1}{n} \sum_{i=1}^{n} e_i
\end{aligned}
\tag{10.6}
$$

Comparing equations 10.5 and 10.6, we see that the portfolio has a sensitivity to the market given by

$$\beta_P = \frac{1}{n} \sum_{i=1}^{n} \beta_i$$

which is the average of the individual $\beta_i$s. It has a nonmarket return component of a constant (intercept)

$$\alpha_P = \frac{1}{n} \sum_{i=1}^{n} \alpha_i$$

which is the average of the individual alphas, plus the zero mean variable

$$e_P = \frac{1}{n} \sum_{i=1}^{n} e_i$$

which is the average of the firm-specific components. Hence the portfolio's variance is

$$\sigma_P^2 = \beta_P^2 \sigma_M^2 + \sigma^2(e_P) \tag{10.7}$$

The systematic risk component of the portfolio variance, which we defined as the component that depends on marketwide movements, is $\beta_P^2 \sigma_M^2$ and depends on the sensitivity coefficients of the individual securities. This part of the risk depends on portfolio beta and $\sigma_M^2$ and will persist regardless of the extent of portfolio diversification. No matter how many

---

[6] William F. Sharpe, "A Simplified Model of Portfolio Analysis," *Management Science*, January 1963.

**Figure 10.2**
**The variance of a portfolio with risk coefficient $\beta_P$ in the single-factor economy**

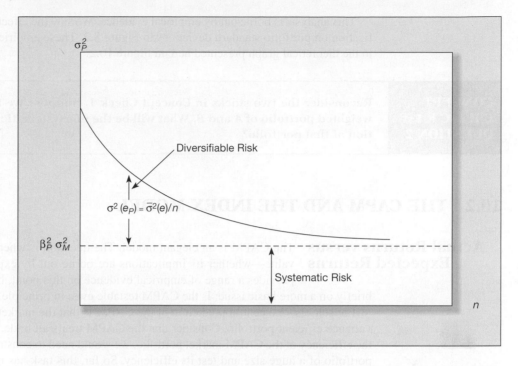

stocks are held, their common exposure to the market will be reflected in portfolio systematic risk.[7]

In contrast, the nonsystematic component of the portfolio variance is $\sigma^2(e_P)$ and is attributable to firm-specific components, $e_i$. Because these $e_i$s are independent, and all have zero expected value, the law of averages can be applied to conclude that as more and more stocks are added to the portfolio, the firm-specific components tend to cancel out, resulting in ever-smaller nonmarket risk. Such risk is thus termed *diversifiable*. To see this more rigorously, examine the formula for the variance of the equally weighted "portfolio" of firm-specific components. Because the $e_i$s are uncorrelated,

$$\sigma^2(e_P) = \sum_{i=1}^{n} \left(\frac{1}{n}\right)^2 \sigma^2(e_i) = \frac{1}{n}\,\bar{\sigma}^2(e)$$

where $\bar{\sigma}^2(e)$ is the average of the firm-specific variances. Because this average is independent of $n$, when $n$ gets large, $\sigma^2(e_P)$ becomes negligible.

To summarize, as diversification increases, the total variance of a portfolio approaches the systematic variance, defined as the variance of the market factor multiplied by the square of the portfolio sensitivity coefficient, $\beta_P^2$. This is shown in Figure 10.2.

Figure 10.2 shows that as more and more securities are combined into a portfolio, the portfolio variance decreases because of the diversification of firm-specific risk. However, the power of diversification is limited. Even for very large $n$, part of the risk remains because of the exposure of virtually all assets to the common, or market, factor. Therefore, this systematic risk is said to be nondiversifiable.

---

[7] Of course, one can construct a portfolio with zero systematic risk by mixing negative $\beta$ and positive $\beta$ assets. The point of our discussion is that the vast majority of securities have a positive $\beta$, implying that well-diversified portfolios with small holdings in large numbers of assets will indeed have positive systematic risk.

This analysis is borne out by empirical evidence. We saw the effect of portfolio diversification on portfolio standard deviations in Figure 8.2. These empirical results are similar to the theoretical graph presented here in Figure 10.2.

| CONCEPT CHECK ☞ QUESTION 2 | Reconsider the two stocks in Concept Check 1. Suppose we form an equally weighted portfolio of A and B. What will be the nonsystematic standard deviation of that portfolio? |
|---|---|

## 10.2    THE CAPM AND THE INDEX MODEL

**Actual Returns versus Expected Returns**    The CAPM is an elegant model. The question is whether it has real-world value—whether its implications are borne out by experience. Chapter 13 provides a range of empirical evidence on this point, but for now we focus briefly on a more basic issue: Is the CAPM testable even in principle?

For starters, one central prediction of the CAPM is that the market portfolio is a mean-variance efficient portfolio. Consider that the CAPM treats all traded risky assets. To test the efficiency of the CAPM market portfolio, we would need to construct a value-weighted portfolio of a huge size and test its efficiency. So far, this task has not been feasible. An even more difficult problem, however, is that the CAPM implies relationships among *expected* returns, whereas all we can observe are actual or realized holding-period returns, and these need not equal prior expectations. Even supposing we could construct a portfolio to represent the CAPM market portfolio satisfactorily, how would we test its mean-variance efficiency? We would have to show that the reward-to-variability ratio of the market portfolio is higher than that of any other portfolio. However, this reward-to-variability ratio is set in terms of expectations, and we have no way to observe these expectations directly.

The problem of measuring expectations haunts us as well when we try to establish the validity of the second central set of CAPM predictions, the expected return–beta relationship. This relationship is also defined in terms of expected returns $E(r_i)$ and $E(r_M)$:

$$E(r_i) = r_f + \beta_i [E(r_M) - r_f] \tag{10.8}$$

The upshot is that, as elegant and insightful as the CAPM is, we must make additional assumptions to make it implementable and testable.

**The Index Model and Realized Returns**    We have said that the CAPM is a statement about ex ante or expected returns, whereas in practice all anyone can observe directly are ex post or realized returns. To make the leap from expected to realized returns, we can employ the index model, which we will use in excess return form as

$$R_i = \alpha_i + \beta_i R_M + e_i \tag{10.9}$$

We saw in Section 10.1 how to apply standard regression analysis to estimate equation 10.9 using observable realized returns over some sample period. Let us now see how this framework for statistically decomposing actual stock returns meshes with the CAPM.

We start by deriving the covariance between the returns on stock $i$ and the market index. By definition, the firm-specific or nonsystematic component is independent of the marketwide or systematic component, that is, $Cov(R_M, e_i) = 0$. From this relationship, it follows that the covariance of the excess rate of return on security $i$ with that of the market index is

$$\begin{aligned} Cov(R_i, R_M) &= Cov(\beta_i R_M + e_i, R_M) \\ &= \beta_i Cov(R_M, R_M) + Cov(e_i, R_M) \\ &= \beta_i \sigma_M^2 \end{aligned}$$

Note that we can drop $\alpha_i$ from the covariance terms because $\alpha_i$ is a constant and thus has zero covariance with all variables.

Because $Cov(R_i, R_M) = \beta_i \sigma_M^2$, the sensitivity coefficient, $\beta_i$, in equation 10.9, which is the slope of the regression line representing the index model, equals

$$\beta_i = \frac{Cov(R_i, R_M)}{\sigma_M^2}$$

The index model beta coefficient turns out to be the same beta as that of the CAPM expected return–beta relationship, except that we replace the (theoretical) market portfolio of the CAPM with the well-specified and observable market index.

---

**CONCEPT CHECK☞ QUESTION 3**

The data below describe a three-stock financial market that satisfies the single-index model.

| Stock | Capitalization | Beta | Mean Excess Return | Standard Deviation |
|-------|---------------|------|-------------------|-------------------|
| A | $3,000 | 1.0 | 10% | 40% |
| B | $1,940 | 0.2 | 2 | 30 |
| C | $1,360 | 1.7 | 17 | 50 |

The single factor in this economy is perfectly correlated with the value-weighted index of the stock market. The standard deviation of the market index portfolio is 25%.

a. What is the mean excess return of the index portfolio?

b. What is the covariance between stock B and the index?

c. Break down the variance of stock B into its systematic and firm-specific components.

---

**The Index Model and the Expected Return–Beta Relationship**

Recall that the CAPM expected return–beta relationship is, for any asset $i$ and the (theoretical) market portfolio,

$$E(r_i) - r_f = \beta_i[E(r_M) - r_f]$$

where $\beta_i = Cov(R_i, R_M)/\sigma_M^2$. This is a statement about the mean of expected excess returns of assets relative to the mean excess return of the (theoretical) market portfolio.

If the index $M$ in equation 10.9 represents the true market portfolio, we can take the expectation of each side of the equation to show that the index model specification is

$$E(r_i) - r_f = \alpha_i + \beta_i[E(r_M) - r_f]$$

**Figure 10.3
Frequency
distribution
of alphas**

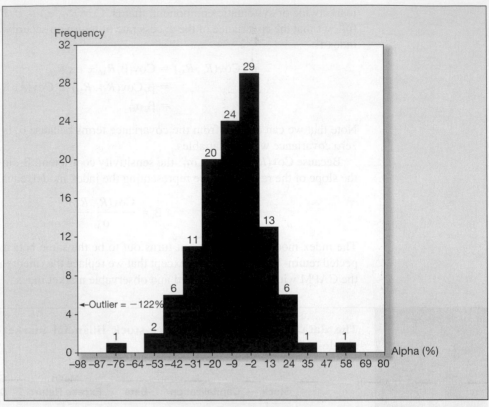

Source: Michael C. Jensen, "The Performance of Mutual Funds in the Period 1945–1964," *Journal of Finance* 23 (May 1968).

A comparison of the index model relationship to the CAPM expected return–beta relationship (equation 10.8) shows that the CAPM predicts that $\alpha_i$ should be zero for all assets. The alpha of a stock is its expected return in excess of (or below) the fair expected return as predicted by the CAPM. If the stock is fairly priced, its alpha must be zero.

We emphasize again that this is a statement about *expected* returns on a security. After the fact, of course, some securities will do better or worse than expected and will have returns higher or lower than predicted by the CAPM; that is, they will exhibit positive or negative alphas over a sample period. But this superior or inferior performance could not have been forecast in advance.

Therefore, if we estimate the index model for several firms, using equation 10.9 as a regression equation, we should find that the ex post or realized alphas (the regression intercepts) for the firms in our sample center around zero. If the initial expectation for alpha were zero, as many firms would be expected to have a positive as a negative alpha for some sample period. The CAPM states that the *expected* value of alpha is zero for all securities, whereas the index model representation of the CAPM holds that the *realized* value of alpha should average out to zero for a sample of historical observed returns. Just as important, the sample alphas should be unpredictable, that is, independent from one sample period to the next.

Some interesting evidence on this property was first compiled by Michael Jensen,[8] who examined the alphas realized by mutual funds over the period 1945 to 1964. Figure 10.3

---

[8] Michael C. Jensen, "The Performance of Mutual Funds in the Period 1945–1964," *Journal of Finance* 23 (May 1968).

shows the frequency distribution of these alphas, which do indeed seem to be distributed around zero. We will see in Chapter 12 (Figure 12.8) that more recent studies come to the same conclusion.

There is yet another applicable variation on the intuition of the index model, the **market model**. Formally, the market model states that the return "surprise" of any security is proportional to the return surprise of the market, plus a firm-specific surprise:

$$r_i - E(r_i) = \beta_i[r_M - E(r_M)] + e_i$$

This equation divides returns into firm-specific and systematic components somewhat differently from the index model. If the CAPM is valid, however, you can confirm that, substituting for $E(r_i)$ from equation 10.8, the market model equation becomes identical to the index model. For this reason the terms "index model" and "market model" often are used interchangeably.

<table>
<tr><td>

**CONCEPT CHECK☞ QUESTION 4**

</td><td>

**Can you sort out the nuances of the following maze of models?**

*a.* **CAPM**

*b.* **Single-factor model**

*c.* **Single-index model**

*d.* **Market model**

</td></tr>
</table>

## 10.3   THE INDUSTRY VERSION OF THE INDEX MODEL

Not surprisingly, the index model has attracted the attention of practitioners. To the extent that it is approximately valid, it provides a convenient benchmark for security analysis.

A modern practitioner using the CAPM, who has neither special information about a security nor insight that is unavailable to the general public, will conclude that the security is "properly" priced. By properly priced, the analyst means that the expected return on the security is commensurate with its risk, and therefore plots on the security market line. For instance, if one has no private information about GM's stock, then one should expect

$$E(r_{GM}) = r_f + \beta_{GM}[E(r_M) - r_f]$$

A portfolio manager who has a forecast for the market index, $E(r_M)$, and observes the risk-free T-bill rate, $r_f$, can use the model to determine the benchmark expected return for any stock. The beta coefficient, the market risk, $\sigma_M^2$, and the firm-specific risk, $\sigma^2(e)$, can be estimated from historical SCLs, that is, from regressions of security excess returns on market index excess returns.

There are many sources for such regression results. One widely used source is Research Computer Services Department of Merrill Lynch, which publishes a monthly *Security Risk Evaluation* book, commonly called the "beta book." The websites listed at the end of the chapter also provide security betas.

*Security Risk Evaluation* uses the S&P 500 as the proxy for the market portfolio. It relies on the 60 most recent monthly observations to calculate regression parameters. Merrill Lynch and most services[9] use total returns, rather than excess returns (deviations from

---

[9] Value Line is another common source of security betas. Value Line uses weekly rather than monthly data and uses the New York Stock Exchange index instead of the S&P 500 as the market proxy.

T-bill rates), in the regressions. In this way they estimate a variant of our index model, which is

$$r = a + br_M + e^* \tag{10.10}$$

instead of

$$r - r_f = \alpha + \beta(r_M - r_f) + e \tag{10.11}$$

To see the effect of this departure, we can rewrite equation 10.11 as

$$r = r_f + \alpha + \beta r_M - \beta r_f + e = \alpha + r_f(1 - \beta) + \beta r_M + e \tag{10.12}$$

Comparing equations 10.10 and 10.12, you can see that if $r_f$ is constant over the sample period, both equations have the same independent variable, $r_M$, and residual, $e$. Therefore, the slope coefficient will be the same in the two regressions.[10]

However, the intercept that Merrill Lynch calls alpha is really an estimate of $\alpha + r_f(1 - \beta)$. The apparent justification for this procedure is that, on a monthly basis, $r_f(1 - \beta)$ is small and is apt to be swamped by the volatility of actual stock returns. But it is worth noting that for $\beta \neq 1$, the regression intercept in equation 10.10 will not equal the index model alpha as it does when excess returns are used as in equation 10.11.

Another way the Merrill Lynch procedure departs from the index model is in its use of percentage changes in price instead of total rates of return. This means that the index model variant of Merrill Lynch ignores the dividend component of stock returns.

Table 10.2 illustrates a page from the beta book which includes estimates for GM. The third column, Close Price, shows the stock price at the end of the sample period. The next two columns show the beta and alpha coefficients. Remember that Merrill Lynch's alpha is actually an estimate of $\alpha + r_f(1 - \beta)$.

The next column, R-SQR, shows the square of the correlation between $r_i$ and $r_M$. The R-square statistic, $R^2$, which is sometimes called the *coefficient of determination*, gives the fraction of the variance of the dependent variable (the return on the stock) that is explained by movements in the independent variable (the return on the S&P 500 index). Recall from Section 10.1 that the part of the total variance of the rate of return on an asset, $\sigma^2$, that is explained by market returns is the systematic variance, $\beta^2\sigma_M^2$. Hence the R-square is systematic variance over total variance, which tells us what fraction of a firm's volatility is attributable to market movements:

$$R^2 = \frac{\beta^2\sigma_M^2}{\sigma^2}$$

The firm-specific variance, $\sigma^2(e)$, is the part of the asset variance that is unexplained by the market index. Therefore, because

$$\sigma^2 = \beta^2\sigma_M^2 + \sigma^2(e)$$

the coefficient of determination also may be expressed as

$$R^2 = 1 - \frac{\sigma^2(e)}{\sigma^2} \tag{10.13}$$

Accordingly, the column following R-SQR reports the standard deviation of the non-systematic component, $\sigma(e)$, calling it RESID STD DEV-N, in reference to the fact

---

[10] Actually, $r_f$ does vary over time and so should not be grouped casually with the constant term in the regression. However, variations in $r_f$ are tiny compared with the swings in the market return. The actual volatility in the T-bill rate has only a small impact on the estimated value of $\beta$.

## Table 10.2  Market Sensitivity Statistics

| Ticker Symbol | Security Name | June 1994 Close Price | Beta | Alpha | R-SQR | RESID STD DEV-N | Standard Error | | Adjusted Beta | Number of Observations |
|---|---|---|---|---|---|---|---|---|---|---|
| | | | | | | | Beta | Alpha | | |
| GBND | General Binding Corp | 18.375 | 0.52 | −0.06 | 0.02 | 10.52 | 0.37 | 1.38 | 0.68 | 60 |
| GBDC | General Bldrs Corp | 0.930 | 0.58 | −1.03 | 0.00 | 17.38 | 0.62 | 2.28 | 0.72 | 60 |
| GNCMA | General Communication Inc Class A | 3.750 | 1.54 | 0.82 | 0.12 | 14.42 | 0.51 | 1.89 | 1.36 | 60 |
| GCCC | General Computer Corp | 8.375 | 0.93 | 1.67 | 0.06 | 12.43 | 0.44 | 1.63 | 0.95 | 60 |
| GDC | General Datacomm Inds Inc | 16.125 | 2.25 | 2.31 | 0.16 | 18.32 | 0.65 | 2.40 | 1.83 | 60 |
| GD | General Dynamics Corp | 40.875 | 0.54 | 0.63 | 0.03 | 9.02 | 0.32 | 1.18 | 0.69 | 60 |
| GE | General Elec Co | 46.625 | 1.21 | 0.39 | 0.61 | 3.53 | 0.13 | 0.46 | 1.14 | 60 |
| JOB | General Employment Enterpris | 4.063 | 0.91 | 1.20 | 0.01 | 20.50 | 0.73 | 2.69 | 0.94 | 60 |
| GMCC | General Magnaplate Corp | 4.500 | 0.97 | 0.00 | 0.04 | 14.18 | 0.50 | 1.86 | 0.98 | 60 |
| GMW | General Microwave Corp | 8.000 | 0.95 | 0.16 | 0.12 | 8.83 | 0.31 | 1.16 | 0.97 | 60 |
| GIS | General MLS Inc | 54.625 | 1.01 | 0.42 | 0.37 | 4.82 | 0.17 | 0.63 | 1.01 | 60 |
| GM | General MTRS Corp | 50.250 | 0.80 | 0.14 | 0.11 | 7.78 | 0.28 | 1.02 | 0.87 | 60 ← |
| GPU | General Pub Utils Cp | 26.250 | 0.52 | 0.20 | 0.20 | 3.69 | 0.13 | 0.48 | 0.68 | 60 |
| GRN | General RE Corp | 108.875 | 1.07 | 0.42 | 0.31 | 5.75 | 0.20 | 0.75 | 1.05 | 60 |
| GSX | General SIGNAL Corp | 33.000 | 0.86 | −0.01 | 0.22 | 5.85 | 0.21 | 0.77 | 0.91 | 60 |

Source: Modified from *Security Risk Evaluation*, 1994, Research Computer Services Department of Merrill Lynch, Pierce, Fenner and Smith, Inc., pp. 9–17. Based on S&P 500 index, using straight regression.

that the $e$ is estimated from the regression residuals. This variable is an estimate of firm-specific risk.

The following two columns appear under the heading of Standard Error. These are statistics that allow us to test the precision and significance of the regression coefficients. The standard error of an estimate is the standard deviation of the possible estimation error of the coefficient. A rule of thumb is that if an estimated coefficient is less than twice its standard error, we cannot reject the hypothesis that the true coefficient is zero. The ratio of the coefficient to its standard error is the $t$-statistic. A $t$-statistic greater than 2 is the traditional cutoff for statistical significance. The two columns of the standard error of the estimated beta and alpha allow us a quick check on the statistical significance of these estimates.

The next-to-last column is called Adjusted Beta. The motivation for adjusting beta estimates is that, on average, the beta coefficients of stocks seem to move toward 1 over time. One explanation for this phenomenon is intuitive. A business enterprise usually is established to produce a specific product or service, and a new firm may be more unconventional than an older one in many ways, from technology to management style. As it grows, however, a firm often diversifies, first expanding to similar products and later to more diverse operations. As the firm becomes more conventional, it starts to resemble the rest of the economy even more. Thus its beta coefficient will tend to change in the direction of 1.

Another explanation for this phenomenon is statistical. We know that the average beta over all securities is 1. Thus, before estimating the beta of a security, our best forecast of the beta would be that it is 1. When we estimate this beta coefficient over a particular sample period, we sustain some unknown sampling error of the estimated beta. The greater the difference between our beta estimate and 1, the greater is the chance that we incurred a large estimation error and that beta in a subsequent sample period will be closer to 1.

| E-INVESTMENTS | Go to one of the sites listed in the Related Websites section. Find the betas of 10 stocks from |
| Beta Estimates | different industries. What sorts of factors might explain the differences among these betas? |
| | Do the firms in industries that are more sensitive to the business cycle appear to have higher |
| | betas? Find betas of four firms in the same industry. Are the beta estimates for firms within an |
| | industry more similar than beta estimates across industries? |

The sample estimate of the beta coefficient is the best guess for that sample period. Given that beta has a tendency to evolve toward 1, however, a forecast of the future beta coefficient should adjust the sample estimate in that direction.

Merrill Lynch adjusts beta estimates in a simple way.[11] It takes the sample estimate of beta and averages it with 1, using weights of two-thirds and one-third:

$$\text{Adjusted beta} = \tfrac{2}{3}\text{ sample beta} + \tfrac{1}{3}(1)$$

## EXAMPLE 10.1    Adjusted Beta

For the 60 months used in Table 10.2, GM's beta was estimated at .80. Therefore, its adjusted beta is $\tfrac{2}{3} \times .80 + \tfrac{1}{3} = .87$, taking it a third of the way toward 1.

In the absence of special information concerning GM, if our forecast for the market index is 14% and T-bills pay 6%, we learn from the Merrill Lynch beta book that the CAPM forecast for the rate of return on GM stock is

$$E(r_{GM}) = r_f + \text{adjusted beta} \times [E(r_M) - r_f]$$
$$= 6 + .87 (14 - 6) = 12.96\%$$

The sample period regression alpha is .14%. Because GM's beta is less than 1, we know that this means that the index model alpha estimate is somewhat smaller. As in equation 10.12, we have to subtract $(1 - \beta)r_f$ from the regression alpha to obtain the index model alpha. Even so, the standard error of the alpha estimate is 1.02. The estimate of alpha is far less than twice its standard error. Consequently, we cannot reject the hypothesis that the true alpha is zero.

| CONCEPT CHECK ☞ QUESTION 5 | What was GM's CAPM alpha per month during the period covered by the Merrill Lynch regression if during this period the average monthly rate of return on T-bills was .6%? |

Always remember that these alpha estimates are ex post (after the fact) measures. They do not mean that anyone could have forecast these alpha values ex ante (before the fact). In fact, the name of the game in security analysis is to forecast alpha values ahead of time. A well-constructed portfolio that includes long positions in future positive-alpha stocks and short positions in future negative-alpha stocks will outperform the market index. The key term here is "well constructed," meaning that the portfolio has to balance concentration on high-alpha stocks with the need for risk-reducing diversification. The beta and residual variance estimates from the index model regression make it possible to achieve this goal. (We examine this technique in more detail in Part 7 on active portfolio management.)

---

[11] A more sophisticated method is described in Oldrich A. Vasicek, "A Note on Using Cross-Sectional Information in Bayesian Estimation of Security Betas," *Journal of Finance* 28 (1973), pp. 1233–39.

Note that GM's RESID STD DEV-$N$ is 7.78% per month and its $R^2$ is .11. This tells us that $\sigma_{GM}^2(e) = 7.78^2 = 60.53$ and, because $R^2 = 1 - \sigma^2(e)/\sigma^2$, we can solve for the estimate of GM's total standard deviation by rearranging equation 10.13 as follows:

$$\sigma_{GM} = \left[ \frac{\sigma_{GM}^2(e)}{1 - R^2} \right]^{1/2} = \left( \frac{60.53}{.89} \right)^{1/2} = 8.25\% \text{ per month}$$

This is GM's monthly standard deviation for the sample period. Therefore, the annualized standard deviation for that period was $8.25 \sqrt{12} = 28.58\%$.

Finally, the last column shows the number of observations, which is 60 months, unless the stock is newly listed and fewer observations are available.

## Predicting Betas

We saw in the previous section that betas estimated from past data may not be the best estimates of future betas: Betas seem to drift toward 1 over time. This suggests that we might want a forecasting model for beta.

One simple approach would be to collect data on beta in different periods and then estimate a regression equation:

$$\text{Current beta} = a + b \text{ (Past beta)} \tag{10.14}$$

Given estimates of $a$ and $b$, we would then forecast future betas using the rule

$$\text{Forecast beta} = a + b \text{ (Current beta)}$$

There is no reason, however, to limit ourselves to such simple forecasting rules. Why not also investigate the predictive power of other financial variables in forecasting beta? For example, if we believe that firm size and debt ratios are two determinants of beta, we might specify an expanded version of equation 10.14 and estimate

$$\text{Current beta} = a + b_1 \text{ (Past beta)} + b_2 \text{ (Firm size)} + b_3 \text{ (Debt ratio)}$$

Now we would use estimates of $a$ and $b_1$ through $b_3$ to forecast future betas.

Such an approach was followed by Rosenberg and Guy[12] who found the following variables to help predict betas:

1. Variance of earnings.
2. Variance of cash flow.
3. Growth in earnings per share.
4. Market capitalization (firm size).
5. Dividend yield.
6. Debt-to-asset ratio.

Rosenberg and Guy also found that even after controlling for a firm's financial characteristics, industry group helps to predict beta. For example, they found that the beta values of gold mining companies are on average .827 lower than would be predicted based on financial characteristics alone. This should not be surprising; the $-.827$ "adjustment factor" for the gold industry reflects the fact that gold values are inversely related to market returns.

Table 10.3 presents beta estimates and adjustment factors for a subset of firms in the Rosenberg and Guy study.

---

[12] Barr Rosenberg and J. Guy, "Prediction of Beta from Investment Fundamentals, Parts 1 and 2," *Financial Analysts Journal*, May–June and July–August 1976.

**Table 10.3    Industry Betas and Adjustment Factors**

| Industry | Beta | Adjustment Factor |
|---|---|---|
| Agriculture | 0.99 | −.140 |
| Drugs and medicine | 1.14 | −.099 |
| Telephone | 0.75 | −.288 |
| Energy utilities | 0.60 | −.237 |
| Gold | 0.36 | −.827 |
| Construction | 1.27 | .062 |
| Air transport | 1.80 | .348 |
| Trucking | 1.31 | .098 |
| Consumer durables | 1.44 | .132 |

**CONCEPT CHECK ☞ QUESTION 6**

Compare the first five and last four industries in Table 10.3. What characteristic seems to determine whether the adjustment factor is positive or negative?

## 10.4    INDEX MODELS AND TRACKING PORTFOLIOS

Suppose a portfolio manager believes she has identified an underpriced portfolio. Her security analysis team estimates the index model equation for this portfolio (using the S&P 500 index) in excess return form and obtains the following estimates:

$$R_P = .04 + 1.4R_{\text{S\&P500}} + e_P \qquad (10.15)$$

Therefore, $P$ has an alpha value of 4% (which measures the extent of mispricing) and a beta of 1.4. The manager is confident in the quality of her security analysis but is wary about the performance of the broad market in the near term. If she buys the portfolio, and the market as a whole turns down, she still could lose money on her investment (which has a large positive beta) even if her team is correct that the portfolio is underpriced on a relative basis. She would like a position that takes advantage of her team's analysis but is independent of the performance of the overall market.

To this end, a **tracking portfolio** ($T$) can be constructed. A tracking portfolio for portfolio $P$ is a portfolio designed to match the systematic component of $P$'s return. The idea is for the portfolio to "track" the market-sensitive component of $P$'s return. This means the tracking portfolio must have the same beta on the index portfolio as $P$ and as little nonsystematic risk as possible.

A tracking portfolio for $P$ will have a levered position in the S&P 500 to achieve a beta of 1.4. Therefore, $T$ includes positions of 1.4 in the S&P 500 and −0.4 in T-bills. Because $T$ is constructed from the index and bills, it has an alpha value of zero.

Now consider buying portfolio $P$ but at the same time offsetting systematic risk by assuming a short position in the tracking portfolio. The short position in $T$ cancels out the systematic exposure of the long position in $P$: the overall combined position is thus *market neutral*. Therefore, even if the market does poorly, the combined position should not be affected. But the alpha on portfolio $P$ will remain intact. The combined portfolio, $C$, provides a return per dollar of

$$R_C = R_P - R_T = (.04 + 1.4R_{\text{S\&P500}} + e_P) - 1.4R_{\text{S\&P500}} = .04 + e_P \qquad (10.16)$$

# EXCEL APPLICATION

# ESTIMATING BETA COEFFICIENTS

The spreadsheet Betas, which you will find on the Online Learning Center (www.mhhe.com/bkm), contains 60 months' returns for 10 individual stocks. Returns are calculated over the 5 years ending in December 2000. The spreadsheet also contains returns for S&P 500 Index and the observed risk-free rates as measured by the 1-year Treasury bill. With this data, monthly excess returns for the individual securities and the market as measured by the S&P 500 Index can be used with the regression module in Excel. The spreadsheet also contains returns on an equally weighted portfolio of the individual securities. The regression module is available under Tools Data Analysis. The dependent variable is the security excess return. The independent variable is the market excess return.

A sample of the output from the regression is shown below. The estimated beta coefficient for American Express is 1.21, and 48% of the variance in returns for American Express can be explained by the returns on the S&P 500 Index.

|    | A | B | C | D | E | F |
|----|---|---|---|---|---|---|
| 1  | SUMMARY OUTPUT | AXP | | | | |
| 2  | | | | | | |
| 3  | *Regression Statistics* | | | | | |
| 4  | Multiple R | 0.69288601 | | | | |
| 5  | R Square | 0.48009103 | | | | |
| 6  | Adjusted R Square | 0.47112708 | | | | |
| 7  | Standard Error | 0.05887426 | | | | |
| 8  | Observations | 60 | | | | |
| 9  | | | | | | |
| 10 | ANOVA | | | | | |
| 11 | | *df* | *SS* | *MS* | *F* | *Significance F* |
| 12 | Regression | 1 | 0.185641557 | 0.1856416 | 53.55799 | 8.55186E-10 |
| 13 | Residual | 58 | 0.201038358 | 0.0034662 | | |
| 14 | Total | 59 | 0.386679915 | | | |
| 15 | | | | | | |
| 16 | | *Coefficients* | *Standard* | *t Stat* | *P-value* | *Lower 95%* |
| 17 | | | *Error* | | | |
| 18 | Intercept | 0.01181687 | 0.00776211 | 1.522379 | 0.133348 | -0.003720666 |
| 19 | X Variable 1 | 1.20877413 | 0.165170705 | 7.3183324 | 8.55E-10 | 0.878149288 |

While this portfolio is still risky (due to the residual risk, $e_P$), the systematic risk has been eliminated, and if $P$ is reasonably well-diversified, the remaining nonsystematic risk will be small. Thus the objective is achieved: the manager can take advantage of the 4% alpha without inadvertently taking on market exposure.

This "long-short strategy" is characteristic of the activity of many *hedge funds*. Hedge fund managers identify an underpriced security and then try to attain a "pure play" on the perceived underpricing. They hedge out all extraneous risk, focusing the bet only on the perceived "alpha." Tracking funds are the vehicle used to hedge the exposures to which they do *not* want exposure. Hedge fund managers use index regressions such as those discussed here, as well as more-sophisticated variations, to create the tracking portfolios at the heart of their hedging strategies.

## SUMMARY

1. A single-factor model of the economy classifies sources of uncertainty as systematic (macroeconomic) factors or firm-specific (microeconomic) factors. The index model assumes that the macro factor can be represented by a broad index of stock returns.

2. The single-index model drastically reduces the necessary inputs in the Markowitz portfolio selection procedure. It also aids in specialization of labor in security analysis.

3. According to the index model specification, the systematic risk of a portfolio or asset equals $\beta^2 \sigma_M^2$ and the covariance between two assets equals $\beta_i \beta_j \sigma_M^2$.

4. The index model is estimated by applying regression analysis to excess rates of return. The slope of the regression curve is the beta of an asset, whereas the intercept is the asset's alpha during the sample period. The regression line is also called the *security characteristic line*. The regression beta is equivalent to the CAPM beta, except that the regression uses actual returns and the CAPM is specified in terms of expected returns. The CAPM predicts that the average value of alphas measured by the index model regression will be zero.

5. Practitioners routinely estimate the index model using total rather than excess rates of return. This makes their estimate of alpha equal to $\alpha + r_f(1 - \beta)$.

6. Betas show a tendency to evolve toward 1 over time. Beta forecasting rules attempt to predict this drift. Moreover, other financial variables can be used to help forecast betas.

## KEY TERMS

| | | |
|---|---|---|
| single-factor model | regression equation | market model |
| single-index model | residuals | tracking portfolio |
| scatter diagram | security characteristic line | |

## WEBSITES

## PROBLEMS

1. A portfolio management organization analyzes 60 stocks and constructs a mean-variance efficient portfolio using only these 60 securities.

   a. How many estimates of expected returns, variances, and covariances are needed to optimize this portfolio?

   b. If one could safely assume that stock market returns closely resemble a single-index structure, how many estimates would be needed?

2. The following are estimates for two of the stocks in problem 1.

| Stock | Expected Return | Beta | Firm-Specific Standard Deviation |
|-------|-----------------|------|----------------------------------|
| A | 13 | 0.8 | 30 |
| B | 18 | 1.2 | 40 |

The market index has a standard deviation of 22% and the risk-free rate is 8%.

   a. What is the standard deviation of stocks A and B?
   b. Suppose that we were to construct a portfolio with proportions:

> Stock A:    .30
> Stock B:    .45
> T-bills:    .25

Compute the expected return, standard deviation, beta, and nonsystematic standard deviation of the portfolio.

3. Consider the following two regression lines for stocks A and B in the following figure.

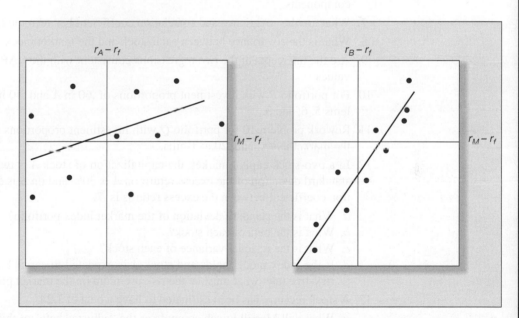

   a. Which stock has higher firm-specific risk?
   b. Which stock has greater systematic (market) risk?
   c. Which stock has higher $R^2$?
   d. Which stock has higher alpha?
   e. Which stock has higher correlation with the market?

4. Consider the two (excess return) index model regression results for A and B:

   $R_A = 1\% + 1.2R_M$
   R-SQR = .576

Visit us at www.mhhe.com/bkm

RESID STD DEV-$N$ = 10.3%

$R_B = -2\% + .8R_M$

R-SQR = .436

RESID STD DEV-$N$ = 9.1%

a. Which stock has more firm-specific risk?

b. Which has greater market risk?

c. For which stock does market movement explain a greater fraction of return variability?

d. Which stock had an average return in excess of that predicted by the CAPM?

e. If $r_f$ were constant at 6% and the regression had been run using total rather than excess returns, what would have been the regression intercept for stock $A$?

Use the following data for problems 5 through 11. Suppose that the index model for stocks $A$ and $B$ is estimated from excess returns with the following results:

$$R_A = 3\% + .7R_M + e_A$$
$$R_B = -2\% + 1.2R_M + e_B$$
$$\sigma_M = 20\%; \quad \text{R-SQR}_A = .20; \quad \text{R-SQR}_B = .12$$

5. What is the standard deviation of each stock?

6. Break down the variance of each stock to the systematic and firm-specific components.

7. What are the covariance and correlation coefficient between the two stocks?

8. What is the covariance between each stock and the market index?

9. Are the intercepts of the two regressions consistent with the CAPM? Interpret their values.

10. For portfolio $P$ with investment proportions of .60 in $A$ and .40 in $B$, rework problems 5, 6, and 8.

11. Rework problem 10 for portfolio $Q$ with investment proportions of .50 in $P$, .30 in the market index, and .20 in T-bills.

12. In a two-stock capital market, the capitalization of stock $A$ is twice that of $B$. The standard deviation of the excess return on $A$ is 30% and on $B$ is 50%. The correlation coefficient between the excess returns is .7.

a. What is the standard deviation of the market index portfolio?

b. What is the beta of each stock?

c. What is the residual variance of each stock?

d. If the index model holds and stock $A$ is expected to earn 11% in excess of the risk-free rate, what must be the risk premium on the market portfolio?

13. A stock recently has been estimated to have a beta of 1.24:

a. What will Merrill Lynch compute as the "adjusted beta" of this stock?

b. Suppose that you estimate the following regression describing the evolution of beta over time:

$$\beta_t = .3 + .7\beta_{t-1}$$

What would be your predicted beta for next year?

14. When the annualized monthly percentage rates of return for a stock market index were regressed against the returns for ABC and XYZ stocks over the period

1992–2001 in an ordinary least squares regression, the following results were obtained:

| Statistic | ABC | XYZ |
|---|---|---|
| Alpha | −3.20% | 7.3% |
| Beta | 0.60 | 0.97 |
| $R^2$ | 0.35 | 0.17 |
| Residual standard deviation | 13.02% | 21.45% |

Explain what these regression results tell the analyst about risk–return relationships for each stock over the 1992–2001 period. Comment on their implications for future risk–return relationships, assuming both stocks were included in a diversified common stock portfolio, especially in view of the following additional data obtained from two brokerage houses, which are based on 2 years of weekly data ending in December 2001.

| Brokerage House | Beta of ABC | Beta of XYZ |
|---|---|---|
| A | .62 | 1.45 |
| B | .71 | 1.25 |

15. Based on current dividend yields and expected growth rates, the expected rates of return on stocks A and B are 11% and 14%, respectively. The beta of stock A is .8, while that of stock B is 1.5. The T-bill rate is currently 6%, while the expected rate of return on the S&P 500 index is 12%. The standard deviation of stock A is 10% annually, while that of stock B is 11%.

   a. If you currently hold a well-diversified portfolio, would you choose to add either of these stocks to your holdings?

   b. If instead you could invest only in bills and *one* of these stocks, which stock would you choose? Explain your answer using either a graph or a quantitative measure of the attractiveness of the stocks.

16. Assume the correlation coefficient between Baker Fund and the S&P 500 Stock Index is .70. What percentage of Baker Fund's total risk is specific (i.e., nonsystematic)?

   a. 35%
   b. 49%
   c. 51%
   d. 70%

17. The correlation between the Charlottesville International Fund and the EAFE Market Index is 1.0. The expected return on the EAFE Index is 11%, the expected return on Charlottesville International Fund is 9%, and the risk-free return in EAFE countries is 3%. Based on this analysis, the implied beta of Charlottesville International is:

   a. Negative
   b. .75
   c. .82
   d. 1.00

18. The concept of *beta* is most closely associated with:
    a. Correlation coefficients.
    b. Mean-variance analysis.
    c. Nonsystematic risk.
    d. The capital asset pricing model.

19. Beta and standard deviation differ as risk measures in that beta measures:
    a. Only unsystematic risk, while standard deviation measures total risk.
    b. Only systematic risk, while standard deviation measures total risk.
    c. Both systematic and unsystematic risk, while standard deviation measures only unsystematic risk.
    d. Both systematic and unsystematic risk, while standard deviation measures only systematic risk.

---

**STANDARD &POOR'S**

Go to **www.mhhe.com/business/finance/edumarketinsight** to obtain monthly rates of return on AT&T and the S&P 500 over the last 3 years. Save these returns in an Excel spreadsheet. Calculate AT&T's beta over this time period using the index model. (You can use the regression feature of Excel to perform the calculation.) What is the intercept of the regression? If your regression specification is in total returns rather than excess returns (see the section in the chapter on the industry version of the index model), what was the CAPM alpha of the stock over the time period? You can find recent interest rates at **www.stls.frb.org**.

---

**E-INVESTMENTS**
**Comparing Volatilities and Beta Coefficients**

Go to Yahoo finance at the following address: **finance.yahoo.com**. Using the *Symbol Lookup* function, find the ticker symbols for Texas Instruments, Intel Corporation, and Advanced Energy Industries.

Once you have the tickers, return to the home page for Yahoo finance and get quotes for all of the stocks by entering the ticker symbol in the *Get Quote* function dialog box and use the pull down menu to the right of the *Get Quotes* box to ask for *Charts*.

When the chart appears change the period from 1 to 2 years and use the *Compare* function, adding the other two ticker symbols and the S&P index. Hit the Compare button and examine your results. You should get a graph that looks similar to the one printed below.

Using the graph for comparison, which of the securities would you predict to have a beta coefficient in excess of 1.0? Which of the companies would you expect to have the highest beta coefficient?

Get the company profile by clicking *Profile*, which appears next to the company name at the top of the chart. Look through the data in the profile report until you find the beta coefficient. When in *Profile*, you can request the profile for the other companies. Are the betas as you predicted?

**SOLUTIONS
TO CONCEPT
CHECKS**

1. The variance of each stock is $\beta^2\sigma_M^2 + \sigma^2(e)$.

   For stock $A$, we obtain

   $$\sigma_A^2 = .9^2(20)^2 + 30^2 = 1,224$$
   $$\sigma_A = 35$$

   For stock $B$,

   $$\sigma_B^2 = 1.1^2(20)^2 + 10^2 = 584$$
   $$\sigma_B = 24$$

   The covariance is

   $$\beta_A\beta_B\sigma_M^2 = .9 \times 1.1 \times 20^2 = 396$$

2. $\sigma^2(e_P) = (1/2)^2[\sigma^2(e_A) + \sigma^2(e_B)]$
   $= (1/4)(30^2 + 10^2)$
   $= 250$

   Therefore $\sigma(e_P) = 15.8$

**SOLUTIONS
TO CONCEPT
CHECKS**
*(Concluded)*

3. *a.* Total market capitalization is $3,000 + 1,940 + 1,360 = 6,300$. Therefore, the mean excess return of the index portfolio is

$$\frac{3,000}{6,300} \times 10 + \frac{1,940}{6,300} \times 2 + \frac{1,360}{6,300} \times 17 = 10$$

*b.* The covariance between stock $B$ and the index portfolio equals

$$\text{Cov}(R_B, R_M) = \beta_B \sigma_M^2 = .2 \times 25^2 = 125$$

*c.* The total variance of $B$ equals

$$\sigma_B^2 = \text{Var}(\beta_B, R_M + e_B) = \beta_B^2 \sigma_M^2 + \sigma^2(e_B)$$

Systematic risk equals $\beta_B^2 \sigma_M^2 = .2^2 \times 25^2 = 25$.
Thus the firm-specific variance of $B$ equals

$$\sigma^2(e_B) = \sigma_B^2 - \beta_B^2 \sigma_M^2 = 30^2 - .2^2 \times 25^2 = 875$$

4. The CAPM is a model that relates expected rates of return to risk. It results in the expected return–beta relationship, where the expected risk premium on any asset is proportional to the expected risk premium on the market portfolio with beta as the proportionality constant. As such the model is impractical for two reasons: (i) expectations are unobservable, and (ii) the theoretical market portfolio includes every risky asset and is in practice unobservable. The next three models incorporate additional assumptions to overcome these problems.

The single-factor model assumes that one economic factor, denoted $F$, exerts the only common influence on security returns. Beyond it, security returns are driven by independent, firm-specific factors. Thus for any security, $i$,

$$r_i = E(r_i) + \beta_i F + e_i$$

The single-index model assumes that in the single-factor model, the factor $F$ can be replaced by a broad-based index of securities that can proxy for the CAPM's theoretical market portfolio. The index model can be stated as $R_i = \alpha_i + \beta_i R_M + e_i$.

At this point it should be said that many interchange the meaning of the index and market models. The concept of the market model is that rate of return *surprises* on a stock are proportional to corresponding surprises on the market index portfolio, again with proportionality constant $\beta$.

5. Merrill Lynch's alpha is related to the CAPM alpha by

$$\alpha_{\text{Merrill}} = \alpha_{\text{CAPM}} + (1 - \beta)r_f$$

For GM, $\alpha_{\text{Merrill}} = .14\%$, $\beta = .80$, and we are told that $r_f$ was .6%. Thus

$$\alpha_{\text{CAPM}} = .14\% - (1 - .80).6\% = .02\%$$

GM still performed well relative to the market and the index model. It beat its "benchmark" return by an average of .02% per month.

6. The industries with positive adjustment factors are most sensitive to the economy. Their betas would be expected to be higher because the business risk of the firms is higher. In contrast, the industries with negative adjustment factors are in business fields with a lower sensitivity to the economy. Therefore, for any given financial profile, their betas are lower.

# ARBITRAGE PRICING THEORY AND MULTIFACTOR MODELS OF RISK AND RETURN

The exploitation of security mispricing in such a way that risk-free profits can be earned is called arbitrage. It involves the simultaneous purchase and sale of equivalent securities in order to profit from discrepancies in their prices. Perhaps the most basic principle of capital market theory is that equilibrium market prices are rational in that they rule out arbitrage opportunities. If actual security prices allow for arbitrage, the result will be strong pressure to restore equilibrium. Therefore, security markets ought to satisfy a "no-arbitrage condition." In this chapter, we show how such no-arbitrage conditions together with the factor model introduced in Chapter 10 allow us to generalize the security market line of the CAPM to gain richer insight into the risk-return relationship.

We begin by showing how the decomposition of risk into market versus firm-specific influences introduced in earlier chapters can be extended to deal with the multifaceted nature of systematic risk. Multifactor models of security returns can be used to measure and manage exposure to each of many economy-wide factors such as business-cycle risk, interest or inflation rate risk, energy price risk, and so on. These models also lead us to a multifactor version of the security market line in which risk premiums derive from exposure to multiple risk sources, each with their own risk premium.

We show how factor models combined with a no-arbitrage condition lead to a simple relationship between expected return and risk. This approach to the risk-return tradeoff is called Arbitrage Pricing Theory or APT. We derive the APT, and show why it implies a multifactor security market line. We ask next what factors are likely to be the most important sources of risk. These will be factors that generate substantial hedging demands. This discussion brings us to a multifactor CAPM, similar to the multifactor APT. Both the APT and the CAPM lead to multiple-risk versions of the security market line, thereby enriching the insights we can derive about the risk-return relationship.

# 11.1   MULTIFACTOR MODELS: AN OVERVIEW

The index model introduced in Chapter 10 gave us a way of decomposing stock variability into market or systematic risk, due largely to macroeconomic events, versus firm-specific or idiosyncratic effects that can be diversified in large portfolios. In the index model, the return on the market portfolio summarized the broad impact of macro factors. Sometimes, however, rather than using a market proxy, it is more useful to focus directly on the ultimate sources of risk. This can be useful in risk assessment, for example, when measuring one's exposures to particular sources of uncertainty. Factor models are tools that allow us to describe and quantify the different factors that affect the rate of return on a security during any time period.

**Factor Models of Security Returns**    To illustrate, we will start by examining a single-factor model like the one introduced in Chapter 10. As noted there, uncertainty in asset returns has two sources: a common or macroeconomic factor, and firm-specific events. The common factor is constructed to have zero expected value, since we use it to measure *new* information concerning the macroeconomy which, by definition, has zero expected value.

If we call $F$ the deviation of the common factor from its expected value, $\beta_i$ the sensitivity of firm $i$ to that factor, and $e_i$ the firm-specific disturbance, the factor model states that the actual return on firm $i$ will equal its initially expected return plus a (zero expected value) random amount attributable to unanticipated economywide events, plus another (zero expected value) random amount attributable to firm-specific events.

Formally, the **single-factor model** is described by equation 11.1:

$$r_i = E(r_i) + \beta_i F + e_i \tag{11.1}$$

where $E(r_i)$ is the expected return on stock $i$. Notice that if the macro factor has a value of 0 in any particular period (i.e., no macro surprises), the return on the security will equal its previously expected value, $E(r_i)$, plus the effect of firm-specific events only. All the nonsystematic components of returns, the $e_i$s, are uncorrelated among themselves and uncorrelated with the factor $F$.

## EXAMPLE 11.1    Factor Models

To make the factor model more concrete, consider an example. Suppose that the macro factor, $F$, is taken to be news about the state of the business cycle, measured by the unexpected percentage change in gross domestic product (GDP), and that the consensus is that GDP will increase by 4% this year. Suppose also that a stock's β value is 1.2. If GDP increases by only 3%, then the value of $F$ would be $-1\%$, representing a 1% disappointment in actual growth versus expected growth. Given the stock's beta value, this disappointment would translate into a return on the stock that is 1.2% lower than previously expected. This macro surprise, together with the firm-specific disturbance, $e_i$, determine the total departure of the stock's return from its originally expected value.

**CONCEPT CHECK ☞ QUESTION 1**

Suppose you currently expect the stock in Example 11.1 to earn a 10% rate of return. Then some macroeconomic news suggests that GDP growth will come in at 5% instead of 4%. How will you revise your estimate of the stock's expected rate of return?

The factor model's decomposition of returns into systematic and firm-specific components is compelling, but confining systematic risk to a single factor is not. Indeed, when we motivated the index model in Chapter 10, we noted that the systematic or macro factor summarized by the market return arises from a number of sources, for example, uncertainty about the business cycle, interest rates, inflation, and so on. The market return reflects both macro factors as well as the average sensitivity of firms to those factors. When we estimate a single-index regression, therefore, we implicitly impose an (incorrect) assumption that each stock has the same relative sensitivity to each risk factor. If stocks actually differ in their betas relative to the various macroeconomic factors, then lumping all systematic sources of risk into one variable such as the return on the market index will ignore the nuances that better explain individual-stock returns.

It stands to reason that a more explicit representation of systematic risk, allowing for the possibility that different stocks exhibit different sensitivities to its various components, would constitute a useful refinement of the single-factor model. It is easy to see that models that allow for several factors—**multifactor models**—can provide better descriptions of security returns.

Apart from their use in building models of equilibrium security pricing, multifactor models are useful in risk management applications. These models give us a simple way to measure our exposure to various macroeconomic risks, and construct portfolios to hedge those risks.

Let's start with a two-factor model. Suppose the two most important macroeconomic sources of risk are uncertainties surrounding the state of the business cycle, news of which we will again measure by unanticipated growth in GDP and changes in interest rates. We will call any unexpected decline in interest rates, which ought to be good news for stocks, IR. The return on any stock will respond both to sources of macro risk as well as to its own firm-specific influences. We therefore can write a two-factor model describing the rate of return on stock $i$ in some time period as follows:

$$r_i = E(r_i) + \beta_{i\,GDP}GDP + \beta_{i\,IR}IR + e_i \tag{11.2}$$

The two macro factors on the right-hand side of the equation comprise the systematic factors in the economy. As in the single-factor model, both of these macro factors have zero expectation: they represent changes in these variables that have not already been anticipated. The coefficients of each factor in equation 11.2 measure the sensitivity of share returns to that factor. For this reason the coefficients are sometimes called **factor sensitivities, factor loadings,** or, equivalently, **factor betas.** Also as before, $e_i$ reflects firm-specific influences.

To illustrate the advantages of multifactor models in understanding the sources of macro risk, consider two firms, one a regulated electric-power utility in a mostly residential area, the other an airline. Because residential demand for electricity is not very sensitive to the business cycle, the utility is likely to have a low beta on GDP. But the utility's stock price may have a relatively high sensitivity to interest rates. Since the cash flow generated by the utility is relatively stable, its present value behaves much like that of a bond, varying inversely with interest rates. Conversely, the performance of the airline is very sensitive to economic activity but is less sensitive to interest rates. It will have a high GDP beta and a lower interest rate beta. Suppose that on a particular day, there is a piece of news suggesting that the economy will expand. GDP is expected to increase, but so are interest rates. Is the "macro news" on this day good or bad? For the utility, this is bad news: its dominant sensitivity is to rates. But for the airline, which responds more to GDP, this is good news. Clearly a one-factor or single-index model cannot capture such differential responses to varying sources of macroeconomic uncertainty.

## EXAMPLE 11.2    Risk Assessment Using Multifactor Models

Suppose we estimate the two-factor model in equation 11.2 for Northeast Airlines and find the following result:

$$r = .10 + 1.8(GDP) + .7(IR) + e$$

This tells us that based on currently available information, the expected rate of return for Northeast is 10%, but that for every percentage point increase in GDP beyond current expectations, the return on Northeast shares increases on average by 1.8%, while for every unanticipated percentage point that interest rates decreases, Northeast's shares rise on average by .7%.

The factor betas can provide a framework for a hedging strategy. The idea for an investor who wishes to hedge a source of risk is to establish an opposite factor exposure to offset that particular source of risk. Often, futures contracts can be used to hedge particular factor exposures. We explore this application in Chapter 22.

**A Multifactor Security Market Line**    As it stands, the multifactor model is no more than a *description* of the factors that affect security returns. There is no "theory" in the equation. The obvious question left unanswered by a factor model like equation 11.2 is where

$E(r)$ comes from, in other words, what determines a security's expected rate of return. This is where we need a theoretical model of equilibrium security returns.

In the previous two chapters we developed one example of such a model: the Security Market Line of the Capital Asset Pricing Model. The CAPM asserts that securities will be priced to give investors an expected return comprised of two components: the risk-free rate, which is compensation for the time value of money, and a risk premium, determined by multiplying a benchmark risk premium (i.e., the risk premium offered by the market portfolio) times the relative measure of risk, beta:

$$E(r) = r_f + \beta[E(r_M) - r_f] \tag{11.3}$$

If we denote the risk premium of the market portfolio by $RP_M$, then a useful way to rewrite equation 11.3 is as follows:

$$E(r) = r_f + \beta RP_M \tag{11.4}$$

We pointed out in Chapter 10 that you can think of beta as measuring the exposure of a stock or portfolio to marketwide or macroeconomic risk factors. Therefore, one interpretation of the SML is that investors are rewarded with a higher expected return for their exposure to macro risk, based on both the sensitivity to that risk (beta) as well as the compensation for bearing each unit of that source of risk (i.e., the risk premium, $RP_M$), but are *not* rewarded for exposure to firm-specific uncertainty (the residual term $e_i$ in equation 11.1).

How might this single-factor view of the world generalize once we recognize the presence of multiple sources of systematic risk? We will work out the details of the argument in the next section, but before getting lost in the trees, we will start with the lay of the forest, motivating intuitively the results that are to come. Perhaps not surprisingly, a multifactor index model gives rise to a multifactor security market line in which the risk premium is determined by the exposure to *each* systematic risk factor, and by a risk premium associated with each of those factors.

For example, in a two-factor economy in which risk exposures can be measured by equation 11.2, we would conclude that the expected rate of return on a security would be the sum of:

1. The risk-free rate of return.
2. The sensitivity to GDP risk (i.e., the GDP beta) times the risk premium for GDP risk.
3. The sensitivity to interest rate risk (i.e., the interest rate beta) times the risk premium for interest rate risk.

This assertion is expressed as follows in equation 11.5. In that equation, for example, $\beta_{GDP}$ denotes the sensitivity of the security return to unexpected changes in GDP growth, and $RP_{GDP}$ is the risk premium associated with "one unit" of GDP exposure, i.e., the exposure corresponding to a GDP beta of 1.0. Here then is a two-factor security market line.

$$E(r) = r_f + \beta_{GDP} RP_{GDP} + \beta_{IR} RP_{IR} \tag{11.5}$$

If you look back at equation 11.4, you will see that equation 11.5 is a generalization of the simple security market line. In the usual SML, the benchmark risk premium is given by the market portfolio, $RP_M = E(r_M) - r_f$, but once we generalize to multiple risk sources, each with its own risk premium, we see that the insights are highly similar.

We still need to specify how to estimate the risk premium for each factor. Analogously to the simple CAPM, the risk premium associated with each factor can be thought of as the risk premium of a portfolio that has a beta of 1.0 on that particular factor and a beta of zero on all other factors. In other words, it is the risk premium one might expect to earn by taking a "pure play" on that factor. We will return to this below, but for now, let's just take the factor risk premia as given and see how a multifactor SML might be used.

---

**EXAMPLE 11.3     A Multifactor SML**

Think about our regression estimates for Northeast Airlines in Example 11.2. Northeast has a GDP beta of 1.8 and an interest rate beta of .7. Suppose the risk premium for one unit of exposure to GDP risk is 6%, while the risk premium for one unit of exposure to interest rate risk is 3%. Then the overall risk premium on the Northeast portfolio should equal the sum of the risk premiums required as compensation for each source of systematic risk.

The risk premium attributable to GDP risk should be the stock's exposure to that risk multiplied by the risk premium of the first factor portfolio, 6%. Therefore, the portion of the firm's risk premium that is compensation for its exposure to the first factor is $1.8 \times 6\% = 10.8\%$. Similarly, the risk premium attributable to interest rate risk is $.7 \times 3\% = 2.1\%$. The total risk premium should be $10.8 + 2.1 = 12.9\%$. Therefore, if the risk-free rate is 4%, the total return on the portfolio should be

| 4.0% | Risk-free rate |
|---|---|
| + 10.8 | + Risk premium for exposure to GDP risk |
| + 2.1 | + Risk premium for exposure to interest rate risk |
| 16.9% | Total expected return |

More concisely,

$$E(r) = 4\% + 1.8 \times 6\% + .7 \times 3\% = 16.9\%$$

---

The multifactor model clearly gives us a much richer way to think about risk exposures and compensation for those exposures than the single-index model or CAPM. Let us now fill in some of the gaps in the argument and more carefully explore the link between multifactor models of security returns and multifactor security market lines.

 **CONCEPT CHECK QUESTION 2**

Suppose the risk premia in Example 11.3 were $RP_{GDP} = 4\%$ and $RP_{IR} = 2\%$. What would be the new value for the equilibrium expected rate of return on Northeast Airlines?

## 11.2   ARBITRAGE PRICING THEORY

Stephen Ross developed the **arbitrage pricing theory** (APT) in 1976.[1] Like the CAPM, the APT predicts a Security Market Line linking expected returns to risk, but the path it takes to its SML is quite different. Ross's APT relies on three key propositions: (i) security returns can be described by a factor model; (ii) there are sufficient securities to diversify

[1] Stephen A. Ross, "Return, Risk and Arbitrage," in I. Friend and J. Bicksler, eds., *Risk and Return in Finance* (Cambridge, MA: Ballinger, 1976).

away idiosyncratic risk; and (iii) well-functioning security markets do not allow for the persistence of arbitrage opportunities. We begin with a simple version of Ross's model, which assumes that only one systematic factor affects security returns. However, the usual discussion of the APT is concerned with the multifactor case, so we treat this more general case as well.

## Arbitrage, Risk Arbitrage, and Equilibrium

An **arbitrage** opportunity arises when an investor can earn riskless profits without making a net investment. A trivial example of an arbitrage opportunity would arise if shares of a stock sold for different prices on two different exchanges. For example, suppose IBM sold for $60 on the NYSE but only $58 on Nasdaq. Then you could buy the shares on Nasdaq and simultaneously sell them on the NYSE, clearing a riskless profit of $2 per share without tying up any of your own capital. The **Law of One Price** states that if two assets are equivalent in all economically relevant respects, then they should have the same market price. The Law of One Price is enforced by arbitrageurs: if they observe a violation of the law, they will engage in *arbitrage activity*—simultaneously buying the asset where it is cheap and selling where it is expensive. In the process, they will bid up the price where it is low and force it down where it is high until the arbitrage opportunity is eliminated.

The idea that market prices will move to rule out arbitrage opportunities is perhaps the most fundamental concept in capital market theory. Violation of this restriction would indicate the grossest form of market irrationality.

The critical property of a risk-free arbitrage portfolio is that any investor, regardless of risk aversion or wealth, will want to take an infinite position in it. Because those large positions will quickly force prices up or down until the opportunity vanishes, security prices should satisfy a "no-arbitrage condition," that is, a condition that rules out the existence of arbitrage opportunities.

There is an important difference between arbitrage and risk–return dominance arguments in support of equilibrium price relationships. A dominance argument holds that when an equilibrium price relationship is violated, many investors will make limited portfolio changes, depending on their degree of risk aversion. Aggregation of these limited portfolio changes is required to create a large volume of buying and selling, which in turn restores equilibrium prices. By contrast, when arbitrage opportunities exist each investor wants to take as large a position as possible; hence it will not take many investors to bring about the price pressures necessary to restore equilibrium. Therefore, implications for prices derived from no-arbitrage arguments are stronger than implications derived from a risk–return dominance argument.

The CAPM is an example of a dominance argument, implying that all investors hold mean-variance efficient portfolios. If a security is mispriced, then investors will tilt their portfolios toward the underpriced and away from the overpriced securities. Pressure on equilibrium prices results from many investors shifting their portfolios, each by a relatively small dollar amount. The assumption that a large number of investors are mean-variance sensitive is critical. In contrast, the implication of a no-arbitrage condition is that a few investors who identify an arbitrage opportunity will mobilize large dollar amounts and quickly restore equilibrium.

Practitioners often use the terms "arbitrage" and "arbitrageurs" more loosely than our strict definition. "Arbitrageur" often refers to a professional searching for mispriced securities in specific areas such as merger-target stocks, rather than to one who seeks strict (risk-free) arbitrage opportunities. Such activity is sometimes called **risk arbitrage** to distinguish it from pure arbitrage.

To leap ahead, in Part 4 we will discuss "derivative" securities such as futures and options, whose market values are determined by prices of other securities. For example, the value of a call option on a stock is determined by the price of the stock. For such securities, strict arbitrage is a practical possibility, and the condition of no-arbitrage leads to exact pricing. In the case of stocks and other "primitive" securities whose values are not determined strictly by another asset or bundle of assets, no-arbitrage conditions must be obtained by appealing to diversification arguments.

## Well-Diversified Portfolios

Now we look at the risk of a portfolio of stocks. We first show that if a portfolio is well diversified, its firm-specific or nonfactor risk becomes negligible, so that only factor (or systematic) risk remains. If we construct an $n$-stock portfolio with weights $w_i$, $\Sigma w_i = 1$, then the rate of return on this portfolio is as follows:

$$r_P = E(r_P) + \beta_P F + e_P \tag{11.6}$$

where

$$\beta_P = \Sigma w_i \beta_i$$

is the weighted average of the $\beta_i$ of the $n$ securities. The portfolio nonsystematic component (which is uncorrelated with $F$) is $e_P = \Sigma w_i e_i$ which similarly is a weighted average of the $e_i$ of the $n$ securities.

We can divide the variance of this portfolio into systematic and nonsystematic sources, as we saw in Chapter 10. The portfolio variance is

$$\sigma_P^2 = \beta_P^2 \sigma_F^2 + \sigma^2(e_P)$$

where $\sigma_F^2$ is the variance of the factor $F$ and $\sigma^2(e_P)$ is the nonsystematic risk of the portfolio, which is given by

$$\sigma^2(e_P) = \text{Variance}(\Sigma w_i e_i) = \Sigma w_i^2 \sigma^2(e_i)$$

Note that in deriving the nonsystematic variance of the portfolio, we depend on the facts that the firm-specific $e_i$s are uncorrelated and hence that the variance of the "portfolio" of nonsystematic $e_i$s is the weighted sum of the individual nonsystematic variances with the square of the investment proportions as weights.

If the portfolio were equally weighted, $w_i = 1/n$, then the nonsystematic variance would be

$$\sigma^2(e_P) = \text{Variance}(\Sigma w_i e_i) = \sum \left(\frac{1}{n}\right)^2 \sigma^2(e_i) = \frac{1}{n} \sum \frac{\sigma^2(e_i)}{n} = \frac{1}{n} \overline{\sigma}^2(e_i)$$

where the last term is the average value across securities of nonsystematic variance. In words, the nonsystematic variance of the portfolio equals the average nonsystematic variance divided by $n$. Therefore, when the portfolio gets large in the sense that $n$ is large, its nonsystematic variance approaches zero. This is the effect of diversification.

We conclude that for the equally weighted portfolio, the nonsystematic variance approaches zero as $n$ becomes ever larger. This property is true of portfolios other than the equally weighted one. *Any* portfolio for which each $w_i$ becomes consistently smaller as $n$ gets large (more precisely, for which each $w_i^2$ approaches zero as $n$ increases) will satisfy the condition that the portfolio nonsystematic risk will approach zero. In fact, this property motivates us to define a **well-diversified portfolio** as one that is diversified over a large enough number of securities with each weight, $w_i$, small enough that for practical purposes the nonsystematic variance, $\sigma^2(e_P)$, is negligible.

---

**CONCEPT CHECK☞ QUESTION 3**

a. A portfolio is invested in a very large number of shares ($n$ is large). However, one-half of the portfolio is invested in stock 1, and the rest of the portfolio is equally divided among the other $n - 1$ shares. Is this portfolio well diversified?

b. Another portfolio also is invested in $n$ shares, where $n$ is very large. Instead of equally weighting with portfolio weights of $1/n$ in each stock, the weights in half the securities are $1.5/n$ while the weights in the other shares are $.5/n$. Is this portfolio well diversified?

---

Because the expected value of $e_P$ for any well-diversified portfolio is zero, and its variance also is effectively zero, we can conclude that any realized value of $e_P$ will be virtually zero. Rewriting equation 11.1, we conclude that for a well-diversified portfolio, for all practical purposes

$$r_P = E(r_P) + \beta_P F$$

Large (mostly institutional) investors can hold portfolios of hundreds and even thousands of securities; thus the concept of well-diversified portfolios clearly is operational in contemporary financial markets.

### Betas and Expected Returns

Because nonfactor risk can be diversified away, only factor risk should command a risk premium in market equilibrium. Nonsystematic risk across firms cancels out in well-diversified portfolios; one would not expect investors to be rewarded for bearing risk that can be eliminated through diversification. Instead, only the systematic risk of a portfolio of securities should be related to its expected returns.

The solid line in Figure 11.1A plots the return of a well-diversified Portfolio $A$ with $\beta_A = 1$ for various realizations of the systematic factor. The expected return of Portfolio $A$ is 10%; this is where the solid line crosses the vertical axis. At this point the systematic factor is zero, implying no macro surprises. If the macro factor is positive, the portfolio's

**Figure 11.1**
**Returns as a function of the systematic factor. Panel A, well-diversified Portfolio A. Panel B, single stock (S).**

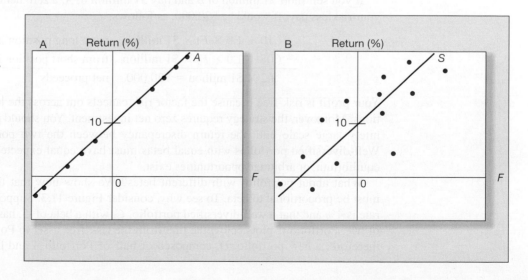

**Figure 11.2
Returns as a
function of the
systematic factor:
an arbitrage
opportunity**

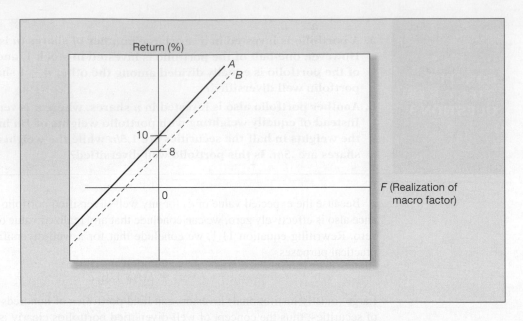

return exceeds its expected value; if it is negative, the portfolio's return falls short of its mean. The return on the portfolio is therefore

$$E(r_A) + \beta_A F = 10\% + 1.0 \times F$$

Compare Figure 11.1A with Figure 11.1B, which is a similar graph for a single stock ($S$) with $\beta_s = 1$. The undiversified stock is subject to nonsystematic risk, which is seen in a scatter of points around the line. The well-diversified portfolio's return, in contrast, is determined completely by the systematic factor.

Now consider Figure 11.2, where the dashed line plots the return on another well-diversified portfolio, Portfolio $B$, with an expected return of 8% and $\beta_B$ also equal to 1.0. Could Portfolios $A$ and $B$ coexist with the return pattern depicted? Clearly not: No matter what the systematic factor turns out to be, Portfolio $A$ outperforms Portfolio $B$, leading to an arbitrage opportunity.

If you sell short $1 million of $B$ and buy $1 million of $A$, a zero net investment strategy, your riskless payoff would be $20,000, as follows:

$$
\begin{array}{ll}
(.10 + 1.0 \times F) \times \$1 \text{ million} & \text{from long position in } A \\
- (.08 + 1.0 \times F) \times \$1 \text{ million} & \text{from short position in } B \\
\hline
.02 \times \$1 \text{ million} = \$20,000 & \text{net proceeds}
\end{array}
$$

Your profit is risk-free because the factor risk cancels out across the long and short positions. Moreover, the strategy requires zero net investment. You should pursue it on an infinitely large scale until the return discrepancy between the two portfolios disappears. Well-diversified portfolios with equal betas must have equal expected returns in market equilibrium, or arbitrage opportunities exist.

What about portfolios with different betas? We show now that their risk premiums must be proportional to beta. To see why, consider Figure 11.3. Suppose that the risk-free rate is 4% and that a well-diversified portfolio, $C$, with a beta of .5, has an expected return of 6%. Portfolio $C$ plots below the line from the risk-free asset to Portfolio $A$. Consider, therefore, a new portfolio, $D$, composed of half of Portfolio $A$ and half of the risk-free

**Figure 11.3**
**An arbitrage**
**opportunity**

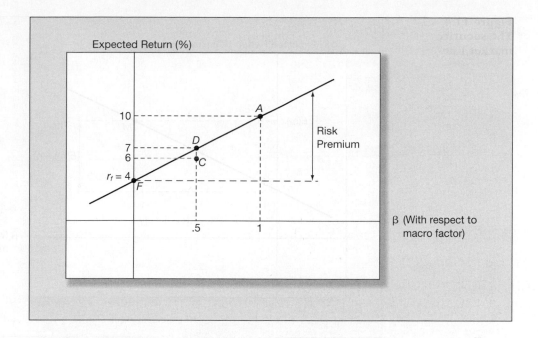

asset. Portfolio $D$'s beta will be $(.5 \times 0 + .5 \times 1.0) = .5$, and its expected return will be $(.5 \times 4 + .5 \times 10) = 7\%$. Now Portfolio $D$ has an equal beta but a greater expected return than Portfolio $C$. From our analysis in the previous paragraph we know that this constitutes an arbitrage opportunity.

We conclude that, to preclude arbitrage opportunities, the expected return on all well-diversified portfolios must lie on the straight line from the risk-free asset in Figure 11.3. The equation of this line will dictate the expected return on all well-diversified portfolios.

Notice in Figure 11.3 that risk premiums are indeed proportional to portfolio betas. The risk premium is depicted by the vertical arrow, which measures the distance between the risk-free rate and the expected return on the portfolio. The risk premium is zero for $\beta = 0$ and rises in direct proportion to $\beta$.

**The One-Factor**
**Security Market Line**
Now consider the market index portfolio, $M$, as a well-diversified portfolio, and let us measure the systematic factor as the unexpected return on that portfolio. Because the index portfolio must be on the line in Figure 11.4 and the beta of the index portfolio is 1, we can determine the equation describing that line. As Figure 11.4 shows, the intercept is $r_f$ and the slope is $E(r_M) - r_f$ [rise $= E(r_M) - r_f$; run $= 1$], implying that the equation of the line is

$$E(r_P) = r_f + [E(r_M) - r_f]\beta_P \tag{11.7}$$

Hence, Figures 11.3 and 11.4 imply an SML relation equivalent to that of the CAPM.

**EXAMPLE 11.4**   **Arbitrage and the Security Market Line**

Suppose the market index is a well-diversified portfolio with expected return 10% and that deviations of its return from expectation (i.e., $r_M - 10\%$) can serve as the systematic factor. The T-bill rate is 4%. Then the SML (equation 11.7) implies that the expected rate of

**Figure 11.4
The security
market line**

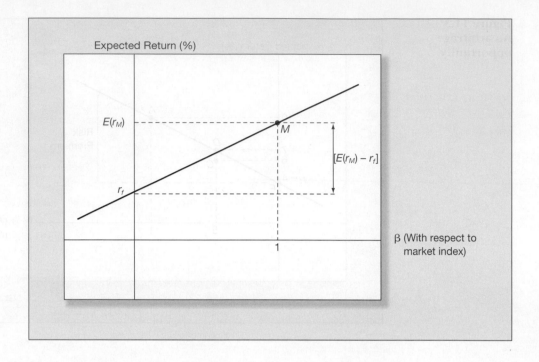

return on well-diversified Portfolio $E$ with a beta of $\frac{2}{3}$ should be $4\% + \frac{2}{3}(10 - 4) = 8\%$. What if its expected return actually is 9%? Then there will be an arbitrage opportunity.

Buy $1 of the stock and sell $1 of a portfolio that is invested $\frac{1}{3}$ in T-bills and $\frac{2}{3}$ in the market. This portfolio by construction has the same beta as Portfolio $E$. The return on this portfolio is $\frac{1}{3} r_f + \frac{2}{3} r_M = \frac{1}{3} \times 4\% + \frac{2}{3} r_M$. The net return on the combined position is:

| | |
|---|---|
| $1 \times [.09 + \frac{2}{3}(r_M - .10)]$ | Invest $1 in portfolio $E$, with expected return 9% and beta of $\frac{2}{3}$ on surprise in market return. |
| $- \$1 (\frac{1}{3} \times .04 + \frac{2}{3} r_M)$ | Sell portfolio invested $\frac{1}{3}$ in T-bills and $\frac{2}{3}$ in the market index. |
| $1 \times .01$ | Total |

The profit per dollar invested is risk-free and precisely equal to the deviation of expected return from the SML.

**CONCEPT
C H E C K** ☞
**QUESTION 4**

Continue to use the data in Example 11.4. Now consider Portfolio $G$ which is well diversified with a beta of $\frac{1}{3}$ and expected return of 5%. Does an arbitrage opportunity exist? If so, what is the arbitrage strategy? Show that the strategy results in risk-free profits with zero net investment.

We have used the no-arbitrage condition to obtain an expected return–beta relationship identical to that of the CAPM, without the restrictive assumptions of the CAPM. As noted, this derivation depends on three assumptions: a factor model describing security returns, a sufficient number of securities to form well-diversified portfolios, and the absence of arbitrage opportunities. This last restriction gives rise to the name of the approach: Arbitrage Pricing Theory. Our demonstration suggests that despite its restrictive assumptions, the main conclusion of the CAPM, namely, the SML expected return–beta relationship, should be at least approximately valid.

It is worth noting that in contrast to the CAPM, the APT does not require that the benchmark portfolio in the SML relationship be the true market portfolio. Any well-diversified portfolio lying on the SML of Figure 11.4 may serve as the benchmark portfolio. For example, one might define the benchmark portfolio as the well-diversified portfolio most highly correlated with whatever systematic factor is thought to affect stock returns. Accordingly, the APT has more flexibility than does the CAPM because problems associated with an unobservable market portfolio are not a concern.

In addition, the APT provides further justification for use of the index model in the practical implementation of the SML relationship. Even if the index portfolio is not a precise proxy for the true market portfolio, which is a cause of considerable concern in the context of the CAPM, we now know that if the index portfolio is sufficiently well diversified, the SML relationship should still hold true according to the APT.

So far we have demonstrated the APT relationship for well-diversified portfolios only. The CAPM expected return–beta relationship applies to single assets, as well as to portfolios. In the next section we generalize the APT result one step further.

## 11.3    INDIVIDUAL ASSETS AND THE APT

We have demonstrated that if arbitrage opportunities are to be ruled out, each well-diversified portfolio's expected excess return must be proportional to its beta. The question is whether this relationship tells us anything about the expected returns on the component stocks. The answer is that if this relationship is to be satisfied by all well-diversified portfolios, it must be satisfied by *almost* all individual securities, although a full proof of this proposition is somewhat difficult. We can illustrate the argument less formally.

Suppose that the expected return–beta relationship is violated for all single assets. Now create a pair of well-diversified portfolios from these assets. What are the chances that in spite of the fact that for any pair of assets the relationship does *not* hold, the relationship *will* hold for both well-diversified portfolios? The chances are small, but it is possible that the relationships among the single securities are violated in offsetting ways so that somehow it holds for the pair of well-diversified portfolios.

Now construct yet a third well-diversified portfolio. What are the chances that the violations of the relationships for single securities are such that the third portfolio also will fulfill the no-arbitrage expected return–beta relationship? Obviously, the chances are smaller still, but the relationship is possible. Continue with a fourth well-diversified portfolio, and so on. If the no-arbitrage expected return–beta relationship has to hold for infinitely many different, well-diversified portfolios, it must be virtually certain that the relationship holds for all but a small number of individual securities.

We use the term *virtually certain* advisedly because we must distinguish this conclusion from the statement that all securities surely fulfill this relationship. The reason we cannot make the latter statement has to do with a property of well-diversified portfolios.

Recall that to qualify as well diversified, a portfolio must have very small positions in all securities. If, for example, only one security violates the expected return–beta relationship, then the effect of this violation on a well-diversified portfolio will be too small to be of importance for any practical purpose, and meaningful arbitrage opportunities will not arise. But if many securities violate the expected return–beta relationship, the relationship will no longer hold for well-diversified portfolios, and arbitrage opportunities will be available. Consequently, we conclude that imposing the no-arbitrage condition on a single-factor security market implies maintenance of the expected return–beta relationship for all well-diversified portfolios and for all but possibly a *small* number of individual securities.

**The APT and the CAPM**    The APT serves many of the same functions as the CAPM. It gives us a benchmark for rates of return that can be used in capital budgeting, security evaluation, or investment performance evaluation. Moreover, the APT highlights the crucial distinction between nondiversifiable risk (factor risk) that requires a reward in the form of a risk premium and diversifiable risk that does not.

The APT is an extremely appealing model. It depends on the assumption that a rational equilibrium in capital markets precludes arbitrage opportunities. A violation of the APT's pricing relationships will cause extremely strong pressure to restore them even if only a limited number of investors become aware of the disequilibrium. Furthermore, the APT yields an expected return–beta relationship using a well-diversified portfolio that practically can be constructed from a large number of securities.

In contrast, the CAPM is derived assuming an inherently unobservable "market" portfolio. The CAPM argument rests on mean-variance efficiency; that is, if any security violates the expected return–beta relationship, then many investors (each relatively small) will tilt their portfolios so that their combined overall pressure on prices will restore an equilibrium that satisfies the relationship.

In spite of these apparent advantages, the APT does not fully dominate the CAPM. The CAPM provides an unequivocal statement on the expected return–beta relationship for all securities, whereas the APT implies that this relationship holds for all but perhaps a small number of securities. Because it focuses on the no-arbitrage condition, without the further assumptions of the market or index model, the APT cannot rule out a violation of the expected return–beta relationship for any particular asset. For this, we need the CAPM assumptions and its dominance arguments.

## 11.4    A MULTIFACTOR APT

We have assumed so far that there is only one systematic factor affecting stock returns. This simplifying assumption is in fact too simplistic. We've noted that it is easy to think of several factors driven by the business cycle that might affect stock returns: interest rate fluctuations, inflation rates, oil prices, and so on. Presumably, exposure to any of these factors will affect a stock's risk and hence its expected return. We can derive a multifactor version of the APT to accommodate these multiple sources of risk.

Suppose that we generalize the factor model expressed in equation 11.1 to a two-factor model:

$$r_i = E(r_i) + \beta_{i1}F_1 + \beta_{i2}F_2 + e_i \tag{11.8}$$

In Example 11.2, Factor 1 was the departure of GDP growth from expectations, and Factor 2 was the unanticipated decline in interest rates. Each factor has zero expected value because each measures the *surprise* in the systematic variable rather than the level of the variable. Similarly, the firm-specific component of unexpected return, $e_i$, also has zero expected value. Extending such a two-factor model to any number of factors is straightforward.

Establishing a multifactor APT is similar to the one-factor case. But first we must introduce the concept of a **factor portfolio,** which is a well-diversified portfolio constructed to have a beta of 1 on one of the factors and a beta of 0 on any other factor. We can think of a factor portfolio as a *tracking portfolio*. That is, the returns on such a portfolio track the evolution of particular sources of macroeconomic risk, but are uncorrelated with other sources of risk. It is possible to form such factor portfolios because we have a large number of securities to choose from, and a relatively small number of factors. Factor portfolios will serve as the benchmark portfolios for a multifactor security market line.

## EXAMPLE 11.5    Multifactor SML

Suppose that the two factor portfolios, Portfolios 1 and 2, have expected returns $E(r_1) = 10\%$ and $E(r_2) = 12\%$. Suppose further that the risk-free rate is 4%. The risk premium on the first factor portfolio is $10\% - 4\% = 6\%$, whereas that on the second factor portfolio is $12\% - 4\% = 8\%$.

Now consider a well-diversified portfolio, Portfolio A, with beta on the first factor, $\beta_{A1} = .5$, and beta on the second factor, $\beta_{A2} = .75$. The multifactor APT states that the overall risk premium on this portfolio must equal the sum of the risk premiums required as compensation for each source of systematic risk. The risk premium attributable to risk factor 1 should be the portfolio's exposure to factor 1, $\beta_{A1}$, multiplied by the risk premium earned on the first factor portfolio, $E(r_1) - r_f$. Therefore, the portion of Portfolio A's risk premium that is compensation for its exposure to the first factor is $\beta_{A1}[E(r_1) - r_f] = .5(10\% - 4\%) = 3\%$, whereas the risk premium attributable to risk factor 2 is $\beta_{A2}[E(r_2) - r_f] = .75(12\% - 4\%) = 6\%$. The total risk premium on the portfolio should be $3 + 6 = 9\%$ and the total return on the portfolio should be $4\% + 9\% = 13\%$.

To generalize the argument in Example 11.5, note that the factor exposures of any portfolio, $P$, are given by its betas, $\beta_{P1}$ and $\beta_{P2}$. A competing portfolio, $Q$, can be formed by investing in factor portfolios with the following weights: $\beta_{P1}$ in the first factor portfolio, $\beta_{P2}$ in the second factor portfolio, and $1 - \beta_{P1} - \beta_{P2}$ in T-bills. By construction, portfolio $Q$ will have betas equal to those of Portfolio $P$ and expected return of

$$E(r_Q) = \beta_{P1}E(r_1) + \beta_{P2}E(r_2) + (1 - \beta_{P1} - \beta_{P2})r_f$$
$$= r_f + \beta_{P1}[E(r_1) - r_f] + \beta_{P2}[E(r_2) - r_f] \tag{11.9}$$

Using the numbers in Example 11.5:

$$E(r_Q) = 4 + .5 \times (10 - 4) + .75 \times (12 - 4) = 13\%$$

Because Portfolio $Q$ has precisely the same exposures as Portfolio $A$ to the two sources of risk, their expected returns also ought to be equal. So Portfolio $A$ also ought to have an expected return of 13%. If it does not, then there will be an arbitrage opportunity.

## EXAMPLE 11.6    Mispricing and Arbitrage

Suppose that the expected return on Portfolio A were 12% rather than 13%. This return would give rise to an arbitrage opportunity. Form a portfolio from the factor portfolios with the same betas as Portfolio A. This requires weights of .5 on the first factor portfolio, .75 on the second factor portfolio, and −.25 on the risk-free asset. This portfolio has exactly the same factor betas as Portfolio A: It has a beta of .5 on the first factor because of its

.5 weight on the first factor portfolio, and a beta of .75 on the second factor. (The weight of $-.25$ on risk-free T-bills does not affect the sensitivity to either factor.)

Now invest \$1 in Portfolio $Q$ and sell (short) \$1 in Portfolio $A$. Your net investment is zero, but your expected dollar profit is positive and equal to

$$\$1 \times E(r_Q) - \$1 \times E(r_A) = \$1 \times .13 - \$1 \times .12 = \$.01$$

Moreover, your net position is riskless. Your exposure to each risk factor cancels out because you are long \$1 in Portfolio $Q$ and short \$1 in Portfolio $A$, and both of these well-diversified portfolios have exactly the same factor betas. Thus, if Portfolio $A$'s expected return differs from that of Portfolio $Q$'s, you can earn positive risk-free profits on a zero net investment position. This is an arbitrage opportunity.

| CONCEPT CHECK ☞ QUESTION 5 | Using the factor portfolios of Example 11.5, find the equilibrium rate of return on a portfolio with $\beta_1 = .2$ and $\beta_2 = 1.4$. |
| --- | --- |

We conclude that any well-diversified portfolio with betas $\beta_{P1}$ and $\beta_{P2}$ must have the return given in equation 11.9 if arbitrage opportunities are to be precluded. If you compare equations 11.3 and 11.9, you will see that equation 11.9 is simply a generalization of the one-factor SML.

Finally, the extension of the multifactor SML of equation 11.9 to individual assets is precisely the same as for the one-factor APT. Equation 11.9 cannot be satisfied by every well-diversified portfolio unless it is satisfied by virtually every security taken individually. Equation 11.9 thus represents the multifactor SML for an economy with multiple sources of risk.

We pointed out earlier that one application of the CAPM is to provide "fair" rates of return for regulated utilities. The multifactor APT can be used to the same ends. The nearby box summarizes a study in which the APT was applied to find the cost of capital for regulated electric companies.

# 11.5   WHERE SHOULD WE LOOK FOR FACTORS?

One shortcoming of the multifactor APT is that it gives no guidance concerning the determination of the relevant risk factors or their risk premiums. Two principles guide us when we specify a reasonable list of factors. First, we want to limit ourselves to systematic factors with considerable ability to explain security returns. If our model calls for hundreds of explanatory variables, it does little to simplify our description of security returns. Second, we wish to choose factors that seem likely to be important risk factors, i.e., factors that concern investors sufficiently that they will demand meaningful risk premiums to bear exposure to those sources of risk.

One example of the multifactor approach is the work of Chen, Roll, and Ross[2] who chose the following set of factors based on the ability of these factors to paint a broad picture of the macroeconomy. Their set is obviously but one of many possible sets that might be considered.

---

[2] N. Chen, R. Roll, and S. Ross, "Economic Forces and the Stock Market," *Journal of Business* 59 (1986), pp. 383–403.

Elton, Gruber, and Mei* use the APT to derive the cost of capital for electric utilities. They assume that the relevant risk factors are unanticipated developments in the term structure of interest rates, the level of interest rates, inflation rates, the business cycle (measured by GDP), foreign exchange rates, and a summary measure they devise to measure other macro factors.

Their first step is to estimate the risk premium associated with exposure to each risk source. They accomplish this in a two-step strategy (which we will describe in considerable detail in the next chapter):

1. *Estimate "factor loadings" (i.e., betas) of a large sample of firms.* Regress returns of 100 randomly selected stocks against the systematic risk factors. They use a time-series regression for each stock (e.g., 60 months of data), therefore estimating 100 regressions, one for each stock.

2. *Estimate the reward earned per unit of exposure to each risk factor.* For each month, regress the return of each stock against the five betas estimated. The coefficient on each beta is the extra average return earned as beta increases, i.e., it is an estimate of the risk premium for that risk factor from that month's data. These estimates are of course subject to sampling error. Therefore, average the risk premium estimates across the 12 months in each year. The *average* response of return to risk is less subject to sampling error.

The risk premia found for 1990 are in the second column of the table at the top of the next column.

Notice that some risk premia are negative. The interpretation of this result is that risk premium should be positive for risk factors you don't want exposure to, but *negative* for factors you *do* want exposure to. For example, you should desire securities that have higher returns when inflation in-

| Factor | Factor Risk Premium | Factor Betas for Niagra Mohawk |
|---|---|---|
| Term structure | .425 | 1.0615 |
| Interest rates | −.051 | −2.4167 |
| Exchange rates | −.049 | 1.3235 |
| Business cycle | .041 | .1292 |
| Inflation | −.069 | −.5220 |
| Other macro factors | .530 | .3046 |

creases and be willing to accept lower expected returns on such securities; this shows up as a negative risk premium.

Therefore, the expected return on any security should be related to its factor betas as follows:

$$r_f + .425\beta_{\text{term struc}} - .051\beta_{\text{int rate}} - .049\beta_{\text{ex rate}} + .041\beta_{\text{bus cycle}} - .069\beta_{\text{inflation}} + .530\beta_{\text{other}}$$

Finally, to obtain the cost of capital for a particular firm, the authors estimate the firm's betas against each source of risk, multiply each factor beta by the "cost of factor risk" from the table above, sum over all risk sources to obtain the total risk premium, and add the risk-free rate.

For example, the beta estimates for Niagra Mohawk appear in the last column of the table above. Therefore its cost of capital is

$$
\begin{aligned}
\text{Cost of capital} &= r_f + .425 \times 1.0615 - .051(-2.4167) \\
&\quad - .049(1.3235) + .041(.1292) \\
&\quad - .069(-.5220) + .530(.3046) \\
&= r_f + .72
\end{aligned}
$$

In other words, the monthly cost of capital for Niagra Mohawk is .72% above the monthly risk-free rate. Its annualized risk premium is therefore .72% × 12 = 8.64%.

* Edwin J. Elton, Martin J. Gruber, and Jianping Mei, "Cost of Capital Using Arbitrage Pricing Theory: A Case Study of Nine New York Utilities," *Financial Markets, Institutions, and Instruments* 3 (August 1994), pp. 46–68.

IP = % change in industrial production
EI = % change in expected inflation
UI = % change in unanticipated inflation
CG = excess return of long-term corporate bonds over long-term government bonds
GB = excess return of long-term government bonds over T-bills

This list gives rise to the following five-factor model of security returns during holding period $t$ as a function of the change in the set of macroeconomic indicators:

$$r_{it} = \alpha_i + \beta_{i\,\text{IP}}\text{IP}_t + \beta_{i\,\text{EI}}\text{EI}_t + \beta_{i\,\text{UI}}\text{UI}_t + \beta_{i\,\text{CG}}\text{CG}_t + \beta_{i\,\text{GB}}\text{GB}_t + e_{it} \quad (11.10)$$

Equation 11.10 is a multidimensional security characteristic line (SCL), with five factors. As before, to estimate the betas of a given stock we can use regression analysis. Here, however, because there is more than one factor, we estimate a *multiple* regression of the returns of the stock in each period on the five macroeconomic factors. The residual variance of the regression estimates the firm-specific risk. We discuss the results of this model in the next chapter, which focuses on empirical evidence on security pricing.

An alternative approach to specifying macroeconomic factors as candidates for relevant sources of systematic risk uses firm characteristics that seem on empirical grounds to proxy for exposure to systematic risk. In other words, the factors are chosen as variables that on past evidence seem to predict high average returns and therefore may be capturing risk premiums. One example of this approach is the so-called Fama and French three-factor model,[3]

$$r_{it} = \alpha_i + \beta_{iM}R_{Mt} + \beta_{iSMB}SMB_t + \beta_{iHML}HML_t + e_{it} \tag{11.11}$$

where

SMB = Small Minus Big, i.e., the return of a portfolio of small stocks in excess of the return on a portfolio of large stocks

HML = High Minus Low, i.e., the return of a portfolio of stocks with a high book-to-market ratio in excess of the return on a portfolio of stocks with a low book-to-market ratio

Note that in this model the market index does play a role and is expected to capture systematic risk originating from macroeconomic factors.

These two firm-characteristic variables are chosen because of long-standing observations that corporate capitalization (firm size) and book-to-market ratio seem to be predictive of average stock returns. Fama and French justify this model on empirical grounds: while SMB and HML are not themselves obvious candidates for relevant risk factors, the hope is that these variables proxy for yet-unknown more-fundamental variables. For example, Fama and French point out that firms with high ratios of book to market value are more likely to be in financial distress and that small stocks may be more sensitive to changes in business conditions. Thus, these variables may capture sensitivity to risk factors in the macroeconomy. Evidence on the Fama-French model also appears in the next chapter.

The problem with empirical approaches such as the Fama-French model, which use proxies for extramarket sources of risk, is that none of the factors in the proposed models can be clearly identified as hedging a significant source of uncertainty. Black[4] points out that when researchers scan and rescan the database of security returns in search of explanatory factors (an activity often called data-snooping), they may eventually uncover past "patterns" that are due purely to chance. Black observes that return premiums to factors such as firm size have largely vanished since first discovered. However, Fama and French point out that size and book-to-market ratios have predicted average returns in various time periods and in markets all over the world, thus mitigating potential effects of data-snooping.

---

[3] Eugene F. Fama and Kenneth R. French, "Multifactor Explanations of Asset Pricing Anomalies," *The Journal of Finance* 51 (1996), pp. 55–84.
[4] Fischer Black, "Beta and Return," *Journal of Portfolio Management* 20 (1993), pp. 8–18.

## 11.6   A MULTIFACTOR CAPM

The CAPM presupposes that the only relevant source of risk arises from variations in security returns, and therefore a representative (market) portfolio can capture this entire risk. As a result, individual-stock risk can be defined by the contribution to overall portfolio risk; hence, the risk premium on an individual stock is solely determined by its beta on the market portfolio. But is this narrow view of risk warranted?

Consider a relatively young investor whose future wealth is determined in large part by labor income. The stream of future labor income is also risky and may be intimately tied to the fortunes of the company for which the investor works. Such an investor might choose an investment portfolio that will help to diversify labor-income risk. For that purpose, stocks with lower-than-average correlation with future labor income would be favored, that is, such stocks will receive higher weights in the individual portfolio than their weights in the market portfolio. Put another way, using this broader notion of risk, these investors no longer consider the market portfolio as efficient and the rationale for the CAPM expected return–beta relationship no longer applies.

In principle, the CAPM may still hold if the hedging demands of various investors are equally distributed across different types of securities so that deviations of portfolio weights from those of the market portfolio are offsetting. But if hedging demands are common to many investors, the prices of securities with desirable hedging characteristics will be bid up and the expected return reduced, which will invalidate the CAPM expected return–beta relationship. For example, suppose the prices of energy stocks were driven up by investors who buy such stocks to hedge uncertainty about energy expenditures. At those higher stock prices, expected rates of return will be lower than dictated by the expected return–beta relationship of the CAPM. The simple SML relationship needs to be generalized to account for the effects of extramarket hedging demands on equilibrium rates of return.

Merton[5] has shown that these hedging demands will result in an expanded or multifactor version of the CAPM that recognizes the multidimensional nature of risk. His model is called the multifactor CAPM or, alternatively, the Intertemporal CAPM (ICAPM for short). The focal point of Merton's model is not dollar returns per se, but the consumption and investment made possible by the investor's wealth. Each source of risk to consumption or investment opportunities may in principle command its own risk premium.

In the case of energy price risk, for example, Merton's model would imply that the expected return–beta relationship of the single-factor CAPM would be generalized to the following two-factor relationship:

$$E(r_i) = r_f + \beta_{iM} [E(r_M) - r_f] + \beta_{ie} [E(r_e) - r_f]$$

where $\beta_{iM}$ is the beta of security $i$ with respect to the market portfolio, and $\beta_{ie}$ is the beta with respect to energy price risk. Similarly, $E(r_e) - r_f$ is the risk premium associated with exposure to energy price uncertainty. The rate of return of the portfolio that best hedges energy price uncertainty is $r_e$. This equation, therefore, is a two-factor CAPM. More generally, we will have a beta and a risk premium for every significant source of risk that consumers try to hedge.

Notice that this expanded version of the CAPM provides a prediction for security returns identical to that of the multifactor APT. Therefore, there is no contradiction between these two theories of the risk premium. The CAPM approach does offer one notable advantage, however. In contrast to the APT, which is silent on the relevant systematic factors,

---

[5] Robert C. Merton, "An Intertemporal Capital Asset Pricing Model," *Econometrica* 41 (1973), pp. 867–87.

the CAPM provides guidance as to where to look for those factors. The important factors will be those sources of risk that large groups of investors try to offset by establishing extramarket hedge portfolios. By specifying the likely sources of risk against which dominant groups of investors attempt to hedge, we identify the dimensions along which the CAPM needs to be generalized.

When a source of risk has an effect on expected returns, we say that this risk "is priced." While the single-factor CAPM predicts that only market risk will be priced, the ICAPM predicts that other sources of risk also may be priced. Merton suggested a list of possible common sources of uncertainty that might affect expected security returns. Among these are uncertainties in labor income, prices of important consumption goods (e.g., energy prices), or changes in future investment opportunities (e.g., changes in the riskiness of various asset classes). However, it is difficult to predict whether there exists sufficient demand for hedging these sources of uncertainty to affect security returns.

**CONCEPT CHECK☞ QUESTION 6**

Consider the following regression results for Stock X.

$$r_X = 2\% + 1.2 \text{ (percentage change in oil prices)}$$

a. If I live in Louisiana, where the local economy is heavily dependent on oil industry profits, does Stock X represent a useful asset to hedge my overall economic well-being?

b. What if I live in Massachusetts, where most individuals and firms are energy *consumers*?

c. If energy consumers are far more numerous than energy producers, will high oil-beta stocks have higher or lower expected rates of return in market equilibrium than low oil-beta stocks?

## SUMMARY

1. Multifactor models seek to improve the explanatory power of single-factor models by explicitly accounting for the various systematic components of security risk. These models use indicators intended to capture a wide range of macroeconomic risk factors.

2. Once we allow for multiple risk factors, we conclude that the security market line also ought to be multidimensional, with exposure to each risk factor contributing to the total risk premium of the security.

3. A (risk-free) arbitrage opportunity arises when two or more security prices enable investors to construct a zero net investment portfolio that will yield a sure profit. The presence of arbitrage opportunities will generate a large volume of trades that puts pressure on security prices. This pressure will continue until prices reach levels that preclude such arbitrage.

4. When securities are priced so that there are no risk-free arbitrage opportunities, we say that they satisfy the no-arbitrage condition. Price relationships that satisfy the no-arbitrage condition are important because we expect them to hold in real-world markets.

5. Portfolios are called "well-diversified" if they include a large number of securities and the investment proportion in each is sufficiently small. The proportion of a security in a

well-diversified portfolio is small enough so that for all practical purposes a reasonable change in that security's rate of return will have a negligible effect on the portfolio's rate of return.

6. In a single-factor security market, all well-diversified portfolios have to satisfy the expected return–beta relationship of the CAPM to satisfy the no-arbitrage condition. If all well-diversified portfolios satisfy the expected return–beta relationship, then all but a small number of securities also must satisfy this relationship.

7. The APT does not require the restrictive assumptions of the CAPM and its (unobservable) market portfolio. The price of this generality is that the APT does not guarantee this relationship for all securities at all times.

8. A multifactor APT generalizes the single-factor model to accommodate several sources of systematic risk. The multidimensional security market line predicts that exposure to each risk factor contributes to the security's total risk premium by an amount equal to the factor beta times the risk premium of the factor portfolio that tracks that source of risk.

9. A multifactor extension of the single-factor CAPM, the ICAPM, is a model of the risk–return trade-off that predicts the same multidimensional security market line as the APT. The ICAPM suggests that priced risk factors will be those sources of risk that lead to significant hedging demand by a substantial fraction of investors.

| KEY TERMS | | |
|---|---|---|
| single-factor model | factor beta | risk arbitrage |
| multifactor model | arbitrage pricing theory | well-diversified portfolio |
| factor sensitivity | arbitrage | factor portfolio |
| factor loading | Law of One Price | |

**WEBSITES**

www.onelook.com/?w=arbitrage+pricing+theory
APT is defined here.

www.aimr.com/pdf/apgapt.pdf
This site serves as a practitioner's guide to APT.

www.bus.ed.ac.uk/cfm/cfmr021.htm
This site offers an application of CAPM and APT to the Italian stock market.

www.datalife.com/mall/pages/glossary/GLOSS_R.HTM
Visit this site for a discussion of several risks that generate return volatility.

**PROBLEMS**

1. Suppose that two factors have been identified for the U.S. economy: the growth rate of industrial production, IP, and the inflation rate, IR. IP is expected to be 3%, and IR 5%. A stock with a beta of 1 on IP and .5 on IR currently is expected to provide

a rate of return of 12%. If industrial production actually grows by 5%, while the inflation rate turns out to be 8%, what is your revised estimate of the expected rate of return on the stock?

2. Suppose that there are two independent economic factors, $F_1$ and $F_2$. The risk-free rate is 6%, and all stocks have independent firm-specific components with a standard deviation of 45%. The following are well-diversified portfolios:

| Portfolio | Beta on $F_1$ | Beta on $F_2$ | Expected Return |
|-----------|---------------|---------------|-----------------|
| A | 1.5 | 2.0 | 31 |
| B | 2.2 | -0.2 | 27 |

What is the expected return–beta relationship in this economy?

3. Consider the following data for a one-factor economy. All portfolios are well diversified.

| Portfolio | $E(r)$ | Beta |
|-----------|--------|------|
| A | 12% | 1.2 |
| F | 6% | 0.0 |

Suppose that another portfolio, Portfolio $E$, is well diversified with a beta of .6 and expected return of 8%. Would an arbitrage opportunity exist? If so, what would be the arbitrage strategy?

4. Jeffrey Bruner, CFA, uses the capital asset pricing model (CAPM) to help identify mispriced securities. A consultant suggests Bruner use arbitrage pricing theory (APT) instead. In comparing CAPM and APT, the consultant made the following arguments:

   a. Both the CAPM and APT require a mean-variance efficient market portfolio.
   b. Neither the CAPM nor APT assumes normally distributed security returns.
   c. The CAPM assumes that one specific factor explains security returns but APT does not.

   State whether each of the consultant's arguments is correct or incorrect. Indicate, for each incorrect argument, why the argument is incorrect.

5. Assume that both Portfolios $A$ and $B$ are well diversified, that $E(r_A) = 12\%$, and $E(r_B) = 9\%$. If the economy has only one factor, and $\beta_A = 1.2$, whereas $\beta_B = .8$, what must be the risk-free rate?

6. Assume that stock market returns have the market index as a common factor, and that all stocks in the economy have a beta of 1 on the market index. Firm-specific returns all have a standard deviation of 30%.

   Suppose that an analyst studies 20 stocks, and finds that one-half have an alpha of 2%, and the other half an alpha of −2%. Suppose the analyst buys $1 million of an equally weighted portfolio of the positive alpha stocks, and shorts $1 million of an equally weighted portfolio of the negative alpha stocks.

   a. What is the expected profit (in dollars) and standard deviation of the analyst's profit?
   b. How does your answer change if the analyst examines 50 stocks instead of 20 stocks? 100 stocks?

7. Assume that security returns are generated by the single-index model,

$$R_i = \alpha_i + \beta_i R_M + e_i$$

where $R_i$ is the excess return for security $i$ and $R_M$ is the market's excess return. The risk-free rate is 2%. Suppose also that there are three securities $A$, $B$, and $C$, characterized by the following data:

| Security | $\beta_i$ | $E(R_i)$ | $\sigma(e_i)$ |
|---|---|---|---|
| A | 0.8 | 10% | 25% |
| B | 1.0 | 12% | 10% |
| C | 1.2 | 14% | 20% |

a. If $\sigma_M = 20\%$, calculate the variance of returns of Securities $A$, $B$, and $C$.
b. Now assume that there are an infinite number of assets with return characteristics identical to those of $A$, $B$, and $C$, respectively. If one forms a well-diversified portfolio of type $A$ securities, what will be the mean and variance of the portfolio's excess returns? What about portfolios composed only of type $B$ or $C$ stocks?
c. Is there an arbitrage opportunity in this market? What is it? Analyze the opportunity graphically.

8. The SML relationship states that the expected risk premium on a security in a one-factor model must be directly proportional to the security's beta. Suppose that this were not the case. For example, suppose that expected return rises more than proportionately with beta as in the figure below.

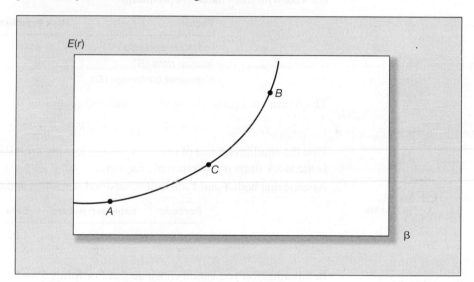

a. How could you construct an arbitrage portfolio? (Hint: Consider combinations of Portfolios $A$ and $B$, and compare the resultant portfolio to $C$.)
b. We will see in Chapter 13 that some researchers have examined the relationship between average return on diversified portfolios and the $\beta$ and $\beta^2$ of those portfolios. What should they have discovered about the effect of $\beta^2$ on portfolio return?

9. If the APT is to be a useful theory, the number of systematic factors in the economy must be small. Why?

10. The APT itself does not provide guidance concerning the factors that one might expect to determine risk premiums. How should researchers decide which factors to investigate? Why, for example, is industrial production a reasonable factor to test for a risk premium?

11. Consider the following multifactor (APT) model of security returns for a particular stock.

| Factor | Factor Beta | Factor Risk Premium |
|---|---|---|
| Inflation | 1.2 | 6% |
| Industrial production | 0.5 | 8 |
| Oil prices | 0.3 | 3 |

a. If T-bills currently offer a 6% yield, find the expected rate of return on this stock if the market views the stock as fairly priced.

b. Suppose that the market expected the values for the three macro factors given in column 1 below, but that the actual values turn out as given in column 2. Calculate the revised expectations for the rate of return on the stock once the "surprises" become known.

| Factor | Expected Rate of Change | Actual Rate of Change |
|---|---|---|
| Inflation | 5% | 4% |
| Industrial production | 3 | 6 |
| Oil prices | 2 | 0 |

12. Suppose that the market can be described by the following three sources of systematic risk with associated risk premiums.

| Factor | Risk Premium |
|---|---|
| Industrial production ($I$) | 6% |
| Interest rates ($R$) | 2 |
| Consumer confidence ($C$) | 4 |

The return on a particular stock is generated according to the following equation:

$$r = 15\% + 1.0I + .5R + .75C + e$$

Find the equilibrium rate of return on this stock using the APT. The T-bill rate is 6%. Is the stock over- or underpriced? Explain.

13. Assume that both $X$ and $Y$ are well-diversified portfolios and the risk-free rate is 8%.

| Portfolio | Expected Return | Beta |
|---|---|---|
| $X$ | 16% | 1.00 |
| $Y$ | 12 | 0.25 |

In this situation you would conclude that Portfolios $X$ and $Y$:

a. Are in equilibrium.
b. Offer an arbitrage opportunity.
c. Are both underpriced.
d. Are both fairly priced.

14. According to the theory of arbitrage:

a. High-beta stocks are consistently overpriced.
b. Low-beta stocks are consistently overpriced.
c. Positive alpha investment opportunities will quickly disappear.
d. Rational investors will pursue arbitrage consistent with their risk tolerance.

15. A zero-investment portfolio with a positive alpha could arise if:

a. The expected return of the portfolio equals zero.
b. The capital market line is tangent to the opportunity set.

c.  The Law of One Price remains unviolated.

d.  A risk-free arbitrage opportunity exists.

16. The arbitrage pricing theory (APT) differs from the single-factor capital asset pricing model (CAPM) because the APT:

a.  Places more emphasis on market risk.

b.  Minimizes the importance of diversification.

c.  Recognizes multiple unsystematic risk factors.

d.  Recognizes multiple systematic risk factors.

17. An investor takes as large a position as possible when an equilibrium price relationship is violated. This is an example of:

a.  A dominance argument.

b.  The mean-variance efficient frontier.

c.  Arbitrage activity.

d.  The capital asset pricing model.

18. The feature of arbitrage pricing theory (APT) that offers the greatest potential advantage over the *simple* CAPM is the:

a.  Identification of anticipated changes in production, inflation, and term structure of interest rates as key factors explaining the risk–return relationship.

b.  Superior measurement of the risk-free rate of return over historical time periods.

c.  Variability of coefficients of sensitivity to the APT factors for a given asset over time.

d.  Use of several factors instead of a single market index to explain the risk–return relationship.

19. In contrast to the capital asset pricing model, arbitrage pricing theory:

a.  Requires that markets be in equilibrium.

b.  Uses risk premiums based on micro variables.

c.  Specifies the number and identifies specific factors that determine expected returns.

d.  Does not require the restrictive assumptions concerning the market portfolio.

20. As a finance intern at Pork Products, Jennifer Wainwright's assignment is to come up with fresh insights concerning the firm's cost of capital. She decides that this would be a good opportunity to try out the new material on the APT that she learned last semester. She decides that three promising factors would be (i) the return on a broad-based index such as the S&P 500; (ii) the level of interest rates, as represented by the yield to maturity on 10-year Treasury bonds; and (iii) the price of hogs, which are particularly important to her firm. Her plan is to find the beta of Pork Products against each of these factors by using a multiple regression and to estimate the risk premium associated with each exposure factor. Comment on Jennifer's choice of factors. Which are most promising with respect to the likely impact on her firm's cost of capital? Can you suggest improvements to her specification?

Enter the Market Insight database at **www.mhhe.com/business/finance/edumarket insight** and link to *Industry*. From the pull-down menu link to the *Computer Hardware* industry and *GO*. Review the latest S&P Industry Survey on that industry. What are the current major "industry" risk factors pertinent to the Computer Hardware industry? Which of these factors would you expect to be priced, that is, command a significant risk premium?

Visit us at www.mhhe.com/bkm

**E-INVESTMENTS
APT versus
CAPM**

The APT attempts to estimate the risk premium by identifying multiple systematic factors. See the interview with William Sharpe (**www.stanford.edu/~wfsharpe/art/djam/djam.htm**) where he discusses the CAPM as well as APT methods. To whom does Dr. Sharpe give credit for providing the basis of his CAPM theory and what are his comments concerning the APT?

**SOLUTIONS
TO CONCEPT
CHECKS**

1. The GDP beta is 1.2 and GDP growth is 1% better than previously expected. So you will increase your forecast for the stock return by $1.2 \times 1\% = 1.2\%$. The revised forecast is for an 11.2% return.

2. With these lower risk premia, the expected return on the stock will be lower:

$$E(r) = 4\% + 1.8 \times 4\% + .7 \times 2\% = 12.6\%$$

3. *a.* This portfolio is not well diversified. The weight on the first security does not decline as $n$ increases. Regardless of how much diversification there is in the rest of the portfolio, you will not shed the firm-specific risk of this security.

   *b.* This portfolio is well diversified. Even though some stocks have three times the weight as other stocks ($1.5/n$ versus $.5/n$), the weight on all stocks approaches zero as $n$ increases. The impact of any individual stock's firm-specific risk will approach zero as $n$ becomes ever larger.

4. The SML says that the expected return on the portfolio should be $4\% + (\frac{1}{3})(10 - 4) = 6\%$. The return actually expected is only 5%, implying that the stock is overpriced and that there is an arbitrage opportunity. Buy $1 of a portfolio that is $\frac{2}{3}$ invested in T-bills and $\frac{1}{3}$ in the market. The return on this portfolio is $\frac{2}{3} r_f + \frac{1}{3} r_M = \frac{2}{3} \times 4\% + \frac{1}{3} r_M$. Sell $1 of Portfolio $G$. The net return on the combined position is:

| | |
|---|---|
| $1 \times [\frac{2}{3} \times .04 + \frac{1}{3} r_M]$ | Buy portfolio invested $\frac{2}{3}$ in T-bills and $\frac{1}{3}$ in the market index. |
| $- \$1 \times [.05 + \frac{1}{3} (r_M - .10)]$ | Sell $1 in portfolio $G$, with expected return of 5% and beta of $\frac{1}{3}$ on surprise in market return. |
| $1 \times .01$ | Total |

   The profit per dollar invested is risk-free and precisely equal to the deviation of expected return from the SML.

5. The equilibrium return is $E(r) = r_f + \beta_{P1} [E(r_1) - r_f] + \beta_{P2} [E(r_2) - r_f]$

   Using the data in Example 11.5:

$$E(r) = 4 + .2 \times (10 - 4) + 1.4 \times (12 - 4) = 16.4\%$$

6. *a.* For Louisiana residents, the stock is not a hedge. When their economy does poorly (low energy prices), the stock also does poorly, thereby aggravating their problems.

   *b.* For Massachusetts residents, the stock is a hedge. When energy prices increase, the stock will provide greater wealth with which to purchase energy.

   *c.* If energy consumers (who are willing to bid up the price of the stock for its hedge value) dominate the economy, then high oil-beta stocks will have lower expected rates of return than would be predicted by the simple CAPM.

# MARKET EFFICIENCY AND BEHAVIORAL FINANCE

One of the early applications of computers in economics in the 1950s was to analyze economic time series. Business cycle theorists felt that tracing the evolution of several economic variables over time would clarify and predict the progress of the economy through boom and bust periods. A natural candidate for analysis was the behavior of stock market prices over time. Assuming that stock prices reflect the prospects of the firm, recurrent patterns of peaks and troughs in economic performance ought to show up in those prices.

Maurice Kendall examined this proposition in 1953.[1] He found to his great surprise that he could identify no predictable patterns in stock prices. Prices seemed to evolve randomly. They were as likely to go up as they were to go down on any particular day, regardless of past performance. The data provided no way to predict price movements.

At first blush, Kendall's results were disturbing to some financial economists. They seemed to imply that the stock market is dominated by erratic market psychology, or "animal spirits"—that it follows no logical rules. In short, the results appeared to confirm the irrationality of the market. On further reflection, however, economists came to reverse their interpretation of Kendall's study.

---

[1] Maurice Kendall, "The Analysis of Economic Time Series, Part I: Prices," *Journal of the Royal Statistical Society* 96 (1953).

It soon became apparent that random price movements indicated a well-functioning or efficient market, not an irrational one. In this chapter we explore the reasoning behind what may seem a surprising conclusion. We show how competition among analysts leads naturally to market efficiency, and we examine the implications of the efficient market hypothesis for investment policy. We also consider empirical evidence that supports and contradicts the notion of market efficiency. Many researchers have interpreted the body of evidence at odds with efficient markets as indicative of systematic irrationalities in how individuals make their investment decisions. This approach focuses on identifying investors' behavioral patterns, and we evaluate the behavioral critique of efficient market theory in the context of evidence on security returns.

## 12.1    RANDOM WALKS AND THE EFFICIENT MARKET HYPOTHESIS

Suppose Kendall had discovered that stock prices are predictable. What a gold mine this would have been. If they could use Kendall's equations to predict stock prices, investors would reap unending profits simply by purchasing stocks that the computer model implied were about to increase in price and by selling those stocks about to fall in price.

A moment's reflection should be enough to convince yourself that this situation could not persist for long. For example, suppose that the model predicts with great confidence that XYZ stock price, currently at $100 per share, will rise dramatically in 3 days to $110. What would all investors with access to the model's prediction do today? Obviously, they would place a great wave of immediate buy orders to cash in on the prospective increase in stock price. No one holding XYZ, however, would be willing to sell. The net effect would be an *immediate* jump in the stock price to $110. The forecast of a future price increase will lead instead to an immediate price increase. In other words, the stock price will immediately reflect the "good news" implicit in the model's forecast.

This simple example illustrates why Kendall's attempt to find recurrent patterns in stock price movements was likely to fail. A forecast about favorable *future* performance leads instead to favorable *current* performance, as market participants all try to get in on the action before the price jump.

More generally, one might say that any information that could be used to predict stock performance should already be reflected in stock prices. As soon as there is any information indicating that a stock is underpriced and therefore offers a profit opportunity, investors flock to buy the stock and immediately bid up its price to a fair level, where only ordinary rates of return can be expected. These "ordinary rates" are simply rates of return commensurate with the risk of the stock.

However, if prices are bid immediately to fair levels, given all available information, it must be that they increase or decrease only in response to new information. New information, by definition, must be unpredictable; if it could be predicted, then the prediction would be part of today's information. Thus stock prices that change in response to new (unpredictable) information also must move unpredictably.

**Figure 12.1
Cumulative
abnormal returns
before takeover
attempts: Target
companies**

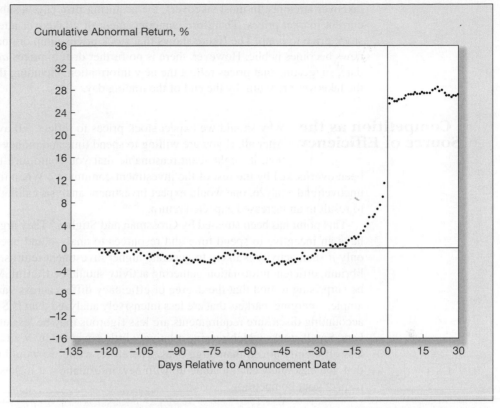

Source: Arthur Keown and John Pinkerton, "Merger Announcements and Insider Trading Activity," *Journal of Finance* 36
(September 1981).

This is the essence of the argument that stock prices should follow a **random walk**, that is, that price changes should be random and unpredictable.[2] Far from a proof of market irrationality, randomly evolving stock prices would be the necessary consequence of intelligent investors competing to discover relevant information on which to buy or sell stocks before the rest of the market becomes aware of that information.

Don't confuse randomness in price *changes* with irrationality in the *level* of prices. If prices are determined rationally, then only new information will cause them to change. Therefore, a random walk would be the natural result of prices that always reflect all current knowledge. Indeed, if stock price movements were predictable, that would be damning evidence of stock market inefficiency, because the ability to predict prices would indicate that all available information was not already reflected in stock prices. Therefore, the notion that stocks already reflect all available information is referred to as the **efficient market hypothesis** (EMH).[3]

Figure 12.1 illustrates the response of stock prices to new information in an efficient market. The graph plots the price response of a sample of 194 firms that were targets of

---

[2] Actually, we are being a little loose with terminology here. Strictly speaking, we should characterize stock prices as following a submartingale, meaning that the expected change in the price can be positive, presumably as compensation for the time value of money and systematic risk. Moreover, the expected return may change over time as risk factors change. A random walk is more restrictive in that it constrains successive stock returns to be independent *and* identically distributed. Nevertheless, the term "random walk" is commonly used in the looser sense that price changes are essentially unpredictable. We will follow this convention.
[3] Market efficiency should not be confused with the idea of efficient portfolios introduced in Chapter 8. An informationally efficient *market* is one in which information is rapidly disseminated and reflected in prices. An efficient *portfolio* is one with the highest expected return for a given level of risk.

takeover attempts. In most takeovers, the acquiring firm pays a substantial premium over current market prices. Therefore, announcement of a takeover attempt should cause the stock price to jump. The figure shows that stock prices jump dramatically on the day the news becomes public. However, there is no further drift in prices *after* the announcement date, suggesting that prices reflect the new information, including the likely magnitude of the takeover premium, by the end of the trading day.

## Competition as the Source of Efficiency

Why should we expect stock prices to reflect "all available information"? After all, if you are willing to spend time and money on gathering information, it might seem reasonable that you could turn up something that has been overlooked by the rest of the investment community. When information is costly to uncover and analyze, one would expect investment analysis calling for such expenditures to result in an increased expected return.

This point has been stressed by Grossman and Stiglitz.[4] They argued that investors will have an incentive to spend time and resources to analyze and uncover new information only if such activity is likely to generate higher investment returns. Thus, in market equilibrium, efficient information-gathering activity should be fruitful. Moreover, it would not be surprising to find that the degree of efficiency differs across various markets. For example, emerging markets that are less intensively analyzed than U.S. markets and in which accounting disclosure requirements are less rigorous may be less efficient than U.S. markets. Small stocks which receive relatively little coverage by Wall Street analysts may be less efficiently priced than large ones. Therefore, while we would not go so far as to say that you absolutely cannot come up with new information, it makes sense to consider and respect your competition.

## EXAMPLE 12.1    Rewards for Incremental Performance

Consider an investment management fund currently managing a $5 billion portfolio. Suppose that the fund manager can devise a research program that could increase the portfolio rate of return by one-tenth of 1% per year, a seemingly modest amount. This program would increase the dollar return to the portfolio by $5 billion × .001, or $5 million. Therefore, the fund would be willing to spend up to $5 million per year on research to increase stock returns by a mere tenth of 1% per year. With such large rewards for such small increases in investment performance, it should not be surprising that professional portfolio managers are willing to spend large sums on industry analysts, computer support, and research effort, and therefore that price changes are, generally speaking, difficult to predict.

With so many well-backed analysts willing to spend considerable resources on research, easy pickings in the market are rare. Moreover, the incremental rates of return on research activity may be so small that only managers of the largest portfolios will find them worth pursuing.

Although it may not literally be true that "all" relevant information will be uncovered, it is virtually certain that there are many investigators hot on the trail of most leads that seem likely to improve investment performance. Competition among these many well-backed, highly paid, aggressive analysts ensures that, as a general rule, stock prices ought to reflect available information regarding their proper levels.

---

[4] Sanford J. Grossman and Joseph E. Stiglitz, "On the Impossibility of Informationally Efficient Markets," *American Economic Review* 70 (June 1980).

## Versions of the Efficient Market Hypothesis

It is common to distinguish among three versions of the EMH: the weak, semistrong, and strong forms of the hypothesis. These versions differ by their notions of what is meant by the term "all available information."

The **weak-form** hypothesis asserts that stock prices already reflect all information that can be derived by examining market trading data such as the history of past prices, trading volume, or short interest. This version of the hypothesis implies that trend analysis is fruitless. Past stock price data are publicly available and virtually costless to obtain. The weak-form hypothesis holds that if such data ever conveyed reliable signals about future performance, all investors already would have learned to exploit the signals. Ultimately, the signals lose their value as they become widely known because a buy signal, for instance, would result in an immediate price increase.

The **semistrong-form** hypothesis states that all publicly available information regarding the prospects of a firm must be reflected already in the stock price. Such information includes, in addition to past prices, fundamental data on the firm's product line, quality of management, balance sheet composition, patents held, earning forecasts, and accounting practices. Again, if investors have access to such information from publicly available sources, one would expect it to be reflected in stock prices.

Finally, the **strong-form** version of the efficient market hypothesis states that stock prices reflect all information relevant to the firm, even including information available only to company insiders. This version of the hypothesis is quite extreme. Few would argue with the proposition that corporate officers have access to pertinent information long enough before public release to enable them to profit from trading on that information. Indeed, much of the activity of the Securities and Exchange Commission is directed toward preventing insiders from profiting by exploiting their privileged situation. Rule 10b-5 of the Security Exchange Act of 1934 sets limits on trading by corporate officers, directors, and substantial owners, requiring them to report trades to the SEC. These insiders, their relatives, and any associates who trade on information supplied by insiders are considered in violation of the law.

Defining insider trading is not always easy, however. After all, stock analysts are in the business of uncovering information not already widely known to market participants. As we saw in Chapter 3, the distinction between private and inside information is sometimes murky.

---

**CONCEPT CHECK☞ QUESTION 1**

*a.* **Suppose you observed that high-level managers make superior returns on investments in their company's stock. Would this be a violation of weak-form market efficiency? Would it be a violation of strong-form market efficiency?**

*b.* **If the weak form of the efficient market hypothesis is valid, must the strong form also hold? Conversely, does strong-form efficiency imply weak-form efficiency?**

---

## 12.2    IMPLICATIONS OF THE EMH

### Technical Analysis

**Technical analysis** is essentially the search for recurrent and predictable patterns in stock prices. Although technicians recognize the value of information regarding future economic prospects of the firm, they believe that such information

**Figure 12.2**
**Dow theory trends**

Source: Melanie F. Bowman and Thom Hartle, "Dow Theory," *Technical Analysis of Stocks and Commodities,* September 1990, p. 690.

is not necessary for a successful trading strategy. This is because whatever the fundamental reason for a change in stock price, if the stock price responds slowly enough, the analyst will be able to identify a trend that can be exploited during the adjustment period. The key to successful technical analysis is a sluggish response of stock prices to fundamental supply-and-demand factors. This prerequisite, of course, is diametrically opposed to the notion of an efficient market.

Technical analysts are sometimes called *chartists* because they study records or charts of past stock prices, hoping to find patterns they can exploit to make a profit. The **Dow theory**, named after its creator Charles Dow (who established *The Wall Street Journal*), is the grandfather of most technical analysis. The Dow theory posits three forces simultaneously affecting stock prices:

1.  The *primary trend* is the long-term movement of prices, lasting from several months to several years.
2.  *Secondary* or *intermediate trends* are caused by short-term deviations of prices from the underlying trend line. These deviations are eliminated via *corrections*, when prices revert back to trend values.
3.  *Tertiary* or *minor trends* are daily fluctuations of little importance.

Figure 12.2 represents these three components of stock price movements. In this figure, the primary trend is upward, but intermediate trends result in short-lived market declines lasting a few weeks. The intraday minor trends have no long-run impact on price.

Figure 12.3 depicts the course of the DJIA during 1988, a year that seems to provide a good example of price patterns consistent with Dow theory. The primary trend is upward, as evidenced by the fact that each market peak is higher than the previous peak (point *F* versus *D* versus *B*). Similarly, each low is higher than the previous low (*E* versus *C* versus *A*). This pattern of upward-moving "tops" and "bottoms" is one of the key ways to identify the underlying primary trend. Notice in Figure 12.3 that, despite the upward primary trend, intermediate trends still can lead to short periods of declining prices (points *B* through *C*, or *D* through *E*).

More-recent variations on the Dow theory are the Elliott wave theory and the theory of Kondratieff waves. Like the Dow theory, the idea behind Elliott waves is that stock prices can be described by a set of wave patterns. Long-term and short-term wave cycles are

**Figure 12.3**
**Dow Jones**
**Industrial**
**Average**
**in 1988**

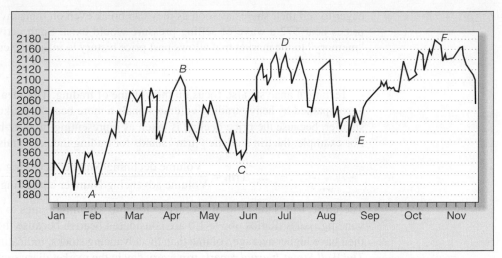

Source: Melanie F. Bowman and Thom Hartle, "Dow Theory," *Technical Analysis of Stocks and Commodities*, September 1990, p. 690.

superimposed and result in a complicated pattern of price movements, but by interpreting the cycles, one can, according to the theory, predict broad movements. Similarly, Kondratieff waves are named after a Russian economist who asserted that the macroeconomy (and thus the stock market) moves in broad waves lasting between 48 and 60 years. The Kondratieff waves are therefore analogous to Dow's primary trend, although of far longer duration. Kondratieff's assertion is hard to evaluate empirically, however, because cycles that last about 50 years can provide only two independent data points per century, which is hardly enough data to test the predictive power of the theory.

Other chartist techniques involve moving averages. In one version of this approach average prices over the past several months are taken as indicators of the "true value" of the stock. If the stock price is above this value, it may be expected to fall. In another version, the moving average is taken as indicative of long-run trends. If the trend has been downward and if the current stock price is below the moving average, then a subsequent increase in the stock price above the moving average line (a "breakthrough") might signal a reversal of the downward trend.

Another technique is called the *relative strength* approach. The chartist compares stock performance over a recent period to performance of the market or other stocks in the same industry. A simple version of relative strength takes the ratio of the stock price to a market indicator such as the S&P 500 index. If the ratio increases over time, the stock is said to exhibit relative strength because its price performance is better than that of the broad market. Such strength presumably may continue for a long enough period of time to offer profit opportunities.

One of the most commonly heard components of technical analysis is the notion of **resistance levels** or **support levels**. These values are said to be price levels above which it is difficult for stock prices to rise, or below which it is unlikely for them to fall, and they are believed to be levels determined by market psychology.

## EXAMPLE 12.2   Resistance Levels

Consider stock XYZ, which traded for several months at a price of $72, and then declined to $65. If the stock eventually begins to increase in price, $72 is considered a resistance level (according to this theory) because investors who bought originally at $72 will be eager to sell their shares as soon as they can break even on their investment. Therefore, at prices near $72 a wave of selling pressure would exist. Such activity imparts a type of "memory" to the market that allows past price history to influence current stock prospects.

Technical analysts also focus on the volume of trading. The idea is that a price decline accompanied by heavy trading volume signals a more bearish market than if volume were smaller, because the price decline is taken as representing broader-based selling pressure. For example, the trin statistic ("trin" stands for trading index) equals

$$\text{Trin} = \frac{\text{Volume declining/Number declining}}{\text{Volume advancing/Number advancing}}$$

Therefore, trin is the ratio of average volume in declining issues to average volume in advancing issues. Ratios above 1.0 are considered bearish because the falling stocks would then have higher average volume than the advancing stocks, indicating net selling pressure. *The Wall Street Journal* reports trin every day in the market diary section, as in Figure 12.4.

Note, however, for every buyer there must be a seller of stock. High volume in a falling market should not necessarily indicate a larger imbalance of buyers versus sellers. For example, a trin statistic above 1.0, which is considered bearish, could equally well be interpreted as indicating that there is more *buying* activity in declining issues.

The efficient market hypothesis implies that technical analysis is without merit. The past history of prices and trading volume is publicly available at minimal cost. Therefore, any information that was ever available from analyzing past prices has already been reflected in stock prices. As investors compete to exploit their common knowledge of a stock's price history, they necessarily drive stock prices to levels where expected rates of return are exactly commensurate with risk. At those levels one cannot expect abnormal returns.

As an example of how this process works, consider what would happen if the market believed that a level of $72 truly were a resistance level for stock XYZ in Example 12.2. No one would be willing to purchase the stock at a price of $71.50, because it would have

**Figure 12.4**
**Market diary**

**Diaries**

| | MON | FRI | WK AGO |
|---|---|---|---|
| Issues traded | 3,414 | 3,404 | 3,414 |
| Advances | 1,056 | 2,269 | 2,054 |
| Declines | 2,204 | 963 | 1,171 |
| Unchanged | 154 | 172 | 189 |
| New highs | 57 | 58 | 24 |
| New lows | 87 | 60 | 82 |
| zAdv vol (000s) | 228,902 | 980,705 | 1,060,698 |
| zDecl vol (000s) | 982,362 | 375,893 | 289,135 |
| zTotal vol (000s) | 1,217,204 | 1,369,653 | 1,365,946 |
| Closing Tick[1] | -44 | +582 | +257 |
| Closing Arms[2] (trin) | 2.06 | .90 | .48 |
| zBlock trades | 17,893 | 21,403 | 21,488 |

NYSE first crossing 5,331,700 shares, value n.a.
Second (basket) 9,989,746 shares, value $330,899,224
[1]The net difference of the number of stocks closing higher than their previous trade from those closing lower.
[2]A comparison of the number of advancing and declining issues with the volume of shares rising and falling. Generally, an Arms of less than 1.00 indicates buying demand; above 1.00 indicates selling pressure.
z-primary market

Source: *The Wall Street Journal*, February 25, 2003. Reprinted by permission of *The Wall Street Journal*, © 2003 Dow Jones & Company, Inc. All Rights Reserved Worldwide.

almost no room to increase in price, but ample room to fall. However, if no one would buy it at $71.50, then $71.50 would become a resistance level. But then, using a similar analysis, no one would buy it at $71, or $70, and so on. The notion of a resistance level is a logical conundrum. Its simple resolution is the recognition that if the stock is ever to sell at $71.50, investors *must* believe that the price can as easily increase as fall. The fact that investors are willing to purchase (or even hold) the stock at $71.50 is evidence of their belief that they can earn a fair expected rate of return at that price.

---

**CONCEPT CHECK☞ QUESTION 2**

**If everyone in the market believes in resistance levels, why do these beliefs not become self-fulfilling prophecies?**

---

An interesting question is whether a technical rule that seems to work will continue to work in the future once it becomes widely recognized. A clever analyst may occasionally uncover a profitable trading rule, but the real test of efficient markets is whether the rule itself becomes reflected in stock prices once its value is discovered.

Suppose, for example, that the Dow theory predicts an upward primary trend. If the theory is widely accepted, it follows that many investors will attempt to buy stocks immediately in anticipation of the price increase; the effect would be to bid up prices sharply and immediately rather than at the gradual, long-lived pace initially expected. The Dow theory's predicted trend would be replaced by a sharp jump in prices. It is in this sense that price patterns ought to be *self-destructing*. Once a useful technical rule (or price pattern) is discovered, it ought to be invalidated when the mass of traders attempts to exploit it.

Thus the market dynamic is one of a continual search for profitable trading rules, followed by destruction by overuse of those rules found to be successful, followed by more search for yet-undiscovered rules.

## Fundamental Analysis

**Fundamental analysis** uses earnings and dividend prospects of the firm, expectations of future interest rates, and risk evaluation of the firm to determine proper stock prices. Ultimately, it represents an attempt to determine the present discounted value of all the payments a stockholder will receive from each share of stock. If that value exceeds the stock price, the fundamental analyst would recommend purchasing the stock.

Fundamental analysts usually start with a study of past earnings and an examination of company balance sheets. They supplement this analysis with further detailed economic analysis, ordinarily including an evaluation of the quality of the firm's management, the firm's standing within its industry, and the prospects for the industry as a whole. The hope is to attain insight into future performance of the firm that is not yet recognized by the rest of the market. Chapters 17 through 19 provide a detailed discussion of the types of analyses that underlie fundamental analysis.

Once again, the efficient market hypothesis predicts that *most* fundamental analysis also is doomed to failure. If the analyst relies on publicly available earnings and industry information, his or her evaluation of the firm's prospects is not likely to be significantly more accurate than those of rival analysts. There are many well-informed, well-financed firms conducting such market research, and in the face of such competition it will be difficult to uncover data not also available to other analysts. Only analysts with a unique insight will be rewarded.

Fundamental analysis is much more difficult than merely identifying well-run firms with good prospects. Discovery of good firms does an investor no good in and of itself if the rest of the market also knows those firms are good. If the knowledge is already public, the investor will be forced to pay a high price for those firms and will not realize a superior rate of return.

The trick is not to identify firms that are good, but to find firms that are *better* than everyone else's estimate. Similarly, poorly run firms can be great bargains if they are not quite as bad as their stock prices suggest.

This is why fundamental analysis is difficult. It is not enough to do a good analysis of a firm; you can make money only if your analysis is better than that of your competitors because the market price will already reflect all commonly available information.

## Active versus Passive Portfolio Management

By now it is apparent that casual efforts to pick stocks are not likely to pay off. Competition among investors ensures that any easily implemented stock evaluation technique will be used widely enough so that any insights derived will be reflected in stock prices. Only serious analysis and uncommon techniques are likely to generate the *differential* insight necessary to yield trading profits.

Moreover, these techniques are economically feasible only for managers of large portfolios. If you have only $100,000 to invest, even a 1% per year improvement in performance generates only $1,000 per year, hardly enough to justify herculean efforts. The billion-dollar manager, however, reaps extra income of $10 million annually from the same 1% increment.

If small investors are not in a favored position to conduct active portfolio management, what are their choices? The small investor probably is better off investing in mutual funds. By pooling resources in this way, small investors can gain from economies of scale.

More difficult decisions remain, though. Can investors be sure that even large mutual funds have the ability or resources to uncover mispriced stocks? Furthermore, will any mispricing be sufficiently large to repay the costs entailed in active portfolio management?

Proponents of the efficient market hypothesis believe that active management is largely wasted effort and unlikely to justify the expenses incurred. Therefore, they advocate a **passive investment strategy** that makes no attempt to outsmart the market. A passive strategy aims only at establishing a well-diversified portfolio of securities without attempting to find under- or overvalued stocks. Passive management is usually characterized by a buy-and-hold strategy. Because the efficient market theory indicates that stock prices are at fair levels, given all available information, it makes no sense to buy and sell securities frequently, which generates large brokerage fees without increasing expected performance. The nearby box is a parable illustrating this point.

One common strategy for passive management is to create an **index fund**, which is a fund designed to replicate the performance of a broad-based index of stocks. For example, in 1976 the Vanguard Group of mutual funds introduced a mutual fund called the Index 500 Portfolio, which holds stocks in direct proportion to their weight in the Standard & Poor's 500 stock price index. The performance of the Index 500 fund therefore replicates the performance of the S&P 500. Investors in this fund obtain broad diversification with relatively low management fees. The fees can be kept to a minimum because Vanguard does not need to pay analysts to assess stock prospects and does not incur transaction costs from high portfolio turnover. Indeed, while the typical annual charge for an actively managed equity fund is more than 1% of assets, Vanguard charges a bit less than .2% for the Index 500 Portfolio.

Some years ago, in a land called Indicia, revolution led to the overthrow of a socialist regime and the restoration of a system of private property. Former government enterprises were reformed as corporations, which then issued stocks and bonds. These securities were given to a central agency, which offered them for sale to individuals, pension funds, and the like (all armed with newly printed money).

Almost immediately a group of money managers came forth to assist these investors. Recalling the words of a venerated elder, uttered before the previous revolution ("Invest in Corporate Indicia"), they invited clients to give them money, with which they would buy a cross-section of all the newly issued securities. Investors considered this a reasonable idea, and soon everyone held a piece of Corporate Indicia.

Before long the money managers became bored because there was little for them to do. Soon they fell into the habit of gathering at a beachfront casino where they passed the time playing roulette, craps, and similar games, for low stakes, with their own money.

After a while, the owner of the casino suggested a new idea. He would furnish an impressive set of rooms which would be designated the Money Managers' Club. There the members could place bets with one another about the fortunes of various corporations, industries, the level of the Gross National Product, foreign trade, etc. To make the betting more exciting, the casino owner suggested that the managers use their clients' money for this purpose.

The offer was immediately accepted, and soon the money managers were betting eagerly with one another. At the end of each week, some found that they had won money for their clients, while others found that they had lost. But the losses always exceeded the gains, for a certain amount was deducted from each bet to cover the costs of the elegant surroundings in which the gambling took place.

Before long a group of professors from Indicia U. suggested that investors were not well served by the activities being conducted at the Money Managers' Club. "Why pay people to gamble with your money? Why not just hold your own piece of Corporate Indicia?" they said.

This argument seemed sensible to some of the investors, and they raised the issue with their money managers. A few capitulated, announcing that they would henceforth stay away from the casino and use their clients' money only to buy proportionate shares of all the stocks and bonds issued by corporations.

The converts, who became known as managers of Indicia funds, were initially shunned by those who continued to frequent the Money Managers' Club, but in time, grudging acceptance replaced outright hostility. The wave of puritan reform some had predicted failed to materialize, and gambling remained legal. Many managers continued to make their daily pilgrimage to the casino. But they exercised more restraint than before, placed smaller bets, and generally behaved in a manner consonant with their responsibilities. Even the members of the Lawyers' Club found it difficult to object to the small amount of gambling that still went on.

And everyone but the casino owner lived happily ever after.

Source: William F. Sharpe, "The Parable of the Money Managers," *The Financial Analysts' Journal* 32 (July/August 1976), p. 4. [Copyright 1976, Association for Investment Management and Research, Charlottesville, VA]

Indexing has grown in appeal considerably since 1976. Vanguard's Index 500 Portfolio was vying with Fidelity's Magellan fund for bragging rights as the largest equity mutual fund with about $70 billion in assets in early 2003. Several other firms have introduced S&P 500 index funds, but Vanguard still dominates the retail market for indexing. Including pension funds and mutual funds, more than $1 trillion was indexed to the S&P 500 by 2001. Many institutional investors now hold indexed bond as well as indexed stock portfolios.

Mutual funds offer portfolios that match a wide variety of market indexes. For example, some of the funds offered by the Vanguard Group track the Wilshire 5000 index, the Salomon Brothers Broad Investment Grade Bond Index, the MSCI index of small-capitalization U.S. companies, the European equity market, and the Pacific Basin equity market.

A hybrid strategy also is fairly common, where the fund maintains a *passive core*, which is an indexed position, and augments that position with one or more actively managed portfolios.

## The Role of Portfolio Management in an Efficient Market

If the market is efficient, why not throw darts at *The Wall Street Journal* instead of trying rationally to choose a stock portfolio? This is a tempting conclusion to draw from the notion that security prices are fairly set, but it is far too facile. There is a role for rational portfolio management, even in perfectly efficient markets.

You have learned that a basic principle in portfolio selection is diversification. Even if all stocks are priced fairly, each still poses firm-specific risk that can be eliminated through diversification. Therefore, rational security selection, even in an efficient market, calls for the selection of a well-diversified portfolio providing the systematic risk level that the investor wants.

Rational investment policy also requires that tax considerations be reflected in security choice. High-tax-bracket investors generally will not want the same securities that low-bracket investors find favorable. At an obvious level high-bracket investors find it advantageous to buy tax-exempt municipal bonds despite their relatively low pretax yields, whereas those same bonds are unattractive to low-tax-bracket investors. At a more subtle level high-bracket investors might want to tilt their portfolios in the direction of capital gains as opposed to dividend or interest income, because the option to defer the realization of capital gains income is more valuable the higher the current tax bracket. Hence these investors may prefer stocks that yield low dividends yet offer greater expected capital gain income. They also will be more attracted to investment opportunities for which returns are sensitive to tax benefits, such as real estate ventures.

A third argument for rational portfolio management relates to the particular risk profile of the investor. For example, a General Motors executive whose annual bonus depends on GM's profits generally should not invest additional amounts in auto stocks. To the extent that his or her compensation already depends on GM's well-being, the executive is already overinvested in GM and should not exacerbate the lack of diversification.

Investors of varying ages also might warrant different portfolio policies with regard to risk bearing. For example, older investors who are essentially living off savings might choose to avoid long-term bonds whose market values fluctuate dramatically with changes in interest rates (discussed in Part 4). Because these investors are living off accumulated savings, they require conservation of principal. In contrast, younger investors might be more inclined toward long-term inflation-indexed bonds. The steady flow of real income over long periods of time that is locked in with these bonds can be more important than preservation of principal to those with long life expectancies.

In conclusion, there is a role for portfolio management even in an efficient market. Investors' optimal positions will vary according to factors such as age, tax bracket, risk aversion, and employment. The role of the portfolio manager in an efficient market is to tailor the portfolio to these needs, rather than to beat the market.

## Resource Allocation

We've focused so far on the investments implications of the efficient market hypothesis. Deviations from efficiency may offer profit opportunities to better-informed traders at the expense of less-informed traders.

However, deviations from informational efficiency would also result in a large cost that will be borne by all citizens, namely, inefficient resource allocation. Recall that in a capitalist economy, investments in *real* assets such as plant, equipment, and know-how are guided in large part by the prices of financial assets. For example, if the values of biotech assets as reflected in the stock market prices of biotech firms exceed the cost of acquiring those assets, the managers of such firms have a strong signal that further investments in the firm will be regarded by the market as a positive net present value venture. In this manner, capital market prices guide resource allocation. Security mispricing thus could entail severe social costs by fostering inappropriate investments on the real side of the economy.

The Appendix to Chapter 9 demonstrates how security analysis impounds information into security prices. To the extent that only part of this information is reflected in prices, corporations with overpriced securities will be able to obtain capital too cheaply and corporations with undervalued securities might forego investment opportunities because the cost of raising capital will be too high. Therefore, inefficient capital markets would diminish one of the most potent benefits of a market economy.

## 12.3   EVENT STUDIES

The notion of informationally efficient markets leads to a powerful research methodology. If security prices reflect all currently available information, then price changes must reflect new information. Therefore, it seems that one should be able to measure the importance of an event of interest by examining price changes during the period in which the event occurs.

An **event study** describes a technique of empirical financial research that enables an observer to assess the impact of a particular event on a firm's stock price. A stock market analyst might want to study the impact of dividend changes on stock prices, for example. An event study would quantify the relationship between dividend changes and stock returns. Using the results of such a study together with a superior means of predicting dividend changes, the analyst could in principle earn superior trading profits.

Analyzing the impact of an announced change in dividends is more difficult than it might at first appear. On any particular day stock prices respond to a wide range of economic news such as updated forecasts for GDP, inflation rates, interest rates, or corporate profitability. Isolating the part of a stock price movement that is attributable to a dividend announcement is not a trivial exercise.

The statistical approach that researchers commonly use to measure the impact of a particular information release, such as the announcement of a dividend change, is a marriage of efficient market theory with the index model discussed in Chapter 10. We want to measure the unexpected return that results from an event. This is the difference between the actual stock return and the return that might have been expected given the performance of the market. This expected return can be calculated using the index model.

Recall that a single-index model holds that stock returns are determined by a market factor and a firm-specific factor. The stock return, $r_t$, during a given period $t$, would be expressed mathematically as

$$r_t = a + br_{Mt} + e_t \tag{12.1}$$

where $r_{Mt}$ is the market's rate of return during the period and $e_t$ is the part of a security's return resulting from firm-specific events. The parameter $b$ measures sensitivity to the market return, and $a$ is the average rate of return the stock would realize in a period with a zero market return.[5] Equation 12.1 therefore provides a decomposition of $r_t$ into market and firm-specific factors. The firm-specific return may be interpreted as the unexpected return that results from the event.

Determination of the firm-specific return in a given period requires that we obtain an estimate of the term $e_t$. Therefore, we rewrite equation 12.1:

$$e_t = r_t - (a + br_{Mt}) \tag{12.2}$$

Equation 12.2 has a simple interpretation: To determine the firm-specific component of a stock's return, subtract the return that the stock ordinarily would earn for a given level of market performance from the actual rate of return on the stock. The residual, $e_t$, is the stock's return over and above what one would predict based on broad market movements in that period, given the stock's sensitivity to the market. We sometimes refer to the term $e_t$ in equation 12.2 as the **abnormal return**—the return beyond what would be predicted from market movements alone.

## EXAMPLE 12.3    Abnormal Returns

Suppose that the analyst has estimated that $a = .05\%$ and $b = .8$. On a day that the market goes up by 1%, you would predict from equation 12.1 that the stock should rise by an expected value of $.05\% + .8 \times 1\% = .85\%$. If the stock actually rises by 2%, the analyst would infer that firm-specific news that day caused an additional stock return of $2\% - .85\% = 1.15\%$. This is the abnormal return for the day.

The general strategy in event studies is to estimate the abnormal return around the date that new information about a stock is released to the market and attribute the abnormal stock performance to the new information. The first step in the study is to estimate parameters $a$ and $b$ for each security in the study. These typically are calculated using index model regressions as described in Chapter 10 in a period before that in which the event occurs. The prior period is used for estimation so that the impact of the event will not affect the estimates of the parameters. Next, the information release dates for each firm are recorded. For example, in a study of the impact of merger attempts on the stock prices of target firms, the announcement date is the date on which the public is informed that a merger is to be attempted. Finally, the abnormal returns of each firm surrounding the announcement date are computed, and the statistical significance and magnitude of the typical abnormal return is assessed to determine the impact of the newly released information.

One concern that complicates event studies arises from *leakage* of information. Leakage occurs when information regarding a relevant event is released to a small group of investors before official public release. In this case the stock price might start to increase (in the case of a "good news" announcement) days or weeks before the official announcement date. Any abnormal return on the announcement date is then a poor indicator of the total impact of the information release. A better indicator would be the **cumulative abnormal return**, which is simply the sum of all abnormal returns over the time period of interest.

---

[5] We know from Chapter 10, Section 10.3, that the CAPM implies that the intercept $a$ in equation 12.1 should equal $r_f(1 - \beta)$. Nevertheless, it is customary to estimate the intercept in this equation empirically rather than imposing the CAPM value. One justification for this practice is that empirically fitted security market lines seem flatter than predicted by the CAPM (see the next chapter), which would make the intercept implied by the CAPM too small.

The cumulative abnormal return thus captures the total firm-specific stock movement for an entire period when the market might be responding to new information.

Figure 12.1 (earlier in the chapter) presents the results from a fairly typical event study. The authors of this study were interested in leakage of information before merger announcements and constructed a sample of 194 firms that were targets of takeover attempts. In most takeovers, stockholders of the acquired firms sell their shares to the acquirer at substantial premiums over market value. Announcement of a takeover attempt is good news for shareholders of the target firm and therefore should cause stock prices to jump.

Figure 12.1 confirms the good-news nature of the announcements. On the announcement day, called day 0, the average cumulative abnormal return (CAR) for the sample of takeover candidates increases substantially, indicating a large and positive abnormal return on the announcement date. Notice that immediately after the announcement date the CAR no longer increases or decreases significantly. This is in accord with the efficient market hypothesis. Once the new information became public, the stock prices jumped almost immediately in response to the good news. With prices once again fairly set, reflecting the effect of the new information, further abnormal returns on any particular day are equally likely to be positive or negative. In fact, for a sample of many firms, the average abnormal return will be extremely close to zero, and thus the CAR will show neither upward nor downward drift. This is precisely the pattern shown in Figure 12.1.

The pattern of returns for the days preceding the public announcement date yields some interesting evidence about efficient markets and information leakage. If insider trading rules were perfectly obeyed and perfectly enforced, stock prices should show no abnormal returns on days before the public release of relevant news, because no special firm-specific information would be available to the market before public announcement. Instead, we should observe a clean jump in the stock price only on the announcement day. In fact, Figure 12.1 shows that the prices of the takeover targets clearly start an upward drift 30 days before the public announcement. There are two possible interpretations of this pattern. One is that information is leaking to some market participants who then purchase the stocks before the public announcement. At least some abuse of insider trading rules is occurring.

Another interpretation is that in the days before a takeover attempt the public becomes suspicious of the attempt as it observes someone buying large blocks of stock. As acquisition intentions become more evident, the probability of an attempted merger is gradually revised upward so that we see a gradual increase in CARs. Although this interpretation is certainly possible, evidence of leakage appears almost universally in event studies, even in cases where the public's access to information is not gradual.

Actually, the SEC itself can take some comfort from patterns such as that in Figure 12.1. If insider trading rules were widely and flagrantly violated, we would expect to see abnormal returns earlier than they appear in these results. For example, in the case of mergers, the CAR would turn positive as soon as acquiring firms decided on their takeover targets, because insiders would start trading immediately. By the time of the public announcement, the insiders would have bid up the stock prices of target firms to levels reflecting the merger attempt, and the abnormal returns on the actual public announcement date would be close to zero. The dramatic increase in the CAR that we see on the announcement date indicates that a good deal of these announcements are indeed news to the market and that stock prices did not already reflect complete knowledge about the takeovers. It would appear, therefore, that SEC enforcement does have a substantial effect on restricting insider trading, even if some amount of it still persists.

Event study methodology has become a widely accepted tool to measure the economic impact of a wide range of events. For example, the SEC regularly uses event studies to measure illicit gains captured by traders who may have violated insider trading or other securities laws.[6] Event studies are also used in fraud cases, where the courts must assess damages caused by a fraudulent activity.

## EXAMPLE 12.4    Using Abnormal Returns to Infer Damages

Suppose the stock of a company with market value of $100 million falls by 4% on the day that news of an accounting scandal surfaces. The rest of the market, however, generally did well that day. The market indexes were up sharply, and based on the usual relationship between the stock and the market, one would have expected a 2% gain on the stock. We would conclude that the impact of the scandal was a 6% drop in value, the difference between the 2% gain that we would have expected and the 4% drop actually observed. One might then infer that the damages sustained from the scandal were $6 million, because the value of the firm (after adjusting for general market movements) fell by 6% of $100 million when investors became aware of the news and reassessed the value of the stock.

---

**CONCEPT CHECK  QUESTION 4**

Suppose that we see negative abnormal returns (declining CARs) after an announcement date. Is this a violation of efficient markets?

---

## 12.4    ARE MARKETS EFFICIENT?

**The Issues**    Not surprisingly, the efficient market hypothesis does not exactly arouse enthusiasm in the community of professional portfolio managers. It implies that a great deal of the activity of portfolio managers—the search for undervalued securities—is at best wasted effort, and quite probably harmful to clients because it costs money and leads to imperfectly diversified portfolios. Consequently, the EMH has never been widely accepted on Wall Street, and debate continues today on the degree to which security analysis can improve investment performance. Before discussing empirical tests of the hypothesis, we want to note three factors that together imply that the debate probably never will be settled: the *magnitude issue*, the *selection bias issue*, and the *lucky event issue*.

**The Magnitude Issue.**    We noted that an investment manager overseeing a $5 billion portfolio who can improve performance by only 0.1% per year will increase investment earnings by .001 × $5 billion = $5 million annually. This manager clearly would be worth her salary! Yet can we, as observers, statistically measure her contribution? Probably not: A 0.1% contribution would be swamped by the yearly volatility of the market. Remember, the annual standard deviation of the well-diversified S&P 500 index has been around 20% per year. Against these fluctuations a small increase in performance would be hard to detect. Nevertheless, $5 million remains an extremely valuable improvement in performance.

---

[6] For a review of SEC applications of this technique, see Mark Mitchell and Jeffry Netter, "The Role of Financial Economics in Securities Fraud Cases: Applications at the Securities and Exchange Commission," School of Business Administration, The University of Michigan, working paper No. 93-25, October 1993.

# HOW TO GUARANTEE A SUCCESSFUL MARKET NEWSLETTER

Suppose you want to make your fortune publishing a market newsletter. You need first to convince potential subscribers that you have talent worth paying for. But what if you have no talent? The solution is simple: start eight newsletters.

In year 1, let four of your newsletters predict an up-market and four a down-market. In year 2, let half of the originally optimistic group of newsletters continue to predict an up-market and the other half a down-market. Do the same for the originally pessimistic group. Continue in this manner to obtain the pattern of predictions in the table that follows (U = prediction of an up-market, D = prediction of a down-market).

After 3 years, no matter what has happened to the market, one of the newsletters would have had a perfect prediction record. This is because after 3 years there are $2^3 = 8$ outcomes for the market, and we have covered all eight possibilities with the eight newsletters. Now, we simply slough off the seven unsuccessful newsletters, and market the eighth newsletter based on its perfect track record. If we want to establish a newsletter with a perfect track record over a 4-year period, we need $2^4 = 16$ newsletters. A 5-year period requires 32 newsletters, and so on.

After the fact, the one newsletter that was always right will attract attention for your uncanny foresight and investors will rush to pay large fees for its advice. Your fortune is made, and you have never even researched the market!

*WARNING:* This scheme is illegal! The point, however, is that with hundreds of market newsletters, you can find one that has stumbled onto an apparently remarkable string of successful predictions without any real degree of skill. After the fact, *someone's* prediction history can seem to imply great forecasting skill. This person is the one we will read about in *The Wall Street Journal;* the others will be forgotten.

| Newsletter Predictions | | | | | | | | |
|---|---|---|---|---|---|---|---|---|
| Year | 1 | 2 | 3 | 4 | 5 | 6 | 7 | 8 |
| 1 | U | U | U | U | D | D | D | D |
| 2 | U | U | D | D | U | U | D | D |
| 3 | U | D | U | D | U | D | U | D |

All might agree that stock prices are very close to fair values and that only managers of large portfolios can earn enough trading profits to make the exploitation of minor mispricing worth the effort. According to this view, the actions of intelligent investment managers are the driving force behind the constant evolution of market prices to fair levels. Rather than ask the qualitative question, Are markets efficient? we ought instead to ask a more quantitative question: How efficient are markets?

**The Selection Bias Issue.** Suppose that you discover an investment scheme that could really make money. You have two choices: either publish your technique in *The Wall Street Journal* to win fleeting fame, or keep your technique secret and use it to earn millions of dollars. Most investors would choose the latter option, which presents us with a conundrum. Only investors who find that an investment scheme cannot generate abnormal returns will be willing to report their findings to the whole world. Hence opponents of the efficient markets view of the world always can use evidence that various techniques do not provide investment rewards as proof that the techniques that do work simply are not being reported to the public. This is a problem in *selection bias;* the outcomes we are able to observe have been preselected in favor of failed attempts. Therefore, we cannot fairly evaluate the true ability of portfolio managers to generate winning stock market strategies.

**The Lucky Event Issue.** In virtually any month it seems we read an article about some investor or investment company with a fantastic investment performance over the recent past. Surely the superior records of such investors disprove the efficient market hypothesis.

Yet this conclusion is far from obvious. As an analogy to the investment game, consider a contest to flip the most number of heads out of 50 trials using a fair coin. The expected outcome for any person is, of course, 50% heads and 50% tails. If 10,000 people, however, compete in this contest, it would not be surprising if at least one or two contestants flipped more than 75% heads. In fact, elementary statistics tells us that the expected number of contestants flipping 75% or more heads would be two. It would be silly, though, to crown these people the "head-flipping champions of the world." Obviously, they are simply the contestants who happened to get lucky on the day of the event. (See the nearby box.)

The analogy to efficient markets is clear. Under the hypothesis that any stock is fairly priced given all available information, any bet on a stock is simply a coin toss. There is equal likelihood of winning or losing the bet. However, if many investors using a variety of schemes make fair bets, statistically speaking, *some* of those investors will be lucky and win a great majority of the bets. For every big winner, there may be many big losers, but we never hear of these managers. The winners, though, turn up in *The Wall Street Journal* as the latest stock market gurus; then they can make a fortune publishing market newsletters.

Our point is that after the fact there will have been at least one successful investment scheme. A doubter will call the results luck, the successful investor will call.it skill. The proper test would be to see whether the successful investors can repeat their performance in another period, yet this approach is rarely taken.

With these caveats in mind, we turn now to some of the empirical tests of the efficient market hypothesis.

| CONCEPT · CHECK ☞ QUESTION 5 | Fidelity's Magellan Fund outperformed the S&P 500 in 11 of the 13 years that Peter Lynch managed the fund, resulting in an average annual return more than 10% better than that of the index. Is Lynch's performance sufficient to dissuade you from a belief in efficient markets? If not, would *any* performance record be sufficient to dissuade you? |
| --- | --- |

### Weak-Form Tests: Patterns in Stock Returns

**Returns over Short Horizons.** Early tests of efficient markets were tests of the weak form. Could speculators find trends in past prices that would enable them to earn abnormal profits? This is essentially a test of the efficacy of technical analysis.

One way of discerning trends in stock prices is by measuring the *serial correlation* of stock market returns. Serial correlation refers to the tendency for stock returns to be related to past returns. Positive serial correlation means that positive returns tend to follow positive returns (a momentum type of property). Negative serial correlation means that positive returns tend to be followed by negative returns (a reversal or "correction" property). Both Conrad and Kaul[7] and Lo and MacKinlay[8] examine weekly returns of NYSE stocks and find positive serial correlation over short horizons. However, the correlation coefficients of weekly returns tend to be fairly small, at least for large stocks for which price data are the most reliably up-to-date. Thus, while these studies demonstrate weak price trends over short periods,[9] the evidence does not clearly suggest the existence of trading opportunities.

---

[7] Jennifer Conrad and Gautam Kaul, "Time-Variation in Expected Returns," *Journal of Business* 61 (October 1988), pp. 409–25.
[8] Andrew W. Lo and A. Craig MacKinlay, "Stock Market Prices Do Not Follow Random Walks: Evidence from a Simple Specification Test," *Review of Financial Studies* 1 (1988), pp. 41–66.
[9] On the other hand, there is evidence that share prices of individual securities (as opposed to broad market indexes) are more prone to reversals than continuations at very short horizons. See, for example, B. Lehmann, "Fads, Martingales and Market Efficiency," *Quarterly Journal of Economics* 105 (February 1990), pp. 1–28; and N. Jegadeesh, "Evidence of Predictable Behavior of Security Returns," *Journal of Finance* 45 (September 1990), pp. 881–98. However, as Lehmann notes, this is probably best interpreted as due to liquidity problems after big movements in stock prices as market makers adjust their positions in the stock.

While broad market indexes demonstrate only weak serial correlation, there appears to be stronger momentum in performance across market sectors exhibiting the best and worst recent returns. In an investigation of intermediate-horizon stock price behavior (using 3- to 12-month holding periods), Jegadeesh and Titman[10] found a **momentum effect** in which good or bad recent performance of particular stocks continues over time. They conclude that while the performance of individual stocks is highly unpredictable, *portfolios* of the best-performing stocks in the recent past appear to outperform other stocks with enough reliability to offer profit opportunities. Thus, it appears that there is evidence of short- to intermediate-horizon price momentum in both the aggregate market and cross-sectionally (i.e., across particular stocks).

**Returns over Long Horizons.** Although studies of short-horizon returns have detected momentum in stock market prices, tests[11] of long-horizon returns (i.e., returns over multiyear periods) have found suggestions of pronounced *negative* long-term serial correlation in the performance of the aggregate market. The latter result has given rise to a "fads hypothesis," which asserts that the stock market might overreact to relevant news. Such overreaction leads to positive serial correlation (momentum) over short time horizons. Subsequent correction of the overreaction leads to poor performance following good performance and vice versa. The corrections mean that a run of positive returns eventually will tend to be followed by negative returns, leading to negative serial correlation over longer horizons. These episodes of apparent overshooting followed by correction gives the stock market the appearance of fluctuating around its fair value.

These long-horizon results are dramatic, but the studies offer far from conclusive evidence regarding efficient markets. First, the study results need not be interpreted as evidence for stock market fads. An alternative interpretation of these results holds that they indicate only that the market risk premium varies over time. For example, when the risk premium and the required return on the market rises, stock prices will fall. When the market then rises (on average) at this higher rate of return, the data convey the impression of a stock price recovery. The impression of overshooting and correction is in fact no more than a rational response of market prices to changes in discount rates.

In addition to studies suggestive of overreaction in overall stock market returns over long horizons, many other studies suggest that over long horizons, extreme performance in particular securities also tends to reverse itself: The stocks that have performed best in the recent past seem to underperform the rest of the market in following periods, while the worst past performers tend to offer above-average future performance. DeBondt and Thaler[12] and Chopra, Lakonishok, and Ritter[13] find strong tendencies for poorly performing stocks in one period to experience sizable reversals over the subsequent period, while the best-performing stocks in a given period tend to follow with poor performance in the following period.

For example, the DeBondt and Thaler study found that if one were to rank order the performance of stocks over a 5-year period and then group stocks into portfolios based on investment performance, the base-period "loser" portfolio (defined as the 35 stocks with the worst investment performance) outperformed the "winner" portfolio (the top 35 stocks) by

[10] Narasimhan Jegadeesh and Sheridan Titman, "Returns to Buying Winners and Selling Losers: Implications for Stock Market Efficiency," *Journal of Finance* 48 (March 1993), pp. 65–91.

[11] Eugene F. Fama and Kenneth R. French, "Permanent and Temporary Components of Stock Prices," *Journal of Political Economy* 96 (April 1988), pp. 24–73; James Poterba and Lawrence Summers, "Mean Reversion in Stock Prices: Evidence and Implications," *Journal of Financial Economics* 22 (October 1988), pp. 27–59.

[12] Werner F. M. DeBondt and Richard Thaler, "Does the Stock Market Overreact?" *Journal of Finance* 40 (1985), pp. 793–805.

[13] Navin Chopra, Josef Lakonishok, and Jay R. Ritter, "Measuring Abnormal Performance: Do Stocks Overreact?" *Journal of Financial Economics* 31 (1992), pp. 235–68.

an average of 25% (cumulative return) in the following 3-year period. This **reversal effect**, in which losers rebound and winners fade back, suggests that the stock market overreacts to relevant news. After the overreaction is recognized, extreme investment performance is reversed. This phenomenon would imply that a *contrarian* investment strategy—investing in recent losers and avoiding recent winners—should be profitable.

It would be hard to explain apparent overreaction in the cross section of stocks by appealing to time-varying risk premiums. Moreover, these returns seem pronounced enough to be exploited profitably.

Thus it appears that there may be short-run momentum but long-run reversal patterns in price behavior both for the market as a whole and across sectors of the market. One interpretation of this pattern is that short-run overreaction (which causes momentum in prices) may lead to long-term reversals (when the market recognizes its past error). This interpretation is emphasized by Haugen.[14]

### Predictors of Broad Market Returns

Several studies have documented the ability of easily observed variables to predict market returns. For example, Fama and French[15] showed that the return on the aggregate stock market tends to be higher when the dividend/price ratio, the dividend yield, is high. Campbell and Shiller[16] found that the earnings yield can predict market returns. Keim and Stambaugh[17] showed that bond market data such as the spread between yields on high- and low-grade corporate bonds also help predict broad market returns.

Again, the interpretation of these results is difficult. On the one hand, they may imply that stock returns can be predicted, in violation of the efficient market hypothesis. More probably, however, these variables are proxying for variation in the market risk premium. For example, given a level of dividends or earnings, stock prices will be lower and dividend and earnings yields will be higher when the risk premium (and therefore the expected market return) is higher. Thus a high dividend or earnings yield will be associated with higher market returns. This does not indicate a violation of market efficiency. The predictability of market returns is due to predictability in the risk premium, not in risk-adjusted abnormal returns.

Fama and French[18] showed that the yield spread between high- and low-grade bonds has greater predictive power for returns on low-grade bonds than for returns on high-grade bonds, and greater predictive power for stock returns than for bond returns, suggesting that the predictability in returns is in fact a risk premium rather than evidence of market inefficiency. Similarly, the fact that the dividend yield on stocks helps to predict bond market returns suggests that the yield captures a risk premium common to both markets rather than mispricing in the equity market.

### Semistrong Tests: Market Anomalies

Fundamental analysis uses a much wider range of information to create portfolios than does technical analysis. Investigations of the efficacy of fundamental analysis ask whether publicly available information beyond the

---

[14] Robert A. Haugen, *The New Finance: The Case against Efficient Markets* (Englewood Cliffs, NJ: Prentice Hall, 1995).

[15] Eugene F. Fama and Kenneth R. French, "Dividend Yields and Expected Stock Returns," *Journal of Financial Economics* 22 (October 1988), pp. 3–25.

[16] John Y. Campbell and Robert Shiller, "Stock Prices, Earnings and Expected Dividends," *Journal of Finance* 43 (July 1988), pp. 661–76.

[17] Donald B. Keim and Robert F. Stambaugh, "Predicting Returns in the Stock and Bond Markets," *Journal of Financial Economics* 17 (1986), pp. 357–90.

[18] Eugene F. Fama and Kenneth R. French, "Business Conditions and Expected Returns on Stocks and Bonds," *Journal of Financial Economics* 25 (November 1989), pp. 3–22.

trading history of a security can be used to improve investment performance, and therefore are tests of semistrong-form market efficiency. Surprisingly, several easily accessible statistics, for example a stock's price-earnings ratio or its market capitalization, seem to predict abnormal risk-adjusted returns. Findings such as these, which we will review in the following pages, are difficult to reconcile with the efficient market hypothesis, and therefore are often referred to as efficient market **anomalies.**

A difficulty in interpreting these tests is that we usually need to adjust for portfolio risk before evaluating the success of an investment strategy. Many tests, for example, use the CAPM to adjust for risk. However, we know that even if beta is a relevant descriptor of stock risk, the empirically measured quantitative trade-off between risk as measured by beta and expected return differs from the predictions of the CAPM. (We review this evidence in the next chapter.) If we use the CAPM to adjust portfolio returns for risk, inappropriate adjustments may lead to the conclusion that various portfolio strategies can generate superior returns, when in fact it simply is the risk adjustment procedure that has failed.

Another way to put this is to note that tests of risk-adjusted returns are *joint tests* of the efficient market hypothesis *and* the risk adjustment procedure. If it appears that a portfolio strategy can generate superior returns, we must then choose between rejecting the EMH and rejecting the risk adjustment technique. Usually, the risk adjustment technique is based on more-questionable assumptions than is the EMH; by opting to reject the procedure, we are left with no conclusion about market efficiency.

An example of this issue is the discovery by Basu[19] that portfolios of low price-earnings (P/E) ratio stocks have higher returns than do high P/E portfolios. The **P/E effect** holds up even if returns are adjusted for portfolio beta. Is this a confirmation that the market systematically misprices stocks according to P/E ratio? This would be an extremely surprising and, to us, disturbing conclusion, because analysis of P/E ratios is such a simple procedure. Although it may be possible to earn superior returns by using hard work and much insight, it hardly seems possible that such a simplistic technique is enough to generate abnormal returns.

One possible interpretation of these results is that the model of capital market equilibrium is at fault in that the returns are not properly adjusted for risk. This makes sense, because if two firms have the same expected earnings, then the riskier stock will sell at a lower price and lower P/E ratio. Because of its higher risk, the low P/E stock also will have higher expected returns. Therefore, unless the CAPM beta fully adjusts for risk, P/E will act as a useful additional descriptor of risk, and will be associated with abnormal returns if the CAPM is used to establish benchmark performance.

**The Small-Firm-in-January Effect.** The so-called size or **small-firm effect**, originally documented by Banz,[20] is illustrated in Figure 12.5. It shows the historical performance of portfolios formed by dividing the NYSE stocks into 10 portfolios each year according to firm size (i.e., the total value of outstanding equity). Average annual returns are consistently higher on the small-firm portfolios. The difference in average annual return between portfolio 10 (with the largest firms) and portfolio 1 (with the smallest firms) is 8.59%. Of course, the smaller-firm portfolios tend to be riskier. But even when returns are

---

[19] Sanjoy Basu, "The Investment Performance of Common Stocks in Relation to Their Price-Earnings Ratios: A Test of the Efficient Market Hypothesis," *Journal of Finance* 32 (June 1977), pp. 663–82; and "The Relationship between Earnings Yield, Market Value, and Return for NYSE Common Stocks: Further Evidence," *Journal of Financial Economics* 12 (June 1983).

[20] Rolf Banz, "The Relationship between Return and Market Value of Common Stocks," *Journal of Financial Economics* 9 (March 1981).

**Figure 12.5**
**Returns in excess of risk-free rate and in excess of the Security Market Line for 10 size-based portfolios, 1926–2000**

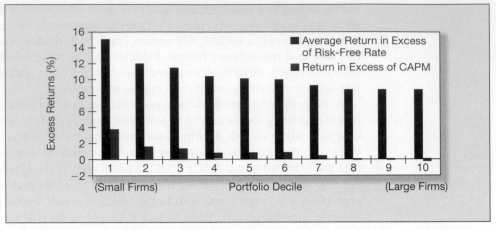

Source: *Stocks, Bonds, Bills, and Inflation 2000 Yearbook*, Ibbotson Associates, 2000.

adjusted for risk using the CAPM, there is still a consistent premium for the smaller-sized portfolios. Even on a risk-adjusted basis, the smallest-size portfolio outperforms the largest-firm portfolio by an average of 4.3% annually.

This is a huge premium; imagine earning a premium of this size on a billion-dollar portfolio. Yet it is remarkable that following a simple (even simplistic) rule such as "invest in low-capitalization stocks" should enable an investor to earn excess returns. After all, any investor can measure firm size at little cost. One would not expect such minimal effort to yield such large rewards.

Later studies (Keim,[21] Reinganum,[22] and Blume and Stambaugh[23]) showed that the small-firm effect occurs virtually entirely in January, in fact, in the first 2 weeks of January. The size effect is in fact a "small-firm-in-January" effect.

Some researchers believe that the January effect is tied to tax-loss selling at the end of the year. The hypothesis is that many people sell stocks that have declined in price during the previous months to realize their capital losses before the end of the tax year. Such investors do not put the proceeds from these sales back into the stock market until after the turn of the year. At that point the rush of demand for stock places an upward pressure on prices that results in the January effect. Indeed, Ritter[24] showed that the ratio of stock purchases to sales of individual investors reaches an annual low at the end of December and an annual high at the beginning of January.

The January effect is said to show up most dramatically for the smallest firms because the small-firm group includes, as an empirical matter, stocks with the greatest variability of prices during the year. The group therefore includes a relatively large number of firms that have declined sufficiently to induce tax-loss selling.

Still, this theory is unsatisfying. First, if the positive January effect is a manifestation of buying pressure, it should be matched by a symmetric negative December effect when the

---

[21] Donald B. Keim, "Size Related Anomalies and Stock Return Seasonality: Further Empirical Evidence," *Journal of Financial Economics* 12 (June 1983).

[22] Marc R. Reinganum, "The Anomalous Stock Market Behavior of Small Firms in January: Empirical Tests for Tax-Loss Effects," *Journal of Financial Economics* 12 (June 1983).

[23] Marshall E. Blume and Robert F. Stambaugh, "Biases in Computed Returns: An Application to the Size Effect," *Journal of Financial Economics*, 1983.

[24] Jay R. Ritter, "The Buying and Selling Behavior of Individual Investors at the Turn of the Year," *Journal of Finance* 43 (July 1988), pp. 701–17.

tax-loss incentives induce selling pressure. Second, if investors who do not already hold these firms know that January will bring abnormal returns to the small-firm group, they should rush to purchase stock in December to capture those returns. This would push buying pressure from January to December. Rational investors should not "allow" such predictable abnormal January returns to persist.

**The Neglected-Firm Effect and Liquidity Effects.** Arbel and Strebel[25] gave another interpretation of the small-firm-in-January effect. Because small firms tend to be neglected by large institutional traders, information about smaller firms is less available. This information deficiency makes smaller firms riskier investments that command higher returns. "Brand-name" firms, after all, are subject to considerable monitoring from institutional investors, which promises high-quality information, and presumably investors do not purchase "generic" stocks without the prospect of greater returns.

As evidence for the **neglected-firm effect**, Arbel[26] divided firms into highly researched, moderately researched, and neglected groups based on the number of institutions holding the stock. The January effect was in fact largest for the neglected firms. An article by Merton[27] shows that neglected firms might be expected to earn higher equilibrium returns as compensation for the risk associated with limited information. In this sense the neglected firm premium is not strictly a market inefficiency, but is a type of risk premium.

Work by Amihud and Mendelson[28] on the effect of liquidity on stock returns might be related to both the small-firm and neglected-firm effects. They argue that investors will demand a rate-of-return premium to invest in less-liquid stocks that entail higher trading costs. (See Chapter 9 for more details.) Indeed, spreads for the least-liquid stocks easily can be more than 5% of stock value. In accord with their hypothesis, Amihud and Mendelson showed that these stocks show a strong tendency to exhibit abnormally high risk-adjusted rates of return. Because small and less-analyzed stocks as a rule are less liquid, the liquidity effect might be a partial explanation of their abnormal returns. However, this theory does not explain why the abnormal returns of small firms should be concentrated in January. In any case, exploiting these effects can be more difficult than it would appear. The high trading costs on small stocks can easily wipe out any apparent abnormal profit opportunity.

**Book-to-Market Ratios.** Fama and French[29] and Reinganum[30] showed that a powerful predictor of returns across securities is the ratio of the book value of the firm's equity to the market value of equity. Fama and French stratified firms into 10 groups according to book-to-market ratios and examined the average monthly rate of return of each of the 10 groups during the period July 1963 through December 1990. The decile with the highest book-to-market ratio had an average monthly return of 1.65%, while the lowest-ratio decile averaged only .72% per month. Figure 12.6 shows the pattern of returns across deciles. The dramatic dependence of returns on book-to-market ratio is independent of beta, suggesting either that high book-to-market ratio firms are relatively underpriced, or

[25] Avner Arbel and Paul J. Strebel, "Pay Attention to Neglected Firms," *Journal of Portfolio Management*, Winter 1983.

[26] Avner Arbel, "Generic Stocks: An Old Product in a New Package," *Journal of Portfolio Management*, Summer 1985.

[27] Robert C. Merton, "A Simple Model of Capital Market Equilibrium with Incomplete Information," *Journal of Finance* 42 (1987), pp. 483–510.

[28] Yakov Amihud and Haim Mendelson, "Asset Pricing and the Bid–Ask Spread," *Journal of Financial Economics* 17 (December 1986), pp. 223–50; and "Liquidity, Asset Prices, and Financial Policy," *Financial Analysts Journal* 47 (November/December 1991), pp. 56–66.

[29] Eugene F. Fama and Kenneth R. French, "The Cross Section of Expected Stock Returns," *Journal of Finance* 47 (1992), pp. 427–65

[30] Marc R. Reinganum, "The Anatomy of a Stock Market Winner," *Financial Analysts Journal*, March–April 1988, pp. 272–84.

**Figure 12.6 Average rate of return as a function of the book-to-market ratio**

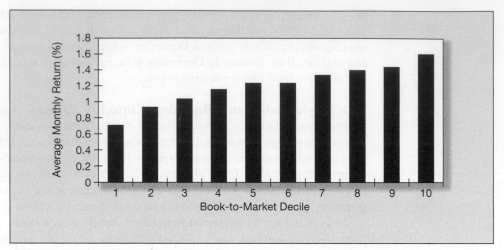

Source: Eugene F. Fama and Kenneth R. French, "The Cross Section of Expected Stock Returns," *Journal of Finance* 47 (1992), pp. 427–65.

that the book-to-market ratio is serving as a proxy for a risk factor that affects equilibrium expected returns.

In fact, Fama and French found that after controlling for the size and **book-to-market effects**, beta seemed to have no power to explain average security returns.[31] This finding is an important challenge to the notion of rational markets, since it seems to imply that a factor that should affect returns—systematic risk—seems not to matter, while a factor that should not matter—the book-to-market ratio—seems capable of predicting future returns. We will return to the interpretation of this anomaly.

**Post–Earnings-Announcement Price Drift.** A fundamental principle of efficient markets is that any new information ought to be reflected in stock prices very rapidly. When good news is made public, for example, the stock price should jump immediately. A puzzling anomaly, therefore, is the apparently sluggish response of stock prices to firms' earnings announcements.

The "news content" of an earnings announcement can be evaluated by comparing the announcement of actual earnings to the value previously expected by market participants. The difference is the "earnings surprise." (Market expectations of earnings can be roughly measured by averaging the published earnings forecasts of Wall Street analysts or by applying trend analysis to past earnings.) Foster, Olsen, and Shevlin[32] have examined the impact of earnings announcements on stock returns.

Each earnings announcement for a large sample of firms was placed in 1 of 10 deciles ranked by the magnitude of the earnings surprise, and the abnormal returns of the stock in

---

[31] However, a study by S. P. Kothari, Jay Shanken, and Richard G. Sloan, "Another Look at the Cross-Section of Expected Stock Returns," *Journal of Finance* 50 (March 1995), pp. 185–224, finds that when betas are estimated using annual rather than monthly returns, securities with high beta values do in fact have higher average returns. Moreover, the authors find a book-to-market effect that is attenuated compared to the results in Fama and French and furthermore is inconsistent across different samples of securities. They conclude that the empirical case for the importance of the book-to-market ratio may be somewhat weaker than the Fama and French study would suggest.

[32] George Foster, Chris Olsen, and Terry Shevlin, "Earnings Releases, Anomalies, and the Behavior of Securities Returns," *Accounting Review* 59 (October 1984).

**Figure 12.7
Cumulative
abnormal returns
in response
to earnings
announcements**

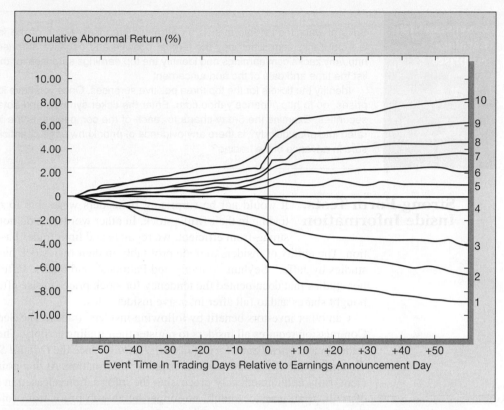

Source: George Foster, Chris Olsen, and Terry Shevlin, "Earnings Releases, Anomalies, and the Behavior of Security Returns,"
*Accounting Review* 59 (October 1984).

each decile were calculated. The abnormal return in a period is the return of a portfolio of
all stocks in a given decile after adjusting for both the market return in that period and the
portfolio beta. It measures return over and above what would be expected given market
conditions in that period. Figure 12.7 is a graph of the cumulative abnormal returns for
each decile.

The results of this study are dramatic. The correlation between ranking by earnings surprise and abnormal returns across deciles is as predicted. There is a large abnormal return
(a large increase in cumulative abnormal return) on the earnings announcement day (time
0). The abnormal return is positive for positive-surprise firms and negative for negative-
surprise firms.

The more remarkable, and interesting, result of the study concerns stock price movement *after* the announcement date. The cumulative abnormal returns of positive-surprise
stocks continue to rise—in other words, exhibit momentum—even after the earnings information becomes public, while the negative-surprise firms continue to suffer negative abnormal returns. The market appears to adjust to the earnings information only gradually,
resulting in a sustained period of abnormal returns.

Evidently, one could have earned abnormal profits simply by waiting for earnings announcements and purchasing a stock portfolio of positive-earnings-surprise companies.
These are precisely the types of predictable continuing trends that ought to be impossible
in an efficient market.

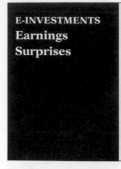

Several websites list information on earnings surprises. Much of the information supplied is from Zacks.com. Each day the largest positive and negative surprises are listed. Go to http://my.zacks.com/earnings and identify the top earnings surprises for the day. The table will list the time and date of the announcement.

Identify the tickers for the top three positive surprises. Once you have identified the top surprises, go to http://finance.yahoo.com. Enter the ticker symbols and obtain quotes for these securities. Examine the 5-day charts for each of the companies. Is the information incorporated into price quickly? Is there any evidence of prior knowledge or anticipation of the disclosure in advance of the trading?

## Strong-Form Tests: Inside Information

It would not be surprising if insiders were able to make superior profits trading in their firm's stock. In other words, we do not expect markets to be strong-from efficient; we regulate and limit trades based on inside information. The ability of insiders to trade profitably in their own stock has been documented in studies by Jaffe,[33] Seyhun,[34] Givoly and Palmon,[35] and others. Jaffe's was one of the earlier studies that documented the tendency for stock prices to rise after insiders intensively bought shares and to fall after intensive insider sales.

Can other investors benefit by following insiders' trades? The Securities and Exchange Commission requires all insiders to register their trading activity. The SEC publishes these trades in an *Official Summary of Insider Trading*. Once the *Official Summary* is published, the knowledge of the trades becomes public information. At that point, if markets are efficient, fully and immediately processing the information released in the *Official Summary* of trading, an investor should no longer be able to profit from following the pattern of those trades.

The study by Seyhun, which carefully tracked the public release dates of the *Official Summary*, found that following insider transactions would be to no avail. Although there is some tendency for stock prices to increase even after the *Official Summary* reports insider buying, the abnormal returns are not of sufficient magnitude to overcome transaction costs.

## Interpreting the Evidence

How should we interpret the ever-growing anomalies literature? Does it imply that markets are grossly inefficient, allowing for simplistic trading rules to offer large profit opportunities? Or are there other, more-subtle interpretations?

**Risk Premiums or Inefficiencies?**  The price-earnings, small-firm, market-to-book, momentum, and long-term reversal effects are currently among the most puzzling phenomena in empirical finance. There are several interpretations of these effects. First note that to some extent, some of these phenomena may be related. The feature that small firms, low-market-to-book firms, and recent "losers" seem to have in common is a stock price that has fallen considerably in recent months or years. Indeed, a firm can become a small firm or a low-market-to-book firm by suffering a sharp drop in price. These groups therefore may contain a relatively high proportion of distressed firms that have suffered recent difficulties.

[33] Jeffrey F. Jaffe, "Special Information and Insider Trading," *Journal of Business* 47 (July 1974).

[34] H. Nejat Seyhun, "Insiders' Profits, Costs of Trading and Market Efficiency," *Journal of Financial Economics* 16 (1986).

[35] Dan Givoly and Dan Palmon, "Insider Trading and Exploitation of Inside Information: Some Empirical Evidence," *Journal of Business* 58 (1985).

Fama and French[36] argue that these effects can be explained as manifestations of risk premiums. Using an arbitrage pricing type of model they show that stocks with higher "betas" (also known as factor loadings) on size or market-to-book factors have higher average returns; they interpret these returns as evidence of a risk premium associated with the factor. Fama and French propose a *three-factor model*, in the spirit of arbitrage pricing theory. Risk is determined by the sensitivity of a stock to three factors: (1) the market portfolio, (2) a portfolio that reflects the relative returns of small versus large firms, and (3) a portfolio that reflects the relative returns of firms with high versus low ratios of book value to market value. This model does a good job in explaining security returns. While size or book-to-market ratios per se are obviously not risk factors, they perhaps might act as proxies for more fundamental determinants of risk. Fama and French argue that these patterns of returns may therefore be consistent with an efficient market in which expected returns are consistent with risk. We examine this paper in more detail in the next chapter.

The opposite interpretation is offered by Lakonishok, Shleifer, and Vishney,[37] who argue that these phenomena are evidence of inefficient markets, more specifically, of systematic errors in the forecasts of stock analysts. They believe that analysts extrapolate past performance too far into the future, and therefore overprice firms with recent good performance and underprice firms with recent poor performance. Ultimately, when market participants recognize their errors, prices reverse. This explanation is consistent with the reversal effect and also, to a degree, is consistent with the small-firm and book-to-market effects because firms with sharp price drops may tend to be small or have high book-to-market ratios.

If Lakonishok, Shleifer, and Vishney are correct, we ought to find that analysts systematically err when forecasting returns of recent "winner" versus "loser" firms. A study by La Porta[38] is consistent with this pattern. He finds that equity of firms for which analysts predict low growth rates of earnings actually perform better than those with high expected earnings growth. Analysts seem overly pessimistic about firms with low growth prospects and overly optimistic about firms with high growth prospects. When these too-extreme expectations are "corrected," the low-expected-growth firms outperform high-expected-growth firms.

Daniel and Titman[39] attempt to test whether the size and book-to-market effects can in fact be explained as risk premia. They classify firms according to size and book-to-market ratio, and further stratify portfolios based on the betas of each stock on size and book-to-market factors. They find that once size and book-to-market ratio are held fixed, the betas on these factors do not add any additional information about expected returns. They conclude that the characteristics per se, and not the betas on the size or book-to-market factors, influence returns. This result is inconsistent with the Fama-French interpretation that the high returns on these portfolios may reflect risk premia.

The Daniel and Titman results do not *necessarily* imply irrational markets. As noted, it might be that these characteristics per se measure a distressed condition that itself commands a return premium. Moreover, as we have noted, a good part of these apparently abnormal returns may be reflective of an illiquidity premium since small and low-priced firms tend to have bigger bid–asked spreads. Nevertheless, a compelling explanation of these results has yet to be offered.

[36] Eugene F. Fama and Kenneth R. French, "Common Risk Factors in the Returns on Stocks and Bonds," *Journal of Financial Economics* 33 (1993), pp. 3–56.

[37] Josef Lakonishok, Andrei Shleifer, and Robert W. Vishney, "Contrarian Investment, Extrapolation, and Risk," *Journal of Finance* 50 (1995), pp. 541–78.

[38] Raphael La Porta, "Expectations and the Cross Section of Stock Returns," *Journal of Finance* 51 (December 1996), pp. 1715–42.

[39] Kent Daniel and Sheridan Titman, "Evidence of the Characteristics of Cross Sectional Variation in Common Stock Returns," *Journal of Finance* 40 (1995), pp. 383–99.

**Anomalies or Data Mining?**  We have covered many of the so-called anomalies cited in the literature, but our list could go on and on. Some wonder whether these anomalies are really unexplained puzzles in financial markets, or whether they instead are an artifact of data mining. After all, if one reruns the computer database of past returns over and over and examines stock returns along enough dimensions, simple chance will cause some criteria to *appear* to predict returns.

In this regard, it is noteworthy that some anomalies have not shown much staying power after being reported in the academic literature. For example, after the small-firm effect was published in the early 1980s, it promptly disappeared for much of the rest of the decade. Similarly, the book-to-market strategy, which commanded considerable attention in the early 1990s, was ineffective for the rest of that decade.

Still, even acknowledging the potential for data mining, a common thread seems to run through many of the anomalies we have considered, lending support to the notion that there is a real puzzle to explain. Value stocks—defined by low P/E ratio, high book-to-market ratio, or depressed prices relative to historic levels—seem to have provided higher average returns than "glamour" or growth stocks.

One way to address the problem of data mining is to find a data set that has not already been researched and see whether the relationship in question shows up in the new data. Such studies have revealed size, momentum, and book-to-market effects in other security markets around the world. While these phenomena may be a manifestation of a systematic risk premium, the precise nature of that risk is not fully understood.

## 12.5    A BEHAVIORAL INTERPRETATION

The premise of **behavioral finance** is that conventional financial theory ignores how real people make decisions and that people make a difference.[40] A growing number of economists have come to interpret the anomalies literature as consistent with several "irrationalities" individuals exhibit when making complicated decisions. These irrationalities stem from two main premises: first, that investors do not always process information correctly and therefore infer incorrect probability distributions about future rates of return; and second, that even given a probability distribution of returns, investors often make inconsistent or systematically suboptimal decisions.

Of course, the existence of irrational investors would not by itself be sufficient to render capital markets inefficient. If such irrationalities did affect prices, then sharp-eyed arbitrageurs taking advantage of profit opportunities might be expected to push prices back to their proper values. Thus, the second leg of the behavioral critique is that in practice the actions of such arbitrageurs are limited.

This leg of the argument is important when we interpret tests of market efficiency. Virtually everyone agrees that if prices are right (i.e., price = intrinsic value), then there are no easy profit opportunities. But the reverse is not necessarily true. If behaviorists are correct about limits to arbitrage activity, then the absence of profit opportunities does not necessarily imply that markets are efficient. Most tests of the efficient market hypothesis have

---

[40] The discussion in this section is based on two excellent survey articles: Nicholas Barberis and Richard Thaler, "A Survey of Behavioral Finance," forthcoming in the *Handbook of the Economics of Finance*, eds. G. Constantinides, M. Harris, and R. Stulz; and W. F. M. De Bondt and R. H. Thaler, "Financial Decision Making in Markets and Firms," in *Handbooks in Operations Research and Management Science, Volume 9: Finance*, eds. R. A. Jarrow, V. Maksimovic, W. T. Ziemba (Amsterdam, Elsevier: 1995).

focused on the existence of profit opportunities, often as reflected in the performance of money managers. But their failure to perform well (see Chapter 4 and the next section) need not imply that markets are in fact efficient.

We will examine some of the information-processing and behavioral irrationalities documented by psychologists and show how these tendencies might be consistent with the anomalies discussed earlier in this chapter. We will then briefly consider limits to arbitrage, and finally evaluate the import of the behavioral debate.

## Information Processing

Errors in information processing can lead investors to misestimate the true probabilities of possible events or associated rates or return. Several such biases have been catalogued. Here are four of the more important ones.

**Forecasting Errors.** A series of experiments by Kahneman and Tversky[41] indicates that people give too much weight to recent experience compared to prior beliefs when making forecasts (sometimes dubbed a *memory bias*) and tend to make forecasts that are too extreme given the uncertainty inherent in their information. DeBondt and Thaler[42] argue that the P/E effect can be explained by earnings expectations that are too extreme. In this view, when forecasts of a firm's future earnings are high, perhaps due to favorable recent performance, they tend to be *too* high relative to the objective prospects of the firm. This results in a high initial P/E (due to the optimism built into the stock price) and poor subsequent performance when investors recognize their error. Thus, high P/E firms tend to be poor investments.

**Overconfidence.** People tend to overestimate the precision of their beliefs or forecasts, and they tend to overestimate their abilities. In one famous survey, 90% of drivers in Sweden ranked themselves as better-than-average drivers. Such overconfidence may be responsible for the prevalence of active versus passive investment management—itself an anomaly to an adherent of the efficient market hypothesis. Despite the recent growth in indexing, less than 10% of the equity in the mutual fund industry is held in indexed accounts. The dominance of active management in the face of the typical underperformance of such strategies (consider the disappointing performance of actively managed mutual funds documented in Chapter 4 as well as in the following section) is consistent with a tendency to overestimate ability.

An interesting example of overconfidence in financial markets is provided by Barber and Odean,[43] who compare trading activity and average returns in brokerage accounts of men and women. They find that men (in particular single men) trade far more actively than women, consistent with the greater overconfidence among men well-documented in the psychology literature. They also find that high trading activity is highly predictive of poor investment performance. The top 20% of accounts ranked by portfolio turnover had average returns 7 percentage points lower than the 20% of the accounts with the lowest turnover rates. As they conclude, "Trading [and by implication, overconfidence] is hazardous to your wealth."

---

[41] D. Kahneman and A. Tversky, "On the Psychology of Prediction," *Psychology Review* 80 (1973), pp. 237–51; and "Subjective Probability: A Judgment of Representativeness," *Cognitive Psychology* 3 (1972), pp. 430–54.
[42] W. F. M. DeBondt and R. H. Thaler, "Do Security Analysts Overreact?" *American Economic Review* 80 (1990), pp. 52–57.
[43] Brad Barber and Terrance Odean, "Boys Will Be Boys: Gender, Overconfidence, and Common Stock Investment," *Quarterly Journal of Economics* 16 (2001), pp. 262–92, and "Trading is Hazardous to your Wealth: The Common Stock Investment Performance of Individual Investors," *Journal of Finance* 55 (2000), pp. 773–806.

**Conservatism.**   A conservatism bias means that investors are too slow (too conservative) in updating their beliefs in response to recent evidence. This means that they might initially underreact to news about a firm, so that prices will fully reflect new information only gradually. Such a bias would give rise to momentum in stock market returns.

**Sample Size Neglect and Representativeness.**   It seems that people commonly do not take into account the size of a sample, apparently reasoning that a small sample is just as representative of a population as a large one. They may therefore infer a pattern too quickly based on a small sample and extrapolate apparent trends too far into the future. It is easy to see how such a pattern would be consistent with overreaction and correction anomalies. A short-lived run of good earnings reports or high returns on a stock would lead such investors to revise their assessments of likely future performance, and thus generate buying pressure that exaggerates the price run-up. Eventually, the gap between price and intrinsic value becomes glaring and the market corrects its initial error.

Interestingly, there is evidence[44] that stocks with the best recent performance show reversals precisely in the few days surrounding earnings announcements, suggesting that the correction occurs just as investors learn that their initial beliefs were too extreme. Combining the conservatism and representativeness biases, we can obtain a pattern of short-to-middle–term momentum, along with long-term reversals, broadly consistent with much of the literature.

**Behavioral Biases**   Even if information processing were perfect, individuals might make less-than-fully rational decisions using that information. These behavioral biases largely affect how investors frame questions of risk versus return and therefore make risk–return trade-offs.

**Framing.**   Decisions seem to be affected by how choices are framed. For example, famous studies by Kahneman and Tversky[45] find an individual may reject a bet when it is posed in terms of the risk surrounding possible gains but may accept that same bet when described in terms of the risk surrounding potential losses. In other words, individuals may act risk-averse in terms of gains but risk-seeking in terms of losses. But in many cases, the choice of how to frame a risky venture—as involving gains or losses—can be arbitrary.

**EXAMPLE 12.5    Framing**

Consider a coin toss with a payoff of $50 for tails. Now consider a gift of $50 that is bundled with a bet that imposes a loss of $50 if the coin comes up heads. In both cases, you end up with zero for heads, and $50 for tails. But the former description frames the coin toss as posing a risky gain while the latter frames the coin toss in terms of risky losses. The difference in framing can lead to different attitudes toward the bet.

**Mental Accounting.**   Mental accounting is a specific form of framing in which people segregate certain decisions. For example, an investor may take a lot of risk with one investment account but establish a very conservative position with another account that is

---

[44] N. Chopra, J. Lakonishok, and J. Ritter, "Measuring Abnormal Performance: Do Stocks Overreact?" *Journal of Financial Economics* 31 (1992), pp. 235-68.

[45] D. Kahneman and A. Tversky, "Prospect Theory: An Analysis of Choice Under Risk," *Econometrica* 47 (March 1979), pp. 263–91.

dedicated to her child's education. Rationally, it might be better to view both accounts as part of the investor's overall portfolio with the risk-return profiles of each integrated into a unified framework. Statman[46] argues that mental accounting is consistent with some investors' irrational preference for stocks with high cash dividends (they feel free to spend dividend income, but would not "dip into capital" by selling a few shares of another stock with the same total rate of return) and with a tendency to ride losing stock positions for too long (since "behavioral investors" are reluctant to realize losses). Odean[47] documents that investors are more likely to sell stocks with gains than those with losses, precisely contrary to a tax-minimization strategy.

Mental accounting effects also can help explain momentum in stock prices. The "house money effect" refers to gamblers' greater willingness to accept new bets if they currently are ahead. They think of (i.e., frame) the bet as being made with their "winnings account," that is, with the casino's and not with their own money, and thus are more willing to accept risk. Analogously, after a stock market run-up, they view investments as largely funded out of a "capital gains account," become more tolerant of risk, discount future cash flows at a lower rate, and thus further push up prices.

**Regret Avoidance.**  Psychologists have found that individuals who make decisions that turn out badly have more regret (blame themselves more) when that decision was more unconventional. For example, buying a blue-chip portfolio that turns down is not as painful as experiencing the same losses on an unknown start-up firm. Any losses on the blue-chip stocks can be more easily attributed to bad luck rather than bad decision-making and cause less regret. De Bondt and Thaler[48] argue that such regret avoidance is consistent with both the size and book-to-market effect. Higher book-to-market firms tend to have lower stock prices. These firms are "out of favor" and more likely to be in a financially precarious position. Similarly, smaller less-well-known firms are also less conventional investments. Such firms require more "courage" on the part of the investor, which increases the required rate of return. Mental accounting can add to this effect. If investors focus on the gains or losses of individual stocks, rather than on broad portfolios, then they can become more risk-averse concerning stocks with recent poor performance, discount their cash flows at a higher rate, and thereby create a "value stock risk premium."

**Limits to Arbitrage**  These behavioral biases would not matter for stock pricing if rational investors could fully profit from the mistakes of behavioral investors. As soon as prices went out of alignment, rational profit-seeking trading would re-establish proper pricing. However, behavioral advocates argue that in practice, several factors limit the ability to profit from mispricing.[49]

**Fundamental Risk.**  Suppose that a share of IBM is underpriced. Buying it may present a profit opportunity, but it is hardly risk-free, since the presumed market underpricing can get worse. While price eventually should converge to intrinsic value, this may not

[46] Meir Statman, "Behavioral Finance," *Contemporary Finance Digest* 1 (Winter 1997), pp. 5–22.

[47] T. Odean, "Are Investors Reluctant to Realize their Losses," *Journal of Finance* 53 (1998), pp. 1775–98.

[48] W. F. M. DeBondt and R. H. Thaler, "Further Evidence on Investor Overreaction and Stock Market Seasonality," *Journal of Finance* 42 (1987), pp. 557–81.

[49] Some of the more influential references on limits to arbitrage are: J. Bradford De Long, Andrei Shleifer, Lawrence H. Summers, and Robert J. Waldmann, "Noise Trader Risk in Financial Markets," *Journal of Political Economy* 98 (August 1990), pp. 704–38; Andrei Shleifer and Robert W. Vishny, "Equilibrium Short Horizons of Investors and Firms," *American Economic Review* 80 (May 1990), pp. 148–53; and Andrei Shleifer and Robert W. Vishny, "The Limits of Arbitrage," *Journal of Finance* 52 (March 1997), pp. 35–55.

happen until after the investor's investment horizon. For example, the investor may be a mutual fund manager who may lose clients (not to mention a job) if short-term performance is poor or a trader who may run through her capital if the market turns against her even temporarily. Risk incurred in exploiting the apparent profit opportunity presumably will limit both the activity and effectiveness of these arbitrage traders.

**Implementation Costs.** Exploiting overpricing can be particularly difficult. Short selling a security entails costs; short-sellers may have to return the borrowed security on little notice, rendering the horizon of the short sale uncertain; and some investors such as pension or mutual fund managers are simply not allowed to short securities. This can limit the ability of arbitrage activity to force prices to fair value. For example, Pontiff[50] demonstrates that deviations of price from net asset value in closed-end funds tend to be higher in funds that are more costly to arbitrage, for example those with high nonsystematic risk, making it difficult to hedge the risk incurred by taking a position in the fund. On the other hand, Ross[51] illustrates that premiums and discounts on closed-end funds can be explained in a "rational framework." Initial expectations of abnormal returns due to skilled management can drive price above net asset value. But management fees that reduce investors' net returns can drive price below the net asset value of the portfolio.

**Model Risk.** One always has to worry that an apparent profit opportunity is more apparent than real. Perhaps you are using a faulty model to value the security, and the price actually is right. This possibility, again, makes the trading activity risky and limits the extent to which it will be pursued.

## Evaluating the Behavioral Critique

The efficient market hypothesis implies that prices usually "are right" and *therefore* there are no easy profit opportunities. Behaviorists emphasize that these two implications (correct prices and no profit opportunities) can be severed: prices can be wrong, but still not give rise to easy profit opportunities. Thus, evidence that profit opportunities are scarce does not necessarily imply that prices are right.

As investors, we are concerned with the existence of profit opportunities. The behavioral explanations of efficient market anomalies do not give guidance as to how to exploit any irrationality. For investors, the question is still whether there is money to be made from mispricing, and the behavioral literature is largely silent on this point.

However, as we pointed out earlier, one of the important implications of the efficient market hypothesis is that security prices serve as reliable guides to the allocation of real capital. If prices are distorted, then capital markets will give misleading signals as to where the resources are best allocated. In this important sense, the behavioral critique of the efficient market hypothesis is potentially important.

There is considerable debate among financial economists concerning the strength of the behavioral critique. Many believe that the behavioral approach is too unstructured, in effect allowing virtually any anomaly to be explained by some combination of irrationalities chosen from a laundry list of behavioral biases.

More fundamentally, others are not convinced that the anomalies literature as a whole is a convincing indictment of the efficient market hypothesis. Fama[52] reviews the anomalies

[50] Jeffrey Pontiff, "Costly Arbitrage: Evidence from Closed-End Funds," *Quarterly Journal of Economics* 111 (November 1996), pp. 1135–51.

[51] Stephen A. Ross, "Neoclassical Finance, Alternative Finance and the Closed End Fund Puzzle, "Keynote Address, *European Financial Management* 8 (2002), pp. 129–38.

[52] Eugene F. Fama, "Market Efficiency, Long-Term Returns, and Behavioral Finance," *Journal of Financial Economics* 49 (September 1998), pp. 283–306.

literature and mounts a counterchallenge to the behavioral school. He argues that the anomalies are inconsistent in terms of their support for one type of irrationality versus another. For example, many papers document long-term corrections (consistent with overreaction) while many others document long-term continuations of abnormal returns (consistent with underreaction). Moreover, the statistical significance of many of these results is less than meets the eye. Even small errors in choosing a benchmark against which to compare returns can cumulate to large apparent abnormalities when applied to long-term returns. Therefore, many of the results in these studies are sensitive to small benchmarking errors, and Fama finds that seemingly minor changes in methodology can have big impacts on conclusions. We will return to some of these issues in the next chapter.

Behavioral finance is still in its infancy. Its critique of full rationality in investor decision-making is well-taken, but the extent to which limited rationality affects asset pricing is controversial. It is probably still too early to pass judgment on the behavioral approach, specifically, which behavioral models will "stick" and become part of the standard toolkit of financial analysts.

## 12.6   MUTUAL FUND PERFORMANCE

We have documented some of the apparent chinks in the armor of efficient market proponents. For investors, the issue of market efficiency boils down to whether skilled investors can make consistent abnormal trading profits. The best test is to look at the performance of market professionals to see if their performance is superior to that of a passive index fund that buys and holds the market.

As we pointed out in Chapter 4, casual evidence does not support the claim that professionally managed portfolios can consistently beat the market. Figure 4.3 in that chapter demonstrated that between 1972 and 2001 the returns of a passive portfolio indexed to the Wilshire 5000 typically would have been better than those of the average equity fund. On the other hand, there was some (admittedly inconsistent) evidence of persistence in performance, meaning that the better managers in one period tended to be better managers in following periods. Such a pattern would suggest that the better managers can with some consistency outperform their competitors, and it would be inconsistent with the notion that market prices already reflect all relevant information.

The analyses cited in Chapter 4 were based on total returns; they did not properly adjust returns for exposure to systematic risk factors. In this section we revisit the question of mutual fund performance, paying more attention to the benchmark against which performance ought to be evaluated.

As a first pass, we can examine the risk-adjusted returns (i.e., the alpha, or return in excess of required return based on beta and the market return in each period) of a large sample of mutual funds. Malkiel[53] computed these abnormal returns for a large sample of mutual funds between 1972 and 1991. The results, which appear in Figure 12.8, show that the distribution of alphas is roughly bell shaped, with a mean that is slightly negative but statistically indistinguishable from zero. On average, it does not appear that these funds outperform the market index (the S&P 500) on a risk-adjusted basis.

One problem in interpreting these alphas is that the S&P 500 may not be an adequate benchmark against which to evaluate mutual fund returns. Because mutual funds tend to maintain considerable holdings in equity of small firms, whereas the S&P 500 is exclusively comprised of large firms, mutual funds as a whole will tend to outperform the S&P

---

[53] Burton G. Malkiel, "Returns from Investing in Equity Mutual Funds 1971–1991," *Journal of Finance* 50 (June 1995), pp. 549–72.

**Figure 12.8    Estimates of individual mutual fund alphas, 1972–1991**

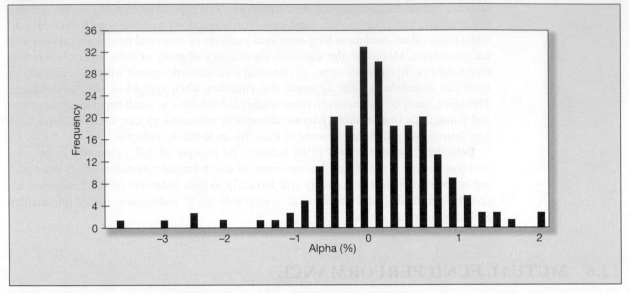

Note: The frequency distribution of estimated alphas for all equity mutual funds with 10-year continuous records.
Source: Burton G. Malkiel, "Returns from Investing in Equity Mutual Funds 1971–1991," *Journal of Finance* 50 (June 1995), pp. 549–72.

when small firms outperform large ones and underperform when small firms fare worse. Thus a better benchmark for the performance of funds would be an index that incorporates the stock market performance of smaller firms.

The importance of the benchmark can be illustrated by examining the returns on small stocks in various subperiods.[54] In the 20-year period between 1945 and 1964, a small-stock index underperformed the S&P 500 by about 4% per year (i.e., the alpha of the small-stock index after adjusting for systematic risk was −4%). In the following 20-year period between 1965 and 1984, small stocks outperformed the S&P index by 10%. Thus if one were to examine mutual fund returns in the earlier period, they would tend to look poor, not necessarily because small-fund managers were poor stock pickers, but simply because mutual funds as a group tend to hold more small stocks than are represented in the S&P 500. In the later period, funds would look better on a risk-adjusted basis relative to the S&P 500 because small funds performed better. The "style choice," that is, the exposure to small stocks (which is an asset allocation decision) would dominate the evaluation of performance even though it has little to do with managers' stock-picking ability.[55]

Elton, Gruber, Das, and Hlavka attempted to control for the impact of non–S&P assets on mutual fund performance. They used a multifactor version of the index model of security returns and calculated fund alphas by using regressions that include as explanatory variables the excess returns of three benchmark portfolios rather than just one proxy for the market index. Their three factors are the excess return on the S&P 500 index, the excess return on an equity index of non–S&P low capitalization (i.e., small) firms, and the excess return on a bond market index. Some of their results are presented in Table 12.1, which

---

[54] This illustration and the statistics cited are based on E. J. Elton, M. J. Gruber, S. Das, and M. Hlavka, "Efficiency with Costly Information: A Reinterpretation of Evidence from Managed Portfolios," *Review of Financial Studies* 6 (1993), pp. 1–22, which is discussed shortly.

[55] Remember that the asset allocation decision is usually in the hands of the individual investor. Investors allocate their investment portfolios to funds in asset classes they desire to hold, and they can reasonably expect only that mutual fund portfolio managers will choose stocks advantageously *within* those asset classes.

## Table 12.1   Performance of Mutual Funds Based on Three-Index Model

| Type of Fund (Wiesenberger Classification) | Number of Funds | Alpha (%) | t-Statistic for Alpha |
|---|---|---|---|
| Equity funds | | | |
|    Maximum capital gain | 12 | −4.59 | −1.87 |
|    Growth | 33 | −1.55 | −1.23 |
|    Growth and income | 40 | −0.68 | −1.65 |
| Balanced funds | 31 | −1.27 | −2.73 |

Note: The three-index model calculates the alpha of each fund as the intercept of the following regression:

$$r - r_f = \alpha + \beta_M(r_M - r_f) + \beta_S(r_S - r_f) + \beta_D(r_D - r_f) + e$$

where $r$ is the return on the fund, $r_f$ is the risk-free rate, $r_M$ is the return on the S&P 500 index, $r_S$ is the return on a non–S&P small-stock index, $r_D$ is the return on a bond index, $e$ is the fund's residual return, and the betas measure the sensitivity of fund returns to the various indexes.
Source: E. J. Elton, M. J. Gruber, S. Das, and M. Hlavka, "Efficiency with Costly Information: A Reinterpretation of Evidence from Managed Portfolios," *Review of Financial Studies* 6 (1993), pp. 1–22.

shows that average alphas are negative for each type of equity fund, although generally not of statistically significant magnitude. They concluded that after controlling for the relative performance of these three asset classes—large stocks, small stocks, and bonds—mutual fund managers as a group do not demonstrate an ability to beat passive index strategies that would simply mix index funds from among these asset classes. They also found that mutual fund performance is worse for firms that have higher expense ratios and higher turnover ratios. Thus it appears that funds with higher fees do not increase gross returns by enough to justify those fees.

Carhart[56] reexamined the issue of consistency in mutual fund performance—sometimes called the "hot hands" phenomenon—controlling for non–S&P factors in a manner similar to Elton, Gruber, Das, and Hlavka. Carhart used a four-factor extension of the index model in which the four benchmark portfolios are the S&P 500 index and portfolios based on book-to-market ratio, size, and prior-year stock market return. These portfolios capture the impacts of the major anomalies discussed earlier: the small-firm effect, the book-to-market effect, and the intermediate-term momentum effect.

Carhart found that there is some persistence in relative performance across managers. However, much of that persistence seems due to expenses and transactions costs rather than gross investment returns. This last point is important; while there can be no consistently superior performers in a fully efficient market, there *can* be consistently inferior performers. Repeated weak performance would not be due to an ability to pick bad stocks consistently (that would be impossible in an efficient market!) but could result from a consistently high expense ratio, high portfolio turnover, or higher-than-average transaction costs per trade. In this regard, it is interesting that in another study documenting apparent consistency across managers, Hendricks, Patel, and Zeckhauser[57] also found the strongest consistency among the weakest performers.

Even allowing for expenses and turnover, some amount of performance persistence seems to be due to differences in investment strategy. Carhart found, however, that the evidence of persistence is concentrated at the two extremes. Figure 12.9 from Carhart's study documents performance persistence. Equity funds are ranked into one of 10 groups

---

[56] Mark M. Carhart, "On Persistence in Mutual Fund Performance," *Journal of Finance* 52 (1997), pp. 57–82.
[57] Darryll Hendricks, Jayendu Patel, and Richard Zeckhauser, "Hot Hands in Mutual Funds: Short-Run Persistence of Relative Performance, 1974–1988," *Journal of Finance* 43 (March 1993), pp. 93–130.

**Figure 12.9
Persistence of
mutual fund
performance.
Performance
over time of
mutual fund
groups ranked
by initial year
performance**

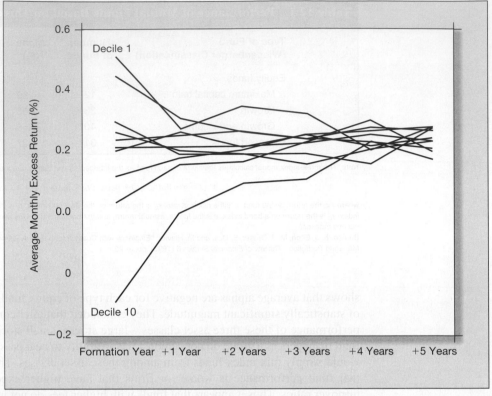

Source: Marc M. Carhart, "On Persistence in Mutual Fund Performance," *Journal of Finance* 52 (March 1997), pp. 57–82.

by performance in the formation year, and the performance of each group in the following years is plotted. It is clear that except for the best-performing top-decile group and the worst-performing 10th decile group, performance in future periods is almost independent of earlier-year returns. Carhart's results suggest that there may be a small group of exceptional managers who can with some consistency outperform a passive strategy, but that for the majority of managers over- or underperformance in any period is largely a matter of chance.

In contrast to the extensive studies of equity fund managers, there have been few studies of the performance of bond fund managers. Blake, Elton, and Gruber[58] examined the performance of fixed-income mutual funds. They found that, on average, bond funds underperform passive fixed-income indexes by an amount roughly equal to expenses, and that there is no evidence that past performance can predict future performance. Their evidence is consistent with the hypothesis that bond managers operate in an efficient market in which performance before expenses is only as good as that of a passive index.

Thus the evidence on the risk-adjusted performance of professional managers is mixed at best. We conclude that the performance of professional managers is broadly consistent with market efficiency. The amounts by which professional managers as a group beat or are beaten by the market fall within the margin of statistical uncertainty. In any event, it is quite clear that performance superior to passive strategies is far from routine. Studies show either that most managers cannot outperform passive strategies or that if there is a margin of superiority, it is small.

---

[58] Christopher R. Blake, Edwin J. Elton, and Martin J. Gruber, "The Performance of Bond Mutual Funds," *Journal of Business* 66 (July 1993), pp. 371–404.

On the other hand, a small number of investment superstars—Peter Lynch (formerly of Fidelity's Magellan Fund), Warren Buffet (of Berkshire Hathaway), John Templeton (of Templeton Funds), and John Neff (of Vanguard's Windsor Fund) among them—have compiled career records that show a consistency of superior performance hard to reconcile with absolutely efficient markets. Nobel Prize winner Paul Samuelson[59] reviewed this investment hall of fame but pointed out that the records of the vast majority of professional money managers offer convincing evidence that there are no easy strategies to guarantee success in the securities markets.

**So, Are Markets Efficient?** There is a telling joke about two economists walking down the street. They spot a $20 bill on the sidewalk. One starts to pick it up, but the other one says, "Don't bother; if the bill were real someone would have picked it up already."

The lesson is clear. An overly doctrinaire belief in efficient markets can paralyze the investor and make it appear that no research effort can be justified. This extreme view is probably unwarranted. There are enough anomalies in the empirical evidence to justify the search for underpriced securities that clearly goes on.

The bulk of the evidence, however, suggests that any supposedly superior investment strategy should be taken with many grains of salt. The market is competitive *enough* that only differentially superior information or insight will earn money; the easy pickings have been picked. In the end it is likely that the margin of superiority that any professional manager can add is so slight that the statistician will not easily be able to detect it.

We conclude that markets are very efficient, but that rewards to the especially diligent, intelligent, or creative may in fact be waiting.

## SUMMARY

1. Statistical research has shown that to a close approximation stock prices seem to follow a random walk with no discernible predictable patterns that investors can exploit. Such findings are now taken to be evidence of market efficiency, that is, evidence that market prices reflect all currently available information. Only new information will move stock prices, and this information is equally likely to be good news or bad news.

2. Market participants distinguish among three forms of the efficient market hypothesis. The weak form asserts that all information to be derived from past trading data already is reflected in stock prices. The semistrong form claims that all publicly available information is already reflected. The strong form, which generally is acknowledged to be extreme, asserts that all information, including insider information, is reflected in prices.

3. Technical analysis focuses on stock price patterns and on proxies for buy or sell pressure in the market. Fundamental analysis focuses on the determinants of the underlying value of the firm, such as current profitability and growth prospects. Because both types of analysis are based on public information, neither should generate excess profits if markets are operating efficiently.

4. Proponents of the efficient market hypothesis often advocate passive as opposed to active investment strategies. The policy of passive investors is to buy and hold a broad-based market index. They expend resources neither on market research nor on frequent purchase and sale of stocks. Passive strategies may be tailored to meet individual investor requirements.

---

[59] Paul Samuelson, "The Judgment of Economic Science on Rational Portfolio Management," *Journal of Portfolio Management* 16 (Fall 1989), pp. 4–12.

5. Event studies are used to evaluate the economic impact of events of interest, using abnormal stock returns. Such studies usually show that there is some leakage of inside information to some market participants before the public announcement date. Therefore, insiders do seem to be able to exploit their access to information to at least a limited extent.

6. Empirical studies of technical analysis do not generally support the hypothesis that such analysis can generate superior trading profits. One notable exception to this conclusion is the apparent success of momentum-based strategies over intermediate-term horizons.

7. Several anomalies regarding fundamental analysis have been uncovered. These include the P/E effect, the small-firm-in-January effect, the neglected-firm effect, post–earnings-announcement price drift, and the book-to-market effect. Whether these anomalies represent market inefficiency or poorly understood risk premia is still a matter of debate.

8. Behavioral finance focuses on systematic irrationalities that characterize investor decision making. These "behavioral shortcomings" may be consistent with some of the efficient market anomalies uncovered by several researchers.

9. By and large, the performance record of professionally managed funds lends little credence to claims that most professionals can consistently beat the market.

**KEY TERMS**

| | | |
|---|---|---|
| random walk | support levels | reversal effect |
| efficient market hypothesis | fundamental analysis | anomalies |
| weak-form EMH | passive investment strategy | P/E effect |
| semistrong-form EMH | index fund | small-firm effect |
| strong-form EMH | event study | neglected-firm effect |
| technical analysis | abnormal return | book-to-market effect |
| Dow theory | cumulative abnormal return | behavioral finance |
| resistance levels | momentum effect | |

**WEBSITES**

The following website contains an online journal entitled *Efficient Frontier: An Online Journal of Practical Asset Allocation*. It contains short articles related to assessment of investment strategies that can be downloaded in *Adobe Acrobat*.

www.efficientfrontier.com/ef/index.shtml

These sites provide extended analysis of behavioral finance:

www.investorhome.com/psych.htm
www.perso.wanadoo.fr/pgreenfinch/behavioral-finance.htm
www.investopedia.com/terms/b/behavioralfinance.asp
econpapers.hhs.se/paper/cwlcwldpp/1385.htm

The following sites contain information on market efficiency, individual stocks, and mutual funds. Enter the stock ticker symbol for easy access.

www.wallpost.com
www.wsrn.com
www.marketguide.com/home.asp
www.corporateinformation.com (Free but requires registration)
www.businessweek.com

## PROBLEMS

1. If markets are efficient, what should be the correlation coefficient between stock returns for two nonoverlapping time periods?

2. Which of the following most appears to contradict the proposition that the stock market is *weakly* efficient? Explain.
   a. Over 25% of mutual funds outperform the market on average.
   b. Insiders earn abnormal trading profits.
   c. Every January, the stock market earns abnormal returns.

3. Suppose that, after conducting an analysis of past stock prices, you come up with the following observations. Which would appear to *contradict* the *weak form* of the efficient market hypothesis? Explain.
   a. The average rate of return is significantly greater than zero.
   b. The correlation between the return during a given week and the return during the following week is zero.
   c. One could have made superior returns by buying stock after a 10% rise in price and selling after a 10% fall.
   d. One could have made higher-than-average capital gains by holding stocks with low dividend yields.

4. Which of the following statements are true if the efficient market hypothesis holds?
   a. It implies that future events can be forecast with perfect accuracy.
   b. It implies that prices reflect all available information.
   c. It implies that security prices change for no discernible reason.
   d. It implies that prices do not fluctuate.

5. Which of the following observations would provide evidence *against* the *semistrong form* of the efficient market theory? Explain.
   a. Mutual fund managers do not on average make superior returns.
   b. You cannot make superior profits by buying (or selling) stocks after the announcement of an abnormal rise in dividends.
   c. Low P/E stocks tend to have positive abnormal returns.
   d. In any year approximately 50% of pension funds outperform the market.

Problems 6–12 are taken from past CFA exams.

6. The semistrong form of the efficient market hypothesis asserts that stock prices:
   a. Fully reflect all historical price information.
   b. Fully reflect all publicly available information.
   c. Fully reflect all relevant information including insider information.
   d. May be predictable.

7. Assume that a company announces an unexpectedly large cash dividend to its shareholders. In an efficient market *without* information leakage, one might expect:
   a. An abnormal price change at the announcement.
   b. An abnormal price increase before the announcement.
   c. An abnormal price decrease after the announcement.
   d. No abnormal price change before or after the announcement.

8. Which one of the following would provide evidence *against* the *semistrong form* of the efficient market theory?
   a. About 50% of pension funds outperform the market in any year.
   b. All investors have learned to exploit signals about future performance.
   c. Trend analysis is worthless in determining stock prices.
   d. Low P/E stocks tend to have positive abnormal returns over the long run.

9. According to the efficient market hypothesis:

   a. High-beta stocks are consistently overpriced.

   b. Low-beta stocks are consistently overpriced.

   c. Positive alphas on stocks will quickly disappear.

   d. Negative alpha stocks consistently yield low returns for arbitrageurs.

10. A "random walk" occurs when:

    a. Stock price changes are random but predictable.

    b. Stock prices respond slowly to both new and old information.

    c. Future price changes are uncorrelated with past price changes.

    d. Past information is useful in predicting future prices.

11. Two basic assumptions of technical analysis are that security prices adjust:

    a. Gradually to new information, and study of the economic environment provides an indication of future market movements.

    b. Rapidly to new information, and study of the economic environment provides an indication of future market movements.

    c. Rapidly to new information, and market prices are determined by the interaction between supply and demand.

    d. Gradually to new information, and prices are determined by the interaction between supply and demand.

12. When technical analysts say a stock has good "relative strength," they mean:

    a. The ratio of the price of the stock to a market or industry index has trended upward.

    b. The recent trading volume in the stock has exceeded the normal trading volume.

    c. The total return on the stock has exceeded the total return on T-bills.

    d. The stock has performed well recently compared to its past performance.

13. Which one of the following would be a bullish signal to a technical analyst using contrary opinion rules?

    a. The level of credit balances in investor accounts declines.

    b. The ratio of bearish investment advisors to the number of advisory services expressing an optimistic opinion is historically quite high.

    c. A large proportion of speculators expect the price of stock index futures to rise.

    d. The ratio of over the counter (OTC) volume to New York Stock Exchange (NYSE) volume is relatively high.

14. A successful firm like Microsoft has consistently generated large profits for years. Is this a violation of the EMH?

15. Suppose you find that prices of stocks before large dividend increases show on average consistently positive abnormal returns. Is this a violation of the EMH?

16. "If the business cycle is predictable, and a stock has a positive beta, the stock's returns also must be predictable." Respond.

17. Which of the following phenomena would be either consistent with or a violation of the efficient market hypothesis? Explain briefly.

    a. Nearly half of all professionally managed mutual funds are able to outperform the S&P 500 in a typical year.

    b. Money managers that outperform the market (on a risk-adjusted basis) in one year are likely to outperform in the following year.

    c. Stock prices tend to be predictably more volatile in January than in other months.

     *d.* Stock prices of companies that announce increased earnings in January tend to outperform the market in February.

     *e.* Stocks that perform well in one week perform poorly in the following week.

18. "If all securities are fairly priced, all must offer equal expected rates of return." Comment.

19. An index model regression applied to past monthly returns in General Motors' stock price produces the following estimates, which are believed to be stable over time:

$$r_{GM} = .10\% + 1.1r_M$$

If the market index subsequently rises by 8% and General Motors' stock price rises by 7%, what is the abnormal change in General Motors' stock price?

20. The monthly rate of return on T-bills is 1%. The market went up this month by 1.5%. In addition, AmbChaser, Inc., which has an equity beta of 2, surprisingly just won a lawsuit that awards it $1 million immediately.

     *a.* If the original value of AmbChaser equity were $100 million, what would you guess was the rate of return of its stock this month?

     *b.* What is your answer to (*a*) if the market had expected AmbChaser to win $2 million?

21. In a recent closely contested lawsuit, Apex sued Bpex for patent infringement. The jury came back today with its decision. The rate of return on Apex was $r_A = 3.1\%$. The rate of return on Bpex was only $r_B = 2.5\%$. The market today responded to very encouraging news about the unemployment rate, and $r_M = 3\%$. The historical relationship between returns on these stocks and the market portfolio has been estimated from index model regressions as:

$$\text{Apex: } r_A = .2\% + 1.4r_M$$
$$\text{Bpex: } r_B = -.1\% + .6r_M$$

Based on these data, which company do you think won the lawsuit?

22. Investors *expect* the market rate of return in the coming year to be 12%. The T-bill rate is 4%. Changing Fortunes Industries' stock has a beta of .5. The market value of its outstanding equity is $100 million.

     *a.* What is your best guess currently as to the expected rate of return on Changing Fortunes' stock? You believe that the stock is fairly priced.

     *b.* If the market return in the coming year actually turns out to be 10%, what is your best guess as to the rate of return that will be earned on Changing Fortunes' stock?

     *c.* Suppose now that Changing Fortunes wins a major lawsuit during the year. The settlement is $5 million. Changing Fortunes' stock return during the year turns out to be 10%. What is your best guess as to the settlement the market previously *expected* Changing Fortunes to receive from the lawsuit? (Continue to assume that the market return in the year turned out to be 10%.) The magnitude of the settlement is the only unexpected firm-specific event during the year.

23. Dollar-cost averaging means that you buy equal dollar amounts of a stock every period, for example, $500 per month. The strategy is based on the idea that when the stock price is low, your fixed monthly purchase will buy more shares, and when the price is high, fewer shares. Averaging over time, you will end up buying more shares when the stock is cheaper and fewer when it is relatively expensive. Therefore, by design, you will exhibit good market timing. Evaluate this strategy.

24. Steady Growth Industries has never missed a dividend payment in its 94-year history. Does this make it more attractive to you as a possible purchase for your stock portfolio?

25. We know that the market should respond positively to good news and that good-news events such as the coming end of a recession can be predicted with at least some accuracy. Why, then, can we not predict that the market will go up as the economy recovers?

26. If prices are as likely to increase as decrease, why do investors earn positive returns from the market on average?

27. You know that firm XYZ is very poorly run. On a scale of 1 (worst) to 10 (best), you would give it a score of 3. The market consensus evaluation is that the management score is only 2. Should you buy or sell the stock?

28. Examine the accompanying figure,[60] which presents cumulative abnormal returns both before and after dates on which insiders buy or sell shares in their firms. How do you interpret this figure? What are we to make of the pattern of CARs before and after the event date?

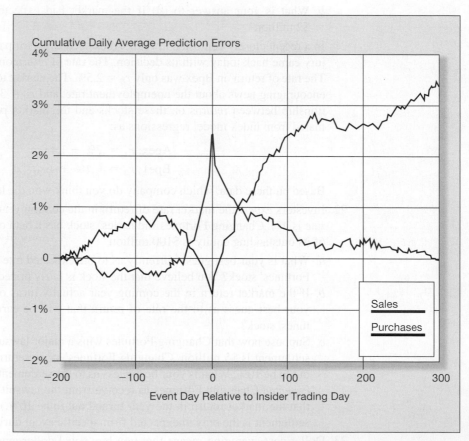

29. Suppose that during a certain week the Fed announces a new monetary growth policy, Congress surprisingly passes legislation restricting imports of foreign automobiles, and Ford comes out with a new car model that it believes will increase

[60] From Nejat H. Seyhun, "Insiders, Profits, Costs of Trading and Market Efficiency," *Journal of Financial Economics* 16 (1986).

profits substantially. How might you go about measuring the market's assessment of Ford's new model?

30. Good News, Inc., just announced an increase in its annual earnings, yet its stock price fell. Is there a rational explanation for this phenomenon?

31. Your investment client asks for information concerning the benefits of active portfolio management. She is particularly interested in the question of whether active managers can be expected to consistently exploit inefficiencies in the capital markets to produce above-average returns without assuming higher risk.

   The semistrong form of the efficient market hypothesis asserts that all publicly available information is rapidly and correctly reflected in securities prices. This implies that investors cannot expect to derive above-average profits from purchases made after information has become public because security prices already reflect the information's full effects.

   *a.* Identify and explain two examples of empirical evidence that tend to support the EMH implication stated above.

   *b.* Identify and explain two examples of empirical evidence that tend to refute the EMH implication stated above.

   *c.* Discuss reasons why an investor might choose not to index even if the markets were, in fact, semistrong-form efficient.

32. *a.* Briefly explain the concept of the efficient market hypothesis (EMH) and each of its three forms—weak, semistrong, and strong—and briefly discuss the degree to which existing empirical evidence supports each of the three forms of the EMH.

   *b.* Briefly discuss the implications of the efficient market hypothesis for investment policy as it applies to:

   i. Technical analysis in the form of charting.

   ii. Fundamental analysis.

   *c.* Briefly explain the roles or responsibilities of portfolio managers in an efficient market environment.

33. Growth and value can be defined in several ways. "Growth" usually conveys the idea of a portfolio emphasizing or including only issues believed to possess above-average future rates of per-share earnings growth. Low current yield, high price-to-book ratios, and high price-to-earnings ratios are typical characteristics of such portfolios. "Value" usually conveys the idea of portfolios emphasizing or including only issues currently showing low price-to-book ratios, low price-to-earnings ratios, above-average levels of dividend yield, and market prices believed to be below the issues' intrinsic values.

   *a.* Identify and provide reasons why, over an extended period of time, value-stock investing might outperform growth-stock investing.

   *b.* Explain why the outcome suggested in (a) should not be possible in a market widely regarded as being highly efficient.

34. Don Sampson begins a meeting with his financial advisor by outlining his investment philosophy as shown below:

| Statement Number | Statement |
|---|---|
| 1 | Investments should offer strong return potential but with very limited risk. I prefer to be conservative and to minimize losses, even if I miss out on substantial growth opportunities. |

Visit us at www.mhhe.com/bkm

| Statement Number | Statement |
|---|---|
| 2 | All nongovernmental investments should be in industry-leading and financially strong companies. |
| 3 | Income needs should be met entirely through interest income and cash dividends. All equity securities held should pay cash dividends. |
| 4 | Investment decisions should be based primarily on consensus forecasts of general economic conditions and company-specific growth. |
| 5 | If an investment falls below the purchase price, that security should be retained until it returns to its original cost. Conversely, I prefer to take quick profits on successful investments. |
| 6 | I will direct the purchase of investments, including derivative securities, periodically. These aggressive investments result from personal research and may not prove consistent with my investment policy. I have not kept records on the performance of similar past investments, but I have had some "big winners". |

Select the statement from the table above that best illustrates each of the following behavioral finance concepts. Justify your selection.

  i.  Mental accounting.

  ii.  Overconfidence (illusion of control).

  iii.  Reference dependence (framing).

35. Monty Frost's tax-deferred retirement account is invested entirely in equity securities. Because the international portion of his portfolio has performed poorly in the past, he has reduced his international equity exposure to 2%. Frost's investment adviser has recommended an increased international equity exposure. Frost responds with the following comments:

  *a.*  Based on past poor performance, I want to sell all my remaining international equity securities once their market prices rise to equal their original cost.

  *b.*  Most diversified international portfolios have had disappointing results over the past 5 years. During that time, however, the market in Country XYZ has outperformed all other markets, even our own. If I do increase my international equity exposure, I would prefer that the entire exposure consist of securities from Country XYZ.

  *c.*  International investments are inherently more risky. Therefore, I prefer to purchase any international equity securities in my "speculative" account, my best chance at becoming rich. I do not want them in my retirement account, which has to protect me from poverty in my old age.

Frost's adviser is familiar with behavioral finance concepts but prefers a traditional or standard finance approach (modern portfolio theory) to investments.

Indicate the behavioral finance concept that Frost most directly exhibits in each of his three comments. Explain how each of Frost's comments can be countered by using an argument from standard finance.

1. Use data from Market Insight (**www.mhhe.com/business/finance/edumarket insight**) to rank firms based on one of these criteria:
   *a.* Market-to-book ratio.
   *b.* Price-earnings ratio.
   *c.* Market capitalization (size).
   *d.* Another criterion that interests you.

   Divide the firms into five groups based on their ranking for the criterion that you choose, and calculate the average rate of return of the firms in each group. Do you confirm or reject any of the anomalies cited in this chapter? Can you uncover a new anomaly? Note: For your test to be valid, you must form your portfolios based on criteria observed at the *beginning* of the period when you form the stock groups. Why?

2. Now form stock groups that use more than one criterion simultaneously. For example, form a portfolio of stocks that are both in the lowest quintile of price-earnings ratios and in the lowest quintile of market-to-book ratio. Does selecting stocks based on more than one characteristic improve your ability to devise portfolios with abnormal returns?

**E-INVESTMENTS
Efficient
Markets and
Insider Trading**

Do restrictions on insider trading limit strong-form market efficiency? Go to Wallpost.com and pull down the *Insiders* and *Insiders-Stock of the Day*. Read the Insider analysis for the stock of the day. Enter the stock symbol for the stock of the day and review a price chart for the time period mentioned in the stock-of-the-day article. What do you conclude about the investment timing of the insiders?

**SOLUTIONS
TO CONCEPT
CHECKS**

1. *a.* A high-level manager might well have private information about the firm. Her ability to trade profitably on that information is not surprising. This ability does not violate weak-form efficiency: The abnormal profits are not derived from an analysis of past price and trading data. If they were, this would indicate that there is valuable information that can be gleaned from such analysis. But this ability does violate strong-form efficiency. Apparently, there is some private information that is not already reflected in stock prices.

   *b.* The information sets that pertain to the weak, semistrong, and strong form of the EMH can be described by the following illustration:

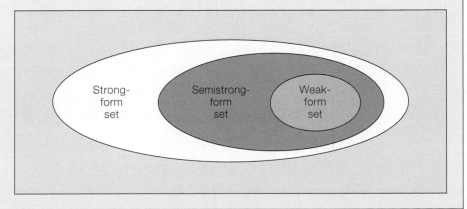

Strong-form set

Semistrong-form set

Weak-form set

Visit us at www.mhhe.com/bkm

**SOLUTIONS TO CONCEPT CHECKS**
*(Concluded)*

The weak-form information set includes only the history of prices and volumes. The semistrong-form set includes the weak form set *plus* all publicly available information. In turn, the strong-form set includes the semistrong set *plus* insiders' information. It is illegal to act on this incremental information (insiders' private information). The direction of *valid* implication is

Strong-form EMH ⇒ Semistrong-form EMH ⇒ Weak-form EMH

The reverse direction implication is *not* valid. For example, stock prices may reflect all past price data (weak-form efficiency) but may not reflect relevant fundamental data (semistrong-form inefficiency).

2. The point we made in the preceding discussion is that the very fact that we observe stock prices near so-called resistance levels belies the assumption that the price can be a resistance level. If a stock is observed to sell *at any price*, then investors must believe that a fair rate of return can be earned if the stock is purchased at that price. It is logically impossible for a stock to have a resistance level *and* offer a fair rate of return at prices just below the resistance level. If we accept that prices are appropriate, we must reject any presumption concerning resistance levels.

3. If *everyone* follows a passive strategy, sooner or later prices will fail to reflect new information. At this point there are profit opportunities for active investors who uncover mispriced securities. As they buy and sell these assets, prices again will be driven to fair levels.

4. Predictably declining CARs do violate the EMH. If one can predict such a phenomenon, a profit opportunity emerges: Sell (or short sell) the affected stocks on an event date just before their prices are predicted to fall.

5. The answer depends on your prior beliefs about market efficiency. Magellan's record was incredibly strong. On the other hand, with so many funds in existence, it is less surprising that *some* fund would appear to be consistently superior after the fact. Still, Magellan's record was so good that even accounting for its selection as the "winner" of an investment "contest," it still appears to be too good to be attributed to chance.

# EMPIRICAL EVIDENCE ON SECURITY RETURNS

In this chapter, we consider the empirical evidence in support of the CAPM and APT. At the outset, however, it is worth noting that many of the implications of these models already have been accepted in widely varying applications. Consider the following:

1. Many professional portfolio managers use the expected return–beta relationship of security returns. Furthermore, many firms rate the performance of portfolio managers according to the reward-to-variability ratios they maintain and the average rates of return they realize relative to the CML or SML.

2. Regulatory commissions use the expected return–beta relationship along with forecasts of the market index return as one factor in determining the cost of capital for regulated firms.

3. Court rulings on torts cases sometimes use the expected return–beta relationship to determine discount rates to evaluate claims of lost future income.

4. Many firms use the SML to obtain a benchmark hurdle rate for capital budgeting decisions.

These practices show that the financial community has passed a favorable judgment on the CAPM and the APT, if only implicitly.

In this chapter we consider the evidence along more explicit and rigorous lines. The first part of the chapter presents the methodology that has been deployed in testing the single-factor CAPM and APT and assesses the results. The second part of the chapter provides an overview of current efforts to establish the validity of the multifactor versions of the CAPM and APT. In the third part, we discuss recent literature on so-called anomalies in patterns of security returns and some of the responses to these puzzling findings. We briefly discuss evidence on how the volatility of asset returns evolves over time. Finally, we present interesting research on stock returns that examines the size of the equity risk premium. Conventional wisdom has held for a long time that the history of returns on equities is quite puzzling. Recent studies address the puzzle.

Why lump together empirical works on the CAPM and APT? The CAPM is a theoretical construct that predicts *expected* rates of return on assets, relative to a market portfolio of all risky assets. It is difficult to test these predictions empirically because expected returns, covariances, and the exact market portfolio are unobservable (see Chapter 10). To overcome this difficulty, a single-factor or multifactor capital market usually is postulated, where a broad-based market index portfolio (such as the S&P 500) is assumed to represent the factor, or one of the factors. Furthermore, to obtain more reliable statistics, most tests have been conducted with the rates of return on highly diversified portfolios rather than on individual securities. For both of these reasons, tests that have been directed at the CAPM actually have been more suitable to establish the validity of the APT. We will see that it is more important to distinguish the empirical work on the basis of the factor structure that is assumed or estimated than to distinguish between tests of the CAPM and the APT.

## 13.1   THE INDEX MODEL AND THE SINGLE-FACTOR APT

**The Expected Return–Beta Relationship**   Recall that if the expected return–beta relationship holds with respect to an observable ex ante efficient index, $M$, the expected rate of return on any security $i$ is

$$E(r_i) = r_f + \beta_i [E(r_M) - r_f] \tag{13.1}$$

where $\beta_i$ is defined as $\text{Cov}(r_i, r_M)/\sigma_M^2$.

This is the most commonly tested implication of the CAPM. Early simple tests followed three basic steps: establishing sample data, estimating the SCL (security characteristic line), and estimating the SML (security market line).

**Setting Up the Sample Data.** Determine a sample period of, for example, 60 monthly holding periods (5 years). For each of the 60 holding periods, collect the rates of return on 100 stocks, a market portfolio proxy (e.g., the S&P 500), and 1-month (risk-free) T-bills. Your data thus consist of

$r_{it}$   Returns on the 100 stocks over the 60-month sample period; $i = 1, \ldots, 100$, and $t = 1, \ldots, 60$.

$r_{Mt}$   Returns on the S&P 500 index over the sample period.

$r_{ft}$   Risk-free rate each month.

This constitutes a table of $102 \times 60 = 6{,}120$ rates of return.

**Estimating the SCL.** View equation 13.1 as a security characteristic line (SCL), as in Chapter 10. For each stock, $i$, you estimate the beta coefficient as the slope of a **first-pass regression** equation. (The terminology *first-pass* regression is due to the fact that the estimated coefficients will be used as input into a **second-pass regression**.)

$$r_{it} - r_{ft} = a_i + b_i(r_{Mt} - r_{ft}) + e_{it}$$

You will use the following statistics in later analysis:

$\overline{r_i - r_f}$   Sample averages (over the 60 observations) of the excess return on each of the 100 stocks.

$b_i$   Sample estimates of the beta coefficients of each of the 100 stocks.

$\overline{r_M - r_f}$   Sample average of the excess return of the market index.

$\sigma^2(e_i)$   Estimates of the variance of the residuals for each of the 100 stocks.

The sample average excess returns on each stock and the market portfolio are taken as estimates of expected excess returns, and the values of $b_i$ are estimates of the true beta coefficients for the 100 stocks during the sample period. The $\sigma^2(e_i)$ estimates the nonsystematic risk of each of the 100 stocks.

**CONCEPT CHECK☞ QUESTION 1**

*a.* **How many regression estimates of the SCL do we have from the sample?**
*b.* **How many observations are there in each of the regressions?**
*c.* **According to the CAPM, what should be the intercept in each of these regressions?**

**Estimating the SML.** Now view equation 13.1 as a security market line (SML) with 100 observations for the stocks in your sample. You can estimate $\gamma_0$ and $\gamma_1$ in the following second-pass regression equation with the estimates $b_i$ from the first pass as the independent variable:

$$\overline{r_i - r_f} = \gamma_0 + \gamma_1 b_i \qquad i = 1, \ldots, 100 \tag{13.2}$$

Compare equations 13.1 and 13.2; you should conclude that if the CAPM is valid, then $\gamma_0$ and $\gamma_1$ should satisfy

$$\gamma_0 = 0 \quad \text{and} \quad \gamma_1 = \overline{r_M - r_f}$$

In fact, however, you can go a step further and argue that the key property of the expected return–beta relationship described by the SML is that the expected excess return on securities is determined *only* by the systematic risk (as measured by beta) and should be independent of the nonsystematic risk, as measured by the variance of the residuals, $\sigma^2(e_i)$, which also were estimated from the first-pass regression. These estimates can be added as a variable in equation 13.2 of an expanded SML that now looks like this:

$$\overline{r_i - r_f} = \gamma_0 + \gamma_1 b_i + \gamma_2 \sigma^2(e_i) \tag{13.3}$$

This *second-pass* regression is estimated with the hypotheses

$$\gamma_0 = 0; \qquad \gamma_1 = \overline{r_M - r_f}; \qquad \gamma_2 = 0$$

The hypothesis that $\gamma_2 = 0$ is consistent with the notion that nonsystematic risk should not be "priced," that is, that there is no risk premium earned for bearing nonsystematic risk. More generally, according to the CAPM, the risk premium depends only on beta. Therefore, *any* additional right-hand-side variable in equation 13.3 beyond beta should have a coefficient that is insignificantly different from zero in the second-pass regression.

## Tests of the CAPM

Early tests of the CAPM performed by John Lintner,[1] and later replicated by Merton Miller and Myron Scholes,[2] used annual data on 631 NYSE stocks for 10 years, 1954 to 1963, and produced the following estimates (with returns expressed as decimals rather than percentages):

| Coefficient: | $\gamma_0 = .127$ | $\gamma_1 = .042$ | $\gamma_2 = .310$ |
|---|---|---|---|
| Standard error: | .006 | .006 | .026 |
| Sample average: | | $\overline{r_M - r_f} = .165$ | |

These results are inconsistent with the CAPM. First, the estimated SML is "too flat;" that is, the $\gamma_1$ coefficient is too small. The slope should be $\overline{r_M - r_f} = .165$ (16.5% per year), but it is estimated at only .042. The difference, .122, is about 20 times the standard error of the estimate, .006, which means that the measured slope of the SML is less than it should be by a statistically significant margin. At the same time, the intercept of the estimated SML, $\gamma_0$, which is hypothesized to be zero, in fact equals .127, which is more than 20 times its standard error of .006.

---

[1] John Lintner, "Security Prices, Risk and Maximal Gains from Diversification," *Journal of Finance* 20 (December 1965).
[2] Merton H. Miller and Myron Scholes, "Rate of Return in Relation to Risk: A Reexamination of Some Recent Findings," in Michael C. Jensen, ed., *Studies in the Theory of Capital Markets* (New York: Praeger, 1972).

*a.* **What is the implication of the empirical SML being "too flat"?**
*b.* **Do high- or low-beta stocks tend to outperform the predictions of the
    CAPM?**
*c.* **What is the implication of the estimate of $\gamma_2$?**

The two-stage procedure employed by these researchers (i.e., first estimate security
betas using a time-series regression and then use those betas to test the SML relationship
between risk and average return) seems straightforward, and the rejection of the CAPM
using this approach is disappointing. However, it turns out that there are several difficulties
with this approach. First and foremost, stock returns are extremely volatile, which lessens
the precision of any tests of average return. For example, the average standard deviation of
annual returns of the stocks in the S&P 500 is about 40%; the average standard deviation
of annual returns of the stocks included in these tests is probably even higher.

In addition, there are fundamental concerns about the validity of the tests. First, the market index used in the tests is surely not the "market portfolio" of the CAPM. Second, in
light of asset volatility, the security betas from the first-stage regressions are necessarily estimated with substantial sampling error and therefore cannot readily be used as inputs to the
second-stage regression. Finally, investors cannot borrow at the risk-free rate, as assumed
by the simple version of the CAPM. Let us investigate the implications of these problems
in turn.

### The Market Index    In what has become known as *Roll's critique*, Richard Roll[3] pointed out that:

1. There is a single testable hypothesis associated with the CAPM: The market
   portfolio is mean-variance efficient.

2. All the other implications of the model, the best known being the linear relation
   between expected return and beta, follow from the market portfolio's efficiency
   and therefore are not independently testable. There is an "if and only if " relation
   between the expected return–beta relationship and the efficiency of the market
   portfolio.

3. In any sample of observations of individual returns there will be an infinite number
   of ex post (i.e., after the fact) mean-variance efficient portfolios using the sample-
   period returns and covariances (as opposed to the ex ante expected returns and
   covariances). Sample betas calculated between each such portfolio and individual
   assets will be exactly linearly related to sample average returns. In other words,
   if betas are calculated against such portfolios, they will satisfy the SML relation
   exactly whether or not the true market portfolio is mean-variance efficient in an
   ex ante sense.

4. The CAPM is not testable unless we know the exact composition of the true market
   portfolio and use it in the tests. This implies that the theory is not testable unless
   *all* individual assets are included in the sample.

5. Using a proxy such as the S&P 500 for the market portfolio is subject to two
   difficulties. First, the proxy itself might be mean-variance efficient even when the
   true market portfolio is not. Conversely, the proxy may turn out to be inefficient,

---

[3] Richard Roll, "A Critique of the Asset Pricing Theory's Tests: Part I: On Past and Potential Testability of the Theory," *Journal of Financial Economics* 4 (1977).

but obviously this alone implies nothing about the true market portfolio's efficiency. Furthermore, most reasonable market proxies will be very highly correlated with each other and with the true market portfolio whether or not they are mean-variance efficient. Such a high degree of correlation will make it seem that the exact composition of the market portfolio is unimportant, whereas the use of different proxies can lead to quite different conclusions. This problem is referred to as **benchmark error**, because it refers to the use of an incorrect benchmark (market proxy) portfolio in the tests of the theory.

Roll and Ross[4] and Kandel and Stambaugh[5] expanded Roll's critique. Essentially, they argued that tests that reject a positive relationship between average return and beta point to inefficiency of the market proxy used in those tests, rather than refuting the theoretical expected return–beta relationship. Their work demonstrates that it is plausible that even highly diversified portfolios, such as the value- or equally weighted portfolios of all stocks in the sample, will fail to produce a significant average return–beta relationship.

Roll and Ross (RR) derived an analytical characterization of market indexes (proxies for the market portfolio) that produce an *arbitrary* cross-sectional slope coefficient in the regression of average asset returns on beta. Their derivation applies to any universe of assets and requires only that the market proxy be constructed from that universe or one of its subsets. They show that the set of indexes that produces a zero second-pass slope lies within a parabola that is tangent to the efficient frontier at the point corresponding to the global minimum variance portfolio.

Figure 13.1 shows one such configuration. In this plausible universe, where "plausible" is taken to mean that the return distribution is not extraordinary, the set of portfolios with zero slope coefficient in the return–beta regression lies near the efficient frontier. Thus even portfolios that are "nearly efficient" do not necessarily support the expected return–beta relationship.

RR concluded that the slope coefficient in the average return–beta regression cannot be relied on to test the theoretical expected return–beta relationship. It can indicate only that the market proxy that produces this result is inefficient in the second-pass regression. Many studies use the more sophisticated regression procedure called generalized least squares (GLS) to improve on statistical reliability. Can the use of GLS overcome the problems raised by Roll and Ross?

Kandel and Stambaugh (KS) extended this analysis and considered whether the use of generalized least squares regressions can overcome some of the problems identified by Roll and Ross. They found that GLS does help, but only to the extent that the researcher can obtain a nearly efficient market index.

KS considered the properties of the usual two-pass test of the CAPM in an environment in which borrowing is restricted but the zero-beta version of the CAPM holds. In this case, you will recall that the expected return–beta relationship describes the expected returns on a stock, a portfolio $E$ on the efficient frontier, and that portfolio's zero-beta companion, $Z$ (see equation 9.9):

$$E(r_i) - E(r_Z) = \beta_i [E(r_E) - E(r_Z)] \tag{13.4}$$

where $\beta_i$ denotes the beta of security $i$ on efficient portfolio $E$.

[4] Richard Roll and Stephen A. Ross, "On the Cross-Sectional Relation between Expected Return and Betas," *Journal of Finance* 50 (1995), pp. 185–224.

[5] Schmuel Kandel and Robert F. Stambaugh, "Portfolio Inefficiency and the Cross-Section of Expected Returns," *Journal of Finance* 50 (1995), pp. 185–224; "A Mean-Variance Framework for Tests of Asset Pricing Models," *Review of Financial Studies* 2 (1989), pp. 125–56; "On Correlations and Inferences about Mean-Variance Efficiency," *Journal of Financial Economics* 18 (1987), pp. 61–90.

**Figure 13.1   Market index proxies that produce betas having no relation to expected returns**

These proxies are located within a restricted region of the mean-variance space, a region bounded by a parabola that lies inside the efficient frontier except for a tangency at the global minimum variance point. The market proxy is located on the boundary at a distance of $M = 22$ basis points below the efficient frontier. While betas against this market proxy have zero cross-sectional correlation with expected returns, a market proxy on the efficient frontier just 22 basis points above it would produce betas that are perfectly positively collinear with expected returns.
Source: Richard Roll and Stephen A. Ross, "On the Cross-Sectional Relation between Expected Return and Betas," *Journal of Finance* 49 (1994), pp. 101–21.

We cannot construct or observe the efficient portfolio $E$ (since we do not know expected returns and covariances of all assets), and so we cannot estimate equation 13.4 directly. KS asked what would happen if we followed the common procedure of using a market proxy portfolio $M$ in place of $E$, and used as well the more efficient GLS regression procedure in estimating the second-pass regression for the zero-beta version of the CAPM, that is,

$$r_i - r_Z = \gamma_0 + \gamma_1 \times (\text{Estimated } \beta_i)$$

They showed that the estimated values of $\gamma_0$ and $\gamma_1$ will be biased by a term proportional to the relative efficiency of the market proxy. If the market index used in the regression is fully efficient, the test will be well specified. But the second-pass regression will provide a poor test of the CAPM if the proxy for the market portfolio is not efficient. Thus, while GLS regressions may not give totally arbitrary results, as Roll and Ross demonstrate may occur using standard OLS regressions, we still cannot test the model in a meaningful way without a reasonably efficient market proxy. Unfortunately, it is difficult to tell how efficient our market index is relative to the theoretical true market portfolio, so we cannot tell how good our tests are.

**Measurement Error in Beta**  Roll's critique tells us that CAPM tests are handicapped from the outset. But suppose that we could get past Roll's problem by obtaining data on the returns of the true market portfolio. We still would have to deal with the statistical problems caused by measurement error in the estimates of beta from the first-stage regressions.

It is well known in statistics that if the right-hand-side variable of a regression equation is measured with error (in our case, beta is measured with error and is the right-hand-side variable in the second-pass regression), then the slope coefficient of the regression equation will be biased downward and the intercept biased upward. This is consistent with the findings cited above, which found that the estimate of $\gamma_0$ was higher than predicted by the CAPM and that the estimate of $\gamma_1$ was lower than predicted.

Indeed, a well-controlled simulation test by Miller and Scholes[6] confirms these arguments. In this test a random-number generator simulated rates of return with covariances similar to observed ones. The average returns were made to agree exactly with the CAPM expected return–beta relationship. Miller and Scholes then used these randomly generated rates of return in the tests we have described as if they were observed from a sample of stock returns. The results of this "simulated" test were virtually identical to those reached using real data, despite the fact that the simulated returns were *constructed* to obey the SML, that is, the true $\gamma$ coefficients were $\gamma_0 = 0$, $\gamma_1 = \overline{r_M - r_f}$, and $\gamma_2 = 0$.

This postmortem of the early test gets us back to square one. We can explain away the disappointing test results, but we have no positive results to support the CAPM-APT implications.

The next wave of tests was designed to overcome the measurement error problem that led to biased estimates of the SML. The innovation in these tests, pioneered by Black, Jensen, and Scholes (BJS),[7] was to use portfolios rather than individual securities. Combining securities into portfolios diversifies away most of the firm-specific part of returns, thereby enhancing the precision of the estimates of beta and the expected rate of return of the portfolio of securities. This mitigates the statistical problems that arise from measurement error in the beta estimates.

Obviously, however, combining stocks into portfolios reduces the number of observations left for the second-pass regression. For example, suppose that we group our sample of 100 stocks into five portfolios of 20 stocks each. If the assumption of a single-factor market is reasonably accurate, then the residuals of the 20 stocks in each portfolio will be practically uncorrelated and, hence, the variance of the portfolio residual will be about one-twentieth the residual variance of the average stock. Thus the portfolio beta in the first-pass regression will be estimated with far better accuracy. However, now consider the second-pass regression. With individual securities we had 100 observations to estimate the second-pass coefficients. With portfolios of 20 stocks each we are left with only five observations for the second-pass regression.

To get the best of this trade-off, we need to construct portfolios with the largest possible dispersion of beta coefficients. Other things being equal, a sample yields more accurate regression estimates the more widely spaced are the observations of the independent variables. Consider the first-pass regressions where we estimate the SCL, that is, the relationship between the excess return on each stock and the market's excess return. If we have a sample with a great dispersion of market returns, we have a greater chance of accurately estimating the effect of a change in the market return on the return of the stock. In

[6] Miller and Scholes, "Rate of Return in Relation to Risk: A Reexamination of Some Recent Findings."
[7] Fischer Black, Michael C. Jensen, and Myron Scholes, "The Capital Asset Pricing Model: Some Empirical Tests," in Michael C. Jensen, ed., *Studies in the Theory of Capital Markets* (New York: Praeger, 1972).

**Table 13.1   Summary of Fama and MacBeth (1973) Study (all rates in basis points per month)**

| Period | 1935/6–1968 | 1935–1945 | 1946–1955 | 1956/6–1968 |
|---|---|---|---|---|
| Av. $r_f$ | 13 | 2 | 9 | 26 |
| Av. $\gamma_0 - r_f$ | 8 | 10 | 8 | 5 |
| Av. $t(\gamma_0 - r_f)$ | 0.20 | 0.11 | 0.20 | 0.10 |
| Av. $r_M - r_f$ | 130 | 195 | 103 | 95 |
| Av. $\gamma_1$ | 114 | 118 | 209 | 34 |
| Av. $t(\gamma_1)$ | 1.85 | 0.94 | 2.39 | 0.34 |
| Av. $\gamma_2$ | −26 | −9 | −76 | 0 |
| Av. $t(\gamma_2)$ | −0.86 | −0.14 | −2.16 | 0 |
| Av. $\gamma_3$ | 516 | 817 | −378 | 960 |
| Av. $t(\gamma_3)$ | 1.11 | 0.94 | −0.67 | 1.11 |
| Av. $R$-SQR | 0.31 | 0.31 | 0.32 | 0.29 |

our case, however, we have no control over the range of the market returns. But we can control the range of the independent variable of the second-pass regression, the portfolio betas. Rather than allocate 20 stocks to each portfolio randomly, we can rank portfolios by betas. Portfolio 1 will include the 20 highest-beta stocks and Portfolio 5 the 20 lowest-beta stocks. In that case a set of portfolios with small nonsystematic components, $e_P$, and widely spaced betas will yield reasonably powerful tests of the SML.

Fama and MacBeth[8] used this methodology to verify that the observed relationship between average excess returns and beta is indeed linear and that nonsystematic risk does not explain average excess returns. Using 20 portfolios constructed according to the BJS methodology, Fama and MacBeth expanded the estimation of the SML equation to include the square of the beta coefficient (to test for linearity of the relationship between returns and betas) and the estimated standard deviation of the residual (to test for the explanatory power of nonsystematic risk). For a sequence of many subperiods they estimated for each subperiod, the equation

$$r_i = \gamma_0 + \gamma_1\beta_i + \gamma_2\beta_i^2 + \gamma_3\sigma(e_i) \tag{13.5}$$

The term $\gamma_2$ measures potential nonlinearity of return, and $\gamma_3$ measures the explanatory power of nonsystematic risk, $\sigma(e_i)$. According to the CAPM, both $\gamma_2$ and $\gamma_3$ should have coefficients of zero in the second-pass regression.

Fama and MacBeth estimated equation 13.5 for every month of the period January 1935 through June 1968. The results are summarized in Table 13.1, which shows average coefficients and $t$-statistics for the overall period as well as for three subperiods. Fama and MacBeth observed that the coefficients on residual standard deviation (nonsystematic risk), denoted by $\gamma_3$, fluctuate greatly from month to month and were insignificant, consistent with the hypothesis that nonsystematic risk is not rewarded by higher average returns. Likewise, the coefficients on the square of beta, denoted by $\gamma_2$, were insignificant, consistent with the hypothesis that the expected return–beta relationship is linear.

---

[8] Eugene Fama and James MacBeth, "Risk, Return, and Equilibrium: Empirical Tests," *Journal of Political Economy* 81 (March 1973).

With respect to the expected return–beta relationship, however, the picture is mixed. The estimated SML is too flat, consistent with previous studies, as can be seen from the fact that $\gamma_0 - r_f$ is positive, and that $\gamma_1$ is, on average, less than $r_M - r_f$. On the positive side, the difference does not appear to be significant, so that the CAPM is not clearly rejected.

---

**CONCEPT CHECK
QUESTION 3**

**According to the CAPM, what are the predicted values of $\gamma_0$, $\gamma_1$, $\gamma_2$, and $\gamma_3$ in the Fama-MacBeth regressions for the period 1946–1955?**

---

In conclusion, these tests of the CAPM provide mixed evidence on the validity of the theory. We can summarize the results as follows:

1. The insights that are supported by the single-factor CAPM and APT are as follows:
   a. Expected rates of return are linear and increase with beta, the measure of systematic risk.
   b. Expected rates of return are not affected by nonsystematic risk.
2. The single-variable expected return–beta relationship predicted by either the risk-free rate or the zero-beta version of the CAPM is not fully consistent with empirical observation.

Thus, although the CAPM seems *qualitatively* correct in that $\beta$ matters and $\sigma(e_i)$ does not, empirical tests do not validate its *quantitative* predictions.

---

**CONCEPT CHECK
QUESTION 4**

**What would you conclude if you performed the Fama and MacBeth tests and found that the coefficients on $\beta^2$ and $\sigma(e)$ were positive?**

---

**The EMH and the CAPM**

Roll's critique also provides a positive avenue to view the empirical content of the CAPM and APT. Recall, as Roll pointed out, that the CAPM and the expected return–beta relationship follow directly from the efficiency of the market portfolio. This means that if we can establish that the market portfolio is efficient, we would have no need to further test the expected return–beta relationship.

As demonstrated in Chapter 12 on the efficient market hypothesis, proxies for the market portfolio such as the S&P 500 and the NYSE index have proven hard to beat by professional investors. This is perhaps the strongest evidence for the empirical content of the CAPM and APT.

**Accounting for Human Capital and Cyclical Variations in Asset Betas**

We are reminded of two important deficiencies of the tests of the single-index models:

1. Only a fraction of the value of assets in the United States is traded in capital markets; perhaps the most important nontraded asset is human capital.
2. There is ample evidence that asset betas are cyclical and that accounting for this cyclicality may improve the predictive power of the CAPM.

One of the CAPM assumptions is that all assets are traded and accessible to all investors. Mayers[9] proposed a version of the CAPM that accounts for a violation of this assumption; this requires an additional term in the expected return–beta relationship.

An important nontraded asset that may partly account for the deficiency of standard market proxies such as the S&P 500 is human capital. The value of future wages and compensation for expert services is a significant component of the wealth of investors who expect years of productive careers prior to retirement. Moreover, it is reasonable to expect that changes in human capital are far less than perfectly correlated with asset returns, and hence they diversify the risk of investor portfolios.

Jaganathan and Wang (JW)[10] used a proxy for changes in the value of human capital based on the rate of change in aggregate labor income. In addition to the standard security betas estimated using the value-weighted stock market index, which we denote $\beta^{vw}$, JW also estimated the betas of assets with respect to labor income growth, which we denote $\beta^{labor}$. Finally, they considered the possibility that business cycles affect asset betas, an issue that has been examined in a number of other studies.[11] They used the difference between the yields on low- and high-grade corporate bonds as a proxy for the state of the business cycle and estimate asset betas relative to this business cycle variable; we denote this beta as $\beta^{prem}$.

With the estimates of these three betas for several stock portfolios, JW estimated a second-pass regression which includes firm size (market value of equity, denoted ME):

$$E(R_i) = c_0 + c_{size}\log(ME) + c_{vw}\beta^{vw} + c_{prem}\beta^{prem} + c_{labor}\beta^{labor} \tag{13.6}$$

Table 13.2 shows the results of various versions of the second-pass estimates. These results are far more supportive of the CAPM than earlier tests. The explanatory power of the equations that include JW's expanded set of explanatory variables (which they call a "conditional" CAPM because beta is conditional on the state of the economy) is much greater than in earlier tests, and the significance of the size variable disappears.

Figure 13.2 shows the improvements of these tests more dramatically. Figure 13.2A shows that the conventional CAPM indeed works poorly. The figure compares predicted security returns fitted using the firm's beta versus actual returns. There is obviously almost no relationship between the two. This is indicative of the weak performance of the conventional CAPM in empirical tests. But if we use the conditional CAPM to compare fitted to actual returns, as in Figure 13.2B, we get a dramatically improved fit. Moreover, adding firm size to this model turns out to do nothing to improve the fit. We conclude that firm size does not improve return predictions once we account for the variables addressed in the conditional CAPM.

JW also compare the conditional CAPM to the Fama and French 3-factor model and find that the significance of the book-to-market and size factors disappears once we account for human capital and cyclical variation of the single-index betas.

[9] David Mayers, "Nonmarketable Assets and Capital Market Equilibrium under Uncertainty," in Michael C. Jensen, ed., *Studies in the Theory of Capital Markets* (New York: Praeger, 1972), pp. 223–48.

[10] Ravi Jaganathan and Zhenyu Wang, "The Conditional CAPM and the Cross-Section of Expected Returns," *Journal of Finance* 51 (March 1996), pp. 3–54.

[11] For example, Campbell Harvey, "Time-Varying Conditional Covariances in Tests of Asset Pricing Models," *Journal of Financial Economics* 24 (October 1989), pp. 289–317; Wayne Ferson and Campbell Harvey, "The Variation of Economic Risk Premiums," *Journal of Political Economy* 99 (April 1991), pp. 385–415; and Wayne Ferson and Robert Korajczyk, "Do Arbitrage Pricing Models Explain the Predictability of Stock Returns?" *Journal of Business* 68 (July 1995), pp. 309–49.

## Table 13.2  Evaluation of Various CAPM Specifications

This table gives the estimates for the cross-sectional regression model

$$E(R_{it}) = c_0 + c_{size}\log(ME_i) + c_{vw}\beta_i^{vw} + c_{prem}\beta_i^{prem} + c_{labor}\beta_i^{labor}$$

with either a subset or all of the variables. Here, $R_{it}$ is the return on portfolio $i$ ($i = 1, 2, \ldots, 100$) in month $t$ (July 1963–December 1990), $R_t^{vw}$ is the return on the value-weighted index of stocks, $R_{t-1}^{prem}$ is the yield spread between low- and high-grade corporate bonds, and $R_t^{labor}$ is the growth rate in per capita labor income. The $\beta_i^{vw}$ is the slope coefficient in the OLS regression of $R_{it}$ on a constant and $R_t^{vw}$. The other betas are estimated in a similar way. The portfolio size, $\log(ME_i)$, is calculated as the equally weighted average of the logarithm of the market value (in millions of dollars) of the stocks in portfolio $i$. The regression models are estimated by using the Fama-MacBeth procedure. The "corrected $t$-values" take sampling errors in the estimated betas into account. All $R^2$s are reported as percentages.

| Coefficient | $c_0$ | $c_{vw}$ | $c_{prem}$ | $c_{labor}$ | $c_{size}$ | $R^2$ |
|---|---|---|---|---|---|---|
| **A. The Static CAPM without Human Capital** | | | | | | |
| Estimate | 1.24 | −0.10 | | | | 1.35 |
| $t$-value | 5.17 | −0.28 | | | | |
| Estimate | 2.08 | −0.32 | | | −0.11 | 57.56 |
| $t$-value | 5.79 | −0.94 | | | −2.30 | |
| **B. The Conditional CAPM with Human Capital** | | | | | | |
| Estimate | 1.24 | −0.40 | 0.34 | 0.22 | | 55.21 |
| $t$-value | 5.51 | −1.18 | 3.31 | 2.31 | | |
| Estimate | 1.70 | −0.40 | 0.20 | 0.10 | −0.07 | 64.73 |
| $t$-value | 4.61 | −1.18 | 3.00 | 2.09 | −1.45 | |

# 13.2  TESTS OF MULTIFACTOR CAPM AND APT

The multifactor CAPM and APT are elegant theories of how exposure to systematic risk factors should influence expected returns, but they provide little guidance concerning which factors (sources of risk) ought to result in risk premiums. A test of this hypothesis would require three stages:

1. Specification of risk factors.
2. Identification of portfolios that hedge these fundamental risk factors.
3. Test of the explanatory power and risk premiums of the hedge portfolios.

**A Macro Factor Model**   Chen, Roll, and Ross,[12] identify several possible variables that might proxy for systematic factors:

IP = Growth rate in industrial production

EI = Changes in expected inflation measured by changes in short-term (T-bill) interest rates

UI = Unexpected inflation defined as the difference between actual and expected inflation

CG = Unexpected changes in risk premiums measured by the difference between the returns on corporate Baa-rated bonds and long-term government bonds

GB = Unexpected changes in the term premium measured by the difference between the returns on long- and short-term government bonds

---

[12] Nai-Fu Chen, Richard Roll, and Stephen Ross, "Economic Forces and the Stock Market," *Journal of Business* 59 (1986).

**Figure 13.2   Fitted expected returns versus realized average returns**

Each scatter point in the graph represents a portfolio, with the realized average return as the horizontal axis and the fitted expected return as the vertical axis. For each portfolio $i$, the realized average return is the time-series average of the portfolio return, and the fitted expected return is the fitted value for the expected return, $E(R_i)$, in the following regression model:

$$E(R_i) = c_0 + c_{vw}\beta_i^{vw}$$

where $\beta_i^{vw}$ is the slope coefficient in the OLS regression of the portfolio return on a constant and the return on the value-weighted index portfolio of stocks. The straight line in the graph is the 45° line from the origin.

Each scatter point in the graph represents a portfolio, with the realized average return as the horizontal axis and the fitted expected return as the vertical axis. For each portfolio $i$, the realized average return is the time-series average of the portfolio return, and the fitted expected return is the fitted value for the expected return, $E(R_i)$, in the following regression model:

$$E(R_i) = c_0 + c_{vw}\beta_i^{vw} + c_{prem}\beta_i^{prem} + c_{labor}\beta_i^{labor}$$

where $\beta_i^{vw}$ is the slope coefficient in the OLS regression of the portfolio return on a constant and the return on the value-weighted index portfolio of stocks, $\beta_i^{prem}$ is the slope coeficient in the OLS regression of the portfolio return on a constant and the yield spread between low- and high-grade corporate bonds, and $\beta_i^{labor}$ is the slope coefficient in the OLS regression of the portfolio return on a constant and the growth rate in per capita labor income. The straight line in the graph is the 45° line from the origin.

With the identification of these potential economic factors, Chen, Roll, and Ross skipped the procedure of identifying factor portfolios (the portfolios that have the highest correlation with the factors). Instead, by using the factors themselves, they implicitly assumed that factor portfolios exist that can proxy for the factors. They use these factors in a test similar to that of Fama and MacBeth.

A critical part of the methodology is the grouping of stocks into portfolios. Recall that in the single-factor tests, portfolios were constructed to span a wide range of betas to enhance the power of the test. In a multifactor framework the efficient criterion for grouping is less obvious. Chen, Roll, and Ross chose to group the sample stocks into 20 portfolios by size (market value of outstanding equity), a variable that is known to be associated with average stock returns.

They first used 5 years of monthly data to estimate the factor betas of the 20 portfolios in a first-pass regression. This is accomplished by estimating the following regressions for each portfolio:

$$r = a + \beta_M r_M + \beta_{IP}IP + \beta_{EI}EI + \beta_{UI}UI + \beta_{CG}CG + \beta_{GB}GB + e \qquad (13.7a)$$

**Table 13.3 Economic Variables and Pricing (percent per month × 10), Multivariate Approach**

| A | YP | IP | EI | UI | CG | GB | Constant |
|---|---|---|---|---|---|---|---|
| | 4.341 | 13.984 | −0.111 | −0.672 | 7.941 | −5.8 | 4.112 |
| | (0.538) | (3.727) | (−1.499) | (−2.052) | (2.807) | (−1.844) | (1.334) |

| B | IP | EI | UI | CG | GB | Constant |
|---|---|---|---|---|---|---|
| | 13.589 | −0.125 | −6.29 | 7.205 | −5.211 | 4.124 |
| | (3.561) | (−1.640) | (−1.979) | (2.590) | (−1.690) | (1.361) |

| C | EWNY | IP | EI | UI | CG | GB | Constant |
|---|---|---|---|---|---|---|---|
| | 5.021 | 14.009 | −0.128 | −0.848 | 0.130 | −5.017 | 6.409 |
| | (1.218) | (3.774) | (−1.666) | (−2.541) | (2.855) | (−1.576) | (1.848) |

| D | VWNY | IP | EI | UI | CG | GB | Constant |
|---|---|---|---|---|---|---|---|
| | −2.403 | 11.756 | −0.123 | −0.795 | 8.274 | −5.905 | 10.713 |
| | (−0.633) | (3.054) | (−1.600) | (−2.376) | (2.972) | (−1.879) | (2.755) |

VWNY = Return on the value-weighted NYSE index; EWNY = Return on the equally weighted NYSE index; IP = Monthly growth rate in industrial production; EI = Change in expected inflation; UI = Unanticipated inflation; CG = Unanticipated change in the risk premium (Baa and under return − long-term government bond return); GB = Unanticipated change in the term structure (long-term government bond return − Treasury-bill rate); and YP = Yearly growth rate in industrial production. Note that $t$-statistics are in parentheses.

Source: Modified from Nai-Fu Chen, Richard Roll, and Stephen Ross, "Economic Forces and the Stock Market," *Journal of Business* 59 (1986); published by the University of Chicago.

where $M$ stands for the stock market index. Chen, Roll, and Ross used as the market index both the value-weighted NYSE index (VWNY) and the equally weighted NYSE index (EWNY).

Using the 20 sets of first-pass estimates of factor betas as the independent variables, they now estimated the second-pass regression (with 20 observations, one for each portfolio):

$$r = \gamma_0 + \gamma_M \beta_M + \gamma_{IP} \beta_{IP} + \gamma_{EI} \beta_{EI} + \gamma_{UI} \beta_{UI} + \gamma_{CG} \beta_{CG} + \gamma_{GB} \beta_{GB} + e \quad (13.7b)$$

where the gammas become estimates of the risk premiums on the factors.

Chen, Roll, and Ross ran this second-pass regression for every month of their sample period, reestimating the first-pass factor betas once every 12 months. They ran the second-pass tests in four variations. First (Table 13.3, parts A and B), they excluded the market index altogether and used two alternative measures of industrial production (YP based on annual growth of industrial production and MP based on monthly growth). Finding that MP is a more effective measure, they next included the two versions of the market index, EWNY and VWNY, one at a time (Table 13.3, parts C and D). The estimated risk premiums (the values for the parameters, $\gamma$) were averaged over all the second-pass regressions.

Note in Table 13.3, parts C and D, that the two market indexes EWNY (equally weighted index of NYSE) and VWNY (the value-weighted NYSE index) are not statistically significant (their $t$-statistics of 1.218 and −.633 are less than 2). Note also that the VWNY factor has the "wrong" sign in that it seems to imply a negative market-risk premium. Industrial production (MP), the risk premium on corporate bonds (CG), and unanticipated inflation (UI) are the factors that appear to have significant explanatory power.

These results indicate that it may be possible to hedge some economic factors that affect future consumption risk with appropriate portfolios. A CAPM or APT multifactor equilibrium expected return–beta relationship may one day supersede the now widely used single-factor model.

## 13.3  THE FAMA-FRENCH THREE-FACTOR MODEL

The multifactor model that occupies center stage these days is the three-factor model introduced by Fama and French, briefly discussed in Chapters 11 and 12. The systematic factors in the Fama-French model are firm size and book-to-market ratio as well as the market index. These additional factors are empirically motivated by the observations that historical-average returns on stocks of small firms and on stocks with high ratios of book equity to market equity (B/M) are higher than predicted by the security market line of the CAPM. These observations suggest that size or the book-to-market ratio may be proxies for exposures to sources of systematic risk not captured by the CAPM beta and thus result in the return premiums we see associated with these factors.

To create portfolios that track the firm size and book-to-market factors, Davis, Fama, and French[13] (DFF) sorted industrial firms annually by size (market capitalization) and by book-to-market (B/M) ratio. The small-firm group (group S) includes all firms with capitalization below the median, while big (group B) firms have above-median capitalization. Similarly, firms are annually sorted into three groups based on book-to-market ratio: a low-ratio group (group L) with the 33% lowest B/M ratio, a medium-ratio group (group M), and a high-ratio group (group H). The high-ratio firms often are called *value firms,* since they appear to be "good values," selling at low multiples of book value. The intersections of the two size groups with the three value groups results in six groups of firms. Six such portfolios (S/L, S/M, S/H, B/L, B/M, B/H) were constructed each year throughout the period, and the monthly returns of each were recorded. This procedure generated six time series of monthly returns for the years 1929 to 1997.

For each year, the size premium is constructed as the difference in returns between small and large firms. Specifically, the difference in returns of an equally-weighted long position in the three small-firm portfolios and an equally-weighted short position in the three big-firm portfolios are computed. SMB (for small minus big) is the return difference. Thus, SMB is calculated from the monthly returns of the six portfolios as

$$\text{SMB} = \tfrac{1}{3}(\text{S/L} + \text{S/M} + \text{S/H}) - \tfrac{1}{3}(\text{B/L} + \text{B/M} + \text{B/H}) \qquad (13.8a)$$

Similarly, the book-to-market effect is calculated from the difference in returns between high B/M ratio and low B/M ratio firms. HML (for high minus low ratio) is constructed as the difference in returns between an equally weighted long position in the high B/M portfolios and an equally weighted short position in the low B/M portfolios. The monthly values of HML were calculated from the monthly returns on the low and high B/M portfolios as

$$\text{HML} = \tfrac{1}{2}(\text{S/H} + \text{B/H}) - \tfrac{1}{2}(\text{S/L} + \text{B/L}) \qquad (13.8b)$$

---

[13] James L. Davis, Eugene F. Fama, and Kenneth R. French, "Characteristics, Covariances, and Average Returns, 1929 to 1997," *Journal of Finance* 55, no. 1, (2000), pp. 389–406.

**Table 13.4    Summary Statistics for Monthly Percent Three-Factor Explanatory Returns**

|  | $R_M - R_f$ | SMB | HML | S/L | S/M | S/H | B/L | B/M | B/H |
|---|---|---|---|---|---|---|---|---|---|
| **7/29–6/97: 816 months** | | | | | | | | | |
| Ave | 0.67 | 0.20 | 0.46 | 1.05 | 1.30 | 1.53 | 0.89 | 1.04 | 1.34 |
| Std | 5.75 | 3.26 | 3.11 | 7.89 | 7.49 | 8.38 | 5.65 | 6.19 | 7.41 |
| $t$(Ave) | 3.34 | 1.78 | 4.24 | 3.80 | 4.96 | 5.21 | 4.52 | 4.78 | 5.16 |
| **7/29–6/63: 408 months** | | | | | | | | | |
| Ave | 0.82 | 0.19 | 0.50 | 1.09 | 1.22 | 1.49 | 0.81 | 1.01 | 1.40 |
| Std | 6.89 | 3.65 | 3.59 | 9.01 | 9.13 | 10.57 | 6.50 | 7.73 | 9.52 |
| $t$(Ave) | 2.41 | 1.07 | 2.80 | 2.44 | 2.71 | 2.85 | 2.52 | 2.64 | 2.98 |
| **7/63–6/97: 408 months** | | | | | | | | | |
| Ave | 0.52 | 0.21 | 0.43 | 1.01 | 1.38 | 1.57 | 0.98 | 1.06 | 1.27 |
| Std | 4.32 | 2.83 | 2.54 | 6.60 | 5.38 | 5.37 | 4.65 | 4.12 | 4.38 |
| $t$(Ave) | 2.44 | 1.53 | 3.38 | 3.10 | 5.17 | 5.88 | 4.24 | 5.20 | 5.87 |
| **7/73–12/93: 246 months** | | | | | | | | | |
| Ave | 0.51 | 0.33 | 0.50 | 1.23 | 1.60 | 1.76 | 0.96 | 1.20 | 1.44 |
| Std | 4.79 | 2.75 | 2.74 | 6.88 | 5.64 | 5.68 | 5.22 | 4.53 | 4.67 |
| $t$(Ave) | 1.68 | 1.88 | 2.87 | 2.81 | 4.46 | 4.87 | 2.90 | 4.17 | 4.83 |

Source: James L. Davis, Eugene F. Fama, and Kenneth R. French, "Characteristics, Covariances, and Average Returns, 1929 to 1999," *Journal of Finance* 55, no. 1, (2000), pp. 393.

The monthly returns on the market portfolio were calculated from the value-weighted portfolio of all firms listed on the NYSE, AMEX, and Nasdaq. The risk-free rate was the return on 1-month T-bills.

The Fama-French three-factor asset pricing model equation is

$$E(r_i) - r_f = a_i + b_i[E(r_M) - r_f] + s_i E(\text{SMB}) + h_i E(\text{HML}) \tag{13.9a}$$

The coefficients $b_i$, $s_i$, and $h_i$, are the factor loadings (equivalently, factor betas) on the three relevant risk factors. According to the APT, the intercept $a_i$ should be zero, since a portfolio with zero loading on all three factors should have an expected excess return of zero. This equation is estimated as a first-pass regression for each portfolio over the 816 months between 1929 and 1997 using the regression model

$$r_i - r_f = a_i + b_i(r_M - r_f) + s_i \text{SMB} + h_i \text{HML} + e_i \tag{13.9b}$$

Summary statistics for the market excess return, the factor portfolio returns, and the six size-value portfolios are shown in Table 13.4. The data clearly indicate that the small firms and high book-to-market firms have significantly higher average returns. SMB and HML are both reliably positive. Portfolios of small firm (S) and value firms (H) earned significantly higher average returns.

To estimate the regressions (13.9b) for a somewhat larger number of portfolios (nine) and secure an equal number of stocks in each group to equalize diversification, DFF repeat the sorts on both size and B/M, but this time they allocate a third of the sample to small, medium, and large firms in the size sort, as well as to low, medium, and high B/M ratio firms in an independent sort. The intersections of these groups lead to nine portfolios containing equal numbers of stocks.

The estimation results of the nine regressions (equation 13.9b) for the overall sample period and for the early and late half-periods are presented in Table 13.5. The $R$-square

**Table 13.5    Three-Factor Regressions for Portfolios Formed from Independent Sorts on Size and BE/ME**

|        | BE/ME | Size  | Ex Ret | a     | b    | s     | h     | t(a)  | t(b)   | t(s)   | t(h)   | R² |
|--------|-------|-------|--------|-------|------|-------|-------|-------|--------|--------|--------|------|
| **7/29–6/97** | | | | | | | | | | | | |
| S/L    | 0.55  | 22.39 | 0.61   | −0.42 | 1.06 | 1.39  | 0.09  | −4.34 | 30.78  | 19.23  | 1.73   | 0.91 |
| S/M    | 1.11  | 22.15 | 1.05   | −0.01 | 0.97 | 1.16  | 0.37  | −0.18 | 53.55  | 19.49  | 9.96   | 0.96 |
| S/H    | 2.83  | 19.05 | 1.24   | −0.03 | 1.03 | 1.12  | 0.77  | −0.73 | 67.32  | 39.21  | 26.97  | 0.98 |
| M/L    | 0.53  | 55.85 | 0.70   | −0.06 | 1.04 | 0.59  | −0.12 | −1.29 | 55.83  | 18.01  | −4.30  | 0.96 |
| M/M    | 1.07  | 55.06 | 0.95   | −0.01 | 1.05 | 0.47  | 0.34  | −0.15 | 32.98  | 17.50  | 9.50   | 0.96 |
| M/H    | 2.18  | 53.21 | 1.13   | −0.04 | 1.08 | 0.53  | 0.73  | −0.90 | 47.85  | 8.99   | 11.12  | 0.97 |
| B/L    | 0.43  | 94.65 | 0.58   | 0.02  | 1.02 | −0.10 | −0.23 | 0.88  | 148.09 | −6.88  | −13.52 | 0.98 |
| B/M    | 1.04  | 92.06 | 0.72   | −0.09 | 1.01 | −0.14 | 0.34  | −1.76 | 61.61  | −4.96  | 13.66  | 0.95 |
| B/H    | 1.87  | 89.53 | 1.00   | −0.09 | 1.06 | −0.07 | 0.84  | −1.40 | 52.12  | −0.86  | 21.02  | 0.93 |
| **7/29–6/63** | | | | | | | | | | | | |
| S/L    | 0.68  | 23.83 | 0.69   | −0.53 | 1.01 | 1.47  | 0.23  | −3.04 | 18.66  | 15.72  | 2.82   | 0.90 |
| S/M    | 1.35  | 23.63 | 1.21   | −0.01 | 0.96 | 1.24  | 0.38  | −0.07 | 34.72  | 15.60  | 6.21   | 0.95 |
| S/H    | 3.96  | 20.23 | 1.44   | −0.03 | 1.02 | 1.17  | 0.83  | −0.40 | 44.71  | 28.80  | 17.76  | 0.98 |
| M/L    | 0.64  | 55.20 | 0.84   | 0.08  | 0.98 | 0.56  | 0.01  | −1.14 | 37.44  | 12.26  | 0.39   | 0.96 |
| M/M    | 1.28  | 54.20 | 1.13   | 0.00  | 1.07 | 0.47  | 0.33  | 0.07  | 26.38  | 11.77  | 7.73   | 0.97 |
| M/H    | 2.83  | 51.59 | 1.30   | −0.07 | 1.07 | 0.50  | 0.79  | −0.92 | 52.49  | 5.44   | 7.74   | 0.97 |
| B/L    | 0.48  | 94.92 | 0.72   | −0.01 | 1.02 | −0.08 | −0.20 | −0.20 | 131.66 | −4.89  | −8.09  | 0.99 |
| B/M    | 1.21  | 91.97 | 0.89   | −0.09 | 1.00 | −0.12 | 0.37  | −1.20 | 43.96  | −2.90  | 10.08  | 0.96 |
| B/H    | 2.33  | 88.91 | 1.30   | 0.00  | 1.02 | −0.12 | 0.97  | −0.01 | 34.28  | −0.96  | 17.99  | 0.94 |
| **7/63–6/97** | | | | | | | | | | | | |
| S/L    | 0.42  | 20.94 | 0.54   | −0.22 | 1.06 | 1.22  | −0.14 | −3.31 | 60.47  | 39.87  | −4.51  | 0.96 |
| S/M    | 0.87  | 20.68 | 0.89   | 0.03  | 0.97 | 1.02  | 0.31  | 0.71  | 74.53  | 52.41  | 13.82  | 0.98 |
| S/H    | 1.71  | 17.88 | 1.04   | 0.04  | 0.99 | 1.03  | 0.62  | 1.27  | 75.12  | 64.49  | 25.86  | 0.98 |
| M/L    | 0.42  | 56.51 | 0.56   | −0.02 | 1.07 | 0.58  | −0.24 | −0.33 | 71.73  | 27.08  | −9.73  | 0.96 |
| M/M    | 0.87  | 55.93 | 0.77   | 0.02  | 1.00 | 0.48  | 0.30  | 0.31  | 64.36  | 22.60  | 11.22  | 0.95 |
| M/H    | 1.54  | 54.83 | 0.96   | 0.03  | 1.05 | 0.55  | 0.63  | 0.53  | 69.16  | 28.08  | 24.23  | 0.96 |
| B/L    | 0.38  | 94.38 | 0.45   | 0.10  | 0.99 | −0.15 | −0.32 | 2.89  | 91.73  | −8.92  | −16.53 | 0.98 |
| B/M    | 0.86  | 92.14 | 0.54   | −0.04 | 0.99 | −0.19 | 0.25  | −0.70 | 55.19  | −6.91  | 8.53   | 0.91 |
| B/H    | 1.41  | 90.16 | 0.70   | −0.13 | 1.04 | −0.01 | 0.69  | −2.59 | 76.64  | −0.36  | 28.53  | 0.94 |

Source: James L. Davis, Eugene F. Fama, and Kenneth R. French, "Characteristics, Covariances, and Average Returns, 1929 to 1999," *Journal of Finance* 55, no. 1, (2000), pp. 396.

statistics, all in excess of 0.91, show that returns are well explained by the three factor portfolios, and the *t*-statistics of the loadings on the size and value factors show that these factors contribute significantly to explanatory power. Moreover, for the full sample period, only one of the nine portfolios has an economically and statistically significant intercept.

How should we interpret these results? One argument is that size and relative value (as measured by the B/M ratio) proxy for risk not captured by the CAPM beta alone.[14] This explanation is consistent with the APT in that it implies that size and value are priced risk

[14] Maria Vassalou and Yuhang Xing, "Default Risk and Equity Returns," *Journal of Finance* (forthcoming), show that these factors contain information on return beyond default risk.

factors and, hence, that these premiums do not represent mispricing. Another explanation attributes these premiums to irrational investor preferences for large size or low B/M firms, which drives up their prices and drives down the returns on these firms. This question may be more relevant for the B/M or "value" factor in light of evidence that the size premium has largely vanished in recent years.

The question about the source of the value premium must be resolved by testing whether, within each group, portfolios with larger loadings on the value factor (larger *h* coefficient on the HML portfolio) do indeed earn a higher average return. If they do not, then it appears that firms with these *characteristics* (i.e., a higher ratio of B/M) earn higher returns but that a greater *exposure* to the B/M factor per se does not itself predict higher returns. This would be evidence of mispricing.[15]

To address this issue, DFF sort each of the portfolios into three subgroups according to their *h* value over the previous 3 years and show that higher *h* portfolios (with greater exposure to HML) earned a higher average return over the full sample period. But DFF also found that this was not the case in the 20-year period between 1973 and 1993. Thus, the important question of whether the model is consistent with a three-factor version of the APT, or instead suggests irrational investor behavior, is not categorically resolved. See the nearby box for further recent approaches to the risk-return tradeoff.

# 13.4 TIME-VARYING VOLATILITY

We may associate the variance of the rate of return on the stock with the rate of arrival of new information because new information may lead investors to revise their assessment of intrinsic value. As a casual survey of the media would indicate, the rate of revision in predictions of business cycles, industry ascents or descents, and the fortunes of individual enterprises fluctuates regularly; in other words, the rate of arrival of new information is time varying. Consequently, we should expect the variances of the rates of return on stocks (as well as the covariances among them) to be time varying.

In an exploratory study of the volatility of NYSE stocks over more than 150 years (using monthly returns over 1835–1987), Pagan and Schwert[16] computed estimates of the variance of monthly returns. Their results, depicted in Figure 13.3 on page 434, show just how important it may be to consider time variation in stock variance. The centrality of the risk-return trade-off suggests that once we make sufficient progress in the modeling, estimation, and prediction of the time variation in return variances and covariances, we should expect a significant refinement in our understanding of expected returns as well.

When we consider a time-varying return distribution, we must refer to the *conditional* mean, variance, and covariance, that is, the mean, variance, or covariance conditional on currently available information. The "conditions" that vary over time are the values of variables that determine the level of these parameters. In contrast, the usual estimate of return variance, the average of squared deviations over the sample period, provides an *unconditional* estimate, because it treats the variance as constant over time.

In 1982 Robert F. Engle published a study[17] of U.K. inflation rates that measured their time-varying volatility. His model, named ARCH (autoregressive conditional heteroskedasticity), is based on the idea that a natural way to update a variance forecast is to

---

[15] This point is emphasized in Kent Daniel and Sheridan Titman, "Evidence on the Characteristics of Cross Sectional Variation in Common Stock Returns," *Journal of Finance* 40 (1995), pp. 383–99.

[16] Adrian Pagan and G. William Schwert, "Alternative Models for Conditional Stock Volatility," *Journal of Econometrics* 45 (1990), pp. 267–90.

[17] Robert F. Engle, "Autoregressive Conditional Heteroskedasticity with Estimates of the Variance of U.K. Inflation," *Econometrica* 50 (1982), pp. 987–1008.

Since the stock market bubble burst more than 3 years ago, investors have had ample time to ponder where to put the remains of their money. Economists and analysts too have been revisiting old ideas. None has been dearer to them than the capital asset pricing model (CAPM), a formula linking movements in a single share price to those of the market as a whole. The key statistic there is "beta."

However, many investors and managers have given up on beta. Although it is useful for working out overall correlation with the market, it tells you little about share-price performance in absolute terms. In fact, the CAPM's obituary was already being written more than a decade ago when a paper by Eugene Fama and Kenneth French showed that the shares of small companies and "value stocks" do much better over time than their betas would predict.

Another new paper, by John Campbell and Tuomo Vuolteenaho of Harvard University, tries to resuscitate beta by splitting it into two.* The authors start from first principles. In essence, the value of a company depends on two things; its expected profits and the interest rate used to discount these profits. Changes in share prices therefore stem from changes in one of these factors.

From this observation, they propose two types of beta: one to gauge shares' responses to changes in profits; the other to pick up the effects of changes in the interest rate. Allowing for separate cash flow versus interest rate betas helps better explain the performance of small and value companies. Shares of such companies are more sensitive than the average to news about profits, in part because they are bets on future growth. Shares with high price–earnings ratios vary more with the discount rate. In all cases, above-average returns compensate investors for above-average risks.

## Equity's Allure

Beta is a tool for comparing shares with each other. Recently, however, investors have been worried about equity as an asset class. The crash has left investors asking what became of the fabled equity premium, the amount by which they can expect returns on shares to exceed those from government bonds.

History says that shareholders have a lot to be optimistic about. Over the past 100 years, investors in American shares have enjoyed a premium, relative to Treasury bonds, of around seven percentage points. Similar effects have been seen in other countries. Some studies have reached less optimistic conclusions, suggesting a premium of four or five points. But even this premium seems generous.

Many answers have been put forward to explain the premium. One is that workers cannot hedge against many risks, such as losing their jobs, which tend to hit at the same time as stock market crashes; this means that buying shares would increase the volatility of their income, so that investors require a premium to be persuaded to hold them. Another is that shares, especially in small companies, are much less liquid than government debt. It is also sometimes argued that in extreme times—in depression or war, or after bubbles—equities fare much worse than bonds, so that equity investors demand higher returns to compensate them for the risk of catastrophe.

Yes, over long periods equities have done better than bonds. But the equity "premium" is unpredictable. Searching for a consistent, God-given premium is a fool's errand.

*"Bad Beta, Good Beta," John Y. Campbell and Tuomo Vuolteenaho, Harvard University mimeo, 2003.

average it with the most recent squared "surprise" (i.e., the squared deviation of the rate of return from its mean).

Today, the most widely used model to estimate the conditional (hence time-varying) variance of stocks and stock-index returns is the *generalized* autoregressive conditional heteroskedasticity (GARCH) model, also pioneered by Robert F. Engle.[18] (The generalized ARCH model allows greater flexibility in the specification of how volatility evolves over time.)

The GARCH model uses rate-of-return history as the information set used to form our estimates of variance. The model posits that the forecast of market volatility evolves relatively smoothly each period in response to new observations on market returns. The updated estimate of market-return variance in each period depends on both the previous

---

[18] Ibid.

**Figure 13.3    Estimates of the monthly stock return variance, 1835–1987**

Source: Adrian R. Pagan and G. William Schwert, "Alternative Models for Conditional Stock Volatility," *Journal of Econometrics* 45 (1990), pp. 267–90.

estimate and the most recent squared residual return on the market. The squared residual is an unbiased estimate of variance, so this technique essentially mixes in a statistically efficient manner the previous volatility estimate with an unbiased estimate based on the new observation of market return. The updating formula is

$$\sigma_t^2 = a_0 + a_1\epsilon_{t-1}^2 + a_2\sigma_{t-1}^2 \tag{13.10}$$

As noted, equation 13.8 asserts that the updated forecast of variance is a function of the most recent variance forecast $\sigma_{t-1}^2$, and the most recent squared prediction error in market return, $\epsilon_{t-1}^2$. The parameters $a_0$, $a_1$, and $a_2$ are estimated from past data.

Evidence on the relationship between mean and variance has been mixed. Whitelaw[19] found that average returns and volatility are negatively related, but Kane, Marcus, and Noh[20] found a positive relationship.

ARCH-type models clearly capture much of the variation in stock market volatility. Figure 13.4 compares volatility estimates from an ARCH model to volatility estimates derived from prices on market-index options.[21] The variation in volatility, as well as the close agreement between the estimates, is evident.

---

[19] Robert F. Whitelaw, "Time Variation and Covariations in the Expectation and Volatility of Stock Returns," *Journal of Finance* 49 (1994), pp. 515–42.

[20] Alex Kane, Alan J. Marcus, and Jaesun Noh, "The P/E Multiple and Market Volatility," *Financial Analysts Journal* 52 (July–August 1996), pp. 16–24.

[21] We will show you how such estimates can be derived from option prices in Chapter 21.

**Figure 13.4
Implied
versus estimated
volatility. Implied
volatility is
derived from
options on the
S&P 100 index.
Estimated
volatility is
derived from an
ARCH-M model.**

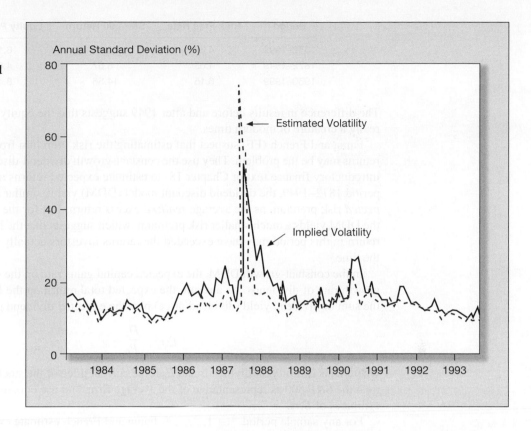

## 13.5  THE EQUITY PREMIUM PUZZLE

In an intriguing article[22] Mehra and Prescott examined the excess returns earned on equity portfolios over the risk-free rate during the period 1889–1978. They concluded that the historical-average excess return has been too large to be consistent with reasonable levels of risk aversion. In other words, it appears that the reward investors have received for bearing risk has been so generous that it is hard to reconcile with rational security pricing. This research has since engendered a large body of literature attempting to explain this puzzle.

Two recent explanations for the puzzle deserve special attention, as they utilize important insights into the difficulties of obtaining inferences from observations of realized returns.

**Expected versus
Realized Returns**   Fama and French[23] offer one possible interpretation of the puzzle. They use the sample period, 1872–1999, and report the average risk-free rates, average return on equity (represented by the S&P 500 index), and the resultant risk premium for the overall period and subperiods:

[22] Jarnish Mehra and Edward Prescott, "The Equity Premium: A Puzzle," *Journal of Monetary Economics*, March 1985.
[23] Eugene Fama and Kenneth French, "The Equity Premium," *Journal of Finance* 57, no. 2 (2002).

| Period | Risk-Free Rate | S&P 500 Return | Equity Premium |
|--------|---------------|----------------|----------------|
| 1872–1999 | 4.87 | 10.97 | 6.10 |
| 1872–1949 | 4.05 | 8.67 | 4.62 |
| 1950–1999 | 6.15 | 14.56 | 8.41 |

The difference in results before and after 1949 suggests that the equity premium puzzle is really a creature of modern times.

Fama and French (FF) suspect that estimating the risk premium from average realized returns may be the problem. They use the constant-growth dividend-discount model (see an introductory finance text or Chapter 18) to estimate expected returns and find that for the period 1872–1949, the dividend discount model (DDM) yields similar estimates of the *expected* risk premium as the average *realized* excess return. But for the period 1950–1999, the DDM yields a much smaller risk premium, which suggests that the high average excess return in this period may have exceeded the returns investors actually expected to earn at the time.

In the constant-growth DDM, the expected capital gains rate on the stock will equal the growth rate of dividends. As a result, the expected total return on the firm's stock will be the sum of dividend yield (dividend/price) plus the expected dividend growth rate, $g$:

$$E(r) = \frac{D_1}{P_0} + g \tag{13.11}$$

where $D_1$ is end-of-year dividends and $P_0$ is the current price of the stock. Fama and French treat the S&P 500 as representative of the average firm, and use equation 13.11 to produce estimates of $E(r)$.

For any sample period, $t = 1, \ldots, T$, Fama and French estimate expected return from the arithmetic average of the dividend yield $(D_t/P_{t-1})$ plus the dividend growth rate $(g_t = D_t/D_{t-1})$. In contrast, the *realized* return is the dividend yield plus the rate of capital gains $(P_t/P_{t-1} - 1)$. Because the dividend yield is common to both estimates, the difference between the expected and realized return equals the difference between the dividend growth and capital gains rates. While dividend growth and capital gains were similar in the earlier period, capital gains significantly exceeded the dividend growth rate in modern times. Hence, FF conclude that the equity premium puzzle may be due at least in part to unanticipated capital gains in the latter period.

FF argue that dividend growth rates produce more reliable estimates of expected capital gains than the average of realized capital gains. They point to three reasons:

1. Average realized returns over 1950–1999 exceeded the internal rate of return on corporate investments. If those returns were representative of expectations, we would have to conclude that firms were willingly engaging in negative NPV investments.

2. The statistical precision of estimates from the DDM are far higher than those using average historical returns. The standard error of the estimates of the risk premium from realized returns is about 2.5 times the standard error from the dividend discount model (see the following table).

3. The reward-to-variability (Sharpe) ratio derived from the DDM is far more stable than that derived from realized returns. If risk aversion remains the same over time, we would expect the Sharpe ratio to be stable.

The evidence for the second and third points is shown in the following table, where estimates from the dividend model (DDM) and from realized returns (Realized) are shown side by side.

**Figure 13.5
Real returns
on global stock
markets. The
figure displays
average real
returns for
39 markets over
the period 1921 to
1996. Markets are
sorted by years
of existence. The
graph shows that
markets with long
histories typically
have higher
returns. An
asterisk indicates
that the market
suffered a long-
term break.**

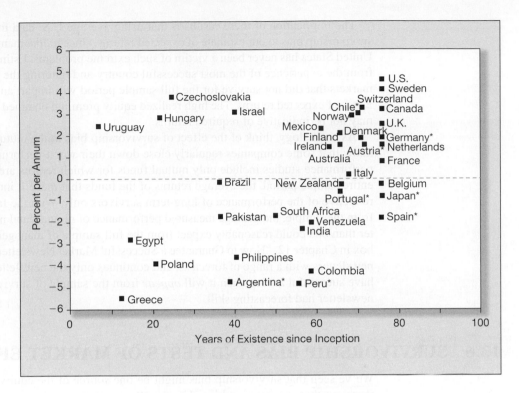

| | Mean Return | | Standard Error | | t-statistic | | Sharpe Ratio | |
|---|---|---|---|---|---|---|---|---|
| Period | DDM | Realized | DDM | Realized | DDM | Realized | DDM | Realized |
| 1872–1999 | 4.03 | 6.10 | 1.14 | 1.65 | 3.52 | 3.70 | 0.22 | 0.34 |
| 1872–1949 | 4.35 | 4.62 | 1.76 | 2.20 | 2.47 | 2.10 | 0.23 | 0.24 |
| 1950–1999 | 3.54 | 8.41 | 1.03 | 2.45 | 3.42 | 3.43 | 0.21 | 0.51 |

FF's innovative study thus provides a possible explanation of the equity premium puzzle. Another implication from the study may be even more important for today's investor: The study predicts that future excess returns will be significantly lower than those experienced in recent decades.

**Survivorship Bias**   The equity premium puzzle emerged from long-term averages of U.S. stock returns. There are reasons to suspect that these estimates of the risk premium are subject to survivorship bias, as the United States has arguably been the most successful capitalist system in the world, an outcome that probably would not have been anticipated several decades ago. Jurion and Goetzmann[24] assembled a database of capital appreciation indexes for the stock markets of 39 countries over the period 1926–1996. Figure 13.5 shows that U.S. equities had the highest real return of all countries, at 4.3% annually, versus a median of 0.8% for other countries. Moreover, unlike the United States, many other countries have had equity markets that actually closed, either permanently, or for extended periods of time.

---

[24] Philippe Jurion and William N. Goetzmann, "Global Stock Markets in the Twentieth Century," *Journal of Finance* 54, no. 3 (June 1999).

The implication of these results is that using average U.S. data may induce a form of survivorship bias to our estimate of expected returns, since unlike many other countries, the United States has never been a victim of such extreme problems. Estimating risk premiums from the experience of the most successful country and ignoring the evidence from stock markets that did not survive for the full sample period will impart an upward bias in estimates of expected returns. The high realized equity premium obtained for the United States may not be indicative of required returns.

As an analogy, think of the effect of survivorship bias in the mutual fund industry. We know that some companies regularly close down their worst-performing mutual funds. If performance studies include only mutual funds for which returns are available during an entire sample period, the average returns of the funds that make it into the sample will be reflective of the performance of long-term survivors only. With the failed funds excluded from the sample, the average measured performance of mutual fund managers will be better than one could reasonably expect from the full sample of managers. Think back to the box in Chapter 12, "How to Guarantee a Successful Market Newsletter." If one starts many newsletters with a range of forecasts, and continues only the newsletters that turned out to have successful advice, then it will *appear* from the sample of survivors that the average newsletter had forecasting skill.

## 13.6 SURVIVORSHIP BIAS AND TESTS OF MARKET EFFICIENCY

We've seen that survivorship bias might be one source of the equity premium puzzle. It turns out that survivorship bias also can affect our measurement of *persistence* in stock market returns, an issue that is crucial for tests of market efficiency. For a demonstration of the potential impact of survivorship bias, imagine that a new group of mutual funds is set up. Half the funds are managed aggressively and the other conservatively; however, none of the managers are able to beat the market in expectation. The probability distribution of alpha values is given by

| | Probability | |
|---|---|---|
| Alpha Value (%) | Conservative Manager | Aggressive Manager |
| 3 | 0 | 0.5 |
| 1 | 0.5 | 0 |
| −1 | 0.5 | 0 |
| −3 | 0 | 0.5 |

Because there are an equal number of aggressive and conservative managers, the frequency distribution of alphas in a given period is:

| | Relative Frequency of Funds | |
|---|---|---|
| Alpha Value (%) | Conservative Manager | Aggressive Manager |
| 3 | 0 | .25 |
| 1 | .25 | 0 |
| −1 | .25 | 0 |
| −3 | 0 | .25 |
| Total | .5 | .5 |

Define a "winner" fund as one in the top-half of the distribution of returns in a given period; a "loser" is one in the bottom half of the sample. Manager alphas are assumed to be serially uncorrelated. Therefore, the probability of being a winner or a loser in the second quarter is the same regardless of first-quarter performance. A $2 \times 2$ tabulation of performance in two consecutive periods, such as in the following table, will show absence of any persistence in performance.

**Distribution of Two-Period Performance: Full Sample**

| | Second Period | |
|---|---|---|
| First Period | Winners | Losers |
| Winners | .25 | .25 |
| Losers | .25 | .25 |

But now assume that in each quarter funds are ranked by returns and the bottom 5% are closed down. A researcher obtains a sample of four quarters of fund returns and ranks the semiannual performance of funds that survived the entire sample. The following table, based only on surviving funds, seems to show that first-period winners are far more likely to be second-period winners as well. Despite lack of true persistence in performance, the loss of just a few funds each period induces an appearance of significant persistence.

**Distribution of Two-Period Performance: Surviving Sample**

| | Second Period | | |
|---|---|---|---|
| First Period | Winners | Losers | Row Total |
| Winners | .3893 | .1401 | .5294 |
| Losers | .1107 | .4706 | .4706 |
| Column total | .5001 | .4999 | 1.0000 |

The degree of survivorship bias depends first and foremost on how aggressively poorly performing funds are shut down. (In this example, the worst 5% of performers were shut down.) The bias increases enormously with the cut-off rate. Other factors affecting bias are correlation across manager portfolios, serial correlation of returns, the dispersion of style across managers, and the strategic response of managers to the possibility of cut-off.

To assess the potential effect of actual survivorship bias, Brown, Goetzmann, Ibbotson, and Ross[25] conducted a simulation using observed characteristics of mutual fund returns. Their results demonstrate that actual survivorship bias could be strong enough to create apparent persistence in the performance of portfolio managers. They simulate annual returns over a 4-year period for 600 mutual fund managers, drawing from distributions that are constructed to mimic observed equity returns in the United States over the period 1926–1989,[26] and mutual fund returns reported in a performance study by Goetzmann and Ibbotson.[27] Four annual returns for each manager are generated independently so that

---

[25] Stephen J. Brown, William Goetzmann, Roger G. Ibbotson, and Stephen A. Ross, "Survivorship Bias in Performance Studies," *Review of Financial Studies* 5, no. 4 (1992).

[26] They draw market risk premiums from a normal distribution with mean 8.6% and standard deviation 20.8%. The 600 manager betas are drawn from a normal distribution with mean .95 and standard deviation .25. The residual standard deviation for each manager is estimated from actual data.

[27] William Goetzmann and Roger Ibbotson, "Do Winners Repeat? Predicting Mutual Fund Performance," *Journal of Portfolio Management* 20 (1994).

relative performance over the first 2-year period does not persist in the following 2-year pe-riod. The simulated returns of the funds and the market index are used to compute four risk-adjusted annual returns (alphas) for each of the 600 managers. Winners (losers) are identified by positive (negative) alphas.

Two-by-two tabulations of the frequency of first-period/second-period winners and losers are shown in Table 13.6. When all 600 managers are included in the 4-year sample, no persistence in performance can be detected. But when the poor performers in each year are eliminated from the sample, performance persistence shows up. Elimination of even a small number of poor performers can generate a significant level of apparent persistence.

The results for a 5% cut-off rate in Table 13.6 are not as strong as in the "clean" exam-ple we presented above; apparently, other factors mitigate the effect somewhat. Still, sur-vivorship bias is sufficient to create an appearance of significant performance persistence even when actual returns are consistent with efficient markets.

**Table 13.6   Two-Way Table of Managers Classified by Risk-Adjusted Returns over Successive Intervals, a Summary of 20,000 Simulations Assuming 0, 5, 10, and 20% Cut-offs**

|  | Second-Period Winners | Second-Period Losers |
|---|---|---|
| No cut-off ($n = 600$) | | |
| First-period winners | 150.09 | 149.51 |
| First-period losers | 149.51 | 150.09 |
| | | Average cross-section $t$-value $= -.004$ |
| | | Average annual excess return $= 0.0\%$ |
| | | Average $\beta = 0.950$ |
| 5% cut-off ($n = 494$) | | |
| First-period winners | 127.49 | 119.51 |
| First-period losers | 119.51 | 127.49 |
| | | Average cross-section $t$-value $= 2.046$ |
| | | Average annual excess return $= 0.44\%$ |
| | | Average $\beta = 0.977$ |
| 10% cut-off ($n = 398$) | | |
| First-period winners | 106.58 | 92.42 |
| First-period losers | 92.42 | 106.58 |
| | | Average cross-section $t$-value $= 3.356$ |
| | | Average annual excess return $= 0.61\%$ |
| | | Average $\beta = 0.994$ |
| 20% cut-off ($n = 249$) | | |
| First-period winners | 71.69 | 53.31 |
| First-period losers | 53.31 | 70.69 |
| | | Average cross-section $t$-value $= 4.679$ |
| | | Average annual excess return $= 0.80\%$ |
| | | Average $\beta = 1.018$ |

In each of the 4 years, managers who experience returns in the lowest percentile indicated by the cut-off value are excluded from the sample, and this experiment is repeated 20,000 times. Thus, the numbers in the first 2 × 2 table give the average frequency with which the 600 managers fall into the respective classifications. The second panel shows the average frequencies for the 494 managers who survive the performance cut, while the third and fourth panels give corresponding results for 398 and 249 managers. For each simulation, the winners are defined as those managers whose average 2-year Jensen's $\alpha$ measure was greater than or equal to that of the median manager in that sample.

**SUMMARY**

1. Although the single-factor expected return–beta relationship has not yet been confirmed by scientific standards, its use is already commonplace in economic life.

2. Early tests of the single-factor CAPM rejected the SML, finding that nonsystematic risk did explain average security returns.

3. Later tests controlling for the measurement error in beta found that nonsystematic risk does not explain portfolio returns but also that the estimated SML is too flat compared with what the CAPM would predict.

4. Roll's critique implied that the usual CAPM test is a test only of the mean-variance efficiency of a prespecified market *proxy* and therefore that tests of the linearity of the expected return–beta relationship do not bear on the validity of the model.

5. Tests of the mean-variance efficiency of professionally managed portfolios against the benchmark of a prespecified market index conform with Roll's critique in that they provide evidence on the efficiency of the prespecific market index.

6. Empirical evidence suggests that most professionally managed portfolios are outperformed by market indexes, which lends weight to acceptance of the efficiency of those indexes and hence the CAPM.

7. Work with economic factors suggests that factors such as unanticipated inflation do play a role in the expected return–beta relationship of security returns.

8. Recent tests of the single-index model, accounting for human capital and cyclical variations in asset betas, are far more consistent with the single-index CAPM and APT. These tests suggest that macroeconomic variables are not necessary to explain expected returns. Moreover, anomalies such as effects of size and book-to-market ratios disappear once these variables are accounted for.

9. Volatility of stock returns is constantly changing. Empirical evidence on stock returns must account for this phenomenon. Contemporary researchers use the variations of the ARCH algorithm to estimate the level of volatility and its effect on mean returns.

10. The equity premium puzzle originates from the observation that equity returns exceeded the risk-free rate to an extent that is inconsistent with reasonable levels of risk aversion—at least when average rates of return are taken to represent expectations. Fama and French show that the puzzle emerges primarily from excess returns over the last 50 years. Alternative estimates of expected returns using the dividend growth model instead of average returns suggest that excess returns on stocks were high because of unexpected large capital gains. The study suggests that future excess returns will be lower than realized in recent decades.

**KEY TERMS**    first-pass regression         second-pass regression         benchmark error

**WEBSITES**

www.efficientfrontier.com
This website gives you access to *Efficient Frontier: An Online Journal of Practical Asset Allocation,* which contains articles related to performance and efficiency.

www.morningstar.com
Morningstar reports longer-term performance of mutual funds. Rankings for all types of mutual funds and performance measures are also available. Link to *Funds,* and then *Mutual Fund Performance.*

Visit us at www.mhhe.com/bkm

**WEBSITES**

www.anderson.ucla.edu/acad_unit/finance/wp/2001/10-01.pdf
This site provides an example using the Fama-French three-factor model.

cepa.newschool.edu/het/schools/finance.htm
Visit this site to review a short history of the development of portfolio theory.

**PROBLEMS**    The following annual excess rates of return were obtained for nine individual stocks and a market index:

| | Market | Stock Excess Returns (%) | | | | | | | | |
|---|---|---|---|---|---|---|---|---|---|---|
| Year | Index | A | B | C | D | E | F | G | H | I |
| 1 | 29.65 | 33.88 | −25.20 | 36.48 | 42.89 | −39.89 | 39.67 | 74.57 | 40.22 | 90.19 |
| 2 | −11.91 | −49.87 | 24.70 | −25.11 | −54.39 | 44.92 | −54.33 | −79.76 | −71.58 | −26.64 |
| 3 | 14.73 | 65.14 | −25.04 | 18.91 | −39.86 | −3.91 | −5.69 | 26.73 | 14.49 | 18.14 |
| 4 | 27.68 | 14.46 | −38.64 | −23.31 | −0.72 | −3.21 | 92.39 | −3.82 | 13.74 | 0.09 |
| 5 | 5.18 | 15.67 | 61.93 | 63.95 | −32.82 | 44.26 | −42.96 | 101.67 | 24.24 | 8.98 |
| 6 | 25.97 | −32.17 | 44.94 | −19.56 | 69.42 | 90.43 | 76.72 | 1.72 | 77.22 | 72.38 |
| 7 | 10.64 | −31.55 | −74.65 | 50.18 | 74.52 | 15.38 | 21.95 | −43.95 | −13.40 | 28.95 |
| 8 | 1.02 | −23.79 | 47.02 | −42.28 | 28.61 | −17.64 | 28.83 | 98.01 | 28.12 | 39.41 |
| 9 | 18.82 | −4.59 | 28.69 | −0.54 | 2.32 | 42.36 | 18.93 | −2.45 | 37.65 | 94.67 |
| 10 | 23.92 | −8.03 | 48.61 | 23.65 | 26.26 | −3.65 | 23.31 | 15.36 | 80.59 | 52.51 |
| 11 | −41.61 | 78.22 | −85.02 | −0.79 | −68.70 | −85.71 | −45.64 | 2.27 | −72.47 | −80.26 |
| 12 | −6.64 | 4.75 | 42.95 | −48.60 | 26.27 | 13.24 | −34.34 | −54.47 | −1.50 | −24.46 |

1. Perform the first-pass regressions and tabulate the summary statistics.

2. Specify the hypotheses for a test of the second-pass regression for the SML.

3. Perform the second-pass SML regression by regressing the average excess return of each portfolio on its beta.

4. Summarize your test results and compare them to the results reported in the text.

5. Group the nine stocks into three portfolios, maximizing the dispersion of the betas of the three resultant portfolios. Repeat the test and explain any changes in the results.

6. Explain Roll's critique as it applies to the tests performed in problems 1 to 5.

7. Plot the capital market line (CML), the nine stocks, and the three portfolios on a graph of average returns versus standard deviation. Compare the mean-variance efficiency of the three portfolios and the market index. Does the comparison support the CAPM?

Suppose that, in addition to the market factor that has been considered in problems 1 to 7, a second factor is considered. The values of this factor for years 1 to 12 were as follows:

| Year | % Change in Factor Value | Year | % Change in Factor Value |
|------|--------------------------|------|--------------------------|
| 1 | −9.84 | 7 | −3.52 |
| 2 | 6.46 | 8 | 8.43 |
| 3 | 16.12 | 9 | 8.23 |
| 4 | −16.51 | 10 | 7.06 |
| 5 | 17.82 | 11 | −15.74 |
| 6 | −13.31 | 12 | 2.03 |

8. Perform the first-pass regressions as did Chen, Roll, and Ross and tabulate the relevant summary statistics. (Hint: Use a multiple regression as in a standard spreadsheet package. Estimate the betas of the 12 stocks on the two factors.)

9. Specify the hypothesis for a test of a second-pass regression for the two-factor SML.

10. Do the data suggest a two-factor economy?

11. Can you identify a factor portfolio for the second factor?

12. Identify and briefly discuss three criticisms of beta as used in the capital asset pricing model.

13. Richard Roll, in an article on using the capital asset pricing model (CAPM) to evaluate portfolio performance, indicated that it may not be possible to evaluate portfolio management ability if there is an error in the benchmark used.

    a. In evaluating portfolio performance, describe the general procedure, with emphasis on the benchmark employed.

    b. Explain what Roll meant by the benchmark error and identify the specific problem with this benchmark.

    c. Draw a graph that shows how a portfolio that has been judged as superior relative to a "measured" security market line (SML) can be inferior relative to the "true" SML.

    d. Assume that you are informed that a given portfolio manager has been evaluated as superior when compared to the Dow Jones Industrial Average, the S&P 500, and the NYSE Composite Index. Explain whether this consensus would make you feel more comfortable regarding the portfolio manager's true ability.

    e. Although conceding the possible problem with benchmark errors as set forth by Roll, some contend this does not mean the CAPM is incorrect, but only that there is a measurement problem when implementing the theory. Others contend that because of benchmark errors the whole technique should be scrapped. Take and defend one of these positions.

14. Bart Campbell, CFA, is a portfolio manager who has recently met with a prospective client, Jane Black. After conducting a Survey Market Line (SML) performance analysis using the Dow Jones Industrial Average as her market proxy, Black claims that her portfolio has experienced superior performance. Campbell uses the Capital Asset Pricing Model as an investment performance measure and finds that Black's portfolio plots below the SML. Campbell concludes that Black's apparent superior performance is a function of an incorrectly specified market proxy, not superior investment management. Justify Campbell conclusion, by addressing the likely effects of an incorrectly specified market proxy on both beta and the slope of the SML.

First obtain monthly returns for a sample of 10 firms and the S&P 500 from the Market Insight database at **www.mhhe.com/business/finance/edumarketinsight**. Then obtain the corresponding returns on the HML (high minus low book value) and SMB (small minus big) portfolios from Ken French's website at **mba.tuck.dartmouth.du/pages/faculty/ken.french/data_library.html**. Finally, obtain monthly interest rates from the Fed's website at **www.federalreserve.gov/releases/h15/data.htm**. Evaluate the alphas of each firm over the last 3 years as the intercept in a first-pass regression using excess returns in a single-index model. Then evaluate the alphas using a first-pass Fama-French three-factor multiple regression. Under which model is alpha more variable across firms? What do you conclude?

---

**E-INVESTMENTS**
**Portfolio Theory**

The History of Economic Thought website presents a concise history of portfolio theory development and the research contributors at **cepa.newschool.edu/net/schools/finance.htm**. Who would you list as major contributors to the development of modern portfolio theory? Why?

---

**SOLUTIONS TO CONCEPT CHECKS**

1. The SCL is estimated for each stock; hence we need to estimate 100 equations. Our sample consists of 60 monthly rates of return for each of the 100 stocks and for the market index. Thus each regression is estimated with 60 observations. Equation 13.1 in the text shows that when stated in excess return form, the SCL should pass through the origin, that is, have a zero intercept.

2. When the SML has a positive intercept and its slope is less than the mean excess return on the market portfolio, it is flatter than predicted by the CAPM. Low-beta stocks therefore have yielded returns that, on average, were higher than they should have been on the basis of their beta. Conversely, high-beta stocks were found to have yielded, on average, lower returns than they should have on the basis of their betas. The positive coefficient on $\gamma_2$ implies that stocks with higher values of firm-specific risk had on average higher returns. This pattern, of course, violates the predictions of the CAPM.

3. According to equation 13.5, $\gamma_0$ is the average return earned on a stock with zero beta and zero firm-specific risk. According to the CAPM, this should be the risk-free rate, which for the 1946–1955 period was 9 basis points, or .09% per month (see Table 13.1). According to the CAPM, $\gamma_1$ should equal the average market risk premium, which for the 1946–1955 period was 103 basis points, or 1.03% per month. Finally, the CAPM predicts that $\gamma_3$, the coefficient on firm-specific risk, should be zero.

4. A positive coefficient on beta-squared would indicate that the relationship between risk and return is nonlinear. High-beta securities would provide expected returns more than proportional to risk. A positive coefficient on $\sigma(e)$ would indicate that firm-specific risk affects expected return, a direct contradiction of the CAPM and APT.

# FIXED-INCOME SECURITIES

www.mhhe.com/bkm

# BOND PRICES AND YIELDS

In the previous chapters on risk and return relationships, we have treated securities at a high level of abstraction. We assumed implicitly that a prior, detailed analysis of each security already had been performed, and that its risk and return features had been assessed.

We turn now to specific analyses of particular security markets. We examine valuation principles, determinants of risk and return, and portfolio strategies commonly used within and across the various markets.

We begin by analyzing **debt securities**. A debt security is a claim on a specified periodic stream of income. Debt securities are often called *fixed-income securities* because they promise either a fixed stream of income or a stream of income that is determined according to a specified formula. These securities have the advantage of being relatively easy to understand because the payment formulas are specified in advance. Risk considerations are minimal as long as the issuer of the security is sufficiently creditworthy. That makes these securities a convenient starting point for our analysis of the universe of potential investment vehicles.

The bond is the basic debt security, and this chapter starts with an overview of the universe of bond markets, including Treasury, corporate, and international bonds. We turn next to bond pricing, showing how bond prices are set in accordance with market interest rates and why bond prices change with those rates. Given this background, we can compare the myriad measures of bond returns such as yield to maturity, yield to call, holding-period return, or realized compound yield to maturity. We show how bond prices evolve over time, discuss certain tax rules that apply to debt securities, and show how to calculate after-tax returns. Finally, we consider the impact of default or credit risk on bond pricing and look at the determinants of credit risk and the default premium built into bond yields.

## 14.1    BOND CHARACTERISTICS

A **bond** is a security that is issued in connection with a borrowing arrangement. The borrower issues (i.e., sells) a bond to the lender for some amount of cash; the bond is the "IOU" of the borrower. The arrangement obligates the issuer to make specified payments to the bondholder on specified dates. A typical coupon bond obligates the issuer to make semiannual payments of interest to the bondholder for the life of the bond. These are called *coupon payments* because in precomputer days, most bonds had coupons that investors would clip off and mail to the issuer of the bond to claim the interest payment. When the bond matures, the issuer repays the debt by paying the bondholder the bond's **par value** (equivalently, its **face value**). The **coupon rate** of the bond serves to determine the interest payment: The annual payment is the coupon rate times the bond's par value. The coupon rate, maturity date, and par value of the bond are part of the **bond indenture**, which is the contract between the issuer and the bondholder.

To illustrate, a bond with par value of $1,000 and coupon rate of 8% might be sold to a buyer for $1,000. The bondholder is then entitled to a payment of 8% of $1,000, or $80 per year, for the stated life of the bond, say 30 years. The $80 payment typically comes in two semiannual installments of $40 each. At the end of the 30-year life of the bond, the issuer also pays the $1,000 par value to the bondholder.

Bonds usually are issued with coupon rates set high enough to induce investors to pay par value to buy the bond. Sometimes, however, **zero-coupon bonds** are issued that make no coupon payments. In this case, investors receive par value at the maturity date but receive no interest payments until then: The bond has a coupon rate of zero. These bonds are issued at prices considerably below par value, and the investor's return comes solely from the difference between issue price and the payment of par value at maturity. We will return to these bonds later.

### Treasury Bonds and Notes

Figure 14.1 is an excerpt from the listing of Treasury issues in *The Wall Street Journal*. Treasury note maturities range up to 10 years, while Treasury bonds with maturities ranging from 10 to 30 years appear in the figure. In 2001, the Treasury suspended new issues of 30-year bonds, making the 10-year bond the longest currently issued Treasury. As of 2003, there have been no announcements of any plans to resume issuing the 30-year bond. Both bonds and notes are issued in denominations of $1,000 or more. Both make semiannual coupon payments. Aside from their differing initial maturities, the only major distinction between T-notes and T-bonds is that in the past, some T-bonds were *callable* for a given period, usually during the last 5 years of the bond's life. The call provision gives the Treasury the right to repurchase the bond at par value during the call period. The Treasury no longer issues callable bonds, but some previously issued callable bonds still are outstanding.

**Figure 14.1
Listing of
Treasury
issues**

## Treasury Bonds, Notes and Bills

February 14, 2003

### Explanatory Notes

Representative Over-the-Counter quotation based on transactions of $1 million or more. Treasury bond, note and bill quotes are as of mid-afternoon. Colons in bid-and-asked quotes represent 32nds; 101:01 means 101 1/32. Net changes in 32nds. n-Treasury note. i-Inflation-Indexed issue. Treasury bill quotes in hundredths, quoted on terms of a rate of discount. Days to maturity calculated from settlement date. All yields are to maturity and based on the asked quote. Latest 13-week and 26-week bills are boldfaced. For bonds callable prior to maturity, yields are computed to the earliest call date for issues quoted above par and to the maturity date for issues below par. *When issued.

Source: eSpeed/Cantor Fitzgerald

U.S. Treasury strips as of 2 p.m. Eastern time, also based on transactions of $1 million or more. Colons in bid and asked quotes represent 32nds; 99:01 means 99 1/32. Net changes in 32nds. Yields calculated on the asked quotation. ci-stripped coupon interest. bp-Treasury bond, stripped principal. np-Treasury note, stripped principal. For bonds callable prior to maturity, yields are computed to the earliest call date for issues quoted above par and to the maturity date for issues below par.

Source: Bear, Stearns & Co. via Street Software Technology Inc.

| RATE | MATURITY MO/YR | BID | ASKED | CHG | ASK YLD |
|---|---|---|---|---|---|
| **Government Bonds & Notes** | | | | | |
| 4.625 | Feb 03n | 100:02 | 100:03 | -2 | 0.65 |
| 5.500 | Feb 03n | 100:03 | 100:04 | -2 | 0.40 |
| 4.250 | Mar 03n | 100:11 | 100:12 | -1 | 0.90 |
| 5.500 | Mar 03n | 100:15 | 100:16 | -1 | 0.90 |
| 4.000 | Apr 03n | 100:17 | 100:18 | -1 | 1.03 |
| 5.750 | Apr 03n | 100:28 | 100:29 | -1 | 1.10 |
| 10.750 | May 03 | 102:07 | 102:08 | -4 | 1.15 |
| 13.750 | Aug 04 | 118:07 | 118:08 | -6 | 1.34 |
| 1.875 | Sep 04n | 100:21 | 100:22 | -3 | 1.44 |
| 2.125 | Oct 04n | 101:02 | 101:03 | -3 | 1.47 |
| 5.875 | Nov 04n | 107:15 | 107:16 | -5 | 1.48 |
| 7.875 | Nov 04n | 110:29 | 110:30 | -5 | 1.47 |
| 11.625 | Nov 04 | 117:10 | 117:11 | -6 | 1.48 |
| 2.000 | Nov 04n | 100:26 | 100:27 | -3 | 1.52 |
| 1.750 | Dec 04n | 100:09 | 100:10 | -4 | 1.57 |
| 1.625 | **Jan 05n** | 100:00 | 100:00 | -4 | 1.62 |
| 7.500 | Feb 05n | 111:15 | 111:16 | -7 | 1.60 |
| 6.500 | May 05n | 110:14 | 110:15 | -7 | 1.70 |
| 6.750 | May 05n | 110:29 | 110:30 | -7 | 1.74 |
| 12.000 | May 05 | 122:15 | 122:16 | -11 | 1.70 |
| 6.500 | Aug 05n | 111:02 | 111:00 | 7 | 1.01 |
| 10.750 | Aug 05 | 121:17 | 121:18 | -8 | 1.85 |
| 5.750 | Nov 05n | 110:01 | 110:02 | -7 | 1.95 |
| 5.875 | Nov 05 | 110:11 | 110:12 | -8 | 1.96 |
| 5.625 | Feb 06n | 110:06 | 110:07 | -9 | 2.08 |
| 9.375 | Feb 06 | 121:02 | 121:03 | -8 | 2.06 |
| 4.625 | May 06n | 107:13 | 107:14 | -9 | 2.23 |
| 6.875 | May 06n | 114:12 | 114:13 | -10 | 2.24 |
| 7.000 | Jul 06n | 115:06 | 115:07 | -11 | 2.32 |
| 6.500 | Oct 06n | 114:03 | 114:04 | -11 | 2.44 |
| 3.500 | Nov 06n | 103:19 | 103:20 | -10 | 2.48 |
| 3.375 | Jan 07i | 109:13 | 109:14 | -4 | 0.91 |
| 6.250 | Feb 07n | 113:18 | 113:19 | -22 | 2.64 |
| 6.625 | May 07n | 115:19 | 115:20 | -20 | 2.70 |
| 4.375 | May 07n | 106:17 | 106:18 | -19 | 2.72 |
| 3.250 | Aug 07n | 101:30 | 101:31 | -13 | 2.78 |
| 6.125 | Aug 07n | 114:04 | 114:05 | -14 | 2.75 |
| 3.000 | Nov 07n | 100:19 | 100:20 | -13 | 2.85 |
| 3.625 | Jan 08i | 111:06 | 111:07 | -1 | 1.26 |
| **3.000** | **Feb 08i** | **100:09** | **100:10** | **-12** | **2.93** |
| 5.500 | Feb 08n | 111:29 | 111:30 | -14 | 2.91 |

| RATE | MATURITY MO/YR | BID | ASKED | CHG | ASK YLD |
|---|---|---|---|---|---|
| 5.625 | May 08n | 112:16 | 112:17 | -15 | 3.02 |
| 8.375 | Aug 08 | 103:16 | 103:17 | 1 | 1.15 |
| 4.750 | Nov 08n | 108:07 | 108:08 | -15 | 3.16 |
| 8.750 | Nov 08 | 105:09 | 105:10 | -8 | 1.48 |
| 3.875 | Jan 09i | 113:07 | 113:08 | -1 | 1.52 |
| 5.500 | May 09n | 112:15 | 112:16 | -14 | 3.26 |
| 9.125 | May 09 | 109:11 | 109:12 | -5 | 1.44 |
| 6.000 | Aug 09n | 115:08 | 115:09 | -16 | 3.36 |
| 10.375 | Nov 09 | 114:30 | 114:31 | -6 | 1.60 |
| 4.250 | Jan 10i | 116:05 | 116:06 | -5 | 1.75 |
| 6.500 | Feb 10n | 118:16 | 118:17 | -19 | 3.49 |
| 11.750 | Feb 10 | 119:16 | 119:17 | -7 | 1.72 |
| 10.000 | May 10 | 117:22 | 117:23 | -6 | 1.87 |
| 5.750 | Aug 10n | 114:00 | 114:01 | -18 | 3.60 |
| 12.750 | Nov 10 | 128:02 | 128:03 | -11 | 2.13 |
| 3.500 | Jan 11i | 111:26 | 111:27 | -5 | 1.88 |
| 5.000 | Feb 11n | 109:00 | 109:00 | -19 | 3.69 |
| 13.875 | May 11 | 135:24 | 135:25 | -11 | 2.33 |
| 5.000 | Aug 11n | 108:24 | 108:25 | -20 | 3.78 |
| 14.000 | Nov 11 | 140:18 | 140:19 | -15 | 2.54 |
| 3.375 | Jan 12i | 111:21 | 111:22 | -5 | 1.94 |
| 4.875 | Feb 12n | 107:20 | 107:21 | -20 | 3.86 |
| 3.000 | Jul 12i | 108:22 | 108:23 | -4 | 1.98 |
| 4.375 | Aug 12n | 103:18 | 103:19 | -20 | 3.92 |
| 4.000 | Nov 12n | 100:15 | 100:16 | -20 | 3.94 |
| 10.375 | Nov 12 | 132:12 | 132:13 | -17 | 2.98 |
| 3.875 | Feb 13n | 99:10 | 99:11 | -18 | 3.96 |
| 12.000 | Aug 13 | 144:07 | 144:08 | -14 | 3.16 |
| 13.250 | May 14 | 155:05 | 155:06 | -24 | 3.36 |
| 6.500 | Nov 26 | 120:12 | 120:13 | -40 | 5.02 |
| 6.625 | Feb 27 | 122:05 | 122:06 | -39 | 5.02 |
| 6.375 | Aug 27 | 118:25 | 118:26 | -38 | 5.03 |
| 6.125 | Nov 27 | 115:12 | 115:13 | -39 | 5.03 |
| 3.625 | Apr 28i | 120:01 | 120:02 | -18 | 2.54 |
| 5.500 | Aug 28 | 106:20 | 106:21 | -37 | 5.03 |
| 5.250 | Nov 28 | 103:03 | 103:04 | -36 | 5.03 |
| 5.250 | Feb 29 | 103:06 | 103:07 | -36 | 5.03 |
| 3.875 | Apr 29i | 125:18 | 125:19 | -19 | 2.53 |
| 6.125 | Aug 29 | 116:00 | 116:00 | -39 | 5.03 |
| 6.250 | May 30 | 118:06 | 118:07 | -39 | 5.02 |
| 5.375 | Feb 31 | 107:14 | 107:15 | -35 | 4.88 |
| 3.375 | Apr 32i | 119:08 | 119:09 | -19 | 2.45 |

### U.S. Treasury Strips

| MATURITY | TYPE | BID | ASKED | CHG | ASK YLD |
|---|---|---|---|---|---|
| Apr 03 | ci | 99:16 | 99:16 | -1 | 3.32 |
| May 03 | ci | 99:24 | 99:24 | ... | 1.07 |
| Jul 03 | ci | 99:17 | 99:17 | ... | 1.13 |
| Aug 03 | ci | 99:15 | 99:15 | ... | 1.07 |
| Aug 03 | np | 99:13 | 99:14 | ... | 1.17 |
| Oct 03 | ci | 98:30 | 98:30 | ... | 1.64 |
| Nov 03 | ci | 99:07 | 99:08 | ... | 1.04 |
| Nov 03 | np | 99:04 | 99:04 | ... | 1.20 |
| Jan 04 | ci | 99:02 | 99:03 | -2 | 1.02 |
| Feb 04 | ci | 98:28 | 98:29 | -2 | 1.12 |
| Feb 04 | np | 98:26 | 98:26 | -2 | 1.20 |
| Apr 04 | ci | 97:27 | 97:27 | ... | 1.89 |
| May 04 | ci | 98:12 | 98:13 | -2 | 1.32 |
| May 04 | np | 98:13 | 98:14 | -2 | 1.27 |
| Jul 04 | ci | 98:08 | 98:08 | -2 | 1.25 |
| Aug 04 | ci | 98:00 | 98:00 | -3 | 1.35 |
| Aug 04 | np | 98:00 | 98:01 | -3 | 1.34 |
| Oct 04 | ci | 96:13 | 96:14 | -1 | 2.21 |
| Nov 04 | ci | 97:13 | 97:14 | -3 | 1.50 |
| Nov 04 | bp | 97:13 | 97:14 | -3 | 1.49 |
| Nov 04 | np | 97:14 | 97:15 | -3 | 1.48 |
| Jan 05 | ci | 97:18 | 97:19 | -3 | 1.28 |
| Feb 05 | ci | 96:25 | 96:26 | -3 | 1.64 |
| Feb 05 | np | 96:26 | 96:27 | -3 | 1.62 |
| Apr 05 | ci | 95:08 | 95:10 | -1 | 2.25 |
| May 05 | ci | 96:02 | 96:03 | -4 | 1.78 |
| May 05 | bp | 96:07 | 96:09 | -4 | 1.71 |
| May 05 | np | 96:07 | 96:08 | -4 | 1.72 |
| Jul 05 | ci | 96:04 | 96:05 | -4 | 1.76 |
| Jul 05 | ci | 96:15 | 96:17 | -4 | 1.48 |
| Aug 05 | ci | 95:16 | 95:18 | -4 | 1.84 |
| Aug 05 | bp | 95:13 | 95:15 | -4 | 1.87 |
| Aug 05 | ci | 95:13 | 95:15 | -4 | 1.88 |
| Aug 05 | ci | 94:19 | 94:20 | -1 | 2.09 |
| Nov 05 | ci | 94:30 | 95:00 | -4 | 1.00 |
| Nov 05 | np | 94:23 | 94:24 | -6 | 1.98 |
| Nov 05 | np | 94:22 | 94:24 | -6 | 1.98 |
| Jan 06 | ci | 94:21 | 94:22 | -6 | 1.89 |
| Feb 06 | ci | 93:23 | 93:25 | -6 | 2.16 |
| Feb 06 | np | 93:28 | 93:30 | -6 | 2.10 |
| Feb 06 | np | 93:30 | 94:00 | -6 | 2.08 |
| Apr 06 | ci | 92:10 | 92:11 | -1 | 2.54 |
| May 06 | ci | 92:28 | 92:30 | -7 | 2.27 |
| May 06 | np | 92:27 | 92:29 | -7 | 2.29 |
| Jul 06 | ci | 93:10 | 93:12 | -7 | 2.03 |
| Jul 06 | np | 92:12 | 92:14 | -7 | 2.33 |
| Aug 06 | ci | 92:08 | 92:10 | -7 | 2.31 |
| Oct 06 | np | 90:30 | 91:01 | -1 | 2.59 |
| Oct 06 | ci | 91:03 | 91:05 | -1 | 2.55 |
| Nov 06 | ci | 91:06 | 91:08 | -8 | 2.46 |
| Nov 06 | np | 91:04 | 91:06 | -8 | 2.48 |
| Feb 07 | ci | 90:03 | 90:06 | -8 | 2.61 |
| Feb 07 | np | 90:03 | 90:05 | -8 | 2.61 |
| May 07 | ci | 89:02 | 89:04 | -9 | 2.73 |
| May 07 | np | 89:06 | 89:08 | -9 | 2.70 |

The highlighted bond in Figure 14.1 matures in February 2012. Its coupon rate is 4.875%. Par value is $1,000; thus the bond pays interest of $48.75 per year in two semi-annual payments of $24.375. Payments are made in February and August of each year. The bid and asked prices[1] are quoted in points plus fractions of 1/32 of a point (the numbers after the colons are the fractions of a point). Although bonds are sold in denominations of $1,000 par value, the prices are quoted as a percentage of par value. Therefore, the bid price of the

---

[1] Recall that the bid price is the price at which you can sell the bond to a dealer. The asked price, which is slightly higher, is the price at which you can buy the bond from a dealer.

bond is 107:20 = 107²⁰⁄₃₂ = 107.625 of par value, or $1076.25, whereas the asked price is 107²¹⁄₃₂% of par, or $1076.5625.

The last column, labeled "Ask Yld," is the yield to maturity on the bond based on the asked price. The yield to maturity is a measure of the average rate of return to an investor who purchases the bond for the asked price and holds it until its maturity date. We will have much to say about yield to maturity below.

**Accrued Interest and Quoted Bond Prices.** The bond prices that you see quoted in the financial pages are not actually the prices that investors pay for the bond. This is because the quoted price does not include the interest that accrues between coupon payment dates.

If a bond is purchased between coupon payments, the buyer must pay the seller for accrued interest, the prorated share of the upcoming semiannual coupon. For example, if 40 days have passed since the last coupon payment, and there are 182 days in the semiannual coupon period, the seller is entitled to a payment of accrued interest of 40/182 of the semiannual coupon. The sale, or *invoice price*, of the bond would equal the stated price plus the accrued interest.

In general, the formula for the amount of accrued interest between two dates is

$$\text{Accrued interest} = \frac{\text{Annual coupon payment}}{2} \times \frac{\text{Days since last coupon payment}}{\text{Days separating coupon payments}}$$

**EXAMPLE 14.1    Accrued Interest**

Suppose that the coupon rate is 8%. Then the annual coupon is $80 and the semiannual coupon payment is $40. Because 40 days have passed since the last coupon payment, the accrued interest on the bond is $40 × (40/182) = $8.79. If the quoted price of the bond is $990, then the invoice price will be $990 + $8.79 = $998.79.

The practice of quoting bond prices net of accrued interest explains why the price of a maturing bond is listed at $1,000 rather than $1,000 plus one coupon payment. A purchaser of an 8% coupon bond 1 day before the bond's maturity would receive $1,040 (par value plus semiannual interest) on the following day and so should be willing to pay a total price of $1,040 for the bond. The bond price is quoted net of accrued interest in the financial pages and thus appears as $1,000.

**Corporate Bonds**    Like the government, corporations borrow money by issuing bonds. Figure 14.2 is a sample of corporate bond listings in *The Wall Street Journal*, which lists only the most actively traded corporate bonds. Although some bonds trade on a formal exchange operated by the New York Stock Exchange, most bonds are traded over the counter in a network of bond dealers linked by a computer quotation system. (See Chapter 3 for a comparison of exchange versus OTC trading.) In practice, the bond market can be quite "thin," in that there are few investors interested in trading a particular issue at any particular time.

The highlighted Ford bond in Figure 14.2 has a coupon rate of 7.45% and matures on July 16, 2031. The last price at which the bond traded was 85.417% of par value, or

**Figure 14.2
Corporate
bonds
listings**

## Corporate Bonds

Monday, August 4, 2003

Forty most active fixed-coupon corporate bonds

| COMPANY (TICKER) | COUPON | MATURITY | LAST PRICE | LAST YIELD | *EST SPREAD | UST† | EST $ VOL (000's) |
|---|---|---|---|---|---|---|---|
| General Motors (GM) | 8.375 | Jul 15, 2033 | 94.229 | 8.929 | 368 | 30 | 138,007 |
| Liberty Media (L) | 5.700 | May 15, 2013 | 95.615 | 6.306 | 199 | 10 | 131,245 |
| Walt Disney (DIS)-c | 2.125 | Apr 15, 2023 | 104.590 | 1.117 | n.a. | n.a. | 95,518 |
| General Motors Acceptance (GMAC) | 8.000 | Nov 01, 2031 | 92.866 | 8.679 | 342 | 30 | 50,355 |
| J.P. Morgan Chase (JPM) | 5.250 | May 30, 2007 | 105.957 | 3.564 | 43 | 5 | 50,154 |
| AT&T Wireless Services (AWE) | 8.125 | May 01, 2012 | 114.500 | 5.968 | 164 | 10 | 49,789 |
| General Motors (GM) | 7.125 | Jul 15, 2013 | 98.349 | 7.360 | 308 | 10 | 48,806 |
| Ford Motor (F) | 7.450 | Jul 16, 2031 | 85.417 | 8.868 | 362 | 30 | 47,835 |
| Bank One (ONE) | 7.625 | Aug 01, 2005 | 110.622 | 2.127 | 44 | 2 | 47,750 |
| General Motors (GM) | 8.250 | Jul 15, 2023 | 94.719 | 8.815 | 350 | 30 | 46,444 |
| Ford Motor Credit (F) | 7.500 | Mar 15, 2005 | 105.822 | 3.727 | 205 | 2 | 45,866 |
| CIT Group (CIT) | 4.000 | May 08, 2008 | 99.997 | 4.007 | 90 | 5 | 42,215 |
| Avon Products (AVP) | 7.150 | Nov 15, 2009 | 115.371 | 4.324 | 122 | 5 | 30,000 |

Volume represents total volume for each issue; price/yield data are for trades of $1 million and greater. * Estimated spreads, in basis points (100 basis points is one percentage point), over the 2, 3, 5, 10 or 30-year hot run Treasury note/bond. 2-year: 1.500 07/05; 3-year: 2.000 05/06; 5-year: 2.625 05/08; 10-year: 3.625 05/13; 30-year: 5.375 02/31. †Comparable U.S. Treasury issue. c-Convertible bond.

Source: MarketAxess Corporate BondTicker

$854.17, and the yield to maturity based on this price was 8.868%. The next column shows the difference or "spread" between the yield to maturity on this bond, and the yield to maturity of a comparable-maturity U.S. Treasury bond. The spread is given in terms of basis points (1 basis point is .01%). Therefore, the spread for the Ford bond is 362 basis points, or 3.62%. The maturity of the Treasury bond against which the Ford bond is compared is 30 years. The yield spread reflects the default or *credit risk* of the Ford bond. We will have much to say about the determinants of credit risk later in the chapter.

Bonds issued in the United States today are *registered*, meaning that the issuing firm keeps records of the owner of the bond and can mail interest checks to the owner. Registration of bonds is helpful to tax authorities in the enforcement of tax collection. *Bearer bonds* are those traded without any record of ownership. The investor's physical possession of the bond certificate is the only evidence of ownership. These are now rare in the United States, but less rare in Europe.

**Call Provisions on Corporate Bonds.** Although the Treasury no longer issues callable bonds, some corporate bonds are issued with call provisions allowing the issuer to repurchase the bond at a specified *call price* before the maturity date. For example, if a company issues a bond with a high coupon rate when market interest rates are high, and interest rates later fall, the firm might like to retire the high-coupon debt and issue new bonds at a lower coupon rate to reduce interest payments. This is called *refunding*. Callable bonds typically come with a period of call protection, an initial time during which the bonds are not callable. Such bonds are referred to as *deferred* callable bonds.

The option to call the bond is valuable to the firm, allowing it to buy back the bonds and refinance at lower interest rates when market rates fall. Of course, the firm's benefit is the bondholder's burden. Holders of called bonds forfeit their bonds for the call price, thereby giving up the prospect of an attractive coupon rate on their original investment. To compensate investors for this risk, callable bonds are issued with higher coupons and promised yields to maturity than noncallable bonds.

| CONCEPT CHECK ☞ QUESTION 1 | Suppose that General Motors issues two bonds with identical coupon rates and maturity dates. One bond is callable, however, whereas the other is not. Which bond will sell at a higher price? |
|---|---|

**Convertible Bonds.**  **Convertible bonds** give bondholders an option to exchange each bond for a specified number of shares of common stock of the firm. The *conversion ratio* is the number of shares for which each bond may be exchanged. Suppose a convertible bond is issued at par value of $1,000 and is convertible into 40 shares of a firm's stock. The current stock price is $20 per share, so the option to convert is not profitable now. Should the stock price later rise to $30, however, each bond may be converted profitably into $1,200 worth of stock. The *market conversion value* is the current value of the shares for which the bonds may be exchanged. At the $20 stock price, for example, the bond's conversion value is $800. The *conversion premium* is the excess of the bond value over its conversion value. If the bond were selling currently for $950, its premium would be $150.

Convertible bondholders benefit from price appreciation of the company's stock. Again, this benefit comes at a price: Convertible bonds offer lower coupon rates and stated or promised yields to maturity than do nonconvertible bonds. However, the actual return on the convertible bond may exceed the stated yield to maturity if the option to convert becomes profitable.

We discuss convertible and callable bonds further in Chapter 20.

**Puttable Bonds.**  While the callable bond gives the issuer the option to extend or retire the bond at the call date, the *extendable* or **put bond** gives this option to the bondholder. If the bond's coupon rate exceeds current market yields, for instance, the bondholder will choose to extend the bond's life. If the bond's coupon rate is too low, it will be optimal not to extend; the bondholder instead reclaims principal, which can be invested at current yields.

**Floating-Rate Bonds.**  **Floating-rate bonds** make interest payments that are tied to some measure of current market rates. For example, the rate might be adjusted annually to the current T-bill rate plus 2%. If the 1-year T-bill rate at the adjustment date is 4%, the bond's coupon rate over the next year would then be 6%. This arrangement means that the bond always pays approximately current market rates.

The major risk involved in floaters has to do with changes in the firm's financial strength. The yield spread is fixed over the life of the security, which may be many years. If the financial health of the firm deteriorates, then a greater yield premium would be called for than is offered by the security. In this case, the price of the bond would fall. Although the coupon rate on floaters adjusts to changes in the general level of market interest rates, it does not adjust to changes in the financial condition of the firm.

## Preferred Stock

Although preferred stock strictly speaking is considered to be equity, it often is included in the fixed-income universe. This is because, like bonds, preferred stock promises to pay a specified stream of dividends. However, unlike bonds, the failure to pay the promised dividend does not result in corporate bankruptcy. Instead, the dividends owed simply cumulate, and the common stockholders may not receive any dividends until the preferred stockholders have been paid in full. In the event of bankruptcy, preferred stockholders' claims to the firm's assets have lower priority than those of bondholders, but higher priority than those of common stockholders.

Preferred stock commonly pays a fixed dividend. Therefore, it is in effect a perpetuity, providing a level cash flow indefinitely. In the last two decades, however, adjustable or floating-rate preferred stock has become popular, in some years accounting for about half of new issues. Floating-rate preferred stock is much like floating-rate bonds. The dividend rate is linked to a measure of current market interest rates and is adjusted at regular intervals.

Unlike interest payments on bonds, dividends on preferred stock are not considered tax-deductible expenses to the firm. This reduces their attractiveness as a source of capital to issuing firms. On the other hand, there is an offsetting tax advantage to preferred stock. When one corporation buys the preferred stock of another corporation, it pays taxes on only 30% of the dividends received. For example, if the firm's tax bracket is 35%, and it receives $10,000 in preferred dividend payments, it will pay taxes on only $3,000 of that income: Total taxes owed on the income will be .35 × $3,000 = $1,050. The firm's effective tax rate on preferred dividends is therefore only .30 × 35% = 10.5%. Given this tax rule, it is not surprising that most preferred stock is held by corporations.

Preferred stock rarely gives its holders full voting privileges in the firm. However, if the preferred dividend is skipped, the preferred stockholders will then be provided some voting power.

**Other Issuers** There are, of course, several issuers of bonds in addition to the Treasury and private corporations. For example, state and local governments issue municipal bonds. The outstanding feature of these is that interest payments are tax-free. We examined municipal bonds and the value of the tax exemption in Chapter 2.

Government agencies such as the Federal Home Loan Bank Board, the Farm Credit agencies, and the mortgage pass-through agencies Ginnie Mae, Fannie Mae, and Freddie Mac, also issue considerable amounts of bonds. These too were reviewed in Chapter 2.

**International Bonds** International bonds are commonly divided into two categories, *foreign bonds* and *Eurobonds*. Foreign bonds are issued by a borrower from a country other than the one in which the bond is sold. The bond is denominated in the currency of the country in which it is marketed. For example, if a German firm sells a dollar-denominated bond in the United States, the bond is considered a foreign bond. These bonds are given colorful names based on the countries in which they are marketed. For example, foreign bonds sold in the United States are called *Yankee bonds*. Like other bonds sold in the United States, they are registered with the Securities and Exchange Commission. Yen-denominated bonds sold in Japan by non-Japanese issuers are called *Samurai bonds*. British pound-denominated foreign bonds sold in the United Kingdom are called *bulldog bonds*.

In contrast to foreign bonds, Eurobonds are bonds issued in the currency of one country but sold in other national markets. For example, the Eurodollar market refers to dollar-denominated bonds sold outside the United States (not just in Europe), although London is the largest market for Eurodollar bonds. Because the Eurodollar market falls outside U.S. jurisdiction, these bonds are not regulated by U.S. federal agencies. Similarly, Euroyen bonds are yen-denominated bonds selling outside Japan, Eurosterling bonds are pound-denominated Eurobonds selling outside the United Kingdom, and so on.

**Innovation in the Bond Market** Issuers constantly develop innovative bonds with unusual features; these issues illustrate that bond design can be extremely flexible. Here are examples of some novel bonds. They should give you a sense of the potential variety in security design.

**Inverse Floaters.** These are similar to the floating-rate bonds we described earlier, except that the coupon rate on these bonds *falls* when the general level of interest rates rises. Investors in these bonds suffer doubly when rates rise. Not only does the present value of each dollar of cash flow from the bond fall as the discount rate rises, but the level of those cash flows falls as well. Of course, investors in these bonds benefit doubly when rates fall.

**Asset-Backed Bonds.** Walt Disney has issued bonds with coupon rates tied to the financial performance of several of its films. Similarly, "David Bowie bonds" have been issued with payments that will be tied to royalties on some of his albums. These are examples of asset-backed securities. The income from a specified group of assets is used to service the debt. More conventional asset-backed securities are mortgage-backed securities or securities backed by auto or credit card loans, as we discussed in Chapter 2.

**Catastrophe Bonds.** Electrolux once issued a bond with a final payment that depended on whether there had been an earthquake in Japan. Winterthur has issued a bond whose payments depend on whether there has been a severe hailstorm in Switzerland. These bonds are a way to transfer "catastrophe risk" from the firm to the capital markets. They represent a novel way of obtaining insurance from the capital markets against specified disasters. Investors in these bonds receive compensation for taking on the risk in the form of higher coupon rates.

**Indexed Bonds.** Indexed bonds make payments that are tied to a general price index or the price of a particular commodity. For example, Mexico has issued 20-year bonds with payments that depend on the price of oil. Some bonds are indexed to the general price level. The United States Treasury started issuing such inflation-indexed bonds in January 1997. They are called Treasury Inflation Protected Securities (TIPS). By tying the par value of the bond to the general level of prices, coupon payments as well as the final repayment of par value on these bonds increase in direct proportion to the consumer price index. Therefore, the interest rate on these bonds is a risk-free real rate.

To illustrate how TIPS work, consider a newly issued bond with a 3-year maturity, par value of $1,000, and a coupon rate of 4%. For simplicity, we will assume the bond makes annual coupon payments. Assume that inflation turns out to be 2%, 3%, and 1% in the next 3 years. Table 14.1 shows how the bond cash flows will be calculated. The first payment comes at the end of the first year, at $t = 1$. Because inflation over the year was 2%, the par value of the bond increases from $1,000 to $1,020; since the coupon rate is 4%, the coupon payment is 4% of this amount, or $40.80. Notice that par value increases by the inflation rate, and because the coupon payments are 4% of par, they too increase in proportion to the general price level. Therefore, the cash flows paid by the bond are fixed in *real* terms. When the bond matures, the investor receives a final coupon payment of $42.44 plus the (price-level-indexed) repayment of principal, $1,061.11.[2]

The *nominal* rate of return on the bond in the first year is

$$\text{Nominal return} = \frac{\text{Interest} + \text{Price Appreciation}}{\text{Initial Price}} = \frac{40.80 + 20}{1000} = 6.08\%.$$

[2] By the way, total nominal income (i.e., coupon plus that year's increase in principal) is treated as taxable income in each year.

| Table 14.1 | Principal and Interest Payments for a Treasury Inflation Protected Security | | | | | | |
|---|---|---|---|---|---|---|---|
| Time | Inflation in Year Just Ended | Par Value | Coupon Payment | + | Principal Repayment | = | Total Payment |
| 0 |  | $1,000.00 |  |  |  |  |  |
| 1 | 2% | 1,020.00 | $40.80 |  | $    0 |  | $    40.80 |
| 2 | 3 | 1,050.60 | 42.02 |  | 0 |  | 42.02 |
| 3 | 1 | 1,061.11 | 42.44 |  | 1,061.11 |  | 1,103.55 |

The real rate of return is precisely the 4% real yield on the bond:

$$\text{Real return} = \frac{1 + \text{Nominal return}}{1 + \text{Inflation}} - 1 = \frac{1.0608}{1.02} = .04, \text{ or } 4\%$$

One can show in a similar manner (see problem 17 in the end-of-chapter problems) that the rate of return in each of the 3 years is 4% as long as the real yield on the bond remains constant. If real yields do change, then there will be capital gains or losses on the bond. In early 2003, the real yield on TIPS bonds was about 2.8%.

## 14.2  BOND PRICING

Because a bond's coupon and principal repayments all occur months or years in the future, the price an investor would be willing to pay for a claim to those payments depends on the value of dollars to be received in the future compared to dollars in hand today. This "present value" calculation depends in turn on market interest rates. As we saw in Chapter 5, the nominal risk-free interest rate equals the sum of (1) a real risk-free rate of return and (2) a premium above the real rate to compensate for expected inflation. In addition, because most bonds are not riskless, the discount rate will embody an additional premium that reflects bond-specific characteristics such as default risk, liquidity, tax attributes, call risk, and so on.

We simplify for now by assuming there is one interest rate that is appropriate for discounting cash flows of any maturity, but we can relax this assumption easily. In practice, there may be different discount rates for cash flows accruing in different periods. For the time being, however, we ignore this refinement.

To value a security, we discount its expected cash flows by the appropriate discount rate. The cash flows from a bond consist of coupon payments until the maturity date plus the final payment of par value. Therefore,

Bond value = Present value of coupons + Present value of par value

If we call the maturity date $T$ and call the interest rate $r$, the bond value can be written as

$$\text{Bond value} = \sum_{t=1}^{T} \frac{\text{Coupon}}{(1+r)^t} + \frac{\text{Par value}}{(1+r)^T} \qquad (14.1)$$

The summation sign in equation 14.1 directs us to add the present value of each coupon payment; each coupon is discounted based on the time until it will be paid. The first term on the right-hand side of equation 14.1 is the present value of an annuity. The second term is the present value of a single amount, the final payment of the bond's par value.

You may recall from an introductory finance class that the present value of a $1 annuity that lasts for $T$ periods when the interest rate equals $r$ is $\frac{1}{r}\left(1 - \frac{1}{(1+r)^T}\right)$. We call this expression the $T$-period *annuity factor* for an interest rate of $r$.[3] Similarly, we call $\frac{1}{(1+r)^T}$ the *PV factor*, that is the present value of a single payment of $1 to be received in $T$ periods. Therefore, we can write the price of the bond as

$$\text{Price} = \text{Coupon} \times \frac{1}{r}\left(1 - \frac{1}{(1+r)^T}\right) + \text{Par value} \times \frac{1}{(1+r)^T} \tag{14.2}$$
$$= \text{Coupon} \times \text{Annuity factor}(r, T) + \text{Par value} \times \text{PV factor}(r, T)$$

## EXAMPLE 14.2    Bond Pricing

We discussed earlier an 8% coupon, 30-year maturity bond with par value of $1,000 paying 60 semiannual coupon payments of $40 each. Suppose that the interest rate is 8% annually, or $r = 4\%$ per 6-month period. Then the value of the bond can be written as

$$\text{Price} = \sum_{t=1}^{60} \frac{\$40}{(1.04)^t} + \frac{\$1,000}{(1.04)^{60}} \tag{14.3}$$
$$= \$40 \times \text{Annuity factor}(4\%, 60) + \$1,000 \times \text{PV factor}(4\%, 60)$$

It is easy to confirm that the present value of the bond's 60 semiannual coupon payments of $40 each is $904.94 and that the $1,000 final payment of par value has a present value of $95.06, for a total bond value of $1,000. You can either calculate the value directly from equation 14.2, perform these calculations on any financial calculator,[4] use a spreadsheet program (see box on page 460), or a set of present value tables.

In this example, the coupon rate equals the market interest rate and the bond price equals par value. If the interest rate were not equal to the bond's coupon rate, the bond would not sell at par value. For example, if the interest rate were to rise to 10% (5% per 6 months), the bond's price would fall by $189.29 to $810.71, as follows:

$$\$40 \times \text{Annuity factor}(5\%, 60) + \$1,000 \times \text{PV factor}(5\%, 60)$$
$$= \$757.17 + \$53.54 = \$810.71$$

At a higher interest rate, the present value of the payments to be received by the bondholder is lower. Therefore, the bond price will fall as market interest rates rise. This illustrates a crucial general rule in bond valuation. When interest rates rise, bond prices must fall because the present value of the bond's payments are obtained by discounting at a higher interest rate.

---

[3] Here is a quick derivation of the formula for the present value of an annuity. An annuity lasting $T$ periods can be viewed as equivalent to a perpetuity whose first payment comes at the end of the current period *less* another perpetuity whose first payment comes at the end of the $(T + 1)$st period. The immediate perpetuity net of the delayed perpetuity provides exactly $T$ payments. We know that the value of a $1 per period perpetuity is $1/r. Therefore, the present value of the delayed perpetuity is $1/r discounted for $T$ additional periods, or $\frac{1}{r}\frac{1}{(1+r)^T}$. The present value of the annuity is the present value of the first perpetuity minus the present value of the delayed perpetuity, or $\frac{1}{r}\left(1 - \frac{1}{(1+r)^T}\right)$.

[4] On your financial calculator, you would enter the following inputs: $n$ (number of periods) = 60; FV (face or future value) = 1000; PMT (payment each period) = 40; $i$ (per period interest rate) = 4%; then you would compute the price of the bond (COMP PV or CPT PV). You should find that the price is $1,000. Actually, most calculators will display the result as *minus* $1,000. This is because most (but not all) calculators treat the initial purchase price of the bond as a cash *outflow*.

**Figure 14.3 The inverse relationship between bond prices and yields. Price of an 8% coupon bond with 30-year maturity making semiannual payments**

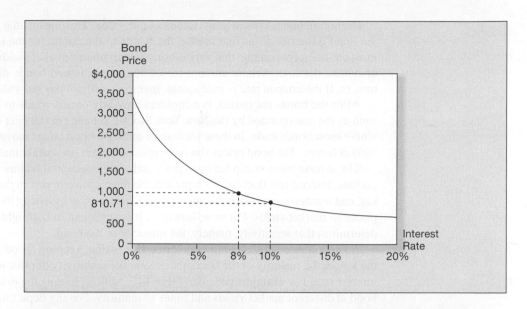

| Table 14.2 | **Bond Prices at Different Interest Rates** (8% coupon bond, coupons paid semiannually) | | | | |
|---|---|---|---|---|---|
| **Time to Maturity** | **Bond Price at Given Market Interest Rate** | | | | |
| | **4%** | **6%** | **8%** | **10%** | **12%** |
| 1 year | 1,038.83 | 1,029.13 | 1,000.00 | 981.41 | 963.33 |
| 10 years | 1,327.03 | 1,148.77 | 1,000.00 | 875.35 | 770.00 |
| 20 years | 1,547.11 | 1,231.15 | 1,000.00 | 828.41 | 699.07 |
| 30 years | 1,695.22 | 1,276.76 | 1,000.00 | 810.71 | 676.77 |

Figure 14.3 shows the price of the 30-year, 8% coupon bond for a range of interest rates, including 8%, at which the bond sells at par, and 10%, at which it sells for $810.71. The negative slope illustrates the inverse relationship between prices and yields. Note also from the figure (and from Table 14.2) that the shape of the curve implies that an increase in the interest rate results in a price decline that is smaller than the price gain resulting from a decrease of equal magnitude in the interest rate. This property of bond prices is called *convexity* because of the convex shape of the bond price curve. This curvature reflects the fact that progressive increases in the interest rate result in progressively smaller reductions in the bond price.[5] Therefore, the price curve becomes flatter at higher interest rates. We return to the issue of convexity in Chapter 16.

**CONCEPT CHECK ☞ QUESTION 2**   Calculate the price of the 30-year, 8% coupon bond for a market interest rate of 3% per half-year. Compare the capital gains for the interest rate decline to the losses incurred when the rate increases to 5%.

---

[5] The progressively smaller impact of interest increases results from the fact that at higher rates the bond is worth less. Therefore, an additional increase in rates operates on a smaller initial base, resulting in a smaller price reduction.

Corporate bonds typically are issued at par value. This means that the underwriters of the bond issue (the firms that market the bonds to the public for the issuing corporation) must choose a coupon rate that very closely approximates market yields. In a primary issue of bonds, the underwriters attempt to sell the newly issued bonds directly to their customers. If the coupon rate is inadequate, investors will not pay par value for the bonds.

After the bonds are issued, bondholders may buy or sell bonds in secondary markets, such as the one operated by the New York Stock Exchange or the over-the-counter market, where most bonds trade. In these secondary markets, bond prices move in accordance with market forces. The bond prices fluctuate inversely with the market interest rate.

The inverse relationship between price and yield is a central feature of fixed-income securities. Interest rate fluctuations represent the main source of risk in the fixed-income market, and we devote considerable attention in Chapter 16 to assessing the sensitivity of bond prices to market yields. For now, however, it is sufficient to highlight one key factor that determines that sensitivity, namely, the maturity of the bond.

A general rule in evaluating bond price risk is that, keeping all other factors the same, the longer the maturity of the bond, the greater the sensitivity of price to fluctuations in the interest rate. For example, consider Table 14.2, which presents the price of an 8% coupon bond at different market yields and times to maturity. For any departure of the interest rate from 8% (the rate at which the bond sells at par value), the change in the bond price is smaller for shorter times to maturity.

This makes sense. If you buy the bond at par with an 8% coupon rate, and market rates subsequently rise, then you suffer a loss: You have tied up your money earning 8% when alternative investments offer higher returns. This is reflected in a capital loss on the bond—a fall in its market price. The longer the period for which your money is tied up, the greater the loss, and correspondingly the greater the drop in the bond price. In Table 14.2, the row for 1-year maturity bonds shows little price sensitivity—that is, with only 1 year's earnings at stake, changes in interest rates are not too threatening. But for 30-year maturity bonds, interest rate swings have a large impact on bond prices.

This is why short-term Treasury securities such as T-bills are considered to be the safest. They are free not only of default risk but also largely of price risk attributable to interest rate volatility.

**Bond Pricing between Coupon Dates**    Equation 14.2 for bond prices assumes that the next coupon payment is in precisely one payment period, either a year for an annual payment bond or 6 months for a semiannual payment bond. But you probably want to be able to price bonds all 365 days of the year, not just on the one or two dates each year that it makes a coupon payment!

We apply the same principles to pricing regardless of the date: we simply compute the present value of the remaining payments. However, if we are between coupon dates, there will be fractional periods remaining until each payment. Even if the principles are no more complicated, this certainly complicates the arithmetic computations.

Fortunately, bond pricing functions are included in most spreadsheet programs such as Excel. The spreadsheet allows you to enter today's date as well as the maturity date of the bond, and so can provide prices for bonds at any date. The box on page 460 shows you how.

As we pointed out earlier, bond prices are typically quoted net of accrued interest. These prices, which appear in the financial press, are called *flat prices*. The actual *invoice price* that a buyer pays for the bond includes accrued interest. Thus,

$$\text{Invoice price} = \text{Flat price} + \text{Accrued interest}$$

When a bond pays its coupon, flat price equals invoice price, since at that moment accrued interest reverts to zero. However, this will be the exceptional case, not the rule.

The Excel pricing function provides the flat price of the bond. To find the invoice price, we need to add accrued interest. Fortunately, Excel also provides functions that count the days since the last coupon payment date and thus can be used to compute accrued interest. The nearby box also illustrates how to use these functions. The box provides examples using bonds that have just paid a coupon and so have zero accrued interest, as well as a bond that is between coupon dates.

## 14.3   BOND YIELDS

We have noted that the current yield of a bond measures only the cash income provided by the bond as a percentage of bond price and ignores any prospective capital gains or losses. We would like a measure of rate of return that accounts for both current income and the price increase or decrease over the bond's life. The yield to maturity is the standard measure of the total rate of return. However, it is far from perfect, and we will explore several variations of this measure.

### Yield to Maturity

In practice, an investor considering the purchase of a bond is not quoted a promised rate of return. Instead, the investor must use the bond price, maturity date, and coupon payments to infer the return offered by the bond over its life. The **yield to maturity** (YTM) is defined as the interest rate that makes the present value of a bond's payments equal to its price. This interest rate is often viewed as a measure of the average rate of return that will be earned on a bond if it is bought now and held until maturity. To calculate the yield to maturity, we solve the bond price equation for the interest rate given the bond's price.

### EXAMPLE 14.3   Yield to Maturity

Suppose an 8% coupon, 30-year bond is selling at $1,276.76. What average rate of return would be earned by an investor purchasing the bond at this price? We find the interest rate at which the present value of the remaining 60 semiannual payments equals the bond price. This is the rate consistent with the observed price of the bond. Therefore, we solve for $r$ in the following equation:

$$\$1,276.76 = \sum_{t=1}^{60} \frac{\$40}{(1+r)^t} + \frac{\$1,000}{(1+r)^{60}}$$

or, equivalently,

$$1,276.76 = 40 \times \text{Annuity factor}(r, 60) + 1,000 \times \text{PV factor}(r, 60)$$

These equations have only one unknown variable, the interest rate, $r$. You can use a financial calculator or spreadsheet to confirm that the solution is $r = .03$, or 3% per half-year.[6] This is considered the bond's yield to maturity.

The financial press reports yields on an annualized basis, and annualizes the bond's semiannual yield using simple interest techniques, resulting in an annual percentage rate, or APR. Yields annualized using simple interest are also called "bond equivalent yields."

---

[6] On your financial calculator, you would enter the following inputs: $n = 60$ periods; PV = $-1,276.76$; FV = 1000; PMT = 40; then you would compute the interest rate (COMP $i$ or CPT $i$). Notice that we enter the present value, or PV, of the bond as *minus* $1,000. Again, this is because most calculators treat the initial purchase price of the bond as a cash outflow. Without a financial calculator, you still could solve the equation, but you would need to use a trial-and-error approach.

# BOND PRICING

Excel and most other spreadsheet programs provide built-in functions to compute bond prices and yields. They typically ask you to input both the date you buy the bond (called the *settlement date*) and the maturity date of the bond. The Excel function for bond price is

=PRICE(settlement date, maturity date, annual coupon rate, yield to maturity, redemption value as percent of par value, number of coupon payments per year)

For the 4.875% coupon 2012 maturity bond highlighted in Figure 14.1, we would enter the values in the following spreadsheet. Alternatively, we could simply enter the following function in Excel:

=PRICE(DATE(2003,02,15), DATE(2012,02,15), .04875, .0386, 100, 2)

| | A | B | C | D | E | F |
|---|---|---|---|---|---|---|
| 1 | | | | | | |
| 2 | | | | | | |
| 3 | | | | | | |
| 4 | | 4.875% coupon | | 4% coupon | | 8% coupon |
| 5 | | maturing | | maturing | | 30-year |
| 6 | | Feb 2012 | | Feb 2012 | | maturity |
| 7 | | | | | | |
| 8 | Settlement date | 2/15/2003 | | 2/15/2003 | | 1/1/2000 |
| 9 | Maturity date | 2/15/2012 | | 11/15/2012 | | 1/1/2030 |
| 10 | Annual coupon rate | 0.04875 | | 0.04 | | 0.08 |
| 11 | Yield to maturity | 0.0386 | | 0.0394 | | 0.1 |
| 12 | Redemption value (% of par value) | 100 | | 100 | | 100 |
| 13 | Coupon payments per year | 2 | | 2 | | 2 |
| 14 | | | | | | |
| 15 | | | Formula in column B | | | |
| 16 | Flat price (% of par) | 107.655 | =PRICE(B8,B9,B10,B11,B12,B13) | 100.477 | | 81.071 |
| 17 | Days since last coupon | 0 | =COUPDAYBS(B8,B9,2,1) | 92 | | 0 |
| 18 | Days in coupon period | 181 | =COUPDAYS(B8,B9,2,1) | 181 | | 182 |
| 19 | Accrued interest | 0 | =(B17/B18)*B10*100/2 | 1.017 | | 0 |
| 20 | Invoice price | 107.655 | =B16+B19 | 101.494 | | 81.071 |

Therefore, the semiannual yield would be doubled and reported in the newspaper as a bond equivalent yield of 6%. The *effective* annual yield of the bond, however, accounts for compound interest. If one earns 3% interest every 6 months, then after 1 year, each dollar invested grows with interest to $1 \times (1.03)^2 = \$1.0609$, and the effective annual interest rate on the bond is 6.09%.

The bond's yield to maturity is the internal rate of return on an investment in the bond. The yield to maturity can be interpreted as the compound rate of return over the life of the bond under the assumption that all bond coupons can be reinvested at that yield.[7] Yield to maturity is widely accepted as a proxy for average return.

---

[7] If the reinvestment rate does not equal the bond's yield to maturity, the compound rate of return will differ from YTM. This is demonstrated later.

The DATE function in Excel, which we use for both the settlement and maturity date, uses the format DATE(year,month,day). The first date is February 15, 2003, when the bond is purchased, and the second is February 15, 2012, when it matures. Most bonds pay coupons on the 15th of the month.

Notice that the coupon rate and yield to maturity are expressed as decimals, not percentages. In most cases, redemption value is 100 (i.e., 100% of par value), and the resulting price similarly is expressed as a percent of par value. Occasionally, however, you may encounter bonds that pay off at a premium or discount to par value. One example would be callable bonds, discussed shortly.

The value of the bond returned by the pricing function is 107.655 (cell B16), which matches the price reported in *The Wall Street Journal* to the nearest 32nd of a point. This bond has just paid a coupon. In other words, the settlement date is precisely at the beginning of the coupon period, so no adjustment for accrued interest is necessary.

To illustrate the procedure for bonds between coupon payments, let us apply the spreadsheet to the 4% coupon November 2012 bond directly below the highlighted bond in Figure 14.1. Using the entries in column D of the spreadsheet, we find in cell D16 that the (flat) price of the bond is 100.477, which matches the actual price of the bond except for a few cents rounding error.

What about the bond's invoice price? Rows 17 through 20 make the necessary adjustments. The function described in cell C17 counts the days since the last coupon. This day count is based on the bond's settlement date, maturity date, coupon period (1 = annual; 2 = semiannual), and day count convention (choice 1 uses actual days). The function described in cell C18 counts the total days in each coupon payment period. Therefore, the entries in row 19 are the semiannual coupon multiplied by the fraction of a coupon period that has elapsed since the last payment. Finally, the invoice prices in row 20 are the sum of flat price plus accrued interest.

As a final example, suppose you wish to find the price of the bond in Example 14.2. It is a 30-year maturity bond with a coupon rate of 8% (paid semiannually). The market interest rate given in the latter part of the example is 10%. However, you are not given a specific settlement or maturity date. You can still use the PRICE function to value the bond. Simply choose an *arbitrary* settlement date (January 1, 2000, is convenient) and let the maturity date be 30 years hence. The appropriate inputs appear in column F of the spreadsheet, with the resulting price, 81.071% of face value, appearing in cell F20.

---

Yield to maturity is different from the **current yield** of a bond, which is the bond's annual coupon payment divided by the bond price. For example, for the 8%, 30-year bond currently selling at $1,276.76, the current yield would be $80/$1,276.76 = .0627, or 6.27% per year. In contrast, recall that the effective annual yield to maturity is 6.09%. For this bond, which is selling at a premium over par value ($1,276 rather than $1,000), the coupon rate (8%) exceeds the current yield (6.27%), which exceeds the yield to maturity (6.09%). The coupon rate exceeds current yield because the coupon rate divides the coupon payments by par value ($1,000) rather than by the bond price ($1,276). In turn, the current yield exceeds yield to maturity because the yield to maturity accounts for the built-in capital loss on the bond; the bond bought today for $1,276 will eventually fall in value to $1,000 at maturity.

Example 14.3 illustrates a general rule: for **premium bonds** (bonds selling above par value), coupon rate is greater than current yield, which in turn is greater than yield to

**Spreadsheet 14.1**

|    | A | B | C | D | E | F | G | H |
|----|---|---|---|---|---|---|---|---|
| 1  |   |   |   |   |            |   |         |   |
| 2  |   |   |   |   |            |   |         |   |
| 3  |   |   |   |   |            |   |         |   |
| 4  |   |   |   |   | Semiannual |   | Annual  |   |
| 5  |   |   |   |   | coupons    |   | coupons |   |
| 6  |   |   |   |   |            |   |         |   |
| 7  | Settlement date |   |   |   | 1/1/2000 |   | 1/1/2000 |   |
| 8  | Maturity date |   |   |   | 1/1/2030 |   | 1/1/2030 |   |
| 9  | Annual coupon rate |   |   |   | 0.08 |   | 0.08 |   |
| 10 | Bond price |   |   |   | 127.676 |   | 127.676 |   |
| 11 | Redemption value (% of face value) |   |   |   | 100 |   | 100 |   |
| 12 | Coupon payments per year |   |   |   | 2 |   | 1 |   |
| 13 |   |   |   |   |            |   |         |   |
| 14 | **Yield to maturity (decimal)** |   |   |   | **0.0600** |   | **0.0599** |   |
| 15 |   |   |   |   |            |   |         |   |
| 16 |   |   |   |   |            |   |         |   |
| 17 |   | The formula entered here is: =YIELD(E7,E8,E9,E10,E11,E12) |   |   |   |   |   |   |

maturity. For **discount bonds** (bonds selling below par value), these relationships are reversed (see Concept Check 3).

It is common to hear people talking loosely about the yield on a bond. In these cases, it is almost always the case that they are referring to the yield to maturity.

**CONCEPT CHECK ☞ QUESTION 3**

What will be the relationship among coupon rate, current yield, and yield to maturity for bonds selling at discounts from par? Illustrate using the 8% (semiannual payment) coupon bond assuming it is selling at a yield to maturity of 10%.

Excel also provides a function for yield to maturity. It is

= YIELD(settlement date, maturity date, annual coupon rate, bond price, redemption value as percent of par value, number of coupon payments per year)

The bond price used in the function should be the reported flat price, without accrued interest. For example, to find the yield to maturity of the bond in Example 14.3, we would use column E of Spreadsheet 14.1. If the coupons were paid only annually, we would change the entry for payments per year to 1 (see cell G12), and the yield would fall slightly to 5.99%.

### Yield to Call

Yield to maturity is calculated on the assumption that the bond will be held until maturity. What if the bond is callable, however, and may be retired prior to the maturity date? How should we measure average rate of return for bonds subject to a call provision?

Figure 14.4 illustrates the risk of call to the bondholder. The colored line is the value at various market interest rates of a "straight" (i.e., noncallable) bond with par value $1,000, an 8% coupon rate, and a 30-year time to maturity. If interest rates fall, the bond price, which equals the present value of the promised payments, can rise substantially.

**Figure 14.4
Bond prices:
Callable and
straight debt.
Coupon = 8%;
maturity =
30 years;
semiannual
payments.**

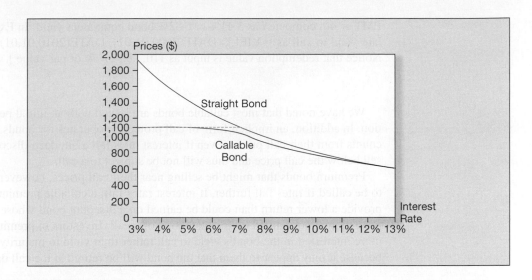

Now consider a bond that has the same coupon rate and maturity date but is callable at 110% of par value, or $1,100. When interest rates fall, the present value of the bond's *scheduled* payments rises, but the call provision allows the issuer to repurchase the bond at the call price. If the call price is less than the present value of the scheduled payments, the issuer can call the bond back from the bondholder.

The dark line in Figure 14.4 is the value of the callable bond. At high interest rates, the risk of call is negligible, and the values of the straight and callable bonds converge. At lower rates, however, the values of the bonds begin to diverge, with the difference reflecting the value of the firm's option to reclaim the callable bond at the call price. At very low rates, the bond is called, and its value is simply the call price, $1,100.

This analysis suggests that bond market analysts might be more interested in a bond's yield to call rather than yield to maturity if the bond is especially vulnerable to being called. The yield to call is calculated just like the yield to maturity except that the time until call replaces time until maturity, and the call price replaces the par value. This computation is sometimes called "yield to first call," as it assumes the bond will be called as soon as the bond is first callable.

**EXAMPLE 14.4**  |  ## Yield to Call

Suppose the 8% coupon, 30-year maturity bond sells for $1,150 and is callable in 10 years at a call price of $1,100. Its yield to maturity and yield to call would be calculated using the following inputs:

|                               | Yield to Call | Yield to Maturity |
| ----------------------------- | ------------- | ----------------- |
| Coupon payment                | $40           | $40               |
| Number of semiannual periods  | 20 periods    | 60 periods        |
| Final payment                 | $1,100        | $1,000            |
| Price                         | $1,150        | $1,150            |

Yield to call is then 6.64%. [To confirm this on your calculator, input *n* = 20; PV = (−)1,150; FV = 1100; PMT = 40; compute *i* as 3.32%, or 6.64% bond equivalent yield]. Yield to maturity is 6.82%. [To confirm, input *n* = 60; PV = (−)1,150; FV = 1000;

PMT = 40; compute *i* as 3.41% or 6.82% bond equivalent yield. In Excel, you can calculate yield to call as =YIELD(DATE(2000,01,01), DATE(2010,01,01), .08, 115, 110, 2). Notice that redemption value is input as 110, i.e., 110% of par value.].

We have noted that most callable bonds are issued with an initial period of call protection. In addition, an implicit form of call protection operates for bonds selling at deep discounts from their call prices. Even if interest rates fall a bit, deep-discount bonds still will sell below the call price and thus will not be subject to a call.

Premium bonds that might be selling near their call prices, however, are especially apt to be called if rates fall further. If interest rates fall, a callable premium bond is likely to provide a lower return than could be earned on a discount bond whose potential price appreciation is not limited by the likelihood of a call. Investors in premium bonds often are more interested in the bond's yield to call rather than yield to maturity as a consequence, because it may appear to them that the bond will be retired at the call date.

**CONCEPT CHECK ☞ QUESTIONS 4 and 5**

4. The yield to maturity on two 10-year maturity bonds currently is 7%. Each bond has a call price of $1,100. One bond has a coupon rate of 6%, the other 8%. Assume for simplicity that bonds are called as soon as the present value of their remaining payments exceeds their call price. What will be the capital gain on each bond if the market interest rate suddenly falls to 6%?

5. A 20-year maturity 9% coupon bond paying coupons semiannually is callable in 5 years at a call price of $1,050. The bond currently sells at a yield to maturity of 8%. What is the yield to call?

### Realized Compound Yield versus Yield to Maturity

We have noted that yield to maturity will equal the rate of return realized over the life of the bond if all coupons are reinvested at an interest rate equal to the bond's yield to maturity. Consider, for example, a 2-year bond selling at par value paying a 10% coupon once a year. The yield to maturity is 10%. If the $100 coupon payment is reinvested at an interest rate of 10%, the $1,000 investment in the bond will grow after 2 years to $1,210, as illustrated in Figure 14.5, panel A. The coupon paid in the first year is reinvested and grows with interest to a second-year value of $110, which together with the second coupon payment and payment of par value in the second year results in a total value of $1,210. The compound growth rate of invested funds, therefore, is calculated from

$$\$1,000 \, (1 + y_{realized})^2 = \$1,210$$
$$y_{realized} = .10 = 10\%$$

With a reinvestment rate equal to the 10% yield to maturity, the *realized* compound yield equals yield to maturity.

But what if the reinvestment rate is not 10%? If the coupon can be invested at more than 10%, funds will grow to more than $1,210, and the realized compound return will exceed 10%. If the reinvestment rate is less than 10%, so will be the realized compound return. Consider the following example.

**Figure 14.5**
**Growth of invested funds**

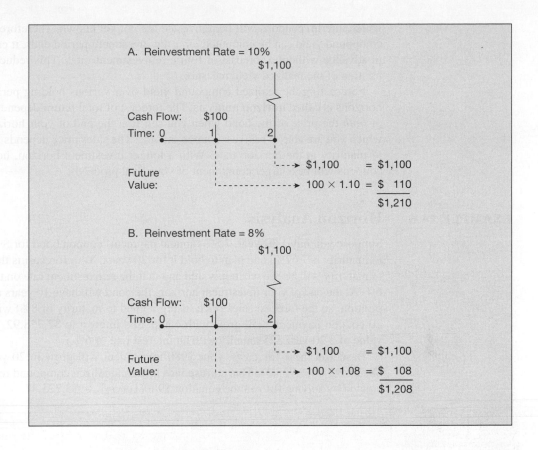

## EXAMPLE 14.5    Realized Compound Yield

If the interest rate earned on the first coupon is less than 10%, the final value of the investment will be less than $1,210, and the realized compound yield will be less than 10%. To illustrate, suppose the interest rate at which the coupon can be invested equals 8%. The following calculations are illustrated in Figure 14.5, panel B.

| | |
|---|---:|
| Future value of first coupon payment with interest earnings $100 × 1.08 = | $ 108 |
| Cash payment in second year (final coupon plus par value) | $1,100 |
| Total value of investment with reinvested coupons | $1,208 |

The realized compound yield is computed by calculating the compound rate of growth of invested funds, assuming that all coupon payments are reinvested. The investor purchased the bond for par at $1,000, and this investment grew to $1,208.

$$\$1,000(1 + y_{realized})^2 = \$1,208$$

$$y_{realized} = .0991 = 9.91\%$$

Example 14.5 highlights the problem with conventional yield to maturity when reinvestment rates can change over time. Conventional yield to maturity will not equal realized compound return. However, in an economy with future interest rate uncertainty, the rates at which interim coupons will be reinvested are not yet known. Therefore, although realized compound yield can be computed *after* the investment period ends, it cannot be computed in advance without a forecast of future reinvestment rates. This reduces much of the attraction of the realized yield measure.

Forecasting the realized compound yield over various holding periods or investment horizons is called **horizon analysis.** The forecast of total return depends on your forecasts of *both* the price of the bond when you sell it at the end of your horizon *and* the rate at which you are able to reinvest coupon income. The sales price depends in turn on the yield to maturity at the horizon date. With a longer investment horizon, however, reinvested coupons will be a larger component of your final proceeds.

**EXAMPLE 14.6**    **Horizon Analysis**

Suppose you buy a 30-year, 7.5% (annual payment) coupon bond for $980 (when its yield to maturity is 7.67%) and plan to hold it for 20 years. Your forecast is that the bond's yield to maturity will be 8% when it is sold and that the reinvestment rate on the coupons will be 6%. At the end of your investment horizon, the bond will have 10 years remaining until expiration, so the forecast sales price (using a yield to maturity of 8%) will be $966.45. The 20 coupon payments will grow with compound interest to $2,758.92. (This is the future value of a 20-year $75 annuity with an interest rate of 6%.)

Based on these forecasts, your $980 investment will grow in 20 years to $966.45 + $2,758.92 = $3,725.37. This corresponds to an annualized compound return of 6.90%, calculated by solving for $r$ in the equation $980(1 + r)^{20} = \$3,725.37$.

## 14.4    BOND PRICES OVER TIME

As we noted earlier, a bond will sell at par value when its coupon rate equals the market interest rate. In these circumstances, the investor receives fair compensation for the time value of money in the form of the recurring interest payments. No further capital gain is necessary to provide fair compensation.

When the coupon rate is lower than the market interest rate, the coupon payments alone will not provide investors as high a return as they could earn elsewhere in the market. To receive a fair return on such an investment, investors also need to earn price appreciation on their bonds. The bonds, therefore, would have to sell below par value to provide a "built-in" capital gain on the investment.

To illustrate this point, suppose a bond was issued several years ago when the interest rate was 7%. The bond's annual coupon rate was thus set at 7%. (We will suppose for simplicity that the bond pays its coupon annually.) Now, with 3 years left in the bond's life, the interest rate is 8% per year. The bond's market price is the present value of the remaining annual coupons plus payment of par value. That present value is

$$\$70 \times \text{Annuity factor}(8\%, 3) + \$1,000 \times \text{PV factor}(8\%, 3) = \$974.23$$

which is less than par value.

In another year, after the next coupon is paid, the bond would sell at

$$\$70 \times \text{Annuity factor}(8\%, 2) + \$1,000 \times \text{PV factor}(8\%, 2) = \$982.17$$

thereby yielding a capital gain over the year of $7.94. If an investor had purchased the bond at $974.23, the total return over the year would equal the coupon payment plus capital gain,

**Figure 14.6**
**Prices over time of 30-year maturity, 6.5% coupon bonds. Bond price approaches par value as maturity approaches.**

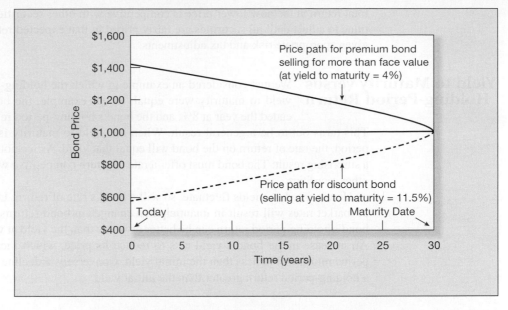

or $70 + $7.94 = $77.94$. This represents a rate of return of $77.94/$974.23, or 8%, exactly the current rate of return available elsewhere in the market.

| CONCEPT CHECK ☞ QUESTION 6 | What will the bond price be in yet another year, when only 1 year remains until maturity? What is the rate of return to an investor who purchases the bond at $982.17 and sells it 1 year hence? |
|---|---|

When bond prices are set according to the present value formula, any discount from par value provides an anticipated capital gain that will augment a below-market coupon rate just sufficiently to provide a fair total rate of return. Conversely, if the coupon rate exceeds the market interest rate, the interest income by itself is greater than that available elsewhere in the market. Investors will bid up the price of these bonds above their par values. As the bonds approach maturity, they will fall in value because fewer of these above-market coupon payments remain. The resulting capital losses offset the large coupon payments so that the bondholder again receives only a fair rate of return.

Problem 12 at the end of the chapter asks you to work through the case of the high-coupon bond. Figure 14.6 traces out the price paths of high- and low-coupon bonds (net of accrued interest) as time to maturity approaches, at least for the case in which the market interest rate is constant. The low-coupon bond enjoys capital gains, whereas the high-coupon bond suffers capital losses.[8]

We use these examples to show that each bond offers investors the same total rate of return. Although the capital gain versus income components differ, the price of each bond is set to provide competitive rates, as we should expect in well-functioning capital markets. Security returns all should be comparable on an after-tax risk-adjusted basis. It they are not, investors will try to sell low-return securities, thereby driving down their prices until the

---

[8] If interest rates are volatile, the price path will be "jumpy," vibrating around the price path in Figure 14.6 and reflecting capital gains or losses as interest rates fall or rise. Ultimately, however, the price must reach par value at the maturity date, so the price of the premium bond will fall over time while that of the discount bond will rise.

total return at the now lower price is competitive with other securities. Prices should continue to adjust until all securities are fairly priced in that expected returns are comparable, given appropriate risk and tax adjustments.

**Yield to Maturity versus Holding-Period Return**    We just considered an example in which the holding-period return and the yield to maturity were equal: In our example, the bond yield started and ended the year at 8%, and the bond's holding-period return also equaled 8%. This turns out to be a general result. When the yield to maturity is unchanged over the period, the rate of return on the bond will equal that yield. As we noted, this should not be a surprising result: The bond must offer a rate of return competitive with those available on other securities.

However, when yields fluctuate, so will a bond's rate of return. Unanticipated changes in market rates will result in unanticipated changes in bond returns, and after the fact, a bond's holding-period return can be better or worse than the yield at which it initially sells. An increase in the bond's yield acts to reduce its price, which means that the holding-period return will be less than the initial yield. Conversely, a decline in yield will result in a holding-period return greater than the initial yield.

**EXAMPLE 14.7    Yield to Maturity versus Holding-Period Return**

Consider a 30-year bond paying an annual coupon of $80 and selling at par value of $1,000. The bond's initial yield to maturity is 8%. If the yield remains at 8% over the year, the bond price will remain at par, so the holding-period return also will be 8%. But if the yield falls below 8%, the bond price will increase. Suppose the yield falls and the price increases to $1,050. Then the holding-period return is greater than 8%:

$$\text{Holding-period return} = \frac{\$80 + (\$1{,}050 - \$1{,}000)}{\$1{,}000} = .13 \text{ or } 13\%$$

**CONCEPT CHECK ☞ QUESTION 7**

Show that if yield to maturity increases, then holding-period return is *less* than initial yield. For example, suppose that by the end of the first year, the bond's yield to maturity is 8.5%. Find the 1-year holding-period return and compare it to the bond's initial 8% yield to maturity.

Here is another way to think about the difference between yield to maturity and holding-period return. Yield to maturity depends only on the bond's coupon, *current* price, and par value at maturity. All of these values are observable today, so yield to maturity can be easily calculated. Yield to maturity can be interpreted as a measure of the *average* rate of return if the investment in the bond is held until the bond matures. In contrast, holding-period return is the rate of return over a particular investment period and depends on the market price of the bond at the end of that holding period; of course this price is *not* known today. Since bond prices over the holding period will respond to unanticipated changes in interest rates, holding-period return can at most be forecast.

**Zero-Coupon Bonds**    *Original issue discount bonds* are less common than coupon bonds issued at par. These are bonds that are issued intentionally with low coupon rates that cause the bond to sell at a discount from par value. An extreme example of this type of bond is the *zero-coupon bond*, which carries no coupons and provides all its return in the form of price appreciation. Zeros provide only one cash flow to their owners, on the maturity date of the bond.

U.S. Treasury bills are examples of short-term zero-coupon instruments. The Treasury issues or sells a bill for some amount less than $10,000, agreeing to repay $10,000 at the bill's maturity. All of the investor's return comes in the form of price appreciation over time.

Longer-term zero-coupon bonds are commonly created from coupon-bearing notes and bonds with the help of the U.S. Treasury. A bond dealer who purchases a Treasury coupon bond may ask the Treasury to break down the cash flows to be paid by the bond into a series of independent securities, where each security is a claim to one of the payments of the original bond. For example, a 10-year coupon bond would be "stripped" of its 20 semi-annual coupons, and each coupon payment would be treated as a stand-alone zero-coupon bond. The maturities of these bonds would thus range from 6 months to 10 years. The final payment of principal would be treated as another stand-alone zero-coupon security. Each of the payments is now treated as an independent security and is assigned its own CUSIP number (by the Committee on Uniform Securities Identification Procedures), the security identifier that allows for electronic trading over the Fedwire system, a network that connects all Federal Reserve banks and their branches. The payments are still considered obligations of the U.S. Treasury. The Treasury program under which coupon stripping is performed is called STRIPS (Separate Trading of Registered Interest and Principal of Securities), and these zero-coupon securities are called Treasury *strips*. Turn back to Figure 14.1 to see the listing of these bonds in *The Wall Street Journal*.

What should happen to prices of zeros as time passes? On their maturity dates, zeros must sell for par value. Before maturity, however, they should sell at discounts from par, because of the time value of money. As time passes, price should approach par value. In fact, if the interest rate is constant, a zero's price will increase at exactly the rate of interest.

To illustrate this property, consider a zero with 30 years until maturity, and suppose the market interest rate is 10% per year. The price of the bond today will be $\$1,000/(1.10)^{30} = \$57.31$. Next year, with only 29 years until maturity, if the yield is still 10%, the price will be $\$1,000/(1.10)^{29} = \$63.04$, a 10% increase over its previous-year value. Because the par value of the bond is now discounted for 1 year fewer, its price has increased by the 1-year discount factor.

Figure 14.7 presents the price path of a 30-year zero-coupon bond until its maturity date for an annual market interest rate of 10%. The bond prices rise exponentially, not linearly, until its maturity.

**After-Tax Returns**   The tax authorities recognize that the "built-in" price appreciation on original issue discount (OID) bonds such as zero-coupon bonds represents an implicit interest payment to the holder of the security. The IRS, therefore, calculates a price appreciation schedule to impute taxable interest income for the built-in appreciation during a tax year, even if the asset is not sold or does not mature until a future year. Any additional gains or losses that arise from changes in market interest rates are treated as capital gains or losses if the OID bond is sold during the tax year.

---

**EXAMPLE 14.8**   **Taxation of OID Bonds**

If the interest rate originally is 10%, the 30-year zero would be issued at a price of $\$1,000/(1.10)^{30} = \$57.31$. The following year, the IRS calculates what the bond price would be if the yield were still 10%. This is $\$1,000/(1.10)^{29} = \$63.04$. Therefore, the IRS

**Figure 14.7
The price of
a 30-year zero-
coupon bond over
time at a yield to
maturity of 10%.
Price equals
$1,000/(1.10)^T$,
where $T$ is time
until maturity.**

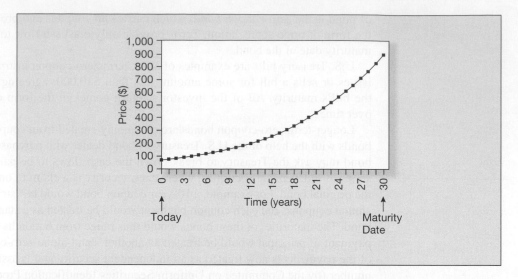

imputes interest income of $63.04 − $57.31 = $5.73. This amount is subject to tax. Notice that the *imputed* interest income is based on a "constant yield method" that ignores any changes in market interest rates.

If interest rates actually fall, let's say to 9.9%, the bond price actually will be $1,000/(1.099)^{29} = $64.72. If the bond is sold, then the difference between $64.72 and $63.04 is treated as capital gains income and taxed at the capital gains tax rate. If the bond is not sold, then the price difference is an unrealized capital gain and does not result in taxes in that year. In either case, the investor must pay taxes on the $5.73 of imputed interest at the rate on ordinary income.

The procedure illustrated in Example 14.8 applies as well to the taxation of other original-issue discount bonds, even if they are not zero-coupon bonds. Consider, as an example, a 30-year maturity bond that is issued with a coupon rate of 4% and a yield to maturity of 8%. For simplicity, we will assume that the bond pays coupons once annually. Because of the low coupon rate, the bond will be issued at a price far below par value, specifically at a price of $549.69. If the bond's yield to maturity is still 8%, then its price in 1 year will rise to $553.66. (Confirm this for yourself.) This would provide a pretax holding-period return (HPR) of exactly 8%:

$$\text{HPR} = \frac{\$40 + (\$553.66 - \$549.69)}{\$549.69} = .08$$

The increase in the bond price based on a constant yield, however, is treated as interest income, so the investor is required to pay taxes on imputed interest income of $553.66 − $549.69 = $3.97. If the bond's yield actually changes during the year, the difference between the bond's price and the constant-yield value of $553.66 would be treated as capital gains income if the bond is sold.

**CONCEPT
CHECK ☞
QUESTION 8**

Suppose that the yield to maturity of the 4% coupon, 30-year maturity bond falls to 7% by the end of the first year and that the investor sells the bond after the first year. If the investor's federal plus state tax rate on interest income is 38% and the combined tax rate on capital gains is 20%, what is the investor's after-tax rate of return?

## 14.5   DEFAULT RISK AND BOND PRICING

Although bonds generally *promise* a fixed flow of income, that income stream is not risk-less unless the investor can be sure the issuer will not default on the obligation. While U.S. government bonds may be treated as free of default risk, this is not true of corporate bonds. Therefore, the actual payments on these bonds are uncertain, for they depend to some degree on the ultimate financial status of the firm.

Bond default risk, usually called **credit risk,** is measured by Moody's Investor Services, Standard & Poor's Corporation, Duff & Phelps, and Fitch Investors Service, all of which provide financial information on firms as well as quality ratings of large corporate and municipal bond issues. Each firm assigns letter grades to the bonds of corporations and municipalities to reflect their assessment of the safety of the bond issue. The top rating is AAA or Aaa. Moody's modifies each rating class with a 1, 2, or 3 suffix (e.g., Aaa1, Aaa2, Aaa3) to provide a finer gradation of ratings. The other agencies use a + or − modification.

Those rated BBB or above (S&P, Duff & Phelps, Fitch) or Baa and above (Moody's) are considered **investment-grade bonds,** whereas lower-rated bonds are classified as **speculative-grade or junk bonds.** Defaults on low-grade issues are not uncommon. For example, almost half of the bonds that were rated CCC by Standard & Poor's at issue have defaulted within 10 years. Highly rated bonds rarely default, but even these bonds are not free of credit risk. For example, in May 2001 WorldCom sold $11.8 billion of bonds with an investment-grade rating. Only a year later, the firm filed for bankruptcy and its bondholders lost more than 80% of their investment. Certain regulated institutional investors such as insurance companies have not always been allowed to invest in speculative-grade bonds.

Figure 14.8 provides the definitions of each bond rating classification.

### Junk Bonds

Junk bonds, also known as *high-yield bonds*, are nothing more than speculative-grade (low-rated or unrated) bonds. Before 1977, almost all junk bonds were "fallen angels," that is, bonds issued by firms that originally had investment-grade ratings but that had since been downgraded. In 1977, however, firms began to issue "original-issue junk."

Much of the credit for this innovation is given to Drexel Burnham Lambert, and especially its trader Michael Milken. Drexel had long enjoyed a niche as a junk bond trader and had established a network of potential investors in junk bonds. Firms not able to muster an investment-grade rating were happy to have Drexel (and other investment bankers) market their bonds directly to the public, as this opened up a new source of financing. Junk issues were a lower-cost financing alternative than borrowing from banks.

High-yield bonds gained considerable notoriety in the 1980s when they were used as financing vehicles in leveraged buyouts and hostile takeover attempts. Shortly thereafter, however, the junk bond market suffered. The legal difficulties of Drexel and Michael Milken in connection with Wall Street's insider trading scandals of the late 1980s tainted the junk bond market.

At the height of Drexel's difficulties, the high-yield bond market nearly dried up. Since then, the market has rebounded dramatically. However, it is worth noting that the average credit quality of high-yield debt issued today is higher than the average quality in the boom years of the 1980s.

### Determinants of Bond Safety

Bond rating agencies base their quality ratings largely on an analysis of the level and trend of some of the issuer's financial ratios. The key ratios used to evaluate safety are:

**Figure 14.8
Definitions
of each bond
rating class**

| Bond Ratings | | | | |
|---|---|---|---|---|
| | **Very High Quality** | **High Quality** | **Speculative** | **Very Poor** |
| Standard & Poor's | AAA    AA | A    BBB | BB    B | CCC    D |
| Moody's | Aaa    Aa | A    Baa | Ba    B | Caa    C |

At times both Moody's and Standard & Poor's have used adjustments to these ratings: S&P uses plus and minus signs: A+ is the strongest A rating and A– the weakest. Moody's uses a 1, 2, or 3 designation, with 1 indicating the strongest.

| Moody's | S&P | |
|---|---|---|
| Aaa | AAA | Debt rated Aaa and AAA has the highest rating. Capacity to pay interest and principal is extremely strong. |
| Aa | AA | Debt rated Aa and AA has a very strong capacity to pay interest and repay principal. Together with the highest rating, this group comprises the high-grade bond class. |
| A | A | Debt rated A has a strong capacity to pay interest and repay principal, although it is somewhat more susceptible to the adverse effects of changes in circumstances and economic conditions than debt in higher-rated categories. |
| Baa | BBB | Debt rated Baa and BBB is regarded as having an adequate capacity to pay interest and repay principal. Whereas it normally exhibits adequate protection parameters, adverse economic conditions or changing circumstances are more likely to lead to a weakened capacity to pay interest and repay principal for debt in this category than in higher-rated categories. These bonds are medium-grade obligations. |
| Ba<br>B<br>Caa<br>Ca | BB<br>B<br>CCC<br>CC | Debt rated in these categories is regarded, on balance, as predominantly speculative with respect to capacity to pay interest and repay principal in accordance with the terms of the obligation. BB and Ba indicate the lowest degree of speculation, and CC and Ca the highest degree of speculation. Although such debt will likely have some quality and protective characteristics, these are outweighed by large uncertainties or major risk exposures to adverse conditions. Some issues may be in default. |
| C | C | This rating is reserved for income bonds on which no interest is being paid. |
| D | D | Debt rated D is in default, and payment of interest and/or repayment of principal is in arrears. |

Source: Stephen A. Ross and Randolph W. Westerfield, *Corporate Finance* (St. Louis: Times Mirror/Mosby College Publishing, 1988). Data from various editions of *Standard & Poor's Bond Guide* and *Moody's Bond Guide*.

1. *Coverage ratios*—Ratios of company earnings to fixed costs. For example, the *times-interest-earned ratio* is the ratio of earnings before interest payments and taxes to interest obligations. The *fixed-charge coverage ratio* includes lease payments and sinking fund payments with interest obligations to arrive at the ratio of earnings to all fixed cash obligations (sinking funds are described below). Low or falling coverage ratios signal possible cash flow difficulties.

2. *Leverage ratio*—*Debt-to-equity ratio.* A too-high leverage ratio indicates excessive indebtedness, signaling the possibility the firm will be unable to earn enough to satisfy the obligations on its bonds.

3. *Liquidity ratios*—The two common liquidity ratios are the *current ratio* (current assets/current liabilities) and the *quick ratio* (current assets excluding inventories/current liabilities). These ratios measure the firm's ability to pay bills coming due with its most liquid assets.

## Table 14.3   Rating on Long-Term Debt and Financial Ratios

| 3-Year (1998–2000) Medians | AAA | AA | A | BBB | BB | B | CCC |
|---|---|---|---|---|---|---|---|
| EBIT interest coverage ratio | 21.4 | 10.1 | 6.1 | 3.7 | 2.1 | 0.8 | 0.1 |
| EBITDA interest coverage | 26.5 | 12.9 | 9.1 | 5.8 | 3.4 | 1.8 | 1.3 |
| Funds flow/total debt (%) | 84.2 | 25.2 | 15.0 | 8.5 | 2.6 | (3.2) | (12.9) |
| Free oper. cash flow/total debt (%) | 128.8 | 55.4 | 43.2 | 30.8 | 18.8 | 7.8 | 1.6 |
| Return on capital (%) | 34.9 | 21.7 | 19.4 | 13.6 | 11.6 | 6.6 | 1.0 |
| Oper. income/sales (%) | 27.0 | 22.1 | 18.6 | 15.4 | 15.9 | 11.9 | 11.9 |
| Long-term debt/capital (%) | 13.3 | 28.2 | 33.9 | 42.5 | 57.2 | 69.7 | 68.8 |
| Total debt/capital (incl. STD) (%) | 22.9 | 37.7 | 42.5 | 48.2 | 62.6 | 74.8 | 87.7 |

Note: EBITDA, earnings before interest, taxes, depreciation, and amortization; STD, short-term debt.
Source: From Standard & Poor's *Credit Week,* July 28, 2001. Used by permission of Standard & Poor's.

4. *Profitability ratios*—Measures of rates of return on assets or equity. Profitability ratios are indicators of a firm's overall financial health. The *return on assets* (earnings before interest and taxes divided by total assets) is the most popular of these measures. Firms with higher return on assets should be better able to raise money in security markets because they offer prospects for better returns on the firm's investments.

5. *Cash flow–to–debt ratio*—This is the ratio of total cash flow to outstanding debt.

Standard & Poor's periodically computes median values of selected ratios for firms in several rating classes, which we present in Table 14.3. Of course, ratios must be evaluated in the context of industry standards, and analysts differ in the weights they place on particular ratios. Nevertheless, Table 14.3 demonstrates the tendency of ratios to improve along with the firm's rating class.

Many studies have tested whether financial ratios can in fact be used to predict default risk. One of the best-known series of tests was conducted by Edward Altman, who used discriminant analysis to predict bankruptcy. With this technique a firm is assigned a score based on its financial characteristics. If its score exceeds a cut-off value, the firm is deemed creditworthy. A score below the cut-off value indicates significant bankruptcy risk in the near future.

To illustrate the technique, suppose that we were to collect data on the return on equity (ROE) and coverage ratios of a sample of firms, and then keep records of any corporate bankruptcies. In Figure 14.9 we plot the ROE and coverage ratios for each firm using $X$ for firms that eventually went bankrupt and $O$ for those that remained solvent. Clearly, the $X$ and $O$ firms show different patterns of data, with the solvent firms typically showing higher values for the two ratios.

The discriminant analysis determines the equation of the line that best separates the $X$ and $O$ observations. Suppose that the equation of the line is $.75 = .9 \times \text{ROE} + .4 \times \text{Coverage}$. Then, based on its own financial ratios, each firm is assigned a "Z-score" equal

| E-INVESTMENTS **Default Risk** | Go to Bondsonline (**www.bondsonline.com**) and link to *Corporate Bonds* under the *Bond Search/Quote Center.* Under the *Express Search* in the *Issue* box, enter and review the bonds issued by Disney, Delta Air, and Goodyear. What explains the differences in yield to maturity (market rate) on the bonds of these three companies? |
|---|---|

**Figure 14.9    Discriminant analysis**

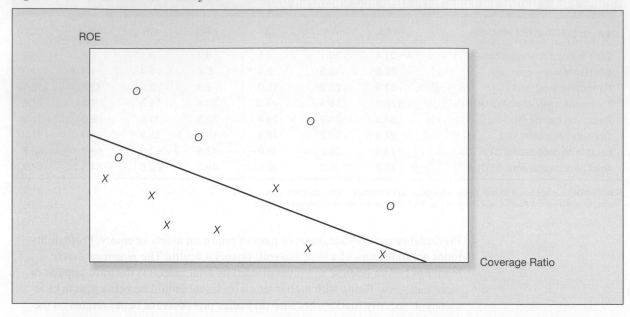

to $.9 \times$ ROE $+ .4 \times$ Coverage. If its Z-score exceeds .75, the firm plots above the line and is considered a safe bet; Z-scores below .75 foretell financial difficulty.

Altman[9] found the following equation to best separate failing and nonfailing firms:

$$Z = 3.3 \frac{\text{EBIT}}{\text{Total assets}} + 99.9 \frac{\text{Sales}}{\text{Assets}} + .6 \frac{\text{Market value of equity}}{\text{Book value of debt}}$$
$$+ 1.4 \frac{\text{Retained earnings}}{\text{Total assets}} + 1.2 \frac{\text{Working capital}}{\text{Total assets}}$$

where EBIT = earnings before interest and taxes.

**CONCEPT CHECK☞ QUESTION 9**    **Suppose we add a new variable equal to current liabilities/current assets to Altman's equation. Would you expect this variable to receive a positive or negative coefficient?**

## Bond Indentures

A bond is issued with an *indenture*, which is the contract between the issuer and the bondholder. Part of the indenture is a set of restrictions that protect the rights of the bondholders. Such restrictions include provisions relating to collateral, sinking funds, dividend policy, and further borrowing. The issuing firm agrees to these *protective covenants* in order to market its bonds to investors concerned about the safety of the bond issue.

**Sinking Funds.**    Bonds call for the payment of par value at the end of the bond's life. This payment constitutes a large cash commitment for the issuer. To help ensure the

[9] Edward I. Altman, "Financial Ratios, Discriminant Analysis, and the Prediction of Corporate Bankruptcy," *Journal of Finance* 23 (September 1968).

commitment does not create a cash flow crisis, the firm agrees to establish a **sinking fund** to spread the payment burden over several years. The fund may operate in one of two ways:

1. The firm may repurchase a fraction of the outstanding bonds in the open market each year.
2. The firm may purchase a fraction of the outstanding bonds at a special call price associated with the sinking fund provision. The firm has an option to purchase the bonds at either the market price or the sinking fund price, whichever is lower. To allocate the burden of the sinking fund call fairly among bondholders, the bonds chosen for the call are selected at random based on serial number.[10]

The sinking fund call differs from a conventional bond call in two important ways. First, the firm can repurchase only a limited fraction of the bond issue at the sinking fund call price. At best, some indentures allow firms to use a *doubling option*, which allows repurchase of double the required number of bonds at the sinking fund call price. Second, while callable bonds generally have call prices above par value, the sinking fund call price usually is set at the bond's par value.

Although sinking funds ostensibly protect bondholders by making principal repayment more likely, they can hurt the investor. The firm will choose to buy back discount bonds (selling below par) at market price, while exercising its option to buy back premium bonds (selling above par) at par. Therefore, if interest rates fall and bond prices rise, firms will benefit from the sinking fund provision that enables them to repurchase their bonds at below-market prices. In these circumstances, the firm's gain is the bondholder's loss.

One bond issue that does not require a sinking fund is a *serial bond* issue. In a serial bond issue, the firm sells bonds with staggered maturity dates. As bonds mature sequentially, the principal repayment burden for the firm is spread over time, just as it is with a sinking fund. One advantage of serial bonds over sinking fund issues is that there is no uncertainty introduced by the possibility that a particular bond will be called for the sinking fund. The disadvantage of serial bonds, however, is that bonds of different maturity dates are not interchangeable, which reduces the liquidity of the issue.

**Subordination of Further Debt.**   One of the factors determining bond safety is total outstanding debt of the issuer. If you bought a bond today, you would be understandably distressed to see the firm tripling its outstanding debt tomorrow. Your bond would be of lower credit quality than it appeared when you bought it. To prevent firms from harming bondholders in this manner, **subordination clauses** restrict the amount of additional borrowing. Additional debt might be required to be subordinated in priority to existing debt; that is, in the event of bankruptcy, *subordinated* or *junior* debtholders will not be paid unless and until the prior senior debt is fully paid off. For this reason, subordination is sometimes called a "me-first rule," meaning the senior (earlier) bondholders are to be paid first in the event of bankruptcy.

**Dividend Restrictions.**   Covenants also limit the dividends firms are allowed to pay. These limitations protect the bondholders because they force the firm to retain assets rather than paying them out to stockholders. A typical restriction disallows payments of dividends if cumulative dividends paid since the firm's inception exceed cumulative retained earnings plus proceeds from sales of stock.

---

[10] Although it is less common, the sinking fund provision also may call for periodic payments to a trustee, with the payments invested so that the accumulated sum can be used for retirement of the entire issue at maturity.

**Collateral.** Some bonds are issued with specific collateral behind them. **Collateral** can take several forms, but it represents a particular asset of the firm that the bondholders receive if the firm defaults on the bond. If the collateral is property, the bond is called a *mortgage bond*. If the collateral takes the form of other securities held by the firm, the bond is a *collateral trust bond*. In the case of equipment, the bond is known as an *equipment obligation bond*. This last form of collateral is used most commonly by firms such as railroads, where the equipment is fairly standard and can be easily sold to another firm should the firm default and the bondholders acquire the collateral.

Because of the specific collateral that backs them, collateralized bonds generally are considered the safest variety of corporate bonds. General **debenture** bonds by contrast do not provide for specific collateral; they are *unsecured* bonds. The bondholder relies solely on the general earning power of the firm for the bond's safety. If the firm defaults, debenture owners become general creditors of the firm. Because they are safer, collateralized bonds generally offer lower yields than general debentures.

Figure 14.10 shows the terms of a bond issued by Mobil as described in *Moody's Industrial Manual*. The terms of the bond are typical and illustrate many of the indenture provisions we have mentioned. The bond is registered and listed on the NYSE. Although it was issued in 1991, it was not callable until 2002. Although the call price started at 105.007% of par value, it falls gradually until it reaches par after 2020.

**Figure 14.10**
**Callable bond**
**issued by Mobil**

> **& Mobil Corp. debenture 8s, due 2032:**
> **Rating — Aa2**
>
> AUTH — $250,000,000.
> OUTSTG — Dec. 31, 1993, $250,000,000.
> DATED — Oct. 30, 1991.
> INTEREST — F&A 12.
> TRUSTEE — Chemical Bank.
> DENOMINATION — Fully registered, $1,000 and integral multiples thereof. Transferable and exchangeable without service charge.
> CALLABLE — As a whole or in part, at any time, on or after Aug. 12, 2002, at the option of Co. on at least 30 but not more than 60 days' notice to each Aug. 11 as follows:
>
> | | | | | | |
> |---|---|---|---|---|---|
> | 2003 | 105.007 | 2004 | 104.756 | 2005 | 104.506 |
> | 2006 | 104.256 | 2007 | 104.005 | 2008 | 103.755 |
> | 2009 | 103.505 | 2010 | 103.254 | 2011 | 103.004 |
> | 2012 | 102.754 | 2013 | 102.503 | 2014 | 102.253 |
> | 2015 | 102.003 | 2016 | 101.752 | 2017 | 101.502 |
> | 2018 | 101.252 | 2019 | 101.001 | 2020 | 100.751 |
> | 2021 | 100.501 | 2022 | 100.250 | | |
>
> and thereafter at 100 plus accrued interest.
> SECURITY — Not secured. Ranks equally with all other unsecured and unsubordinated indebtedness of Co. Co. nor any Affiliate will not incurr any indebtedness; provided that Co. will not create as security for any indebtedness for borrowed money, any mortgage, pledge, security interest or lien on any stock or indebtedness is directly owned by Co., without effectively providing that the debt securities shall be secured equally and ratably with such indebtedness, so long as such indebtedness shall be so secured.
> INDENTURE    MODIFICATION — Indenture may be modified, except as provided with, consent of 66⅔% of debs. outstg.
> RIGHTS ON DEFAULT — Trustee, or 25% of debs. outstg., may declare principal dua nad payable (30 days' grace for payment of interest).
> LISTED — On New York Stock Exchange.
> PURPOSE — Proceeds used for general corporate purposes.
> OFFERED — ($250,000,000) at 99.51 plus accrued interest (proceeds to Co., 99.11) on Aug. 5, 1992 thru Merrill Lynch & Co., Donaldson, Lufkin & Jenerette Securities Corp., PaineWebber Inc., Prudential Securities Inc., Smith Barney, Harris Upham & Co. Inc. and associates.

Source: *Moody's Industrial Manual*, Moody's Investor Services, 1994.

**Yield to Maturity and Default Risk**    Because corporate bonds are subject to default risk, we must distinguish between the bond's promised yield to maturity and its expected yield. The promised or stated yield will be realized only if the firm meets the obligations of the bond issue. Therefore, the stated yield is the *maximum possible* yield to maturity of the bond. The expected yield to maturity must take into account the possibility of a default.

For example, in November 2001, as Enron approached bankruptcy, its 6.4% coupon bonds due in 2006 were selling at about 20% of par value, resulting in a yield to maturity of about 57%. Investors did not really expect these bonds to provide a 57% rate of return. They recognized that bondholders were very unlikely to receive all the payments promised in the bond contract and that the yield based on *expected* cash flows was far less than the yield based on *promised* cash flows.

**EXAMPLE 14.9**    **Expected vs. Promised Yield to Maturity**

Suppose a firm issued a 9% coupon bond 20 years ago. The bond now has 10 years left until its maturity date but the firm is having financial difficulties. Investors believe that the firm will be able to make good on the remaining interest payments, but that at the maturity date, the firm will be forced into bankruptcy, and bondholders will receive only 70% of par value. The bond is selling at $750.

Yield to maturity (YTM) would then be calculated using the following inputs:

|                              | Expected YTM | Stated YTM |
|------------------------------|--------------|------------|
| Coupon payment               | $45          | $45        |
| Number of semiannual periods | 20 periods   | 20 periods |
| Final payment                | $700         | $1,000     |
| Price                        | $750         | $750       |

The yield to maturity based on promised payments is 13.7%. Based on the expected payment of $700 at maturity, however, the yield to maturity would be only 11.6%. The stated yield to maturity is greater than the yield investors actually expect to receive.

**CONCEPT CHECK☞ QUESTION 10**    **What is the expected yield to maturity if the firm is in even worse condition and investors expect a final payment of only $600?**

To compensate for the possibility of default, corporate bonds must offer a **default premium**. The default premium is the difference between the promised yield on a corporate bond and the yield of an otherwise-identical government bond that is riskless in terms of default. If the firm remains solvent and actually pays the investor all of the promised cash flows, the investor will realize a higher yield to maturity than would be realized from the government bond. If, however, the firm goes bankrupt, the corporate bond is likely to provide a lower return than the government bond. The corporate bond has the potential for both better and worse performance than the default-free Treasury bond. In other words, it is riskier.

The pattern of default premiums offered on risky bonds is sometimes called the *risk structure of interest rates*. The greater the default risk, the higher the default premium.

**Figure 14.11 Yields on long-term bonds, 1954–2003**

Figure 14.11 shows yield to maturity of bonds of different risk classes since 1954 and yields on junk bonds since 1986. You can see here clear evidence of credit-risk premiums on promised yields.

One particular manner in which yield spreads seem to vary over time is related to the business cycle. Yield spreads tend to be wider when the economy is in a recession. Apparently, investors perceive a higher probability of bankruptcy when the economy is faltering, even holding bond rating constant. They require a commensurately higher default premium. This is sometimes termed a *flight to quality*, meaning that investors move their funds into safer bonds unless they can obtain larger premiums on lower-rated securities.

## SUMMARY

1. Fixed-income securities are distinguished by their promise to pay a fixed or specified stream of income to their holders. The coupon bond is a typical fixed-income security.

2. Treasury notes and bonds have original maturities greater than 1 year. They are issued at or near par value, with their prices quoted net of accrued interest. T-bonds may be callable during their last 5 years of life.

3. Callable bonds should offer higher promised yields to maturity to compensate investors for the fact that they will not realize full capital gains should the interest rate fall and the bonds be called away from them at the stipulated call price. Bonds often are issued with a period of call protection. In addition, discount bonds selling significantly below their call price offer implicit call protection.

4. Put bonds give the bondholder rather than the issuer the option to terminate or extend the life of the bond.

5. Convertible bonds may be exchanged, at the bondholder's discretion, for a specified number of shares of stock. Convertible bondholders "pay" for this option by accepting a lower coupon rate on the security.

6. Floating-rate bonds pay a coupon rate at a fixed premium over a reference short-term interest rate. Risk is limited because the rate is tied to current market conditions.

7. The yield to maturity is the single interest rate that equates the present value of a security's cash flows to its price. Bond prices and yields are inversely related. For premium bonds, the coupon rate is greater than the current yield, which is greater than the yield to maturity. The order of these inequalities is reversed for discount bonds.

8. The yield to maturity is often interpreted as an estimate of the average rate of return to an investor who purchases a bond and holds it until maturity. This interpretation is subject to error, however. Related measures are yield to call, realized compound yield, and expected (versus promised) yield to maturity.

9. Prices of zero-coupon bonds rise exponentially over time, providing a rate of appreciation equal to the interest rate. The IRS treats this price appreciation as imputed taxable interest income to the investor.

10. When bonds are subject to potential default, the stated yield to maturity is the maximum possible yield to maturity that can be realized by the bondholder. In the event of default, however, that promised yield will not be realized. To compensate bond investors for default risk, bonds must offer default premiums, that is, promised yields in excess of those offered by default-free government securities. If the firm remains healthy, its bonds will provide higher returns than government bonds. Otherwise the returns may be lower.

11. Bond safety is often measured using financial ratio analysis. Bond indentures are another safeguard to protect the claims of bondholders. Common indentures specify sinking fund requirements, collateralization of the loan, dividend restrictions, and subordination of future debt.

**KEY TERMS**

| | | |
|---|---|---|
| debt securities | put bond | investment-grade bonds |
| bond | floating-rate bonds | speculative-grade or junk |
| par value | yield to maturity | bonds |
| face value | current yield | sinking fund |
| coupon rate | premium bonds | subordination clauses |
| bond indenture | discount bonds | collateral |
| zero-coupon bonds | horizon analysis | debenture |
| convertible bonds | credit risk | default premium |

**WEBSITES**

General bond yield data may be found at these sites:
   www.bloomberg.com
   www.money.cnn.com/markets/bondcenter
   www.smartmoney.com/bondmarketup

Detailed information on bonds may be found at these comprehensive sites:
   www.investinginbonds.com
   www.bondsonline.com
   bonds.yahoo.com
   www.fool.com/school/basics/investingbasics005.htm
   www.fintools.com

Visit us at www.mhhe.com/bkm

**PROBLEMS**

1. Which security has a higher *effective* annual interest rate?
   a. A 3-month T-bill selling at $97,645 with par value $100,000.
   b. A coupon bond selling at par and paying a 10% coupon semiannually.

2. Treasury bonds paying an 8% coupon rate with *semiannual* payments currently sell at par value. What coupon rate would they have to pay in order to sell at par if they paid their coupons *annually*? (Hint: what is the effective annual yield on the bond?)

3. Two bonds have identical times to maturity and coupon rates. One is callable at 105, the other at 110. Which should have the higher yield to maturity? Why?

4. Consider a bond with a 10% coupon and with yield to maturity = 8%. If the bond's yield to maturity remains constant, then in 1 year, will the bond price be higher, lower, or unchanged? Why?

5. Consider an 8% coupon bond selling for $953.10 with 3 years until maturity making *annual* coupon payments. The interest rates in the next 3 years will be, with certainty, $r_1 = 8\%$, $r_2 = 10\%$, and $r_3 = 12\%$. Calculate the yield to maturity and realized compound yield of the bond.

6. Philip Morris may issue a 10-year maturity fixed-income security, which might include a sinking fund provision and either refunding or call protection.
   a. Describe a sinking fund provision.
   b. Explain the impact of a sinking-fund provision on:
      i. The expected average life of the proposed security.
      ii. Total principal and interest payments over the life of the proposed security.
   c. From the investor's point of view, explain the rationale for demanding a sinking fund provision.

7. Bonds of Zello Corporation with a par value of $1,000 sell for $960, mature in 5 years, and have a 7% annual coupon rate paid semiannually.
   a. Calculate the:
      i. Current yield.
      ii. Yield to maturity (to the nearest whole percent, i.e., 3%, 4%, 5%, etc.).
      iii. Realized compound yield for an investor with a 3-year holding period and a reinvestment rate of 6% over the period. At the end of 3 years the 7% coupon bonds with 2 years remaining will sell to yield 7%.
   b. Cite one major shortcoming for each of the following fixed-income yield measures:
      i. Current yield.
      ii. Yield to maturity.
      iii. Realized compound yield.

8. Assume you have a 1-year investment horizon and are trying to choose among three bonds. All have the same degree of default risk and mature in 10 years. The first is a zero-coupon bond that pays $1,000 at maturity. The second has an 8% coupon rate and pays the $80 coupon once per year. The third has a 10% coupon rate and pays the $100 coupon once per year.

*a.* If all three bonds are now priced to yield 8% to maturity, what are their prices?

*b.* If you expect their yields to maturity to be 8% at the beginning of next year, what will their prices be then? What is your before-tax holding-period return on each bond? If your tax bracket is 30% on ordinary income and 20% on capital gains income, what will your after-tax rate of return be on each?

*c.* Recalculate your answer to (*b*) under the assumption that you expect the yields to maturity on each bond to be 7% at the beginning of next year.

9. A 20-year maturity bond with par value of $1,000 makes semiannual coupon payments at a coupon rate of 8%. Find the bond equivalent and effective annual yield to maturity of the bond if the bond price is:

*a.* $950.

*b.* $1,000.

*c.* $1,050.

10. Repeat problem 9 using the same data, but assuming that the bond makes its coupon payments annually. Why are the yields you compute lower in this case?

11. Fill in the table below for the following zero-coupon bonds, all of which have par values of $1,000.

| Price | Maturity (years) | Bond-Equivalent Yield to Maturity |
|---|---|---|
| $400 | 20 | ___ |
| $500 | 20 | ___ |
| $500 | 10 | ___ |
| | 10 | 10% |
| | 10 | 8% |
| $400 | ___ | 8% |

12. Consider a bond paying a coupon rate of 10% per year semiannually when the market interest rate is only 4% per half year. The bond has 3 years until maturity.

*a.* Find the bond's price today and 6 months from now after the next coupon is paid.

*b.* What is the total (6 month) rate of return on the bond?

13. A newly issued bond pays its coupons once annually. Its coupon rate is 5%, its maturity is 20 years, and its yield to maturity is 8%.

*a.* Find the holding-period return for a 1-year investment period if the bond is selling at a yield to maturity of 7% by the end of the year.

*b.* If you sell the bond after 1 year, what taxes will you owe if the tax rate on interest income is 40% and the tax rate on capital gains income is 30%? The bond is subject to original-issue discount tax treatment.

*c.* What is the after-tax holding-period return on the bond?

*d.* Find the realized compound yield *before taxes* for a 2-year holding period, assuming that (1) you sell the bond after 2 years, (2) the bond yield is 7% at the end of the second year, and (3) the coupon can be reinvested for 1 year at a 3% interest rate.

*e.* Use the tax rates in (*b*) above to compute the *after-tax* 2-year realized compound yield. Remember to take account of OID tax rules.

14. A bond with a coupon rate of 7% makes semiannual coupon payments on January 15 and July 15 of each year. *The Wall Street Journal* reports the asked price for the bond on January 30 at 100:02. What is the invoice price of the bond? The coupon period has 182 days.

Visit us at www.mhhe.com/bkm

15. A bond has a current yield of 9% and a yield to maturity of 10%. Is the bond selling above or below par value? Explain.

16. Is the coupon rate of the bond in problem 15 more or less than 9%?

17. Return to Table 14.1 and calculate both the real and nominal rates of return on the TIPS bond in the second and third years.

18. A newly issued 20-year maturity, zero-coupon bond is issued with a yield to maturity of 8% and face value $1,000. Find the imputed interest income in the first, second, and last year of the bond's life.

19. A newly issued 10-year maturity, 4% coupon bond making *annual* coupon payments is sold to the public at a price of $800. What will be an investor's taxable income from the bond over the coming year? The bond will not be sold at the end of the year. The bond is treated as an original issue discount bond.

20. A 30-year maturity, 8% coupon bond paying coupons semiannually is callable in 5 years at a call price of $1,100. The bond currently sells at a yield to maturity of 7% (3.5% per half-year).
    a. What is the yield to call?
    b. What is the yield to call if the call price is only $1,050?
    c. What is the yield to call if the call price is $1,100, but the bond can be called in 2 years instead of 5 years?

21. A 10-year bond of a firm in severe financial distress has a coupon rate of 14% and sells for $900. The firm is currently renegotiating the debt, and it appears that the lenders will allow the firm to reduce coupon payments on the bond to one-half the originally contracted amount. The firm can handle these lower payments. What is the stated and expected yield to maturity of the bonds? The bond makes its coupon payments annually.

22. A 2-year bond with par value $1,000 making annual coupon payments of $100 is priced at $1,000. What is the yield to maturity of the bond? What will be the realized compound yield to maturity if the 1-year interest rate next year turns out to be (*a*) 8%, (*b*) 10%, (*c*) 12%?

23. The stated yield to maturity and realized compound yield to maturity of a (default-free) zero-coupon bond will always be equal. Why?

24. Suppose that today's date is April 15. A bond with a 10% coupon paid semiannually every January 15 and July 15 is listed in *The Wall Street Journal* as selling at an asked price of 101:04. If you buy the bond from a dealer today, what price will you pay for it?

25. Assume that two firms issue bonds with the following characteristics. Both bonds are issued at par.

| | ABC Bonds | XYZ Bonds |
|---|---|---|
| Issue size | $1.2 billion | $150 million |
| Maturity | 10 years* | 20 years |
| Coupon | 9% | 10% |
| Collateral | First mortgage | General debenture |
| Callable | Not callable | In 10 years |
| Call price | None | 110 |
| Sinking fund | None | Starting in 5 years |

*Bond is extendible at the discretion of the bondholder for an additional 10 years.

Ignoring credit quality, identify four features of these issues that might account for the lower coupon on the ABC debt. Explain.

26. A large corporation issued both fixed and floating-rate notes 5 years ago, with terms given in the following table:

|  | 9% Coupon Notes | Floating-Rate Note |
|---|---|---|
| Issue size | $250 million | $280 million |
| Original Maturity | 20 years | 10 years |
| Current price (% of par) | 93 | 98 |
| Current coupon | 9% | 8% |
| Coupon adjusts | Fixed coupon | Every year |
| Coupon reset rule | — | 1-year T-bill rate + 2% |
| Callable | 10 years after issue | 10 years after issue |
| Call price | 106 | 102.50 |
| Sinking fund | None | None |
| Yield to maturity | 9.9% | — |
| Price range since issued | $85–$112 | $97–$102 |

a. Why is the price range greater for the 9% coupon bond than the floating-rate note?
b. What factors could explain why the floating-rate note is not always sold at par value?
c. Why is the call price for the floating-rate note not of great importance to investors?
d. Is the probability of call for the fixed-rate note high or low?
e. If the firm were to issue a fixed-rate note with a 15-year maturity, what coupon rate would it need to offer to issue the bond at par value?
f. Why is an entry for yield to maturity for the floating-rate note not appropriate?

27. On May 30, 1999, Janice Kerr is considering one of the newly issued 10-year AAA corporate bonds shown in the following exhibit.

| Description | Coupon | Price | Callable | Call Price |
|---|---|---|---|---|
| Sentinal, due May 30, 2009 | 6.00% | 100 | Noncallable | NA |
| Colina, due May 30, 2009 | 6.20% | 100 | Currently callable | 102 |

a. Suppose that market interest rates decline by 100 basis points (i.e., 1%). Contrast the effect of this decline on the price of each bond.
b. Should Kerr prefer the Colina over the Sentinal bond when rates are expected to rise or to fall?
c. What would be the effect, if any, of an increase in the *volatility* of interest rates on the prices of each bond?

28. Masters Corp. issues two bonds with 20-year maturities. Both bonds are callable at $1,050. The first bond is issued at a deep discount with a coupon rate of 4% and a price of $580 to yield 8.4%. The second bond is issued at par value with a coupon rate of 8¾%.

a. What is the yield to maturity of the par bond? Why is it higher than the yield of the discount bond?

b. If you expect rates to fall substantially in the next 2 years, which bond would you prefer to hold?

c. In what sense does the discount bond offer "implicit call protection"?

29. A convertible bond has the following features:

| | |
|---|---|
| Coupon | 5.25% |
| Maturity | June 15, 2027 |
| Market price of bond | $77.50 |
| Market price of underlying common stock | $28.00 |
| Annual dividend | $1.20 |
| Conversion ratio | 20.83 shares |

Calculate the conversion premium for this bond.

30. a. Explain the impact on the offering yield of adding a call feature to a proposed bond issue.

b. Explain the impact on the bond's expected life of adding a call feature to a proposed bond issue.

c. Describe one advantage and one disadvantage of including callable bonds in a portfolio.

31. The multiple-choice problems following are based on questions that appeared in past CFA examinations.

a. An investment in a coupon bond will provide the investor with a return equal to the bond's yield to maturity at the time of purchase if:

   i. The bond is not called for redemption at a price that exceeds its par value.

   ii. All sinking fund payments are made in a prompt and timely fashion over the life of the issue.

   iii. The reinvestment rate is the same as the bond's yield to maturity and the bond is held until maturity.

   iv. All of the above.

b. A bond with a call feature:

   i. Is attractive because the immediate receipt of principal plus premium produces a high return.

   ii. Is more apt to be called when interest rates are high because the interest savings will be greater.

   iii. Will usually have a higher yield than a similar noncallable bond.

   iv. None of the above.

c. The yield to maturity on a bond is:

   i. Below the coupon rate when the bond sells at a discount, and above the coupon rate when the bond sells at a premium.

   ii. The discount rate that will set the present value of the payments equal to the bond price.

   iii. The current yield plus the average annual capital gain rate.

   iv. Based on the assumption that any payments received are reinvested at the coupon rate.

d. In which *one* of the following cases is the bond selling at a discount?

   i. Coupon rate is greater than current yield, which is greater than yield to maturity.

   ii. Coupon rate, current yield, and yield to maturity are all the same.

   iii. Coupon rate is less than current yield, which is less than yield to maturity.

   iv. Coupon rate is less than current yield, which is greater than yield to maturity.

e. Consider a 5-year bond with a 10% coupon that has a present yield to maturity of 8%. If interest rates remain constant, 1 year from now the price of this bond will be:
   i. Higher
   ii. Lower
   iii. The same
   iv. Par

f. The call feature of a bond means the:
   i. Investor can call for payment on demand.
   ii. Investor can call only if the firm defaults on an interest payment.
   iii. Issuer can call the bond issue before the maturity date.
   iv. Issuer can call the issue during the first 3 years.

---

Go to **www.mhhe.com/business/finance/edumarketinsight**. Find the bond ratings of Southwest Airlines (LUV) and Northwest Airlines (NWAC) in the *Financial Highlights* section. Which has higher-rated bonds? Now compare the financial ratios of the two firms. Are the relative bond ratings of the two firms consistent with their financial ratios?

---

**E-INVESTMENTS**
**Credit**
**Spreads**

At **www.bondsonline.com** review the *Industrial Spreads* for various ratings (at the menu under *Corporate/Agency Bonds*). These are spreads above U.S. Treasuries of comparable maturity. What factors tend to explain the yield differences? How might these yield spreads differ during an economic boom versus a recession? From the home page, analyze and summarize the historic bond spreads and current yield curves (see the *Composite Bond Yields* under *Today's Bond News*).

---

**SOLUTIONS**
**TO CONCEPT**
**C H E C K S**

1. The callable bond will sell at the *lower* price. Investors will not be willing to pay as much if they know that the firm retains a valuable option to reclaim the bond for the call price if interest rates fall.

2. At a semiannual interest rate of 3%, the bond is worth $40 × Annuity factor (3%, 60) + $1,000 × PV factor(3%, 60) = $1,276.76, which results in a capital gain of $276.76. This exceeds the capital loss of $189.29 ($1,000 − $810.71) when the semiannual interest rate increased to 5%.

3. Yield to maturity exceeds current yield, which exceeds coupon rate. Take as an example the 8% coupon bond with a yield to maturity of 10% per year (5% per half year). Its price is $810.71, and therefore its current yield is 80/810.71 = .0987, or 9.87%, which is higher than the coupon rate but lower than the yield to maturity.

4. The bond with the 6% coupon rate currently sells for 30 × Annuity factor (3.5%, 20) + 1,000 × PV factor(3.5%, 20) = $928.94. If the interest rate immediately drops to 6% (3% per half-year), the bond price will rise to $1,000, for a capital gain of $71.06, or 7.65%. The 8% coupon bond currently sells for $1,071.06. If the interest rate falls to 6%, the present value of the *scheduled* payments increases to $1,148.77. However, the bond will be called at $1,100, for a capital gain of only $28.94, or 2.70%.

**SOLUTIONS
TO CONCEPT
CHECKS
*(Concluded)***

5. The current price of the bond can be derived from the yield to maturity. Using your calculator, set: $n = 40$ (semiannual periods); payment = $45 per period; future value = $1000; interest rate = 4% per semiannual period. Calculate present value as $1,098.96. Now we can calculate yield to call. The time to call is 5 years, or 10 semiannual periods. The price at which the bond will be called is $1,050. To find yield to call, we set: $n = 10$ (semiannual periods); payment = $45 per period; future value = $1050; present value = $1098.96. Calculate yield to call as 3.72%.

6. Price = $70 × Annuity factor(8%, 1) + $1,000 × PV factor(8%, 1) = $990.74

$$\text{Rate of return to investor} = \frac{70 + (\$990.74 - \$982.17)}{\$982.17} = .080 = 8\%$$

7. By year-end, remaining maturity is 29 years. If the yield to maturity were still 8%, the bond would still sell at par and the holding-period return would be 8%. At a higher yield, price and return will be lower. Suppose, for example, that the yield to maturity rises to 8.5%. With annual payments of $80 and a face value of $1,000, the price of the bond will be $946.70 [$n = 29$; $i = 8.5\%$; PMT = $80; FV = $1,000]. The bond initially sold at $1,000 when issued at the start of the year. The holding-period return is

$$\text{HPR} = \frac{80 + (946.70 - 1000)}{1000} = .0267 = 2.67\%$$

which is less than the initial yield to maturity of 8%.

8. At the lower yield, the bond price will be $631.67 [$n = 29$, $i = 7\%$, FV = $1,000, PMT = $40]. Therefore, total after-tax income is

| | | |
|---|---|---|
| Coupon | $40 × (1 − .38) = | $24.80 |
| Imputed interest | ($553.66 − $549.69) × (1 − .38) = | 2.46 |
| Capital gains | ($631.67 − $553.66) × (1 − .20) = | 62.41 |
| Total income after taxes | | $89.67 |

Rate of return = 89.67/549.69 = .163 = 16.3%.

9. It should receive a negative coefficient. A high ratio of liabilities to assets is a poor omen for a firm that should lower its credit rating.

10. The coupon payment is $45. There are 20 semiannual periods. The final payment is assumed to be $600. The present value of expected cash flows is $750. The expected yield to maturity is 5.42% semiannual or annualized, 10.84%, bond equivalent yield.

## CHAPTER FIFTEEN

# THE TERM STRUCTURE OF INTEREST RATES

In Chapter 14 we assumed for the sake of simplicity that the same constant interest rate is used to discount cash flows of any maturity. In the real world this is rarely the case. We have seen, for example, that in early 2003 short-term bonds and notes carried yields to maturity of about 1.5% while the longest-term bonds offered yields of about 5%. At the time when these bond prices were quoted, anyway, the longer-term securities had higher yields. This, in fact, is a typical pattern, but as we shall see below, the relationship between time to maturity and yield to maturity can vary dramatically from one period to another.

In this chapter we explore the pattern of interest rates for different-term assets. We attempt to identify the factors that account for that pattern and determine what information may be derived from an analysis of the so-called **term structure of interest rates,** the structure of interest rates for discounting cash flows of different maturities.

We show how traders can use the term structure to compute forward rates that represent interest rates on "forward" or deferred loans, and consider the relationship between forward rates and future interest rates. Finally, we give an overview of some issues involved in measuring the term structure.

# 15.1   THE TERM STRUCTURE UNDER CERTAINTY

What might one conclude from the observation that longer-term bonds usually offer higher yields to maturity? One possibility is that longer-term bonds are riskier and that the higher yields are evidence of a risk premium that compensates for interest rate risk. Another possibility is that at these times investors expect interest rates to rise and that the higher average yields on long-term bonds reflect the anticipation of high interest rates in the latter years of the bond's life. We start our analysis of these possibilities with the easiest case: a world with no uncertainty where investors already know the path of future interest rates.

**Bond Pricing**   The interest rate for a given time interval is called the **short interest rate** for that period. Suppose that all participants in the bond market are convinced that the short rates for the next 4 years will follow the pattern in Table 15.1

Of course, market participants cannot look up such a sequence of short rates in *The Wall Street Journal*. All they observe there are prices and yields of bonds of various maturities. Nevertheless, we can think of the short-rate sequence of Table 15.1 as the series of interest rates that investors keep in the back of their minds when they evaluate prices of bonds of various maturities. Given this pattern of rates, what prices might we observe on these bonds? To keep the algebra simple, for now we will treat only zero-coupon bonds.

A zero-coupon bond paying $1,000 in 1 year would sell today for $1,000/1.08 = $925.93. Similarly, a 2-year maturity bond would sell today for

$$P = \frac{\$1,000}{(1.08)(1.10)} = \$841.75 \tag{15.1}$$

This is the present value of the future $1,000 cash flow, because $841.75 would need to be set aside now to provide a $1,000 payment in 2 years. After 1 year, the $841.75 set aside would grow to $841.75(1.08) = $909.09 and after the second year to $909.09(1.10) = $1,000.

In general we may write the present value of $1 to be received after $n$ periods as

$$\text{PV of \$1 in } n \text{ periods} = \frac{1}{(1 + r_1)(1 + r_2) \cdots (1 + r_n)}$$

where $r_i$ is the 1-year interest rate that will prevail in year $i$. Continuing in this manner, we find the values of the 3- and 4-year bonds as shown in the middle column of Table 15.2.

From the bond prices we can calculate the yield to maturity on each bond. Recall that the yield is the *single* interest rate that equates the present value of the bond's payments to the bond's price. Although interest rates may vary over time, the yield to maturity is calculated as one "average" rate that is applied to discount all of the bond's payments. For example, the yield to maturity of the 2-year zero-coupon bond, which we will call $y_2$, is the interest rate that satisfies

$$841.75 = 1,000/(1 + y_2)^2 \tag{15.2}$$

| Table 15.1    Interest Rates on 1-Year Bonds in Coming Years | |
| --- | --- |
| Year | Interest Rate |
| 0 (Today) | 8% |
| 1 | 10 |
| 2 | 11 |
| 3 | 11 |

which we solve for $y_2 = .08995$. We repeat the process for the two other bonds, with results as reported in Table 15.2. For example, we find $y_3$ by solving

$$758.33 = 1,000/(1 + y_3)^3$$

Now we can make a graph of the yield to maturity on the four bonds as a function of time to maturity. This graph, which is called the **yield curve,** appears in Figure 15.1.

While the yield curve in Figure 15.1 rises smoothly, a wide range of curves may be observed in practice. Figure 15.2 presents four such curves. Panel A is a downward-sloping or "inverted" yield curve. Panel B is an upward-sloping yield curve, and Panel C is a hump-shaped curve, first rising and then falling. Finally, the yield curve in Panel D is essentially flat.

The yield to maturity on zero-coupon bonds is sometimes called the **spot rate** that prevails today for a period corresponding to the maturity of the zero. The yield curve, or, equivalently, the last column of Table 15.2, thus presents the spot rates for four maturities. Note that the spot rates, or yields to maturity, do *not* equal the 1-year interest rates for each year.

To emphasize the difference between the sequence of *short* rates for each future year and current *spot* rates for different maturity dates, examine Figure 15.3. The first line of data presents the short rate for each annual period. The lower lines present the spot rates,

| Table 15.2 | Prices and Yields of Zero-Coupon Bonds | | |
|---|---|---|---|
| | Time to Maturity | Price | Yield to Maturity |
| | 1 | $925.93 | 8.000% |
| | 2 | 841.75 | 8.995 |
| | 3 | 758.33 | 9.660 |
| | 4 | 683.18 | 9.993 |

**Figure 15.1**
**Yield curve**

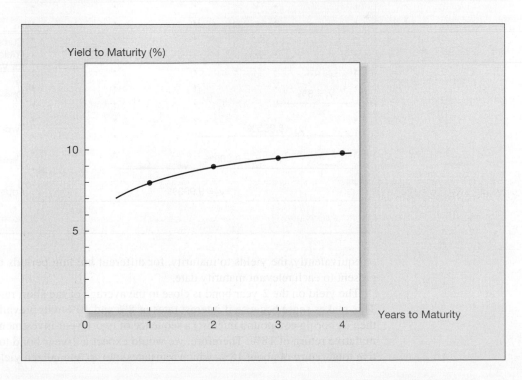

**Figure 15.2    Treasury yield curves**

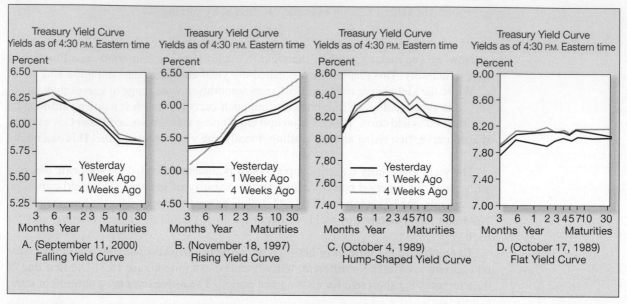

A. (September 11, 2000)
Falling Yield Curve

B. (November 18, 1997)
Rising Yield Curve

C. (October 4, 1989)
Hump-Shaped Yield Curve

D. (October 17, 1989)
Flat Yield Curve

**Figure 15.3
Short rates
versus spot rates**

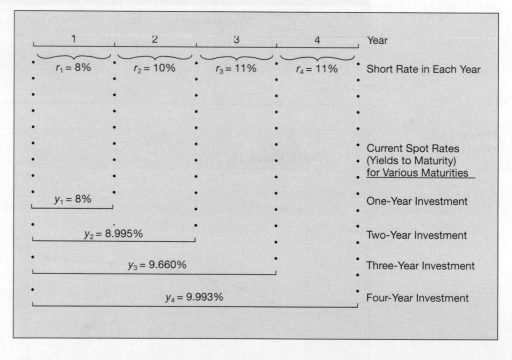

or equivalently, the yields to maturity, for different holding periods that extend from the present to each relevant maturity date.

The yield on the 2-year bond is close to the average of the short rates for years 1 and 2. This makes sense because if interest rates of 8% and 10% will prevail in the next 2 years, then (ignoring compound interest) a sequence of two 1-year investments will provide a cumulative return of 18%. Therefore, we would expect a 2-year bond to provide a competitive total return of about 18%, which translates into an annualized yield to maturity of 9%, just about equal to the 8.995% yield we derived in Table 15.2. Because the yield is a measure of the average return over the life of the bond, it should be determined by the market interest rates available in both years 1 and 2.

In fact, we can be more precise. Notice that equations 15.1 and 15.2 each relate the 2-year bond's price to appropriate interest rates. Combining equations 15.1 and 15.2, we find

$$841.75 = \frac{1,000}{(1.08)(1.10)} = \frac{1,000}{(1 + y_2)^2}$$

so that

$$(1 + y_2)^2 = (1.08)(1.10)$$

and

$$1 + y_2 = [(1.08)(1.10)]^{1/2} = 1.08995$$

Similarly,

$$1 + y_3 = [(1 + r_1)(1 + r_2)(1 + r_3)]^{1/3}$$

and

$$1 + y_4 = [(1 + r_1)(1 + r_2)(1 + r_3)(1 + r_4)]^{1/4} \tag{15.3}$$

and so on. Thus the yields are in fact averages of the interest rates in each period. However, because of compound interest, the relationship is not an arithmetic average but a geometric one.

**Bond Stripping and Pricing of Coupon Bonds**   We've seen that the prices of zero-coupon bonds are found by discounting their face value at the spot rate appropriate to the bond's maturity. What about coupon bonds, which make several payments over time? Our approach generalizes: we simply discount each payment by the spot rate corresponding to the time until that payment. To illustrate, consider a 3-year bond with par value $1,000, paying an annual coupon rate of 8%. The bond pays $80 at the end of the next 2 years, and $1,080 when it matures in 3 years. Using the spot rates from Table 15.2, the price of this bond is therefore

$$P = \frac{80}{1.08} + \frac{80}{1.08995^2} + \frac{1,080}{1.09660^3} = \$960.41$$

In other words, we can treat each of the bond's payments as in effect a stand-alone zero-coupon security that can be valued independently. The total value of the bond is just the sum of the values of each of its cash flows.

Notice that the yield to maturity of this 3-year coupon bond is 9.58%, a bit less than that of the 3-year zero-coupon bond. This makes sense: if we think of the coupon bond as a "portfolio" of three zeros (corresponding to each of its three coupon payments), then its yield should be a weighted average of the three spot rates for years 1–3. Of course, the yield on the last payment will dominate, since it accounts for the overwhelming proportion of the value of the bond. But as a general rule, we conclude that yields to maturity can differ for bonds of the same maturity if their coupon rates differ.

**CONCEPT CHECK ☞ QUESTION 1**   Find the price and yield to maturity on a 4-year maturity bond with a coupon rate of 8% also making annual payments. How does its yield to maturity compare to the spot rate on the 4-year zero-coupon bond in Table 15.2?

Bond traders often distinguish between the yield curve for zero-coupon bonds and that for coupon-paying bonds. The **pure yield curve** refers to the relationship between yield to maturity and time to maturity for zero-coupon bonds. The coupon-paying curve portrays this relationship for coupon bonds, as in Figure 15.2. The most recently issued Treasuries are said to be **on the run**. On-the-run Treasuries have the greatest liquidity, so traders have keen interest in the on-the-run yield curve.

Turn back to Figure 14.1 in the previous chapter, and you will see the difference between the pure and coupon-paying yield curves. The latter part of the figure shows prices and yields of Treasury strips. As discussed in that chapter, strips are created by breaking down a Treasury bond's coupons and ultimate repayment of par value into a series of independent zero-coupon bonds. Thus, you can plot the pure yield curve by using the data on Treasury strips. You can see from Figure 14.1 that yields on zeros and coupon-paying bonds can differ considerably.

## Holding-Period Returns

What is the rate of return on each of the four bonds in Table 15.2 over a 1-year holding period? You might think at first that higher-yielding bonds would provide higher 1-year rates of return, but this is not the case. In our simple world with no uncertainty all bonds must offer identical rates of return over any holding period. Otherwise, at least one bond would be dominated by the others in the sense that it would offer a lower rate of return than would combinations of other bonds; no one would be willing to hold the bond, and its price would fall. In fact, despite their different yields to maturity, each bond will provide a rate of return over the coming year equal to this year's short interest rate.

### EXAMPLE 15.1    Holding Period Return on Zero-Coupon Bonds

Let's compute the rate of return on each bond. The 1-year bond is bought today for $925.93 and matures in 1 year to its par value of $1,000. Because the bond pays no coupon, total income is $1,000 − $925.93 = $74.07, and the rate of return is $74.07/$925.93 = .08, or 8%. The 2-year bond is bought today for $841.75. Next year the interest rate will be 10%, and the bond will have 1 year left until maturity. It will sell then for $1,000/1.10 = $909.09. Thus the holding-period return is ($909.09 − $841.75)/$841.75 = .08, again implying an 8% rate of return. Similarly, the 3-year bond will be purchased for $758.33 and will be sold at year-end for $1,000/(1.10)(1.11) = $819.00, for a rate of return ($819.00 − $758.33)/$758.33 = .08, again, an 8% return.

**CONCEPT
CHECK ☞
QUESTION 2**

**Confirm that the return on the 4-year zero-coupon bond also will be 8%. Show that the return on a 2-year 8% coupon bond making annual payments also will be 8%.**

We conclude from Example 15.1 that when interest rate movements are known with certainty, and all bonds are properly priced, all will provide equal 1-year rates of return. The higher yields on the longer-term bonds merely reflect the fact that future interest rates are higher than current rates and that the longer bonds are still alive during the higher-rate period. Owners of the short-term bonds receive lower yields to maturity, but they can reinvest, or "roll over," their proceeds for higher yields in later years when rates are higher. In the end, both long-term bonds and short-term rollover strategies provide equal returns over the holding period, at least in a world of interest rate certainty.

**Forward Rates**   Unfortunately, investors do not have access to short-term interest rate quotations for coming years. What they can observe are bond prices and yields to maturity. Can they infer future short rates from the available data?

Suppose we are interested in the interest rate that will prevail during year 3, and we have access only to the data reported in Table 15.2. We start by comparing two alternatives, illustrated in Figure 15.4:

1.  Invest in a 3-year zero-coupon bond.
2.  Invest in a 2-year zero-coupon bond. After 2 years reinvest the proceeds in a 1-year bond.

Assuming an investment of $100, under strategy 1, with a yield to maturity of 9.660% on 3-year zero-coupon bonds, our investment would grow to $100(1.0966)^3 = $131.87. Under strategy 2, the $100 investment in the 2-year bond would grow after 2 years to $100(1.08995)^2 = $118.80. Then in the third year it would grow by an additional factor of $1 + r_3$.

In a world of certainty both of these strategies must yield exactly the same final payoff. If strategy 1 were to dominate strategy 2, no one would hold 2-year bonds; their prices would fall and their yields would rise. Likewise, if strategy 2 dominated strategy 1, no one would hold 3-year bonds. Therefore, we can conclude that $131.87 = $118.80(1 + r_3)$, which implies that $(1 + r_3) = 1.11$, or $r_3 = 11\%$. This is in fact the rate that will prevail in year 3, as Table 15.1 indicates. Thus our method of obtaining the third-period interest rate does provide the correct solution in the certainty case.

More generally, the comparison of the two strategies establishes that the return on a 3-year bond equals that on a 2-year bond and rollover strategy:

$$100(1 + y_3)^3 = 100(1 + y_2)^2(1 + r_3)$$

**Figure 15.4   Two 3-year investment programs**

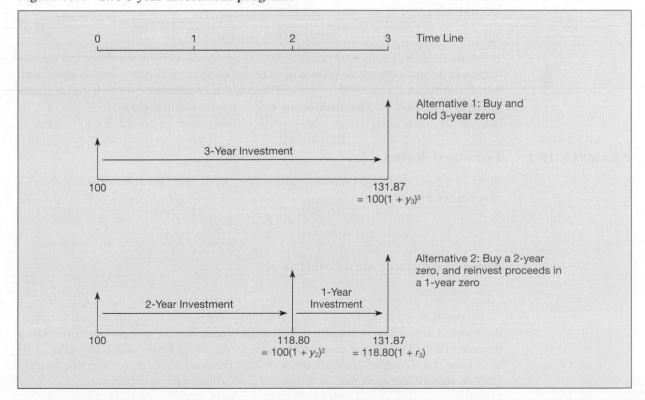

so that $1 + r_3 = (1 + y_3)^3/(1 + y_2)^2$. Generalizing, for the certainty case, a simple rule for inferring a future short interest rate from the yield curve of zero-coupon bonds is to use the following formula:

$$(1 + r_n) = \frac{(1 + y_n)^n}{(1 + y_{n-1})^{n-1}} \tag{15.4}$$

where $n$ denotes the period in question and $y_n$ is the yield to maturity of a zero-coupon bond with an $n$-period maturity.

Equation 15.4 has a simple interpretation. The numerator on the right-hand side is the total growth factor of an investment in an $n$-year zero held until maturity. Similarly, the denominator is the growth factor of an investment in an $(n - 1)$-year zero. Because the former investment lasts for one more year than the latter, the difference in these growth factors must be the rate of return available in year $n$ when the $(n - 1)$-year zero can be rolled over into a 1-year investment.

Of course, when future interest rates are uncertain, as they are in reality, there is no meaning to inferring "the" future short rate. No one knows today what the future interest rate will be. At best, we can speculate as to its expected value and associated uncertainty. Nevertheless, it still is common to use equation 15.4 to investigate the implications of the yield curve for future interest rates. In recognition of the fact that future interest rates are uncertain, we call the interest rate that we infer in this matter the **forward interest rate** rather than the *future short rate,* because it need not be the interest rate that actually will prevail at the future date.

If the forward rate for period $n$ is denoted $f_n$, we then define $f_n$ by the equation

$$(1 + f_n) = \frac{(1 + y_n)^n}{(1 + y_{n-1})^{n-1}}$$

Equivalently, we may rewrite the equation as

$$(1 + y_n)^n = (1 + y_{n-1})^{n-1} (1 + f_n) \tag{15.5}$$

In this formulation, the forward rate is *defined* as the "break-even" interest rate that equates the return on an $n$-period zero-coupon bond to that of an $(n - 1)$-period zero-coupon bond rolled over into a 1-year bond in year $n$. The actual total returns on the two $n$-year strategies will be equal if the short interest rate in year $n$ turns out to equal $f_n$.

## EXAMPLE 15.2 Forward Rates

Suppose a bond trader uses the data presented in Table 15.2. The forward rate for year 4 would be computed as

$$1 + f_4 = \frac{(1 + y_4)^4}{(1 + y_3)^3} = \frac{1.09993^4}{1.09660^3} = 1.11$$

Therefore, the forward rate is $f_4 = .11$, or 11%.

We emphasize that the interest rate that actually will prevail in the future need not equal the forward rate, which is calculated from today's data. Indeed, it is not even necessarily the case that the forward rate equals the expected value of the future short interest rate. This is an issue that we address in much detail shortly. For now, however, we note that forward rates do equal future short rates in the special case of interest rate certainty.

**CONCEPT**
**CHECK** ☞
**QUESTION 3**

You've been exposed to many "rates" in the last few pages. Explain the differences between spot rates, short rates, and forward rates.

## 15.2    INTEREST RATE UNCERTAINTY AND FORWARD RATES

Let us turn now to the more difficult analysis of the term structure when future interest rates are uncertain. We have argued so far that, in a certain world, different investment strategies with common terminal dates must provide equal rates of return. For example, two consecutive 1-year investments in zeros would need to offer the same total return as an equal-sized investment in a 2-year zero. Therefore, under certainty,

$$(1 + r_1)(1 + r_2) = (1 + y_2)^2$$

What can we say when $r_2$ is not known today?

For example, referring once again to Table 15.1, suppose that today's rate, $r_1 = 8\%$, and that the *expected* short rate next year is $E(r_2) = 10\%$. If bonds were priced based only on the expected value of the interest rate, a 1-year zero would sell for $\$1,000/1.08 = \$925.93$, and a 2-year zero would sell for $\$1,000/[(1.08)(1.10)] = \$841.75$, just as in Table 15.2.

But now consider a short-term investor who wishes to invest only for 1 year. She can purchase the 1-year zero and lock in a riskless 8% return because she knows that at the end of the year, the bond will be worth its maturity value of $\$1,000$. She also can purchase the 2-year zero. Its *expected* rate of return also is 8%: Next year, the bond will have 1 year to maturity, and we expect that the 1-year interest rate will be 10%, implying a price of $\$909.09$ and a holding-period return of 8%.

But the rate of return on the 2-year bond is risky. If next year's interest rate turns out to be above expectations, that is, greater than 10%, the bond price will be below $\$909.09$, and conversely if $r_2$ turns out to be less than 10%, the bond price will exceed $\$909.09$. Why should this short-term investor buy the *risky* 2-year bond when its expected return is 8%, no better than that of the *risk-free* 1-year bond? Clearly, she would not hold the 2-year bond unless it offered an expected rate of return greater than the riskless 8% return available on the competing 1-year bond. This requires that the 2-year bond sell at a price lower than the $\$841.75$ value we derived when we ignored risk.

**EXAMPLE 15.3**    **Bond Prices and Forward Rates with Interest Rate Risk**

Suppose that most investors have short-term horizons and therefore are willing to hold the 2-year bond only if its price falls to $\$819$. At this price, the expected holding-period return on the 2-year bond is 11% (because $909.09/819 = 1.11$). The risk premium of the 2-year bond, therefore, is 3%; it offers an expected rate of return of 11% versus the 8% risk-free return on the 1-year bond. At this risk premium, investors are willing to bear the price risk associated with interest rate uncertainty.

In this environment, the forward rate, $f_2$, no longer equals the expected short rate, $E(r_2)$. Although we have assumed that $E(r_2) = 10\%$, it is easy to confirm that $f_2 = 13\%$. The yield to maturity on the 2-year zeros selling at $\$819$ is 10.5%, and

$$1 + f_2 = \frac{(1 + y_2)^2}{1 + y_1} = \frac{1.105^2}{1.08} = 1.13$$

The result in Example 15.3—that the forward rate exceeds the expected short rate—should not surprise us. We defined the forward rate as the interest rate that would need to prevail in the second year to make the long- and short-term investments equally attractive, ignoring risk. When we account for risk, it is clear that short-term investors will shy away from the long-term bond unless it offers an expected return greater than that of the 1-year bond. Another way of putting this is to say that investors will require a risk premium to hold the longer-term bond. The risk-averse investor would be willing to hold the long-term bond only if $E(r_2)$ is less than the break-even value, $f_2$, because the lower the expectation of $r_2$, the greater the anticipated return on the long-term bond.

Therefore, if most individuals are short-term investors, bonds must have prices that make $f_2$ greater than $E(r_2)$. The forward rate will embody a premium compared with the expected future short-interest rate. This **liquidity premium** compensates short-term investors for the uncertainty about the price at which they will be able to sell their long-term bonds at the end of the year.[1]

| CONCEPT CHECK ☞ QUESTION 4 | **Suppose that the required liquidity premium for the short-term investor is 1%. What must $E(r_2)$ be if $f_2$ is 10%?** |
| --- | --- |

Perhaps surprisingly, we also can imagine scenarios in which long-term bonds can be perceived by investors to be *safer* than short-term bonds. To see how, we now consider a "long-term" investor, who wishes to invest for a full 2-year period. Suppose that the investor can purchase a $1,000 par value 2-year zero-coupon bond for $841.75 and lock in a guaranteed yield to maturity of $y_2 = 9\%$. Alternatively, the investor can roll over two 1-year investments. In this case an investment of $841.75 would grow in 2 years to $841.75 \times (1.08) \times (1 + r_2)$, which is an uncertain amount today because $r_2$ is not yet known. The break-even year-2 interest rate is, once again, the forward rate, 10%, because the forward rate is defined as the rate that equates the terminal value of the two investment strategies.

The expected value of the payoff of the rollover strategy is $841.75(1.08)[1 + E(r_2)]$. If $E(r_2)$ equals the forward rate, $f_2$, then the expected value of the payoff from the rollover strategy will equal the *known* payoff from the 2-year maturity bond strategy.

Is this a reasonable presumption? Once again, it is only if the investor does not care about the uncertainty surrounding the final value of the rollover strategy. Whenever that risk is important, the long-term investor will not be willing to engage in the rollover strategy unless its expected return exceeds that of the 2-year bond. In this case the investor would require that

$$(1.08)[1 + E(r_2)] > (1.09)^2 = (1.08)(1 + f_2)$$

which implies that $E(r_2)$ exceeds $f_2$. The investor would require that the expected period 2 interest rate exceed the break-even value of 10%, which is the forward rate.

Therefore, if all investors were long-term investors, no one would be willing to hold short-term bonds unless those bonds offered a reward for bearing interest rate risk. In this situation bond prices would be set at levels such that rolling over short bonds resulted in

---

[1]*Liquidity* refers to the ability to sell an asset easily at a predictable price. Because long-term bonds have greater price risk, they are considered less liquid in this context and thus must offer a premium.

greater expected return than holding long bonds. This would cause the forward rate to be less than the expected future spot rate.

For example, suppose that in fact $E(r_2) = 11\%$. The liquidity premium therefore is negative: $f_2 - E(r_2) = 10\% - 11\% = -1\%$. This is exactly opposite from the conclusion that we drew in the first case of the short-term investor. Clearly, whether forward rates will equal expected future short rates depends on investors' readiness to bear interest rate risk, as well as their willingness to hold bonds that do not correspond to their investment horizons.

## 15.3   THEORIES OF THE TERM STRUCTURE

**The Expectations Hypothesis**     The simplest theory of the term structure is the **expectations hypothesis.** A common version of this hypothesis states that the forward rate equals the market consensus expectation of the future short interest rate; in other words, $f_2 = E(r_2)$ and liquidity premiums are zero. Because $f_2 = E(r_2)$, we may relate yields on long-term bonds to expectations of future interest rates. In addition, we can use the forward rates derived from the yield curve to infer market expectations of future short rates. For example, with $(1 + y_2)^2 = (1 + r_1)(1 + f_2)$ from equation 15.5, we may also write that $(1 + y_2)^2 = (1 + r_1)[1 + E(r_2)]$ if the expectations hypothesis is correct. The yield to maturity would thus be determined solely by current and expected future one-period interest rates. An upward-sloping yield curve would be clear evidence that investors anticipate increases in interest rates.

> **CONCEPT CHECK ☞ QUESTION 5**
>
> **If the expectations hypothesis is valid, what can we conclude about the premiums necessary to induce investors to hold bonds of different maturities from their investment horizons?**

**Liquidity Preference**     We noted in our discussion of the long- and short-term investors that short-term investors will be unwilling to hold long-term bonds unless the forward rate exceeds the expected short interest rate, $f_2 > E(r_2)$, whereas long-term investors will be unwilling to hold short bonds unless $E(r_2) > f_2$. In other words, both groups of investors require a premium to induce them to hold bonds with maturities different from their investment horizons. Advocates of the **liquidity preference theory** of the term structure believe that short-term investors dominate the market so that, generally speaking, the forward rate exceeds the expected short rate. The excess of $f_2$ over $E(r_2)$, the **liquidity premium,** is predicted to be positive.

> **CONCEPT CHECK ☞ QUESTION 6**
>
> **The liquidity premium hypothesis also holds that *issuers* of bonds prefer to issue long-term bonds. How would this preference contribute to a positive liquidity premium?**

To illustrate the differing implications of these theories for the term structure of interest rates, consider a situation in which the short interest rate is expected to be constant indefinitely. Suppose that $r_1 = 10\%$ and that $E(r_2) = 10\%$, $E(r_3) = 10\%$, and so on. Under the expectations hypothesis the 2-year yield to maturity could be derived from the following:

$$(1 + y_2)^2 = (1 + r_1)[1 + E(r_2)]$$
$$= (1.10)(1.10)$$

so that $y_2$ equals 10%. Similarly, yields on bonds of all maturities would equal 10%.

In contrast, under the liquidity preference theory $f_2$ would exceed $E(r_2)$. To illustrate, suppose that $f_2$ is 11%, implying a 1% liquidity premium. Then, for 2-year bonds:

$$(1 + y_2)^2 = (1 + r_1)(1 + f_2)$$
$$= (1.10)(1.11) = 1.221$$

implying that $1 + y_2 = 1.105$. Similarly, if $f_3$ also equals 11%, then the yield on 3-year bonds would be determined by

$$(1 + y_3)^3 = (1 + r_1)(1 + f_2)(1 + f_3)$$
$$= (1.10)(1.11)(1.11) = 1.35531$$

implying that $1 + y_3 = 1.1067$. The plot of the yield curve in this situation would be given as in Figure 15.5, panel A, on page 500. Such an upward-sloping yield curve is commonly observed in practice.

If interest rates are expected to change over time, then the liquidity premium may be overlaid on the path of expected spot rates to determine the forward interest rate. Then the yield to maturity for each date will be an average of the single-period forward rates. Several such possibilities for increasing and declining interest rates appear in Figure 15.5, panels B to D.

# 15.4    INTERPRETING THE TERM STRUCTURE

We have seen that under certainty, 1 plus the yield to maturity on a zero-coupon bond is simply the geometric average of 1 plus the future short rates that will prevail over the life of the bond. This is the meaning of equation 15.3, which we give in general form here:

$$1 + y_n = [(1 + r_1)(1 + r_2) \cdots (1 + r_n)]^{1/n}$$

When future rates are uncertain, we modify equation 15.3 by replacing future short rates with forward rates:

$$1 + y_n = [(1 + r_1)(1 + f_2)(1 + f_3) \cdots (1 + f_n)]^{1/n} \tag{15.6}$$

Thus there is a direct relationship between yields on various maturity bonds and forward interest rates. This relationship is the source of the information that can be gleaned from an analysis of the yield curve.

First, we ask what factors can account for a rising yield curve. Mathematically, if the yield curve is rising, $f_{n+1}$ must exceed $y_n$. In words, the yield curve is upward sloping at any maturity date, $n$, for which the forward rate for the coming period is greater than the yield at that maturity. This rule follows from the notion of the yield to maturity as an average (albeit a geometric average) of forward rates.

If the yield curve is to rise as one moves to longer maturities, it must be the case that extension to a longer maturity results in the inclusion of a "new" forward rate that is higher than the average of the previously observed rates. This is analogous to the observation that if a new student's test score is to increase the class average, that student's score must exceed the class's average without her score. To raise the yield to maturity, an above-average forward rate must be added to the other rates in the averaging computation.

**EXAMPLE 15.4**

## Forward Rates and the Slopes of the Yield Curve

If the yield to maturity on 3-year zero-coupon bonds is 9%, then the yield on 4-year bonds will satisfy the following equation:

$$(1 + y_4)^4 = (1.09)^3(1 + f_4)$$

If $f_4 = .09$, then $y_4$ also will equal .09. (Confirm this!) If $f_4$ is greater than 9%, $y_4$ will exceed 9%, and the yield curve will slope upward. For example, if $f_4 = .10$, then $(1 + y_4)^4 = (1.09)^3(1.10) = 1.4245$, and $y_4 = .0925$.

---

**CONCEPT CHECK☞ QUESTION 7**

Look back at Tables 15.1 and 15.2. Show that $y_4$ would exceed $y_3$ if and only if the interest rate for period 4 had been greater than 9.66%, which was the yield to maturity on the 3-year bond, $y_3$.

---

Given that an upward-sloping yield curve is always associated with a forward rate higher than the spot, or current, yield to maturity, we ask next what can account for that higher forward rate. Unfortunately, there always are two possible answers to this question. Recall that the forward rate can be related to the expected future short rate according to this equation:

$$f_n = E(r_n) + \text{Liquidity premium}$$

where the liquidity premium might be necessary to induce investors to hold bonds of maturities that do not correspond to their preferred investment horizons.

By the way, the liquidity premium need not be positive, although that is the position generally taken by advocates of the liquidity premium hypothesis. We showed previously that if most investors have long-term horizons, the liquidity premium in principle could be negative.

In any case, the equation shows that there are two reasons that the forward rate could be high. Either investors expect rising interest rates, meaning that $E(r_n)$ is high, or they require a large premium for holding longer-term bonds. Although it is tempting to infer from a rising yield curve that investors believe that interest rates will eventually increase, this is not a valid inference. Indeed, panel A in Figure 15.5, provides a simple counterexample to this line of reasoning. There, the spot rate is expected to stay at 10% forever. Yet there is a constant 1% liquidity premium so that all forward rates are 11%. The result is that the yield curve continually rises, starting at a level of 10% for 1-year bonds, but eventually approaching 11% for long-term bonds as more and more forward rates at 11% are averaged into the yields to maturity.

Therefore, although it is true that expectations of increases in future interest rates can result in a rising yield curve, the converse is not true: A rising yield curve does not in and of itself imply expectations of higher future interest rates. This is the heart of the difficulty in drawing conclusions from the yield curve. The effects of possible liquidity premiums confound any simple attempt to extract expectations from the term structure. But estimating

**Figure 15.5
Yield curves.
A, Constant
expected short
rate. Liquidity
premium of 1%.
Result is a rising
yield curve.
B, Declining
expected short
rates. Increasing
liquidity
premiums.
Result is a
rising yield
curve despite
falling expected
interest rates.**

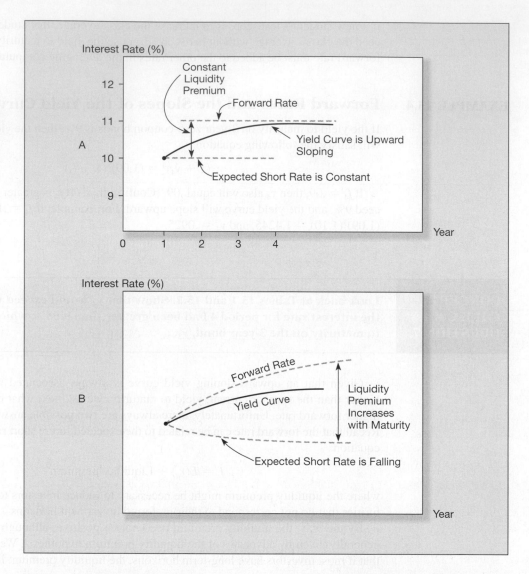

the market's expectations is a crucial task, because only by comparing your own expectations to those reflected in market prices can you determine whether you are relatively bullish or bearish on interest rates.

One very rough approach to deriving expected future spot rates is to assume that liquidity premiums are constant. An estimate of that premium can be subtracted from the forward rate to obtain the market's expected interest rate. For example, again making use of the example plotted in panel A of Figure 15.5, the researcher would estimate from historical data that a typical liquidity premium in this economy is 1%. After calculating the forward rate from the yield curve to be 11%, the expectation of the future spot rate would be determined to be 10%.

**Figure 15.5 (Concluded) C, Declining expected short rates. Constant liquidity premiums. Result is a hump-shaped yield curve. D, Increasing expected short rates. Increasing liquidity premiums. Result is a sharply increasing yield curve.**

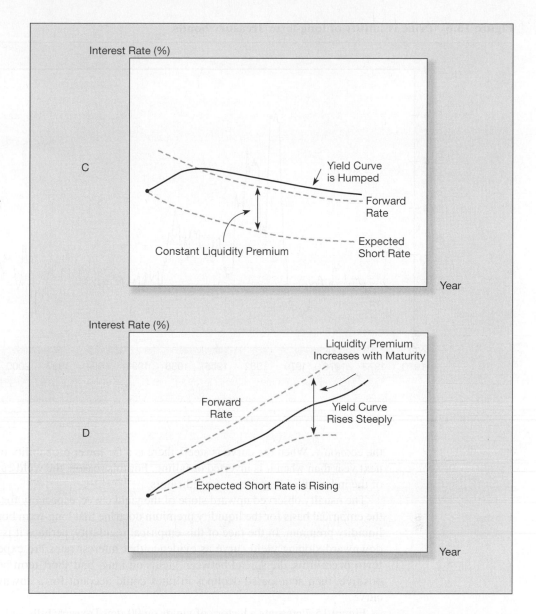

This approach has little to recommend it for two reasons. First, it is next to impossible to obtain precise estimates of a liquidity premium. The general approach to doing so would be to compare forward rates and eventually realized future short rates and to calculate the average difference between the two. However, the deviations between the two values can be quite large and unpredictable because of unanticipated economic events that affect the realized short rate. The data do not contain enough information to calculate a reliable estimate of the expected premium. Second, there is no reason to believe that the liquidity premium should be constant. Figure 15.6 shows the rate of return variability of prices of long-term Treasury bonds since 1971. Interest rate risk fluctuated dramatically during the period. So we might expect risk premiums on various maturity bonds to fluctuate, and empirical evidence suggests that term premiums do in fact fluctuate over time.

Still, very steep yield curves are interpreted by many market professionals as warning signs of impending rate increases. In fact, the yield curve is a good predictor of the business cycle as a whole, since long-term rates tend to rise in anticipation of an expansion in

**Figure 15.6    Price volatility of long-term Treasury bonds**

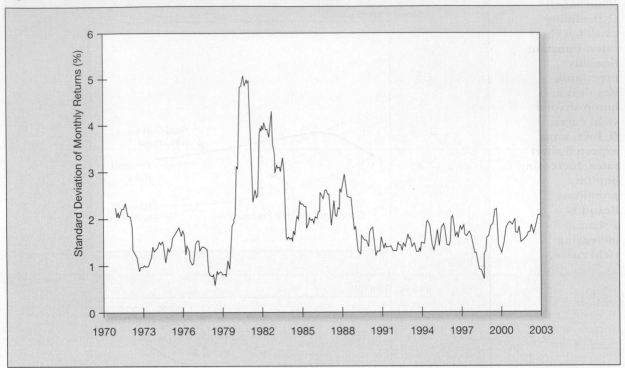

the economy. When the curve is steep, there is a far lower probability of a recession in the next year than when it is inverted or falling. For this reason, the yield curve is a component of the index of leading economic indicators.

The usually observed upward slope of the yield curve, especially for short maturities, is the empirical basis for the liquidity premium doctrine that long-term bonds offer a positive liquidity premium. In the face of this empirical regularity, perhaps it is valid to interpret a downward-sloping yield curve as evidence that interest rates are expected to decline. If **term premiums,** the spread between yields on long- and short-term bonds, generally are positive, then anticipated declines in rates could account for a downward-sloping yield curve.

Figure 15.7 presents a history of yields on 90-day Treasury bills and long-term Treasury bonds. Yields on the longer-term bonds *generally* exceed those on the bills, meaning that the yield curve generally slopes upward. Moreover, the exceptions to this rule seem to precede episodes of falling short rates, which if anticipated, would induce a downward-sloping yield curve. For example, the figure shows that 1980–82 were years in which 90-day yields exceeded long-term yields. These years preceded a drastic drop in the general level of rates.

Why might interest rates fall? There are two factors to consider: the real rate and the inflation premium. Recall that the nominal interest rate is composed of the real rate plus a factor to compensate for the effect of inflation:

$$1 + \text{Nominal rate} = (1 + \text{Real rate})(1 + \text{Inflation rate})$$

or approximately,

$$\text{Nominal rate} \approx \text{Real rate} + \text{Inflation rate}$$

**Figure 15.7**
**Yields on long-term versus 90-day Treasury securities: term spread**

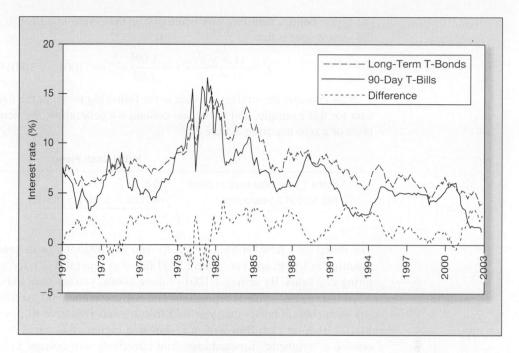

Therefore, an expected change in interest rates can be due to changes in either expected real rates or expected inflation rates. Usually, it is important to distinguish between these two possibilities because the economic environments associated with them may vary substantially. High real rates may indicate a rapidly expanding economy, high government budget deficits, and tight monetary policy. Although high inflation rates can arise out of a rapidly expanding economy, inflation also may be caused by rapid expansion of the money supply or supply-side shocks to the economy such as interruptions in oil supplies. These factors have very different implications for investments. Even if we conclude from an analysis of the yield curve that rates will fall, we need to analyze the macroeconomic factors that might cause such a decline.

## 15.5   FORWARD RATES AS FORWARD CONTRACTS

We have seen that forward rates may be derived from the yield curve, using equation 15.5. In general, forward rates will not equal the eventually realized short rate, or even today's expectation of what that short rate will be. But there is still an important sense in which the forward rate is a market interest rate. Suppose that you wanted to arrange *now* to make a loan at some future date. You would agree today on the interest rate that will be charged, but the loan would not commence until some time in the future. How would the interest rate on such a "forward loan" be determined? Perhaps not surprisingly, it would be the forward rate of interest for the period of the loan. Let's use an example to see how this might work.

**EXAMPLE 15.5**   **Forward Interest Rate Contract**

Suppose the price of 1-year maturity zero-coupon bonds with face value $1,000 is 925.93 and the price of 2-year zeros with $1,000 face value is $841.68. The yield to maturity on the 1-year bond is therefore 8%, while that on the 2-year bond is 9%. The forward rate for the second year is thus

$$f_2 = \frac{(1 + y_2)^2}{(1 + y_1)} - 1 = \frac{1.09^2}{1.08} - 1 = .1001, \text{ or } 10.01\%$$

Now consider the strategy laid out in the following table. In the first column we present data for this example, and in the last column we generalize. We denote by $B_0(T)$ today's price of a zero maturing at time $T$.

|  | Initial Cash Flow | In General |
|---|---|---|
| Buy a 1-year zero-coupon bond | −925.93 | −$B_0(1)$ |
| Sell 1.1001 2-year zeros | +841.68 × 1.1001 = 925.93 | +$B_0(2) \times (1 + f_2)$ |
|  | 0 | 0 |

The initial cash flow (at time 0) is zero. You pay $925.93, or in general $B_0(1)$, for a zero maturing in 1 year, and you receive $841.68, or in general $B_0(2)$, for each zero you sell maturing in 2 years. By selling 1.1001 of these bonds, you set your initial cash flow to zero.[2]

At time 1, the 1-year bond matures and you receive $1,000. At time 2, the 2-year maturity zero-coupon bonds that you sold mature, and you have to pay 1.1001 × $1,000 = $1,100.10. Your cash flow stream is shown in Figure 15.8, panel A. Notice that you have created a "synthetic" forward loan: You effectively *will* borrow $1,000 a year from now, and repay $1,100.10 a year later. The rate on this forward loan is therefore 10.01%, precisely equal to the forward rate for the second year.

In general, to construct the synthetic forward loan, you sell $(1 + f_2)$ 2-year zeros for every 1-year zero that you buy. This makes your initial cash flow zero because the prices of the 1- and 2-year zeros differ by the factor $(1 + f_2)$; notice that

$$B_0(1) = \frac{\$1,000}{(1 + y_1)} \quad \text{while} \quad B_0(2) = \frac{\$1,000}{(1 + y_2)^2} = \frac{\$1,000}{(1 + y_1)(1 + f_2)}$$

Therefore, when you sell $(1 + f_2)$ 2-year zeros you generate just enough cash to buy one 1-year zero. Both zeros mature to a face value of $1,000, so the difference between the cash inflow at time 1 and the cash outflow at time 2 is the same factor, $1 + f_2$, as illustrated in Figure 15.8, panel B. As a result, $f_2$ is the rate on the forward loan.

Obviously, you can construct a synthetic forward loan for periods beyond the second year, and you can construct such loans for multiple periods. Problems 23 and 24 at the end of the chapter lead you through some of these variants.

**CONCEPT CHECK☞ QUESTION 8**    Suppose that the price of 3-year zero coupon bonds is $761.65. What is the forward rate for the third year? How would you construct a synthetic 1-year forward loan that commences at $t = 2$ and matures at $t = 3$?

---

[2] Of course, in reality one cannot sell a fraction of a bond, but you can think of this part of the transaction as follows. If you sold one of these bonds, you would effectively be borrowing $841.68 for a 2-year period. Selling 1.1001 of these bonds simply means that you are borrowing $841.68 × 1.1001 = $925.93.

**Figure 15.8
Engineering
a synthetic
forward loan**

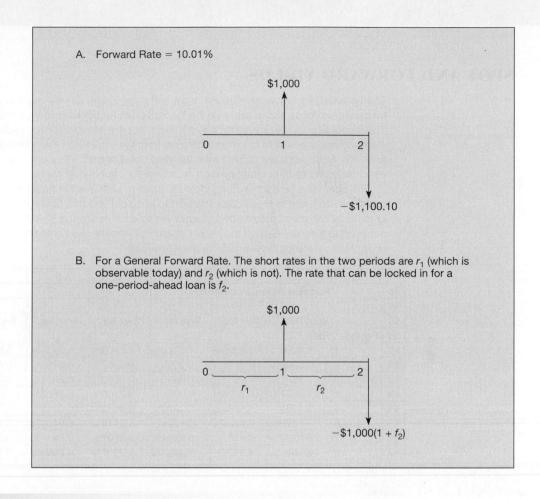

A.   Forward Rate = 10.01%

$1,000

0               1               2

−$1,100.10

B.   For a General Forward Rate. The short rates in the two periods are $r_1$ (which is observable today) and $r_2$ (which is not). The rate that can be locked in for a one-period-ahead loan is $f_2$.

$1,000

0 _____ 1 _____ 2
      $r_1$        $r_2$

−$1,000(1 + $f_2$)

## 15.6   MEASURING THE TERM STRUCTURE

Thus far we have focused on default-free zero-coupon bonds. These bonds are easiest to analyze because their maturity is given by their single payment. In practice, however, the great majority of bonds pay coupons, so we must develop a general approach to calculate spot and forward rates from prices of coupon bonds.

Equations 15.4 and 15.5 for the determination of the forward rate from available yields apply only to zero-coupon bonds. They were derived by equating the returns to competing investment strategies that both used zeros. If coupon bonds had been used in those strategies, we would have had to deal with the issue of coupons paid and reinvested during the investment period, which complicates the analysis.

A further complication arises from the fact that bonds with different coupon rates can have different yields even if their maturities are equal. For example, consider two bonds, each with a two-year time to maturity and annual coupon payments. Bond $A$ has a 3% coupon; bond $B$ a 12% coupon. Using the interest rates of Table 15.1, we see that bond $A$ will sell for

$$\frac{\$30}{1.08} + \frac{\$1,030}{(1.08)(1.10)} = \$894.78$$

# SPOT AND FORWARD YIELDS

The spreadsheet below (available at www.mhhe.com/bkm) can be used to estimate spot rates from coupon bonds and to calculate the forward rates for both single-year and multiyear periods. The model sequentially solves for the spot rates that are associated with each of the periods. The methodology is similar to but slightly different from the regression methodology described in Section 15.6. Spot yields are derived from the yield curve of bonds that are selling at their par value, also referred to as the current coupon or "on-the-run" bond yield curve.

The spot rates for each maturity date are used to calculate the present value of each period's cash flow. The sum of these cash flows is the price of the bond. Given its price, the bond's yield to maturity can then be computed. If you were to err and use the yield to maturity of the on-the-run bond to discount each of the bond's coupon payments, you could find a significantly different price. That difference is calculated in the worksheet.

| | A | B | C | D | E | F | G | H |
|---|---|---|---|---|---|---|---|---|
| 56 | | **Forward Rate Calculations** | | | | | | |
| 57 | | | | | | | | |
| 58 | | **Spot Rate** | **1-yr for.** | **2-yr for.** | **3-yr for.** | **4-yr for.** | **5-yr for.** | **6-yr for.** |
| 59 | **Period** | **Rate** | | | | | | |
| 60 | 1 | 8.0000% | 7.9792% | 7.6770% | 7.2723% | 6.9709% | 6.8849% | 6.7441% |
| 61 | 2 | 7.9896% | 7.3757% | 6.9205% | 6.6369% | 6.6131% | 6.4988% | 6.5520% |
| 62 | 3 | 7.7846% | 6.4673% | 6.2695% | 6.3600% | 6.2807% | 6.3880% | 6.1505% |
| 63 | 4 | 7.4537% | 6.0720% | 6.3065% | 6.2186% | 6.3682% | 6.0872% | 6.0442% |
| 64 | 5 | 7.1760% | 6.5414% | 6.2920% | 6.4671% | 6.0910% | 6.0387% | 5.8579% |
| 65 | 6 | 7.0699% | 6.0432% | 6.4299% | 5.9413% | 5.9134% | 5.7217% | 5.6224% |
| 66 | 7 | 6.9227% | 6.8181% | 5.8904% | 5.8701% | 5.6414% | 5.5384% | 5.3969% |
| 67 | 8 | 6.9096% | 4.9707% | 5.3993% | 5.2521% | 5.2209% | 5.1149% | 5.1988% |

At this price its yield to maturity is 8.98%. Bond $B$ will sell for

$$\frac{\$120}{1.08} + \frac{\$1,120}{(1.08)(1.10)} = \$1,053.87$$

at which price its yield to maturity is 8.94%. Because bond $B$ makes a greater share of its payments in the first year when the interest rate is lower, its yield to maturity is slightly lower. Because bonds with the same maturity can have different yields, we conclude that a single yield curve relating yields and times to maturity cannot be appropriate for all bonds.

The solution to this ambiguity is to perform all of our analysis by using the yield curve for zero-coupon bonds, sometimes called the *pure yield curve*. Our goal, therefore, is to calculate the pure yield curve even if we have to use data on more-common coupon-paying bonds.

The trick we use to infer the pure yield curve from data on coupon bonds is to treat each coupon payment as a separate "mini"–zero-coupon bond. A coupon bond then becomes just a "portfolio" of many zeros. Indeed, we have noted that most zero-coupon bonds are created by stripping coupon payments from coupon bonds and repackaging the separate payments from many bonds into portfolios with common maturity dates. By determining the price of each of these "zeros" we can calculate the yield to that maturity date for a single-payment security and thereby construct the pure yield curve.

## EXAMPLE 15.6   Yields and Forward Rates on Coupon Bonds

Suppose that we observe an 8% coupon bond making semiannual payments with 1 year until maturity, selling at $986.10, and a 10% coupon bond, also with a year until maturity, selling at $1,004.78. To infer the short rates for the next two 6-month periods, we first attempt to find the present value of each coupon payment taken individually, that is, treated as a mini–zero-coupon bond. Call $d_1$ the present value of $1 to be received in half a year and $d_2$ the present value of a dollar to be received in 1 year. (The $d$ stands for discounted values; therefore, $d_1 = 1/(1 + r_1)$, where $r_1$ is the short rate for the first 6-month period.) Then our two bonds must satisfy the simultaneous equations

$$986.10 = d_1 \times 40 + d_2 \times 1{,}040$$
$$1{,}004.78 = d_1 \times 50 + d_2 \times 1{,}050$$

In each equation the bond's price is set equal to the discounted value of all of its remaining cash flows. Solving these equations we find that $d_1 = .95694$ and $d_2 = .91137$. Thus if $r_1$ is the short rate for the first 6-month period, then $d_1 = 1/(1 + r_1) = .95694$, so that $r_1 = .045$, and $d_2 = 1/[(1 + r_1)(1 + f_2)] = 1/[(1.045)(1 + f_2)] = .91137$, so that $f_2 = .05$. Thus the two short rates are shown to be 4.5% for the first half-year period and 5% for the second.

**CONCEPT CHECK ☞ QUESTION 9** A T-bill with 6-month maturity and $10,000 face value sells for $9,700. A 1-year maturity T-bond paying semiannual coupons of $40 sells for $1,000. Find the current 6-month short rate and the forward rate for the following 6-month period.

When we analyze many bonds, the procedure in Example 15.6 is more difficult, in part because of the greater number of bonds and time periods, but also because not all bonds give rise to identical estimates for the discounted value of a future $1 payment. In other words, there seem to be apparent error terms in the pricing relationship.[3] Nevertheless, treating these errors as random aberrations, we can use a statistical approach to infer the pattern of forward rates embedded in the yield curve.

To see how the statistical procedure would operate, suppose that we observe many coupon bonds, indexed by $i$, selling at prices $P_i$. The coupon and/or principal payment (the cash flow) of bond $i$ at time $t$ is denoted $CF_{it}$, and the present value of a $1 payment at time $t$, which is the implied price of a zero-coupon bond that we are trying to determine, is denoted $d_t$. Then for each bond we may write the following:

$$
\begin{aligned}
P_1 &= d_1 CF_{11} + d_2 CF_{12} + d_3 CF_{13} + \cdots + e_1 \\
P_2 &= d_1 CF_{21} + d_2 CF_{22} + d_3 CF_{23} + \cdots + e_2 \\
P_3 &= d_1 CF_{31} + d_2 CF_{32} + d_3 CF_{33} + \cdots + e_3 \\
&\;\;\vdots \qquad\qquad\qquad\qquad\qquad\quad \vdots \\
P_n &= d_1 CF_{n1} + d_2 CF_{n2} + d_3 CF_{n3} + \cdots + e_n
\end{aligned}
\tag{15.7}
$$

---

[3] We will consider shortly some of the reasons for the appearance of these error terms.

Each line of equation system 15.7 equates the price of the bond to the sum of its cash flows, discounted according to time until payment. The last term in each equation, $e_i$, represents the error term that accounts for the deviations of a bond's price from the prediction of the equation.

Students of statistics will recognize that equation 15.7 is a simple system of equations that can be estimated by regression analysis. The dependent variables are the bond prices, the independent variables are the cash flows, and the coefficients $d_t$ are to be estimated from the observed data.[4] The estimates of $d_t$ are our inferences of the present value of $1 to be paid at time $t$. The pattern of $d_t$ for various times to payment is called the *discount function,* because it gives the discounted value of $1 as a function of time until payment. From the discount function, which is equivalent to a list of zero-coupon bond prices for various maturity dates, we can calculate the yields on pure zero-coupon bonds. We would use Treasury securities in this procedure to avoid complications arising from default risk.

Before leaving the issue of the measurement of the yield curve, it is worth pausing briefly to discuss the error terms. Why is it that all bond prices do not conform exactly to a common discount function that sets price equal to present value? Two of the reasons relate to factors not accounted for in the regression analysis of equation 15.7: taxes and options associated with the bond.

Taxes affect bond prices because investors care about their after-tax return on investment. Therefore, the coupon payments should be treated as net of taxes. Similarly, if a bond is not selling at par value, the IRS may impute a "built-in" interest payment by amortizing the difference between the price and the par value of the bond. These considerations are difficult to capture in a mathematical formulation because different individuals are in different tax brackets, meaning that the net-of-tax cash flows from a given bond depend on the identity of the owner. Moreover, the specification of equation 15.7 implicitly assumes that the bond is held until maturity: It discounts *all* the bond's coupon and principal payments. This, of course, ignores the investor's option to sell the bond before maturity and so to realize a different stream of income from that described by equation 15.7. Moreover, it ignores the investor's ability to engage in *tax-timing options.* For example, an investor whose tax bracket is expected to change over time may benefit by realizing capital gains during the period when the tax rate is the lowest.

Another feature affecting bond pricing is the call provision. First, if the bond is callable, how do we know whether to include in equation 15.7 coupon payments in years following the first call date? Similarly, the date of the principal repayment becomes uncertain. More important, one must realize that the issuer of the callable bond will exercise the option to call only when it is profitable to do so. Conversely, the call provision is a transfer of value away from the bondholder who has "sold" the option to call to the bond issuer. The call feature therefore will affect the bond's price and introduce further error terms in the simple specification of equation 15.7.

Finally, we must recognize that the yield curve is based on price quotes that often are somewhat inaccurate. Price quotes used in the financial press may be stale (i.e., out of date), even if only by a few hours. Moreover, they may not represent prices at which dealers actually are willing to trade.

---

[4] In practice, variations of regression analysis called "splining techniques" are usually used to estimate the coefficients. This method was first suggested by McCulloch in the following two articles: J. Huston McCulloch, "Measuring the Term Structure of Interest Rates," *Journal of Business* 44 (January 1971); and "The Tax Adjusted Yield Curve," *Journal of Finance* 30 (June 1975).

**SUMMARY**

1. The term structure of interest rates refers to the interest rates for various terms to maturity embodied in the prices of default-free zero-coupon bonds.

2. In a world of certainty all investments must provide equal total returns for any investment period. Short-term holding-period returns on all bonds would be equal in a risk-free economy, and all equal to the rate available on short-term bonds. Similarly, total returns from rolling over short-term bonds over longer periods would equal the total return available from long-maturity bonds.

3. The forward rate of interest is the break-even future interest rate that would equate the total return from a rollover strategy to that of a longer-term zero-coupon bond. It is defined by the equation

$$(1 + y_n)^n(1 + f_{n+1}) = (1 + y_{n+1})^{n+1}$$

   where $n$ is a given number of periods from today. This equation can be used to show that yields to maturity and forward rates are related by the equation

$$(1 + y_n)^n = (1 + r_1)(1 + f_2)(1 + f_3) \cdots (1 + f_n)$$

4. A common version of the expectations hypothesis holds that forward interest rates are unbiased estimates of expected future interest rates. However, there are good reasons to believe that forward rates differ from expected short rates because of a risk premium known as a *liquidity premium*. A liquidity premium can cause the yield curve to slope upward even if no increase in short rates is anticipated.

5. The existence of liquidity premiums makes it extremely difficult to infer expected future interest rates from the yield curve. Such an inference would be made easier if we could assume the liquidity premium remained reasonably stable over time. However, both empirical and theoretical considerations cast doubt on the constancy of that premium.

6. Forward rates are market interest rates in the important sense that commitments to forward (i.e., deferred) borrowing or lending arrangements can be made at these rates.

7. A pure yield curve could be plotted easily from a complete set of zero-coupon bonds. In practice, however, most bonds carry coupons, payable at different future times, so that yield-curve estimates are often inferred from prices of coupon bonds. Measurement of the term structure is complicated by tax issues such as tax timing options and the different tax brackets of different investors.

**KEY TERMS**

| | | |
|---|---|---|
| term structure of interest rates | pure yield curve | liquidity preference theory |
| short interest rate | on the run | liquidity premium |
| yield curve | forward interest rate | term premiums |
| spot rate | liquidity premium | |
| | expectations hypothesis | |

**WEBSITES**

www.smartmoney.com/bonds
This is a good source for current rates, and current and past yield curves. (Be sure to check out *The Living Yield Curve*.) Review the current factors influencing bond prices and yields under *Bond Market Updates*.

*(continued)*

Visit us at www.mhhe.com/bkm

## PROBLEMS

1. Briefly explain why bonds of different maturities have different yields in terms of the expectations and liquidity preference hypotheses. Briefly describe the implications of each hypothesis when the yield curve is (1) upward sloping and (2) downward sloping.

2. Which one of the following statements about the term structure of interest rates is true?
    a. The expectations hypothesis indicates a flat yield curve if anticipated future short-term rates exceed current short-term rates.
    b. The expectations hypothesis contends that the long-term rate is equal to the anticipated short-term rate.
    c. The liquidity premium theory indicates that, all else being equal, longer maturities will have lower yields.
    d. The liquidity preference theory contends that lenders prefer to buy securities at the short end of the yield curve.

3. What is the relationship between forward rates and the market's expectation of future short rates? Explain in the context of both the expectations and liquidity preference theories of the term structure of interest rates.

4. Under the expectations hypothesis, if the yield curve is upward sloping, the market must expect an increase in short-term interest rates. True/false/uncertain? Why?

5. Under the liquidity preference theory, if inflation is expected to be falling over the next few years, long-term interest rates will be higher than short-term rates. True/false/uncertain? Why?

6. The following is a list of prices for zero-coupon bonds of various maturities. Calculate the yields to maturity of each bond and the implied sequence of forward rates.

| Maturity (Years) | Price of Bond ($) |
| --- | --- |
| 1 | $943.40 |
| 2 | 898.47 |
| 3 | 847.62 |
| 4 | 792.16 |

7. Assuming that the expectations hypothesis is valid, compute the expected price path of the 4-year bond in problem 6 as time passes. What is the rate of return of the bond in each year? Show that the expected return equals the forward rate for each year.

8. Suppose the following table shows yields to maturity of zero coupon U.S. Treasury securities as of January 1, 1996:

| Term to Maturity (Years) | Yield to Maturity |
|:---:|:---:|
| 1 | 3.50% |
| 2 | 4.50 |
| 3 | 5.00 |
| 4 | 5.50 |
| 5 | 6.00 |
| 10 | 6.60 |

a. Based on the data in the table, calculate the implied forward 1-year rate of interest at January 1, 1999.

b. Describe the conditions under which the calculated forward rate would be an unbiased estimate of the 1-year spot rate of interest at January 1, 1999.

c. Assume that 1 year earlier, at January 1, 1995, the prevailing term structure for U.S. Treasury securities was such that the implied forward 1-year rate of interest at January 1, 1999, was significantly higher than the corresponding rate implied by the term structure at January 1, 1996. On the basis of the pure expectations theory of the term structure, briefly discuss *two* factors that could account for such a decline in the implied forward rate.

9. Would you expect the yield on a callable bond to lie above or below a yield curve fitted from noncallable bonds?

10. The 6-month Treasury bill spot rate is 4%, and the 1-year Treasury bill spot rate is 5%. The implied 6-month forward rate for 6 months from now is:

   a. 3.0%
   b. 4.5%
   c. 5.5%
   d. 6.0%

11. The tables below show, respectively, the characteristics of two annual-pay bonds from the same issuer with the same priority in the event of default, and spot interest rates. Neither bond's price is consistent with the spot rates. Using the information in these tables, recommend either bond *A* or bond *B* for purchase. Justify your choice.

### Bond Characteristics

|  | Bond *A* | Bond *B* |
|---|:---:|:---:|
| Coupons | Annual | Annual |
| Maturity | 3 years | 3 years |
| Coupon rate | 10% | 6% |
| Yield to maturity | 10.65% | 10.75% |
| Price | 98.40 | 88.34 |

### Spot Interest Rates

| Term (Years) | Spot Rates (Zero Coupon) |
|:---:|:---:|
| 1 | 5% |
| 2 | 8 |
| 3 | 11 |

12. The current yield curve for default-free zero-coupon bonds is as follows:

| Maturity (Years) | YTM |
|---|---|
| 1 | 10% |
| 2 | 11 |
| 3 | 12 |

   *a.* What are the implied 1-year forward rates?

   *b.* Assume that the pure expectations hypothesis of the term structure is correct. If market expectations are accurate, what will the pure yield curve (that is, the yields to maturity on 1- and 2-year zero coupon bonds) be next year?

   *c.* If you purchase a 2-year zero-coupon bond now, what is the expected total rate of return over the next year? What if you purchase a 3-year zero-coupon bond? (Hint: Compute the current and expected future prices.) Ignore taxes.

   *d.* What should be the current price of a 3-year maturity bond with a 12% coupon rate paid annually? If you purchased it at that price, what would your total expected rate of return be over the next year (coupon plus price change)? Ignore taxes.

13. The term structure for zero-coupon bonds is currently:

| Maturity (Years) | YTM |
|---|---|
| 1 | 4% |
| 2 | 5 |
| 3 | 6 |

Next year at this time, *you* expect it to be:

| Maturity (Years) | YTM |
|---|---|
| 1 | 5% |
| 2 | 6 |
| 3 | 7 |

   *a.* What do *you* expect the rate of return to be over the coming year on a 3-year zero-coupon bond?

   *b.* Under the expectations theory, what yields to maturity does *the market* expect to observe on 1- and 2-year zeros next year? Is the market's expectation of the return on the 3-year bond greater or less than yours?

14. The yield to maturity on 1-year zero-coupon bonds is currently 7%; the YTM on 2-year zeros is 8%. The Treasury plans to issue a 2-year maturity *coupon* bond, paying coupons once per year with a coupon rate of 9%. The face value of the bond is $100.

   *a.* At what price will the bond sell?

   *b.* What will the yield to maturity on the bond be?

   *c.* If the expectations theory of the yield curve is correct, what is the market expectation of the price that the bond will sell for next year?

   *d.* Recalculate your answer to (*c*) if you believe in the liquidity preference theory and you believe that the liquidity premium is 1%.

15. A portfolio manager at Superior Trust Company is structuring a fixed-income portfolio to meet the objectives of a client. This client plans on retiring in 15 years and wants a substantial lump sum at that time. The client has specified the use of AAA-rated securities.

    The portfolio manager compares coupon U.S. Treasuries with zero-coupon stripped U.S. Treasuries and observes a significant yield advantage for the stripped bonds:

| Term (Years) | Coupon U.S. Treasuries | Zero-Coupon Stripped U.S. Treasuries |
|---|---|---|
| 3 | 5.50% | 5.80% |
| 5 | 6.00 | 6.60 |
| 7 | 6.75 | 7.25 |
| 10 | 7.25 | 7.60 |
| 15 | 7.40 | 7.80 |
| 30 | 7.75 | 8.20 |

Briefly discuss why zero-coupon stripped U.S. Treasuries could yield more than coupon U.S. Treasuries with the same final maturity.

16. Below is a list of prices for zero-coupon bonds of various maturities.

| Maturity (Years) | Price of $1,000 Par Bond (Zero Coupon) |
|---|---|
| 1 | 943.40 |
| 2 | 873.52 |
| 3 | 816.37 |

   a. An 8.5% coupon $1,000 par bond pays an annual coupon and will mature in 3 years. What should the yield to maturity on the bond be?
   b. If at the end of the first year the yield curve flattens out at 8%, what will be the 1-year holding-period return on the coupon bond?

17. Prices of zero-coupon bonds reveal the following pattern of forward rates:

| Year | Forward Rate |
|---|---|
| 1 | 5% |
| 2 | 7 |
| 3 | 8 |

In addition to the zero-coupon bond, investors also may purchase a 3-year bond making annual payments of $60 with par value $1,000.

   a. What is the price of the coupon bond?
   b. What is the yield to maturity of the coupon bond?
   c. Under the expectations hypothesis, what is the expected realized compound yield of the coupon bond?
   d. If you forecast that the yield curve in 1 year will be flat at 7%, what is your forecast for the expected rate of return on the coupon bond for the 1-year holding period?

18. The shape of the U.S. Treasury yield curve appears to reflect two expected Federal Reserve reductions in the Federal Funds rate. The current short-term interest rate is

5%. The first reduction of approximately 50 basis points (bp) is expected 6 months from now and the second reduction of approximately 50 bp is expected 1 year from now. The current U.S. Treasury term premiums are 10 bp per year for each of the next 3 years (out through the 3-year benchmark).

However, the market also believes that the Federal Reserve reductions will be reversed in a single 100 bp increase in the Federal Funds rate 2½ years from now. You expect term premiums to remain 10 bp per year for each of the next 3 years (out through the 3-year benchmark).

Describe or draw the shape of the Treasury yield curve out through the 3-year benchmark. State which term structure theory supports the shape of the U.S. Treasury yield curve you've described.

19. You observe the following term structure:

|  | Effective Annual YTM |
|---|---|
| 1-year zero-coupon bond | 6.1% |
| 2-year zero-coupon bond | 6.2 |
| 3-year zero-coupon bond | 6.3 |
| 4-year zero-coupon bond | 6.4 |

   a. If you believe that the term structure next year will be the same as today's, will the 1-year or the 4-year zeros provide a greater expected 1-year return?

   b. What if you believe in the expectations hypothesis?

20. U.S. Treasuries represent a significant holding in many pension portfolios. You decide to analyze the yield curve for U.S. Treasury notes.

   a. Using the data in the table below, calculate the 5-year spot and forward rates assuming annual compounding. Show your calculations.

### U.S. Treasury Note Yield Curve Data

| Years to Maturity | Par Coupon Yield to Maturity | Calculated Spot Rates | Calculated Forward Rates |
|---|---|---|---|
| 1 | 5.00 | 5.00 | 5.00 |
| 2 | 5.20 | 5.21 | 5.42 |
| 3 | 6.00 | 6.05 | 7.75 |
| 4 | 7.00 | 7.16 | 10.56 |
| 5 | 7.00 | ? | ? |

   b. Define and describe each of the following three concepts:
      i. Yield to maturity.
      ii. Spot rate.
      iii. Forward rate.
      Explain how these concepts are related.

   c. You are considering the purchase of a zero-coupon U.S. Treasury note with 4 years to maturity. Based on the above yield-curve analysis, calculate both the expected yield to maturity and the price for the security. Show your calculations.

21. The yield to maturity (YTM) on 1-year zero-coupon bonds is 5% and the YTM on 2-year zeros is 6%. The yield to maturity on 2-year-maturity coupon bonds with coupon rates of 12% (paid annually) is 5.8%. What arbitrage opportunity is available for an investment banking firm? What is the profit on the activity?

22. Suppose that a 1-year zero-coupon bond with face value $100 currently sells at $94.34, while a 2-year zero sells at $84.99. You are considering the purchase of a 2-year-maturity bond making *annual* coupon payments. The face value of the bond is $100, and the coupon rate is 12% per year.

    a. What is the yield to maturity of the 2-year zero? The 2-year coupon bond?

    b. What is the forward rate for the second year?

    c. If the expectations hypothesis is accepted, what are (1) the expected price of the coupon bond at the end of the first year and (2) the expected holding-period return on the coupon bond over the first year?

    d. Will the expected rate of return be higher or lower if you accept the liquidity preference hypothesis?

23. Suppose that the prices of zero-coupon bonds with various maturities are given in the following table. The face value of each bond is $1,000.

| Maturity (Years) | Price |
|---|---|
| 1 | $925.93 |
| 2 | 853.39 |
| 3 | 782.92 |
| 4 | 715.00 |
| 5 | 650.00 |

    a. Calculate the forward rate of interest for each year.

    b. How could you construct a 1-year forward loan beginning in year 3? Confirm that the rate on that loan equals the forward rate.

    c. Repeat (*b*) for a 1-year forward loan beginning in year 4.

24. Continue to use the data in the preceding problem. Suppose that you want to construct a *2-year* maturity forward loan commencing in 3 years.

    a. Suppose that you buy *today* one 3-year maturity zero-coupon bond. How many 5-year maturity zeros would you have to sell to make your initial cash flow equal to zero?

    b. What are the cash flows on this strategy in each year?

    c. What is the effective 2-year interest rate on the effective 3-year-ahead forward loan?

    d. Confirm that the effective 2-year interest rate equals $(1 + f_4) \times (1 + f_5) - 1$. You therefore can interpret the 2-year loan rate as a 2-year forward rate for the last 2 years. Alternatively, show that the effective 2-year forward rate equals

$$\frac{(1 + y_5)^5}{(1 + y_3)^3} - 1$$

25. The spot rates of interest for five U.S. Treasury Securities are shown in the following exhibit. Assume all securities pay interest annually.

### Spot Rates of Interest

| Term to Maturity (years) | Spot Rate of Interest |
|---|---|
| 1 | 13.00% |
| 2 | 12.00 |
| 3 | 11.00 |
| 4 | 10.00 |
| 5 | 9.00 |

   *a.*  i.  Compute the 2-year implied forward rate for a deferred loan beginning in 3 years.
        ii.  Explain your answer by using the expectations theory.
   *b.*  Compute the price of a 5-year annual-pay Treasury security with a coupon rate of 9% by using the information in the exhibit.

---

**E-INVESTMENTS**
**Expectations and Term Spreads**

Go to the St. Louis Fed's FRED database at **research.stlouisfed.org/fred/data/irates.html**. Examine the spread between short- and long-term yields in the early 1980s when rates were generally high but the slope of the yield curve turned steeply negative. What happened to yields in the next several years? How does this square with the expectations hypothesis?

---

**SOLUTIONS TO CONCEPT CHECKS**

1.  Using the spot rates from Table 15.2, the price of the 4-year coupon bond is

$$P = \frac{80}{1.08} + \frac{80}{1.08995^2} + \frac{80}{1.09660^3} + \frac{1,080}{1.09993^4} = \$939.92$$

The yield to maturity on this bond is 9.891%. [On the calculator, enter $n = 4$; PV = $-939.92$; FV = 1000; pmt = 80.] This yield to maturity is less than that of the 4-year zero-coupon bond in Table 15.2.

2.  The zero-coupon bond sells today for $683.18 (from Table 15.2). Next year, it will sell for $\$1,000/[(1.10)(1.11)(1.11)] = \$737.84$, for a return $1 + r = 737.84/683.18 = 1.08$, or $r = 8\%$.

    The 2-year bond will sell today for

$$P = \frac{80}{1.08} + \frac{1,080}{1.08995^2} = 983.17$$

Next year, it will have one remaining payment of $1,080, and so will sell for $\$1,080/1.10 = \$981.82$. The rate of return is

$$\frac{\text{Coupon} + P_1 - P_0}{P_0} = \frac{80 + 981.82 - 983.17}{983.17} = .08$$

3.  The *n*-period *spot* rate is the yield to maturity on a zero-coupon bond with a maturity of *n* periods. The *short* rate for period *n* is the *one-period* interest rate that will prevail in period *n*. Finally, the *forward* rate for period *n* is the short rate that would satisfy a "break-even condition" equating the total returns on two *n*-period investment strategies. The first strategy is an investment in an *n*-period zero-coupon bond; the second is an investment in an *n* − 1 period zero-coupon bond "rolled over" into an investment in a one-period zero. Spot rates and forward rates are observable today, but because interest rates evolve with uncertainty, future short rates are not. *In the special case* in which there is no uncertainty in future interest rates, the forward rate calculated from the yield curve would equal the short rate that will prevail in that period.

4.  $10\% - 1\% = 9\%$.

5.  The risk premium will be zero.

6.  If issuers prefer to issue long-term bonds, they will be willing to accept higher expected interest costs on long bonds over short bonds. This willingness combines with investors' demands for higher rates on long-term bonds to reinforce the tendency toward a positive liquidity premium.

Visit us at www.mhhe.com/bkm

**SOLUTIONS
TO CONCEPT
CHECKS
*(Concluded)***

7. If $r_4$ equaled 9.66%, then the 4-year bond would sell for $1,000/ $[(1.08)(1.10)(1.11)(1.0966)] = \$691.53$. The yield to maturity would satisfy the equation $691.53(1 + y_4)^4 = 1,000$, or $y_4 = 9.66\%$. At a lower value of $r_4$, the bond would sell for a higher price and offer a lower yield. At a higher value of $r_4$, the yield would be greater.

8. The 3-year yield to maturity is $\left(\dfrac{1,000}{761.65}\right)^{1/3} - 1 = .095 = 9.5\%$.

   The forward rate for the third year is therefore

   $$f_3 = \frac{(1 + y_3)^3}{(1 + y_2)^2} - 1 = \frac{1.095^3}{1.09^2} - 1 = .1051 = 10.51\%$$

   (Alternatively, note that the ratio of the price of the 2-year zero to the price of the 3-year zero is $1 + f_3 = 1.1051$.) To construct the synthetic loan, buy one 2-year maturity zero, and sell 1.1051 3-year maturity zeros. Your initial cash flow is zero, your cash flow at time 2 is $+\$1,000$, and your cash flow at time 3 is $-\$1,105.10$, which corresponds to the cash flows on a 1-year forward loan commencing at time 2 with an interest rate of 10.51%.

9. The data pertaining to the T-bill imply that the 6-month interest rate is $300/ $9,700 = .03093$, or 3.093%. To obtain the forward rate, we look at the 1-year T-bond: The pricing formula

   $$1,000 = \frac{40}{1.03093} + \frac{1040}{(1.03093)(1 + f)}$$

   implies that $f = .04952$, or 4.952%.

# MANAGING BOND PORTFOLIOS

In this chapter we turn to various strategies that bond portfolio managers can pursue, making a distinction between passive and active strategies. A *passive investment strategy* takes market prices of securities as fairly set. Rather than attempting to beat the market by exploiting superior information or insight, passive managers act to maintain an appropriate risk–return balance given market opportunities. One special case of passive management is an immunization strategy that attempts to insulate or immunize the portfolio from interest rate risk. In contrast, an *active investment strategy* attempts to achieve returns greater than those commensurate with the risk borne. In the context of bond management this style of management can take two forms. Active managers use either interest rate forecasts to predict movements in the entire bond market or some form of intramarket analysis to identify particular sectors of the market or particular bonds that are relatively mispriced.

Because interest rate risk is crucial to formulating both active and passive strategies, we begin our discussion with an analysis of the sensitivity of bond prices to interest rate fluctuations. This sensitivity is measured by the duration of the bond, and we devote considerable attention to what determines bond duration. We discuss several passive investment strategies, and show how duration-matching techniques can be used to immunize the holding-period return of a portfolio from interest rate risk. After examining the broad range of applications of the duration measure, we consider refinements in the way that interest rate sensitivity is measured, focusing on the concept of bond convexity. Duration is important in formulating active investment strategies as well, and we next explore several of these strategies. We consider strategies based on intramarket analysis as well as on interest rate forecasting. We also show how interest rate swaps may be used in bond portfolio management. We conclude the chapter with a discussion of financial engineering and derivatives in the bond market, and the novel risk profiles that can be achieved through such techniques.

# 16.1    INTEREST RATE RISK

We have seen already that an inverse relationship exists between bond prices and yields, and we know that interest rates can fluctuate substantially. As interest rates rise and fall, bondholders experience capital losses and gains. These gains or losses make fixed-income investments risky, even if the coupon and principal payments are guaranteed, as in the case of Treasury obligations.

Why do bond prices respond to interest rate fluctuations? Remember that in a competitive market all securities must offer investors fair expected rates of return. If a bond is issued with an 8% coupon when competitive yields are 8%, then it will sell at par value. If the market rate rises to 9%, however, who would purchase an 8% coupon bond at par value? The bond price must fall until its expected return increases to the competitive level of 9%. Conversely, if the market rate falls to 7%, the 8% coupon on the bond is attractive compared to yields on alternative investments. In response, investors eager for that return would bid the bond price above its par value until the total rate of return falls to the market rate.

**Interest Rate Sensitivity**    The sensitivity of bond prices to changes in market interest rates is obviously of great concern to investors. To gain some insight into the determinants of interest rate risk, turn to Figure 16.1, which presents the percentage change in price corresponding to changes in yield to maturity for four bonds that differ according to coupon rate, initial yield to maturity, and time to maturity. All four bonds illustrate that bond prices decrease when yields rise, and that the price curve is convex, meaning that decreases in yields have bigger impacts on price than increases in yields of equal magnitude. We summarize these observations in the following two propositions:

1. *Bond prices and yields are inversely related: as yields increase, bond prices fall; as yields fall, bond prices rise.*
2. *An increase in a bond's yield to maturity results in a smaller price change than a decrease in yield of equal magnitude.*

Now compare the interest rate sensitivity of bonds *A* and *B*, which are identical except for maturity. Figure 16.1 shows that bond *B*, which has a longer maturity than bond *A*, exhibits greater sensitivity to interest rate changes. This illustrates another general property:

3. *Prices of long-term bonds tend to be more sensitive to interest rate changes than prices of short-term bonds.*

This is not surprising. If rates increase, for example, the bond is less valuable as its cash flows are discounted at a now-higher rate. The impact of the higher discount rate will be greater as that rate is applied to more-distant cash flows.

Although bond *B* has six times the maturity of bond *A*, it has less than six times the interest rate sensitivity. Although interest rate sensitivity seems to increase with maturity, it

**Figure 16.1   Change in bond price as a function of change in yield to maturity**

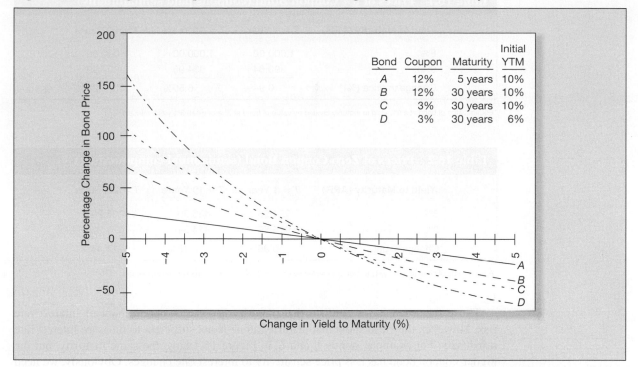

| Bond | Coupon | Maturity | Initial YTM |
|------|--------|----------|-------------|
| A | 12% | 5 years | 10% |
| B | 12% | 30 years | 10% |
| C | 3% | 30 years | 10% |
| D | 3% | 30 years | 6% |

does so less than proportionally as bond maturity increases. Therefore, our fourth property is that:

4. *The sensitivity of bond prices to changes in yields increases at a decreasing rate as maturity increases. In other words, interest rate risk is less than proportional to bond maturity.*

Bonds *B* and *C,* which are alike in all respects except for coupon rate, illustrate another point. The lower-coupon bond exhibits greater sensitivity to changes in interest rates. This turns out to be a general property of bond prices:

5. *Interest rate risk is inversely related to the bond's coupon rate. Prices of high-coupon bonds are less sensitive to changes in interest rates than prices of low-coupon bonds.*

Finally, bonds *C* and *D* are identical except for the yield to maturity at which the bonds currently sell. Yet bond *C,* with a higher yield to maturity, is less sensitive to changes in yields. This illustrates our final property:

6. *The sensitivity of a bond's price to a change in its yield is inversely related to the yield to maturity at which the bond currently is selling.*

The first five of these general properties were described by Malkiel[1] and are sometimes known as Malkiel's bond-pricing relationships. The last property was demonstrated by Homer and Liebowitz.[2]

[1] Burton G. Malkiel, "Expectations, Bond Prices, and the Term Structure of Interest Rates," *Quarterly Journal of Economics* 76 (May 1962), pp. 197–218.
[2] Sidney Homer and Martin L. Liebowitz, *Inside the Yield Book: New Tools for Bond Market Strategy* (Englewood Cliffs, NJ: Prentice Hall, 1972).

### Table 16.1    Prices of 8% Coupon Bond (coupons paid semiannually)

| Yield to Maturity (APR) | $T = 1$ Year | $T = 10$ Years | $T = 20$ Years |
|---|---|---|---|
| 8% | 1,000.00 | 1,000.00 | 1,000.00 |
| 9% | 990.64 | 934.96 | 907.99 |
| Change in price (%)* | 0.94% | 6.50% | 9.20% |

*Equals value of bond at a 9% yield to maturity divided by value of bond at (the original) 8% yield, minus 1.

### Table 16.2    Prices of Zero-Coupon Bond (semiannual compounding)

| Yield to Maturity (APR) | $T = 1$ Year | $T = 10$ Years | $T = 20$ Years |
|---|---|---|---|
| 8% | 924.56 | 456.39 | 208.29 |
| 9% | 915.73 | 414.64 | 171.93 |
| Change in price (%)* | 0.96% | 9.15% | 17.46% |

*Equals value of bond at a 9% yield to maturity divided by value of bond at (the original) 8% yield, minus 1.

These six propositions confirm that maturity is a major determinant of interest rate risk. However, they also show that maturity alone is not sufficient to measure interest rate sensitivity. For example, bonds B and C in Figure 16.1 have the same maturity, but the higher-coupon bond has less price sensitivity to interest rate changes. Obviously, we need to know more than a bond's maturity to quantify its interest rate risk.

To see why bond characteristics such as coupon rate or yield to maturity affect interest rate sensitivity, let's start with a simple numerical example. Table 16.1 gives bond prices for 8% semiannual coupon bonds at different yields to maturity and times to maturity, $T$. [The interest rates are expressed as annual percentage rates (APRs), meaning that the true 6-month yield is doubled to obtain the stated annual yield.] The shortest-term bond falls in value by less than 1% when the interest rate increases from 8% to 9%. The 10-year bond falls by 6.5%, and the 20-year bond by over 9%.

Let us now look at a similar computation using a zero-coupon bond rather than the 8% coupon bond. The results are shown in Table 16.2. Notice that for each maturity, the price of the zero-coupon bond falls by a greater proportional amount than the price of the 8% coupon bond. Because we know that long-term bonds are more sensitive to interest rate movements than are short-term bonds, this observation suggests that in some sense a zero-coupon bond represents a longer-term bond than an equal-time-to-maturity coupon bond.

In fact, this insight about the effective maturity of a bond is a useful one that we can make mathematically precise. To start, note that the times to maturity of the two bonds in this example are not perfect measures of the long- or short-term nature of the bonds. The 20-year 8% bond makes many coupon payments, most of which come years before the bond's maturity date. Each of these payments may be considered to have its own "maturity date." In this sense, it is often useful to view a coupon bond as a "portfolio" of coupon payments. The effective maturity of the bond is therefore some sort of average of the maturities of *all* the cash flows paid out by the bond. The zero-coupon bond, by contrast, makes only one payment at maturity. Its time to maturity is, therefore, a well-defined concept.

Higher-coupon-rate bonds have a higher fraction of value tied to coupons rather than final payment of par value, and so the "portfolio of coupons" is more heavily weighted

**Figure 16.2**
**Cash flows paid by 9% coupon, annual payment bond with 8-year maturity and 10% yield to maturity. The height of each bar is the total of interest and principal. The lower portion of each bar is the present value of that total cash flow. The fulcrum point is Macaulay's duration, the weighted average of the time until each payment.**

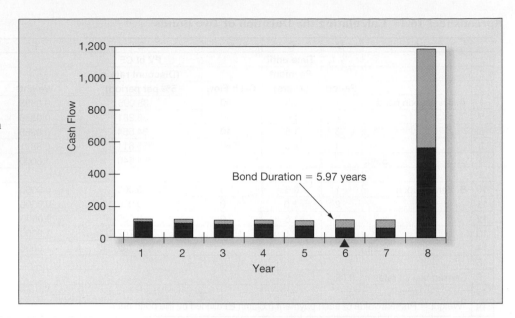

toward the earlier, short-maturity payments, which give it lower "effective maturity." This explains Malkiel's fifth rule, that price sensitivity falls with coupon rate.

Similar logic explains our sixth rule, that price sensitivity falls with yield to maturity. A higher yield reduces the present value of all of the bond's payments, but more so for more-distant payments. Therefore, at a higher yield, a higher fraction of the bond's value is due to its earlier payments, which have lower effective maturity and interest rate sensitivity. The overall sensitivity of the bond price to changes in yields is thus lower.

**Duration**   To deal with the ambiguity of the "maturity" of a bond making many payments, we need a measure of the average maturity of the bond's promised cash flows to serve as a useful summary statistic of the effective maturity of the bond. We would like also to use the measure as a guide to the sensitivity of a bond to interest rate changes, because we have noted that price sensitivity tends to increase with time to maturity.

Frederick Macaulay[3] termed the effective maturity concept the duration of the bond. **Macaulay's duration** is computed as the weighted average of the times to each coupon or principal payment made by the bond. The weight associated with each payment time clearly should be related to the "importance" of that payment to the value of the bond. Therefore, the weight applied to each payment time should be the proportion of the total value of the bond accounted for by that payment. This proportion is just the present value of the payment divided by the bond price.

Figure 16.2 can help us interpret Macaulay's duration. The figure shows the cash flows made by an 8-year maturity annual payment bond with a coupon rate of 9%, selling at a yield to maturity of 10%. In the first 7 years, cash flow is simply the $90 coupon payment; in the last year, cash flow is the sum of coupon plus par value, or $1,090. The height of each bar is the size of the cash flow; the shaded part of each bar is the *present value* of that

---

[3] Frederick Macaulay, *Some Theoretical Problems Suggested by the Movements of Interest Rates, Bond Yields, and Stock Prices in the United States since 1856* (New York: National Bureau of Economic Research, 1938).

**Spreadsheet 16.1    Calculating the Duration of Two Bonds**

| | A | B | C | D | E | F | G |
|---|---|---|---|---|---|---|---|
| 1 | | | Time until | | PV of CF | | Column (C) |
| 2 | | | Payment | | (Discount rate = | | times |
| 3 | | Period | (Years) | Cash Flow | 5% per period) | Weight* | Column (F) |
| 4 | A. 8% coupon bond | 1 | 0.5 | 40 | 38.095 | 0.0395 | 0.0197 |
| 5 | | 2 | 1.0 | 40 | 36.281 | 0.0376 | 0.0376 |
| 6 | | 3 | 1.5 | 40 | 34.554 | 0.0358 | 0.0537 |
| 7 | | 4 | 2.0 | 1040 | 855.611 | 0.8871 | 1.7741 |
| 8 | Sum: | | | | 964.540 | 1.0000 | 1.8852 |
| 9 | | | | | | | |
| 10 | B. Zero-coupon | 1 | 0.5 | 0 | 0.000 | 0.0000 | 0.0000 |
| 11 | | 2 | 1.0 | 0 | 0.000 | 0.0000 | 0.0000 |
| 12 | | 3 | 1.5 | 0 | 0.000 | 0.0000 | 0.0000 |
| 13 | | 4 | 2.0 | 1000 | 822.702 | 1.0000 | 2.0000 |
| 14 | Sum: | | | | 822.702 | 1.0000 | 2.0000 |
| 15 | | | | | | | |
| 16 | Semiannual int rate: | 0.05 | | | | | |
| 17 | | | | | | | |
| 18 | *Weight = Present value of each payment (column E) divided by the bond price. | | | | | | |

Column sums subject to rounding error.

cash flow using a discount rate of 10%. If you view the cash flow diagram as a balancing scale, like a child's see-saw, the duration of the bond is the fulcrum point where the scale would be balanced using present values of each cash flow as weights. The balancing point in Figure 16.2 is at 5.97 years, which in fact is the weighted average of the times until each payment, with weights proportional to the present value of each cash flow. The coupon payments made prior to maturity make the effective (i.e., weighted average) maturity of the bond less than its actual time to maturity.

To calculate the weighted average directly, we define the weight, $w_t$, associated with the cash flow made at time $t$ (denoted $CF_t$) as:

$$w_t = \frac{CF_t/(1 + y)^t}{\text{Bond price}}$$

where $y$ is the bond's yield to maturity. The numerator on the right-hand side of this equation is the present value of the cash flow occurring at time $t$ while the denominator is the value of all the payments forthcoming from the bond. These weights sum to 1.0 because the sum of the cash flows discounted at the yield to maturity equals the bond price.

Using these values to calculate the weighted average of the times until the receipt of each of the bond's payments, we obtain Macaulay's duration formula:

$$D = \sum_{t=1}^{T} t \times w_t \qquad (16.1)$$

As an example of the application of equation 16.1, we derive in Spreadsheet 16.1 the durations of an 8% coupon and zero-coupon bond, each with 2 years to maturity. We assume that the yield to maturity on each bond is 10%, or 5% per half-year. The present value of each payment is discounted at 5% per period for the number of (semiannual) periods shown in column B. The weight associated with each payment time (column F) is the present value of the payment for that period (column E) divided by the bond price (the sum of the present values in column E).

**Spreadsheet 16.2    Spreadsheet formulas for calculating duration**

| | A | B | C | D | E | F | G |
|---|---|---|---|---|---|---|---|
| 1 | | | Time until | | PV of CF | | Column (C) |
| 2 | | | Payment | | (Discount rate = | | times |
| 3 | | Period | (Years) | Cash Flow | 5% per period) | Weight | Column (F) |
| 4 | **A.** 8% coupon bond | 1 | 0.5 | 40 | =D4/(1+$B$16)^B4 | =E4/E$8 | =F4*C4 |
| 5 | | 2 | 1 | 40 | =D5/(1+$B$16)^B5 | =E5/E$8 | =F5*C5 |
| 6 | | 3 | 1.5 | 40 | =D6/(1+$B$16)^B6 | =E6/E$8 | =F6*C6 |
| 7 | | 4 | 2 | 1040 | =D7/(1+$B$16)^B7 | =E7/E$8 | =F7*C7 |
| 8 | Sum: | | | | =SUM(E4:E7) | =SUM(F4:F7) | =SUM(G4:G7) |
| 9 | | | | | | | |
| 10 | **B.** Zero-coupon | 1 | 0.5 | 0 | =D10/(1+$B$16)^B10 | =E10/E$14 | =F10*C10 |
| 11 | | 2 | 1 | 0 | =D11/(1+$B$16)^B11 | =E11/E$14 | =F11*C11 |
| 12 | | 3 | 1.5 | 0 | =D12/(1+$B$16)^B12 | =E12/E$14 | =F12*C12 |
| 13 | | 4 | 2 | 1000 | =D13/(1+$B$16)^B13 | =E13/E$14 | =F13*C13 |
| 14 | Sum: | | | | =SUM(E10:E13) | =SUM(F10:F13) | =SUM(G10:G13) |
| 15 | | | | | | | |
| 16 | Semiannual int rate: | 0.05 | | | | | |

The numbers in column G are the products of time to payment and payment weight. Each of these products corresponds to one of the terms in equation 16.1. According to that equation, we can calculate the duration of each bond by adding the numbers in column G.

The duration of the zero-coupon bond is exactly equal to its time to maturity, 2 years. This makes sense, because with only one payment, the average time until payment must be the bond's maturity. In contrast, the 2-year coupon bond has a shorter duration of 1.8852 years.

Spreadsheet 16.2 shows the spreadsheet formulas used to produce the entries in Spreadsheet 16.1. The inputs in the spreadsheet—specifying the cash flows the bond will pay—are given in columns B–D. In column E we calculate the present value of each cash flow using the assumed yield to maturity, in column F we calculate the weights for equation 16.1, and in column G we compute the product of time to payment and payment weight. Each of these terms corresponds to one of the values that are summed in equation 16.1. The sums computed in cells G8 and G14 are therefore the durations of each bond. Using the spreadsheet, you can easily answer several "what if" questions such as the one in Concept Check 1.

**CONCEPT CHECK ☞ QUESTION 1**

Suppose the interest rate decreases to 9% at an annual percentage rate. What will happen to the prices and durations of the two bonds in Spreadsheet 16.1?

Duration is a key concept in fixed-income portfolio management for at least three reasons. First, as we have noted, it is a simple summary statistic of the effective average maturity of the portfolio. Second, it turns out to be an essential tool in immunizing portfolios from interest rate risk. We explore this application in Section 16.3. Third, duration is a measure of the interest rate sensitivity of a portfolio, which we explore here.

We have seen that long-term bonds are more sensitive to interest rate movements than are short-term bonds. The duration measure enables us to quantify this relationship.

Specifically, it can be shown that when interest rates change, the proportional change in a bond's price can be related to the change in its yield to maturity, $y$, according to the rule

$$\frac{\Delta P}{P} = -D \times \left[ \frac{\Delta(1 + y)}{1 + y} \right] \qquad (16.2)$$

The proportional price change equals the proportional change in 1 plus the bond's yield times the bond's duration.

Practitioners commonly use equation 16.2 in a slightly different form. They define **modified duration** as $D^* = D/(1 + y)$, note that $\Delta(1 + y) = \Delta y$, and rewrite equation 16.2 as

$$\frac{\Delta P}{P} = -D^* \Delta y \qquad (16.3)$$

The percentage change in bond price is just the product of modified duration and the change in the bond's yield to maturity. Because the percentage change in the bond price is proportional to modified duration, modified duration is a natural measure of the bond's exposure to changes in interest rates. Actually, as we will see below, equation 16.2, or equivalently 16.3, is only approximately valid for large changes in the bond's yield. The approximation becomes exact as one considers smaller, or localized, changes in yields.[4]

## EXAMPLE 16.1     Duration

Consider the 2-year maturity, 8% coupon bond in Spreadsheet 16.1 making semiannual coupon payments and selling at a price of $964.540, for a yield to maturity of 10%. The duration of this bond is 1.8852 years. For comparison, we will also consider a zero-coupon bond with maturity *and duration* of 1.8852 years. As we found in Spreadsheet 16.1, because the coupon bond makes payments semiannually, it is best to treat one "period" as a half-year. So the duration of each bond is $1.8852 \times 2 = 3.7704$ (semiannual) periods, with a per period interest rate of 5%. The modified duration of each bond is therefore $3.7704/1.05 = 3.591$ periods.

Suppose the semiannual interest rate increases from 5% to 5.01%. According to equation 16.3, the bond prices should fall by

$$\Delta P/P = -D^* \Delta y = -3.591 \times .01\% = -.03591\%$$

Now compute the price change of each bond directly. The coupon bond, which initially sells at $964.540, falls to $964.1942 when its yield increases to 5.01%, which is a percentage decline of .0359%. The zero-coupon bond initially sells for $1,000/1.05^{3.7704} = 831.9704$. At the higher yield, it sells for $1,000/1.0501^{3.7704} = 831.6717$. This price also falls by .0359%.

We conclude that bonds with equal durations do in fact have equal interest rate sensitivity and that (at least for small changes in yields) the percentage price change is the modified duration times the change in yield.

---

[4] Students of calculus will recognize that modified duration is proportional to the derivative of the bond's price with respect to changes in the bond's yield:

$$D^* = -\frac{1}{P}\frac{dP}{dy}$$

As such, it gives a measure of the slope of the bond price curve only in the neighborhood of the current price.

*a.* In Concept Check 1, you calculated the price and duration of a 2-year maturity, 8% coupon bond making semiannual coupon payments when the market interest rate is 9%. Now suppose the interest rate increases to 9.05%. Calculate the new value of the bond and the percentage change in the bond's price.

*b.* Calculate the percentage change in the bond's price predicted by the duration formula in equation 16.2 or 16.3. Compare this value to your answer for (*a*).

## What Determines Duration?

Malkiel's bond price relations, which we laid out in the previous section, characterize the determinants of interest rate sensitivity. Duration allows us to quantify that sensitivity, which greatly enhances our ability to formulate investment strategies. For example, if we wish to speculate on interest rates, duration tells us how strong a bet we are making. Conversely, if we wish to remain "neutral" on rates, and simply match the interest rate sensitivity of a chosen bond-market index, duration allows us to measure that sensitivity and mimic it in our own portfolio. For these reasons, it is crucial to understand the determinants of duration, and convenient to have formulas to calculate the duration of some commonly encountered securities. Therefore, in this section, we present several "rules" that summarize most of the important properties of duration.

The sensitivity of a bond's price to changes in market interest rates is influenced by three key factors: time to maturity, coupon rate, and yield to maturity. These determinants of price sensitivity are important to fixed-income portfolio management. Therefore, we summarize some of the important relationships in the following eight rules. These rules are also illustrated in Figure 16.3, where durations of bonds of various coupon rates, yields to maturity, and times to maturity are plotted.

**Figure 16.3  Bond duration versus bond maturity**

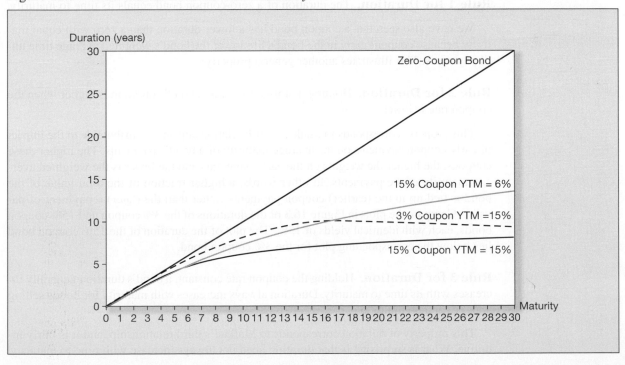

# BOND PRICING AND DURATION

Bond pricing and duration calculations can be cumbersome. The calculations are set up in a spreadsheet that is available on the Online Learning Center (www.mhhe.com/bkm). The models allow you to calculate the price and duration for bonds of different maturities. The models also allow you to examine the sensitivity of the calculations to changes in coupon rate and yield to maturity.

|   | A | B | C | D | E |
|---|---|---|---|---|---|
| 1 | Duration Example: Using Data Tables | | | | |
| 2 | | | | | |
| 3 | Bond | | | | |
| 4 | Coupon Rate | 0.08 | | | |
| 5 | Par Value | 1000 | | | |
| 6 | Years Mat | 10 | | | |
| 7 | YTM | 0.06 | | | |
| 8 | | | | | |
| 9 | Bond Price | Years | Cash Flow | PVCF | PVCF×t |
| 10 | | 1 | 80 | 75.4717 | 75.4717 |
| 11 | | 2 | 80 | 71.19972 | 142.3994 |
| 12 | | 3 | 80 | 67.16954 | 201.5086 |
| 13 | | 4 | 80 | 63.36749 | 253.47 |
| 14 | | 5 | 80 | 59.78065 | 298.9033 |
| 15 | | 6 | 80 | 56.39684 | 338.3811 |

We have already established:

**Rule 1 for Duration.** The duration of a zero-coupon bond equals its time to maturity.

We have also seen that a coupon bond has a lower duration than a zero with equal maturity because coupons early in the bond's life lower the bond's weighted average time until payments. This illustrates another general property:

**Rule 2 for Duration.** Holding maturity constant, a bond's duration is higher when the coupon rate is lower.

This property corresponds to Malkiel's fifth relationship and is attributable to the impact of early coupon payments on the average maturity of a bond's payments. The higher these coupons, the higher the weights on the early payments and the lower is the weighted average maturity of the payments. In other words, a higher fraction of the total value of the bond is tied up in the (earlier) coupon payments rather than the (later) repayment of par value. Compare the plots in Figure 16.3 of the durations of the 3% coupon and 15% coupon bonds, each with identical yields of 15%. The plot of the duration of the 15% coupon bond lies below the corresponding plot for the 3% coupon bond.

**Rule 3 for Duration.** Holding the coupon rate constant, a bond's duration generally increases with its time to maturity. Duration always increases with maturity for bonds selling at par or at a premium to par.

This property of duration corresponds to Malkiel's third relationship, and it is fairly intuitive. What is surprising is that duration need not always increase with time to maturity.

It turns out that for some deep-discount bonds, duration may fall with increases in maturity. However, for virtually all traded bonds it is safe to assume that duration increases with maturity.

Notice in Figure 16.3 that for the zero-coupon bond, maturity and duration are equal. However, for coupon bonds duration increases by less than a year with a year's increase in maturity. The slope of the duration graph is less than 1.0.

Although long-maturity bonds generally will be high-duration bonds, duration is a better measure of the long-term nature of the bond because it also accounts for coupon payments. Time to maturity is an adequate statistic only when the bond pays no coupons; then, maturity and duration are equal.

Notice also in Figure 16.3 that the two 15% coupon bonds have different durations when they sell at different yields to maturity. The lower-yield bond has longer duration. This makes sense, because at lower yields the more distant payments made by the bond have relatively greater present values and account for a greater share of the bond's total value. Thus in the weighted-average calculation of duration the distant payments receive greater weights, which results in a higher duration measure. This establishes rule 4:

**Rule 4 for Duration.**  Holding other factors constant, the duration of a coupon bond is higher when the bond's yield to maturity is lower.

As we noted above, the intuition for this property is that while a higher yield reduces the present value of all of the bond's payments, it reduces the value of more-distant payments by a greater proportional amount. Therefore, at higher yields a higher fraction of the total value of the bond lies in its earlier payments, thereby reducing effective maturity. Rule 4, which is the sixth bond-pricing relationship above, applies to coupon bonds. For zeros, of course, duration equals time to maturity, regardless of the yield to maturity.

Finally, we develop some algebraic rules for the duration of securities of special interest. These rules are derived from and consistent with the formula for duration given in equation 16.1 but may be easier to use for long-term bonds.

**Rule 5 for Duration.**  The duration of a level perpetuity is

$$\text{Duration of perpetuity} = \frac{1 + y}{y} \tag{16.4}$$

For example, at a 10% yield, the duration of a perpetuity that pays $100 once a year forever is 1.10/.10 = 11 years, but at an 8% yield it is 1.08/.08 = 13.5 years.

Equation 16.4 makes it obvious that maturity and duration can differ substantially. The maturity of the perpetuity is infinite, whereas the duration of the instrument at a 10% yield is only 11 years. The present-value-weighted cash flows early on in the life of the perpetuity dominate the computation of duration.

Notice from Figure 16.3 that as their maturities become ever longer, the durations of the two coupon bonds with yields of 15% both converge to the duration of the perpetuity with the same yield, 7.67 years.

**CONCEPT CHECK ☞ QUESTION 3**    **Show that the duration of the perpetuity increases as the interest rate decreases in accordance with rule 4.**

**Rule 6 for Duration.** The duration of a level annuity is equal to the following:

$$\text{Duration of annuity} = \frac{1+y}{y} - \frac{T}{(1+y)^T - 1} \tag{16.5}$$

where $T$ is the number of payments and $y$ is the annuity's yield per payment period. For example, a 10-year annual annuity with a yield of 8% will have duration

$$\frac{1.08}{.08} - \frac{10}{1.08^{10} - 1} = 4.87 \text{ years}$$

**Rule 7 for Duration.** The duration of a coupon bond equals

$$\text{Duration of coupon bond} = \frac{1+y}{y} - \frac{(1+y) + T(c-y)}{c[(1+y)^T - 1] + y} \tag{16.6}$$

where $c$ is the coupon rate per payment period, $T$ is the number of payment periods, and $y$ is the bond's yield per payment period. For example, a 10% coupon bond with 20 years until maturity, paying coupons semiannually, would have a 5% semiannual coupon and 40 payment periods. If the yield to maturity were 4% per half-year period, the bond's duration would be

$$\frac{1.04}{.04} - \frac{1.04 + 40(.05 - .04)}{.05[1.04^{40} - 1] + .04} = 19.74 \text{ half-years} = 9.87 \text{ years}$$

This calculation reminds us again of the importance of maintaining consistency between the time units of the payment period and interest rate. When the bond pays a coupon semiannually, we must use the effective semiannual interest rate and semiannual coupon rate in all calculations. This unit of time (a half-year) is then carried into the duration measure, when we calculate duration to be 19.74 half-year periods.

**Rule 8 for Duration.** For coupon bonds selling at par value, rule 7 simplifies to the following formula for duration:

$$\text{Duration of coupon bond at par} = \frac{1+y}{y}\left[1 - \frac{1}{(1+y)^T}\right] \tag{16.7}$$

The equations for the durations of coupon bonds are somewhat tedious. Moreover, they assume that the bond is at the beginning of a coupon payment period. Fortunately, spreadsheet programs such as Excel come with generalizations of these equations that can accommodate bonds between coupon payment dates. Spreadsheet 16.3 illustrates how to use

**Spreadsheet 16.3**
**Using Excel to**
**Compute Duration**

| | A | B | C |
|---|---|---|---|
| 1 | **Using Excel to compute duration** | | |
| 2 | | | |
| 3 | **Inputs** | | Formula in column B |
| 4 | Settlement date | 1/1/2000 | =DATE(2000,1,1) |
| 5 | Maturity date | 1/1/2008 | =DATE(2008,1,1) |
| 6 | Coupon rate | 0.09 | 0.09 |
| 7 | Yield to maturity | 0.1 | 0.1 |
| 8 | Coupons per year | 1 | 1 |
| 9 | | | |
| 10 | **Outputs** | | |
| 11 | Macaulay Duration | 5.9735 | =DURATION(B4,B5,B6,B7,B8) |
| 12 | Modified Duration | 5.4304 | =MDURATION(B4,B5,B6,B7,B8) |

Excel to compute duration. The spreadsheet uses many of the same conventions as the bond-pricing spreadsheets described in Chapter 14.

The settlement date (i.e., today's date) and maturity date are entered in cells B4 and B5 using Excel's date function, DATE(year, month, day). The coupon and maturity rates are entered as decimals in cells B6 and B7, and the payment periods per year are entered in cell B8. Macaulay and modified duration appear in cells B11 and B12. The spreadsheet shows that the duration of the bond in Figure 16.2 is indeed 5.97 years. For this 8-year maturity bond, we don't have a specific settlement date. We arbitrarily set the settlement date to January 1, 2000, and use a maturity date precisely 8 years later.

Durations can vary widely among traded bonds. Table 16.3 presents durations computed from equation 16.6 for several bonds all assumed to pay semiannual coupons and to yield 4% per half-year. Notice that duration decreases as coupon rates increase, and duration generally increases with time to maturity. According to Table 16.3 and equation 16.2, if the interest rate were to increase from 8% to 8.1%, the 6% coupon 20-year bond would fall in value by about 1.01% (10.922 × .1%/1.08), whereas the 10% coupon 1-year bond would fall by only .090%. Notice also from Table 16.3 that duration is independent of coupon rate only for perpetuities.

## 16.2   CONVEXITY

As a measure of interest rate sensitivity, duration clearly is a key tool in fixed-income portfolio management. Yet the duration rule for the impact of interest rates on bond prices is only an approximation. Equation 16.2, or its equivalent, 16.3, which we repeat here, states that the percentage change in the value of a bond approximately equals the product of modified duration times the change in the bond's yield:

$$\frac{\Delta P}{P} = -D^*\Delta y \qquad (16.3)$$

This equation asserts that the percentage price change is directly proportional to the change in the bond's yield. If this were *exactly* so, however, a graph of the percentage change in bond price as a function of the change in its yield would plot as a straight line, with slope equal to $-D^*$. Yet we know from Figure 16.1, and more generally from Malkiel's five rules (specifically rule 2), that the relationship between bond prices and yields is *not* linear. The duration rule is a good approximation for small changes in bond yield, but it is less accurate for larger changes.

Figure 16.4 illustrates this point. Like Figure 16.1, the figure presents the percentage change in bond price in response to a change in the bond's yield to maturity. The curved line is the percentage price change for a 30-year maturity, 8% coupon bond, selling at an

### Table 16.3   Bond Durations (initial bond yield = 8% APR)

| Years to Maturity | Coupon Rates (per Year) | | | |
| --- | --- | --- | --- | --- |
| | 6% | 8% | 10% | 12% |
| 1 | 0.985 | 0.980 | 0.976 | 0.972 |
| 5 | 4.361 | 4.218 | 4.095 | 3.990 |
| 10 | 7.454 | 7.067 | 6.772 | 6.541 |
| 20 | 10.922 | 10.292 | 9.870 | 9.568 |
| Infinite (perpetuity) | 13.000 | 13.000 | 13.000 | 13.000 |

**Figure 16.4    Bond price convexity. 30-year maturity, 8% coupon bond; initial yield to maturity = 8%**

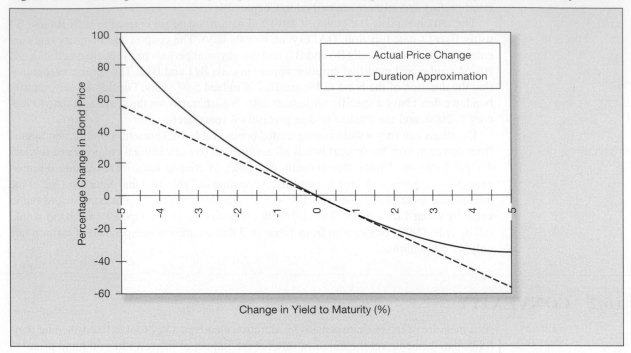

initial yield to maturity of 8%. The straight line is the percentage price change predicted by the duration rule: The modified duration of the bond at its initial yield is 11.26 years, so the straight line is a plot of $-D^*\Delta y = -11.26 \times \Delta y$. Notice that the two plots are tangent at the initial yield. Thus for small changes in the bond's yield to maturity, the duration rule is quite accurate. However, for larger changes in yield, there is progressively more "daylight" between the two plots, demonstrating that the duration rule becomes progressively less accurate.

Notice from Figure 16.4 that the duration approximation (the straight line) always understates the value of the bond; it underestimates the increase in bond price when the yield falls, and it overestimates the decline in price when the yield rises. This is due to the curvature of the true price-yield relationship. Curves with shapes such as that of the price-yield relationship are said to be *convex*, and the curvature of the price-yield curve is called the **convexity** of the bond.

We can quantify convexity as the rate of change of the slope of the price-yield curve, expressed as a fraction of the bond price.[5] As a practical rule, you can view bonds with higher convexity as exhibiting higher curvature in the price-yield relationship. The convexity of noncallable bonds such as that in Figure 16.4 is positive: The slope increases (i.e., becomes less negative) at higher yields.

---

[5] We pointed out in footnote 4 that equation 16.2 for modified duration can be written as $dP/P = -D^*dy$. Thus $D^* = -1/P \times dP/dy$ is the slope of the price-yield curve expressed as a fraction of the bond price. Similarly, the convexity of a bond equals the second derivative (the rate of change of the slope) of the price-yield curve divided by bond price: $1/P \times d^2P/dy^2$. The formula for the convexity of a bond with a maturity of $T$ years making annual coupon payments is

$$\text{Convexity} = \frac{1}{P \times (1+y)^2} \sum_{t=1}^{T} \left[ \frac{CF_t}{(1+y)^t} (t^2 + t) \right]$$

where $CF_t$ is the cash flow paid to the bondholder at date $t$; $CF_t$ represents either a coupon payment before maturity or final coupon plus par value at the maturity date.

Convexity allows us to improve the duration approximation for bond price changes. Accounting for convexity, equation 16.3 can be modified as follows:[6]

$$\frac{\Delta P}{P} = -D^*\Delta y + \frac{1}{2} \times \text{Convexity} \times (\Delta y)^2 \tag{16.8}$$

The first term on the right-hand side is the same as the duration rule, equation 16.3. The second term is the modification for convexity. Notice that for a bond with positive convexity, the second term is positive, regardless of whether the yield rises or falls. This insight corresponds to the fact noted just above that the duration rule always underestimates the new value of a bond following a change in its yield. The more accurate equation 16.8, which accounts for convexity, always predicts a higher bond price than equation 16.2. Of course, if the change in yield is small, the convexity term, which is multiplied by $(\Delta y)^2$ in equation 16.8, will be extremely small and will add little to the approximation. In this case, the linear approximation given by the duration rule will be sufficiently accurate. Thus convexity is more important as a practical matter when potential interest rate changes are large.

**EXAMPLE 16.2    Convexity**

The bond in Figure 16.4 has a 30-year maturity, an 8% coupon, and sells at an initial yield to maturity of 8%. Because the coupon rate equals yield to maturity, the bond sells at par value, or $1,000. The modified duration of the bond at its initial yield is 11.26 years, and its convexity is 212.4 (which can be verified using the formula in footnote 5). If the bond's yield increases from 8% to 10%, the bond price will fall to $811.46, a decline of 18.85%. The duration rule, equation 16.2, would predict a price decline of

$$\frac{\Delta P}{P} = -D^*\Delta y = -11.26 \times .02 = -.2252, \text{ or } -22.52\%$$

which is considerably more than the bond price actually falls. The duration-with-convexity rule, equation 16.4, is more accurate:[7]

$$\frac{\Delta P}{P} = -D^*\Delta y + \frac{1}{2} \times \text{Convexity} \times (\Delta y)^2$$
$$= -11.26 \times .02 + \frac{1}{2} \times 212.4 \times (.02)^2 = -.1827, \text{ or } -18.27\%$$

which is far closer to the exact change in bond price.

Notice that if the change in yield were smaller, say .1%, convexity would matter less. The price of the bond actually would fall to $988.85, a decline of 1.115%. Without accounting for convexity, we would predict a price decline of

$$\frac{\Delta P}{P} = -D^*\Delta y = -11.26 \times .001 = -.01126, \text{ or } -1.126\%$$

Accounting for convexity, we get almost the precisely correct answer:

$$\frac{\Delta P}{P} = -11.26 \times .001 + \frac{1}{2} \times 212.4 \times (.001)^2 = -.01115, \text{ or } -1.115\%$$

Nevertheless, the duration rule is quite accurate in this case, even without accounting for convexity.

[6] To use the convexity rule, you must express interest rates as decimals rather than percentages.
[7] Notice that when we use equation 16.4, we express interest rates as decimals rather than percentages. The change in rates from 8% to 10% is represented as $\Delta y = .02$.

**Figure 16.5   Convexity of two bonds**

Why Do Investors
Like Convexity?

Convexity is generally considered a desirable trait. Bonds with greater curvature gain more in price when yields fall than they lose when yields rise. For example in Figure 16.5 bonds *A* and *B* have the same duration at the initial yield. The plots of their proportional price changes as a function of interest rate changes are tangent, meaning that their sensitivities to changes in yields at that point are equal. However, bond *A* is more convex than bond *B*. It enjoys greater price increases and smaller price decreases when interest rates fluctuate by larger amounts. If interest rates are volatile, this is an attractive asymmetry that increases the expected return on the bond, since bond *A* will benefit more from rate decreases and suffer less from rate increases. Of course, if convexity is desirable, it will not be available for free: investors will have to pay more and accept lower yields on bonds with greater convexity.

Duration and Convexity
of Callable Bonds

Look at Figure 16.6, which depicts the price-yield curve for a callable bond. When interest rates are high, the curve is convex, as it would be for a straight bond. For example, at an interest rate of 10%, the price-yield curve lies above its tangency line. But as rates fall, there is a ceiling on the possible price: The bond cannot be worth more than its call price. So as rates fall, we sometimes say that the bond is subject to price compression—its value is "compressed" to the call price. In this region, for example at an interest rate of 5%, the price-yield curve lies *below* its tangency line, and the curve is said to have *negative convexity*.[8]

Notice that in the region of negative convexity, the price-yield curve exhibits an *unattractive* asymmetry. Interest rate increases result in a larger price decline than the price gain corresponding to an interest rate decrease of equal magnitude. The asymmetry arises

---

[8] If you've taken a calculus course, you will recognize that the curve is *concave* in this region. However, rather than saying that these bonds exhibit concavity, bond traders prefer the terminology negative convexity.

**Figure 16.6   Price-yield curve for a callable bond**

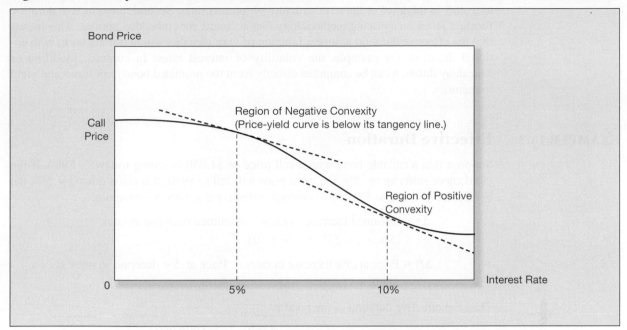

from the fact that the bond issuer has retained an option to call back the bond. If rates rise, the bondholder loses, as would be the case for a straight bond. But if rates fall, rather than reaping a large capital gain, the investor may have the bond called back from her. The bondholder is thus in a "heads I lose, tails I don't win" position. Of course, she was compensated for this unattractive situation when she purchased the bond. Callable bonds sell at lower initial prices (higher initial yields) than otherwise comparable straight bonds.

The effect of negative convexity is highlighted in equation 16.8. When convexity is negative, the second term on the right-hand side is necessarily negative, meaning that bond price performance will be worse than would be predicted by the duration approximation. However, callable bonds, or more generally, bonds with "embedded options," are difficult to analyze in terms of Macaulay's duration. This is because in the presence of such options, the future cash flows provided by the bonds are no longer known. If the bond may be called, for example, its cash flow stream may be terminated and its principal repaid earlier than was initially anticipated. Because cash flows are random, we can hardly take a weighted average of times until each future cash flow, as would be necessary to compute Macaulay's duration.

The convention on Wall Street is to compute the **effective duration** of bonds with embedded options. Effective duration cannot be computed with a simple formula such as 16.1 for Macaulay's duration. Instead, more complex bond valuation approaches that account for the embedded options are used, and effective duration is *defined* as the proportional change in the bond price per unit change in market interest rates:

$$\text{Effective duration} = -\frac{\Delta P/P}{\Delta r} \qquad (16.9)$$

This equation *seems* merely like a slight manipulation of the modified duration formula 16.3. However, there are important differences. First, note that we do not compute effective duration relative to a change in the bond's own yield to maturity. (The denominator is $\Delta r$, not $\Delta y$.) This is because for bonds with embedded options, which may be called early, the yield to maturity is often not a relevant statistic. Instead, we calculate price change relative to a shift in the level of the term structure of interest rates. Second, the effective duration formula relies on a pricing methodology that accounts for embedded options. This means that the effective duration will be a function of variables that would not matter to conventional duration, for example, the volatility of interest rates. In contrast, modified or Macaulay duration can be computed directly from the promised bond cash flows and yield to maturity.

**EXAMPLE 16.3**    **Effective Duration**

Suppose that a callable bond with a call price of $1,050 is selling today for $980. If the yield curve shifts up by .5%, the bond price will fall to $930. If it shifts down by .5%, the bond price will rise to $1,010. To compute effective duration, we compute:

$$\Delta r = \text{Assumed increase in rates} - \text{Assumed decrease in rates}$$
$$= .5\% - (-.5\%) = 1\% = .01$$

$$\Delta P = \text{Price at .5\% increase in rates} - \text{Price at .5\% decrease in rates}$$
$$= \$930 - \$1,010 = -\$80$$

Then the effective duration of the bond is

$$\text{Effective duration} = -\frac{\Delta P/P}{\Delta r} = -\frac{-\$80/\$980}{.01} = 8.16 \text{ years}$$

In other words, the bond price changes by 8.16% for a 1 percentage point swing in rates around current values.

**CONCEPT CHECK☞ QUESTION 4**

**What are the differences between Macaulay duration, modified duration, and effective duration?**

## 16.3  PASSIVE BOND MANAGEMENT

Passive managers take bond prices as fairly set and seek to control only the risk of their fixed-income portfolio. Two broad classes of passive management are pursued in the fixed-income market. The first is an indexing strategy that attempts to replicate the performance of a given bond index. The second broad class of passive strategies is known as immunization techniques; they are used widely by financial institutions such as insurance companies and pension funds, and are designed to shield the overall financial status of the institution from exposure to interest rate fluctuations.

Although indexing and immunization strategies are alike in that they accept market prices as correctly set, they are very different in terms of risk exposure. A bond-index portfolio will have the same risk–reward profile as the bond market index to which it is tied. In contrast, immunization strategies seek to establish a virtually zero-risk profile, in which interest rate movements have no impact on the value of the firm. We discuss both types of strategies in this section.

**Bond-Index Funds**  In principle, bond market indexing is similar to stock market indexing. The idea is to create a portfolio that mirrors the composition of an index that measures the broad market. In the U.S. equity market, for example, the S&P 500 is the most commonly used index for stock-index funds, and these funds simply buy shares of each firm in the S&P 500 in proportion to the market value of outstanding equity. A similar strategy is used for bond-index funds, but as we shall see shortly, several modifications are required because of difficulties unique to the bond market and its indexes.

Three major indexes of the broad bond market are the Salomon Smith Barney Broad Investment Grade (BIG) index, the Lehman Aggregate Bond Index, and the Merrill Lynch Domestic Master Index. All three are market-value-weighted indexes of total returns. All three include government, corporate, mortgage-backed, and Yankee bonds in their universes. (Yankee bonds are dollar-denominated, SEC-registered bonds of foreign issuers sold in the United States.) All three indexes include only bonds with maturities greater than 1 year. As time passes, and the maturity of a bond falls below 1 year, the bond is dropped from the index. Table 16.4 presents some summary statistics pertaining to each index.

The first problem that arises in the formation of a bond index is apparent from Table 16.4. Each of these indexes includes more than 5,000 securities, making it quite difficult to purchase each security in the index in proportion to its market value. Moreover, many bonds are very thinly traded, meaning that identifying their owners and purchasing the securities at a fair market price can be difficult.

Bond-index funds also present more difficult rebalancing problems than do stock-index funds. Bonds are continually dropped from the index as their maturities fall below 1 year. Moreover, as new bonds are issued, they are added to the index. Therefore, in contrast to equity indexes, the securities used to compute bond indexes constantly change. As they do, the manager must update or rebalance the portfolio to ensure a close match between the composition of the portfolio and the bonds included in the index. The fact that bonds generate considerable interest income that must be reinvested further complicates the job of the index fund manager.

In practice, it is deemed infeasible to precisely replicate the broad bond indexes. Instead, a stratified sampling or *cellular* approach is often pursued. Figure 16.7 illustrates the idea behind the cellular approach. First, the bond market is stratified into several subclasses. Figure 16.7 shows a simple two-way breakdown by maturity and issuer; in practice, however, criteria such as the bond's coupon rate or the credit risk of the issuer also would be

### Table 16.4  Profile of Bond Indexes

|  | Lehman | Merrill Lynch | Salomon Smith Barney |
|---|---|---|---|
| Number of issues | Over 6,500 | Over 5,000 | Over 5,000 |
| Maturity of included bonds | ≥ 1 year | ≥ 1 year | ≥ 1 year |
| Excluded issues | Junk bonds | Junk bonds | Junk bonds |
|  | Convertibles | Convertibles | Convertibles |
|  | Floating-rate bonds |  | Floating-rate bonds |
| Weighting | Market value | Market value | Market value |
| Reinvestment of intramonth cash flows | No | Yes (in specific bond) | Yes (at 1-month T-bill rate) |
| Daily availability | Yes | Yes | Yes |

Source: Frank K. Reilly, G. Wenchi Kao, and David J. Wright, "Alternative Bond Market Indexes," *Financial Analysts Journal* (May–June 1992), pp. 44–58.

**Figure 16.7
Stratification of
bonds into cells**

| Term to Maturity \ Sector | Treasury | Agency | Mortgage-Backed | Industrial | Finance | Utility | Yankee |
|---|---|---|---|---|---|---|---|
| <1 year | 12.1% | | | | | | |
| 1–3 years | 5.4% | | | | | | |
| 3–5 years | | | 4.1% | | | | |
| 5–7 years | | | | | | | |
| 7–10 years | | 0.1% | | | | | |
| 10–15 years | | | | | | | |
| 15–30 years | | | 9.2% | | | 3.4% | |
| 30+ years | | | | | | | |

used to form cells. Bonds falling within each cell are then considered reasonably homogeneous. Next, the percentages of the entire universe (i.e., the bonds included in the index that is to be matched) falling within each cell are computed and reported, as we have done for a few cells in Figure 16.7. Finally, the portfolio manager establishes a bond portfolio with representation for each cell that matches the representation of that cell in the bond universe. In this way, the characteristics of the portfolio in terms of maturity, coupon rate, credit risk, industrial representation, and so on, will match the characteristics of the index, and the performance of the portfolio likewise should match the index.

## Immunization

In contrast to indexing strategies, many institutions try to insulate their portfolios from interest rate risk altogether. Generally, there are two ways of viewing this risk, depending on the circumstances of the particular investor. Some institutions, such as banks, are concerned with protecting the current net worth or net market value of the firm against interest rate fluctuations. Other investors, such as pension funds, may face an obligation to make payments after a given number of years. These investors are more concerned with protecting the future values of their portfolios.

What is common to the bank and the pension fund, however, is interest rate risk. The net worth of the firm or the ability to meet future obligations fluctuates with interest rates. These institutions presumably might be interested in methods to control that risk. We will see that, by properly adjusting the maturity structure of their portfolios, these institutions can shed their interest rate risk. **Immunization** techniques refer to strategies used by such investors to shield their overall financial status from exposure to interest rate fluctuations.

Many banks and thrift institutions have a natural mismatch between asset and liability maturity structures. Bank liabilities are primarily the deposits owed to customers, most of which are very short-term in nature and, consequently, of low duration. Bank assets by contrast are composed largely of outstanding commercial and consumer loans or mortgages. These assets are of longer duration than are deposits, and their values are correspondingly more sensitive to interest rate fluctuations. In periods when interest rates increase unexpectedly, banks can suffer serious decreases in net worth—their assets fall in value by more than their liabilities.

Similarly, a pension fund may have a mismatch between the interest rate sensitivity of the assets held in the fund and the present value of its liabilities—the promise to make payments to retirees. The box on page 541 illustrates the dangers that pension funds face when they neglect the interest rate exposure of *both* assets and liabilities. The article points out that when interest rates change, the present value of the fund's liabilities change. For example, in some recent years pension funds lost ground despite the fact that they enjoyed excellent investment returns. As interest rates fell, the value of their liabilities grew even faster than the value of their assets. The article concludes that funds should match the interest rate exposure of assets and liabilities so that the value of assets will track the value of liabilities whether rates rise or fall. In other words, the financial manager might want to *immunize* the fund against interest rate volatility.

Pension funds are not alone in this concern. Any institution with a future fixed obligation might consider immunization a reasonable risk management policy. Insurance companies, for example, also pursue immunization strategies. Indeed, the notion of immunization was introduced by F. M. Redington,[9] an actuary for a life insurance company. The idea behind immunization is that duration-matched assets and liabilities let the asset portfolio meet the firm's obligations despite interest rate movements.

Consider, for example, an insurance company that issues a guaranteed investment contract, or GIC, for $10,000. (Essentially, GICs are zero-coupon bonds issued by the insurance company to its customers. They are popular products for individuals' retirement-savings accounts.) If the GIC has a 5-year maturity and a guaranteed interest rate of 8%, the insurance company is obligated to pay $10,000 \times (1.08)^5 = \$14,693.28$ in 5 years.

Suppose that the insurance company chooses to fund its obligation with $10,000 of 8% *annual* coupon bonds, selling at par value, with 6 years to maturity. As long as the market interest rate stays at 8%, the company has fully funded the obligation, as the present value of the obligation exactly equals the value of the bonds.

Table 16.5A shows that if interest rates remain at 8%, the accumulated funds from the bond will grow to exactly the $14,693.28 obligation. Over the 5-year period, the year-end coupon income of $800 is reinvested at the prevailing 8% market interest rate. At the end of the period, the bonds can be sold for $10,000; they still will sell at par value because the coupon rate still equals the market interest rate. Total income after 5 years from reinvested coupons and the sale of the bond is precisely $14,693.28.

If interest rates change, however, two offsetting influences will affect the ability of the fund to grow to the targeted value of $14,693.28. If interest rates rise, the fund will suffer a capital loss, impairing its ability to satisfy the obligation. The bonds will be worth less in 5 years than if interest rates had remained at 8%. However, at a higher interest rate, reinvested coupons will grow at a faster rate, offsetting the capital loss. In other words, fixed-income investors face two offsetting types of interest rate risk: *price risk* and *reinvestment rate risk*. Increases in interest rates cause capital losses but at the same time increase the rate at which reinvested income will grow. If the portfolio duration is chosen appropriately, these two effects will cancel out exactly. When the portfolio duration is set equal to the investor's horizon date, the accumulated value of the investment fund at the horizon date will be unaffected by interest rate fluctuations. *For a horizon equal to the portfolio's duration, price risk and reinvestment risk exactly cancel out.*

In the example we are discussing, the duration of the 6-year maturity bonds used to fund the GIC is 5 years. You can confirm this using equation 16.7. Because the fully funded plan has equal duration for its assets and liabilities, the insurance company should be immunized against interest rate fluctuations. To confirm that this is the case, let us now

---

[9] F. M. Redington, "Review of the Principle of Life-Office Valuations," *Journal of the Institute of Actuaries* 78 (1952).

**Table 16.5    Terminal Value of a Bond Portfolio after 5 Years (all proceeds reinvested)**

| Payment Number | Years Remaining until Obligation | Accumulated Value of Invested Payment | | |
|---|---|---|---|---|
| **A. Rates remain at 8%** | | | | |
| 1 | 4 | $800 \times (1.08)^4$ | = | 1,088.39 |
| 2 | 3 | $800 \times (1.08)^3$ | = | 1,007.77 |
| 3 | 2 | $800 \times (1.08)^2$ | = | 933.12 |
| 4 | 1 | $800 \times (1.08)^1$ | = | 864.00 |
| 5 | 0 | $800 \times (1.08)^0$ | = | 800.00 |
| Sale of bond | 0 | 10,800/1.08 | = | 10,000.00 |
| | | | | 14,693.28 |
| **B. Rates fall to 7%** | | | | |
| 1 | 4 | $800 \times (1.07)^4$ | = | 1,048.64 |
| 2 | 3 | $800 \times (1.07)^3$ | = | 980.03 |
| 3 | 2 | $800 \times (1.07)^2$ | = | 915.92 |
| 4 | 1 | $800 \times (1.07)^1$ | = | 856.00 |
| 5 | 0 | $800 \times (1.07)^0$ | = | 800.00 |
| Sale of bond | 0 | 10,800/1.07 | = | 10,093.46 |
| | | | | 14,694.05 |
| **C. Rates increase to 9%** | | | | |
| 1 | 4 | $800 \times (1.09)^4$ | = | 1,129.27 |
| 2 | 3 | $800 \times (1.09)^3$ | = | 1,036.02 |
| 3 | 2 | $800 \times (1.09)^2$ | = | 950.48 |
| 4 | 1 | $800 \times (1.09)^1$ | = | 872.00 |
| 5 | 0 | $800 \times (1.09)^0$ | = | 800.00 |
| Sale of bond | 0 | 10,800/1.09 | = | 9,908.26 |
| | | | | 14,696.02 |

Note: The sale price of the bond portfolio equals the portfolio's final payment ($10,800) divided by $1 + r$, because the time to maturity of the bonds will be 1 year at the time of sale.

investigate whether the bond can generate enough income to pay off the obligation 5 years from now regardless of interest rate movements.

Tables 16.5B and C consider two possible interest rate scenarios: Rates either fall to 7%, or increase to 9%. In both cases, the annual coupon payments from the bond are reinvested at the new interest rate, which is assumed to change before the first coupon payment, and the bond is sold in year 5 to help satisfy the obligation of the GIC.

Table 16.5B shows that if interest rates fall to 7%, the total funds will accumulate to $14,694.05, providing a small surplus of $.77. If rates increase to 9% as in Table 16.5C, the fund accumulates to $14,696.02, providing a small surplus of $2.74.

Several points are worth highlighting. First, duration matching balances the difference between the accumulated value of the coupon payments (reinvestment rate risk) and the sale value of the bond (price risk). That is, when interest rates fall, the coupons grow less than in the base case, but the gain on the sale of the bond offsets this. When interest rates rise, the resale value of the bond falls, but the coupons more than make up for this loss because they are reinvested at the higher rate. Figure 16.8 illustrates this case. The solid curve traces out the accumulated value of the bonds if interest rates remain at 8%. The dashed curve shows that value if interest rates happen to increase. The initial impact is a capital

In one of the happiest reports to come out of Detroit lately, General Motors proclaimed Tuesday that its U.S. pension funds are now "fully funded on an economic basis." Less noticed was GM's admission that, in accounting terms, it is still a few cents—well, $3 billion—shy of the mark.

Wait a minute. If GM's pension plans were $9.3 billion in the hole when the year began, and if the company, to its credit, shoveled in $10.4 billion more during the year, how come its pension deficit wasn't wiped out in full?

We'll get to that, but the real news here is broader than GM. According to experts, most pension funds actually *lost* ground,…even though, as you may recall, it was a rather good year for stocks and bonds.

True, pension-fund assets did have a banner year. But as is sometimes overlooked, pension funds also have liabilities (their obligations to retirees). And at most funds, liabilities grew at a rate that put asset growth to shame. At the margin, that means more companies' pension plans will be "underfunded." And down the road, assuming no reversal in the trend, more companies will have to pony up more cash.

What's to blame? The sharp decline in interest rates that brought joy to everyone else. As rates fall, pension funds have to set aside more money today to pay off a fixed obli-gation tomorrow. In accounting-speak, this "discounted present value" of their liabilities rises.

By now, maybe you sense that pension liabilities swing more, in either direction, than assets. How come? In a phrase, most funds are "mismatched," meaning their liabilities are longer-lived than their investments. The longer an obligation, the more its present value reacts to changes in rates. And at a typical pension fund, even though the average obligation is 15 years away, the average duration of its bond portfolio is roughly five years.

If this seems to defy common sense, it does. No sensible family puts its grocery money (a short-term obligation) into common stocks (a long-term asset). Ordinary Joes and Janes grasp the principle of "matching" without even thinking about it.

But fund managers—the pros—insist on shorter, un-matching bond portfolios for a simple, stupefying reason. They are graded—usually by consultants—according to how they perform against standard (and shorter-term) bond indexes. Thus, rather than invest to keep up with liabilities, managers are investing so as to avoid lagging behind the popular index in any year.

loss, but this loss eventually is offset by the now-faster growth rate of reinvested funds. At the 5-year horizon date, the two effects just cancel, leaving the company able to satisfy its obligation with the accumulated proceeds from the bond. The above box discusses this

**Figure 16.8 Growth of invested funds.** The solid colored curve represents the growth of portfolio value at the original interest rate. If interest rates increase at time $t^*$, the portfolio value initially falls but increases thereafter at the faster rate represented by the broken curve. At time $D$ (duration) the curves cross.

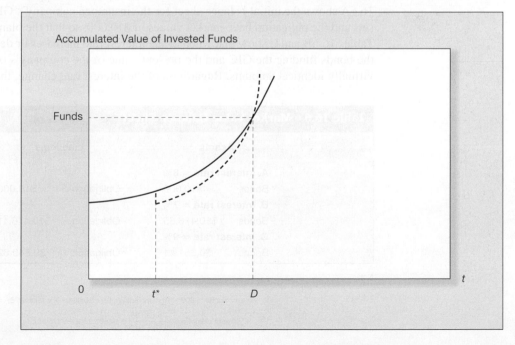

# EXCEL APPLICATION

## HOLDING-PERIOD IMMUNIZATION

The Online Learning Center (www.mhhe.com/bkm) contains a spreadsheet that is useful in understanding the concept of holding-period immunization. The spreadsheet calculates duration and holding-period returns on bonds of any maturity. The spreadsheet shows how price risk and reinvestment risk offset if a bond is sold at its duration.

| | A | B | C | D | E | F | F | H |
|---|---|---|---|---|---|---|---|---|
| 1 | **Holding Period Immunization Example:** | | | | | | | |
| 2 | | | | | | | | |
| 3 | Yield to Maturity | 11.580% | | | | | | |
| 4 | Coupon Rate | 14.000% | | | | | | |
| 5 | Years to Maturity | 7.0 | | | | | | |
| 6 | Par Value | $1,000.00 | | | | | | |
| 7 | Holding Period | 5.0 | | | | | | |
| 8 | Duration | 5.000251 | | 5.000251 | | | | |
| 9 | Market Price | $1,111.929 | | $1,111.929 | | | | |
| 10 | | | | | | | | |
| 11 | If YTM increases 200 basis points: | | | 2.00% | | If YTM increases 200 basis points: | | |
| 12 | Yield to Maturity | 13.580% | | | | Yield to Maturity | 12.580% | |
| 13 | Future Value of Coupons | $917.739 | | $917.739 | | Future Value of Coupons | $899.705 | |
| 14 | Sale of Bond | $1,006.954 | | 1,006.954 | | Sale of Bond | $1,023.817 | |
| 15 | Accumulated Value | $1,924.693 | | | | Accumulated Value | $1,923.522 | |
| 16 | Internal Rate of Return | 11.5981% | | | | Internal Rate of Return | 11.5845% | |
| 17 | | | | | | | | |

trade-off between price and reinvestment rate risk, suggesting how duration can be used to tailor a fixed-income portfolio to the horizon of the investor.

We can also analyze immunization in terms of present as opposed to future values. Table 16.6A shows the initial balance sheet for the insurance company's GIC account. Both assets and the obligation have market values of $10,000, so that the plan is just fully funded. Tables 16.6B and C show that whether the interest rate increases or decreases, the value of the bonds funding the GIC and the present value of the company's obligation change by virtually identical amounts. Regardless of the interest rate change, the plan remains fully

### Table 16.6   Market Value Balance Sheet

| Assets | | Liabilities | |
|---|---|---|---|
| **A. Interest rate = 8%** | | | |
| Bonds | $10,000 | Obligation | $10,000 |
| **B. Interest rate = 7%** | | | |
| Bonds | $10,476.65 | Obligation | $10,476.11 |
| **C. Interest rate = 9%** | | | |
| Bonds | $9,551.41 | Obligation | $9,549.62 |

Notes:

Value of bonds = $800 \times$ Annuity factor($r$, 6) + 10,000 $\times$ PV factor($r$, 6)

Value of obligation = $\dfrac{14,693.28}{(1 + r)^5}$ = 14,693.28 $\times$ PV factor($r$, 5)

funded, with the surplus in Table 16.6B and C just about zero. The duration-matching strategy has ensured that both assets and liabilities react equally to interest rate fluctuations.

Figure 16.9 is a graph of the present values of the bond and the single-payment obligation as a function of the interest rate. At the current rate of 8%, the values are equal, and the obligation is fully funded by the bond. Moreover, the two present value curves are tangent at $y = 8\%$. As interest rates change, the change in value of both the asset and the obligation is equal, so the obligation remains fully funded. For greater changes in the interest rate, however, the present value curves diverge. This reflects the fact that the fund actually shows a small surplus in Table 16.5 at market interest rates other than 8%.

If the obligation was immunized, why is there any surplus in the fund? The answer is convexity. Figure 16.9 shows that the coupon bond has greater convexity than the obligation it funds. Hence, when rates move substantially, the bond value exceeds the present value of the obligation by a noticeable amount. Another way to think about it is that although the duration of the bond is indeed equal to 5 years at a yield to maturity of 8%, it rises to 5.02 years when its yield falls to 7% and drops to 4.97 years at $y = 9\%$; that is, the bond and the obligation were not duration-matched *across* the interest rate shift.

This example highlights the importance of **rebalancing** immunized portfolios. As interest rates and asset durations change, a manager must rebalance the portfolio of fixed-income assets continually to realign its duration with the duration of the obligation. Moreover, even if interest rates do not change, asset durations *will* change solely because of the passage of time. Recall from Figure 16.3 that duration generally decreases less rapidly than does maturity. Thus, even if an obligation is immunized at the outset, as time passes the durations of the asset and liability will fall at different rates. Without portfolio rebalancing, durations will become unmatched and the goals of immunization will not be

**Figure 16.9**
**Immunization.**
**The coupon bond**
**fully funds the**
**obligation at**
**an interest rate**
**of 8%. Moreover,**
**the present value**
**curves are tangent**
**at 8%, so the**
**obligation will**
**remain fully**
**funded even if**
**rates change by**
**a small amount.**

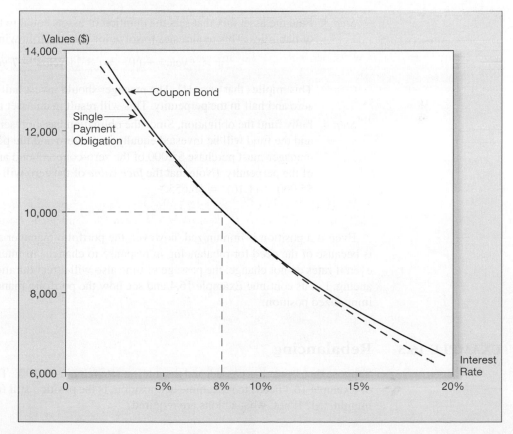

realized. Obviously, immunization is a passive strategy only in the sense that it does not involve attempts to identify undervalued securities. Immunization managers still actively update and monitor their positions.

## EXAMPLE 16.4    Constructing an Immunized Portfolio

An insurance company must make a payment of $19,487 in 7 years. The market interest rate is 10%, so the present value of the obligation is $10,000. The company's portfolio manager wishes to fund the obligation using 3-year zero-coupon bonds and perpetuities paying annual coupons. (We focus on zeros and perpetuities to keep the algebra simple.) How can the manager immunize the obligation?

Immunization requires that the duration of the portfolio of assets equal the duration of the liability. We can proceed in four steps:

*Step 1.*  Calculate the duration of the liability. In this case, the liability duration is simple to compute. It is a single-payment obligation with duration of 7 years.

*Step 2.*  Calculate the duration of the asset portfolio. The portfolio duration is the weighted average of duration of each component asset, with weights proportional to the funds placed in each asset. The duration of the zero-coupon bond is simply its maturity, 3 years. The duration of the perpetuity is $1.10/.10 = 11$ years. Therefore, if the fraction of the portfolio invested in the zero is called $w$, and the fraction invested in the perpetuity is $(1 - w)$, the portfolio duration will be

$$\text{Asset duration} = w \times 3 \text{ years} + (1 - w) \times 11 \text{ years}$$

*Step 3.*  Find the asset mix that sets the duration of assets equal to the 7-year duration of liabilities. This requires us to solve for $w$ in the following equation:

$$w \times 3 \text{ years} + (1 - w) \times 11 \text{ years} = 7 \text{ years}$$

This implies that $w = 1/2$. The manager should invest half the portfolio in the zero and half in the perpetuity. This will result in an asset duration of 7 years.

*Step 4.*  Fully fund the obligation. Since the obligation has a present value of $10,000, and the fund will be invested equally in the zero and the perpetuity, the manager must purchase $5,000 of the zero-coupon bond and $5,000 of the perpetuity. (Note that the *face value* of the zero will be $5,000 \times (1.10)^3 = $6,655.)

Even if a position is immunized, however, the portfolio manager still cannot rest. This is because of the need for rebalancing in response to changes in interest rates. Moreover, even if rates do not change, the passage of time also will affect duration and require rebalancing. Let us continue Example 16.4 and see how the portfolio manager can maintain an immunized position.

## EXAMPLE 16.5    Rebalancing

Suppose that 1 year has passed, and the interest rate remains at 10%. The portfolio manager of Example 16.4 needs to reexamine her position. Is the position still fully funded? Is it still immunized? If not, what actions are required?

First, examine funding. The present value of the obligation will have grown to $11,000, as it is 1 year closer to maturity. The manager's funds also have grown to $11,000: The zero-coupon bonds have increased in value from $5,000 to $5,500 with the passage of time, while the perpetuity has paid its annual $500 coupons and remains worth $5,000. Therefore, the obligation is still fully funded.

The portfolio weights must be changed, however. The zero-coupon bond now will have a duration of 2 years, while the perpetuity duration remains at 11 years. The obligation is now due in 6 years. The weights must now satisfy the equation

$$w \times 2 + (1 - w) \times 11 = 6$$

which implies that $w = 5/9$. To rebalance the portfolio and maintain the duration match, the manager now must invest a total of $11,000 \times 5/9 = $6,111.11 in the zero-coupon bond. This requires that the entire $500 coupon payment be invested in the zero, with an additional $111.11 of the perpetuity sold and invested in the zero-coupon bond.

Of course, rebalancing of the portfolio entails transaction costs as assets are bought or sold, so one cannot rebalance continuously. In practice, an appropriate compromise must be established between the desire for perfect immunization, which requires continual rebalancing, and the need to control trading costs, which dictates less frequent rebalancing.

| CONCEPT CHECK ☞ QUESTION 5 | **Look again at Example 16.5. What would be the immunizing weights in the second year if the interest rate had fallen to 8%?** |
|---|---|

## Cash Flow Matching and Dedication

The problems associated with immunization seem to have a simple solution. Why not simply buy a zero-coupon bond that provides a payment in an amount exactly sufficient to cover the projected cash outlay? If we follow the principle of **cash flow matching** we automatically immunize the portfolio from interest rate movement because the cash flow from the bond and the obligation exactly offset each other.

Cash flow matching on a multiperiod basis is referred to as a **dedication strategy**. In this case, the manager selects either zero-coupon or coupon bonds that provide total cash flows in each period that match a series of obligations. The advantage of dedication is that it is a once-and-for-all approach to eliminating interest rate risk. Once the cash flows are matched, there is no need for rebalancing. The dedicated portfolio provides the cash necessary to pay the firm's liabilities regardless of the eventual path of interest rates.

Cash flow matching is not more widely pursued probably because of the constraints that it imposes on bond selection. Immunization or dedication strategies are appealing to firms that do not wish to bet on general movements in interest rates, but these firms may want to immunize using bonds that they perceive are undervalued. Cash flow matching, however, places so many more constraints on the bond selection process that it can be impossible to pursue a dedication strategy using only "underpriced" bonds. Firms looking for underpriced bonds give up exact and easy dedication for the possibility of achieving superior returns from the bond portfolio.

Sometimes, cash flow matching is simply not possible. To cash flow match for a pension fund that is obligated to pay out a perpetual flow of income to current and future retirees, the pension fund would need to purchase fixed-income securities with maturities ranging up to hundreds of years. Such securities do not exist, making exact dedication infeasible.

---

**CONCEPT CHECK☞ QUESTION 6**

How would an increase in trading costs affect the attractiveness of dedication versus immunization?

---

## Other Problems with Conventional Immunization

If you look back at the definition of duration in equation 16.1, you note that it uses the bond's yield to maturity to calculate the weight applied to the time until each coupon payment. Given this definition and limitations on the proper use of yield to maturity, it is perhaps not surprising that this notion of duration is strictly valid only for a flat yield curve for which all payments are discounted at a common interest rate.

If the yield curve is not flat, then the definition of duration must be modified and $CF_t/(1 + y)^t$ replaced with the present value of $CF_t$, where the present value of each cash flow is calculated by discounting with the appropriate interest rate from the yield curve corresponding to the date of the *particular* cash flow, instead of by discounting with the *bond's* yield to maturity. Moreover, even with this modification, duration matching will immunize

---

**E-INVESTMENTS Immunization and Zero Coupon Bonds**

Go to **www.investinginbonds.com** to review the information about zero-coupon bonds. Pull down the menu tab to the *Zero Coupon Bonds* link. What are the advantages and disadvantages of zeros for the personal investor? In what situation and for what strategies would an individual bond investor consider zero-coupon bonds?

portfolios only for parallel shifts in the yield curve. Clearly, this sort of restriction is un-realistic. As a result, much work has been devoted to generalizing the notion of duration. Multifactor duration models have been developed to allow for tilts and other distortions in the shape of the yield curve, in addition to shifts in its level. However, it does not appear that the added complexity of such models pays off in terms of substantially greater effectiveness.[10]

Finally, immunization can be an inappropriate goal in an inflationary environment. Immunization is essentially a nominal notion and makes sense only for nominal liabilities. It makes no sense to immunize a projected obligation that will grow with the price level using nominal assets such as bonds. For example, if your child will attend college in 15 years and if the annual cost of tuition is expected to be $40,000 at that time, immunizing your portfolio at a locked-in terminal value of $40,000 is not necessarily a risk-reducing strategy. The tuition obligation will vary with the realized inflation rate, whereas the asset portfolio's final value will not. In the end, the tuition obligation will not necessarily be matched by the value of the portfolio.

## 16.4   ACTIVE BOND MANAGEMENT

### Sources of Potential Profit

Broadly speaking, there are two sources of potential value in active bond management. The first is interest rate forecasting, which tries to anticipate movements across the entire spectrum of the fixed-income market. If interest rate declines are anticipated, managers will increase portfolio duration (and vice versa). The second source of potential profit is identification of relative mispricing within the fixed-income market. An analyst, for example, might believe that the default premium on one particular bond is unnecessarily large and therefore that the bond is underpriced.

These techniques will generate abnormal returns only if the analyst's information or insight is superior to that of the market. You cannot profit from knowledge that rates are about to fall if prices already reflect this information. You know this from our discussion of market efficiency. Valuable information is differential information. In this context it is worth noting that interest rate forecasters have a notoriously poor track record. If you consider this record, you will approach attempts to time the bond market with caution.

Homer and Liebowitz (see footnote 2) coined a popular taxonomy of active bond portfolio strategies. They characterize portfolio rebalancing activities as one of four types of *bond swaps*. In the first two swaps the investor typically believes that the yield relationship between bonds or sectors is only temporarily out of alignment. When the aberration is eliminated, gains can be realized on the underpriced bond. The period of realignment is called the *workout period*.

1. The **substitution swap** is an exchange of one bond for a nearly identical substitute. The substituted bonds should be of essentially equal coupon, maturity, quality, call features, sinking fund provisions, and so on. This swap would be motivated by a belief that the market has temporarily mispriced the two bonds, and that the discrepancy between the prices of the bonds represents a profit opportunity.

   An example of a substitution swap would be a sale of a 20-year maturity, 9% coupon Ford bond callable after 5 years at $1,050 that is priced to provide a yield to

---

[10] G. O. Bierwag, G. C. Kaufman, and A. Toevs, eds., *Innovations in Bond Portfolio Management: Duration Analysis and Immunization* (Greenwich, CT: JAI Press, 1983).

maturity of 9.05%, coupled with a purchase of a 9% coupon GM bond with the same call provisions and time to maturity that yields 9.15%. If the bonds have about the same credit rating, there is no apparent reason for the GM bonds to provide a higher yield. Therefore, the higher yield actually available in the market makes the GM bond seem relatively attractive. Of course, the equality of credit risk is an important condition. If the GM bond is in fact riskier, then its higher yield does not represent a bargain.

2. The **intermarket spread swap** is pursued when an investor believes that the yield spread between two sectors of the bond market is temporarily out of line. For example, if the current spread between corporate and government bonds is considered too wide and is expected to narrow, the investor will shift from government bonds into corporate bonds. If the yield spread does in fact narrow, corporates will outperform governments. For example, if the yield spread between 10-year Treasury bonds and 10-year Baa-rated corporate bonds is now 3%, and the historical spread has been only 2%, an investor might consider selling holdings of Treasury bonds and replacing them with corporates. If the yield spread eventually narrows, the Baa-rated corporate bonds will outperform the Treasuries.

   Of course, the investor must consider carefully whether there is a good reason that the yield spread seems out of alignment. For example, the default premium on corporate bonds might have increased because the market is expecting a severe recession. In this case, the wider spread would not represent attractive pricing of corporates relative to Treasuries, but would simply be an adjustment for a perceived increase in credit risk.

3. The **rate anticipation swap** is pegged to interest rate forecasting. In this case if investors believe that rates will fall, they will swap into bonds of longer duration. Conversely, when rates are expected to rise, they will swap into shorter duration bonds. For example, the investor might sell a 5-year maturity Treasury bond, replacing it with a 25-year maturity Treasury bond. The new bond has the same lack of credit risk as the old one, but has longer duration.

4. The **pure yield pickup swap** is pursued not in response to perceived mispricing, but as a means of increasing return by holding higher-yield bonds. When the yield curve is upward sloping, the yield pickup swap entails moving into longer-term bonds. This must be viewed as an attempt to earn an expected term premium in higher-yield bonds. The investor is willing to bear the interest rate risk that this strategy entails. The investor who swaps the shorter-term bond for the longer one will earn a higher rate of return as long as the yield curve does not shift up during the holding period. Of course if it does, the longer-duration bond will suffer a greater capital loss.

We can add a fifth swap, called a **tax swap**, to this list. This simply refers to a swap to exploit some tax advantage. For example, an investor may swap from one bond that has decreased in price to another if realization of capital losses is advantageous for tax purposes.

**Horizon Analysis**    One form of interest rate forecasting is called **horizon analysis**. The analyst using this approach selects a particular holding period and predicts the yield curve at the end of that period. Given a bond's time to maturity at the end of the holding period, its yield can be read from the predicted yield curve and its end-of-period price calculated. Then the analyst adds the coupon income and prospective capital gain of the bond to obtain the total return on the bond over the holding period.

**EXAMPLE 16.6    Horizon Analysis**

A 20-year maturity bond with a 10% coupon rate (paid annually) currently sells at a yield to maturity of 9%. A portfolio manager with a 2-year horizon needs to forecast the total return on the bond over the coming 2 years. In 2 years, the bond will have an 18-year maturity. The analyst forecasts that 2 years from now, 18-year bonds will sell at yields to maturity of 8%, and that coupon payments can be reinvested in short-term securities over the coming 2 years at a rate of 7%.

To calculate the 2-year return on the bond, the analyst would perform the following calculations:

1. Current price = $100 × Annuity factor(9%, 20 years) + $1,000 × PV factor
(9%, 20 years)
= $1,091.29

2. Forecast price = $100 × Annuity factor(8%, 18 years) + $1,000 × PV factor
(8%, 18 years)
= $1,187.44

3. The future value of reinvested coupons will be ($100 × 1.07) + $100 = $207

4. The 2-year return is $\dfrac{\$207 + (\$1,187.44 - \$1,091.29)}{\$1,091.29} = 0.278$, or 27.8%

The annualized rate of return over the 2-year period would then be $(1.278)^{1/2} - 1 = 0.13$, or 13%.

---

**CONCEPT CHECK ☞ QUESTION 7**

Consider a 30-year, annual pay 8% coupon bond currently selling at $925. The analyst believes that in 2 years the yield on 28-year bonds will be 8.3%. Should she purchase the 20-year bond of Example 16.6 or the 30-year bond?

---

**Contingent Immunization**

**Contingent immunization** is a mixed passive-active strategy suggested by Liebowitz and Weinberger.[11] To illustrate, suppose that interest rates currently are 10% and that a manager's portfolio is worth $10 million right now. At current rates the manager could lock in, via conventional immunization techniques, a future portfolio value of $12.1 million after 2 years. Now suppose that the manager wishes to pursue active management but is willing to risk losses only to the extent that the terminal value of the portfolio would not drop lower than $11 million. Because only $9.09 million (i.e., the present value of $11 million, or $11 million/1.10²) is required to achieve this minimum acceptable terminal value, and the portfolio currently is worth $10 million, the manager can afford to risk some losses at the outset and might start off with an active strategy rather than immediately immunizing.

The key is to calculate the funds required to lock in via immunization a future value of $11 million at current rates. If $T$ denotes the time left until the horizon date, and $r$ is the market interest rate at any particular time, then the value of the fund necessary to guarantee an ability to reach the minimum acceptable terminal value is $11 million/$(1 + r)^T$, because this size portfolio, if immunized, will grow risk-free to $11 million by the horizon date.

---

[11] Martin L. Liebowitz and Alfred Weinberger, "Contingent Immunization—Part I: Risk Control Procedures," *Financial Analysts Journal* 38 (November–December 1982).

This value becomes the trigger point: If and when the actual portfolio value dips to the trigger point, active management will cease. *Contingent* upon reaching the trigger, an immunization strategy is initiated instead, guaranteeing that the minimal acceptable performance can be realized.

Figure 16.10 illustrates two possible outcomes in a contingent immunization strategy. In Figure 16.10A, the portfolio falls in value and hits the trigger at time $t^*$. At that point, immunization is pursued and the portfolio rises smoothly to the $11 million terminal value. In Figure 16.10B, the portfolio does well, never reaches the trigger point, and is worth more than $11 million at the horizon date.

<table>
<tr><td>**CONCEPT CHECK ☞ QUESTION 8**</td><td>**What would be the trigger point with a 3-year horizon, an interest rate of 12%, and a minimum acceptable terminal value of $10 million?**</td></tr>
</table>

**Figure 16.10 Contingent immunization**

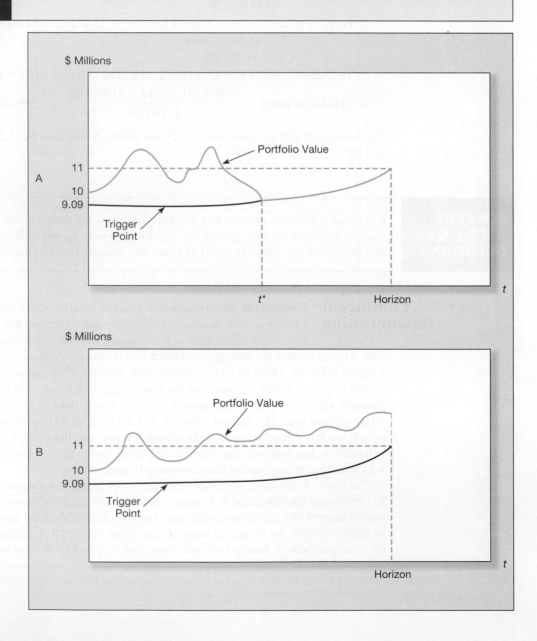

# 16.5    INTEREST RATE SWAPS

An **interest rate swap** is a contract between two parties to exchange a series of cash flows similar to those that would result if the parties instead were to exchange equal dollar values of different types of bonds. Swaps arose originally as a means of managing interest rate risk. The volume of swaps has increased from virtually zero in 1980 to about $60 trillion today. (Interest rate swaps do not have anything to do with the Homer-Liebowitz bond swap taxonomy set out earlier.)

**EXAMPLE 16.7**    **Interest Rate Swap**

Consider the manager of a large portfolio that currently includes $100 million par value of long-term bonds paying an average coupon rate of 7%. The manager believes that interest rates are about to rise. As a result, he would like to sell the bonds and replace them with either short-term or floating-rate issues. However, it would be exceedingly expensive in terms of transaction costs to replace the portfolio every time the forecast for interest rates is updated. A cheaper and more flexible way to modify the portfolio is for the managers to "swap" the $7 million a year in interest income the portfolio currently generates for an amount of money that is tied to the short-term interest rate. That way, if rates do rise, so will the portfolio's interest income.

A swap dealer might advertise its willingness to exchange, or "swap," a cash flow based on the 6-month LIBOR rate for one based on a fixed rate of 7%. (The LIBOR, or London Interbank Offered Rate, is the interest rate at which banks borrow from each other in the Eurodollar market. It is the most commonly used short-term interest rate in the swap market.) The portfolio manager would then enter into a swap agreement with the dealer to *pay* 7% on **notional principal** of $100 million and *receive* payment of the LIBOR rate on that amount of notional principal.[12] In other words, the manager swaps a payment of .07 × $100 million for a payment of LIBOR × $100 million. The manager's *net* cash flow from the swap agreement is therefore (LIBOR − .07) × $100 million. Note that the swap arrangement does not mean that a loan has been made. The participants have agreed only to exchange a fixed cash flow for a variable one.

Now consider the net cash flow to the manager's portfolio in three interest rate scenarios:

|  | LIBOR Rate | | |
| --- | :---: | :---: | :---: |
|  | **6.5%** | **7.0%** | **7.5%** |
| Interest income from bond portfolio<br>(= 7% of $100 million bond portfolio) | $7,000,000 | $7,000,000 | $7,000,000 |
| Cash flow from swap<br>[= (LIBOR − 7%) × notional principal of $100 million] | (500,000) | 0 | 500,000 |
| Total (= LIBOR × $100 million) | $6,500,000 | $7,000,000 | $7,500,000 |

Notice that the total income on the overall position—bonds plus swap agreement—is now equal to the LIBOR rate in each scenario times $100 million. The manager has, in effect, converted a fixed-rate bond portfolio into a synthetic floating-rate portfolio.

---

[12] The participants to the swap do not loan each other money. They agree only to exchange a fixed cash flow for a variable cash flow that depends on the short-term interest rate. This is why the principal is described as *notional*. The notional principal is simply a way to describe the size of the swap agreement. In this example, the parties to the swap exchange a 7% fixed rate for the LIBOR rate; the difference between LIBOR and 7% is multiplied by notional principal to determine the cash flow exchanged by the parties.

## Swaps and Balance Sheet Restructuring

Example 16.7 illustrates why swaps have tremendous appeal to fixed-income managers. These contracts provide a means to quickly, cheaply, and anonymously restructure the balance sheet. Suppose a corporation that has issued fixed-rate debt believes that interest rates are likely to fall; it might prefer to have issued floating-rate debt. In principle, it could issue floating-rate debt and use the proceeds to buy back the outstanding fixed-rate debt. In practice, however, this would be enormously expensive in terms of transaction costs. Instead, the firm can convert the outstanding fixed-rate debt into synthetic floating-rate debt by entering a swap to receive a fixed interest rate (offsetting its fixed-rate coupon obligation) and paying a floating rate.

Conversely, a bank that pays current market interest rates to its depositors, and thus is exposed to increases in rates, might wish to convert some of its financing to a fixed-rate basis. It would enter a swap to receive a floating rate and pay a fixed rate on some amount of notional principle. This swap position, added to its floating-rate deposit liability, would result in a net liability of a fixed stream of cash. The bank might then be able to invest in long-term fixed-rate loans without encountering interest rate risk.

As a final example, consider a fixed-income portfolio manager. Swaps enable the manager to switch back and forth between a fixed- or floating-rate profile quickly and cheaply as forecast for interest rate changes. A manager who holds a fixed-rate portfolio can transform it into a synthetic floating-rate portfolio by entering a pay fixed–receive floating swap and can later transform it back by entering the opposite side of a similar swap.

## The Swap Dealer

What about the swap dealer? Why is the dealer, which is typically a financial intermediary such as a bank, willing to take on the opposite side of the swaps desired by these participants in these hypothetical swaps?

Consider a dealer who takes on one side of a swap, let's say paying LIBOR and receiving a fixed rate. The dealer will search for another trader in the swap market who wishes to receive a fixed rate and pay LIBOR. For example, Company A may have issued a 7% coupon fixed-rate bond that it wishes to convert into synthetic floating-rate debt, while Company B may have issued a floating-rate bond tied to LIBOR that it wishes to convert into synthetic fixed-rate debt. The dealer will enter a swap with Company A in which it pays a fixed rate and receives LIBOR, and will enter another swap with Company B in which it pays LIBOR and receives a fixed rate. When the two swaps are combined, the dealer's position is effectively neutral on interest rates, paying LIBOR on one swap and receiving it on another. Similarly, the dealer pays a fixed rate on one swap and receives it on another. The dealer becomes little more than an intermediary, funneling payments from one party to the other.[13] The dealer finds this activity profitable because it will charge a bid–asked spread on the transaction.

This rearrangement is illustrated in Figure 16.11. Company A has issued 7% fixed-rate debt (the leftmost arrow in the figure) but enters a swap to pay the dealer LIBOR and receive a 6.95% fixed rate. Therefore, the company's net payment is 7% + (LIBOR − 6.95%) = LIBOR + .05%. It has thus transformed its fixed-rate debt into synthetic floating-rate debt. Conversely, Company B has issued floating-rate debt paying LIBOR (the rightmost arrow), but enters a swap to pay a 7.05% fixed rate in return for LIBOR. Therefore, its net payment is LIBOR + (7.05% − LIBOR) = 7.05%. It has thus transformed its

---

[13] Actually, things are a bit more complicated. The dealer is more than just an intermediary because it bears the credit risk that one or the other of the parties to the swap might default on the obligation. Referring to Figure 16.11, if firm A defaults on its obligation, for example, the swap dealer still must maintain its commitment to firm B. In this sense, the dealer does more than simply pass through cash flows to the other swap participants.

**Figure 16.11   Interest rate swap. Company B pays a fixed rate of 7.05% to the swap dealer in return for LIBOR. Company A receives 6.95% from the dealer in return for LIBOR. The swap dealer realizes a cash flow each period equal to .10% of notional principal.**

floating-rate debt into synthetic fixed-rate debt. The bid–asked spread, the source of the dealer's profit, in the example illustrated in Figure 16.11 is .10% of notional principal each year.

**CONCEPT CHECK☞ QUESTION 9**

A pension fund holds a portfolio of money market securities that the manager believes are paying excellent yields compared to other comparable-risk short-term securities. However, the manager believes that interest rates are about to fall. What type of swap will allow the fund to continue to hold its portfolio of short-term securities while at the same time benefiting from a decline in rates?

## 16.6   FINANCIAL ENGINEERING AND INTEREST RATE DERIVATIVES

New financial instruments created through financial engineering can have highly unusual risk and return characteristics that offer both opportunities and challenges for fixed-income portfolio managers. To illustrate the possibilities opened up by financial engineering, consider the inverse floater, which is a bond that pays a *lower* coupon payment when a reference interest rate rises. For example, an inverse floater may pay a coupon rate equal to 10% *minus* the rate on 1-year Treasury bills. Therefore, if the T-bill rate is 4%, the bond will pay interest income equal to 10% − 4% = 6% of par value. You can see that such a bond will have an interest rate sensitivity much greater than that of a fixed-rate bond with comparable maturity. If the T-bill rate rises, say to 7%, the inverse floater's coupon payments fall to 3% of par value; in addition, as other interest rates rise along with the T-bill rate, the bond price falls as well for the usual reason that future cash flows are discounted at higher rates. Therefore, there is a dual impact on value and these securities perform especially poorly when interest rates rise. Conversely, inverse floaters perform especially well when rates fall: Coupon payments rise, even as the discount rate falls.

While firms do not commonly issue inverse floaters, they may be created synthetically by allocating the cash flows from a fixed-rate security into two *derivative* securities. An investment banking firm can buy a bond issue and carve the original security into a floating-rate note and an inverse floater. The floater will receive interest payments that rise when the

T-bill rate rises; the inverse floater will receive interest payments that fall when the T-bill rate rises. The sum of the interest payments due to the two classes of securities is fixed and equal to the interest from the original bond, the primary asset.

**EXAMPLE 16.8    Inverse Floater**

Consider a $100 million par value, 20-year maturity bond with a coupon rate of 8%. The bond issue therefore pays total interest of $8 million annually. An investment banking firm might arrange to use the cash flows from the underlying bond to support issues of a floating-rate note and an inverse floater. The floating-rate notes might be issued with aggregate par value of $60 million and a coupon level equal to the T-bill rate plus 1%. If the T-bill rate currently is 6%, therefore, the coupon rate on the floater would be 7% and total interest payments would be $.07 \times \$60$ million $= \$4.2$ million. This leaves $8 million − $4.2 million = $3.8 million available to pay interest on the interest floater. The coupon rate on the inverse floater might be set at $18.5\% - 1.5 \times$ (T-bill rate), which at the current T-bill rate equals 9.5%. Therefore, the coupon income flowing to the inverse floater is 9.5% of $40 million, or $3.8 million, which just absorbs the remaining interest flowing from the original bond.

Now suppose that in 1 year, the T-bill rate has increased by 1%. The coupon rate on the floater increases to 8%, while the coupon rate on the inverse floater falls to $18.5\% - 1.5 \times 7\% = 8\%$. Again, total interest paid on the two derivative securities sums to $8 million: $.08 \times \$60$ million $+ .08 \times \$40$ million $= \$8$ million. However, the value of the inverse floater falls precipitously: Not only are market interest rates higher (which makes the present value of any future cash flow lower), but the coupon rate on the bond has fallen from 9.5% to 8%.[14] Therefore, the inverse floater will have extreme interest rate sensitivity. When rates fall, its performance will be spectacular, but when rates rise, its performance will be disastrous.

The inverse floater is an example of an interest rate derivative product created by financial engineering in which the cash flows from the original bond are unbundled and reallocated to the floater and inverse floater. Because of the impact of interest rates on its coupon rate, the inverse floater will have a very large effective duration, in fact much longer than the maturity of the bond. This property can be useful to investors who wish to immunize very long duration liabilities; it is also obviously useful to investors who wish to speculate on decreases in interest rates.

Inverse floaters are not the only financially engineered products with dramatic dependence on interest rates. In Chapters 1 and 2, we introduced you to derivative securities created by allocating the cash flows from mortgage-backed securities into various CMO (collateralized mortgage obligation) tranches. Some of the more popular mortgage derivative products are interest-only and principal-only strips. The interest-only (IO) strip gets all the interest payments from the mortgage pool and the principal-only (PO) strip gets all the principal payments. Both of these mortgage strips have extreme and interesting interest rate exposures. In both cases, the sensitivity is due to the effect of mortgage prepayments on the cash flows accruing to the security holder.

---

[14] If the T-bill rate increases beyond 12.33%, the formula for the inverse floater's coupon would call for a negative coupon rate. However, in practice, the inverse floater provides that the coupon rate may never fall below zero. This floor on the coupon rate of the inverse floater necessitates a ceiling on the coupon rate of the floater. The total interest paid by the two securities is constrained to equal the interest provided by the underlying bond.

PO securities, like inverse floaters, exhibit very long effective durations; that is, their values are very sensitive to interest rate fluctuations. When interest rates fall and mortgage holders prepay their mortgages, PO holders receive their principal payments much earlier than initially anticipated. Therefore, the payments are discounted for fewer years than expected and have much higher present value. Hence PO strips perform extremely well when rates fall. Conversely, interest rate increases slow mortgage prepayments and reduce the value of PO strips.

The prices of interest-only strips, on the other hand, fall when interest rates fall. This is because mortgage prepayments abruptly end the flow of interest payments accruing to IO security holders. Because rising rates discourage prepayments, they increase the value of IO strips. Thus IOs have *negative* effective durations. They are good investments for an investor who wishes to bet on an increase in rates, or they can be useful for hedging the value of a conventional fixed-income portfolio.

There are still other ways to make highly sensitive bets on the direction of interest rates. Some of these are custom-designed swaps in which the cash flow paid by one party to the swap varies dramatically with the level of some reference interest rate. Such swaps made news in 1994 when Procter & Gamble lost more than $100 million in an interest rate swap that obligated it to make payments that exploded when interest rates increased. In the wake of its losses, P&G sued Bankers Trust, which sold it the swap, claiming that it was misled about the risks of the swap.

Interest rate derivatives are not necessarily bad, or even dangerous, investments. The dramatic sensitivity of their prices to interest rate fluctuations can be useful for hedging as well as for speculation. They can be potent risk management as well as risk-increasing tools. One Wall Street observer has compared them to power tools: When used well by a trained expert, they can serve a valuable function, but in untrained hands, they can lead to severe damage.

## SUMMARY

1. Even default free bonds such as Treasury issues are subject to interest rate risk. Longer-term bonds generally are more sensitive to interest rate shifts than are short-term bonds. A measure of the average life of a bond is Macaulay's duration, defined as the weighted average of the times until each payment made by the security, with weights proportional to the present value of the payment.

2. Duration is a direct measure of the sensitivity of a bond's price to a change in its yield. The proportional change in a bond's price equals the negative of duration multiplied by the proportional change in $1 + y$.

3. Convexity refers to the curvature of a bond's price-yield relationship. Accounting for convexity can substantially improve on the accuracy of the duration approximation for bond price sensitivity to changes in yields.

4. Immunization strategies are characteristic of passive fixed-income portfolio management. Such strategies attempt to render the individual or firm immune from movements in interest rates. This may take the form of immunizing net worth or, instead, immunizing the future accumulated value of a fixed-income portfolio.

5. Immunization of a fully funded plan is accomplished by matching the durations of assets and liabilities. To maintain an immunized position as time passes and interest rates change, the portfolio must be periodically rebalanced. Classic immunization also depends on parallel shifts in a flat yield curve. Given that this assumption is unrealistic, immunization generally will be less than complete. To mitigate the problem, multifactor duration models can be used to allow for variation in the shape of the yield curve.

Visit us at www.mhhe.com/bkm

6. A more direct form of immunization is dedication, or cash flow matching. If a portfolio is perfectly matched in cash flow with projected liabilities, rebalancing will be unnecessary.

7. Active bond management consists of interest rate forecasting techniques and intermarket spread analysis. One popular taxonomy classifies active strategies as substitution swaps, intermarket spread swaps, rate anticipation swaps, or pure yield pickup swaps.

8. Horizon analysis is a type of interest rate forecasting. In this procedure the analyst forecasts the position of the yield curve at the end of some holding period, and from that yield curve predicts corresponding bond prices. Bonds then can be ranked according to expected total returns (coupon plus capital gain) over the holding period.

9. Interest rate swaps are major recent developments in the fixed-income market. In these arrangements parties trade the cash flows of different securities without actually exchanging any securities directly. This is a useful tool to manage the interest-rate exposure of a portfolio.

10. Financial engineering has created many new fixed-income derivative assets with novel risk characteristics.

## KEY TERMS

| | | |
|---|---|---|
| Macaulay's duration | cash flow matching | tax swap |
| modified duration | dedication strategy | horizon analysis |
| convexity | substitution swap | contingent immunization |
| effective duration | intermarket spread swap | interest rate swap |
| immunization | rate anticipation swap | notional principal |
| rebalancing | pure yield pickup swap | |

## WEBSITES

www.about.com
This site contains links to many facets of the fixed-income market. Enter "bonds" in the input box.

bonds.yahoo.com/calculator.html
bonds.yahoo.com
Yahoo! has general information, a bond market glossary, and several bond calculators.

www.smartmoney.com/bonds
This site has several tools that apply to concepts covered in this chapter, among them a template for analyzing interest rate swaps and a portfolio allocation model that allows you to enter information concerning your expectations and risk aversion.

webster.directhit.com/webster/search.aspx?qry=Bond+Duration
webster.directhit.com/webster/search.aspx?qry=Bond+Portfolio+Management&meta=rs
*Ask Jeeves* about bond duration. This site provides helpful information and discussions about duration, and bond portfolio management.

**PROBLEMS**

1. A 9-year bond has a yield of 10% and a duration of 7.194 years. If the market yield changes by 50 basis points, what is the percentage change in the bond's price?

2. Find the duration of a 6% coupon bond making *annual* coupon payments if it has 3 years until maturity and has a yield to maturity of 6%. What is the duration if the yield to maturity is 10%?

3. Find the duration of the bond in problem 2 if the coupons are paid semiannually.

4. Rank the durations or effective durations of the following pairs of bonds:

   *a.* Bond *A* is an 8% coupon bond, with a 20-year time to maturity selling at par value. Bond *B* is an 8% coupon bond, with a 20-year maturity time selling below par value.

   *b.* Bond *A* is a 20-year noncallable coupon bond with a coupon rate of 8%, selling at par. Bond *B* is a 20-year callable bond with a coupon rate of 9%, also selling at par.

5. An insurance company must make payments to a customer of $10 million in 1 year and $4 million in 5 years. The yield curve is flat at 10%.

   *a.* If it wants to fully fund and immunize its obligation to this customer with a *single* issue of a zero-coupon bond, what maturity bond must it purchase?

   *b.* What must be the face value and market value of that zero-coupon bond?

6. *a.* Explain the impact on the offering yield of adding a call feature to a proposed bond issue.

   *b.* Explain the impact on *both* effective bond duration and convexity of adding a call feature to a proposed bond issue.

7. Long-term Treasury bonds currently are selling at yields to maturity of nearly 8%. You expect interest rates to fall. The rest of the market thinks that they will remain unchanged over the coming year. In each question, choose the bond that will provide the higher holding-period return over the next year if you are correct. Briefly explain your answer.

   *a.*  i. A Baa-rated bond with coupon rate 8% and time to maturity 20 years.
       ii. An Aaa-rated bond with coupon rate of 8% and time to maturity 20 years.

   *b.*  i. An A-rated bond with coupon rate 4% and maturity 20 years, callable at 105.
       ii. An A-rated bond with coupon rate 8% and maturity 20 years, callable at 105.

   *c.*  i. A 6% coupon noncallable T-bond with maturity 20 years and YTM = 8%.
       ii. A 9% coupon noncallable T-bond with maturity 20 years and YTM = 8%.

8. The following questions are from past CFA examinations.

   *a.* A 6% coupon bond paying interest annually has a modified duration of 10 years, sells for $800, and is priced at a yield to maturity of 8%. If the YTM increases to 9%, the predicted change in price, using the duration concept, decreases by:

    i. $76.56
    ii. $76.92
    iii. $77.67
    iv. $80.00

  *b.* A 6% coupon bond with semiannual coupons has a convexity (in years) of 120, sells for 80% of par, and is priced at a yield to maturity of 8%. If the YTM increases to 9.5%, the predicted contribution to the percentage change in price, due to convexity, would be:
    i. 1.08%
    ii. 1.35%
    iii. 2.48%
    iv. 7.35%

  *c.* Which statement is true for the Macaulay duration of a zero-coupon bond? The Macaulay duration of a zero-coupon bond:
    i. Is equal to the bond's maturity in years.
    ii. Is equal to one-half the bond's maturity in years.
    iii. Is equal to the bond's maturity in years divided by its yield to maturity.
    iv. Cannot be calculated because of the lack of coupons.

  *d.* A bond with annual coupon payments has a coupon rate of 8%, yield to maturity of 10%, and Macaulay duration of 9. The bond's modified duration is:
    i. 8.18
    ii. 8.33
    iii. 9.78
    iv. 10.00

  *e.* The interest rate risk of a bond normally is:
    i. Greater for shorter maturities.
    ii. Lower for longer duration.
    iii. Lower for higher coupons.
    iv. None of the above.

  *f.* When interest rates decline, the duration of a 30-year bond selling at a premium:
    i. Increases.
    ii. Decreases.
    iii. Remains the same.
    iv. Increases at first, then declines.

  *g.* If a bond manager swaps a bond for one that is identical in terms of coupon rate, maturity, and credit quality but offers a higher yield to maturity, the swap is:
    i. A substitution swap.
    ii. An interest rate anticipation swap.
    iii. A tax swap.
    iv. An intermarket spread swap.

  *h.* Which bond has the longest duration?
    i. 8-year maturity, 6% coupon.
    ii. 8-year maturity, 11% coupon.
    iii. 15-year maturity, 6% coupon.
    iv. 15-year maturity, 11% coupon.

9. Currently, the term structure is as follows: 1-year bonds yield 7%, 2-year bonds yield 8%, 3-year bonds and longer maturity bonds all yield 9%. An investor is choosing between 1-, 2-, and 3-year maturity bonds all paying annual coupons of 8%, once a year. Which bond should you buy if you strongly believe that at year-end the yield curve will be flat at 9%?

10. Philip Morris has issued bonds that pay annually with the following characteristics:

| Coupon | Yield to Maturity | Maturity | Macaulay Duration |
|---|---|---|---|
| 8% | 8% | 15 years | 10 years |

  a. Calculate modified duration using the information above.
  b. Explain why modified duration is a better measure than maturity when calculating the bond's sensitivity to changes in interest rates.
  c. Identify the direction of change in modified duration if:
   i. The coupon of the bond were 4%, not 8%.
   ii. The maturity of the bond were 7 years, not 15 years.
  d. Define convexity and explain how modified duration and convexity are used to approximate the bond's percentage change in price, given a change in interest rates.

11. You will be paying $10,000 a year in tuition expenses at the end of the next 2 years. Bonds currently yield 8%.

  a. What is the present value and duration of your obligation?
  b. What maturity zero-coupon bond would immunize your obligation?
  c. Suppose you buy a zero-coupon bond with value and duration equal to your obligation. Now suppose that rates immediately increase to 9%. What happens to your net position, that is, to the difference between the value of the bond and that of your tuition obligation? What if rates fall to 7%?

12. Several Investment Committee members have asked about interest rate swap agreements and how are they used in the management of domestic fixed-income portfolios.

  a. Define an interest rate swap and briefly describe the obligation of each party involved.
  b. Cite and explain two examples of how interest rate swaps could be used by a fixed-income portfolio manager to control risk or improve return.

13. What type of interest rate swap would be appropriate for a corporation holding long-term assets that it funded with floating-rate bonds?

14. Bonds of Zello Corporation with a par value of $1,000 sell for $960, mature in 5 years, and have a 7% annual coupon rate paid semiannually.

  a. Calculate the:
   i. Current yield;
   ii. Yield-to-maturity (to the nearest whole percent, i.e., 3%, 4%, 5%, etc.); and
   iii. Horizon yield (also called total return) for an investor with a 3-year holding period and a reinvestment rate of 6% over the period. At the end of 3 years the 7% coupon bonds with 2 years remaining will sell to yield 7%.
  b. Cite one major shortcoming for each of the following fixed-income yield measures:
   i. Current yield;
   ii. Yield to maturity; and
   iii. Horizon yield (also called total return).

15. A corporation has issued a $10 million issue of floating-rate bonds on which it pays an interest rate 1% over the LIBOR rate. The bonds are selling at par value. The firm is worried that rates are about to rise, and it would like to lock in a fixed interest rate on its borrowings. The firm sees that dealers in the swap market are offering

Visit us at www.mhhe.com/bkm

swaps of LIBOR for 7%. What interest rate swap will convert the firm's interest obligation into one resembling a synthetic fixed-rate loan? What interest rate will it pay on that synthetic fixed-rate loan?

16. Pension funds pay lifetime annuities to recipients. If a firm will remain in business indefinitely, the pension obligation will resemble a perpetuity. Suppose, therefore, that you are managing a pension fund with obligations to make perpetual payments of $2 million per year to beneficiaries. The yield to maturity on all bonds is 16%.

    a. If the duration of 5-year maturity bonds with coupon rates of 12% (paid annually) is 4 years and the duration of 20-year maturity bonds with coupon rates of 6% (paid annually) is 11 years, how much of each of these coupon bonds (in market value) will you want to hold to both fully fund and immunize your obligation?

    b. What will be the par value of your holdings in the 20-year coupon bond?

17. You are managing a portfolio of $1 million. Your target duration is 10 years, and you can choose from two bonds: a zero-coupon bond with maturity of 5 years, and a perpetuity, each currently yielding 5%.

    a. How much of each bond will you hold in your portfolio?

    b. How will these fractions change *next year* if target duration is now 9 years?

18. My pension plan will pay me $10,000 once a year for a 10-year period. The first payment will come in exactly 5 years. The pension fund wants to immunize its position.

    a. What is the duration of its obligation to me? The current interest rate is 10% per year.

    b. If the plan uses 5-year and 20-year zero-coupon bonds to construct the immunized position, how much money ought to be placed in each bond? What will be the *face value* of the holdings in each zero?

19. One common goal among fixed-income portfolio managers is to earn high incremental returns on corporate bonds versus government bonds of comparable durations. The approach of some corporate-bond portfolio managers is to find and purchase those corporate bonds having the largest initial spreads over comparable-duration government bonds. John Ames, HFS's fixed-income manager, believes that a more rigorous approach is required if incremental returns are to be maximized.

    The following table presents data relating to one set of corporate/government spread relationships present in the market at a given date:

### Current and Expected Spreads and Durations of High-Grade Corporate Bonds (1-Year Horizon)

| Bond Rating | Initial Spread over Governments | Expected Horizon Spread | Initial Duration | Expected Duration 1 Year from Now |
|---|---|---|---|---|
| Aaa | 31 b.p. | 31 b.p. | 4 years | 3.1 years |
| Aa | 40 b.p. | 50 b.p. | 4 years | 3.1 years |

Note: 1 b.p. means 1 basis point, or .01%.

    a. Recommend purchase of *either* Aaa *or* Aa bonds for a 1-year investment horizon given a goal of maximizing incremental returns.

Ames chooses not to rely *solely* on initial spread relationships. His analytical framework considers a full range of other key variables likely to impact realized incremental returns, including call provisions and potential changes in interest rates.

b. Describe variables, *in addition to those identified above,* that Ames should include in his analysis *and* explain how *each* of these could cause realized incremental returns to differ from those indicated by initial spread relationships.

20. A 30-year maturity bond making annual coupon payments with a coupon rate of 12% has duration of 11.54 years and convexity of 192.4. The bond currently sells at a yield to maturity of 8%. Use a financial calculator or spreadsheet to find the price of the bond if its yield to maturity falls to 7% or rises to 9%. What prices for the bond at these new yields would be predicted by the duration rule and the duration-with-convexity rule? What is the percentage error for each rule? What do you conclude about the accuracy of the two rules?

21. A 12.75-year maturity zero-coupon bond selling at a yield to maturity of 8% (effective annual yield) has convexity of 150.3 and modified duration of 11.81 years. A 30-year maturity 6% coupon bond making annual coupon payments also selling at a yield to maturity of 8% has nearly identical duration—11.79 years—but considerably higher convexity of 231.2.

a. Suppose the yield to maturity on both bonds increases to 9%. What will be the actual percentage capital loss on each bond? What percentage capital loss would be predicted by the duration-with-convexity rule?

b. Repeat part (*a*), but this time assume the yield to maturity decreases to 7%.

c. Compare the performance of the two bonds in the two scenarios, one involving an increase in rates, the other a decrease. Based on the comparative investment performance, explain the attraction of convexity.

d. In view of your answer to (*c*), do you think it would be possible for two bonds with equal duration but different convexity to be priced initially at the same yield to maturity if the yields on both bonds always increased or decreased by equal amounts, as in this example? Would anyone be willing to buy the bond with lower convexity under these circumstances?

22. A newly issued bond has a maturity of 10 years and pays a 7% coupon rate (with coupon payments coming once annually). The bond sells at par value.

a. What are the convexity and the duration of the bond? Use the formula for convexity in footnote 5.

b. Find the actual price of the bond assuming that its yield to maturity immediately increases from 7% to 8% (with maturity still 10 years).

c. What price would be predicted by the duration rule (equation 16.3)? What is the percentage error of that rule?

d. What price would be predicted by the duration-with-convexity rule (equation 16.8)? What is the percentage error of that rule?

23. Patrick Wall is considering the purchase of one of the two bonds described in the following table. Wall realizes his decision will depend primarily on effective duration, and he believes that interest rates will decline by 50 basis points at all maturities over the next 6 months.

| Characteristic | CIC | PTR |
|---|---|---|
| Market price | 101.75 | 101.75 |
| Maturity date | June 1, 2012 | June 1, 2012 |
| Call date | Noncallable | June 1, 2007 |
| Annual coupon | 6.25% | 7.35% |
| Interest payment | Semiannual | Semiannual |
| Effective duration | 7.35 | 5.40 |
| Yield to maturity | 6.02% | 7.10% |
| Credit rating | A | A |

a. Calculate the percentage price change forecasted by effective duration for *both* the CIC and PTR bonds if interest rates decline by 50 basis points over the next 6 months.

b. Calculate the 6-month horizon return (in percent) for *each* bond, if the actual CIC bond price equals 105.55 and the actual PTR bond price equals 104.15 at the end of 6 months. Assume you purchased the bonds to settle on June 1, 2002.

c. Wall is surprised by the fact that although interest rates fell by 50 basis points, the actual price change for the CIC bond was greater than the price change forecasted by effective duration, whereas the actual price change for the PTR bond was less than the price change forecasted by effective duration. Explain why the actual price change would be greater for the CIC bond and the actual price change would be less for the PTR bond.

24. You are the manager for the bond portfolio of a pension fund. The policies of the fund allow for the use of active strategies in managing the bond portfolio.

It appears that the economic cycle is beginning to mature, inflation is expected to accelerate, and in an effort to contain the economic expansion, central bank policy is moving toward constraint. For each of the situations below, state which one of the two bonds you would prefer. Briefly justify your answer in each case.

a. Government of Canada (Canadian pay) 7% due in 2006 and priced at 98.75 to yield 7.50% to maturity.

or

Government of Canada (Canadian pay) 7% due in 2014 and priced at 91.75 to yield 8.19% to maturity.

b. Texas Power and Light Co., 6½ due in 2006, rated AAA, and priced at 90 to yield 8.02% to maturity.

or

Arizona Public Service Co. 6.45 due in 2006, rated A–, and priced at 85 to yield 9.05% to maturity.

c. Commonwealth Edison 2¾ due in 2006, rated Baa, and priced at 81 to yield 9.2% to maturity.

or

Commonwealth Edison 12⅜ due in 2006, rated Baa, and priced at 114.40 to yield 9.2% to maturity.

d. Shell Oil Co. 7½ sinking fund debentures due in 2020, rated AAA (sinking fund begins September 2004 at par), and priced at 78 to yield 10.91% to maturity.

or

Warner-Lambert 7⅞ sinking fund debentures due in 2020, rated AAA (sinking fund begins April 2009 at par), and priced at 84 to yield 10.31% to maturity.

e. Bank of Montreal (Canadian pay) 5% certificates of deposit due in 2006, rated AAA, and priced at 100 to yield 5% to maturity.

or

Bank of Montreal (Canadian pay) floating rate-note due in 2011, rated AAA. Coupon currently set at 4.1% and priced at 100 (coupon adjusted semiannually to .5% above the 3-month Government of Canada Treasury bill rate).

25. A member of a firm's investment committee is very interested in learning about the management of fixed-income portfolios. He would like to know how fixed-income managers position portfolios to capitalize on their expectations concerning three factors which influence interest rates:

a. Changes in the level of interest rates.
b. Changes in yield spreads across/between sectors.
c. Changes in yield spreads as to a particular instrument.

Formulate and describe a fixed-income portfolio management strategy for each of these factors that could be used to exploit a portfolio manager's expectations about that factor. (Note: Three strategies are required, one for each of the listed factors.)

26. Prices of long-term bonds are more volatile than prices of short-term bonds. However, yields to maturity of short-term bonds fluctuate more than yields of long-term bonds. How do you reconcile these two empirical observations?

27. A fixed-income portfolio manager is unwilling to realize a rate of return of less than 3% annually over a 5-year investment period on a portfolio currently valued at $1 million. Three years later, the interest rate is 8%. What is the trigger point of the portfolio at this time, that is, how low can the value of the portfolio fall before the manager will be forced to immunize to be assured of achieving the minimum acceptable return?

28. A 30-year maturity bond has a 7% coupon rate, paid annually. It sells today for $867.42. A 20-year maturity bond has 6.5% coupon rate, also paid annually. It sells today for $879.50. A bond market analyst forecasts that in 5 years, 25-year maturity bonds will sell at yields to maturity of 8% and 15-year maturity bonds will sell at yields of 7.5%. Because the yield curve is upward sloping, the analyst believes that coupons will be invested in short-term securities at a rate of 6%. Which bond offers the higher expected rate of return over the 5-year period?

29. Carol Harrod is the investment officer for a $100 million U.S. pension fund. The fixed-income portion of the portfolio is actively managed, and a substantial portion of the fund's large capitalization U.S. equity portfolio is indexed and managed by Webb Street Advisors.

Harrod has been impressed with the investment results of Webb Street's equity index strategy and is considering asking Webb Street to index a portion of the actively managed fixed-income portfolio.

a. Describe advantages and disadvantages of bond indexing relative to active bond management.
b. Webb Street manages indexed bond portfolios. Discuss how an indexed bond portfolio is constructed under stratified sampling (cellular) methods.
c. Describe the main source of tracking error for the cellular method.

30. Fran Arseneault manages investment assets and liabilities for Allied Corporation. Allied's portfolio currently has the following characteristics:
   - $300 million of the assets must be invested short term. These assets currently earn a 6-month LIBOR rate of 5%.
   - $300 million in debt is outstanding; $100 million is 7-year-term fixed at a 6.5% rate and $200 million is short term at the 6-month LIBOR rate.
   a. Describe Arseneault's asset/liability exposure to declining interest rates.
   b. Allied has been unable to issue additional variable rate debt at reasonable fees. Hogan Stanfield Investment Bank stands ready to swap intermediate-term 6.5% fixed for 6-month LIBOR. Devise an appropriate interest rate swap to hedge the firm's interest rate exposure.

31. Acree Corporation issued a floating-rate note that pays 1-year LIBOR + 1% annually. The note has a par value of $100 million and a remaining term of 5 years.
   a. Describe the interest rate risk that Acree faces.
   b. Explain how a plain vanilla interest rate swap can eliminate Acree's interest rate risk.

32. Noah Kramer, a fixed-income portfolio manager based in the country of Sevista, is considering the purchase of a Sevista government bond. Kramer decides to evaluate two strategies for implementing his investment in Sevista bonds. Table 16A gives the details of the two strategies, and Table 16B contains the assumptions that apply to both strategies.

   Before choosing one of the two bond investment strategies, Kramer wants to analyze how the market value of the bonds will change if an instantaneous interest rate shift occurs immediately after his investment. The details of the interest rate shift are shown in Table 16C. Calculate, for the instantaneous interest rate shift shown in Table 16C, the percent change in the market value of the bonds that will occur under each strategy.

33. As part of your analysis of debt issued by Monticello Corporation, you are asked to evaluate two specific bond issues, shown in the table below.

| | Monticello Corporation Bond Information | |
| --- | --- | --- |
| | Bond A (Callable) | Bond B (Noncallable) |
| Maturity | 2010 | 2010 |
| Coupon | 11.50% | 7.25% |
| Current price | 125.75 | 100.00 |
| Yield to maturity | 7.70% | 7.25% |
| Modified duration to maturity | 6.20 | 6.80 |
| Call date | 2004 | — |
| Call price | 105 | — |
| Yield to call | 5.10% | — |
| Modified duration to call | 3.10 | — |

   a. Using the duration and yield information in the table, compare the price and yield behavior of the two bonds under each of the following two scenarios:

**Table 16A   Investment Strategies (amounts are market value invested)**

| Strategy | 5-Year Maturity (Modified Duration = 4.83) | 15-Year Maturity (Modified Duration = 14.35) | 25-Year Maturity (Modified Duration = 23.81) |
|---|---|---|---|
| I | $5 million | 0 | $5 million |
| II | 0 | $10 million | 0 |

**Table 16B   Investment Strategy Assumptions**

| | |
|---|---|
| Market value of bonds | $10 million |
| Bond maturities | 5 and 25 years or 15 years |
| Bond coupon rates | 0.00% |
| Target modified duration | 15 years |

**Table 16C   Instantaneous Interest Rate Shift Immediately After Investment**

| Maturity | Interest Rate Change |
|---|---|
| 5 year | Down 75 basis points (bps) |
| 15 year | Up 25 bps |
| 25 year | Up 50 bps |

    i. Strong economic recovery with rising inflation expectations.
   ii. Economic recession with reduced inflation expectations.
 b. Using the information in the table, calculate the projected price change for bond
    B if the yield-to-maturity for this bond falls by 75 basis points.
 c. Describe the shortcoming of analyzing bond A strictly to call or to maturity.

34. a. Use a spreadsheet to calculate the durations of the two bonds in Spreadsheet 16.1
    if the annual interest rate increases to 12%. Why does the duration of the coupon
    bond fall while that of the zero remains unchanged? (Hint: examine what hap-
    pens to the weights computed in column F.)
 b. Use the same spreadsheet to calculate the duration of the coupon bond if the
    coupon were 12% instead of 8% and the semiannual interest rate is again 5%.
    Explain why duration is lower than in Spreadsheet 16.1. (Again, start by looking
    at column F.)

35. a. Footnote 5 presents the formula for the convexity of a bond. Build a spreadsheet
    to calculate the convexity of a 5-year, 8% coupon bond making annual payments
    at the initial yield to maturity of 10%.
 b. What is the convexity of a 5-year zero-coupon bond?

Go to **www.mhhe.com/business/finance/edumarketinsight/**. At the Market Insight Company page, enter the stock ticker symbol, "*T*," for AT&T and review the recent *Industry Outlook* report for the telecom industry. Review the variety of AT&T bonds outstanding by reviewing the latest *EDGAR 10K* report for AT&T. (Bonds are listed in the first few pages). Then go to **www.bondsonline.com,** and search AT&T (enter under *issue*) at the *Bond Search/Quote Center* link under *Corporate*. What is the current rating and yield to maturity for AT&T debt securities? What explains the yield level? For what type of investor or bond portfolio would AT&T bonds be most interesting?

**E-INVESTMENTS**
**Bond Calculations**

Go to **www.derivativesmodels.com**. Choose the link for the classic page. You can also experiment with the enhanced page, which requires you first to establish a (free) user account. This site has a wealth of calculators. Scroll down to find *Bond Calculators,* and choose the link for *calculator*. The calculator provides yield to maturity, modified duration, and bond convexity as the bond's price changes. Experiment by trying different inputs. What happens to duration and convexity as coupon increases? As maturity increases? As price increases (holding coupon fixed)?

**SOLUTIONS TO CONCEPT CHECKS**

1. Use Spreadsheet 16.1 with a semiannual discount rate of 4.5%.

| | Period | Time until Payment (Years) | Cash Flow | PV of CF (Discount rate = 5% per period) | Weight | Weight × Time |
|---|---|---|---|---|---|---|
| **A. 8% coupon bond** | 1 | 0.5 | 40 | 38.278 | 0.0390 | 0.0195 |
| | 2 | 1.0 | 40 | 36.629 | 0.0373 | 0.0373 |
| | 3 | 1.5 | 40 | 35.052 | 0.0357 | 0.0535 |
| | 4 | 2.0 | 1040 | 872.104 | 0.8880 | 1.7761 |
| Sum: | | | | 982.062 | 1.0000 | 1.8864 |
| **B. Zero-coupon** | 1 | 0.5 | 0 | 0.000 | 0.0000 | 0.0000 |
| | 2 | 1.0 | 0 | 0.000 | 0.0000 | 0.0000 |
| | 3 | 1.5 | 0 | 0.000 | 0.0000 | 0.0000 |
| | 4 | 2.0 | 1000 | 838.561 | 1.0000 | 2.0000 |
| Sum: | | | | 838.561 | 1.0000 | 2.0000 |

The duration of the 8% coupon bond rises to 1.8864 years. Price increases to $982.062. The duration of the zero-coupon bond is unchanged at 2 years, although its price also increases (to $838.561) when the interest rate falls.

2. *a.* If the interest rate increases from 9% to 9.05%, the bond price falls from $982.062 to $981.177. The percentage change in price is −0.0901%.

*b.* Using the initial semiannual rate of 4.5%, duration is 1.8864 years (see Concept Check 1), so the duration formula would predict a price change of

$$-\frac{1.8864}{1.045} \times .0005 = -.000903 = -.0903\%$$

which is almost the same answer that we obtained from direct computation in part (*a*).

3. The duration of a level perpetuity is $(1 + y)/y$ or $1 + 1/y$, which clearly falls as $y$ increases. Tabulating duration as a function of $y$ we get

| y | D |
|---|---|
| .01 | 101 years |
| .02 | 51 |
| .05 | 21 |
| .10 | 11 |
| .20 | 6 |
| .25 | 5 |
| .40 | 3.5 |

4. Macaulay's duration is defined as the weighted average of the time until receipt of each bond payment. Modified duration is defined as Macaulay's duration divided by $1 + y$ (where $y$ is yield per payment period, e.g., a semiannual yield if the bond pays semiannual coupons). One can demonstrate that for a straight bond, modified duration equals the percentage change in bond price per change in yield. Effective duration captures this last property of modified duration. It is *defined* as percentage change in bond price per change in market interest rates. Effective duration for a bond with embedded options requires a valuation method that allows for such options in computing price changes. Effective duration cannot be related to a weighted average of times until payments, since those payments are themselves uncertain.

5. The perpetuity's duration now would be 1.08/.08 = 13.5. We need to solve the following equation for $w$:

$$w \times 2 + (1 - w) \times 13.5 = 6$$

Therefore $w = .6522$

**SOLUTIONS
TO CONCEPT
CHECKS**
*(Continued)*

**SOLUTIONS
TO CONCEPT
CHECKS**
*(Concluded)*

6. Dedication would be more attractive. Cash flow matching eliminates the need for re-balancing and thus saves transaction costs.

7. The 30-year 8% coupon bond will provide a stream of coupons of $80 per year, which invested at the assumed rate of 7% will accumulate to $165.60. The bond will sell in 2 years at a price equal to $80 × Annuity factor(8.3%, 28) + $1,000 × PV factor(8.3%, 28), or $967.73, for a capital gain of $42.73. The total 2-year income is $42.73 + $165.60 = $208.33, for a 2-year return of $208.33/$925 = .2252, or 22.52%. Based on this scenario, the 20-year 10% coupon bond of Example 16.6 offers a higher projected return for a 2-year horizon.

8. The trigger point is $10 million/$(1.12)^3$ = $7.118 million.

9. The manager would like to hold on to the money market securities because of their attractive relative pricing compared to other short-term assets. However, there is an expectation that rates will fall. The manager can hold this *particular* portfolio of short-term assets and still benefit from the drop in interest rates by entering a swap to pay a short-term interest rate and receive a fixed interest rate. The resulting synthetic fixed-rate portfolio will increase in value if rates do fall.

# SECURITY ANALYSIS

www.mhhe.com/bkm

# MACROECONOMIC AND INDUSTRY ANALYSIS

To determine a proper price for a firm's stock, the security analyst must forecast the dividend and earnings that can be expected from the firm. This is the heart of **fundamental analysis**—that is, the analysis of the determinants of value such as earnings prospects. Ultimately, the business success of the firm determines the dividends it can pay to shareholders and the price it will command in the stock market. Because the prospects of the firm are tied to those of the broader economy, however, fundamental analysis must consider the business environment in which the firm operates. For some firms, macroeconomic and industry circumstances might have a greater influence on profits than the firm's relative performance within its industry. In other words, investors need to keep the big economic picture in mind.

Therefore, in analyzing a firm's prospects it often makes sense to start with the broad economic environment, examining the state of the aggregate economy and even the international economy. From there, one considers the implications of the outside environment on the industry in which the firm operates. Finally, the firm's position within the industry is examined.

This chapter treats the broad-based aspects of fundamental analysis— macroeconomic and industry analysis. The two chapters following cover firm-specific analysis. We begin with a discussion of international factors relevant to firm performance, and move on to an overview of the significance of the key variables usually used to summarize the state of the macro-economy. We then discuss government macroeconomic policy. We conclude the analysis of the macroenvironment with a discussion of business cycles. Finally, we move to industry analysis, treating issues concerning the sensitivity of the firm to the business cycle, the typical life cycle of an industry, and strategic issues that affect industry performance.

# 17.1   THE GLOBAL ECONOMY

A top-down analysis of a firm's prospects must start with the global economy. The international economy might affect a firm's export prospects, the price competition it faces from competitors, or the profits it makes on investments abroad. Certainly, despite the fact that the economies of most countries are linked in a global macroeconomy, there is considerable variation in the economic performance across countries at any time. Consider, for example, Table 17.1, which presents data on several so-called emerging economies. The table documents striking variation in growth rates of economic output in 2002. For example, while the Chinese economy grew by 11.2%, Venezuelan output fell by 16.7%. Similarly, there was considerable variation in stock market returns in these countries in 2002, ranging from a 52.5% loss in Brazil (in dollar terms) to a 45.7% gain in Russia.

These data illustrate that the national economic environment can be a crucial determinant of industry performance. It is far harder for businesses to succeed in a contracting economy than in an expanding one. This observation highlights the role of a big-picture macroeconomic analysis as a fundamental part of the investment process.

In addition, the global environment presents political risks of far greater magnitude than are typically encountered in U.S.-based investments. In the last decade, we have seen

**Table 17.1   Economic Performance in Selected Emerging Markets**

|  | Growth in Real GDP | Stock Market Return | |
|---|---|---|---|
|  |  | Local Currency | $ Terms |
| China | 11.2 | −7.6 | −7.6 |
| Hong Kong | 3.3 | −20.0 | −20.0 |
| India | 5.8 | −0.1 | +1.0 |
| Indonesia | 3.8 | +1.4 | +18.7 |
| Singapore | 3.0 | −20.7 | −15.6 |
| South Korea | 5.8 | −14.9 | −5.7 |
| Taiwan | 4.2 | −19.7 | −19.1 |
| Brazil | 2.4 | −26.4 | −52.5 |
| Colombia | 1.9 | +49.4 | +15.3 |
| Mexico | 1.9 | −7.9 | −23.5 |
| Venezuela | −16.7 | +24.0 | −41.2 |
| Argentina | −10.1 | +98.3 | −37.5 |
| South Africa | 3.0 | −20.7 | +19.5 |
| Turkey | 7.9 | −18.1 | −26.2 |
| Russia | 4.3 | +50.9 | +45.7 |

Source: *The Economist*, March 1, 2003.

several instances where political developments had major impacts on economic prospects. For example, in 1992 and 1993, the Mexican stock market responded dramatically to changing assessments regarding the prospect of the passage of the North American Free Trade Association by the U.S. Congress. In 1997, the Hong Kong stock market was extremely sensitive to political developments leading up to the transfer of governance to China. The biggest international economic story in late 1997 and 1998 was the turmoil in several Asian economies, notably Thailand, Indonesia, and South Korea. The close interplay between politics and economics was also highlighted by these episodes, as both currency and stock values swung with enormous volatility in response to developments concerning the prospects for aid from the International Monetary Fund. In August 1998, the shockwaves following Russia's devaluation of the ruble and its default on some of its debt created havoc in world security markets, ultimately requiring a rescue of the giant hedge fund Long Term Capital Management to avoid further major disruptions. Currently, the aftermath of the 2003 war in Iraq is weighing heavily on stock markets around the world.

Other political issues that are less sensational but still extremely important to economic growth and investment returns include issues of protectionism and trade policy, the free flow of capital, and the status of a nation's workforce.

One obvious factor that affects the international competitiveness of a country's industries is the exchange rate between that country's currency and other currencies. The **exchange rate** is the rate at which domestic currency can be converted into foreign currency. For example, in early 2003, it took about 118 Japanese yen to purchase 1 U.S. dollar. We would say that the exchange rate is ¥118 per dollar or, equivalently, $.0085 per yen.

As exchange rates fluctuate, the dollar value of goods priced in foreign currency similarly fluctuates. For example, in 1980, the dollar–yen exchange rate was about $.0045 per yen. Because the exchange rate today is $.0085 per yen, a U.S. citizen would need almost twice as many dollars in 2003 to buy a product selling for ¥10,000 as would have been required in 1980. If the Japanese producer were to maintain a fixed yen price for its product, the price expressed in U.S. dollars would nearly double. This would make Japanese products more expensive to U.S. consumers, however, and result in lost sales. Obviously, appreciation of the yen creates a problem for Japanese producers that must compete with U.S. producers.

Figure 17.1 shows the change in the purchasing power of the U.S. dollar relative to the purchasing power of the currencies of several major industrial countries in the period between 1986 and 2002. The ratio of purchasing powers is called the "real," or inflation-adjusted, exchange rate. The change in the real exchange rate measures how much more or

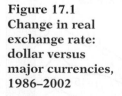

**Figure 17.1
Change in real
exchange rate:
dollar versus
major currencies,
1986–2002**

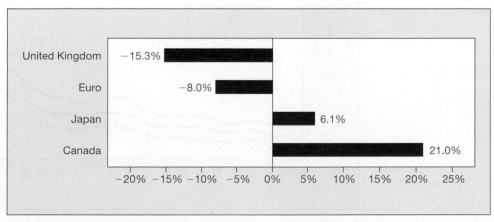

Source: Economic Report of the President, 2003.
Note: Data for the euro prior to 1999 are inferred from deutschemark inflation and exchange rates.

less expensive foreign goods have become to U.S. citizens, accounting for both exchange rate fluctuations and inflation differentials across countries. A positive value in Figure 17.1 means that the dollar has gained purchasing power relative to another currency; a negative number indicates a depreciating dollar. For example, the figure shows that goods priced in terms of the British pound have become far more expensive to U.S. consumers but that goods priced in Canadian dollars have become cheaper. Conversely, goods priced in U.S. dollars have become more affordable to British consumers, but more expensive to Canadian consumers.

## 17.2   THE DOMESTIC MACROECONOMY

The macroeconomy is the environment in which all firms operate. The importance of the macroeconomy in determining investment performance is illustrated in Figure 17.2, which compares the level of the S&P 500 stock price index to forecasts of earnings per share of the S&P 500 companies. The graph shows that stock prices tend to rise along with earnings. While the exact ratio of stock price to earnings varies with factors such as interest rates, risk, inflation rates, and other variables, the graph does illustrate that as a general rule the ratio has tended to be in the range of 10 to 20. Given "normal" price–earnings ratios, we would expect the S&P 500 index to fall within these boundaries. Although the earnings-multiplier rule clearly is not perfect—note the dramatic increase in the price-earnings multiple in the 1990s—it also seems clear that the level of the broad market and aggregate earnings do trend together. Thus the first step in forecasting the performance of the broad market is to assess the status of the economy as a whole.

The ability to forecast the macroeconomy can translate into spectacular investment performance. But it is not enough to forecast the macroeconomy well. You must forecast it *better* than your competitors to earn abnormal profits.

In this section, we will review some of the key economic statistics used to describe the state of the macroeconomy. Some of these key variables are:

**Gross Domestic Product. Gross domestic product**, or GDP, is the measure of the economy's total production of goods and services. Rapidly growing GDP indicates an

**Figure 17.2
S&P 500 index
versus earnings
per share estimate**

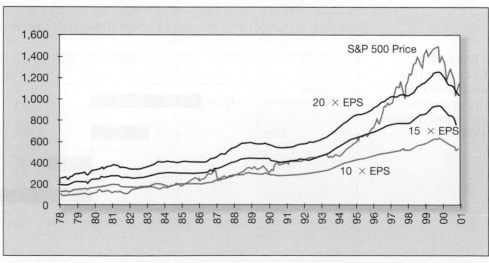

Source: Thomson Financial, *Global Comments*, December 3, 2001.

expanding economy with ample opportunity for a firm to increase sales. Another popular measure of the economy's output is *industrial production*. This statistic provides a measure of economic activity more narrowly focused on the manufacturing side of the economy.

**Employment.** The **unemployment rate** is the percentage of the total labor force (i.e., those who are either working or actively seeking employment) yet to find work. The unemployment rate measures the extent to which the economy is operating at full capacity. The unemployment rate is a factor related to workers only, but further insight into the strength of the economy can be gleaned from the unemployment rate for other factors of production. Analysts also look at the factory *capacity utilization rate*, which is the ratio of actual output from factories to potential output.

**Inflation. Inflation** is the rate at which the general level of prices is rising. High rates of inflation often are associated with "overheated" economies, that is, economies where the demand for goods and services is outstripping productive capacity, which leads to upward pressure on prices. Most governments walk a fine line in their economic policies. They hope to stimulate their economies enough to maintain nearly full employment, but not so much as to bring on inflationary pressures. The perceived trade-off between inflation and unemployment is at the heart of many macroeconomic policy disputes. There is considerable room for disagreement as to the relative costs of these policies as well as the economy's relative vulnerability to these pressures at any particular time.

**Interest Rates.** High interest rates reduce the present value of future cash flows, thereby reducing the attractiveness of investment opportunities. For this reason, real interest rates are key determinants of business investment expenditures. Demand for housing and high-priced consumer durables such as automobiles, which are commonly financed, also is highly sensitive to interest rates because interest rates affect interest payments. (In Chapter 5, Section 5.1, we examined the determinants of interest rates.)

**Budget Deficit.** The **budget deficit** of the federal government is the difference between government spending and revenues. Any budgetary shortfall must be offset by government borrowing. Large amounts of government borrowing can force up interest rates by increasing the total demand for credit in the economy. Economists generally believe excessive government borrowing will "crowd out" private borrowing and investing by forcing up interest rates and choking off business investment.

**Sentiment.** Consumers' and producers' optimism or pessimism concerning the economy is an important determinant of economic performance. If consumers have confidence in their future income levels, for example, they will be more willing to spend on big-ticket items. Similarly, businesses will increase production and inventory levels if they anticipate higher demand for their products. In this way, beliefs influence how much consumption and investment will be pursued and affect the aggregate demand for goods and services.

---

**CONCEPT CHECK ☞ QUESTION 1**   Consider an economy where the dominant industry is automobile production for domestic consumption as well as export. Now suppose the auto market is hurt by an increase in the length of time people use their cars before replacing them. Describe the probable effects of this change on (*a*) GDP, (*b*) unemployment, (*c*) the government budget deficit, and (*d*) interest rates.

## 17.3    DEMAND AND SUPPLY SHOCKS

A useful way to organize your analysis of the factors that might influence the macroeconomy is to classify any impact as a supply or demand shock. A **demand shock** is an event that affects the demand for goods and services in the economy. Examples of positive demand shocks are reductions in tax rates, increases in the money supply, increases in government spending, or increases in foreign export demand. A **supply shock** is an event that influences production capacity and costs. Examples of supply shocks are changes in the price of imported oil; freezes, floods, or droughts that might destroy large quantities of agricultural crops; changes in the educational level of an economy's workforce; or changes in the wage rates at which the labor force is willing to work.

Demand shocks are usually characterized by aggregate output moving in the same direction as interest rates and inflation. For example, a big increase in government spending will tend to stimulate the economy and increase GDP. It also might increase interest rates by increasing the demand for borrowed funds by the government as well as by businesses that might desire to borrow to finance new ventures. Finally, it could increase the inflation rate if the demand for goods and services is raised to a level at or beyond the total productive capacity of the economy.

Supply shocks are usually characterized by aggregate output moving in the opposite direction of inflation and interest rates. For example, a big increase in the price of imported oil will be inflationary because costs of production will rise, which eventually will lead to increases in prices of finished goods. The increase in inflation rates over the near term can lead to higher nominal interest rates. Against this background, aggregate output will be falling. With raw materials more expensive, the productive capacity of the economy is reduced, as is the ability of individuals to purchase goods at now-higher prices. GDP, therefore, tends to fall.

How can we relate this framework to investment analysis? You want to identify the industries that will be most helped or hurt in any macroeconomic scenario you envision. For example, if you forecast a tightening of the money supply, you might want to avoid industries such as automobile producers that might be hurt by the likely increase in interest rates. We caution you again that these forecasts are no easy task. Macroeconomic predictions are notoriously unreliable. And again, you must be aware that in all likelihood your forecast will be made using only publicly available information. Any investment advantage you have will be a result only of better analysis—not better information.

An example of how investment advice is tied to macroeconomic forecasts is given in the nearby box. The article features advice at the end of 2002 by an investment strategist at Standard & Poor's. Given a moderately bullish forecast for the economy, S&P recommended a mild shift in asset allocation from cash equivalents toward stocks. Similarly, within the stock market, S&P recommended an emphasis on economically sensitive sectors such as discretionary consumer items. The strategy guidelines also reflected political risks. Domestic political uncertainties at the time centered on the prospects of the Bush administration's proposal to cut or eliminate taxes on dividends. International political risk factors revolved around the impact of the looming war in Iraq on various sectors of the U.S. economy.

## 17.4    FEDERAL GOVERNMENT POLICY

As the previous section would suggest, the government has two broad classes of macroeconomic tools—those that affect the demand for goods and services and those that affect the supply. For much of postwar history, demand-side policy was of primary interest. The

# S&P'S MARKET OUTLOOK FOR 2003

Look for a good but not great year in 2003. That's the essence of the message from Sam Stovall, senior investment strategist for Standard & Poor's who sees 3% growth in real GDP. Stovall reports that S&P's investment-policy committee has just voted to up its recommended asset allocation for stocks to 65% of a portfolio from 60%. Given an expectation of improvement in both the economy and corporate earnings, Stovall says S&P encourages investors to overweight consumer-discretionary and staples stocks, as well as the energy and materials sectors.

**Q: Sam, what are the sectors to be in for 2003?**
**A:** Because we're looking for a recovery in both the economy and earnings, we believe it best to emphasize the economically sensitive areas, such as the consumer-discretionary, energy, and materials sectors. But just to be on the safe side, we also advise a hefty exposure to consumer staples because of their reliable and transparent earnings growth.

**Q: Would the possible end of the double taxation of dividends be an opportunity to invest in dividend-bearing funds (or stocks)?**
**A:** It seems as if Congress and the White House are willing to come up with some way to either end or ease the burden of double taxation of dividends (once at the corporate level and once at the individual level). Year-to-date, while the S&P 500 declined 18%, the average dividend-paying stock fell only 8%, while the average non-dividend-paying stock dropped 26%.

**Q: How will a war in Iraq affect your outlook?**
**A:** That's certainly a wild card that has been with us for quite some time, but it's also a scenario that all investors have been aware of for at least the past 12 months. Should the bombs start falling, more casualties than victors are likely to be seen on the equity front. One group that could be hit hard is transportation, which is made up of air freight, airlines, railroads, shipping lines, and truckers. Each may initially be hurt by the prospects for rising fuel costs amid concerns of oil-supply disruptions.

In addition, airlines and cruise lines could feel the added pinch of declining travel due to concerns about the possibility of renewed terrorist activity. Of course, if this conflict is rapidly resolved, as was Desert Storm, any downward movement in share prices would represent a buying opportunity.

focus was on government spending, tax levels, and monetary policy. Since the 1980s, however, increasing attention has been focused on supply-side economics. Broadly interpreted, supply-side concerns have to do with enhancing the productive capacity of the economy, rather than increasing the demand for the goods and services the economy can produce. In practice, supply-side economists have focused on the appropriateness of the incentives to work, innovate, and take risks that result from our system of taxation. However, issues such as national policies on education, infrastructure (such as communication and transportation systems), and research and development also are properly regarded as part of supply-side macroeconomic policy.

**Fiscal Policy**    **Fiscal policy** refers to the government's spending and tax actions and is part of "demand-side management." Fiscal policy is probably the most direct way either to stimulate or to slow the economy. Decreases in government spending directly deflate the demand for goods and services. Similarly, increases in tax rates immediately siphon income from consumers and result in fairly rapid decreases in consumption.

Ironically, although fiscal policy has the most immediate impact on the economy, the formulation and implementation of such policy is usually painfully slow and involved. This is because fiscal policy requires enormous amounts of compromise between the executive and legislative branches. Tax and spending policy must be initiated and voted on by Congress, which requires considerable political negotiations, and any legislation passed must be signed by the president, requiring more negotiation. Thus, although the impact of fiscal policy is relatively immediate, its formulation is so cumbersome that fiscal policy cannot in practice be used to fine-tune the economy.

Moreover, much of government spending, such as that for Medicare or social security, is nondiscretionary, meaning that it is determined by formula rather than policy and cannot be changed in response to economic conditions. This places even more rigidity into the formulation of fiscal policy.

A common way to summarize the net impact of government fiscal policy is to look at the government's budget deficit or surplus, which is simply the difference between revenues and expenditures. A large deficit means the government is spending considerably more than it is taking in by way of taxes. The net effect is to increase the demand for goods (via spending) by more than it reduces the demand for goods (via taxes), thereby stimulating the economy.

## Monetary Policy

**Monetary policy** refers to the manipulation of the money supply to affect the macroeconomy and is the other main leg of demand-side policy. Monetary policy works largely through its impact on interest rates. Increases in the money supply lower short-term interest rates, ultimately encouraging investment and consumption demand. Over longer periods, however, most economists believe a higher money supply leads only to a higher price level and does not have a permanent effect on economic activity. Thus the monetary authorities face a difficult balancing act. Expansionary monetary policy probably will lower interest rates and thereby stimulate investment and some consumption demand in the short run, but these circumstances ultimately will lead only to higher prices. The stimulation/inflation trade-off is implicit in all debate over proper monetary policy.

Fiscal policy is cumbersome to implement but has a fairly direct impact on the economy, whereas monetary policy is easily formulated and implemented but has a less immediate impact. Monetary policy is determined by the Board of Governors of the Federal Reserve System. Board members are appointed by the president for 14-year terms and are reasonably insulated from political pressure. The board is small enough, and often sufficiently dominated by its chairperson, that policy can be formulated and modulated relatively easily.

Implementation of monetary policy also is quite direct. The most widely used tool is the open market operation, in which the Fed buys or sells bonds for its own account. When the Fed buys securities, it simply "writes a check," thereby increasing the money supply. (Unlike us, the Fed can pay for the securities without drawing down funds at a bank account.) Conversely, when the Fed sells a security, the money paid for it leaves the money supply. Open market operations occur daily, allowing the Fed to fine-tune its monetary policy.

Other tools at the Fed's disposal are the discount rate, which is the interest rate it charges banks on short-term loans, and the reserve requirement, which is the fraction of deposits that banks must hold as cash on hand or as deposits with the Fed. Reductions in the discount rate signal a more expansionary monetary policy. Lowering reserve requirements allows banks to make more loans with each dollar of deposits and stimulates the economy by increasing the effective money supply.

Monetary policy affects the economy in a more roundabout way than fiscal policy. Whereas fiscal policy directly stimulates or dampens the economy, monetary policy works largely through its impact on interest rates. Increases in the money supply lower interest rates, which stimulates investment demand. As the quantity of money in the economy increases, investors will find that their portfolios of assets include too much money. They will rebalance their portfolios by buying securities such as bonds, forcing bond prices up and interest rates down. In the longer run, individuals may increase their holdings of stocks as well and ultimately buy real assets, which stimulates consumption demand directly. The ultimate effect of monetary policy on investment and consumption demand, however, is less immediate than that of fiscal policy.

**CONCEPT CHECK ☞ QUESTION 2**

Suppose the government wants to stimulate the economy without increasing interest rates. What combination of fiscal and monetary policy might accomplish this goal?

### Supply-Side Policies

Fiscal and monetary policy are demand-oriented tools that affect the economy by stimulating the total demand for goods and services. The implicit belief is that the economy will not by itself arrive at a full employment equilibrium and that macroeconomic policy can push the economy toward this goal. In contrast, supply-side policies treat the issue of the productive capacity of the economy. The goal is to create an environment in which workers and owners of capital have the maximum incentive and ability to produce and develop goods.

Supply-side economists also pay considerable attention to tax policy. Whereas demand-siders look at the effect of taxes on consumption demand, supply-siders focus on incentives and marginal tax rates. They argue that lowering tax rates will elicit more investment and improve incentives to work, thereby enhancing economic growth. Some go so far as to claim that reductions in tax rates can lead to increases in tax revenues because the lower tax rates will cause the economy and the revenue tax base to grow by more than the tax rate is reduced.

**CONCEPT CHECK ☞ QUESTION 3**

Large tax cuts in the 1980s were followed by rapid growth in GDP. How would demand-side and supply-side economists differ in their interpretations of this phenomenon?

## 17.5   BUSINESS CYCLES

We've looked at the tools the government uses to fine-tune the economy, attempting to maintain low unemployment and low inflation. Despite these efforts, economies repeatedly seem to pass through good and bad times. One determinant of the broad asset allocation decision of many analysts is a forecast of whether the macroeconomy is improving or deteriorating. A forecast that differs from the market consensus can have a major impact on investment strategy.

### The Business Cycle

The economy recurrently experiences periods of expansion and contraction, although the length and depth of those cycles can be irregular. This recurring pattern of recession and recovery is called the **business cycle**. Figure 17.3 presents graphs of several measures of production and output. The production series all show clear variation around a generally rising trend. The bottom graph of capacity utilization also evidences a clear cyclical (although irregular) pattern.

The transition points across cycles are called peaks and troughs, labeled P and T at the top of the graph. A **peak** is the transition from the end of an expansion to the start of a contraction. A **trough** occurs at the bottom of a recession just as the economy enters a recovery. The shaded areas in Figure 17.3 all represent periods of recession.

As the economy passes through different stages of the business cycle, the relative performance of different industry groups might be expected to vary. For example, at a trough, just before the economy begins to recover from a recession, one would expect that **cyclical industries**, those with above-average sensitivity to the state of the economy, would tend to

**Figure 17.3   Cyclical indicators**

Source: The Conference Board, *Business Cycle Indicators*, February 2002.

outperform other industries. Examples of cyclical industries are producers of durable goods such as automobiles or washing machines. Because purchases of these goods can be deferred during a recession, sales are particularly sensitive to macroeconomic conditions. Other cyclical industries are producers of capital goods, that is, goods used by other firms to produce their own products. When demand is slack, few companies will be expanding and purchasing capital goods. Therefore, the capital goods industry bears the brunt of a slowdown but does well in an expansion.

In contrast to cyclical firms, **defensive industries** have little sensitivity to the business cycle. These are industries that produce goods for which sales and profits are least sensitive to the state of the economy. Defensive industries include food producers and processors, pharmaceutical firms, and public utilities. These industries will outperform others when the economy enters a recession.

The cyclical/defensive classification corresponds well to the notion of systematic or market risk introduced in our discussion of portfolio theory. When perceptions about the health of the economy become more optimistic, for example, the prices of most stocks will increase as forecasts of profitability rise. Because the cyclical firms are most sensitive to such developments, their stock prices will rise the most. Thus firms in cyclical industries will tend to have high-beta stocks. In general, then, stocks of cyclical firms will show the best results when economic news is positive but the worst results when that news is bad. Conversely, defensive firms will have low betas and performance that is relatively unaffected by overall market conditions.

If your assessments of the state of the business cycle were reliably more accurate than those of other investors, you would simply choose cyclical industries when you are relatively more optimistic about the economy and defensive firms when you are relatively more pessimistic. Unfortunately, it is not so easy to determine when the economy is passing through a peak or a trough. It if were, choosing between cyclical and defensive industries would be easy. As we know from our discussion of efficient markets, however, attractive investment choices will rarely be obvious. It usually is not apparent that a recession or expansion has started or ended until several months after the fact. With hindsight, the transitions from expansion to recession and back might be apparent, but it is often quite difficult to say whether the economy is heating up or slowing down at any moment.

## Economic Indicators

Given the cyclical nature of the business cycle, it is not surprising that to some extent the cycle can be predicted. A set of cyclical indicators computed by the Conference Board helps forecast, measure, and interpret short-term fluctuations in economic activity. **Leading economic indicators** are those economic series that tend to rise or fall in advance of the rest of the economy. *Coincident* and *lagging indicators*, as their names suggest, move in tandem with or somewhat after the broad economy.

Ten series are grouped into a widely followed composite index of leading economic indicators. Similarly, four coincident and seven lagging indicators form separate indexes. The composition of these indexes appears in Table 17.2.

Figure 17.4 graphs these three series. The numbers on the charts near the turning points of each series indicate the length of the lead time or lag time (in months) from the turning point to the designated peak or trough of the corresponding business cycle. Although the index of leading indicators consistently turns before the rest of the economy, the lead time is somewhat erratic. Moreover, the lead time for peaks is consistently longer than that for troughs.

The stock market price index is a leading indicator. This is as it should be, as stock prices are forward-looking predictors of future profitability. Unfortunately, this makes the series of leading indicators much less useful for investment policy—by the time the series predicts an upturn, the market has already made its move. Although the business cycle may

**Table 17.2    Indexes of Economic Indicators**

**A. Leading indicators**
1. Average weekly hours of production workers (manufacturing)
2. Initial claims for unemployment insurance
3. Manufacturers' new orders (consumer goods and materials industries)
4. Vendor performance—slower deliveries diffusion index
5. New orders for nondefense capital goods
6. New private housing units authorized by local building permits
7. Yield curve slope: 10-year Treasury minus federal funds rate
8. Stock prices, 500 common stocks
9. Money supply (M2)
10. Index of consumer expectations

**B. Coincident indicators**
1. Employees on nonagricultural payrolls
2. Personal income less transfer payments
3. Industrial production
4. Manufacturing and trade sales

**C. Lagging indicators**
1. Average duration of unemployment
2. Ratio of trade inventories to sales
3. Change in index of labor cost per unit of output
4. Average prime rate charged by banks
5. Commercial and industrial loans outstanding
6. Ratio of consumer installment credit outstanding to personal income
7. Change in consumer price index for services

Source: The Conference Board, *Business Cycle Indicators*, February 2002.

be somewhat predictable, the stock market may not be. This is just one more manifestation of the efficient markets hypothesis.

The money supply is another leading indicator. This makes sense in light of our earlier discussion concerning the lags surrounding the effects of monetary policy on the economy. An expansionary monetary policy can be observed fairly quickly, but it might not affect the economy for several months. Therefore, today's monetary policy might well predict future economic activity.

Other leading indicators focus directly on decisions made today that will affect production in the near future. For example, manufacturers' new orders for goods, contracts and orders for plant and equipment, and housing starts all signal a coming expansion in the economy.

A wide range of economic indicators are released to the public on a regular "economic calendar." Table 17.3 is an "economic calendar," listing the public announcement dates and sources for about 20 statistics of interest. These announcements are reported in the financial press, for example *The Wall Street Journal,* as they are released. They also are available at many sites on the World Wide Web, for example, at the Yahoo! website. Figure 17.5 is an excerpt from the Economic Calendar page at Yahoo! The page gives a list of the announcements released the week of January 22. Notice that recent forecasts of each variable

**Figure 17.4   Indexes of leading, coincident, and lagging indicators**

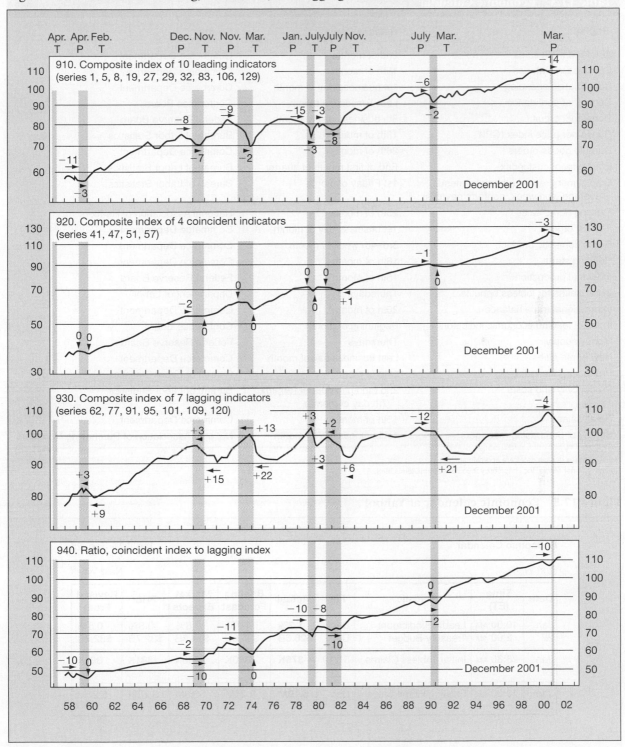

Source: The Conference Board, *Business Cycle Indicators*, February 2002.

## Table 17.3 Economic Calendar

| Statistic | Release Date* | Source |
|---|---|---|
| Auto and truck sales | 2nd of month | Commerce Department |
| Business inventories | 15th of month | Commerce Department |
| Construction spending | 1st business day of month | Commerce Department |
| Consumer confidence | Last Tuesday of month | Conference Board |
| Consumer credit | 5th business day of month | Federal Reserve Board |
| Consumer price index (CPI) | 13th of month | Bureau of Labor Statistics |
| Durable goods orders | 26th of month | Commerce Department |
| Employment cost index | End of first month of quarter | Bureau of Labor Statistics |
| Employment record (unemployment, average workweek, nonfarm payrolls) | 1st Friday of month | Bureau of Labor Statistics |
| Existing home sales | 25th of month | National Association of Realtors |
| Factory orders | 1st business day of month | Commerce Department |
| Gross domestic product | 3rd–4th week of month | Commerce Department |
| Housing starts | 16th of month | Commerce Department |
| Industrial production | 15th of month | Federal Reserve Board |
| Initial claims for jobless benefits | Thursdays | Department of Labor |
| International trade balance | 20th of month | Commerce Department |
| Index of leading economic indicators | Beginning of month | Conference Board |
| Money supply | Thursdays | Federal Reserve Board |
| New home sales | Last business day of month | Commerce Department |
| Producer price index | 11th of month | Bureau of Labor Statistics |
| Productivity and costs | 2nd month in quarter (approx. 7th day of month) | Bureau of Labor Statistics |
| Retail sales | 13th of month | Commerce Department |
| Survey of purchasing managers | 1st business day of month | National Association of Purchasing Managers |

*Many of these release dates are approximate.
Source: Charter Media, Inc., http://biz.yahoo.com/c/terms/terms.html.

## Figure 17.5 Economic calendar at Yahoo!

**Economic Calendar**                                          Jan. 22 – Jan. 25

Last Week                                                      Next Week

| Date | Time (ET) | Statistic | For | Actual | Briefing Forecast | Market Expects | Prior | Revised From |
|---|---|---|---|---|---|---|---|---|
| Jan 22 | 10:00 AM | Leading Indicators | Dec | **1.2%** | 1.1% | 0.8% | 0.8% | 0.5% |
| | 2:00 AM | Treasury Budget | Dec | **$26.6B** | $24.0B | $24.0B | $32.7B | $32.7B |
| Jan 24 | 8:30 AM | Initial Jobless Claims | 01/19 | **376K** | 380K | 395K | 391K | 384K |
| Jan 25 | 10:00 AM | Existing Home Sales | Dec | **5.19M** | 5.25M | 5.18M | 5.23M | 5.21M |

are provided along with the actual value of each statistic. This is useful, because in an efficient market, security prices already will reflect market expectations. The *new* information in the announcement will determine the market response.

**Figure 17.6    Estimates of earnings growth rates in several industries, 2001 and 2002**

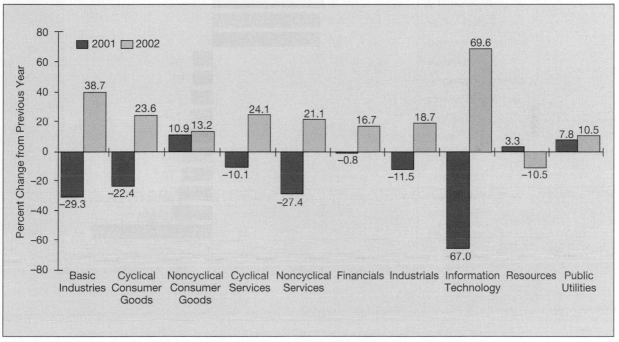

Source: Thomson Financial.

# 17.6    INDUSTRY ANALYSIS

Industry analysis is important for the same reason that macroeconomic analysis is. Just as it is difficult for an industry to perform well when the macroeconomy is ailing, it is unusual for a firm in a troubled industry to perform well. Similarly, just as we have seen that economic performance can vary widely across countries, performance also can vary widely across industries. Figure 17.6 illustrates the dispersion of industry performance. It shows projected growth in earnings per share in 2001 and 2002 for several major industry groups. The forecasts for 2002, which come from a survey of industry analysts, range from −10.5% for natural resources to 69.6% for information technology.

Not surprisingly, industry groups exhibit considerable dispersion in their stock market performance. Figure 17.7 illustrates the performance of the 10 best- and 10 worst-performing industries in 2002. The spread in performance is remarkable, ranging from a 40.5% return for the precious metals industry to a 60.0% loss in the wireless communications industry.

**Figure 17.7   Industry stock price performance, 2002**

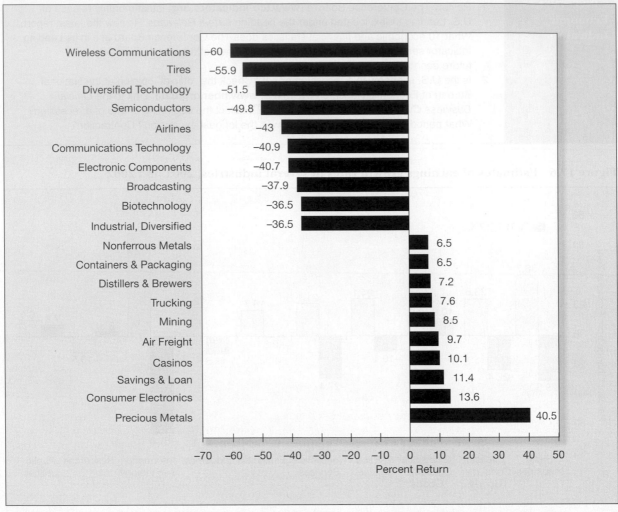

Even small investors can easily take positions in industry performance by using mutual funds with an industry focus. For example, Fidelity offers about 40 Select Funds, each of which is invested in a particular industry.

**Defining an Industry**     Although we know what we mean by an "industry," it can be difficult in practice to decide where to draw the line between one industry and another. Consider, for example, the financial industry. Figure 17.6 shows that the forecast for 2002 growth in industry earnings per share was 16.7%. But the financial "industry" contains firms with widely differing products and prospects. Figure 17.8 breaks down the industry into six subgroups. The forecasted performance on these more narrowly defined groups differs widely, from −0.9% to 60.5%, suggesting that they are not members of a homogeneous industry. Similarly, most of these subgroups in Figure 17.8 could be divided into even smaller and more homogeneous groups.

A useful way to define industry groups in practice is given by *Standard Industry Classification*, or **SIC codes,** and, more recently, North American Industry Classification System or **NAICS codes.** The SIC codes are assigned by the U.S. government for the purpose of

**Figure 17.8
Estimates of
earnings growth
for finance firms,
2002**

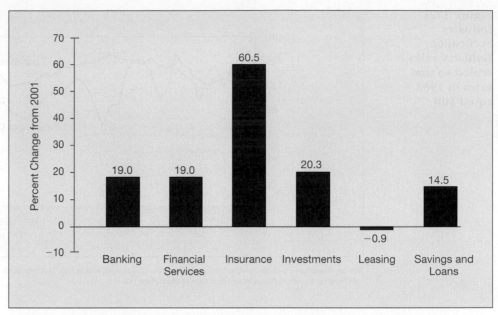

Source: Thomson Financial.

grouping firms for statistical analysis. The first two digits of the SIC codes denote very broad industry classifications. For example, the SIC codes assigned to any type of building contractor all start with 15. The third and fourth digits define the industry grouping more narrowly. For example, codes starting with 152 denote *residential* building contractors, and group 1521 contains *single-family* building contractors. Firms with the same four-digit SIC code, therefore, are commonly taken to be in the same industry. Many statistics are computed for even more narrowly defined five-digit SIC groups. NAICS codes similarly group firms operating inside the NAFTA (North American Free Trade Agreement) region, which includes the United States, Mexico, and Canada.

Neither NAICS nor SIC industry classifications are perfect. For example, both J.C. Penney and Neiman Marcus can be classified as "Department Stores." Yet the former is a high-volume "value" store, whereas the latter is a high-margin elite retailer. Are they really in the same industry? Still, SIC and NAICS classifications are a tremendous aid in conducting industry analysis since they provide a means of focusing on very broad or fairly narrowly defined groups of firms.

Several other industry classifications are provided by other analysts; for example, Standard & Poor's reports on the performance of about 100 industry groups. S&P computes stock price indexes for each group, which is useful in assessing past investment performance. The *Value Line Investment Survey* reports on the conditions and prospects of about 1,700 firms, grouped into about 90 industries. Value Line's analysts prepare forecasts of the performance of industry groups as well as of each firm.

**Sensitivity to the
Business Cycle**
Once the analyst forecasts the state of the macroeconomy, it is necessary to determine the implication of that forecast for specific industries. Not all industries are equally sensitive to the business cycle. For example, consider Figure 17.9, which is a graph of automobile production and shipments of cigarettes, both scaled so that 1963 has a value of 100.

Clearly, the cigarette industry is largely independent of the business cycle. Demand for cigarettes does not seem affected by the state of the macroeconomy in any meaningful way.

**Figure 17.9
Industry
cyclicality.
Industry sales,
scaled so that
sales in 1963
equal 100**

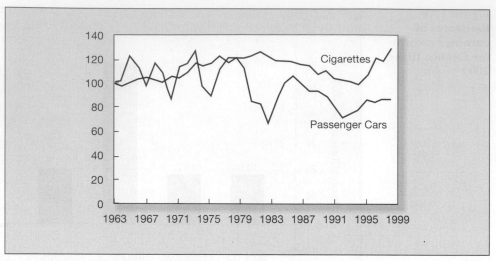

Source: Passenger car sales: *Ward's Automobile Yearbook*, 1994 and www.nada.org. Cigarette sales: Department of Alcohol, Tobacco, and Firearms Statistical Releases and Statistical Abstract of the U.S.

This is not surprising. Cigarette consumption is determined largely by habit and is a small enough part of most budgets that it will not be given up in hard times.

Auto production, by contrast, is highly volatile. In recessions, consumers can try to prolong the lives of their cars until their income is higher. For example, the worst year for auto production, according to Figure 17.9, was 1982. This was also a year of deep recession, with the unemployment rate at 9.5%.

Three factors will determine the sensitivity of a firm's earnings to the business cycle. First is the sensitivity of sales. Necessities will show little sensitivity to business conditions. Examples of industries in this group are food, drugs, and medical services. Other industries with low sensitivity are those for which income is not a crucial determinant of demand. As we noted, tobacco products are examples of this type of industry. Another industry in this group is movies, because consumers tend to substitute movies for more expensive sources of entertainment when income levels are low. In contrast, firms in industries such as machine tools, steel, autos, and transportation are highly sensitive to the state of the economy.

The second factor determining business cycle sensitivity is operating leverage, which refers to the division between fixed and variable costs. (Fixed costs are those the firm incurs regardless of its production levels. Variable costs are those that rise or fall as the firm produces more or less product.) Firms with greater amounts of variable as opposed to fixed costs will be less sensitive to business conditions. This is because in economic downturns, these firms can reduce costs as output falls in response to falling sales. Profits for firms with high fixed costs will swing more widely with sales because costs do not move to offset revenue variability. Firms with high fixed costs are said to have high operating leverage, as small swings in business conditions can have large impacts on profitability.

**EXAMPLE 17.1    Operating Leverage**

Consider two firms operating in the same industry with identical revenues in all phases of the business cycle: recession, normal, and expansion. Firm A has short-term leases on most of its equipment and can reduce its lease expenditures when production slackens. It has fixed costs of $5 million and variable costs of $1 per unit of output. Firm B has long-term

## Table 17.4 Operating Leverage

| Scenario: | Recession | | Normal | | Expansion | |
|---|---|---|---|---|---|---|
| Firm: | A | B | A | B | A | B |
| Sales (million units) | 5 | 5 | 6 | 6 | 7 | 7 |
| Price per unit | $ 2 | $ 2 | $ 2 | $ 2 | $ 2 | $ 2 |
| Revenue ($ million) | 10 | 10 | 12 | 12 | 14 | 14 |
| Fixed costs ($ million) | 5 | 8 | 5 | 8 | 5 | 8 |
| Variable costs ($ million) | 5 | 2.5 | 6 | 3 | 7 | 3.5 |
| Total costs ($ million) | $10 | $10.5 | $11 | $11 | $12 | $11.5 |
| Profits | $ 0 | $ (0.5) | $ 1 | $ 1 | $ 2 | $ 2.5 |

leases on most of its equipment and must make lease payments regardless of economic conditions. Its fixed costs are higher, $8 million, but its variable costs are only $.50 per unit. Table 17.4 shows that Firm A will do better in recessions than Firm B, but not as well in expansions. A's costs move in conjunction with its revenues to help performance in downturns and impede performance in upturns.

We can quantify operating leverage by measuring how sensitive profits are to changes in sales. The **degree of operating leverage**, or DOL, is defined as

$$DOL = \frac{\text{Percentage change in profits}}{\text{Percentage change in sales}}$$

DOL greater than 1 indicates some operating leverage. For example, if DOL = 2, then for every 1% change in sales, profits will change by 2% in the same direction, either up or down.

We have seen that the degree of operating leverage increases with a firm's exposure to fixed costs. In fact, one can show that DOL depends on fixed costs in the following manner:[1]

$$DOL = 1 + \frac{\text{Fixed costs}}{\text{Profits}}$$

## EXAMPLE 17.2 Degree of Operating Leverage

Return to the two firms illustrated in Table 17.4 and compare profits and sales in the "normal" scenario for the economy with those in a recession. Profits of Firm A fall by 100% (from $1 million to zero) when sales fall by 16.7% (from $6 million to $5 million):

$$DOL(\text{Firm A}) = \frac{\text{Percentage change in profits}}{\text{Percentage change in sales}} = \frac{-100\%}{-16.7\%} = 6$$

We can confirm the relationship between DOL and fixed costs as follows:

$$DOL(\text{Firm A}) = 1 + \frac{\text{Fixed costs}}{\text{Profits}} = 1 + \frac{\$5 \text{ million}}{\$1 \text{ million}} = 6$$

---

[1] Operating leverage and DOL are treated in more detail in most corporate finance texts.

Firm B has higher fixed costs, and its operating leverage is higher. Again, compare data for a normal scenario to a recession. Profits for Firm B fall by 150%, from $1 million to −$.5 million. Operating leverage for Firm B is therefore

$$DOL(\text{Firm B}) = \frac{\text{Percentage change in profits}}{\text{Percentage change in sales}} = \frac{-150\%}{-16.7\%} = 9$$

which reflects its higher level of fixed costs:

$$DOL(\text{Firm B}) = 1 + \frac{\text{Fixed costs}}{\text{Profits}} = 1 + \frac{\$8 \text{ million}}{\$1 \text{ million}} = 9$$

The third factor influencing business cycle sensitivity is financial leverage, which is the use of borrowing. Interest payments on debt must be paid regardless of sales. They are fixed costs that also increase the sensitivity of profits to business conditions. (We will have more to say about financial leverage in Chapter 19.)

Investors should not always prefer industries with lower sensitivity to the business cycle. Firms in sensitive industries will have high-beta stocks and are riskier. But while they swing lower in downturns, they also swing higher in upturns. As always, the issue you need to address is whether the expected return on the investment is fair compensation for the risks borne.

| CONCEPT CHECK☞ QUESTION 4 | What will be profits in the three scenarios for Firm C with fixed costs of $2 million and variable costs of $1.50 per unit? What are your conclusions regarding operating leverage and business risk? |
|---|---|

**Sector Rotation**    One way that many analysts think about the relationship between industry analysis and the business cycle is the notion of **sector rotation.** The idea is to shift the portfolio more heavily into industry or sector groups that are expected to outperform based on one's assessment of the state of the business cycle.

Figure 17.10 is a stylized depiction of the business cycle. Near the peak of the business cycle, the economy might be overheated with high inflation and interest rates, and price

**Figure 17.10**
**A stylized depiction of the business cycle**

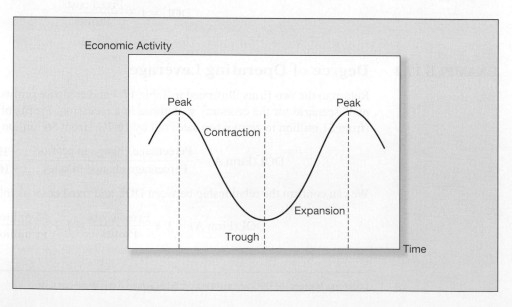

pressures on basic commodities. This might be a good time to invest in firms engaged in natural resource extraction and processing such as minerals or petroleum.

Following a peak, when the economy enters a contraction or recession, one would expect defensive industries that are less sensitive to economic conditions, for example, pharmaceuticals, food, and other necessities, to be the best performers. At the height of the contraction, financial firms will be hurt by shrinking loan volume and higher default rates. Toward the end of the recession, however, contractions induce lower inflation and interest rates, which favor financial firms.

At the trough of a recession, the economy is poised for recovery and subsequent expansion. Firms might thus be spending on purchases of new equipment to meet anticipated increases in demand. This, then, would be a good time to invest in capital goods industries, such as equipment, transportation, or construction.

Finally, in an expansion, the economy is growing rapidly. Cyclical industries such as consumer durables and luxury items will be most profitable in this stage of the cycle. Banks might also do well in expansions, since loan volume will be high and default exposure low when the economy is growing rapidly.

Let us emphasize again that sector rotation, like any other form of market timing, will be successful only if one anticipates the next stage of the business cycle better than other investors. The business cycle depicted in Figure 17.10 is highly stylized. In real life, it is never as clear how long each phase of the cycle will last, nor how extreme it will be. These forecasts are where analysts need to earn their keep.

---

**CONCEPT CHECK☞ QUESTION 5**

In which phase of the business cycle would you expect the following industries to enjoy their best performance?

*a.* Newspapers

*b.* Machine tools

*c.* Beverages

*d.* Timber

---

**Industry Life Cycles**   Examine the biotechnology industry and you will find many firms with high rates of investment, high rates of return on investment, and low dividend payout rates. Do the same for the public utility industry and you will find lower rates of return, lower investment rates, and higher dividend payout rates. Why should this be?

The biotech industry is still new. Recently, available technologies have created opportunities for highly profitable investment of resources. New products are protected by patents, and profit margins are high. With such lucrative investment opportunities, firms find it advantageous to put all profits back into the firm. The companies grow rapidly on average.

Eventually, however, growth must slow. The high profit rates will induce new firms to enter the industry. Increasing competition will hold down prices and profit margins. New technologies become proven and more predictable, risk levels fall, and entry becomes even easier. As internal investment opportunities become less attractive, a lower fraction of profits are reinvested in the firm. Cash dividends increase.

Ultimately, in a mature industry, we observe "cash cows," firms with stable dividends and cash flows and little risk. Growth rates might be similar to that of the overall economy. Industries in early states of their life cycles offer high-risk/high-potential-return investments. Mature industries offer lower-risk, lower-return profiles.

This analysis suggests that a typical **industry life cycle** might be described by four stages: a start-up stage, characterized by extremely rapid growth; a consolidation stage, characterized by growth that is less rapid but still faster than that of the general economy; a maturity state, characterized by growth no faster than the general economy; and a stage of relative decline, in which the industry grows less rapidly than the rest of the economy, or actually shrinks. This industry life cycle is illustrated in Figure 17.11. Let us turn to an elaboration of each of these stages.

**Start-Up Stage.**  The early stages of an industry are often characterized by a new technology or product such as VCRs or personal computers in the 1980s, or wireless communication more recently. At this stage, it is difficult to predict which firms will emerge as industry leaders. Some firms will turn out to be wildly successful, and others will fail altogether. Therefore, there is considerable risk in selecting one particular firm within the industry.

At the industry level, however, sales and earnings will grow at an extremely rapid rate, because the new product has not yet saturated its market. For example, in 1980 very few households had VCRs. The potential market for the product therefore was the entire set of television-watching households. In contrast to this situation, consider the market for a mature product like refrigerators. Almost all households in the United States already have refrigerators, so the market for this good is primarily comprised of households replacing old refrigerators. Obviously, the growth rate in this market will be far lower.

**Consolidation Stage.**  After a product becomes established, industry leaders begin to emerge. The survivors from the start-up stage are more stable, and market share is easier to predict. Therefore, the performance of the surviving firms will more closely track the performance of the overall industry. The industry still grows faster than the rest of the economy as the product penetrates the marketplace and becomes more commonly used.

**Maturity Stage.**  At this point, the product has reached its full potential for use by consumers. Further growth might merely track growth in the general economy. The product has become far more standardized, and producers are forced to compete to a greater extent on the basis of price. This leads to narrower profit margins and further pressure on profits. Firms at this stage sometimes are characterized as cash cows, having reasonably stable cash

**Figure 17.11**
**The industry**
**life cycle**

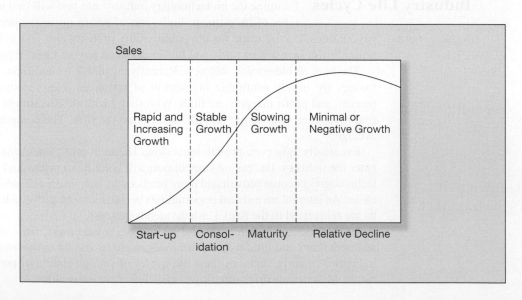

flow but offering little opportunity for profitable expansion. The cash flow is best "milked from" rather than reinvested in the company.

We pointed to VCRs as a start-up industry in the 1980s. By now, it is certainly a mature or even declining industry, with high market penetration, considerable price competition, low profit margins, and slowing or even declining sales. In September of 2001, monthly sales of DVD players, which seem to be the start-up product that will eventually replace VCRs, surpassed those of VCRs for the first time.

**Relative Decline.** In this stage, the industry might grow at less than the rate of the overall economy, or it might even shrink. This could be due to obsolescence of the product, competition from new products, or competition from new low-cost suppliers.

At which stage in the life cycle are investments in an industry most attractive? Conventional wisdom is that investors should seek firms in high-growth industries. This recipe for success is simplistic, however. If the security prices already reflect the likelihood for high growth, then it is too late to make money from that knowledge. Moreover, high growth and fat profits encourage competition from other producers. The exploitation of profit opportunities brings about new sources of supply that eventually reduce prices, profits, investment returns, and finally growth. This is the dynamic behind the progression from one stage of the industry life cycle to another. The famous portfolio manager Peter Lynch makes this point in *One Up on Wall Street*:

> Many people prefer to invest in a high-growth industry, where there's a lot of sound and fury. Not me. I prefer to invest in a low-growth industry. . . . In a low-growth industry, especially one that's boring and upsets people [such as funeral homes or the oil-drum retrieval business], there's no problem with competition. You don't have to protect your flanks from potential rivals . . . and this gives you the leeway to continue to grow. [p. 131]

In fact, Lynch uses an industry classification system in a very similar spirit to the life-cycle approach we have described. He places firms in the following six groups:

*Slow Growers.* Large and aging companies that will grow only slightly faster than the broad economy. These firms have matured from their earlier fast-growth phase. They usually have steady cash flow and pay a generous dividend, indicating that the firm is generating more cash than can be profitably reinvested in the firm.

*Stalwarts.* Large, well-known firms like Coca-Cola, Hershey's, or Colgate-Palmolive. They grow faster than the slow growers, but are not in the very rapid growth start-up stage. They also tend to be in noncyclical industries that are relatively unaffected by recessions.

*Fast Growers.* Small and aggressive new firms with annual growth rates in the neighborhood of 20% to 25%. Company growth can be due to broad industry growth or to an increase in market share in a more mature industry.

*Cyclicals.* These are firms with sales and profits that regularly expand and contract along with the business cycle. Examples are auto companies (see Figure 17.9 again), steel companies, or the construction industry.

*Turnarounds.* These are firms that are in bankruptcy or soon might be. If they can recover from what might appear to be imminent disaster, they can offer tremendous investment returns. A good example of this type of firm would be Chrysler in 1982, when it required a government guarantee on its debt to avoid bankruptcy. The stock price rose fifteenfold in the next 5 years.

***Asset Plays.***    These are firms that have valuable assets not currently reflected in the stock price. For example, a company may own or be located on valuable real estate that is worth as much or more than the company's business enterprises. Sometimes the hidden asset can be tax-loss carryforwards. Other times the assets may be intangible. For example, a cable company might have a valuable list of cable subscribers. These assets do not immediately generate cash flow, and so may be more easily overlooked by other analysts attempting to value the firm.

## Industry Structure and Performance

The maturation of an industry involves regular changes in the firm's competitive environment. As a final topic, we examine the relationship among industry structure, competitive strategy, and profitability. Michael Porter[2] has highlighted these five determinants of competition: threat of entry from new competitors, rivalry between existing competitors, price pressure from substitute products, bargaining power of buyers, and bargaining power of suppliers.

**Threat of Entry.**    New entrants to an industry put pressure on price and profits. Even if a firm has not yet entered an industry, the potential for it to do so places pressure on prices, because high prices and profit margins will encourage entry by new competitors. Therefore, barriers to entry can be a key determinant of industry profitability. Barriers can take many forms. For example, existing firms may already have secure distribution channels for their products based on longstanding relationships with customers or suppliers that would be costly for a new entrant to duplicate. Brand loyalty also makes it difficult for new entrants to penetrate a market and gives firms more pricing discretion. Proprietary knowledge or patent protection also may give firms advantages in serving a market. Finally, an existing firm's experience in a market may give it cost advantages due to the learning that takes place over time.

**Rivalry between Existing Competitors.**    When there are several competitors in an industry, there will generally be more price competition and lower profit margins as competitors seek to expand their share of the market. Slow industry growth contributes to this competition, because expansion must come at the expense of a rival's market share. High fixed costs also create pressure to reduce prices, because fixed costs put greater pressure on firms to operate near full capacity. Industries producing relatively homogeneous goods are also subject to considerable price pressure, because firms cannot compete on the basis of product differentiation.

**Pressure from Substitute Products.**    Substitute products means that the industry faces competition from firms in related industries. For example, sugar producers compete with corn syrup producers. Wool producers compete with synthetic fiber producers. The availability of substitutes limits the prices that can be charged to customers.

**Bargaining Power of Buyers.**    If a buyer purchases a large fraction of an industry's output, it will have considerable bargaining power and can demand price concessions. For example, auto producers can put pressure on suppliers of auto parts. This reduces the profitability of the auto parts industry.

---

[2] Michael Porter, *Competitive Advantage: Creating and Sustaining Superior Performance* (New York: Free Press, 1985).

**Bargaining Power of Suppliers.** If a supplier of a key input has monopolistic control over the product, it can demand higher prices for the good and squeeze profits out of the industry. One special case of this issue pertains to organized labor as a supplier of a key input to the production process. Labor unions engage in collective bargaining to increase the wages paid to workers. When the labor market is highly unionized, a significant share of the potential profits in the industry can be captured by the workforce.

The key factor determining the bargaining power of suppliers is the availability of substitute products. If substitutes are available, the supplier has little clout and cannot extract higher prices.

## SUMMARY

1. Macroeconomic policy aims to maintain the economy near full employment without aggravating inflationary pressures. The proper trade-off between these two goals is a source of ongoing debate.

2. The traditional tools of macropolicy are government spending and tax collection, which comprise fiscal policy, and manipulation of the money supply via monetary policy. Expansionary fiscal policy can stimulate the economy and increase GDP but tends to increase interest rates. Expansionary monetary policy works by lowering interest rates.

3. The business cycle is the economy's recurring pattern of expansions and recessions. Leading economic indicators can be used to anticipate the evolution of the business cycle because their values tend to change before those of other key economic variables.

4. Industries differ in their sensitivity to the business cycle. More sensitive industries tend to be those producing high-priced durable goods for which the consumer has considerable discretion as to the timing of purchase. Examples are automobiles or consumer durables. Other sensitive industries are those that produce capital equipment for other firms. Operating leverage and financial leverage increase sensitivity to the business cycle.

## KEY TERMS

| | | |
|---|---|---|
| fundamental analysis | fiscal policy | SIC codes |
| exchange rate | monetary policy | NAICS codes |
| gross domestic product | business cycle | degree of operating |
| unemployment rate | peak | leverage |
| inflation | trough | sector rotation |
| budget deficit | cyclical industries | industry life cycle |
| demand shock | defensive industries | |
| supply shock | leading economic indicators | |

## WEBSITES

205.232.165.149
This site, supported by Dr. Ed Yardeni of Prudential Financial, is a comprehensive site with complete analysis of economic indicators for both the United States and global economies.

www.federalreserve.gov/otherfrb.htm
The banks of the Federal Reserve System provide significant economic data for the domestic and international economy. Most of the regional banks also provide economic analysis for their regions. The above site links to each of the regional banks.

Visit us at www.mhhe.com/bkm

## WEBSITES

www.federalreserve.gov/policy.htm
Review the minutes from recent Federal Open Market Committee meetings, upcoming meeting dates, and recent Beige Book economic analysis from around the United States.

www.economagic.com
Economagic offers current economic data and reports.

www.tcb-indicators.org
The Conference Board provides business cycles indicators.

online.wsj.com/public/us
www.smartmoney.com
www.barrons.com
Current news and analysis of the economy, industries, and individual companies are available with an online subscription to *The Wall Street Journal.* Subscribers gain access to *Barron's* and *Smart Money* as well. More-limited information is available for free at the above sites.

www.economics.about.com
www.investormap.com/data-econ.htm
moneycentral.msn.com/investor/research/profile.asp
www.bloomberg.com
www.hoovers.com
Visit these sites for general information on the economy.

## PROBLEMS

1. What monetary and fiscal policies might be prescribed for an economy in a deep recession?

2. Unlike other investors, you believe the Fed is going to loosen monetary policy. What would be your recommendations about investments in the following industries?

   *a.* Gold mining.

   *b.* Construction.

3. Briefly discuss what actions the U.S. Federal Reserve would likely take in pursuing an *expansionary* monetary policy using each of the following three monetary tools:

   *a.* Reserve requirements.

   *b.* Open market operations.

   *c.* Discount rate.

4. An unanticipated expansionary monetary policy has been implemented. Indicate the impact of this policy on each of the following four variables:

   *a.* Inflation rate.

   *b.* Real output and employment.

   *c.* Real interest rate.

   *d.* Nominal interest rate.

5. If you believe the U.S. dollar will depreciate more dramatically than do other investors, what will be your stance on investments in U.S. auto producers?

6. According to supply-side economists, what will be the long-run impact on prices of a reduction in income tax rates?

7. Consider two firms producing videocassette recorders. One uses a highly automated robotics process, whereas the other uses workers on an assembly line and pays overtime when there is heavy production demand.

   *a.* Which firm will have higher profits in a recession? In a boom?

   *b.* Which firm's stock will have a higher beta?

8. Here are four industries and four forecasts for the macroeconomy. Match the industry to the scenario in which it is likely to be the best performer.

| Industry | Economic Forecast |
|---|---|
| *a.* Housing construction | (i) *Deep recession:* falling inflation, interest rates, and GDP |
| *b.* Health care | (ii) *Superheated economy:* rapidly rising GDP, increasing inflation and interest rates |
| *c.* Gold mining | |
| *d.* Steel production | (iii) *Healthy expansion:* rising GDP, mild inflation, low unemployment |
| | (iv) *Stagflation:* falling GDP, high inflation |

9. In which stage of the industry life cycle would you place the following industries? (Note: There is considerable room for disagreement concerning the "correct" answers to this question.)

   *a.* Oil well equipment.

   *b.* Computer hardware.

   *c.* Computer software.

   *d.* Genetic engineering.

   *e.* Railroads.

10. For each pair of firms, choose the one that you think would be more sensitive to the business cycle.

   *a.* General Autos or General Pharmaceuticals.

   *b.* Friendly Airlines or Happy Cinemas.

11. Choose an industry and identify the factors that will determine its performance in the next 3 years. What is your forecast for performance in that time period?

12. Why do you think the index of consumer expectations is a useful leading indicator of the macroeconomy? (See Table 17.2.)

13. Why do you think the change in the index of labor cost per unit of output is a useful lagging indicator of the macroeconomy? (See Table 17.2.)

14. Universal Auto is a large multinational corporation headquartered in the United States. For segment reporting purposes, the company is engaged in two businesses: production of motor vehicles and information processing services.

   The motor vehicle business is by far the larger of Universal's two segments. It consists mainly of domestic U.S. passenger car production, but it also includes small truck manufacturing operations in the United States and passenger car production in other countries. This segment of Universal has had weak operating results for the past several years, including a large loss in 2002. Although the company does not reveal the operating results of its domestic passenger car segments, that part of Universal's business is generally believed to be primarily responsible for the weak performance of its motor vehicle segment.

Visit us at www.mhhe.com/bkm

**Table 17A    Ratios for Electric Toothbrush Industry Index and Broad Stock Market Index**

|  | 1996 | 1997 | 1998 | 1999 | 2000 | 2001 |
|---|---|---|---|---|---|---|
| **Return on equity** | | | | | | |
| Electric toothbrush industry index | 12.5% | 12.0% | 15.4% | 19.6% | 21.6% | 21.6% |
| Market index | 10.2 | 12.4 | 14.6 | 19.9 | 20.4 | 21.2 |
| **Average P/E** | | | | | | |
| Electric toothbrush industry index | 28.5× | 23.2× | 19.6× | 18.7× | 18.5× | 16.2× |
| Market index | 10.2 | 12.4 | 14.6 | 19.9 | 18.1 | 19.1 |
| **Dividend payout ratio** | | | | | | |
| Electric toothbrush industry index | 8.8% | 8.0% | 12.1% | 12.1% | 14.3% | 17.1% |
| Market index | 39.2 | 40.1 | 38.6 | 43.7 | 41.8 | 39.1 |
| **Average dividend yield** | | | | | | |
| Electric toothbrush industry index | 0.3% | 0.3% | 0.6% | 0.7% | 0.8% | 1.0% |
| Market index | 3.8 | 3.2 | 2.6 | 2.2 | 2.3 | 2.1 |

Idata, the information processing services segment of Universal, was started by Universal about 15 years ago. This business has shown strong, steady growth that has been entirely internal; no acquisitions have been made.

An excerpt from a research report on Universal prepared by Paul Adams, a CFA candidate, states: "Based on our assumption that Universal will be able to increase prices significantly on U.S. passenger cars in 2004, we project a multibillion dollar profit improvement."

*a.* Discuss the concept of an industrial life cycle by describing each of its four phases.

*b.* Identify where each of Universal's two primary businesses—passenger cars and information processing—is in such a cycle.

*c.* Discuss how product pricing should differ between Universal's two businesses, based on the location of each in the industrial life cycle.

15. Adams's research report (see the preceding problem) continued as follows: "With a business recovery already under way, the expected profit surge should lead to a much higher price for Universal Auto stock. We strongly recommend purchase."

*a.* Discuss the business cycle approach to investment timing. (Your answer should describe actions to be taken on both stocks and bonds at different points over a typical business cycle.)

*b.* Assuming Adams's assertion is correct (that a business recovery is already under-way), evaluate the timeliness of his recommendation to purchase Universal Auto, a cyclical stock, based on the business cycle approach to investment timing.

16. General Weedkillers dominates the chemical weed control market with its patented product Weed-ex. The patent is about to expire, however. What are your forecasts for changes in the industry? Specifically, what will happen to industry prices, sales, the profit prospects of General Weedkillers, and the profit prospects of its competitors? What stage of the industry life cycle do you think is relevant for the analysis of this market?

Problem 17 has two parts.

17. Janet Ludlow is preparing a report on U.S.-based manufacturers in the electric toothbrush industry and has gathered the information shown in Tables 17A and 17B.

CFA®
PROBLEMS

**Table 17B    Characteristics of the Electric Toothbrush Manufacturing Industry**

- **Industry Sales Growth**—Industry sales have grown at 15–20% per year in recent years and are expected to grow at 10–15% per year over the next 3 years.
- **Non-U.S. Markets**—Some U.S. manufacturers are attempting to enter fast-growing non-U.S. markets, which remain largely unexploited.
- **Mail Order Sales**—Some manufacturers have created a new niche in the industry by selling electric toothbrushes directly to customers through mail order. Sales for this industry segment are growing at 40% per year.
- **U.S. Market Penetration**—The current penetration rate in the United States is 60% of households and will be difficult to increase.
- **Price Competition**—Manufacturers compete fiercely on the basis of price, and price wars within the industry are common.
- **Niche Markets**—Some manufacturers are able to develop new, unexploited niche markets in the United States based on company reputation, quality, and service.
- **Industry Consolidation**—Several manufacturers have recently merged, and it is expected that consolidation in the industry will increase.
- **New Entrants**—New manufacturers continue to enter the market.

Ludlow's report concludes that the electric toothbrush industry is in the maturity (i.e., late) phase of its industry life cycle.

*a.* Select and justify three factors from Table 17A that *support* Ludlow's conclusion.

*b.* Select and justify three factors from Table 17B that *refute* Ludlow's conclusion.

18. Your business plan for your proposed start-up firm envisions first-year revenues of $120,000, fixed costs of $30,000, and variable costs equal to one-third of revenue.

*a.* What are expected profits based on these expectations?

*b.* What is the degree of operating leverage based on the estimate of fixed costs and expected profits?

*c.* If sales are 10% below expectation, what will be the decrease in profits?

*d.* Show that the percentage decrease in profits equals DOL times the 10% drop in sales.

*e.* Based on the DOL, what is the largest percentage shortfall in sales relative to original expectations that the firm can sustain before profits turn negative? What are break-even sales at this point?

*f.* Confirm that your answer to (*e*) is correct by calculating profits at the break-even level of sales.

19. As a securities analyst you have been asked to review a valuation of a closely held business, Wigwam Autoparts Heaven, Inc. (WAH), prepared by the Red Rocks Group (RRG). You are to give an opinion on the valuation and to support your opinion by analyzing each part of the valuation. WAH's sole business is automotive parts retailing. The RRG valuation includes a section called "Analysis of the Retail Autoparts Industry," based completely on the data in Table 17C and the following additional information:

- WAH and its principal competitors each operated more than 150 stores at year-end 1999.
- The average number of stores operated per company engaged in the retail autoparts industry is 5.3.
- The major customer base for auto parts sold in retail stores consists of young owners of old vehicles. These owners do their own automotive maintenance out of economic necessity.

*a.* One of RRG's conclusions is that the retail autoparts industry as a whole is in the maturity stage of the industry life cycle. Discuss three relevant items of data from Table 17C that support this conclusion.

**Table 17C    Selected Retail Autoparts Industry Data**

| | 1999 | 1998 | 1997 | 1996 | 1995 | 1994 | 1993 | 1992 | 1991 | 1990 |
|---|---|---|---|---|---|---|---|---|---|---|
| Population 18–29 years old (percentage change) | −1.8% | −2.0% | −2.1% | −1.4% | −0.8% | −0.9% | −1.1% | −0.9% | −0.7% | −0.3% |
| Number of households with income more than $35,000 (percentage change) | 6.0% | 4.0% | 8.0% | 4.5% | 2.7% | 3.1% | 1.6% | 3.6% | 4.2% | 2.2% |
| Number of households with income less than $35,000 (percentage change) | 3.0% | −1.0% | 4.9% | 2.3% | −1.4% | 2.5% | 1.4% | −1.3% | 0.6% | 0.1% |
| Number of cars 5–15 years old (percentage change) | 0.9% | −1.3% | −6.0% | 1.9% | 3.3% | 2.4% | −2.3% | −2.2% | −8.0% | 1.6% |
| Automotive aftermarket industry retail sales (percentage change) | 5.7% | 1.9% | 3.1% | 3.7% | 4.3% | 2.6% | 1.3% | 0.2% | 3.7% | 2.4% |
| Consumer expenditures on automotive parts and accessories (percentage change) | 2.4% | 1.8% | 2.1% | 6.5% | 3.6% | 9.2% | 1.3% | 6.2% | 6.7% | 6.5% |
| Sales growth of retail autoparts companies with 100 or more stores | 17.0% | 16.0% | 16.5% | 14.0% | 15.5% | 16.8% | 12.0% | 15.7% | 19.0% | 16.0% |
| Market share of retail autoparts companies with 100 or more stores | 19.0% | 18.5% | 18.3% | 18.1% | 17.0% | 17.2% | 17.0% | 16.9% | 15.0% | 14.0% |
| Average operating margin of retail autoparts companies with 100 or more stores | 12.0% | 11.8% | 11.2% | 11.5% | 10.6% | 10.6% | 10.0% | 10.4% | 9.8% | 9.0% |
| Average operating margin of all retail autoparts companies | 5.5% | 5.7% | 5.6% | 5.8% | 6.0% | 6.5% | 7.0% | 7.2% | 7.1% | 7.2% |

b. Another RRG conclusion is that WAH and its principal competitors are in the consolidation stage of their life cycle.

   i. Cite three relevant items of data from Table 17C that support this conclusion.

   ii. Explain how WAH and its principal competitors can be in a consolidation stage while their industry as a whole is in the maturity stage.

20. The following problems appeared on past CFA examinations.

   a. The supply-side view stresses that:

      i. Aggregate demand is the major determinant of real output and aggregate employment.

      ii. An increase in government expenditures and tax rates will cause real income to rise.

      iii. Tax rates are a major determinant of real output and aggregate employment.

      iv. Expansionary monetary policy will cause real output to expand without causing the rate of inflation to accelerate.

   b. In macroeconomics, the crowding-out effect refers to:

      i. The impact of government deficit spending on inflation.

      ii. Increasing population pressures and associated movements toward zero population growth.

      iii. A situation where the unemployment rate is below its natural rate.

iv. The impact of government borrowing on interest rates and private investment.

c. Based on historical data and assuming less-than-full employment, periods of sharp acceleration in the growth rate of the money supply tend to be associated *initially* with:

   i. Periods of economic recession.

   ii. An increase in the velocity of money.

   iii. A rapid growth of gross domestic product.

   iv. Reductions in real gross domestic product.

d. If the exchange rate value of the British pound goes from U.S.$1.80 to U.S.$1.60, then the pound has:

   i. Appreciated and the British will find U.S. goods cheaper.

   ii. Appreciated and the British will find U.S. goods more expensive.

   iii. Depreciated and the British will find U.S. goods more expensive.

   iv. Depreciated and the British will find U.S. goods cheaper.

e. The consumer price index is:

   i. A measure of the increase in the prices of the goods that are included in the calculation of GDP.

   ii. The ratio of the average price of a typical market basket of goods compared to the cost of producing those goods during the previous year.

   iii. A comparison of the cost of a typical bundle of goods during a given period with the cost of the same bundle during a prior base period.

   iv. Computed in the same manner as the GDP deflator.

f. Changes in which of the following are likely to affect interest rates?

   I. Inflation expectations.

   II. Size of the federal deficit.

   III. Money supply.

   i. I and II only.

   ii. II and III only.

   iii. I and III only.

   iv. I, II, and III.

g. According to the supply-side view of fiscal policy, if the impact on total tax revenues is the same, does it make any difference whether the government cuts taxes by either reducing marginal tax rates or increasing the personal exemption allowance?

   i. No, both methods of cutting taxes will exert the same impact on aggregate supply.

   ii. No, people in both cases will increase their saving, expecting higher future taxes, and thereby offset the stimulus effect of lower current taxes.

   iii. Yes, the lower marginal tax rates alone will increase the incentive to earn marginal income and thereby stimulate aggregate supply.

   iv. Yes, interest rates will increase if marginal tax rates are lowered, whereas they will tend to decrease if the personal exemption allowance is raised.

h. If the Federal Reserve wanted to reduce the supply of money as part of an anti-inflation policy, it might:

   i. Increase the reserve requirements.

   ii. Buy U.S. securities on the open market.

   iii. Lower the discount rate.

   iv. Buy U.S. securities directly from the Treasury.

Visit us at www.mhhe.com/bkm

1. Go to **www.mhhe.com/business/finance/edumarketinsight**. Access the Industry Profile for the biotechnology and the water utility industries. Compare the price-to-book ratios for the two industries. (Price-to-book is price per share divided by book value per share.) Do the differences make sense to you in light of the different stages of these industries in terms of the typical industry life cycle?

2. Compare the price-to-earnings (P/E) ratios for these industries. Why might biotech have a negative P/E ratio in some periods? Why is its P/E ratio (when positive) so much higher than that of water utilities? Again, think in terms of where these industries stand in their life cycle.

**E-INVESTMENTS**
**The Macro-economy**

Go to **www.prudential.com** and under the tab for *Markets and Research* select *Opinions and Analysis.* You can *View the Economics Network* of Dr. Ed Yardeni, chief investment strategist of the Prudential Equity Group, which contains a wealth of market commentaries, charts, and other analysis. What current economic issues are uppermost in his mind? How will they affect potential returns in stock and bond markets? Also take a look at the links to recent news and numbers from the Fed, Treasury, Congress, and the White House.

**SOLUTIONS TO CONCEPT CHECKS**

1. The downturn in the auto industry will reduce the demand for the product of this economy. The economy will, at least in the short term, enter a recession. This would suggest that:
   *a.* GDP will fall.
   *b.* The unemployment rate will rise.
   *c.* The government deficit will increase. Income tax receipts will fall, and government expenditures on social welfare programs probably will increase.
   *d.* Interest rates should fall. The contraction in the economy will reduce the demand for credit. Moreover, the lower inflation rate will reduce nominal interest rates.

2. Expansionary fiscal policy coupled with expansionary monetary policy will stimulate the economy, with the loose monetary policy keeping down interest rates.

3. A traditional demand-side interpretation of the tax cuts is that the resulting increase in after-tax income increased consumption demand and stimulated the economy. A supply-side interpretation is that the reduction in marginal tax rates made it more attractive for businesses to invest and for individuals to work, thereby increasing economic output.

4. Firm C has the lowest fixed cost and highest variable costs. It should be least sensitive to the business cycle. In fact, it is. Its profits are highest of the three firms in recessions but lowest in expansions.

| | Recession | Normal | Expansion |
|---|---|---|---|
| Revenue | $10 | $12 | $14 |
| Fixed cost | 2 | 2 | 2 |
| Variable cost | 7.5 | 9 | 10.5 |
| Profits | $ 0.5 | $ 1 | $ 1.5 |

**SOLUTIONS
TO CONCEPT
CHECKS**
*(Concluded)*

5.  *a.*  Newspapers will do best in an expansion when advertising volume is increasing.
    *b.*  Machine tools are a good investment at the trough of a recession, just as the economy is about to enter an expansion and firms may need to increase capacity.
    *c.*  Beverages are defensive investments, with demand that is relatively insensitive to the business cycle. Therefore, they are relatively attractive investments if a recession is forecast.
    *d.*  Timber is a good investment at a peak period, when natural resource prices are high and the economy is operating at full capacity.

# EQUITY VALUATION MODELS

As our discussion of market efficiency indicated, finding undervalued securities is hardly easy. At the same time, there are enough chinks in the armor of the efficient market hypothesis that the search for such securities should not be dismissed out of hand. Moreover, it is the ongoing search for mispriced securities that maintains a nearly efficient market. Even infrequent discoveries of minor mispricing would justify the salary of a stock market analyst.

This chapter describes the valuation models that stock market analysts use to uncover mispriced

securities. The models presented are those used by *fundamental analysts,* those analysts who use information concerning the current and prospective profitability of a company to assess its fair market value. We start with a discussion of alternative measures of the value of a company. From there, we progress to quantitative tools called *dividend discount models,* which security analysts commonly use to measure the value of a firm as an ongoing concern. Next we turn to price–earnings, or P/E, ratios, explaining why they are of such interest to analysts but also highlighting some of their shortcomings. We explain how P/E ratios are tied to dividend valuation models and, more generally, to the growth prospects of the firm.

# 18.1  VALUATION BY COMPARABLES

The purpose of fundamental analysis is to identify stocks that are mispriced relative to some measure of "true" value that can be derived from observable financial data. A clear example of mispricing occurs when there is a violation of the *Law of One Price,* which was discussed in Chapter 11. The law states that if two assets are equivalent in all economically relevant respects, then they should have the same market price. The Law of One Price is enforced by the process of *arbitrage*—simultaneously buying an underpriced asset and selling its overpriced equivalent to achieve a positive profit with no net outlay of cash.

For example, suppose we observe that shares of Microsoft stock are priced at $50 on the Nasdaq stock exchange. A small regional firm called Dealertown is offering to sell us Microsoft shares at $49. The only difference between the Microsoft shares selling on Nasdaq and those being offered by Dealertown is their serial number, a feature that has no economic relevance. If we can truly buy shares from Dealertown at $49 and simultaneously sell them on the Nasdaq exchange for $50, then we can unambiguously affirm that Microsoft is mispriced by Dealertown.

Arbitrage opportunities like this are exceedingly rare. In general, stock analysts have a much more difficult task than simply comparing the observable prices of the stock in two different markets that are geographically separate. To accomplish this task they use models to estimate the "fundamental" value of a corporation's stock from observable market data and from the financial statements of the firm and its competitors. These valuation models differ in the specific data they use and in the level of their theoretical sophistication.

The Internet makes it convenient for anyone with a device connected to an online information service to obtain relevant data at low cost. For U.S. companies, the Securities and Exchange Commission provides information for free at its EDGAR website, www.sec.gov/edgar.shtml. The SEC requires all public companies (except foreign companies and companies with less than $10 million in assets and 500 shareholders) to file registration statements, periodic reports, and other forms electronically through EDGAR. Anyone can access and download this information for free.

Many websites provide analysis of the data. An example is Standard and Poor's Market Insight service, which includes COMPUSTAT.[1] Table 18.1 shows COMPUSTAT's selection of financial highlights for Microsoft Corporation on February 14, 2003.

The price of a share of Microsoft common stock on that day is shown as $46.99, and the total market value of all 5,351 million shares outstanding was $251,443.49 million. Under the heading Valuation, Table 18.1 reports the ratios of Microsoft's stock price to four different items taken from its latest financial statements (each divided by the number of outstanding shares): operating earnings, book value, sales revenue, and cash flow. Microsoft's price-to-earnings (P/E) ratio is 29.4, the price-to-book value is 4.5, and price-to-sales is 8.2. Such comparative valuation ratios are used to assess the valuation of one firm versus others in the same industry. In the column to the right in Table 18.1 are comparable ratios for the average firm in the PC software industry.

For example, an analyst might compare the P/E ratio for Microsoft—29.4, to the industry average ratio of 34.6. By comparison with this standard, Microsoft appears to be relatively underpriced. The price-to-sales ratio is useful for firms and industries that are in a start-up phase. Earnings figures for start-up firms are often negative and not reported, so analysts shift their focus from earnings per share to sales revenue per share.

The market price of a share of Microsoft stock on February 14, 2003, was 4.5 times its book value at the end of December 2002. **Book value** is the net worth of a company as

---

[1] A free subscription to S&P Market Insight's educational version comes with this textbook.

**Table 18.1    Financial Highlights for Microsoft Corporation, February 14, 2003**

| Current Qtr Ended: | Dec. 2002 | Current Year Ended: | Jun. 2002 |
|---|---|---|---|
| **Miscellaneous** | | | |
| Current price | 46.990000 | Comn Shareholdrs (actual) | 117730 |
| Comn shares outstdg (mil) | 5351.000 | Employees (actual) | 50500 |
| Market capitalization (mil) | 251443.490 | S&P Issuer Credit Rating | AA |
| **Latest 12 Months** | **Company** | **1 Yr Change (%)** | |
| Sales (mil) | 30785.000 | 14.7 | |
| EBITDA (mil) | 14580.000 | 5.9 | |
| Net income (mil) | 9541.000 | 56.9 | |
| EPS from ops | 1.60 | 32.2 | |
| Dividends/share | 0.000000 | | |
| **Valuation** | **Company** | **Industry Avg** | |
| Price/EPS from ops | 29.4 | 34.6 | |
| Price/book | 4.5 | 4.9 | |
| Price/sales | 8.2 | 7.1 | |
| Price/cash flow | 23.6 | | |
| **Profitability (%)** | | | |
| Return on equity | 17.1 | 14.9 | |
| Return on assets | 13.2 | 10.2 | |
| Oper profit margin | 43.8 | | |
| Net profit margin | 31.0 | 21.5 | |
| **Financial Risk** | | | |
| Debt/equity | 0.0 | 6.2 | |

Source: COMPUSTAT Company Profiles.

reported on its balance sheet. For the average firm in the PC software industry it was 4.9. By comparison with this standard, again Microsoft seems undervalued.

## Limitations of Book Value

The book value of a firm is the result of applying a set of arbitrary accounting rules to spread the acquisition cost of assets over a specified number of years, whereas the market price of a stock takes account of the firm's value as a going concern. In other words, the market price reflects the present value of its expected future cash flows. It would be unusual if the market price of a stock were exactly equal to its book value.

Can book value represent a "floor" for the stock's price, below which level the market price can never fall? Although Microsoft's book value per share in December 2002 was less than its market price, other evidence disproves this notion. While it is not common, there are always some firms selling at a market price below book value.

A better measure of a floor for the stock price is the **liquidation value** per share of the firm. This represents the amount of money that could be realized by breaking up the firm, selling its assets, repaying its debt, and distributing the remainder to the shareholders. The reasoning behind this concept is that if the market price of equity drops below the liquidation value of the firm, the firm becomes attractive as a takeover target. A corporate raider would find it profitable to buy enough shares to gain control and then actually to liquidate, because the liquidation value exceeds the value of the business as a going concern.

Another balance sheet concept that is of interest in valuing a firm is the **replacement cost** of its assets less its liabilities. Some analysts believe the market value of the firm cannot remain for long too far above its replacement cost because if it did, competitors would try to replicate the firm. The competitive pressure of other similar firms entering the same industry would drive down the market value of all firms until they came into equality with replacement cost.

This idea is popular among economists, and the ratio of market price to replacement cost is known as **Tobin's $q$**, after the Nobel Prize–winning economist James Tobin. In the long run, according to this view, the ratio of market price to replacement cost will tend toward 1, but the evidence is that this ratio can differ significantly from 1 for very long periods of time.

Although focusing on the balance sheet can give some useful information about a firm's liquidation value or its replacement cost, the analyst must usually turn to expected future cash flows for a better estimate of the firm's value as a going concern. We now examine the quantitative models that analysts use to value common stock in terms of the future earnings and dividends the firm will yield.

## 18.2  INTRINSIC VALUE VERSUS MARKET PRICE

The most popular model for assessing the value of a firm as a going concern starts from the observation that an investor in stock expects a return consisting of cash dividends and capital gains or losses. We begin by assuming a 1-year holding period and supposing that ABC stock has an expected dividend per share, $E(D_1)$, of \$4, the current price of a share, $P_0$, is \$48, and the expected price at the end of a year, $E(P_1)$, is \$52. For now, don't worry about how you derive your forecast of next year's price. At this point we ask only whether the stock seems attractively priced *today* given your forecast of *next year's* price.

The *expected* holding-period return is $E(D_1)$ plus the expected price appreciation, $E(P_1) - P_0$, all divided by the current price, $P_0$:

$$\text{Expected HPR} = E(r) = \frac{E(D_1) + [E(P_1) - P_0]}{P_0}$$

$$= \frac{4 + (52 - 48)}{48} = .167, \text{ or } 16.7\%$$

Thus, the stock's expected holding-period return is the sum of the expected dividend yield, $E(D_1)/P_0$, and the expected rate of price appreciation, the capital gains yield, $[E(P_1) - P_0]/P_0$.

But what is the required rate of return for ABC stock? We know from the CAPM that when stock market prices are at equilibrium levels, the rate of return that investors can expect to earn on a security is $r_f + \beta[E(r_M) - r_f]$. Thus, the CAPM may be viewed as providing the rate of return an investor can expect to earn on a security given its risk as measured by beta. This is the return that investors will require of any other investment with equivalent risk. We will denote this required rate of return as $k$. If a stock is priced "correctly," its *expected* return will equal the *required* return. Of course, the goal of a security analyst is to find stocks that are mispriced. For example, an underpriced stock will provide an expected return greater than the "fair," or required, return.

Suppose that $r_f = 6\%$, $E(r_M) - r_f = 5\%$, and the beta of ABC is 1.2. Then the value of $k$ is

$$k = 6\% + 1.2 \times 5\% = 12\%$$

The rate of return the investor expects exceeds the required rate based on ABC's risk by a margin of 4.7%. Naturally, the investor will want to include more of ABC stock in the portfolio than a passive strategy would indicate.

Another way to see this is to compare the intrinsic value of a share of stock to its market price. The **intrinsic value**, denoted $V_0$, of a share of stock is defined as the present value of all cash payments to the investor in the stock, including dividends as well as the proceeds from the ultimate sale of the stock, discounted at the appropriate risk-adjusted interest rate, $k$. Whenever the intrinsic value, or the investor's own estimate of what the stock is really worth, exceeds the market price, the stock is considered undervalued and a good investment. In the case of ABC, using a 1-year investment horizon and a forecast that the stock can be sold at the end of the year at price $P_1 = \$52$, the intrinsic value is

$$V_0 = \frac{E(D_1) + E(P_1)}{1 + k} = \frac{\$4 + \$52}{1.12} = \$50$$

Because intrinsic value, $50, exceeds current price, $48, we conclude the stock is undervalued in the market. We again conclude investors will want to buy more ABC than they would following a passive strategy.

If the intrinsic value turns out to be lower than the current market price, investors should buy less of it than under the passive strategy. It might even pay to go short on ABC stock, as we discussed in Chapter 3.

In market equilibrium, the current market price will reflect the intrinsic value estimates of all market participants. This means the individual investor whose $V_0$ estimate differs from the market price, $P_0$, in effect must disagree with some or all of the market consensus estimates of $E(D_1)$, $E(P_1)$, or $k$. A common term for the market consensus value of the required rate of return, $k$, is the **market capitalization rate**, which we use often throughout this chapter.

---

**CONCEPT CHECK☞ QUESTION 1**

You expect the price of IBX stock to be $59.77 per share a year from now. Its current market price is $50, and you expect it to pay a dividend 1 year from now of $2.15 per share.

*a.* What is the stock's expected dividend yield, rate of price appreciation, and holding-period return?

*b.* If the stock has a beta of 1.15, the risk-free rate is 6% per year, and the expected rate of return on the market portfolio is 14% per year, what is the required rate of return on IBX stock?

*c.* What is the intrinsic value of IBX stock, and how does it compare to the current market price?

---

# 18.3   DIVIDEND DISCOUNT MODELS

Consider an investor who buys a share of Steady State Electronics stock, planning to hold it for 1 year. The intrinsic value of the share is the present value of the dividend to be received at the end of the first year, $D_1$, and the expected sales price, $P_1$. We will henceforth use the simpler notation $P_1$ instead of $E(P_1)$ to avoid clutter. Keep in mind, though, that future prices and dividends are unknown, and we are dealing with expected values, not certain values. We've already established

$$V_0 = \frac{D_1 + P_1}{1 + k} \tag{18.1}$$

Although this year's dividends are fairly predictable given a company's history, you might ask how we can estimate $P_1$, the year-end price. According to equation 18.1, $V_1$ (the year-end intrinsic value) will be

$$V_1 = \frac{D_2 + P_2}{1 + k}$$

If we assume the stock will be selling for its intrinsic value next year, then $V_1 = P_1$, and we can substitute this value for $P_1$ into equation 18.1 to find

$$V_0 = \frac{D_1}{1 + k} + \frac{D_2 + P_2}{(1 + k)^2}$$

This equation may be interpreted as the present value of dividends plus sales price for a 2-year holding period. Of course, now we need to come up with a forecast of $P_2$. Continuing in the same way, we can replace $P_2$ by $(D_3 + P_3)/(1 + k)$, which relates $P_0$ to the value of dividends plus the expected sales price for a 3-year holding period.

More generally, for a holding period of $H$ years, we can write the stock value as the present value of dividends over the $H$ years, plus the ultimate sale price, $P_H$:

$$V_0 = \frac{D_1}{1 + k} + \frac{D_2}{(1 + k)^2} + \cdots + \frac{D_H + P_H}{(1 + k)^H} \tag{18.2}$$

Note the similarity between this formula and the bond valuation formula developed in Chapter 14. Each relates price to the present value of a stream of payments (coupons in the case of bonds, dividends in the case of stocks) and a final payment (the face value of the bond, or the sales price of the stock). The key differences in the case of stocks are the uncertainty of dividends, the lack of a fixed maturity date, and the unknown sales price at the horizon date. Indeed, one can continue to substitute for price indefinitely, to conclude

$$V_0 = \frac{D_1}{1 + k} + \frac{D_2}{(1 + k)^2} + \frac{D_3}{(1 + k)^3} + \cdots \tag{18.3}$$

Equation 18.3 states that the stock price should equal the present value of all expected future dividends into perpetuity. This formula is called the **dividend discount model (DDM)** of stock prices.

It is tempting, but incorrect, to conclude from equation 18.3 that the DDM focuses exclusively on dividends and ignores capital gains as a motive for investing in stock. Indeed, we assume explicitly in equation 18.1 that capital gains (as reflected in the expected sales price, $P_1$) are part of the stock's value. Our point is that the price at which you can sell a stock in the future depends on dividend forecasts at that time.

The reason only dividends appear in equation 18.3 is not that investors ignore capital gains. It is instead that those capital gains will be determined by dividend forecasts at the time the stock is sold. That is why in equation 18.2 we can write the stock price as the present value of dividends plus sales price for *any* horizon date. $P_H$ is the present value at time $H$ of all dividends expected to be paid after the horizon date. That value is then discounted back to today, time 0. The DDM asserts that stock prices are determined ultimately by the cash flows accruing to stockholders, and those are dividends.[2]

---

[2] If investors never expected a dividend to be paid, then this model implies that the stock would have no value. To reconcile the DDM with the fact that non-dividend-paying stocks do have a market value, one must assume that investors expect that some day it may pay out some cash, even if only a liquidating dividend.

**The Constant-Growth DDM**   Equation 18.3 as it stands is still not very useful in valuing a stock because it requires dividend forecasts for every year into the indefinite future. To make the DDM practical, we need to introduce some simplifying assumptions. A useful and common first pass at the problem is to assume that dividends are trending upward at a stable growth rate that we will call $g$. Then if $g = .05$, and the most recently paid dividend was $D_0 = 3.81$, expected future dividends are

$$D_1 = D_0(1 + g) = 3.81 \times 1.05 = 4.00$$
$$D_2 = D_0(1 + g)^2 = 3.81 \times (1.05)^2 = 4.20$$
$$D_3 = D_0(1 + g)^3 = 3.81 \times (1.05)^3 = 4.41$$

and so on. Using these dividend forecasts in equation 18.3, we solve for intrinsic value as

$$V_0 = \frac{D_0(1 + g)}{1 + k} + \frac{D_0(1 + g)^2}{(1 + k)^2} + \frac{D_0(1 + g)^3}{(1 + k)^3} + \cdots$$

This equation can be simplified to[3]

$$V_0 = \frac{D_0(1 + g)}{k - g} = \frac{D_1}{k - g} \tag{18.4}$$

Note in equation 18.4 that we divide $D_1$ (not $D_0$) by $k - g$ to calculate intrinsic value. If the market capitalization rate for Steady State is 12%, now we can use equation 18.4 to show that the intrinsic value of a share of Steady State stock is

$$\frac{\$4.00}{.12 - .05} = \$57.14$$

Equation 18.4 is called the **constant-growth DDM**, or the Gordon model, after Myron J. Gordon, who popularized the model. It should remind you of the formula for the present value of a perpetuity. If dividends were expected not to grow, then the dividend stream would be a simple perpetuity, and the valuation formula would be[4] $V_0 = D_1/k$. Equation 18.4 is a generalization of the perpetuity formula to cover the case of a *growing* perpetuity. As $g$ increases (for a given value of $D_1$), the stock price also rises.

---

[3] We prove that the intrinsic value, $V_0$, of a stream of cash dividends growing at a constant rate $g$ is equal to $\dfrac{D_1}{(k - g)}$ as follows. By definition,

$$V_0 = \frac{D_1}{1 + k} + \frac{D_1(1 + g)}{(1 + k)^2} + \frac{D_1(1 + g)^2}{(1 + k)^3} + \cdots \tag{a}$$

Multiplying through by $(1 + k)/(1 + g)$, we obtain

$$\frac{(1 + k)}{(1 + g)} V_0 = \frac{D_1}{(1 + g)} + \frac{D_1}{(1 + k)} + \frac{D_1(1 + g)}{(1 + k)^2} + \cdots \tag{b}$$

Subtracting equation a from equation b, we find that

$$\frac{1 + k}{1 + g} V_0 - V_0 = \frac{D_1}{(1 + g)}$$

which implies

$$\frac{(k - g)V_0}{(1 + g)} = \frac{D_1}{(1 + g)}$$

$$V_0 = \frac{D_1}{k - g}$$

[4] Recall from introductory finance that the present value of a $1 per year perpetuity is $1/k$. For example, if $k = 10\%$, the value of the perpetuity is $1/.10 = $10. Notice that if $g = 0$ in equation 18.4, the constant-growth DDM formula is the same as the perpetuity formula.

**EXAMPLE 18.1**   **Preferred Stock and the DDM**

Preferred stock that pays a fixed dividend can be valued using the constant growth dividend discount model. The constant growth rate of dividends is simply zero. For example, to value a preferred stock paying a fixed dividend of $2 per share when the discount rate is 8%, we compute

$$V_0 = \frac{\$2}{0.08 - 0} = \$25$$

**EXAMPLE 18.2**   **The Constant Growth DDM**

High Flyer Industries has just paid its annual dividend of $3 per share. The dividend is expected to grow at a constant rate of 8% indefinitely. The beta of High Flyer stock is 1.0, the risk-free rate is 6%, and the market risk premium is 8%. What is the intrinsic value of the stock? What would be your estimate of intrinsic value if you believed that the stock was riskier, with a beta of 1.25?

Because a $3 dividend has just been paid and the growth rate of dividends is 8%, the forecast for the year-end dividend is $3 × 1.08 = $3.24. The market capitalization rate is 6% + 1.0 × 8% = 14%. Therefore, the value of the stock is

$$V_0 = \frac{D_1}{k - g} = \frac{\$3.24}{0.14 - 0.08} = \$54$$

If the stock is perceived to be riskier, its value must be lower. At the higher beta, the market capitalization rate is 6% + 1.25 × 8% = 16%, and the stock is worth only

$$\frac{\$3.24}{0.16 - 0.08} = \$40.50$$

The constant-growth DDM is valid only when $g$ is less than $k$. If dividends were expected to grow forever at a rate faster than $k$, the value of the stock would be infinite. If an analyst derives an estimate of $g$ that is greater than $k$, that growth rate must be unsustainable in the long run. The appropriate valuation model to use in this case is a multistage DDM such as that discussed below.

The constant-growth DDM is so widely used by stock market analysts that it is worth exploring some of its implications and limitations. The constant-growth rate DDM implies that a stock's value will be greater:

1. The larger its expected dividend per share.
2. The lower the market capitalization rate, $k$.
3. The higher the expected growth rate of dividends.

Another implication of the constant-growth model is that the stock price is expected to grow at the same rate as dividends. To see this, suppose Steady State stock is selling at its intrinsic value of $57.14, so that $V_0 = P_0$. Then

$$P_0 = \frac{D_1}{k - g}$$

Note that price is proportional to dividends. Therefore, next year, when the dividends paid to Steady State stockholders are expected to be higher by $g = 5\%$, price also should increase by 5%. To confirm this, note

$$D_2 = \$4(1.05) = \$4.20$$

$$P_1 = \frac{D_2}{k - g} = \frac{\$4.20}{.12 - .05} = \$60.00$$

which is 5% higher than the current price of $57.14. To generalize,

$$P_1 = \frac{D_2}{k - g} = \frac{D_1(1 + g)}{k - g} = \frac{D_1}{k - g}(1 + g)$$
$$= P_0(1 + g)$$

Therefore, the DDM implies that in the case of constant growth of dividends, the rate of price appreciation in any year will equal that constant-growth rate, $g$. Note that for a stock whose market price equals its intrinsic value ($V_0 = P_0$), the expected holding-period return will be

$$E(r) = \text{Dividend yield} + \text{Capital gains yield}$$

$$= \frac{D_1}{P_0} + \frac{P_1 - P_0}{P_0} = \frac{D_1}{P_0} + g \qquad (18.5)$$

This formula offers a means to infer the market capitalization rate of a stock, for if the stock is selling at its intrinsic value, then $E(r) = k$, implying that $k = D_1/P_0 + g$. By observing the dividend yield, $D_1/P_0$, and estimating the growth rate of dividends, we can compute $k$. This equation is also known as the *discounted cash flow (DCF) formula*.

This is an approach often used in rate hearings for regulated public utilities. The regulatory agency responsible for approving utility pricing decisions is mandated to allow the firms to charge just enough to cover costs plus a "fair" profit, that is, one that allows a competitive return on the investment the firm has made in its productive capacity. In turn, that return is taken to be the expected return investors require on the stock of the firm. The $D_1/P_0 + g$ formula provides a means to infer that required return.

## EXAMPLE 18.3    The Constant Growth Model

Suppose that Steady State Electronics wins a major contract for its revolutionary computer chip. The very profitable contract will enable it to increase the growth rate of dividends from 5% to 6% without reducing the current dividend from the projected value of $4.00 per share. What will happen to the stock price? What will happen to future expected rates of return on the stock?

The stock price ought to increase in response to the good news about the contract, and indeed it does. The stock price rises from its original value of $57.14 to a postannouncement price of

$$\frac{D_1}{k - g} = \frac{\$4.00}{0.12 - 0.06} = \$66.67$$

Investors who are holding the stock when the good news about the contract is announced will receive a substantial windfall.

On the other hand, at the new price the expected rate of return on the stock is 12%, just as it was before the new contract was announced.

$$E(r) = \frac{D_1}{P_0} + g = \frac{\$4.00}{\$66.67} + 0.06 = 0.12, \text{ or } 12\%$$

This result makes sense, of course. Once the news about the contract is reflected in the stock price, the expected rate of return will be consistent with the risk of the stock. Since the risk of the stock has not changed, neither should the expected rate of return.

*a.* **IBX's stock dividend at the end of this year is expected to be $2.15, and it is expected to grow at 11.2% per year forever. If the required rate of return on IBX stock is 15.2% per year, what is its intrinsic value?**

*b.* **If IBX's current market price is equal to this intrinsic value, what is next year's expected price?**

*c.* **If an investor were to buy IBX stock now and sell it after receiving the $2.15 dividend a year from now, what is the expected capital gain (i.e., price appreciation) in percentage terms? What is the dividend yield, and what would be the holding-period return?**

## Convergence of Price to Intrinsic Value

Now suppose that the current market price of ABC stock is only $48 per share and, therefore, that the stock now is undervalued by $2 per share. In this case the expected rate of price appreciation depends on an additional assumption about whether the discrepancy between the intrinsic value and the market price will disappear, and if so, when.

One fairly common assumption is that the discrepancy will never disappear and that the market price will continue to grow at rate *g* forever. This implies that the discrepancy between intrinsic value and market price also will grow at the same rate. In our example:

| Now | Next Year |
|---|---|
| $V_0 = \$50$ | $V_1 = \$50 \times 1.04 = \$52$ |
| $P_0 = \$48$ | $P_1 = \$48 \times 1.04 = \$49.92$ |
| $V_0 - P_0 = \$2$ | $V_1 - P_1 = \$2 \times 1.04 = \$2.08$ |

Under this assumption the expected HPR will exceed the required rate, because the dividend yield is higher than it would be if $P_0$ were equal to $V_0$. In our example the dividend yield would be 8.33% instead of 8%, so that the expected HPR would be 12.33% rather than 12%:

$$E(r) = \frac{D_1}{P_0} + g = \frac{\$4}{\$48} + .04 = .0833 + .04 = .1233$$

An investor who identifies this undervalued stock can get an expected dividend that exceeds the required yield by 33 basis points. This excess return is earned each year, and the market price never catches up to intrinsic value.

A second possible assumption is that the gap between market price and intrinsic value will disappear by the end of the year. In that case we would have $P_1 = V_1 = \$52$, and

$$E(r) = \frac{D_1}{P_0} + \frac{P_1 - P_0}{P_0} = \frac{4}{48} + \frac{52 - 48}{48} = .0833 + .0833 = .1667$$

The assumption of complete catch-up to intrinsic value produces a much larger 1-year HPR. In future years the stock is expected to generate only fair rates of return.

**Figure 18.1
Dividend growth
for two earnings
reinvestment
policies**

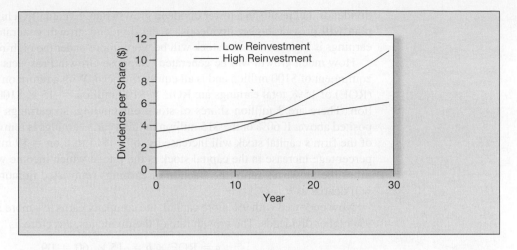

Many stock analysts assume that a stock's price will approach its intrinsic value gradually over time—for example, over a 5-year period. This puts their expected 1-year HPR somewhere between the bounds of 12.33% and 16.67%.

**Stock Prices
and Investment
Opportunities**

Consider two companies, Cash Cow, Inc., and Growth Prospects, each with expected earnings in the coming year of $5 per share. Both companies could in principle pay out all of these earnings as dividends, maintaining a perpetual dividend flow of $5 per share. If the market capitalization rate were $k = 12.5\%$, both companies would then be valued at $D_1/k = \$5/.125 = \$40$ per share. Neither firm would grow in value, because with all earnings paid out as dividends, and no earnings reinvested in the firm, both companies' capital stock and earnings capacity would remain unchanged over time; earnings[5] and dividends would not grow.

Now suppose one of the firms, Growth Prospects, engages in projects that generate a return on investment of 15%, which is greater than the required rate of return, $k = 12.5\%$. It would be foolish for such a company to pay out all of its earnings as dividends. If Growth Prospects retains or plows back some of its earnings into its highly profitable projects, it can earn a 15% rate of return for its shareholders, whereas if it pays out all earnings as dividends, it forgoes the projects, leaving shareholders to invest the dividends in other opportunities at a fair market rate of only 12.5%. Suppose, therefore, that Growth Prospects chooses a lower **dividend payout ratio** (the fraction of earnings paid out as dividends), reducing payout from 100% to 40%, maintaining a **plowback ratio** (the fraction of earnings reinvested in the firm) at 60%. The plowback ratio is also referred to as the **earnings retention ratio**.

The dividend of the company, therefore, will be $2 (40% of $5 earnings) instead of $5. Will share price fall? No—it will rise! Although dividends initially fall under the earnings reinvestment policy, subsequent growth in the assets of the firm because of reinvested profits will generate growth in future dividends, which will be reflected in today's share price.

Figure 18.1 illustrates the dividend streams generated by Growth Prospects under two dividend policies. A low-reinvestment-rate plan allows the firm to pay higher initial

[5] Actually, we are referring here to earnings net of the funds necessary to maintain the productivity of the firm's capital, that is, earnings net of "economic depreciation." In other words, the earnings figure should be interpreted as the maximum amount of money the firm could pay out each year in perpetuity without depleting its productive capacity. For this reason, the net earnings number may be quite different from the accounting earnings figure that the firm reports in its financial statements. We explore this further in the next chapter.

dividends, but results in a lower dividend growth rate. Eventually, a high-reinvestment-rate plan will provide higher dividends. If the dividend growth generated by the reinvested earnings is high enough, the stock will be worth more under the high-reinvestment strategy.

How much growth will be generated? Suppose Growth Prospects starts with plant and equipment of $100 million and is all equity financed. With a return on investment or equity (ROE) of 15%, total earnings are ROE × $100 million = .15 × $100 million = $15 million. There are 3 million shares of stock outstanding, so earnings per share are $5, as posited above. If 60% of the $15 million in this year's earnings is reinvested, then the value of the firm's capital stock will increase by .60 × $15 million = $9 million, or by 9%. The percentage increase in the capital stock is the rate at which income was generated (ROE) times the plowback ratio (the fraction of earnings reinvested in more capital), which we will denote as $b$.

Now endowed with 9% more capital, the company earns 9% more income, and pays out 9% higher dividends. The growth rate of the dividends, therefore, is[6]

$$g = \text{ROE} \times b = .15 \times .60 = .09$$

If the stock price equals its intrinsic value, it should sell at

$$P_0 = \frac{D_1}{k - g} = \frac{\$2}{.125 - .09} = \$57.14$$

When Growth Prospects pursued a no-growth policy and paid out all earnings as dividends, the stock price was only $40. Therefore, you can think of $40 as the value per share of the assets the company already has in place.

When Growth Prospects decided to reduce current dividends and reinvest some of its earnings in new investments, its stock price increased. The increase in the stock price reflects the fact that the planned investments provide an expected rate of return greater than the required rate. In other words, the investment opportunities have positive net present value. The value of the firm rises by the NPV of these investment opportunities. This net present value is also called the **present value of growth opportunities,** or **PVGO.**

Therefore, we can think of the value of the firm as the sum of the value of assets already in place, or the no-growth value of the firm, plus the net present value of the future investments the firm will make, which is the PVGO. For Growth Prospects, PVGO = $17.14 per share:

Price = No-growth value per share + PVGO

$$P_0 = \frac{E_1}{k} + \text{PVGO} \tag{18.6}$$

$$57.14 = 40 + 17.14$$

We know that in reality, dividend cuts almost always are accompanied by steep drops in stock prices. Does this contradict our analysis? Not necessarily: Dividend cuts are usually taken as bad news about the future prospects of the firm, and it is the *new information* about the firm—not the reduced dividend yield per se—that is responsible for the stock price decline. The stock price history of Microsoft (which until recently paid no dividends)

---

[6] We can derive this relationship more generally by noting that with a fixed ROE, earnings (which equal ROE × book value) will grow at the same rate as the book value of the firm. Abstracting from net new investment in the firm, the growth rate of book value equals reinvested earnings/book value. Therefore,

$$g = \frac{\text{Reinvested earnings}}{\text{Book value}} = \frac{\text{Reinvested earnings}}{\text{Total earnings}} \times \frac{\text{Total earnings}}{\text{Book value}} = b \times \text{ROE}$$

proves that investors do not demand generous dividends if they are convinced that the funds are better deployed to new investments in the firm.

In one well-known case, Florida Power & Light announced a cut in its dividend, not because of financial distress but because it wanted to better position itself for a period of deregulation. At first, the stock market did not believe this rationale—the stock price dropped 14% on the day of the announcement. But within a month, the market became convinced that the firm had in fact made a strategic decision that would improve growth prospects, and the share price actually rose *above* its preannouncement value. Even including the initial price drop, the share price outperformed both the S&P 500 and the S&P utility index in the year following the dividend cut.

It is important to recognize that growth per se is not what investors desire. Growth enhances company value only if it is achieved by investment in projects with attractive profit opportunities (i.e., with ROE $> k$). To see why, let's now consider Growth Prospects's unfortunate sister company, Cash Cow, Inc. Cash Cow's ROE is only 12.5%, just equal to the required rate of return, $k$. The net present value of its investment opportunities is zero. We've seen that following a zero-growth strategy with $b = 0$ and $g = 0$, the value of Cash Cow will be $E_1/k = \$5/.125 = \$40$ per share. Now suppose Cash Cow chooses a plowback ratio of $b = .60$, the same as Growth Prospects's plowback. Then $g$ would increase to

$$g = \text{ROE} \times b = .125 \times .60 = .075$$

but the stock price is still

$$P_0 = \frac{D_1}{k - g} = \frac{\$2}{.125 - .075} = \$40$$

no different from the no-growth strategy.

In the case of Cash Cow, the dividend reduction used to free funds for reinvestment in the firm generates only enough growth to maintain the stock price at the current level. This is as it should be: If the firm's projects yield only what investors can earn on their own, shareholders cannot be made better off by a high reinvestment rate policy. This demonstrates that "growth" is not the same as growth opportunities. To justify reinvestment, the firm must engage in projects with better prospective returns than those shareholders can find elsewhere. Notice also that the PVGO of Cash Cow is zero: PVGO = $P_0 - E_1/k = 40 - 40 = 0$. With ROE $= k$, there is no advantage to plowing funds back into the firm; this shows up as PVGO of zero. In fact, this is why firms with considerable cash flow but limited investment prospects are called "cash cows." The cash these firms generate is best taken out of, or "milked from," the firm.

## EXAMPLE 18.4   Growth Opportunities

Takeover Target is run by entrenched management that insists on reinvesting 60% of its earnings in projects that provide an ROE of 10%, despite the fact that the firm's capitalization rate is $k = 15\%$. The firm's year-end dividend will be $2 per share, paid out of earnings of $5 per share. At what price will the stock sell? What is the present value of growth opportunities? Why would such a firm be a takeover target for another firm?

Given current management's investment policy, the dividend growth rate will be

$$g = \text{ROE} \times b = 10\% \times 0.6 = 6\%$$

and the stock price should be

$$P_0 = \frac{\$2}{0.15 - 0.06} = \$22.22$$

The present value of growth opportunities is

$$PVGO = \text{Price per share} - \text{No-growth value per share}$$
$$= \$22.22 - E_1/k = \$22.22 - \$5/0.15 = -\$11.11$$

PVGO is *negative*. This is because the net present value of the firm's projects is negative: The rate of return on those assets is less than the opportunity cost of capital.

Such a firm would be subject to takeover, because another firm could buy the firm for the market price of $22.22 per share and increase the value of the firm by changing its investment policy. For example, if the new management simply paid out all earnings as dividends, the value of the firm would increase to its no-growth value, $E_1/k = \$5/0.15 = \$33.33$.

**CONCEPT CHECK☞ QUESTION 3**

*a.* **Calculate the price of a firm with a plowback ratio of 0.60 if its ROE is 20%. Current earnings, $E_1$, will be $5 per share, and $k = 12.5\%$.**

*b.* **What if ROE is 10%, which is less than the market capitalization rate? Compare the firm's price in this instance to that of a firm with the same ROE and $E_1$, but a plowback ratio of $b = 0$.**

## Life Cycles and Multistage Growth Models

As useful as the constant-growth DDM formula is, you need to remember that it is based on a simplifying assumption, namely, that the dividend growth rate will be constant forever. In fact, firms typically pass through life cycles with very different dividend profiles in different phases. In early years, there are ample opportunities for profitable reinvestment in the company. Payout ratios are low, and growth is correspondingly rapid. In later years, the firm matures, production capacity is sufficient to meet market demand, competitors enter the market, and attractive opportunities for reinvestment may become harder to find. In this mature phase, the firm may choose to increase the dividend payout ratio, rather than retain earnings. The dividend level increases, but thereafter it grows at a slower rate because the company has fewer growth opportunities.

Table 18.2 illustrates this pattern. It gives Value Line's forecasts of return on assets, dividend payout ratio, and 3-year growth rate in earnings per share of a sample of the firms included in the semiconductor industry versus those of East Coast electric utilities. (We compare return on assets rather than return on equity because the latter is affected by leverage, which tends to be far greater in the electric utility industry than in the semiconductor industry. Return on assets measures operating income per dollar of total assets, regardless of whether the source of the capital supplied is debt or equity. We will return to this issue in the next chapter.)

Despite recent problems, the semiconductor firms as a group have attractive investment opportunities. The average return on assets of these firms is forecast to be 15.6%, and the firms have responded with high plowback ratios. Many of these firms pay no dividends at all. The high return on assets and high plowback result in rapid growth. The average growth rate of earnings per share in this group is projected at 20.2%.

In contrast, the electric utilities are more representative of mature firms. Their return on assets is lower, 7.2%; dividend payout is higher, 55.6%; and average growth is lower, 6.5%.

To value companies with temporarily high growth, analysts use a multistage version of the dividend discount model. Dividends in the early high-growth period are forecast and

## Table 18.2   Financial Ratios in Two Industries

|  | Return on Assets | Payout Ratio | Growth Rate* 2003–2006 |
|---|---|---|---|
| **Semiconductors** | | | |
| Analog Devices | 15.5% | 0.0% | 21.7% |
| Cirrus Logic | 11.0 | 0.0 | 11.5 |
| Intel | 20.0 | 8.0 | 20.1 |
| LSI Logic Corp. | 18.0 | 0.0 | 23.0 |
| Micron Technologies | 12.5 | 0.0 | 22.5 |
| National Semiconductor | 15.5 | 0.0 | 18.5 |
| NVIDIA | 20.0 | 0.0 | 21.5 |
| Semtech | 17.0 | 0.0 | 18.5 |
| Texas Instruments | 11.0 | 9.0 | 24.6 |
| *Average* | 15.6% | 1.9% | 20.2% |
| **Electric Utilities** | | | |
| Allegheny Energy | 6.0% | 78.0% | 5.0% |
| Central Vermont | 8.0 | 48.0 | 11.2 |
| Consolidated Edison | 7.5 | 68.0 | 2.0 |
| Energy East | 6.5 | 51.0 | 5.8 |
| Green Mountain Power | 7.5 | 35.0 | 5.0 |
| Northeast Utilities | 6.0 | 39.0 | 18.6 |
| Nstar | 8.0 | 62.0 | 3.8 |
| Public Services Enter. | 8.5 | 50.0 | 2.4 |
| United Illuminating | 6.5 | 69.0 | 4.4 |
| *Average* | 7.2% | 55.6% | 6.5% |

*Year 2003 earnings for some semiconductor firms were negative, which would make growth rates meaningless. In these cases, we used longer-term growth estimates from Value Line.
Source: *Value Line Investment Survey,* 2003.

their combined present value is calculated. Then, once the firm is projected to settle down to a steady-growth phase, the constant-growth DDM is applied to value the remaining stream of dividends.

We can illustrate this with a real-life example. Figure 18.2 is a Value Line Investment Survey report on the defense contractor Raytheon. Some of the relevant information at the end of 2002 is highlighted.

Raytheon's beta appears at the circled A, its recent stock price at the B, the per-share dividend payments at the C, the ROE (referred to as "return on shareholder equity") at the D, and the dividend payout ratio (referred to as "all dividends to net profits") at the E. The rows ending at C, D, and E are historical time series. The boldfaced, italicized entries under 2003 are estimates for that year. Similarly, the entries in the far right column (labeled 05–07) are forecasts for some time between 2005 and 2007, which we will take to be 2006.

Value Line projects rapid growth in the near term, with dividends rising from $.80 in 2003 to $1.20 in 2006. This rapid growth rate cannot be sustained indefinitely. We can obtain dividend inputs for this initial period by using the explicit forecasts for 2003 and 2006 and linear interpolation for the years between:

| | | | | |
|---|---|---|---|---|
| 2003 | $.80 | | 2005 | $1.06 |
| 2004 | $.93 | | 2006 | $1.20 |

## Figure 18.2    Value Line Investment Survey report on Raytheon

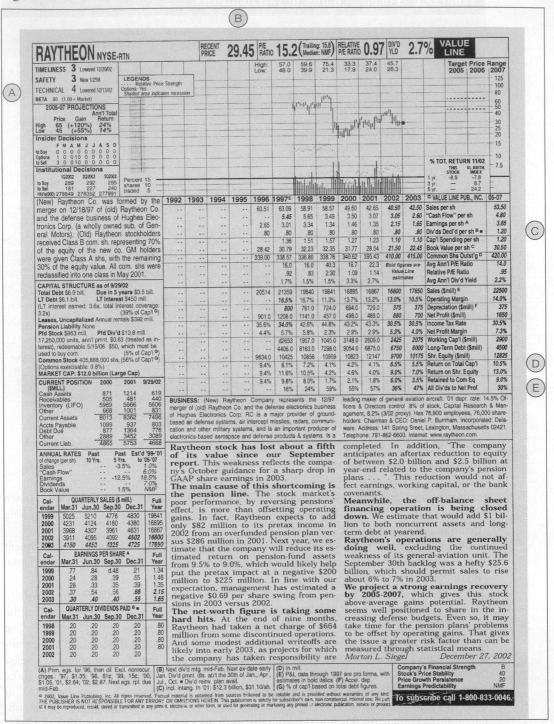

Now let us assume the dividend growth rate levels off in 2006. What is a good guess for that steady-state growth rate? Value Line forecasts a dividend payout ratio of 0.30 and an ROE of 13.0%, implying long-term growth will be

$$g = \text{ROE} \times b = 13.0\% \times (1 - 0.30) = 9.1\%$$

Our estimate of Raytheon's intrinsic value using an investment horizon of 2006 is therefore obtained from Equation 18.2, which we restate here:

$$
\begin{aligned}
V_{2002} &= \frac{D_{2003}}{1 + k} + \frac{D_{2004}}{(1 + k)^2} + \frac{D_{2005}}{(1 + k)^3} + \frac{D_{2006} + P_{2006}}{(1 + k)^4} \\
&= \frac{.80}{1 + k} + \frac{.93}{(1 + k)^2} + \frac{1.06}{(1 + k)^3} + \frac{1.20 + P_{2006}}{(1 + k)^4}
\end{aligned}
$$

Here, $P_{2006}$ represents the forecast price at which we can sell our shares of Raytheon at the end of 2006, when dividends enter their constant-growth phase. That price, according to the constant-growth DDM, should be

$$P_{2006} = \frac{D_{2007}}{k - g} = \frac{D_{2006}\,(1 + g)}{k - g} = \frac{1.20 \times 1.091}{k - .091}$$

The only variable remaining to be determined to calculate intrinsic value is the market capitalization rate, $k$.

One way to obtain $k$ is from the CAPM. Observe from the Value Line data that Raytheon's beta is 0.80. The risk-free rate on longer-term bonds in 2002 was about 5%. Suppose that the market risk premium were forecast at 8.0%. This would imply that the forecast for the market return was

$$\text{Risk-free rate} + \text{Market risk premium} = 5.0\% + 8.0\% = 13.0\%$$

Therefore, we can solve for the market capitalization rate for Raytheon as

$$k = r_f + \beta[E(r_M) - r_f] = 5\% + .80(13.0 - 5.0) = 11.4\%$$

Our forecast for the stock price in 2006 is thus

$$P_{2006} = \frac{\$1.20 \times 1.091}{.114 - .091} = \$56.92$$

And today's estimate of intrinsic value is

$$V_{2002} = .80/1.114 + .93/(1.114)^2 + 1.06/(1.114)^3 + (1.20 + 56.92)/(1.114)^4 = \$39.97$$

We know from the Value Line report that Raytheon's actual price was $29.45 (at the circled B). Our intrinsic value analysis indicates Raytheon was underpriced. Should we increase our holdings of Raytheon?

Perhaps. But before betting the farm, stop to consider how firm our estimate is. We've had to guess at dividends in the near future, the ultimate growth rate of those dividends, and the appropriate discount rate. Moreover, we've assumed Raytheon will follow a relatively simple two-stage growth process. In practice, the growth of dividends can follow more complicated patterns. Even small errors in these approximations could upset a conclusion.

For example, suppose that we have overestimated Raytheon's growth prospects and that the actual ROE in the post-2006 period will be 11% rather than 13%, a seemingly minor change. Using the lower return on equity in the dividend discount model would result in an intrinsic value in 2002 of $25.69, which actually is less than the stock price. Our conclusion regarding intrinsic value versus price is reversed.

This exercise shows that finding bargains is not as easy as it seems. Although the DDM is easy to apply, establishing its inputs is more of a challenge. This should not be surprising. In even a moderately efficient market, finding profit opportunities has to be more involved than sitting down with Value Line for a half-hour.

The exercise also highlights the importance of performing sensitivity analysis when you attempt to value stocks. Your estimates of stock values are no better than your assumptions. Sensitivity analysis will highlight the inputs that need to be most carefully examined. For example, we just found that very small changes in the estimated ROE for the post-2006 period would result in big changes in intrinsic value. Similarly, small changes in the assumed capitalization rate would change intrinsic value substantially. On the other hand, reasonable changes in the dividends forecast between 2003 and 2006 would have a small impact on intrinsic value.

| CONCEPT CHECK☞ QUESTION 4 | Confirm that the intrinsic value of Raytheon using ROE = 11% is $25.69. (Hint: First calculate the stock price in 2006. Then calculate the present value of all interim dividends plus the present value of the 2006 sales price.) |

## Multistage Growth Models

The two-stage growth model that we just considered for Raytheon is a good start toward realism, but clearly we could do even better if our valuation model allowed for more-flexible patterns of growth. Multistage growth models allow dividends per share to grow at several different rates as the firm matures. Many analysts use three-stage growth models. They may assume an initial period of high dividend growth (or instead make year-by-year forecasts of dividends for the short term), a final period of sustainable growth, and a transition period between, during which dividend growth rates taper off from the initial rapid rate to the ultimate sustainable rate. These models are conceptually no harder to work with than a two-stage model, but they require many more calculations and can be tedious to do by hand. It is easy, however, to build an Excel spreadsheet for such a model. We refer you to the nearby Excel application for an example of a two-stage spreadsheet. A three-stage spreadsheet appears later in the chapter.

## 18.4   PRICE–EARNINGS RATIO

### The Price–Earnings Ratio and Growth Opportunities

Much of the real-world discussion of stock market valuation concentrates on the firm's **price–earnings multiple**, the ratio of price per share to earnings per share, commonly called the P/E ratio. Our discussion of growth opportunities shows why stock market analysts focus on the P/E ratio. Both companies considered, Cash Cow and Growth Prospects, had earnings per share (EPS) of $5, but Growth Prospects reinvested 60% of earnings in prospects with an ROE of 15%, whereas Cash Cow paid out all earnings as dividends. Cash Cow had a price of $40, giving it a P/E multiple of 40/5 = 8.0, whereas Growth Prospects sold for $57.14, giving it a multiple of 57.14/5 = 11.4. This observation suggests the P/E ratio might serve as a useful indicator of expectations of growth opportunities.

# TWO-STAGE GROWTH MODEL

The spreadsheet in this box is a two-stage dividend discount model. Rather than forecasting year-by-year dividends in the first stage, in this version of the model the analyst forecasts an initial high-dividend growth rate. In the second stage, dividends are forecast to grow indefinitely at a constant rate. This spreadsheet is available at **www.mhhe.com/bkm**. A three-stage dividend growth model is also available at the OnLine Learning Center and is presented in a box later in the chapter.

| | A | B |
|---|---|---|
| 1 | **Two Stage Growth Model** | |
| 2 | | |
| 3 | Initial Earnings ($E_0$) | $4.00 |
| 4 | Initial Dividend ($D_0$) | $2.00 |
| 5 | Stage 1 Growth rate ($g_1$) | 13.00% |
| 6 | Duration of Stage 1 growth (years) | 10.0 |
| 7 | Stage 2 growth rate ($g_2$) | 8.00% |
| 8 | Beta Coefficient ($\beta$) | 1.25 |
| 9 | T-Bill Rate ($r_f$) | 5.00% |
| 10 | Market Risk Premium ($r_M - r_f$) | 8.00% |
| 11 | | |
| 12 | Required Return (k) | 15.00% |
| 13 | Ratio of $[(1+g_1)/(1+k)]$ | 0.98261 |
| 14 | Present value of a growing annuity | 8.04574 |
| 15 | | |
| 16 | Present Value of the Stage 1 Dividends | $18.183 |
| 17 | Present Value of the Stage 2 Dividends | $25.892 |
| 18 | Value of the Stock | $44.075 |
| 19 | | |
| 20 | **Analysis of Growth Opportunities** | |
| 21 | No-Growth value of the Firm | $26.667 |
| 22 | Present Value of Growth Opportunities | $17.408 |
| 23 | | |
| 24 | **Price-to-Earnings Ratios** | |
| 25 | Price/Current Earnings | 11.0188 |
| 26 | Price/Next Year's Expected Earnings | 9.7511 |
| 27 | | |
| 28 | | |

We can see how growth opportunities are reflected in P/E ratios by rearranging equation 18.6 to

$$\frac{P_0}{E_1} = \frac{1}{k}\left(1 + \frac{PVGO}{E/k}\right) \tag{18.7}$$

When PVGO = 0, equation 18.7 shows that $P_0 = E_1/k$. The stock is valued like a nongrowing perpetuity of $E_1$. The P/E ratio is just $1/k$. However, as PVGO becomes an increasingly dominant contributor to price, the P/E ratio can rise dramatically.

The ratio of PVGO to $E/k$ has a simple interpretation. It is the ratio of the component of firm value due to growth opportunities to the component of value due to assets already in place (i.e., the no-growth value of the firm, $E/k$). When future growth opportunities dominate the estimate of total value, the firm will command a high price relative to current earnings. Thus a high P/E multiple indicates that a firm enjoys ample growth opportunities.

Let's see if P/E multiples do vary with growth prospects. Between 1992 and 2001, Intel's P/E ratio averaged about 35 while AEP's (an electric utility) average P/E was only about half of that. These numbers do not necessarily imply that Intel was overpriced compared to AEP. If investors believed Intel would grow faster than AEP, the higher price per dollar of earnings would be justified. That is, an investor might well pay a higher price per dollar of *current* earnings if he or she expects that earnings stream to grow more rapidly. In fact, Intel's growth rate has been consistent with its higher P/E multiple. In the decade ending 2000, its earnings per share grew more than 8-fold (before turning down sharply in 2001, which was a difficult year for the entire high-tech sector), while AEP's earnings were essentially unchanged. Figure 18.4, page 631, shows the EPS history of the two companies.

Clearly, it is differences in expected growth opportunities that justify particular differentials in P/E ratios across firms. The P/E ratio actually is a reflection of the market's optimism concerning a firm's growth prospects. In their use of a P/E ratio, analysts must decide whether they are more or less optimistic than the market. If they are more optimistic, they will recommend buying the stock.

There is a way to make these insights more precise. Look again at the constant-growth DDM formula, $P_0 = D_1/(k - g)$. Now recall that dividends equal the earnings that are *not* reinvested in the firm: $D_1 = E_1(1 - b)$. Recall also that $g = \text{ROE} \times b$. Hence, substituting for $D_1$ and $g$, we find that

$$P_0 = \frac{E_1(1 - b)}{k - \text{ROE} \times b}$$

implying the P/E ratio is

$$\frac{P_0}{E_1} = \frac{1 - b}{k - \text{ROE} \times b} \tag{18.8}$$

It is easy to verify that the P/E ratio increases with ROE. This makes sense, because high-ROE projects give the firm good opportunities for growth.[7] We also can verify that the P/E ratio increases for higher plowback, *b,* as long as ROE exceeds *k*. This too makes sense. When a firm has good investment opportunities, the market will reward it with a higher P/E multiple if it exploits those opportunities more aggressively by plowing back more earnings into those opportunities.

Remember, however, that growth is not desirable for its own sake. Examine Table 18.3 where we use equation 18.8 to compute both growth rates and P/E ratios for different combinations of ROE and *b*. Although growth always increases with the plowback rate (move across the rows in Table 18.3A), the P/E ratio does not (move across the rows in panel B). In the top row of Table 18.3B, the P/E falls as the plowback rate increases. In the middle row, it is unaffected by plowback. In the third row, it increases.

This pattern has a simple interpretation. When the expected ROE is less than the required return, *k*, investors prefer that the firm pay out earnings as dividends rather than reinvest earnings in the firm at an inadequate rate of return. That is, for ROE lower than *k*, the value of the firm falls as plowback increases. Conversely, when ROE exceeds *k*, the firm offers attractive investment opportunities, so the value of the firm is enhanced as those opportunities are more fully exploited by increasing the plowback rate.

Finally, where ROE just equals *k*, the firm offers "break-even" investment opportunities with a fair rate of return. In this case, investors are indifferent between reinvestment of

---

[7] Note that equation 18.8 is a simple rearrangement of the DDM formula, with $\text{ROE} \times b = g$. Because that formula requires that $g < k$, equation 18.8 is valid only when $\text{ROE} \times b < k$.

### Table 18.3   Effect of ROE and Plowback on Growth and the P/E Ratio

| ROE | Plowback Rate (b) | | | |
|---|---|---|---|---|
| | 0 | .25 | .50 | .75 |
| **A. Growth rate, g** | | | | |
| 10% | 0 | 2.5% | 5.0% | 7.5% |
| 12 | 0 | 3.0 | 6.0 | 9.0 |
| 14 | 0 | 3.5 | 7.0 | 10.5 |
| **B. P/E ratio** | | | | |
| 10% | 8.33 | 7.89 | 7.14 | 5.56 |
| 12 | 8.33 | 8.33 | 8.33 | 8.33 |
| 14 | 8.33 | 8.82 | 10.00 | 16.67 |

Assumption: $k = 12\%$ per year.

earnings in the firm or elsewhere at the market capitalization rate, because the rate of return in either case is 12%. Therefore, the stock price is unaffected by the plowback rate.

One way to summarize these relationships is to say the higher the plowback rate, the higher the growth rate, but a higher plowback rate does not necessarily mean a higher P/E ratio. A higher plowback rate increases P/E only if investments undertaken by the firm offer an expected rate of return higher than the market capitalization rate. Otherwise, higher plowback hurts investors because it means more money is sunk into projects with inadequate rates of return.

Notwithstanding these fine points, P/E ratios commonly are taken as proxies for the expected growth in dividends or earnings. In fact, a common Wall Street rule of thumb is that the growth rate ought to be roughly equal to the P/E ratio. In other words, the ratio of P/E to g, often called the *PEG ratio,* should be about 1.0. Peter Lynch, the famous portfolio manager, puts it this way in his book *One Up on Wall Street*:

> The P/E ratio of any company that's fairly priced will equal its growth rate. I'm talking here about growth rate of earnings here. . . . If the P/E ratio of Coca Cola is 15, you'd expect the company to be growing at about 15% per year, etc. But if the P/E ratio is less than the growth rate, you may have found yourself a bargain. [p. 198]

## EXAMPLE 18.5   P/E Ratio versus Growth Rate

Let's try Lynch's rule of thumb. Assume that

$$r_f = 8\% \quad \text{(roughly the value when Peter Lynch was writing)}$$
$$r_M - r_f = 8\% \quad \text{(about the historical average market risk premium)}$$
$$b = .4 \quad \text{(a typical value for the plowback ratio in the United States)}$$

Therefore, $r_M = r_f +$ market risk premium $= 8\% + 8\% = 16\%$, and $k = 16\%$ for an average ($\beta = 1$) company. If we also accept as reasonable that ROE = 16% (the same value as the expected return on the stock), we conclude that

$$g = \text{ROE} \times b = 16\% \times .4 = 6.4\%$$

and

$$\frac{P}{E} = \frac{1 - .4}{.16 - .064} = 6.26$$

Thus, the P/E ratio and $g$ are about equal using these assumptions, consistent with the rule of thumb.

However, note that this rule of thumb, like almost all others, will not work in all circumstances. For example, the value of $r_f$ today is more like 5%, so a comparable forecast of $r_M$ today would be

$$r_f + \text{Market risk premium} = 5\% + 8\% = 13\%$$

If we continue to focus on a firm with $\beta = 1$, and if ROE still is about the same as $k$, then

$$g = 13\% \times .4 = 5.2\%$$

while

$$\frac{P}{E} = \frac{1 - .4}{.13 - .052} = 7.69$$

The P/E ratio and $g$ now diverge and the PEG ratio is now 1.5. Nevertheless, it still is the case that high P/E stocks are almost invariably expected to show rapid earnings growth, even if the expected growth rate does not equal the P/E ratio.

The importance of growth opportunities is nowhere more evident than in the valuation of Internet firms. Many companies that had yet to turn a profit were valued by the market in the late 1990s at billions of dollars. The perceived value of these companies was *exclusively* as growth opportunities. Of course, when company valuation is determined primarily by growth opportunities, those values can be very sensitive to reassessments of such prospects. In 2001 and 2002 the high-tech sector crashed as the market became more skeptical of the prospects of these businesses, that is, as it revised the estimates of growth opportunities downward. The nearby box discusses how stock market analysts became part of what is now regarded as the (burst) Internet bubble. "The Day the Nasdaq Died" (see the other nearby box) is a musical review of these years.

**CONCEPT CHECK☞ QUESTION 5**

**ABC stock has an expected ROE of 12% per year, expected earnings per share of $2, and expected dividends of $1.50 per share. Its market capitalization rate is 10% per year.**

*a.* **What are its expected growth rate, its price, and its P/E ratio?**

*b.* **If the plowback rate were .4, what would be the expected dividend per share, the growth rate, price, and the P/E ratio?**

**P/E Ratios and Stock Risk**   One important implication of any stock valuation model is that (holding all else equal) riskier stocks will have lower P/E multiples. We can see this quite easily in the context of the constant-growth model by examining the formula for the P/E ratio (equation 18.8):

$$\frac{P}{E} = \frac{1 - b}{k - g}$$

Riskier firms will have higher required rates of return, that is, higher values of $k$. Therefore, the P/E multiple will be lower. This is true even outside the context of the constant-growth model. For *any* expected earnings and dividend stream, the present value of those cash

Analysts are far from perfect, and in the days of the bubble some were careless or complacent, but their activities are more varied, benign and valuable than commonly portrayed. Analysts are daily reminded that the stock market will make a fool of you. Predicting stock prices is predicting the future, and being wrong is part of the job.

Analysts dedicate almost all their time and energy to serving institutional investors—the people who manage mutual funds, pension funds and hedge funds. Analysts furiously compete to be the most useful voice to fund managers on Disney, say, or General Electric. Analysts whose research fails to hold up quickly find that fund managers will no longer return their calls. Then they quickly find themselves out of work, especially these days. Analysts whose research is valuable find themselves voted onto Institutional Investor's annual poll of "All-Star" analysts, an honor that results in lots of prestige and lots of money. It is this competition, more than anything else, that keeps analysts honest.

Analysts have succeeded in making themselves necessary for institutional investors. Few of the recent caricatures of Jack Grubman, for example, note that the former Salomon Smith Barney analyst reached his position of power—with the obscenity of his compensation—because he was institutional investors' favorite telecom analyst. These investors weren't tricked. They were aware of Mr. Grubman's well-deserved reputation for investment banking hanky-panky, his too-convenient ratings changes and his penchant for recommending companies all the way into bankruptcy. But as a friend who met with him earlier this year told me, Mr. Grubman's insights were perceptive. After the meeting, my friend's firm was better equipped to invest in telecom companies.

But someone forgot to tell small investors how all this worked. When analysts, more out of laziness than corruption, allowed reports or ratings to persist that didn't reflect their latest views, they misled investors who didn't have access to the financial world's cozy candor. For this, analysts deserve part of the blame for the losses amateur investors incurred. More blame, however, should go to those who never explained to small investors how even the best Wall Street research is conditional, fluid and fallible. In their celebration of the limitless possibilities of stock ownership, online brokers, traditional brokers and the press created a culture of reckless, ill-informed investing.

If regulators really want to help small investors, they should find a way to remind them that professionals are frequently wrong and that amateurs cannot regularly beat the market on their own. Regulators, perhaps, should take a cue from cigarette packaging. On every page of every analyst report, in bold letters, the message should be blunt: The person who wrote this report is a fallible human being. And in even bolder letters: Small investors should not buy individual stocks.

Source: Excerpted from Gary Sernovitz, "Don't Shoot the Analyst," *The New York Times,* November 15, 2002.

flows will be lower when the stream is perceived to be riskier. Hence the stock price and the ratio of price to earnings will be lower.

Of course, if you scan *The Wall Street Journal,* you will observe many small, risky, start-up companies with very high P/E multiples. This does not contradict our claim that P/E multiples should fall with risk; instead it is evidence of the market's expectations of high growth rates for those companies. This is why we said that high-risk firms will have lower P/E ratios *holding all else equal*. Given a growth projection, the P/E multiple will be lower when risk is perceived to be higher.

## Pitfalls in P/E Analysis

No description of P/E analysis is complete without mentioning some of its pitfalls. First, consider that the denominator in the P/E ratio is accounting earnings, which are influenced by somewhat arbitrary accounting rules such as the use of historical cost in depreciation and inventory valuation. In times of high inflation, historic cost depreciation and inventory costs will tend to underrepresent true economic values, because the replacement cost of both goods and capital equipment will rise with the general level of prices. As Figure 18.3 on page 630 demonstrates, P/E ratios have tended to be lower when inflation has been higher. This reflects the market's assessment that earnings in these periods are of "lower quality," artificially distorted by inflation, and warranting lower P/E ratios.

**Humble Pie (sung to the tune of "American Pie")**
A long, long week ago
I can still remember how the market used to make me smile
What I'd do when I had the chance
Is get myself a cash advance
And add another tech stock to the pile.

But Alan Greenspan made me shiver
With every speech that he delivered
Bad news on the rate front
Still I'd take one more punt

I can't remember if I cried
When I heard about the CPI
I lost my fortune and my pride
The day the NASDAQ died

So bye-bye to my piece of the pie
I poured by paycheck into Datek
Now my cash account's dry
It's just two weeks from a new all-time high
And now we're right back where we were in July
We're right back where we were in July

Did you buy stocks you never heard of?
Q COM at 150 or above?
'Cause your plumber told you so
Now do you believe in Home Depot?
Can Wal-Mart save your portfolio?
And can you teach me what's a P/E ratio?

Well, I know that you were leveraged too
So you can't just take a long-term view

Your broker shut you down
No more margin could be found

I never worried on the whole way up
Buying dot coms from the back of a pickup truck
But Friday I ran out of luck
It was the day the NAAAASDAQ died

I started singin'
Bye-bye to my piece of the pie
I poured by paycheck into Datek
Now my cash account's dry
It's just two weeks from a new all-time high
And now we're right back where we were in July
Yeah we're right back where we were in July

Now for ten days, we've been on our own
And E-trade won't pick up the phone
But that's not how it used to be
When investors snapped up EMC
With cash they borrowed easily
And a quote that flashed up permanently green

Oh, and just as things were turning 'round
Joel Klein slapped Mister Softee down
The courtroom was adjourned
A guilty verdict was returned
And while Gilder read a book on quarks
Buffet smirked and Greenspan barked
The bulls were eaten by the sharks
The day, the NASDAQ died

I started singin' . . .

---

**Earnings management** is the practice of using flexibility in accounting rules to improve the apparent profitability of the firm. We will have much to say on this topic in the next chapter on interpreting financial statements. A version of earnings management that became common in the 1990s was the reporting of "pro forma earnings" measures. These measures are sometimes called *operating earnings,* a term with no generally accepted definition.

Pro forma earnings are calculated ignoring certain expenses, for example, restructuring charges, stock-option expenses, or write-downs of assets from continuing operations. Firms argue that ignoring these expenses gives a clearer picture of the underlying profitability of the firm. Comparisons with earlier periods probably would make more sense if those costs were excluded.

But there is so much leeway for choosing what to exclude that it becomes hard for investors or analysts to interpret the numbers or to compare them across firms. The lack of standards gives firms considerable leeway to manage earnings. One analyst calculated that in the first three quarters of 2001, the companies that comprise the Nasdaq 100 index reported collective pro forma earnings of $82.3 billion, but GAAP losses of $19.1 billion, a difference of over $100 billion—for only these 100 firms![8]

---

[8] Reported in *The Economist,* February 23, 2002, p. 77.

Manic panic, it's just like the *Titanic*
Unsinkable and now under the Atlantic
We're at four thou and falling fast
All at once the bottom-fishers pounced
But that just caused a dead-cat bounce
'Cause Mister Softee, from the sidelines, preannounced

Now the graph-lines showed complete collapse
While the margin calls were coming fast
We all were forced to sell
Our Apple, E-Bay and Intel
Then the bear funds moved to take the field
And the long bond shed a point of yield
Was Glass-Steagall ever really repealed?
The day, the NASDAQ died

We started singing . . .

Oh, and suddenly we're underwater
Millionaires all hot and bothered
With no cash left to buy again
So come on, Fed be anxious, com-pen-sate
By lowering the discount rate
'Cause easy money is a bubble's only friend

Oh, and as I watched the index fall
I received the dreaded margin call
No broker born in hell
Could make me want to sell
But as my gains fell fast into the crash

E-Trade began demanding cash
The talking heads were talking trash
The day, the NASDAQ died

They were singing . . .

I met an analyst for Micromuse
I asked him for their earning news
But he just smiled and turned away
I logged on to the trading floor
Where I made my fortune weeks before
But they demanded to see cash before I played

And on T.V. the ticker streamed
Kudlow cried and Barton dreamed
Not a bullish word was spoken
The daytraders were choking

And the three stocks I acquired last
AMAT, Dell and Infocast
Couldn't catch a bid and faded fast
The day the NASDAQ died

And they were singing . . .
Bye-bye to my piece of the pie
I poured by paycheck into Datek
Now my cash account's dry
It's just two weeks from a new all-time high
And now we're right back where we were in July
Yeah we're right back where we were in July

Even GAAP allows firms considerable discretion to manage earnings. For example, in the late 1990s, Kellogg took restructuring charges, which are supposed to be one-time events, nine quarters in a row. Were these really one-time events, or were they more appropriately treated as ordinary expenses? Given the available leeway in managing earnings, the justified P/E multiple becomes difficult to gauge.

Another confounding factor in the use of P/E ratios is related to the business cycle. We were careful in deriving the DDM to define earnings as being net of *economic* depreciation, that is, the maximum flow of income that the firm could pay out without depleting its productive capacity. But reported earnings are computed in accordance with generally accepted accounting principles and need not correspond to economic earnings. Beyond this, however, notions of a normal or justified P/E ratio, as in equations 18.7 or 18.8, assume implicitly that earnings rise at a constant rate, or, put another way, on a smooth trend line. In contrast, reported earnings can fluctuate dramatically around a trend line over the course of the business cycle.

Another way to make this point is to note that the "normal" P/E ratio predicted by equation 18.8 is the ratio of today's price to the trend value of future earnings, $E_1$. The P/E ratio reported in the financial pages of the newspaper, by contrast, is the ratio of price to the most recent *past* accounting earnings. Current accounting earnings can differ considerably from future economic earnings. Because ownership of stock conveys the right to future as well

**Figure 18.3**
**P/E ratios**
**and inflation**

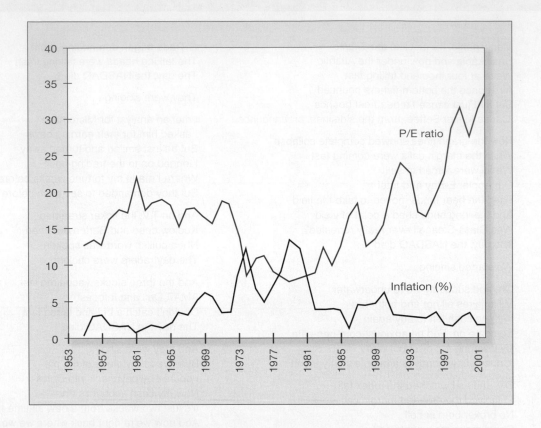

as current earnings, the ratio of price to most recent earnings can vary substantially over the business cycle, as accounting earnings and the trend value of economic earnings diverge by greater and lesser amounts.

As an example, Figure 18.4 graphs the earnings per share of Intel and AEP since 1992. Note that Intel's EPS fluctuate considerably. This reflects the company's relatively high degree of sensitivity to the business cycle. Value Line estimates its beta at 1.25. AEP, by contrast, shows much less variation in earnings per share around a smoother and flatter trend line. Its beta was only .75.

Because the market values the entire stream of future dividends generated by the company, when earnings are temporarily depressed, the P/E ratio should tend to be high—that is, the denominator of the ratio responds more sensitively to the business cycle than the numerator. This pattern is borne out well.

Figure 18.5 graphs the Intel and AEP P/E ratios. Intel, with the more volatile earnings profile, also has a more volatile P/E profile. For example, in 2001, when earnings fell below the trend line (Figure 18.4), the P/E ratio correspondingly jumped (Figure 18.5). The market clearly recognized that earnings were depressed only temporarily.

This example shows why analysts must be careful in using P/E ratios. There is no way to say P/E ratio is overly high or low without referring to the company's long-run growth prospects, as well as to current earnings per share relative to the long-run trend line.

Nevertheless, Figures 18.4 and 18.5 demonstrate a clear relationship between P/E ratios and growth. Despite considerable short-run fluctuations, Intel's EPS clearly trended upward over the period. AEP's earnings were essentially flat. Intel's growth prospects are reflected in its consistently higher P/E multiple.

This analysis suggests that P/E ratios should vary across industries, and in fact they do. Figure 18.6 shows P/E ratios in early 2003 for a sample of industries. P/E ratios for each

**Figure 18.4
Earnings growth
for two companies**

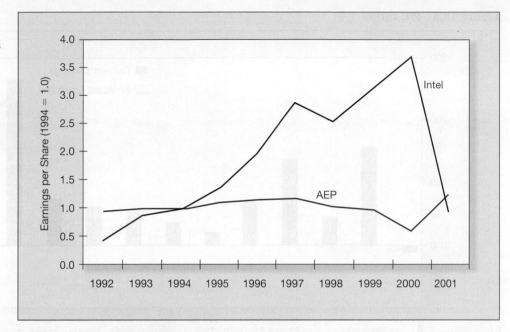

**Figure 18.5
Price–
earnings
ratios**

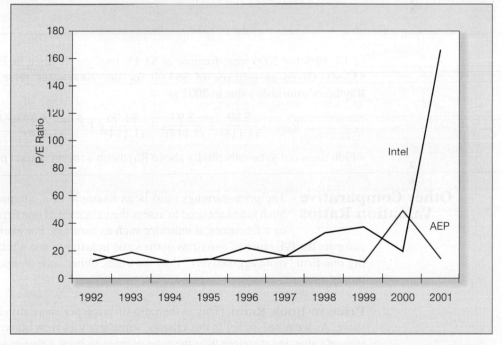

industry are computed in two ways: by taking the ratio of price to previous year earnings, and projected next-year earnings. Notice that although the ratios based on last year's earnings appear quite high, the ratios are more moderate when prices are compared to forecasted earnings. This should not surprise you, because stock market prices are based on firms' future earnings prospects.

# Combining P/E Analysis and the DDM

Some analysts use P/E ratios in conjunction with earnings forecasts to estimate the price of a stock at an investor's horizon date. The Raytheon analysis in Figure 18.2 shows that Value Line forecasted a P/E ratio for 2006

**Figure 18.6**  P/E ratios

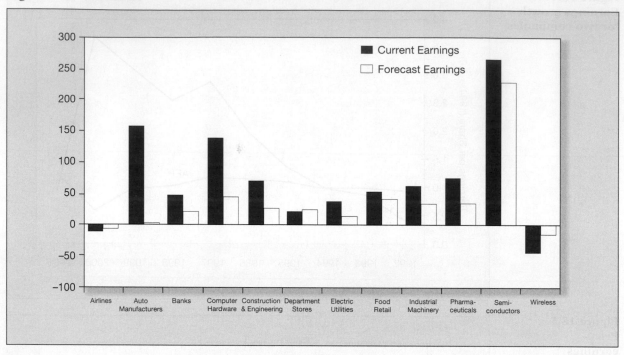

of 14. EPS for 2006 were forecast at \$3.85, implying a price in 2006 of 14 × \$3.85 = \$53.90. Given an estimate of \$53.90 for the 2006 sales price, we would compute Raytheon's intrinsic value in 2002 as

$$V_{2002} = \frac{\$.80}{(1.114)} + \frac{\$.93}{(1.114)^2} + \frac{\$1.06}{(1.114)^3} + \frac{\$1.20 + \$53.90}{(1.114)^4} = \$35.13$$

which turns out to be only mildly above Raytheon's recent market price.

### Other Comparative Valuation Ratios

The price–earnings ratio is an example of a comparative valuation ratio. Such ratios are used to assess the valuation of one firm versus another based on a fundamental indicator such as earnings. For example, an analyst might compare the P/E ratios of two firms in the same industry to test whether the market is valuing one firm "more aggressively" than the other. Other such comparative ratios are commonly used:

**Price-to-Book Ratio.** This is the ratio of price per share divided by book value per share. As we noted earlier in this chapter, some analysts view book value as a useful measure of value and therefore treat the ratio of price to book value as an indicator of how aggressively the market values the firm.

**Price-to-Cash-Flow Ratio.** Earnings as reported on the income statement can be affected by the company's choice of accounting practices, and thus are commonly viewed as subject to some imprecision and even manipulation. In contrast, cash flow—which tracks cash actually flowing into or out of the firm—is less affected by accounting decisions. As a result, some analysts prefer to use the ratio of price to cash flow per share rather than price to earnings per share. Some analysts use operating cash flow when calculating this ratio; others prefer "free cash flow," that is, operating cash flow net of new investment.

**Figure 18.7 Market valuation statistics**

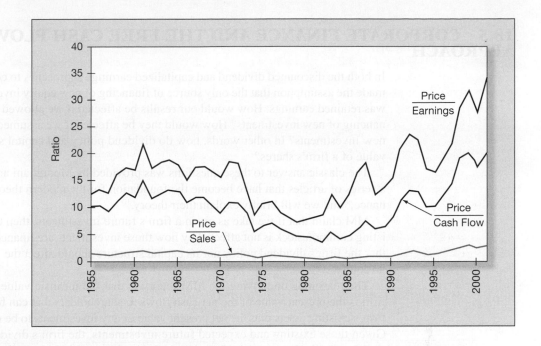

**Price-to-Sales Ratio.**    Many start-up firms have no earnings. As a result, the price–earnings ratio for these firms is meaningless. The price-to-sales ratio (the ratio of stock price to the annual sales per share) has recently become a popular valuation benchmark for these firms. Of course, price-to-sales ratios can vary markedly across industries, since profit margins vary widely.

**Be Creative.**    Sometimes a standard valuation ratio will simply not be available, and you will have to devise your own. In the 1990s, some analysts valued retail Internet firms based on the number of Web hits their sites received. As it turns out, they valued these firms using too-generous "price-to-hits" ratios. Nevertheless, in a new investment environment, these analysts used the information available to them to devise the best valuation tools they could.

Figure 18.7 presents the behavior of several valuation measures since 1955. While the levels of these ratios differ considerably, for the most part, they track each other fairly closely, with upturns and downturns at the same times.

# 18.5  CORPORATE FINANCE AND THE FREE CASH FLOW APPROACH

In both the discounted dividend and capitalized earnings approaches to equity valuation we made the assumption that the only source of financing of new equity investment in the firm was retained earnings. How would our results be affected if we allowed external equity financing of new investments? How would they be affected if we assumed debt financing of new investments? In other words, how do dividend policy and capital structure affect the value of a firm's shares?

The classic answer to these questions was provided by Modigliani and Miller (MM) in a series of articles that have become the foundation for the modern theory of corporate finance,[9] and we will briefly explain their theory.[10]

MM claim that if we take as given a firm's future investments, then the value of its existing common stock is not affected by how those investments are financed. Therefore, neither the firm's dividend policy nor its capital structure should affect the value of a share of its equity.

The reasoning underlying the MM theory is that the intrinsic value of the equity in a firm is the present value of the net cash flows to shareholders that can be produced by the firm's existing assets plus the net present value of any investments to be made in the future. Given those existing and expected future investments, the firm's dividend and financing decisions will affect only the form in which existing shareholders will receive their future returns, that is, as dividends or capital gains, but not their present value.

As a by-product of their proof of these propositions, MM show the equivalence of three seemingly different approaches to valuing the equity in a firm. The first two are the discounted dividend and capitalized earnings approaches presented in the earlier parts of this chapter. The third is the free cash flow approach.

This third approach starts with an estimate of the value of the firm as a whole and derives the value of the equity by subtracting the market value of all nonequity claims. The estimate of the value of the firm is found as the present value of cash flows, assuming all-equity financing plus the net present value of tax shields created by using debt. This approach is similar to that used by the firm's own management in capital budgeting, or the valuation approach that another firm would use in assessing the firm as a possible acquisition target.

## EXAMPLE 18.6    Free Cash Flow Valuation

Consider the MiMo Corporation. Its cash flow from operations before interest and taxes was $1 million in the year just ended, and it expects that this will grow by 6% per year forever. To make this happen, the firm will have to invest an amount equal to 15% of pretax cash flow each year. The tax rate is 30%. Depreciation was $100,000 in the year just ended and is expected to grow at the same rate as the operating cash flow. The appropriate market capitalization rate for the unleveraged cash flow is 10% per year, and the firm currently has debt of $2 million outstanding.

---

[9] The original two papers are M. Miller and F. Modigliani, "Dividend Policy, Growth and the Valuation of Shares," *Journal of Business,* October 1961; and F. Modigliani and M. Miller, "The Cost of Capital, Corporation Finance, and the Theory of Investment," *American Economic Review,* June 1958. Miller has revised his views in "Debt and Taxes," *Journal of Finance,* May 1976, and Modigliani his in "Debt, Dividend Policy, Taxes, Inflation and Market Valuation," *Journal of Finance,* May 1982.

[10] For a more complete treatment see Stephen A. Ross, Randolph W. Westerfield, and Jeffrey F. Jaffe, *Corporate Finance,* 6th ed. (New York: McGraw-Hill/Irwin, 2002), Chapters 15 and 16; or Richard A. Brealey and Stewart C. Myers, *Principles of Corporate Finance,* 7th ed. (New York: McGraw-Hill/Irwin, 2003), Chapters 17 and 18.

# MULTI-STAGE GROWTH MODELS

The spreadsheets at the Online Learning Center for this chapter contain two- and three-stage dividend discount models. Rather than forecasting year-by-year dividends in the first stage, in this version of the model the analyst forecasts an initial high dividend growth rate. In the last stage, dividends are forecast to grow indefinitely at a constant rate. In the transition years, the analyst forecasts a dividend growth rate in between the initial high rate and the more moderate sustainable rate. This spreadsheet is available at **www.mhhe.com/bkm**.

|   | A | B |
|---|---|---|
| 1 | | |
| 2 | | |
| 3 | | |
| 4 | Initial Earnings ($E_0$) | $4.00 |
| 5 | Initial Dividend ($D_0$) | $2.00 |
| 6 | Stage 1 growth rate ($g_1$) | 35.00% |
| 7 | Duration of Stage1 growth (years) | 10.0 |
| 8 | Stage 2 growth rate ($g_2$) | 14.00% |
| 9 | Duration of Stage 2 growth (years) | 10.0 |
| 10 | Stage 3 growth rate ($g_3$) | 8.00% |
| 11 | Beta Coefficient ($\beta$) | 1.25 |
| 12 | T-Bill Rate ($r_f$) | 5.00% |
| 13 | Market Risk Premium ($r_M - r_f$) | 8.00% |
| 14 | | |
| 15 | Required Return (k) | 15.00% |
| 16 | Ratio of $[(1+g^1)/(1+k)]$ | 1.17391 |
| 17 | Ratio of $[(1+g^2)/(1+k)]$ | 0.99130 |
| 18 | Present Value of Stage 1 growing annuity | 19.85017 |
| 19 | Present Value of Stage 2 growing annuity | 1.19474 |
| 20 | | |
| 21 | Present Value of Stage 1 Dividends | $53.595 |
| 22 | Present Value of Stage 2 Dividends | $13.538 |
| 23 | Present Value of Stage 3 Dividends | $140.535 |
| 24 | Value of the Stock | $207.669 |
| 25 | | |
| 26 | **Analysis of Growth Opportunities** | |
| 27 | No-Growth value of the firm | $26.667 |
| 28 | Present Value of Growth Opportunities | $181.002 |
| 29 | | |
| 30 | **Price-to-Earnings Ratios** | |
| 31 | Price/Current Earnings | 51.9173 |
| | Price/Next Year's Expected Earnings | 38.4572 |

MiMo's projected free cash flow for the coming year is

| | |
|---|---|
| Before-tax cash flow from operations | $1,060,000 |
| Depreciation | 106,000 |
| Taxable income | 954,000 |
| Taxes (at 30%) | 286,200 |
| After-tax unleveraged income | 667,800 |
| After-tax cash flow from operations (after-tax unleveraged income plus depreciation) | 773,800 |
| New investment (15% of cash flow from operations) | 159,000 |
| Free cash flow (after-tax cash flow from operations minus new investment) | 614,800 |

It is important to realize that this projected free cash flow is what the firm's cash flow would be under all-equity financing. It ignores the interest expense on the debt, as well as any tax savings resulting from the deductibility of the interest expense.

The present value of all future free cash flows is

$$V_0 = \frac{C_1}{k - g} = \frac{\$614,800}{.10 - .06} = \$15,370,000$$

Thus the value of the whole firm, debt plus equity, is $15,370,000. Because the value of the debt is $2 million, the value of the equity is $13,370,000.

If we believe that the use of financial leverage enhances the total value of the firm, then we should add to the $15,370,000 estimate of the firm's unleveraged value the gain from leverage. Thus if in Example 18.6 we believe that the tax shield provided by the deductibility of interest payments on the debt increases the firm's total value by $.5 million, the value of the firm would be $15,870,000 and the value of the equity $13,870,000.

In reconciling this free cash flow approach with either the discounted dividend or the capitalized earnings approach, it is important to realize that the capitalization rate to be used in the present value calculation is different. In the free cash flow approach it is the rate appropriate for unleveraged equity, whereas in the other two approaches, it is the rate appropriate for leveraged equity. Because leverage affects the stock's beta, these two capitalization rates will be different.

## 18.6    INFLATION AND EQUITY VALUATION

What about the effects of inflation on stock prices? We start with an "inflation-neutral" case in which all *real* variables, and therefore the stock price, are unaffected by inflation. We then explore the ways in which reality might differ.

Consider the case of Inflatotrend, a firm that in the absence of inflation pays out all earnings as dividends. Earnings and dividends per share are $1, and there is no growth. We will use asterisked (*) letters to denote variables in the no-inflation case, or what represents the real value of variables. We consider an equilibrium real capitalization rate, $k^*$, of 10% per year. The price per share of this stock should be $10:

$$P_0 = \frac{\$1}{.10} = \$10$$

Now imagine that inflation, $i$, is 6% per year, but that the values of the other economic variables adjust so as to leave their real values unchanged. Specifically, the *nominal* capitalization rate, $k$, becomes $(1 + k^*)(1 + i) - 1 = 1.10 \times 1.06 - 1 = .166$, or 16.6%, and the expected nominal growth rate of dividends, $g$, is now 6%, which is necessary to maintain a constant level of real dividends. The *nominal* dividend expected at the end of this year is therefore $1.06 per share.

If we apply the constant-growth DDM to these nominal variables we get the same price as in the no-inflation case:

$$P_0 = \frac{D_1}{k - g} = \frac{\$1.06}{.166 - .060} = \$10$$

Thus, as long as real values are unaffected, the stock's current price is unaffected by inflation.

Note that the expected nominal dividend yield, $D_1/P_0$, is 10.6% and the expected nominal capital gains rate, $(P_1 - P_0)/P_0$, is 6%. Almost the entire 6.6% increase in nominal return comes in the form of expected capital gains. A capital gain is necessary if the real value of the stock is to remain unaffected by inflation.

Let us see how these assumptions affect the other variables: earnings and the plowback ratio. To illuminate what otherwise may be confusing implications, we can explore a simplified story behind the examples above.

Inflatotrend produces a product that requires purchase of inventory at the beginning of each year, and sells the finished product at the end of the year. Last year there was no inflation. The inventory cost $10 million. Labor, rent, and other processing costs (paid at year-end) were $1 million, and revenue was $12 million. Assuming no taxes, earnings were $1 million:

| | |
|---|---|
| Revenue | $12 million |
| − Labor and rent | 1 million |
| − Cost of goods sold | 10 million |
| Earnings | $ 1 million |

All earnings are distributed as dividends to the 1 million shareholders. Because the only invested capital is the $10 million in inventory, the ROE is 10%.

This year, inflation of 6% is expected, and all prices are expected to rise at that rate. Because inventory is paid for at the beginning of the year, it will still cost $10 million. However, revenue will be $12.72 million instead of $12 million, and other costs will be $1.06 million.

**Nominal Earnings**

| | |
|---|---|
| Revenue | $12.72 million |
| − Labor and rent | 1.06 million |
| − Cost of goods sold | 10.00 million |
| Earnings | $ 1.66 million |
| ROE | 16.6% |

Note that the amount required to *replace* inventory at year's end is $10.6 million, rather than the beginning *cost* of $10 million, so the amount of cash available to distribute as dividends is $1.06 million, not the reported earnings of $1.66 million.

A dividend of $1.06 million would be just enough to keep the real value of dividends unchanged and at the same time allow for maintenance of the same real value of inventory. The reported earnings of $1.66 million overstate true economic earnings, in other words.

We thus have the following set of relationships:

| | No Inflation | 6% Inflation |
|---|---|---|
| Dividends | $1 million | $1.06 million |
| Reported earnings | $1 million | $1.66 million |
| ROE | 10% | 16.6% |
| Plowback ratio | 0 | .36145 |
| Price of a share | $10 | $10 |
| P/E ratio | 10 | 6.0241 |

There are some surprising findings in this case of "neutral" inflation, that is, inflation that leaves the real interest rate and real earnings unaffected. Although nominal dividends rise at the rate of inflation, 6%, reported earnings increase initially by 66%. In subsequent years, as long as inflation remains at a constant rate of 6%, earnings will grow at 6%.

Note also that the plowback ratio rises from 0 to .36145. Although plowback in the no-inflation case was zero, positive plowback of reported earnings now becomes necessary to maintain the level of inventory at a constant real value. Inventory must rise from a nominal level of $10 million to a level of $10.6 million to maintain its real value. This inventory investment requires reinvested earnings of $.6 million.

Thus, the proportion of reported income that must be retained and reinvested to keep the real growth rate of earnings at zero is .36145 if inflation is 6% per year. Multiplying this plowback ratio by the nominal ROE of 16.6% produces a nominal growth rate of dividends of 6%, which is equal to the inflation rate:

$$g = b \times \text{ROE}$$
$$= .36145 \times 16.6\% = 6\% \text{ per year}$$

More generally, the relationship between nominal and real variables is:

| Variable | Real | Nominal |
|---|---|---|
| Growth rate | $g^*$ | $g = (1 + g^*)(1 + i) - 1$ |
| Capitalization rate | $k^*$ | $k = (1 + k^*)(1 + i) - 1$ |
| Return on equity | ROE* | $\text{ROE} = (1 + \text{ROE}^*)(1 + i) - 1$ |
| Expected dividend | $D_1^*$ | $D_1 = (1 + i)D_1^*$ |
| Plowback ratio | $b^*$ | $b = \dfrac{(1 + b^* \times \text{ROE}^*)(1 + i) - 1}{(1 + \text{ROE}^*)(1 + i) - 1}$ |

Note that it is not true that $E_1 = (1 + i)E_1^*$. That is, expected reported earnings do not, in general, equal expected real earnings times one plus the inflation rate. The reason, as you have seen, is that stated earnings do not accurately measure the cost of replenishing assets.

For example, cost of goods sold is treated as if it were $10 million, even though it now costs $10.6 million to replace the inventory. Historical cost accounting in this case distorts the measured cost of goods sold, which in turn distorts the reported earnings figures. We will return to this point in Chapter 19.

Note also the effect of inflation on the P/E ratio. In our example the P/E ratio drops from 10 in the no-inflation scenario to 6.0241 in the 6% inflation scenario. This is entirely a result of the fact that the reported earnings figure gets distorted by inflation and overstates true economic earnings.

This is true in the real world too, not just in our simplified example. Look back at Figure 18.3 and you will see that P/E ratios fall dramatically when the inflation rate increases. Many companies show gains in reported earnings during inflationary periods, even though real earnings may be unaffected. This is one reason analysts must interpret data on the past behavior of P/E ratios over time with great care.

**CONCEPT CHECK ☞ QUESTION 6**

Assume that Inflatotrend has a 4% annual expected constant growth rate of earnings if there is no inflation. $E_1^* = \$1$ per share; ROE* = 10% per year; $b^* = .4$; and $k^* = 10\%$ per year.

a. What is the current price of a share?

b. What are the expected real dividend yield and rate of capital appreciation?

c. If the firm's real revenues and dividends are unaffected by inflation, and expected inflation is 6% per year, what should be the nominal growth rate of dividends, the expected nominal dividend yield, the expected ROE, and the nominal plowback ratio?

For many years economists thought that stocks ought to be an inflation-neutral investment in the sense that we have described. They believed, and many of them still believe, that changes in the rate of inflation, whether expected or unexpected, ought to have no effect on the expected real rate of return on common stocks.

Recent empirical research, however, seems to indicate that real rates of return are negatively correlated with inflation. In terms of the simple constant-growth-rate DDM, this would mean that an increase in inflation is associated with a decrease in $D_1$, an increase in $k$, a decrease in $g$, or some combination of all three.

One school of thought[11] believes that economic "shocks" such as oil price hikes can cause a simultaneous increase in the inflation rate and decline of expected real earnings (and dividends). This would result in a negative correlation between inflation and real stock returns.

A second view[12] is that the higher the rate of inflation, the riskier real stock returns are perceived to be. The reasoning here is that higher inflation is associated with greater uncertainty about the economy, which tends to induce a higher required rate of return on equity. In addition, a higher $k$ implies a lower level of stock prices.

A third perspective[13] is that higher inflation results in lower real dividends because our tax system results in lower after-tax real earnings as the inflation rate rises.

Finally, there is the view[14] that many investors in the stock market suffer from a form of "money illusion." Investors mistake the rise in nominal rate of interest for a rise in the real rate. As a result, they undervalue stocks in a period of higher inflation.

# 18.7   THE AGGREGATE STOCK MARKET

**Explaining**
**Past Behavior**

It has been well documented that the stock market is a leading economic indicator.[15] This means that it tends to fall before a recession and to rise before an economic recovery. However, the relationship is far from perfectly reliable.

Most scholars and serious analysts would agree that, although the stock market sometimes appears to have a substantial life of its own, responding perhaps to bouts of mass euphoria and then panic, economic events and the anticipation of such events do have a substantial effect on stock prices. Perhaps the two factors with the greatest impact are interest rates and corporate profits.

Figure 18.8 shows the behavior of the earnings-to-price ratio (i.e., the earnings yield) of the S&P 500 stock index versus the yield to maturity on long-term Treasury bonds since 1955. Clearly, the two series track each other quite closely. This is to be expected: The two variables that affect a firm's value are earnings (and implicitly the dividends they can support) and the discount rate, which "translates" future income into present value. Thus, it should not be surprising that the ratio of earnings to stock price (the inverse of the P/E ratio) varies with the interest rate.

---

[11] See Eugene F. Fama, "Stock Returns, Real Activity, Inflation, and Money," *American Economic Review*, September 1981.
[12] See Burton Malkiel, *A Random Walk Down Wall Street*, 6th ed. (New York: W. W. Norton, 1996).
[13] See Martin Feldstein, "Inflation and the Stock Market," *American Economic Review*, December 1980.
[14] See Franco Modigliani and Richard Cohn, "Inflation, Rational Valuation, and the Market," *Financial Analysts Journal*, March–April 1979.
[15] See, for example, Stanley Fischer and Robert C. Merton, "Macroeconomics and Finance: The Role of the Stock Market," *Carnegie-Rochester Conference Series on Public Policy* 21 (1984).

**Figure 18.8    Earnings yield of S&P 500 versus 10-year Treasury-bond yield**

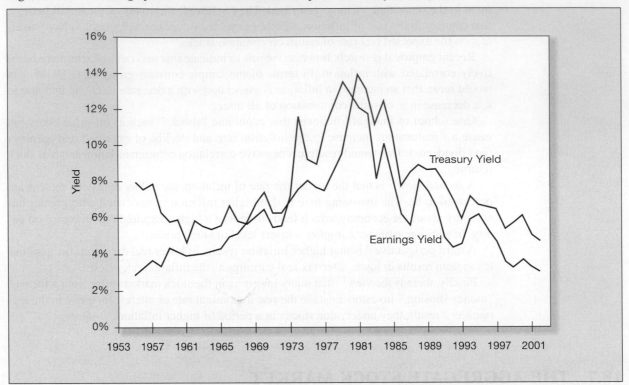

### Forecasting the Stock Market

What can we learn from all of this about the future rate of return on stocks? First, a note of optimism. Although timing the stock market is a very difficult and risky game, it may not be impossible. For example, we saw in Chapter 12 that some variables such as the market dividend yield seem to predict market returns.

However, if market history teaches us anything at all, it is that the market has great variability. Thus, although we can use a variety of methods to derive a best forecast of the expected holding-period return on the market, the uncertainty surrounding that forecast will always be high.

The most popular approach to forecasting the overall stock market is the earnings multiplier approach applied at the aggregate level. The first step is to forecast corporate profits for the coming period. Then we derive an estimate of the earnings multiplier, the aggregate P/E ratio, based on a forecast of long-term interest rates. The product of the two forecasts is the estimate of the end-of-period level of the market.

The forecast of the P/E ratio of the market is sometimes derived from a graph similar to that in Figure 18.8, which plots the *earnings yield* (earnings per share divided by price per share, the reciprocal of the P/E ratio) of the S&P 500 and the yield to maturity on 10-year Treasury bonds. The figure shows that both yields rose dramatically in the 1970s. In the case of Treasury bonds, this was because of an increase in the inflationary expectations built into interest rates. The earnings yield on the S&P 500, however, probably rose because of inflationary distortions that artificially increased reported earnings. We have already seen that P/E ratios tend to fall when inflation rates increase. When inflation moderated in the 1980s, both Treasury and earnings yields fell. For most of the last 20 years, the earnings yield ran about 1 percentage point below the T-bond rate.

| Table 18.4   S&P 500 Price Forecasts under Various Scenarios | | | |
|---|---|---|---|
| | **Most Likely Scenario** | **Pessimistic Scenario** | **Optimistic Scenario** |
| Treasury bond yield | 5.2% | 5.7% | 4.7% |
| Earnings yield | 4.2% | 4.7% | 3.7% |
| Resulting P/E ratio | 23.8 | 21.3 | 27.0 |
| EPS forecast | $53 | $53 | $53 |
| Forecast for S&P 500 | 1,261 | 1,129 | 1,431 |

Forecast for the earnings yield on the S&P 500 equals Treasury bond yield minus 1%. The P/E ratio is the reciprocal of the forecasted earnings yield.

One might use this relationship and the current yield on 10-year Treasury bonds to forecast the earnings yield on the S&P 500. Given that earnings yield, a forecast of earnings could be used to predict the level of the S&P in some future period. Let's consider a simple example of this procedure.

**EXAMPLE 18.7**   **Forecasting the Aggregate Stock Market**

The early 2002 forecast for 2002 earnings per share for the S&P 500 portfolio was about $53.[16] The 10-year Treasury bond yield was about 5.2%. Because the earnings yield on the S&P 500 has been about 1 percentage point below the 10-year Treasury yield, a first guess for the earnings yield on the S&P 500 might be 4.2%. This would imply a P/E ratio of $1/.042 = 23.8$. Our forecast for the S&P 500 index would then be $23.8 \times 53 = 1,261$.

Of course, there is uncertainty regarding all three inputs into this analysis: the actual earnings on the S&P 500 stocks, the level of Treasury yields at year end, and the spread between the Treasury yield and the earnings yield. One would wish to perform sensitivity or scenario analysis to examine the impact of changes in all of these variables. To illustrate, consider Table 18.4, which shows a simple scenario analysis treating possible effects of variation in the Treasury bond yield. The scenario analysis shows that forecasted level of the stock market varies inversely and with dramatic sensitivity to interest rate changes.

Some analysts use an aggregate version of the dividend discount model rather than an earnings multiplier approach. All of these models, however, rely heavily on forecasts of such macroeconomic variables as GDP, interest rates, and the rate of inflation, which are difficult to predict accurately.

Because stock prices reflect expectations of future dividends, which are tied to the economic fortunes of firms, it is not surprising that the performance of a broad-based stock index like the S&P 500 is taken as a leading economic indicator, that is, a predictor of the performance of the aggregate economy. Stock prices are viewed as embodying consensus forecasts of economic activity and are assumed to move up or down in anticipation of movements in the economy. The government's index of leading economic indicators, which is taken to predict the progress of the business cycle, is made up in part of recent stock market performance. However, the predictive value of the market is far from perfect. A well-known joke, often attributed to Paul Samuelson, is that the market has forecast eight of the last five recessions.

---

[16] According to Institutional Brokers Estimate System (I/B/E/S). I/B/E/S surveys a large sample of stock analysts and reports several analyses of their forecasts for both the economy and individual stocks.

# SUMMARY

1. One approach to firm valuation is to focus on the firm's book value, either as it appears on the balance sheet or as adjusted to reflect current replacement cost of assets or liquidation value. Another approach is to focus on the present value of expected future dividends.

2. The dividend discount model holds that the price of a share of stock should equal the present value of all future dividends per share, discounted at an interest rate commensurate with the risk of the stock.

3. The constant-growth version of the DDM asserts that if dividends are expected to grow at a constant rate forever, the intrinsic value of the stock is determined by the formula

$$V_0 = \frac{D_1}{k - g}$$

This version of the DDM is simplistic in its assumption of a constant value of $g$. There are more-sophisticated multistage versions of the model for more-complex environments. When the constant-growth assumption is reasonably satisfied and the stock is selling for its intrinsic value, the formula can be inverted to infer the market capitalization rate for the stock:

$$k = \frac{D_1}{P_0} + g$$

4. The constant growth dividend discount model is best suited for firms that are expected to exhibit stable growth rates over the foreseeable future. In reality, however, firms progress through lifecycles. In early years, attractive investment opportunities are ample and the firm responds with high plowback ratios and rapid dividend growth. Eventually, however, growth rates level off to more sustainable values. Three-stage growth models are well-suited to such a pattern. These models allow for an initial period of rapid growth, a final period of steady dividend growth, and a middle, or transition, period in which the dividend growth rate declines from its initial high rate to the lower sustainable rate.

5. Dividend growth models give estimates of the intrinsic value of a stock. If price does not equal intrinsic value, the rate of return will differ from the equilibrium return based on the stock's risk. The actual return will depend on the rate at which the stock price is predicted to revert to its intrinsic value.

6. Stock market analysts devote considerable attention to a company's price-to-earnings ratio. The P/E ratio is a useful measure of the market's assessment of the firm's growth opportunities. Firms with no growth opportunities should have a P/E ratio that is just the reciprocal of the capitalization rate, $k$. As growth opportunities become a progressively more important component of the total value of the firm, the P/E ratio will increase.

7. The expected growth rate of earnings is related both to the firm's expected profitability and to its dividend policy. The relationship can be expressed as

$$g = (\text{ROE on new investment}) \times (1 - \text{Dividend payout ratio})$$

8. You can relate any DDM to a simple capitalized earnings model by comparing the expected ROE on future investments to the market capitalization rate, $k$. If the two rates are equal, then the stock's intrinsic value reduces to expected earnings per share (EPS) divided by $k$.

9. Many analysts form their estimate of a stock's value by multiplying their forecast of next year's EPS by a P/E multiple derived from some empirical rule. This rule can be consistent with some version of the DDM, although often it is not.

10. The free cash flow approach is the one used most often in corporate finance. The analyst first estimates the value of the entire firm as the present value of expected future free cash flows, assuming all-equity financing, then adds the value of tax shields arising from debt financing, and finally subtracts the value of all claims other than equity. This approach will be consistent with the DDM and capitalized earnings approaches as long as the capitalization rate is adjusted to reflect financial leverage.

11. We explored the effects of inflation on stock prices in the context of the constant-growth DDM. Although traditional theory has been that inflation should have a neutral effect on real stock returns, historical evidence shows a striking negative correlation between inflation and real stock market returns. There are four different explanations that may account for this negative correlation:

    a. Economic "shocks" that simultaneously produce high inflation and lower real earnings.
    b. Increased riskiness of stocks in a more inflationary environment.
    c. Lower real after-tax earnings and dividends attributable to inflation-induced distortions in the tax system.
    d. Money "illusion."

12. The models presented in this chapter can be used to explain and forecast the behavior of the aggregate stock market. The key macroeconomic variables that determine the level of stock prices in the aggregate are interest rates and corporate profits.

**KEY TERMS**

| | | |
|---|---|---|
| book value | dividend discount model | present value of growth |
| liquidation value | (DDM) | opportunities |
| replacement cost | constant-growth DDM | price–earnings multiple |
| Tobin's $q$ | dividend payout ratio | earnings management |
| intrinsic value | plowback ratio | |
| market capitalization rate | earnings retention ratio | |

**WEBSITES**

Go to the following sites for information on earnings announcements and other material announcements.

www.fulldisclosure.com/highlight.asp?client=cb
www.earningswhispers.com

These websites make it possible to listen in on conference calls related to earnings announcements.
platinum.yahoo.com
www.bestcalls.com
www.investorbroadcast.com

You can research specific company information at the following sites:
www.fool.com/community/resource/company_research.htm

These websites provide stock screeners:
moneycentral.msn.com/investor (See lower-left menu.)
screen.yahoo.com/stocks.html
www.stocktables.com

## PROBLEMS

1. A common stock pays an annual dividend per share of $2.10. The risk-free rate is 7%, and the risk premium for this stock is 4%. If the annual dividend is expected to remain at $2.10, the value of the stock is *closest* to:
   a. $19.09
   b. $30.00
   c. $52.50
   d. $70.00

2. Which of the following assumptions does the constant-growth dividend discount model require?
      I. Dividends grow at a constant rate.
     II. The dividend growth rate continues indefinitely.
    III. The required rate of return is less than the dividend growth rate.
   a. I only.
   b. III only.
   c. I and II only.
   d. I, II, and III.

3. a. Computer stocks currently provide an expected rate of return of 16%. MBI, a large computer company, will pay a year-end dividend of $2 per share. If the stock is selling at $50 per share, what must be the market's expectation of the growth rate of MBI dividends?
   b. If dividend growth forecasts for MBI are revised downward to 5% per year, what will happen to the price of MBI stock? What (qualitatively) will happen to the company's price–earnings ratio?

4. *a.* MF Corp. has an ROE of 16% and a plowback ratio of 50%. If the coming year's earnings are expected to be $2 per share, at what price will the stock sell? The market capitalization rate is 12%.

   *b.* What price do you expect MF shares to sell for in 3 years?

5. At Litchfield Chemical Corp. (LCC), a director of the company said that the use of dividend discount models by investors is "proof" that the higher the dividend, the higher the stock price.

   *a.* Using a constant-growth dividend discount model as a basis of reference, evaluate the director's statement.

   *b.* Explain how an increase in dividend payout would affect each of the following (holding all other factors constant):
   
   i.  Sustainable growth rate.
   
   ii. Growth in book value.

6. The market consensus is that Analog Electronic Corporation has an ROE = 9%, has a beta of 1.25, and plans to maintain indefinitely its traditional plowback ratio of 2/3. This year's earnings were $3 per share. The annual dividend was just paid. The consensus estimate of the coming year's market return is 14%, and T-bills currently offer a 6% return.

   *a.* Find the price at which Analog stock should sell.

   *b.* Calculate the P/E ratio.

   *c.* Calculate the present value of growth opportunities.

   *d.* Suppose your research convinces you Analog will announce momentarily that it will immediately reduce its plowback ratio to 1/3. Find the intrinsic value of the stock. The market is still unaware of this decision. Explain why $V_0$ no longer equals $P_0$ and why $V_0$ is greater or less than $P_0$.

7. If the expected rate of return of the market portfolio is 15% and a stock with a beta of 1.0 pays a dividend yield of 4%, what must the market believe is the expected rate of price appreciation on that stock?

8. The FI Corporation's dividends per share are expected to grow indefinitely by 5% per year.

   *a.* If this year's year-end dividend is $8 and the market capitalization rate is 10% per year, what must the current stock price be according to the DDM?

   *b.* If the expected earnings per share are $12, what is the implied value of the ROE on future investment opportunities?

   *c.* How much is the market paying per share for growth opportunities (i.e., for an ROE on future investments that exceeds the market capitalization rate)?

9. Helen Morgan, CFA, has been asked to use the DDM to determine the value of Sundanci, Inc. Morgan anticipates that Sundanci's earnings and dividends will grow at 32% for 2 years and 13% thereafter.

   Calculate the current value of a share of Sundanci stock by using a two-stage dividend discount model and the data from Tables 18A and 18B.

10. Abbey Naylor, CFA, has been directed to determine the value of Sundanci's stock using the Free Cash Flow to Equity (FCFE) model. Naylor believes that Sundanci's FCFE will grow at 27% for 2 years and 13% thereafter. Capital expenditures, depreciation, and working capital are all expected to increase proportionately with FCFE.

    *a.* Calculate the amount of FCFE per share for the year 2000, using the data from Table 18A.

**Table 18A    Sundanci Actual 1999 and 2000 Financial Statements for Fiscal Years Ending May 31 ($ million, except per-share data)**

| Income Statement | 1999 | 2000 |
|---|---|---|
| Revenue | $474 | $598 |
| Depreciation | 20 | 23 |
| Other operating costs | 368 | 460 |
| Income before taxes | 86 | 115 |
| Taxes | 26 | 35 |
| Net income | 60 | 80 |
| Dividends | 18 | 24 |
| Earnings per share | $0.714 | $0.952 |
| Dividend per share | $0.214 | $0.286 |
| Common shares outstanding (millions) | 84.0 | 84.0 |
| **Balance Sheet** | **1999** | **2000** |
| Current assets | $201 | $326 |
| Net property, plant and equipment | 474 | 489 |
| Total assets | 675 | 815 |
| Current liabilities | 57 | 141 |
| Long-term debt | 0 | 0 |
| Total liabilities | 57 | 141 |
| Shareholders' equity | 618 | 674 |
| Total liabilities and equity | 675 | 815 |
| Capital expenditures | 34 | 38 |

**Table 18B    Selected Financial Information**

| | |
|---|---|
| Required rate of return on equity | 14% |
| Growth rate of industry | 13% |
| Industry P/E ratio | 26 |

  *b.* Calculate the current value of a share of Sundanci stock based on the two-stage FCFE model.

  *c.* i. Describe one limitation of the two-stage DDM model that is addressed by using the two-stage FCFE model.

   ii. Describe one limitation of the two-stage DDM model that is *not* addressed by using the two-stage FCFE model.

11. Christie Johnson, CFA, has been assigned to analyze Sundanci using the constant dividend growth price/earnings (P/E) ratio model. Johnson assumes that Sundanci's earnings and dividends will grow at a constant rate of 13%.

  *a.* Calculate the P/E ratio based on information in Tables 18A and 18B and on Johnson's assumptions for Sundanci.

  *b.* Identify, within the context of the constant dividend growth model, how each of the following factors would affect the P/E ratio.
- Risk (beta) of Sundanci.
- Estimated growth rate of earnings and dividends.
- Market risk premium.

12. The risk-free rate of return is 10%, the required rate of return on the market is 15%, and High-Flyer stock has a beta coefficient of 1.5. If the dividend per share expected during the coming year, $D_1$, is $2.50 and $g = 5\%$, at what price should a share sell?

13. Your preliminary analysis of two stocks has yielded the information set forth below. The market capitalization rate for both Stock A and Stock B is 10% per year.

| | Stock A | Stock B |
|---|---|---|
| Expected return on equity, ROE | 14% | 12% |
| Estimated earnings per share, $E_1$ | $ 2.00 | $ 1.65 |
| Estimated dividends per share, $D_1$ | $ 1.00 | $ 1.00 |
| Current market price per share, $P_0$ | $27.00 | $25.00 |

   a. What are the expected dividend payout ratios for the two stocks?
   b. What are the expected dividend growth rates of each?
   c. What is the intrinsic value of each stock?
   d. In which, if either, of the two stocks would you choose to invest?

14. Peninsular Research is initiating coverage of a mature manufacturing industry. John Jones, CFA, head of the research department, gathered the following fundamental industry and market data to help in his analysis:

| | |
|---|---|
| Forecast industry earnings retention rate | 40% |
| Forecast industry return on equity | 25% |
| Industry beta | 1.2 |
| Government bond yield | 6% |
| Equity risk premium | 5% |

   a. Compute the price-to-earnings ($P_0/E_1$) ratio for the industry based on this fundamental data.
   b. Jones wants to analyze how fundamental P/E ratios might differ among countries. He gathered the following economic and market data:

| Fundamental Factors | Country A | Country B |
|---|---|---|
| Forecast growth in real GDP | 5% | 2% |
| Government bond yield | 10% | 6% |
| Equity risk premium | 5% | 4% |

   Determine whether each of these fundamental factors would cause P/E ratios to be generally higher for Country A or higher for Country B.

15. "Growth" and "value" can be defined in several ways, but "growth" usually conveys the idea of a portfolio emphasizing or including only issues believed to possess above-average future rates of per-share earnings growth. Low current yield, high price-to-book ratios, and high price-to-earnings ratios are typical characteristics of such portfolios.

   "Value" usually conveys the idea of portfolios emphasizing or including only issues currently showing low price-to-book ratios, low price-to-earnings ratios, above-average levels of dividend yield, and market prices believed to be below the issues' intrinsic values.

   a. Identify and explain three reasons why, over an extended period of time, value stock investing might outperform growth stock investing.

b. Explain why the outcome suggested in part (*a*) above should *not* be possible in a market widely regarded as being highly efficient.

16. The stock of Nogro Corporation is currently selling for $10 per share. Earnings per share in the coming year are expected to be $2. The company has a policy of paying out 50% of its earnings each year in dividends. The rest is retained and invested in projects that earn a 20% rate of return per year. This situation is expected to continue indefinitely.

    a. Assuming the current market price of the stock reflects its intrinsic value as computed using the constant-growth DDM, what rate of return do Nogro's investors require?

    b. By how much does its value exceed what it would be if all earnings were paid as dividends and nothing were reinvested?

    c. If Nogro were to cut its dividend payout ratio to 25%, what would happen to its stock price? What if Nogro eliminated the dividend?

17. Chiptech, Inc., is an established computer chip firm with several profitable existing products as well as some promising new products in development. The company earned $1 a share last year, and just paid out a dividend of $.50 per share. Investors believe the company plans to maintain its dividend payout ratio at 50%. ROE equals 20%. Everyone in the market expects this situation to persist indefinitely.

    a. What is the market price of Chiptech stock? The required return for the computer chip industry is 15%, and the company has just gone ex-dividend (i.e., the next dividend will be paid a year from now, at $t = 1$).

    b. Suppose you discover that Chiptech's competitor has developed a new chip that will eliminate Chiptech's current technological advantage in this market. This new product, which will be ready to come to the market in 2 years, will force Chiptech to reduce the prices of its chips to remain competitive. This will decrease ROE to 15%, and, because of falling demand for its product, Chiptech will decrease the plowback ratio to .40. The plowback ratio will be decreased at the end of the second year, at $t = 2$: The annual year-end dividend for the second year (paid at $t = 2$) will be 60% of that year's earnings. What is your estimate of Chiptech's intrinsic value per share? (Hint: Carefully prepare a table of Chiptech's earnings and dividends for each of the next 3 years. Pay close attention to the change in the payout ratio in $t = 2$.)

    c. No one else in the market perceives the threat to Chiptech's market. In fact, you are confident that no one else will become aware of the change in Chiptech's competitive status until the competitor firm publicly announces its discovery near the end of year 2. What will be the rate of return on Chiptech stock in the coming year (i.e., between $t = 0$ and $t = 1$)? In the second year (between $t = 1$ and $t = 2$)? The third year (between $t = 2$ and $t = 3$)? (Hint: Pay attention to when the *market* catches on to the new situation. A table of dividends and market prices over time might help.)

18. The risk-free rate of return is 8%, the expected rate of return on the market portfolio is 15%, and the stock of Xyrong Corporation has a beta coefficient of 1.2. Xyrong pays out 40% of its earnings in dividends, and the latest earnings announced were $10 per share. Dividends were just paid and are expected to be paid annually. You expect that Xyrong will earn an ROE of 20% per year on all reinvested earnings forever.

    a. What is the intrinsic value of a share of Xyrong stock?

b. If the market price of a share is currently $100, and you expect the market price to be equal to the intrinsic value 1 year from now, what is your expected 1-year holding-period return on Xyrong stock?

19. Janet Ludlow's firm requires all its analysts to use a two-stage dividend discount model (DDM) and the Capital Asset Pricing Model (CAPM) to value stocks. Using the CAPM and DDM, Ludlow has valued QuickBrush Company at $63 per share. She now must value SmileWhite Corporation.

   a. Calculate the required rate of return for SmileWhite by using the information in the following table:

| | QuickBrush | SmileWhite |
|---|---|---|
| Beta | 1.35 | 1.15 |
| Market price | $45.00 | $30.00 |
| Intrinsic value | $63.00 | ? |
| *Notes:* | | |
| Risk-free rate | 4.50% | |
| Expected market return | 14.50% | |

   b. Ludlow estimates the following EPS and dividend growth rates for SmileWhite:

| First 3 years | 12% per year |
|---|---|
| Years thereafter | 9% per year |

   Estimate the intrinsic value of SmileWhite by using the table above, and the two-stage DDM. Dividends per share in the most recent year were $1.72.

   c. Recommend QuickBrush or SmileWhite stock for purchase by comparing each company's intrinsic value with its current market price.

   d. Describe one strength of the two-stage DDM in comparison with the constant-growth DDM. Describe one weakness inherent in all DDMs.

20. The Digital Electronic Quotation System (DEQS) Corporation pays no cash dividends currently and is not expected to for the next 5 years. Its latest EPS was $10, all of which was reinvested in the company. The firm's expected ROE for the next 5 years is 20% per year, and during this time it is expected to continue to reinvest all of its earnings. Starting 6 years from now the firm's ROE on new investments is expected to fall to 15%, and the company is expected to start paying out 40% of its earnings in cash dividends, which it will continue to do forever after. DEQS's market capitalization rate is 15% per year.

   a. What is your estimate of DEQS's intrinsic value per share?

   b. Assuming its current market price is equal to its intrinsic value, what do you expect to happen to its price over the next year? The year after?

   c. What effect would it have on your estimate of DEQS's intrinsic value if you expected DEQS to pay out only 20% of earnings starting in year 6?

21. At year-end 1991, the Wall Street consensus was that Philip Morris's earnings and dividends would grow at 20% for 5 years, after which growth would fall to a marketlike 7%. Analysts also projected a required rate of return of 10% for the U.S. equity market.

   a. Using the data in the accompanying table and the multistage dividend discount model, calculate the intrinsic value of Philip Morris stock at year-end 1991. Assume a similar level of risk for Philip Morris stock as for the typical U.S. stock.

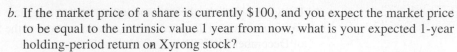

b. Using the data in the accompanying table, calculate Philip Morris's price–earnings ratio and the price–earnings ratio relative to the S&P 500 Stock Index as of December 31, 1991.

c. Using the data in the accompanying table, calculate Philip Morris's price–book ratio (i.e., ratio of market value to book value) and the price–book ratio relative to the S&P 500 Stock Index as of December 31, 1991.

**Philip Morris Corporation**
**Selected Financial Data**
**Years Ending December 31**
**($ millions except per share data)**

|  | 1991 | 1981 |
| --- | --- | --- |
| Earnings per share | $4.24 | $0.66 |
| Dividends per share | $1.91 | $0.25 |
| Stockholders' equity | 12,512 | 3,234 |
| Total liabilities and stockholders' equity | $47,384 | $9,180 |
| **Other data** | | |
| Philip Morris | | |
| Common shares outstanding (millions) | 920 | 1,003 |
| Closing price common stock | $80.250 | $6.125 |
| S&P 500 Stock Index: | | |
| Closing price | 417.09 | 122.55 |
| Earnings per share | 16.29 | 15.36 |
| Book value per share | 161.08 | 109.43 |

22. a. State one major advantage and one major disadvantage of each of the three valuation methodologies you used to value Philip Morris in the previous problem.

b. State whether Philip Morris stock was undervalued or overvalued as of December 31, 1991. Support your conclusion using your answers to previous questions and any data provided. (The past 10-year average S&P 500 Stock Index relative price–earnings and price–book ratios for Philip Morris were .80 and 1.61, respectively.)

23. The Duo Growth Company just paid a dividend of $1 per share. The dividend is expected to grow at a rate of 25% per year for the next 3 years and then to level off to 5% per year forever. You think the appropriate market capitalization rate is 20% per year.

a. What is your estimate of the intrinsic value of a share of the stock?

b. If the market price of a share is equal to this intrinsic value, what is the expected dividend yield?

c. What do you expect its price to be 1 year from now? Is the implied capital gain consistent with your estimate of the dividend yield and the market capitalization rate?

24. The Generic Genetic (GG) Corporation pays no cash dividends currently and is not expected to for the next 4 years. Its latest EPS was $5, all of which was reinvested in the company. The firm's expected ROE for the next 4 years is 20% per year, during which time it is expected to continue to reinvest all of its earnings. Starting 5 years from now, the firm's ROE on new investments is expected to fall to 15% per year. GG's market capitalization rate is 15% per year.

     *a.* What is your estimate of GG's intrinsic value per share?

     *b.* Assuming its current market price is equal to its intrinsic value, what do you expect to happen to its price over the next year?

25. The MoMi Corporation's cash flow from operations before interest and taxes was $2 million in the year just ended, and it expects that this will grow by 5% per year forever. To make this happen, the firm will have to invest an amount equal to 20% of pretax cash flow each year. The tax rate is 34%. Depreciation was $200,000 in the year just ended and is expected to grow at the same rate as the operating cash flow. The appropriate market capitalization rate for the unleveraged cash flow is 12% per year, and the firm currently has debt of $4 million outstanding. Use the free cash flow approach to value the firm's equity.

26. The CPI Corporation is expected to pay a real dividend of $1 per share this year. Its expected growth rate of real dividends is 4% per year, and its current market price per share is $20.

     *a.* Assuming the constant-growth DDM is applicable, what must be the real market capitalization rate for CPI?

     *b.* If the expected rate of inflation is 6% per year, what must be the nominal capitalization rate, the nominal dividend yield, and the growth rate of nominal dividends?

     *c.* If the expected real earnings per share are $1.80, what would be your estimate of intrinsic value if you used a simple capitalized earnings model?

Access the Market Insight database at **www.mhhe.com/business/finance/edumarket insight**.

1. Find ROE and calculate the plowback ratio for 20 firms. (Use the data in the financial highlights section.)

     *a.* Compute sustainable growth, $g = b \times$ ROE.

     *b.* Compare the growth rate computed in (a) with the P/E ratio of the firms. (It would be useful to plot P/E against *g* in a scatter diagram. This is easy to do in Excel.) Is there a relationship between *g* and P/E?

     *c.* What is the average PEG ratio for the firms in your sample? How much variation is there across firms?

     *d.* Find the price-to-book, price-to-sales, and price-to-cash flow ratios for your sample of firms. Plot a scatter diagram of P/E against these three ratios. What do you conclude?

     *e.* Calculate the historical growth rate of earnings per share, using the longest possible historical period. Is the actual rate of earnings growth correlated with the sustainable growth rate computed in part (a)?

2. *a.* Use the data from Market Insight to estimate the intrinsic value of a firm in the sample. You will need to calculate the beta from the historical return series, and you will need to make reasonable judgments about the market risk premium, long-term growth rates based on recent profitability, and plowback.

     *b.* How sensitive are our estimates to your assumptions? Which assumptions are most critical?

     *c.* Try using a three-stage growth model and comparing the values derived to a two-stage model. Which estimates seem more reasonable?

**E-INVESTMENTS**
**Equity Valuation**

Go to the MoneyCentral Investor page at **moneycentral.msn.com/investor/home.asp**. Use the Research Wizard function to obtain fundamentals, price history, price target, catalysts, and comparison for EMC Corporation (EMC). For comparison, use Network Appliance Inc. (NTAP) and Silicon Storage (SSTI).

1. What has been the 1-year sales and income growth for EMC?
2. What has been the company's 5-year profit margin percentage? How does that compare with the comparison firms?
3. What have been the percentage price changes for the last 3, 6, and 12 months? How do they compare with the comparison firms?
4. What is the estimated high and low price for EMC for the coming year using EMC's current P/E multiple?
5. Compare the price performance of EMC with NTAP and SSTI. Which of the companies appears to be the most expensive in terms of current earnings? Which of the companies is the least expensive in terms of current earnings?

**SOLUTIONS TO CONCEPT CHECKS**

1. *a.* Dividend yield = $2.15/$50 = 4.3%.
   Capital gains yield = (59.77 − 50)/50 = 19.54%.
   Total return = 4.3% + 19.54% = 23.84%.
   *b.* $k = 6\% + 1.15(14\% - 6\%) = 15.2\%$.
   *c.* $V_0 = (\$2.15 + \$59.77)/1.152 = \$53.75$, which exceeds the market price. This would indicate a "buy" opportunity.

2. *a.* $D_1/(k - g) = \$2.15/(.152 - .112) = \$53.75$.
   *b.* $P_1 = P_0(1 + g) = \$53.75(1.112) = \$59.77$.
   *c.* The expected capital gain equals $59.77 − $53.75 = $6.02, for a percentage gain of 11.2%. The dividend yield is $D_1/P_0 = 2.15/53.75 = 4\%$, for a holding-period return of 4% + 11.2% = 15.2%.

3. *a.* $g = \text{ROE} \times b = 20\% \times .60 = 12\%$.
   $D_1 = .4 \times E_1 = .4 \times \$5 = \$2$.
   $P_0 = 2/(.125 - .12) = 400$.
   *b.* When the firm invests in projects with ROE less than *k,* its stock price falls. If $b = 0.60$, the $g = 10\% \times 0.60 = 6\%$ and $P_0 = \$2/(0.125 - 0.06) = \$30.77$. In contrast, if $b = 0$, then $P_0 = \$5/0.125 = \$40$.

4. $V_{2002} = \dfrac{.80}{(1.114)} + \dfrac{.93}{(1.114)^2} + \dfrac{1.06}{(1.114)^3} + \dfrac{1.20 + P_{2006}}{(1.114)^4}$

   Now compute the sales price in 2006 using the constant-growth dividend discount model. The growth rate will be $g = \text{ROE} \times b = 11\% \times .7 = 7.7\%$.

   $$P_{2006} = \frac{1.20 \times (1 + g)}{k - g} = \frac{\$1.20 \times 1.077}{.114 - .077} = \$34.92$$

   Therefore, $V_{2002} = \$25.69$.

**SOLUTIONS
TO CONCEPT
CHECKS**
*(Concluded)*

5. *a.* ROE = 12%.

   $b = \$.50/\$2.00 = .25.$

   $g = \text{ROE} \times b = 12\% \times .25 = 3\%.$

   $P_0 = D_1/(k - g) = \$1.50/(.10 - .03) = \$21.43.$

   $P_0/E_1 = \$21.43/\$2.00 = 10.71.$

   *b.* If $b = .4$, then $.4 \times \$2 = \$.80$ would be reinvested and the remainder of earnings, or \$1.20, would be paid as dividends.

   $g = 12\% \times .4 = 4.8\%.$

   $P_0 = D_1/(k - g) = \$1.20/(.10 - .048) = \$23.08.$

   $P_0/E_1 = \$23.08/\$2.00 = 11.54.$

6. *a.* $P_0 = \dfrac{(1 - b)E_1}{k - g} = \dfrac{.6 \times \$1}{.10 - .04} = \$10$

   *b.* $\dfrac{D_1^*}{P_0} = \dfrac{(1 - b)E_1^*}{P_0} = \dfrac{(1 - .4) \times \$1}{\$10} = .06$, or 6% per year. The rate of price

   appreciation $= g^* = b^* \times \text{ROE}^* = 4\%$ per year.

   *c.*  i. $g = (1.04)(1.06) - 1 = .1024$, or 10.24%.

   ii. $\dfrac{D_1}{P_0} = \dfrac{D_1^*(1 + i)}{P_0} = .06 \times 1.06 = .0636$, or 6.36%.

   iii. ROE = 16.6%.

   iv. $b = \dfrac{g}{\text{ROE}} = \dfrac{.1024}{.166} = .6169.$

# FINANCIAL STATEMENT ANALYSIS

In the previous chapter, we explored equity valuation techniques. These techniques take the firm's dividends and earnings prospects as inputs. Although the valuation analyst is interested in economic earnings streams, only financial accounting data are readily available. What can we learn from a company's accounting data that can help us estimate the intrinsic value of its common stock? In this chapter, we show how investors can use financial data as inputs into stock valuation analysis. We start by reviewing the basic sources of such data—the income statement, the balance sheet, and the statement of cash flows. We next discuss the difference between economic and accounting earnings. Although economic earnings are more important for issues of valuation, we examine evidence suggesting that, whatever their shortcomings, accounting data still are useful in assessing the economic prospects of the firm. We show how analysts use financial ratios to explore the sources of a firm's profitability and evaluate the "quality" of its earnings in a systematic fashion. We also examine the impact of debt policy on various financial ratios. Finally, we conclude with a discussion of the limitations of financial statement analysis as a tool in uncovering mispriced securities. Some of these limitations are due to differences in firms' accounting procedures. Others arise from inflation-induced distortions in accounting numbers.

## 19.1    THE MAJOR FINANCIAL STATEMENTS

**The Income Statement**    The **income statement** is a summary of the profitability of the firm over a period of time, such as a year. It presents revenues generated during the operating period, the expenses incurred during that same period, and the company's net earnings or profits, which are simply the difference between revenues and expenses.

It is useful to distinguish four broad classes of expenses: cost of goods sold, which is the direct cost attributable to producing the product sold by the firm; general and administrative expenses, which correspond to overhead expenses, salaries, advertising, and other costs of operating the firm that are not directly attributable to production; interest expense on the firm's debt; and taxes on earnings owed to federal and local governments.

Table 19.1 presents a 2002 income statement for Alcoa. At the top are revenues from operations. Next come operating expenses, the costs incurred in the course of generating those revenues, including a depreciation allowance. The difference between operating revenues and operating costs is called *operating income.* Income or expenses from other, primarily nonrecurring, sources are then added or subtracted to obtain earnings before interest and taxes (EBIT), which is what the firm would have earned if not for obligations to its creditors and the tax authorities. EBIT is a measure of the profitability of the firm's operations, ignoring any interest burden attributable to debt financing. The income statement then goes on to subtract net interest expense from EBIT to arrive at taxable income. Finally, the income tax due the government is subtracted to arrive at net income, the "bottom line" of the income statement.

| Table 19.1    Consolidated Statement of Income for Alcoa, Inc., for the Year Ended December 31, 2002 (figures in $ millions) | |
| --- | --- |
| **Operating Revenues** | |
| Net sales | $20,263 |
| **Operating Expenses** | |
| Cost of goods sold | $16,247 |
| Selling, general, & administrative expense | 1,147 |
| Depreciation and amortization | 1,108 |
| Research & Development expense | 214 |
| Other expenses | 451 |
| Total operating expenses | $19,167 |
| **Operating income** | $ 1,096 |
| Nonoperating income | 179 |
| **Earning before interest and income tax** | $ 1,275 |
| Net interest expense | 350 |
| **Earning before income taxes** | $ 925 |
| Income taxes | 292 |
| Minority interests | 135 |
| Extraordinary items & discontinued operation | 78 |
| **Net income** | $ 420 |

Source: Alcoa *Annual Report,* 2002.

**The Balance Sheet**  While the income statement provides a measure of profitability over a period of time, the **balance sheet** provides a "snapshot" of the financial condition of the firm at a particular moment. The balance sheet is a list of the firm's assets and liabilities at that moment. The difference in assets and liabilities is the net worth of the firm, also called *shareholders'* or *stockholders' equity*. Like income statements, balance sheets are reasonably standardized in presentation. Table 19.2 is the balance sheet of Alcoa for the year-end 2002.

### Table 19.2   Consolidated Balance Sheet for Alcoa, Inc., as of December 31, 2002

|  | Dollars (millions) | Percent of Total Assets |
|---|---|---|
| **Assets** | | |
| Current assets: | | |
| Cash and cash equivalents | $    344 | 1% |
| Other short-term investments | 69 | 0 |
| Receivables | 2,552 | 9 |
| Inventories | 2,441 | 8 |
| Deferred income taxes | 468 | 2 |
| Prepaid taxes and other expenses | 439 | 1 |
| Total current assets | 6,313 | 21% |
| Property, plant, and equipment (net of depreciation) | 12,111 | 41 |
| Net intangible assets | 6,365 | 21 |
| Other assets | 5,021 | 17 |
| Total assets | $29,810 | 100% |
| **Liabilities and Stockholders' Equity** | | |
| Current liabilities: | | |
| Loans payable | $      37 | 0% |
| Accounts payable and other current liabilities | 3,521 | 12 |
| Income taxes due | 818 | 3 |
| Long-term debt due within 1 year | 85 | 0 |
| Total current liabilities | 4,461 | 15 |
| Long-term debt | 8,365 | 28 |
| Deferred income taxes | 502 | 2 |
| Other long-term liabilities | 5,262 | 18 |
| Total liabilities | $18,590 | 62 |
| Minority interests | $  1,293 | 4 |
| Stockholders' equity: | | |
| Preferred stock | $      55 | 0% |
| Common stock | 925 | 3 |
| Additional paid-in capital | 6,101 | 20 |
| Retained earnings | 7,428 | 25 |
| Accumulated other comprehensive loss | (1,754) | −6 |
| Treasury stock (at cost) | (2,828) | −9 |
| Total stockholders' equity | 9,927 | 33 |
| Total liabilities and stockholders' equity | $29,810 | 100% |

Note: Column sums subject to rounding error.
Source: Alcoa *Annual Report*, 2002.

The first section of the balance sheet gives a listing of the assets of the firm. Current assets are presented first. These are cash and other items such as accounts receivable or inventories that will be converted into cash within 1 year. Next comes a listing of long-term assets, which consists primarily of the company's property, plant, and equipment. The sum of current and long-term assets is total assets, the last line of the assets section of the balance sheet.

The liability and stockholders' equity section is arranged similarly. First come short-term, or "current," liabilities such as accounts payable, accrued taxes, and debts that are due within 1 year. Following this is long-term debt and other liabilities due in more than 1 year. The difference between total assets and total liabilities is stockholders' equity. This is the net worth, or book value, of the firm. Stockholders' equity is divided into par value of stock, additional paid-in capital, and retained earnings, although this division is usually unimportant. Briefly, par value plus additional paid-in capital represent the proceeds realized from the sale of stock to the public, whereas retained earnings represent the buildup of equity from profits plowed back into the firm. Even if the firm issues no new equity, book value will increase each year by those reinvested earnings.

The first column of numbers in the balance sheet in Table 19.2 presents the dollar value of each asset. To make it easier to compare firms of different sizes, analysts sometimes present each item on the balance sheet as a percentage of total assets. This is called a *common-size balance sheet*, and it is presented in the last column of the table.

## The Statement of Cash Flows

The **statement of cash flows** details the cash flow generated by the firm's operations, investments, and financial activities. This statement was mandated by the Financial Accounting Standards Board in 1987 and is sometimes called the *FASB Statement No. 95*, or *FAS 95*.

Although the income statement and balance sheets are based on accrual methods of accounting, which means that revenues and expenses are recognized when incurred even if no cash has yet been exchanged, the statement of cash flows recognizes only transactions in which cash changes hands. For example, if goods are sold now, with payment due in 60 days, the income statement will treat the revenue as generated when the sale occurs, and the balance sheet will be immediately augmented by accounts receivable, but the statement of cash flows will not recognize the transaction until the bill is paid and the cash is in hand.

Table 19.3 is the 2002 statement of cash flows for Alcoa. The first entry listed under cash flows from operations is net income. The next entries modify that figure by components of income that have been recognized but for which cash has not yet changed hands. Increases in accounts receivable, for example, mean that income has been claimed on the income statement, but cash has not yet been collected. Hence increases in accounts receivable reduce the cash flows realized from operations in this period. Similarly, increases in accounts payable mean that expenses have been incurred, but cash has not yet left the firm. Any payment delay increases the company's net cash flows in this period.

Another major difference between the income statement and the statement of cash flows involves depreciation, which is a major addition to income in the adjustment section of the statement of cash flows in Table 19.3. The income statement attempts to "smooth" large capital expenditures over time to reflect a measure of profitability not distorted by large, infrequent expenditures. The depreciation expense on the income statement is a way of doing this by recognizing capital expenditures over a period of many years rather than at the specific time of those expenditures.

The statement of cash flows, however, recognizes the cash implication of a capital expenditure when it occurs. It will ignore the depreciation "expense" over time but will account for the full capital expenditure when it is paid.

**Table 19.3    Consolidated Statement of Cash Flows for Alcoa, Inc.,
for the Year Ended December 31, 2002 (figures in $ millions)**

**Cash Flows from Operating Activities**

| | |
|---|---:|
| Net income | $    420 |
| *Adjustments to reconcile net income provided by operating activities* | |
| Depreciation and amortization | $ 1,116 |
| Change in deferred income taxes | (178) |
| Gains from sale of assets | (52) |
| Changes in operating assets and liabilities: | |
| Reduction (increase) in receivables | 411 |
| Reduction (increase) in inventories | 202 |
| Reduction (increase) in prepaid expenses and other assets | 36 |
| Reduction in accounts payable and accrued expenses | (318) |
| (Reduction) increase in taxes, including taxes on income | (232) |
| Net change in noncurrent assets and liabilities | (239) |
| Reduction (increase) in net assets held for sale | 113 |
| Other | 560 |
| Total adjustments | $1,419 |
| Net cash provided by operating activities | $1,839 |

**Cash Flows from Investing Activities**

| | |
|---|---:|
| Capital expenditures (including discontinued operations) | $(1,270) |
| Acquisitions of business | (1,253) |
| Proceeds from the sale of assets | 127 |
| Short-term investments | (54) |
| Other | (94) |
| Net cash provided (used) in investing activities | $(2,544) |

**Cash Flow from Financing Activities**

| | |
|---|---:|
| Net changes to short-term borrowing | $  (382) |
| Common stock issued for stock compensation plans | 55 |
| Repayment of long-term debt | (231) |
| Additions to long-term debt | 1,636 |
| Dividends paid | (509) |
| Repurchase of common stock | (224) |
| Other | 248 |
| Net cash provided by (used in) financing activities | $  593 |
| Effect of exchange rate changes | (56) |
| Net increase (decrease) in cash and cash equivalents | $  (168) |

Source: Alcoa *Annual Report,* 2002.

Rather than smooth or allocate expenses over time, as in the income statement, the statement of cash flows reports cash flows separately for operations, investing, and financing activities. This way, any large cash flows, such as those for big investments, can be recognized explicitly as nonrecurring without affecting the measure of cash flow generated by operating activities.

The second section of the statement of cash flows is the accounting of cash flows from investing activities. These entries are investments in the capital stock necessary for the firm to maintain or enhance its productive capacity.

Finally, the last section of the statement lists the cash flows realized from financing activities. Issuance of securities will contribute positive cash flows, and redemption of outstanding securities will use up cash. For Alcoa financing activities in 2002 resulted in a net increase in cash of $593 million.

The statement of cash flows provides evidence on the well-being of a firm. If a company cannot pay its dividends and maintain the productivity of its capital stock out of cash flow from operations, for example, and it must resort to borrowing to meet these demands, this is a serious warning that the firm cannot maintain the dividend payout at its current level in the long run. The statement of cash flows will reveal this developing problem when it shows that cash flow from operations is inadequate and that borrowing is being used to maintain dividend payments at unsustainable levels.

# 19.2    ACCOUNTING VERSUS ECONOMIC EARNINGS

We've seen that stock valuation models require a measure of **economic earnings**—the sustainable cash flow that can be paid out to stockholders without impairing the productive capacity of the firm. In contrast, **accounting earnings** are affected by several conventions regarding the valuation of assets such as inventories (e.g., LIFO versus FIFO treatment), and by the way some expenditures such as capital investments are recognized over time (as depreciation expenses). We discuss problems with some of these accounting conventions in greater detail later in the chapter. In addition to these accounting issues, as the firm makes its way through the business cycle, its earnings will rise above or fall below the trend line that might more accurately reflect sustainable economic earnings. This introduces an added complication in interpreting net income figures. One might wonder how closely accounting earnings approximate economic earnings and, correspondingly, how useful accounting data might be to investors attempting to value the firm.

In fact, the net income figure on the firm's income statement does convey considerable information concerning a firm's prospects. We see this in the fact that stock prices tend to increase when firms announce earnings greater than market analysts or investors had anticipated.

# 19.3    RETURN ON EQUITY

**Past versus Future ROE**    We noted in Chapter 18 that **return on equity** (ROE) is one of the two basic factors in determining a firm's growth rate of earnings. Sometimes it is reasonable to assume that future ROE will approximate its past value, but a high ROE in the past does not necessarily imply a firm's future ROE will be high. A declining ROE, on the other hand, is evidence that the firm's new investments have offered a lower ROE than its past investments. The vital point for a security analyst is not to accept historical values as indicators of future values. Data from the recent past may provide information regarding future performance, but the analyst should always keep an eye on the future. Expectations of *future* dividends and earnings determine the intrinsic value of the company's stock.

**Financial Leverage and ROE**    An analyst interpreting the past behavior of a firm's ROE or forecasting its future value must pay careful attention to the firm's debt-equity mix and to the interest rate on its debt. An example will show why. Suppose Nodett is a firm that is all-equity financed and has total assets of $100 million. Assume it pays corporate taxes at the rate of 40% of taxable earnings.

**Table 19.4   Nodett's Profitability over the Business Cycle**

| Scenario | Sales ($ millions) | EBIT ($ millions) | ROA (% per year) | Net Profit ($ millions) | ROE (% per year) |
|---|---|---|---|---|---|
| Bad year | 80 | 5 | 5 | 3 | 3 |
| Normal year | 100 | 10 | 10 | 6 | 6 |
| Good year | 120 | 15 | 15 | 9 | 9 |

**Table 19.5   Impact of Financial Leverage on ROE**

| | Nodett | | | Somdett | |
|---|---|---|---|---|---|
| Scenario | EBIT ($ millions) | Net Profits ($ millions) | ROE (%) | Net Profit* ($ millions) | ROE† (%) |
| Bad year | 5 | 3 | 3 | 1.08 | 1.8 |
| Normal year | 10 | 6 | 6 | 4.08 | 6.8 |
| Good year | 15 | 9 | 9 | 7.08 | 11.8 |

*Somdett's after-tax profits are given by .6(EBIT − $3.2 million).
†ROE = net profit/equity. Somdett's equity is only $60 million.

Table 19.4 shows the behavior of sales, earnings before interest and taxes, and net profits under three scenarios representing phases of the business cycle. It also shows the behavior of two of the most commonly used profitability measures: operating **return on assets** (ROA), which equals EBIT/assets, and ROE, which equals net profits/equity.

Somdett is an otherwise identical firm to Nodett, but $40 million of its $100 million of assets are financed with debt bearing an interest rate of 8%. It pays annual interest expenses of $3.2 million. Table 19.5 shows how Somdett's ROE differs from Nodett's.

Note that annual sales, EBIT, and therefore ROA for both firms are the same in each of the three scenarios; that is, business risk for the two companies is identical. It is their financial risk that differs. Although Nodett and Somdett have the same ROA in each scenario, Somdett's ROE exceeds that of Nodett in normal and good years and is lower in bad years.

We can summarize the exact relationship among ROE, ROA, and leverage in the following equation:[1]

$$\text{ROE} = (1 - \text{Tax rate})\left[\text{ROA} + (\text{ROA} - \text{Interest rate})\frac{\text{Debt}}{\text{Equity}}\right] \qquad (19.1)$$

---

[1] The derivation of equation 19.1 is as follows:

$$\text{ROE} = \frac{\text{Net profit}}{\text{Equity}}$$

$$= \frac{\text{EBIT} - \text{Interest} - \text{Taxes}}{\text{Equity}}$$

$$= \frac{(1 - \text{Tax rate})(\text{EBIT} - \text{Interest})}{\text{Equity}}$$

$$= (1 - \text{Tax rate})\left[\frac{(\text{ROA} \times \text{Assets}) - (\text{Interest rate} \times \text{Debt})}{\text{Equity}}\right]$$

$$= (1 - \text{Tax rate})\left[\text{ROA} \times \frac{\text{Equity} + \text{Debt}}{\text{Equity}} - \text{Interest rate} \times \frac{\text{Debt}}{\text{Equity}}\right]$$

$$= (1 - \text{Tax rate})\left[\text{ROA} + (\text{ROA} - \text{Interest rate})\frac{\text{Debt}}{\text{Equity}}\right]$$

The relationship has the following implications. If there is no debt or if the firm's ROA equals the interest rate on its debt, its ROE will simply equal (1 minus the tax rate) times ROA. If its ROA exceeds the interest rate, then its ROE will exceed (1 minus the tax rate) times ROA by an amount that will be greater the higher the debt-to-equity ratio.

This result makes intuitive sense: If ROA exceeds the borrowing rate, the firm earns more on its money than it pays out to creditors. The surplus earnings are available to the firm's owners, the equityholders, which increases ROE. If, on the other hand, ROA is less than the interest rate, then ROE will decline by an amount that depends on the debt-to-equity ratio.

**EXAMPLE 19.1    Leverage and ROE**

To illustrate the application of equation 19.1, we can use the numerical example in Table 19.5. In a normal year, Nodett has an ROE of 6%, which is .6 (i.e., 1 minus the tax rate) times its ROA of 10%. However, Somdett, which borrows at an interest rate of 8% and maintains a debt-to-equity ratio of ⅔, has an ROE of 6.8%. The calculation using equation 19.1 is

$$ROE = .6[10\% + (10\% - 8\%)\tfrac{2}{3}]$$
$$= .6[10\% + \tfrac{4}{3}\%] = 6.8\%$$

The important point is that increased debt will make a positive contribution to a firm's ROE only if the firm's ROA exceeds the interest rate on the debt.

Note also that financial leverage increases the risk of the equityholder returns. Table 19.5 shows that ROE on Somdett is worse than that of Nodett in bad years. Conversely, in good years, Somdett outperforms Nodett because the excess of ROA over ROE provides additional funds for equityholders. The presence of debt makes Somdett more sensitive to the business cycle than Nodett. Even though the two companies have equal business risk (reflected in their identical EBITs in all three scenarios), Somdett carries greater financial risk than Nodett.

Even if financial leverage increases the expected ROE of Somdett relative to Nodett (as it seems to in Table 19.5), this does not imply that the market value of Somdett's equity will be higher. Financial leverage increases the risk of the firm's equity as surely as it raises the expected ROE.

| CONCEPT CHECK☞ QUESTION 1 | Mordett is a company with the same assets as Nodett and Somdett but a debt-to-equity ratio of 1.0 and an interest rate of 9%. What would its net profit and ROE be in a bad year, a normal year, and a good year? |
|---|---|

## 19.4    RATIO ANALYSIS

**Decomposition of ROE**    To understand the factors affecting a firm's ROE, including its trend over time and its performance relative to competitors, analysts often "decompose" ROE into the product of a series of ratios. Each component ratio is in itself meaningful, and the process serves to focus the analyst's attention on the separate factors influencing performance. This kind of decomposition of ROE is often called the **Du Pont system.**

One useful decomposition of ROE is

$$ROE = \frac{\text{Net profits}}{\text{Pretax Profits}} \times \frac{\text{Pretax profits}}{\text{EBIT}} \times \frac{\text{EBIT}}{\text{Sales}} \times \frac{\text{Sales}}{\text{Assets}} \times \frac{\text{Assets}}{\text{Equity}}$$

$$(1) \quad \times \quad (2) \quad \times \quad (3) \times \quad (4) \quad \times \quad (5)$$

Table 19.6 shows all these ratios for Nodett and Somdett Corporations under the three different economic scenarios. Let us first focus on factors 3 and 4. Notice that their product, EBIT/Assets, gives us the firm's ROA.

Factor 3 is known as the firm's operating **profit margin** or **return on sales** (ROS). ROS shows operating profit per dollar of sales. In a normal year, ROS is .10, or 10%; in a bad year, it is .0625, or 6.25%, and in a good year, .125, or 12.5%.

Factor 4, the ratio of sales to assets, is known as **asset turnover** (ATO). It indicates the efficiency of the firm's use of assets in the sense that it measures the annual sales generated by each dollar of assets. In a normal year, Nodett's ATO is 1.0 per year, meaning that sales of $1 per year were generated per dollar of assets. In a bad year, this ratio declines to .8 per year, and in a good year, it rises to 1.2 per year.

Comparing Nodett and Somdett, we see that factors 3 and 4 do not depend on a firm's financial leverage. The firms' ratios are equal to each other in all three scenarios.

Similarly, factor 1, the ratio of net income after taxes to pretax profit, is the same for both firms. We call this the *tax-burden ratio*. Its value reflects both the government's tax code and the policies pursued by the firm in trying to minimize its tax burden. In our example it does not change over the business cycle, remaining a constant .6.

Although factors 1, 3, and 4 are not affected by a firm's capital structure, factors 2 and 5 are. Factor 2 is the ratio of pretax profits to EBIT. The firm's pretax profits will be greatest when there are no interest payments to be made to debtholders. In fact, another way to express this ratio is

$$\frac{\text{Pretax profits}}{\text{EBIT}} = \frac{\text{EBIT} - \text{Interest expense}}{\text{EBIT}}$$

We will call this factor the *interest-burden ratio* (*IB*). It takes on its highest possible value, 1, for Nodett, which has no financial leverage. The higher the degree of financial leverage, the lower the IB ratio. Nodett's IB ratio does not vary over the business cycle. It is fixed at 1.0, reflecting the total absence of interest payments. For Somdett, however,

**Table 19.6   Ratio Decomposition Analysis for Nodett and Somdett**

|  | ROE | (1) Net Profit/ Pretax Profit | (2) Pretax Profit/ EBIT | (3) EBIT/ Sales (ROS) | (4) Sales/ Assets (ATO) | (5) Assets/ Equity | (6) Compound Leverage Factor (2) × (5) |
|---|---|---|---|---|---|---|---|
| **Bad year** | | | | | | | |
| Nodett | .030 | .6 | 1.000 | .0625 | 0.800 | 1.000 | 1.000 |
| Somdett | .018 | .6 | 0.360 | .0625 | 0.800 | 1.667 | 0.600 |
| **Normal year** | | | | | | | |
| Nodett | .060 | .6 | 1.000 | .1000 | 1.000 | 1.000 | 1.000 |
| Somdett | .068 | .6 | 0.680 | .1000 | 1.000 | 1.667 | 1.134 |
| **Good year** | | | | | | | |
| Nodett | .090 | .6 | 1.000 | .1250 | 1.200 | 1.000 | 1.000 |
| Somdett | .118 | .6 | 0.787 | .1250 | 1.200 | 1.667 | 1.311 |

| Table 19.7 | Differences between ROS and ATO across Industries | | |
|---|---|---|---|
| | **ROS × ATO = ROA** | | |
| Supermarket chain | 2% | 5.0 | 10% |
| Utility | 20% | 0.5 | 10% |

because interest expense is fixed in a dollar amount while EBIT varies, the IB ratio varies from a low of .36 in a bad year to a high of .787 in a good year.

Factor 5, the ratio of assets to equity, is a measure of the firm's degree of financial leverage. It is called the **leverage ratio** and is equal to 1 plus the debt-to-equity ratio.[2] In our numerical example in Table 19.6, Nodett has a leverage ratio of 1, while Somdett's is 1.667.

From our discussion in Section 19.2, we know that financial leverage helps boost ROE only if ROA is greater than the interest rate on the firm's debt. How is this fact reflected in the ratios of Table 19.6?

The answer is that to measure the full impact of leverage in this framework, the analyst must take the product of the IB and leverage ratios (i.e., factors 2 and 5, shown in Table 19.6 as column 6). For Nodett, factor 6, which we call the *compound leverage factor*, remains a constant 1.0 under all three scenarios. But for Somdett, we see that the compound leverage factor is greater than 1 in normal years (1.134) and in good years (1.311), indicating the positive contribution of financial leverage to ROE. It is less than 1 in bad years, reflecting the fact that when ROA falls below the interest rate, ROE falls with increased use of debt.

We can summarize all of these relationships as follows:

$$\text{ROE} = \text{Tax burden} \times \text{Interest burden} \times \text{Margin} \times \text{Turnover} \times \text{Leverage}$$

Because

$$\text{ROA} = \text{Margin} \times \text{Turnover}$$

and

$$\text{Compound leverage factor} = \text{Interest burden} \times \text{Leverage}$$

we can decompose ROE equivalently as follows:

$$\text{ROE} = \text{Tax burden} \times \text{ROA} \times \text{Compound leverage factor}$$

Comparison of ROS and ATO usually is meaningful only in evaluating firms in the same industry. Cross-industry comparisons of these two ratios are often meaningless and can even be misleading.

## EXAMPLE 19.2　Margin versus Turnover

Consider two firms with the same ROA of 10% per year. The first is a supermarket chain, the second is a gas and electric utility.

As Table 19.7 shows, the supermarket chain has a "low" ROS of 2% and achieves a 10% ROA by "turning over" its assets five times per year. The capital-intensive utility, on the other hand, has a "low" ATO of only .5 times per year and achieves its 10% ROA by

---

[2] $\dfrac{\text{Assets}}{\text{Equity}} = \dfrac{\text{Equity} + \text{Debt}}{\text{Equity}} = 1 + \dfrac{\text{Debt}}{\text{Equity}}$

having an ROS of 20%. The point here is that a "low" ROS or ATO ratio need not indicate a troubled firm. Each ratio must be interpreted in light of industry norms.

Even within an industry, ROS and ATO sometimes can differ markedly among firms pursuing different marketing strategies. In the retailing industry, for example, Neiman Marcus pursues a high-margin, low-ATO policy compared to Wal-Mart, which pursues a low-margin, high-ATO policy.

| CONCEPT CHECK☞ QUESTION 2 | Do a ratio decomposition analysis for the Mordett corporation of Question 1, preparing a table similar to Table 19.6. |
| --- | --- |

## Turnover and Other Asset Utilization Ratios

It is often helpful in understanding a firm's ratio of sales to assets to compute comparable efficiency-of-utilization, or turnover, ratios for subcategories of assets. For example, *fixed-asset turnover* would be

$$\frac{\text{Sales}}{\text{Fixed assets}}$$

This ratio measures sales per dollar of the firm's money tied up in fixed assets.

To illustrate how you can compute this and other ratios from a firm's financial statements, consider Growth Industries, Inc. (GI). GI's income statement and opening and closing balance sheets for the years 2005, 2006, and 2007 appear in Table 19.8.

GI's total asset turnover in 2007 was .303, which was below the industry average of .4. To understand better why GI underperformed, we can compute asset utilization ratios separately for fixed assets, inventories, and accounts receivable.

GI's sales in 2007 were $144 million. Its only fixed assets were plant and equipment, which were $216 million at the beginning of the year and $259.2 million at year's end. Average fixed assets for the year were, therefore, $237.6 million [($216 million + $259.2 million)/2]. GI's fixed-asset turnover for 2007 therefore was $144 million per year/$237.6 million = .606 per year. In other words, for every dollar of fixed assets, there were $.606 in sales during the year 2007.

Comparable figures for the fixed-asset turnover ratio for 2005 and 2006 and the 2007 industry average are

| 2005 | 2006 | 2007 | 2007 Industry Average |
| --- | --- | --- | --- |
| .606 | .606 | .606 | .700 |

GI's fixed asset turnover has been stable over time and below the industry average.

Whenever a financial ratio includes one item from the income statement, which covers a period of time, and another from a balance sheet, which is a "snapshot" at a particular time, the practice is to take the average of the beginning and end-of-year balance sheet figures. Thus in computing the fixed-asset turnover ratio we divided sales (from the income statement) by average fixed assets (from the balance sheet).

Another widely followed turnover ratio is the inventory turnover ratio, which is the ratio of cost of goods sold per dollar of average inventory. The numerator is cost of goods sold instead of sales revenue because inventory is valued at cost. This ratio measures the speed with which inventory is turned over.

**Table 19.8   Growth Industries Financial Statements, 2004–2007 ($ thousands)**

|  | 2004 | 2005 | 2006 | 2007 |
|---|---|---|---|---|
| **Income Statements** | | | | |
| Sales revenue | | $100,000 | $120,000 | $144,000 |
| Cost of goods sold (including depreciation) | | 55,000 | 66,000 | 79,200 |
| Depreciation | | 15,000 | 18,000 | 21,600 |
| Selling and administrative expenses | | 15,000 | 18,000 | 21,600 |
| Operating income | | 30,000 | 36,000 | 43,200 |
| Interest expense | | 10,500 | 19,095 | 34,391 |
| Taxable income | | 19,500 | 16,905 | 8,809 |
| Income tax (40% rate) | | 7,800 | 6,762 | 3,524 |
| Net income | | $ 11,700 | $ 10,143 | $  5,285 |
| **Balance Sheets (end of year)** | | | | |
| Cash and marketable securities | $ 50,000 | $ 60,000 | $ 72,000 | $ 86,400 |
| Accounts receivable | 25,000 | 30,000 | 36,000 | 43,200 |
| Inventories | 75,000 | 90,000 | 108,000 | 129,600 |
| Net plant and equipment | 150,000 | 180,000 | 216,000 | 259,200 |
| Total assets | $300,000 | $360,000 | $432,000 | $518,400 |
| Accounts payable | $ 30,000 | $ 36,000 | $ 43,200 | $ 51,840 |
| Short-term debt | 45,000 | 87,300 | 141,957 | 214,432 |
| Long-term debt (8% bonds maturing in 2025) | 75,000 | 75,000 | 75,000 | 75,000 |
| Total liabilities | $150,000 | $198,300 | $260,157 | $341,272 |
| Shareholders' equity (1 million shares outstanding) | $150,000 | $161,700 | $171,843 | $177,128 |
| **Other Data** | | | | |
| Market price per common share at year-end | | $93.60 | $61.00 | $21.00 |

In 2005, GI's cost of goods sold (excluding depreciation) was $40 million, and its average inventory was $82.5 million [($75 million + $90 million)/2]. Its inventory turnover was .485 per year ($40 million/$82.5 million). In 2006 and 2007, inventory turnover remained the same, which was below the industry average of .5 per year.

Another measure of efficiency is the ratio of accounts receivable to sales. The accounts receivable ratio usually is computed as average accounts receivable/sales × 365. The result is a number called the **average collection period,** or **days receivables,** which equals the total credit extended to customers per dollar of daily sales. It is the number of days' worth of sales tied up in accounts receivable. You can also think of it as the average lag between the date of sale and the date payment is received.

For GI in 2007 this number was 100.4 days:

$$\frac{(\$36 \text{ million} + \$43.2 \text{ million})/2}{\$144 \text{ million}} \times 365 = 100.4 \text{ days}$$

The industry average was 60 days.

In summary, these ratios show us that GI's poor total asset turnover relative to the industry is in part caused by lower-than-average fixed-asset turnover and inventory turnover and higher-than-average days receivables. This suggests GI may be having problems with excess plant capacity along with poor inventory and receivables management procedures.

**Liquidity and Coverage Ratios**  Liquidity and interest coverage ratios are of great importance in evaluating the riskiness of a firm's securities. They aid in assessing the financial strength of the firm. Liquidity ratios include the current ratio, quick ratio, and interest coverage ratio.

1. **Current ratio:** Current assets/current liabilities. This ratio measures the ability of the firm to pay off its current liabilities by liquidating its current assets (i.e., turning them into cash). It indicates the firm's ability to avoid insolvency in the short run. GI's current ratio in 2005, for example, was (60 + 30 + 90)/(36 + 87.3) = 1.46. In other years, it was

| 2005 | 2006 | 2007 | 2007 Industry Average |
|---|---|---|---|
| 1.46 | 1.17 | .97 | 2.0 |

This represents an unfavorable time trend and poor standing relative to the industry.

2. **Quick ratio:** (Cash + receivables)/current liabilities. This ratio is also called the **acid test ratio.** It has the same denominator as the current ratio, but its numerator includes only cash, cash equivalents, and receivables. The quick ratio is a better measure of liquidity than the current ratio for firms whose inventory is not readily convertible into cash. GI's quick ratio shows the same disturbing trends as its current ratio:

| 2005 | 2006 | 2007 | 2007 Industry Average |
|---|---|---|---|
| .73 | .58 | .49 | 1.0 |

3. **Interest coverage ratio:** EBIT/interest expense. This ratio is often called **times interest earned.** It is closely related to the interest-burden ratio discussed in the previous section. A high coverage ratio tells the firm's shareholders and lenders that the likelihood of bankruptcy is low because annual earnings are significantly greater than annual interest obligations. It is widely used by both lenders and borrowers in determining the firm's debt capacity and is a major determinant of the firm's bond rating. GI's interest coverage ratios are

| 2005 | 2006 | 2007 | 2007 Industry Average |
|---|---|---|---|
| 2.86 | 1.89 | 1.26 | 5 |

GI's interest coverage ratio has fallen dramatically over this 3-year period, and by 2003 it is far below the industry average. Probably its credit rating has been declining as well, and no doubt GI is considered a relatively poor credit risk in 2003.

**Market Price Ratios**  Two important market price ratios are the market–book-value ratio and the price–earnings ratio.

The **market–book-value ratio** (P/B) equals the market price of a share of the firm's common stock divided by its *book value*, that is, shareholders' equity per share. Analysts sometimes consider the stock of a firm with a low market–book value to be a "safer" investment, seeing the book value as a "floor" supporting the market price.

Analysts presumably view book value as the level below which market price will not fall because the firm always has the option to liquidate, or sell, its assets for their book values. However, this view is questionable. In fact, some firms sell for less than book value. Nevertheless, low market–book-value ratio is seen by some as providing a "margin of safety," and some analysts will screen out or reject high P/B firms in their stock selection process.

Proponents of the P/B screen would argue that if all other relevant attributes are the same for two stocks, the one with the lower P/B ratio is safer. Although there may be firms for which this approach has some validity, book value does not necessarily represent liquidation value, which renders the margin of safety notion unreliable.

The theory of equity valuation offers some insight into the significance of the P/B ratio. A high P/B ratio is an indication that investors think a firm has opportunities of earning a rate of return on their investment in excess of the market capitalization rate, $k$.

---

**EXAMPLE 19.3**   **Price-to-Book Ratio and Investment Opportunities**

Return to the numerical example in Chapter 18, Table 18.3. That example assumes the market capitalization rate is 12% per year. Now add the assumptions that the book value per share is $8.33 and that the coming year's expected EPS is $1, so that in the case for which the expected ROE on future investments also is 12%, the stock would sell at $1/.12 = $8.33, and the P/B ratio would be 1.

Table 19.9 shows the P/B ratio for alternative assumptions about future ROE and plowback ratio. Reading down any column, you can see how the P/B ratio changes with ROE. The numbers reveal that for a given plowback ratio, the P/B ratio is higher, the higher the expected ROE. This makes sense, because the greater the expected profitability of the firm's future investment opportunities, the greater its market value as an ongoing enterprise compared with the cost of acquiring its assets.

---

We've noted that the **price–earnings ratio** that is based on the firm's financial statements and reported in newspaper stock listings is not the same as the price–earnings multiple that emerges from a dividend discount model. The numerator is the same (the market price of the stock), but the denominator is different. The reported P/E ratio uses the most recent past accountings earnings, whereas the P/E multiple predicted by valuation models uses expected future economic earnings.

Many security analysts pay careful attention to the accounting P/E ratio in the belief that among low P/E stocks they are more likely to find bargains than with high P/E stocks. The idea is that you can acquire a claim on a dollar of earnings more cheaply if the P/E ratio is low. For example, if the P/E ratio is 8, you pay $8 per share per $1 of *current* earnings, whereas if P/E is 12, you must pay $12 for a claim on $1 of current earnings.

**Table 19.9   Effect of ROE and Plowback Ratio on P/B**

| | | Plowback Ratio, $b$ | | |
|---|---|---|---|---|
| ROE | 0 | 25% | 50% | 75% |
| 10% | 1.00 | 0.95 | 0.86 | 0.67 |
| 12% | 1.00 | 1.00 | 1.00 | 1.00 |
| 14% | 1.00 | 1.06 | 1.20 | 2.00 |

The assumptions and formulas underlying this table are: $E_1 = \$1$; book value per share $= \$8.33$; $k = 12\%$ per year; and

$$g = b \times ROE \qquad P_0 = \frac{(1-b)E}{k-g} \qquad P/B = \frac{P_0}{\$8.33}$$

Note, however, that current earnings may differ substantially from future earnings. The higher P/E stock still may be a bargain relative to the low P/E stock if its earnings and dividends are expected to grow at a faster rate. Our point is that ownership of the stock conveys the right to future earnings, as well as to current earnings. An exclusive focus on the commonly reported accounting P/E ratio can he shortsighted, because by its nature it ignores future growth in earnings.

An efficient markets adherent will be skeptical of the notion that a strategy of investment in low P/E stocks would result in an expected rate of return greater than that of investing in high or medium P/E stocks having the same risk. The empirical evidence on this question is mixed, but even if the strategy has worked in the past, it still should not work in the future because too many investors would be following it. This is the lesson of market efficiency.

Before leaving the P/B and P/E ratios, it is worth pointing out the relationship among these ratios and ROE:

$$ROE = \frac{\text{Earnings}}{\text{Book value}}$$

$$= \frac{\text{Market price}}{\text{Book value}} \div \frac{\text{Market price}}{\text{Earnings}}$$

$$= \text{P/B ratio} \div \text{P/E ratio}$$

By rearranging the terms, we find that a firm's **earnings yield,** the ratio of earnings to price, is equal to its ROE divided by the market–book-value ratio:

$$\frac{E}{P} = \frac{\text{ROE}}{\text{P/B}}$$

Thus a company with a high ROE can have a relatively low earnings yield because its P/B ratio is high. This indicates that a high ROE does not in and of itself imply the stock is a good buy: The price of the stock already may be bid up to reflect an attractive ROE. If so, the P/B ratio will be above 1.0, and the earnings yield to stockholders will be below the ROE, as the equation demonstrates. The relationship shows that a strategy of investing in the stock of high ROE firms may produce a lower holding-period return than investing in those with a low ROE.

Clayman[3] found that investing in the stocks of 29 "excellent" companies, with mean reported ROE of 19.05% during the period of 1976 to 1980, produced results much inferior to investing in 39 "unexcellent" companies, those with a mean ROE of 7.09% during the period. An investor putting equal dollar amounts in the stocks of unexcellent companies would have earned a portfolio rate of return over the 1981 to 1985 period that was 11.3% higher per year than the rate of return on a comparable portfolio of excellent company stocks.

| CONCEPT CHECK☞ QUESTION 3 | **What were GI's ROE, P/E, and P/B ratios in the year 2007? How do they compare to the industry average ratios, which were:**<br><br>**ROE = 8.64%     P/E = 8     P/B = .69**<br><br>**How does GI's earnings yield in 2007 compare to the industry average?** |
| --- | --- |

[3] Michelle Clayman, "In Search of Excellence: The Investor's Viewpoint," *Financial Analysts Journal*, May–June 1987.

**Choosing a Benchmark**   We have discussed how to calculate the principal financial ratios. To evaluate the performance of a given firm, however, you need a benchmark to which you can compare its ratios. One obvious benchmark is the ratio for the same company in earlier years. For example, Figure 19.1 shows Alcoa's return on assets, profit margin, and asset turnover ratio for the last few years. You can see there that all of these ratios have declined in the last four years.

It is also helpful to compare financial ratios to those of other firms in the same industry. Financial ratios for industries are published by the U.S. Department of Commerce (see Table 19.10), Dun & Bradstreet (*Industry Norms and Key Business Ratios*), and the Risk Management Association, or RMA (*Annual Statement Studies*). A broad range of financial ratios is also easily accessible on the Web. Standard & Poor's Market Insight is a good source of industry average ratios. (See **www.mhhe.com/edumarketinsight**).

Table 19.10 presents ratios for a sample of major industry groups to give you a feel for some of the differences across industries. You should note that while some ratios such as asset turnover or total debt ratio tend to be relatively stable over time, others such as return on assets or equity will be more sensitive to the state of the economy.

**Figure 19.1
Alcoa
financial
ratios**

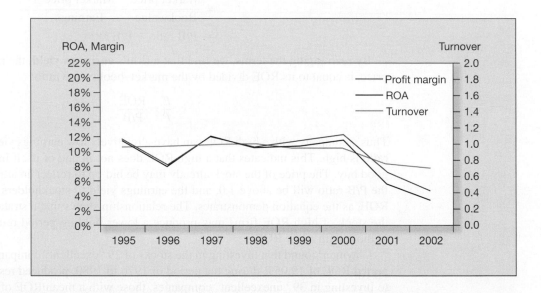

**Table 19.10    Financial Ratios for Selected Industry Groups, Fourth Quarter, 2001**

|  | All Manufacturing | Food | Retail Trade | Pharmaceuticals | Petroleum | Aerospace |
|---|---|---|---|---|---|---|
| LT Debt ratio | 0.48 | 0.55 | 0.46 | 0.46 | 0.41 | 0.52 |
| Total debt ratio | 0.61 | 0.67 | 0.62 | 0.63 | 0.51 | 0.69 |
| NWC/Assets | 0.06 | 0.08 | 0.15 | 0.02 | 0.01 | 0.05 |
| Current ratio | 1.22 | 1.30 | 1.48 | 1.06 | 1.04 | 1.14 |
| Cash ratio | 0.24 | 0.19 | 0.18 | 0.29 | 0.21 | 0.05 |
| Asset turnover | 0.88 | 1.44 | 2.29 | 0.72 | 0.90 | 0.98 |
| Net profit margin | 3.0% | 1.9% | 4.2% | 22.7% | 1.5% | 2.5% |
| ROA | 0.7% | 0.7% | 2.4% | 4.1% | 0.3% | 0.6% |
| ROE | 0.2% | 0.2% | 3.7% | 7.6% | 0.5% | 1.5% |

Source: U.S. Department of Commerce, *Quarterly Report for Manufacturing, Mining and Trade Corporations,* fourth quarter 2001.

## 19.5    ECONOMIC VALUE ADDED

One common use of financial ratios is to evaluate the performance of the firm. While profitability is typically used to measure that performance, profitability is really not enough. A firm should be viewed as successful only if the return on its projects is better than the rate investors could expect to earn for themselves (on a risk-adjusted basis) in the capital market. Think back to Table 19.9, where we showed that plowing back funds into the firm increases stock price *only* if the firm earns a higher rate of return on the reinvested funds than the opportunity cost of capital, that is, the market capitalization rate. To account for this opportunity cost, we might measure the success of the firm using the *difference* between the return on assets, ROA, and the opportunity cost of capital, $k$. **Economic value added** is the spread between ROA and $k$ multiplied by the capital invested in the firm. It therefore measures the dollar value of the firm's return in excess of its opportunity cost.

Table 19.11 shows EVA for a small sample of firms drawn from a larger study of 1,000 firms by Stern Stewart, a consulting firm that has done much to develop and promote the concept of EVA. Another term for EVA (the term coined by Stern Stewart) is **residual income.**

**EXAMPLE 19.4    Economic Value Added**

Microsoft had one of the highest returns on assets, at 39.1%. Since the cost of capital for Microsoft was only about 14.3%, each dollar invested by Microsoft was earning about

**Table 19.11    Measures of Company Performance, 2000**

|  | Market-to-Book Ratio | Return on Assets, % | Economic Value Added (billions of dollars) |
|---|---|---|---|
| General Electric | 6.6 | 20.4 | $5.94 |
| Microsoft | 8.8 | 39.1 | 5.92 |
| Wal-Mart Stores | 4.4 | 12.8 | 1.60 |
| Merck & Co | 7.1 | 24.0 | 4.84 |
| Philip Morris | 2.1 | 17.4 | 6.08 |
| ExxonMobil | 1.9 | 10.5 | 5.36 |
| Viacom | 1.3 | 2.0 | −4.37 |
| General Motors | 0.7 | 5.7 | −1.07 |
| WorldCom | 0.7 | 6.3 | −5.39 |
| AT&T | 0.6 | 4.5 | −9.97 |

Source: Data provided by Stern Stewart & Co.

24.8 cents more than the return that investors could have expected by investing in equivalent-risk stocks. Applying this 24.8% margin of superiority to Microsoft's capital base of $23.89 billion, we calculate economic value added in 2000 as $5.92 billion. GE's EVA was slightly larger than Microsoft's, despite a far smaller margin between ROA and cost of capital. This is because GE applied this margin to a larger capital base. At the other extreme, AT&T earned less than its opportunity cost on a very large capital base, which resulted in a large negative EVA.

Notice that even the EVA "losers" in Table 19.11 generally had positive profits. For example, AT&T's ROA was 4.5%. The problem is that its profits were not high enough to compensate for the opportunity cost of funds. EVA treats the opportunity cost of capital as a real cost that, like other costs, should be deducted from revenues to arrive at a more meaningful "bottom line." A firm that is earning profits but is not covering its opportunity cost might be able to redeploy its capital to better uses. Therefore, a growing number of firms now calculate EVA and tie managers' compensation to it.

# 19.6   AN ILLUSTRATION OF FINANCIAL STATEMENT ANALYSIS

In her 2007 annual report to the shareholders of Growth Industries, Inc., the president wrote: "2007 was another successful year for Growth Industries. As in 2006, sales, assets, and operating income all continued to grow at a rate of 20%."

Is she right?

We can evaluate her statement by conducting a full-scale ratio analysis of Growth Industries. Our purpose is to assess GI's performance in the recent past, to evaluate its future prospects, and to determine whether its market price reflects its intrinsic value.

Table 19.12 shows the key financial ratios we can compute from GI's financial statements. The president is certainly right about the growth rate in sales, assets, and operating income. Inspection of GI's key financial ratios, however, contradicts her first sentence: 2007 was not another successful year for GI—it appears to have been another miserable one.

ROE has been declining steadily from 7.51% in 2005 to 3.03% in 2007. A comparison of GI's 2007 ROE to the 2007 industry average of 8.64% makes the deteriorating time trend appear especially alarming. The low and falling market to book-value ratio and the falling price–earnings ratio indicate investors are less and less optimistic about the firm's future profitability.

The fact that ROA has not been declining, however, tells us that the source of the declining time trend in GI's ROE must be inappropriate use of financial leverage. And we see that as GI's leverage ratio climbed from 2.117 in 2005 to 2.723 in 2007, its interest-burden

| Table 19.12 | Key Financial Ratios of Growth Industries, Inc. | | | | | | | | |
|---|---|---|---|---|---|---|---|---|---|
| | | (1) Net Profit/ Pretax Profit | (2) Pretax Profit/ EBIT | (3) EBIT/ Sales (ROS) | (4) Sales/ Assets (ATO) | (5) Assets/ Equity | (6) Compound Leverage Factor (2) × (5) | (7) ROA (3) × (4) | | |
| Year | ROE | | | | | | | | P/E | P/B |
| 2005 | 7.51% | .6 | .650 | 30% | .303 | 2.117 | 1.376 | 9.09% | 8 | .58 |
| 2006 | 6.08 | .6 | .470 | 30 | .303 | 2.375 | 1.116 | 9.09 | 6 | .35 |
| 2007 | 3.03 | .6 | .204 | 30 | .303 | 2.723 | 0.556 | 9.09 | 4 | .12 |
| Industry average | 8.64 | .6 | .800 | 30 | .400 | 1.500 | 1.200 | 12.00 | 8 | .69 |

ratio (column 2) fell from .650 to .204—with the net result that the compound leverage factor fell from 1.376 to .556.

The rapid increase in short-term debt from year to year and the concurrent increase in interest expense make it clear that to finance its 20% growth rate in sales, GI has incurred sizable amounts of short-term debt at high interest rates. The firm is paying rates of interest greater than the ROA it is earning on the investment financed with the new borrowing. As the firm has expanded, its situation has become ever more precarious.

In 2007, for example, the average interest rate on short-term debt was 20% versus an ROA of 9.09%. (We compute the average interest rate on short-term debt by taking the total interest expense of $34,391,000, subtracting the $6 million in interest on the long-term bonds, and dividing by the beginning-of-year short-term debt of $141,957,000.)

GI's problems become clear when we examine its statement of cash flows in Table 19.13. The statement is derived from the income statement and balance sheet in Table 19.8. GI's cash flow from operations is falling steadily, from $12,700,000 in 2005 to $6,725,000 in 2007. The firm's investment in plant and equipment, by contrast, has increased greatly. Net plant and equipment (i.e., net of depreciation) rose from $150,000,000 in 2004 to $259,200,000 in 2007 (see Table 19.8). This near doubling of the capital assets makes the decrease in cash flow from operations all the more troubling.

The source of the difficulty is GI's enormous amount of short-term borrowing. In a sense, the company is being run as a pyramid scheme. It borrows more and more each year to maintain its 20% growth rate in assets and income. However, the new assets are not generating enough cash flow to support the extra interest burden of the debt, as the falling cash flow from operations indicates. Eventually, when the firm loses its ability to borrow further, its growth will be at an end.

At this point GI stock might be an attractive investment. Its market price is only 12% of its book value, and with a P/E ratio of 4 its earnings yield is 25% per year. GI is a likely candidate for a takeover by another firm that might replace GI's management and build shareholder value through a radical change in policy.

| Table 19.13   Growth Industries Statement of Cash Flows ($ thousands) | | | |
|---|---|---|---|
| | **2005** | **2006** | **2007** |
| **Cash Flow from Operating Activities** | | | |
| Net income | $ 11,700 | $ 10,143 | $  5,285 |
| + Depreciation | 15,000 | 18,000 | 21,600 |
| + Decrease (increase) in accounts receivable | (5,000) | (6,000) | (7,200) |
| + Decrease (increase) in inventories | (15,000) | (18,000) | (21,600) |
| + Increase in accounts payable | 6,000 | 7,200 | 8,640 |
| | $ 12,700 | $ 11,343 | $  6,725 |
| **Cash Flow from Investing Activities** | | | |
| Investment in plant and equipment* | $(45,000) | $(54,000) | $(64,800) |
| **Cash Flow from Financing Activities** | | | |
| Dividends paid† | $      0 | $      0 | $      0 |
| Short-term debt issued | 42,300 | 54,657 | 72,475 |
| Change in cash and marketable securities‡ | $ 10,000 | $ 12,000 | $ 14,400 |

*Gross investment equals increase in net plant and equipment plus depreciation.
†We can conclude that no dividends are paid because stockholders' equity increases each year by the full amount of net income, implying a plowback ratio of 1.0.
‡Equals cash flow from operations plus cash flow from investment activities plus cash flow from financing activities. Note that this equals the yearly change in cash and marketable securities on the balance sheet.

**CONCEPT CHECK☞ QUESTION 4**

You have the following information for IBX Corporation for the years 2005 and 2007 (all figures are in $ millions):

|  | 2005 | 2007 |
|---|---|---|
| Net income | $ 253.7 | $ 239.0 |
| Pretax income | 411.9 | 375.6 |
| EBIT | 517.6 | 403.1 |
| Average assets | 4,857.9 | 3,459.7 |
| Sales | 6,679.3 | 4,537.0 |
| Shareholders' equity | 2,233.3 | 2,347.3 |

What is the trend in IBX's ROE, and how can you account for it in terms of tax burden, margin, turnover, and financial leverage?

## 19.7  COMPARABILITY PROBLEMS

Financial statement analysis gives us a good amount of ammunition for evaluating a company's performance and future prospects. But comparing financial results of different companies is not so simple. There is more than one acceptable way to represent various items of revenue and expense according to generally accepted accounting principles (GAAP). This means two firms may have exactly the same economic income yet very different accounting incomes.

Furthermore, interpreting a single firm's performance over time is complicated when inflation distorts the dollar measuring rod. Comparability problems are especially acute in this case because the impact of inflation on reported results often depends on the particular method the firm adopts to account for inventories and depreciation. The security analyst must adjust the earnings and the financial ratio figures to a uniform standard before attempting to compare financial results across firms and over time.

Comparability problems can arise out of the flexibility of GAAP guidelines in accounting for inventories and depreciation and in adjusting for the effects of inflation. Other important potential sources of noncomparability include the capitalization of leases and other expenses and the treatment of pension costs, but they are beyond the scope of this book.

**Inventory Valuation**   There are two commonly used ways to value inventories: **LIFO** (last-in first-out) and **FIFO** (first-in first-out). We can explain the difference using a numerical example.

Suppose Generic Products, Inc. (GPI), has a constant inventory of 1 million units of generic goods. The inventory turns over once per year, meaning the ratio of cost of goods sold to inventory is 1.

The LIFO system calls for valuing the million units used up during the year at the current cost of production, so that the last goods produced are considered the first ones to be sold. They are valued at today's cost.

The FIFO system assumes that the units used up or sold are the ones that were added to inventory first, and goods sold should be valued at original cost.

If the price of generic goods has been constant, at the level of $1, say, the book value of inventory and the cost of goods sold would be the same, $1 million under both systems. But suppose the price of generic goods rises by 10 cents per unit during the year as a result of general inflation.

LIFO accounting would result in a cost of goods sold of $1.1 million, whereas the end-of-year balance sheet value of the 1 million units in inventory remains $1 million. The balance sheet value of inventories is given as the cost of the goods still in inventory. Under LIFO the last goods produced are assumed to be sold at the current cost of $1.10; the goods remaining are the previously produced goods, at a cost of only $1. You can see that although LIFO accounting accurately measures the cost of goods sold today, it understates the current value of the remaining inventory in an inflationary environment.

In contrast, under FIFO accounting, the cost of goods sold would be $1 million, and the end-of-year balance sheet value of the inventory would be $1.1 million. The result is that the LIFO firm has both a lower reported profit and a lower balance sheet value of inventories than the FIFO firm.

LIFO is preferred over FIFO in computing economic earnings (i.e., real sustainable cash flow) because it uses up-to-date prices to evaluate the cost of goods sold. A disadvantage is that LIFO accounting induces balance sheet distortions when it values investment in inventories at original cost. This practice results in an upward bias in ROE because the investment base on which return is earned is undervalued.

In computing the gross national product, the U.S. Department of Commerce has to make an inventory valuation adjustment (IVA) to eliminate the effects of FIFO accounting on the cost of goods sold. In effect, it puts all firms in the aggregate onto a LIFO basis.

## Depreciation

Another source of problems is the measurement of depreciation, which is a key factor in computing true earnings. The accounting and economic measures of depreciation can differ markedly. According to the *economic* definition, depreciation is the amount of a firm's operating cash flow that must be reinvested in the firm to sustain its real productive capacity at the current level.

The *accounting* measurement is quite different. Accounting depreciation is the amount of the original acquisition cost of an asset that is allocated to each accounting period over an arbitrarily specified life of the asset. This is the figure reported in financial statements. Assume, for example, that a firm buys machines with a useful economic life of 20 years at $100,000 apiece. In its financial statements, however, the firm can depreciate the machines over 10 years using the straight-line method, for $10,000 per year in depreciation. Thus after 10 years a machine will be fully depreciated on the books, even though it remains a productive asset that will not need replacement for another 10 years.

In computing accounting earnings, this firm will overestimate depreciation in the first 10 years of the machine's economic life and underestimate it in the last 10 years. This will cause reported earnings to be understated compared with economic earnings in the first 10 years and overstated in the last 10 years.

Depreciation comparability problems add one more wrinkle. A firm can use different depreciation methods for tax purposes than for other reporting purposes. Most firms use accelerated depreciation methods for tax purposes and straight-line depreciation in published financial statements. There also are differences across firms in their estimates of the depreciable life of plant, equipment, and other depreciable assets.

The major problem related to depreciation, however, is caused by inflation. Because conventional depreciation is based on historical costs rather than on the current replacement cost of assets, measured depreciation in periods of inflation is understated relative to replacement cost, and *real* economic income (sustainable cash flow) is correspondingly overstated.

The situation is similar to what happens in FIFO inventory accounting. Conventional depreciation and FIFO both result in an inflation-induced overstatement of real income because both use original cost instead of current cost to calculate net income.

For example, suppose Generic Products, Inc., has a machine with a 3-year useful life that originally cost $3 million. Annual straight-line depreciation is $1 million, regardless of what happens to the replacement cost of the machine. Suppose inflation in the first year turns out to be 10%. Then the true annual depreciation expense is $1.1 million in current terms, whereas conventionally measured depreciation remains fixed at $1 million per year. Accounting income overstates *real* economic income by $.1 million.

**Inflation and Interest Expense**    Although inflation can cause distortions in the measurement of a firm's inventory and depreciation costs, it has perhaps an even greater effect on calculation of *real* interest expense. Nominal interest rates include an inflation premium that compensates the lender for inflation-induced erosion in the real value of principal. From the perspective of both lender and borrower, therefore, part of what is conventionally measured as interest expense should be treated more properly as repayment of principal.

**EXAMPLE 19.5    Inflation and Real Income**

Suppose Generic Products has debt outstanding with a face value of $10 million at an interest rate of 10% per year. Interest expense as conventionally measured is $1 million per year. However, suppose inflation during the year is 6%, so that the real interest rate is 4%. Then $.6 million of what appears as interest expense on the income statement is really an inflation premium, or compensation for the anticipated reduction in the real value of the $10 million principal; only $.4 million is *real* interest expense. The $.6 million reduction in the purchasing power of the outstanding principal may be thought of as repayment of principal, rather than as an interest expense. Real income of the firm is, therefore, understated by $.6 million.

Mismeasurement of real interest means inflation deflates the computation of real income. The effects of inflation on the reported values of inventories and depreciation that we have discussed work in the opposite direction.

---

**CONCEPT CHECK☞ QUESTION 5**

In a period of rapid inflation, companies ABC and XYZ have the same *reported* earnings. ABC uses LIFO inventory accounting, has relatively fewer depreciable assets, and has more debt than XYZ. XYZ uses FIFO inventory accounting. Which company has the higher *real* income, and why?

---

**Quality of Earnings**    Many firms will make accounting choices that present their financial statements in the best possible light. The different choices that firms can make give rise to the comparability problems we have discussed. As a result, earnings statements for different companies may be more or less rosy presentations of true economic earnings—sustainable cash flow that can be paid to shareholders without impairing the firm's productive capacity. Analysts commonly evaluate the **quality of earnings** reported by a firm. This concept refers to the realism and conservatism of the earnings number, in other words, the extent to which we might expect the reported level of earnings to be sustained.

Examples of the types of factors that influence quality of earnings are:

- *Allowance for bad debt.* Most firms sell goods using trade credit and must make an allowance for bad debt. An unrealistically low allowance reduces the quality of reported earnings.

- *Nonrecurring items.* Some items that affect earnings should not be expected to recur regularly. These include asset sales, effects of accounting changes, effects of exchange rate movements, or unusual investment income. For example, in 1999, which was a banner year for equity returns, some firms enjoyed large investment returns on securities held. These contributed to that year's earnings, but should not be expected to repeat regularly. They would be considered a "low-quality" component of 1999 earnings. Similarly, investment gains in corporate pension plans generated large but one-off contributions to reported earnings.

- *Stock options.* Many firms compensate employees in large part with stock options. To the extent that these options replace cash salary that otherwise would need to be paid, the value of the options should be considered as one component of the firm's labor expense. But GAAP accounting rules do not require such treatment. Therefore, all else equal, earnings of firms with large employee stock option programs should be considered of lower quality. We return to this issue in Chapter 20 on options.

- *Revenue recognition.* Under GAAP accounting, a firm is allowed to recognize a sale before it is paid. This is why firms have accounts receivable. But sometimes it can be hard to know when to recognize sales. For example, suppose a computer firm signs a contract to provide products and services over a 5-year period. Should the revenue be booked immediately or spread out over 5 years? A more extreme version of this problem is called "channel stuffing," in which firms "sell" large quantities of goods to customers, but give them the right to later either refuse delivery or return the product. The revenue from the "sale" is booked now, but the likely returns are not recognized until they occur (in a future accounting period). According to the SEC, Sunbeam, which filed for bankruptcy in 2001, generated $60 million in fraudulent profits in 1999 using this technique. If you see accounts receivable increasing far faster than sales, or becoming a larger percentage of total assets, beware of these practices. Global Crossing, which filed for bankruptcy in 2002, illustrates a similar problem in revenue recognition. It swapped capacity on its network for capacity of other companies for periods of up to 20 years. But while it seems to have booked the *sale* of its capacity as immediate revenue, it treated the *acquired* capacity as capital assets that could be expensed over time. Given the wide latitude firms have to manipulate revenue, many analysts choose instead to concentrate on cash flow, which is far harder for a company to manipulate.

- *Off-balance-sheet assets and liabilities.* Suppose that one firm guarantees the outstanding debt of another firm, perhaps a firm in which it has an ownership stake. That obligation ought to be disclosed as a *contingent liability,* since it may require payments down the road. But these obligations may not be reported as part of the firm's outstanding debt. Similarly, leasing may be used to manage off-balance-sheet assets and liabilities. Airlines, for example, may show no aircraft on their balance sheets but have long-term leases that are virtually equivalent to debt-financed ownership. However, if the leases are treated as operating rather than capital leases, they may appear only as footnotes to the financial statements.

The nearby box discusses proposals to make financial statements more informative.

# TRUE AND FAIR IS NOT HARD AND FAST

The procession of companies admitting to having lied in their reported accounts has undermined faith in corporate numbers. The first priority for those who set accounting rules has been to try to choke off the most obvious loopholes.

Looking further into the future, however, some see the crisis in accounting as an opportunity to change the shape and content of accounts more fundamentally. The growing use of market values for assets and liabilities (instead of the accidental "historic cost" at which they were obtained) is going to make shareholders' equity and profits swing around far more than in the past. Under such circumstances, profits may come to be stated as a range of figures, each of them arrived at by using different accounting assumptions.

For the moment though, the efforts of regulators and standard-setters are focused on five main areas:

- **Pro-forma accounts.** These are the first sets of results produced by companies in America: they are unaudited and do not follow America's GAAP (Generally Accepted Accounting Principles). In the years of the stockmarket bubble they were shamelessly abused. Companies regularly reported huge profits in their pro-forma earnings statements, only to register even larger losses in their official filings.

- **Off-balance-sheet vehicles.** These include the "special-purpose entities" made famous by Enron. They allowed the Houston oil trader to hide hundreds of millions of dollars of liabilities from investors' eyes.

- **Stock options.** Most significant of all, perhaps, is the attempt to force companies to account for stock options granted to their employees. This week, FASB agreed that the cost of employee stock options should be treated as an expense. The question is, how to value them.

- **Pension funds.** Another controversial aim is to make companies change the way they account for their employee pension schemes. In March, FASB said it would start examining ways to improve accounting for employee pension plans.

- **Revenue recognition.** This is the vexed issue of when precisely to include revenue in the accounts—for example, when an order is made, when it is shipped, or when payment is received.

## Future Standards

Yet another goal is to shift the world's body of accounting standards away from rules (the approach favored in America) towards principles (more influential in Britain). The hard rules embedded in America's GAAP have helped devious financiers to design structures that obey the letter of the law but ignore the spirit.

The way to make accounts more relevant (and to stop executives from fiddling them) is, standard-setters believe, to force companies to value more of their assets and liabilities at market prices, to "mark them to market." Instead of holding assets and liabilities at historic cost, and depreciating assets by a set amount each year, they maintain that companies should be required to mark them to market at the end of each reporting period. The slow march to market value is probably unstoppable in the long run, because so many accountants now believe that it is the most intellectually valid way to value assets.

Some accountants, however, would like to see a far more radical rethink of accounts. To start with the basics, what are accounts for? Most accountants would probably reply that they are there to give a true picture of a company's performance during a particular period of time. Investors, however, want far more than that: they want a sense of the company's future prospects.

Regulators also believe that companies should be obliged to give out new sorts of information. There should be new sections in annual reports on companies' intangible assets and on "key performance indicators"—such as employee turnover, customer acquisition cost, or inventory turnover.

None of this, however, will address the deepest flaw in accounts, says Baruch Lev, a professor of accounting and finance at the New York University Stern School of Business. This is the reality that most of the numbers in accounts are not facts but estimates.

Mr. Lev's remedy is to separate company accounts into two pieces: one "core" and one "satellite." The core part would have the most reliable numbers, or the ones that rely the least on estimates—cash flow would go here, for instance, and perhaps property. The satellite part would contain fair-value numbers and intangible assets, as well as other items.

Although companies and their auditors pretend that they can work out a single profit figure and a single net-assets number, the truth is that accountants do not know exactly how much money a company has made, nor exactly how much it is worth at any one moment. Realistically, the best they can hope for is a range—"X corporation made somewhere between $600m and $800m"—depending on, for instance, what assumption is made about the likelihood that its customers will pay all the money that they owe.

**International Accounting Conventions**   The examples cited above illustrate some of the problems that analysts can encounter when attempting to interpret financial data. Even greater problems arise in the interpretation of the financial statements of foreign firms. This is because these firms do not follow GAAP guidelines. Accounting practices in various countries differ to greater or lesser extents from U.S. standards. Here are some of the major issues that you should be aware of when using the financial statements of foreign firms:

**Reserving Practices.** Many countries allow firms considerably more discretion in setting aside reserves for future contingencies than is typical in the United States. Because additions to reserves result in a charge against income, reported earnings are far more subject to managerial discretion than in the United States.

Germany is a country that allows particularly wide discretion in reserve practice. When Daimler-Benz AG (producer of the Mercedes-Benz) decided to issue shares on the New York Stock Exchange in 1993, it had to revise its accounting statements in accordance with U.S. standards. The revisions transformed a small profit for the first half of 1993 using German accounting rules into a *loss* of a $592 million under more stringent U.S. rules.

**Depreciation.** In the United States, firms typically maintain separate sets of accounts for tax and reporting purposes. For example, accelerated depreciation is typically used for tax purposes, whereas straight-line depreciation is used for reporting purposes. In contrast, most other countries do not allow dual sets of accounts, and most firms in foreign countries use accelerated depreciation to minimize taxes despite the fact that it results in lower reported earnings. This makes reported earnings of foreign firms lower than they would be if the firms were allowed to use the U.S. practice.

**Intangibles.** Treatment of intangibles such as goodwill can vary widely. Are they amortized or expensed? If amortized, over what period? Such issues can have a large impact on reported profits.

Figure 19.2 summarizes some of the major differences in accounting rules in various countries. The effect of different accounting practices can be substantial. Figure 19.3 compares P/E ratios in different countries as reported and restated on a common basis. The variation is considerable.

Such differences in international accounting standards become more of a problem as the drive to globally integrated capital markets progresses. For example, many foreign firms would like to list their shares on the New York Stock Exchange to more easily tap U.S. equity markets, and the NYSE would like to have those firms listed. But the SEC will not allow such shares to be listed unless the firms prepare their financial statements in accordance with U.S. GAAP standards. This has limited listing of non-U.S. companies dramatically.

In contrast to the United States, most other large national stock exchanges allow foreign firms to be listed if their financial statements conform to International Accounting Standards (IAS) rules. IAS disclosure requirements tend to be far more rigorous than those of most countries, and these standards impose greater uniformity in accounting practices. Its advocates argue that IAS rules are at least as revealing as GAAP rules, providing high-quality financial information about the firm. See the nearby box for more information on the IASB.

**Figure 19.2    Comparative accounting rules**

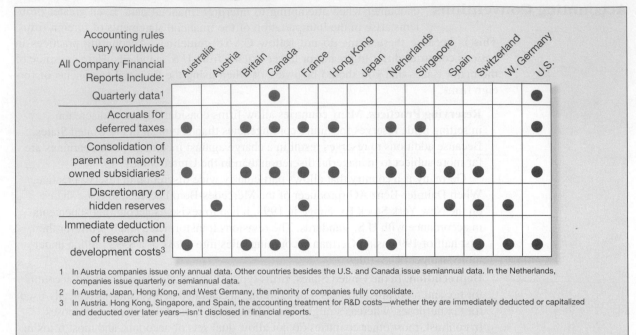

| Accounting rules vary worldwide<br>All Company Financial Reports Include: | Australia | Austria | Britain | Canada | France | Hong Kong | Japan | Netherlands | Singapore | Spain | Switzerland | W. Germany | U.S. |
|---|---|---|---|---|---|---|---|---|---|---|---|---|---|
| Quarterly data[1] | | | | ● | | | | | | | | | ● |
| Accruals for deferred taxes | ● | | ● | ● | ● | | | ● | | | | | ● |
| Consolidation of parent and majority owned subsidiaries[2] | ● | | ● | ● | ● | | | ● | ● | ● | | | ● |
| Discretionary or hidden reserves | | ● | | | ● | | | | | ● | ● | ● | |
| Immediate deduction of research and development costs[3] | ● | | ● | ● | ● | | ● | ● | | ● | ● | ● | ● |

1  In Austria companies issue only annual data. Other countries besides the U.S. and Canada issue semiannual data. In the Netherlands, companies issue quarterly or semiannual data.
2  In Austria, Japan, Hong Kong, and West Germany, the minority of companies fully consolidate.
3  In Austria, Hong Kong, Singapore, and Spain, the accounting treatment for R&D costs—whether they are immediately deducted or capitalized and deducted over later years—isn't disclosed in financial reports.

Source: Center for International Financial Analysis and Research, Princeton, NJ; and Frederick D. S. Choi and Gerhard G. Mueller, *International Accounting*, 2d, ed. (Englewood Cliffs, NJ: Prentice Hall, 1992).

**Figure 19.3    Adjusted versus reported price–earnings ratios**

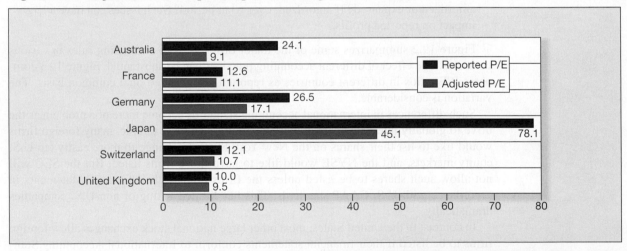

| Country | Reported P/E | Adjusted P/E |
|---|---|---|
| Australia | 24.1 | 9.1 |
| France | 12.6 | 11.1 |
| Germany | 26.5 | 17.1 |
| Japan | 78.1 | 45.1 |
| Switzerland | 12.1 | 10.7 |
| United Kingdom | 10.0 | 9.5 |

Source: Lawrence S. Speidell and Vinod Bavishi, "GAAP Arbitrage: Valuation Opportunities in International Accounting Standards," *Financial Analysts Journal*, November–December 1992, pp. 58–66.

# 19.8    VALUE INVESTING: THE GRAHAM TECHNIQUE

No presentation of fundamental security analysis would be complete without a discussion of the ideas of Benjamin Graham, the greatest of the investment "gurus." Until the evolution of modern portfolio theory in the latter half of this century, Graham was the single most important thinker, writer, and teacher in the field of investment analysis. His influence on investment professionals remains very strong.

Graham's magnum opus is *Security Analysis*, written with Columbia Professor David Dodd in 1934. Its message is similar to the ideas presented in this chapter. Graham believed careful analysis of a firm's financial statements could turn up bargain stocks. Over the years, he developed many different rules for determining the most important financial ratios and the critical values for judging a stock to be undervalued. Through many editions, his book has been so influential and successful that widespread adoption of Graham's techniques has led to elimination of the very bargains they are designed to identify.

In a 1976 seminar Graham said:[4]

> I am no longer an advocate of elaborate techniques of security analysis in order to find superior value opportunities. This was a rewarding activity, say, forty years ago, when our textbook "Graham and Dodd" was first published; but the situation has changed a good deal since then. In the old days any well-trained security analyst could do a good professional job of selecting undervalued issues through detailed studies; but in the light of the enormous amount of research now being carried on, I doubt whether in most cases such extensive efforts will generate sufficiently superior selections to justify their cost. To that very limited extent I'm on the side of the "efficient market" school of thought now generally accepted by the professors.

Nonetheless, in that same seminar, Graham suggested a simplified approach to identify bargain stocks:

> My first, more limited, technique confines itself to the purchase of common stocks at less than their working-capital value, or net current-asset value, giving no weight to the plant and other fixed assets, and deducting all liabilities in full from the current assets. We used this approach extensively in managing investment funds, and over a 30-odd-year period we must have earned an average of some 20 percent per year from this source. I consider it a foolproof method of systematic investment—once again, not on the basis of individual results but in terms of the expectable group income.

There are two convenient sources of information for those interested in trying out the Graham technique: Both Standard & Poor's *Outlook* and *The Value Line Investment Survey* carry lists of stocks selling below net working capital value.

## SUMMARY

1. The primary focus of the security analyst should be the firm's real economic earnings rather than its reported earnings. Accounting earnings as reported in financial statements can be a biased estimate of real economic earnings, although empirical studies reveal that reported earnings convey considerable information concerning a firm's prospects.

---

[4] As cited by John Train in *Money Masters* (New York: Harper & Row, 1987).

2. A firm's ROE is a key determinant of the growth rate of its earnings. ROE is affected profoundly by the firm's degree of financial leverage. An increase in a firm's debt-to-equity ratio will raise its ROE and hence its growth rate only if the interest rate on the debt is less than the firm's return on assets.

3. It is often helpful to the analyst to decompose a firm's ROE ratio into the product of several accounting ratios and to analyze their separate behavior over time and across companies within an industry. A useful breakdown is

$$\text{ROE} = \frac{\text{Net profits}}{\text{Pretax profits}} \times \frac{\text{Pretax profits}}{\text{EBIT}} \times \frac{\text{EBIT}}{\text{Sales}} \times \frac{\text{Sales}}{\text{Assets}} \times \frac{\text{Assets}}{\text{Equity}}$$

4. Other accounting ratios that have a bearing on a firm's profitability and/or risk are fixed-asset turnover, inventory turnover, days receivables, and the current, quick, and interest coverage ratios.

5. Two ratios that make use of the market price of the firm's common stock in addition to its financial statements are the ratios of market to book value and price to earnings. Analysts sometimes take low values for these ratios as a margin of safety or a sign that the stock is a bargain.

6. A strategy of investing in stocks with high reported ROE seems to have produced a lower rate of return to the investor than investing in low ROE stocks. This implies that high reported ROE stocks were overpriced compared with low ROE stocks.

7. A major problem in the use of data obtained from a firm's financial statements is comparability. Firms have a great deal of latitude in how they choose to compute various items of revenue and expense. It is, therefore, necessary for the security analyst to adjust accounting earnings and financial ratios to a uniform standard before attempting to compare financial results across firms.

8. Comparability problems can be acute in a period of inflation. Inflation can create distortions in accounting for inventories, depreciation, and interest expense.

## KEY TERMS

| | | |
|---|---|---|
| income statement | return on sales | times interest earned |
| balance sheet | asset turnover | market–book-value ratio |
| statement of cash flows | leverage ratio | price–earnings ratio |
| economic earnings | average collection period | earnings yield |
| accounting earnings | days receivables | economic value added |
| return on equity | current ratio | residual income |
| return on assets | quick ratio | LIFO |
| Du Pont system | acid test ratio | FIFO |
| profit margin | interest coverage ratio | quality of earnings |

## WEBSITES

www.sec.gov
www.cfo.com
www.fei.org
www.aicpa.org/index.htm
Visit these sites for articles about financial accounting issues.

**WEBSITES**

www.nasdaq.com
moneycentral.msn.com/investor/home.asp
yahoo.marketguide.com
www.edgar-online.com
www.hoovers.com
www.freeedgar.com
www.smartmoney.com
www.executivelibrary.com/Research.asp

Financial statement data is available at the websites listed above. Enter the stock symbol and look for ratios.

edgarscan.pwcglobal.com/servlets/edgarscan

Examine financial ratios for time trend and cross-company comparisons. Compare a company's financials with an industry or a company of choice. Use EdgarScan and the Benchmarking Assistant.

gozips.uakron.edu/~drd/cs4.html

Visit this site for general industry information.

gozips.uakron.edu/~drd/cs5.html

This site offers stock performance updates and charting services.

**PROBLEMS**

1. An analyst applies the Du Pont system of financial analysis to the following data for a company:

   - Leverage ratio (assets/equity)        2.2
   - Total asset turnover                   2.0
   - Net profit margin                      5.5%
   - Dividend payout ratio                  31.8%

   What is the company's return on equity?

2. The Crusty Pie Co., which specializes in apple turnovers, has a return on sales higher than the industry average, yet its ROA is the same as the industry average. How can you explain this?

3. The ABC Corporation has a profit margin on sales below the industry average, yet its ROA is above the industry average. What does this imply about its asset turnover?

4. Firm A and Firm B have the same ROA, yet Firm A's ROE is higher. How can you explain this?

Problems 5 through 21 are from past CFA examinations.

5. The information in the following exhibit comes from the financial statements of QuickBrush Company and SmileWhite Corporation:

|  | QuickBrush | SmileWhite |
|---|---|---|
| Goodwill | The company amortizes goodwill over 20 years. | The company amortizes goodwill over 5 years. |
| Property, plant, and equipment | The company uses a straight-line depreciation method over the economic lives of the assets, which range from 5 to 20 years for buildings. | The company uses an accelerated depreciation method over the economic lives of the assets, which range from 5 to 20 years for buildings. |
| Accounts receivable | The company uses a bad debt allowance of 2% of accounts receivable. | The company uses a bad debt allowance of 5% of accounts receivable. |

Determine which company has the higher quality of earnings by discussing each of the three notes.

6. Scott Kelly is reviewing MasterToy's financial statements in order to estimate its sustainable growth rate. Using the information presented in the following exhibit.

   *a.* Identify and calculate the components of the Du Pont formula.
   *b.* Calculate the ROE for 1999 using the components of the Du Pont formula.
   *c.* Calculate the sustainable growth rate for 1999 from the firm's ROE and plowback ratios.

**MasterToy, Inc.: Actual 1998 and Estimated 1999 Financial Statements for Fiscal Year Ending December 31 ($ millions, except per-share data)**

|  | 1998 | 1999e | Change (%) |
|---|---|---|---|
| *Income Statement* |  |  |  |
| Revenue | $4,750 | $5,140 | 7.6% |
| Cost of goods sold | 2,400 | 2,540 |  |
| Selling, general, and administrative | 1,400 | 1,550 |  |
| Depreciation | 180 | 210 |  |
| Goodwill amortization | 10 | 10 |  |
| Operating income | $ 760 | $ 830 | 8.4 |
| Interest expense | 20 | 25 |  |
| Income before taxes | $ 740 | $ 805 |  |
| Income taxes | 265 | 295 |  |
| Net income | $ 475 | $ 510 |  |
| Earnings per share | $1.79 | $1.96 | 8.6 |
| Averages shares outstanding (millions) | 265 | 260 |  |
| *Balance Sheet* |  |  |  |
| Cash | $ 400 | $ 400 |  |
| Accounts receivable | 680 | 700 |  |
| Inventories | 570 | 600 |  |
| Net property, plant, and equipment | 800 | 870 |  |
| Intangibles | 500 | 530 |  |
| Total assets | $2,950 | $3,100 |  |
| Current liabilities | 550 | 600 |  |
| Long-term debt | 300 | 300 |  |
| Total liabilities | $ 850 | $ 900 |  |
| Stockholders' equity | 2,100 | 2,200 |  |
| Total liabilities and equity | $2,950 | $3,100 |  |
| Book value per share | $7.92 | $8.46 |  |
| Annual dividend per share | $0.55 | $0.60 |  |

7. The cash flow data of Palomba Pizza Stores for the year ended December 31, 1999, are as follows:

| | |
|---|---:|
| Cash payment of dividends | $ 35,000 |
| Purchase of land | 14,000 |
| Cash payments for interest | 10,000 |
| Cash payments for salaries | 45,000 |
| Sale of equipment | 38,000 |
| Retirement of common stock | 25,000 |
| Purchase of equipment | 30,000 |
| Cash payments to suppliers | 85,000 |
| Cash collections from customers | 250,000 |
| Cash at beginning of year | 50,000 |

a. Prepare a statement of cash flows for Palomba showing:
   - Net cash provided by operating activities.
   - Net cash provided by or used in investing activities.
   - Net cash provided by or used in financing activities.

b. Discuss, from an analyst's viewpoint, the purpose of classifying cash flows into the three categories listed above.

8. This problem should be solved using the following data:

| | |
|---|---:|
| Cash payments for interest | $(12) |
| Retirement of common stock | (32) |
| Cash payments to merchandise suppliers | (85) |
| Purchase of land | (8) |
| Sale of equipment | 30 |
| Payments of dividends | (37) |
| Cash payment for salaries | (35) |
| Cash collection from customers | 260 |
| Purchase of equipment | (40) |

a. What are cash flows from operating activities?

b. Using the data above, calculate cash flows from investing activities.

c. Using the data above, calculate cash flows from financing activities.

9. Janet Ludlow is a recently hired analyst. After describing the electric toothbrush industry, her first report focuses on two companies, QuickBrush Company and Smile-White Corporation, and concludes:

QuickBrush is a more profitable company than SmileWhite, as indicated by the 40% sales growth and substantially higher margins it has produced over the last few years. Smile-White's sales and earnings are growing at a 10% rate and produce much lower margins. We do not think SmileWhite is capable of growing faster than its recent growth rate of 10% whereas QuickBrush can sustain a 30% long-term growth rate.

a. Criticize Ludlow's analysis and conclusion that QuickBrush is more profitable, as defined by return on equity (ROE), than SmileWhite and that it has a higher sustainable growth rate. Use only the information provided in Tables 19A and 19B. Support your criticism by calculating and analyzing:
   - the five components that determine ROE.
   - the two ratios that determine sustainable growth: ROE and plowback.

Visit us at www.mhhe.com/bkm

| Table 19A | | QuickBrush Company Financial Statements: Yearly Data ($000 except per share data) | | |
|---|---|---|---|---|

| Income Statement | December 2000 | December 2001 | December 2002 | |
|---|---|---|---|---|
| Revenue | $3,480 | $5,400 | $7,760 | |
| Cost of goods sold | 2,700 | 4,270 | 6,050 | |
| Selling, general, and admin. expense | 500 | 690 | 1,000 | |
| Depreciation and amortization | 30 | 40 | 50 | |
| Operating income (EBIT) | $ 250 | $ 400 | $ 660 | |
| Interest expense | 0 | 0 | 0 | |
| Income before taxes | $ 250 | $ 400 | $ 660 | |
| Income taxes | 60 | 110 | 215 | |
| Income after taxes | $ 190 | $ 290 | $ 445 | |
| Diluted EPS | $0.60 | $0.84 | $1.18 | |
| Average shares outstanding (000) | 317 | 346 | 376 | |

| Financial Statistics | December 2000 | December 2001 | December 2002 | 3-Year Average |
|---|---|---|---|---|
| COGS as % of sales | 77.59% | 79.07% | 77.96% | 78.24% |
| General & admin. as % of sales | 14.37 | 12.78 | 12.89 | 13.16 |
| Operating margin | 7.18 | 7.41 | 8.51 | |
| Pretax income/EBIT | 100.00 | 100.00 | 100.00 | |
| Tax rate | 24.00 | 27.50 | 32.58 | |

| Balance Sheet | December 2000 | December 2001 | December 2002 | |
|---|---|---|---|---|
| Cash and cash equivalents | $ 460 | $ 50 | $ 480 | |
| Accounts receivable | 540 | 720 | 950 | |
| Inventories | 300 | 430 | 590 | |
| Net property, plant, and equipment | 760 | 1,830 | 3,450 | |
| Total assets | $2,060 | $3,030 | $5,470 | |
| Current liabilities | $ 860 | $1,110 | $1,750 | |
| Total liabilities | $ 860 | $1,110 | $1,750 | |
| Stockholders' equity | 1,200 | 1,920 | 3,720 | |
| Total liabilities and equity | $2,060 | $3,030 | $5,470 | |
| Market price per share | $21.00 | $30.00 | $45.00 | |
| Book value per share | $3.79 | $5.55 | $9.89 | |
| Annual dividend per share | $0.00 | $0.00 | $0.00 | |

b. Explain how QuickBrush has produced an average annual earnings per share (EPS) growth rate of 40% over the last 2 years with an ROE that has been declining. Use only the information provided in Table 19A.

The following case should be used to solve problems 10–13.

10. Eastover Company (EO) is a large, diversified forest products company. Approximately 75% of its sales are from paper and forest products, with the remainder from

**Table 19B**
**SmileWhite Corporation**
**Financial Statements: Yearly Data**
**($000 except per share data)**

| Income Statement | December 2000 | December 2001 | December 2002 | |
|---|---|---|---|---|
| Revenue | $104,000 | $110,400 | $119,200 | |
| Cost of goods sold | 72,800 | 75,100 | 79,300 | |
| Selling, general, and admin. expense | 20,300 | 22,800 | 23,900 | |
| Depreciation and amortization | 4,200 | 5,600 | 8,300 | |
| Operating income | $ 6,700 | $ 6,900 | $ 7,700 | |
| Interest expense | 600 | 350 | 350 | |
| Income before taxes | $ 6,100 | $ 6,550 | $ 7,350 | |
| Income taxes | 2,100 | 2,200 | 2,500 | |
| Income after taxes | $ 4,000 | $ 4,350 | $ 4,850 | |
| Diluted EPS | $2.16 | $2.35 | $2.62 | |
| Average shares outstanding (000) | 1,850 | 1,850 | 1,850 | |

| Financial Statistics | December 2000 | December 2001 | December 2002 | 3-Year Average |
|---|---|---|---|---|
| COGS as % of sales | 70.00% | 68.00% | 66.53% | 68.10% |
| General & admin. as % of sales | 19.52 | 20.64 | 20.05 | 20.08 |
| Operating margin | 6.44 | 6.25 | 6.46 | |
| Pretax income/EBIT | 91.04 | 94.93 | 95.45 | |
| Tax rate | 34.43 | 33.59 | 34.01 | |

| Balance Sheet | December 2000 | December 2001 | December 2002 | |
|---|---|---|---|---|
| Cash and cash equivalents | $ 7,900 | $ 3,300 | $ 1,700 | |
| Accounts receivable | 7,500 | 8,000 | 9,000 | |
| Inventories | 6,300 | 6,300 | 5,900 | |
| Net property, plant, and equipment | 12,000 | 14,500 | 17,000 | |
| Total assets | $33,700 | $32,100 | $33,600 | |
| Current liabilities | $ 6,200 | $ 7,800 | $ 6,600 | |
| Long-term debt | 9,000 | 4,300 | 4,300 | |
| Total liabilities | $15,200 | $12,100 | $10,900 | |
| Stockholders' equity | 18,500 | 20,000 | 22,700 | |
| Total liabilities and equity | $33,700 | $32,100 | $33,600 | |
| Market price per share | $23.00 | $26.00 | $30.00 | |
| Book value per share | $10.00 | $10.81 | $12.27 | |
| Annual dividend per share | $1.42 | $1.53 | $1.72 | |

financial services and real estate. The company owns 5.6 million acres of timberland, which is carried at very low historical cost on the balance sheet.

Peggy Mulroney, CFA, is an analyst at the investment counseling firm of Centurion Investments. She is assigned the task of assessing the outlook for Eastover, which is being considered for purchase, and comparing it to another forest products company in Centurion's portfolios, Southampton Corporation (SHC). SHC is a

### Table 19C    Eastover Company ($ millions, except shares outstanding)

|  | 1998 | 1999 | 2000 | 2001 | 2002 |
|---|---|---|---|---|---|
| **Income Statement Summary** | | | | | |
| Sales | $5,652 | $6,990 | $7,863 | $8,281 | $7,406 |
| Earnings before interest and taxes (EBIT) | $ 568 | $ 901 | $1,037 | $ 708 | $ 795 |
| Interest expense (net) | (147) | (188) | (186) | (194) | (195) |
| Income before taxes | $ 421 | $ 713 | $ 851 | $ 514 | $ 600 |
| Income taxes | (144) | (266) | (286) | (173) | (206) |
| Tax rate | 34% | 37% | 33% | 34% | 34% |
| Net income | $ 277 | $ 447 | $ 565 | $ 341 | $ 394 |
| Preferred dividends | (28) | (17) | (17) | (17) | (0) |
| Net income to common | $ 249 | $ 430 | $ 548 | $ 324 | $ 394 |
| Common shares outstanding (millions) | 196 | 204 | 204 | 205 | 201 |
| **Balance Sheet Summary** | | | | | |
| Current assets | $1,235 | $1,491 | $1,702 | $1,585 | $1,367 |
| Timberland assets | 649 | 625 | 621 | 612 | 615 |
| Property, plant, and equipment | 4,370 | 4,571 | 5,056 | 5,430 | 5,854 |
| Other assets | 360 | 555 | 473 | 472 | 429 |
| Total assets | $6,614 | $7,242 | $7,852 | $8,099 | $8,265 |
| Current liabilities | $1,226 | $1,186 | $1,206 | $1,606 | $1,816 |
| Long-term debt | 1,120 | 1,340 | 1,585 | 1,340 | 1,585 |
| Deferred taxes | 1,000 | 1,000 | 1,016 | 1,000 | 1,000 |
| Equity-preferred | 364 | 350 | 350 | 400 | 0 |
| Equity-common | 2,904 | 3,366 | 3,695 | 3,747 | 3,864 |
| Total liabilities and equity | $6,614 | $7,242 | $7,852 | $8,099 | $8,265 |

major producer of lumber products in the United States. Building products, primarily lumber and plywood, account for 89% of SHC's sales, with pulp accounting for the remainder. SHC owns 1.4 million acres of timberland, which is also carried at historical cost on the balance sheet. In SHC's case, however, that cost is not as far below current market as Eastover's.

Mulroney began her examination of Eastover and Southampton by looking at the five components of return on equity (ROE) for each company. For her analysis, Mulroney elected to define equity as total shareholders' equity, including preferred stock. She also elected to use year-end data rather than averages for the balance sheet items.

*a.* Based on the data shown in Tables 19C and 19D, calculate each of the five ROE components for Eastover and Southampton in 2002. Using the five components, calculate ROE for both companies in 2002.

*b.* Referring to the components calculated in part (*b*), explain the difference in ROE for Eastover and Southampton in 2002.

*c.* Using 2002 data, calculate the sustainable growth rate for both Eastover and Southampton. Discuss the appropriateness of using these calculations as a basis for estimating future growth.

11. *a.* Mulroney (see the previous problem) recalled from her CFA studies that the constant-growth discounted dividend model was one way to arrive at a valuation

| Table 19D | Southampton Corporation | | | | |
| --- | --- | --- | --- | --- | --- |
| ($ millions, except shares outstanding) | | | | | |
| | **1998** | **1999** | **2000** | **2001** | **2002** |
| **Income Statement Summary** | | | | | |
| Sales | $1,306 | $1,654 | $1,799 | $2,010 | $1,793 |
| Earnings before interest and taxes (EBIT) | $  120 | $  230 | $  221 | $  304 | $  145 |
| Interest expense (net) | (13) | (36) | (7) | (12) | (8) |
| Income before taxes | $  107 | $  194 | $  214 | $  292 | $  137 |
| Income taxes | (44) | (75) | (79) | (99) | (46) |
| Tax rate | 41% | 39% | 37% | 34% | 34% |
| Net income | $   63 | $  119 | $  135 | $  193 | $   91 |
| Common shares outstanding (millions) | 38 | 38 | 38 | 38 | 38 |
| **Balance Sheet Summary** | | | | | |
| Current assets | $  487 | $  504 | $  536 | $  654 | $  509 |
| Timberland assets | 512 | 513 | 508 | 513 | 518 |
| Property, plant, and equipment | 648 | 681 | 718 | 827 | 1,037 |
| Other assets | 141 | 151 | 34 | 38 | 40 |
| Total assets | $1,788 | $1,849 | $1,796 | $2,032 | $2,104 |
| Current liabilities | $  185 | $  176 | $  162 | $  180 | $  195 |
| Long-term debt | 536 | 493 | 370 | 530 | 589 |
| Deferred taxes | 123 | 136 | 127 | 146 | 153 |
| Equity | 944 | 1,044 | 1,137 | 1,176 | 1,167 |
| Total liabilities and equity | $1,788 | $1,849 | $1,796 | $2,032 | $2,104 |

for a company's common stock. She collected current dividend and stock price data for Eastover and Southampton, shown in Table 19E. Using 11% as the required rate of return (i.e., discount rate) and a projected growth rate of 8%, compute a constant-growth DDM value for Eastover's stock and compare the computed value for Eastover to its stock price indicated in Table 19F.

b. Mulroney's supervisor commented that a two-stage DDM may be more appropriate for companies such as Eastover and Southampton. Mulroney believes that Eastover and Southampton could grow more rapidly over the next 3 years and then settle in at a lower but sustainable rate of growth beyond 2006. Her estimates are indicated in Table 19G. Using 11% as the required rate of return, compute the two-stage DDM value of Eastover's stock and compare that value to its stock price indicated in Table 19F.

c. Discuss advantages and disadvantages of using a constant-growth DDM. Briefly discuss how the two-stage DDM improves upon the constant-growth DDM.

12. In addition to the discounted dividend model approach, Mulroney (see previous problem) decided to look at the price–earnings ratio and price–book ratio, relative to the S&P 500, for both Eastover and Southampton. Mulroney elected to perform this analysis using 1999–2003 and current data.

a. Using the data in Tables 19E and 19F, compute both the current and the 5-year (1999–2003) average relative price–earnings ratios and relative price–book ratios for Eastover and Southampton (i.e., ratios relative to those for the S&P 500). Discuss each company's current relative price–earnings ratio compared to its 5-year

**Table 19E    Valuation of Eastover Company and Southampton Corporation Compared to S&P 500**

|  | 1998 | 1999 | 2000 | 2001 | 2002 | 2003 | 5-Year Average (1999–2003) |
|---|---|---|---|---|---|---|---|
| **Eastover Company** | | | | | | | |
| Earnings per share | $ 1.27 | $ 2.12 | $ 2.68 | $ 1.56 | $ 1.87 | $ 0.90 | |
| Dividends per share | 0.87 | 0.90 | 1.15 | 1.20 | 1.20 | 1.20 | |
| Book value per share | 14.82 | 16.54 | 18.14 | 18.55 | 19.21 | 17.21 | |
| Stock price | | | | | | | |
| High | 28 | 40 | 30 | 33 | 28 | 30 | |
| Low | 20 | 20 | 23 | 25 | 18 | 20 | |
| Close | 25 | 26 | 25 | 28 | 22 | 27 | |
| Average P/E | 18.9 | 14.2 | 9.9 | 18.6 | 12.3 | 27.8 | |
| Average P/B | 1.6 | 1.8 | 1.5 | 1.6 | 1.2 | 1.5 | |
| **Southampton Corporation** | | | | | | | |
| Earnings per share | $ 1.66 | $ 3.13 | $ 3.55 | $ 5.08 | $ 2.46 | $ 1.75 | |
| Dividends per share | 0.77 | 0.79 | 0.89 | 0.98 | 1.04 | 1.08 | |
| Book value per share | 24.84 | 27.47 | 29.92 | 30.95 | 31.54 | 32.21 | |
| Stock price | | | | | | | |
| High | 34 | 40 | 38 | 43 | 45 | 46 | |
| Low | 21 | 22 | 26 | 28 | 20 | 26 | |
| Close | 31 | 27 | 28 | 39 | 27 | 44 | |
| Average P/E | 16.6 | 9.9 | 9.0 | 7.0 | 13.2 | 20.6 | |
| Average P/B | 1.1 | 1.1 | 1.1 | 1.2 | 1.0 | 1.1 | |
| **S&P 500** | | | | | | | |
| Average P/E | 15.8 | 16.0 | 11.1 | 13.9 | 15.6 | 19.2 | 15.2 |
| Average P/B | 1.8 | 2.1 | 1.9 | 2.2 | 2.1 | 2.3 | 2.1 |

**Table 19F    Current Information**

|  | Current Share Price | Current Dividends Per Share | 2004 EPS Estimate | Current Book Value Per Share |
|---|---|---|---|---|
| Eastover | $ 28 | $ 1.20 | $ 1.60 | $ 17.32 |
| Southampton | 48 | 1.08 | 3.00 | 32.21 |
| S&P 500 | 830 | 24.00 | 41.08 | 319.66 |

**Table 19G    Projected Growth Rates as of 2003**

|  | Next Three Years (2004, 2005, 2006) | Growth Beyond 2006 |
|---|---|---|
| Eastover | 12% | 8% |
| Southampton | 13% | 7% |

average relative price–earnings ratio and each company's current relative price–book ratio as compared to its 5-year average relative price–book ratio.

b. Briefly discuss one disadvantage for each of the relative price–earnings and relative price–book approaches to valuation.

13. Mulroney (see problems 10–12) previously calculated a valuation for Southampton for both the constant-growth and two-stage DDM as shown below:

| Constant Growth Approach | Two-Stage Approach |
|---|---|
| $29 | $35.50 |

Using only the information provided and your answers to problems 10–12, select the stock (EO or SHC) that Mulroney should recommend as the better value, and justify your selection.

14. In reviewing the financial statements of the Graceland Rock Company, you note that net income increased while cash flow from operations decreased from 1999 to 2000.

*a.* Explain how net income could increase for Graceland Rock Company while cash flow from operations decreased. Give some illustrative examples.

*b.* Explain why cash flow from operations may be a good indicator of a firm's "quality of earnings."

15. A firm has net sales of $3,000, cash expenses (including taxes) of $1,400, and depreciation of $500. If accounts receivable increase over the period by $400, what would be cash flow from operations?

16. A company's current ratio is 2.0. If the company uses cash to retire notes payable due within 1 year, would this transaction increase or decrease the current ratio and asset turnover ratio?

| | Current Ratio | Asset Turnover Ratio |
|---|---|---|
| *a.* | Increase | Increase |
| *b.* | Increase | Decrease |
| *c.* | Decrease | Increase |
| *d.* | Decrease | Decrease |

17. During a period of rising prices, the financial statements of a firm using FIFO reporting instead of LIFO reporting would show:

*a.* Higher total assets and higher net income.
*b.* Higher total assets and lower net income.
*c.* Lower total assets and higher net income.
*d.* Lower total assets and lower net income.

18. In an inflationary period, the use of FIFO will make which one of the following more realistic than the use of LIFO?

*a.* Balance sheet.
*b.* Income statement.
*c.* Cash flow statement.
*d.* None of the above.

19. All other things being equal, what effect will the payment of a cash dividend have on the following ratios?

| | Times Interest Earned | Debt/Equity Ratio |
|---|---|---|
| *a.* | Increase | Increase |
| *b.* | No effect | Increase |
| *c.* | No effect | No effect |
| *d.* | Decrease | Decrease |

### Table 19H  Income Statements and Balance Sheets

| | 2005 | 2009 |
|---|---|---|
| **Income Statement Data** | | |
| Revenues | $542 | $979 |
| Operating income | 38 | 76 |
| Depreciation and amortization | 3 | 9 |
| Interest expense | 3 | 0 |
| Pretax income | 32 | 67 |
| Income taxes | 13 | 37 |
| Net income after tax | 19 | 30 |
| **Balance Sheet Data** | | |
| Fixed assets | $ 41 | $ 70 |
| Total assets | 245 | 291 |
| Working capital | 123 | 157 |
| Total debt | 16 | 0 |
| Total shareholders' equity | 159 | 220 |

20. The Du Pont formula defines the net return on shareholders' equity as a function of the following components:
    - Operating margin.
    - Asset turnover.
    - Interest burden.
    - Financial leverage.
    - Income tax rate.

    Using only the data in Table 19H:

    a. Calculate each of the five components listed above for 2005 and 2009, and calculate the return on equity (ROE) for 2005 and 2009, using all of the five components.
    b. Briefly discuss the impact of the changes in asset turnover and financial leverage on the change in ROE from 2005 to 2009.

Enter the Market Insight database at **www.mhhe.com/business/finance/edumarket insight** and link to *Company,* then *Population.* Select a company of interest to you and link to the *Company Research* page with a menu of company information reports on the left. Link to the *Excel Analytics Reports,* then, under *Annual,* the *Ratios Report.* What is the 5-year trend in the ROE? Look over the trends of the net margin, asset turnover, and leverage, the primary ROE decomposition ratios. Which of these ratios had the greatest impact on ROE changes? What might explain these trends?

| E-INVESTMENTS | Go to **moneycentral.msn.com/investor** and review the financial results for EMC Corporation |
|---|---|

**E-INVESTMENTS**
**Financial Statement Analysis**

Go to **moneycentral.msn.com/investor** and review the financial results for EMC Corporation (EMC) and Network Appliance Inc. (NTAP). The financial result area has sections on highlights, key ratios, and statements. You will need information on all three to answer the following questions.

1. Compare the price-to-book and price-to-sales ratios of the companies. How do they compare with the average for the S&P 500?
2. Are there any substantial differences in the gross and net profit margins for the companies?
3. Compare the profitability ratios of the companies as measured by return on equity and return on assets.
4. Are there any significant differences in efficiency ratios?
5. Are there any significant differences in the financial condition ratios?
6. Compare the growth in sales and income for the two companies over the last 5 years.

**SOLUTIONS TO CONCEPT CHECKS**

1. A debt-to-equity ratio of 1 implies that Mordett will have $50 million of debt and $50 million of equity. Interest expense will be .09 × $50 million, or $4.5 million per year. Mordett's net profits and ROE over the business cycle will therefore be

|  |  | Nodett | | Mordett | |
|---|---|---|---|---|---|
| Scenario | EBIT | Net Profits | ROE | Net Profits* | ROE† |
| Bad year | $ 5 million | $3 million | 3% | $0.3 million | .6% |
| Normal year | 10 | 6 | 6 | 3.3 | 6.6 |
| Good year | 15 | 9 | 9 | 6.3 | 12.6 |

*Mordett's after-tax profits are given by .6(EBIT − $4.5 million).
†Mordett's equity is only $50 million.

2. 

**Ratio Decomposition Analysis for Mordett Corporation**

|  | ROE | (1) Net Profit/ Pretax Profit | (2) Pretax Profit/ EBIT | (3) EBIT/ Sales (ROS) | (4) Sales/ Assets (ATO) | (5) Assets/ Equity | (6) Combined Leverage Factor (2) × (5) |
|---|---|---|---|---|---|---|---|
| **Bad year** | | | | | | | |
| Nodett | .030 | .6 | 1.000 | .0625 | 0.800 | 1.000 | 1.000 |
| Somdett | .018 | .6 | 0.360 | .0625 | 0.800 | 1.667 | 0.600 |
| Mordett | .006 | .6 | 0.100 | .0625 | 0.800 | 2.000 | 0.200 |
| **Normal year** | | | | | | | |
| Nodett | .060 | .6 | 1.000 | .100 | 1.000 | 1.000 | 1.000 |
| Somdett | .068 | .6 | 0.680 | .100 | 1.000 | 1.667 | 1.134 |
| Mordett | .066 | .6 | 0.550 | .100 | 1.000 | 2.000 | 1.100 |
| **Good year** | | | | | | | |
| Nodett | .090 | .6 | 1.000 | .125 | 1.200 | 1.000 | 1.000 |
| Somdett | .118 | .6 | 0.787 | .125 | 1.200 | 1.667 | 1.311 |
| Mordett | .126 | .6 | 0.700 | .125 | 1.200 | 2.000 | 1.400 |

**SOLUTIONS
TO CONCEPT
C H E C K S
*(Concluded)*

3. GI's ROE in 2007 was 3.03%, computed as follows:

$$ROE = \frac{\$5,285}{.5(\$171,843 + \$177,128)} = .0303, \text{ or } 3.03\%$$

Its P/E ratio was 4 = $21/$5.285 and its P/B ratio was .12 = $21/$177. Its earnings yield was 25% compared with an industry average of 12.5%.

Note that in our calculations the earnings yield will not equal ROE/(P/B) because we have computed ROE with average shareholders' equity in the denominator and P/B with end-of-year shareholders' equity in the denominator.

4.

**IBX Ratio Analysis**

| Year | ROE | (1) Net Profit/ Pretax Profit | (2) Pretax Profit/ EBIT | (3) EBIT/ Sales (ROS) | (4) Sales/ Assets (ATO) | (5) Assets/ Equity | (6) Combined Leverage Factor (2) × (5) | (7) ROA (3) × (4) |
|------|-----|------|------|------|------|------|------|------|
| 2007 | 11.4% | .616 | .796 | 7.75% | 1.375 | 2.175 | 1.731 | 10.65% |
| 2005 | 10.2 | .636 | .932 | 8.88 | 1.311 | 1.474 | 1.374 | 11.65 |

ROE went up despite a decline in operating margin and a decline in the tax burden ratio because of increased leverage and turnover. Note that ROA declined from 11.65% in 2005 to 10.65% in 2007.

5. LIFO accounting results in lower reported earnings than does FIFO. Fewer assets to depreciate results in lower reported earnings because there is less bias associated with the use of historic cost. More debt results in lower reported earnings because the inflation premium in the interest rate is treated as part of interest expense and not as repayment of principal. If ABC has the same reported earnings as XYZ despite these three sources of downward bias, its real earnings must be greater.

# OPTIONS, FUTURES, AND OTHER DERIVATIVES

www.mhhe.com/bkm

# OPTIONS MARKETS: INTRODUCTION

Derivative securities, or more simply *derivatives,* play a large and increasingly important role in financial markets. These are securities whose prices are determined by, or "derive from," the prices of other securities. These assets are also called *contingent claims* because their payoffs are contingent on the prices of other securities. Options and futures contracts are both derivative securities. We will see that their payoffs depend on the value of other securities. Swaps, which we discussed in Chapter 16, also are derivatives. Because the value of derivatives depends on the value of other securities, they can be powerful tools for both hedging and speculation. We will investigate these applications in the next four chapters, starting in this chapter with options.

Trading of standardized options contracts on a national exchange started in 1973 when the Chicago Board Options Exchange (CBOE) began listing call options. These contracts were almost immediately a great success, crowding out the previously existing over-the-counter trading in stock options. Option contracts are traded now on several exchanges. They are written on common stock, stock indexes, foreign exchange, agricultural commodities, precious metals, and interest rate futures. In addition, the over-the-counter market has enjoyed a tremendous resurgence in recent years as trading in custom-tailored options has exploded. Popular and potent tools in modifying portfolio characteristics, options have become essential tools a portfolio manager must understand.

This chapter is an introduction to options markets. It explains how puts and calls work and examines their investment characteristics. Popular option strategies are considered next. Finally, we examine a range of securities with embedded options such as callable or convertible bonds, and we take a quick look at some so-called exotic options.

## 20.1    THE OPTION CONTRACT

A **call option** gives its holder the right to purchase an asset for a specified price, called the **exercise**, or **strike price**, on or before some specified expiration date. For example, a March call option on Microsoft stock with exercise price $25 entitles its owner to purchase Microsoft stock for a price of $25 at any time up to and including the expiration date in March. The holder of the call is not required to exercise the option. The holder will choose to exercise only if the market value of the asset to be purchased exceeds the exercise price. When the market price does exceed the exercise price, the option holder may "call away" the asset for the exercise price. Otherwise, the option may be left unexercised. If it is not exercised before the expiration date of the contract, a call option simply expires and no longer has value. Therefore, if the stock price is greater than the exercise price on the expiration date, the value of the call option equals the difference between the stock price and the exercise price; but if the stock price is less than the exercise price at expiration, the call will be worthless. The *net profit* on the call is the value of the option minus the price originally paid to purchase it.

The purchase price of the option is called the **premium.** It represents the compensation the purchaser of the call must pay for the right to exercise the option if exercise becomes profitable.

Sellers of call options, who are said to *write* calls, receive premium income now as payment against the possibility they will be required at some later date to deliver the asset in return for an exercise price lower than the market value of the asset. If the option is left to expire worthless because the exercise price remains above the market price of the asset, then the writer of the call clears a profit equal to the premium income derived from the sale of the option. But if the call is exercised, the profit to the option writer is the premium income derived when the option was initially sold minus the difference between the value of the stock that must be delivered and the exercise price that is paid for those shares. If that difference is larger than the initial premium, the writer will incur a loss.

**EXAMPLE 20.1    Profits and Losses on a Call Option**

Consider the March 2003 maturity call option on a share of Microsoft stock with an exercise price of $22.50 per share selling on March 4, 2003, for $1.15. Exchange-traded options expire on the third Friday of the expiration month, which for this option was March 21. Until the expiration day, the purchaser of the calls was entitled to buy shares of Microsoft for $22.50. On March 4, Microsoft sold for $23.07, which was $.57 more than the exercise price. Obviously, an investor who paid $1.15 for the call had no intention of exercising it immediately.

On the expiration date of the option, if Microsoft stock had fallen below $22.50, the call would have been left to expire worthless. If, on the other hand, Microsoft was selling above

$22.50 at expiration, the call holder would have found it optimal to exercise. For example, if Microsoft sold for $23.50 on March 20, the option would be exercised since it would give its holder the right to pay $22.50 for a stock worth $23.50. The value of the option on the expiration date would be

$$\text{Value at expiration} = \text{Stock price} - \text{Exercise price} = \$23.50 - \$22.50 = \$1$$

Despite the $1 payoff at maturity, the investor still realizes a loss of $.15 on the call because it cost $1.15 to purchase:

$$\text{Profit} = \text{Final value} - \text{Original investment} = \$1 - \$1.15 = -\$.15$$

Nevertheless, exercise of the call is optimal at maturity if the stock price exceeds the exercise price because the exercise proceeds will offset at least part of the investment in the option. The investor in the call will clear a profit if Microsoft is selling above $23.65 at the maturity date. At that price, the proceeds from exercise will just cover the original cost of the call.

A **put option** gives its holder the right to *sell* an asset for a specified exercise or strike price on or before some expiration date. A March put on Microsoft with exercise price $22.50 entitles its owner to sell Microsoft stock to the put writer at a price of $22.50 at any time before expiration in March even if the market price of Microsoft is less than $22.50. While profits on call options increase when the asset increases in value, profits on put options increase when the asset value falls. A put will be exercised only if the exercise price is greater than the price of the underlying asset, that is, only if its holder can deliver for the exercise price an asset with market value less than the exercise price. (One doesn't need to own the shares of Microsoft to exercise the Microsoft put option. Upon exercise, the investor's broker purchases the necessary shares of Microsoft at the market price and immediately delivers, or "puts them," to an option writer for the exercise price. The owner of the put profits by the difference between the exercise price and market price.)

**EXAMPLE 20.2**    **Profits and Losses on a Put Option**

Now consider the March 2003 maturity put option on Microsoft with an exercise price of $22.50, selling on March 4, 2003, for $.55. It entitled its owner to sell a share of Microsoft for $22.50 at any time until March 21. Since the stock was then selling for more than $22.50, it clearly would not make sense at the moment to exercise the right to sell at $22.50. If, on the other hand, Microsoft sold for $21.50 at expiration, the put would turn out to be a profitable investment. The option value at expiration would be

$$\text{Value at expiration} = \text{Exercise price} - \text{Stock price} = \$22.50 - \$21.50 = \$1$$

and the investor's profit would be $1 − $.55 = $.45. This is a holding-period return of $.45/$.55 = .818, or 81.8%—over only 17 days! Obviously, put option sellers on March 4 did not consider this outcome very likely.

An option is described as **in the money** when its exercise would produce profits for its holder. An option is **out of the money** when exercise would be unprofitable. Therefore, a call option is in the money when the exercise price is below the asset's value. It is out of the money when the exercise price exceeds the asset value; no one would exercise the right to purchase for the strike price an asset worth less than that price. Conversely, put options are in the money when the exercise price exceeds the asset's value, because delivery of the lower-valued asset in exchange for the exercise price is profitable for the holder. Options are **at the money** when the exercise price and asset price are equal.

## Options Trading

Some options trade on over-the-counter markets. The OTC market offers the advantage that the terms of the option contract—the exercise price, maturity date, and number of shares committed—can be tailored to the needs of the traders. The costs of establishing an OTC option contract, however, are higher than for exchange-traded options.

Options contracts traded on exchanges are standardized by allowable maturity dates and exercise prices for each listed option. Each stock option contract provides for the right to buy or sell 100 shares of stock (except when stock splits occur after the contract is listed and the contract is adjusted for the terms of the split).

Standardization of the terms of listed option contracts means all market participants trade in a limited and uniform set of securities. This increases the depth of trading in any particular option, which lowers trading costs and results in a more competitive market. Exchanges, therefore, offer two important benefits: ease of trading, which flows from a central marketplace where buyers and sellers or their representatives congregate; and a liquid secondary market where buyers and sellers of options can transact quickly and cheaply.

Until recently, most options trading in the United States took place on the Chicago Board Options Exchange. However, by 2003 the International Securities Exchange, an electronic exchange based in New York, displaced the CBOE as the largest options market. Options trading in Europe is uniformly transacted in electronic exchanges.

Figure 20.1 is a reproduction of listed stock option quotations from *The Wall Street Journal*. The highlighted options are for shares of Microsoft. The numbers in the column below the company name represent the last recorded price on the New York Stock Exchange for Microsoft stock, $23.07 per share.[1] The first column shows that options are traded on Microsoft at exercise prices of $22.50 through $27.50. These values are also called the *strike price*.

The exercise or strike prices bracket the stock price. While exercise prices generally are set at five-point intervals, larger intervals may be set for stocks selling above $200, and intervals of $2.50 may be used for stocks selling below $30. If the stock price moves outside the range of exercise prices of the existing set of options, new options with appropriate exercise prices may be offered. Therefore, at any time, both in-the-money and out-of-the-money options will be listed, as in the Microsoft example.

The next column in Figure 20.1 gives the maturity month of each contract, followed by two pairs of columns showing the number of contracts traded on that day and the closing price for the call and put, respectively. When we compare prices of call options with the same maturity date but different exercise prices in Figure 20.1, we see that the value of a call is lower when the exercise price is higher. This makes sense, because the right to purchase a share at a given exercise price is not as valuable when the purchase price is higher. Thus the March maturity Microsoft call option with strike price $22.50 sells for $1.15, whereas the $25 exercise price March call sells for only $0.20. Conversely, put options are worth *more* when the exercise price is higher: You would rather have the right to sell Microsoft shares for $25 than for $22.50, and this is reflected in the prices of the puts. The

---

[1] Occasionally, this price may not match the closing price listed for the stock on the stock market page. This is because some NYSE stocks also trade on the Pacific Stock Exchange, which closes after the NYSE, and the stock pages may reflect the more recent Pacific Exchange closing price. The options exchanges, however, close with the NYSE, so the closing NYSE stock price is appropriate for comparison with the closing option price.

**Figure 20.1
Stock options**

# LISTED OPTIONS QUOTATIONS

**Tuesday, March 4, 2003**

Composite volume and close for actively traded equity and LEAPS, or long-term options, with results for the corresponding put or call contract. Volume figures are unofficial. Open interest is total outstanding for all exchanges and reflects previous trading day. Close when possible is shown for the underlying stock or primary market. **XC**-Composite. **p**-Put. **o**-Strike price adjusted for split.

| OPTION/STRIKE | | EXP | -CALL- VOL | LAST | -PUT- VOL | LAST |
|---|---|---|---|---|---|---|
| A M R | 5 | Aug | 6600 | 0.40 | 40 | 2.90 |
| Amazon | 17.50 | Jul | ... | ... | 16000 | 0.95 |
| 22.27 | 22.50 | Mar | 2676 | 0.65 | 2001 | 0.90 |
| 22.27 | 22.50 | Apr | 16169 | 1.30 | 66 | 1.60 |
| Amgen | 50 | Apr | 312 | 5.80 | 2742 | 1.25 |
| 54.12 | 55 | Mar | 3638 | 1.10 | 523 | 2 |
| AppldMat | 12.50 | Apr | 1467 | 0.45 | 3362 | 0.65 |
| BP PLC | 40 | Mar | 4400 | 0.85 | ... | ... |
| Bk of Am | 60 | Mar | 4456 | 8.20 | 550 | 0.20 |
| 68.05 | 70 | Mar | 5505 | 0.60 | 2461 | 3.10 |
| 68.05 | 70 | Apr | 11060 | 1.60 | 252 | 4 |
| 68.05 | 70 | May | 5025 | 2.40 | 70 | 4.50 |
| Blckbstr | 15 | Apr | 2793 | 1.50 | ... | ... |
| BrownFB | 75 | Mar | 4275 | 0.25 | 3585 | 6.80 |
| BurlRs | 50 | Aug | 4002 | 2.20 | ... | ... |
| CapOne | 22.50 | Apr | 75 | 5.80 | 8372 | 0.75 |
| 27.37 | 25 | Mar | 76 | 3.10 | 13927 | 0.60 |
| 27.37 | 30 | Mar | 7719 | 0.60 | 2909 | 3 |
| 27.37 | 32.50 | Jun | 8883 | 1.55 | 44 | 6.40 |
| Celestica | 10 | Apr | ... | ... | 3110 | 0.30 |
| Cisco | 12.50 | Mar | 1381 | 1.35 | 4065 | 0.20 |
| 13.63 | 12.50 | Apr | 336 | 1.65 | 12633 | 0.50 |
| 13.63 | 15 | Apr | 14215 | 0.45 | 273 | 1.75 |
| Citigrp o | 30 | Apr | 1513 | 3.40 | 3170 | 0.90 |
| 32.37 | 30 | Jun | 11 | 4.60 | 6356 | 1.80 |
| 32.37 | 32.50 | Mar | 1333 | 1.05 | 4162 | 1.10 |

| OPTION/STRIKE | | EXP | -CALL- VOL | LAST | -PUT- VOL | LAST |
|---|---|---|---|---|---|---|
| 31.27 | 35 | Apr | 382 | 0.55 | 4279 | 4.20 |
| GM H | 10 | Mar | 121 | 0.30 | 4299 | 0.50 |
| GoldmnS | 70 | Mar | 7607 | 0.65 | 203 | 4.70 |
| 65.69 | 85 | Apr | 2926 | 0.05 | ... | ... |
| Halbtn | 20 | Mar | 4975 | 0.60 | 278 | 0.65 |
| HarleyDav | 40 | Mar | 373 | 0.40 | 3115 | 3 |
| HewlettPk | 17.50 | Mar | 7962 | 0.15 | 215 | 2.05 |
| 15.54 | 17.50 | May | 4067 | 0.70 | 30 | 2.55 |
| Intel | 17.50 | Mar | 3831 | 0.35 | 6042 | 1.20 |
| I B M | 80 | Mar | 2257 | 1 | 3263 | 4.40 |
| JPMorgCh | 22.50 | Mar | 8100 | 0.80 | 594 | 0.90 |
| 22.40 | 22.50 | Apr | 6196 | 1.35 | 636 | 1.75 |
| JohnJn | 50 | Apr | 284 | 3.40 | 8843 | 1.60 |
| 51.69 | 55 | Apr | 12186 | 0.95 | 39 | 4 |
| LamRsch | 12.50 | Mar | 5034 | 0.70 | 32 | 0.75 |
| Level3 | 5 | Jun | 10 | 0.50 | 5262 | 0.60 |
| Lyondl | 10 | Sep | ... | ... | 3025 | 1.65 |
| Merck | 45 | Apr | 2 | 7.30 | 6765 | 0.60 |
| Microsft | 22.50 | Mar | 3005 | 1.15 | 3269 | 0.55 |
| 23.07 | 22.50 | Jul | 247 | 2.70 | 17079 | 1.90 |
| 23.07 | 23.75 | Jul | 10420 | 2.05 | 6296 | 2.50 |
| 23.07 | 25 | Mar | 9304 | 0.20 | 960 | 2.10 |
| 23.07 | 25 | Jul | 3223 | 1.50 | 85 | 3.10 |
| 23.07 | 27.50 | Jul | 1273 | 0.75 | 19300 | 4.80 |
| Nasd100Tr | 20 | Jun | 5 | 5.30 | 13230 | 0.60 |
| 24.50 | 21 | Mar | 30 | 3.50 | 17653 | 0.10 |

| OPTION/STRIKE | | EXP | -CALL- VOL | LAST | -PUT- VOL | LAST |
|---|---|---|---|---|---|---|
| 13.08 | 12.50 | Jul | 12 | 1.85 | 5757 | 1.55 |
| 13.08 | 15 | Jul | 3036 | 0.95 | ... | ... |
| 13.08 | 17.50 | Jul | 5009 | 0.40 | ... | ... |
| Peoplesoft | 15 | Apr | 25 | 2.35 | 2806 | 0.90 |
| Sap AG | 22.50 | Mar | 19 | 0.25 | 9193 | 3.30 |
| 19.40 | 25 | Mar | 177 | 0.05 | 9020 | 5.70 |
| Sears | 20 | Apr | 5511 | 1.80 | 598 | 1.70 |
| SemiHTr | 22.50 | Mar | 1690 | 0.95 | 2916 | 1 |
| Symntc | 45 | Jul | 6155 | 3.40 | 1018 | 6.50 |
| Target | 25 | Apr | 13 | 2.65 | 2737 | 1 |
| 26.50 | 30 | Apr | 2869 | 0.50 | 92 | 3.80 |
| TexasInst | 17.50 | Apr | 6125 | 0.65 | 35 | 2.10 |
| 16.00 | 17.50 | Jul | 4109 | 1.50 | 15 | 3 |
| 3M Co | 120 | Mar | 685 | 5.10 | 3326 | 1.35 |
| WalMart | 45 | Apr | 17 | 3.30 | 5459 | 1.20 |
| 46.90 | 50 | Apr | 8107 | 0.85 | 160 | 3.70 |
| Yahoo | 17.50 | Apr | 150 | 3 | 10494 | 0.50 |
| 19.87 | 17.50 | Jul | 1 | 3.90 | 3010 | 1.45 |

Source: *The Wall Street Journal*, March 4, 2003. Reprinted by permission of *The Wall Street Journal*, © 2003 Dow Jones & Company, Inc. All Rights Reserved Worldwide.

March maturity put options with strike price $25 sells for $2.10, whereas the $22.50 exercise price March put sells for only $.55.

Throughout Figure 20.1, you will see that some options may go an entire day without trading. Lack of trading is denoted by three dots in the volume and price columns. Because trading is infrequent, it is not unusual to find option prices that appear out of line with other prices. You might see, for example, two calls with different exercise prices that seem to sell for the same price. This discrepancy arises because the last trades for these options may have occurred at different times during the day. At any moment, the call with the lower exercise price must be worth more than an otherwise-identical call with a higher exercise price.

Figure 20.1 illustrates that the maturities of most exchange-traded options tend to be fairly short, ranging up to only several months. For larger firms and several stock indexes, however, longer-term options are traded with maturities ranging up to several years. These options are called LEAPS (for *L*ong-*T*erm *E*quity *A*ntici*P*ation *S*ecurities).

**CONCEPT CHECK☞ QUESTION 1**

*a.* **What will be the proceeds and net profits to an investor who purchases the March maturity Microsoft calls with exercise price $22.50 if the stock price at maturity is $25? What if the stock price at maturity is $20?**

*b.* **Now answer part (*a*) for an investor who purchases a March maturity Microsoft put option with exercise price $22.50.**

## American and European Options

An **American option** allows its holder to exercise the right to purchase (if a call) or sell (if a put) the underlying asset on *or before* the expiration date. **European options** allow for exercise of the option only on the expiration date. American options, because they allow more leeway than their European counterparts, generally will be more valuable. Virtually all traded options in the United States are American style. Foreign currency options and CBOE stock index options are notable exceptions to this rule, however.

## Adjustments in Option Contract Terms

Because options convey the right to buy or sell shares at a stated price, stock splits would radically alter their value if the terms of the options contract were not adjusted to account for the stock split. For example, reconsider the Microsoft call options in Figure 20.1. If Microsoft were to announce a 2-for-1 split, its share price would fall from about $23 to about $11.50. A call option with exercise price $22.50 would be just about worthless, with virtually no possibility that the stock would sell at more than $22.50 before the options expired.

To account for a stock split, the exercise price is reduced by a factor of the split, and the number of options held is increased by that factor. For example, each original Microsoft call option with exercise price of $22.50 would be altered after a 2-for-1 split to 2 new options, with each new option carrying an exercise price of $11.25. A similar adjustment is made for stock dividends of more than 10%; the number of shares covered by each option is increased in proportion to the stock dividend, and the exercise price is reduced by that proportion.

In contrast to stock dividends, cash dividends do not affect the terms of an option contract. Because payment of a cash dividend reduces the selling price of the stock without inducing offsetting adjustments in the option contract, the value of the option is affected by dividend policy. Other things being equal, call option values are lower for high-dividend-payout policies, because such policies slow the rate of increase of stock prices; conversely, put values are higher for high-dividend payouts. (Of course, the option values do not necessarily rise or fall on the dividend payment or ex-dividend dates. Dividend payments are anticipated, so the effect of the payment already is built into the original option price.)

---

**CONCEPT CHECK☞ QUESTION 2**

Suppose that Microsoft's stock price at the exercise date is $25, and the exercise price of the call is $22.50. What is the payoff on one option contract? After a 2-for-1 split, the stock price is $12.50, the exercise price is $11.25, and the option holder now can purchase 200 shares. Show that the split leaves the payoff from the option unaffected.

---

## The Option Clearing Corporation

The Option Clearing Corporation (OCC), the clearinghouse for options trading, is jointly owned by the exchanges on which stock options are traded. Buyers and sellers of options who agree on a price will strike a deal. At this point, the OCC steps in. The OCC places itself between the two traders, becoming the effective buyer of the option from the writer and the effective writer of the option to the buyer. All individuals, therefore, deal only with the OCC, which effectively guarantees contract performance.

When an option holder exercises an option, the OCC arranges for a member firm with clients who have written that option to make good on the option obligation. The member firm selects from its clients who have written that option to fulfill the contract. The selected client must deliver 100 shares of stock at a price equal to the exercise price for each call

**E-INVESTMENTS**
**The Options Clearing Corporation**

Most of your education in finance and financial markets focuses on the "front office" activities of investment analysis, trading, and broker or dealer interaction with investing customers. For every trade there is a "clearing" and, a few days later, "settlement." This "back office" area of financial markets, though not in the spotlight, is an enormous operation, and a source of considerable employment. The Option Clearing Corporation, **www.optionsclearing.com**, discussed in the chapter, is an excellent example. Go to the OCC home page and answer the following questions:

a. How many equity option contracts were cleared by the OCC yesterday?

b. What percent of the total contract clearings were equity contracts? Index contracts? (See *Historical volume statistics*.)

c. Examine the *Who We Are* link. How does the "Three Tiered Backup System" provide the OCC with a AAA rating?

d. What are the current employment opportunities with the OCC? Where is the OCC located?

option contract written or must purchase 100 shares at the exercise price for each put option contract written.

Because the OCC guarantees contract performance, option writers are required to post margin to guarantee that they can fulfill their contract obligations. The margin required is determined in part by the amount by which the option is in the money, because that value is an indicator of the potential obligation of the option writer upon exercise of the option. When the required margin exceeds the posted margin, the writer will receive a margin call. The holder of the option need not post margin because the holder will exercise the option only if it is profitable to do so. After purchasing the option, no further money is at risk.

Margin requirements are determined in part by the other securities held in the investor's portfolio. For example, a call option writer owning the stock against which the option is written can satisfy the margin requirement simply by allowing a broker to hold that stock in the brokerage account. The stock is then guaranteed to be available for delivery should the call option be exercised. If the underlying security is not owned, however, the margin requirement is determined by the value of the underlying security as well as by the amount by which the option is in or out of the money. Out-of-the-money options require less margin from the writer, for expected payouts are lower.

## Other Listed Options

Options on assets other than stocks are also widely traded. These include options on market indexes and industry indexes, on foreign currency, and even on the futures prices of agricultural products, gold, silver, fixed-income securities, and stock indexes. We will discuss these in turn.

**Index Options.** An index option is a call or put based on a stock market index such as the S&P 500 or the Nasdaq 100. Index options are traded on several broad-based indexes as well as on several industry-specific indexes and even commodity price indexes. We discussed many of these indexes in Chapter 2.

The construction of the indexes can vary across contracts or exchanges. For example, the S&P 100 index is a value-weighted average of the 100 stocks in the Standard & Poor's 100 stock group. The weights are proportional to the market value of outstanding equity for each stock. The Dow Jones Industrial Index, by contrast, is a price-weighted average of 30 stocks.

Option contracts on many foreign stock indexes also trade. For example, options on the (Japanese) Nikkei Stock Index trade on the Chicago Mercantile Exchange, and options on the Eurotop 100, Hong Kong, and Japan indexes trade on the American Stock Exchange. The Chicago Board Options Exchange as well as the Amex lists options on industry indexes such as the hightech, pharmaceutical, or banking industries.

Figure 20.2 is a reproduction of the listings of index options from *The Wall Street Journal*. The listings for index options are similar to those of stock options. However, instead of supplying separate columns for puts and calls, the index options are all listed in one column, and the letter *p* or *c* is used to denote puts or calls. The index options listings also report the *open interest* for each contract, which is the number of contracts currently outstanding. Options on the major indexes, that is, the S&P 100 (often called the OEX after its ticker symbol), the S&P 500 (the SPX), and the Dow Jones Industrials (the DJX) are the most actively traded contracts on the CBOE. Together, these contracts dominate CBOE volume.

In contrast to stock options, index options do not require that the call writer actually "deliver the index" upon exercise or that the put writer "purchase the index." Instead, a cash settlement procedure is used. The payoff that would accrue upon exercise of the option is calculated, and the option writer simply pays that amount to the option holder. The payoff is equal to the difference between the exercise price of the option and the value of the

**Figure 20.2   Index options**

# INDEX OPTIONS TRADING

Monday, February 26, 2001

Volume, last, net change and open interest for all contracts. Volume figures are unofficial. Open interest reflects previous trading day. p-Put c-Call

**CHICAGO**

### DJ INDUS AVG(DJX)

| STRIKE | | VOL. | LAST | NET CHG. | | OPEN INT. |
|---|---|---|---|---|---|---|
| Mar | 76 c | 10 | 30¹⁰ | + | 1¹⁰ | 10 |
| Mar | 88 p | 350 | 0⁰⁵ | – | 0¹⁵ | 2,207 |
| Jun | 90 p | 1 | 1⁹⁰ | + | 0⁷⁰ | 98 |
| Mar | 92 p | 77 | 0¹⁰ | – | 0²⁰ | 2,459 |
| Apr | 92 p | 121 | 0⁴⁰ | – | 0²⁰ | 1,845 |
| Mar | 96 c | 20 | 9⁹⁰ | + | 0⁸⁰ | 91 |
| Mar | 96 p | 105 | 0²⁰ | – | 0¹⁵ | 11,296 |
| Apr | 96 p | 34 | 1⁰⁵ | + | 0¹⁵ | 3,788 |
| May | 96 p | 38 | 1⁸⁵ | – | 0¹⁰ | 2,677 |
| Jun | 96 p | 8 | 3³⁰ | + | 0¹⁰ | 678 |
| Mar | 98 p | 145 | 0⁴⁰ | – | 0⁰⁵ | 1,529 |
| Apr | 112 c | 50 | 6⁵⁰ | + | 0⁵⁰ | 28 |
| May | 112 c | 2 | 2⁶⁵ | + | 0⁰⁵ | 1,566 |
| Mar | 116 c | 40 | 0⁰⁵ | | | 5,939 |
| Apr | 116 c | 10 | 0³⁵ | – | 0⁰⁵ | 2,283 |
| Jun | 116 c | 5 | 1 | – | 1⁶⁵ | 387 |

Call Vol. ...... 2,770  Open Int. ...... 124,054
Put Vol. ...... 9,764  Open Int. ...... 189,107

### DJ TRANP AVG(DTX)

| Apr | 310 c | 15 | 4⁸⁰ | | | ... |
| Sep | 360 p | 3 | 59⁴⁰ | – | 5⁴⁰ | ... |

Call Vol. ...... 15  Open Int. ...... 920
Put Vol. ...... 3  Open Int. ...... 98

### DJ UTIL AVG(DUX)

| Mar | 380 p | 1 | 4⁹⁰ | – | 2 | 1 |
| Mar | 390 p | 1 | 9 | + | 0⁸⁸ | 20 |

Call Vol. ...... 0  Open Int. ...... 45
Put Vol. ...... 2  Open Int. ...... 55

### NASDAQ-MINI(MNX)

| Apr | 80 p | 150 | 7⁷⁰ | – | 3³⁰ | 927 |
| Mar | 90 p | 2,515 | 4²⁰ | – | 5⁷⁰ | 3,799 |
| Apr | 160 p | 3 | 3⁸⁰ | – | 1²⁰ | 3,175 |

| STRIKE | | VOL. | LAST | NET CHG. | | OPEN INT. |
|---|---|---|---|---|---|---|
| Mar | 170 p | 20 | 1⁵⁰ | – | 1⁵⁰ | 2,804 |
| Mar | 270 c | 3,031 | 0⁴⁰ | + | 0¹⁰ | 10,122 |
| May | 300 c | 200 | 1⁷⁵ | ... | | ... |

Call Vol. ...... 33,843  Open Int. ...... 235,268
Put Vol. ...... 16,670  Open Int. ...... 201,178

### NASDAQ-100(NDX)

| Mar | 1400 p | 9 | 2⁴⁰ | – | 0²⁵ | 297 |
| Mar | 1500 p | 238 | 4⁸⁰ | + | 0²⁰ | 272 |
| Apr | 1500 p | 200 | 21 | – | 7 | 200 |
| Mar | 1600 p | 39 | 8 | – | 11 | 368 |
| Mar | 1650 p | 12 | 9 | – | 9 | 740 |
| Mar | 1700 p | 7 | 12 | – | 16 | 1,123 |
| Apr | 1700 p | 4 | 56 | – | 19 | 82 |
| Mar | 1750 p | 7 | 20 | – | 23⁹⁰ | 729 |
| Mar | 1800 c | 11 | 3³⁰ | + | 27 | 20 |
| Apr | 3200 c | 10 | 2⁴⁵ | – | 1⁵⁵ | 568 |
| Jun | 3300 c | 1 | 13⁵⁰ | + | 4 | 161 |
| Apr | 3400 c | 280 | 1⁵⁰ | – | 3⁵⁰ | 1,622 |

Call Vol. ...... 2,544  Open Int. ...... 47,050
Put Vol. ...... 1,772  Open Int. ...... 39,457

### RUSSELL 2000(RUT)

| Mar | 460 p | 1 | 4⁸⁰ | – | 4³⁰ | 155 |
| Mar | 480 c | 40 | 16⁷⁰ | + | 2⁶⁰ | 821 |
| Mar | 490 c | 10 | 10 | + | 3⁸⁰ | 12 |
| Mar | 490 p | 2 | 13¹⁰ | + | 3²⁰ | 18 |
| Mar | 500 c | 133 | 7⁵⁰ | + | 2⁴⁰ | 1,163 |
| May | 500 c | 65 | 25⁴⁰ | ... | | ... |
| Jun | 520 p | 11 | 18⁹⁰ | – | 6⁷⁰ | 2 |
| Mar | 540 c | 5 | 0⁹⁰ | – | 1⁶⁰ | 1,000 |

Call Vol. ...... 264  Open Int. ...... 5,721
Put Vol. ...... 13  Open Int. ...... 14,402

### S & P 100(OEX)

| Apr | 540 p | 38 | 2²⁵ | ... | | ... |
| Mar | 550 p | 1,501 | 0⁶⁰ | ... | | ... |
| Mar | 560 p | 829 | 0⁵⁵ | – | 1⁰⁵ | 6,362 |
| Mar | 560 p | 685 | 3⁵⁰ | – | 2⁷⁰ | 1,173 |
| May | 560 p | 1 | 7 | – | 1⁵⁰ | 91 |
| Mar | 570 p | 401 | 0⁸⁵ | ... | | 2,647 |
| Apr | 570 p | 21 | 4⁴⁰ | ... | | 10 |
| Mar | 580 p | 364 | 1 | – | 2 | 5,962 |
| Apr | 580 p | 217 | 5 | – | 5⁹⁰ | 732 |

| STRIKE | | VOL. | LAST | NET CHG. | | OPEN INT. |
|---|---|---|---|---|---|---|
| May | 580 p | 3 | 9⁸⁰ | – | 0⁴⁰ | 114 |
| Jun | 580 p | 18 | 10⁷⁰ | – | 4⁷⁰ | 86 |
| Jun | 1650 p | 5 | 374¹⁰ | + | 87¹⁰ | 2,629 |
| Mar | 1800 p | 2 | 5²⁵ | – | 15 | 3,812 |
| Jun | 1800 p | 1 | 5⁰⁶ | + | 84 | 1,198 |
| Mar | 1995 p | 80 | 7⁴⁰ | – | 15⁷⁰ | 11,012 |
| Jun | 1995 p | 80 | 716⁵⁰ | + | 54⁵⁰ | 193 |

Call Vol. ...... 62,086  Open Int. ...... 788,750
Put Vol. ...... 25,533  Open Int. ...... 777,239

## AMERICAN

### HONG KONG INDEX(HKO)

| Mar | 250 p | 20 | 0⁷⁵ | + | 0³⁰ | 110 |

Call Vol. ...... 0  Open Int. ...... 159
Put Vol. ...... 20  Open Int. ...... 162

### INTERNET(IIX)

| Mar | 260 c | 4 | 7 | + | 1 | 10 |
| Mar | 260 p | 4 | 27⁹⁰ | – | 4⁹⁰ | 10 |

Call Vol. ...... 5  Open Int. ...... 185
Put Vol. ...... 4  Open Int. ...... 469

### JAPAN INDEX(JPN)

| Mar | 130 p | 9 | 0⁶⁵ | – | 0³⁰ | 5 |
| Jun | 135 p | 20 | 4⁶⁰ | ... | | 15 |
| Mar | 140 p | 4 | 2⁴⁵ | – | 0⁶⁵ | 1,630 |
| Jun | 140 p | 4 | 6³⁰ | – | 0⁶⁰ | 1,321 |

Call Vol. ...... 0  Open Int. ...... 5,226
Put Vol. ...... 37  Open Int. ...... 3,294

### MAJOR MARKET(XMI)

| Mar | 970 p | 1 | 3³⁰ | + | 1⁹⁰ | 10 |
| Mar | 990 p | 1 | 5⁷⁰ | + | 1⁹⁰ | 5 |
| Mar | 1060 c | 16 | 8⁵⁰ | – | 14⁵⁰ | 16 |
| Mar | 1080 p | 6 | 39²⁰ | – | 10³⁰ | 1 |

Call Vol. ...... 16  Open Int. ...... 24,079
Put Vol. ...... 8  Open Int. ...... 24,161

### MORGAN STANLEY(MOX)

| Mar | 30 p | 16 | 4⁷⁰ | – | 2¹⁰ | 1,791 |

Call Vol. ...... 0  Open Int. ...... 222
Put Vol. ...... 16  Open Int. ...... 1,889

index. For example, if the S&P index is at 900 when a call option on the index with exercise price 890 is exercised, the holder of the call receives a cash payment of the difference, 900 − 890, times the contract multiplier of $100, or $1,000 per contract.

**Futures Options.**  Futures options give their holders the right to buy or sell a specified futures contract, using as a futures price the exercise price of the option. Although the delivery process is slightly complicated, the terms of futures options contracts are designed in effect to allow the option to be written on the futures price itself. The option holder receives upon exercise a net payoff equal to the difference between the current futures price on the specified asset and the exercise price of the option. Thus if the futures price is, say, $37, and the call has an exercise price of $35, the holder who exercises the call option on the futures gets a payoff of $2.

**Foreign Currency Options.**  A currency option offers the right to buy or sell a quantity of foreign currency for a specified amount of domestic currency. Currency option contracts call for purchase or sale of the currency in exchange for a specified number of U.S. dollars. Contracts are quoted in cents or fractions of a cent per unit of foreign currency.

There is an important difference between currency options and currency *futures* options. The former provide payoffs that depend on the difference between the exercise price and the exchange rate at maturity. The latter are foreign exchange futures options that provide payoffs that depend on the difference between the exercise price and the exchange rate *futures price* at maturity. Because exchange rates and exchange rate futures prices generally are not equal, the options and futures-options contracts will have different values, even with identical expiration dates and exercise prices. Today, trading volume in currency futures options dominates by far trading in currency options.

**Interest Rate Options.**  Options are traded on Treasury notes and bonds, Treasury bills, certificates of deposit, GNMA pass-through certificates, and yields on Treasury and Eurodollar securities of various maturities. Options on several interest rate futures also trade. Among these are contracts on Treasury bond, Treasury note, municipal bond, LIBOR, Euribor,[2] Eurodollar, and German euro-denominated government bond futures.

## 20.2   VALUES OF OPTIONS AT EXPIRATION

**Call Options**   Recall that a call option gives the right to purchase a security at the exercise price. Suppose you hold a call option on IBM stock with an exercise price of $100, and IBM is now selling at $110. You can exercise your option to purchase the stock at $100 and simultaneously sell the shares at the market price of $110, clearing $10 per share. Yet if the shares sell below $100, you can sit on the option and do nothing, realizing no further gain or loss. The value of the call option at expiration equals

$$\text{Payoff to call holder} = \begin{array}{ll} S_T - X & \text{if } S_T > X \\ 0 & \text{if } S_T \le X \end{array}$$

where $S_T$ is the value of the stock at expiration and $X$ is the exercise price. This formula emphasizes the option property because the payoff cannot be negative. That is, the option is

[2] The Euribor market is similar to the LIBOR market (see Chapter 2), but the interest rate charged in the Euribor market is the interbank rate for euro-denominated deposits.

**Figure 20.3   Payoff and profit to call option at expiration**

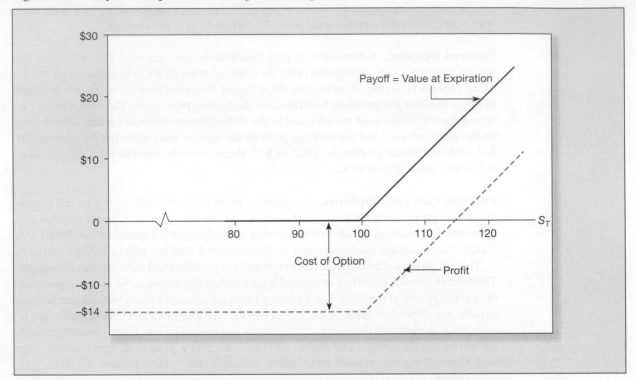

exercised only if $S_T$ exceeds $X$. If $S_T$ is less than $X$, exercise does not occur, and the option expires with zero value. The loss to the option holder in this case equals the price originally paid for the option. More generally, the *profit* to the option holder is the value of the option at expiration minus the original purchase price.

The value at expiration of the call on IBM with exercise price $100 is given by the schedule:

| IBM value: | $90 | $100 | $110 | $120 | $130 |
|---|---|---|---|---|---|
| Option value: | 0 | 0 | 10 | 20 | 30 |

For IBM prices at or below $100, the option is worthless. Above $100, the option is worth the excess of IBM's price over $100. The option's value increases by $1 for each dollar increase in the IBM stock price. This relationship can be depicted graphically as in Figure 20.3.

The solid line in Figure 20.3 depicts the value of the call at maturity. The net *profit* to the holder of the call equals the gross payoff less the initial investment in the call. Suppose the call cost $14. Then the profit to the call holder would be as given in the dashed (bottom) line of Figure 20.3. At option expiration, the investor has suffered a loss of $14 if the stock price is less than or equal to $100.

Profits do not become positive unless the stock price at expiration exceeds $114. The break-even point is $114, because at that price the payoff to the call, $S_T - X = \$114 - \$100 = \$14$, equals the cost paid to acquire the call. Hence the call holder shows a profit only if the stock price is higher.

Conversely, the writer of the call incurs losses if the stock price is high. In that scenario, the writer will receive a call and will be obligated to deliver a stock worth $S_T$ for only $X$ dollars:

**Figure 20.4  Payoff and profit to call writers at expiration**

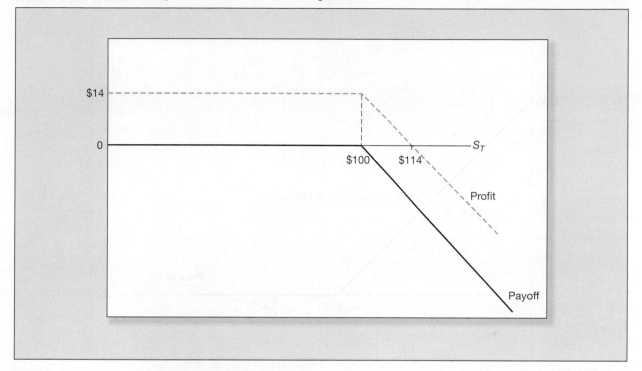

$$\text{Payoff to call writer} = \begin{array}{ll} -(S_T - X) & \text{if } S_T > X \\ 0 & \text{if } S_T \le X \end{array}$$

The call writer, who is exposed to losses if IBM increases in price, is willing to bear this risk in return for the option premium.

Figure 20.4 depicts the payoff and profit diagrams for the call writer. These are the mirror images of the corresponding diagrams for call holders. The break-even point for the option writer also is $114. The (negative) payoff at that point just offsets the premium originally received when the option was written.

**Put Options**    A put option conveys the right to sell an asset at the exercise price. In this case, the holder will not exercise the option unless the asset sells for *less* than the exercise price. For example, if IBM shares were to fall to $90, a put option with exercise price $100 could be exercised to clear $10 for its holder. The holder would purchase a share of IBM for $90 and simultaneously deliver it to the put option writer for the exercise price of $100.

The value of a put option at expiration is

$$\text{Payoff to put holder} = \begin{array}{ll} 0 & \text{if } S_T \ge X \\ X - S_T & \text{if } S_T < X \end{array}$$

The solid line in Figure 20.5 illustrates the payoff at maturity to the holder of a put option on IBM stock with an exercise price of $100. If the stock price at option maturity is above $100, the put has no value, as the right to sell the shares at $100 would not be exercised. Below a price of $100, the put value at expiration increases by $1 for each dollar the stock price falls. The dashed line in Figure 20.5 is a graph of the put option owner's profit at expiration, net of the initial cost of the put.

**Figure 20.5   Payoff and profit to put option at expiration**

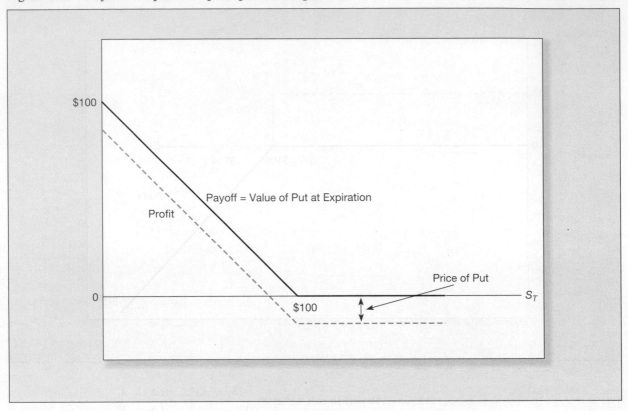

Writing puts *naked* (i.e., writing a put without an offsetting short position in the stock for hedging purposes) exposes the writer to losses if the market falls. Writing naked out-of-the-money puts was once considered an attractive way to generate income, as it was believed that as long as the market did not fall sharply before the option expiration, the option premium could be collected without the put holder ever exercising the option against the writer. Because only sharp drops in the market could result in losses to the writer of the put, the strategy was not viewed as overly risky. However, in the wake of the market crash of October 1987, such put writers suffered huge losses. Participants now perceive much greater risk to this strategy.

**CONCEPT CHECK ☞ QUESTION 3**

Consider these four option strategies: (i) buy a call; (ii) write a call; (iii) buy a put; (iv) write a put.

*a.* For each strategy, plot both the payoff and profit diagrams as a function of the final stock price.

*b.* Why might one characterize both buying calls and writing puts as "bullish" strategies? What is the difference between them?

*c.* Why might one characterize both buying puts and writing calls as "bearish" strategies? What is the difference between them?

## Option versus Stock Investments

Purchasing call options is a bullish strategy; that is, the calls provide profits when stock prices increase. Purchasing puts, in contrast, is a bearish strategy. Symmetrically, writing calls is bearish, whereas writing puts is bullish. Because option values depend on the price of the underlying stock, purchase of options may be viewed as a substitute for direct purchase or sale of a stock. Why might an option strategy be preferable to direct stock transactions?

For example, why would you purchase a call option rather than buy IBM stock directly? Maybe you have some information that leads you to believe IBM stock will increase in value from its current level, which in our examples we will take to be $100. You know your analysis could be incorrect, however, and that IBM also could fall in price. Suppose a 6-month maturity call option with exercise price $100 currently sells for $10, and the interest rate for the period is 3%. Consider these three strategies for investing a sum of money, say, $10,000. For simplicity, suppose IBM will not pay any dividends until after the 6-month period.

Strategy A:    Purchase 100 shares of IBM stock.

Strategy B:    Purchase 1,000 call options on IBM with exercise price $100. (This would require 10 contracts, each for 100 shares.)

Strategy C:    Purchase 100 call options for $1,000. Invest the remaining $9,000 in 6-month T-bills, to earn 3% interest. The bills will grow in value from $9,000 to $9,000 × 1.03 = $9,270.

Let us trace the possible values of these three portfolios when the options expire in 6 months as a function of IBM stock price at that time:

| Portfolio | IBM Price | | | | | |
|---|---|---|---|---|---|---|
| | $95 | $100 | $105 | $110 | $115 | $120 |
| Portfolio A: All stock | $9,500 | $10,000 | $10,500 | $11,000 | $11,500 | $12,000 |
| Portfolio B: All options | 0 | 0 | 5,000 | 10,000 | 15,000 | 20,000 |
| Portfolio C: Call plus bills | 9,270 | 9,270 | 9,770 | 10,270 | 10,770 | 11,270 |

Portfolio A will be worth 100 times the share value of IBM. Portfolio B is worthless unless IBM sells for more than the exercise price of the call. Once that point is reached, the portfolio is worth 1,000 times the excess of the stock price over the exercise price. Finally, Portfolio C is worth $9,270 from the investment in T-bills plus any profits from the 100 call options. Remember that each of these portfolios involves the same $10,000 initial investment. The rates of return on these three portfolios are as follows:

| Portfolio | IBM Price | | | | | |
|---|---|---|---|---|---|---|
| | $95 | $100 | $105 | $110 | $115 | $120 |
| Portfolio A: All stock | −5.0% | 0.0% | 5.0% | 10.0% | 15.0% | 20.0% |
| Portfolio B: All options | −100.0 | −100.0 | −50.0 | 0.0 | 50.0 | 100.0 |
| Portfolio C: Call plus bills | −7.3 | −7.3 | −2.3 | 2.7 | 7.7 | 12.7 |

These rates of return are graphed in Figure 20.6.

Comparing the returns of Portfolios B and C to those of the simple investment in IBM stock represented by Portfolio A, we see that options offer two interesting features. First, an option offers leverage. Compare the returns of Portfolios B and A. Unless IBM stock

**Figure 20.6**
**Rate of return to**
**three strategies**

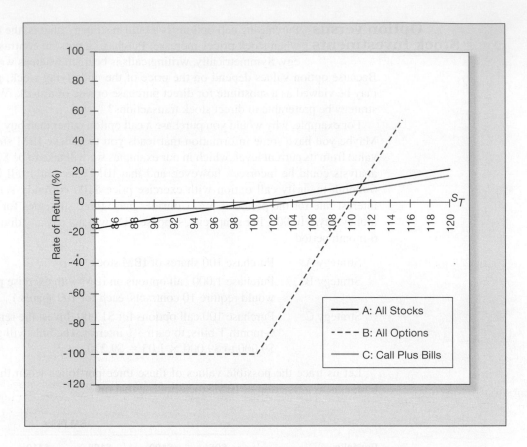

increases from its initial value of $100, the value of Portfolio B falls precipitously to zero—a rate of return of negative 100%. Conversely, modest increases in the rate of return on the stock result in disproportionate increases in the option rate of return. For example, a 4.3% increase in the stock price from $115 to $120 would increase the rate of return on the call from 50% to 100%. In this sense, calls are a levered investment on the stock. Their values respond more than proportionately to changes in the stock value.

Figure 20.6 vividly illustrates this point. The slope of the all-option portfolio is far steeper than that of the all-stock portfolio, reflecting its greater proportional sensitivity to the value of the underlying security. The leverage factor is the reason investors (illegally) exploiting inside information commonly choose options as their investment vehicle.

The potential insurance value of options is the second interesting feature, as Portfolio C shows. The T-bill-plus-option portfolio cannot be worth less than $9,270 after 6 months, as the option can always be left to expire worthless. The worst possible rate of return on Portfolio C is −7.3%, compared to a (theoretically) worst possible rate of return of IBM stock of −100% if the company were to go bankrupt. Of course, this insurance comes at a price: When IBM does well, Portfolio C, the option-plus-bills portfolio, does not perform quite as well as Portfolio A, the all-stock portfolio.

This simple example makes an important point. Although options can be used by speculators as effectively leveraged stock positions, as in Portfolio B, they also can be used by investors who desire to tailor their risk exposures in creative ways, as in Portfolio C. For example, the call-plus-bills strategy of Portfolio C provides a rate of return profile quite unlike that of the stock alone. The absolute limitation on downside risk is a novel and attractive feature of this strategy. We next discuss several option strategies that provide other novel risk profiles that might be attractive to hedgers and other investors.

## 20.3   OPTION STRATEGIES

An unlimited variety of payoff patterns can be achieved by combining puts and calls with various exercise prices. We explain in this section the motivation and structure of some of the more popular ones.

**Protective Put**   Imagine you would like to invest in a stock, but you are unwilling to bear potential losses beyond some given level. Investing in the stock alone seems risky to you because in principle you could lose all the money you invest. You might consider instead investing in stock and purchasing a put option on the stock. Table 20.1 shows the total value of your portfolio at option expiration: Whatever happens to the stock price, you are guaranteed a payoff equal to the put option's exercise price because the put gives you the right to sell IBM for the exercise price even if the stock price is below that value.

**EXAMPLE 20.3**   **Protective Put**

Suppose the strike price is $X = \$100$ and IBM is selling at $97 at option expiration. Then the value of your total portfolio is $100. The stock is worth $97 and the value of the expiring put option is

$$X - S_T = \$100 - \$97 = \$3$$

Another way to look at it is that you are holding the stock and a put contract giving you the right to sell the stock for $100. The right to sell locks in a minimum portfolio value of $100. On the other hand, if the stock price is above $100, say $104, then the right to sell a share at $100 is worthless. You allow the put to expire unexercised, ending up with a share of stock worth $S_T = \$104$.

Figure 20.7 illustrates the payoff and profit to this **protective put** strategy. The solid line in Figure 20.7C is the total payoff. The dashed line is displaced downward by the cost of establishing the position, $S_0 + P$. Notice that potential losses are limited.

It is instructive to compare the profit on the protective put strategy with that of the stock investment. For simplicity, consider an at-the-money protective put, so that $X = S_0$. Figure 20.8 compares the profits for the two strategies. The profit on the stock is zero if the stock price remains unchanged and $S_T = S_0$. It rises or falls by $1 for every dollar swing in the ultimate stock price. The profit on the protective put is negative and equal to the cost of the put if $S_T$ is below $S_0$. The profit on the protective put increases one for one with increases in the stock price once $S_T$ exceeds $S_0$.

Figure 20.8 makes it clear that the protective put offers some insurance against stock price declines in that it limits losses. Therefore, protective put strategies provide a form of *portfolio insurance*. The cost of the protection is that, in the case of stock price increases, your profit is reduced by the cost of the put, which turned out to be unneeded.

This example also shows that despite the common perception that derivatives mean risk, derivative securities can be used effectively for *risk management*. In fact, such risk management is becoming accepted as part of the fiduciary responsibility of financial managers. Indeed, in one court case, *Brane* v. *Roth*, a company's board of directors was successfully sued for failing to use derivatives to hedge the price risk of grain held in storage. Such hedging might have been accomplished using protective puts. Some observers believe that this case will soon lead to a broad legal obligation for firms to use derivatives and other techniques to manage risk.

| Table 20.1 | Value of Protective Put Portfolio at Option Expiration | |
| --- | --- | --- |
| | $S_T \le X$ | $S_T > X$ |
| Stock | $S_T$ | $S_T$ |
| + Put | $X - S_T$ | 0 |
| = TOTAL | $X$ | $S_T$ |

**Figure 20.7**
**Value of a protective put position at option expiration**

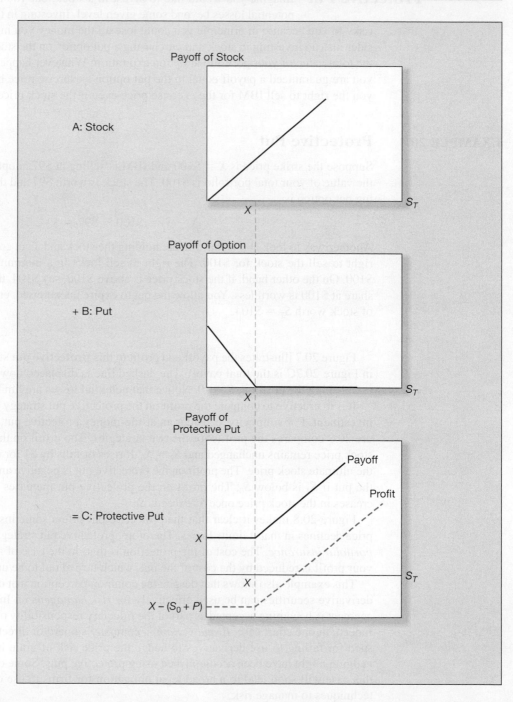

**Figure 20.8
Protective put
versus stock
investment**

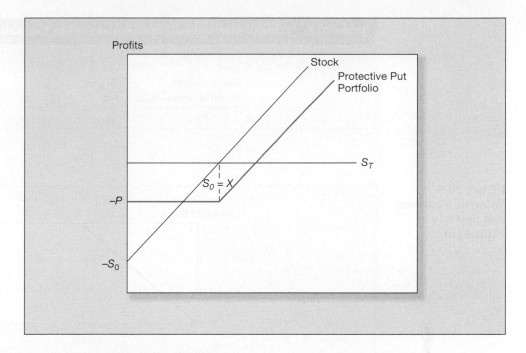

**Covered Calls**    A **covered call** position is the purchase of a share of stock with a simultaneous sale of a call on that stock. The call is "covered" because the potential
obligation to deliver the stock is covered by the stock held in the portfolio. Writing an option without an offsetting stock position is called by contrast *naked option writing*. The
value of a covered call position at the expiration of the call, presented in Table 20.2, equals
the stock value minus the value of the call. The call value is *subtracted* because the covered
call position involves issuing a call to another investor who can choose to exercise it to
profit at your expense.

The solid line in Figure 20.9C illustrates the payoff pattern. You see that the total position is worth $S_T$ when the stock price at time $T$ is below $X$ and rises to a maximum of $X$
when $S_T$ exceeds $X$. In essence, the sale of the call options means the call writer has sold the
claim to any stock value above $X$ in return for the initial premium (the call price). Therefore, at expiration, the position is worth at most $X$. The dashed line of Figure 20.9C is the
net profit to the covered call.

Writing covered call options has been a popular investment strategy among institutional
investors. Consider the managers of a fund invested largely in stocks. They might find it
appealing to write calls on some or all of the stock in order to boost income by the premiums collected. Although they thereby forfeit potential capital gains should the stock price
rise above the exercise price, if they view $X$ as the price at which they plan to sell the stock
anyway, then the call may be viewed as a kind of "sell discipline." The written call guarantees the stock sale will occur as planned.

**EXAMPLE 20.4    Covered Call**

Assume a pension fund holds 1,000 shares of IBM stock, with a current price of $100 per
share. Suppose management intends to sell all 1,000 shares if the share price hits $110, and
a call expiring in 60 days with an exercise price of $110 currently sells for $5. By writing
10 IBM call contracts (100 shares each) the fund can pick up $5,000 in extra income. The

### Table 20.2    Value of Covered Call Position at Option Expiration

|  | $S_T \leq X$ | $S_T > X$ |
|---|---|---|
| Payoff of stock | $S_T$ | $S_T$ |
| + Payoff of written call | $-0$ | $-(S_T - X)$ |
| = TOTAL | $S_T$ | $X$ |

**Figure 20.9
Value of a covered
call position at
expiration**

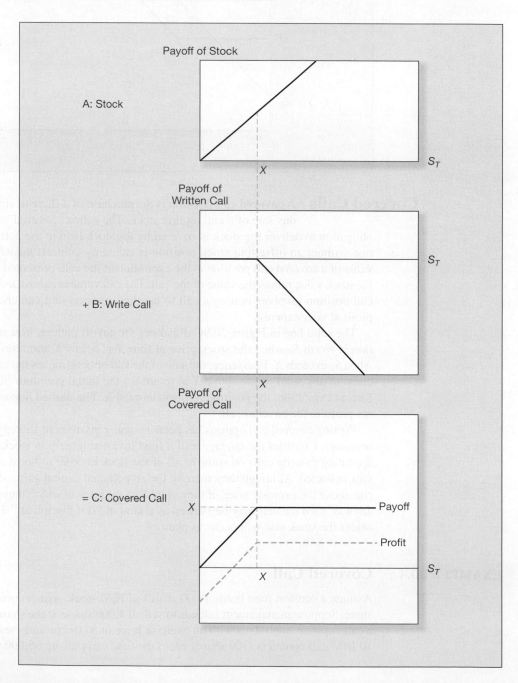

# STOCK, OPTIONS, AND COMBINED LENDING AND OPTIONS

The Options, Stock, and Lending spreadsheet extends the analysis presented in this section. The model facilitates comparison of alternative investment strategies involving options, stock, and lending. The spreadsheet allows you to use various combinations of options, stock, and T-bills to explore the flexibility made possible by options. It is built using the data table function so that it allows comparison of investment values and rates of return on investments over a range of ending stock prices.

The full spreadsheet model can be found on the OnLine Learning Center (**www.mhhe. com/bkm**).

| | A | B | C | D | E | F | G | H | I | J | K |
|---|---|---|---|---|---|---|---|---|---|---|---|
| 1 | Chapter 20 Solution to Problems | | | | | | LEGEND: | | | | |
| 2 | Comparison of Options, Equity and Combined Bills and Options | | | | | | Enter data | | | | |
| 3 | | | | | | | Value calculated | | | | |
| 4 | Current stock price ($S_0$) | $150.00 | | | | | See comment | | | | |
| 5 | Option premium | $20.00 | | | | | | | | | |
| 6 | Exercise price(X) | $150.00 | | | | | | | | | |
| 7 | Risk-free interest rate (annual)($r_f$) | 4.00% | | One-Way Data Table | | Value of stock at expiration | | | | | |
| 8 | Value of stock at expiration ($S_T$) | $170.00 | | Options Only Strategy | | $120 | $130 | $140 | $150 | $160 | $170 |
| 9 | Option premium at expiration | $20.00 | | Total value at expiration | $30,000 | $0 | $0 | $0 | $0 | $16,000 | $30,000 |
| 10 | Investment amount | $30,000.00 | | | | | | | | | |
| 11 | | | | One-Way Data Table | | Value of stock at expiration | | | | | |
| 12 | Options Only Strategy | | | Stock Only Strategy | | $120 | $130 | $140 | $150 | $160 | $170 |
| 13 | Number of options purchased | $500.00 | | Total value at expiration | $34,000 | $24,000 | $26,000 | $28,000 | $30,000 | $32,000 | $34,000 |
| 14 | Option premium at expiration | $20.00 | | | | | | | | | |
| 15 | Total value at expiration | $30,000.00 | | One-Way Data Table | | Value of stock at expiration | | | | | |
| 16 | Total profit | $0.00 | | Bills and Options Strategy | | $120 | $130 | $140 | $150 | $160 | $170 |
| 17 | Return on Investment | 0.00% | | Total value at expiration | $31,040 | $27,040 | $27,040 | $27,040 | $27,040 | $29,040 | $31,040 |
| 18 | | | | | | | | | | | |
| 19 | | | | | | | | | | | |

fund would lose its share of profits from any movement of IBM stock above $110 per share, but given that it would have sold its shares at $110, it would not have realized those profits anyway.

### Straddle

A long **straddle** is established by buying both a call and a put on a stock, each with the same exercise price, X, and the same expiration date, T. Straddles are useful strategies for investors who believe a stock will move a lot in price but are uncertain about the direction of the move. For example, suppose you believe an important court case that will make or break a company is about to be settled, and the market is not yet aware of the situation. The stock will either double in value if the case is settled favorably or will drop by half if the settlement goes against the company. The straddle position will do well regardless of the outcome because its value is highest when the stock price makes extreme upward or downward moves from X.

The worst-case scenario for a straddle is no movement in the stock price. If $S_T$ equals X, both the call and the put expire worthless, and the investor's outlay for the purchase of both options is lost. Straddle positions, therefore, are bets on volatility. An investor who establishes a straddle must view the stock as more volatile than the market does. Conversely, investors who *write* straddles—selling both a call and a put—must believe the stock is less volatile. They accept the option premiums now, hoping the stock price will not change much before option expiration.

The payoff to a straddle is presented in Table 20.3. The solid line of Figure 20.10C illustrates this payoff. Notice the portfolio payoff is always positive, except at the one point where the portfolio has zero value, $S_T = X$. You might wonder why all investors don't pursue such a seemingly "no-lose" strategy. The reason is that the straddle requires that both the put and call be purchased. The value of the portfolio at expiration, while never negative, still must exceed the initial cash outlay for a straddle investor to clear a profit.

The dashed line of Figure 20.10C is the profit to the straddle. The profit line lies below the payoff line by the cost of purchasing the straddle, $P + C$. It is clear from the diagram that the straddle position generates a loss unless the stock price deviates substantially from $X$. The stock price must depart from $X$ by the total amount expended to purchase the call and the put in order for the purchaser of the straddle to clear a profit.

*Strips* and *straps* are variations of straddles. A strip is two puts and one call on a security with the same exercise price and maturity date. A strap is two calls and one put.

---

**CONCEPT CHECK☞ QUESTION 4**

Graph the profit and payoff diagrams for strips and straps.

---

**Spreads**    A **spread** is a combination of two or more call options (or two or more puts) on the same stock with differing exercise prices or times to maturity. Some options are bought, whereas others are sold, or written. A *money spread* involves the purchase of one option and the simultaneous sale of another with a different exercise price. A *time spread* refers to the sale and purchase of options with differing expiration dates.

Consider a money spread in which one call option is bought at an exercise price $X_1$, whereas another call with identical expiration date, but higher exercise price, $X_2$, is written. The payoff to this position will be the difference in the value of the call held and the value of the call written, as in Table 20.4.

There are now three instead of two outcomes to distinguish: the lowest-price region where $S_T$ is below both exercise prices, a middle region where $S_T$ is between the two exercise prices, and a high-price region where $S_T$ exceeds both exercise prices. Figure 20.11 illustrates the payoff and profit to this strategy, which is called a *bullish spread* because the payoff either increases or is unaffected by stock price increases. Holders of bullish spreads benefit from stock price increases.

One motivation for a bullish spread might be that the investor thinks one option is overpriced relative to another. For example, an investor who believes an $X = \$100$ call is cheap compared to an $X = \$110$ call might establish the spread, even without a strong desire to take a bullish position in the stock.

**Collars**    A **collar** is an options strategy that brackets the value of a portfolio between two bounds. Suppose that an investor currently is holding a large position in IBM, which is currently selling at $100 per share. A lower bound of $90 can be placed on the value of the portfolio by buying a protective put with exercise price $90. This protection, however, requires that the investor pay the put premium. To raise the money to pay for the put, the investor might write a call option, say with exercise price $110. The call might sell for roughly the same price as the put, meaning that the net outlay for the two options positions is approximately zero. Writing the call limits the portfolio's upside potential. Even if the stock price moves above $110, the investor will do no better than $110, because at a higher price the stock will be called away. Thus the investor obtains the downside protection represented by the exercise price of the put by selling her claim to any upside potential beyond the exercise price of the call.

**Table 20.3   Value of a Straddle Position at Option Expiration**

|  | $S_T < X$ | $S_T \geq X$ |
|---|---|---|
| Payoff of call | 0 | $S_T - X$ |
| + Payoff of put | $X - S_T$ | 0 |
| = TOTAL | $X - S_T$ | $S_T - X$ |

**Figure 20.10
Value of a straddle
at expiration**

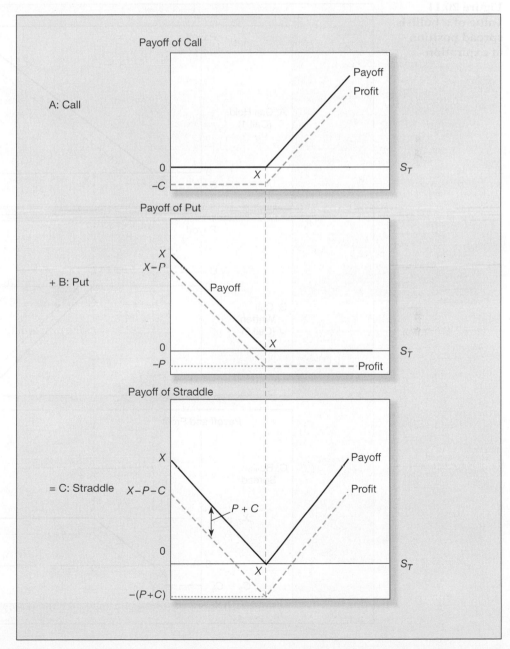

**Table 20.4    Value of a Bullish Spread Position at Expiration**

| | $S_T \leq X_1$ | $X_1 < S_T \leq X_2$ | $S_T \geq X_2$ |
|---|---|---|---|
| Payoff of purchased call, exercise price = $X_1$ | 0 | $S_T - X_1$ | $S_T - X_1$ |
| + Payoff of written call, exercise price = $X_2$ | − 0 | − 0 | − $(S_T - X_2)$ |
| = *TOTAL* | 0 | $S_T - X_1$ | $X_2 - X_1$ |

**Figure 20.11
Value of a bullish
spread position
at expiration**

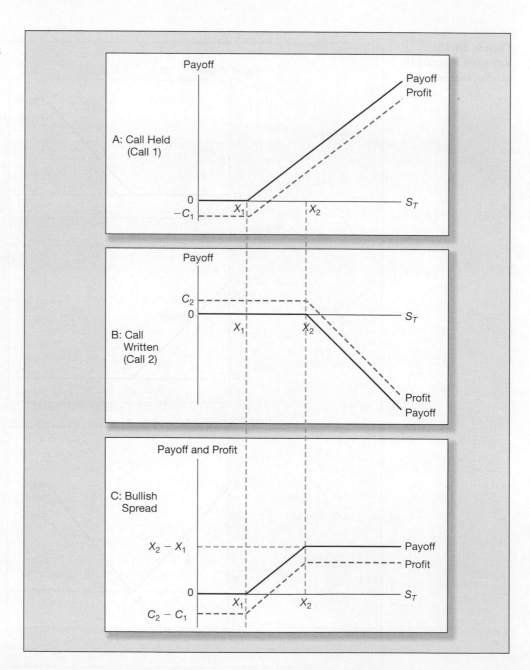

A collar would be appropriate for an investor who has a target wealth goal in mind but is unwilling to risk losses beyond a certain level. If you are contemplating buying a house for $220,000, for example, you might set this figure as your goal. Your current wealth may be $200,000, and you are unwilling to risk losing more than $20,000. A collar established by (1) purchasing 2,000 shares of stock currently selling at $100 per share, (2) purchasing 2,000 put options (20 option contracts) with exercise price $90, and (3) writing 2,000 calls with exercise price $110 would give you a good chance to realize the $20,000 capital gain without risking a loss of more than $20,000.

| CONCEPT CHECK☞ QUESTION 5 | Graph the payoff diagram for the collar described in the paragraph above for the investor contemplating the purchase of a house. |
| --- | --- |

## 20.4   THE PUT-CALL PARITY RELATIONSHIP

We saw in the previous section that a protective put portfolio, comprising a stock position and a put option on that position, provides a payoff with a guaranteed minimum value, but with unlimited upside potential. This is not the only way to achieve such protection, however. A call-plus-bills portfolio also can provide limited downside risk with unlimited upside potential.

Consider the strategy of buying a call option and, in addition, buying Treasury bills with face value equal to the exercise price of the call, and with maturity date equal to the expiration date of the option. For example, if the exercise price of the call option is $100, then each option contract (which is written on 100 shares) would require payment of $10,000 upon exercise. Therefore, you would purchase one T-bill, which also has a maturity value of $10,000. More generally, for each option that you hold with exercise price $X$, you would purchase a risk-free zero-coupon bond with face value $X$.

Examine the value of this position at time $T$, when the options expire and the zero-coupon bond matures:

|  | $S_T \leq X$ | $S_T > X$ |
| --- | --- | --- |
| Value of call option | 0 | $S_T - X$ |
| Value of riskless bond | $X$ | $X$ |
| TOTAL | $X$ | $S_T$ |

If the stock price is below the exercise price, the call is worthless, but the riskless bond matures to its face value, $X$. The bond therefore provides a floor value to the portfolio. If the stock price exceeds $X$, then the payoff to the call, $S_T - X$, is added to the face value of the bond to provide a total payoff of $S_T$. The payoff to this portfolio is precisely identical to the payoff of the protective put that we derived in Table 20.1.

If two portfolios always provide equal values, then they must cost the same amount to establish. Therefore, the call-plus-bond portfolio must cost the same as the stock-plus-put portfolio. Each call costs $C$. The riskless zero-coupon bond costs $X/(1 + r_f)^T$. Therefore, the call-plus-bond portfolio costs $C + X/(1 + r_f)^T$ to establish. The stock costs $S_0$ to purchase now (at time zero), while the put costs $P$. Therefore, we conclude that

$$C + \frac{X}{(1 + r_f)^T} = S_0 + P \qquad (20.1)$$

Equation 20.1 is called the **put-call parity theorem** because it represents the proper relationship between put and call prices. If the parity relation is ever violated, an arbitrage opportunity arises. For example, suppose you confront these data for a certain stock:

| | |
|---|---|
| Stock price | $110 |
| Call price (6-month maturity, $X$ = $105) | $ 17 |
| Put price (6-month maturity, $X$ = $105) | $ 5 |
| Risk-free interest rate | 10.25% per year |

We can use these data in equation 20.1 to see if parity is violated:

$$C + \frac{X}{(1 + r_f)^T} \overset{?}{=} S_0 + P$$

$$17 + \frac{105}{1.1025^{1/2}} \overset{?}{=} 110 + 5$$

$$117 \overset{?}{=} 115$$

This result, a violation of parity—117 does not equal 115—indicates mispricing. To exploit the mispricing you buy the relatively cheap portfolio (the stock-plus-put position represented on the right-hand side of the equation), and sell the relatively expensive portfolio (the call-plus-bond position corresponding to the left-hand side). Therefore, if you *buy* the stock, *buy* the put, *write* the call, and *borrow* $100 for 6 months (because borrowing money is the opposite of buying a bond), you should earn arbitrage profits.

Let's examine the payoff to this strategy. In 6 months, the stock will be worth $S_T$. The $100 borrowed will be paid back with interest, resulting in a cash flow of $105. The written call will result in a cash outflow of $S_T - $105 if $S_T$ exceeds $105. The purchased put pays off $105 - S_T$ if the stock price is below $105.

Table 20.5 summarizes the outcome. The immediate cash inflow is $2. In 6 months, the various positions provide exactly offsetting cash flows: The $2 inflow is realized without any offsetting outflows. This is an arbitrage opportunity that investors will pursue on a large scale until buying and selling pressure restores the parity condition expressed in equation 20.1.

Equation 20.1 actually applies only to options on stocks that pay no dividends before the maturity date of the option. The extension of the parity condition for European call options on dividend-paying stocks is, however, straightforward. Problem 5 at the end of the chapter leads you through the extension of the parity relationship. The more general formulation of the *put-call parity* condition is

$$P = C - S_0 + PV(X) + PV(\text{dividends}) \qquad (20.2)$$

**Table 20.5   Arbitrage Strategy**

| | | Cash Flow in 6 Months | |
|---|---|---|---|
| Position | Immediate Cash Flow | $S_T < 105$ | $S_T \geq 105$ |
| Buy stock | −110 | $S_T$ | $S_T$ |
| Borrow $105/1.1025^{1/2}$ = $100 | +100 | −105 | −105 |
| Sell call | +17 | 0 | − $(S_T − 105)$ |
| Buy put | −5 | $105 − S_T$ | 0 |
| TOTAL | 2 | 0 | 0 |

where PV(dividends) is the present value of the dividends that will be paid by the stock during the life of the option. If the stock does not pay dividends, equation 20.2 becomes identical to equation 20.1.

Notice that this generalization would apply as well to European options on assets other than stocks. Instead of using dividend income per se in equation 20.2, we would let any income paid out by the underlying asset play the role of the stock dividends. For example, European put and call options on bonds would satisfy the same parity relationship, except that the bond's coupon income would replace the stock's dividend payments in the parity formula.

Even this generalization, however, applies only to European options, as the cash flow streams from the two portfolios represented by the two sides of equation 20.2 will match only if each position is held until maturity. If a call and a put may be optimally exercised at different times before their common expiration date, then the equality of payoffs cannot be assured, or even expected, and the portfolios will have different values.

## EXAMPLE 20.5   Put-Call Parity

Let's see how well parity works using real data on the Microsoft options in Figure 20.1. The March maturity call with exercise price $22.50 and time to expiration of 17 days cost $1.15 while the corresponding put option cost $.55. Microsoft was selling for $23.07, and the annualized short-term interest rate on this date was 1.2%. There are no dividends to be paid to a stock purchaser between the date of the listing, March 4, and the option maturity date. According to parity, we should find that

$$P = C + PV(X) - S_0 + PV(\text{dividends})$$

$$.55 = 1.15 + \frac{22.50}{(1.012)^{17/365}} - 23.07 + 0$$

$$.55 = 1.15 + 22.49 - 23.07$$

$$.55 = .57$$

So parity is violated by about $.02 per share, not even close to a big enough difference to exploit. You have to weigh the potential profit against the trading costs of the call, put, and stock. More important, given the fact that options trade relatively infrequently, this deviation from parity might not be "real," but may instead be attributable to "stale" price quotes at which you cannot actually trade.

## 20.5   OPTIONLIKE SECURITIES

Suppose you never traded an option directly. Why do you need to appreciate the properties of options in formulating an investment plan? Many financial instruments and agreements have features that convey implicit or explicit options to one or more parties. If you are to value and use these securities correctly, you must understand these embedded option attributes.

**Callable Bonds**   You know from Chapter 14 that many corporate bonds are issued with call provisions entitling the issuer to buy bonds back from bondholders at some time in the future at a specified call price. A call provision conveys a call option to the issuer, where the exercise price is equal to the price at which the bond can be repurchased. A callable bond arrangement is essentially a sale of a *straight bond* (a bond with no option features such as callability or convertibility) to the investor and the concurrent issuance of a call option by the investor to the bond-issuing firm.

There must be some compensation for conveying this implicit call option to the firm. If the callable bond were issued with the same coupon rate as a straight bond, we would expect it to sell at a lower price than the straight bond. In fact, we would expect the price difference to equal the value of the call. To sell callable bonds at par, firms must issue them with coupon rates higher than the coupons on straight debt. The higher coupons are the investor's compensation for the call option retained by the issuer. Coupon rates usually are selected so that the newly issued bond will sell at par value.

Figure 20.12 illustrates this optionlike property. The horizontal axis is the value of a straight bond with otherwise identical terms as the callable bond. The dashed 45-degree line represents the value of straight debt. The solid line is the value of the callable bond, and the dotted line is the value of the call option retained by the firm. A callable bond's potential for capital gains is limited by the firm's option to repurchase at the call price.

| CONCEPT CHECK☞ QUESTION 6 | How is a callable bond similar to a covered call strategy on a straight bond? |
| --- | --- |

The option inherent in callable bonds actually is more complex than an ordinary call option, because usually it may be exercised only after some initial period of call protection. The price at which the bond is callable may change over time also. Unlike exchange-listed options, these features are defined in the initial bond covenant and will depend on the needs of the issuing firm and its perception of the market's tastes.

**Figure 20.12 Values of callable bonds compared with straight bonds**

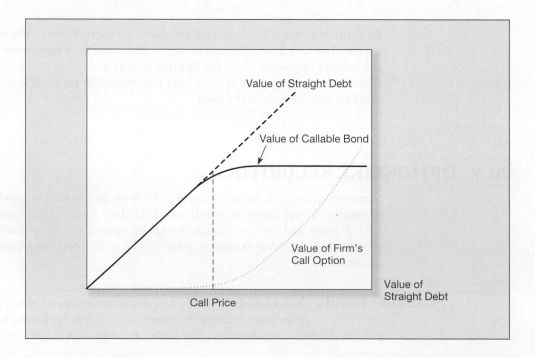

**CONCEPT
C H E C K ☞
QUESTION 7**

Suppose the period of call protection is extended. How will the coupon rate the company needs to offer on its bonds change to enable the issuer to sell the bonds at par value?

## Convertible Securities

Convertible bonds and convertible preferred stock convey options to the holder of the security rather than to the issuing firm. A convertible security typically gives its holder the right to exchange each bond or share of preferred stock for a fixed number of shares of common stock, regardless of the market prices of the securities at the time.

**CONCEPT
C H E C K ☞
QUESTION 8**

Should a convertible bond issued at par value have a higher or lower coupon rate than a nonconvertible bond at par?

For example, a bond with a *conversion ratio* of 10 allows its holder to convert one bond of par value $1,000 into 10 shares of common stock. Alternatively, we say the *conversion price* in this case is $100: To receive 10 shares of stock, the investor sacrifices bonds with face value $1,000 or, put another way, $100 of face value per share. If the present value of the bond's scheduled payments is less than 10 times the value of one share of stock, it may pay to convert; that is, the conversion option is in the money. A bond worth $950 with a conversion ratio of 10 could be converted profitably if the stock were selling above $95, as the value of the 10 shares received for each bond surrendered would exceed $950. Most convertible bonds are issued "deep out of the money." That is, the issuer sets the conversion ratio so that conversion will not be profitable unless there is a substantial increase in stock prices and/or decrease in bond prices from the time of issue.

A bond's *conversion value* equals the value it would have if you converted it into stock immediately. Clearly, a bond must sell for at least its conversion value. If it did not, you could purchase the bond, convert it, and clear an immediate profit. This condition could never persist, for all investors would pursue such a strategy and ultimately would bid up the price of the bond.

The straight bond value, or "bond floor," is the value the bond would have if it were not convertible into stock. The bond must sell for more than its straight bond value because a convertible bond has more value; it is in fact a straight bond plus a valuable call option. Therefore, the convertible bond has two lower bounds on its market price: the conversion value and the straight bond value.

Figure 20.13 illustrates the optionlike properties of the convertible bond. Figure 20.13A shows the value of the straight debt as a function of the stock price of the issuing firm. For healthy firms, the straight debt value is almost independent of the value of the stock because default risk is small. However, if the firm is close to bankruptcy (stock prices are low), default risk increases, and the straight bond value falls. Panel B shows the conversion value of the bond. Panel C compares the value of the convertible bond to these two lower bounds.

When stock prices are low, the straight bond value is the effective lower bound, and the conversion option is nearly irrelevant. The convertible will trade like straight debt. When stock prices are high, the bond's price is determined by its conversion value. With conversion all but guaranteed, the bond is essentially equity in disguise.

We can illustrate with two examples:

**Figure 20.13
Value of a
convertible bond
as a function of
stock price.
A, Straight
debt value,
or bond floor.
B, Conversion
value of the bond.
C, Total value of
convertible bond.**

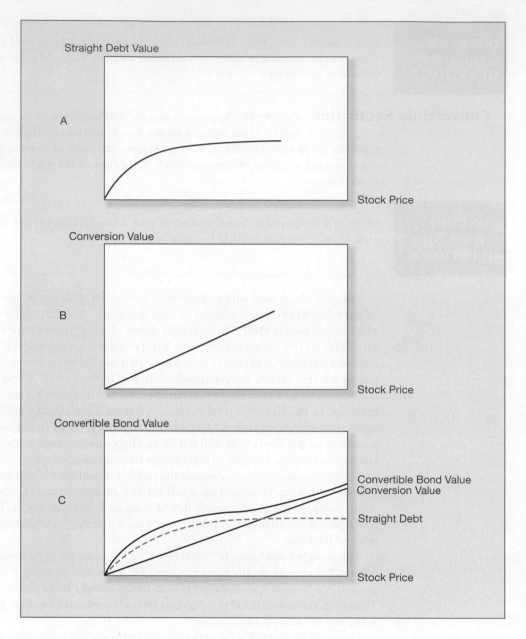

| | Bond A | Bond B |
|---|---|---|
| Annual coupon | $80 | $80 |
| Maturity date | 10 years | 10 years |
| Quality rating | Baa | Baa |
| Conversion ratio | 20 | 25 |
| Stock price | $30 | $50 |
| Conversion value | $600 | $1,250 |
| Market yield on 10-year Baa-rated bonds | 8.5% | 8.5% |
| Value as straight debt | $967 | $967 |
| Actual bond price | $972 | $1,255 |
| Reported yield to maturity | 8.42% | 4.76% |

Bond A has a conversion value of only $600. Its value as straight debt, in contrast, is $967. This is the present value of the coupon and principal payments at a market rate for straight debt of 8.5%. The bond's price is $972, so the premium over straight bond value is only $5, reflecting the low probability of conversion. Its reported yield to maturity based on scheduled coupon payments and the market price of $972 is 8.42%, close to that of straight debt.

The conversion option on Bond B is in the money. Conversion value is $1,250, and the bond's price, $1,255, reflects its value as equity (plus $5 for the protection the bond offers against stock price declines). The bond's reported yield is 4.76%, far below the comparable yield on straight debt. The big yield sacrifice is attributable to the far greater value of the conversion option.

In theory, we could value convertible bonds by treating them as straight debt plus call options. In practice, however, this approach is often impractical for several reasons:

1. The conversion price frequently increases over time, which means the exercise price of the option changes.

2. Stocks may pay several dividends over the life of the bond, further complicating the option valuation analysis.

3. Most convertibles also are callable at the discretion of the firm. In essence, both the investor and the issuer hold options on each other. If the issuer exercises its call option to repurchase the bond, the bondholders typically have a month during which they still can convert. When issuers use a call option, knowing bondholders will choose to convert, the issuer is said to have *forced a conversion*. These conditions together mean the actual maturity of the bond is indeterminate.

## Warrants

**Warrants** are essentially call options issued by a firm. One important difference between calls and warrants is that exercise of a warrant requires the firm to issue a new share of stock—the total number of shares outstanding increases. Exercise of a call option requires only that the writer of the call deliver an already-issued share of stock to discharge the obligation. In that case, the number of shares outstanding remains fixed. Also unlike call options, warrants result in a cash flow to the firm when the warrant holder pays the exercise price. These differences mean that warrant values will differ somewhat from the values of call options with identical terms.

Like convertible debt, warrant terms may be tailored to meet the needs of the firm. Also like convertible debt, warrants generally are protected against stock splits and dividends in that the exercise price and the number of warrants held are adjusted to offset the effects of the split.

Warrants are often issued in conjunction with another security. Bonds, for example, may be packaged together with a warrant "sweetener," frequently a warrant that may be sold separately. This is called a *detachable warrant*.

Issue of warrants and convertible securities creates the potential for an increase in outstanding shares of stock if exercise occurs. Exercise obviously would affect financial statistics that are computed on a per-share basis, so annual reports must provide earnings per share figures under the assumption that all convertible securities and warrants are exercised. These figures are called *fully diluted earnings per share*.[3]

The executive and employee stock options that became so popular in the last decade actually were warrants. We saw in Chapter 1, Table 1.4, that some of these grants were huge, with payoffs to top executives in excess of $100 million. Yet firms almost uniformly chose

---

[3] We should note that the exercise of a convertible bond need not reduce EPS. Diluted EPS will be less than undiluted EPS only if interest saved (per share) on the convertible bonds is less than the prior EPS.

# OPTIONS SHOULD BE REFLECTED IN THE BOTTOM LINE

There are some issues on which accounting and finance professors disagree, but the expensing of employee stock options is not one of them. We believe there is near unanimity of opinion that the value of employee stock options should be expensed on a firm's income statement at the time they are granted.

Stock options have a market price, so when a company grants options to employees, the company has given up something that has considerable value. This is the amount the company would have received had these options been underwritten and sold for cash in a competitive options market. Yet many executives, venture capitalists, politicians, journalists, and even some professional economists have voiced their opposition to proposals that companies reflect the cost of employee stock options on their income statements. We think their arguments make one or more errors in reasoning.

First, some argue that grants of stock options do not involve cash outlays, and therefore no expense should be recorded. This reasoning violates the basic accrual principle of accounting. Not every cash outflow is recorded as an expense in the period in which it occurs, nor does every expense recognized in a period involve a cash outflow. For example, when a company compensates employees by making outright grants of stock, no cash outflows occur. Yet the company would record, as compensation expense, the value of the stock granted. Stock-option grants should receive comparable treatment.

A second error is to argue that the expensing of stock options would be double counting because the diluting effect of granting the options is recognized by an increase in the number of shares in the denominator of a fully diluted earnings-per-share calculation. But this erroneous argument would also enable a company to issue stock options to, say, a supplier of materials, and not record the materials as an expense because the effect would show up in the higher number of shares in an earnings-per-share calculation. Curious reasoning.

Some opponents of expensing employee stock options make two arguments that actually conflict with each other. First, they claim that it is enough to disclose the information in the footnotes to corporate financial statements as is done now. And second, they claim that requiring options to be expensed would hurt companies. But if deducting the expenses of options that are already disclosed in footnotes would drive a company's stock price down, then we have proof that the disclosure alone was inadequate to capture the underlying economic reality.

The accounting for employee stock options on a firm's income statement should be decided according to economic and accounting principles, not by dubious rationalizations. If the following true-or-false question appeared on an accounting exam, the answer is quite clear: Employee stock options should be expensed on a firm's income statement. True.

Zvi Bodie, Robert S. Kaplan, and Robert C. Merton, "Options Should be Reflected in The Bottom Line," *The Wall Street Journal*, August 1, 2002.

---

not to acknowledge these grants as expenses on their income statements. This dubious practice finally may be changing. The nearby box makes the case for recognizing employee option grants as an expense, just as it does other components of compensation such as salary or promised pension benefits.

## Collateralized Loans

Many loan arrangements require that the borrower put up collateral to guarantee the loan will be paid back. In the event of default, the lender takes possession of the collateral. A nonrecourse loan gives the lender no recourse beyond the right to the collateral. That is, the lender may not sue the borrower for further payment if the collateral turns out not to be valuable enough to repay the loan.

This arrangement gives an implicit call option to the borrower. Assume the borrower is obligated to pay back $L$ dollars at the maturity of the loan. The collateral will be worth $S_T$ dollars at maturity. (Its value today is $S_0$.) The borrower has the option to wait until loan maturity and repay the loan only if the collateral is worth more than the $L$ dollars necessary to satisfy the loan. If the collateral is worth less than $L$, the borrower can default on the loan, discharging the obligation by forfeiting the collateral, which is worth only $S_T$.[4]

---

[4] In reality, of course, defaulting on a loan is not so simple. There are losses of reputation involved as well as considerations of ethical behavior. This is a description of a pure nonrecourse loan where both parties agree from the outset that only the collateral backs the loan and that default is not to be taken as a sign of bad faith if the collateral is insufficient to repay the loan.

Another way of describing such a loan is to view the borrower as turning over the collateral to the lender but retaining the right to reclaim it by paying off the loan. The transfer of the collateral with the right to reclaim it is equivalent to a payment of $S_0$ dollars, less a simultaneous recovery of a sum that resembles a call option with exercise price $L$. Basically, the borrower turns over collateral and keeps an option to "repurchase" it for $L$ dollars at the maturity of the loan if $L$ turns out to be less than $S_T$. This is a call option.

A third way to look at a collateralized loan is to assume that the borrower will repay the $L$ dollars with certainty but also retain the option to sell the collateral to the lender for $L$ dollars, even if $S_T$ is less than $L$. In this case, the sale of the collateral would generate the cash necessary to satisfy the loan. The ability to "sell" the collateral for a price of $L$ dollars represents a put option, which guarantees the borrower can raise enough money to satisfy the loan simply by turning over the collateral.

It is perhaps surprising to realize that we can describe the same loan as involving either a put option or a call option, as the payoffs to calls and puts are so different. Yet the equivalence of the two approaches is nothing more than a reflection of the put-call parity relationship. In our call-option description of the loan, the value of the borrower's liability is $S_0 - C$: The borrower turns over the asset, which is a transfer of $S_0$ dollars, but retains a call worth $C$ dollars. In the put-option description, the borrower is obligated to pay $L$ dollars but retains the put, which is worth $P$: The present value of this net obligation is $L/(1 + r_f)^T - P$. Because these alternative descriptions are equivalent ways of viewing the same loan, the value of the obligations must be equal:

$$S_0 - C = \frac{L}{(1 + r_f)^T} - P \qquad (20.3)$$

Treating $L$ as the exercise price of the option, equation 20.3 is simply the put-call parity relationship.

Figure 20.14 illustrates this fact. Figure 20.14A is the value of the payment to be received by the lender, which equals the minimum of $S_T$ or $L$. Panel B shows that this amount can be expressed as $S_T$ minus the payoff of the call implicitly written by the lender and held by the borrower. Panel C shows it also can be viewed as a receipt of $L$ dollars minus the proceeds of a put option.

## Levered Equity and Risky Debt

Investors holding stock in incorporated firms are protected by limited liability, which means that if the firm cannot pay its debts, the firm's creditors may attach only the firm's assets, not sue the corporation's equityholders for further payment. In effect, any time the corporation borrows money, the maximum possible collateral for the loan is the total of the firm's assets. If the firm declares bankruptcy, we can interpret this as an admission that the assets of the firm are insufficient to satisfy the claims against it. The corporation may discharge its obligations by transferring ownership of the firm's assets to the creditors.

Just as is true for nonrecourse collateralized loans, the required payment to the creditors represents the exercise price of the implicit option, while the value of the firm is the underlying asset. The equityholders have a put option to transfer their ownership claims on the firm to the creditors in return for the face value of the firm's debt.

Alternatively, we may view the equityholders as retaining a call option. They have, in effect, already transferred their ownership claim to the firm to the creditors but have retained the right to reacquire that claim by paying off the loan. Hence the equityholders have the option to "buy back" the firm for a specified price: They have a call option.

The significance of this observation is that analysts can value corporate bonds using option pricing techniques. The default premium required of risky debt in principle can be

**Figure 20.14
Collateralized
loan**

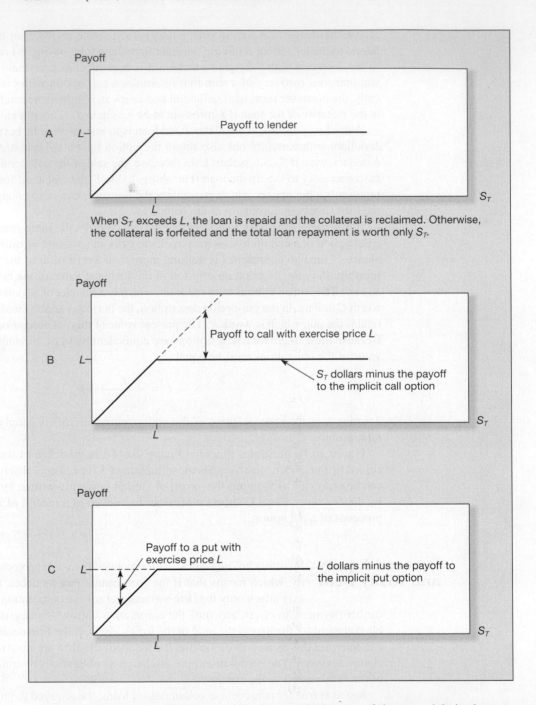

When $S_T$ exceeds $L$, the loan is repaid and the collateral is reclaimed. Otherwise, the collateral is forfeited and the total loan repayment is worth only $S_T$.

estimated using option valuation models. We consider some of these models in the next chapter.

## 20.6  FINANCIAL ENGINEERING

One of the attractions of options is the ability they provide to create investment positions with payoffs that depend in a variety of ways on the values of other securities. We have seen evidence of this capability in the various options strategies examined in Section 20.4.

Options also can be used to custom design new securities or portfolios with desired patterns of exposure to the price of an underlying security. In this sense, options (and futures contracts, to be discussed in Chapters 22 and 23) provide the ability to engage in *financial engineering*, the creation of portfolios with specified payoff patterns.

Most financial engineering takes place for institutional investors. However, some applications have been designed for the retail market. One highly successful retail product of financial engineering, first introduced by Merrill Lynch in 1985, is the liquid-yield option note, or LYON.[5] A LYON is a *zero-coupon, convertible, callable*, and *puttable* bond. To illustrate how the bond works, consider the first LYON issued, by Waste Management, Inc. The bond paid no coupon income and was priced at $250 in 1985, with a maturity value of $1,000 in 2001. If the security is not called, converted, or redeemed, it provides a yield to maturity of about 9%. However, three options may result in early retirement of the issue.

First, the investor can convert each bond into 4.36 shares of Waste Management stock. Second, the investor can put (sell) the bond back to Waste Management at a predetermined exercise price that rises over time according to a schedule detailed in the bond indenture. Finally, Waste Management can call the bond back from the investor at fixed exercise prices that also increase over time.

This combination of options results in risk-sharing attributes that seem to be attractive to both the issuer and investors. The convertibility feature provides the opportunity to profit from price advances in Waste Management stock. At the same time, the embedded put option provides the LYON holder a protective floor. Finally, the call feature allows Waste Management to call the bonds back for refinancing if interest rates drop considerably. The Waste Management LYON was a big success for Merrill Lynch. Although only 10% of a convertible bond typically is purchased by individual investors, they purchased approximately 40% of the LYON issue. Although other underwriters have since brought LYON competitors to the market, Merrill Lynch remains dominant in the field.

A simpler product also engineered with options is the index-linked certificate of deposit. Index-linked CDs enable retail investors to take small positions in index options. Unlike conventional CDs, which pay a fixed rate of interest, these CDs pay depositors a specified fraction of the rate of return on a market index such as the S&P 500, while guaranteeing a minimum rate of return should the market fall. For example, the index-linked CD may offer 70% of any market increase, but protect its holder from any market decrease by guaranteeing at least no loss.

The index-linked CD is clearly a type of call option. If the market rises, the depositor profits according to the *participation rate* or *multiplier*, in this case 70%; if the market falls, the investor is insured against loss. Just as clearly, the bank offering these CDs is in effect writing call options and can hedge its position by buying index calls in the options market. Figure 20.15 shows the nature of the bank's obligation to its depositors.

How might the bank set the appropriate multiplier? To answer this, note various features of the option:

1. The price the depositor is paying for the options is the forgone interest on the conventional CD that could be purchased. Because interest is received at the end of the period, the present value of the interest payment on each dollar invested is $r_f/(1 + r_f)$. Therefore, the depositor trades a sure payment with present value per dollar invested of $r_f/(1 + r_f)$ for a return that depends on the market's performance. Conversely, the bank can fund its obligation using the interest that it would have paid on a conventional CD.

[5] This discussion is based on a paper by John J. McConnell and Eduardo S. Schwartz, "The Origins of LYONs: A Case Study in Financial Innovation," *Journal of Applied Corporate Finance*, Winter 1992.

**Figure 20.15
Return on
index-linked CD**

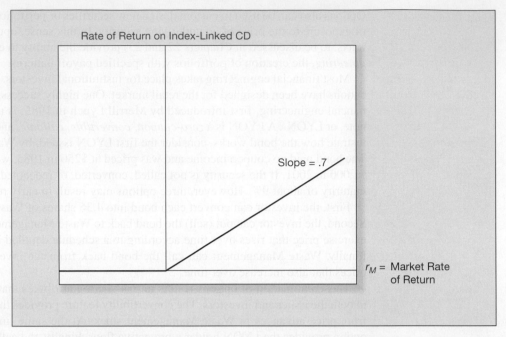

2. The option we have described is an at-the-money option, meaning that the exercise price equals the current value of the stock index. The option goes into the money as soon as the market index increases from its level at the inception of the contract.

3. We can analyze the option on a per-dollar-invested basis. For example, the option costs the depositor $r_f/(1 + r_f)$ dollars per dollar placed in the index-linked CD. The market price of the option per dollar invested is $C/S_0$: The at-the-money option costs $C$ dollars and is written on one unit of the market index, currently at $S_0$.

Now it is easy to determine the multiplier that the bank can offer on the CDs. It receives from its depositors a "payment" of $r_f/(1 + r_f)$ per dollar invested. It costs the bank $C/S_0$ to purchase the call option on a \$1 investment in the market index. Therefore, if $r_f/(1 + r_f)$ is, for example, 70% of $C/S_0$, the bank can purchase at most .7 call option on the \$1 investment and the multiplier will be .7. More generally, the break-even multiplier on an index-linked CD is $r_f/(1 + r_f)$ divided by $C/S_0$.

**EXAMPLE 20.6    Indexed-Linked CDs**

Suppose that $r_f = 6\%$ per year, and that 6-month maturity at-the-money calls on the market index currently cost \$50. The index is at 1,000. Then the option costs 50/1,000 = \$.05 per dollar of market value. The CD rate is 3% per 6 months, meaning that $r_f/(1 + r_f) =$ .03/1.03 = .0291. Therefore, the multiplier would be .0291/.05 = .5825.

The index-linked CD has several variants. Investors can purchase similar CDs that guarantee a positive minimum return if they are willing to settle for a smaller multiplier. In this case, the option is "purchased" by the depositor for $(r_f - r_{min})/(1 + r_f)$ dollars per dollar invested, where $r_{min}$ is the guaranteed minimum return. Because the purchase price is lower, fewer options can be purchased, which results in a lower multiplier. Another variant of the "bullish" CD we have described is the *bear CD*, which pays depositors a fraction of any *fall* in the market index. For example, a bear CD might offer a rate of return of .6 times any percentage decline in the S&P 500.

CONCEPT
CHECK ☞
QUESTION 9

Continue to assume that $r_f$ = 3% per half-year, that at-the-money calls sell for $50, and that the market index is at 1,000. What would be the multiplier for 6-month bullish equity-linked CDs offering a guaranteed minimum return of .5% over the term of the CD?

## 20.7   EXOTIC OPTIONS

Options markets have been tremendously successful. Investors clearly value the portfolio strategies made possible by trading options; this is reflected in the heavy trading volume in these markets. Success breeds imitation, and in recent years we have witnessed considerable innovation in the range of option instruments available to investors. Part of this innovation has occurred in the market for customized options, which now trade in active over-the-counter markets. Many of these options have terms that would have been highly unusual even a few years ago; they are therefore called "exotic options." In this section we survey some of the more interesting variants of these new instruments.

**Asian Options**   You already have been introduced to American and European style options. Asian style options are options with payoffs that depend on the *average* price of the underlying asset during at least some portion of the life of the option. For example, an Asian call option may have a payoff equal to the average stock price over the last 3 months minus the strike price if that value is positive, and zero otherwise. These options may be of interest, for example, to firms that wish to hedge a profit stream that depends on the average price of a commodity over some period of time.

**Barrier Options**   Barrier options have payoffs that depend not only on some asset price at option expiration, but also on whether the underlying asset price has crossed through some "barrier." For example, a down-and-out option is one type of barrier option that automatically expires worthless if and when the stock price falls below some barrier price. Similarly, down-and-in options will not provide a payoff unless the stock price *does* fall below some barrier at least once during the life of the option. These options also are referred to as knock-out and knock-in options.

**Lookback Options**   Lookback options have payoffs that depend in part on the minimum or maximum price of the underlying asset during the life of the option. For example, a lookback call option might provide a payoff equal to the *maximum* stock price during the life of the option minus the exercise price, instead of the *final* stock price minus the exercise price. Such an option provides (for a price, of course) a form of perfect market timing, providing the call holder with a payoff equal to the one that would accrue if the asset were purchased for $X$ dollars and later sold at what turns out to be its high price.

**Currency-Translated Options**   Currency-translated options have either asset or exercise prices denominated in a foreign currency. A good example of such an option is the *quanto*, which allows an investor to fix in advance the exchange rate at which an investment in a foreign currency can be converted back into dollars. The right to translate a fixed amount of foreign currency into dollars at a given exchange rate is a simple foreign exchange option. Quantos are more interesting, however, because the amount of currency that will be translated into dollars depends on the investment performance of the foreign security. Therefore, a quanto in effect provides a *random number* of options.

**Binary Options** Binary, or "bet," options have fixed payoffs that depend on whether a condition is satisfied by the price of the underlying asset. For example, a binary call option might pay off a fixed amount of $100 if the stock price at maturity exceeds the exercise price.

## SUMMARY

1. A call option is the right to buy an asset at an agreed-upon exercise price. A put option is the right to sell an asset at a given exercise price.

2. American style options allow exercise on or before the exercise date. European options allow exercise only on the expiration date. Most traded options are American in nature.

3. Options are traded on stocks, stock indexes, foreign currencies, fixed-income securities, and several futures contracts.

4. Options can be used either to lever up an investor's exposure to an asset price or to provide insurance against volatility of asset prices. Popular option strategies include covered calls, protective puts, straddles, spreads, and collars.

5. The put-call parity theorem relates the prices of put and call options. If the relationship is violated, arbitrage opportunities will result. Specifically, the relationship that must be satisfied is

$$P = C - S_0 + PV(X) + PV(\text{dividends})$$

where $X$ is the exercise price of both the call and the put options, $PV(X)$ is the present value of a claim to $X$ dollars to be paid at the expiration date of the options and $PV(\text{dividends})$ is the present value of dividends to be paid before option expiration.

6. Many commonly traded securities embody option characteristics. Examples of these securities are callable bonds, convertible bonds, and warrants. Other arrangements such as collateralized loans and limited-liability borrowing can be analyzed as conveying implicit options to one or more parties.

7. Trading in so-called exotic options now takes place in an active over-the-counter market.

## KEY TERMS

| | | |
|---|---|---|
| call option | at the money | spread |
| exercise or strike price | American option | collar |
| premium | European option | put-call parity theorem |
| put option | protective put | warrant |
| in the money | covered call | |
| out of the money | straddle | |

## WEBSITES

www.cboe.com/Home/Default.asp
The Chicago Board Options Exchange site is an excellent site for learning how options are used in risk management.

www.amex.com
The American Stock Exchange has excellent general information on options. Link to Options, and then to Education.

## WEBSITES

www.cme.com
The Chicago Mercantile Exchange offers excellent information on options and futures.
See the Getting Started and Education links.

www.duke.edu/~charvey/Classes/glossary/g_index.htm
This site offers a glossary of option terms.

www.nymex.com/jsp/index.jsp
This is the New York Mercantile Exchange website. Review the Reference links.

commoditytrader.net
Access information on commodities, options, and futures.

www.optionscentral.com
The Options Industry Council site contains extensive educational material, including access to an Options Toolbox. The toolbox is an excellent source that allows you to simulate different options positions and examine the pricing of options.

www.numa.com
www.phlx.com/educat/index.html (Philadelphia Stock Exchange)
The two sites above have extensive links to many derivatives-related websites.

The following are exchange sites:
www.cme.com
www.amex.com
www.cboe.com
www.nasdaq.com
www.cbt.com
www.numa.com/ref/exchange.htm. (This site offers links to options and futures exchanges around the world.)

## PROBLEMS

1. Turn back to Figure 20.1, which lists prices of various Microsoft options. Use the data in the figure to calculate the payoff and the profits for investments in each of the following July maturity options, assuming that the stock price on the maturity date is $25.
   a. Call option, $X = \$22.50$.
   b. Put option, $X = \$22.50$.
   c. Call option, $X = \$25$.
   d. Put option, $X = \$25$.
   e. Call option, $X = \$27.50$.
   f. Put option, $X = \$27.50$.

2. Suppose you think Wal-Mart stock is going to appreciate substantially in value in the next 6 months. Say the stock's current price, $S_0$, is $100, and the call option expiring in 6 months has an exercise price, $X$, of $100 and is selling at a price, $C$, of $10. With $10,000 to invest, you are considering three alternatives.

a.  Invest all $10,000 in the stock, buying 100 shares.

b.  Invest all $10,000 in 1,000 options (10 contracts).

c.  Buy 100 options (one contract) for $1,000, and invest the remaining $9,000 in a money market fund paying 4% in interest over 6 months (8% per year).

What is your rate of return for each alternative for the following four stock prices 6 months from now? Summarize your results in the table and diagram below.

| | Price of Stock 6 Months from Now | | | |
|---|---|---|---|---|
| | $80 | $100 | $110 | $120 |
| a.  All stocks (100 shares) | | | | |
| b.  All options (1,000 shares) | | | | |
| c.  Bills + 100 options | | | | |

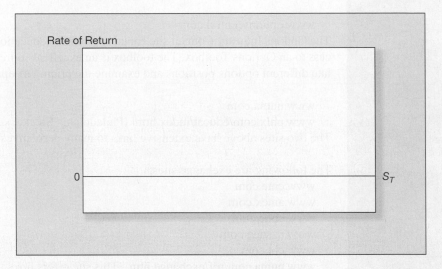

3.  The common stock of the P.U.T.T. Corporation has been trading in a narrow price range for the past month, and you are convinced it is going to break far out of that range in the next 3 months. You do not know whether it will go up or down, however. The current price of the stock is $100 per share, and the price of a 3-month call option at an exercise price of $100 is $10.

a.  If the risk-free interest rate is 10% per year, what must be the price of a 3-month put option on P.U.T.T. stock at an exercise price of $100? (The stock pays no dividends.)

b.  What would be a simple options strategy to exploit your conviction about the stock price's future movements? How far would it have to move in either direction for you to make a profit on your initial investment?

4.  The common stock of the C.A.L.L. Corporation has been trading in a narrow range around $50 per share for months, and you believe it is going to stay in that range for the next 3 months. The price of a 3-month put option with an exercise price of $50 is $4.

a.  If the risk-free interest rate is 10% per year, what must be the price of a 3-month call option on C.A.L.L. stock at an exercise price of $50 if it is at the money? (The stock pays no dividends.)

b.  What would be a simple options strategy using a put and a call to exploit your conviction about the stock price's future movement? What is the most money you can make on this position? How far can the stock price move in either direction before you lose money?

   *c.* How can you create a position involving a put, a call, and riskless lending that would have the same payoff structure as the stock at expiration? What is the net cost of establishing that position now?

5. In this problem, we derive the put-call parity relationship for European options on stocks that pay dividends before option expiration. For simplicity, assume that the stock makes one dividend payment of $D per share at the expiration date of the option.

   *a.* What is the value of a stock-plus-put position on the expiration date of the option?

   *b.* Now consider a portfolio comprising a call option and a zero-coupon bond with the same maturity date as the option and with face value $(X + D)$. What is the value of this portfolio on the option expiration date? You should find that its value equals that of the stock-plus-put portfolio regardless of the stock price.

   *c.* What is the cost of establishing the two portfolios in parts (*a*) and (*b*)? Equate the costs of these portfolios, and you will derive the put-call parity relationship, equation 20.2.

6. *a.* A butterfly spread is the purchase of one call at exercise price $X_1$, the sale of two calls at exercise price $X_2$, and the purchase of one call at exercise price $X_3$. $X_1$ is less than $X_2$, and $X_2$ is less than $X_3$ by equal amounts, and all calls have the same expiration date. Graph the payoff diagram to this strategy.

   *b.* A vertical combination is the purchase of a call with exercise price $X_2$ and a put with exercise price $X_1$, with $X_2$ greater than $X_1$. Graph the payoff to this strategy.

7. A bearish spread is the purchase of a call with exercise price $X_2$ and the sale of a call with exercise price $X_1$, with $X_2$ greater than $X_1$. Graph the payoff to this strategy and compare it to Figure 20.11.

8. Joseph Jones, a manager at Computer Science, Inc. (CSI), received 10,000 shares of company stock as part of his compensation package. The stock currently sells at $40 a share. Joseph would like to defer selling the stock until the next tax year. In January, however, he will need to sell all his holdings to provide for a down payment on his new house. Joseph is worried about the price risk involved in keeping his shares. At current prices, he would receive $400,000 for the stock. If the value of his stock holdings falls below $350,000, his ability to come up with the necessary down payment would be jeopardized. On the other hand, if the stock value rises to $450,000, he would be able to maintain a small cash reserve even after making the down payment. Joseph considers three investment strategies:

   *a.* Strategy A is to write January call options on the CSI shares with strike price $45. These calls are currently selling for $3 each.

   *b.* Strategy B is to buy January put options on CSI with strike price $35. These options also sell for $3 each.

   *c.* Strategy C is to establish a zero-cost collar by writing the January calls and buying the January puts.

Evaluate each of these strategies with respect to Joseph's investment goals. What are the advantages and disadvantages of each? Which would you recommend?

9. You are attempting to formulate an investment strategy. On the one hand, you think there is great upward potential in the stock market and would like to participate in the upward move if it materializes. However, you are not able to afford substantial stock market losses and so cannot run the risk of a stock market collapse, which

you also think is a possibility. Your investment adviser suggests a protective put position: Buy both shares in a market index stock fund and put options on those shares with 3-month maturity and exercise price of $780. The stock index fund is currently selling for $900. However, your uncle suggests you instead buy a 3-month call option on the index fund with exercise price $840 and buy 3-month T-bills with face value $840.

a. On the same graph, draw the *payoffs* to each of these strategies as a function of the stock fund value in 3 months. (Hint: Think of the options as being on one "share" of the stock index fund, with the current price of each share of the fund equal to $900.)

b. Which portfolio must require a greater initial outlay to establish? (Hint: Does either portfolio provide a final payout that is always at least as great as the payoff of the other portfolio?)

c. Suppose the market prices of the securities are as follows:

| | |
|---|---|
| Stock fund | $900 |
| T-bill (face value $840) | $810 |
| Call (exercise price $840) | $120 |
| Put (exercise price $780) | $ 6 |

Make a table of the profits realized for each portfolio for the following values of the stock price in 3 months: $S_T = $700, $840, $900, $960.

Graph the profits to each portfolio as a function of $S_T$ on a single graph.

d. Which strategy is riskier? Which should have a higher beta?

e. Explain why the data for the securities given in part (c) do *not* violate the put-call parity relationship.

**CFA® PROBLEMS**

10. Donna Donie, CFA, has a client who believes the common stock price of TRT Materials (currently $58 per share) could move substantially in either direction in reaction to an expected court decision involving the company. The client currently owns no TRT shares, but asks Donie for advice about implementing a strangle strategy to capitalize on the possible stock price movement. A strangle is a portfolio of a put and a call with different exercise prices but the same expiration date. Donie gathers the TRT option pricing data shown on the following page:

| Characteristic | Call Option | Put Option |
|---|---|---|
| Price | $ 5 | $ 4 |
| Strike Price | $60 | $55 |
| Time to expiration | 90 days from now | 90 days from now |

a. Recommend whether Donie should choose a long strangle strategy or a short strangle strategy to achieve the client's objective.

b. Calculate, at expiration for the appropriate strangle strategy in part a, the:
   i. Maximum possible loss per share.
   ii. Maximum possible gain per share.
   iii. Breakeven stock price(s).

11. The agricultural price support system guarantees farmers a minimum price for their output. Describe the program provisions as an option. What is the asset? The exercise price?

12. In what ways is owning a corporate bond similar to writing a put option? A call option?

13. An executive compensation scheme might provide a manager a bonus of $1,000 for every dollar by which the company's stock price exceeds some cutoff level. In what way is this arrangement equivalent to issuing the manager call options on the firm's stock?

14. Martin Bowman is preparing a report distinguishing traditional debt securities from structured note securities. Discuss how the following structured note securities differ from a traditional debt security with respect to coupon and principal payments:
    i. Equity index-linked notes.
    ii. Commodity- linked bear bond.

15. Consider the following options portfolio. You write a March maturity call option on Microsoft with exercise price 25. You write a March Microsoft put option with exercise price 22.50.

    a. Graph the payoff of this portfolio at option expiration as a function of Microsoft's stock price at that time.
    b. What will be the profit/loss on this position if Microsoft is selling at 23 on the option maturity date? What if Microsoft is selling at 30? Use *The Wall Street Journal* listing from Figure 20.1 to answer this question.
    c. At what two stock prices will you just break even on your investment?
    d. What kind of "bet" is this investor making; that is, what must this investor believe about Microsoft's stock price to justify this position?

16. Consider the following portfolio. You write a put option with exercise price 90 and buy a put option on the same stock with the same maturity date with exercise price 95.

    a. Plot the value of the portfolio at the maturity date of the options.
    b. On the same graph, plot the profit of the portfolio. Which option must cost more?

17. A Ford put option with strike price 60 trading on the Acme options exchange sells for $2. To your amazement, a Ford put with the same maturity selling on the Apex options exchange but with strike price 62 also sells for $2. If you plan to hold the options positions to maturity, devise a zero-net-investment arbitrage strategy to exploit the pricing anomaly. Draw the profit diagram at maturity for your position.

18. Using the Microsoft option prices in Figure 20.1, calculate the market price of a riskless zero-coupon bond with face value $23.75 that matures in July on the same date as the listed options.

19. You buy a share of stock, write a 1-year call option with $X = \$10$, and buy a 1-year put option with $X = \$10$. Your net outlay to establish the entire portfolio is $9.50. What is the risk-free interest rate? The stock pays no dividends.

20. Demonstrate that an at-the-money call option on a given stock must cost more than an at-the-money put option on that stock with the same maturity. (Hint: Use put-call parity.)

21. You write a put option with $X = 100$ and buy a put with $X = 110$. The puts are on the same stock and have the same maturity date.

    a. Draw the payoff graph for this strategy.
    b. Draw the profit graph for this strategy.
    c. If the underlying stock has positive beta, does this portfolio have positive or negative beta?

22. Joe Finance has just purchased a stock index fund, currently selling at $400 per share. To protect against losses, Joe also purchased an at-the-money European put option on the fund for $20, with exercise price $400, and 3-month time to expiration. Sally Calm, Joe's financial adviser, points out that Joe is spending a lot of

money on the put. She notes that 3-month puts with strike prices of $390 cost only $15, and suggests that Joe use the cheaper put.

*a.* Analyze Joe's and Sally's strategies by drawing the *profit* diagrams for the stock-plus-put positions for various values of the stock fund in 3 months.

*b.* When does Sally's strategy do better? When does it do worse?

*c.* Which strategy entails greater systematic risk?

23. You write a call option with $X = 50$ and buy a call with $X = 60$. The options are on the same stock and have the same maturity date. One of the calls sells for $3; the other sells for $9.

*a.* Draw the payoff graph for this strategy at the option maturity date.

*b.* Draw the profit graph for this strategy.

*c.* What is the break-even point for this strategy? Is the investor bullish or bearish on the stock?

24. Devise a portfolio using only call options and shares of stock with the following value (payoff) at the option maturity date. If the stock price is currently 53, what kind of bet is the investor making?

25. Suresh Singh, CFA, is analyzing a convertible bond. The characteristics of the bond and the underlying common stock are given in the following exhibit:

**Convertible Bond Characteristics**

| | |
|---|---|
| Par value | $1,000 |
| Annual coupon rate (annual pay) | 6.5% |
| Conversion ratio | 22 |
| Market price | 105% of par value |
| Straight value | 99% of par value |

**Underlying Stock Characteristics**

| | |
|---|---|
| Current market price | $40 per share |
| Annual cash dividend | $1.20 per share |

Compute the bond's:

  i. Conversion value.

  ii. Market conversion price.

26. Rich McDonald, CFA, is evaluating his investment alternatives in Ytel Incorporated by analyzing a Ytel convertible bond and Ytel common equity. Characteristics of the two securities are given in the following exhibit:

| Characteristics | Convertible Bond | Common Equity |
|---|---|---|
| Par value | $1,000 | — |
| Coupon (annual payment) | 4% | — |
| Current market price | $980 | $35 per share |
| Straight bond value | $925 | — |
| Conversion ratio | 25 | — |
| Conversion option | At any time | — |
| Dividend | — | $0 |
| Expected market price in 1 year | $1,125 | $45 per share |

a. Calculate, based on the exhibit the:
   i. Current market conversion price for the Ytel convertible bond.
   ii. Expected 1-year rate of return for the Ytel convertible bond.
   iii. Expected 1-year rate of return for the Ytel common equity.

One year has passed and Ytel's common equity price has increased to $51 per share. Also, over the year, the interest rate on Ytel's nonconvertible bonds of the same maturity increased, while credit spreads remained unchanged.

b. Name the two components of the convertible bond's value. Indicate whether the value of each component should decrease, stay the same, or increase in response to the:
   i. Increase in Ytel's common equity price.
   ii. Increase in interest rates.

27. The following questions appeared in past CFA Level I examinations.

a. Consider a bullish spread option strategy using a call option with a $25 exercise price priced at $4 and a call option with a $40 exercise price priced at $2.50. If the price of the stock increases to $50 at expiration and the option is exercised on the expiration date, the net profit per share at expiration (ignoring transaction costs) is:
   i. $8.50
   ii. $13.50
   iii. $16.50
   iv. $23.50

b. A put on XYZ stock with a strike price of $40 is priced at $2.00 per share, while a call with a strike price of $40 is priced at $3.50. What is the maximum per-share loss to the writer of the uncovered put and the maximum per-share gain to the writer of the uncovered call?

| | Maximum Loss to Put Writer | Maximum Gain to Call Writer |
|---|---|---|
| i. | $38.00 | $ 3.50 |
| ii. | $38.00 | $36.50 |
| iii. | $40.00 | $ 3.50 |
| iv. | $40.00 | $40.00 |

**1.** Look back at the March 2003 expiration Microsoft call and put options, discussed in Examples 20.1 and 20.2 of the chapter. Then go to **www.mhhe.com/business/finance/edumarketinsight**. Using the *Monthly Adjusted Prices* Excel Analytic report (closing prices), were these options ever in the money?

---

**E-INVESTMENTS**
**Options and Straddles**

Go to **www.nasdaq.com** and enter EMC in the quote section and obtain an information quote. Once you have the information quote, request the information on options. You will be able to access the prices and market characteristics for all put and call options for EMC. Select the two expiration months that follow the closest expiration month and obtain the prices for the calls and puts that are closest to being at the money. For example, if you are in February, you would select the April and July expirations. If the price of EMC was $56.40, you would choose the options with the 55 strike or exercise price. Answer the following questions.

What are the prices for the put and call with the nearest expiration date?

What would be the cost of a straddle using the above options?

At expiration, what would be the break-even stock prices for the above straddle?

What would be the percentage increase or decrease in the stock price required to break even?

What are the prices for the put and call with a later expiration date?

What would be the cost of a straddle using the later expiration date?

At expiration, what would be the break-even stock prices for the above straddle?

What would be the percentage increase or decrease in the stock price required to break even?

---

**SOLUTIONS TO CONCEPT CHECKS**

1. *a.* Denote the stock price at option expiration by $S_T$, and the exercise price by $X$. Value at expiration = $S_T - X = S_T - \$22.50$ if this value is positive; otherwise the call expires worthless.

Profit = Final value − Price of call option = Proceeds − $1.15.

|  | $S_T = \$20$ | $S_T = \$25$ |
|---|---|---|
| Proceeds | $0 | $2.50 |
| Profits | −$1.15 | $1.35 |

*b.* Value at expiration = $X - S_T = \$22.50 - S_T$ if this value is positive; otherwise the put expires worthless.

Profit = Final value − Price of put option = Proceeds − $.55.

|            | $S_T = \$20$ | $S_T = \$25$ |
|------------|--------------|--------------|
| Proceeds   | $2.50        | $0           |
| Profits    | $1.95        | -$.55        |

2. Before the split, the final payoff would have been $100 \times (\$25 - \$22.50) = \$250$. After the split, the payoff is $200 \times (\$12.50 - \$11.25) = \$250$. The payoff is unaffected.

3. *a.*

**SOLUTIONS TO CONCEPT CHECKS** *(Continued)*

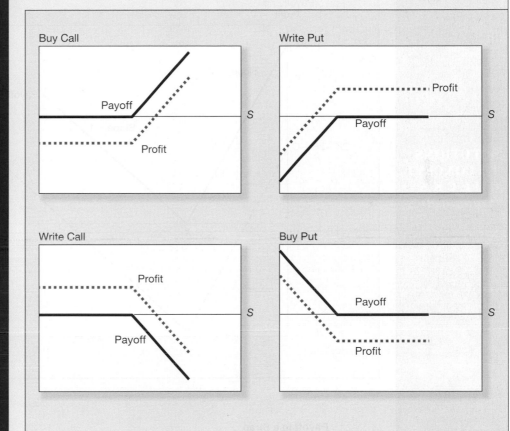

  *b.* The payoffs and profits to both buying calls and writing puts generally are higher when the stock price is higher. In this sense, both positions are bullish. Both involve potentially taking delivery of the stock. However, the call holder will *choose* to take delivery when the stock price is high, while the put writer *is obligated* to take delivery when the stock price is low.
  *c.* The payoffs and profits to both writing calls and buying puts generally are higher when the stock price is lower. In this sense, both positions are bearish. Both involve potentially making delivery of the stock. However, the put holder will *choose* to make delivery when the stock price is low, while the call writer *is obligated* to make delivery when the stock price is high.

**SOLUTIONS
TO CONCEPT
CHECKS**
*(Continued)*

4.

**Payoff to a Strip**

|  | $S_T \leq X$ | $S_T > X$ |
|---|---|---|
| 2 Puts | $2(X - S_T)$ | 0 |
| 1 Call | 0 | $S_T - X$ |

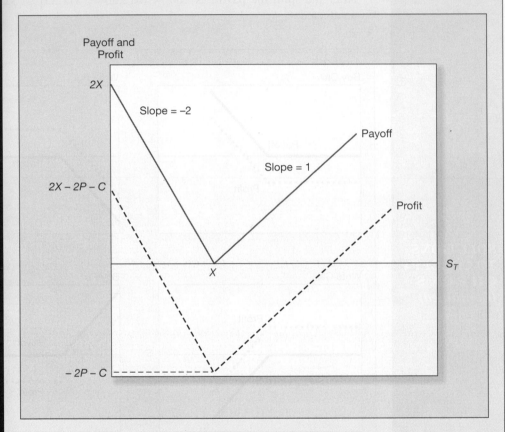

**Payoff to a Strap**

|  | $S_T \leq X$ | $S_T > X$ |
|---|---|---|
| 1 Put | $X - S_T$ | 0 |
| 2 Calls | 0 | $2(S_T - X)$ |

**SOLUTIONS
TO CONCEPT
CHECKS**
*(Continued)*

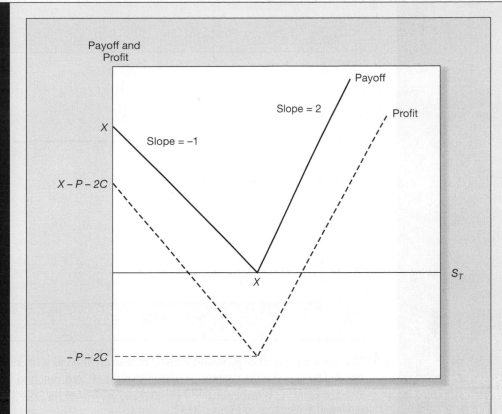

5. The payoff table on a per share basis is as follows:

| | $S_T \leq 90$ | $90 \leq S_T \leq 110$ | $S_T > 110$ |
|---|---|---|---|
| Buy put (X = 90) | $90 - S_T$ | 0 | 0 |
| Share | $S_T$ | $S_T$ | $S_T$ |
| Write call (X = 110) | 0 | 0 | $-(S_T - 110)$ |
| *TOTAL* | 90 | $S_T$ | 110 |

The graph of the payoff is as follows. If you multiply the per share values by 2,000, you will see that the collar provides a minimum payoff of $180,000 (representing a maximum loss of $20,000) and a maximum payoff of $220,000 (which is the cost of the house).

**SOLUTIONS
TO CONCEPT
CHECKS**
*(Concluded)*

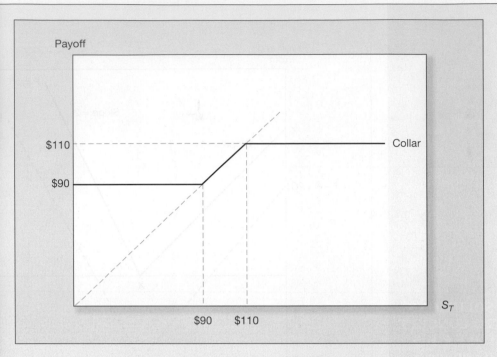

6. The covered call strategy would consist of a straight bond with a call written on the bond. The value of the strategy at option expiration as a function of the value of the straight bond is given by the solid colored payoff line in the figure following, which is virtually identical to Figure 20.12.

7. The call option is worth less as call protection is expanded. Therefore, the coupon rate need not be as high.

8. Lower. Investors will accept a lower coupon rate in return for the conversion option.

9. The depositor's implicit cost per dollar invested is now only ($.03 − $.005)/1.03 = $.02427 per 6-month period. Calls cost 50/1,000 = $.05 per dollar invested in the index. The multiplier falls to .02427/.05 = .4854.

# OPTION VALUATION

In the previous chapter we examined option markets and strategies. We noted that many securities contain embedded options that affect both their values and their risk–return characteristics. In this chapter, we turn our attention to option valuation issues. To understand most option valuation models requires considerable mathematical and statistical background. Still, many of the ideas and insights of these models can be demonstrated in simple examples, and we will concentrate on these.

We start with a discussion of the factors that ought to affect option prices. After this discussion, we present several bounds within which option prices must lie. Next we turn to quantitative models, starting with a simple "two-state" option valuation model, and then showing how this approach can be generalized into a useful and accurate pricing tool. We then move on to one particular valuation formula, the famous Black-Scholes model, one of the most significant break-throughs in finance theory in the past three decades. Finally, we look at some of the more important applications of option-pricing theory in portfolio management and control.

## 21.1   OPTION VALUATION: INTRODUCTION

**Intrinsic
and Time Values**
Consider a call option that is out of the money at the moment, with the stock price below the exercise price. This does not mean the option is valueless. Even though immediate exercise today would be unprofitable, the call retains a positive value because there is always a chance the stock price will increase sufficiently by the expiration date to allow for profitable exercise. If not, the worst that can happen is that the option will expire with zero value.

The value $S_0 - X$ is sometimes called the **intrinsic value** of in-the-money call options because it gives the payoff that could be obtained by immediate exercise. Intrinsic value is set equal to zero for out-of-the-money or at-the-money options. The difference between the actual call price and the intrinsic value is commonly called the *time value* of the option.

"Time value" is an unfortunate choice of terminology, because it may confuse the option's time value with the time value of money. Time value in the options context refers simply to the difference between the option's price and the value the option would have if it were expiring immediately. It is the part of the option's value that may be attributed to the fact that it still has positive time to expiration.

Most of an option's time value typically is a type of "volatility value." As long as the option holder can choose not to exercise, the payoff cannot be worse than zero. Even if a call option is out of the money now, it still will sell for a positive price because it offers the potential for a profit if the stock price increases, while imposing no risk of additional loss should the stock price fall. The volatility value lies in the value of the right *not* to exercise the call if that action would be unprofitable. The option to exercise, as opposed to the obligation to exercise, provides insurance against poor stock price performance.

As the stock price increases substantially, it becomes more likely that the call option will be exercised by expiration. In this case, with exercise all but assured, the volatility value becomes minimal. As the stock price gets ever larger, the option value approaches the "adjusted" intrinsic value, the stock price minus the present value of the exercise price, $S_0 - PV(X)$.

Why should this be? If you are virtually certain the option will be exercised and the stock purchased for $X$ dollars, it is as though you own the stock already. The stock certificate, with a value today of $S_0$, might as well be sitting in your safe-deposit box now, as it will be there in only a few months. You just haven't paid for it yet. The present value of your obligation is the present value of $X$, so the net value of the call option is $S_0 - PV(X)$.[1]

Figure 21.1 illustrates the call option valuation function. The value curve shows that when the stock price is very low, the option is nearly worthless, because there is almost no chance that it will be exercised. When the stock price is very high, the option value approaches adjusted intrinsic value. In the midrange case, where the option is approximately at the money, the option curve diverges from the straight lines corresponding to adjusted intrinsic value. This is because although exercise today would have a negligible (or negative) payoff, the volatility value of the option is quite high in this region.

The option always increases in value with the stock price. The slope is greatest, however, when the option is deep in the money. In this case, exercise is all but assured, and the option increases in price one for one with the stock price.

---

[1] This discussion presumes that the stock pays no dividends until after option expiration. If the stock does pay dividends before maturity, then there *is* a reason you would care about getting the stock now rather than at expiration—getting it now entitles you to the interim dividend payments. In this case, the adjusted intrinsic value of the option must subtract the value of the dividends the stock will pay out before the call is exercised. Adjusted intrinsic value would more generally be defined as $S_0 - PV(X) - PV(D)$ where $D$ is the dividend to be paid before option expiration.

**Figure 21.1   Call option value before expiration**

## Determinants of Option Values

We can identify at least six factors that should affect the value of a call option: the stock price, the exercise price, the volatility of the stock price, the time to expiration, the interest rate, and the dividend rate of the stock. The call option should increase in value with the stock price and decrease in value with the exercise price because the payoff to a call, if exercised, equals $S_T - X$. The magnitude of the expected payoff from the call increases with the difference $S_0 - X$.

Call option values also increase with the volatility of the underlying stock price. To see why, consider circumstances where possible stock prices at expiration may range from $10 to $50 compared to a situation where stock prices may range only from $20 to $40. In both cases, the expected, or average, stock price will be $30. Suppose the exercise price on a call option is also $30. What are the option payoffs?

**High-Volatility Scenario**

| Stock price | $10 | $20 | $30 | $40 | $50 |
|---|---|---|---|---|---|
| Option payoff | 0 | 0 | 0 | 10 | 20 |

**Low-Volatility Scenario**

| Stock price | $20 | $25 | $30 | $35 | $40 |
|---|---|---|---|---|---|
| Option payoff | 0 | 0 | 0 | 5 | 10 |

If each outcome is equally likely, with probability .2, the expected payoff to the option under high-volatility conditions will be $6, but under low-volatility conditions the expected payoff to the call option is half as much, only $3.

Despite the fact that the average stock price in each scenario is $30, the average option payoff is greater in the high-volatility scenario. The source of this extra value is the limited loss an option holder can suffer, or the volatility value of the call. No matter how far below $30 the stock price drops, the option holder will get zero. Obviously, extremely poor stock price performance is no worse for the call option holder than moderately poor performance.

In the case of good stock performance, however, the call option will expire in the money, and it will be more profitable the higher the stock price. Thus extremely good stock outcomes can improve the option payoff without limit, but extremely poor outcomes cannot worsen the payoff below zero. This asymmetry means that volatility in the underlying stock price increases the expected payoff to the option, thereby enhancing its value.

Similarly, longer time to expiration increases the value of a call option. For more distant expiration dates, there is more time for unpredictable future events to affect prices, and the range of likely stock prices increases. This has an effect similar to that of increased volatility. Moreover, as time to expiration lengthens, the present value of the exercise price falls, thereby benefiting the call option holder and increasing the option value. As a corollary to this issue, call option values are higher when interest rates rise (holding the stock price constant) because higher interest rates also reduce the present value of the exercise price.

Finally, the dividend payout policy of the firm affects option values. A high-dividend payout policy puts a drag on the rate of growth of the stock price. For any expected total rate of return on the stock, a higher dividend yield must imply a lower expected rate of capital gain. This drag on stock price appreciation decreases the potential payoff from the call option, thereby lowering the call value. Table 21.1 summarizes these relationships.

| CONCEPT CHECK☞ QUESTION 1 | Prepare a table like Table 21.1 for the determinants of put option values. How should American put values respond to increases in $S$, $X$, $\sigma$, $T$, $r_f$, and dividend payouts? |
|---|---|

## 21.2    RESTRICTIONS ON OPTION VALUES

Several quantitative models of option pricing have been devised, and we will examine some of them in this chapter. All models, however, rely on simplifying assumptions. You might wonder which properties of option values are truly general and which depend on the particular simplifications. To start with, we will consider some of the more important general properties of option prices. Some of these properties have important implications for the effect of stock dividends on option values and the possible profitability of early exercise of an American option.

**Table 21.1    Determinants of Call Option Values**

| If This Variable Increases . . . | The Value of a Call Option |
|---|---|
| Stock price, $S$ | Increases |
| Exercise price, $X$ | Decreases |
| Volatility, $\sigma$ | Increases |
| Time to expiration, $T$ | Increases |
| Interest rate, $r_f$ | Increases |
| Dividend payouts | Decreases |

## Restrictions on the Value of a Call Option

The most obvious restriction on the value of a call option is that its value cannot be negative. Because the option need not be exercised, it cannot impose any liability on its holder; moreover, as long as there is any possibility that at some point the option can be exercised profitably, the option will command a positive price. Its payoff is zero at worst, and possibly positive, so that investors are willing to pay some amount to purchase it.

We can place another lower bound on the value of a call option. Suppose that the stock will pay a dividend of $D$ dollars just before the expiration date of the option, denoted by $T$ (where today is time 0). Now compare two portfolios, one consisting of a call option on one share of stock and the other a leveraged equity position consisting of that share and borrowing of $(X + D)/(1 + r_f)^T$ dollars. The loan repayment is $X + D$ dollars, due on the expiration date of the option. For example, for a half-year maturity option with exercise price $70, dividends to be paid of $5, and effective annual interest of 10%, you would purchase one share of stock and borrow $75/(1.10)^{1/2} = \$71.51$. In 6 months, when the loan matures, the payment due is $75.

At that time, the payoff to the leveraged equity position would be

|                    | In General | Our Numbers |
|--------------------|:----------:|:-----------:|
| Stock value        | $S_T + D$  | $S_T + 5$   |
| − Payback of loan  | $-(X + D)$ | $-75$       |
| TOTAL              | $S_T - X$  | $S_T - 70$  |

where $S_T$ denotes the stock price at the option expiration date. Notice that the payoff to the stock is the ex-dividend stock value plus dividends received. Whether the total payoff to the stock-plus-borrowing position is positive or negative depends on whether $S_T$ exceeds $X$. The net cash outlay required to establish this leveraged equity position is $S_0 - \$71.51$, or, more generally, $S_0 - (X + D)/(1 + r_f)^T$, that is, the current price of the stock, $S_0$, less the initial cash inflow from the borrowing position.

The payoff to the call option will be $S_T - X$ if the option expires in the money and zero otherwise. Thus the option payoff is equal to the leveraged equity payoff when that payoff is positive and is greater when the leveraged equity position has a negative payoff. Because the option payoff is always greater than or equal to that of the leveraged equity position, the option price must exceed the cost of establishing that position.

Therefore, the value of the call must be greater than $S_0 - (X + D)/(1 + r_f)^T$, or, more generally,

$$C \geq S_0 - \text{PV}(X) - \text{PV}(D)$$

where $\text{PV}(X)$ denotes the present value of the exercise price and $\text{PV}(D)$ is the present value of the dividends the stock will pay at the option's expiration. More generally, we can interpret $\text{PV}(D)$ as the present value of any and all dividends to be paid prior to the option expiration date. Because we know already that the value of a call option must be nonnegative, we may conclude that $C$ is greater than the *maximum* of either 0 or $S_0 - \text{PV}(X) - \text{PV}(D)$.

We also can place an upper bound on the possible value of the call; this bound is simply the stock price. No one would pay more than $S_0$ dollars for the right to purchase a stock currently worth $S_0$ dollars. Thus $C \leq S_0$.

Figure 21.2 demonstrates graphically the range of prices that is ruled out by these upper and lower bounds for the value of a call option. Any option value outside the shaded area is not possible according to the restrictions we have derived. Before expiration, the call option value normally will be *within* the allowable range, touching neither the upper nor lower bound, as in Figure 21.3.

**Figure 21.2
Range of possible
call option values**

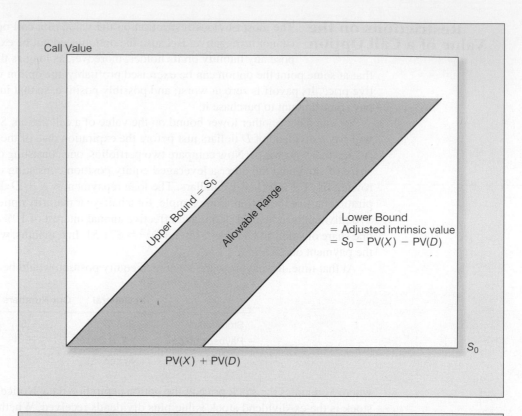

**Figure 21.3
Call option
value as a
function of
the current
stock price**

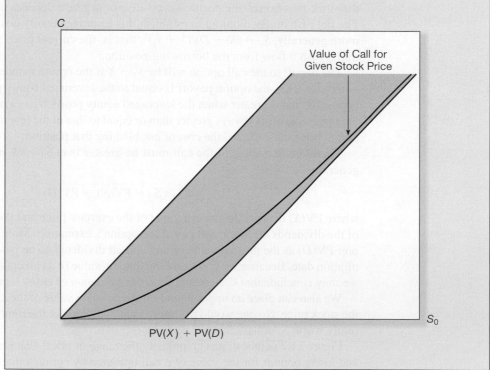

**Early Exercise and Dividends**

A call option holder who wants to close out that position has two choices: exercise the call or sell it. If the holder exercises at time $t$, the call will provide a payoff of $S_t - X$, assuming, of course, that the option is in the money. We have just seen that the option can be sold for at least $S_t - PV(X) - PV(D)$. Therefore, for an option on a non-dividend-paying stock, $C$ is greater than $S_t - PV(X)$. Because the present value of $X$ is less than $X$ itself, it follows that

$$C \geq S_t - PV(X) > S_t - X$$

The implication here is that the proceeds from a sale of the option (at price $C$) must exceed the proceeds from an exercise ($S_t - X$). It is economically more attractive to sell the call, which keeps it alive, than to exercise and thereby end the option. In other words, calls on non-dividend-paying stocks are "worth more alive than dead."

If it never pays to exercise a call option before maturity, the right to exercise early actually must be valueless. The right to exercise an American call early is irrelevant because it will never pay to exercise early. We therefore conclude that the values of otherwise identical American and European call options on stocks paying no dividends are equal. If we can find the value for the European call, we also will have found the value of the American call. This simplifies matters, because any valuation formula that applies to the European call, for which only one exercise date need be considered, also must apply to an American call.

As most stocks do pay dividends, you may wonder whether this result is just a theoretical curiosity. It is not: Reconsider our argument and you will see that all that we really require is that the stock pay no dividends *until the option expires*. This condition will be true for many real-world options.

**Early Exercise of American Puts**

For American *put options*, the optimality of early exercise is most definitely a possibility. To see why, consider a simple example. Suppose that you purchase a put option on a stock. Soon the firm goes bankrupt, and the stock price falls to zero. Of course you want to exercise now, because the stock price can fall no lower. Immediate exercise gives you immediate receipt of the exercise price, which can be invested to start generating income. Delay in exercise means a time-value-of-money cost. The right to exercise a put option before maturity must have value.

Now suppose instead that the firm is only *nearly* bankrupt, with the stock selling at just a few cents. Immediate exercise may still be optimal. After all, the stock price can fall by only a very small amount, meaning that the proceeds from future exercise cannot be more than a few cents greater than the proceeds from immediate exercise. Against this possibility of a tiny increase in proceeds must be weighed the time-value-of-money cost of deferring exercise. Clearly, there is some stock price below which early exercise is optimal.

This argument also proves that the American put must be worth more than its European counterpart. The American put allows you to exercise anytime before maturity. Because the right to exercise early may be useful in some circumstances, it will command a positive price in the capital market. The American put therefore will sell for a higher price than a European put with otherwise identical terms.

Figure 21.4A illustrates the value of an American put option as a function of the current stock price, $S_0$. Once the stock price drops below a critical value, denoted $S^*$ in the figure, exercise becomes optimal. At that point the option-pricing curve is tangent to the straight line depicting the intrinsic value of the option. If and when the stock price reaches $S^*$, the put option is exercised and its payoff equals its intrinsic value.

**Figure 21.4    Put option values as a function of the current stock price**

In contrast, the value of the European put, which is graphed in Figure 21.4B, is not asymptotic to the intrinsic value line. Because early exercise is prohibited, the maximum value of the European put is PV(X), which occurs at the point $S_0 = 0$. Obviously, for a long enough horizon, PV(X) can be made arbitrarily small.

**CONCEPT CHECK☞ QUESTION 2**

In light of this discussion, explain why the put-call parity relationship is valid only for European options on non-dividend-paying stocks. If the stock pays no dividends, what *inequality* for American options would correspond to the parity theorem?

## 21.3    BINOMIAL OPTION PRICING

**Two-State Option Pricing**    A complete understanding of commonly used option valuation formulas is difficult without a substantial mathematics background. Nevertheless, we can develop valuable insight into option valuation by considering a simple special case. Assume that a stock price can take only two possible values at option expiration: The stock will either increase to a given higher price or decrease to a given lower price. Although this may seem an extreme simplification, it allows us to come closer to understanding more complicated and realistic models. Moreover, we can extend this approach to describe far more reasonable specifications of stock price behavior. In fact, several major financial firms employ variants of this simple model to value options and securities with optionlike features.

Suppose the stock now sells at $S_0 = \$100$, and the price will either increase by a factor of $u = 2$ to $200 (u$ stands for "up") or fall by a factor of $d = .5$ to $50 (d$ stands for "down") by year-end. A call option on the stock might specify an exercise price of $125 and a time to expiration of 1 year. The interest rate is 8%. At year-end, the payoff to the holder of the call option will be either zero, if the stock falls, or $75, if the stock price goes to $200.

These possibilities are illustrated by the following value "trees":

| Stock price | Call option value |

Compare the payoff of the call to that of a portfolio consisting of one share of the stock and borrowing of $46.30 at the interest rate of 8%. The payoff of this portfolio also depends on the stock price at year-end:

|  | $50 | $200 |
|---|---|---|
| Value of stock at year-end | $50 | $200 |
| − Repayment of loan with interest | −50 | −50 |
| TOTAL | $ 0 | $150 |

We know the cash outlay to establish the portfolio is $53.70: $100 for the stock, less the $46.30 proceeds from borrowing. Therefore the portfolio's value tree is

The payoff of this portfolio is exactly twice that of the call option for either value of the stock price. In other words, two call options will exactly replicate the payoff to the portfolio; it follows that two call options should have the same price as the cost of establishing the portfolio. Hence the two calls should sell for the same price as the "replicating portfolio." Therefore,

$$2C = \$53.70$$

or each call should sell at $C = \$26.85$. Thus, given the stock price, exercise price, interest rate, and volatility of the stock price (as represented by the magnitude of the up or down movements), we can derive the fair value for the call option.

This valuation approach relies heavily on the notion of *replication*. With only two possible end-of-year values of the stock, the payoffs to the levered stock portfolio replicate the payoffs to two call options and, therefore, command the same market price. This notion of replication is behind most option-pricing formulas. For more complex price distributions for stocks, the replication technique is correspondingly more complex, but the principles remain the same.

One way to view the role of replication is to note that, using the numbers assumed for this example, a portfolio made up of one share of stock and two call options written is perfectly hedged. Its year-end value is independent of the ultimate stock price:

|  | $50 | $200 |
|---|---|---|
| Stock value | $50 | $200 |
| − Obligations from 2 calls written | −0 | −150 |
| Net payoff | $50 | $ 50 |

The investor has formed a riskless portfolio, with a payout of $50. Its value must be the present value of $50, or $50/1.08 = $46.30. The value of the portfolio, which equals $100 from the stock held long, minus $2C$ from the two calls written, should equal $46.30. Hence $100 − 2C = \$46.30$, or $C = \$26.85$.

The ability to create a perfect hedge is the key to this argument. The hedge locks in the end-of-year payout, which can be discounted using the risk-free interest rate. To find the value of the option in terms of the value of the stock, we do not need to know either the option's or the stock's beta or expected rate of return. The perfect hedging, or replication, approach enables us to express the value of the option in terms of the current value of the stock without this information. With a hedged position, the final stock price does not affect the investor's payoff, so the stock's risk and return parameters have no bearing.

The hedge ratio of this example is one share of stock to two calls, or one-half. For every call option written, one-half share of stock must be held in the portfolio to hedge away risk. This ratio has an easy interpretation in this context: It is the ratio of the range of the values of the option to those of the stock across the two possible outcomes. The stock, which originally sells for $S_0 = 100$, will be worth either $d \times \$100 = \$50$ or $u \times \$100 = \$200$, for a range of $150. If the stock price increases, the call will be worth $C_u = \$75$, whereas if the stock price decreases, the call will be worth $C_d = 0$, for a range of $75. The ratio of ranges, 75/150, is one-half, which is the hedge ratio we have established.

The hedge ratio equals the ratio of ranges because the option and stock are perfectly correlated in this two-state example. When the returns of the option and stock are perfectly correlated, a perfect hedge requires that the option and stock be held in a fraction determined only by relative volatility.

We can generalize the hedge ratio for other two-state option problems as

$$H = \frac{C_u - C_d}{uS_0 - dS_0}$$

where $C_u$ or $C_d$ refers to the call option's value when the stock goes up or down, respectively, and $uS_0$ and $dS_0$ are the stock prices in the two states. The hedge ratio, $H$, is the ratio of the swings in the possible end-of-period values of the option and the stock. If the investor writes one option and holds $H$ shares of stock, the value of the portfolio will be unaffected by the stock price. In this case, option pricing is easy: Simply set the value of the hedged portfolio equal to the present value of the known payoff.

Using our example, the option-pricing technique would proceed as follows:

1. Given the possible end-of-year stock prices, $uS_0 = 200$ and $dS_0 = 50$, and the exercise price of 125, calculate that $C_u = 75$ and $C_d = 0$. The stock price range is 150, while the option price range is 75.
2. Find that the hedge ratio of 75/150 = .5.
3. Find that a portfolio made up of .5 share with one written option would have an end-of-year value of $25 with certainty.
4. Show that the present value of $25 with a 1-year interest rate of 8% is $23.15.
5. Set the value of the hedged position to the present value of the certain payoff:

$$.5S_0 - C_0 = \$23.15$$
$$\$50 - C_0 = \$23.15$$

6. Solve for the call's value, $C_0 = \$26.85$.

What if the option were overpriced, perhaps selling for $30? Then you can make arbitrage profits. Here is how:

| | Initial Cash Flow | Cash Flow in 1 Year for Each Possible Stock Price | |
| --- | --- | --- | --- |
| | | $S_1 = 50$ | $S_1 = 200$ |
| 1. Write 2 options | $ 60 | $ 0 | $−150 |
| 2. Purchase 1 share | −100 | 50 | 200 |
| 3. Borrow $40 at 8% interest | 40 | −43.20 | −43.20 |
| Repay in 1 year | | | |
| TOTAL | $ 0 | $ 6.80 | $ 6.80 |

Although the net initial investment is zero, the payoff in 1 year is positive and riskless. If the option were underpriced, one would simply reverse this arbitrage strategy: Buy the option, and sell the stock short to eliminate price risk. Note, by the way, that the present value of the profit to the arbitrage strategy above exactly equals twice the amount by which the option is overpriced. The present value of the risk-free profit of $6.80 at an 8% interest rate is $6.30. With two options written in the strategy above, this translates to a profit of $3.15 per option, exactly the amount by which the option was overpriced: $30 versus the "fair value" of $26.85.

| CONCEPT CHECK ☞ QUESTION 3 | Suppose the call option had been underpriced, selling at $24. Formulate the arbitrage strategy to exploit the mispricing, and show that it provides a riskless cash flow in 1 year of $3.08 per option purchased. |

### Generalizing the Two-State Approach

Although the two-state stock price model seems simplistic, we can generalize it to incorporate more realistic assumptions. To start, suppose we were to break up the year into two 6-month segments, and then assert that over each half-year segment the stock price could take on two values. Here we will say it can increase 10% (i.e., $u = 1.10$) or decrease 5% (i.e., $d = .95$). A stock initially selling at 100 could follow these possible paths over the course of the year:

The midrange value of 104.50 can be attained by two paths: an increase of 10% followed by a decrease of 5%, or a decrease of 5% followed by a 10% increase.

There are now three possible end-of-year values for the stock and three for the option:

Using methods similar to those we followed above, we could value $C_u$ from knowledge of $C_{uu}$ and $C_{ud}$, then value $C_d$ from knowledge of $C_{du}$ and $C_{dd}$, and finally value $C$ from knowledge of $C_u$ and $C_d$. And there is no reason to stop at 6-month intervals. We could next break the year into four 3-month units, or 12 1-month units, or 365 1-day units, each of which would be posited to have a two-state process. Although the calculations become quite numerous and correspondingly tedious, they are easy to program into a computer, and such computer programs are used widely by participants in the options market.

### EXAMPLE 21.1    Binomial Option Pricing

Suppose that the risk-free interest rate is 5% per 6-month period and we wish to value a call option with exercise price $110 on the stock described in the two-period price tree just above. We start by finding the value of $C_u$. From this point, the call can rise to an expiration-date value of $C_{uu} = $11 (since at this point the stock price is $u \times u \times S_0 = $121) or fall to a final value of $C_{ud} = 0$ (since at this point, the stock price is $u \times d \times S_0 = \$104.50$, which is less than the $110 exercise price). Therefore the hedge ratio at this point is

$$H = \frac{C_{uu} - C_{ud}}{uuS_0 - udS_0} = \frac{\$11 - 0}{\$121 - 104.50} = \frac{2}{3}$$

Thus, the following portfolio will be worth $209 at option expiration regardless of the ultimate stock price:

|  | $udS_0 = \$104.50$ | $uuS_0 = \$121$ |
|---|---|---|
| Buy 2 shares at price $uS_0 = \$110$ | $209 | $242 |
| Write 3 calls at price $C_u$ | 0 | −33 |
| TOTAL | $209 | $209 |

The portfolio must have a current market value equal to the present value of $209:

$$2 \times 110 - 3\, C_u = \$209/1.05 = \$199.047$$

Solve to find that $C_u = \$6.984$.

Next we find the value of $C_d$. It is easy to see that this value must be zero. If we reach this point (corresponding to a stock price of $95), the stock price at option maturity will be either $104.50 or $90.25; in either case, the option will expire out of the money. (More formally, we could note that with $C_{ud} = C_{dd} = 0$, the hedge ratio is zero, and a portfolio of *zero* shares will replicate the payoff of the call!)

Finally, we solve for $C$ using the values of $C_u$ and $C_d$. Concept Check 4 leads you through the calculations that show the option value to be $4.434.

As we break the year into progressively finer subintervals, the range of possible year-end stock prices expands and, in fact, will ultimately take on a familiar bell-shaped distribution. This can be seen from an analysis of the event tree for the stock for a period with three subintervals:

First, notice that as the number of subintervals increases, the number of possible stock prices also increases. Second, notice that extreme events such as $u^3 S_0$ or $d^3 S_0$ are relatively rare, as they require either three consecutive increases or decreases in the three subintervals. More moderate, or midrange, results such as $u^2 dS_0$ can be arrived at by more than one path—any combination of two price increases and one decrease will result in stock price $u^2 dS_0$. Thus the midrange values will be more likely. The probability of each outcome is described by the binomial distribution, and this multiperiod approach to option pricing is called the **binomial model.**

For example, using our initial stock price of $100, equal probability of stock price increases or decreases, and three intervals for which the possible price increase is 5% and decrease is 3%, we can obtain the probability distribution of stock prices from the following calculations. There are eight possible combinations for the stock price movements in the three periods: *uuu, uud, udu, duu, udd, dud, ddu, ddd.* Each has probability of 1/8. Therefore, the probability distribution of stock prices at the end of the last interval would be:

| Event | Probability | Final Stock Price | |
|---|---|---|---|
| 3 up movements | 1/8 | $100 \times 1.05^3$ | $= 115.76$ |
| 2 up and 1 down | 3/8 | $100 \times 1.05^2 \times .97$ | $= 106.94$ |
| 1 up and 2 down | 3/8 | $100 \times 1.05 \times .97^2$ | $= 98.79$ |
| 3 down movements | 1/8 | $100 \times .97^3$ | $= 91.27$ |

The midrange values are three times as likely to occur as the extreme values. Figure 21.5A is a graph of the frequency distribution for this example. The graph approaches the appearance of the familiar bell-shaped curve. In fact, as the number of intervals increases, as in Figure 21.5B, the frequency distribution progressively approaches the lognormal distribution rather than the normal distribution.[2]

Suppose we were to continue subdividing the interval in which stock prices are posited to move up or down. Eventually, each node of the event tree would correspond to an infinitesimally small time interval. The possible stock price movement within that time interval would be correspondingly small. As those many intervals passed, the end-of-period stock price would more and more closely resemble a lognormal distribution. Thus the apparent oversimplification of the two-state model can be overcome by progressively subdividing any period into many subperiods.

At any node, one still could set up a portfolio that would be perfectly hedged over the next tiny time interval. Then, at the end of that interval, on reaching the next node, a new hedge ratio could be computed and the portfolio composition could be revised to remain hedged over the coming small interval. By continuously revising the hedge position, the portfolio would remain hedged and would earn a riskless rate of return over each interval. This is called *dynamic hedging*, the continued updating of the hedge ratio as time passes. As the dynamic hedge becomes ever finer, the resulting option valuation procedure becomes more precise.

---

[2] Actually, more complex considerations enter here. The limit of this process is lognormal only if we assume also that stock prices move continuously, by which we mean that over small time intervals only small price movements can occur. This rules out rare events such as sudden, extreme price moves in response to dramatic information (like a takeover attempt). For a treatment of this type of "jump process," see John C. Cox and Stephen A. Ross, "The Valuation of Options for Alternative Stochastic Processes," *Journal of Financial Economics* 3 (January–March 1976), pp. 145–66, or Robert C. Merton, "Option Pricing when Underlying Stock Returns Are Discontinuous," *Journal of Financial Economics* 3 (January–March 1976), pp. 125–44.

**Figure 21.5
Probability
distributions
A. Possible
outcomes and
associated
probabilities for
stock prices after
three periods. The
stock price starts
at $100, and in
each period it can
increase by 5% or
decrease by 3%.
B, Each period is
subdivided into
two smaller
subperiods.
Now there are six
periods, and in
each of these the
stock price can
increase by 2.5%
or fall by 1.5%.
As the number of
periods increases,
the stock price
distribution
approaches the
familiar bell-
shaped curve.**

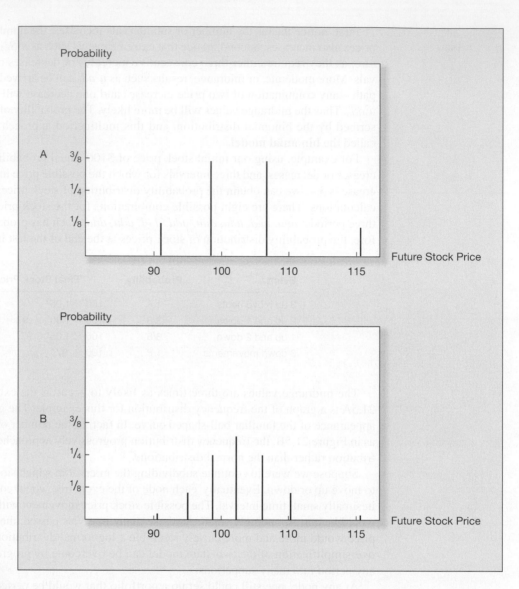

**CONCEPT
C H E C K ☞
QUESTION 5**

Would you expect the hedge ratio to be higher or lower when the call option is more in the money? (Hint: Remember that the hedge ratio is the change in the option price divided by the change in the stock price. When is the option price most sensitive to the stock price?)

## 21.4    BLACK-SCHOLES OPTION VALUATION

Although the binomial model we have described is extremely flexible, a computer is needed for it to be useful in actual trading. An option-pricing *formula* would be far easier to use than the complex algorithm involved in the binomial model. It turns out that such a formula can be derived if one is willing to make just two more assumptions: that both the risk-free interest rate and stock price volatility are constant over the life of the option.

**Figure 21.6
A standard
normal curve**

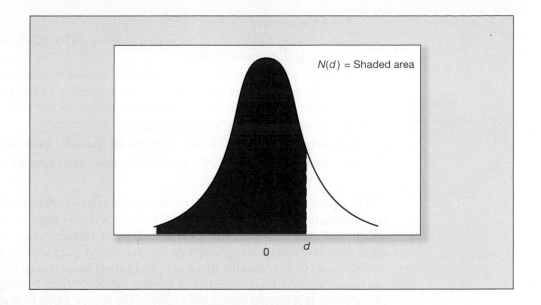

$N(d)$ = Shaded area

0    $d$

**E-INVESTMENTS
Nobel Prizes
in Financial
Economics**

Robert Merton and Myron Scholes won the Nobel Prize in Economic Sciences in 1997. (Fisher Black was deceased.) Link to **www.almaz.com/nobel/economics** and review the Nobel Prize winners since 1969. What other "finance economics" concepts (that are associated with this course) and their associated authors have won Nobel Prizes?

## The Black-Scholes Formula

Financial economists searched for years for a workable option-pricing model before Black and Scholes[3] and Merton[4] derived a formula for the value of a call option. Scholes and Merton shared the 1997 Nobel Prize in economics for their accomplishment.[5] Now widely used by options market participants, the **Black-Scholes pricing formula** for a call option is

$$C_0 = S_0 N(d_1) - X e^{-rT} N(d_2) \tag{21.1}$$

where

$$d_1 = \frac{\ln(S_0/X) + (r + \sigma^2/2)T}{\sigma\sqrt{T}}$$

$$d_2 = d_1 - \sigma\sqrt{T}$$

and where

$C_0$ = Current call option value.

$S_0$ = Current stock price.

$N(d)$ = The probability that a random draw from a standard normal distribution will be less than $d$. This equals the area under the normal curve up to $d$, as in the shaded area of Figure 21.6. In Excel, this function is called NORMSDIST ( ).

[3] Fischer Black and Myron Scholes, "The Pricing of Options and Corporate Liabilities," *Journal of Political Economy* 81 (May–June 1973).
[4] Robert C. Merton, "Theory of Rational Option Pricing," *Bell Journal of Economics and Management Science* 4 (Spring 1973).
[5] Fischer Black died in 1995.

$X$ = Exercise price.

$e$ = 2.71828, the base of the natural log function. In Excel, $e^x$ can be evaluated using the function EXP($x$).

$r$ = Risk-free interest rate (the annualized continuously compounded rate on a safe asset with the same maturity as the expiration of the option, which is to be distinguished from $r_f$, the discrete period interest rate).

$T$ = Time to maturity of option, in years.

ln = Natural logarithm function. In Excel, ln($x$) can be calculated as LN($x$).

$\sigma$ = Standard deviation of the annualized continuously compounded rate of return of the stock.

The option value does *not* depend on the expected rate of return on the stock. In a sense, this information is already built into the formula with the inclusion of the stock price, which itself depends on the stock's risk and return characteristics. This version of the Black-Scholes formula is predicated on the assumption that the stock pays no dividends.

Although you may find the Black-Scholes formula intimidating, we can explain it at a somewhat intuitive level. The trick is to view the $N(d)$ terms (loosely) as risk-adjusted probabilities that the call option will expire in the money. First, look at equation 21.1 assuming both $N(d)$ terms are close to 1.0, that is, when there is a very high probability the option will be exercised. Then the call option value is equal to $S_0 - Xe^{-rT}$, which is what we called earlier the adjusted intrinsic value, $S_0 - PV(X)$. This makes sense; if exercise is certain, we have a claim on a stock with current value $S_0$, and an obligation with present value $PV(X)$, or, with continuous compounding, $Xe^{-rT}$.

Now look at equation 21.1 assuming the $N(d)$ terms are close to zero, meaning the option almost certainly will not be exercised. Then the equation confirms that the call is worth nothing. For middle-range values of $N(d)$ between 0 and 1, equation 21.1 tells us that the call value can be viewed as the present value of the call's potential payoff adjusting for the probability of in-the-money expiration.

How do the $N(d)$ terms serve as risk-adjusted probabilities? This question quickly leads us into advanced statistics. Notice, however, that $\ln(S_0/X)$, which appears in the numerator of $d_1$ and $d_2$, is approximately the percentage amount by which the option is currently in or out of the money. For example, if $S_0 = 105$ and $X = 100$, the option is 5% in the money, and $\ln(105/100) = .049$. Similarly, if $S_0 = 95$, the option is 5% out of the money, and $\ln(95/100) = -.051$. The denominator, $\sigma\sqrt{T}$, adjusts the amount by which the option is in or out of the money for the volatility of the stock price over the remaining life of the option. An option in the money by a given percent is more likely to stay in the money if both stock price volatility and time to maturity are small. Therefore, $N(d_1)$ and $N(d_2)$ increase with the probability that the option will expire in the money.

## EXAMPLE 21.2    Black-Scholes Valuation

You can use the Black-Scholes formula fairly easily. Suppose you want to value a call option under the following circumstances:

| | |
|---|---|
| Stock price | $S_0 = 100$ |
| Exercise price | $X = 95$ |
| Interest rate | $r = .10$ (10% per year) |
| Time to expiration | $T = .25$ (one-quarter of a year) |
| Standard deviation | $\sigma = .50$ (50% per year) |

First calculate

$$d_1 = \frac{\ln(100/95) + (.10 + .5^2/2).25}{.5\sqrt{.25}} = .43$$
$$d_2 = .43 - .5\sqrt{.25} = .18$$

Next find $N(d_1)$ and $N(d_2)$. The values of the normal distribution are tabulated and may be found in many statistics textbooks. A table of $N(d)$ is provided here as Table 21.2. The normal distribution function, $N(d)$, is also provided in any spreadsheet program. In Microsoft Excel, for example, the function name is NORMSDIST. Using either Excel or Table 21.2 we find that

$$N(.43) = .6664$$
$$N(.18) = .5714$$

Thus the value of the call option is

$$C = 100 \times .6664 - 95e^{-.10 \times .25} \times .5714$$
$$= 66.64 - 52.94 = \$13.70$$

**CONCEPT CHECK☞ QUESTION 6**

**Calculate the call option value if the standard deviation on the stock were .6 instead of .5. Confirm that the option is worth more using this higher volatility.**

What if the option price in Example 21.2 were $15 rather than $13.70? Is the option mispriced? Maybe, but before betting your fortune on that, you may want to reconsider the valuation analysis. First, like all models, the Black-Scholes formula is based on some simplifying abstractions that make the formula only approximately valid.

Some of the important assumptions underlying the formula are the following:

1. The stock will pay no dividends until after the option expiration date.
2. Both the interest rate, $r$, and variance rate, $\sigma^2$, of the stock are constant (or in slightly more general versions of the formula, both are *known* functions of time—any changes are perfectly predictable).
3. Stock prices are continuous, meaning that sudden extreme jumps such as those in the aftermath of an announcement of a takeover attempt are ruled out.

Variants of the Black-Scholes formula have been developed to deal with some of these limitations.

Second, even within the context of the Black-Scholes model, you must be sure of the accuracy of the parameters used in the formula. Four of these—$S_0$, $X$, $T$, and $r$—are straightforward. The stock price, exercise price, and time to maturity are readily determined. The interest rate used is the money market rate for a maturity equal to that of the option, and the dividend payout is reasonably predictable, at least over short horizons.

The last input, though, the standard deviation of the stock return, is not directly observable. It must be estimated from historical data, from scenario analysis, or from the prices of other options, as we will describe momentarily.

## Table 21.2   Cumulative Normal Distribution

| d | N(d) | d | N(d) | d | N(d) |
|---|------|---|------|---|------|
| −3.00 | .0013 | −1.58 | .0571 | −0.76 | .2236 |
| −2.95 | .0016 | −1.56 | .0594 | −0.74 | .2297 |
| −2.90 | .0019 | −1.54 | .0618 | −0.72 | .2358 |
| −2.85 | .0022 | −1.52 | .0643 | −0.70 | .2420 |
| −2.80 | .0026 | −1.50 | .0668 | −0.68 | .2483 |
| −2.75 | .0030 | −1.48 | .0694 | −0.66 | .2546 |
| −2.70 | .0035 | −1.46 | .0721 | −0.64 | .2611 |
| −2.65 | .0040 | −1.44 | .0749 | −0.62 | .2676 |
| −2.60 | .0047 | −1.42 | .0778 | −0.60 | .2743 |
| −2.55 | .0054 | −1.40 | .0808 | −0.58 | .2810 |
| −2.50 | .0062 | −1.38 | .0838 | −0.56 | .2877 |
| −2.45 | .0071 | −1.36 | .0869 | −0.54 | .2946 |
| −2.40 | .0082 | −1.34 | .0901 | −0.52 | .3015 |
| −2.35 | .0094 | −1.32 | .0934 | −0.50 | .3085 |
| −2.30 | .0107 | −1.30 | .0968 | −0.48 | .3156 |
| −2.25 | .0122 | −1.28 | .1003 | −0.46 | .3228 |
| −2.20 | .0139 | −1.26 | .1038 | −0.44 | .3300 |
| −2.15 | .0158 | −1.24 | .1075 | −0.42 | .3373 |
| −2.10 | .0179 | −1.22 | .1112 | −0.40 | .3446 |
| −2.05 | .0202 | −1.20 | .1151 | −0.38 | .3520 |
| −2.00 | .0228 | −1.18 | .1190 | −0.36 | .3594 |
| −1.98 | .0239 | −1.16 | .1230 | −0.34 | .3669 |
| −1.96 | .0250 | −1.14 | .1271 | −0.32 | .3745 |
| −1.94 | .0262 | −1.12 | .1314 | −0.30 | .3821 |
| −1.92 | .0274 | −1.10 | .1357 | −0.28 | .3897 |
| −1.90 | .0287 | −1.08 | .1401 | −0.26 | .3974 |
| −1.88 | .0301 | −1.06 | .1446 | −0.24 | .4052 |
| −1.86 | .0314 | −1.04 | .1492 | −0.22 | .4129 |
| −1.84 | .0329 | −1.02 | .1539 | −0.20 | .4207 |
| −1.82 | .0344 | −1.00 | .1587 | −0.18 | .4286 |
| −1.80 | .0359 | −0.98 | .1635 | −0.16 | .4365 |
| −1.78 | .0375 | −0.96 | .1685 | −0.14 | .4443 |
| −1.76 | .0392 | −0.94 | .1736 | −0.12 | .4523 |
| −1.74 | .0409 | −0.92 | .1788 | −0.10 | .4602 |
| −1.72 | .0427 | −0.90 | .1841 | −0.08 | .4681 |
| −1.70 | .0446 | −0.88 | .1894 | −0.06 | .4761 |
| −1.68 | .0465 | −0.86 | .1949 | −0.04 | .4841 |
| −1.66 | .0485 | −0.84 | .2005 | −0.02 | .4920 |
| −1.64 | .0505 | −0.82 | .2061 | 0.00 | .5000 |
| −1.62 | .0526 | −0.80 | .2119 | 0.02 | .5080 |
| −1.60 | .0548 | −0.78 | .2177 | 0.04 | .5160 |

We saw in Chapter 5 that the historical variance of stock market returns can be calculated from $n$ observations as follows:

$$\sigma^2 = \frac{n}{n-1} \sum_{t=1}^{n} \frac{(r_t - \bar{r})^2}{n}$$

**Table 21.2   (Concluded)**

| d | N(d) | d | N(d) | d | N(d) |
|------|-------|------|-------|------|-------|
| 0.06 | .5239 | 0.86 | .8051 | 1.66 | .9515 |
| 0.08 | .5319 | 0.88 | .8106 | 1.68 | .9535 |
| 0.10 | .5398 | 0.90 | .8159 | 1.70 | .9554 |
| 0.12 | .5478 | 0.92 | .8212 | 1.72 | .9573 |
| 0.14 | .5557 | 0.94 | .8264 | 1.74 | .9591 |
| 0.16 | .5636 | 0.96 | .8315 | 1.76 | .9608 |
| 0.18 | .5714 | 0.98 | .8365 | 1.78 | .9625 |
| 0.20 | .5793 | 1.00 | .8414 | 1.80 | .9641 |
| 0.22 | .5871 | 1.02 | .8461 | 1.82 | .9656 |
| 0.24 | .5948 | 1.04 | .8508 | 1.84 | .9671 |
| 0.26 | .6026 | 1.06 | .8554 | 1.86 | .9686 |
| 0.28 | .6103 | 1.08 | .8599 | 1.88 | .9699 |
| 0.30 | .6179 | 1.10 | .8643 | 1.90 | .9713 |
| 0.32 | .6255 | 1.12 | .8686 | 1.92 | .9726 |
| 0.34 | .6331 | 1.14 | .8729 | 1.94 | .9738 |
| 0.36 | .6406 | 1.16 | .8770 | 1.96 | .9750 |
| 0.38 | .6480 | 1.18 | .8810 | 1.98 | .9761 |
| 0.40 | .6554 | 1.20 | .8849 | 2.00 | .9772 |
| 0.42 | .6628 | 1.22 | .8888 | 2.05 | .9798 |
| 0.44 | .6700 | 1.24 | .8925 | 2.10 | .9821 |
| 0.46 | .6773 | 1.26 | .8962 | 2.15 | .9842 |
| 0.48 | .6844 | 1.28 | .8997 | 2.20 | .9861 |
| 0.50 | .6915 | 1.30 | .9032 | 2.25 | .9878 |
| 0.52 | .6985 | 1.32 | .9066 | 2.30 | .9893 |
| 0.54 | .7054 | 1.34 | .9099 | 2.35 | .9906 |
| 0.56 | .7123 | 1.36 | .9131 | 2.40 | .9918 |
| 0.58 | .7191 | 1.38 | .9162 | 2.45 | .9929 |
| 0.60 | .7258 | 1.40 | .9192 | 2.50 | .9938 |
| 0.62 | .7324 | 1.42 | .9222 | 2.55 | .9946 |
| 0.64 | .7389 | 1.44 | .9251 | 2.60 | .9953 |
| 0.66 | .7454 | 1.46 | .9279 | 2.65 | .9960 |
| 0.68 | .7518 | 1.48 | .9306 | 2.70 | .9965 |
| 0.70 | .7580 | 1.50 | .9332 | 2.75 | .9970 |
| 0.72 | .7642 | 1.52 | .9357 | 2.80 | .9974 |
| 0.74 | .7704 | 1.54 | .9382 | 2.85 | .9978 |
| 0.76 | .7764 | 1.56 | .9406 | 2.90 | .9981 |
| 0.78 | .7823 | 1.58 | .9429 | 2.95 | .9984 |
| 0.80 | .7882 | 1.60 | .9452 | 3.00 | .9986 |
| 0.82 | .7939 | 1.62 | .9474 | 3.05 | .9989 |
| 0.84 | .7996 | 1.64 | .9495 | | |

where $\bar{r}$ is the average return over the sample period. The rate of return on day $t$ is defined to be consistent with continuous compounding as $r_t = \ln(S_t/S_{t-1})$. [We note again that the natural logarithm of a ratio is approximately the percentage difference between the numerator and denominator so that $\ln(S_t/S_{t-1})$ is a measure of the rate of return of the stock from time $t - 1$ to time $t$.] Historical variance commonly is computed using daily returns over

**Figure 21.7   S&P 500 implied and historical volatility comparison**

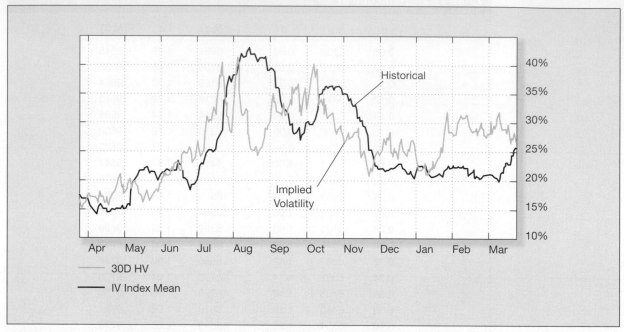

Source: IVolatility website: www.ivolatility.com

periods of several months. Because the standard deviation of stock returns must be estimated, however, it is always possible that discrepancies between an option price and its Black-Scholes value are simply artifacts of error in the estimation of the stock's volatility.

In fact, market participants often give the option valuation problem a different twist. Rather than calculating a Black-Scholes option value for a given stock's standard deviation, they ask instead: What standard deviation would be necessary for the option price that I observe to be consistent with the Black-Scholes formula? This is called the **implied volatility** of the option, the volatility level for the stock that the option price implies.[6] Investors can then judge whether they think the actual stock standard deviation exceeds the implied volatility. If it does, the option is considered a good buy; if actual volatility seems greater than the implied volatility, its fair price would exceed the observed price.

Another variation is to compare two options on the same stock with equal expiration dates but different exercise prices. The option with the higher implied volatility would be considered relatively expensive, because a higher standard deviation is required to justify its price. The analyst might consider buying the option with the lower implied volatility and writing the option with the higher implied volatility.

Figure 21.7 presents plots of the historical and implied standard deviation of the rate of return on the S&P 500 Index. The implied volatility is derived from prices of option contracts traded on the index. Notice that although both series have considerable tendency to move together, there is occasionally dramatic slippage between the two estimates of volatility. Notice also that both volatility series vary considerably over time. Therefore, choosing the proper volatility value to use in any option-pricing model always presents a formidable challenge. A considerable amount of recent research has been devoted to new techniques to predict changes in volatility. These techniques, which go by the name ARCH models and stochastic volatility models, posit that changes in stock volatility are partially

---

[6] This concept was introduced in Richard E. Schmalensee and Robert R. Trippi, "Common Stock Volatility Expectations Implied by Option Premia," *Journal of Finance* 33 (March 1978), pp. 129–47.

**Figure 21.8   Spreadsheet to calculate Black-Scholes call option values**

| | A | B | C | D | E | F | G | H | I | J |
|---|---|---|---|---|---|---|---|---|---|---|
| 1 | INPUTS | | | OUTPUTS | | | FORMULA FOR OUTPUT IN COLUMN E | | | |
| 2 | standard deviation (annual) | 0.2783 | | d1 | 0.0029 | | LN(B5/B6)+(B4–B7+5*B2^2)*B3)/(B2*SQRT(B3)) | | | |
| 3 | Maturity (in years) | 0.5 | | d2 | –0.1939 | | E2–B2*SQRT(B3) | | | |
| 4 | Risk-free rate (annual) | 0.06 | | N(d1) | 0.5012 | | NORMDIST(E2) | | | |
| 5 | Stock price | 100 | | N(d2) | 0.4231 | | NORMDIST(E3) | | | |
| 6 | Exercise price | 105 | | B/S call value | 7.0000 | | B5*EXP(–B7*B3)*E4–B6*EXP(–B4*B3)*E5 | | | |
| 7 | Dividend yield (annual) | 0 | | B/S put value | 8.8968 | | B6*EXP(–B4*B3)*(1–E5)–B5*EXP(–B7*B3)*(1–E4) | | | |

predictable and that by analyzing recent levels and trends in volatility, one can improve predictions of future volatility.

The Black-Scholes valuation formula, as well as implied volatilities, are easily calculated using an Excel spreadsheet, as in Figure 21.8. The model inputs are provided in column B, and the outputs are given in column E. The formulas for $d_1$ and $d_2$ are provided in the spreadsheet, and the Excel formula NORMSDIST($d_1$) is used to calculate $N(d_1)$. Cell E6 contains the Black-Scholes formula. (The formula in the spreadsheet actually includes an adjustment for dividends, as described in the next section.)

To compute an implied volatility, we can use the Goal Seek command from the Tools menu in Excel. Goal Seek asks us to change the value of one cell to make the value of another cell (called the target cell) equal to a specific value. For example, if we observe a call option selling for $7 with other inputs as given in the spreadsheet, we can use Goal Seek to find the value for cell B2 (the standard deviation of the stock) that will make the option value in cell E6 equal to $7. In this case, the target cell, E6, is the call price, and the spreadsheet manipulates cell B2. When you ask the spreadsheet to "Solve," it finds that a standard deviation equal to .2783 is consistent with a call price of $7; this would be the option's implied volatility if it were selling at $7.

**CONCEPT CHECK☞ QUESTION 7**   Consider the call option in the example above selling for $15 with Black-Scholes value of $13.70. Is its implied volatility more or less than 50%?

**Dividends and Call Option Valuation**   We noted earlier that the Black-Scholes call option formula applies to stocks that do not pay dividends. When dividends are to be paid before the option expires, we need to adjust the formula. The payment of dividends raises the possibility of early exercise, and for most realistic dividend payout schemes the valuation formula becomes significantly more complex than the Black-Scholes equation.

We can apply some simple rules of thumb to approximate the option value, however. One popular approach, originally suggested by Black, calls for adjusting the stock price downward by the present value of any dividends that are to be paid before option expiration.[7] Therefore, we would simply replace $S_0$ with $S_0 -$ PV(dividends) in the Black-Scholes formula. Such an adjustment will take dividends into account by reflecting their eventual impact on the stock price. The option value then may be computed as before, assuming that the option will be held to expiration.

---

[7] Fischer Black, "Fact and Fantasy in the Use of Options," *Financial Analysts Journal* 31 (July–August 1975).

In one special case, the dividend adjustment takes a simple form. Suppose the underlying asset pays a continuous flow of income. This might be a reasonable assumption for options on a stock index, where different stocks in the index pay dividends on different days, so that dividend income arrives in a more or less continuous flow. If the dividend yield, denoted $\delta$, is constant, one can show that the present value of that dividend flow accruing until the option maturity date is $S_0(1 - e^{-\delta T})$. (For intuition, notice that $e^{-\delta T}$ approximately equals $1 - \delta T$, so the value of the dividend is approximately $\delta T S_0$.) In this case, $S_0 - \text{PV(Div)} = S_0 e^{-\delta T}$, and we can derive a Black-Scholes call option formula on the dividend-paying asset simply by substituting $S_0 e^{-\delta T}$ for $S_0$ in the original formula. This approach is used in Figure 21.8.

These procedures would yield a very good approximation of option value for European call options that must be held until maturity but they do not allow for the fact that the holder of an American call option might choose to exercise the option just before a dividend. The current value of a call option, assuming that the option will be exercised just before the ex-dividend date, might be greater than the value of the option assuming it will be held until maturity. Although holding the option until maturity allows greater effective time to expiration, which increases the option value, it also entails more dividend payments, lowering the expected stock price at maturity and thereby lowering the current option value.

For example, suppose that a stock selling at $20 will pay a $1 dividend in 4 months, whereas the call option on the stock does not expire for 6 months. The effective annual interest rate is 10%, so that the present value of the dividend is $1/(1.10)^{1/3} = \$0.97$. Black suggests that we can compute the option value in one of two ways:

1. Apply the Black-Scholes formula assuming early exercise, thus using the actual stock price of $20 and a time to expiration of 4 months (the time until the dividend payment).

2. Apply the Black-Scholes formula assuming no early exercise, using the dividend-adjusted stock price of $20 − \$.97 = \$19.03$ and a time to expiration of 6 months.

The greater of the two values is the estimate of the option value, recognizing that early exercise might be optimal. In other words, the so-called **pseudo-American call option value** is the maximum of the value derived by assuming that the option will be held until expiration and the value derived by assuming that the option will be exercised just before an ex-dividend date. Even this technique is not exact, however, for it assumes that the option holder makes an irrevocable decision now on when to exercise, when in fact the decision is not binding until exercise notice is given.[8]

**Put Option Valuation**    We have concentrated so far on call option valuation. We can derive Black-Scholes European put option values from call option values using the put-call parity theorem. To value the put option, we simply calculate the value of the corresponding call option in equation 21.1 from the Black-Scholes formula, and solve for the put option value as

$$P = C + \text{PV}(X) - S_0$$
$$= C + Xe^{-rT} - S_0 \tag{21.2}$$

---

[8] An exact formula for American call valuation on dividend-paying stocks has been developed in Richard Roll, "An Analytic Valuation Formula for Unprotected American Call Options on Stocks with Known Dividends," *Journal of Financial Economics* 5 (November 1977). The technique has been discussed and revised in Robert Geske, "A Note on an Analytical Formula for Unprotected American Call Options on Stocks with Known Dividends," *Journal of Financial Economics* 7 (December 1979), and Robert E. Whaley, "On the Valuation of American Call Options on Stocks with Known Dividends," *Journal of Financial Economics* 9 (June 1981). These are difficult papers, however.

We must calculate the present value of the exercise price using continuous compounding to be consistent with the Black-Scholes formula.

Sometimes, it is easier to work with a put option valuation formula directly. If we substitute the Black-Scholes formula for a call in equation 21.2, we obtain the value of a European put option as

$$P = Xe^{-rT}[1 - N(d_2)] - S_0[1 - N(d_1)] \tag{21.3}$$

**EXAMPLE 21.3**    **Black-Scholes Put Valuation**

Using data from Example 21.2 ($C = \$13.70$, $X = \$95$, $S = \$100$, $r = .10$, $\sigma = .50$, and $T = .25$), we find that a European put option on that stock with identical exercise price and time to maturity is worth

$$\$95e^{-.10 \times .25}(1 - .5714) - \$100(1 - .6664) = \$6.35$$

Notice that this value is consistent with put-call parity:

$$P = C + \text{PV}(X) - S_0 = 13.70 + 95e^{-.10 \times .25} - 100 = 6.35$$

As we noted traders can do, we might then compare this formula value to the actual put price as one step in formulating a trading strategy.

Equation 21.2 or 21.3 is valid for European puts on non-dividend-paying stocks. As for calls, if the underlying asset pays a dividend, we can find European put values by substituting $S_0 - \text{PV}(\text{div})$ for $S_0$. Cell E7 in Figure 21.8 allows for a continuous dividend flow with a dividend yield of $\delta$. In that case $S_0 - \text{PV}(\text{div}) = S_0 e^{-\delta T}$.

However, listed put options on stocks are American options that offer the opportunity of early exercise, and we have seen that the right to exercise puts early can turn out to be valuable. This means that an American put option must be worth more than the corresponding European option. Therefore, equation 21.2 or 21.3 describes only the lower bound on the true value of the American put. However, in many applications the approximation is very accurate.[9]

## 21.5   USING THE BLACK-SCHOLES FORMULA

**Hedge Ratios and the Black-Scholes Formula**    In the last chapter, we considered two investments in IBM: 100 shares of IBM stock or 1,000 call options on IBM. We saw that the call option position was more sensitive to swings in IBM's stock price than was the all-stock position. To analyze the overall exposure to a stock price more precisely, however, it is necessary to quantify these relative sensitivities. A tool that enables us to summarize the overall exposure of portfolios of options with various exercise prices and times to maturity is the hedge ratio. An option's **hedge ratio** is the change in the price of an option for a $1 increase in the stock price. A call option, therefore, has a positive hedge ratio and a put option a negative hedge ratio. The hedge ratio is commonly called the option's **delta.**

---

[9] For a more complete treatment of American put valuation, see R. Geske and H. E. Johnson, "The American Put Valued Analytically," *Journal of Finance* 39 (December 1984), pp. 1511–24.

# BLACK-SCHOLES OPTION VALUATION

The spreadsheet below can be used to determine option values using the Black-Scholes model. The inputs are the stock price, standard deviation, maturity of the option, exercise price, risk-free rate, and dividend yield. The call option is valued using equation 21.1 and the put is valued using equation 21.3. For both calls and puts, the dividend-adjusted Black-Scholes formula substitutes $Se^{-\delta T}$ for $S$, as outlined on page 766. The model also calculates the intrinsic and time value for both puts and calls.

The model also presents sensitivity analysis using the one-way data table. The first workbook presents the analysis of calls while the second workbook presents similar analysis of puts. You can find these spreadsheets at the OnLine Learning Center at **www.mhhe.com/bkm**.

| | A | B | C | D | E | F | G | H | I | J | K | L | M | N |
|---|---|---|---|---|---|---|---|---|---|---|---|---|---|---|
| 1 | Chapter 21- Black-Scholes Option Pricing | | | | | | LEGEND: | | | | | | | |
| 2 | Call Valuation & Call Time Premiums | | | | | | Enter data | | | | | | | |
| 3 | | | | | | | Value calculated | | | | | | | |
| 4 | | | | | | | See comment | | | | | | | |
| 5 | Standard Deviation (σ) | 0.27830 | | | | | | | | | | | | |
| 6 | Variance (annual, σ²) | 0.07745 | | | Call | | | Call | | | Call | | | Call |
| 7 | Time to expiration (years, T) | 0.50 | | Standard | Option | | Standard | Time | | Stock | Option | | Stock | Time |
| 8 | Risk-free rate (annual, r) | 6.00% | | Deviation | Value | | Deviation | Value | | Price | Value | | Price | Value |
| 9 | Current stock price (S₀) | $100.00 | | | 7.000 | | | 7.000 | | | 7.000 | | | 7.000 |
| 10 | Exercise price (X) | $105.00 | | 0.15 | 3.388 | | 0.150 | 3.388 | | $60 | 0.017 | | $60 | 0.017 |
| 11 | Dividend Yield (annual, δ) | 0.00% | | 0.18 | 4.089 | | 0.175 | 4.089 | | $65 | 0.061 | | $65 | 0.061 |
| 12 | | | | 0.20 | 4.792 | | 0.200 | 4.792 | | $70 | 0.179 | | $70 | 0.179 |
| 13 | d₁ | 0.0029095 | | 0.23 | 5.497 | | 0.225 | 5.497 | | $75 | 0.440 | | $75 | 0.440 |
| 14 | d₂ | -0.193878 | | 0.25 | 6.202 | | 0.250 | 6.202 | | $80 | 0.935 | | $80 | 0.935 |
| 15 | N(d₁) | 0.50116 | | 0.28 | 6.907 | | 0.275 | 6.907 | | $85 | 1.763 | | $85 | 1.763 |
| 16 | N(d₂) | 0.42314 | | 0.30 | 7.612 | | 0.300 | 7.612 | | $90 | 3.014 | | $90 | 3.014 |
| 17 | Black-Scholes Call Value | $6.99992 | | 0.33 | 8.317 | | 0.325 | 8.317 | | $95 | 4.750 | | $95 | 4.750 |
| 18 | Black-Scholes Put Value | $8.89670 | | 0.35 | 9.022 | | 0.350 | 9.022 | | $100 | 7.000 | | $100 | 7.000 |
| 19 | | | | 0.38 | 9.726 | | 0.375 | 9.726 | | $105 | 9.754 | | $105 | 9.754 |
| 20 | | | | 0.40 | 10.429 | | 0.400 | 10.429 | | $110 | 12.974 | | $110 | 7.974 |
| 21 | Intrinsic Value of Call | $0.00000 | | 0.43 | 11.132 | | 0.425 | 11.132 | | $115 | 16.602 | | $115 | 6.602 |
| 22 | Time Value of Call | 6.99992 | | 0.45 | 11.834 | | 0.450 | 11.834 | | $120 | 20.572 | | $120 | 5.572 |
| 23 | | | | 0.48 | 12.536 | | 0.475 | 12.536 | | $125 | 24.817 | | $125 | 4.817 |
| 24 | Intinsic Value of Put | $5.00000 | | 0.50 | 13.236 | | 0.500 | 13.236 | | $130 | 29.275 | | $130 | 4.275 |
| 25 | Time Value of Put | 3.89670 | | | | | | | | $135.00 | 33.893 | | $135 | 3.893 |

If you were to graph the option value as a function of the stock value as we have done for a call option in Figure 21.9, the hedge ratio is simply the slope of the value curve evaluated at the current stock price. For example, suppose the slope of the curve at $S_0 = \$120$ equals .60. As the stock increases in value by $1, the option increases by approximately $.60, as the figure shows.

For every call option written, .60 share of stock would be needed to hedge the investor's portfolio. For example, if one writes 10 options and holds six shares of stock, according to the hedge ratio of .6, a $1 increase in stock price will result in a gain of $6 on the stock holdings, whereas the loss on the 10 options written will be $10 \times \$.60$, an equivalent $6. The stock price movement leaves total wealth unaltered, which is what a hedged position is intended to do. The investor holding the stock and an option in proportions dictated by their relative price movements hedges the portfolio.

Black-Scholes hedge ratios are particularly easy to compute. The hedge ratio for a call is $N(d_1)$, whereas the hedge ratio for a put is $N(d_1) - 1$. We defined $N(d_1)$ as part of the Black-Scholes formula in equation 21.1. Recall that $N(d)$ stands for the area under the standard normal curve up to $d$. Therefore, the call option hedge ratio must be positive and less than 1.0, whereas the put option hedge ratio is negative and of smaller absolute value than 1.0.

**Figure 21.9**
**Call option value**
**and hedge ratio**

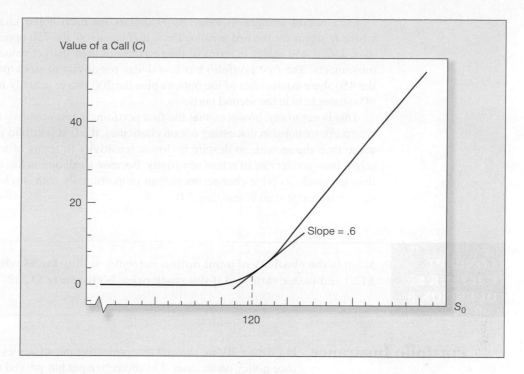

Figure 21.9 verifies the insight that the slope of the call option valuation function is less than 1.0, approaching 1.0 only as the stock price becomes much greater than the exercise price. This tells us that option values change less than one for one with changes in stock prices. Why should this be? Suppose an option is so far in the money that you are absolutely certain it will be exercised. In that case, every dollar increase in the stock price would increase the option value by $1. But if there is a reasonable chance the call option will expire out of the money, even after a moderate stock price gain, a $1 increase in the stock price will not necessarily increase the ultimate payoff to the call; therefore, the call price will not respond by a full dollar.

The fact that hedge ratios are less than 1.0 does not contradict our earlier observation that options offer leverage and are sensitive to stock price movements. Although *dollar* movements in option prices are less than dollar movements in the stock price, the *rate of return* volatility of options remains greater than stock return volatility because options sell at lower prices. In our example, with the stock selling at $120, and a hedge ratio of .6, an option with exercise price $120 may sell for $5. If the stock price increases to $121, the call price would be expected to increase by only $.60 to $5.60. The percentage increase in the option value is $.60/$5.00 = 12%, however, whereas the stock price increase is only $1/$120 = .83%. The ratio of the percentage changes is 12%/.83% = 14.4. For every 1% increase in the stock price, the option price increases by 14.4%. This ratio, the percentage change in option price per percentage change in stock price, is called the **option elasticity.**

The hedge ratio is an essential tool in portfolio management and control. An example will show why.

**EXAMPLE 21.4**   **Hedge Ratios**

Consider two portfolios, one holding 750 IBM calls and 200 shares of IBM and the other holding 800 shares of IBM. Which portfolio has greater dollar exposure to IBM price movements? You can answer this question easily using the hedge ratio.

Each option changes in value by $H$ dollars for each dollar change in stock price, where $H$ stands for the hedge ratio. Thus, if $H$ equals .6, the 750 options are equivalent to $.6 \times 750 = 450$ shares in terms of the response of their market value to IBM stock price movements. The first portfolio has less dollar sensitivity to stock price change because the 450 share-equivalents of the options plus the 200 shares actually held are less than the 800 shares held in the second portfolio.

This is not to say, however, that the first portfolio is less sensitive to the stock's rate of return. As we noted in discussing option elasticities, the first portfolio may be of lower total value than the second, so despite its lower sensitivity in terms of total market value, it might have greater rate of return sensitivity. Because a call option has a lower market value than the stock, its price changes more than proportionally with stock price changes, even though its hedge ratio is less than 1.0.

---

**CONCEPT CHECK☞ QUESTION 8**

**What is the elasticity of a put option currently selling for $4 with exercise price $120 and hedge ratio −.4 if the stock price is currently $122?**

---

**Portfolio Insurance**    In Chapter 20, we showed that protective put strategies offer a sort of insurance policy on an asset. The protective put has proved to be extremely popular with investors. Even if the asset price falls, the put conveys the right to sell the asset for the exercise price, which is a way to lock in a minimum portfolio value. With an at-the-money put ($X = S_0$), the maximum loss that can be realized is the cost of the put. The asset can be sold for $X$, which equals its original value, so even if the asset price falls, the investor's net loss over the period is just the cost of the put. If the asset value increases, however, upside potential is unlimited. Figure 21.10 graphs the profit or loss on a protective put position as a function of the change in the value of the underlying asset, $P$.

While the protective put is a simple and convenient way to achieve **portfolio insurance,** that is, to limit the worst-case portfolio rate of return, there are practical difficulties in

**Figure 21.10 Profit on a protective put strategy**

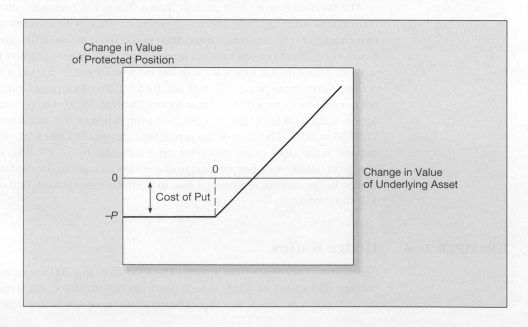

trying to insure a portfolio of stocks. First, unless the investor's portfolio corresponds to a standard market index for which puts are traded, a put option on the portfolio will not be available for purchase. And if index puts are used to protect a non-indexed portfolio, tracking error can result. For example, if the portfolio falls in value while the market index rises, the put will fail to provide the intended protection. Tracking error limits the investor's freedom to pursue active stock selection because such error will be greater as the managed portfolio departs more substantially from the market index.

Moreover, the desired horizon of the insurance program must match the maturity of a traded put option in order to establish the appropriate protective put position. Today long-term options on market indexes and several larger stocks called LEAPS (for *long-term equity anticipation securities*) trade on the CBOE with maturities of several years. However, in the mid-1980s, while most investors pursuing insurance programs had horizons of several years, actively traded puts were limited to maturities of less than a year. Rolling over a sequence of short-term puts, which might be viewed as a response to this problem, introduces new risks because the prices at which successive puts will be available in the future are not known today.

Providers of portfolio insurance who had horizons of several years, therefore, could not rely on the simple expedient of purchasing protective puts for their clients' portfolios. Instead, they followed trading strategies to replicate the payoffs to the protective put position.

Here is the general idea. Even if a put option on the desired portfolio with the desired expiration date does not exist, a theoretical option-pricing model (such as the Black-Scholes model) can be used to determine how that option's price would respond to the portfolio's value if the option did trade. For example, if stock prices were to fall, the put option would increase in value. The option model could quantify this relationship. The net exposure of the (hypothetical) protective put portfolio to swings in stock prices is the sum of the exposures of the two components of the portfolio, the stock and the put. The net exposure of the portfolio equals the equity exposure less the (offsetting) put option exposure.

We can create "synthetic" protective put positions by holding a quantity of stocks with the same net exposure to market swings as the hypothetical protective put position. The key to this strategy is the option delta, or hedge ratio, that is, the change in the price of the protective put option per change in the value of the underlying stock portfolio.

EXAMPLE 21.5   Synthetic Protective Put Options

Suppose a portfolio is currently valued at $100 million. An at-the-money put option on the portfolio might have a hedge ratio or delta of −.6, meaning the option's value swings $.60 for every dollar change in portfolio value, but in an opposite direction. Suppose the stock portfolio falls in value by 2%. The profit on a hypothetical protective put position (if the put existed) would be as follows (in millions of dollars):

| | | |
|---|---|---|
| Loss on stocks: | 2% of $100 = | $2.00 |
| Gain on put: | .6 × $2.00 = | 1.20 |
| Net loss | | = $ .80 |

We create the synthetic option position by selling a proportion of shares equal to the put option's delta (i.e., selling 60% of the shares) and placing the proceeds in risk-free T-bills. The rationale is that the hypothetical put option would have offset 60% of any change in the stock portfolio's value, so one must reduce portfolio risk directly by selling 60% of the equity and putting the proceeds into a risk-free asset. Total return on a synthetic protective put position with $60 million in risk-free investments such as T-bills and $40 million in equity is

Loss on stocks:      2% of $40 = $.80
+ Loss on bills:                  =    0
Net loss              = $.80

The synthetic and actual protective put positions have equal returns. We conclude that if you sell a proportion of shares equal to the put option's delta and place the proceeds in cash equivalents, your exposure to the stock market will equal that of the desired protective put position.

The difficulty with this procedure is that deltas constantly change. Figure 21.11 shows that as the stock price falls, the magnitude of the appropriate hedge ratio increases. Therefore, market declines require extra hedging, that is, additional conversion of equity into cash. This constant updating of the hedge ratio is called **dynamic hedging** (alternatively, delta hedging)

Dynamic hedging is one reason portfolio insurance has been said to contribute to market volatility. Market declines trigger additional sales of stock as portfolio insurers strive to increase their hedging. These additional sales are seen as reinforcing or exaggerating market downturns.

In practice, portfolio insurers do not actually buy or sell stocks directly when they update their hedge positions. Instead, they minimize trading costs by buying or selling stock index futures as a substitute for sale of the stocks themselves. As you will see in the next chapter, stock prices and index futures prices usually are very tightly linked by cross-market arbitrageurs so that futures transactions can be used as reliable proxies for stock transactions. Instead of selling equities based on the put option's delta, insurers will sell an equivalent number of futures contracts.[10]

Several portfolio insurers suffered great setbacks during the market crash of October 19, 1987, when the market suffered an unprecedented 1-day loss of about 20%. A description of what happened then should let you appreciate the complexities of applying a seemingly straightforward hedging concept.

1. Market volatility at the crash was much greater than ever encountered before. Put option deltas based on historical experience were too low; insurers underhedged, held too much equity, and suffered excessive losses.

2. Prices moved so fast that insurers could not keep up with the necessary rebalancing. They were "chasing deltas" that kept getting away from them. The futures market also saw a "gap" opening, where the opening price was nearly 10% below the previous day's close. The price dropped before insurers could update their hedge ratios.

3. Execution problems were severe. First, current market prices were unavailable, with trade execution and the price quotation system hours behind, which made computation of correct hedge ratios impossible. Moreover, trading in stocks and stock futures ceased during some periods. The continuous rebalancing capability that is essential for a viable insurance program vanished during the precipitous market collapse.

4. Futures prices traded at steep discounts to their proper levels compared to reported stock prices, thereby making the sale of futures (as a proxy for equity sales) seem

---

[10] Notice, however, that the use of index futures reintroduces the problem of tracking error between the portfolio and the market index.

**Figure 21.11
Hedge ratios
change as the
stock price
fluctuates**

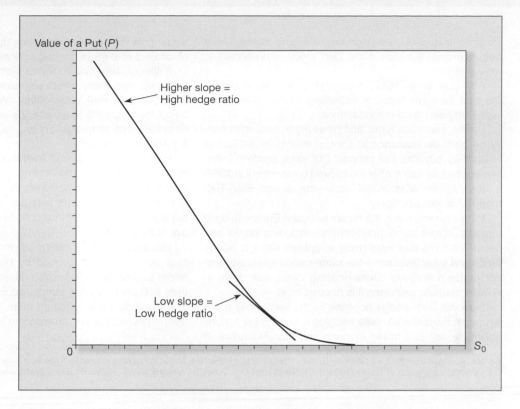

**Figure 21.12
S&P 500 cash-to-
futures spread
in points at
15-minute
intervals**

Note: Trading in futures contracts halted between 12:15 and 1:05.
Source: *The Wall Street Journal.* Reprinted by permission of *The Wall Street Journal,* © 1987 Dow Jones & Company, Inc. All Rights Reserved Worldwide.

expensive. Although you will see in the next chapter that stock index futures prices normally exceed the value of the stock index, Figure 21.12 shows that on October 19, futures sold far below the stock index level. When some insurers gambled that the futures price would recover to its usual premium over the stock index, and chose to defer sales, they remained underhedged. As the market fell farther, their portfolios experienced substantial losses.

# DELTA-HEDGING:
# THE NEW NAME IN PORTFOLIO INSURANCE

Portfolio insurance, the high-tech hedging strategy that helped grease the slide in the 1987 stock-market crash, is alive and well.

And just as in 1987, it doesn't always work out as planned, as some financial institutions found out in the recent European bond-market turmoil.

Banks, securities firms, and other big traders rely heavily on portfolio insurance to contain their potential losses when they buy and sell options. But since portfolio insurance got a bad name after it backfired on investors in 1987, it goes by an alias these days—the sexier, Star Trek moniker of "delta-hedging."

Whatever you call it, the recent turmoil in European bond markets taught some practitioners—including banks and securities firms that were hedging options sales to hedge funds and other investors—the same painful lessons of earlier portfolio insurers: Delta-hedging can break down in volatile markets, just when it is needed most.

How you delta-hedge depends on the bets you're trying to hedge. For instance, delta-hedging would prompt options sellers to sell into falling markets and buy into rallies. It would give the opposite directions to options buyers, such as dealers who might hold big options inventories.

In theory, delta-hedging takes place with computer-timed precision, and there aren't any snags. But in real life, it doesn't always work so smoothly. "When volatility ends up being much greater than anticipated, you can't get your delta trades off at the right points," says an executive at one big derivatives dealer.

How does this happen? Take the relatively simple case of dealers who sell "call" options on long-term Treasury bonds. Such options give buyers the right to buy bonds at a fixed price over a specific time period. And compared with buying bonds outright, these options are much more sensitive to market moves.

Because selling the calls made those dealers vulnerable to a rally, they delta-hedged by buying bonds. As bond prices turned south [and option deltas fell] the dealers shed their hedges by selling bonds, adding to the selling orgy. The plunging markets forced them to sell at lower prices than expected, causing unexpected losses on their hedges.

Source: Abridged from Barbara Donnelly Granito, "Delta-Hedging: The New Name in Portfolio Insurance," *The Wall Street Journal*, March 17, 1994. Excerpted by permission of *The Wall Street Journal*, © 1994 Dow Jones & Company, Inc. All Rights Reserved Worldwide.

Although most observers believe that the portfolio insurance industry will never recover from the market crash, the above box points out that delta hedging is still alive and well on Wall Street. Dynamic hedges are widely used by large firms to hedge potential losses from the options they write. The article also points out, however, that these traders are increasingly aware of the practical difficulties in implementing dynamic hedges in very volatile markets.

**Hedging Bets on Mispriced Options** Suppose you believe that the standard deviation of IBM stock returns will be 35% over the next few weeks, but IBM put options are selling at a price consistent with a volatility of 33%. Because the put's implied volatility is less than your forecast of the stock volatility, you believe the option is underpriced. Using your assessment of volatility in an option-pricing model like the Black-Scholes formula, you would estimate that the fair price for the puts exceeds the actual price.

Does this mean that you ought to buy put options? Perhaps it does, but by doing so, you risk great losses if IBM stock performs well, *even if* you are correct about the volatility. You would like to separate your bet on volatility from the "attached" bet inherent in purchasing a put that IBM's stock price will fall. In other words, you would like to speculate on the option mispricing by purchasing the put option, but hedge the resulting exposure to the performance of IBM stock.

The option *delta* can be interpreted as a hedge ratio that can be used for this purpose. The delta was defined as

$$\text{Delta} = \frac{\text{Change in value of option}}{\text{Change in value of stock}}$$

Therefore, delta is the slope of the option-pricing curve.

This ratio tells us precisely how many shares of stock we must hold to offset our exposure to IBM. For example, if the delta is $-.6$, then the put will fall by $.60 in value for every one-point increase in IBM stock, and we need to hold .6 share of stock to hedge each put. If we purchase 10 option contracts, each for 100 shares, we would need to buy 600 shares of stock. If the stock price rises by $1, each put option will decrease in value by $.60, resulting in a loss of $600. However, the loss on the puts will be offset by a gain on the stock holdings of $1 per share $\times$ 600 shares.

To see how the profits on this strategy might develop, let's use the following example.

**EXAMPLE 21.6**

## Speculating on Mispriced Options

Suppose option maturity, $T$ is 60 days; put price, $P$ is $4.495; exercise price, $X$ is $90; stock price, $S$ is $90; and the risk-free rate, $r$ is 4%. We assume that the stock will not pay a dividend in the next 60 days. Given these data, the implied volatility on the option is 33%, as we posited. However, you believe the true volatility is 35%, implying that the fair put price is $4.785. Therefore, if the market assessment of volatility is revised to the value you believe is correct, your profit will be $.29 per put purchased.

Recall that the hedge ratio, or delta, of a put option equals $N(d_1) - 1$, where $N(\bullet)$ is the cumulative normal distribution function and

$$d_1 = \frac{\ln(S/X) + (r + \sigma^2/2)T}{\sigma\sqrt{T}}$$

Using your estimate of $\sigma = .35$, you find that the hedge ratio $N(d_1) - 1 = -.453$.

Suppose, therefore, that you purchase 10 option contracts (1,000 puts) and purchase 453 shares of stock. Once the market "catches up" to your presumably better volatility estimate, the put options purchased will increase in value. If the market assessment of volatility changes as soon as you purchase the options, your profits should equal 1,000 $\times$ $.29 = $290. The option price will be affected as well by any change in the stock price, but this part of your exposure will be eliminated if the hedge ratio is chosen properly. Your profit should be based solely on the effect of the change in the implied volatility of the put, with the impact of the stock price hedged away.

Table 21.3 illustrates your profits as a function of the stock price assuming that the put price changes to reflect *your* estimate of volatility. Panel B shows that the put option alone can provide profits or losses depending on whether the stock price falls or rises. We see in panel C, however, that each *hedged* put option provides profits nearly equal to the original mispricing, regardless of the change in the stock price.

Notice in Example 21.6 that the profit is not exactly independent of the stock price. This is because as the stock price changes, so do the deltas used to calculate the hedge ratio. The hedge ratio in principle would need to be continually adjusted as deltas evolve. The sensitivity of the delta to the stock price is called the **gamma** of the option. Option gammas are analogous to bond convexity. In both cases, the curvature of the value function means that hedge ratios or durations change with market conditions, making rebalancing a necessary part of hedging strategies.

**CONCEPT CHECK☞ QUESTION 9**

**Suppose you bet on volatility by purchasing calls instead of puts. How would you hedge your exposure to stock-price fluctuations? What is the hedge ratio?**

### Table 21.3   Profit on Hedged Put Portfolio

**A. Cost to establish hedged position**

| | |
|---|---:|
| 1,000 put options @ $4.495/option | $ 4,495 |
| 453 shares @ $90/share | 40,770 |
| *TOTAL* outlay | $45,265 |

**B. Value of put option as a function of the stock price at implied volatility of 35%**

| Stock Price: | 89 | 90 | 91 |
|---|---:|---:|---:|
| Put price | $5.254 | $4.785 | $4.347 |
| Profit (loss) on each put | 0.759 | 0.290 | (0.148) |

**C. Value of and profit on hedged put portfolio**

| Stock Price: | 89 | 90 | 91 |
|---|---:|---:|---:|
| Value of 1,000 put options | $ 5,254 | $ 4,785 | $ 4,347 |
| Value of 453 shares | 40,317 | 40,770 | 41,223 |
| *TOTAL* | $45,571 | $45,555 | $45,570 |
| Profit (= Value − Cost from panel A) | 306 | 290 | 305 |

A variant of the strategy in Example 21.6 involves cross-option speculation. Suppose you observe a 45-day maturity call option on IBM with strike price 95 selling at a price consistent with a volatility of $\sigma = 33\%$ while another 45-day call with strike price 90 has an implied volatility of only 27%. Because the underlying asset and maturity date are identical, you conclude that the call with the higher implied volatility is relatively overpriced. To exploit the mispricing, you might buy the cheap calls (with strike price 90 and implied volatility of 27%) and write the expensive calls (with strike price 95 and implied volatility 33%). If the risk-free rate is 4% and IBM is selling at $90 per share, the calls purchased will be priced at $3.6202 and the calls written will be priced at $2.3735.

Despite the fact that you are long one call and short another, your exposure to IBM stock-price uncertainty will not be hedged using this strategy. This is because calls with different strike prices have different sensitivities to the price of the underlying asset. The lower-strike-price call has a higher delta and therefore greater exposure to the price of IBM. If you take an equal number of positions in these two options, you will inadvertently establish a bullish position in IBM, as the calls you purchase have higher deltas than the calls you write. In fact, you may recall from Chapter 20 that this portfolio (long call with low exercise price and short call with high exercise price) is called a *bullish spread*.

To establish a hedged position, we can use the hedge ratio approach as follows. Consider the 95-strike-price options you write as the asset that hedges your exposure to the 90-strike-price options your purchase. Then the hedge ratio is

$$H = \frac{\text{Change in value of 90-strike-price call for \$1 change in IBM}}{\text{Change in value of 95-strike-price call for \$1 change in IBM}}$$

$$= \frac{\text{Delta of 90-strike-price call}}{\text{Delta of 95-strike-price call}} < 1$$

You need to write *more* than one call with the higher strike price to hedge the purchase of each call with the lower strike price. Because the prices of higher-strike-price calls are less sensitive to IBM prices, more of them are required to offset the exposure.

**Table 21.4   Profits on Delta-Neutral Options Portfolio**

**A. Cash flow when portfolio is established**

Purchase 1,000 calls ($X = 90$) @ $3.6202
(option priced at implied volatility of 27%)                          $3,620.20 cash outflow

Write 1,589 calls ($X = 95$) @ $2.3735
(option priced at implied volatility of 33%)                           3,771.50 cash inflow

    *TOTAL*                                                                        $   151.30 net cash inflow

**B. Option prices at implied volatility of 30%**

| Stock Price: | 89 | 90 | 91 |
|---|---|---|---|
| 90-strike-price calls | $3.478 | $3.997 | $4.557 |
| 95-strike-price calls | 1.703 | 2.023 | 2.382 |

**C. Value of portfolio after implied volatilities converge to 30%**

| Stock Price: | 89 | 90 | 91 |
|---|---|---|---|
| Value of 1,000 calls held | $3,478 | $3,997 | $4,557 |
| − Value of 1,589 calls written | 2,705 | 3,214 | 3,785 |
|     TOTAL | $   773 | $   782 | $   772 |

Suppose the true annual volatility of the stock is midway between the two implied volatilities, so $\sigma = 30\%$. We know that the delta of a call option is $N(d_1)$. Therefore, the deltas of the two options and the hedge ratio are computed as follows:

*Option with strike price 90:*

$$d_1 = \frac{\ln(90/90) + (.04 + .30^2/2) \times 45/365}{.30\sqrt{45/365}} = .0995$$

$$N(d_1) = .5396$$

*Option with strike price 95:*

$$d_1 = \frac{\ln(90/95) + (.04 + .30^2/2) \times 45/365}{.30\sqrt{45/365}} = -.4138$$

$$N(d_1) = .3395$$

*Hedge ratio:*

$$\frac{.5396}{.3395} = 1.589$$

Therefore, for every 1,000 call options purchased with strike price 90, we need to write 1,589 call options with strike price 95. Following this strategy enables us to bet on the relative mispricing of the two options without taking a position on IBM. Panel A of Table 21.4 shows that the position will result in a cash inflow of $151.30. The premium income on the calls written exceeds the cost of the calls purchased.

When you establish a position in stocks and options that is hedged with respect to fluctuations in the price of the underlying asset, your portfolio is said to be **delta neutral,** meaning that the portfolio has no tendency to either increase or decrease in value when the stock price fluctuates.

Let's check that our options position is in fact delta neutral. Suppose that the implied volatilities of the two options come back into alignment just after you establish your position, so that both options are priced at implied volatilities of 30%. You expect to profit from the increase in the value of the call purchased as well as from the decrease in the value of the call written. The option prices at 30% volatility are given in panel B of Table 21.4 and the values of your position for various stock prices are presented in panel C. Although the profit or loss on each option is affected by the stock price, the value of the delta-neutral option portfolio is positive and essentially independent of the price of IBM. Moreover, we saw in panel A that the portfolio would have been established without ever requiring a cash outlay. You would have cash inflows both when you establish the portfolio *and* when you liquidate it after the implied volatilities converge to 30%.

This unusual profit opportunity arises because you have identified prices out of alignment. Such opportunities could not arise if prices were at equilibrium levels. By exploiting the pricing discrepancy using a delta-neutral strategy, you should earn profits regardless of the price movement in IBM stock.

Delta-neutral hedging strategies are also subject to practical problems, the most important of which is the difficulty in assessing the proper volatility for the coming period. If the volatility estimate is incorrect, so will be the deltas, and the overall position will not truly be hedged. Moreover, option or option-plus-stock positions generally will not be neutral with respect to changes in volatility. For example, a put option hedged by a stock might be delta neutral, but it is not volatility neutral. Changes in the market assessments of volatility will affect the option price even if the stock price is unchanged.

These problems can be serious, because volatility estimates are never fully reliable. First, volatility cannot be observed directly, and must be estimated from past data which imparts measurement error to the forecast. Second, we've seen that both historical and implied volatilities fluctuate over time. Therefore, we are always shooting at a moving target. Although delta-neutral positions are hedged against changes in the price of the underlying asset, they still are subject to **volatility risk,** the risk incurred from unpredictable changes in volatility. Thus, although delta-neutral option hedges might eliminate exposure to risk from fluctuations in the value of the underlying asset, they do not eliminate volatility risk.

## 21.6   EMPIRICAL EVIDENCE ON OPTION PRICING

There have been an enormous number of empirical tests of the Black-Scholes option-pricing model. For the most part, the results of the studies have been positive in that the Black-Scholes model generates option values fairly close to the actual prices at which options trade. At the same time, some regular empirical failures of the model have been noted.

Whaley[11] examined the performance of the Black-Scholes formula relative to that of more complicated option formulas that allow for early exercise. His findings indicate that formulas allowing for the possibility of early exercise do better at pricing than the Black-Scholes formula. The Black-Scholes formula seems to perform worst for options on stocks with high dividend payouts. The true American call option formula, on the other hand, seems to fare equally well in the prediction of option prices on stocks with high or low dividend payouts.

Rubinstein[12] has pointed out that the performance of the Black-Scholes model has deteriorated in recent years in the sense that options on the same stock with the same strike

---

[11] Robert E. Whaley, "Valuation of American Call Options on Dividend-Paying Stocks: Empirical Tests," *Journal of Financial Economics* 10 (1982).

[12] Mark Rubinstein, "Implied Binomial Trees," *Journal of Finance* 49 (July 1994), pp. 771–818.

**Figure 21.13   Black-Scholes implied volatilities for options with 30, 45, and 60 days to maturity on May 16, 1996.**

Source: Shiheng Wang, "An Empirical Study on the Implied Volatility Function of S&P 500 Options," Dissertation, Queen's University, Ontario, Canada, August 2002.

price that *should* have the same implied volatility actually exhibit progressively different implied volatilities. He attributed this to an increasing fear of another market crash like that in 1987, and noted that, consistent with this hypothesis, low-strike-price options are priced higher (i.e., with higher implied volatilities) than are other options. The market prices these options as though there is a bigger chance of a large drop in the stock price than would be suggested by the Black-Scholes assumptions.

Figure 21.13, which considers implied volatility of options on the S&P 500, is typical of recent empirical studies. The implied volatility as a function of exercise price would be flat if the Black-Scholes model were perfect. All S&P options with identical expiration dates would have identical implied volatilities since they are all written on the same index for the same horizon. Instead, the figure shows that the implied volatility curve declines as a function of exercise price. Clearly the Black-Scholes model is missing something, and that seems to be related to the probability of a big negative jump in stock prices.

## SUMMARY

1. Option values may be viewed as the sum of intrinsic value plus time or "volatility" value. The volatility value is the right to choose not to exercise if the stock price moves against the holder. Thus the option holder cannot lose more than the cost of the option regardless of stock price performance.

2. Call options are more valuable when the exercise price is lower, when the stock price is higher, when the interest rate is higher, when the time to maturity is greater, when the stock's volatility is greater, and when dividends are lower.

3. Call options must sell for at least the stock price less the present value of the exercise price and dividends to be paid before maturity. This implies that a call option on a non-dividend-paying stock may be sold for more than the proceeds from immediate exercise. Thus European calls are worth as much as American calls on stocks that pay no dividends, because the right to exercise the American call early has no value.

4. Options may be priced relative to the underlying stock price using a simple two-period, two-state pricing model. As the number of periods increases, the binomial model can approximate more realistic stock price distributions. The Black-Scholes formula may be seen as a limiting case of the binomial option model, as the holding period is divided into progressively smaller subperiods when the interest rate and stock volatility are constant.

5. The Black-Scholes formula applies to options on stocks that pay no dividends. Dividend adjustments may be adequate to price European calls on dividend-paying stocks, but the proper treatment of American calls on dividend-paying stocks requires more complex formulas.

6. Put options may be exercised early, whether the stock pays dividends or not. Therefore, American puts generally are worth more than European puts.

7. European put values can be derived from the call value and the put-call parity relationship. This technique cannot be applied to American puts for which early exercise is a possibility.

8. The hedge ratio is the number of shares of stock required to hedge the price risk involved in writing one option. Hedge ratios are near zero for deep out-of-the-money call options and approach 1.0 for deep in-the-money calls.

9. Although hedge ratios are less than 1.0, call options have elasticities greater than 1.0. The rate of return on a call (as opposed to the dollar return) responds more than one for one with stock price movements.

10. Portfolio insurance can be obtained by purchasing a protective put option on an equity position. When the appropriate put is not traded, portfolio insurance entails a dynamic hedge strategy where a fraction of the equity portfolio equal to the desired put option's delta is sold and placed in risk-free securities.

11. The option delta is used to determine the hedge ratio for options positions. Delta-neutral portfolios are independent of price changes in the underlying asset. Even delta-neutral option portfolios are subject to volatility risk, however.

## KEY TERMS

| | | |
|---|---|---|
| intrinsic value | pseudo-American call | portfolio insurance |
| binomial model | option value | dynamic hedging |
| Black-Scholes pricing formula | hedge ratio | gamma |
| | delta | delta neutral |
| implied volatility | option elasticity | volatility risk |

## WEBSITES

stocks.about.com
biz.yahoo.com/opt

These sites have extensive links to many other sites. They include sections on education, exchanges, research, and quotes, as well as extensive sources related to futures markets. From the home page, left margin, link to *Derivatives.*

www.optionscentral.com

The Options Industry Council site "options central" contains comprehensive educational material, including access to the freely available Options Toolbox. The toolbox allows you to simulate different options positions and examine option pricing.

www.numa.com
www.phlx.com

These sites contain extensive links to several derivatives-related websites.

The following sites offer options analysis and calculators:
www.optionstrategist.com
www.schaeffersresearch.com

**WEBSITES**

www.fintools.com/calculators.html
www.optionsclearing.com (See *Education* link for three valuation models.)
www.adamscapital.com/option_valuation3.html

**PROBLEMS**

1. We showed in the text that the value of a call option increases with the volatility of the stock. Is this also true of put option values? Use the put-call parity theorem as well as a numerical example to prove your answer.

2. In each of the following questions, you are asked to compare two options with parameters as given. The risk-free interest rate for *all* cases should be assumed to be 6%. Assume the stocks on which these options are written pay no dividends.

   *a.*
   | Put | T | X | σ | Price of Option |
   |-----|---|---|---|-----------------|
   | A | .5 | 50 | .20 | $10 |
   | B | .5 | 50 | .25 | $10 |

   Which put option is written on the stock with the lower price?
   i.  A.
   ii. B.
   iii. Not enough information.

   *b.*
   | Put | T | X | σ | Price of Option |
   |-----|---|---|---|-----------------|
   | A | .5 | 50 | .2 | $10 |
   | B | .5 | 50 | .2 | $12 |

   Which put option must be written on the stock with the lower price?
   i.  A.
   ii. B.
   iii. Not enough information.

   *c.*
   | Call | S | X | σ | Price of Option |
   |------|---|---|---|-----------------|
   | A | 50 | 50 | .20 | $12 |
   | B | 55 | 50 | .20 | $10 |

   Which call option must have the lower time to maturity?
   i.  A.
   ii. B.
   iii. Not enough information.

   *d.*
   | Call | T | X | S | Price of Option |
   |------|---|---|---|-----------------|
   | A | .5 | 50 | 55 | $10 |
   | B | .5 | 50 | 55 | $12 |

   Which call option is written on the stock with higher volatility?
   i.  A.
   ii. B.
   iii. Not enough information.

| e. Call | T | X | S | Price of Option |
|---------|-----|-----|-----|-----------------|
| A | .5 | 50 | 55 | $10 |
| B | .5 | 50 | 55 | $ 7 |

Which call option is written on the stock with higher volatility?
  i.  A.
  ii.  B.
  iii.  Not enough information.

3. Reconsider the determination of the hedge ratio in the two-state model (page 753), where we showed that one-half share of stock would hedge one option. What is the hedge ratio at the following exercise prices: 115, 100, 75, 50, 25, 10? What do you conclude about the hedge ratio as the option becomes progressively more in the money?

4. Show that Black-Scholes call option hedge ratios also increase as the stock price increases. Consider a 1-year option with exercise price $50, on a stock with annual standard deviation 20%. The T-bill rate is 8% per year. Find $N(d_1)$ for stock prices $45, $50, and $55.

5. We will derive a two-state put option value in this problem. Data: $S_0 = 100$; $X = 110$; $1 + r = 1.10$. The two possibilities for $S_T$ are 130 and 80.
  a. Show that the range of $S$ is 50, whereas that of $P$ is 30 across the two states. What is the hedge ratio of the put?
  b. Form a portfolio of three shares of stock and five puts. What is the (nonrandom) payoff to this portfolio? What is the present value of the portfolio?
  c. Given that the stock currently is selling at 100, solve for the value of the put.

6. Calculate the value of a call option on the stock in the previous problem with an exercise price of 110. Verify that the put-call parity theorem is satisfied by your answers to problems 5 and 6. (Do not use continuous compounding to calculate the present value of $X$ in this example because we are using a two-state model here, not a continuous-time Black-Scholes model.)

7. Use the Black-Scholes formula to find the value of a call option on the following stock:

| | |
|---|---|
| Time to maturity: | 6 months |
| Standard deviation: | 50% per year |
| Exercise price: | $50 |
| Stock price: | $50 |
| Interest rate: | 10% |

8. Find the Black-Scholes value of a put option on the stock in the previous problem with the same exercise price and maturity as the call option.

9. Recalculate the value of the call option in problem 7, successively substituting one of the changes below while keeping the other parameters as in problem 7:
  a. Time to maturity = 3 months.
  b. Standard deviation = 25% per year.
  c. Exercise price = $55.
  d. Stock price = $55.
  e. Interest rate = 15%.

Consider each scenario independently. Confirm that the option value changes in accordance with the prediction of Table 21.1.

10. A call option with $X = \$50$ on a stock currently priced at $S = \$55$ is selling for $10. Using a volatility estimate of $\sigma = .30$, you find that $N(d_1) = .6$ and $N(d_2) = .5$. The risk-free interest rate is zero. Is the implied volatility based on the option price more or less than .30? Explain.

11. What would be the Excel formula in Figure 21.8 for the Black-Scholes value of a straddle position?

12. Would you expect a $1 increase in a call option's exercise price to lead to a decrease in the option's value of more or less than $1?

13. Is a put option on a high-beta stock worth more than one on a low-beta stock? The stocks have identical firm-specific risk.

14. All else equal, is a call option on a stock with a lot of firm-specific risk worth more than one on a stock with little firm-specific risk? The betas of the two stocks are equal.

15. All else equal, will a call option with a high exercise price have a higher or lower hedge ratio than one with a low exercise price?

16. Should the rate of return of a call option on a long-term Treasury bond be more or less sensitive to changes in interest rates than is the rate of return of the underlying bond?

17. If the stock price falls and the call price rises, then what has happened to the call option's implied volatility?

18. If the time to maturity falls and the put price rises, then what has happened to the put option's implied volatility?

19. According to the Black-Scholes formula, what will be the value of the hedge ratio of a call option as the stock price becomes infinitely large? Explain briefly.

20. According to the Black-Scholes formula, what will be the value of the hedge ratio of a put option for a very small exercise price?

21. The hedge ratio of an at-the-money call option on IBM is .4. The hedge ratio of an at-the-money put option is $-.6$. What is the hedge ratio of an at-the-money straddle position on IBM?

22. A collar is established by buying a share of stock for $50, buying a 6-month put option with exercise price $45, and writing a 6-month call option with exercise price $55. Based on the volatility of the stock, you calculate that for a strike price of $45 and maturity of 6 months, $N(d_1) = .60$, whereas for the exercise price of $55, $N(d_1) = .35$.

   a. What will be the gain or loss on the collar if the stock price increases by $1?
   b. What happens to the delta of the portfolio if the stock price becomes very large? Very small?

23. The board of directors of Abco Company is concerned about the downside risk of a $100 million equity portfolio in its pension plan. The board's consultant has proposed temporarily (for 1 month) hedging the portfolio with either futures or options. Referring to the following table, the consultant states:

   a. "The $100 million equity portfolio can be fully protected on the downside by selling (shorting) 2,000 futures contracts."
   b. "The cost of this protection is that the portfolio's expected rate of return will be zero percent."

**Market, Portfolio, and Contract Data**

| | |
|---|---|
| Equity index level | 99.00 |
| Equity futures price | 100.00 |
| Futures contract multiplier | 500 |
| Portfolio beta | 1.20 |
| Contract expiration (months) | 3 |

Critique the accuracy of each of the consultant's two statements.

24. These three put options are all written on the same stock. One has a delta of $-.9$, one a delta of $-.5$, and one a delta of $-.1$. Assign deltas to the three puts by filling in this table.

| Put | X | Delta |
|---|---|---|
| A | 10 | |
| B | 20 | |
| C | 30 | |

25. You are *very* bullish (optimistic) on stock EFG, much more so than the rest of the market. In each question, choose the portfolio strategy that will give you the biggest dollar profit if your bullish forecast turns out to be correct. Explain your answer.

   a. *Choice A:* $10,000 invested in calls with $X = 50$.
      *Choice B:* $10,000 invested in EFG stock.
   b. *Choice A:* 10 call option contracts (for 100 shares each), with $X = 50$.
      *Choice B:* 1,000 shares of EFG stock.

26. Imagine you are a provider of portfolio insurance. You are establishing a 4-year program. The portfolio you manage is currently worth $100 million, and you hope to provide a minimum return of 0%. The equity portfolio has a standard deviation of 25% per year, and T-bills pay 5% per year. Assume for simplicity that the portfolio pays no dividends (or that all dividends are reinvested).

   a. How much should be placed in bills? How much in equity?
   b. What should the manager do if the stock portfolio falls by 3% on the first day of trading?

27. Joel Franklin is a portfolio manager responsible for derivatives. Franklin observes an American-style option and a European-style option with the same strike price, expiration, and underlying stock. Franklin believes that the European-style option will have a higher premium than the American-style option.

   a. Critique Franklin's belief that the European-style option will have a higher premium.

   Franklin is asked to value a 1-year European-style call option for Abaco Ltd. common stock, which last traded at $43.00. He has collected the information in the following table.

| | |
|---|---|
| Closing stock price | $43.00 |
| Call and put option exercise price | 45.00 |
| 1-year put option price | 4.00 |
| 1-year Treasury bill rate | 5.50% |
| Time to expiration | One year |

   b. Calculate, using put-call parity and the information provided in the table, the European-style call option value.

c. State the effect, if any, of each of the following three variables on the value of a call option. (No calculations required.)

   i. an increase in short-term interest rate.

   ii. an increase in stock price volatility.

   iii. a decrease in time to option expiration.

28. You would like to be holding a protective put position on the stock of XYZ Co. to lock in a guaranteed minimum value of $100 at year-end. XYZ currently sells for $100. Over the next year the stock price will increase by 10% or decrease by 10%. The T-bill rate is 5%. Unfortunately, no put options are traded on XYZ Co.

   a. Suppose the desired put option were traded. How much would it cost to purchase?

   b. What would have been the cost of the protective put portfolio?

   c. What portfolio position in stock and T-bills will ensure you a payoff equal to the payoff that would be provided by a protective put with $X = 100$? Show that the payoff to this portfolio and the cost of establishing the portfolio matches that of the desired protective put.

29. Return to Example 21.1. Use the binomial model to value a 1-year European put option with exercise price $110 on the stock in that example. Does your solution for the put price satisfy put-call parity?

30. A stock index is currently trading at 50. Paul Tripp, CFA, wants to value 2-year index options using the binomial model. The stock will either increase in value by 20% or fall in value by 20%. The annual risk-free interest rate is 6%. No dividends are paid on any of the underlying securities in the index.

   a. Construct a two-period binomial tree for the value of the stock index.

   b. Calculate the value of a European call option on the index with an exercise price of 60.

   c. Calculate the value of a European put option on the index with an exercise price of 60.

   d. Confirm that your solutions for the values of the call and the put satisfy put-call parity.

31. Suppose that the risk-free interest rate is zero. Would an American put option ever be exercised early? Explain.

32. Let $p(S, T, X)$ denote the value of a European put on a stock selling at $S$ dollars, with time to maturity $T$, and with exercise price $X$, and let $P(S, T, X)$ be the value of an American put.

   a. Evaluate $p(0, T, X)$.

   b. Evaluate $P(0, T, X)$.

   c. Evaluate $p(S, T, 0)$.

   d. Evaluate $P(S, T, 0)$.

   e. What does your answer to (b) tell you about the possibility that American puts may be exercised early?

33. You are attempting to value a call option with an exercise price of $100 and 1 year to expiration. The underlying stock pays no dividends, its current price is $100, and you believe it has a 50% chance of increasing to $120 and a 50% change of decreasing to $80. The risk-free rate of interest is 10%. Calculate the call option's value using the two-state stock price model.

34. Consider an increase in the volatility of the stock in the previous problem. Suppose that if the stock increases in price, it will increase to $130, and that if it falls, it will

fall to $70. Show that the value of the call option is now higher than the value derived in the previous problem.

35. Calculate the value of a put option with exercise price $100 using the data in problem 33. Show that put-call parity is satisfied by your solution.

36. XYZ Corp. will pay a $2 per share dividend in 2 months. Its stock price currently is $60 per share. A call option on XYZ has an exercise price of $55 and 3-month time to maturity. The risk-free interest rate is .5% per month, and the stock's volatility (standard deviation) = 7% per month. Find the pseudo-American option value. (Hint: Try defining one "period" as a month, rather than as a year.)

37. Ken Webster manages a $100 million equity portfolio benchmarked to the S&P 500 index. Over the past 2 years, the S&P 500 Index has appreciated 60 percent. Webster believes the market is overvalued when measured by several traditional fundamental/economic indicators. He is concerned about maintaining the excellent gains the portfolio has experienced in the past 2 years but recognizes that the S&P 500 Index could still move above its current 668 level.

Webster is considering the following *option collar* strategy:

- Protection for the portfolio can be attained by purchasing an S&P 500 Index put with a strike price of 665 (just out of the money).
- The put can be financed by selling two 675 calls (farther out-of-the-money) for every put purchased.
- Because the combined delta of the two calls (see following table) is less than 1 (that is, $2 \times 0.36 = 0.72$) the options will not lose more than the underlying portfolio will gain if the market advances.

The information in the following table describes the two options used to create the collar.

| Characteristics | 675 Call | 665 Put |
|---|---|---|
| Option price | $4.30 | $8.05 |
| Option implied volatility | 11.00% | 14.00% |
| Option's delta | 0.36 | −0.44 |
| Contracts needed for collar | 602 | 301 |

Notes:
- Ignore transaction costs.
- S&P 500 historical 30-day volatility = 12.00%.
- Time to option expiration = 30 days.

a. Describe the potential returns of the combined portfolio (the underlying portfolio plus the option collar) if after 30 days the S&P 500 index has:
   i. risen approximately 5% to 701.
   ii. remained at 668 (no change).
   iii. declined by approximately 5% to 635.
   (No calculations are necessary.)
b. Discuss the effect on the hedge ratio (delta) of *each* option as the S&P 500 approaches the level for *each* of the potential outcomes listed in part (*a*).
c. Evaluate the pricing of *each* of the following in relation to the volatility data provided:
   i. the put
   ii. the call

38. "The beta of a call option on General Motors is greater than the beta of a share of General Motors." True or false?

39. "The beta of a call option on the S&P 500 index with an exercise price of 1,030 is greater than the beta of a call on the index with an exercise price of 1,040." True or false?

40. What will happen to the hedge ratio of a convertible bond as the stock price becomes very large?

41. Salomon Brothers believes that market volatility will be 20% annually for the next 3 years. Three-year at-the-money call and put options on the market index sell at an implied volatility of 22%. What options portfolio can Salomon Brothers establish to speculate on its volatility belief without taking a bullish or bearish position on the market? Using Salomon's estimate of volatility, 3-year at-the-money options have $N(d_1) = .6$.

42. Suppose that call options on ExxonMobil stock with time to maturity 3 months and strike price $60 are selling at an implied volatility of 30%. ExxonMobil stock currently is $60 per share, and the risk-free rate is 4%. If you believe the true volatility of the stock is 32%, how can you trade on your belief without taking on exposure to the performance of ExxonMobil? How many shares of stock will you hold for each option contract purchased or sold?

43. Using the data in problem 42, suppose that 3-month put options with a strike price of $60 are selling at an implied volatility of 34%. Construct a delta-neutral portfolio comprising positions in calls and puts that will profit when the option prices come back into alignment.

44. Suppose that Salomon Brothers sells call options on $1.25 million worth of a stock portfolio with beta = 1.5. The option delta is .8. It wishes to hedge out its resultant exposure to a market advance by buying market index futures contracts.

    a. If the current value of the market index is 1,000 and the contract multiplier is $250, how many contracts should it buy?

    b. What if Salomon instead uses market index puts to hedge its exposure? Should it buy or sell puts? Each put option is on 100 units of the index, and the index at current prices represents $1,000 worth of stock.

45. You are holding call options on a stock. The stock's beta is .75, and you are concerned that the stock market is about to fall. The stock is currently selling for $5 and you hold 1 million options on the stock (i.e., you hold 10,000 contracts for 100 shares each). The option delta is .8. How many market index futures contracts must you buy or sell to hedge your market exposure if the current value of the market index is 1,000 and the contract multiplier is $250?

**STANDARD &POOR'S**

Option traders love stock volatility. (Why?) From the Market Insight entry page (**www.mhhe.com/business/finance/edumarketinsight**), link to *Industry,* then pull down to the airlines industry. Review the *Industry Profile* for a measure of recent stock price volatility. Then review the S&P Industry Survey for the airlines industry. What factors associated with the industry have produced the recent stock volatility? In the Black-Scholes valuation model, how is volatility associated with option value? What options strategies exploit volatility?

**E-INVESTMENTS**
**Black-Scholes**
**Option Pricing**

Go to options calculator available at **www.schaeffersresearch.com/streetools/calculator. aspx**.

Use EMC Corporation for the firm. Enter the ticker symbol (EMC) and latest price for the firm. Since the company is not paying a cash dividend at this time, enter 0.0 for the quarterly dividend. The calculator will display the current interest rate. Find the prices for call and put options in the 2 months following the closest expiration month. (You can request the options prices directly in the calculator.) For example, if you are in February, you would use the April and July options. Use the options that are closest to being at the money. For example, if the most recent price of EMC was $56.40, you would select the 55 strike price.

Once you have entered the options prices and other data, hit the *Go Figure* button and analyze the results.

Are the calculated prices in line with observed prices?

Compare the implied volatility with the historical volatility.

**SOLUTIONS TO CONCEPT CHECKS**

1. **If This Variable Increases . . . The Value of a Put Option**

| | |
|---|---|
| $S$ | Decreases |
| $X$ | Increases |
| $\sigma$ | Increases |
| $T$ | Increases* |
| $r_f$ | Decreases |
| Dividend payouts | Increases |

*For American puts, increase in time to expiration must increase value. One can always choose to exercise early if this is optimal; the longer expiration date simply expands the range of alternatives open to the option holder which must make the option more valuable. For a European put, where early exercise is not allowed, longer time to expiration can have an indeterminate effect. Longer maturity increases volatility value since the final stock price is more uncertain, but it reduces the present value of the exercise price that will be received if the put is exercised. The net effect on put value is ambiguous.

To understand the impact of higher volatility, consider the same scenarios as for the call. The low volatility scenario yields a lower expected payoff.

| High volatility | Stock price | $10 | $20 | $30 | $40 | $50 |
|---|---|---|---|---|---|---|
| | Put payoff | $20 | $10 | $ 0 | $ 0 | $ 0 |
| Low volatility | Stock price | $20 | $25 | $30 | $35 | $40 |
| | Put payoff | $10 | $ 5 | $ 0 | $ 0 | $ 0 |

2. The parity relationship assumes that all options are held until expiration and that there are no cash flows until expiration. These assumptions are valid only in the special case of European options on non-dividend-paying stocks. If the stock pays no dividends, the American and European calls are equally valuable, whereas the American put is worth more than the European put. Therefore, although the parity theorem for European options states that

$$P = C - S_0 + \text{PV}(X)$$

in fact, *P* will be *greater* than this value if the put is American.

**3.** Because the option now is underpriced, we want to reverse our previous strategy.

| | Initial Cash Flow | Cash Flow in 1 Year for Each Possible Stock Price | |
|---|---|---|---|
| | | $S = 50$ | $S = 200$ |
| Buy 2 options | −48 | 0 | 150 |
| Short-sell 1 share | 100 | −50 | −200 |
| Lend $52 at 8% interest rate | −52 | 56.16 | 56.16 |
| TOTAL | 0 | 6.16 | 6.16 |

**4.** *a.* $C_u - C_d = \$6.984 - 0$

*b.* $uS_0 - dS_0 = \$110 - \$95 = \$15$

*c.* $6.984/15 = .4656$

*d.*

| Action Today (time 0) | Value in Next Period As Function of Stock Price | |
|---|---|---|
| | $dS_0 = \$95$ | $uS_0 = \$110$ |
| Buy .4656 shares at price $S_0 = \$100$ | $\$44.232$ | $\$51.216$ |
| Write 1 call at price $C_0$ | 0 | − 6.984 |
| TOTAL | $\$44.232$ | $\$44.232$ |

The portfolio must have a market value equal to the present value of $44.232.

*e.* $\$44.232/1.05 = \$42.126$

*f.* $.4656 \times \$100 - C_0 = \$42.126$

$C_0 = \$46.56 - \$42.126 = \$4.434$

**5.** Higher. For deep out-of-the-money call options, an increase in the stock price still leaves the option unlikely to be exercised. Its value increases only fractionally. For deep in-the-money options, exercise is likely, and option holders benefit by a full dollar for each dollar increase in the stock, as though they already own the stock.

**6.** Because $\sigma = .6$, $\sigma^2 = .36$.

$$d_1 = \frac{\ln(100/95) + (.10 + .36/2).25}{.6\sqrt{.25}} = .4043$$

$$d_2 = d_1 - .6\sqrt{.25} = .1043$$

Using Table 21.2 and interpolation, or from a spreadsheet function:

$N(d_1) = .6570$

$N(d_2) = .5415$

$C = 100 \times .6570 - 95e^{-.10 \times .25} \times .5415 = 15.53$

**7.** Implied volatility exceeds .5. Given a standard deviation of .5, the option value is $13.70. A higher volatility is needed to justify the actual $15 price.

**8.** A $1 increase in stock price is a percentage increase of $1/122 = .82\%$. The put option will fall by $(.4 \times \$1) = \$.40$, a percentage decrease of $\$.40/\$4 = 10\%$. Elasticity is $-10/.82 = -12.2$.

**9.** The delta for a call option is $N(d_1)$, which is positive, and in this case is .547. Therefore, for every 10 option contracts purchased, you would need to *short* 547 shares of stock.

# FUTURES MARKETS

Futures and forward contracts are like options in that they specify purchase
or sale of some underlying security at some future date. The key difference
is that the holder of an option is not compelled to buy or sell, and will not
do so if the trade is unprofitable. A futures or forward contract, however,
carries the obligation to go through with the agreed-upon transaction.

A forward contract is not an investment in the strict sense that funds are
paid for an asset. It is only a commitment today to transact in the future.
Forward arrangements are part of our study of investments, however,
because they offer powerful
means to hedge other
investments and generally
modify portfolio
characteristics.

Forward markets for
future delivery of various
commodities go back at least
to ancient Greece. Organized
*futures markets*, though, are a
relatively modern development,
dating only to the 19th century.
Futures markets replace
informal forward contracts
with highly standardized,
exchange-traded securities.

This chapter describes the workings of futures markets and the mechanics
of trading in these markets. We show how futures contracts are useful
investment vehicles for both hedgers and speculators and how the futures
price relates to the spot price of an asset. We also show how futures can
be used in several risk-management applications. This chapter deals with
general principles of future markets. Chapter 23 describes specific futures
markets in greater detail.

## 22.1   THE FUTURES CONTRACT

To see how futures and forwards work and how they might be useful, consider the portfolio diversification problem facing a farmer growing a single crop, let us say wheat. The entire planting season's revenue depends critically on the highly volatile crop price. The farmer can't easily diversify his position because virtually his entire wealth is tied up in the crop.

The miller who must purchase wheat for processing faces a portfolio problem that is the mirror image of the farmer's. He is subject to profit uncertainty because of the unpredictable future cost of the wheat.

Both parties can reduce this source of risk if they enter into a **forward contract** requiring the farmer to deliver the wheat when harvested at a price agreed upon now, regardless of the market price at harvest time. No money need change hands at this time. A forward contract is simply a deferred-delivery sale of some asset with the sales price agreed on now. All that is required is that each party be willing to lock in the ultimate price to be paid or received for delivery of the commodity. A forward contract protects each party from future price fluctuations.

Futures markets formalize and standardize forward contracting. Buyers and sellers trade in a centralized futures exchange. The exchange standardizes the types of contracts that may be traded: It establishes contract size, the acceptable grade of commodity, contract delivery dates, and so forth. Although standardization eliminates much of the flexibility available in forward contracting, it has the offsetting advantage of liquidity because many traders will concentrate on the same small set of contracts. Futures contracts also differ from forward contracts in that they call for a daily settling up of any gains or losses on the contract. In the case of forward contracts, no money changes hands until the delivery date.

The centralized market, standardization of contracts, and depth of trading in each contract allows futures positions to be liquidated easily through a broker rather than personally renegotiated with the other party to the contract. Because the exchange guarantees the performance of each party to the contract, costly credit checks on other traders are not necessary. Instead, each trader simply posts a good-faith deposit, called the *margin*, in order to guarantee contract performance.

### The Basics of Futures Contracts

The futures contract calls for delivery of a commodity at a specified delivery or maturity date, for an agreed-upon price, called the **futures price,** to be paid at contract maturity. The contract specifies precise requirements for the commodity. For agricultural commodities, the exchange sets allowable grades (e.g., No. 2 hard winter wheat or No. 1 soft red wheat). The place or means of delivery of the commodity is specified as well. Delivery of agricultural commodities is made by transfer of warehouse receipts issued by approved warehouses. In the case of financial futures, delivery may be made by wire transfer; in the case of index futures, delivery may be accomplished by a cash settlement procedure such as those for index options. (Although the futures contract technically calls for delivery of an asset, delivery rarely occurs. Instead, parties to the contract much more commonly close out their positions before contract maturity, taking gains or losses in cash.)

Because the futures exchange specifies all the terms of the contract, the traders need bargain only over the futures price. The trader taking the **long position** commits to purchasing the commodity on the delivery date. The trader who takes the **short position** commits to delivering the commodity at contract maturity. The trader in the long position is said to "buy" a contract; the short-side trader "sells" a contract. The words *buy* and *sell* are figurative only, because a contract is not really bought or sold like a stock or bond; it is entered into by mutual agreement. At the time the contract is entered into, no money changes hands.

Figure 22.1 shows prices for several futures contracts as they appear in *The Wall Street Journal*. The boldface heading lists in each case the commodity, the exchange where the futures contract is traded in parentheses, the contract size, and the pricing unit. The first contract listed is for corn, traded on the Chicago Board of Trade (CBT). Each contract calls for delivery of 5,000 bushels, and prices in the entry are quoted in cents per bushel.

The next several rows detail price data for contracts expiring on various dates. The May 2003 maturity corn contract, for example, opened during the day at a futures price of 229 cents per bushel. The highest futures price during the day was 229.50, the lowest was 227.25, and the settlement price (a representative trading price during the last few minutes of trading) was 228.25. The settlement price decreased by .75 cents from the previous trading day. The highest futures price over the contract's life to date was 301, the lowest 227.25 cents. Finally, open interest, or the number of outstanding contracts, was 171,705. Similar information is given for each maturity date.

The trader holding the long position, that is, the person who will purchase the good, profits from price increases. Suppose that when the contract matures in May, the price of corn turns out to be 233.25 cents per bushel. The long-position trader who entered the contract at the futures price of 228.25 cents earns a profit of 5 cents per bushel: The eventual price is 5 cents higher than the originally agreed-to futures price. As each contract calls for delivery of 5,000 bushels, the profit to the long position equals $5,000 \times \$.05 = \$250$ per contract. Conversely, the short position loses 5 cents per bushel. The short position's loss equals the long position's gain.

To summarize, at maturity:

$$\text{Profit to long} = \text{Spot price at maturity} - \text{Original futures price}$$
$$\text{Profit to short} = \text{Original futures price} - \text{Spot price at maturity}$$

where the spot price is the actual market price of the commodity at the time of the delivery.

The futures contract is, therefore, a zero-sum game, with losses and gains to all positions netting out to zero. Every long position is offset by a short position. The aggregate profits to futures trading, summing over all investors, also must be zero, as is the net exposure to changes in the commodity price. For this reason, the establishment of a futures market in a commodity should not have a major impact on prices in the spot market for that commodity.

Figure 22.2, panel A, is a plot of the profits realized by an investor who enters the long side of a futures contract as a function of the price of the asset on the maturity date. Notice that profit is zero when the ultimate spot price, $P_T$, equals the initial futures price, $F_0$. Profit per unit of the underlying asset rises or falls one-for-one with changes in the final spot price. Unlike the payoff of a call option, the payoff of the long futures position can be negative: This will be the case if the spot price falls below the original futures price. Unlike the holder of a call, who has an *option* to buy, the long futures position trader cannot simply walk away from the contract. Also unlike options, in the case of futures there is no need to distinguish gross payoffs from net profits. This is because the futures contract is not purchased; it is simply a contract that is agreed to by two parties. The futures price adjusts to make the present value of either side of the contract equal to zero.

The distinction between futures and options is highlighted by comparing panel A of Figure 22.2 to the payoff and profit diagrams for an investor in a call option with exercise price, *X,* chosen equal to the futures price $F_0$ (see panel C). The futures investor is exposed to considerable losses if the asset price falls. In contrast, the investor in the call cannot lose more than the cost of the option.

**Figure 22.1 Futures listings**

FUTURE PRICES

**Figure 22.1**   *(Concluded)*

# FUTURE PRICES

| | OPEN | HIGH | LOW | SETTLE | CHG | LIFETIME HIGH | LIFETIME LOW | OPEN INT |
|---|---|---|---|---|---|---|---|---|
| Sept | 94.84 | 94.86 | 94.75 | 94.79 | ... | 5.21 | ... | 28,160 |
| Dec | 94.72 | 94.74 | 94.63 | 94.68 | ... | 5.32 | ... | 26,512 |
| Mr08 | 94.64 | 94.64 | 94.55 | 94.60 | .01 | 5.40 | -.01 | 14,427 |
| Ju10 | 93.93 | 93.95 | 93.89 | 93.91 | ... | 6.09 | ... | 2,400 |
| Ju11 | 93.69 | 93.69 | 93.63 | 93.65 | ... | 6.35 | ... | 1,555 |

Est vol 803,125; vol Mon 643,177; open int 4,321,619, +13,166.

**Euroyen** (CME)-¥100,000,000; pts of 100%

| | | | | | | | | |
|---|---|---|---|---|---|---|---|---|
| Sept | 99.92 | 99.92 | 99.92 | 99.92 | ... | 99.93 | 98.32 | 11,919 |
| Sept | ... | ... | ... | 99.90 | ... | 99.91 | 99.43 | 3,706 |
| Dec | 99.89 | 99.89 | 99.89 | 99.89 | ... | 99.90 | 99.22 | 2,388 |
| Mr03 | 99.85 | 99.85 | 99.85 | 99.85 | ... | 99.87 | 99.14 | 716 |
| June | 99.85 | 99.85 | 99.85 | 99.85 | -.01 | 99.86 | 99.41 | 791 |

Est vol 527; vol Mon 215; open int 25,080, -193.

**Short Sterling** (LIFFE)-£500,000; pts of 100%

| | | | | | | | | |
|---|---|---|---|---|---|---|---|---|
| Apr | ... | 96.36 | ... | 96.42 | 96.36 | ... | ... | 2,421 |
| June | 96.41 | 96.44 | 96.41 | 96.42 | .03 | 96.81 | 92.77 | 149,897 |
| Sept | 96.42 | 96.45 | 96.39 | 96.41 | .03 | 96.81 | 92.90 | 147,022 |
| Dec | 96.30 | 96.38 | 96.29 | 96.32 | .05 | 96.82 | 92.92 | 138,157 |
| Mr04 | 96.12 | 96.23 | 96.12 | 96.17 | .08 | 96.80 | 93.01 | 101,181 |
| June | 95.93 | 96.03 | 95.93 | 95.98 | .09 | 96.71 | 93.04 | 55,787 |
| Sept | 95.76 | 95.85 | 95.75 | 95.79 | .08 | 96.59 | 93.35 | 44,518 |
| Dec | 95.62 | 95.69 | 95.60 | 95.64 | .07 | 96.48 | 93.25 | 44,076 |
| Mr05 | 95.51 | 95.59 | 95.51 | 95.53 | .06 | 96.34 | 93.29 | 32,678 |
| June | 95.45 | 95.51 | 95.42 | 95.45 | .06 | 96.21 | 93.29 | 22,136 |
| Sept | 95.39 | 95.44 | 95.39 | 95.39 | .06 | 96.08 | 94.06 | 12,117 |
| Dec | 95.32 | 95.38 | 95.30 | 95.33 | .06 | 95.96 | 94.06 | 5,945 |
| Mr06 | 95.33 | 95.33 | 95.29 | 95.29 | .05 | 95.83 | 94.05 | 1,921 |

Est vol 135,784; vol Mon 98,108; open int 774,885, -15,917.

**Long Gilt** (LIFFE)-£100,000; pts of 100%

| | | | | | | | | |
|---|---|---|---|---|---|---|---|---|
| Mar | 120.04 | 120.06 | 119.88 | 119.81 | .21 | 123.68 | 116.85 | 4,925 |
| June | 119.08 | 119.41 | 118.94 | 119.04 | .21 | 122.94 | 118.01 | 81,096 |

Est vol 36,054; vol Mon 27,310; open int 86,026, -2,711.

**3 Month Euribor** (LIFFE)-€1,000,000; pts of 100%

| | | | | | | | | |
|---|---|---|---|---|---|---|---|---|
| Apr | 97.53 | 97.53 | 97.52 | 97.52 | -.01 | 97.66 | 97.39 | 56,405 |
| May | 97.59 | 97.59 | 97.59 | 97.59 | -.01 | 97.71 | 95.77 | 1,851 |
| June | 97.64 | 97.65 | 97.63 | 97.63 | .01 | 97.78 | 93.99 | 543,157 |
| Sept | 97.67 | 97.67 | 97.56 | 97.66 | .01 | 97.91 | 93.80 | 424,354 |
| Dec | 97.57 | 97.60 | 97.56 | 97.56 | .02 | 97.91 | 93.80 | 456,051 |
| Mr04 | 97.41 | 97.45 | 97.40 | 97.41 | .03 | 97.84 | 93.83 | 304,326 |
| June | 97.18 | 97.24 | 97.18 | 97.19 | .03 | 97.70 | 93.79 | 117,813 |
| Sept | 96.95 | 97.01 | 96.95 | 96.96 | .04 | 97.53 | 93.73 | 128,719 |
| Dec | 96.73 | 96.78 | 96.72 | 96.73 | .04 | 97.35 | 93.64 | 85,278 |
| Mr05 | 96.56 | 96.61 | 96.55 | 96.55 | .04 | 97.18 | 94.07 | 73,877 |
| June | 96.40 | 96.45 | 96.40 | 96.40 | .05 | 97.02 | 94.29 | 37,295 |
| Sept | 96.26 | 96.30 | 96.25 | 96.25 | .05 | 96.85 | 94.29 | 23,407 |
| Dec | 96.11 | 96.15 | 96.10 | 96.10 | .05 | 96.69 | 94.41 | 20,486 |
| Mr06 | 96.00 | 96.05 | 95.99 | 95.99 | .05 | 96.59 | 94.40 | 5,856 |

Est vol 394,538; vol Mon 362,531; open int 2,288,881, +18,066.

**3 Month Euroswiss** (LIFFE)-CHF 1,000,000; pts of 100%

| | | | | | | | | |
|---|---|---|---|---|---|---|---|---|
| June | 99.63 | 99.66 | 99.63 | 99.66 | .04 | 99.74 | 93.99 | 90,946 |
| Sept | 99.48 | 99.52 | 99.48 | 99.50 | .04 | 99.70 | 93.91 | 40,544 |
| Dec | 99.20 | 99.29 | 99.25 | 99.27 | .04 | 99.60 | 93.80 | 38,250 |
| Mr04 | 99.07 | 99.07 | 99.00 | 99.02 | .01 | 99.44 | 96.32 | 13,088 |
| June | 98.84 | 98.84 | 98.78 | 98.76 | -.01 | 99.30 | 96.98 | 9,456 |
| Sept | 98.56 | 98.56 | 98.50 | 98.51 | -.03 | 99.06 | 97.60 | 4,017 |
| Dec | 98.36 | 98.36 | 98.27 | 98.27 | -.05 | 98.86 | 98.10 | 5,633 |
| Mr05 | 98.05 | 98.07 | 98.05 | 98.07 | -.05 | 98.13 | 98.05 | 100 |

Est vol 22,997; vol Mon 18,179; open int 202,014, -1,834.

**Canadian Bankers Acceptance** (ME)-CAD 1,000,000

| | | | | | | | | |
|---|---|---|---|---|---|---|---|---|
| Apr | ... | ... | 96.65 | -0.03 | 96.75 | 96.71 | ... | 650 |
| June | 96.51 | 96.51 | 96.48 | -0.02 | 97.13 | 93.96 | ... | 76,682 |
| Sept | 96.31 | 96.32 | 96.27 | -0.05 | 97.07 | 93.82 | ... | 67,360 |
| Dec | 96.12 | 96.13 | 96.04 | 96.06 | -0.06 | 96.90 | 93.88 | 37,993 |
| Mr04 | 95.94 | 95.94 | 95.87 | 95.89 | -0.06 | 96.70 | 93.77 | 7,768 |
| June | 95.68 | 95.68 | 95.64 | 95.61 | -0.06 | 96.13 | 94.22 | 2,995 |
| Sept | 95.51 | 95.51 | 95.51 | 95.51 | -0.06 | 96.03 | 94.10 | 539 |
| Mr05 | 95.39 | 95.39 | 95.39 | 95.39 | -0.06 | 95.83 | 94.45 | 136 |

Est vol 19,954; vol Mon 13,193; open int 200,124, -19,594.

**10 Yr. Canadian Govt. Bonds** (ME)-CAD 100,000

| | | | | | | | | |
|---|---|---|---|---|---|---|---|---|
| June | 105.49 | 105.52 | 105.02 | 105.23 | -0.14 | 108.07 | 104.61 | 100,487 |

Est vol 5,959; vol Mon 6,972; open int 100,487, +2,641.

## Currency Futures

**Japanese Yen** (CME)-¥12,500,000; $ per ¥

| | | | | | | | | |
|---|---|---|---|---|---|---|---|---|
| June | .8304 | .8400 | .8303 | .8347 | .0040 | .8800 | .7769 | 83,876 |
| Sept | .8382 | .8401 | .8330 | .8372 | .0040 | .8815 | .8220 | 590 |

Est vol 4,009; vol Mon 14,229; open int 84,584, -733.

**Canadian Dollar** (CME)-CAD 100,000; $ per CAD

| | | | | | | | | |
|---|---|---|---|---|---|---|---|---|
| June | .6722 | .6757 | .6720 | .6742 | .0016 | .6818 | .6197 | 87,087 |
| Sept | .6692 | .6711 | .6688 | .6704 | .0016 | .6785 | .6185 | 3,324 |
| Dec | .6655 | .6671 | .6655 | .6668 | .0021 | .6750 | .6160 | 1,023 |
| Mr04 | .6627 | .6630 | .6620 | .6631 | .0016 | .6690 | .6150 | 578 |

Est vol 5,050; vol Mon 20,827; open int 93,286, -4,963.

**British Pound** (CME)-£62,500; $ per £

| | | | | | | | | |
|---|---|---|---|---|---|---|---|---|
| June | 1.5666 | 1.5714 | 1.5600 | 1.5636 | -.0020 | 1.6416 | 1.5000 | 19,833 |

Est vol 1,557; vol Mon 6,656; open int 20,339, -1,195.

**Swiss Franc** (CME)-CHF 125,000; $ per CHF

| | | | | | | | | |
|---|---|---|---|---|---|---|---|---|
| June | .7242 | .7296 | .7235 | .7248 | .0010 | .7577 | .5940 | 30,758 |

Est vol 2,989; vol Mon 9,503; open int 31,344, -620.

**Australian Dollar** (CME)-AUD 100,000; $ per AUD

| | | | | | | | | |
|---|---|---|---|---|---|---|---|---|
| June | .5905 | .5931 | .5893 | .5908 | .0007 | .6128 | .5050 | 31,492 |
| Sept | ... | ... | ... | .5857 | .0007 | .6055 | .5075 | 473 |
| Dec | .5830 | .5830 | .5810 | .5806 | .0007 | .6010 | .5025 | 216 |

Est vol 316; vol Mon 3,527; open int 32,283, -554.

**Mexican Peso** (CME)-MXN 500,000; $ per MXN

| | | | | | | | | |
|---|---|---|---|---|---|---|---|---|
| June | .09145 | .09200 | .09145 | .09180 | .00057 | .09600 | .08650 | 20,082 |

Est vol 4,566; vol Mon 3,480; open int 21,583, -427.

**Euro/US Dollar** (CME)-€125,000; $ per €

| | | | | | | | | |
|---|---|---|---|---|---|---|---|---|
| June | 1.0613 | 1.0691 | 1.0600 | 1.0621 | .0007 | 1.1043 | .8615 | 68,954 |
| Sept | 1.0630 | 1.0642 | 1.0575 | 1.0590 | .0007 | 1.1000 | .8780 | 1,577 |

Est vol 10,179; vol Mon 27,154; open int 70,926, -1,067.

**Euro/US Dollar** (FINEX)-€100,000; $ per €

| | | | | | | | | |
|---|---|---|---|---|---|---|---|---|
| June | ... | ... | ... | 1.0619 | .0006 | ... | ... | 976 |

Est vol 141; vol Mon 194; open int 980, +45.

**Euro/Japanese Yen** (FINEX)-€100,000; ¥ per €

| | | | | | | | | |
|---|---|---|---|---|---|---|---|---|
| June | 127.70 | 127.32 | 127.32 | 127.24 | -.49 | 128.66 | 125.37 | 9,669 |

Est vol 642; vol Mon 233; open int 9,695, +49.

**Euro/British Pound** (FINEX)-€100,000; £ per €

| | | | | | | | | |
|---|---|---|---|---|---|---|---|---|
| June | .6780 | .6805 | .6805 | .6794 | .0015 | .6930 | .6738 | 5,422 |

Est vol 423; vol Mon 314; open int 5,423, +32.

## Index Futures

**DJ Industrial Average** (CBT)-$10 x index

| | | | | | | | | |
|---|---|---|---|---|---|---|---|---|
| June | 8184 | 8312 | 8120 | 8242 | 52 | 9452 | 7380 | 28,496 |
| Sept | 8270 | 8285 | 8140 | 8222 | 52 | 8700 | 7460 | 155 |

Est vol 16,634; vol Mon 19,220; open int 28,686, -356.
Idx prl: Hi 8337.72; Lo 8180.72; Close 8280.23, +65.55.

**Mini DJ Industrial Average** (CBT)-$5 x index

| | | | | | | | | |
|---|---|---|---|---|---|---|---|---|
| June | 8184 | 8312 | 8122 | 8242 | 52 | 8835 | 7395 | 14,090 |

Vol Tue 36,419; open int 14,248, -180.

**S&P 500 Index** (CME)-$250 x index

| | | | | | | | | |
|---|---|---|---|---|---|---|---|---|
| June | 86380 | 87930 | 85600 | 87220 | 870 | 133280 | 77050 | 609,138 |
| Sept | 86650 | 87650 | 86100 | 87090 | 800 | 121490 | 77200 | 7,652 |

Est vol 68,308; vol Mon 73,972; open int 619,835, -89,228.
Idx prl: Hi 879.97; Lo 862.59; Close 874.74, +10.51.

**S&P Midcap 400** (CME)-$500 x index

| | | | | | | | | |
|---|---|---|---|---|---|---|---|---|
| June | 410.00 | 417.00 | 409.75 | 415.00 | 5.75 | 497.25 | 374.75 | 12,819 |

Est vol 774; vol Mon 669; open int 12,819, -3,672.
Idx prl: Hi 416.63; Lo 410.22; Close 415.83, +5.59.

**Nasdaq 100** (CME)-$100 x index

| | | | | | | | | |
|---|---|---|---|---|---|---|---|---|
| June | 105000 | 107900 | 104400 | 106550 | 1550 | 113550 | 81850 | 69,040 |
| Sept | 107200 | 107200 | 107200 | 106800 | 1550 | 110500 | 95250 | 1,639 |

Est vol 14,995; vol Mon 17,160; open int 70,691, -46,250.
Idx prl: Hi 1075.43; Lo 1047.06; Close 1066.57, +19.47.

**Russell 2000** (CME)-$500 x index

| | | | | | | | | |
|---|---|---|---|---|---|---|---|---|
| June | 367.00 | 372.50 | 366.00 | 371.40 | 4.40 | 465.90 | 328.85 | 21,415 |

Est vol 1,794; vol Mon 2,112; open int 21,420, -10,348.
Idx prl: Hi 372.22; Lo 367.01; Close 371.79, +4.54.

**Russell 1000** (NYFE)-$500 x index

| | | | | | | | | |
|---|---|---|---|---|---|---|---|---|
| June | 458.25 | 465.00 | 457.50 | 462.25 | 4.50 | 474.50 | 424.00 | 49,954 |

Est vol 113; vol Mon 157; open int 49,954, +32.
Idx prl: Hi 466.28; Lo 457.41; Close 463.80, +5.62.

**NYSE Composite Index** (NYFE)-$500 x index

| | | | | | | | | |
|---|---|---|---|---|---|---|---|---|
| June | 458.75 | 464.00 | 458.25 | 462.25 | 4.50 | 530.20 | 422.00 | 1,700 |

Est vol 682; vol Mon 250; open int 1,710, +151.
Idx prl: Hi 465.75; Lo 457.72; Close 463.68, +5.18.

**U.S. Dollar Index** (FINEX)-$1,000 x index

| | | | | | | | | |
|---|---|---|---|---|---|---|---|---|
| June | 101.40 | 101.49 | 100.82 | 101.37 | -.06 | 110.40 | 98.05 | 10,397 |

Est vol 1,700; vol Mon 2,134; open int 12,428, -561.
Idx prl: Hi 101.02; Lo 100.31; Close 100.87, -.11.

**Nikkei 225 Stock Average** (CME)-$5 x index

| | | | | | | | | |
|---|---|---|---|---|---|---|---|---|
| June | 8260. | 8350. | 8200. | 8325. | 40 | 11050. | 7755. | 18,251 |

Est vol 1,639; vol Mon 3,010; open int 18,252, +68.
Index: Hi 8377.17; Lo 8231.95; Close 8238.76, -196.31.

**Share Price Index** (SFE)-AUD 25 x index

| | | | | | | | | |
|---|---|---|---|---|---|---|---|---|
| Mar | 2860.0 | 2962.0 | 2323.0 | 2851.0 | -14.0 | 3457.0 | 2679.0 | 155,080 |
| June | 2866.0 | 2868.0 | 2830.0 | 2857.0 | -14.0 | 3395.0 | 2684.0 | 53,817 |
| Sept | 2867.0 | 2867.0 | 2846.0 | 2856.0 | -14.0 | 3475.0 | 2717.0 | 1,325 |
| Dec | 2855.0 | 2855.0 | 2855.0 | 2857.0 | -14.0 | 3190.0 | 2743.0 | 2,089 |
| Mr04 | 2850.0 | 2850.0 | 2850.0 | 2858.0 | -14.0 | 2925.0 | 2700.0 | 965 |
| June | 2945.0 | 2865.0 | 2825.0 | 2874.0 | -14.0 | 2920.0 | 2700.0 | 204 |

Est vol 56,517; vol Mon 29,829; open int 213,380, +14,219.
Index: Hi 2858.5; Lo 2829.0; Close 2854.4, -4.1.

**CAC-40 Stock Index** (MATIF)-€10 x index

| | | | | | | | | |
|---|---|---|---|---|---|---|---|---|
| Mar | 2718.0 | 2818.0 | 2643.0 | 2797.0 | 68.0 | 3927.5 | 2388.0 | 734,910 |
| Apr | 2696.0 | 2799.0 | 2646.0 | 2791.0 | 67.5 | 2913.0 | 2380.0 | 27,460 |
| June | 2676.5 | 2753.0 | 2668.0 | 2744.5 | 68.0 | 2817.0 | 2592.0 | 14,161 |

Est vol na; vol Mon 145,462; open int 787,881, +64,262.
Index: Hi 2803.15; Lo 2644.22; Close 2795.79, +88.94.

**Xetra DAX** (EUREX)-€25 x index

| | | | | | | | | |
|---|---|---|---|---|---|---|---|---|
| June | 2557.0 | 2637.0 | 2497.5 | 2645.5 | 61.5 | 3523.5 | 2201.0 | 337,529 |
| Sept | 2569.0 | 2660.0 | 2565.0 | 2661.0 | 61.5 | 3095.0 | 2217.0 | 2,045 |

Vol Tue 134,323; open int 469,782, +3,223.
Index: Hi 2636.72; Lo 2481.71; Close 2636.10, +87.73.

**FTSE 100 Index** (LIFFE)-£10 x index

| | | | | | | | | |
|---|---|---|---|---|---|---|---|---|
| June | 3717.5 | 3768.5 | 3656.0 | 3770.0 | 42.5 | 4699.0 | 3248.5 | 450,554 |
| Sept | 3702.0 | 3778.5 | 3656.5 | 3770.0 | 40.5 | 4220.5 | 3359.0 | 25,357 |

Vol Tue 94,766; open int 478,848, -6,208.
Index: Hi 3782.80; Lo 3660.40; Close 3762.00, +18.70.

**DJ Euro STOXX 50 Index** (EUREX)-€10 x index

| | | | | | | | | |
|---|---|---|---|---|---|---|---|---|
| Ju04 | 2075.0 | 2168.0 | 2017.0 | 2160.0 | 72.0 | 2776.0 | 1792.0 | 1,421,793 |
| Sept | 2072.0 | 2154.0 | 2013.0 | 2154.0 | 73.0 | 2521.0 | 1789.0 | 39,642 |

Vol Tue 657,340; open int 2,375,447, +17,195.
Index: Hi 2189.90; Lo 2058.40; Close 2184.98, +60.20.

**DJ STOXX 50 Index** (EUREX)-€10 x index

| | | | | | | | | |
|---|---|---|---|---|---|---|---|---|
| June | 2180.0 | 2232.0 | 2118.0 | 2225.0 | 45.0 | 2457.0 | 1882.0 | 35,738 |

Vol Tue 6,313; open int 56,822, +82.
Index: Hi 2242.98; Lo 2139.66; Close 2237.92, +33.54.

Figure 22.2, panel B, is a plot of the profits realized by an investor who enters the short side of a futures contract. It is the mirror image of the profit diagram for the long position.

**CONCEPT CHECK☞ QUESTION 1**

*a.* Compare the profit diagram in Figure 22.2B to the payoff diagram for a long position in a put option. Assume the exercise price of the option equals the initial futures price.

*b.* Compare the profit diagram in Figure 22.2B to the payoff diagram for an investor who writes a call option.

**Figure 22.2   Profits to buyers and sellers of futures and options contracts**

A. Long futures profit = $P_T - F_0$

B. Short futures profit = $F_0 - P_T$

C. Buy a call option

**Existing Contracts**   Futures and forward contracts are traded on a wide variety of goods in four broad categories: agricultural commodities, metals and minerals (including energy commodities), foreign currencies, and financial futures (fixed-income securities and stock market indexes). Innovation in financial futures has been rapid and is ongoing. Figure 22.3 illustrates both the tremendous growth in futures trading in the last decade and the preeminent role of financial futures. Table 22.1 enumerates some of the various contracts trading in 2002. Contracts now trade on items that would not have been considered possible only a few years ago. For example, there are now electricity as well as weather futures and options contracts. Weather derivatives (which trade on the Chicago Mercantile Exchange) have payoffs that depend on the number of degree-days by which the temperature in a region exceeds or falls short of 65 degrees Fahrenheit. The potential use of these derivatives in managing the risk surrounding electricity or oil and natural gas use should be evident.

Outside the futures markets, a well-developed network of banks and brokers has established a forward market in foreign exchange. This forward market is not a formal exchange in the sense that the exchange specifies the terms of the traded contract. Instead, participants in a forward contract may negotiate for delivery of any quantity of goods, whereas in the formal futures markets contract size and delivery dates are set by the exchange. In forward arrangements, banks and brokers simply negotiate contracts for clients (or themselves) as needed.

# 22.2   MECHANICS OF TRADING IN FUTURES MARKETS

**The Clearinghouse and Open Interest**   The mechanics of trading in futures contracts are more complex than for ordinary stock transactions. If you want to make a stock purchase, your broker simply acts as an intermediary to enable you to buy shares from or sell to another individual through the stock exchange. In futures trading, however, the clearinghouse plays a more active role.

When an investor contacts a broker to establish a futures position, the brokerage firm wires the order to the firm's trader on the floor of the futures exchange. In contrast to stock trading, which involves either specialists or market makers in each security, most futures trades in the United States traditionally have taken place among floor traders in the "trad-

**Figure 22.3   CBOT trading volume in futures contracts**

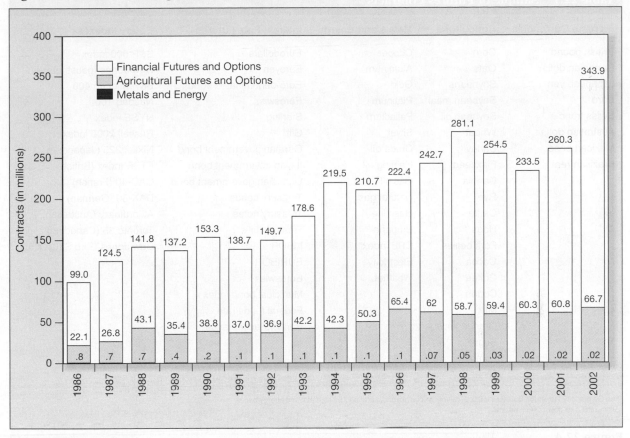

Note: Totals subject to rounding error.
Source: Chicago Board of Trade.

ing pit" for each contract. Traders use voice or hand signals to signify their desire to buy or sell. Once a trader willing to accept the opposite side of a trade is located, the trade is recorded and the investor is notified. This system of "open outcry" is progressively giving way to electronic trading, however. About half the trades on the Chicago Board of Trade today are carried out electronically, and electronic trading is the norm in Europe.

At this point, just as is true for options contracts, the **clearinghouse** enters the picture. Rather than having the long and short traders hold contracts with each other, the clearinghouse becomes the seller of the contract for the long position and the buyer of the contract for the short position. The clearinghouse is obligated to deliver the commodity to the long position and to pay for delivery from the short; consequently, the clearinghouse's position nets to zero. This arrangement makes the clearinghouse the trading partner of each trader, both long and short. The clearinghouse, bound to perform on its side of each contract, is the only party that can be hurt by the failure of any trader to observe the obligations of the futures contract. This arrangement is necessary because a futures contract calls for future performance, which cannot be as easily guaranteed as an immediate stock transaction.

Figure 22.4 illustrates the role of the clearinghouse. Panel A shows what would happen in the absence of the clearinghouse. The trader in the long position would be obligated to pay the futures price to the short-position trader, and the trader in the short position would be obligated to deliver the commodity. Panel B shows how the clearinghouse becomes an intermediary, acting as the trading partner for each side of the contract. The clearinghouse's position is neutral, as it takes a long and a short position for each transaction.

### Table 22.1    Sample of Futures Contracts

| Foreign Currencies | Agricultural | Metals and Energy | Interest Rate Futures | Equity Indexes |
|---|---|---|---|---|
| British pound | Corn | Copper | Eurodollars | S&P 500 index |
| Canadian dollar | Oats | Aluminum | Euroyen | Dow Jones Industrials |
| Japanese yen | Soybeans | Gold | Euro-denominated bond | S&P Midcap 400 |
| Euro | Soybean meal | Platinum | Euroswiss | Nasdaq 100 |
| Swiss franc | Soybean oil | Palladium | Sterling | NYSE index |
| Australian dollar | Wheat | Silver | Gilt† | Russell 2000 index |
| Mexican peso | Barley | Crude oil | German government bond | Nikkei 225 (Japanese) |
| Brazilian real | Flaxseed | Heating oil | Italian government bond | FTSE index (British) |
| | Canola | Gas oil | Canadian government bond | CAC-40 (French) |
| | Rye | Natural gas | Treasury bonds | DAX-30 (German) |
| | Cattle | Gasoline | Treasury notes | All ordinary (Australian) |
| | Hogs | Propane | Treasury bills | Toronto 35 (Canadian) |
| | Pork bellies | CRB index* | LIBOR | Dow Jones Euro STOXX 50 |
| | Cocoa | Electricity | EURIBOR | |
| | Coffee | Weather | Euroswiss | |
| | Cotton | | Municipal bond index | |
| | Milk | | Federal funds rate | |
| | Orange juice | | Bankers' acceptance | |
| | Sugar | | | |
| | Lumber | | | |
| | Rice | | | |

*The Commodity Research Bureau's index of futures prices of agricultural as well as metal and energy prices.
†Gilts are British government bonds.

**Figure 22.4**
**A. Trading without a clearinghouse.**
**B. Trading with a clearinghouse.**

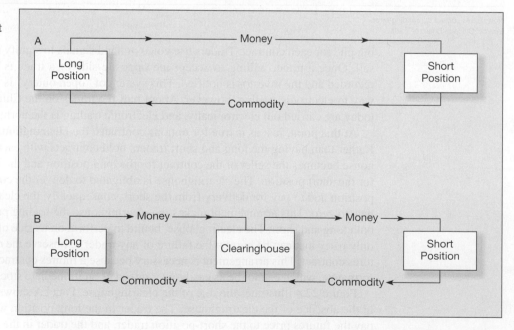

The clearinghouse makes it possible for traders to liquidate positions easily. If you are currently long in a contract and want to undo your position, you simply instruct your broker to enter the short side of a contract to close out your position. This is called a *reversing*

*trade.* The exchange nets out your long and short positions, reducing your net position to zero. Your zero net position with the clearinghouse eliminates the need to fulfill at maturity either the original long or reversing short position.

The **open interest** on the contract is the number of contracts outstanding. (Long and short positions are not counted separately, meaning that open interest can be defined as the number of either long or short contracts outstanding.) The clearinghouse's position nets out to zero, and so is not counted in the computation of open interest. When contracts begin trading, open interest is zero. As time passes, open interest increases as progressively more contracts are entered. Almost all traders, however, liquidate their positions before the contract maturity date.

Instead of actually taking or making delivery of the commodity, virtually all market participants enter reversing trades to cancel their original positions, thereby realizing the profits or losses on the contract. Actual deliveries and purchases of commodities are then made via regular channels of supply, usually via warehouse receipts. The fraction of contracts that result in actual delivery is estimated to range from less than 1% to 3%, depending on the commodity and the activity in the contract. The image of a trader awakening one delivery date with a mountain of wheat in the front yard is amusing, but only fanciful.

You can see the typical pattern of open interest in Figure 22.1. In the silver contract, for example, the March delivery contract is close to maturity, and open interest is small; most contracts have been reversed already. The next few maturities have significant open interest. Finally, the most distant maturity contracts have little open interest, as they have been available only recently, and few participants have yet traded. For other contracts, for example, soybean oil, for which May is the nearest maturity, open interest is typically highest in the nearest contract.

## Marking to Market and the Margin Account

Anyone who saw the film *Trading Places* knows that Eddie Murphy as a trader in orange juice futures had no intention of purchasing or delivering orange juice. Traders simply bet on the futures price of juice. The total profit or loss realized by the long trader who buys a contract at time 0 and closes, or reverses, it at time $t$ is just the change in the futures price over the period, $F_t - F_0$. Symmetrically, the short trader earns $F_0 - F_t$.

The process by which profits or losses accrue to traders is called *marking to market*. At initial execution of a trade, each trader establishes a margin account. The margin is a security account consisting of cash or near-cash securities, such as Treasury bills, that ensures the trader is able to satisfy the obligations of the futures contract. Because both parties to a futures contract are exposed to losses, both must post margin. If the initial margin on corn, for example, is 10%, then the trader must post $1,140 per contract of the margin account. This is 10% of the value of the contract ($2.28 per bushel × 5,000 bushels per contract).

Because the initial margin may be satisfied by posting interest-earning securities, the requirement does not impose a significant opportunity cost of funds on the trader. The initial margin is usually set between 5% and 15% of the total value of the contract. Contracts written on assets with more volatile prices require higher margins.

On any day that futures contracts trade, futures prices may rise or may fall. Instead of waiting until the maturity date for traders to realize all gains and losses, the clearinghouse requires all positions to recognize profits as they accrue daily. If the futures price of corn rises from 228 to 230 cents per bushel, the clearinghouse credits the margin account of the long position for 5,000 bushels times 2 cents per bushel, or $100 per contract. Conversely, for the short position, the clearinghouse takes this amount from the margin account for each contract held. Although the price of corn has changed by only $2/228 = .88\%$, the percentage return on the long corn position on that day is 10 times greater: $\$100/\$1,140 = 8.8\%$. The 10-to-1 ratio of percentage changes reflects the leverage inherent in the futures position, since the corn contract was established with an initial margin of one-tenth the value of the underlying asset.

This daily settling is called **marking to market.** It means the maturity date of the contract does not govern realization of profit or loss. Marking to market ensures that, as futures prices change, the proceeds accrue to the trader's margin account immediately. We will provide a more detailed example of this process shortly.

---

**CONCEPT CHECK ☞ QUESTION 2**

**What must be the net inflow or outlay from marking to market for the clearinghouse?**

---

If a trader accrues sustained losses from daily marking to market, the margin account may fall below a critical value called the **maintenance margin.** Once the value of the account falls below this value, the trader receives a margin call. For example, if the maintenance margin on corn is 5%, then the margin call will go out when the 10% margin initially posted has fallen about in half, to $570 per contract. (This requires that the futures price fall only about 11 cents as each 1-cent drop in the futures price results in a loss of $50 to the long position.) Either new funds must be transferred into the margin account, or the broker will close out enough of the trader's position to meet the required margin for that position. This procedure safeguards the position of the clearinghouse. Positions are closed out before the margin account is exhausted—the trader's losses are covered, and the clearinghouse is not affected.

Marking to market is the major way in which futures and forward contracts differ, besides contract standardization. Futures follow this pay- (or receive-) as-you-go method. Forward contracts are simply held until maturity, and no funds are transferred until that date, although the contracts may be traded.

It is important to note that the futures price on the delivery date will equal the spot price of the commodity on that date. As a maturing contract calls for immediate delivery, the futures price on that day must equal the spot price—the cost of the commodity from the two competing sources is equalized in a competitive market.[1] You may obtain delivery of the commodity either by purchasing it directly in the spot market or by entering the long side of a futures contract.

A commodity available from two sources (spot or futures market) must be priced identically, or else investors will rush to purchase it from the cheap source in order to sell it in the high-priced market. Such arbitrage activity could not persist without prices adjusting to eliminate the arbitrage opportunity. Therefore, the futures price and the spot price must converge at maturity. This is called the **convergence property.**

For an investor who establishes a long position in a contract now (time 0) and holds that position until maturity (time $T$), the sum of all daily settlements will equal $F_T - F_0$, where $F_T$ stands for the futures price at contract maturity. Because of convergence, however, the

---

[1] Small differences between the spot and futures price at maturity may persist because of transportation costs, but this is a minor factor.

futures price at maturity, $F_T$, equals the spot price, $P_T$, so total futures profits also may be expressed as $P_T - F_0$. Thus we see that profits on a futures contract held to maturity perfectly track changes in the value of the underlying asset.

## EXAMPLE 22.1    Marking to Market

Assume the current futures price for silver for delivery 5 days from today is $5.10 per ounce. Suppose that over the next 5 days, the futures price evolves as follows:

| Day | Futures Price |
|---|---|
| 0 (today) | $5.10 |
| 1 | 5.20 |
| 2 | 5.25 |
| 3 | 5.18 |
| 4 | 5.18 |
| 5 (delivery) | 5.21 |

The spot price of silver on the delivery date is $5.21: The convergence property implies that the price of silver in the spot market must equal the futures price on the delivery day.

The daily mark-to-market settlements for each contract held by the long position will be as follows:

| Day | Profit (Loss) per Ounce × 5,000 Ounces/Contract = Daily Proceeds |  |
|---|---|---|
| 1 | 5.20 − 5.10 =   .10 | $500 |
| 2 | 5.25 − 5.20 =   .05 | 250 |
| 3 | 5.18 − 5.25 = −.07 | −350 |
| 4 | 5.18 − 5.18 =   0 | 0 |
| 5 | 5.21 − 5.18 =   .03 | 150 |
|  |  | Sum = $550 |

The profit on Day 1 is the increase in the futures price from the previous day, or ($5.20 − $5.10) per ounce. Because each silver contract on the Commodity Exchange (CMX) calls for purchase and delivery of 5,000 ounces, the total profit per contract is 5,000 times $.10, or $500. On Day 3, when the futures price falls, the long position's margin account will be debited by $350. By Day 5, the sum of all daily proceeds is $550. This is exactly equal to 5,000 times the difference between the final futures price of $5.21 and original futures price of $5.10. Thus the sum of all the daily proceeds (per ounce of silver held long) equals $P_T - F_0$.

**Cash versus Actual Delivery**   Most futures contracts call for delivery of an actual commodity such as a particular grade of wheat or a specified amount of foreign currency if the contract is not reversed before maturity. For agricultural commodities, where quality of the delivered good may vary, the exchange sets quality standards as part of the futures contract. In some cases, contracts may be settled with higher- or lower-grade commodities. In these cases, a premium or discount is applied to the delivered commodity to adjust for the quality difference.

Some futures contracts call for **cash delivery.** An example is a stock index futures contract where the underlying asset is an index such as the Standard & Poor's 500 or the

New York Stock Exchange Index. Delivery of every stock in the index clearly would be impractical. Hence the contract calls for "delivery" of a cash amount equal to the value that the index attains on the maturity date of the contract. The sum of all the daily settlements from marking to market results in the long position realizing total profits or losses of $S_T - F_0$, where $S_T$ is the value of the stock index on the maturity date $T$ and $F_0$ is the original futures price. Cash settlement closely mimics actual delivery, except the cash value of the asset rather than the asset itself is delivered by the short position in exchange for the futures price.

More concretely, the S&P 500 index contract calls for delivery of $250 times the value of the index. At maturity, the index might list at 900, the market-value-weighted index of the prices of all 500 stocks in the index. The cash settlement contract calls for delivery of $250 \times 900$, or $225,000 cash in return for 250 times the futures price. This yields exactly the same profit as would result from directly purchasing 250 units of the index for $225,000 and then delivering it for 250 times the original futures price.

**Regulations**    Futures markets are regulated by the Commodities Futures Trading Commission, a federal agency. The CFTC sets capital requirements for member firms of the futures exchanges, authorizes trading in new contracts, and oversees maintenance of daily trading records.

The futures exchange may set limits on the amount by which futures prices may change from one day to the next. For example, if the price limit on silver contracts traded on the Chicago Board of Trade is $1 and silver futures close today at $5.10 per ounce, then trades in silver tomorrow may vary only between $6.10 and $4.10 per ounce. The exchanges may increase or reduce price limits in response to perceived changes in price volatility of the contract. Price limits are often eliminated as contracts approach maturity, usually in the last month of trading.

Price limits traditionally are viewed as a means to limit violent price fluctuations. This reasoning seems dubious. Suppose an international monetary crisis overnight drives up the spot price of silver to $8.00. No one would sell silver futures at prices for future delivery as low as $5.10. Instead, the futures price would rise each day by the $1 limit, although the quoted price would represent only an unfilled bid order—no contracts would trade at the low quoted price. After several days of limit moves of $1 per day, the futures price would finally reach its equilibrium level, and trading would occur again. This process means no one could unload a position until the price reached its equilibrium level. This example shows that price limits offer no real protection against fluctuations in equilibrium prices.

**Taxation**    Because of the mark-to-market procedure, investors do not have control over the tax year in which they realize gains or losses. Instead, price changes are realized gradually, with each daily settlement. Therefore, taxes are paid at year-end on cumulated profits or losses regardless of whether the position has been closed out.

## 22.3   FUTURES MARKETS STRATEGIES

**Hedging and Speculation**    Hedging and speculating are two polar uses of futures markets. A speculator uses a futures contract to profit from movements in futures prices, a hedger to protect against price movement.

If speculators believe prices will increase, they will take a long position for expected profits. Conversely, they exploit expected price declines by taking a short position.

**EXAMPLE 22.2**     **Speculating with T-Bond Futures**

Let's consider the use of the T-bond futures contract, the listing for which appears in Figure 22.1. Each T-bond contract on the Chicago Board of Trade (CBT) calls for delivery of $100,000 par value of bonds. The listed futures price of 111-02 (i.e., $111^{02}\!/_{32}$) means the market price of the underlying bonds is 111.0625% of par, or $111,062.50. Therefore, for every increase of one point in the T-bond futures price (e.g., to 112-02), the long position gains $1,000, and the short loses that amount. Therefore, if you are bullish on bond prices, you might speculate by buying T-bond futures contracts.

If the T-bond futures price increases by one point to 112-02, then you profit by $1,000 per contract. If the forecast is incorrect, and T-bond futures prices decline, you lose $1,000 times the decrease in the futures price for each contract purchased. Speculators bet on the direction of futures price movements.

Why does a speculator buy a T-bond futures contract? Why not buy T-bonds directly? One reason lies in transaction costs, which are far smaller in futures markets.

Another important reason is the leverage futures trading provides. Recall that each T-bond contract calls for delivery of $100,000 par value, worth $111,062.50 in our example. The initial margin required for this account might be only $10,000. The $1,000 per contract gain translates into a $1,000/$10,000 = 10% return on the money put up, despite the fact that the T-bond futures price increases only 1/111.0625 = 0.9%. Futures margins, therefore, allow speculators to achieve much greater leverage than is available from direct trading in a commodity.

Hedgers by contrast use futures markets to protect themselves against price movements. An investor holding a T-bond portfolio, for example, might anticipate a period of interest rate volatility and want to protect the value of the portfolio against price fluctuations. In this case, the investor has no desire to bet on price movements in either direction. To achieve such protection, a hedger takes a short position in T-bond futures, which obligates him to deliver T-bonds at the contract maturity date for the current futures price. This locks in the sales price for the bonds and guarantees that the total value of the bond-plus-futures position at the maturity date is the futures price.[2]

**EXAMPLE 22.3**     **Hedging with T-Bond Futures**

Suppose as in Figure 22.1 that the futures price for June 2003 delivery (rounding to the nearest dollar) is $111 per $100 par value, and that the only three possible T-bond prices in June are $110, $111, and $112. If the investor currently holds 200 bonds, each with par value $1,000, he would take short positions in two contracts, each for $100,000 par value. Protecting the value of a portfolio with short futures positions is called *short hedging*. Taking the futures position requires no current investment. (The initial margin requirement is small relative to the size of the contract, and because it may be posted in interest-bearing securities, it does not represent a time-value or opportunity cost.)

The profits in June from each of the two short futures contracts will be 1,000 times any decrease in the futures price. At maturity, the convergence property ensures that the final futures price will equal the spot price of the T-bonds. Hence the futures profit will be 2,000

---

[2] To keep things simple, we will assume that the T-bond futures contract calls for delivery of a bond with the same coupon and maturity as that in the investor's portfolio. In practice, a variety of bonds may be delivered to satisfy the contract, and a "conversion factor" is used to adjust for the relative values of the eligible delivery bonds. We will ignore this complication.

times $(F_0 - P_T)$, where $P_T$ is the price of the bonds on the delivery date and $F_0$ is the original futures price, \$111.

Now consider the hedged portfolio consisting of the bonds and the short futures positions. The portfolio value as a function of the bond price in June can be computed as follows:

| | **T-Bond Price in June** | | |
| | **\$110** | **\$111** | **\$112** |
| --- | --- | --- | --- |
| Bond holdings (value = $2,000 P_T$) | \$220,000 | \$222,000 | \$224,000 |
| Futures profits or losses | 2,000 | 0 | −2,000 |
| *TOTAL* | \$222,000 | \$222,000 | \$222,000 |

The total portfolio value is unaffected by the eventual bond price, which is what the hedger wants. The gains or losses on the bond holdings are exactly offset by those on the two contracts held short.

For example, if bond prices fall to \$110, the losses on the bond portfolio are offset by the \$2,000 gain on the futures contracts. That profit equals the difference between the futures price on the maturity date (which equals the spot price on that date of \$110) and the originally contracted futures price of \$111. For short contracts, a profit of \$1 per \$100 par value is realized from the fall in the spot price. Because two contracts call for delivery of \$200,000 par value, this results in a \$2,000 gain that offsets the decline in the value of the bonds held in portfolio. In contrast to a speculator, a hedger is indifferent to the ultimate price of the asset. The short hedger who has in essence arranged to sell the asset for an agreed-upon price need not be concerned about further developments in the market price.

To generalize this example, you can note that the bond will be worth $P_T$ at maturity, whereas the profit on the futures contract is $F_0 - P_T$. The sum of the two positions is $F_0$ dollars, which is independent of the eventual bond price.

A *long hedge* is the analogue to a short hedge for a purchaser of an asset. Consider, for example, a pension fund manager who anticipates a cash inflow in 2 months that will be invested in fixed-income securities. The manager views T-bonds as very attractively priced now and would like to lock in current prices and yields until the investment actually can be made 2 months hence. The manager can lock in the effective cost of the purchase by entering the long side of a contract, which commits her to purchasing at the current futures price.

**CONCEPT CHECK ☞ QUESTION 3**

Suppose, as in our example, that T-bonds will be priced at \$110, \$111, or \$112 in 2 months. Show that the cost in June of purchasing \$200,000 par value of T-bonds net of the profit/loss on two long T-bond contracts will be \$222,000 regardless of the eventual bond price.

Exact futures hedging may be impossible for some goods because the necessary futures contract is not traded. For example, a portfolio manager might want to hedge the value of a diversified, actively managed portfolio for a period of time. However, futures contracts are listed only on indexed portfolios. Nevertheless, because returns on the manager's diversified portfolio will have a high correlation with returns on broad-based indexed portfolios, an effective hedge may be established by selling index futures contracts. Hedging a position using futures on another asset is called *cross-hedging*.

| CONCEPT CHECK ☞ QUESTION 4 | What are the sources of risk to an investor who uses stock index futures to hedge an actively managed stock portfolio? |
|---|---|

Futures contracts may be used also as general portfolio hedges. Bodie and Rosansky[3] found that commodity futures returns have had a negative correlation with the stock market. Investors therefore may add a diversified portfolio of futures contracts to a diversified stock portfolio to lower the standard deviation of the overall rate of return.

Commodity futures are also inflation hedges. When commodity prices increase because of unanticipated inflation, returns from long futures positions will increase because the contracts call for delivery of goods for the price agreed on before the high inflation rate became a reality.

## Basis Risk and Hedging

The **basis** is the difference between the futures price and the spot price.[4] As we have noted, on the maturity date of a contract, the basis must be zero: The convergence property implies that $F_T - P_T = 0$. Before maturity, however, the futures price for later delivery may differ substantially from the current spot price.

We discussed the case of a short hedger who holds an asset (T-bonds, in our example) and a short position to deliver that asset in the future. If the asset and futures contract are held until maturity, the hedger bears no risk, as the ultimate value of the portfolio on the delivery date is determined by the current futures price. Risk is eliminated because the futures price and spot price at contract maturity must be equal: Gains and losses on the futures and the commodity position will exactly cancel. However, if the contract and asset are to be liquidated early, before contract maturity, the hedger bears **basis risk,** because the futures price and spot price need not move in perfect lockstep at all times before the delivery date. In this case, gains and losses on the contract and the asset need not exactly offset each other.

Some speculators try to profit from movements in the basis. Rather than betting on the direction of the futures or spot prices per se, they bet on the changes in the difference between the two. A long spot–short futures position will profit when the basis narrows.

## EXAMPLE 22.4    Speculating on the Basis

Consider an investor holding 100 ounces of gold, who is short one gold-futures contract. Suppose that gold today sells for $291 an ounce, and the futures price for June delivery is $296 an ounce. Therefore, the basis is currently $5. Tomorrow, the spot price might increase to $294, while the futures price increases to $298.50, so the basis narrows to $4.50. The investor gains $3 per ounce on the gold holdings, but loses $2.50 an ounce on the short futures position. The net gain is the decrease in the basis, or $.50 an ounce.

A related strategy is a **calendar spread** position, where the investor takes a long position in a futures contract of one maturity and a short position in a contract on the same commodity, but with a different maturity.[5] Profits accrue if the difference in futures prices

---

[3] Zvi Bodie and Victor Rosansky, "Risk and Return in Commodity Futures." *Financial Analysts Journal*, May–June 1980.

[4] Usage of the word *basis* is somewhat loose. It sometimes is used to refer to the futures-spot difference $F - P$, and sometimes to the spot-futures difference $P - F$. We will consistently call the basis $F - P$.

[5] Another strategy is an *intercommodity spread,* in which the investor buys a contract on one commodity and sells a contract on a different commodity.

between the two contracts changes in the hoped-for direction; that is, if the futures price on the contract held long increases by more (or decreases by less) than the futures price on the contract held short.

**EXAMPLE 22.5    Speculating on the Spread**

Consider an investor who holds a September maturity contract long and a June contract short. If the September futures price increases by 5 cents while the June futures price increases by 4 cents, the net gain will be 5 cents −4 cents, or 1 cent. Like basis strategies, spread positions aim to exploit movements in relative price structures rather than to profit from movements in the general level of prices.

## 22.4   THE DETERMINATION OF FUTURES PRICES

**The Spot-Futures Parity Theorem**    We have seen that a futures contract can be used to hedge changes in the value of the underlying asset. If the hedge is perfect, meaning that the asset-plus-futures portfolio has no risk, then the hedged position must provide a rate of return equal to the rate on other risk-free investments. Otherwise, there will be arbitrage opportunities that investors will exploit until prices are brought back into line. This insight can be used to derive the theoretical relationship between a futures price and the price of its underlying asset.

Suppose, for example, that the S&P 500 index currently is at 900 and an investor who holds $900 in a mutual fund indexed to the S&P 500 wishes to temporarily hedge her exposure to market risk. Assume that the indexed portfolio pays dividends totaling $20 over the course of the year, and for simplicity, that all dividends are paid at year-end. Finally, assume that the futures price for year-end delivery of the S&P 500 contract is 925.[6] Let's examine the end-of-year proceeds for various values of the stock index if the investor hedges her portfolio by entering the short side of the futures contract.

| Final value of stock portfolio, $S_T$ | $885 | $905 | $925 | $945 | $965 | $985 |
|---|---|---|---|---|---|---|
| Payoff from short futures position | 40 | 20 | 0 | −20 | −40 | −60 |
| (equals $F_0 - F_T = \$925 - S_T$) | | | | | | |
| Dividend income | 20 | 20 | 20 | 20 | 20 | 20 |
| TOTAL | $945 | $945 | $945 | $945 | $945 | $945 |

The payoff from the short futures position equals the difference between the original futures price, $925, and the year-end stock price. This is because of convergence: The futures price at contract maturity will equal the stock price at that time.

Notice that the overall position is perfectly hedged. Any increase in the value of the indexed stock portfolio is offset by an equal decrease in the payoff of the short futures position, resulting in a final value independent of the stock price. The $945 total payoff is the sum of the current futures price, $F_0 = \$925$, and the $20 dividend. It is as though the investor arranged to sell the stock at year-end for the current futures price, thereby

---

[6] Actually, the futures contract calls for delivery of $250 times the value of the S&P 500 index, so that each contract would be settled for $250 times the index. We will simplify by assuming that you can buy a contract for one unit rather than 250 units of the index. In practice, one contract would hedge about $250 × 900 = $225,000 worth of stock. Of course, institutional investors would consider a stock portfolio of this size to be quite small.

eliminating price risk and locking in total proceeds equal to the sales price plus dividends paid before the sale.

What rate of return is earned on this riskless position? The stock investment requires an initial outlay of $900, whereas the futures position is established without an initial cash outflow. Therefore, the $900 portfolio grows to a year-end value of $945, providing a rate of return of 5%. More generally, a total investment of $S_0$, the current stock price, grows to a final value of $F_0 + D$, where $D$ is the dividend payout on the portfolio. The rate of return is therefore

$$\text{Rate of return on perfectly hedged stock portfolio} = \frac{(F_0 + D) - S_0}{S_0}$$

This return is essentially riskless. We observe $F_0$ at the beginning of the period when we enter the futures contract. While dividend payouts are not perfectly riskless, they are highly predictable over short periods, especially for diversified portfolios. Any uncertainty is *extremely* small compared to the uncertainty in stock prices.

Presumably, 5% must be the rate of return available on other riskless investments. If not, then investors would face two competing risk-free strategies with different rates of return, a situation that could not last. Therefore, we conclude that

$$\frac{(F_0 + D) - S_0}{S_0} = r_f$$

Rearranging, we find that the futures price must be

$$F_0 = S_0(1 + r_f) - D = S_0(1 + r_f - d) \tag{22.1}$$

where $d$ is the dividend yield on the stock portfolio, defined as $D/S_0$. This result is called the **spot-futures parity theorem.** It gives the normal or theoretically correct relationship between spot and futures prices. Any deviation from parity would give rise to risk-free arbitrage opportunities.

## EXAMPLE 22.6   Futures Market Arbitrage

Suppose that parity were violated. For example, suppose the risk-free interest rate in the economy were only 4% so that according to parity, the futures price should be $900(1.04) − $20 = $916. The actual futures price, $F_0 = $925, is $9 higher than its "appropriate" value. This implies that an investor can make arbitrage profits by shorting the relatively overpriced futures contract and buying the relatively underpriced stock portfolio using money borrowed at the 4% market interest rate. The proceeds from this strategy would be as follows:

| Action | Initial Cash Flow | Cash Flow in 1 Year |
|---|---|---|
| Borrow $900, repay with interest in 1 year | +900 | −900(1.04) = −$936 |
| Buy stock for $900 | −900 | $S_T$ + $20 dividend |
| Enter short futures position ($F_0 = $925) | 0 | $925 − $S_T$ |
| TOTAL | 0 | $9 |

The net initial investment of the strategy is zero. But its cash flow in 1 year is positive and riskless. The payoff is $9 regardless of the stock price. This payoff is precisely equal to the mispricing of the futures contract relative to its parity value.

When parity is violated, the strategy to exploit the mispricing produces an arbitrage profit—a riskless profit requiring no initial net investment. If such an opportunity existed, all market participants would rush to take advantage of it. The results? The stock price would be bid up, and/or the futures price offered down until equation 22.1 is satisfied. A similar analysis applies to the possibility that $F_0$ is less than \$916. In this case, you simply reverse the strategy above to earn riskless profits. We conclude, therefore, that in a well-functioning market in which arbitrage opportunities are competed away, $F_0 = S_0(1 + r_f) - D$.

| CONCEPT CHECK ☞ QUESTION 5 | Return to the arbitrage strategy laid out in Example 22.6. What would be the three steps of the strategy if $F_0$ were too low, say \$905? Work out the cash flows of the strategy now and in 1 year in a table like the one in the example. |
| --- | --- |

The arbitrage strategy of Example 22.6 can be represented more generally as follows:

| Action | Initial Cash Flow | Cash Flow in 1 Year |
| --- | --- | --- |
| 1. Borrow $S_0$ dollars | $S_0$ | $-S_0(1 + r_f)$ |
| 2. Buy stock for $S_0$ | $-S_0$ | $S_T + D$ |
| 3. Enter short futures position | 0 | $F_0 - S_T$ |
| TOTAL | 0 | $F_0 - S_0(1 + r_f) + D$ |

The initial cash flow is zero by construction: The money necessary to purchase the stock in Step 1 is borrowed in Step 2, and the futures position in Step 3, which is used to hedge the value of the stock position, does not require an initial outlay. Moreover, the total cash flow to the strategy at year-end is riskless because it involves only terms that are already known when the contract is entered. If the final cash flow were not zero, all investors would try to cash in on the arbitrage opportunity. Ultimately prices would change until the year-end cash flow is reduced to zero, at which point $F_0$ would equal $S_0(1 + r_f) - D$.

The parity relationship also is called the **cost-of-carry relationship** because it asserts that the futures price is determined by the relative costs of buying a stock with deferred delivery in the futures market versus buying it in the spot market with immediate delivery and "carrying" it in inventory. If you buy stock now, you tie up your funds and incur a time-value-of-money cost of $r_f$ per period. On the other hand, you receive dividend payments with a current yield of $d$. The net carrying cost advantage of deferring delivery of the stock is therefore $r_f - d$ per period. This advantage must be offset by a differential between the futures price and the spot price. The price differential just offsets the cost-of-carry advantage when $F_0 = S_0(1 + r_f - d)$.

The parity relationship is easily generalized to multiperiod applications. We simply recognize that the difference between the futures and spot price will be larger as the maturity of the contract is longer. This reflects the longer period to which we apply the net cost of carry. For contract maturity of $T$ periods, the parity relationship is

$$F_0 = S_0(1 + r_f - d)^T \tag{22.2}$$

Although we have described parity in terms of stocks and stock index futures, it should be clear that the logic applies as well to any financial futures contract. For gold futures, for example, we would simply set the dividend yield to zero. For bond contracts, we would let the coupon income on the bond play the role of dividend payments. In both cases, the parity relationship would be essentially the same as equation 22.2.

The arbitrage strategy described above should convince you that these parity relationships are more than just theoretical results. Any violations of the parity relationship give rise to arbitrage opportunities that can provide large profits to traders. We will see in the next chapter that index arbitrage in the stock market is a tool to exploit violations of the parity relationship for stock index futures contracts.

**Spreads**   Just as we can predict the relationship between spot and futures prices, there are similar ways to determine the proper relationships among futures prices for contracts of different maturity dates. Equation 22.2 shows that the futures price is in part determined by time to maturity. If the risk-free rate is greater than the dividend yield (i.e., $r_f > d$), then the futures price will be higher on longer-maturity contracts. This has been the common pattern in the last several decades. In early 2003, however, interest rates were quite low, actually below the dividend yield on the S&P 500. As a result, you can confirm from Figure 22.1 that longer-maturity contracts had lower future prices. (*A warning to avoid confusion*: You will notice that for some stock index contracts in Figure 22.1, including the S&P 500 contract, the financial pages omit decimal points to save space. Thus, the settlement price for the June maturity S&P contract should be interpreted as 872.20.) For futures on assets like gold, which pay no "dividend yield," we call set $d = 0$ and conclude that $F$ must increase as time to maturity increases.

To be more precise about spread pricing, call $F(T_1)$ the current futures price for delivery at date $T_1$, and $F(T_2)$ the futures price for delivery at $T_2$. Let $d$ be the dividend yield of the stock. We know from the parity equation 22.2 that

$$F(T_1) = S_0(1 + r_f - d)^{T_1}$$
$$F(T_2) = S_0(1 + r_f - d)^{T_2}$$

As a result,

$$F(T_2)/F(T_1) = (1 + r_f - d)^{(T_2 - T_1)}$$

Therefore, the basic parity relationship for spreads is

$$F(T_2) = F(T_1)(1 + r_f - d)^{(T_2 - T_1)} \tag{22.3}$$

Note that equation 22.3 is quite similar to the spot-futures parity relationship. The major difference is in the substitution of $F(T_1)$ for the current spot price. The intuition is also similar. Delaying delivery from $T_1$ to $T_2$ provides the long position the knowledge that the stock will be purchased for $F(T_2)$ dollars at $T_2$ but does not require that money be tied up in the stock until $T_2$. The savings realized are the net cost of carry between $T_1$ and $T_2$. Delaying delivery from $T_1$ until $T_2$ frees up $F(T_1)$ dollars, which earn risk-free interest at $r_f$. The delayed delivery of the stock also results in the lost dividend yield between $T_1$ and $T_2$. The net cost of carry saved by delaying the delivery is thus $r_f - d$. This gives the proportional increase in the futures price that is required to compensate market participants for the delayed delivery of the stock and postponement of the payment of the futures price. If the parity condition for spreads is violated, arbitrage opportunities will arise. (Problem 20 at the end of the chapter explores this possibility.)

**EXAMPLE 22.7**   **Spread Pricing**

To see how to use equation 22.3, consider the following data for a hypothetical contract:

| Contract Maturity Data | Futures Price |
|---|---|
| January 15 | $105.00 |
| March 15 | 105.10 |

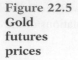

**Figure 22.5**
**Gold**
**futures**
**prices**

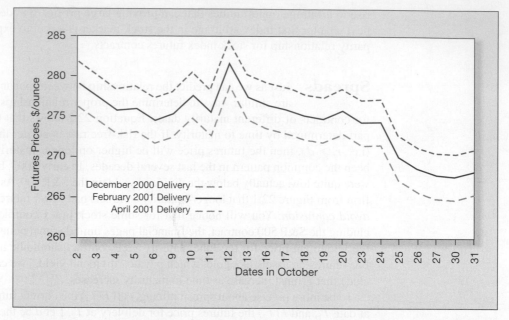

Suppose that the effective annual T-bill rate is expected to persist at 5% and that the dividend yield is 4% per year. The "correct" March futures price relative to the January price is, according to equation 22.3,

$$105(1 + .05 - .04)^{1/6} = 105.174$$

The actual March futures price is 105.10, meaning that the March futures price is slightly underpriced compared to the January futures and that, aside from transaction costs, an arbitrage opportunity seems to be present.

Equation 22.3 shows that futures prices should all move together. Actually, it is not surprising that futures prices for different maturity dates move in unison, because all are linked to the same spot price through the parity relationship. Figure 22.5 plots futures prices on gold for three maturity dates. It is apparent that the prices move in virtual lockstep and that the more distant delivery dates command higher futures prices, as equation 22.3 predicts.

**Forward**        Until now we have paid little attention to the differing time profile of returns
**versus Futures Pricing**  of futures and forward contracts. Instead, we have taken the sum of daily
                    mark-to-market proceeds to the long position as $P_T - F_0$ and assumed for
convenience that the entire profit to the futures contract accrues on the delivery date. The
parity theorems we have derived apply strictly to forward pricing because they are predicated on the assumption that contract proceeds are realized only on delivery. Although this treatment is appropriate for a forward contract, the actual timing of cash flows influences the determination of the futures price.

Futures prices will deviate from parity values when marking to market gives a systematic advantage to either the long or short position. If marking to market tends to favor the long position, for example, the futures price should exceed the forward price, since the long position will be willing to pay a premium for the advantage of marking to market.

When will marking to market favor either a long or short trader? A trader will benefit if daily settlements are received when the interest rate is high and are paid when the interest rate is low. Receiving payments when the interest rate is high allows investment of

**Figure 22.6
Futures price
over time, in the
special case that
the expected spot
price remains
unchanged**

proceeds at a high rate; traders therefore prefer a high correlation between the level of the interest rate and the payments received from marking to market. The long position will benefit if futures prices tend to rise when interest rates are high. In such circumstances the long trader will be willing to accept a higher futures price. Whenever there is a positive correlation between interest rates and changes in futures prices, the "fair" futures price will exceed the forward price. Conversely, a negative correlation means that marking to market favors the short position and implies that the equilibrium futures price should be below the forward price.

For most contracts, the covariance between futures prices and interest rates is so low that the difference between futures and forward prices will be negligible. However, contracts on long-term fixed-income securities are an important exception to this rule. In this case, because prices have a high correlation with interest rates, the covariance can be large enough to generate a meaningful spread between forward and future prices.

## 22.5   FUTURES PRICES VERSUS EXPECTED SPOT PRICES

So far we have considered the relationship between futures prices and the current spot price. One of the oldest controversies in the theory of futures pricing concerns the relationship between the futures price and the expected value of the spot price of the commodity at some *future* date. Three traditional theories have been put forth: the expectations hypothesis, normal backwardation, and contango. Today's consensus is that all of these traditional hypotheses are subsumed by the insights provided by modern portfolio theory. Figure 22.6 shows the expected path of futures under the three traditional hypotheses.

**Expectations
Hypothesis**   The *expectations hypothesis* is the simplest theory of futures pricing. It states that the futures price equals the expected value of the future spot price of the asset: $F_0 = E(P_T)$. Under this theory the expected profit to either position of a futures contract would equal zero: The short position's expected profit is $F_0 - E(P_T)$, whereas the long's is $E(P_T) - F_0$. With $F_0 = E(P_T)$, the expected profit to

either side is zero. This hypothesis relies on a notion of risk neutrality. If all market participants are risk neutral, they should agree on a futures price that provides an expected profit of zero to all parties.

The expectations hypothesis bears a resemblance to market equilibrium in a world with no uncertainty; that is, if prices of goods at all future dates are currently known, then the futures price for delivery at any particular date would equal the currently known future spot price for that date. It is a tempting but incorrect leap to assert next that under uncertainty the futures price should equal the currently expected spot price. This view ignores the risk premiums that must be built into futures prices when ultimate spot prices are uncertain.

## Normal Backwardation

This theory is associated with the famous British economists John Maynard Keynes and John Hicks. They argued that for most commodities there are natural hedgers who desire to shed risk. For example, wheat farmers desire to shed the risk of uncertain wheat prices. These farmers will take short positions to deliver wheat in the future at a guaranteed price; they will short hedge. In order to induce speculators to take the corresponding long positions, the farmers need to offer speculators an expectation of profit. Speculators will enter the long side of the contract only if the futures price is below the expected spot price of wheat, for an expected profit of $E(P_T) - F_0$. The speculators' expected profit is the farmers' expected loss, but farmers are willing to bear the expected loss on the contract in order to shed the risk of uncertain wheat prices. The theory of *normal backwardation* thus suggests that the futures price will be bid down to a level below the expected spot price and will rise over the life of the contract until the maturity date, at which point $F_T = P_T$.

Although this theory recognizes the important role of risk premiums in futures markets, it is based on total variability rather than on systematic risk. (This is not surprising, as Keynes wrote almost 40 years before the development of modern portfolio theory.) The modern view refines the measure of risk used to determine appropriate risk premiums.

## Contango

The polar hypothesis to backwardation holds that the natural hedgers are the purchasers of a commodity, rather than the suppliers. In the case of wheat, for example, we would view grain processors as willing to pay a premium to lock in the price that they must pay for wheat. These processors hedge by taking a long position in the futures market; they are long hedgers, whereas farmers are short hedgers. Because long hedgers will agree to pay high futures prices to shed risk, and because speculators must be paid a premium to enter into the short position, the *contango* theory holds that $F_0$ must exceed $E(P_T)$.

It is clear that any commodity will have both natural long hedgers and short hedgers. The compromise traditional view, called the "net hedging hypothesis," is that $F_0$ will be less than $E(P_T)$ when short hedgers outnumber long hedgers and vice versa. The strong side of the market will be the side (short or long) that has more natural hedgers. The strong side must pay a premium to induce speculators to enter into enough contracts to balance the "natural" supply of long and short hedgers.

## Modern Portfolio Theory

The three traditional hypotheses all envision a mass of speculators willing to enter either side of the futures market if they are sufficiently compensated for the risk they incur. Modern portfolio theory fine-tunes this approach by refining the notion of risk used in the determination of risk premiums. Simply put, if commodity prices pose positive systematic risk, futures prices must be lower than expected spot prices.

As an example of the use of modern portfolio theory to determine the equilibrium futures price, consider once again a stock paying no dividends. If $E(P_T)$ denotes today's expectation of the time $T$ price of the stock, and $k$ denotes the required rate of return on the stock, then the price of the stock today must equal the present value of its expected future payoff as follows:

$$P_0 = \frac{E(P_T)}{(1 + k)^T} \tag{22.4}$$

We also know from the spot-futures parity relationship that

$$P_0 = \frac{F_0}{(1 + r_f)^T} \tag{22.5}$$

Therefore, the right-hand sides of equations 22.4 and 22.5 must be equal. Equating these terms allows us to solve for $F_0$:

$$F_0 = E(P_T)\left(\frac{1 + r_f}{1 + k}\right)^T \tag{22.6}$$

You can see immediately from equation 22.6 that $F_0$ will be less than the expectation of $P_T$ whenever $k$ is greater than $r_f$, which will be the case for any positive-beta asset. This means that the long side of the contract will make an expected profit [$F_0$ will be lower than $E(P_T)$] when the commodity exhibits positive systematic risk ($k$ is greater than $r_f$).

Why should this be? A long futures position will provide a profit (or loss) of $P_T - F_0$. If the ultimate realization of $P_T$ involves positive systematic risk, the profit to the long position also involves such risk. Speculators with well-diversified portfolios will be willing to enter long futures positions only if they receive compensation for bearing that risk in the form of positive expected profits. Their expected profits will be positive only if $E(P_T)$ is greater than $F_0$. The converse is that the short position's profit is the negative of the long's and will have negative systematic risk. Diversified investors in the short position will be willing to suffer an expected loss in order to lower portfolio risk and will be willing to enter the contract even when $F_0$ is less than $E(P_T)$. Therefore, if $P_T$ has positive beta, $F_0$ must be less than the expectation of $P_T$. The analysis is reversed for negative-beta commodities.

> **CONCEPT CHECK☞ QUESTION 6**
>
> **What must be true of the risk of the spot price of an asset if the futures price is an unbiased estimate of the ultimate spot price?**

## SUMMARY

1. Forward contracts are arrangements that call for future delivery of an asset at a currently agreed-on price. The long trader is obligated to purchase the good, and the short trader is obligated to deliver it. If the price of the asset at the maturity of the contract exceeds the forward price, the long side benefits by virtue of acquiring the good at the contract price.

2. A futures contract is similar to a forward contract, differing most importantly in the aspects of standardization and marking to market, which is the process by which gains and losses on futures contract positions are settled daily. In contrast, forward contracts call for no cash transfers until contract maturity.

3. Futures contracts are traded on organized exchanges that standardize the size of the contract, the grade of the deliverable asset, the delivery date, and the delivery location. Traders negotiate only over the contract price. This standardization creates increased liquidity in the marketplace and means that buyers and sellers can easily find many traders for a desired purchase or sale.

4. The clearinghouse acts as an intermediary between each pair of traders, acting as the short position for each long and as the long position for each short. In this way traders need not be concerned about the performance of the trader on the opposite side of the contract. In turn, traders post margins to guarantee their own performance on the contracts.

5. The gain or loss to the long side for the futures contract held between time 0 and $t$ is $F_t - F_0$. Because $F_T = P_T$, the long's profit if the contract is held until maturity is $P_T - F_0$, where $P_T$ is the spot price at time $T$ and $F_0$ is the original futures price. The gain or loss to the short position is $F_0 - P_T$.

6. Futures contracts may be used for hedging or speculating. Speculators use the contracts to take a stand on the ultimate price of an asset. Short hedgers take short positions in contracts to offset any gains or losses on the value of an asset already held in inventory. Long hedgers take long positions to offset gains or losses in the purchase price of a good.

7. The spot-futures parity relationship states that the equilibrium futures price on an asset providing no service or payments (such as dividends) is $F_0 = P_0(1 + r_f)^T$. If the futures price deviates from this value, then market participants can earn arbitrage profits.

8. If the asset provides services or payments with yield $d$, the parity relationship becomes $F_0 = P_0(1 + r_f - d)^T$. This model is also called the cost-of-carry model, because it states that futures price must exceed the spot price by the net cost of carrying the asset until maturity date $T$.

9. The equilibrium futures price will be less than the currently expected time $T$ spot price if the spot price exhibits systematic risk. This provides an expected profit for the long position who bears the risk and imposes an expected loss on the short position who is willing to accept that expected loss as a means to shed systematic risk.

## KEY TERMS

| | | |
|---|---|---|
| forward contract | open interest | basis |
| futures price | marking to market | basis risk |
| long position | maintenance margin | calendar spread |
| short position | convergence property | spot-futures parity theorem |
| clearinghouse | cash delivery | cost-of-carry relationship |

## WEBSITES

The sites listed below are a good place to start looking for websites related to futures and derivatives. They contain information on services as well as other links.

www.stocks.about.com (Link to *Derivatives.*)
www.numa.com

*Exchange sites:*

| | |
|---|---|
| Minneapolis Grain Exchange: | www.mgex.com |
| New York Board of Trade: | www.nybot.com |
| New York Mercantile Exchange: | www.nymex.com |
| Chicago Board of Trade: | www.cbot.com |
| Chicago Mercantile Exchange: | www.cme.com |
| Kansas City Board of Trade: | www.kcbt.com |
| Links to many exchanges: | www.numa.com/ref/exchange.htm |

Commodity Futures Trading Commission:
www.cftc.gov/cftc/cftchome.htm

**PROBLEMS**

1. *a.* Using Figure 22.1, compute the dollar value of the stocks traded on one contract on the Standard & Poor's 500 index. The closing spot price of the S&P 500 index is given in the last line of the listing. If the margin requirement is 10% of the futures price times the multiplier of $250, how much must you deposit with your broker to trade the June contract?

   *b.* If the June futures price were to increase to 880, what percentage return would you earn on your net investment if you entered the long side of the contract at the price shown in the figure?

   *c.* If the June futures price falls by 1%, what is your percentage return?

2. Why is there no futures market in cement?

3. Why might individuals purchase futures contracts rather than the underlying asset?

4. What is the difference in cash flow between short-selling an asset and entering a short futures position?

5. Are the following statements true or false? Why?

   *a.* All else equal, the futures price on a stock index with a high dividend yield should be higher than the futures price on an index with a low dividend yield.

   *b.* All else equal, the futures price on a high-beta stock should be higher than the futures price on a low-beta stock.

   *c.* The beta of a short position in the S&P 500 futures contract is negative.

6. *a.* A hypothetical futures contract on a non-dividend-paying stock with current price $150 has a maturity of 1 year. If the T-bill rate is 6%, what should the futures price be?

   *b.* What should the futures price be if the maturity of the contract is 3 years?

   *c.* What if the interest rate is 8% and the maturity of the contract is 3 years?

7. Your analysis leads you to believe the stock market is about to rise substantially. The market is unaware of this situation. What should you do?

8. How might a portfolio manager use financial futures to hedge risk in each of the following circumstances:

   *a.* You own a large position in a relatively illiquid bond that you want to sell.

   *b.* You have a large gain on one of your Treasuries and want to sell it, but you would like to defer the gain until the next tax year.

   *c.* You will receive your annual bonus next month that you hope to invest in long-term corporate bonds. You believe that bonds today are selling at quite attractive yields, and you are concerned that bond prices will rise over the next few weeks.

9. Suppose the value of the S&P 500 stock index is currently 900. If the 1-year T-bill rate is 6% and the expected dividend yield on the S&P 500 is 2%, what should the 1-year maturity futures price be?

10. Consider a stock that pays no dividends on which a futures contract, a call option, and a put option trade. The maturity date for all three contracts is $T$, the exercise price of the put and the call are both $X$, and the futures price is $F$. Show that if $X = F$, then the call price equals the put price. Use parity conditions to guide your demonstration.

11. It is now January. The current interest rate is 5%. The June futures price for gold is $346.30, whereas the December futures price is $360.00. Is there an arbitrage opportunity here? If so, how would you exploit it?

12. Joan Tam, CFA, believes she has identified an arbitrage opportunity for a commodity as indicated by the information given in the following exhibit:

Visit us at www.mhhe.com/bkm

| | |
|---|---|
| Spot price for commodity | $120 |
| Futures price for commodity expiring in 1 year | $125 |
| Interest rate for 1 year | 8% |

    *a.* Describe the transactions necessary to take advantage of this specific arbitrage opportunity.

    *b.* Calculate the arbitrage profit.

13. The Chicago Board of Trade has just introduced a new futures contract on Brandex stock, a company that currently pays no dividends. Each contract calls for delivery of 1,000 shares of stock in 1 year. The T-bill rate is 6% per year.

    *a.* If Brandex stock now sells at $120 per share, what should the futures price be?

    *b.* If the Brandex price drops by 3%, what will be the change in the futures price and the change in the investor's margin account?

    *c.* If the margin on the contract is $12,000, what is the percentage return on the investor's position?

14. The multiplier for a futures contract on the stock market index is $250. The maturity of the contract is 1 year, the current level of the index is 1,000, and the risk-free interest rate is .5% per month. The dividend yield on the index is .2% per month. Suppose that after 1 month, the stock index is at 1,020.

    *a.* Find the cash flow from the mark-to-market proceeds on the contract. Assume that the parity condition always holds exactly.

    *b.* Find the holding-period return if the initial margin on the contract is $15,000.

15. Michelle Industries issued a Swiss franc–denominated 5-year discount note for SFr200 million. The proceeds were converted to U.S. dollars to purchase capital equipment in the United States. The company wants to hedge this currency exposure and is considering the following alternatives:

    • At-the-money Swiss franc call options.

    • Swiss franc forwards.

    • Swiss franc futures.

    *a.* Contrast the essential characteristics of each of these three derivative instruments.

    *b.* Evaluate the suitability of each in relation to Michelle's hedging objective, including both advantages and disadvantages.

16. You are a corporate treasurer who will purchase $1 million of bonds for the sinking fund in 3 months. You believe rates will soon fall, and you would like to repurchase the company's sinking fund bonds (which currently are selling below par) in advance of requirements. Unfortunately, you must obtain approval from the board of directors for such a purchase, and this can take up to 2 months. What action can you take in the futures market to hedge any adverse movements in bond yields and prices until you can actually buy the bonds? Will you be long or short? Why? A qualitative answer is fine.

17. Identify the fundamental distinction between a futures contract and an option contract, and briefly explain the difference in the manner that futures and options modify portfolio risk.

18. The S&P portfolio pays a dividend yield of 1% annually. Its current value is 900. The T-bill rate is 4%. Suppose the S&P futures price for delivery in 1 year is 930. Construct an arbitrage strategy to exploit the mispricing and show that your profits 1 year hence will equal the mispricing in the futures market.

19. *a.* How should the parity condition (equation 22.2) for stocks be modified for futures contracts on Treasury bonds? What should play the role of the dividend yield in that equation?

   *b.* In an environment with an upward-sloping yield curve, should T-bond futures prices on more distant contracts be higher or lower than those on near-term contracts?

   *c.* Confirm your intuition by examining Figure 22.1.

20. Consider this arbitrage strategy to derive the parity relationship for spreads: (1) enter a long futures position with maturity date $T_1$ and futures price $F(T_1)$; (2) enter a short position with maturity $T_2$ and futures price $F(T_2)$; (3) at $T_1$, when the first contract expires, buy the asset and borrow $F(T_1)$ dollars at rate $r_f$; (4) pay back the loan with interest at time $T_2$.

   *a.* What are the total cash flows to this strategy at times 0, $T_1$, and $T_2$?

   *b.* Why must profits at time $T_2$ be zero if no arbitrage opportunities are present?

   *c.* What must the relationship between $F(T_1)$ and $F(T_2)$ be for the profits at $T_2$ to be equal to zero? This relationship is the parity relationship for spreads.

21. Janice Delsing, a U.S.-based portfolio manager, manages an $800 million portfolio ($600 million in stocks and $200 million in bonds). In reaction to anticipated short-term market events, Delsing wishes to adjust the allocation to 50% stock and 50% bonds through the use of futures. Her position will be held only until "the time is right to restore the original asset allocation." Delsing determines a financial futures-based asset allocation strategy is appropriate. The stock futures index multiplier is $250 and the denomination of the bond futures contract is $100,000. Other information relevant to a futures-based strategy is given in the following exhibit:

| | |
|---|---|
| Bond portfolio modified duration | 5 years |
| Bond portfolio yield to maturity | 7% |
| Basis Point Value (BPV) of bond futures | $97.85 |
| Stock index futures price | 1378 |
| Stock portfolio beta | 1.0 |

   *a.* Describe the financial futures-based strategy needed and explain how the strategy allows Delsing to implement her allocation adjustment. No calculations are necessary.

   *b.* Compute the number of each of the following needed to implement Delsing's asset allocation strategy:
   i. Bond futures contracts.
   ii. Stock index futures contracts.

22. What is the difference between the futures price and the value of the futures contract?

23. Evaluate the criticism that futures markets siphon off capital from more productive uses.

From the Market Insight entry page (**www.mhhe.com/business/finance/edumarket insight**), link to *Industry*, then pull down to the soft drink industry. Open the S&P industry survey for Food and nonalcoholic beverages and review the *Key Industry Ratios and Statistics*. What futures contract might this industry use to hedge its price risk? Where is this contract traded? For information on this market see **www.chdwk.com/sugar.cfm**.

**E-INVESTMENTS**
**Contract Specifications for Financial Futures and Options**

Go to the Chicago Board of Trade site at **www.cbot.com**. Under the *Knowledge Center* item find the contract specifications for the Dow Jones Industrial Average Futures and the Dow Jones Industrial Average Options. Answer the following questions.

What contract months are available for both the futures and the options?

What is the trading unit on the futures contract?

What is the trading unit on the option contract?

Obtain current prices on the Dow Jones Industrial Average Futures Contract. This can be found under Equity Futures quotes.

What is the futures price for the two delivery months that are closest to the current month? (Use the last trade for price.)

How does that compare to the current price of the Dow Jones Industrial Average?

What are the prices for the put and call options that are deliverable in the same months as the futures contracts? Choose exercise prices as close as possible to the futures price.

**SOLUTIONS TO CONCEPT CHECKS**

1.

2. The clearinghouse has a zero net position in all contracts. Its long and short positions are offsetting, so that net cash flow from marking to market must be zero.

3.

|  | T-Bond Price in June | | |
| --- | --- | --- | --- |
|  | **$110** | **$111** | **$112** |
| Cash flow to purchase bonds (= −2,000 $P_T$) | −$220,000 | −$222,000 | −$224,000 |
| Profits on long futures position | −2,000 | 0 | 2,000 |
| *TOTAL* cash flow | −$222,000 | −$222,000 | −$222,000 |

4. The risk would be that the index and the portfolio do not move perfectly together. Thus basis risk involving the spread between the futures price and the portfolio value could persist even if the index futures price were set perfectly relative to the index itself.

**SOLUTIONS
TO CONCEPT
CHECKS**
*(Concluded)*

5.

| Action | Initial Cash Flow | Cash Flow in 1 Year |
|---|---|---|
| Lend $S_0$ dollars | −900 | 900(1.04) = 936 |
| Sell stock short | +900 | $-S_T - 20$ |
| Long futures | 0 | $S_T - 905$ |
| TOTAL | 0 | $11 risklessly |

6. It must have zero beta. If the futures price is an unbiased estimator, then we infer that it has a zero risk premium, which means that beta must be zero.

## CHAPTER TWENTY-THREE

# FUTURES AND SWAPS: A CLOSER LOOK

The previous chapter provided a basic introduction to the operation of futures markets and the principles of futures pricing. This chapter explores both pricing and risk management in selected futures markets in more depth. Most of the growth has been in financial futures, which now dominate trading, so we emphasize these contracts.

**Hedging** refers to techniques that offset *particular* sources of risk, rather than as a more ambitious search for an optimal risk-return profile for an entire portfolio. Because futures contracts are written on particular quantities such as stock index values, foreign exchange rates, commodity prices, and so on, they are ideally suited for these applications. In this chapter we will consider several hedging applications, illustrating general principles using a variety of contracts.

We begin with foreign exchange futures, where we show how forward exchange rates are determined by interest rate differentials across countries, and examine how firms can use futures to manage exchange rate risk. We then move on to stock-index futures, where we focus on program trading and index arbitrage. Next we turn to the most actively traded markets, those for interest rate futures. We also examine commodity futures pricing. Finally, we turn to swaps markets in foreign exchange and fixed-income securities. We will see that swaps can be interpreted as portfolios of forward contracts and valued accordingly.

## 23.1   FOREIGN EXCHANGE FUTURES

**The Markets**   Exchange rates between currencies vary continually and often substantially. This variability can be a source of concern for anyone involved in international business. A U.S. exporter who sells goods in England, for example, will be paid in British pounds, and the dollar value of those pounds depends on the exchange rate at the time payment is made. Until that date, the U.S. exporter is exposed to foreign exchange rate risk. This risk can be hedged through currency futures or forward markets. For example, if you know you will receive £100,000 in 90 days, you can sell those pounds forward today in the forward market and lock in an exchange rate equal to today's forward price.

The forward market in foreign exchange is fairly informal. It is simply a network of banks and brokers that allows customers to enter forward contracts to purchase or sell currency in the future at a currently agreed-upon rate of exchange. The bank market in currencies is among the largest in the world, and most large traders with sufficient creditworthiness execute their trades here rather than in futures markets. Unlike those in futures markets, contracts in forward markets are not standardized in a formal market setting. Instead, each is negotiated separately. Moreover, there is no marking to market, as would occur in futures markets. Currency forward contracts call for execution only at the maturity date.

For currency *futures*, however, there are formal markets on exchanges such as the Chicago Mercantile Exchange (International Monetary Market) or the London International Financial Futures Exchange. Here contracts are standardized by size, and daily marking to market is observed. Moreover, there are standard clearing arrangements that allow traders to enter or reverse positions easily.

Figure 23.1 reproduces *The Wall Street Journal* listing of foreign exchange spot and forward rates. The listing gives the number of U.S. dollars required to purchase some unit of foreign currency and then the amount of foreign currency needed to purchase $1. Figure 23.2 reproduces futures listings, which show the number of dollars needed to purchase a given unit of foreign currency. In Figure 23.1, both spot and forward exchange rates are listed for various delivery dates.

The forward quotations listed in Figure 23.1 always apply to rolling delivery in 30, 90, or 180 days. Thus tomorrow's forward listings will apply to a maturity date 1 day later than today's listing. In contrast, the futures contracts mature at specified dates in March, June, September, and December; these four maturity days are the only dates each year when futures contracts settle.

**Interest Rate Parity**   As is true of stocks and stock futures, there is a spot-futures exchange rate relationship that will prevail in well-functioning markets. Should this so-called interest rate parity relationship be violated, arbitrageurs will be able to make risk-free profits in foreign exchange markets with zero net investment. Their actions will force futures and spot exchange rate back into alignment.

We can illustrate the **interest rate parity theorem** by using two currencies, the U.S. dollar and the British (U.K.) pound. Call $E_0$ the current exchange rate between the two currencies, that is, $E_0$ dollars are required to purchase one pound. $F_0$, the forward price, is the number of dollars that is agreed to today for purchase of one pound at time $T$ in the future. Call the risk-free rates in the United States and United Kingdom $r_{US}$ and $r_{UK}$, respectively.

**Figure 23.1**
**Spot and forward prices in foreign exchange**

Source: Reuters

## Exchange Rates

The foreign exchange mid-range rates below apply to trading among banks in amounts of $1 million and more, as quoted at 4 p.m. Eastern time by Reuters and other sources. Retail transactions provide fewer units of foreign currency per dollar.

| Country | U.S. $ EQUIVALENT Thu | Wed | CURRENCY PER U.S. $ Thu | Wed |
|---|---|---|---|---|
| Argentina (Peso)-y | .3150 | .3150 | 3.1746 | 3.1746 |
| Australia (Dollar) | .6144 | .6165 | 1.6276 | 1.6221 |
| Bahrain (Dinar) | 2.6523 | 2.6523 | .3770 | .3770 |
| Brazil (Real) | .2874 | .2815 | 3.4795 | 3.5524 |
| Canada (Dollar) | .6799 | .6808 | 1.4708 | 1.4689 |
| 1-month forward | .6789 | .6797 | 1.4730 | 1.4712 |
| 3-months forward | .6767 | .6776 | 1.4778 | 1.4758 |
| 6-months forward | .6730 | .6739 | 1.4859 | 1.4839 |
| Chile (Peso) | .001325 | .001322 | 754.72 | 756.43 |
| China (Renminbi) | .1208 | .1208 | 8.2781 | 8.2781 |
| Colombia (Peso) | .0003379 | .0003378 | 2959.46 | 2960.33 |
| Czech. Rep. (Koruna) | | | | |
| Commercial rate | .03450 | .03439 | 28.986 | 29.078 |
| Denmark (Krone) | .1477 | .1476 | 6.7705 | 6.7751 |
| Ecuador (US Dollar) | 1.0000 | 1.0000 | 1.0000 | 1.0000 |
| Hong Kong (Dollar) | .1282 | .1282 | 7.8003 | 7.8003 |
| Hungary (Forint) | .004477 | .004464 | 223.36 | 224.01 |
| India (Rupee) | .02102 | .02099 | 47.574 | 47.642 |
| Indonesia (Rupiah) | .0001128 | .0001131 | 8865 | 8842 |
| Israel (Shekel) | .2065 | .2058 | 4.8426 | 4.8591 |
| Japan (Yen) | .008517 | .008526 | 117.41 | 117.29 |
| 1-month forward | .008527 | .008535 | 117.27 | 117.16 |
| 3-months forward | .008545 | .008554 | 117.03 | 116.90 |
| 6-months forward | .008570 | .008580 | 116.69 | 116.55 |
| Jordan (Dinar) | 1.4094 | 1.4094 | .7095 | .7095 |
| Kuwait (Dinar) | 3.3495 | 3.3473 | .2986 | .2987 |
| Lebanon (Pound) | .0006634 | .0006634 | 1507.39 | 1507.39 |
| Malaysia (Ringgit)-b | .2632 | .2632 | 3.7994 | 3.7994 |
| Malta (Lira) | 2.5871 | 2.5853 | .3865 | .3868 |

| Country | U.S. $ EQUIVALENT Thu | Wed | CURRENCY PER U.S. $ Thu | Wed |
|---|---|---|---|---|
| Mexico (Peso) | | | | |
| Floating rate | .0895 | .0891 | 11.1707 | 11.2208 |
| New Zealand (Dollar) | .5649 | .5671 | 1.7702 | 1.7634 |
| Norway (Krone) | .1400 | .1419 | 7.1429 | 7.0472 |
| Pakistan (Rupee) | .01728 | .01726 | 57.870 | 57.937 |
| Peru (new Sol) | .2874 | .2875 | 3.4795 | 3.4783 |
| Philippines (Peso) | .01822 | .01826 | 54.885 | 54.765 |
| Poland (Zloty) | .2562 | .2560 | 3.9032 | 3.9063 |
| Russia (Ruble)-a | .03166 | .03166 | 31.586 | 31.586 |
| Saudi Arabia (Riyal) | .2667 | .2667 | 3.7495 | 3.7495 |
| Singapore (Dollar) | .5760 | .5774 | 1.7361 | 1.7319 |
| Slovak Rep. (Koruna) | .02625 | .02621 | 38.095 | 38.153 |
| South Africa (Rand) | .1251 | .1256 | 7.9936 | 7.9618 |
| South Korea (Won) | .0008220 | .0008339 | 1216.55 | 1199.18 |
| Sweden (Krona) | .1193 | .1192 | 8.3822 | 8.3893 |
| Switzerland (Franc) | .7497 | .7512 | 1.3339 | 1.3312 |
| 1-month forward | .7503 | .7516 | 1.3328 | 1.3305 |
| 3-months forward | .7515 | .7527 | 1.3307 | 1.3286 |
| 6-months forward | .7532 | .7542 | 1.3277 | 1.3259 |
| Taiwan (Dollar) | .02889 | .02894 | 34.614 | 34.554 |
| Thailand (Baht) | .02347 | .02351 | 42.608 | 42.535 |
| Turkey (Lira) | .00000061 | .00000063 | 1639344 | 1587302 |
| U.K. (Pound) | 1.6037 | 1.6009 | .6236 | .6246 |
| 1-month forward | 1.6005 | 1.5977 | .6248 | .6259 |
| 3-months forward | 1.5944 | 1.5916 | .6272 | .6283 |
| 6-months forward | 1.5858 | 1.5832 | .6306 | .6316 |
| United Arab (Dirham) | .2723 | .2723 | 3.6724 | 3.6724 |
| Uruguay (Peso) | | | | |
| Financial | .03520 | .03510 | 28.409 | 28.490 |
| Venezuela (Bolivar) | .000626 | .000626 | 1597.44 | 1597.44 |
| SDR | 1.3800 | 1.3759 | .7246 | .7268 |
| Euro | 1.0974 | 1.0960 | .9112 | .9124 |

Special Drawing Rights (SDR) are based on exchange rates for the U.S., British, and Japanese currencies. Source: International Monetary Fund.

a-Russian Central Bank rate. b-Government rate. y-Floating rate.

Source: *The Wall Street Journal*, March 7, 2003. Reprinted by permission of *The Wall Street Journal*, © 2003 Dow Jones & Company, Inc. All Rights Reserved Worldwide.

**Figure 23.2**
**Foreign exchange futures**

## Currency Futures

| | OPEN | HIGH | LOW | SETTLE | CHG | LIFETIME HIGH | LOW | OPEN INT |
|---|---|---|---|---|---|---|---|---|
| **Japanese Yen (CME)-¥12,500,000; $ per ¥** | | | | | | | | |
| Mar | .8527 | .8539 | .8506 | .8524 | -.0005 | .8980 | .7482 | 86,729 |
| June | .8550 | .8568 | .8535 | .8551 | -.0005 | .8800 | .7769 | 29,523 |

Est vol 3,955; vol Wed 23,890; open int 116,642, +21.

| | OPEN | HIGH | LOW | SETTLE | CHG | LIFETIME HIGH | LOW | OPEN INT |
|---|---|---|---|---|---|---|---|---|
| **Canadian Dollar (CME)-CAD 100,000; $ per CAD** | | | | | | | | |
| Mar | .6802 | .6809 | .6775 | .6792 | -.0006 | .6809 | .6198 | 78,582 |
| June | .6768 | .6778 | .6743 | .6761 | -.0006 | .6778 | .6197 | 29,409 |
| Sept | .6735 | .6735 | .6712 | .6726 | -.0006 | .6735 | .6185 | 2,512 |
| Dec | .6690 | .6700 | .6680 | .6691 | -.0006 | .6700 | .6160 | 1,350 |
| Mr04 | .6642 | .6650 | .6642 | .6655 | -.0006 | .6655 | .6150 | 521 |

Est vol 10,407; vol Wed 16,585; open int 112,653, -321.

| | OPEN | HIGH | LOW | SETTLE | CHG | LIFETIME HIGH | LOW | OPEN INT |
|---|---|---|---|---|---|---|---|---|
| **British Pound (CME)-£62,500; $ per £** | | | | | | | | |
| Mar | 1.6014 | 1.6054 | 1.5976 | 1.6016 | .0002 | 1.6524 | 1.4360 | 29,586 |
| June | 1.5924 | 1.5966 | 1.5886 | 1.5924 | ... | 1.6416 | 1.5000 | 3,254 |

Est vol 4,498; vol Wed 15,819; open int 32,876, +2,987.

| | OPEN | HIGH | LOW | SETTLE | CHG | LIFETIME HIGH | LOW | OPEN INT |
|---|---|---|---|---|---|---|---|---|
| **Swiss Franc (CME)-CHF 125,000; $ per CHF** | | | | | | | | |
| Mar | .7518 | .7530 | .7479 | .7497 | -.0029 | .7543 | .6470 | 57,883 |
| June | .7537 | .7542 | .7499 | .7515 | -.0026 | .7555 | .5940 | 7,415 |

Est vol 5,030; vol Wed 10,317; open int 65,380, +83.

| | OPEN | HIGH | LOW | SETTLE | CHG | LIFETIME HIGH | LOW | OPEN INT |
|---|---|---|---|---|---|---|---|---|
| **Australian Dollar (CME)-AUD 100,000; $ per AUD** | | | | | | | | |
| Mar | .6153 | .6162 | .6121 | .6139 | -.0017 | .6173 | .5010 | 37,508 |
| June | .6103 | .6109 | .6070 | .6088 | -.0017 | .6121 | .5050 | 9,547 |
| Sept | .6040 | .6040 | .6040 | .6037 | -.0017 | .6055 | .5075 | 447 |

Est vol 4,206; vol Wed 4,119; open int 47,817, -501.

| | OPEN | HIGH | LOW | SETTLE | CHG | LIFETIME HIGH | LOW | OPEN INT |
|---|---|---|---|---|---|---|---|---|
| **Mexican Peso (CME)-MXN 500,000; $ per MXN** | | | | | | | | |
| Mar | .08890 | .08940 | .08850 | .08925 | .00055 | .10495 | .08850 | 25,157 |
| June | .08685 | .08735 | .08650 | .08725 | .00055 | .09600 | .08650 | 12,818 |

Est vol 4,288; vol Wed 10,079; open int 39,222, +1,081.

| | OPEN | HIGH | LOW | SETTLE | CHG | LIFETIME HIGH | LOW | OPEN INT |
|---|---|---|---|---|---|---|---|---|
| **Euro/US Dollar (CME)-€125,000; $ per €** | | | | | | | | |
| Mar | 1.0960 | 1.1007 | 1.0922 | 1.0969 | .0001 | 1.1007 | .8585 | 99,920 |
| June | 1.0929 | 1.0975 | 1.0893 | 1.0936 | -.0001 | 1.0975 | .8615 | 24,149 |
| Sept | 1.0932 | 1.0932 | 1.0908 | 1.0907 | -.0002 | 1.0932 | .8780 | 968 |

Est vol 25,616; vol Wed 52,712; open int 125,467, +2,453.

| | OPEN | HIGH | LOW | SETTLE | CHG | LIFETIME HIGH | LOW | OPEN INT |
|---|---|---|---|---|---|---|---|---|
| **Euro/US Dollar (FINEX)-€200,000; $ per €** | | | | | | | | |
| Mar | | | | 1.0967 | .0003 | 1.0777 | 1.0385 | 1,844 |

Est vol 72; vol Wed 1,152; open int 2,367, +559.

| | OPEN | HIGH | LOW | SETTLE | CHG | LIFETIME HIGH | LOW | OPEN INT |
|---|---|---|---|---|---|---|---|---|
| **Euro/Japanese Yen (FINEX)-€100,000; ¥ per €** | | | | | | | | |
| Mar | 128.55 | 128.82 | 128.55 | 128.66 | .12 | 130.45 | 119.20 | 11,676 |
| June | 127.85 | 127.81 | 127.81 | 127.92 | .09 | 127.81 | ... | 3,506 |

Est vol 2,135; vol Wed 691; open int 15,208, +1,650.

| | OPEN | HIGH | LOW | SETTLE | CHG | LIFETIME HIGH | LOW | OPEN INT |
|---|---|---|---|---|---|---|---|---|
| **Euro/British Pound (FINEX)-€100,000; £ per €** | | | | | | | | |
| Mar | .6840 | .6836 | .6826 | .6850 | .0002 | .6905 | .6393 | 7,579 |
| June | .6860 | .6875 | .6841 | .6869 | -.0001 | .6915 | .6841 | 1,708 |

Est vol 1,735; vol Wed 594; open int 9,287, +1,914.

Source: *The Wall Street Journal*, March 7, 2003. Reprinted by permission of *The Wall Street Journal*, © 2003 Dow Jones & Company, Inc. All Rights Reserved Worldwide.

The interest rate parity theorem then states that the proper relationship between $E_0$ and $F_0$ is given as

$$F_0 = E_0 \left( \frac{1 + r_{US}}{1 + r_{UK}} \right)^T \qquad (23.1)$$

For example, if $r_{US} = .05$ and $r_{UK} = .06$ annually, while $E_0 = \$1.60$ per pound, then the proper futures price for a 1-year contract would be

$$\$1.60 \left( \frac{1.05}{1.06} \right) = \$1.585 \text{ per pound}$$

Consider the intuition behind this result. If $r_{US}$ is less than $r_{UK}$, money invested in the United States will grow at a slower rate than money invested in the United Kingdom. If this is so, why wouldn't all investors decide to invest their money in the United Kingdom? One important reason why not is that the dollar may be appreciating relative to the pound. Although dollar investments in the United States grow slower than pound investments in the United Kingdom, each dollar is worth progressively more pounds as time passes. Such an effect will exactly offset the advantage of the higher U.K. interest rate.

To complete the argument, we need only determine how an appreciating dollar will show up in equation 23.1. If the dollar is appreciating, meaning that progressively fewer dollars are required to purchase each pound, then the forward exchange rate $F_0$ (which equals the dollars required to purchase one pound for delivery in 1 year) must be less than $E_0$, the current exchange rate. This is exactly what equation 23.1 tells us: When $r_{US}$ is less than $r_{UK}$, $F_0$ must be less than $E_0$. The appreciation of the dollar embodied in the ratio of $F_0$ to $E_0$ exactly compensates for the difference in interest rates available in the two countries. Of course, the argument also works in reverse: If $r_{US}$ is greater than $r_{UK}$, then $F_0$ is greater than $E_0$.

## EXAMPLE 23.1    Covered Interest Arbitrage

What if the interest rate parity relationship were violated? For example, suppose the futures price is $\$1.57/£$ instead of $\$1.585/£$. You could adopt the following strategy to reap arbitrage profits. In this example let $E_1$ denote the exchange rate ($\$/£$) that will prevail in 1 year. $E_1$ is, of course, a random variable from the perspective of today's investors.

| Action | Initial Cash Flow ($) | CF in 1 Year ($) |
|---|---|---|
| 1. Borrow 1 U.K. pound in London. Convert to dollars. Repay £1.06 at year end. | 1.60 | $-E_1(£1.06)$ |
| 2. Lend $1.60 in the United States. | −1.60 | $\$1.60(1.05)$ |
| 3. Enter a contract to purchase £1.06 at a (futures) price of $F_0 = \$1.57/£$ | 0 | $£1.06(E_1 - \$1.57/£)$ |
| TOTAL | 0 | $\$.0158$ |

In Step 1, you exchange the one pound borrowed in the United Kingdom for $1.60 at the current exchange rate. After 1 year you must repay the pound borrowed with interest. Because the loan is made in the United Kingdom at the U.K. interest rate, you would repay £1.06, which would be worth $E_1(1.06)$ dollars. The U.S. loan in Step 2 is made at the U.S. interest rate of 5%. The futures position in Step 3 results in receipt of £1.06, for which you would pay $1.57 each, and then convert into dollars at exchange rate $E_1$.

Note that the exchange rate risk here is exactly offset between the pound obligation in Step 1 and the futures position in Step 3. The profit from the strategy is therefore risk-free and requires no net investment.

To generalize the strategy in Example 23.1:

| Action | Initial CF ($) | CF in 1 Year ($) |
|---|---|---|
| 1. Borrow 1 U.K. pound in London. Convert to dollars. | $E_0$ | $-\$E_1(1 + r_{UK})$ |
| 2. Use proceeds of borrowing in London to lend in the U.S. | $-\$E_0$ | $\$E_0(1 + r_{US})$ |
| 3. Enter $(1 + r_{UK})$ futures positions to purchase 1 pound for $F_0$ dollars. | 0 | $(1 + r_{UK})(E_1 - F_0)$ |
| TOTAL | 0 | $E_0(1 + r_{US}) - F_0(1 + r_{UK})$ |

Let us again review the stages of the arbitrage operation. The first step requires borrowing one pound in the United Kingdom. With a current exchange rate of $E_0$, the one pound is converted into $E_0$ dollars, which is a cash inflow. In 1 year the British loan must be paid off with interest, requiring a payment in pounds of $(1 + r_{UK})$, or in dollars of $E_1(1 + r_{UK})$. In the second step the proceeds of the British loan are invested in the United States. This involves an initial cash outflow of $\$E_0$, and a cash inflow of $\$E_0(1 + r_{US})$ in 1 year. Finally, the exchange risk involved in the British borrowing is hedged in Step 3. Here, the $(1 + r_{UK})$ pounds that will need to be delivered to satisfy the British loan are purchased ahead in the futures contract.

The net proceeds to the arbitrage portfolio are risk-free and given by $E_0(1 + r_{US}) - F_0(1 + r_{UK})$. If this value is positive, borrow in the United Kingdom, lend in the United States, and enter a long futures position to eliminate foreign exchange risk. If the value is negative, borrow in the United States, lend in the United Kingdom, and take a short position in pound futures. When prices preclude arbitrage opportunities, the expression must equal zero.

Rearranging this expression gives us the relationship

$$F_0 = \frac{1 + r_{US}}{1 + r_{UK}} E_0 \tag{23.2}$$

which is the interest rate parity theorem for a 1-year horizon, known also as the **covered interest arbitrage relationship.**

---

**CONCEPT CHECK ☞ QUESTION 1**

What are the arbitrage strategy and associated profits if the initial futures price is $F_0 = \$1.62$/pound?

---

Ample empirical evidence bears out this relationship. For example, on March 27, 2003, the interest rate on U.S. Treasury securities with maturity of one-half year was 1.15%, while the comparable rate in the United Kingdom was 3.48%. The spot exchange rate was $1.5563/£. Using these values, we find that interest rate parity implies that the forward exchange rate for delivery in one-half year should have been $1.5563 \times (1.0348/1.0115)^{1/2} = \$1.5741$/£. The actual forward rate was $1.5748/£, which was so close to the parity value that transaction costs would have prevented arbitrageurs from profiting from the discrepancy.

**Direct versus Indirect Quotes**    The exchange rate in Example 23.1 is expressed as dollars per pound. This is an example of what is termed a *direct* exchange rate quote. The euro-dollar exchange rate is also typically expressed as a direct quote. In contrast, exchange rates for other currencies such as the Japanese yen or Swiss franc are typically expressed as *indirect* quotes, that is, as units of foreign currency per dollar, for example 120 yen per dollar. For currencies expressed as indirect quotes, depreciation of the dollar would result in a *decrease* in the quoted exchange rate ($1 buys fewer yen); in contrast, dollar depreciation versus the pound would show up as a *higher* exchange rate (more dollars are required to buy £1). When the exchange rate is quoted as foreign currency per dollar, the domestic and foreign exchange rates in equation 23.3 must be switched: in this case the equation becomes

$$F_0(\text{foreign currency/\$}) = \frac{1 + r_{\text{foreign}}}{1 + r_{\text{US}}} \times E_0(\text{foreign currency/\$})$$

If the interest rate in the U.S. is higher than in Japan, the dollar will sell in the forward market at a lower price than in the spot market.

**Using Futures to Manage Exchange Rate Risk**    Consider a U.S. firm that exports most of its product to Great Britain. The firm is vulnerable to fluctuations in the dollar/pound exchange rate for several reasons. First, the dollar value of the pound-denominated revenue derived from its customers will fluctuate with the exchange rate. Second, the pound price that the firm can charge its customers in the United Kingdom will itself be affected by the exchange rate. For example, if the pound depreciates by 10% relative to the dollar, the firm would need to increase the pound price of its goods by 10% in order to maintain the dollar-equivalent price. However, the firm might not be able to raise the price by 10% if it faces competition from British producers, or if it believes the higher pound-denominated price would reduce demand for its product.

To offset its foreign exchange exposure, the firm might engage in transactions that bring it profits when the pound depreciates. The lost profits from business operations resulting from a depreciation will then be offset by gains on its financial transactions. Suppose, for example, that the firm enters a futures contract to deliver pounds for dollars at an exchange rate agreed to today. Therefore, if the pound depreciates, the futures position will yield a profit.

For example, suppose that the futures price is currently $1.50 per pound for delivery in 3 months. If the firm enters a futures contract with a futures price of $1.50 per pound, and the exchange rate in 3 months is $1.40 per pound, then the profit on the transaction is $.10 per pound. The futures price converges at the maturity date to the spot exchange rate of $1.40 and the profit to the short position is therefore $F_0 - F_T = \$1.50 - \$1.40 = \$.10$ per pound.

How many pounds should be sold in the futures market to most fully offset the exposure to exchange rate fluctuations? Suppose the dollar value of profits in the next quarter will fall by $200,000 for every $.10 depreciation of the pound. We need to find the number of pounds we should commit to delivering in order to provide a $200,000 profit for every $.10 that the pound depreciates. Therefore, we need a futures position to deliver 2,000,000 pounds. As we have just seen, the profit per pound on the futures contract equals the difference in the current futures price and the ultimate exchange rate; therefore, the foreign exchange profits resulting from a $.10 depreciation[1] will equal $.10 \times 2,000,000 = $200,000.

---

[1] Actually, the profit on the contract depends on the changes in the futures price, not the spot exchange rate. For simplicity, we call the decline in the futures price the depreciation in the pound.

The proper hedge position in pound futures is independent of the actual depreciation in the pound as long as the relationship between profits and exchange rates is approximately linear. For example, if the pound depreciates by only half as much, $.05, the firm would lose only $100,000 in operating profits. The futures position would also return half the profits: $.05 × 2,000,000 = $100,000, again just offsetting the operating exposure. If the pound *appreciates,* the hedge position still (unfortunately in this case) offsets the operating exposure. If the pound appreciates by $.05, the firm might gain $100,000 from the enhanced value of the pound; however, it will lose that amount on its obligation to deliver the pounds for the original futures price.

The hedge ratio is the number of futures positions necessary to hedge the risk of the unprotected portfolio, in this case the firm's export business. In general, we can think of the **hedge ratio** as the number of hedging vehicles (e.g., futures contracts) one would establish to offset the risk of a particular unprotected position. The hedge ratio, $H$, in this case is

$$H = \frac{\text{Change in value of unprotected position for a given change in exchange rate}}{\text{Profit derived from one futures position for the same change in exchange rate}}$$

$$= \frac{\$200,000 \text{ per } \$.10 \text{ change in } \$/\pounds \text{ exchange rate}}{\$.10 \text{ profit } per \ pound \text{ delivered per } \$.10 \text{ change in } \$/\pounds \text{ exchange rate}}$$

$$= 2,000,000 \text{ pounds to be delivered}$$

Because each pound-futures contract on the International Monetary Market (a division of the Chicago Mercantile Exchange) calls for delivery of 62,500 pounds, you would need to short 2,000,000/62,500 per contract = 32 contracts.

One interpretation of the hedge ratio is as a ratio of sensitivities to the underlying source of uncertainty. The sensitivity of operating profits is $200,000 per swing of $.10 in the exchange rate. The sensitivity of futures profits is $.10 per pound to be delivered per swing of $.10 in the exchange rate. Therefore, the hedge ratio is 200,000/.10 = 2,000,000 pounds.

We could just as easily have defined the hedge ratio in terms of futures contracts. Because each contract calls for delivery of 62,500 pounds, the profit on each contract per swing of $.10 in the exchange rate is $6,250. Therefore, the hedge ratio defined in units of futures contracts is $200,000/$6,250 = 32 contracts, as derived above.

| CONCEPT CHECK☞ QUESTION 2 | Suppose a multinational firm is harmed when the *dollar* depreciates. Specifically, suppose that its profits decrease by $200,000 for every $.05 rise in the dollar/pound exchange rate. How many contracts should the firm enter? Should it take the long side or the short side of the contracts? |
|---|---|

Given the sensitivity of the unhedged position to changes in the exchange rate, calculating the risk-minimizing hedge position is easy. Far more difficult is the determination of that sensitivity. For the exporting firm, for example, a naive view might hold that one need

| E-INVESTMENTS Foreign Currency Futures | Go to the Chicago Mercantile Exchange website (**www.cme.com**) and link to *Products,* then *Currency.* Link to the *Canadian Dollar* contracts (left margin) and answer the following questions about the futures contract:<br><br>What is the size (units of $CD) of each contract?<br>What is the maximum daily price fluctuation?<br>What time period during the day is the contract traded?<br>If the delivery option is exercised, when and where does delivery take place? |
|---|---|

only estimate the expected pound-denominated revenue, and then contract to deliver that number of pounds in the futures or forward market. This approach, however, fails to recognize that pound revenue is itself a function of the exchange rate because the U.S. firm's competitive position in the United Kingdom is determined in part by the exchange rate.

One approach relies, in part, on historical relationships. Suppose, for example, that the firm prepares a scatter diagram as in Figure 23.3 that relates its business profits (measured in dollars) in each of the last 40 quarters to the dollar/pound exchange rate in that quarter. Profits generally are lower when the exchange rate is lower, that is, when the pound depreciates. To quantify that sensitivity, we might estimate the following regression equation:

$$\text{Profits} = a + b(\$/£ \text{ exchange rate})$$

The slope of the regression, the estimate of $b$, is the sensitivity of quarterly profits to the exchange rate. For example, if the estimate of $b$ turns out to be 2,000,000, as in Figure 23.3, then on average, a $1 *increase* in the value of the pound results in a $2,000,000 *increase* in quarterly profits. This, of course, is the sensitivity we posited when we asserted that a $.10 drop in the dollar/pound exchange rate would decrease profits by $200,000.

Of course, one must interpret regression output with care. For example, one would not want to extrapolate the historical relationship between profitability and exchange rates exhibited in a period when the exchange rate hovered between $1.40 and $1.70 per pound to scenarios in which the exchange rate might be forecast at below $1.10 per pound or above $2.00 per pound.

In addition, one always must use care when extrapolating past relationships into the future. We saw in Chapter 10 that regression betas from the index model tend to vary across time; such problems are not unique to the index model. Moreover, regression estimates are just that—estimates. Parameters of a regression equation are sometimes measured with considerable imprecision.

Still, historical relationships are often a good place to start when looking for the average sensitivity of one variable to another. These slope coefficients are not perfect, but they are still useful indicators of hedge ratios.

**Figure 23.3**
**Profits as a function of the exchange rate**

**CONCEPT CHECK** ☞ **QUESTION 3**

United Millers purchases corn to make cornflakes. When the price of corn increases, the cost of making cereal increases, resulting in lower profits. Historically, profits per quarter have been related to the price of corn according to the equation: Profits = $8 million − 1 million × price per bushel. How many bushels of corn should United Millers purchase in the corn futures market to hedge its corn-price risk?

## 23.2   STOCK-INDEX FUTURES

**The Contracts**   In contrast to most futures contracts, which call for delivery of a specified commodity, stock-index contracts are settled by a cash amount equal to the value of the stock index in question on the contract maturity date times a multiplier that scales the size of the contract. The total profit to the long position is $S_T - F_0$, where $S_T$ is the value of the stock index on the maturity date. Cash settlement avoids the costs that would be incurred if the short trader had to purchase the stocks in the index and deliver them to the long position, and if the long position then had to sell the stocks for cash. Instead, the long trader receives $S_T - F_0$ dollars, and the short trader $F_0 - S_T$ dollars. These profits duplicate those that would arise with actual delivery.

There are several stock-index futures contracts currently traded. Table 23.1 lists some of the major ones, showing under contract size the multiplier used to calculate contract settlements. An S&P 500 contract, for example, with a futures price of 900 and a final index value of 905 would result in a profit for the long side of $250 × (905 − 900) = $1,250. The S&P contract by far dominates the market in stock index futures.

| Table 23.1 | Major Stock-Index Futures | | |
|---|---|---|---|
| **Contract** | **Underlying Market Index** | **Contract Size** | **Exchange** |
| S&P 500 | Standard & Poor's 500 index. A value-weighted arithmetic average of 500 stocks. | $250 times S&P 500 index | Chicago Mercantile Exchange |
| Dow Jones Industrial Average (DJIA) | Dow Jones Industrial Average. Price-weighted average of 30 firms. | $10 times index | Chicago Board of Trade |
| Russell 2000 | Index of 2,000 smaller firms. | $500 times index | Chicago Mercantile Exchange |
| S&P Mid-Cap | Index of 400 firms of midrange market value. | $500 times index | Chicago Mercantile Exchange |
| Nasdaq 100 | Value-weighted arithmetic average of 100 of the largest over-the-counter stocks. | $100 times index | Chicago Mercantile Exchange |
| Nikkei | Nikkei 225 stock average. | $5 times Nikkei Index | Chicago Mercantile Exchange |
| FT-SE 100 | Financial Times–Share Exchange Index of 100 U.K. firms. | £10 times FT-SE Index | London International Financial Futures Exchange |
| DAX-30 | Index of 30 German stocks. | 25 euros times index | Eurex |
| CAC-40 | Index of 40 French stocks. | 10 euros times index | MATIF (Marché à Terme International de France) |
| DJ Euro Stoxx − 50 | Index of blue chip Euro-zone stocks | 10 euros times index | Eurex |

The broad-based stock market indexes are all highly correlated. Table 23.2 presents a correlation matrix for the major U.S. indexes. The smallest correlation is .944.

**Creating Synthetic Stock Positions: An Asset Allocation Tool**

One reason stock-index futures are so popular is that they substitute for holdings in the underlying stocks themselves. Index futures let investors participate in broad market movements without actually buying or selling large amounts of stock.

Because of this, we say futures represent "synthetic" holdings of the market portfolio. Instead of holding the market directly, the investor takes a long futures position in the index. Such a strategy is attractive because the transaction costs involved in establishing and liquidating futures positions are much lower than taking actual spot positions. Investors who wish to frequently buy and sell market positions find it much less costly to play the futures market rather than the underlying spot market. "Market timers," who speculate on broad market moves rather than on individual securities, are large players in stock-index futures for this reason.

One means to market time, for example, is to shift between Treasury bills and broad-based stock market holdings. Timers attempt to shift from bills into the market before market upturns, and to shift back into bills to avoid market downturns, thereby profiting from broad market movements. Market timing of this sort, however, can result in huge brokerage fees with the frequent purchase and sale of many stocks. An attractive alternative is to invest in Treasury bills and hold varying amounts of market-index futures contracts.

The strategy works like this. When timers are bullish, they will establish many long futures positions that they can liquidate quickly and cheaply when expectations turn bearish. Rather than shifting back and forth between T-bills and stocks, they buy and hold T-bills and adjust only the futures position. This minimizes transaction costs. An advantage of this technique for timing is that investors can implicitly buy or sell the market index in its entirety, whereas market timing in the spot market would require the simultaneous purchase or sale of all the stocks in the index. This is technically difficult to coordinate and can lead to slippage in execution of a timing strategy.

You can construct a T-bill plus index futures position that duplicates the payoff to holding the stock index itself. Here is how:

1. Hold as many market-index futures contracts as long as you need to purchase your desired stock position. A desired holding of $1,000 multiplied by the S&P 500 index, for example, would require the purchase of four contracts because each contract calls for delivery of $250 multiplied by the index.

2. Invest enough money in T-bills to cover the payment of the futures price at the contract's maturity date. The necessary investment will equal the present value of the futures price that will be paid to satisfy the contracts. The T-bill holdings will grow by the maturity date to a level equal to the futures price.

**Table 23.2   Correlations among Major U.S. Stock Market Indexes**

|        | S&P | NYSE  | Nasdaq | DJIA  |
|--------|-----|-------|--------|-------|
| S&P    | 1   | 0.988 | 0.980  | 0.992 |
| NYSE   |     | 1     | 0.944  | 0.994 |
| Nasdaq |     |       | 1      | 0.960 |
| DJIA   |     |       |        | 1     |

Note: Correlations were computed from monthly percentage rates of price appreciation between 1992 and 1999.

**EXAMPLE 23.2**

## Synthetic Positions Using Stock Index Futures

Suppose that an institutional investor wants to invest $90 million in the market for 1 month and, to minimize trading costs, chooses to buy the S&P 500 futures contracts as a substitute for actual stock holdings. If the index is now at 900, the 1-month delivery futures price is 909, and the T-bill rate is 1% per month, it would buy 400 contracts. (Each contract controls $250 \times 900 = \$225,000$ worth of stock, and $90$ million/$225,000 = 400$.) The institution thus has a long position on $100,000 times the S&P 500 index (400 contracts times the contract multiplier of $250). To cover payment of the futures price, it must invest 100,000 times the present value of the futures price in T-bills. This equals $100,000 \times (909/1.01) = \$90$ million market value of bills. Notice that the $90 million outlay in bills is precisely equal to the amount that would have been needed to buy the stock directly. (The face value of the bills will be $100,000 \times 909 = \$90.9$ million.)

This is an artificial, or synthetic, stock position. What is the value of this portfolio at the maturity date? Call $S_T$ the value of the stock index on the maturity date $T$, and as usual, let $F_0$ be the original futures price:

|  | In General (Per Unit of the Index) | Our Numbers |
|---|---|---|
| 1. Profits from contract | $S_T - F_0$ | $100,000(S_T - 909)$ |
| 2. Face value of T-bills | $F_0$ | 90,900,000 |
| TOTAL | $S_T$ | $100,000 S_T$ |

The total payoff on the contract maturity date is exactly proportional to the value of the stock index. In other words, adopting this portfolio strategy is equivalent to holding the stock index itself, aside from the issue of interim dividend distributions and tax treatment.

The bills-plus-futures contracts strategy in Example 23.2 may be viewed as a 100% stock strategy. At the other extreme, investing in zero futures results in a 100% bills position. Moreover, a short futures position will result in a portfolio equivalent to that obtained by short selling the stock market index, because in both cases the investor gains from decreases in the stock price. Bills-plus-futures mixtures clearly allow for a flexible and low-transaction-cost approach to market timing. The futures positions may be established or reversed quickly and cheaply. Also, since the short futures position allows the investor to earn interest on T-bills, it is superior to a conventional short sale of the stock, where the investor may earn little or no interest on the proceeds of the short sale.

The box on the next page illustrates that it is now commonplace for money managers to use futures contracts to create synthetic equity positions in stock markets. The article notes that futures positions can be particularly helpful in establishing synthetic positions in foreign equities, where trading costs tend to be greater and markets tend to be less liquid.

**CONCEPT CHECK ☞ QUESTION 4**

The market timing strategy of Example 23.2 also can be achieved by an investor who holds an indexed stock portfolio and "synthetically exits" the position using futures if and when he turns pessimistic concerning the market. Suppose the investor holds $90 million of stock. What futures position added to the stock holdings would create a synthetic T-bill exposure when he is bearish on the market? Confirm that the profits are effectively risk-free using a table like that in Example 23.2.

As investors go increasingly global and market turbulence grows, stock-index futures are emerging as the favorite way for nimble money managers to deploy their funds. Indeed, in most major markets, trading in stock futures now exceeds the buying and selling of actual shares.

What's the big appeal? Speed, ease and cheapness. For most major markets, stock futures not only boast greater liquidity but also lower transaction costs than traditional trading methods.

"When I decide it's time to move into France, Germany or Britain, I don't necessarily want to wait around until I find exactly the right stocks," says Fabrizio Pierallini, manager of New York–based Vontobel Ltd.'s Euro Pacific Fund.

Mr. Pierallini says he later fine-tunes his market picks by gradually shifting out of futures into favorite stocks. To the extent Mr. Pierallini's stocks outperform the market, futures provide a means to preserve those gains, even while hedging against market declines.

For instance, by selling futures equal to the value of the underlying portfolio, a manager can almost completely insulate a portfolio from market moves. Say a manager succeeds in outperforming the market, but still loses 3% while the market as a whole falls 10%. Hedging with futures would capture that margin of outperformance, transforming the loss into a profit of roughly 7%.

Among futures-intensive strategies is "global tactical asset allocation," which involves trading whole markets worldwide as traditional managers might trade stocks. The growing popularity of such asset-allocation strategies has given futures a big boost in recent years.

To capitalize on global market swings, "futures do the job for us better than stocks, and they're cheaper," said Jarrod Wilcox, director of global investments at PanAgora Asset Management, a Boston-based asset allocator. Even when PanAgora does take positions in individual stocks, it often employs futures to modify its position, such as by hedging part of its exposure to that particular stock market.

When it comes to investing overseas, Mr. Wilcox noted, futures are often the only vehicle that makes sense from a cost standpoint. Abroad, transaction taxes and sky-high commissions can wipe out more than 1% of the money deployed on each trade. By contrast, a comparable trade in futures costs as little as 0.05%.

Source: Abridged from Suzanne McGee, *The Wall Street Journal*, February 21, 1995. Reprinted by permission of *The Wall Street Journal*, © 1995 Dow Jones & Company, Inc. All Rights Reserved Worldwide.

## Empirical Evidence on Pricing of Stock-Index Futures

Recall the spot-futures parity relationship between the futures and spot stock price:

$$F_0 = S_0(1 + r_f - d)^T \qquad (23.3)$$

Several investigators have tested this relationship empirically. The general procedure has been to calculate the theoretically appropriate futures price using the current value of the stock index and equation 23.3. The dividend yield of the index in question is approximated using historical data. Although dividends of individual securities may fluctuate unpredictably, the annualized dividend yield of a broad-based index such as the S&P 500 is fairly stable, recently in the neighborhood of 1.5% per year. The yield is seasonal with regular and predictable peaks and troughs, however, so the dividend yield for the relevant months must be the one used. Figure 23.4 illustrates the seasonal pattern of the dividend yield of the S&P 500 index. Notice that some months, such as January or April, have consistently low yields. Others, such as May, have consistently high yields.

If the actual futures price deviates from the value dictated by the parity relationship, then (aside from transaction costs), an arbitrage opportunity arises. Given an estimate of transaction costs, we can bracket the theoretically correct futures price within a band. If the actual futures price lies within that band, the discrepancy between the actual and the proper futures price is too small to exploit because of the transaction costs; if the actual price lies outside the no-arbitrage band, profit opportunities are worth exploiting.

Modest and Sundaresan[2] constructed such a test. Figure 23.5 replicates an example of their results. The figure shows that the futures prices generally did lie in the theoretically

[2] David Modest and Mahadevan Sundaresan, "The Relationship between Spot and Futures Prices in Stock Index Futures Markets: Some Preliminary Evidence," *Journal of Futures Markets* 3 (Spring 1983).

**Figure 23.4   Monthly dividend yield of the S&P 500**

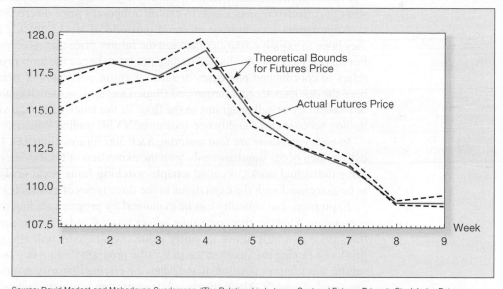

**Figure 23.5
Prices of S&P 500
contract maturing
June 1982.
Data plotted
for April 21–
June 16, 1982**

Source: David Modest and Mahadevan Sundaresan, "The Relationship between Spot and Futures Prices in Stock Index Futures Markets: Some Preliminary Evidence," *Journal of Futures Markets* 3 (Spring 1983).

determined no-arbitrage band, but that profit opportunities occasionally were possible for low-cost transactors.

Modest and Sundaresan pointed out that much of the cost of short selling shares is attributable to the investor's inability to invest the entire proceeds from the short sale. Proceeds must be left on margin account, where they do not earn interest. Arbitrage opportunities, or the width of the no-arbitrage band, therefore depend on assumptions regarding the use of short-sale proceeds. Figure 23.5 assumes that one-half of the proceeds are available to the short-seller.

**CONCEPT CHECK ☞ QUESTION 5**

**What (if anything) would happen to the top of the no-arbitrage band if short-sellers could obtain full use of the proceeds from the short sale? What would happen to the low end of the band? (Hint: When do violations of parity call for a long futures–short stock position versus short futures–long stock?)**

## Index Arbitrage and the Triple-Witching Hour

Whenever the actual futures price falls outside the no-arbitrage band, there is an opportunity for profit. This is why the parity relationships are so important. Far from being theoretical academic constructs, they are in fact a guide to trading rules that can generate large profits. One of the most notable developments in trading activity has been the advent of **index arbitrage,** an investment strategy that exploits divergences between the actual futures price and its theoretically correct parity value.

In theory, index arbitrage is simple. If the futures price is too high, short the futures contract and buy the stocks in the index. If it is too low, go long in futures and short the stocks. You can perfectly hedge your position and should earn arbitrage profits equal to the mispricing of the contract.

In practice, however, index arbitrage is difficult to implement. The problem lies in buying "the stocks in the index." Selling or purchasing shares in all 500 stocks in the S&P 500 is impractical for two reasons. The first is transaction costs, which may outweigh any profits to be made from the arbitrage. Second, it is extremely difficult to buy or sell stock of 500 different firms simultaneously, and any lags in the execution of such a strategy can destroy the effectiveness of a plan to exploit temporary price discrepancies.

Arbitrageurs need to trade an entire portfolio of stocks quickly and simultaneously if they hope to exploit disparities between the futures price and its corresponding stock index. For this they need a coordinated trading program; hence the term **program trading,** which refers to coordinated purchases or sales of entire portfolios of stocks. The response has been the designated order turnaround (SuperDot) system, which enables traders to send coordinated buy or sell programs to the floor of the stock exchange via computer. Program trading accounts for roughly one-quarter of NYSE trading volume.

In each year, there are four maturing S&P 500 futures contracts. Each of these four Fridays, which occur simultaneously with the expiration of S&P index options and options on some individual stocks, is called a **triple-witching hour** because of the volatility believed to be associated with the expirations in the three types of contracts.

Expiration-day volatility can be explained by program trading to exploit arbitrage opportunities. Suppose that some time before a stock-index future contract matures, the futures price is a little above its parity value. Arbitrageurs will attempt to lock in superior profits by buying the stocks in the index (the program trading buy order) and taking an offsetting short futures position. If and when the pricing disparity reverses, the position can be unwound at a profit. Alternatively, arbitrageurs can wait until contract maturity day and realize a profit by simultaneously closing out the offsetting stock and futures positions. By waiting until contract maturity, arbitrageurs can be assured that the futures price and stock-index price will be aligned—they rely on the convergence property.

Obviously, when many program traders follow such a strategy at contract expiration, a wave of program selling passes over the market. The result? Prices go down. This is the *expiration-day effect.* If execution of the arbitrage strategy calls for an initial sale (or short sale) of stocks, unwinding on expiration day requires repurchase of the stocks, with the opposite effect: Prices will increase.

The success of these arbitrage positions and associated program trades depends on only two things: the relative levels of spot and futures prices and synchronized trading in the two markets. Because arbitrageurs exploit disparities in futures and spot prices, absolute price levels are unimportant. This means that large buy or sell programs can hit the floor even if stock prices are at "fair" levels, that is, at levels consistent with fundamental information. The markets in individual stocks may not be sufficiently deep to absorb the arbitrage-based program trades without significant price movements despite the fact that those trades are not informationally motivated.

In an investigation of expiration-day effects on stock prices Stoll and Whaley[3] found that the market is in fact somewhat more volatile at contract expirations. They noted, however, that any expiration-day effects detected in their sample are quite mild, resulting in an increase in standard deviation of returns of less than 0.5% at contract expiration. They concluded that expiration-day effects are small, and that the market seems to handle expirations of index futures contracts reasonably well. Index arbitrage probably does not have a major impact on stock prices, and any impact it does have appears to be extremely short-lived.

## Using Index Futures to Hedge Market Risk

How might a portfolio manager use futures to hedge market exposure? Suppose, for example, that you manage a $30 million portfolio with a beta of .8. You are bullish on the market over the long term, but you are afraid that over the next 2 months, the market is vulnerable to a sharp downturn. If trading were costless, you could sell your portfolio, place the proceeds in T-bills for 2 months, and then reestablish your position after you perceive that the risk of the downturn has passed. In practice, however, this strategy would result in unacceptable trading costs, not to mention tax problems resulting from the realization of capital gains or losses on the portfolio. An alternative approach would be to use stock index futures to hedge your market exposure.

## EXAMPLE 23.3  Hedging Market Risk

Suppose that the S&P 500 index currently is at 1,000. A decrease in the index to 975 would represent a drop of 2.5%. Given the beta of your portfolio, you would expect a loss of $.8 \times 2.5\% = 2\%$, or in dollar terms, $.02 \times \$30$ million $= \$600,000$. Therefore, the sensitivity of your portfolio value to market movements is $600,000 per 25-point movement in the S&P 500 index.

To hedge this risk, you could sell stock index futures. When your portfolio falls in value along with declines in the broad market, the futures contract will provide an offsetting profit.

The sensitivity of a futures contract to market movements is easy to determine. With its contract multiplier of $250, the profit on the S&P 500 futures contract varies by $6,250 for every 25-point swing in the index. Therefore, to hedge your market exposure for 2 months, you could calculate the hedge ratio as follows:

$$H = \frac{\text{Change in portfolio value}}{\text{Profit on one futures contract}} = \frac{\$600,000}{\$6,250} = 96 \text{ contracts (short)}$$

You would enter the short side of the contracts, because you want profits from the contract to offset the exposure of your portfolio to the market. Because your portfolio does poorly when the market falls, you need a position that will do well when the market falls.

---

[3] Hans R. Stoll and Robert E. Whaley, "Program Trading and Expiration-Day Effect," *Financial Analysts Journal*, March–April 1987.

We also could approach the hedging problem in Example 23.3 using a similar regression procedure as that illustrated in Figure 23.3 for foreign exchange risk. The predicted value of the portfolio is graphed in Figure 23.6 as a function of the value of the S&P 500 index. With a beta of .8, the slope of the relationship is 24,000: A 2.5% increase in the index, from 1,000 to 1,025 results in a capital gain of 2% of $30 million, or $600,000. Therefore, your portfolio will increase in value by $24,000 for each increase of one point in the index. As a result, you should enter a short position on 24,000 units of the S&P 500 index to fully off-set your exposure to marketwide movements. Because the contract multiplier is $250 times the index, you need to sell 24,000/250 = 96 contracts.

Notice that when the slope of the regression line relating your unprotected position to the value of an asset is positive, your hedge strategy calls for a *short* position in that asset. The hedge ratio is the negative of the regression slope. This is because the hedge position should offset your initial exposure. If you do poorly when the asset value falls, you need a hedge vehicle that will do well when the asset value falls. This calls for a short position in the asset.

Active managers sometimes believe that a particular asset is underpriced, but that the market as a whole is about to fall. Even if the asset is a good buy relative to other stocks in the market, it still might perform poorly in a broad market downturn. To solve this prob-lem, the manager would like to separate the bet on the firm from the bet on the market: The bet on the company must be offset with a hedge against the market exposure that normally would accompany a purchase of the stock.

Here again, the stock's beta is the key to the hedging strategy. Suppose the beta of the stock is 2/3, and the manager purchases $375,000 worth of the stock. For every 3% drop in the broad market, the stock would be expected to respond with a drop of 2/3 × 3% = 2%, or $7,500. The S&P 500 contract will fall by 30 points from a current value of 1,000 if the market drops 3%. With the contract multiplier of $250, this would entail a profit to a short futures position of 30 × $250 = $7,500 per contract. Therefore, the market risk of the

**Figure 23.6 Predicted value of the portfolio as a function of the market index**

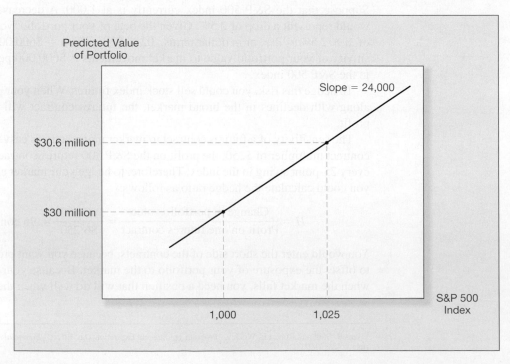

Predicted Value of Portfolio

Slope = 24,000

$30.6 million

$30 million

1,000        1,025

S&P 500 Index

stock can be offset by shorting one S&P contract. More formally, we could calculate the hedge ratio as

$$H = \frac{\text{Expected change in stock value per 3\% market drop}}{\text{Profit on one short contract per 3\% market drop}}$$

$$= \frac{\$7,500 \text{ swing in unprotected position}}{\$7,500 \text{ profit per contract}}$$

$$= 1 \text{ contract}$$

Now that market risk is hedged, the only source of variability in the performance of the stock-plus-futures portfolio will be the firm-specific performance of the stock.

By allowing investors to bet on market performance, the futures contract allows the portfolio manager to make stock picks without concern for the market exposure of the stocks chosen. After the stocks are chosen, the resulting market risk of the portfolio can be modulated to any degree using the stock futures contracts.

## 23.3   INTEREST RATE FUTURES

**Hedging Interest Rate Risk**   Like equity managers, fixed-income managers also desire to separate security-specific decisions from bets on movements in the entire structure of interest rates. Consider, for example, these problems:

1. A fixed-income manager holds a bond portfolio on which considerable capital gains have been earned. She foresees an increase in interest rates but is reluctant to sell her portfolio and replace it with a lower-duration mix of bonds because such rebalancing would result in large trading costs as well as realization of capital gains for tax purposes. Still, she would like to hedge her exposure to interest rate increases.

2. A corporation plans to issue bonds to the public. It believes that now is a good time to act, but it cannot issue the bonds for another 3 months because of the lags inherent in SEC registration. It would like to hedge the uncertainty surrounding the yield at which it eventually will be able to sell the bonds.

3. A pension fund will receive a large cash inflow next month that it plans to invest in long-term bonds. It is concerned that interest rates may fall by the time it can make the investment and would like to lock in the yield currently available on long-term issues.

In each of these cases, the investment manager wishes to hedge interest rate uncertainty. To illustrate the procedures that might be followed, we will focus on the first example, and suppose that the portfolio manager has a $10 million bond portfolio with a modified duration of 9 years.[4] If, as feared, market interest rates increase and the bond portfolio's yield also rises, say by 10 basis points (.1%), the fund will suffer a capital loss. Recall from Chapter 16 that the capital loss in percentage terms will be the product of modified duration, $D^*$, and the change in the portfolio yield. Therefore, the loss will be

$$D^* \times \Delta y = 9 \times .1\% = .9\%$$

---

[4] Recall that modified duration, $D^*$, is related to duration, $D$, by the formula $D^* = D/(1 + y)$, where $y$ is the bond's yield to maturity. If the bond pays coupons semiannually, then $y$ should be measured as a semiannual yield. For simplicity, we will assume annual coupon payments, and treat $y$ as the effective annual yield to maturity.

or $90,000. This establishes that the sensitivity of the value of the unprotected portfolio to changes in market yields is $9,000 per 1 basis point change in the yield. Market practitioners call this ratio the **price value of a basis point,** or PVBP. The PVBP represents the sensitivity of the dollar value of the portfolio to changes in interest rates. Here, we've shown that

$$\text{PVBP} = \frac{\text{Change in portfolio value}}{\text{Predicted change in yield}} = \frac{\$90,000}{10 \text{ basis points}} = \$9,000 \text{ per basis point}$$

One way to hedge this risk is to take an offsetting position in an interest rate futures contract. The Treasury bond contract is the most widely traded contract. The bond nominally calls for delivery of $100,000 par value T-bonds with 6% coupons and 20-year maturity. In practice, the contract delivery terms are fairly complicated because many bonds with different coupon rates and maturities may be substituted to settle the contract. However, we will assume that the bond to be delivered on the contract already is known and has a modified duration of 10 years. Finally, suppose that the futures price currently is $90 per $100 par value. Because the contract requires delivery of $100,000 par value of bonds, the contract multiplier is $1,000.

Given these data, we can calculate the PVBP for the futures contract. If the yield on the delivery bond increases by 10 basis points, the bond value will fall by $D^* \times .1\% = 10 \times .1\% = 1\%$. The futures price also will decline 1% from 90 to 89.10.[5] Because the contract multiplier is $1,000, the gain on each short contract will be $1,000 \times .90 = $900$. Therefore, the PVBP for one futures contract is $900/10-basis-point change, or $90 for a change in yield of 1 basis point.

Now we can easily calculate the hedge ratio as follows:

$$H = \frac{\text{PVBP of portfolio}}{\text{PVBP of hedge vehicle}} = \frac{\$9,000}{\$90 \text{ per contract}} = 100 \text{ contracts}$$

Therefore, 100 T-bond futures contracts will serve to offset the portfolio's exposure to interest rate fluctuations.

| CONCEPT CHECK ☞ QUESTION 6 | Suppose the bond portfolio is twice as large, $20 million, but that its modified duration is only 4.5 years. Show that the proper hedge position in T-bond futures is the same as the value just calculated, 100 contracts. |
|---|---|

Although the hedge ratio is easy to compute, the hedging problem in practice is more difficult. We assumed in our example that the yields on the T-bond contract and the bond portfolio would move perfectly in unison. Although interest rates on various fixed-income instruments do tend to vary in tandem, there is considerable slippage across sectors of the fixed-income market. For example, Figure 23.7 shows that the spread between long-term corporate and 10-year Treasury bond yields has fluctuated considerably over time. Our hedging strategy would be fully effective only if the yield spread across the two sectors of the fixed-income market were constant (or at least perfectly predictable) so that yield changes in both sectors were equal.

This problem highlights the fact that most hedging activity is in fact **cross-hedging,** meaning that the hedge vehicle is a different asset than the one to be hedged. To the extent that there is slippage between prices or yields of the two assets, the hedge will not be per-

---

[5] This assumes the futures price will be exactly proportional to the bond price, which ought to be nearly true.

**Figure 23.7**
**Yield spread between 10-year Treasury and Baa-rated corporate bonds**

**Figure 23.8**
**The Eurodollar futures contract**

**Eurodollar** (CME)–$1,000,000; pts of 100%

| | OPEN | HIGH | LOW | SETTLE | CHG | YIELD | CHG | OPEN INT |
|---|---|---|---|---|---|---|---|---|
| Mar | 98.69 | 98.70 | 98.69 | 98.69 | ... | 1.31 | ... | 668,180 |
| Apr | 98.73 | 98.74 | 98.73 | 98.74 | ... | 1.26 | ... | 19,854 |
| May | 98.78 | 98.78 | 98.77 | 98.78 | .01 | 1.22 | –.01 | 3,105 |
| June | 98.78 | 98.81 | 98.78 | 98.79 | ... | 1.21 | ... | 728,843 |
| July | 98.80 | 98.80 | 98.79 | 98.80 | .02 | 1.20 | –.02 | 201 |
| Sept | 98.76 | 98.79 | 98.75 | 98.77 | ... | 1.23 | ... | 621,423 |
| Dec | 98.61 | 98.64 | 98.59 | 98.62 | ... | 1.38 | ... | 573,959 |
| Mr04 | 98.36 | 98.39 | 98.33 | 98.36 | –.01 | 1.64 | .01 | 402,207 |
| June | 98.05 | 90.07 | 98.01 | 98.04 | –.02 | 1.96 | .02 | 278,510 |
| Sept | 97.72 | 97.75 | 97.67 | 97.71 | –.03 | 2.29 | .03 | 218,632 |
| Dec | 97.38 | 97.42 | 97.33 | 97.36 | –.05 | 2.64 | .05 | 196,799 |
| Mr05 | 97.09 | 97.13 | 97.04 | 97.08 | –.05 | 2.92 | .05 | 138,429 |
| June | 96.86 | 96.88 | 96.79 | 96.82 | –.06 | 3.18 | .06 | 119,414 |
| Sept | 96.62 | 96.64 | 96.55 | 96.58 | –.06 | 3.42 | .06 | 110,403 |
| Dec | 96.39 | 96.41 | 96.32 | 96.35 | –.06 | 3.65 | .06 | 97,741 |
| Mr06 | 96.20 | 96.22 | 96.13 | 96.17 | –.06 | 3.83 | .06 | 81,040 |
| June | 96.02 | 96.04 | 95.95 | 95.99 | –.06 | 4.01 | .06 | 70,071 |
| Sept | 95.86 | 95.88 | 95.79 | 95.82 | –.06 | 4.18 | .06 | 64,099 |
| Dec | 95.69 | 95.71 | 95.62 | 95.65 | –.06 | 4.35 | .06 | 51,260 |
| Mr07 | 95.55 | 95.55 | 95.47 | 95.51 | –.06 | 4.49 | .06 | 49,232 |
| June | 95.42 | 95.42 | 95.33 | 95.37 | –.07 | 4.63 | .07 | 35,148 |
| Sept | 95.30 | 95.30 | 95.21 | 95.25 | –.07 | 4.75 | .07 | 27,409 |
| Dec | 95.17 | 95.17 | 95.09 | 95.13 | –.07 | 4.87 | .07 | 23,368 |
| Mr08 | 95.06 | 95.06 | 95.00 | 95.02 | –.07 | 4.98 | .07 | 9,598 |
| Sp09 | 94.49 | 94.49 | 94.46 | 94.46 | –.06 | 5.54 | .06 | 7,974 |

Est vol 698,991; vol Wed 752,080; open int 4,684,399, +30,901.

fect. Nevertheless, even cross-hedges can eliminate a large fraction of the total risk of the unprotected portfolio.

**Other Interest Rate Futures**   We have just seen how futures contracts on long-term Treasury bonds can be used to manage interest rate risk. These contracts are on the *prices* of interest-rate-dependent securities. Futures contracts also trade on *interest rates* themselves. The biggest of these contracts in terms of trading volume is the Eurodollar contract, the listing for which we reproduce as Figure 23.8. The profit on this contract is proportional to the difference between the LIBOR rate at contract maturity and the contract rate entered into at contract inception. Recall that LIBOR stands for the London Interbank Offer Rate. It is the rate at which large banks in London are willing to lend money among themselves, and it is the premier short-term interest rate quoted in the European dollar-denominated money market. There are analogous rates on interbank loans in other currencies. For example, one close cousin of LIBOR is EURIBOR, which is the rate at which euro-denominated interbank loans within the euro zone are offered by one prime bank to another.

The listing conventions for this contract are a bit peculiar. Consider, for example, the first contract listed, which matures in March 2003. The current futures price is presented as $F_0 = 98.69$. However, this value is not really a price. In effect, participants in the contract negotiate over the contract interest rate, and the so-called "futures price" is actually set equal to $100 -$ contract rate. Since the contract rate is 1.31% (see the next-to-last column), the futures price is listed as $100 - 1.31 = 98.69$. Similarly, the final futures price on contract maturity date will be marked to $F_T = 100 - \text{LIBOR}_T$. Thus, profits to the buyer of the contract will be proportional to

$$F_T - F_0 = (100 - \text{LIBOR}_T) - (100 - \text{Contract rate}) = \text{Contract rate} - \text{LIBOR}_T$$

Thus, the contract design allows participants to trade directly on the LIBOR rate. The contract multiplier is $1 million, but the LIBOR rate on which the contract is written is a 3-month (quarterly) rate; for each basis point that the (annualized) LIBOR increases, the quarterly interest rate increases by only ¼ of a basis point, and the profit to the buyer decreases by

$$.0001 \times \tfrac{1}{4} \times \$1,000,000 = \$25.$$

Examine the payoff on the contract, and you will see that, in effect, the Eurodollar contract allows traders to "swap" a fixed interest rate (the contract rate) for a floating rate (LIBOR). This exchange of interest rates is the building block for long-term interest rate swaps, which is the subject of Section 23.5. Notice in Figure 23.8 that the total open interest on this contract is enormous—almost 5 million contracts—and that contracts with open interest extend out to nearly 10 years maturity. Contracts with such long-term maturities are quite unusual (see the futures listings in Figure 22.1 for a comparison). They reflect the fact that the Eurodollar contract is used by dealers in long-term interest rate swaps as a hedging tool.

## 23.4 COMMODITY FUTURES PRICING

Commodity futures prices are governed by the same general considerations as stock futures. One difference, however, is that the cost of carrying commodities, especially those subject to spoilage, is greater than the cost of carrying financial assets. Moreover, spot prices for some commodities demonstrate marked seasonal patterns that can affect futures pricing.

**Pricing with Storage Costs**   The cost of carrying commodities includes, in addition to interest costs, storage costs, insurance costs, and an allowance for spoilage of goods in storage. To price commodity futures, let us reconsider the earlier arbitrage strategy that calls for holding both the asset and a short position in the futures contract on the asset. In this case we will denote the price of the commodity at time $T$ as $P_T$, and assume for simplicity that all non–interest carrying costs ($C$) are paid in one lump sum at time $T$, the contract maturity. Carrying costs appear in the final cash flow.

| Action | Initial Cash Flow | CF at Time $T$ |
|---|---|---|
| Buy asset; pay carrying costs at $T$ | $-P_0$ | $P_T - C$ |
| Borrow $P_0$; repay with interest at time $T$ | $P_0$ | $-P_0(1 + r_f)$ |
| Short futures position | 0 | $F_0 - P_T$ |
| TOTAL | 0 | $F_0 - P_0(1 + r_f) - C$ |

Because market prices should not allow for arbitrage opportunities, the terminal cash flow of this zero net investment, risk-free strategy should be zero.

If the cash flow were positive, this strategy would yield guaranteed profits for no investment. If the cash flow were negative, the reverse of this strategy also would yield profits. In practice, the reverse strategy would involve a short sale of the commodity. This is unusual but may be done as long as the short sale contract appropriately accounts for storage costs.[6] Thus, we conclude that

$$F_0 = P_0(1 + r_f) + C$$

Finally, if we define $c = C/P_0$, and interpret $c$ as the percentage "rate" of carrying costs, we may write

$$F_0 = P_0(1 + r_f + c) \tag{23.4}$$

which is a (1-year) parity relationship for futures involving storage costs. Compare equation 23.4 to the parity relation for stocks, equation 23.3, and you will see that they are extremely similar. In fact, if we think of carrying costs as a "negative dividend," the equations are identical. This treatment makes intuitive sense because, instead of receiving a dividend yield of $d$, the storer of the commodity must pay a storage cost of $c$. Obviously, this parity relationship is simply an extension of those we have seen already.

Actually, although we have called $c$ the carrying cost of the commodity, we may interpret it more generally as the *net* carrying cost, that is, the carrying cost net of the benefits derived from holding the commodity in inventory. For example, part of the "convenience yield" of goods held in inventory is the protection against stocking out, which may result in lost production or sales.

It is vital to note that we derive equation 23.4 assuming that the asset will be bought and stored; it therefore applies only to goods that currently *are* being stored. Two kinds of commodities cannot be expected to be stored. The first kind is commodities for which storage is technologically not feasible, such as electricity. The second includes goods that are not stored for economic reasons. For example, it would be foolish to buy soybeans now, planning to store them for ultimate use in 3 years. Instead, it is clearly preferable to delay the purchase of the soybeans until after the harvest of the third year. The soybeans are then obtained without incurring the storage costs. Moreover, if the crop in the third year is comparable to this year's, you could obtain it at roughly the same price as you would pay this year. By waiting to purchase, you avoid both interest and storage costs.

Because storage across harvests is costly, equation 23.4 should not be expected to apply for holding periods that span harvest times, nor should it apply to perishable goods that are available only "in season." You can see that this is so if you look at the futures markets page of the newspaper. Figure 23.9, for example, gives futures prices for several times to maturity for soybeans and for gold. Whereas the futures price for gold, which is a stored commodity, increases steadily with the maturity of the contract, the futures price for soybeans is seasonal; it rises within a harvest period as equation 23.4 would predict, but the price falls across harvests as new supplies become available. This sort of pattern is

---

[6] Robert A. Jarrow and George S. Oldfield, "Forward Contracts and Futures Contracts," *Journal of Financial Economics* 9 (1981).

**Figure 23.9
Futures prices for
soybeans and gold**

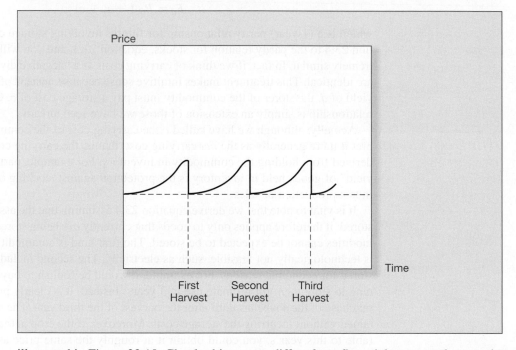

| | OPEN | HIGH | LOW | SETTLE | CHG | LIFETIME HIGH | LIFETIME LOW | OPEN INT |
|---|---|---|---|---|---|---|---|---|
| **Soybeans** (CBT)-5,000 bu.; cents per bu. | | | | | | | | |
| Mar | 568.25 | 570.00 | 562.25 | 562.50 | −6.00 | 593.00 | 449.00 | 6,024 |
| May | 567.50 | 569.00 | 562.00 | 562.25 | −5.25 | 588.00 | 461.00 | 114,251 |
| July | 565.50 | 567.00 | 560.00 | 560.25 | −5.25 | 586.50 | 450.00 | 49,044 |
| Aug | 554.50 | 556.00 | 550.00 | 550.50 | −4.50 | 580.00 | 510.00 | 6,979 |
| Sept | 537.00 | 539.00 | 533.50 | 533.50 | −4.00 | 553.00 | 466.00 | 5,111 |
| Nov | 519.00 | 520.50 | 516.00 | 516.25 | −3.50 | 543.00 | 484.00 | 44,399 |
| Ja04 | 520.00 | 520.50 | 519.00 | 519.50 | −2.50 | 545.00 | 507.00 | 2,064 |
| Mar | 520.00 | 522.00 | 520.00 | 522.50 | −2.00 | 538.00 | 508.00 | 490 |
| Nov | 500.25 | 500.25 | 500.25 | 500.25 | −1.00 | 506.00 | 483.00 | 225 |
| Est vol 50,703; Wed 43,484; open int 228,724, −2,455. | | | | | | | | |
| **Gold** (CMX)-100 troy oz.; $ per troy oz. | | | | | | | | |
| Mar | ... | ... | ... | 356.80 | 3.70 | 460.00 | 346.00 | 61 |
| Apr | 353.50 | 357.40 | 352.60 | 356.90 | 3.70 | 390.80 | 281.50 | 106,349 |
| June | 355.70 | 358.30 | 354.10 | 357.80 | 3.70 | 391.70 | 280.00 | 29,866 |
| Aug | 356.10 | 358.50 | 356.10 | 358.50 | 3.70 | 390.00 | 303.50 | 9,740 |
| Dec | 357.40 | 359.30 | 357.40 | 359.50 | 3.70 | 391.00 | 280.00 | 13,934 |
| Fb04 | 357.50 | 357.50 | 357.50 | 360.00 | 3.70 | 390.60 | 322.00 | 7,261 |
| Dec | 363.80 | 363.80 | 363.80 | 362.90 | 3.50 | 396.30 | 290.00 | 10,514 |
| Est vol 40,000; vol Wed 41,248; open int 191,999, +2,071. | | | | | | | | |

Source: *The Wall Street Journal*, March 7, 2003. Reprinted by permission of *The Wall Street Journal*, © 2003 Dow Jones & Company, Inc. All Rights Reserved Worldwide.

**Figure 23.10
Typical
commodity price
pattern over the
season. Prices
adjusted for
inflation**

Price

First Harvest    Second Harvest    Third Harvest

Time

illustrated in Figure 23.10. Clearly this pattern differs from financial assets such as stocks or gold for which there is no seasonal price movement. Financial assets are priced so that holding them in portfolio produces a fair expected return. Agricultural prices, in contrast, are subject to steep periodic drops as each crop is harvested, which makes storage across harvests generally unprofitable.

**CONCEPT
CHECK ☞
QUESTION 7**

People are willing to buy and "store" shares of stock despite the fact that their purchase ties up capital. Most people, however, are not willing to buy and store soybeans. What is the difference in the properties of the expected evolution of stock prices versus soybean prices that accounts for this result?

**Table 23.3    Commodity Betas**

| Commodity | Beta | Commodity | Beta |
|---|---|---|---|
| Wheat | −0.370 | Orange juice | 0.117 |
| Corn | −0.429 | Propane | −3.851 |
| Oats | 0.000 | Cocoa | −0.291 |
| Soybeans | −0.266 | Silver | −0.272 |
| Soybean oil | −0.650 | Copper | 0.005 |
| Soybean meal | 0.239 | Cattle | 0.365 |
| Broilers | −1.692 | Hogs | −0.148 |
| Plywood | 0.660 | Pork bellies | −0.062 |
| Potatoes | −0.610 | Egg | −0.293 |
| Platinum | 0.221 | Lumber | −0.131 |
| Wool | 0.307 | Sugar | −2.403 |
| Cotton | −0.015 | | |

Source: Zvi Bodie and Victor Rosansky, "Risk and Return in Commodity Futures," *Financial Analysts Journal* 36 (May–June 1980).

Futures pricing across seasons therefore requires a different approach that is not based on storage across harvest periods. In place of general no-arbitrage restrictions we rely instead on risk premium theory and discounted cash flow (DCF) analysis.

**Discounted Cash Flow Analysis for Commodity Futures**

Given the current expectation of the spot price of the commodity at some future date and a measure of the risk characteristics of that price, we can measure the present value of a claim to receive the commodity at that future date. We simply calculate the appropriate risk premium from a model such as the CAPM or APT and discount the expected spot price at the appropriate risk-adjusted interest rate, as illustrated in the following example.

**EXAMPLE 23.4    Commodity Futures Pricing**

Table 23.3, which presents betas on a variety of commodities, shows that the beta of orange juice, for example, was estimated to be .117 over the period. If the T-bill rate is currently 5.5% and the historical market risk premium is about 8.5%, the appropriate discount rate for orange juice would be given by the CAPM as

$$5.5\% + .117(8.5\%) = 6.49\%$$

If the expected spot price for orange juice 6 months from now is $1.45 per pound, the present value of a 6-month deferred claim to a pound of orange juice is simply

$$\$1.45/(1.0649)^{1/2} = \$1.405$$

What would the proper futures price for orange juice be? The contract calls for the ultimate exchange of orange juice for the futures price. We have just shown that the present value of the juice is $1.405. This should equal the present value of the futures price that will be paid for the juice. A commitment to a payment of $F_0$ dollars in 6 months has a present value of $F_0/(1.055)^{1/2} = .974 \times F_0$. (Note that the discount rate is the risk-free rate of 5.5%, because the promised payment is fixed and therefore independent of market conditions.)

To equate the present values of the promised payment of $F_0$ and the promised receipt of orange juice, we would set

$$.974F_0 = \$1.405$$

or $F_0 = \$1.443$.

The general rule, then, to determine the appropriate futures price is to equate the present value of the future payment of $F_0$ and the present value of the commodity to be received. This gives us

$$\frac{F_0}{(1 + r_f)^T} = \frac{E(P_T)}{(1 + k)^T}$$

or

$$F_0 = E(P_T)\left(\frac{1 + r_f}{1 + k}\right)^T \tag{23.5}$$

where $k$ is the required rate of return on the commodity, which may be obtained from a model of asset market equilibrium such as the CAPM.

Note that equation 23.5 is perfectly consistent with the spot-futures parity relationship. For example, apply equation 23.5 to the futures price for a stock paying no dividends. Because the entire return on the stock is in the form of capital gains, the expected rate of capital gains must equal $k$, the required rate of return on the stock. Consequently, the expected price of the stock will be its current price times $(1 + k)^T$, or $E(P_T) = P_0(1 + k)^T$. Substituting this expression into equation 23.5 results in $F_0 = P_0(1 + r_f)^T$, which is exactly the parity relationship. This equilibrium derivation of the parity relationship simply reinforces the no-arbitrage restrictions we derived earlier. The spot-futures parity relationship may be obtained from the equilibrium condition that all portfolios earn fair expected rates of return.

---

**CONCEPT CHECK☞ QUESTION 8**

**Suppose that the systematic risk of orange juice were to increase, holding the expected time $T$ price of juice constant. If the expected spot price is unchanged, would the futures price change? In what direction? What is the intuition behind your answer?**

---

## 23.5    SWAPS

We noted in Chapter 16 that interest rate swaps have become common tools for interest rate risk management. A large and active market also exists for foreign exchange swaps. Recall that a swap arrangement obligates two counterparties to exchange cash flows at one or more future dates. To illustrate, a **foreign exchange swap** might call for one party to exchange $1.6 million for 1 million British pounds in each of the next 5 years. An **interest rate swap** with notional principal of $1 million might call for one party to exchange a variable cash flow equal to $1 million times the LIBOR rate for $1 million times a fixed rate of 8%. In this way the two parties exchange the cash flows corresponding to interest payments on a fixed-rate 8% coupon bond for those corresponding to payments on a floating-rate bond paying LIBOR.

## EXAMPLE 23.5   Balance Sheet Restructuring Using Swaps

Swaps offer participants easy ways to restructure their balance sheets. Consider, for example, a firm that has issued long-term bonds with total par value of $10 million at a fixed coupon rate of 8%. The firm is obligated to make interest payments of $800,000 per year. However, it can change the nature of its interest obligations from fixed rate to floating rate by entering a swap agreement to pay a floating rate of interest and receive a fixed rate.

A swap with notional principal of $10 million that exchanges LIBOR for an 8% fixed rate will bring the firm fixed cash inflows of $800,000 per year and obligate it to pay instead $10 million × LIBOR. The net cash flow from the swap is $10 million × (.08 − LIBOR). The receipt of the fixed payments from the swap agreement offsets the firm's interest obligations on the outstanding bond issue, leaving it with a net obligation to make floating-rate payments. The swap, therefore, is a way for the firm to effectively convert its outstanding fixed-rate debt into synthetic floating-rate debt.

Suppose that the swap is for 3 years and the LIBOR rates turn out to be 7%, 8%, and 9% in the next 3 years. The firm's cash flows would be as illustrated in Table 23.4. The top line of the table shows the cash flow on the fixed-rate debt, equal to 8% of the $10 million bond principal. The cash flow on its $10 million swap position (pay floating, receive fixed rate) equals (.08 − LIBOR) × $10 million. The swap therefore contributes a positive cash flow when LIBOR is only 7% but a negative cash flow when LIBOR rises to 9%. The firm's net payment, in the last line of the table, is simply LIBOR × $10 million. The swap has therefore transformed the firm's fixed rate debt into synthetic floating-rate debt. To see this more generally, note that the firm's net cash flow after entering the swap is as follows:

| | |
|---|---|
| − .08 × principal | Payment on bond |
| + (.08 − LIBOR) × principal | Net cash flow from swap (pay LIBOR, receive 8%) |
| = −LIBOR × principal | |

Therefore, the firm's net cash outflow equals the LIBOR rate times bond principal, just as if it had issued a floating rate bond tied to LIBOR.

---

**CONCEPT CHECK☞ QUESTION 9**

Show how a firm that has issued a floating-rate bond with a coupon equal to the LIBOR rate can use swaps to convert that bond into synthetic fixed-rate debt. Assume the terms of the swap allow an exchange of LIBOR for a fixed rate of 8%.

---

**Table 23.4   Balance Sheet Restructuring (The firm converts an 8% fixed-rate bond into a synthetic floating-rate bond with coupon equal to the LIBOR rate.)**

| | LIBOR | | |
|---|---|---|---|
| | 7% | 8% | 9% |
| As debt payer (8% of $10 million) | −$800,000 | −$800,000 | −$800,000 |
| As floating payer receives $10 million × (.08 − LIBOR) | +$100,000 | +0 | +−$100,000 |
| Net cash flow | −$700,000 | −$800,000 | −$900,000 |

Instead of entering the swap in Example 23.5, the firm could have retired its outstanding debt and issued floating-rate notes. The swap agreement is a far cheaper and quicker way to restructure the balance sheet, however. The swap does not entail trading costs to buy back outstanding bonds or underwriting fees and lengthy registration procedures to issue new debt. In addition, if the firm perceives price advantages in either the fixed- or floating-rate markets, the swap market allows it to issue its debt in the cheaper of the two markets and then "convert" to the financing mode it feels best suits its business needs.

Foreign exchange swaps also enable the firm to quickly and cheaply restructure its balance sheet. Suppose, for example, that the firm that issued the $10 million in debt actually preferred that its interest obligations be denominated in British pounds. For example, the issuing firm might have been a British corporation that perceived advantageous financing opportunities in the United States but prefers pound-denominated liabilities. Then the firm, whose debt currently obliges it to make dollar-denominated payments of $800,000, can agree to swap a given number of pounds each year for $800,000. By so doing, it effectively covers its dollar obligation and replaces it with a new pound-denominated obligation.

## Swap Pricing

How can the fair swap rate be determined? For example, do we know that an exchange of LIBOR is a fair trade for a fixed rate of 8%? Or, what is the fair swap rate between dollars and pounds for the foreign exchange swap we considered? To answer these questions we can exploit the analogy between a swap agreement and forward or futures contract.

Consider a swap agreement to exchange dollars for pounds for one period only. Next year, for example, one might exchange $1 million for £.6 million. This is no more than a simple forward contract in foreign exchange. The dollar-paying party is contracting to buy British pounds in 1 year for a number of dollars agreed to today. The forward exchange rate for 1-year delivery is $F_1 = \$1.67$/pound. We know from the interest rate parity relationship that this forward price should be related to the spot exchange rate, $E_0$, by the formula $F_1 = E_0(1 + r_{US})/(1 + r_{UK})$. Because a one-period swap is in fact a forward contract, the fair swap rate is also given by the parity relationship.

Now consider an agreement to trade foreign exchange for two periods. This agreement could be structured as a portfolio of two separate forward contracts. If so, the forward price for the exchange of currencies in 1 year would be $F_1 = E_0(1 + r_{US})/(1 + r_{UK})$, while the forward price for the exchange in the second year would be $F_2 = E_0[(1 + r_{US})/(1 + r_{UK})]^2$. As an example, suppose that $E_0 = \$1.70$/pound, $r_{US} = 5\%$, and $r_{UK} = 7\%$. Then, using the parity relationship, we would have prices for forward delivery of $F_1 = \$1.70/£ \times (1.05/1.07) = \$1.668/£$ and $F_2 = \$1.70/£ \times (1.05/1.07)^2 = \$1.637/£$. Figure 23.11A illustrates this sequence of cash exchanges assuming that the swap calls for delivery of one pound in each year. Although the dollars to be paid in each of the 2 years are known today, they differ from year to year.

In contrast, a swap agreement to exchange currency for 2 years would call for a fixed exchange rate to be used for the duration of the swap. This means that the same number of dollars would be paid per pound in each year, as illustrated in Figure 23.11B. Because the forward prices for delivery in each of the next 2 years are $1.668/£ and $1.637/£, the fixed exchange rate that makes the two-period swap a fair deal must be between these two values. Therefore, the dollar payer underpays for the pound in the first year (compared to the forward exchange rate) and overpays in the second year. Thus, the swap can be viewed as a portfolio of forward transactions, but instead of each transaction being priced independently, one forward price is applied to all of the transactions.

Given this insight, it is easy to determine the fair swap price. If we were to purchase one pound per year for 2 years using two independent forward agreements, we would pay $F_1$

**Figure 23.11
Forward contracts
versus swaps**

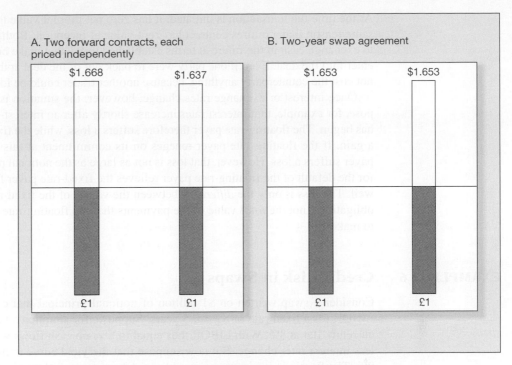

dollars in 1 year and $F_2$ dollars in 2 years. If instead we enter a swap, we pay a constant rate of $F^*$ dollars per pound. Because both strategies must be equally costly, we conclude that

$$\frac{F_1}{1 + y_1} + \frac{F_2}{(1 + y_2)^2} = \frac{F^*}{1 + y_1} + \frac{F^*}{(1 + y_2)^2}$$

where $y_1$ and $y_2$ are the appropriate yields from the yield curve for discounting dollar cash flows of 1- and 2-year maturities, respectively. In our example, where we have assumed a flat U.S. yield curve at 5%, we would solve

$$\frac{1.668}{1.05} + \frac{1.637}{1.05^2} = \frac{F^*}{1.05} + \frac{F^*}{1.05^2}$$

which implies that $F^* = 1.653$. The same principle would apply to a foreign exchange swap of any other maturity. In essence, we need to find the level annuity, $F^*$, with the same present value as the stream of annual cash flows that would be incurred in a sequence of forward rate agreements.

Interest rate swaps can be subjected to precisely the same analysis. Here, the forward contract is on an interest rate. For example, if you swap LIBOR for an 8% fixed rate with notional principal of $100, then you have entered a forward contract for delivery of $100 times LIBOR for a fixed "forward" price of $8. If the swap agreement is for many periods, the fair spread will be determined by the entire sequence of interest rate forward prices over the life of the swap.

**Credit Risk
in the Swap Market**   The rapid growth of the swap market has given rise to increasing concern about credit risk in these markets and the possibility of a default by a major swap trader. Actually, although credit risk in the swap market certainly is not trivial, it is not nearly as large as the magnitude of notional principal in these markets would suggest. To see why, consider a simple interest rate swap of LIBOR for a fixed rate.

At the time the transaction is initiated, it has zero net present value to both parties for the same reason that a futures contract has zero value at inception: Both are simply contracts to exchange cash in the future at terms established today that make both parties willing to enter into the deal. Even if one party were to back out of the deal at this moment, it would not cost the counterparty anything, because another trader could be found to take its place.

Once interest or exchange rates change, however, the situation is not as simple. Suppose, for example, that interest rates increase shortly after an interest-rate swap agreement has begun. The floating-rate payer therefore suffers a loss, while the fixed-rate payer enjoys a gain. If the floating-rate payer reneges on its commitment at this point, the fixed-rate payer suffers a loss. However, that loss is not as large as the notional principal of the swap, for the default of the floating-rate payer relieves the fixed-rate payer from its obligation as well. The loss is only the *difference* between the values of the fixed-rate and floating-rate obligations, not the *total* value of the payments that the floating-rate payer was obligated to make.

**EXAMPLE 23.6    Credit Risk in Swaps**

Consider a swap written on $1 million of notional principal that calls for exchange of LIBOR for a fixed rate of 8% for 5 years. Suppose, for simplicity, that the yield curve is currently flat at 8%. With LIBOR thus equal to 8%, no cash flows will be exchanged unless interest rates change. But now suppose that the yield curve immediately shifts up to 9%. The floating-rate payer now is obligated to pay a cash flow of $(.09 - .08) \times \$1$ million $= \$10,000$ each year to the fixed-rate payer (as long as rates remain at 9%). If the floating-rate payer defaults on the swap, the fixed-rate payer loses the prospect of that 5-year annuity. The present value of that annuity is $\$10,000 \times$ Annuity factor(9%, 5 years) $= \$38,897$. This loss may not be trivial, but it is less than 4% of notional principal. We conclude that the credit risk of the swap is far less than notional principal. Again, this is because the default by the floating-rate payer costs the counterparty only the *difference* between the LIBOR rate and the fixed rate.

**Swap Variations**    Swaps have given rise to a wide range of spinoff products. Many of these add option features to the basic swap agreement. For example, an *interest rate cap* is an agreement in which the buyer makes a payment today in exchange for possible future payments if a reference interest rate (usually LIBOR) exceeds a specified limit— the cap—on a series of settlement dates. For example, if the limit rate is 7%, then the cap holder receives (LIBOR − .07) for each dollar of notional principal if the LIBOR rate exceeds 7%. The purchaser of the cap in effect has entered a swap agreement to exchange the LIBOR rate for a fixed rate of 7% with an option not to do the swap in any period that the transaction is unprofitable. The payoff to the holder of the cap is

(Reference rate − Limit rate) × Notional principal *if* this value is positive

and zero otherwise. This, of course, is the payoff of a call option to purchase a cash flow proportional to the LIBOR rate for an exercise price proportional to the limit rate.

An *interest rate floor,* on the other hand, pays its holder in any period that the reference interest rate falls *below* some limit. This is analogous to a sequence of options to sell the reference rate for a stipulated "strike rate," in other words, a put option.

A *collar* combines interest rate caps and floors. A collar entails the purchase of a cap with one limit rate, and the sale of a floor with a lower limit rate. If a firm issues a floating-rate liability and buys the cap, it achieves protection against rates rising. If rates do rise, the cap provides a cash flow equal to the reference interest rate in exchange for a payment equal to the limit rate. Therefore, the cap places an upper bound equal to the limit rate on the firm's net interest rate expense. The written floor places a limit on how much the firm can benefit from rate declines. Even if interest rates fall dramatically, the firm's savings on its floating-rate obligation will be offset by its obligation to pay the difference between the reference rate and the limit rate. Therefore, the collar limits the firm's net cost of funds to a value between the limit rate on the cap and the limit rate on the floor.

Other option-based variations on the basic swap arrangement are *swaptions*. A swaption is an option on a swap. The buyer of the swaption has the right to enter an interest rate swap on some reference interest rate at a specified fixed interest rate on or before some expiration date. A put swaption (often called a *payer swaption*) is the right to pay the fixed rate in a swap and receive the floating rate. A call swaption is the right to receive the fixed rate and pay the floating rate. An exit option is the right to walk away from a swap without penalty. Swaptions can be European or American style.

There also are futures and forward variations on swaps. A forward swap, for example, obligates both traders to enter a swap at some date in the future with terms agreed to today.

**SUMMARY**

1. Foreign exchange futures trade on several foreign currencies, as well as on a European currency index. The interest rate parity relationship for foreign exchange futures is

$$F_0 = E_0 \left( \frac{1 + r_{US}}{1 + r_{foreign}} \right)^T$$

with exchange rates quoted as dollars per foreign currency. Deviations of the futures price from this value imply arbitrage opportunity. Empirical evidence, however, suggests that generally the parity relationship is satisfied.

2. Futures contracts calling for cash settlement are traded on various stock market indexes. The contracts may be mixed with Treasury bills to construct artificial equity positions, which makes them potentially valuable tools for market timers. Market index contracts are used also by arbitrageurs who attempt to profit from violations of the parity relationship.

3. Hedging requires investors to purchase assets that will offset the sensitivity of their portfolios to particular sources of risk. A hedged position requires that the hedging vehicle provide profits that vary inversely with the value of the position to be protected.

4. The hedge ratio is the number of hedging vehicles such as futures contracts required to offset the risk of the unprotected position. The hedge ratio for systematic market risk is proportional to the size and beta of the underlying stock portfolio. The hedge ratio for fixed-income portfolios is proportional to the price value of a basis point, which in turn is proportional to modified duration and the size of the portfolio.

5. Interest rate futures contracts may be written on the *prices* of debt securities (as in the case of Treasury-bond futures contracts) or on interest rates directly (as in the case of Eurodollar contracts).

6. Commodity futures pricing is complicated by costs for storage of the underlying commodity. When the asset is willingly stored by investors, then the storage costs net of convenience yield enter the futures pricing equation as follows:

$$F_0 = P_0(1 + r_f + c)$$

The non–interest net carrying costs, $c$, play the role of a "negative dividend" in this context.

7. When commodities are not stored for investment purposes, the correct futures price must be determined using general risk–return principles. In this event,

$$F_0 = E(P_T)\left(\frac{1 + r_f}{1 + k}\right)^T$$

The equilibrium (risk–return) and the no-arbitrage predictions of the proper futures price are consistent with one another for stored commodities.

8. Swaps, which call for the exchange of a series of cash flows, may be viewed as portfolios of forward contracts. Each transaction may be viewed as a separate forward agreement. However, instead of pricing each exchange independently, the swap sets one "forward price" that applies to all of the transactions. Therefore, the swap price will be an average of the forward prices that would prevail if each exchange were priced separately.

## KEY TERMS

| | | |
|---|---|---|
| hedging | hedge ratio | price value of a basis point |
| interest rate parity theorem | index arbitrage | cross-hedging |
| covered interest arbitrage relationship | program trading | foreign exchange swap |
| | triple-witching hour | interest rate swap |

## WEBSITES

www.numa.com
NumaWeb calls itself the Internet's home page for financial derivatives. The site has numerous links to other derivatives-related sites. It also has a calendar to track release of economic statistics and contract expiration dates.

stocks.about.com (Link to *Derivatives.*)
This site contains links and references to all types of futures and option contracts.

www.adtrading.com
This applied derivatives site contains articles on current topics related to derivatives. It also has calendar to track release of economic statistics and contract expiration dates.

www.isda.org
The International Swap and Derivatives Organization's Web page contains some basic information on markets for swaps and provides limited educational links.

www.iafe.org
The International Association of Financial Engineers' Web page contains some basic information on derivatives as well as an extensive list of additional sources.

www.cme.com/prd/fx
This site lists the Chicago Mercantile Exchange currency contracts.

The following sites contain information on futures, swaps, and other derivative instruments. Many of the sites also contain general information on risk management.
www.ino.com
www.contingencyanalysis.com

**WEBSITES**      www.finpipe.com/derivatives.htm
                  www.swapsmonitor.com/index.htm
                  www.erisks.com

## PROBLEMS

1. Consider the futures contract written on the S&P 500 index and maturing in 6 months. The interest rate is 3% per 6-month period, and the future value of dividends expected to be paid over the next 6 months is $15. The current index level is 1,425. Assume that you can short sell the S&P index.

   a. Suppose the expected rate of return on the market is 6% per 6-month period. What is the expected level of the index in 6 months?

   b. What is the theoretical no-arbitrage price for a 6-month futures contract on the S&P 500 stock index?

   c. Suppose the futures price is 1,422. Is there an arbitrage opportunity here? If so, how would you exploit it?

2. Suppose that the value of the S&P 500 stock index is 1,350.

   a. If each futures contract costs $25 to trade with a discount broker, how much is the transaction cost per dollar of stock controlled by the futures contract?

   b. If the average price of a share on the NYSE is about $40, how much is the transaction cost per "typical share" controlled by one futures contract?

   c. For small investors, a typical transaction cost per share in stocks directly is about 20 cents per share. How many times the transactions costs in futures markets is this?

3. Suppose the 1-year futures price on a stock-index portfolio is 1,218, the stock index currently is 1,200, the 1-year risk-free interest rate is 3%, and the year-end dividend that will be paid on a $1,200 investment in the market index portfolio is $15.

   a. By how much is the contract mispriced?

   b. Formulate a zero-net-investment arbitrage portfolio and show that you can lock in riskless profits equal to the futures mispricing.

   c. Now assume (as is true for small investors) that if you short sell the stocks in the market index, the proceeds of the short sale are kept with the broker, and you do not receive any interest income on the funds. Is there still an arbitrage opportunity (assuming that you don't already own the shares in the index)? Explain.

   d. Given the short-sale rules, what is the no-arbitrage *band* for the stock-futures price relationship? That is, given a stock index of 1,200, how high and how low can the futures price be without giving rise to arbitrage opportunities?

4. Consider these futures market data for the June delivery S&P 500 contract, exactly 6 months hence. The S&P 500 index is at 1,350, and the June maturity contract is at $F_0 = 1,351$.

   a. If the current interest rate is 2.2% semiannually, and the average dividend rate of the stocks in the index is 1.2% semiannually, what fraction of the proceeds of stock short sales would need to be available to you to earn arbitrage profits?

   b. Suppose that you in fact have access to 90% of the proceeds from a short sale. What is the lower bound on the futures price that rules out arbitrage opportunities? By how much does the actual futures price fall below the no-arbitrage bound? Formulate the appropriate arbitrage strategy, and calculate the profits to that strategy.

5. Donna Doni, CFA, wants to explore potential inefficiencies in the futures market. The TOBEC stock index has a spot value of 185.00 now. TOBEC futures contracts are settled in cash and underlying contract values are determined by multiplying $100 times the index value. The current annual risk-free interest rate is 6.0%.

   a. Calculate the theoretical price of the futures contract expiring 6 months from now, using the cost-of-carry model. The index pays no dividends.

   The total (round-trip) transaction cost for trading a futures contract is $15.00.

   b. Calculate the lower bound for the price of the futures contract expiring 6 months from now.

6. You manage a $13.5 million portfolio, currently all invested in equities, and believe that you have extraordinary market-timing skills. You believe that the market is on the verge of a big but short-lived downturn; you would move your portfolio temporarily into T-bills, but you do not want to incur the transaction costs of liquidating and reestablishing your equity position. Instead, you decide to temporarily hedge your equity holdings with S&P 500 index futures contracts.

   a. Should you be long or short the contracts? Why?

   b. If your equity holdings are invested in a market-index fund, into how many contracts should you enter? The S&P 500 index is now at 1,350 and the contract multiplier is $250.

   c. How does your answer to (b) change if the beta of your portfolio is .6?

7. A manager is holding a $1 million stock portfolio with a beta of 1.25. She would like to hedge the risk of the portfolio using the S&P 500 stock index futures contract. How many dollars' worth of the index should she sell in the futures market to minimize the volatility of her position?

8. You hold a $12 million stock portfolio with a beta of 1.0. You believe that the risk-adjusted abnormal return on the portfolio (the alpha) over the next 3 months is 2%. The S&P 500 index currently is at 1,200 and the risk-free rate is 1% per quarter.

   a. What will be the futures price on the 3-month maturity S&P 500 futures contract?

   b. How many S&P 500 futures contracts are needed to hedge the stock portfolio?

   c. What will be the profit on that futures position in 3 months as a function of the value of the S&P 500 index on the maturity date?

   d. If the alpha of the portfolio is 2%, show that the expected rate of return (in decimal form) on the portfolio as a function of the market return is $r_p = .03 + 1.0 \times (r_M - .01)$.

   e. Call $S_T$ the value of the index in 3 months. Then $S_T/S_0 = S_T/1,200 = 1 + r_M$. (We are ignoring dividends here to keep things simple.) Substitute this expression in the equation for the portfolio return, $r_p$, and calculate the expected value of the hedged stock-plus-futures portfolio in 3 months as a function of the value of the index.

   f. Show that the hedged portfolio provides an expected rate of return of 3% over the next three months.

   g. What is the beta of the hedged portfolio? What is the alpha of the hedged portfolio?

9. Suppose that the relationship between the rate of return on IBM stock, the market index, and a computer industry index can be described by the following regression equation: $r_{IBM} = .5r_M + .75r_{Industry}$. If a futures contract on the computer industry is traded, how would you hedge the exposure to the systematic and industry factors affecting the performance of IBM stock? How many dollars' worth of the market and industry index contracts would you buy or sell for each dollar held in IBM?

10. Suppose your client says, "I am invested in Japanese stocks but want to eliminate my exposure to this market for a period of time. Can I accomplish this without the cost and inconvenience of selling out and buying back in again if my expectations change?"

   a. Briefly describe a strategy to hedge both the local market risk and the currency risk of investing in Japanese stocks.

   b. Briefly explain why the hedge strategy you described in part (a) might not be fully effective.

11. Suppose that the spot price of the euro is currently 90 cents. The 1-year futures price is 93 cents. Is the interest rate higher in the United States or the euro zone?

12. a. The spot price of the British pound is currently $1.60. If the risk-free interest rate on 1-year government bonds is 4% in the United States and 8% in the United Kingdom, what must be the forward price of the pound for delivery 1 year from now?

   b. How could an investor make risk-free arbitrage profits if the forward price were higher than the price you gave in answer to (a)? Give a numerical example.

13. Consider the following information:

$$r_{US} = 4\% \qquad r_{UK} = 7\%$$
$$E_0 = 1.60 \text{ dollars per pound}$$
$$F_0 = 1.58 \text{ (1-year delivery)}$$

where the interest rates are annual yields on U.S. or U.K. bills. Given this information:

   a. Where would you lend?

   b. Where would you borrow?

   c. How could you arbitrage?

14. René Michaels, CFA, plans to invest $1 million in U.S. government cash equivalents for the next 90 days. Michaels's client has authorized her to use non–U.S. government cash equivalents, but only if the currency risk is hedged to U.S. dollars by using forward currency contracts.

   a. Calculate the U.S. dollar value of the hedged investment at the end of 90 days for each of the two cash equivalents in the table below. Show all calculations.

   b. Briefly explain the theory that best accounts for your results.

   c. Based on this theory, estimate the implied interest rate for a 90-day U.S. government cash equivalent.

### Interest Rates
### 90-Day Cash Equivalents

| | |
|---|---|
| Japanese government | 7.6% |
| Swiss government | 8.6% |

### Exchange Rates
### Currency Units per U.S. Dollar

| | Spot | 90-Day Forward |
|---|---|---|
| Japanese yen | 133.05 | 133.47 |
| Swiss franc | 1.5260 | 1.5348 |

15. a. Pamela Itsuji, a currency trader for a Japanese bank, is evaluating the price of a 6-month Japanese yen/U.S. dollar currency futures contract. She gathers the following currency and interest rate data:

| Japanese yen/U.S. dollar spot currency exchange rate | ¥124.30/$1.00 |
|---|---|
| 6-month Japanese interest rate | 0.10% |
| 6-month U.S. interest rate | 3.80% |

Calculate the theoretical price for a 6-month Japanese yen/U.S. dollar currency futures contract, using the data above.

b. Itsuji is also reviewing the price of a 3-month Japanese yen/U.S. dollar currency futures contract, using the currency and interest rate data shown below. Because the 3-month Japanese interest rate has just increased to 0.50%, Itsuji recognizes that an arbitrage opportunity exists and decides to borrow $1 million U.S. dollars to purchase Japanese yen. Calculate the yen arbitrage profit from Itsuji's strategy, using the following data:

| Japanese yen/U.S. dollar spot currency exchange rate | ¥124.30/$1.00 |
|---|---|
| New 3-month Japanese interest rate | 0.50% |
| 3-month U.S. interest rate | 3.50% |
| 3-month currency futures contract value | ¥123.2605/$1.00 |

16. Farmer Brown grows Number 1 red corn and would like to hedge the value of the coming harvest. However, the futures contract is traded on the Number 2 yellow grade of corn. Suppose that yellow corn typically sells for 90% of the price of red corn. If he grows 100,000 bushels, and each futures contract calls for delivery of 5,000 bushels, how many contracts should Farmer Brown buy or sell to hedge his position?

17. You believe that the spread between municipal bond yields and U.S. Treasury bond yields is going to narrow in the coming month. How can you profit from such a change using the municipal bond and T-bond futures contracts?

18. Return to Figure 23.8. Suppose the LIBOR rate when the first listed Eurodollar contract matures in October is 1.71%. What will be the profit or loss to each side of the Eurodollar contract?

19. Yields on short-term bonds tend to be more volatile than yields on long-term bonds. Suppose that you have estimated that the yield on 20-year bonds changes by 10 basis points for every 15-basis-point move in the yield on 5-year bonds. You hold a $1 million portfolio of 5-year maturity bonds with modified duration 4 years and desire to hedge your interest rate exposure with T-bond futures, which currently have modified duration 9 years and sell at $F_0 = \$95$. How many futures contracts should you sell?

20. A manager is holding a $1 million bond portfolio with a modified duration of 8 years. She would like to hedge the risk of the portfolio by short-selling Treasury bonds. The modified duration of T-bonds is 10 years. How many dollars' worth of T-bonds should she sell to minimize the variance of her position?

21. A corporation plans to issue $10 million of 10-year bonds in 3 months. At current yields the bonds would have modified duration of 8 years. The T-note futures contract is selling at $F_0 = 100$ and has modified duration of 6 years. How can the firm use this futures contract to hedge the risk surrounding the yield at which it will be able to sell its bonds? Both the bond and the contract are at par value.

22. If the spot price of gold is $300 per troy ounce, the risk-free interest rate is 10%, and storage and insurance costs are zero, what should the forward price of gold be for delivery in 1 year? Use an arbitrage argument to prove your answer. Include a

numerical example showing how you could make risk-free arbitrage profits if the forward price exceeded its upper bound value.

23. If the corn harvest today is poor, would you expect this fact to have any effect on today's futures prices for corn to be delivered (postharvest) 2 years from today? Under what circumstances will there be no effect?

24. Suppose that the price of corn is risky, with a beta of .5. The monthly storage cost is $.03, and the current spot price is $2.75, with an expected spot price in 3 months of $2.94. If the expected rate of return on the market is 1.8% per month, with a risk-free rate of 1% per month, would you store corn for 3 months?

25. You are provided the information outlined as follows to be used in solving this problem.

| Issue | Price | Yield to Maturity | Modified Duration* |
|---|---|---|---|
| U.S. Treasury bond 11¾% maturing Nov. 15, 2024 | 100 | 11.75% | 7.6 years |
| U.S. Treasury long bond futures contract (contract expiration in 6 months) | 63.33 | 11.85% | 8.0 years |
| XYZ Corporation bond 12½% maturing June 1, 2015 (sinking fund debenture, rated AAA) | 93 | 13.50% | 7.2 years |
| Volatility of AAA corporate bond yields relative to U.S. Treasury bond yields = 1.25 to 1.0 (1.25 times) | | | |

Assume no commission and no margin requirements on U.S. Treasury long bond futures contracts. Assume no taxes.

One U.S. Treasury long bond futures contract is a claim on $100,000 par value long-term U.S. Treasury bonds.

*Modified duration = Duration/(1 + $y$).

*Situation A*    A fixed-income manager holding a $20 million market value position of U.S. Treasury 11¾% bonds maturing November 15, 2024, expects the economic growth rate and the inflation rate to be above market expectations in the near future. Institutional rigidities prevent any existing bonds in the portfolio from being sold in the cash market.

*Situation B*    The treasurer of XYZ Corporation has recently become convinced that interest rates will decline in the near future. He believes it is an opportune time to purchase his company's sinking fund bonds in advance of requirements since these bonds are trading at a discount from par value. He is preparing to purchase in the open market $20 million par value XYZ Corporation 12½% bonds maturing June 1, 2015. A $20 million par value position of these bonds is currently offered in the open market at 93. Unfortunately, the treasurer must obtain approval from the board of directors for such a purchase, and this approval process can take up to 2 months. The board of directors' approval in this instance is only a formality.

For each of these two situations, demonstrate how interest rate risk can be hedged using the Treasury bond futures contract. Show all calculations, including the number of futures contracts used.

26. You ran a regression of the yield of KC Company's 10-year bond on the 10-year U.S. Treasury benchmark's yield using month-end data for the past year. You found the following result:

$$\text{Yield}_{KC} = 0.54 + 1.22\,\text{Yield}_{Treasury}$$

where Yield$_{KC}$ is the yield on the KC bond and Yield$_{Treasury}$ is the yield on the U.S. Treasury bond.

The modified duration on the 10-year U.S. Treasury is 7.0 years, and modified duration on the KC bond is 6.93 years.

   *a.* Calculate the percentage change in the price of the 10-year U.S. Treasury, assuming a 50-basis-point change in the yield on the 10-year U.S. Treasury.

   *b.* Calculate the percentage change in the price of the KC bond, using the regression equation above, assuming a 50-basis-point change in the yield on the 10-year U.S. Treasury.

27. The U.S. yield curve is flat at 5% and the euro yield curve is flat at 8%. The current exchange rate is $.85 per euro. What will be the swap rate on an agreement to exchange currency over a 3-year period? The swap will call for the exchange of 1 million euros for a given number of dollars in each year.

28. Firm ABC enters a 5-year swap with firm XYZ to pay LIBOR in return for a fixed 8% rate on notional principal of $10 million. Two years from now, the market rate on 3-year swaps is LIBOR for 7%; at this time, firm XYZ goes bankrupt and defaults on its swap obligation.

   *a.* Why is firm ABC harmed by the default?

   *b.* What is the market value of the loss incurred by ABC as a result of the default?

   *c.* Suppose instead that ABC had gone bankrupt. How do you think the swap would be treated in the reorganization of the firm?

29. At the present time, one can enter 5-year swaps that exchange LIBOR for 8%. Five-year caps with limit rates of 8% sell for $.30 per dollar of notional principal. What must be the price of 5-year floors with a limit rate of 8%?

30. At the present time, one can enter 5-year swaps that exchange LIBOR for 8%. An *off-market swap* would then be defined as a swap of LIBOR for a fixed rate other than 8%. For example, a firm with 10% coupon debt outstanding might like to convert to synthetic floating-rate debt by entering a swap in which it pays LIBOR and receives a fixed rate of 10%. What up-front payment will be required to induce a counterparty to take the other side of this swap? Assume notional principal is $10 million.

---

From the *Market Insight* entry page (**www.mhhe.com/business/finance/edumarket insight**), link to Coca-Cola (*KO*). From the *EDGAR* link and the latest 10K report, find the proportion of Coke's revenue derived from sales outside the U.S. If Coke expects to transfer funds from Europe to the United States in 90 days, how might it hedge this transaction with currency futures and options on futures contracts? (What contracts might Coke buy or sell? Why?)

---

**E-INVESTMENTS**
**Describing Different Swaps**

Go to **www.finpipe.com/derprem.htm**. Finpipe.com contains excellent discussions on the derivatives markets. From this site, access the descriptions on the following types of swaps: Interest Rate Swaps, Commodity Swaps, Equity Swaps, and Commodity Swaps.

   Describe each of the swaps.

   Give an example of how each of the swaps could be used to hedge risk.

1. According to interest rate parity, $F_0$ should be $1.585. Since the futures price is too high, we should reverse the arbitrage strategy just considered.

|  | CF Now ($) | CF in 1 Year |
|---|---|---|
| 1. Borrow $1.60 in the U.S. Convert to one pound. | +1.60 | −1.60(1.05) |
| 2. Lend the one pound in the U.K. | −1.60 | $1.06E_1$ |
| 3. Enter a contract to sell 1.06 pounds at a futures price of $1.62/£. | 0 | (£1.06)($1.62/£ − $E_1$) |
| _TOTAL_ | 0 | $.0372 |

2. Because the firm does poorly when the dollar depreciates, it hedges with a futures contract that will provide profits in that scenario. It needs to enter a _long_ position in pound futures, which means that it will earn profits on the contract when the futures price increases, that is, when more dollars are required to purchase one pound. The specific hedge ratio is determined by noting that if the number of dollars required to buy one pound rises by $.05, profits decrease by $200,000 at the same time that the profit on a long future contract would be $.05 × 62,500 = $3,125. The hedge ratio is

$$\frac{\$200,000 \text{ per } \$.05 \text{ depreciation in the dollar}}{\$3,125 \text{ per contract per } \$.05 \text{ depreciation}} = 64 \text{ contracts long}$$

**SOLUTIONS TO CONCEPT CHECKS**

3. Each $1 increase in the price of corn reduces profits by $1 million. Therefore, the firm needs to enter futures contracts to purchase 1 million bushels at a price stipulated today. The futures position will profit by $1 million for each increase of $1 in the price of corn. The profit on the contract will offset the lost profits on operations.

4.

|  | In General (per unit of index) | Our Numbers |
|---|---|---|
| Hold 100,000 units of indexed stock portfolio with $S_0 = 900$. | $S_T$ | 100,000 $S_T$ |
| Sell 400 contracts. | $F_0 − S_T$ | 400 × $250 × (909 − $S_T$) |
| _TOTAL_ | $F_0$ | $90,900,000 |

The net cash flow is riskless, and provides a 1% monthly rate of return, equal to the risk-free rate.

5. If the futures price is above the parity level, investors would sell futures and buy stocks. Short-selling would not be necessary. Therefore, the top of the no-arbitrage band would be unaffected by the use of the proceeds. If the futures price is too low, investors would want to short sell stocks and buy futures. Now the costs of short selling are important. If proceeds from the short sale become available, short selling becomes less costly and the bottom of the band will move up.

6. The price value of a basis point is still $9,000, as a one-basis-point change in the interest rate reduces the value of the $20 million portfolio by .01% × 4.5 = .045%. Therefore, the number of futures needed to hedge the interest rate risk is the same as for a portfolio half the size with double the modified duration.

7. Stocks offer a total return (capital gain plus dividends) large enough to compensate investors for the time value of the money tied up in the stock. Agricultural prices do

Visit us at www.mhhe.com/bkm

**SOLUTIONS TO CONCEPT CHECKS** *(Concluded)*

not necessarily increase over time. In fact, across a harvest, crop prices will fall. The returns necessary to make storage economically attractive are lacking.

8. If systematic risk were higher, the appropriate discount rate, $k$, would increase. Referring to equation 23.5, we conclude that $F_0$ would fall. Intuitively, the claim to 1 pound of orange juice is worth less today if its expected price is unchanged, but the risk associated with the value of the claim increases. Therefore, the amount investors are willing to pay today for future delivery is lower.

9.

| | LIBOR | | |
|---|---|---|---|
| | 7% | 8% | 9% |
| As debt payer (LIBOR × $10 million) | −700,000 | −800,000 | −900,000 |
| As fixed payer receives $10 million × (LIBOR − .08) | −100,000 | 0 | +100,000 |
| Net cash flow | −800,000 | −800,000 | −800,000 |

Regardless of the LIBOR rate, the firm's net cash outflow equals .08 × bond principal, just as if it had issued a fixed-rate bond with a coupon of 8%.

# ACTIVE PORTFOLIO MANAGEMENT

www.mhhe.com/bkm

## CHAPTER TWENTY-FOUR

# PORTFOLIO PERFORMANCE EVALUATION

How can we evaluate the performance of a portfolio manager? It turns out that even average portfolio return is not as straightforward to measure as it might seem. In addition, adjusting average returns for risk presents a host of other problems. We begin with the measurement of portfolio returns. From there we move on to conventional approaches to risk adjustment. We identify the problems with these approaches when applied in various situations. We then turn to some procedures for performance evaluation in the field, for example, performance attribution techniques, style analysis, and the Morningstar Star Rating method.

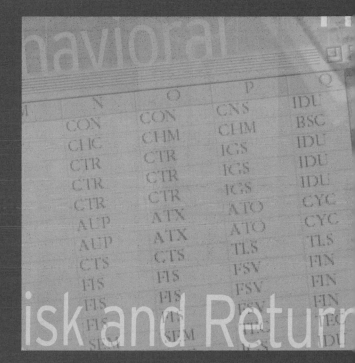

## 24.1    MEASURING INVESTMENT RETURNS

The rate of return of an investment is a simple concept in the case of a one-period investment. It is simply the total proceeds derived from the investment per dollar initially invested. Proceeds must be defined broadly to include both cash distributions and capital gains. For stocks, total returns are dividends plus capital gains. For bonds, total returns are coupon or interest paid plus capital gains.

To set the stage for discussing the more subtle issues that follow, let us start with a trivial example. Consider a stock paying a dividend of $2 annually that currently sells for $50. You purchase the stock today and collect the $2 dividend, and then you sell the stock for $53 at year-end. Your rate of return is

$$\frac{\text{Total proceeds}}{\text{Initial investment}} = \frac{\text{Income} + \text{Capital gain}}{50} = \frac{2+3}{50} = .10, \text{ or } 10\%$$

Another way to derive the rate of return that is useful in the more difficult multiperiod case is to set up the investment as a discounted cash flow problem. Call $r$ the rate of return that equates the present value of all cash flows from the investment with the initial outlay. In our example the stock is purchased for $50 and generates cash flows at year-end of $2 (dividend) plus $53 (sale of stock). Therefore, we solve $50 = (2 + 53)/(1 + r)$ to find again that $r = 10\%$.

**Time-Weighted Returns versus Dollar-Weighted Returns**    When we consider investments over a period during which cash was added to or withdrawn from the portfolio, measuring the rate of return becomes more difficult. To continue our example, suppose that you were to purchase a second share of the same stock at the end of the first year, and hold both shares until the end of Year 2, at which point you sell each share for $54.

Total cash outlays are

| Time | Outlay |
|---|---|
| 0 | $50 to purchase first share |
| 1 | $53 to purchase second share a year later |

| | Proceeds |
|---|---|
| 1 | $2 dividend from initially purchased share |
| 2 | $4 dividend from the 2 shares held in the second year, plus $108 received from selling both shares at $54 each |

Using the discounted cash flow (DCF) approach, we can solve for the average return over the 2 years by equating the present values of the cash inflows and outflows:

$$50 + \frac{53}{1+r} = \frac{2}{1+r} + \frac{112}{(1+r)^2}$$

resulting in $r = 7.117\%$.

This value is called the internal rate of return, or the **dollar-weighted rate of return** on the investment. It is "dollar weighted" because the stock's performance in the second year, when two shares of stock are held, has a greater influence on the average overall return than the first-year return, when only one share is held.

An alternative to the internal, or dollar-weighted, return is the **time-weighted return.** This method ignores the number of shares of stock held in each period. The stock return in the first year was 10%. In the second year the stock had a starting value of $53 and sold at year-end for $54, for a total one-period rate of return of $3 ($2 dividend plus $1 capital gain) divided by $53 (the stock price at the start of the second year), or 5.66%. The time-weighted return is the average of 10% and 5.66%, which is 7.83%. This average return considers only the period-by-period returns without regard to the amounts invested in the stock in each period.

Note that the dollar-weighted return is less than the time-weighted return in this example. The reason is that the stock fared relatively poorly in the second year, when the investor was holding more shares. The greater weight that the dollar-weighted average places on the second-year return results in a lower measure of investment performance. In general, dollar- and time-weighted returns will differ, and the difference can be positive or negative, depending on the configuration of period returns and portfolio composition.

Which measure of performance is superior? At first, it appears that the dollar-weighted return must be more relevant. After all, the more money you invest in a stock when its performance is superior, the more money you end up with. Certainly your performance measure should reflect this fact.

Time-weighted returns have their own use, however, especially in the money management industry. This is so because in many important applications a portfolio manager may not directly control the timing or the amount of money invested in securities. Pension fund management is a good example. A pension fund manager faces cash inflows into the fund when pension contributions are made, and cash outflows when pension benefits are paid. Obviously, the amount of money invested at any time can vary for reasons beyond the manager's control. Because dollars invested do not depend on the manager's choice, it is inappropriate to weight returns by dollars invested when measuring investment ability. Consequently, the money management industry uses time-weighted returns for performance evaluation.

| CONCEPT CHECK ☞ QUESTION 1 | Shares of XYZ Corp. pay a $2 dividend at the end of every year on December 31. An investor buys two shares of the stock on January 1 at a price of $20 each, sells one of those shares for $22 a year later on the next January 1, and sells the second share an additional year later for $19. Find the time- and dollar-weighted rates of return on the 2-year investment. |
| --- | --- |

**Arithmetic versus Geometric Averages**   Our example takes the arithmetic average of the two annual returns, 10% and 5.66%, as the time-weighted average, 7.83%. Another approach is to take a geometric average, denoted $r_G$.

The motivation for this calculation comes from the principle of compounding. If dividend proceeds are reinvested, the accumulated value of an investment in the stock will grow by a factor of 1.10 in the first year and by an additional factor of 1.0566 in the second year. The compound average growth rate, $r_G$, is then calculated as the solution to the following equation:

$$(1 + r_G)^2 = (1.10)(1.0566)$$

This approach would entail computing

$$1 + r_G = [(1.10)(1.0566)]^{1/2} = 1.0781$$

or $r_G = 7.81\%$.

More generally, for an $n$-period investment, the geometric average rate of return is defined by

$$1 + r_G = [(1 + r_1)(1 + r_2) \cdots (1 + r_n)]^{1/n}$$

where $r_t$ is the return in each time period.

**Table 24.1    Average Annual Returns by Investment Class, 1926–2002**

| | Arithmetic Average | Geometric Average | Difference | Standard Deviation |
|---|---|---|---|---|
| Common stocks of small firms* | 17.74 | 11.64 | 6.10 | 39.30 |
| Common stocks of large firms | 12.04 | 10.01 | 2.03 | 20.55 |
| Long-term Treasury bonds | 5.68 | 5.38 | 0.30 | 8.24 |
| U.S. Treasury bills | 3.82 | 3.78 | 0.04 | 3.18 |

*These are firms with relatively low market values of equity. Market capitalization is computed as price per share times shares outstanding.
Source: Authors' calculations based on data in Figure 5.5.

The geometric average return in this example, 7.81%, is slightly less than the arithmetic average return, 7.83%. This is a general property: Geometric averages never exceed arithmetic ones. To see the intuition behind this result, consider a stock that doubles in price in period 1 ($r_1 = 100\%$) and halves in price in period 2 ($r_2 = -50\%$). The arithmetic average is $r_A = [100 + (-50)]/2 = 25\%$, whereas the geometric average is $r_G = [(1 + 1)(1 - .5)]^{1/2} - 1 = 0$. The effect of the $-50\%$ return in period 2 fully offsets the 100% return in period 1 in the calculation of the geometric average, resulting in an average return of zero. This is not true of the arithmetic average. In general, the bad returns have a greater influence on the averaging process in the geometric technique. Therefore, geometric averages are lower.

Moreover, the difference in the two averaging techniques will be greater the greater is the variability of period-by-period returns. The general rule when returns are expressed as decimals (rather than percentages) is as follows:

$$r_G \approx r_A - \tfrac{1}{2}\sigma^2 \tag{24.1}$$

where $\sigma^2$ is the variance of returns. Equation 24.1 is exact when returns are normally distributed.

## EXAMPLE 24.1    Arithmetic versus Geometric Average

Consider Table 24.1, which presents arithmetic and geometric returns over the 1926–2002 period for a variety of investments. The arithmetic averages all exceed the geometric ones, with the difference greatest in the case of stocks of small firms, where annual returns exhibit the greatest standard deviation. The difference between the two averages falls to zero only when there is no variation in yearly returns. The table indicates that when the standard deviation falls to a level characteristic of T-bills, the difference is quite small.

To illustrate equation 24.1, consider the average returns for large stocks. According to the equation,

$$.1001 \approx .1204 - \tfrac{1}{2}(.2055)^2 = .0993$$
$$.1001 \approx .0993$$

As predicted, the arithmetic mean (.1204) exceeded the geometric mean (.1001) by approximately one-half the variance in returns. Clearly, when comparing returns, one never should mix and match the two averaging techniques.[1]

---

[1] In the case of small stocks, $\tfrac{1}{2}(.3930)^2 = .0772$ exceeds the difference, $r_A - r_G = .0610$, by a substantial amount, .0162, or 1.62%, because extreme values in small stock returns are more frequent than would be predicted from a normal distribution.

This last point leads to another question. Which is the superior measure of investment performance, the arithmetic average or the geometric average? The geometric average has considerable appeal because it represents the constant rate of return we would have needed to earn in each year to match actual performance over some past investment period. It is an excellent measure of *past* performance. However, if our focus is on future performance, then the arithmetic average is the statistic of interest because it is an unbiased estimate of the portfolio's expected return (assuming, of course, that the expected return does not change over time). In contrast, because the geometric return over a sample period is always less than the arithmetic mean, it constitutes a downward-biased estimator of the stock's expected return in any future year.

**EXAMPLE 24.2**     **Forecasting Future Returns**

Consider again a stock that will either double in value ($r = 100\%$) with probability of .5, or halve in value ($r = -50\%$) with probability .5. The following table illustrates these outcomes:

| Investment Outcome | Final Value of Each Dollar Invested | 1-Year Rate of Return |
|---|---|---|
| Double | $2.00 | 100% |
| Halve | $0.50 | -50% |

Suppose that the stock's performance over a 2-year period is characteristic of the probability distribution, doubling in 1 year and halving in the other. The stock's price ends up exactly where it started, and the geometric average annual return is zero:

$$1 + r_G = [(1 + r_1)(1 + r_2)]^{1/2}$$
$$= [(1 + 1)(1 - .50)]^{1/2} = 1$$
$$r_G = 0$$

which confirms that a zero year-by-year return would have replicated the total return earned on the stock.

The expected annual future rate of return on the stock, however, is *not* zero; it is the arithmetic average of 100% and $-50\%$: $(100 - 50)/2 = 25\%$. There are two equally likely outcomes per dollar invested: either a gain of $1 (when $r = 100\%$) or a loss of $.50 (when $r = -50\%$). The expected profit is ($1 - $.50)/2 = $.25, for a 25% expected rate of return. The profit in the good year more than offsets the loss in the bad year, despite the fact that the geometric return is zero. The arithmetic average return thus provides the best guide to expected rate of return.

The argument in Example 24.2 carries forward into multiperiod investments. Consider, for example, all the possible outcomes over a 2-year period:

| Investment Outcome | Final Value of Each Dollar Invested | Total Return over 2 Years |
|---|---|---|
| Double, double | $4.00 | 300% |
| Double, halve | 1.00 | 0 |
| Halve, double | 1.00 | 0 |
| Halve, halve | 0.25 | -75% |

The expected final value of each dollar invested is $(4 + 1 + 1 + .25)/4 = \$1.5625$ for 2 years, again indicating an average rate of return of 25% per year, equal to the arithmetic average. Note that an investment yielding 25% per year with certainty will yield the same final compounded value as the expected final value of this investment, as $1.25^2 = 1.5625$.

The arithmetic average return on the stock is $[300 + 0 + 0 + (-75)]/4 = 56.25\%$ per 2 years, for an effective annual return of 25%, that is, $1.5625^{1/2} - 1$. In contrast, the geometric mean return is zero:

$$[(1 + 3)(1 + 0)(1 + 0)(1 - .75)]^{1/4} = 1.0$$

Again, the arithmetic average is the better guide to *future* performance.

There is one important caveat regarding the use of the geometric versus arithmetic mean to forecast future returns. We have assumed in these examples that we know the true distribution of the rate of return. This, of course, is virtually never the case. Most often we rely on past history of returns to provide an *estimate* of the arithmetic or geometric mean return. Estimates are necessarily subject to sampling error, even if they are unbiased. It turns out that compounding at the estimated arithmetic mean will result in an upward bias of future cumulative performance beyond a 1-period horizon. This is so because with compounding, a positive estimation error will have a greater impact on future portfolio value than a negative estimation error of equal magnitude.

It turns out that to forecast future portfolio values over long horizons, its current value should be compounded forward at a *weighted average* of the geometric and arithmetic historical average returns.[2] The proper weight on the geometric average equals the ratio of the investment horizon to the sample estimation period. Suppose we estimate the mean from an average over a sample of $T$ years, and wish to forecast the average annual return over a horizon of $H$ years. When returns are lognormal (that is, short-term returns are normally distributed) and serially uncorrelated, then the unbiased forecast of the compound annual growth rate over the next $H$ years is

$$\text{Arithmetic average} \times (1 - H/T) + \text{Geometric average} \times H/T$$

Note that this formula implies that if the forecast period, $H$, equals the historical estimation period, $T$, then one should compound at the geometric rate.

**CONCEPT CHECK ☞ QUESTION 2**

**Suppose that a stock now selling for \$100 will either increase in value by 15% by year-end with probability .5, or fall in value by 5% with probability .5. The stock pays no dividends.**

*a.* **What are the geometric and arithmetic mean returns on the stock?**

*b.* **What is the expected end-of-year value of the share?**

*c.* **Which measure of expected return is superior?**

# 24.2   THE CONVENTIONAL THEORY OF PERFORMANCE EVALUATION

Calculating average portfolio returns does not mean the task is done. Returns must be adjusted for risk before they can be compared meaningfully. The simplest and most popular way to adjust returns for portfolio risk is to compare rates of return with those of other investment funds with similar risk characteristics. For example, high-yield bond portfolios are grouped into one "universe," growth stock equity funds are grouped into another universe, and so on. Then the (usually time-weighted) average returns of each fund within the universe are ordered, and each portfolio manager receives a percentile ranking depending on relative performance with the **comparison universe.** For example, the manager with the

---

[2] See Eric Jacquier, Alex Kane, and Alan J. Marcus. "Geometric or Arithmetic Mean: A Reconsideration," *Financial Analysts Journal*, November 2003.

**Figure 24.1
Universe
comparison.
Periods ending
December 31,
2004**

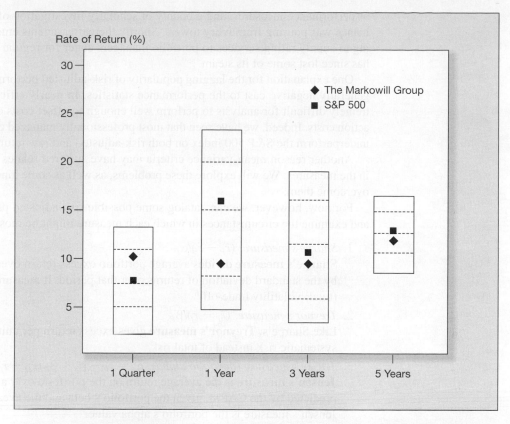

ninth-best performance in a universe of 100 funds would be the 90th percentile manager: Her performance was better than 90% of all competing funds over the evaluation period.

These relative rankings are usually displayed in a chart such as that in Figure 24.1. The chart summarizes performance rankings over four periods: 1 quarter, 1 year, 3 years, and 5 years. The top and bottom lines of each box are drawn at the rate of return of the 95th and 5th percentile managers. The three dashed lines correspond to the rates of return of the 75th, 50th (median), and 25th percentile managers. The diamond is drawn at the average return of a particular fund and the square is drawn at the return of a benchmark index such as the S&P 500. The placement of the diamond within the box is an easy-to-read representation of the performance of the fund relative to the comparison universe.

This comparison of performance with other managers of similar investment style is a useful first step in evaluating performance. However, such rankings can be misleading. For example, within a particular universe, some managers may concentrate on particular subgroups, so that portfolio characteristics are not truly comparable. For example, within the equity universe, one manager may concentrate on high-beta or aggressive growth stocks. Similarly, within fixed-income universes, durations can vary across managers. These considerations suggest that a more precise means for risk adjustment is desirable.

Methods of risk-adjusted performance evaluation using mean-variance criteria came on stage simultaneously with the capital asset pricing model. Jack Treynor,[3] William Sharpe,[4] and Michael Jensen[5] recognized immediately the implications of the CAPM for rating the performance of managers. Within a short time, academicians were in command of a battery

[3] Jack L. Treynor, "How to Rate Management Investment Funds," *Harvard Business Review* 43 (January–February 1966).

[4] William F. Sharpe, "Mutual Fund Performance," *Journal of Business* 39 (January 1966).

[5] Michael C. Jensen, "The Performance of Mutual Funds in the Period 1945–1964," *Journal of Finance*, May 1968; and "Risk, the Pricing of Capital Assets, and the Evaluation of Investment Portfolios," *Journal of Business*, April 1969.

of performance measures, and a bounty of scholarly investigation of mutual fund performance was pouring from ivory towers. Shortly thereafter, agents emerged who were willing to supply rating services to portfolio managers eager for regular feedback. This trend has since lost some of its steam.

One explanation for the lagging popularity of risk-adjusted performance measures is the generally negative cast to the performance statistics. In nearly efficient markets it is extremely difficult for analysts to perform well enough to offset costs of research and transaction costs. Indeed, we have seen that most professionally managed equity funds generally underperform the S&P 500 index on both risk-adjusted and raw return measures.

Another reason mean-variance criteria may have suffered relates to intrinsic problems in the measures. We will explore these problems, as well as some innovations suggested to overcome them.

For now, however, we can catalog some possible risk-adjusted performance measures and examine the circumstances in which each measure might be most relevant.

1. *Sharpe's measure:* $(\bar{r}_P - \bar{r}_f)/\sigma_P$
   **Sharpe's measure** divides average portfolio excess return over the sample period by the standard deviation of returns over that period. It measures the reward to (total) volatility trade-off.[6]

2. *Treynor's measure:* $(\bar{r}_P - \bar{r}_f)/\beta_P$
   Like Sharpe's, **Treynor's measure** gives excess return per unit of risk, but it uses systematic risk instead of total risk.

3. *Jensen's measure (portfolio alpha):* $\alpha_P = \bar{r}_P - [\bar{r}_f + \beta_P(\bar{r}_M - \bar{r}_f)]$
   **Jensen's measure** is the average return on the portfolio over and above that predicted by the CAPM, given the portfolio's beta and the average market return. Jensen's measure is the portfolio's alpha value.

4. *Information ratio (also called appraisal ratio):* $\alpha_P/\sigma(e_P)$
   The **information ratio** divides the alpha of the portfolio by the nonsystematic risk of the portfolio called "tracking error" in the industry. It measures abnormal return per unit of risk that in principle could be diversified away by holding a market index portfolio.

Each measure has some appeal. But each does not necessarily provide consistent assessments of performance, since the risk measures used to adjust returns differ substantially.

---

**CONCEPT CHECK ☞ QUESTION 3**

Consider the following data for a particular sample period:

|                                        | Portfolio *P* | Market *M* |
| -------------------------------------- | ------------- | ---------- |
| Average return                         | 35%           | 28%        |
| Beta                                   | 1.20          | 1.00       |
| Standard deviation                     | 42%           | 30%        |
| Tracking error (nonsystematic risk), $\sigma(e)$ | 18% | 0          |

Calculate the following performance measures for portfolio *P* and the market: Sharpe, Jensen (alpha), Treynor, information ratio. The T-bill rate during the period was 6%. By which measures did portfolio *P* outperform the market?

---

[6] We place bars over $r_f$ as well as $r_P$ to denote the fact that since the risk-free rate may not be constant over the measurement period, we are taking a sample average, just as we do for $r_P$.

## The $M^2$ Measure of Performance

While the Sharpe ratio can be used to rank portfolio performance, its numerical value is not easy to interpret. Comparing the ratios for portfolios $M$ and $P$ in Concept Check 3, you should have found that $S_P = .69$ and $S_M = .73$. This suggests that portfolio $P$ underperformed the market index. But is a difference of .04 in the Sharpe ratio economically meaningful? We often compare rates of return, but these ratios are difficult to interpret.

A variant of Sharpe's measure was proposed by Graham and Harvey, and later popularized by Leah Modigliani of Morgan Stanley and her grandfather Franco Modigliani, past winner of the Nobel Prize for economics.[7] Their approach has been dubbed the $M^2$ measure (for Modigliani-squared). Like the Sharpe ratio, the $M^2$ measure focuses on total volatility as a measure of risk, but its risk-adjusted measure of performance has the easy interpretation of a differential return relative to the benchmark index.

To compute the $M^2$ measure, we imagine that a managed portfolio, $P$, is mixed with a position in T-bills so that the complete, or "adjusted," portfolio matches the volatility of a market index such as the S&P 500. For example, if the managed portfolio has 1.5 times the standard deviation of the index, the adjusted portfolio would be two-thirds invested in the managed portfolio and one-third invested in bills. The adjusted portfolio, which we call $P^*$, would then have the same standard deviation as the index. (If the managed portfolio had *lower* standard deviation than the index, it would be leveraged by borrowing money and investing the proceeds in the portfolio.) Because the market index and portfolio $P^*$ have the same standard deviation, we may compare their performance simply by comparing returns. This is the $M^2$ measure:

$$M^2 = r_{P*} - r_M$$

---

**EXAMPLE 24.3**     $M^2$ **Measure**

Using the data of Concept Check 3, $P$ has a standard deviation of 42% versus a market standard deviation of 30%. Therefore, the adjusted portfolio $P^*$ would be formed by mixing bills and portfolio $P$ with weights 30/42 = .714 in $P$ and $1 - .714 = .286$ in bills. The return on this portfolio would be $(.286 \times 6\%) + (.714 \times 35\%) = 26.7\%$, which is 1.3% less than the market return. Thus portfolio $P$ has an $M^2$ measure of $-1.3\%$.

A graphical representation of the $M^2$ measure appears in Figure 24.2. We move down the capital allocation line corresponding to portfolio $P$ (by mixing $P$ with T-bills) until we reduce the standard deviation of the adjusted portfolio to match that of the market index. The $M^2$ measure is then the vertical distance (i.e., the difference in expected returns) between portfolios $P^*$ and $M$. You can see from Figure 24.2 that $P$ will have a negative $M^2$ measure when its capital allocation line is less steep than the capital market line, that is, when its Sharpe ratio is less than that of the market index.[8]

---

The box on page 871 reports on the growing popularity of the $M^2$ measure in the investment community.

---

[7] John R. Graham and Campbell R. Harvey, "Market Timing Ability and Volatility Implied in Investment Advisors' Asset Allocation Recommendations," National Bureau of Economic Research Working Paper 4890, October 1994. The part of this paper dealing with volatility-adjusted returns was ultimately published as "Grading the Performance of Market Timing Newsletters," *Financial Analysts Journal* 53 (Nov./Dec. 1997), pp. 54–66. Franco Modigliani and Leah Modigliani, "Risk-Adjusted Performance," *Journal of Portfolio Management*, Winter 1997, pp. 45–54.

[8] In fact you use Figure 24.2 to show that the $M^2$ and Sharpe measures are directly related. Letting $R$ denote excess returns and $S$ denote Sharpe measures, the geometry of the figure implies that $R_{P*} = S_P \sigma_M$, and therefore that

$$M^2 = r_{P*} - r_M = R_{P*} - R_M = S_P \sigma_M - S_M \sigma_M = (S_P - S_M)\sigma_M$$

**Figure 24.2**
$M^2$ of portfolio $P$

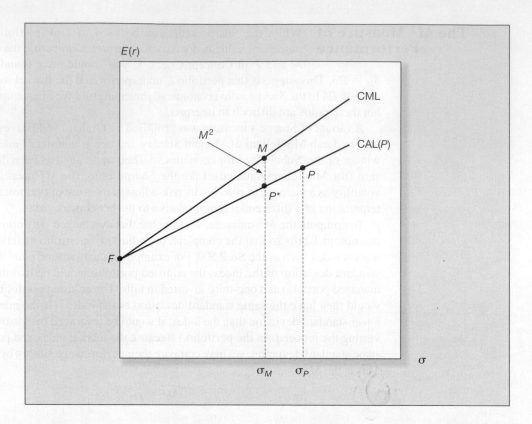

## Sharpe's Measure as the Criterion for Overall Portfolios

Suppose that Jane Close constructs a portfolio and holds it for a considerable period of time. She makes no changes in portfolio composition during the period. In addition, suppose that the daily rates of return on all securities have constant means, variances, and covariances. This assures that the portfolio rate of return also has a constant mean and variance. These assumptions are unrealistic, but they make it easier to highlight the important issues. They are also crucial to understanding the shortcoming of conventional applications of performance measurement.

Now we want to evaluate the performance of Jane's portfolio. Has she made a good choice of securities? This is really a three-pronged question. First, "good choice" compared with what alternatives? Second, in choosing between two distinct alternative portfolios, what are the appropriate criteria to evaluate performance? Finally, having identified the performance criteria, is there a rule that will separate basic ability from the random luck of the draw?

Earlier chapters of this text help to determine portfolio choice criteria. If investor preferences can be summarized by a mean-variance utility function such as that introduced in Chapter 6, we can arrive at a relatively simple criterion. The particular utility function that we used is

$$U = E(r_P) - .005A\sigma_P^2$$

where $A$ is the coefficient of risk aversion. With mean-variance preferences, Jane wants to maximize the Sharpe measure (i.e., the ratio $[E(r_P) - r_f]/\sigma_P$). Recall that this criterion led to the selection of the tangency portfolio in Chapter 8. Jane's problem reduces to the search for the highest possible Sharpe ratio.

# NEW GAUGE MEASURES MUTUAL-FUND RISK

Fidelity Select Electronics Portfolio boasts the best five-year record in the mutual-fund business. But take volatility into account, and it tumbles to 40th place among the top 50 five-year winners. What gives?

At *The Wall Street Journal*'s request, Morgan Stanley Dean Witter strategist Leah Modigliani reshuffled the 50 best-performing funds of the past five years, using a new gauge of risk-adjusted performance she developed with her grandfather, Nobel laureate Franco Modigliani.

Her purpose: to encourage investors to consider not only raw performance but also volatility along the way, and to identify funds that have delivered the best results relative to the risks they took.

The need for fund investors to weigh risk along with potential reward has gotten a lot of attention from investment advisers and fund regulators in recent years. Many fret that investors aren't paying enough attention to risk. Hence, the appeal of risk-adjusted measures such as M-squared.

The Modiglianis define risk as the variability, or unpredictability, in a fund's quarterly returns. They adjust each fund's risk to that of a market benchmark such as the Standard & Poor's 500-stock average. How? By hypothetically blending shares of a volatile fund with cash or by using borrowed money to leverage up the jumpiness of a more sedate fund.

The M-squared figure is the return an investor would have earned in a particular period if the fund had been diluted or leveraged to match the benchmark's risk.

Though there's nothing inherently superior about a high-risk or a low-risk fund, Ms. Modigliani says investors should favor mutual funds that are the most efficient in delivering high returns for the amount of risk they take. Over the past five years, she notes, an aggressive, risk-tolerant investor would have done better by shunning Fidelity Select Electronics in favor of a leveraged bet on an index fund that tracks the S&P 500, or on a fund such as Safeco Equity Fund that has a high M-squared.

Like many other performance and risk measures, M-squared is backward-looking. Steve Lipper, vice president of fund researchers Lipper Analytical Services, in Summit, N.J., complains that risk-adjusted returns can be deceptive because the volatility of an industry or type of investment doesn't stay constant. Several years ago, he says, technology funds appeared to have great risk-adjusted returns. Now they look terrible on a risk-adjusted basis, as the stocks first soared and then plunged in quick succession.

One final thought for investors: While these M-squared rankings address the risk-adjusted performance of individual funds, risky funds can be skillfully blended into a low-risk diversified portfolio. "You should be thinking about the risk of your whole portfolio, not the individual pieces," says Susan Belden of the *No-Load Fund Analyst*.

Source: Karen Damato and Robert McGough, "New Gauge Measures Mutual-Fund Risk," *The Wall Street Journal*, January 9, 1998. Excerpted by permission of *The Wall Street Journal*, © 1998 Dow Jones & Company, Inc. All Rights Reserved Worldwide.

## Appropriate Performance Measures in Three Scenarios

To evaluate Jane's portfolio choice, we first ask whether this portfolio is her exclusive investment vehicle. If the answer is no, we need to know her "complementary" portfolio. The appropriate measure of portfolio performance depends critically on whether the portfolio is the entire investment fund or only a portion of the investor's overall wealth.

**Jane's Portfolio Represents Her Entire Risky Investment Fund.** In this simplest case we need to ascertain only whether Jane's portfolio has the highest Sharpe measure. We can proceed in three steps:

1. Assume that past security performance is representative of expected performance, meaning that realized security returns over Jane's holding period exhibit averages and covariances similar to those that Jane had anticipated.

2. Determine the benchmark (alternative) portfolio that Jane would have held if she had chosen a passive strategy, such as the S&P 500.

3. Compare Jane's Sharpe measure to that of the best portfolio.

In sum, when Jane's portfolio represents her entire investment fund, the benchmark is the market index or another specific portfolio. The performance criterion is the Sharpe measure of the actual portfolio versus the benchmark.

### Jane's Portfolio Is an Active Portfolio and Is Mixed with a Passive Market-Index Portfolio.

How do we evaluate the optimal mix in this case? Call Jane's portfolio $P$, and denote the market portfolio by $M$. When the two portfolios are mixed optimally, we will see in Chapter 27 that the square of the Sharpe measure of the complete portfolio, $C$, is given by

$$S_C^2 = S_M^2 + \left[ \frac{\alpha_P}{\sigma(e_P)} \right]^2 \tag{24.2}$$

where $\alpha_P$, the portfolio's alpha, is the abnormal return of the active portfolio relative to the market-index, and $\sigma(e_P)$ is the standard deviation of tracking error. The information ratio, $\alpha_P/\sigma(e_P)$, is thus the correct performance measure for $P$ in this case, since it gives the improvement in the Sharpe measure of the overall portfolio.

To see this result intuitively, recall the single-index model:

$$r_P - r_f = \alpha_P + \beta_P(r_M - r_f) + e_P$$

If $P$ is fairly priced, then $\alpha_P = 0$, and $e_P$ is just diversifiable risk that can be avoided. If $P$ is mispriced, however, $\alpha_P$ no longer equals zero. Instead, it represents the expected abnormal return. Holding $P$ in addition to the market portfolio thus brings a reward of $\alpha_P$ against the nonsystematic risk (tracking error) voluntarily incurred, $\sigma(e_P)$. Therefore, the information ratio of $\alpha_P/\sigma(e_P)$ is the natural benefit-to-cost ratio for portfolio $P$.

### Jane's Choice Portfolio Is One of Many Portfolios Combined into a Large Investment Fund.

This third case might describe a situation where Jane, as a corporate financial officer, manages the corporate pension fund. She parcels out the entire fund to a number of portfolio managers. Then she evaluates the performance of individual managers to reallocate the fund to improve future performance. What is the correct performance measure?

We would use the information ratio if the complementary portfolio to $P$ (i.e., the part of the fund managed by others) were approximated by the market index. But you can expect other portfolio managers to take offense at this assumption. Jane, too, is likely to respond, "Do you think I am exerting all this effort just to end up with a passive portfolio?"

Although alpha is one basis for performance measurement, it alone is not sufficient to determine $P$'s potential contribution to the overall portfolio. The discussion below shows why, and develops the Treynor measure, the appropriate criterion in this case.

Suppose you determine that portfolio $P$ exhibits an alpha value of 2%. "Not bad," you tell Jane. But she pulls out of her desk a report and informs you that another portfolio, $Q$, has an alpha of 3%. "One hundred basis points is significant," says Jane. "Should I transfer some of my funds from $P$'s manager to $Q$'s?"

You tabulate the relevant data, as in Table 24.2, and graph the results as in Figure 24.3. Note that we plot $P$ and $Q$ in the expected return–beta (rather than the expected return–standard deviation) plane, because we assume that $P$ and $Q$ are two of many sub-portfolios in the fund, and thus that nonsystematic risk will be largely diversified away, leaving beta as the appropriate risk measure. The security market line (SML) shows the value of $\alpha_P$ and $\alpha_Q$ as the distance of $P$ and $Q$ above the SML.

### Table 24.2    Portfolio Performance

|  | Portfolio P | Portfolio Q | Market |
|---|---|---|---|
| Beta | .90 | 1.60 | 1.0 |
| Excess return ($\bar{r} - \bar{r}_f$) | 11% | 19% | 10% |
| Alpha* | 2% | 3% | 0 |

*Alpha = Excess return − (Beta × Market excess return)
$$= (\bar{r} - \bar{r}_f) - \beta(\bar{r}_M - \bar{r}_f) = \bar{r} - [\bar{r}_f + \beta(\bar{r}_M - \bar{r}_f)]$$

**Figure 24.3
Treynor's
measure**

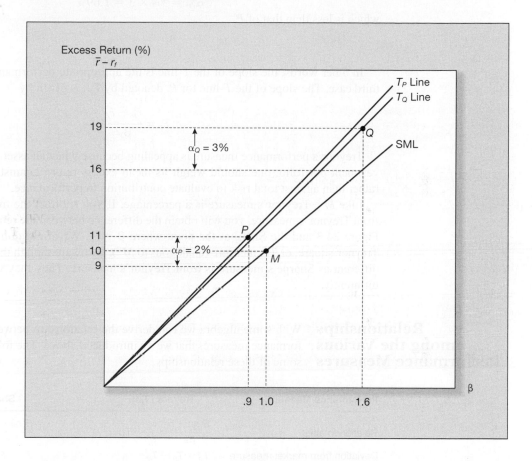

Suppose portfolio $Q$ can be mixed with T-bills. Specifically, if we invest $w_Q$ in $Q$ and $w_F = 1 - w_Q$ in T-bills, the resulting portfolio, $Q^*$, will have alpha and beta values proportional to $Q$'s alpha and beta scaled down by $w_Q$:

$$\alpha_{Q*} = w_Q \alpha_Q$$
$$\beta_{Q*} = w_Q \beta_Q$$

Thus all portfolios $Q^*$ generated from mixing $Q$ with T-bills plot on a straight line from the origin through $Q$. We call it the T-line for the Treynor measure, which is the slope of this line.

Figure 24.3 shows the T-line for portfolio $P$ as well. $P$ has a steeper T-line; despite its lower alpha, $P$ is a better portfolio after all. For any *given* beta, a mixture of $P$ with T-bills will give a better alpha than a mixture of $Q$ with T-bills. Consider an example.

**EXAMPLE 24.4    Equalizing Beta**

Suppose that we choose to mix $Q$ with T-bills to create a portfolio $Q^*$ with a beta equal to that of $P$. We find the necessary proportion by solving for $w_Q$:

$$\beta_{Q^*} = w_Q \beta_Q = 1.6w_Q = \beta_P = .9$$
$$w_Q = \tfrac{9}{16}$$

Portfolio $Q^*$ therefore has an alpha of

$$\alpha_{Q^*} = \tfrac{9}{16} \times 3 = 1.69\%$$

which is less than that of $P$.

In other words, the slope of the $T$-line is the appropriate performance criterion for the third case. The slope of the $T$-line for $P$, denoted by $T_P$, is given by

$$T_P = \frac{\bar{r}_P - \bar{r}_f}{\beta_P}$$

Treynor's performance measure is appealing because when an asset is part of a large investment portfolio, one should weigh its mean excess return against its *systematic* risk rather than against total risk to evaluate contribution to performance.

Like $M^2$, Treynor's measure is a percentage. If you subtract the market excess return from Treynor's measure, you will obtain the difference between the return on the $T_P$ line in Figure 24.3 and the SML, at the point where $\beta = 1$. We might dub this difference the Treynor-square, or $T^2$, measure (analogous to $M^2$). Be aware though that $M^2$ and $T^2$ are as different as Sharpe's measure is from Treynor's measure. They may well rank portfolios differently.

**Relationships among the Various Performance Measures**   With some algebra we can derive the relationship between the various performance measures that we've introduced above. The following table shows some of these relationships.

| Performance Measure: | Treynor ($T_P$) | Sharpe* ($S_P$) |
|---|---|---|
| Relation to alpha | $\dfrac{E(r_P) - r_f}{\beta_P} = \dfrac{\alpha_P}{\beta_P} + T_M$ | $\dfrac{E(r_P) - r_f}{\sigma_P} = \dfrac{\alpha_P}{\sigma_P} + \rho S_M$ |
| Deviation from market measure | $T_P^2 = T_P - T_M$ | $S_P - S_M$ |
|  | $= \dfrac{\alpha_P}{\beta_P}$ | $= \dfrac{\alpha_P}{\sigma_P} + (\rho - 1)S_M$ |

Note: $\rho$ denotes the correlation coefficient between portfolio $P$ and the market, and is less than 1.

All of these models are consistent in that superior performance requires a positive alpha. Hence, alpha is the most widely used performance measure. However, the Treynor and Sharpe measures make different uses of alpha and can therefore rank portfolios differently. A positive alpha alone cannot guarantee a better Sharpe measure of a portfolio, because taking advantage of security mispricing means departing from full diversification which entails a cost (notice in the table that $\rho - 1$ is negative, so that the Sharpe measure can actually fall). However, a positive alpha does imply that if a mispriced security is *optimally* mixed with the market index, the Sharpe measure *will* improve. We will show you how in Chapter 27.

# PERFORMANCE MEASUREMENT

The following performance measurement spreadsheet computes all the performance measures discussed in this section. You can see how relative ranking differs according to the criterion selected. This Excel model is available at the Online Learning Center (**www.mhhe.com/bkm**).

| | A | B | C | D | E | F | G | H | I | J | K |
|---|---|---|---|---|---|---|---|---|---|---|---|
| 1 | Performance Measurement | | | | | | | LEGEND | | | |
| 2 | | | | | | | | Enter data | | | |
| 3 | | | | | | | | Value calculated | | | |
| 4 | | | | | | | | See comment | | | |
| 5 | | | | | | | | | | | |
| 6 | | | | | Non- | | | | | | |
| 7 | | Average | Standard | Beta | systematic | Sharpe's | Treynor's | Jensen's | M2 | T2 | Appraisal |
| 8 | Fund | Return | Deviation | Coefficient | Risk | Measure | Measure | Measure | Measure | Measure | Ratio |
| 9 | Alpha | 28.00% | 27.00% | 1.7000 | 5.00% | 0.8148 | 0.1294 | -0.0180 | -0.0015 | -0.0106 | -0.3600 |
| 10 | Omega | 31.00% | 26.00% | 1.6200 | 6.00% | 0.9615 | 0.1543 | 0.0232 | 0.0235 | 0.0143 | 0.3867 |
| 11 | Omicron | 22.00% | 21.00% | 0.8500 | 2.00% | 0.7619 | 0.1882 | 0.0410 | -0.0105 | 0.0482 | 2.0500 |
| 12 | Millennium | 40.00% | 33.00% | 2.5000 | 27.00% | 1.0303 | 0.1360 | -0.0100 | 0.0352 | -0.0040 | -0.0370 |
| 13 | Big Value | 15.00% | 13.00% | 0.9000 | 3.00% | 0.6923 | 0.1000 | -0.0360 | -0.0223 | -0.0400 | -1.2000 |
| 14 | Momentum Watcher | 29.00% | 24.00% | 1.4000 | 16.00% | 0.9583 | 0.1643 | 0.0340 | 0.0229 | 0.0243 | 0.2125 |
| 15 | Big Potential | 15.00% | 11.00% | 0.5500 | 1.50% | 0.8182 | 0.1636 | 0.0130 | -0.0009 | 0.0236 | 0.8667 |
| 16 | S & P Index Return | 20.00% | 17.00% | 1.0000 | 0.00% | 0.8235 | 0.1400 | 0.0000 | 0.0000 | 0.0000 | 0.0000 |
| 17 | T-Bill Return | 6.00% | | | 0.0000 | | | | | | |
| 18 | | | | | | | | | | | |
| 19 | Ranking By Sharpe's Measure | | | | Non- | | | | | | |
| 20 | | Average | Standard | Beta | systematic | Sharpe's | Treynor's | Jensen's | M2 | T2 | Appraisal |
| 21 | Fund | Return | Deviation | Coefficient | Risk | Measure | Measure | Measure | Measure | Measure | Ratio |
| 22 | Millennium | ?.00% | 33.00% | ? | 27.00% | 1.0303 | ?? | -0.0100 | 0.0?? | ?.0040 | -0.0370 |
| | | 26.00% | | | ?% | ? | | 0.0232 | | | 0.38?? |

## Actual Performance Measurement: An Example

Now that we have examined possible criteria for performance evaluation, we need to deal with a statistical issue: Can we assess the quality of ex ante decisions using ex post data? Before we plunge into a discussion of this problem, let us look at the rate of return on Jane's portfolio over the last 12 months. Table 24.3 shows the excess return recorded each month for Jane's portfolio $P$, one of her alternative portfolios $Q$, and the benchmark index portfolio $M$. The last rows in Table 24.3 give sample average and standard deviations. From these, and regressions of $P$ and $Q$ on $M$, we obtain the necessary performance statistics.

The performance statistics in Table 24.4 show that portfolio $Q$ is more aggressive than $P$, in the sense that its beta is significantly higher (1.40 vs. .69). On the other hand, from its residual standard deviation $P$ appears better diversified (1.95% vs. 8.98%). Both portfolios outperformed the benchmark market index, as is evident from their larger Sharpe measures (and thus positive $M^2$) and their positive alphas.

Which portfolio is more attractive based on reported performance? If $P$ or $Q$ represents the entire investment fund, $Q$ would be preferable on the basis of its higher Sharpe measure (.51 vs. .45) and better $M^2$ (2.69% vs. 2.19%). On the other hand, as an active portfolio to be mixed with the market index, $P$ is preferable to $Q$, as is evident from its appraisal ratio (.84 vs. .59). For the third scenario, where $P$ and $Q$ are competing for a role as one of a number of subportfolios, $Q$ dominates again because its Treynor measure is higher (5.40 versus 4.00). Thus, the example illustrates that the right way to evaluate a portfolio depends in large part how the portfolio fits into the investor's overall wealth.

This analysis is based on 12 months of data only, a period too short to lend statistical significance to the conclusions. Even longer observation intervals may not be enough to make the decision clear-cut, which represents a further problem. A model that calculates these performance measures is available on the Online Learning Center (www.mhhe.com/bkm).

## Realized Returns versus Expected Returns

When evaluating a portfolio, the evaluator knows neither the portfolio manager's original expectations nor whether those expectations made sense. One

**Table 24.3    Excess Returns for Portfolios P and Q and the Benchmark M over 12 Months**

| Month | Jane's Portfolio P | Alternative Q | Benchmark M |
|---|---|---|---|
| 1 | 3.58% | 2.81% | 2.20% |
| 2 | −4.91 | −1.15 | −8.41 |
| 3 | 6.51 | 2.53 | 3.27 |
| 4 | 11.13 | 37.09 | 14.41 |
| 5 | 8.78 | 12.88 | 7.71 |
| 6 | 9.38 | 39.08 | 14.36 |
| 7 | −3.66 | −8.84 | −6.15 |
| 8 | 5.56 | 0.83 | 2.74 |
| 9 | −7.72 | 0.85 | −15.27 |
| 10 | 7.76 | 12.09 | 6.49 |
| 11 | −4.01 | −5.68 | −3.13 |
| 12 | 0.78 | −1.77 | 1.41 |
| Year's average | 2.76 | 7.56 | 1.63 |
| Standard deviation | 6.17 | 14.89 | 8.48 |

**Table 24.4    Performance Statistics**

| | Portfolio P | Portfolio Q | Portfolio M |
|---|---|---|---|
| Sharpe's measure | 0.45 | 0.51 | 0.19 |
| $M^2$ | 2.19 | 2.69 | 0.00 |
| **SCL regression statistics** | | | |
| Alpha | 1.63 | 5.28 | 0.00 |
| Beta | 0.69 | 1.40 | 1.00 |
| Treynor | 4.00 | 5.40 | 1.63 |
| $T^2$ | 2.37 | 3.77 | 0.00 |
| $\sigma(e)$ | 1.95 | 8.98 | 0.00 |
| Appraisal ratio | 0.84 | 0.59 | 0.00 |
| R-SQR | 0.91 | 0.64 | 1.00 |

can only observe performance after the fact and hope that random results are not taken for, or do not hide, true underlying ability. But risky asset returns are "noisy," which complicates the inference problem. To avoid making mistakes, we have to determine the "significance level" of a performance measure to know whether it reliably indicates ability.

Consider Joe Dart, a portfolio manager. Suppose that his portfolio has an alpha of 20 basis points per month, which makes for a hefty 2.4% per year before compounding. Let us assume that the return distribution of Joe's portfolio has constant mean, beta, and alpha, a heroic assumption, but one that is in line with the usual treatment of performance measurement. Suppose that for the measurement period Joe's portfolio beta is 1.2 and the monthly standard deviation of the residual (nonsystematic risk) is .02 (2%). With a market index standard deviation of 6.5% per month (22.5% per year), Joe's portfolio systematic variance is

$$\beta^2 \sigma_M^2 = 1.2^2 \times 6.5^2 = 60.84$$

and hence the correlation coefficient between his portfolio and the market index is

$$\rho = \left[ \frac{\beta^2 \sigma_M^2}{\beta^2 \sigma_M^2 + \sigma^2(e)} \right]^{1/2} = \left[ \frac{60.84}{60.84 + 4} \right]^{1/2} = .97$$

which shows that his portfolio is quite well diversified.

To estimate Joe's portfolio alpha from the security characteristic line (SCL), we regress the portfolio excess returns on the market index. Suppose that we are in luck and the regression estimates yield the true parameters. That means that our SCL estimates for the $N$ months are

$$\hat{\alpha} = .2\%, \qquad \hat{\beta} = 1.2, \qquad \hat{\sigma}(e) = 2\%$$

The evaluator who runs such a regression, however, does not know the true values, and hence must compute the $t$-statistic of the alpha estimate to determine whether to reject the hypothesis that Joe's alpha is zero, that is, that he has no superior ability.

The standard error of the alpha estimate in the SCL regression is approximately

$$\hat{\sigma}(\alpha) = \frac{\hat{\sigma}(e)}{\sqrt{N}}$$

where $N$ is the number of observations and $\sigma(e)$ is the sample estimate of nonsystematic risk. The $t$-statistic for the alpha estimate is then

$$t(\hat{\alpha}) = \frac{\hat{\alpha}}{\hat{\sigma}(\alpha)} = \frac{\hat{\alpha}\sqrt{N}}{\hat{\sigma}(e)} \qquad (24.3)$$

Suppose that we require a significance level of 5%. This requires a $t(\hat{\alpha})$ value of 1.96 if $N$ is large. With $\hat{\alpha} = .2$ and $\hat{\sigma}(e) = 2$, we solve equation 24.3 for $N$ and find that

$$1.96 = \frac{.2\sqrt{N}}{2}$$

$$N = 384 \text{ months}$$

or 32 years!

What have we shown? Here is an analyst who has very substantial ability. The example is biased in his favor in the sense that we have assumed away statistical problems. Nothing changes in the parameters over a long period of time. Furthermore, the sample period "behaves" perfectly. Regression estimates are all perfect. Still, it will take Joe's entire working career to get to the point where statistics will confirm his true ability. We have to conclude that the problem of statistical inference makes performance evaluation extremely difficult in practice.

**CONCEPT CHECK☞ QUESTION 4**   **Suppose an analyst has a measured alpha of .2% with a standard error of 2%, as in our example. What is the probability that the positive alpha is due to luck of the draw and that true ability is zero?**

## 24.3   PERFORMANCE MEASUREMENT WITH CHANGING PORTFOLIO COMPOSITION

We have seen already that the high variance of stock returns requires a very long observation period to determine performance levels with any statistical significance, even if portfolio returns are distributed with constant mean and variance. Imagine how this problem is compounded when portfolio return distributions are constantly changing.

It is acceptable to assume that the return distributions of passive strategies have constant mean and variance when the measurement interval is not too long. However, under an active strategy return distributions change by design, as the portfolio manager updates the portfolio in accordance with the dictates of financial analysis. In such a case estimating various statistics from a sample period assuming a constant mean and variance may lead to substantial errors. Let us look at an example.

**EXAMPLE 24.5**

## Changing Portfolio Risk

Suppose that the Sharpe measure of the market index is .4. Over an initial period of 52 weeks, the portfolio manager executes a low-risk strategy with an annualized mean excess return of 1% and standard deviation of 2%. This makes for a Sharpe measure of .5, which beats the passive strategy. Over the next 52-week period this manager finds that a *high*-risk strategy is optimal, with an annual mean excess return of 9% and standard deviation of 18%. Here, again, the Sharpe measure is .5. Over the 2-year period our manager maintains a better-than-passive Sharpe measure.

Figure 24.4 shows a pattern of (annualized) quarterly returns that are consistent with our description of the manager's strategy of 2 years. In the first four quarters the excess returns are −1%, 3%, −1%, and 3%, making for an average of 1% and standard deviation of 2%. In the next four quarters the returns are −9%, 27%, −9%, 27%, making for an average of 9% and standard deviation of 18%. Thus *both* years exhibit a Sharpe measure of .5. However, over the eight-quarter sequence the mean and standard deviation are 5% and 13.42%, respectively, making for a Sharpe measure of only .37, apparently inferior to the passive strategy!

**Figure 24.4 Portfolio returns. Returns in last four quarters are more variable than in the first four.**

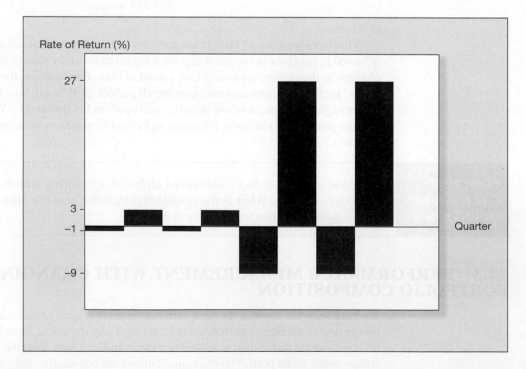

What happened in Example 24.5? The shift of the mean from the first four quarters to the next was not recognized as a shift in strategy. Instead, the difference in mean returns in the 2 years added to the *appearance* of volatility in portfolio returns. The active strategy with shifting means appears riskier than it really is and biases the estimate of the Sharpe measure downward. We conclude that for actively managed portfolios it is helpful to keep track of portfolio composition and changes in portfolio mean and risk. We will see another example of this problem in the next section, which deals with market timing.

## 24.4    MARKET TIMING

In its pure form, market timing involves shifting funds between a market-index portfolio and a safe asset, such as T-bills or a money market fund, depending on whether the market as a whole is expected to outperform the safe asset. In practice, of course, most managers do not shift fully between T-bills and the market. How can we account for partial shifts into the market when it is expected to perform well?

To simplify, suppose that an investor holds only the market-index portfolio and T-bills. If the weight of the market were constant, say, .6, then portfolio beta would also be constant, and the SCL would plot as a straight line with slope .6, as in Figure 24.5A. If, however, the investor could correctly time the market and shift funds into it in periods when the market does well, the SCL would plot as in Figure 24.5B. If bull and bear markets can be predicted, the investor will shift more into the market when the market is about to go up. The portfolio beta and the slope of the SCL will be higher when $r_M$ is higher, resulting in the curved line that appears in Figure 24.5B.

**Figure 24.5    Characteristic lines. A. No market timing, beta is constant. B. Market timing, beta increases with expected market excess return. C. Market timing with only two values of beta**

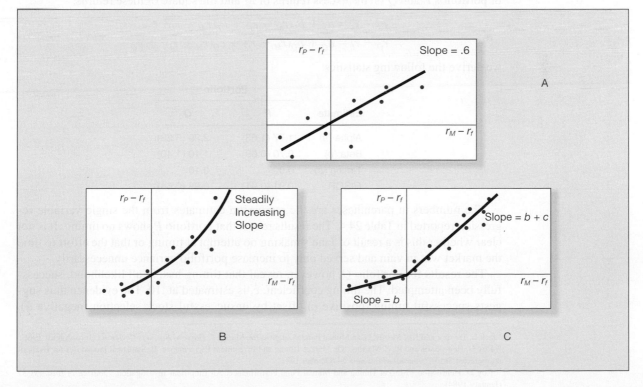

Treynor and Mazuy[9] were the first to propose that such a line can be estimated by adding a squared term to the usual linear index model:

$$r_P - r_f = a + b(r_M - r_f) + c(r_M - r_f)^2 + e_P$$

where $r_P$ is the portfolio return, and $a$, $b$, and $c$ are estimated by regression analysis. If $c$ turns out to be positive, we have evidence of timing ability, because this last term will make the characteristic line steeper as $r_M - r_f$ is larger. Treynor and Mazuy estimated this equation for a number of mutual funds, but found little evidence of timing ability.

A similar and simpler methodology was proposed by Henriksson and Merton.[10] These authors suggested that the beta of the portfolio take only two values: a large value if the market is expected to do well and a small value otherwise. Under this scheme the portfolio characteristic line appears as Figure 24.5C. Such a line appears in regression form as

$$r_P - r_f = a + b(r_M - r_f) + c(r_M - r_f)D + e_P$$

where $D$ is a dummy variable that equals 1 for $r_M > r_f$ and zero otherwise. Hence the beta of the portfolio is $b$ in bear markets and $b + c$ in bull markets. Again, a positive value of $c$ implies market timing ability.

Henriksson[11] estimated this equation for 116 mutual funds over the period 1968 to 1980. He found that the average value of $c$ for the funds was *negative*, and equal to $-.07$, although the value was not statistically significant at the conventional 5% level. Eleven funds had significantly positive values of $c$, while eight had significantly negative values. Overall, 62% of the funds had negative point estimates of timing ability. In sum, the results showed little evidence of market timing ability. Perhaps this should be expected; given the tremendous values to be reaped by a successful market timer, it would be surprising in nearly efficient markets to uncover clear-cut evidence of such skills.

To illustrate a test for market timing, return to Table 24.3. Regressing the excess returns of portfolios $P$ and $Q$ on the excess returns of $M$ and the square of these returns,

$$r_P - r_f = a_P + b_P(r_M - r_f) + c_P(r_M - r_f)^2 + e_P$$
$$r_Q - r_f = a_Q + b_Q(r_M - r_f) + c_Q(r_M - r_f)^2 + e_Q$$

we derive the following statistics:

|  | Portfolio | |
| --- | --- | --- |
| **Estimate** | **P** | **Q** |
| Alpha (a) | 1.77 (1.63) | −2.29 (5.28) |
| Beta (b) | 0.70 (0.69) | 1.10 (1.40) |
| Timing (c) | 0.00 | 0.10 |
| R-SQR | 0.91 (0.91) | 0.98 (0.64) |

The numbers in parentheses are the regression estimates from the single variable regression reported in Table 24.4. The results reveal that portfolio $P$ shows no timing. It is not clear whether this is a result of Jane's making no attempt at timing or that the effort to time the market was in vain and served only to increase portfolio variance unnecessarily.

The results for portfolio $Q$, however, reveal that timing has, in all likelihood, successfully been attempted. The timing coefficient, $c$, is estimated at .10. The evidence thus suggests successful timing (positive $c$) offset by unsuccessful stock selection (negative $a$).

---

[9] Jack L. Treynor and Kay Mazuy, "Can Mutual Funds Outguess the Market?" *Harvard Business Review* 43 (July–August 1966).
[10] Roy D. Henriksson and R. C. Merton, "On Market Timing and Investment Performance. II. Statistical Procedures for Evaluating Forecast Skills," *Journal of Business* 54 (October 1981).
[11] Roy D. Henriksson, "Market Timing and Mutual Fund Performance: An Empirical Investigation," *Journal of Business* 57 (January 1984).

Note that the alpha estimate, $a$, is now $-2.29\%$ as opposed to the $5.28\%$ estimate derived from the regression equation that did not allow for the possibility of timing activity.

This is an example of the inadequacy of conventional performance evaluation techniques that assume constant mean returns and constant risk. The market timer constantly shifts beta and mean return, moving into and out of the market. Whereas the expanded regression captures this phenomenon, the simple SCL does not. The relative desirability of portfolios $P$ and $Q$ remains unclear in the sense that the value of the timing success and selectivity failure of $Q$ compared with $P$ has yet to be evaluated. The important point for performance evaluation, however, is that expanded regressions can capture many of the effects of portfolio composition change that would confound the more conventional mean-variance measures.

## 24.5   PERFORMANCE ATTRIBUTION PROCEDURES

Rather than focus on risk-adjusted returns, practitioners often want simply to ascertain which decisions resulted in superior or inferior performance. Superior investment performance depends on an ability to be in the "right" securities at the right time. Such timing and selection ability may be considered broadly, such as being in equities as opposed to fixed-income securities when the stock market is performing well. Or it may be defined at a more detailed level, such as choosing the relatively better-performing stocks within a particular industry.

Portfolio managers constantly make broad-brush asset allocation decisions as well as more detailed sector and security allocation decisions within asset class. Performance attribution studies attempt to decompose overall performance into discrete components that may be identified with a particular level of the portfolio selection process.

Attribution studies start from the broadest asset allocation choices and progressively focus on ever-finer details of portfolio choice. The difference between a managed portfolio's performance and that of a benchmark portfolio then may be expressed as the sum of the contributions to performance of a series of decisions made at the various levels of the portfolio construction process. For example, one common attribution system decomposes performance into three components: (1) broad asset market allocation choices across equity, fixed-income, and money markets; (2) industry (sector) choice within each market; and (3) security choice within each sector.

The attribution method explains the difference in returns between a managed portfolio, $P$, and a selected benchmark portfolio, $B$, called the **bogey.** Suppose that the universe of assets for $P$ and $B$ includes $n$ asset classes such as equities, bonds, and bills. For each asset class, a benchmark index portfolio is determined. For example, the S&P 500 may be chosen as benchmark for equities. The bogey portfolio is set to have fixed weights in each asset class, and its rate of return is given by

$$r_B = \sum_{i=1}^{n} w_{Bi}\, r_{Bi}$$

where $w_{Bi}$ is the weight of the bogey in asset class $i$, and $r_{Bi}$ is the return on the benchmark portfolio of that class over the evaluation period. The portfolio managers choose weights in each class, $w_{Pi}$, based on their capital market expectations, and they choose a portfolio of the securities within each class based on their security analysis, which earns $r_{Pi}$ over the evaluation period. Thus the return of the managed portfolio will be

$$r_P = \sum_{i=1}^{n} w_{Pi}\, r_{Pi}$$

The difference between the two rates of return, therefore, is

$$r_P - r_B = \sum_{i=1}^{n} w_{Pi} r_{Pi} - \sum_{i=1}^{n} w_{Bi} r_{Bi} = \sum_{i=1}^{n} (w_{Pi} r_{Pi} - w_{Bi} r_{Bi}) \qquad (24.4)$$

Each term in the summation of equation 24.4 can be rewritten in a way that shows how asset allocation decisions versus security selection decisions for each asset class contributed to overall performance. We decompose each term of the summation into a sum of two terms as follows. Note that the two terms we label as contributions from asset allocation and contribution from security selection in the following decomposition do in fact sum to the total contribution of each asset class to overall performance.

| | |
|---|---|
| Contribution from asset allocation | $(w_{Pi} - w_{Bi})r_{Bi}$ |
| + Contribution from security selection | $w_{Pi}(r_{Pi} - r_{Bi})$ |
| = Total contribution from asset class $i$ | $w_{Pi} r_{Pi} - w_{Bi} r_{Bi}$ |

The first term of the sum measures the impact of asset allocation because it shows how deviations of the actual weight from the benchmark weight for that asset class multiplied by the index return for the asset class added to or subtracted from total performance. The second term of the sum measures the impact of security selection because it shows how the manager's excess return *within* the asset class compared to the benchmark return for that class multiplied by the portfolio weight for that class added to or subtracted from total performance. Figure 24.6 presents a graphical interpretation of the attribution of overall performance into security selection versus asset allocation.

To illustrate this method, consider the attribution results for a hypothetical portfolio. The portfolio invests in stocks, bonds, and money market securities. An attribution analysis appears in Tables 24.5 through 24.8. The portfolio return over the month is 5.34%.

The first step is to establish a benchmark level of performance against which performance ought to be compared. This benchmark, again, is called the bogey. It is designed to

**Figure 24.6 Performance attribution of *i*th asset class. Enclosed area indicates total rate of return.**

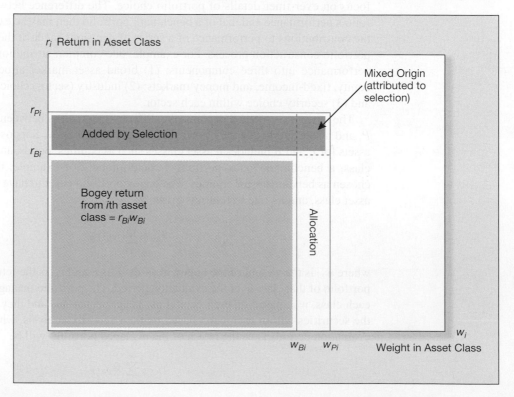

measure the returns the portfolio manager would earn if he or she were to follow a completely passive strategy. "Passive" in this context has two attributes. First, it means that the allocation of funds across broad asset classes is set in accord with a notion of "usual," or neutral, allocation across sectors. This would be considered a passive asset-market allocation. Second, it means that *within* each asset class, the portfolio manager holds an indexed portfolio such as the S&P 500 index for the equity sector. In such a manner, the passive strategy used as a performance benchmark rules out asset allocation as well as security selection decisions. Any departure of the manager's return from the passive benchmark must be due to either asset allocation bets (departures from the neutral allocation across markets) or security selection bets (departures from the passive index within asset classes).

While we have already discussed in earlier chapters the justification for indexing within sectors, it is worth briefly explaining the determination of the neutral allocation of funds across the broad asset classes. Weights that are designated as "neutral" will depend on the risk tolerance of the investor and must be determined in consultation with the client. For example, risk-tolerant clients may place a large fraction of their portfolio in the equity market, perhaps directing the fund manager to set neutral weights of 75% equity, 15% bonds, and 10% cash equivalents. Any deviation from these weights must be justified by a belief that one or another market will either over- or underperform its usual risk–return profile. In contrast, more risk-averse clients may set neutral weights of 45%/35%/20% for the three markets. Therefore, their portfolios in normal circumstances will be exposed to less risk than that of the risk-tolerant client. Only intentional bets on market performance will result in departures from this profile.

In Table 24.5, the neutral weights have been set at 60% equity, 30% fixed income, and 10% cash (money market securities). The bogey portfolio, comprised of investments in each index with the 60/30/10 weights, returned 3.97%. The managed portfolio's measure of performance is positive and equal to its actual return less the return of the bogey: $5.34 - 3.97 = 1.37\%$. The next step is to allocate the 1.37% excess return to the separate decisions that contributed to it.

**Asset Allocation Decisions**   Our hypothetical managed portfolio is invested in the equity, fixed-income, and money markets with weights of 70%, 7%, and 23%, respectively. The portfolio's performance could have to do with the departure of this weighting scheme from the benchmark 60/30/10 weights and/or to superior or inferior results *within* each of the three broad markets.

To isolate the effect of the manager's asset allocation choice, we measure the performance of a hypothetical portfolio that would have been invested in the indexes for each

**Table 24.5   Performance of the Managed Portfolio**

| Component | Benchmark Weight | Return of Index during Month (%) |
|---|---|---|
| Equity (S&P 500) | .60 | 5.81 |
| Bonds (Lehman Brothers Index) | .30 | 1.45 |
| Cash (money market) | .10 | 0.48 |

Bogey = (.60 × 5.81) + (.30 × 1.45) + (.10 × 0.48) = 3.97%

| | |
|---|---|
| Return of managed portfolio | 5.34% |
| − Return of bogey portfolio | 3.97 |
| Excess return of managed portfolio | 1.37% |

market with weights 70/7/23. This return measures the effect of the shift away from the benchmark 60/30/10 weights without allowing for any effects attributable to active management of the securities selected within each market.

Superior performance relative to the bogey is achieved by overweighting investments in markets that turn out to perform well and by underweighting those in poorly performing markets. The contribution of asset allocation to superior performance equals the sum over all markets of the excess weight (sometimes called the *active weight* in the industry) in each market times the return of the market index.

Table 24.6A demonstrates that asset allocation contributed 31 basis points to the portfolio's overall excess return of 137 basis points. The major factor contributing to superior performance in this month is the heavy weighting of the equity market in a month when the equity market has an excellent return of 5.81%.

**Sector and Security Selection Decisions**

If .31% of the excess performance (Table 24.6A) can be attributed to advantageous asset allocation across markets, the remaining 1.06% then must be attributable to sector selection and security selection within each market. Table 24.6B details the contribution of the managed portfolio's sector and security selection to total performance.

Panel B shows that the equity component of the managed portfolio has a return of 7.28% versus a return of 5.81% for the S&P 500. The fixed-income return is 1.89% versus 1.45% for the Lehman Brothers Index. The superior performance in both equity and fixed-income markets weighted by the portfolio proportions invested in each market sums to the 1.06% contribution to performance attributable to sector and security selection.

Table 24.7 documents the sources of the equity market performance by each sector within the market. The first three columns detail the allocation of funds within the equity market compared to their representation in the S&P 500. Column (4) shows the rate of return of each sector. The contribution of each sector's allocation presented in column (5) equals the product of the difference in the sector weight and the sector's performance.

---

### Table 24.6 Performance Attribution

#### A. Contribution of Asset Allocation to Performance

| Market | (1) Actual Weight in Market | (2) Benchmark Weight in Market | (3) Active or Excess Weight | (4) Market Return (%) | (5) = (3) × (4) Contribution to Performance (%) |
|---|---|---|---|---|---|
| Equity | .70 | .60 | .10 | 5.81 | .5810 |
| Fixed-income | .07 | .30 | −.23 | 1.45 | −.3335 |
| Cash | .23 | .10 | .13 | .48 | .0624 |
| Contribution of asset allocation | | | | | .3099 |

#### B. Contribution of Selection to Total Performance

| Market | (1) Portfolio Performance (%) | (2) Index Performance (%) | (3) Excess Performance (%) | (4) Portfolio Weight | (5) = (3) × (4) Contribution (%) |
|---|---|---|---|---|---|
| Equity | 7.28 | 5.81 | 1.47 | .70 | 1.03 |
| Fixed-income | 1.89 | 1.45 | 0.44 | .07 | 0.03 |
| Contribution of selection within markets | | | | | 1.06 |

Note that good performance (a positive contribution) derives from overweighting well-performing sectors such as consumer noncyclicals, as well as underweighting poorly performing sectors such as technology. The excess return of the equity component of the portfolio attributable to sector allocation alone is 1.29%. Table 24.6B, column (3) shows that the equity component of the portfolio outperformed the S&P 500 by 1.47%. We conclude that the effect of security selection *within* sectors must have contributed an additional 1.47% − 1.29%, or 0.18%, to the performance of the equity component of the portfolio.

A similar sector analysis can be applied to the fixed-income portion of the portfolio, but we do not show those results here.

**Summing Up Component Contributions**   In this particular month, all facets of the portfolio selection process were successful. Table 24.8 details the contribution of each aspect of performance. Asset allocation across the major security markets contributes 31 basis points. Sector and security allocation within those markets contributes 106 basis points, for total excess portfolio performance of 137 basis points.

The sector and security allocation of 106 basis points can be partitioned further. Sector allocation within the equity market results in excess performance of 129 basis points, and security selection within sectors contributes 18 basis points. (The total equity excess

**Table 24.7   Sector Selection within the Equity Market**

| Sector | (1) Beginning of Month Weights (%) Portfolio | (2) S&P 500 | (3) Active Weights (%) | (4) Sector Return (%) | (5) = (3) × (4) Sector Allocation Contribution |
|---|---|---|---|---|---|
| Basic materials | 1.96 | 8.3 | 6.34 | 6.9 | −0.4375 |
| Business services | 7.84 | 4.1 | 3.74 | 7.0 | 0.2618 |
| Capital goods | 1.87 | 7.8 | −5.93 | 4.1 | −0.2431 |
| Consumer cyclical | 8.47 | 12.5 | −4.03 | 8.8 | 0.3546 |
| Consumer noncyclical | 40.37 | 20.4 | 19.97 | 10.0 | 1.9970 |
| Credit sensitive | 24.01 | 21.8 | 2.21 | 5.0 | 0.1105 |
| Energy | 13.53 | 14.2 | −0.67 | 2.6 | −0.0174 |
| Technology | 1.95 | 10.9 | −8.95 | 0.3 | −0.0269 |
| TOTAL | | | | | 1.2898 |

**Table 24.8   Portfolio Attribution: Summary**

| | Contribution (basis points) |
|---|---|
| 1. Asset allocation | 31 |
| 2. Selection | |
| a. Equity excess return (basis points) | |
| i. Sector allocation        129 | |
| ii. Security selection       18 | |
| 147 × .70 (portfolio weight) = | 102.9 |
| b. Fixed-income excess return    44 × .07 (portfolio weight) = | 3.1 |
| Total excess return of portfolio | 137.0 |

# PERFORMANCE ATTRIBUTION

The performance attribution spreadsheet develops the attribution analysis that is presented in this section. Additional data can be used in the analysis of performance for other sets of portfolios. The model can be used to analyze performance of mutual funds and other managed portfolios. You can find this Excel model on the Online Learning Center (**www.mhhe.com/bkm**).

| | A | B | C | D | E | F |
|---|---|---|---|---|---|---|
| 1 | **Performance Attribution** | | | | | |
| 2 | | | | | | |
| 3 | | | | | | |
| 4 | **Bogey** | | | | | |
| 5 | **Portfolio** | | **Benchmark** | **Return on** | **Portfolio** | |
| 6 | **Component** | **Index** | **Weight** | **Index** | **Return** | |
| 7 | Equity | S&P 500 | 0.60 | 5.8100% | 3.4860% | |
| 8 | Bonds | Lehman Index | 0.30 | 1.4500% | 0.4350% | |
| 9 | Cash | Money Market | 0.10 | 0.4800% | 0.0480% | |
| 10 | | | Return on Bogey | | 3.9690% | |
| 11 | | | | | | |
| 12 | | **Managed** | | | | |
| 13 | | **Portfolio** | **Portfolio** | **Actual** | **Portfolio** | |
| 14 | | **Component** | **Weight** | **Return** | **Return** | |
| 15 | | Equity | 0.70 | 5.8100% | 5.0960% | |
| 16 | | Bonds | 0.07 | 1.4500% | 0.1323% | |
| 17 | | Cash | 0.23 | 0.4800% | 0.1104% | |
| 18 | | | Return on Managed | | 5.3387% | |
| 19 | | | Excess Return | | 1.3697% | |

performance of 147 basis points is multiplied by the 70% weight in equity to obtain contribution to portfolio performance.) Similar partitioning could be done for the fixed-income sector.

**CONCEPT CHECK☞ QUESTION 5**

*a.* Suppose the benchmark weights had been set at 70% equity, 25% fixed-income, and 5% cash equivalents. What then are the contributions of the manager's asset allocation choices?

*b.* Suppose the S&P 500 return is 5%. Compute the new value of the manager's security selection choices.

## 24.6   STYLE ANALYSIS

*Style analysis* was introduced by Nobel laureate William Sharpe.[12] The popularity of the concept was aided by a well-known study[13] concluding that 91.5% of the variation in

---

[12] William F. Sharpe, "Asset Allocation: Management Style and Performance Evaluation," *Journal of Portfolio Management,* Winter 1992, pp. 7–19.

[13] Gary Brinson, Brian Singer, and Gilbert Beebower, "Determinants of Portfolio Performance," *Financial Analysts Journal,* May/June 1991.

### Table 24.9   Sharpe's Style Portfolios for the Magellan Fund

| | Regression Coefficient* |
|---|---|
| Bills | 0 |
| Intermediate bonds | 0 |
| Long-term bonds | 0 |
| Corporate bonds | 0 |
| Mortgages | 0 |
| Value stocks | 0 |
| Growth stocks | 47 |
| Medium-cap stocks | 31 |
| Small stocks | 18 |
| Foreign stocks | 0 |
| European stocks | 4 |
| Japanese stocks | 0 |
| *TOTAL* | 100.00 |
| R-squared | 97.3 |

*Regressions are constrained to have nonnegative coefficients and to have coefficients that sum to 100%.
Source: William F. Sharpe, "Asset Allocation. Management Style and Performance Evaluation," *Journal of Portfolio Management,* Winter 1992, pp. 7–19.

returns of 82 mutual funds could be explained by the funds' asset allocation to bills, bonds, and stocks. Later studies that considered asset allocation across a broader range of asset classes found that as much as 97% of fund returns can be explained by asset allocation alone.

Sharpe considered 12 asset class (style) portfolios. His idea was to regress fund returns on indexes representing a range of asset classes. The regression coefficient on each index would then measure the implicit allocation to that "style." Because funds are barred from short positions, the regression coefficients are constrained to be either zero or positive and to sum to 100%, so as to represent a complete asset allocation. The $R$-square of the regression would then measure the percentage of return variability attributed to the effects of security selection.

To illustrate the approach, consider Sharpe's study of the monthly returns on Fidelity's Magellan Fund over the period January 1985 through December 1989, shown in Table 24.9. While there are 12 asset classes, each one represented by a stock index, the regression coefficients are positive for only 4 of them. We can conclude that the fund returns are well explained by only four style portfolios. Moreover, these four style portfolios alone explain 97.3% of returns.

The proportion of return variability *not* explained by asset allocation can be attributed to security selection within asset classes. For Magellan, this was $100 - 97.3 = 2.7\%$. To evaluate the average contribution of stock selection to fund performance we track the residuals from the regression, displayed in Figure 24.7. The figure plots the cumulative effect of these residuals; the steady upward trend confirms Magellan's success at stock selection in this period. Notice that the plot in Figure 24.7 is far smoother than the plot in Figure 24.8, which shows Magellan's performance compared to a standard benchmark, the S&P 500. This reflects the fact that the regression-weighted index portfolio tracks Magellan's overall style much better than the S&P 500. The performance spread is much noisier using the S&P as the benchmark.

**Figure 24.7
Fidelity Magellan
Fund cumulative
return difference:
Fund versus style
benchmark**

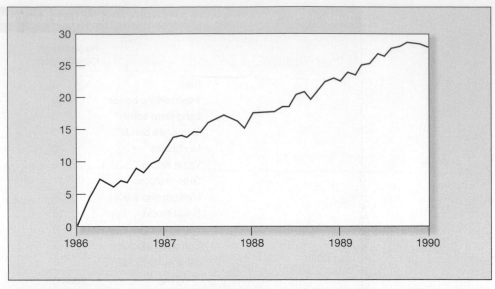

Source: William F. Sharpe, "Asset Allocation: Management Style and Performance Evaluation," *Journal of Portfolio Management*, Winter 1992, pp. 7–19.

**Figure 24.8
Fidelity Magellan
Fund cumulative
return difference:
Fund versus
S&P 500**

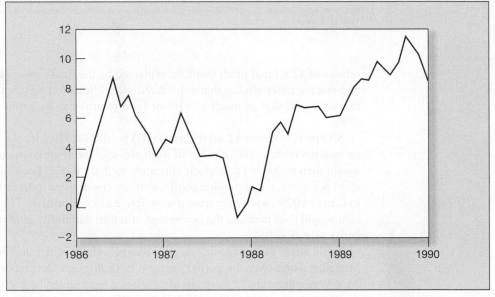

Source: William F. Sharpe, "Asset Allocation: Management Style and Performance Evaluation," *Journal of Portfolio Management*, Winter 1992, pp. 7–19.

Of course, Magellan's consistently positive residual returns (reflected in the steadily increasing plot of cumulative return difference) is hardly common. Figure 24.9 shows the frequency distribution of average residuals across 636 mutual funds. The distribution has the familiar bell shape with a slightly negative mean of −.074% per month. This should remind you of Figure 12.8, where we presented the frequency distribution of CAPM alphas for a large sample of mutual funds. As in Sharpe's study, these risk-adjusted returns plot as a bell-shaped curve with slightly negative mean.

Style analysis has become very popular in the investment management industry and has spawned quite a few variations on Sharpe's methodology. Many portfolio managers utilize websites that help investors identify their style and stock selection performance.

**Figure 24.9
Average tracking
error 636 mutual
funds, 1985–1989**

Average Tracking Error (%/month)

Source: William F. Sharpe, "Asset Allocation: Management Style and Performance Evaluation," *Journal of Portfolio Management,* Winter 1992, pp. 7–19.

---

**E-INVESTMENTS
Performance
and Fees**

Mutual fund loads and especially annual expenses have a tremendous impact on long-term savings or pension fund accumulation. The TIAA-CREF Mutual Fund Expense/Growth Calculator (**www.tiaa-cref.org/mfs/expcalc.html**) provides a look at the impact of expenses on long-term accumulation. The calculator provides an assessment of what a front-end load, back-end load, and/or various annual expense ratios will have on long-term savings. Also considered is the opportunity cost of lost earnings on funds paid for loads and expenses. Enter an original $100,000 invested for 35 years at 8%. What is the differential effect of a 3% front-end versus a 3% back-end load on the portfolio accumulation? (Set other expenses to zero). Finally, note the impact of the expense ratios as they increase beyond .5% per year. This is especially important for bond funds.

---

## 24.7   MORNINGSTAR'S RISK-ADJUSTED RATING

The commercial success of Morningstar, Inc., the premier source of information on mutual funds, has made its *Risk Adjusted Rating* (RAR) among the most widely used performance measures. The Morningstar five-star rating is coveted by the managers of the thousands of funds covered by the service. We reviewed the rating system in Chapter 4.

Morningstar calculates a number of RAR performance measures that are similar, although not identical, to the standard mean/variance measures we discussed in this chapter. The best-known measure, the Morningstar Star Rating, is based on comparison of each fund to a peer group. The peer group for each fund is selected on the basis of the fund's investment universe (e.g., international, growth versus value, fixed income, and so on) as well as portfolio characteristics such as average price-to-book value, price–earnings ratio, and market capitalization.

Morningstar computes fund returns (adjusted for loads) as well as a risk measure based primarily on fund performance in its worst years. The risk-adjusted performance is ranked across funds in a style group and stars are awarded based on the following table:

| Percentile | Stars |
|------------|-------|
| 0–10 | 1 |
| 10–32.5 | 2 |
| 32.5–67.5 | 3 |
| 67.5–90 | 4 |
| 90–100 | 5 |

The Morningstar RAR method produces results that are similar but not identical to that of the mean/variance-based Sharpe ratios. Figure 24.10 demonstrates the fit between ranking by RAR and by Sharpe ratios from the performance of 1,286 diversified equity funds over the period 1994–1996. Sharpe notes that this period is characterized by high returns that contribute to a good fit.

## 24.8    EVALUATING PERFORMANCE EVALUATION

Performance evaluation has two very basic problems:

1. Many observations are needed for significant results even when portfolio mean and variance are constant.

2. Shifting parameters when portfolios are actively managed makes accurate performance evaluation all the more elusive.

Although these objective difficulties cannot be overcome completely, it is clear that to obtain reasonably reliable performance measures we need to do the following:

1. Maximize the number of observations by taking more frequent return readings.

2. Specify the exact makeup of the portfolio to obtain better estimates of the risk parameters at each observation period.

**Figure 24.10 Rankings based on Morningstar's category RARs and excess return Sharpe ratios**

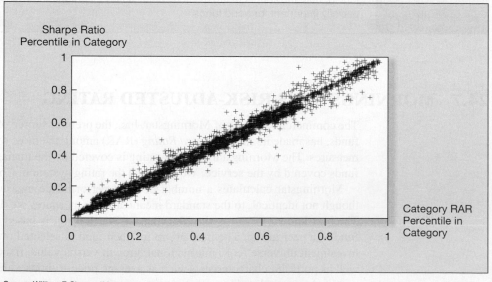

Source: William F. Sharpe, "Morningstar Performance Measures," **www.wsharpe.com**.

# HIGHLIGHTS OF AIMR PERFORMANCE PRESENTATION STANDARDS

- Returns must be total returns, including income and capital appreciation. Income should include accrued interest on securities.

- Annual returns should be reported for all years individually, as well as for longer periods. Firms should present time-weighted average rates of return (with portfolios valued at least quarterly, but preferably monthly or more frequently where feasible) and present geometric average linked returns (compound annualized returns) to summarize average performance. Portfolios should be revalued whenever large cash flows (e.g., more than 10% of the portfolio's value) might affect performance.

- Performance should be reported before fees, except where SEC advertising requirements mandate after-fee performance (because fees are often a function of size of assets). Fee schedules should be clearly presented.

- Composite results should reflect the record of the firm, not of individual managers. A portfolio's return should be included in the firm's composite performance as of the first full reporting period for which the portfolio is under management. Asset weighting within a composite should use beginning-of-period weights based on market value. Composite returns may not be biased by excluding selected portfolios. For example, portfolios no longer under management must be included in historical composites. Composite results may not be adjusted because of changes in the firm's organization or personnel.

- Composite returns should be reported for at least a 10-year period; 20 years is preferable if the company has been in existence for that period. Firms may not link simulated (or model) portfolio returns based on some trading strategy with actual performance.

- Performance results must be presented, including positions in cash and cash equivalents. Cash positions must be assigned to various portfolios at the beginning of each reporting period.

- The total return of multiple-asset portfolios (e.g., balanced accounts) must be included in composite results. If segment returns (i.e., individual asset class returns) from multiple-asset composite portfolios are included in the performance of a single asset class composite, a cash allocation to each segment must be made at the beginning of each reporting period.

- Risk measures such as beta, duration, or standard deviation are encouraged. In addition, benchmarks for performance evaluation such as returns on market indexes or normal portfolios should be chosen to reflect the expected risk or investment style of the client portfolio. Rebalancing of the benchmark asset allocation of multiple-asset portfolios should be agreed to by managers and clients in advance.

- In addition to actual results, performance for accounts utilizing leverage should be restated to an all-cash (no leverage) basis.

Suppose an evaluator knows the exact portfolio composition at the opening of each day. Because the daily return on each security is available, the total daily return on the portfolio can be calculated. Furthermore, the exact portfolio composition allows the evaluator to estimate the risk characteristics (variance, beta, residual variance) for each day. Thus daily risk-adjusted rates of return can be obtained. Although a performance measure for one day is statistically unreliable, the number of days with such rich data accumulates quickly. Performance evaluation that accounts for frequent revision in portfolio composition is superior by far to evaluation that assumes constant risk characteristics over the entire measurement period.

What sort of evaluation takes place in practice? Performance reports for portfolio managers traditionally have been based on quarterly data over 5 to 10 years. Currently, managers of mutual funds are required to disclose the exact composition of their portfolios only quarterly. Trading activity that immediately precedes the reporting date is known as "window dressing." Window dressing involves changes in portfolio composition to make it look as if the manager chose successful stocks. If IBM performed well over the quarter, for example, a portfolio manager might make sure that his or her portfolio includes a lot of IBM on the reporting date whether or not it did during the quarter and whether or not IBM is expected to perform as well over the next quarter. Of course, portfolio managers deny such activity, and we know of no published evidence to substantiate the allegation. However, if window dressing is quantitatively significant, even the reported quarterly composition data can be misleading. Mutual funds publish portfolio values on a daily basis, which means the rate of return for each day is publicly available, but portfolio composition is not.

Moreover, mutual fund managers have had considerable leeway in the presentation of both past investment performance and fees charged for management services. The resultant noncomparability of net-of-expense performance numbers has made it difficult to meaningfully compare funds.

This situation has changed, however. The money management industry has responded to demands for more complete and easily interpretable data on historical performance. For example, the Association of Investment Management and Research (AIMR) has published an extensive set of *Performance Presentation Standards*. The nearby box briefly summarizes some of the highlights of these recommendations. The thrust of these recommendations is that firms are not allowed to "cherry pick" when presenting their performance history: A complete record of performance is required. For example, firms must present returns for all years, as opposed to strategically choosing a starting date that makes subsequent performance look best. They also should provide the investment performance of an index against which their performance may reasonably be compared. Similarly, composite results for the firm must include returns of all of its managers, even those who have since left the firm. The firm, therefore, may not ignore the results of its unsuccessful managers who have since been replaced. The firm, not the individual manager, has the responsibility for performance. Finally, the firm is encouraged to supply risk measures such as beta or duration to make risk–return trade-offs easier to evaluate. Although the AIMR guidelines do not have the force of law, it nevertheless is expected that they will form the basis for industry performance presentation practices.

Still, even with more data, an insidious problem that will continue to complicate performance evaluation is survivorship bias. Since poorly performing mutual funds are regularly closed down, sample data will include only surviving funds, which correspondingly tend to be the more successful ones. At the same time, survivorship bias also affects broad-market indexes used as bogey portfolios and generates upward biased returns that are harder to beat. Several providers supply returns for various indexes that are adjusted for survivorship bias. These providers also attempt to adjust returns for cross holdings of shares that can distort the appropriate weights in the index.

## SUMMARY

1. The appropriate performance measure depends on the role of the portfolio to be evaluated. Appropriate performance measures are as follows:
   a. Sharpe: when the portfolio represents the entire investment fund.
   b. Information ratio: when the portfolio represents the active portfolio to be optimally mixed with the passive portfolio.
   c. Treynor or Jensen: when the portfolio represents one subportfolio of many.

2. Many observations are required to eliminate the effect of the "luck of the draw" from the evaluation process because portfolio returns commonly are very "noisy."

3. The shifting mean and variance of actively managed portfolios make it even harder to assess performance. A typical example is the attempt of portfolio managers to time the market, resulting in ever-changing portfolio betas.

4. A simple way to measure timing and selection success simultaneously is to estimate an expanded security characteristic line, with a quadratic term added to the usual index model.

5. Common attribution procedures partition performance improvements to asset allocation, sector selection, and security selection. Performance is assessed by calculating departures of portfolio composition from a benchmark or neutral portfolio.

6. Style analysis uses a multiple regression model where the factors are category (style) portfolios such as bills, bonds, and stocks. A regression of fund returns on the style portfolio returns generates residuals that represent the value added of stock selection in each period. These residuals can be used to gauge fund performance relative to similar-style funds.

7. The Morningstar Star Rating method compares each fund to a peer group represented by a style portfolio within four asset classes. Risk-adjusted ratings (RAR) are based on fund returns relative to the peer group and used to award each fund one to five stars based on the rank of its RAR.

## KEY TERMS

| | | |
|---|---|---|
| dollar-weighted rate of return | comparison universe | Jensen's measure |
| time-weighted return | Sharpe's measure | information ratio |
| | Treynor's measure | bogey |

## WEBSITES

www.morningstar.com
www.bloomberg.com
www.mutualfunds.about.com/money/mutualfunds
www.fool.com/school/mutualfunds/performance/record.htm
www.thestreet.com/funds/deardagen/10087858.html
www.chicagotribune.com/business/investing/personalfinance/chi-021007qty-fund-graphic,0,3509228.graphic
Visit these sites for information on mutual fund performance.

www.pionline.com
This site gives information on pensions and professional managers.

www.statestreet.com/capabilities/investment_management/institution.html
Review the services provided by State Street for institutional investors.

www.tiaa-cref.org/mfs/expcalc.html
Visit this site for a discussion of the impact of investment expense in pension management.

www.moneychimp.com/articles/risk/riskintro.htm
Review the discussion of the Sharpe ratio and portfolio allocation.

## PROBLEMS

1. Consider the rate of return of stocks ABC and XYZ.

| Year | $r_{ABC}$ | $r_{XYZ}$ |
|---|---|---|
| 1 | 20% | 30% |
| 2 | 12 | 12 |
| 3 | 14 | 18 |
| 4 | 3 | 0 |
| 5 | 1 | −10 |

   a. Calculate the arithmetic average return on these stocks over the sample period.
   b. Which stock has greater dispersion around the mean?
   c. Calculate the geometric average returns of each stock. What do you conclude?
   d. If you were equally likely to earn a return of 20%, 12%, 14%, 3%, or 1%, in each year (these are the five annual returns for stock ABC), what would be your expected rate of return? What if the five possible outcomes were those of stock XYZ?

2. XYZ stock price and dividend history are as follows:

| Year | Beginning-of-Year Price | Dividend Paid at Year-End |
|---|---|---|
| 1998 | $100 | $4 |
| 1999 | 120 | 4 |
| 2000 | 90 | 4 |
| 2001 | 100 | 4 |

   An investor buys three shares of XYZ at the beginning of 1998, buys another two shares at the beginning of 1999, sells one share at the beginning of 2000, and sells all four remaining shares at the beginning of 2001.

   a. What are the arithmetic and geometric average time-weighted rates of return for the investor?
   b. What is the dollar-weighted rate of return? (Hint: Carefully prepare a chart of cash flows for the *four* dates corresponding to the turns of the year for January 1, 1998, to January 1, 2001. If your calculator cannot calculate internal rate of return, you will have to use trial and error.)

3. A manager buys three shares of stock today, and then sells one of those shares each year for the next 3 years. His actions and the price history of the stock are summarized below. The stock pays no dividends.

| Time | Price | Action |
|---|---|---|
| 0 | $ 90 | Buy 3 shares |
| 1 | 100 | Sell 1 share |
| 2 | 100 | Sell 1 share |
| 3 | 100 | Sell 1 share |

   a. Calculate the time-weighted geometric average return on this "portfolio."
   b. Calculate the time-weighted arithmetic average return on this portfolio.
   c. Calculate the dollar-weighted average return on this portfolio.

4. Based on current dividend yields and expected capital gains, the expected rates of return on portfolios A and B are 12% and 16%, respectively. The beta of A is .7, while that of B is 1.4. The T-bill rate is currently 5%, whereas the expected rate of return of the S&P 500 index is 13%. The standard deviation of portfolio A is 12% annually, that of B is 31%, and that of the S&P 500 index is 18%.

    *a.* If you currently hold a market-index portfolio, would you choose to add either of these portfolios to your holdings? Explain.

    *b.* If instead you could invest *only* in T-bills and *one* of these portfolios, which would you choose?

5. Consider the two (excess return) index-model regression results for stocks A and B. The risk-free rate over the period was 6%, and the market's average return was 14%. Performance is measured using an index model regression on excess returns.

| | Stock A | Stock B |
|---|---|---|
| Index model regression estimates | $1\% + 1.2(r_M - r_f)$ | $2\% + .8(r_M - r_f)$ |
| *R*-square | .576 | .436 |
| Residual standard deviation, $\sigma(e)$ | 10.3% | 19.1% |
| Standard deviation of excess returns | 21.6% | 24.9% |

    *a.* Calculate the following statistics for each stock:

       i. Alpha

      ii. Information ratio

     iii. Sharpe measure

     iv. Treynor measure

    *b.* Which stock is the best choice under the following circumstances?

       i. This is the only risky asset to be held by the investor.

      ii. This stock will be mixed with the rest of the investor's portfolio, currently composed solely of holdings in the market index fund.

     iii. This is one of many stocks that the investor is analyzing to form an actively managed stock portfolio.

6. Evaluate the market timing and security selection abilities of four managers whose performances are plotted in the accompanying diagrams.

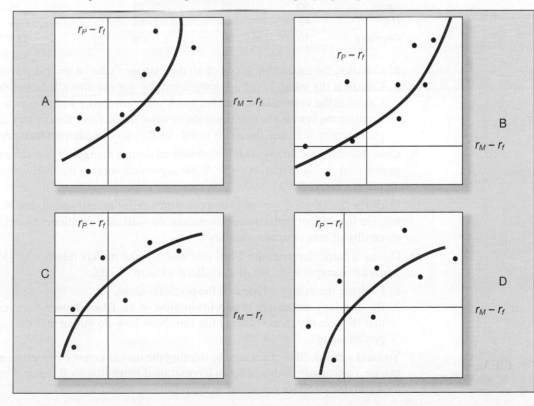

7. Consider the following information regarding the performance of a money manager in a recent month. The table represents the actual return of each sector of the manager's portfolio in column 1, the fraction of the portfolio allocated to each sector in column 2, the benchmark or neutral sector allocations in column 3, and the returns of sector indices in column 4.

|        | Actual Return | Actual Weight | Benchmark Weight | Index Return |
|--------|---------------|---------------|------------------|--------------|
| Equity | 2%            | .70           | .60              | 2.5% (S&P 500) |
| Bonds  | 1             | .20           | .30              | 1.2 (Salomon Index) |
| Cash   | 0.5           | .10           | .10              | 0.5 |

   a. What was the manager's return in the month? What was her overperformance or underperformance?
   b. What was the contribution of security selection to relative performance?
   c. What was the contribution of asset allocation to relative performance? Confirm that the sum of selection and allocation contributions equals her total "excess" return relative to the bogey.

8. A global equity manager is assigned to select stocks from a universe of large stocks throughout the world. The manager will be evaluated by comparing her returns to the return on the MSCI World Market Portfolio, but she is free to hold stocks from various countries in whatever proportions she finds desirable. Results for a given month are contained in the following table:

| Country | Weight In MSCI Index | Manager's Weight | Manager's Return in Country | Return of Stock Index for That Country |
|---------|----------------------|------------------|-----------------------------|----------------------------------------|
| U.K.    | .15                  | .30              | 20%                         | 12% |
| Japan   | .30                  | .10              | 15                          | 15 |
| U.S.    | .45                  | .40              | 10                          | 14 |
| Germany | .10                  | .20              | 5                           | 12 |

   a. Calculate the total value added of all the manager's decisions this period.
   b. Calculate the value added (or subtracted) by her *country* allocation decisions.
   c. Calculate the value added from her stock selection ability within countries. Confirm that the sum of the contributions to value added from her country allocation plus security selection decisions equals total over- or underperformance.

9. Conventional wisdom says that one should measure a manager's investment performance over an entire market cycle. What arguments support this convention? What arguments contradict it?

10. Does the use of universes of managers with similar investment styles to evaluate relative investment performance overcome the statistical problems associated with instability of beta or total variability?

11. During a particular year, the T-bill rate was 6%, the market return was 14%, and a portfolio manager with beta of .5 realized a return of 10%.

   a. Evaluate the manager based on the portfolio alpha.
   b. Reconsider your answer to part (a) in view of the Black-Jensen-Scholes finding that the security market line is too flat. Now how do you assess the manager's performance?

12. You and a prospective client are considering the measurement of investment performance, particularly with respect to international portfolios for the past 5 years. The data you discussed are presented in the following table:

CFA®
PROBLEMS

| International Manager or Index | Total Return | Country and Security Return | Currency Return |
|---|---|---|---|
| Manager A | −6.0% | 2.0% | −8.0% |
| Manager B | −2.0 | −1.0 | −1.0 |
| International Index | −5.0 | 0.2 | −5.2 |

a. Assume that the data for Manager A and Manager B accurately reflect their investment skills and that both managers actively manage currency exposure. Briefly describe one strength and one weakness for each manager.

b. Recommend and justify a strategy that would enable your fund to take advantage of the strengths of each of the two managers while minimizing their weaknesses.

13. Carl Karl, a portfolio manager for the Alpine Trust Company, has been responsible since 2010 for the City of Alpine's Employee Retirement Plan, a municipal pension fund. Alpine is a growing community, and city services and employee payrolls have expanded in each of the past 10 years. Contributions to the plan in fiscal 2015 exceeded benefit payments by a three-to-one ratio.

The plan board of trustees directed Karl 5 years ago to invest for total return over the long term. However, as trustees of this highly visible public fund, they cautioned him that volatile or erratic results could cause them embarrassment. They also noted a state statute that mandated that not more than 25% of the plan's assets (at cost) be invested in common stocks.

At the annual meeting of the trustees in November 2015, Karl presented the following portfolio and performance report to the board:

**Alpine Employee Retirement Plan**

| Asset Mix as of 9/30/15 | At Cost (millions) | | At Market (millions) | |
|---|---|---|---|---|
| Fixed-income assets: | | | | |
| Short-term securities | $ 4.5 | 11.0% | $ 4.5 | 11.4% |
| Long-term bonds and mortgages | 26.5 | 64.7 | 23.5 | 59.5 |
| Common stocks | 10.0 | 24.3 | 11.5 | 29.1 |
| | $41.0 | 100.0% | $39.5 | 100.0% |

**Investment Performance**

| | Annual Rates of Return for Periods Ending 9/30/15 | |
|---|---|---|
| | 5 Years | 1 Year |
| Total Alpine Fund: | | |
| Time-weighted | 8.2% | 5.2% |
| Dollar-weighted (internal) | 7.7% | 4.8% |
| Assumed actuarial return | 6.0% | 6.0% |
| U.S. Treasury bills | 7.5% | 11.3% |
| Large sample of pension funds (average 60% equities, 40% fixed income) | 10.1% | 14.3% |
| Common stocks—Alpine Fund | 13.3% | 14.3% |
| Average portfolio beta coefficient | 0.90 | 0.89 |
| Standard & Poor's 500 Stock Index | 13.8% | 21.1% |
| Fixed-income securities—Alpine Fund | 6.7% | 1.0% |
| Salomon Brothers' Bond Index | 4.0% | −11.4% |

Karl was proud of his performance and was chagrined when a trustee made the following critical observations:

a. "Our 1-year results were terrible, and it's what you've done for us lately that counts most."

b. "Our total fund performance was clearly inferior compared to the large sample of other pension funds for the last 5 years. What else could this reflect except poor management judgment?"

c. "Our common stock performance was especially poor for the 5-year period."

d. "Why bother to compare your returns to the return from Treasury bills and the actuarial assumption rate? What your competition could have earned for us or how we would have fared if invested in a passive index (which doesn't charge a fee) are the only relevant measures of performance."

e. "Who cares about time-weighted return? If it can't pay pensions, what good is it!"

Appraise the merits of each of these statements and give counterarguments that Mr. Karl can use.

14. The Retired Fund is an open-ended mutual fund composed of $500 million in U.S. bonds and U.S. Treasury bills. This fund has had a portfolio duration (including T-bills) of between 3 and 9 years. Retired has shown first-quartile performance over the past 5 years, as measured by an independent fixed-income measurement service. However, the directors of the fund would like to measure the market timing skill of the fund's sole bond investor manager. An external consulting firm has suggested the following three methods:

a. Method I examines the value of the bond portfolio at the beginning of every year, then calculates the return that would have been achieved had that same portfolio been held throughout the year. This return would then be compared with the return actually obtained by the fund.

b. Method II calculates the average weighting of the portfolio in bonds and T-bills for each year. Instead of using the actual bond portfolio, the return on a long-bond market index and T-bill index would be used. For example, if the portfolio on average was 65% in bonds and 35% in T-bills, the annual return on a portfolio invested 65% in a long-bond index and 35% in T-bills would be calculated. This return is compared with the annual return that would have been generated using the indexes and the manager's actual bond/T-bill weighting for each quarter of the year.

c. Method III examines the net bond purchase activity (market value of purchases less sales) for each quarter of the year. If net purchases were positive (negative) in any quarter, the performance of the bonds would be evaluated until the net purchase activity became negative (positive). Positive (negative) net purchases would be viewed as a bullish (bearish) view taken by the manager. The correctness of this view would be measured.

Critique *each* method with regard to market timing measurement problems.

Use the following data in solving problems 15 and 16:

The administrator of a large pension fund wants to evaluate the performance of four portfolio managers. Each portfolio manager invests only in U.S. common stocks. Assume that during the most recent 5-year period, the average annual total rate of return including dividends on the S&P 500 was 14%, and the average nominal rate of return on government Treasury bills was 8%. The following table shows risk and return measures for each portfolio:

| Portfolio | Average Annual Rate of Return | Standard Deviation | Beta |
|-----------|-------------------------------|--------------------|------|
| P | 17% | 20% | 1.1 |
| Q | 24 | 18 | 2.1 |
| R | 11 | 10 | 0.5 |
| S | 16 | 14 | 1.5 |
| S&P 500 | 14 | 12 | 1.0 |

15. What is the Treynor performance measure for Portfolio P?

16. What is the Sharpe performance measure for Portfolio Q?

17. An analyst wants to evaluate Portfolio X, consisting entirely of U.S. common stocks, using both the Treynor and Sharpe measures of portfolio performance. The following table provides the average annual rate of return for Portfolio X, the market portfolio (as measured by the S&P 500), and U.S. Treasury bills during the past 8 years:

|  | Average Annual Rate of Return | Standard Deviation of Return | Beta |
|--|-------------------------------|------------------------------|------|
| Portfolio X | 10% | 18% | 0.60 |
| S&P 500 | 12 | 13 | 1.00 |
| T-bills | 6 | N/A | N/A |

a. Calculate the Treynor and Sharpe measures for both Portfolio X and the S&P 500. Briefly explain whether Portfolio X underperformed, equaled, or outperformed the S&P 500 on a risk-adjusted basis using both the Treynor measure and the Sharpe measure.

b. Based on the performance of Portfolio X relative to the S&P 500 calculated in part (a), briefly explain the reason for the conflicting results when using the Treynor measure versus the Sharpe measure.

18. Assume you invested in an asset for 2 years. The first year you earned a 15% return, and the second year you earned a negative 10% return. What was your annual geometric return?

19. A portfolio of stocks generates a −9% return in 1999, a 23% return in 2000, and a 17% return in 2001. The annualized return (geometric mean) for the entire period is:
a. 7.2%.
b. 9.4%.
c. 10.3%.
d. None of the above.

20. A 2-year investment of $2,000 results in a return of $150 at the end of the first year and a return of $150 at the end of the second year, in addition to the return of the original investment. The internal rate of return on the investment is:
a. 6.4%.
b. 7.5%.
c. 15.0%.
d. None of the above.

21. In measuring the performance of a portfolio, the time-weighted rate of return is superior to the dollar-weighted rate of return because:
a. When the rate of return varies, the time-weighted return is higher.
b. The dollar-weighted return assumes all portfolio deposits are made on Day 1.
c. The dollar-weighted return can only be estimated.

d. The time-weighted return is unaffected by the timing of portfolio contributions and withdrawals.

22. A pension fund portfolio begins with $500,000 and earns 15% the first year and 10% the second year. At the beginning of the second year, the sponsor contributes another $500,000. The time-weighted and dollar-weighted rates of return were:

    a. 12.5% and 11.7%.
    b. 8.7% and 11.7%.
    c. 12.5% and 15.0%.
    d. 15.0% and 11.7%.

23. Pure market timers attempt to maintain a _____ portfolio beta and a _____ portfolio alpha.

    a. Constant; shifting.
    b. Shifting; zero.
    c. Shifting; shifting.
    d. Zero; zero.

24. The difference between an arithmetic average and a geometric average of returns

    a. Increases as the variability of the returns increases.
    b. Increases as the variability of the returns decreases.
    c. Is always negative.
    d. Depends on the specific returns being averaged, but is not necessarily sensitive to their variability.

25. During the annual review of Acme's pension plan, several trustees questioned their investment consultant about various aspects of performance measurement and risk assessment.

    a. Comment on the appropriateness of using each of the following benchmarks for performance evaluation:
       • Market index.
       • Benchmark normal portfolio.
       • Median of the manager universe.
    b. Distinguish among the following performance measures:
       • The Sharpe ratio.
       • The Treynor measure.
       • Jensen's alpha.
       i. Describe how each of the three performance measures is calculated.
       ii. State whether each measure assumes that the relevant risk is systematic, unsystematic, or total. Explain how each measure relates excess return and the relevant risk.

26. Trustees of the Pallor Corp. pension plan ask consultant Donald Millip to comment on the following statements. What should his response be?

    i. Median manager benchmarks are statistically unbiased measures of performance over long periods of time.
    ii. Median manager benchmarks are unambiguous and are therefore easily replicated by managers wishing to adopt a passive/indexed approach.
    iii. Median manager benchmarks are not appropriate in all circumstances because the median manager universe encompasses many investment styles.

27. James Chan is reviewing the performance of the global equity managers of the Jarvis University endowment fund. Williamson Capital is currently the endowment fund's only large-capitalization global equity manager. Performance data for Williamson Capital are shown in Table 24A.

Chan also presents the endowment fund's investment committee with performance information for Joyner Asset Management, which is another large-capitalization global equity manager. Performance data for Joyner Asset Management are shown in Table 24B. Performance data for the relevant risk-free asset and market index are shown in Table 24C.

a. Calculate the Sharpe ratio and Treynor measure for both Williamson Capital and Joyner Asset Management.

b. The Investment Committee notices that using the Sharpe ratio versus the Treynor measure produces different performance rankings of Williamson and Joyner. Explain why these criteria may result in different rankings.

### Table 24A   Williamson Capital Performance Data, 1990–2001

| | |
|---|---|
| Average annual rate of return | 22.1% |
| Beta | 1.2 |
| Standard deviation of returns | 16.8% |

### Table 24B   Joyner Asset Management Performance Data 1990–2001

| | |
|---|---|
| Average annual rate of return | 24.2% |
| Beta | 0.8 |
| Standard deviation of returns | 20.2% |

### Table 24C   Relevant Risk-free Asset and Market Index Performance Data, 1990–2001

| | |
|---|---|
| **Risk-free Asset** | |
| Average annual rate of return | 5.0% |
| **Market Index** | |
| Average annual rate of return | 18.9% |
| Standard deviation of returns | 13.8% |

**STANDARD &POOR'S**

Enter the Market Insight database at **www.mhhe.com/business/finance/edumarket insight** and link to *Commentary,* then *S&P Investment Policy Notes.* Look in the USA IPC *Archives* for the Investment Policy Committee (IPC) Notes of June 25, 2003. The Federal Reserve had just announced a .25% downward adjustment in the Federal funds rate to 1% as a further stimulant to the slow-growing economy. What portfolio allocation actions were taken by the IPC that day? Why? Later that day bond yields increased significantly. Read the current *Trends & Projections* from S&P. What was their forecast for bonds and the stock market at that time?

Visit us at www.mhhe.com/bkm

**E-INVESTMENTS**
**Performance of Mutual Funds**

Go to **money.com/money** and select the Funds tab. On the Funds page you will find a dialog box with a heading of *Find A Fund.* This fund screener has an *Advanced* option. Select that option. You will then find a series of options that allow you to further refine your search.

Under *Expenses,* request funds that have below-average expenses, below-average sales charges, and no redemption fee. For risk, select funds with an above-average risk and an above-average *R*-square with the market. Under the *More* tab, further refine your search to managers that have been with the fund since at least 2000.

When you request the results, the screener will show the top 50 funds and their average 3-year return. Repeat the above steps, but now request results that show the highest average return for both a 5-year period and a 10-year period. In each step you have to reenter the expense, risk, and manager information.

Compare the results in terms of consistency. Are there any managers that are in the top 10 in all three return periods? Are there any managers that are in the top 10 in two of the three periods?

**SOLUTIONS TO CONCEPT CHECKS**

1. 

| Time | Action | Cash Flow |
|------|--------|-----------|
| 0 | Buy two shares | −40 |
| 1 | Collect dividends; then sell one of the shares | 4 + 22 |
| 2 | Collect dividend on remaining share, then sell it | 2 + 19 |

   *a.* Dollar-weighted return:

$$-40 + \frac{26}{1 + r} + \frac{21}{(1 + r)^2} = 0$$

$$r = .1191, \text{ or } 11.91\%$$

   *b.* Time-weighted return:
   The rates of return on the stock in the 2 years were:

$$r_1 = \frac{2 + (22 - 20)}{20} = .20$$

$$r_2 = \frac{2 + (19 - 22)}{22} = -.045$$

$$(r_1 + r_2)/2 = .077, \text{ or } 7.7\%$$

2. *a.* $E(r_A) = [.15 + (-.05)]/2 = .05$
      $E(r_G) = [(1.15)(.95)]^{1/2} - 1 = .045$
   *b.* The expected stock price is $(115 + 95)/2 = 105$.
   *c.* The expected rate of return on the stock is 5%, equal to $r_A$.

3. Sharpe: $(\bar{r} - \bar{r}_f)/\sigma$

   $S_P = (35 - 6)/42 = .69$

   $S_M = (28 - 6)/30 = .733$

   Alpha: $\bar{r} - [\bar{r}_f + \beta(\bar{r}_M - \bar{r}_f)]$

   $\alpha_P = 35 - [6 + 1.2(28 - 6)] = 2.6$

   $\alpha_M = 0$

Treynor: $(\bar{r} - \bar{r}_f)/\beta$

$T_P = (35 - 6)/1.2 = 24.2$

$T_M = (28 - 6)/1.0 = 22$

Information ratio: $\alpha/\sigma(e)$

$I_P = 2.6/18 = .144$

$I_M = 0$

4. The *t*-statistic on $\alpha$ is $.2/2 = .1$. The probability that a manager with a true alpha of zero could obtain a sample period alpha with a *t*-statistic of .1 or better by pure luck depends on the length of the sample period. The smallest probability would occur with a large sample and is found in a table of the normal distribution. That probability is 46%.

5. Performance Attribution

First compute the new bogey performance as $(.70 \times 5.81) + (.25 \times 1.45) + (.05 \times .48) = 4.45$.

   *a.* Contribution of asset allocation to performance:

| Market | (1) Actual Weight in Market | (2) Benchmark Weight in Market | (3) Active or Excess Weight | (4) Market Return (%) | (5) = (3) × (4) Contribution to Performance (%) |
|---|---|---|---|---|---|
| Equity | .70 | .70 | .00 | 5.81 | .00 |
| Fixed-income | .07 | .25 | −.18 | 1.45 | −.26 |
| Cash | .23 | .05 | .18 | 0.48 | .09 |
| Contribution of asset allocation | | | | | −.17 |

   *b.* Contribution of selection to total performance:

| Market | (1) Portfolio Performance (%) | (2) Index Performance (%) | (3) Excess Performance (%) | (4) Portfolio Weight | (5) = (3) × (4) Contribution (%) |
|---|---|---|---|---|---|
| Equity | 7.28 | 5.00 | 2.28 | .70 | 1.60 |
| Fixed-income | 1.89 | 1.45 | 0.44 | .07 | 0.03 |
| Contribution of selection within markets | | | | | 1.63 |

# INTERNATIONAL DIVERSIFICATION

Although we in the United States customarily use a broad index of U.S. equities as the market-index portfolio, the practice is increasingly inappropriate. U.S. equities represent less than 50% of world equities and a far smaller fraction of total world wealth. In this chapter, we look beyond domestic markets to survey issues of international and extended diversification. In one sense, international investing may be viewed as no more than a straightforward generalization of our earlier treatment of portfolio selection with a larger menu of assets from which to construct a portfolio. Similar issues of diversification, security analysis, security selection, and asset allocation face the investor. On the other hand, international investments pose some problems not encountered in domestic markets. Among these are the presence of exchange rate risk, restrictions on capital flows across national boundaries, an added dimension of political risk and country-specific regulations, and differing accounting practices in different countries. Therefore, in this chapter we review the major topics covered in the rest of the book, emphasizing their international aspects. We start with the central concept of portfolio theory—diversification. We will see that global diversification offers opportunities for improving portfolio risk–return trade-offs. We also will see how exchange rate fluctuations and political risk affect the risk of international investments. We next turn to passive and active investment styles in the international context. We will consider some of the special problems involved in the interpretation of passive index portfolios, and we will show how active asset allocation can be generalized to incorporate country and currency choices in addition to traditional domestic asset class choices.

# 25.1   GLOBAL MARKETS FOR EQUITIES

**Developed Countries**    To appreciate the myopia of an exclusive investment focus on U.S. stocks and bonds, consider the data in Table 25.1. Developed (high-income) countries are defined as those with per capita income exceeding $9,300 (in 2000), and their broad stock indexes are generally less risky than those of emerging markets. The World Bank listed 52 developed countries in 2000, many of them with very small exchanges. Our list includes 25 countries with the largest equity capitalization, the smallest of which is New Zealand with a capitalization of $19 billion in 2001. These countries made up 79% of world gross domestic product in 2001.

The first five columns of Table 25.1 show market capitalization over the years 1996–2001. The first line is capitalization for all world exchanges, showing total capitalization of corporate equity in 2001 as $25.7 trillion, of which U.S. stock exchanges made up $13.2 trillion (49%). The figures in these columns demonstrate the volatility of these markets; indeed, world capitalization in 2001 was less than it was 2 years earlier and in the entire Pacific Basin it was less than it was in 1996!

The next three columns of Table 25.1 show country equity capitalization as a percentage of the world's in 2001 and 1996 and the growth in capitalization over the 5 years 1996–2001. The large volatility of country stock indexes resulted in significant changes in relative size. For example, U.S. weight in the world equity portfolio increased from 37% in 1996 to 49% in 2001, while that of Japan decreased from 24% to 11%. The weights of the five largest countries behind the U.S. (Japan, U.K., France, Germany, and Switzerland) added up to 39.2% in 2001, so that in the universe of these six countries alone, the weight of the U.S. was only 62% [49/(49 + 39.2)]. Clearly, U.S. stocks may not comprise a fully diversified portfolio of equities.

Unlike the 1980s and early 1990s, the period 1996–2001 saw a decline in the value of equities of the Pacific Basin (growth of −4%), but a resurgence in North America (growth of 136%) and Europe (104%). These numbers show that economic position of countries is just as variable as the stock prices that capitalize the future value of the particular corporate sectors of these economies.

The last three columns of Table 25.1 show GDP, per capita GDP, and equity capitalization as a percentage of GDP for the year 2001. As we would expect, per capital GDP in developed countries is not as variable across countries as total GDP, which is determined in part by total population. But market capitalization as a percentage of GDP is quite variable, suggesting widespread differences in economic structure even across developed countries. We return to this issue in the next section.

**Emerging Markets**    For a passive strategy one could argue that a portfolio of equities of just the six countries with the largest capitalization would make up 79.2% (in 2001)

## Table 25.1  Market Capitalization of Stock Exchanges in Developed Countries

| | Market Capitalization U.S. Dollars (billions) | | | | | | Percent of World | | Growth 1996–2001 | GDP 2001 | GDP per Capita 2001 | Capitalization as % of GDP 2001 |
|---|---|---|---|---|---|---|---|---|---|---|---|---|
| | 2001 | 2000 | 1999 | 1998 | 1997 | 1996 | 2001 | 1996 | | | | |
| **World** | **$25,711** | **$31,668** | **$26,198** | **$20,703** | **$17,966** | **$14,494** | **100%** | **100%** | **77%** | **30,960** | **5,450** | **83** |
| **North America** | **13,169** | **15,601** | **13,166** | **10,008** | **7,685** | **5,590** | **51.2** | **38.6** | **135.6** | | | |
| United States | 12,597 | 14,882 | 12,623 | 9,528 | 7,271 | 5,294 | 49.0 | 36.5 | 137.9 | 10,208 | 35,900 | 123 |
| Canada | 572 | 719 | 543 | 479 | 413 | 295 | 2.2 | 2.0 | 94.0 | 700 | 22,525 | 82 |
| **Europe** | **7,305** | **9,185** | **7,657** | **6,948** | **4,878** | **3,585** | **28** | **25** | **104** | | | |
| United Kingdom | 2,256 | 2,639 | 2,475 | 2,179 | 1,635 | 1,206 | 8.8 | 8.3 | 87 | 1,424 | 23,750 | 158 |
| France | 1,119 | 1,356 | 937 | 843 | 518 | 427 | 4.4 | 2.9 | 162 | 1,307 | 21,910 | 86 |
| Germany | 896 | 1,204 | 1,062 | 992 | 709 | 481 | 3.5 | 3.3 | 86 | 1,848 | 22,500 | 48 |
| Switzerland | 633 | 712 | 662 | 596 | 447 | 303 | 2.5 | 2.1 | 109 | 247 | 34,019 | 256 |
| Netherlands | 559 | 723 | 634 | 607 | 479 | 339 | 2.2 | 2.3 | 65 | 381 | 23,810 | 147 |
| Italy | 556 | 736 | 526 | 464 | 247 | 214 | 2.2 | 1.5 | 160 | 1,090 | 18,950 | 51 |
| Spain | 336 | 337 | 310 | 311 | 212 | 150 | 1.3 | 1.0 | 124 | 582 | 14,590 | 58 |
| Sweden | 212 | 375 | 253 | 247 | 188 | 139 | 0.8 | 1.0 | 52 | 210 | 23,580 | 101 |
| Finland | 164 | 379 | 173 | 93 | 60 | 42 | 0.6 | 0.3 | 295 | 121 | 23,260 | 136 |
| Belgium | 130 | 158 | 152 | 173 | 105 | 82 | 0.5 | 0.6 | 58 | 230 | 22,420 | 56 |
| Denmark | 90 | 101 | 75 | 88 | 61 | 44 | 0.3 | 0.3 | 103 | 163 | 30,450 | 55 |
| Ireland | 76 | 75 | 58 | 59 | 36 | 27 | 0.3 | 0.2 | 185 | 103 | 27,140 | 73 |
| Norway | 69 | 54 | 52 | 56 | 47 | 35 | 0.3 | 0.2 | 100 | 165 | 36,600 | 42 |
| Greece | 55 | 88 | 83 | 51 | 27 | 17 | 0.2 | 0.1 | 224 | 116 | 11,000 | 47 |
| Portugal | 49 | 74 | 59 | 75 | 47 | 23 | 0.2 | 0.2 | 111 | 110 | 10,940 | 45 |
| Israel | 39 | 47 | 35 | 29 | 24 | 18 | 0.2 | 0.1 | 120 | 110 | 17,159 | 35 |
| Austria | 24 | 28 | 31 | 35 | 27 | 26 | 0.1 | 0.2 | -8 | 189 | 23,078 | 13 |
| New Zealand | 19 | 23 | 26 | 26 | 36 | 29 | 0.1 | 0.2 | -34 | 49 | 12,763 | 39 |
| **Pacific Basin** | **4,642** | **6,184** | **4,764** | **3,201** | **4,729** | **4,830** | **18** | **33** | **-4** | | | |
| Japan | 2,947 | 4,246 | 3,092 | 2,188 | 3,138 | 3,509 | 11 | 24 | -16 | 4,148 | 32,720 | 71 |
| Hong Kong | 532 | 553 | 404 | 254 | 452 | 289 | 2.1 | 2.0 | 84 | 162 | 10,940 | 329 |
| Australia | 363 | 384 | 378 | 249 | 276 | 219 | 1.4 | 1.5 | 65 | 357 | 18,459 | 102 |
| Taiwan | 205 | 331 | 260 | 173 | 232 | 152 | 0.8 | 1.0 | 35 | 282 | 12,620 | 73 |
| Singapore | 113 | 143 | 133 | 72 | 116 | 138 | 0.4 | 0.9 | -18 | 86 | 20,880 | 132 |

Source: Datastream, July 2002.

of the world portfolio and may be sufficiently diversified. This argument will not hold for active portfolios that seek to tilt investments toward promising assets. Active portfolios will naturally include many stocks or even indexes of emerging markets.

Table 25.2 makes the point. Surely, active portfolio managers must prudently scour stocks in markets such as China, Brazil, or Korea. Table 25.2 shows data from the 20 largest emerging markets, the most notable of which is China with equity capitalization of $170 billion (0.66% of world capitalization) in 2001, and growth of 651% over the 5 years 1996–2001. But managers also would not want to have missed a market like Poland (0.09% of world capitalization) with a growth of 287% over the same years.

These 20 emerging markets make up 16% of the world GDP and, together with the 25 developed markets in Table 25.1, make up 95% of the world GDP. Per capita GDP in these countries in 2001 was quite variable, ranging from $470 (India) to $8,870 (Korea); still, no active manager would want to ignore India in an international portfolio. Market capitalization as a percent of GDP, which ranges from 3% (Venezuela) to 90% (South Africa), suggests that these markets are expected to show significant growth over the coming years, even absent spectacular growth in GDP.

The growth of capitalization in emerging markets over 1996–2001 was much more volatile than growth in developed countries (as disastrous as −71% for Thailand), suggesting that both risk and rewards in this segment of the globe may be substantial.

## Market Capitalization and GDP

The contemporary view of economic development (rigorously stated in deSoto[1]) holds that a major requirement for economic advancement is a developed code of business laws, institutions, and regulation that allows citizens to legally own, capitalize, and trade capital assets. As a corollary, we expect that development of equity markets will serve as catalysts for enrichment of the population, that is, that countries with larger relative capitalization of equities will tend to be richer.

Figure 25.1 is a simple (perhaps simplistic, since other relevant explanatory variables are omitted) rendition of the argument that a developed market for corporate equity contributes to the enrichment of the population. The R-square of the regression line shown in Figure 25.1 is 35% and the regression coefficient is .73, suggesting that an increase of 1% in the ratio of market capitalization to GDP is associated with an increase in per capita GDP of 0.73%. It is remarkable that not one of the 25 developed countries is below the regression line; only low-income emerging markets lie below the line. Countries like Venezuela and Norway that lie above the line, that is, exhibit higher per capita GDP than predicted by the regression, enjoy oil wealth that contributes to population income. Countries below the line, such as Indonesia, South Africa, Philippines, and India, suffered from deterioration of the business environment due to political strife and/or government policies that restricted the private sector. China's policies of freeing up economic activities contributed to the remarkable growth in market capitalization over 1996–2001. The expected continuation of this process will likely move China toward the predicted relationship in coming years.

---

[1] Hernando de Soto, *The Mystery of Capital* (New York: Basic Books, 2000).

## Table 25.2  Market Capitalization of Stock Exchanges in Emerging Markets

| | Market Capitalization | | | | | | | Percent of World | | Growth | GDP | GDP per Capita | Capitalization as % of GDP |
| | U.S. Dollars (billions) | | | | | | | | | | | | |
| | 2001 | 2000 | 1999 | 1998 | 1997 | 1996 | | 2001 | 1996 | 1996–2001 | 2001 | 2001 | 2001 |
|---|---|---|---|---|---|---|---|---|---|---|---|---|---|
| China | $170 | $ 94 | $ 78 | $ 67 | $ 48 | $ 23 | | 0.66% | 0.16% | 651% | 1,180 | 928 | 14% |
| Brazil | 169 | 220 | 155 | 135 | 175 | 86 | | 0.66 | 0.59 | 97 | 503 | 2,810 | 34 |
| Korea | 151 | 218 | 181 | 35 | 95 | 104 | | 0.59 | 0.72 | 45 | 423 | 8,870 | 36 |
| Mexico | 140 | 128 | 115 | 96 | 97 | 74 | | 0.55 | 0.51 | 89 | 621 | 6,190 | 23 |
| South Africa | 101 | 123 | 126 | 121 | 148 | 124 | | 0.39 | 0.86 | −19 | 112 | 2,520 | 90 |
| India | 88 | 139 | 93 | 72 | 113 | 88 | | 0.34 | 0.61 | −1 | 485 | 470 | 18 |
| Malaysia | 76 | 98 | 90 | 50 | 170 | 167 | | 0.30 | 1.15 | −54 | 89 | 3,720 | 86 |
| Russia | 66 | 49 | 35 | 44 | 93 | 37 | | 0.26 | 0.25 | 80 | 310 | 2,144 | 21 |
| Chile | 53 | 49 | 47 | 45 | 61 | 48 | | 0.20 | 0.33 | 10 | 64 | 4,170 | 82 |
| Turkey | 36 | 75 | 39 | 54 | 36 | 24 | | 0.14 | 0.16 | 50 | 148 | 2,230 | 24 |
| Argentina | 29 | 37 | 51 | 48 | 56 | 43 | | 0.11 | 0.30 | −31 | 267 | 7,120 | 11 |
| Thailand | 26 | 30 | 46 | 17 | 46 | 89 | | 0.10 | 0.61 | −71 | 115 | 1,820 | 23 |
| Poland | 22 | 29 | 25 | 14 | 7 | 6 | | 0.09 | 0.04 | 287 | 176 | 4,566 | 13 |
| Philippines | 20 | 23 | 41 | 26 | 55 | 62 | | 0.08 | 0.42 | −68 | 71 | 862 | 28 |
| Indonesia | 19 | 32 | 39 | 12 | 76 | 60 | | 0.07 | 0.41 | −68 | 145 | 688 | 13 |
| Czech Republic | 10 | 13 | 12 | 13 | 11 | 13 | | 0.04 | 0.09 | −26 | 52 | 5,137 | 19 |
| Hungary | 9 | 14 | 14 | 15 | 8 | 4 | | 0.04 | 0.03 | 128 | 56 | 5,482 | 16 |
| Peru | 6 | 8 | 7 | 8 | 11 | 10 | | 0.02 | 0.07 | −36 | 54 | 2,070 | 11 |
| Colombia | 6 | 5 | 7 | 10 | 22 | 17 | | 0.02 | 0.12 | −65 | 83 | 1,940 | 7 |
| Venezuela | 4 | 4 | 4 | 4 | 10 | 4 | | 0.02 | 0.03 | 2 | 130 | 5,280 | 3 |

**Figure 25.1
Per capita GDP
tends to be higher
when market
capitalization as
a percentage of
GDP is higher.
(log scale)**

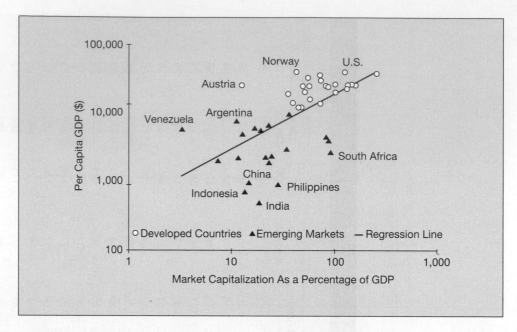

## Home-Country Bias

One would expect that most investors, particularly institutional and professional investors, would be aware of the opportunities offered by international investing. Yet in practice, investor portfolios notoriously overweight home-country stocks compared to a neutral indexing strategy and underweight, or even completely ignore, foreign equities. This has come to be known as the *home-country bias*. Despite a continuous increase in cross-border investing, home-country bias still dominates investor portfolios.

## 25.2    RISK FACTORS IN INTERNATIONAL INVESTING

Opportunities in international investments do not come free of risk or of the cost of specialized analysis. The risk factors that are unique to international investments are exchange rate risk and country-specific risk, discussed in the next two sections.

### Exchange Rate Risk

It is best to begin with a simple example.

### EXAMPLE 25.1    Exchange Rate Risk

Consider an investment in risk-free British government bills paying 10% annual interest in British pounds. While these U.K. bills would be the risk-free asset to a British investor, this is not the case for a U.S. investor. Suppose, for example, the current exchange rate is $2 per pound, and the U.S. investor starts with $20,000. That amount can be exchanged for £10,000 and invested at a riskless 10% rate in the United Kingdom to provide £11,000 in 1 year.

What happens if the dollar–pound exchange rate varies over the year? Say that during the year, the pound depreciates relative to the dollar, so that by year-end only $1.80 is required to purchase £1. The £11,000 can be exchanged at the year-end exchange rate for only $19,800 (= £11,000 × $1.80/£), resulting in a loss of $200 relative to the initial $20,000 investment. Despite the positive 10% pound-denominated return, the dollar-denominated return is a negative 1%.

**Figure 25.2
Stock market
returns in dollars
and local
currencies
for 2001**

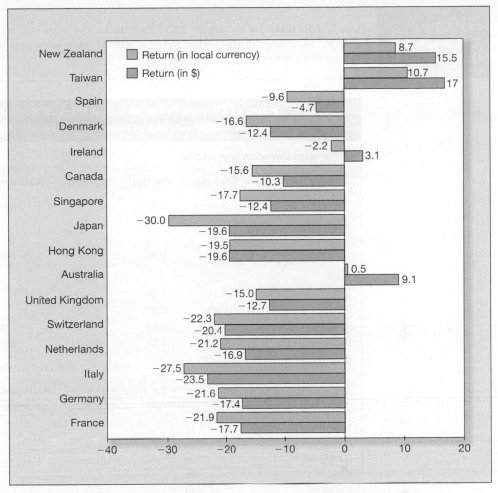

Source: Datastream.

We can generalize from Example 25.1. The $20,000 is exchanged for $20,000/$E_0$ pounds, where $E_0$ denotes the original exchange rate ($2/£). The U.K. investment grows to $(20,000/E_0)[1 + r_f(\text{UK})]$ British pounds, where $r_f$ (UK) is the risk-free rate in the United Kingdom. The pound proceeds ultimately are converted back to dollars at the subsequent exchange rate $E_1$, for total dollar proceeds of $20,000(E_1/E_0)[1 + r_f(\text{UK})]$. The dollar-denominated return on the investment in British bills, therefore, is

$$1 + r(\text{US}) = [1 + r_f(\text{UK})]E_1/E_0 \qquad (25.1)$$

We see in Equation 25.1 that the dollar-denominated return for a U.S. investor equals the pound-denominated return times the exchange rate "return." For a U.S. investor, the investment in British bills is a combination of a safe investment in the United Kingdom and a risky investment in the performance of the pound relative to the dollar. Here, the pound fared poorly, falling from a value of $2.00 to only $1.80. The loss on the pound more than offsets the earnings on the British bill.

Figure 25.2 illustrates this point. It presents rates of returns on stock market indexes in several countries for 2001. The dark boxes depict returns in local currencies, while the light boxes depict returns in dollars, adjusted for exchange rate movements. It's clear that exchange rate fluctuations over this period had large effects on dollar-denominated returns in several countries.

<table>
<tr><td>CONCEPT CHECK☞ QUESTION 1</td><td>Using the data in Example 25.1, calculate the rate of return in dollars to a U.S. investor holding the British bill if the year-end exchange rate is: (a) $E_1 = \$2.00/£$; (b) $E_1 = \$2.20/£$.</td></tr>
</table>

**Table 25.3    Rates of Change in the Value of the U.S. Dollar Against Major World Currencies, 1997–2001 (monthly data)**

**A. Standard Deviation (annualized)**

| Country Currency | Euro (€) | U.K. (£) | Japan (¥) | Australia ($A) | Canada ($C) |
|---|---|---|---|---|---|
| Standard dev. | 9.61 | 6.61 | 14.18 | 11.44 | 5.01 |

**B. Correlation Matrix**

| | Euro | U.K. | Japan | Australia | Canada |
|---|---|---|---|---|---|
| Euro | 1.00 | | | | |
| U.K. | 0.64 | 1.00 | | | |
| Japan | 0.29 | 0.21 | 1.00 | | |
| Australia | 0.29 | 0.22 | 0.35 | 1.00 | |
| Canada | −0.02 | 0.02 | 0.13 | 0.53 | 1.00 |

**C. Average Increases**

| | Average Annualized Dollar Return on Cash Investments | | Average Annualized % Increase in the Value of the U.S. Dollar |
|---|---|---|---|
| U.S. | 5.67 | | |
| France | −2.64 | Euro | 7.28 |
| Germany | −2.82 | Euro | 7.28 |
| Italy | −1.81 | Euro | 7.28 |
| Netherlands | −2.88 | Euro | 7.28 |
| Switzerland | −1.48 | Euro | 7.28 |
| U.K. | 3.34 | U.K. | 3.47 |
| Australia | −2.74 | Australia | 9.46 |
| Japan | −0.97 | Japan | 3.44 |
| Canada | 1.90 | Canada | 3.17 |

Pure **exchange rate risk** is the risk borne by investments in foreign safe assets. The investor in U.K. bills of Example 25.1 bears only the risk of the U.K./U.S. exchange rate. We can assess the magnitude of exchange rate risk by examination of historical rates of change in various exchange rates and their correlations.

Table 25.3A shows historical exchange rate risk measured from monthly percent changes in the exchange rates of major currencies over the period 1997–2001. The data shows that currency risk is quite high. The annualized standard deviation of the percent changes in the exchange rate ranged from 5.01% (Canadian dollar) to 14.18% (Japanese yen). The standard deviation of monthly returns on U.S. large stocks for the same period was 18.81%. Hence, currency exchange risk alone would amount to between 27% (5.01/18.81) and 75% (14.18/18.81) of the risk on stocks. Clearly, an active investor who believes that Japanese stocks are underpriced, but has no information about any mispricing of the Japanese yen, would be advised to hedge the yen risk exposure when tilting the portfolio toward Japanese stocks. Exchange rate risk of the major currencies is quite stable over time. For example, a study by Solnik[2] for the period 1971–1998 finds similar standard deviations, ranging from 4.8% (Canadian dollar) to 12.0% (Japanese yen).

In the context of international portfolios, exchange rate risk may be mostly diversifiable. This is evident from the low correlation coefficients in Table 25.3B. (This observation will be reinforced when we compare the risk of hedged and unhedged country portfolios in a later section.) Thus, passive investors with well-diversified international portfolios need not be concerned with hedging exposure to foreign currencies.

The annualized average monthly increase in the value of the U.S. dollar against the major currencies over the 5-year period and dollar returns on foreign bills (cash investments) appear in Table 25.3C. The table shows that the value of the U.S. dollar consistently increased in this particular period. For example, the total increase against the Japanese yen over the 5 years was 18% and against the Australian dollar, 57%. This currency appreciation of the U.S. dollar was not offset by higher interest rates available in other countries. Had an investor been able to forecast the large exchange rate movements, it would have been a source of great profit. The currency market thus provided attractive opportunities for investors with superior information or analytical ability.

The investor in Example 25.1 could have hedged the exchange rate risk using a forward or futures contract in foreign exchange. Recall that a forward or futures contract on foreign exchange calls for delivery or acceptance of one currency for another at a stipulated exchange rate. Here, the U.S. investor would agree to deliver pounds for dollars at a fixed exchange rate, thereby eliminating the future risk involved with conversion of the pound investment back into dollars.

## EXAMPLE 25.2    Hedging Exchange Rate Risk

If the futures exchange rate had been $F_0 = \$1.93/£$ when the investment was made, the U.S. investor could have assured a riskless dollar-denominated return by locking in the year-end exchange rate at $1.93/£. In this case, the riskless U.S. return would have been 6.15%:

$$[1 + r_f(UK)]F_0/E_0 = (1.10)1.93/2.00 = 1.0615$$

You may recall that the futures hedge underlying Example 25.2 is the same type of hedging strategy at the heart of the spot-futures parity relationship first discussed in Chapter 22. In both instances, futures markets are used to eliminate the risk of holding another asset. The U.S. investor can lock in a riskless dollar-denominated return either by investing in the United Kingdom and hedging exchange rate risk or by investing in riskless U.S. assets. Because the returns on two riskless strategies must provide equal returns, we conclude

$$\frac{F_0}{E_0} = \frac{1 + r_f(US)}{1 + r_f(UK)} \tag{25.2}$$

This relationship is called the **interest rate parity relationship** or **covered interest arbitrage relationship,** which we first encountered in Chapter 23.

Unfortunately, such perfect exchange rate hedging usually is not so easy. In our example, we knew exactly how many pounds to sell in the forward or futures market because the pound-denominated return in the United Kingdom was riskless. If the U.K. investment had not been in bills, but instead had been in risky U.K. equity, we would know neither the ultimate value in pounds of our U.K. investment nor how many pounds to sell forward.

[2] B. Solnik, *International Investing,* 4th ed. (Reading, MA: Addison Wesley, 1999).

That is, the hedging opportunity offered by foreign exchange forward contracts would be imperfect.

To summarize, the generalization of equation 25.1 is that

$$1 + r(\text{US}) = [1 + r(\text{foreign})]E_1/E_0 \tag{25.3}$$

where $r(\text{foreign})$ is the possibly risky return earned in the currency of the foreign investment. You can set up a perfect hedge only in the special case that $r(\text{foreign})$ is itself a known number. In that case, you know you must sell in the forward or futures market an amount of foreign currency equal to $[1 + r(\text{foreign})]$ for each unit of that currency you purchase today.

| CONCEPT CHECK ☞ QUESTION 2 | How many pounds would the investor in Example 25.2 need to sell forward to hedge exchange rate risk if: (a) $r(\text{UK}) = 20\%$; and (b) $r(\text{UK}) = 30\%$? |
|---|---|

**Country-Specific Risk**    In principle, security analysis at the macroeconomic, industry, and firm-specific level is similar in all countries. Such analysis aims to provide estimates of expected returns and risk of individual assets and portfolios. To achieve the same quality of information about assets in a foreign country is by nature more difficult and hence more expensive. Moreover, the risk of coming by false or misleading information is greater.

Consider two investors: an American wishing to invest in Indonesian stocks and an Indonesian wishing to invest in U.S. stocks. While each would have to consider macro-economic analysis of the foreign country, the task would be much more difficult for the American investor. The reason is not that investment in Indonesia is necessarily riskier than investment in the U.S. You can easily find many U.S. stocks that are, in the final analysis, riskier than a number of Indonesian stocks. The difference lies in the fact that the U.S. investment environment is more predictable than that of Indonesia.

In the past, when international investing was novel, the added risk was referred to as **political risk** and its assessment was an art. As cross-border investment has increased and more resources have been utilized, the quality of related analysis has improved. A leading organization in the field (which is quite competitive) is the PRS Group (Political Risk Services) and the presentation here follows the PRS methodology.[3]

PRS's country risk analysis results in a country composite risk rating on a scale of 0 (most risky) to 100 (least risky). Countries are then ranked by composite risk measure and divided into five categories: very low risk (100–80), low risk (79.9–70), moderate risk (69.9–60), high risk (59.9–50), and very high risk (less than 50). To illustrate, Table 25.4 shows the placement of five countries in the September 2001 issue of the PRS *International Country Risk Guide*. The countries shown are the two largest capitalization countries (U.S. and Japan) and the three most populous emerging markets (China, India, and Indonesia). Surprisingly, Table 25.4 shows that the U.S. ranked only 20th in September of 2001, having deteriorated from the 11th rank in the previous year. Japan actually ranked higher at 13. Both these developed countries placed in the "very low risk" category. Of the three emerging markets, it is not surprising to see Indonesia ranked 115th of 140 countries, placing it in the "high risk" category, while China ranked 60th, in the "low risk" category, and India ranked 92nd, in the "moderate risk" category.

---

[3] You can find more information on the website: www.prsgroup.com.

**Table 25.4    Composite Risk Ratings for October 2000 and September 2001**

| Rank, Sept. 2001 | Country | Composite Risk Rating, Sept. 2001 | Composite Risk Rating, Oct. 2000 | Sept. 2001 Rating Minus Oct. 2000 Rating | Rank, Oct. 2000 |
|---|---|---|---|---|---|
| | **Very low risk** | | | | |
| 13 | Japan | 86.5 | 83.5 | 3 | 12 |
| 20 | United States | 83.3 | 83.8 | −0.5 | 11 |
| | **Low risk** | | | | |
| 60 | China | 72.5 | 73.5 | −1 | 47 |
| | **Moderate risk** | | | | |
| 92 | India | 64.8 | 63.3 | 1.5 | 89 |
| | **High risk** | | | | |
| 115 | Indonesia | 59.8 | 56.5 | 3.3 | 118 |

Source: *International Country Risk Guide,* September 2001, Table 1.

**Table 25.5    Variables Used in PRS's Political Risk Score**

| Political Risk Variables | Financial Risk Variables | Economic Risk Variables |
|---|---|---|
| Government stability | Foreign debt (% of GDP) | GDP per capita |
| Socioeconomic conditions | Foreign debt service (% of GDP) | Real annual GDP growth |
| Investment profile | | Annual inflation rate |
| Internal conflicts | Current account (% of exports) | Budget balance (% of GDP) |
| External conflicts | Net liquidity in months of imports | Current account balance (% GDP) |
| Corruption | Exchange rate stability | |
| Military in politics | | |
| Religious tensions | | |
| Law and order | | |
| Ethnic tensions | | |
| Democratic accountability | | |
| Bureaucracy quality | | |

The composite risk rating is an average of three measures: political risk, financial risk, and economic risk. Political risk is measured on a scale of 100–0, while financial and economic risk are measured on a scale of 50–0. The three measures are added and divided by two to obtain the composite rating. This amounts to a weighted average of the three measures with a weight of .5 on political risk and .25 each on financial and economic risk. The variables used by PRS to determine the composite risk rating of the three measured are shown in Table 25.5.

Table 25.6 shows the three risk measures for the five countries in Table 25.4, in order of the September 2001 ranking of the composite risk ratings. The table shows that by political risk, the five countries ranked in the same order. But in the financial risk measure, the U.S. ranked below China and India (!), and by the economic risk measure, the U.S. ranked above Japan, and India ranked below Indonesia. More interesting are the ratings forecasts for 1 and 5 years. These forecasts are quite pessimistic about the U.S., whose composite rating is expected to continue to deteriorate over the years 2002–2006. (This may have been prescient, since it appears this report was prepared prior to the September 11, 2001, attacks.) At the same time, the ratings of three of the other four countries were expected to improve over the next 5 years.

## Table 25.6    Current Risk Ratings and Composite Risk Forecasts

| Country | Current Ratings | | | Composite Ratings | | | |
|---|---|---|---|---|---|---|---|
| | Political Risk, Sept. 2001 | Financial Risk, Sept. 2001 | Economic Risk, Sept. 2001 | Year Ago, Oct. 2000 | Current, Sept. 2001 | 1-Year Forecast | 5-Year Forecast |
| Japan | 90 | 45.5 | 37.5 | 83.5 | 86.5 | 84.5 | 85.5 |
| United States | 89.5 | 37.5 | 39.5 | 83.8 | 83.3 | 82.5 | 80.5 |
| China | 62 | 45 | 38 | 73.5 | 72.5 | 72.5 | 76.5 |
| India | 56 | 40.5 | 33 | 63.3 | 64.8 | 64 | 68 |
| Indonesia | 49.5 | 35 | 35 | 56.5 | 59.8 | 52.5 | 64.5 |

Source: *International Country Risk Guide,* September 2001, Table 2B.

## Table 25.7    Composite and Political Risk Forecasts

### A. Composite Risk Forecasts

| | | 1 Year Ahead | | | | 5 Years Ahead | | | |
|---|---|---|---|---|---|---|---|---|---|
| | Current Rating | Worst Case | Most Probable | Best Case | Risk Stability | Worst Case | Most Probable | Best Case | Risk Stability |
| Japan | **86.5** | 79.5 | 84.5 | 88 | 8.5 | 78.5 | 85.5 | 91 | 12.5 |
| United States | **83.3** | 75 | 82.5 | 85.5 | 10.5 | 73 | 80.5 | 84 | 11 |
| China | **72.5** | 68 | 72.5 | 74.5 | 6.5 | 67 | 76.5 | 81 | 14 |
| India | **64.8** | 58 | 64 | 66.5 | 8.5 | 60 | 68 | 70.5 | 10.5 |
| Indonesia | **59.8** | 45 | 52.5 | 55 | 10 | 46.5 | 64.5 | 68.5 | 22 |

### B. Political Risk Forecasts

| | | 1 Year Ahead | | | | 5 Years Ahead | | | |
|---|---|---|---|---|---|---|---|---|---|
| | Current Rating | Worst Case | Most Probable | Best Case | Risk Stability | Worst Case | Most Probable | Best Case | Risk Stability |
| Japan | **90** | 76 | 83 | 88 | 12 | 76 | 85 | 94 | 18 |
| United States | **89.5** | 78 | 90 | 93 | 15 | 80 | 85 | 88 | 8 |
| China | **62** | 58 | 63 | 65 | 7 | 60 | 70 | 74 | 14 |
| India | **56** | 50 | 60 | 63 | 13 | 58 | 65 | 67 | 9 |
| Indonesia | **49.5** | 40 | 48 | 50 | 10 | 40 | 60 | 64 | 24 |

Sources: A: *International Country Risk Guide,* September 2001, Table 2C; B: *International Country Risk Guide,* September 2001, Table 3C.

The country risk is captured in greater depth by scenario analysis for the composite measure and each of its components. Table 25.7 (A and B) shows 1- and 5-year worst case and best case scenarios for the composite ratings and for the political risk measure. Risk stability is defined as the difference in the rating between the best and worst case scenarios and is quite large in most cases. The worst case scenario is in some cases sufficient to move a country to a higher risk category. Table 25.7B shows that U.S. political risk was forecast to deteriorate in 5 years (2006) to the level of Japan.

Finally, Table 25.8 shows ratings of political risk by each of its 12 components. Corruption (variable F) in China is rated worse than in India and equal to that of Indonesia. In democratic accountability (variable K), China ranked worst and India best, while Indonesia ranked better than both in external conflict (variable E).

## Table 25.8   Political Risk Points by Component, September 2001

This table lists the total points for each of the following political risk components out of the maximum points indicated. The symbol ↑ indicates a rise in the points awarded to that specific risk component from the previous month (an improving risk), while the symbol ↓ indicates a decrease (deteriorating risk). The final columns in the table show the overall political risk rating (the sum of the points awarded to each component) and the change from the preceding month.

| | | | | | | |
|---|---|---|---|---|---|---|
| A | Government stability | 12 | E | External conflict | 12 | J | Ethnic tensions | 6 |
| B | Socioeconomic conditions | 12 | F | Corruption | 6 | K | Democratic accountability | 6 |
| C | Investment profile | 12 | H | Religious tensions | 6 | L | Bureaucracy quality | 4 |
| D | Internal conflict | 12 | I | Law and order | 6 | | | |

| Country | A | B | C | D | E | F | G | H | I | J | K | L | Political Risk Rating | |
|---|---|---|---|---|---|---|---|---|---|---|---|---|---|---|
| United States | 10 | 10.5 | 11 | 12 | 10.5 | 4 | 5.5 | 6 | 6 | 5 | 5 | 4 | **89.5** | 0 |
| Japan | 10.5 | 8.5 | ↑12.0 | 12 | ↓11.0 | 3 | 6 | 5 | 5 | 6 | 5 | 4 | **88** | −0.5 |
| China | 10 | 7 | ↓7.5 | 10 | 9.5 | 1 | 2 | 4 | 4 | 4 | 1 | 2 | **62** | −0.5 |
| India | ↑7.5 | 3.5 | ↓8.0 | ↓7.0 | ↓8.0 | 2 | 3 | 2 | 4 | 2 | 6 | 3 | **56** | −1.5 |
| Indonesia | ↑9.5 | 2 | ↑7.0 | 6.5 | 10 | 1 | 2.5 | 1 | 2 | 2 | 4 | 2 | **49.5** | 2 |

Each monthly issue of the *International Country Risk Guide* of the PRS Group includes great detail and holds some 250 pages. Other organizations compete in supplying such evaluations. The result is that today's investor can become well equipped to properly assess the risks involved in international investing.

# 25.3   INTERNATIONAL INVESTING: RISK, RETURN, AND BENEFITS FROM DIVERSIFICATION

U.S. investors have several avenues through which they can invest internationally. The most obvious method, which is available in practice primarily to larger institutional investors, is to purchase securities directly in the capital markets of other countries. However, even small investors now can take advantage of several investment vehicles with an international focus.

Shares of several foreign firms are traded in U.S. markets in the form of American depository receipts, or ADRs. A U.S. financial institution such as a bank will purchase shares of a foreign firm in that firm's country, then issue claims to those shares in the United States. Each ADR is then a claim on a given number of the shares of stock held by the bank. In this way, the stock of foreign companies can be traded on U.S. stock exchanges. Trading foreign stocks with ADRs has become increasingly easy.

There is also a wide array of mutual funds with an international focus. Single-country funds are mutual funds that invest in the shares of only one country. These tend to be closed-end funds, as the listing of these funds in Table 25.9 indicates. In addition to single-country funds, there are several open-end mutual funds with an international focus. For example, Fidelity offers funds with investments concentrated overseas, generally in Europe, in the Pacific Basin, and in developing economies in an emerging opportunities fund. Vanguard, consistent with its indexing philosophy, offers separate index funds for Europe, the Pacific Basin, and emerging markets. The nearby box (page 921) discusses a wide range of single-country index funds.

U.S. investors also can trade derivative securities based on prices in foreign security markets. For example, they can trade options and futures on the Nikkei stock index of 225 stocks traded on the Tokyo stock exchange, or on FTSE (Financial Times Share Exchange) indexes of U.K. and European stocks.

**Table 25.9   Sampling of Emerging Country Funds**

| Closed-End Funds | | Closed-End Funds | |
| --- | --- | --- | --- |
| Fund Name | Symbol | Fund Name | Symbol |
| **Europe/Middle East** | | **Pacific/Asia** | |
| First Israel | ISL | India Fund | IFN |
| Turkish Inv. | TKF | Jardine Fleming China | JFC |
| **Latin America** | | Korea | KF |
| Brazil | BZF | Malaysia | MF |
| Chile | CH | Scudder New Asia | SAF |
| Latin Amer. Eqty. | LAQ | Taiwan | TWN |
| Mexico | MXF | Thai | TTF |
| **Pacific/Asia** | | **Global** | |
| Asia Pacific | APB | Emerging Markets Tele. | ETF |
| China | CHN | Morgan Stanley EmMkFd | MSF |
| First Philippine | FPF | Templeton Emerging | EMF |

| Open-End Funds | |
| --- | --- |
| Fund Name | Assets (millions) |
| Fidelity Emerging Markets | $  333 |
| Merrill Developing Cap. Market | 87 |
| Merrill Latin Amer. Developing Cap. | 130 |
| Montgomery Emerging Mkt. | 151 |
| Morgan Stanley Dean Witter EM | 785 |
| Scudder Emerging Market Income | 127 |
| Templeton Dev. Mkts. | 1,400 |
| Vanguard Int'l Index: Emerging | 985 |

Source: *The Wall Street Journal*, July 5, 2002.

**Risk and Return: Summary Statistics**     Table 25.10 presents annualized average returns and standard deviations in U.S. dollars and in local currency from monthly returns over the period 1997–2001. Developed countries appear in panel A and emerging markets in panel B. We use this table to develop insights into the risk and reward in international investing. The equity markets in both panels of Table 25.10 are ordered by standard deviation.

**Are Investments in Emerging Markets Riskier?**     In Figure 25.3, countries in both developed and emerging markets are ordered from low to high standard deviation. The standard deviations of investments in emerging markets are charted over those in developed countries. The graphs clearly show that investment in emerging markets is largely riskier than in developed countries, at least as measured by total volatility of returns. Still, you can find emerging markets that appear safer than some developed countries.

**Are Average Returns in Emerging Markets Greater?**     Figure 25.4 repeats the previous exercise for average returns. The graphs show that investing in emerging markets generally provided lower returns than investing in developed countries. Of course these data are far from conclusive since 5-year averages are subject to considerable imprecision. The fact that a number of markets averaged a negative rate of return is proof positive that

## Table 25.10   Risk and Return across the Globe, 1997–2001

| Country | % Per Annum in U.S. Dollars | | % Per Annum in Local Currency | |
| --- | --- | --- | --- | --- |
| | Average | Standard Dev. | Average | Standard Dev. |
| **A. Developed Countries** | | | | |
| U.K. | 5.97 | 15.24 | 9.39 | 16.23 |
| Belgium | 5.36 | 17.98 | 12.42 | 17.58 |
| Austria | −3.09 | 18.41 | 4.00 | 18.32 |
| U.S. | 11.98 | 18.78 | 11.98 | 18.78 |
| Denmark | 8.30 | 19.38 | 15.62 | 21.04 |
| Netherlands | 6.84 | 19.55 | 14.34 | 20.87 |
| Switzerland | 8.74 | 19.86 | 13.31 | 21.05 |
| Ireland | 10.73 | 20.16 | 19.21 | 21.73 |
| Germany | 5.55 | 20.43 | 13.13 | 22.49 |
| Australia | 4.86 | 20.74 | 12.42 | 13.01 |
| France | 11.45 | 21.36 | 18.84 | 22.81 |
| Canada | 10.08 | 22.41 | 12.51 | 19.37 |
| Spain | 8.38 | 24.20 | 15.94 | 25.20 |
| Italy | 12.30 | 24.50 | 20.02 | 26.47 |
| New Zealand | −3.17 | 24.51 | 5.99 | 17.65 |
| Norway | 1.57 | 25.61 | 7.80 | 23.34 |
| Portugal | 6.51 | 25.63 | 14.12 | 26.10 |
| Japan | −3.96 | 25.96 | −2.84 | 19.68 |
| Israel | 15.37 | 28.13 | 20.98 | 26.04 |
| Sweden | 9.25 | 29.10 | 17.45 | 27.61 |
| Singapore | −2.47 | 32.86 | 1.98 | 29.26 |
| Hong Kong | 3.01 | 33.34 | 3.17 | 33.32 |
| Taiwan | 2.89 | 38.28 | 6.67 | 35.41 |
| Greece | 20.50 | 39.70 | 28.83 | 40.64 |
| Finland | 29.99 | 42.09 | 38.10 | 43.33 |
| **B. Emerging Markets** | | | | |
| Peru | −5.61 | 23.15 | −0.36 | 21.74 |
| Chile | 0.39 | 23.85 | 8.64 | 20.89 |
| China | 8.23 | 25.37 | 8.17 | 25.37 |
| Colombia | −15.96 | 29.67 | −0.66 | 27.81 |
| Czech Rep. | 0.54 | 32.66 | 4.60 | 28.71 |
| Mexico | 13.44 | 33.65 | 14.76 | 28.49 |
| India | 4.36 | 33.78 | 9.93 | 32.75 |
| South Africa | −0.33 | 34.06 | 16.77 | 28.22 |
| Argentina | −0.47 | 34.08 | −0.41 | 34.29 |
| Poland | 2.78 | 40.83 | 7.17 | 35.88 |
| Hungary | 10.45 | 41.29 | 20.76 | 40.73 |
| Venezuela | −9.81 | 41.90 | −1.10 | 41.14 |
| Philippines | −20.63 | 41.91 | −9.81 | 34.76 |
| Brazil | 6.09 | 42.40 | 19.38 | 34.91 |
| Malaysia | −4.25 | 51.37 | 0.49 | 43.70 |
| Korea | 18.56 | 56.85 | 22.84 | 49.30 |
| Thailand | −11.92 | 57.27 | −3.08 | 54.66 |
| Russia | 29.23 | 61.25 | 29.23 | 61.25 |
| Turkey | 29.43 | 73.54 | 81.40 | 73.56 |
| Indonesia | −1.67 | 86.11 | −2.41 | 47.37 |

**Figure 25.3
Annualized
standard deviation
of investments
across the globe,
1997–2001**

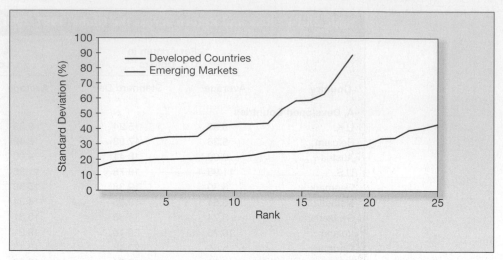

Countries in developed and emerging markets are ranked from low to high standard deviation.

**Figure 25.4
Annualized
average return
of investments
across the globe,
1997–2001**

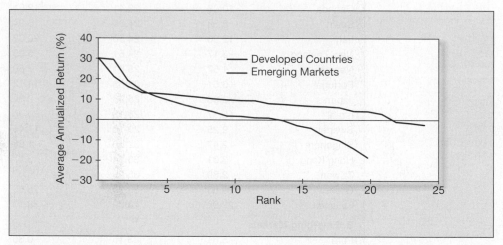

Countries in developed and emerging markets are ranked from high to low average return.

expectations were not realized over the period and hence these data are inadequate for risk-return analysis. But regardless of these qualifications, we should not even expect any clear relationship since the higher standard deviation of emerging market equities is not an adequate measure of risk. In the context of a diversified international portfolio, the risk of any single market is measured by its covariance with the overall portfolio. Assessment of the proportion of systematic risk in country portfolios can be gleaned from the correlation matrix that we will examine shortly. First, though, we inquire about the role of exchange rate risk in overall country risk.

**Is Exchange Rate
Risk Important in
International
Portfolios?**

Table 25.3 revealed that changes in exchange rates are not highly correlated across countries. This feature suggests that when international portfolios are well diversified, the exchange rate component of overall risk will be effectively diminished. Another feature that would render exchange rate risk diversifiable is low correlation between changes in exchange rates and country stock returns in local currencies.

## Low-Cost Foreign Index Funds Called WEBS Eliminate Some of the Guesswork and Costs of Investing Abroad

WEBS, an acronym for World Equity Benchmark Shares, represents an investment in a portfolio of publicly traded foreign stocks in a selected country. Each WEBS Index Series seeks to generate investment results that generally correspond to the price and yield performance of a specific Morgan Stanley Capital International (MSCI) index.

You sell these shares rather than redeeming them, but there the similarity to closed-end country funds ends. WEBS are equity securities, not mutual funds. WEBS shares trade continuously on a secondary market, the Amex, during regular Amex trading hours, like any other publicly traded U.S. stock listed on the exchange. In contrast, mutual fund shares do not trade in the secondary market, and are normally bought and sold from the issuing mutual fund at prices determined only at the end of the day. The new funds create and redeem shares in large blocks as needed, thus preventing the big premiums or discounts to net asset value typical of closed-end country funds. As index portfolios, WEBS are passively managed, so their expenses run much lower than for current open- or closed-end country funds.

WEBS shares offer U.S. investors portfolio exposure to country-specific equity markets, in a single, listed security you can easily buy, sell, or short on the Amex. Unlike American Depository Receipts (ADRs) that give you an investment in just one company, WEBS shares enable you to gain exposure to a broad portfolio of a desired foreign country's stocks. You gain exposure in the country or countries of your choice without the complications usually associated with buying, owning, or monitoring direct investments in foreign countries. You also have the conveniences of trading on a major U.S. exchange and dealing in U.S. dollars.

Some investors may prefer the active management, diversity, and flexibility of open-end international equity index funds as a way to limit currency and political risks of investing in foreign markets. As conventional open-end funds, however, the international funds are sometimes forced by net redemptions to sell stocks at inopportune times, which can be a particular problem in foreign markets with highly volatile stocks.

You pay brokerage commissions on the purchase and sale of WEBS, but since their portfolios are passively managed, their management and administrative fees are relatively low and they eliminate most of the transaction charges typical of managed funds.

### Foreign Index Baskets

| WEBS | Ticker Symbol | WEBS | Ticker Symbol |
|------|---------------|------|---------------|
| Australia | EWA | Malaysia | EWM |
| Austria | EWO | Mexico | EWW |
| Belgium | EWK | Netherlands | EWN |
| Canada | EWC | Singapore | EWS |
| France | EWQ | Spain | EWP |
| Germany | EWG | Sweden | EWD |
| Hong Kong | EWH | Switzerland | EWL |
| Italy | EWI | U.K. | EWU |
| Japan | EWJ | | |

Sources: Modified from *The Outlook*, May 22, 1996, and Amex website, www.amex.com/indexshares/index_shares_webs.stm, February 2000.

In Figure 25.5, all 45 stock markets are ordered from low to high standard deviation of returns in U.S. dollars. The figure contrasts the graph of standard deviation of returns in local currency with that of returns in U.S. dollars. The graphs are quite close in most cases, reinforcing the notion that hedging exchange rate risk is not crucial in well-diversified international portfolios.

## Benefits from International Diversification

Table 25.11 presents correlations between returns on stock and long-term bond portfolios in various countries. Panel A shows correlation of returns in U.S. dollars, that is, returns to a U.S. investor when currency risk is not hedged. Panel B shows correlation of returns in local currencies, that is, returns to a U.S. investor when the exchange risk is hedged. As noted earlier, the correlation coefficients of the hedged (local currency) and unhedged (U.S. dollars) returns are very similar, confirming that hedging currencies is not a significant issue in diversifying internationally.

**Figure 25.5
Standard
deviation of
investments
across the globe
in U.S. dollars vs.
local currency,
1997–2001**

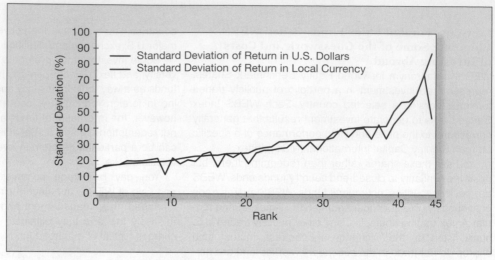

Countries ranked from low to high standard deviation of returns in U.S. dollars.

The correlation coefficients between a stock index of one country and bond portfolios of another are very low, suggesting that income portfolios that are balanced between stocks and bonds would greatly benefit from international diversification. The correlation among unhedged stock portfolios of the countries in Table 25.11A is much larger, in the range of .45 (Japan–Germany) to .89 (France–Germany). These correlation coefficients are much larger than conventional wisdom; they suggest that cross-border correlation of stock indexes has been increasing. For another, independent example, Table 25.12 shows the correlation of various country indexes with U.S. stocks using monthly excess returns over the period 1970–1989, next to correlation coefficients estimated over 1996–2001. The marked increase in correlation with 17 stock indexes and the world portfolio is uniform.

These results raise the question of whether the increase in correlation is an artifact of the sample period or a result of globalization and increased capital market integration that would be expected to increase cross-border correlation. While there is no question that a 5-year sample period is quite short and limits precision, the fact that we find the increase in correlation across the board suggests that globalization and market integration are the more plausible cause, as discussed in the box on page 925.

The observed high correlation across markets calls into question the common claim of large diversification benefits from international investing. This conventional wisdom is depicted in Figure 25.6, which is based on data for the period 1961–1975. Figure 25.6 suggests that international diversification can reduce the standard deviation of a domestic portfolio by as much as half (from about 27% of the standard deviation of a single stock to about 12%). This improvement may well be exaggerated if correlation across markets has markedly increased, as data from recent years suggest. Still, benefits from international diversification are significant, as we will show shortly. But first it is well to dispose of a misleading, yet widespread, representation of benefits from diversification.

**Misleading
Representation of
Diversification Benefits**     The baseline technique for constructing efficient portfolios is the efficient frontier. A useful efficient frontier is constructed from *expected* returns and an estimate of the covariance matrix of returns. This frontier combined with cash assets generates the capital allocation line, the set of efficient complete portfolios, as elaborated in Chapter 7. The benefit from this efficient diversification is reflected in the curvature of the efficient frontier. Other things equal, the lower the covariance

## Table 25.11   Correlations for Asset Returns; Unhedged and Hedged Currencies

### A. Correlation of Monthly Asset Return 1997–2001 in $U.S. (unhedged currencies)

| Asset/Country | Stocks | | | | | | | Bonds | | | | | | |
|---|---|---|---|---|---|---|---|---|---|---|---|---|---|---|
| | U.S. | Germany | U.K. | Japan | Australia | Canada | France | U.S. | Germany | U.K. | Japan | Australia | Canada | France |
| **Stocks** | | | | | | | | | | | | | | |
| U.S. | 1.00 | | | | | | | | | | | | | |
| Germany | 0.75 | 1.00 | | | | | | | | | | | | |
| U.K. | 0.83 | 0.80 | 1.00 | | | | | | | | | | | |
| Japan | 0.58 | 0.45 | 0.57 | 1.00 | | | | | | | | | | |
| Australia | 0.71 | 0.62 | 0.73 | 0.60 | 1.00 | | | | | | | | | |
| Canada | 0.82 | 0.74 | 0.73 | 0.52 | 0.67 | 1.00 | | | | | | | | |
| France | 0.70 | 0.89 | 0.82 | 0.49 | 0.57 | 0.70 | 1.00 | | | | | | | |
| **Bonds** | | | | | | | | | | | | | | |
| U.S. Treas. | 0.09 | 0.17 | 0.08 | 0.00 | −0.11 | 0.11 | 0.08 | 1.00 | | | | | | |
| Germany | 0.00 | 0.06 | −0.03 | −0.25 | −0.19 | −0.01 | −0.02 | 0.77 | 1.00 | | | | | |
| U.K. | 0.11 | 0.17 | 0.13 | −0.07 | −0.08 | 0.00 | 0.06 | 0.83 | 0.76 | 1.00 | | | | |
| Japan | 0.02 | 0.09 | 0.12 | −0.04 | −0.06 | 0.04 | 0.02 | 0.80 | 0.57 | 0.72 | 1.00 | | | |
| Australia | 0.00 | 0.12 | 0.04 | −0.01 | −0.08 | 0.15 | −0.01 | 0.88 | 0.70 | 0.71 | 0.71 | 1.00 | | |
| Canada | 0.00 | 0.08 | 0.00 | −0.03 | −0.05 | 0.12 | −0.03 | 0.88 | 0.75 | 0.65 | 0.64 | 0.90 | 1.00 | |
| France | −0.06 | 0.03 | −0.07 | −0.24 | −0.18 | −0.04 | −0.05 | 0.69 | 0.98 | 0.66 | 0.46 | 0.63 | 0.72 | 1.00 |

### B. Correlation of Monthly Asset Return 1997–2001 in Local Currency (hedged currencies)

| Asset/Country | Stocks | | | | | | | Bonds | | | | | | |
|---|---|---|---|---|---|---|---|---|---|---|---|---|---|---|
| | U.S. | Germany | U.K. | Japan | Australia | Canada | France | U.S. | Germany | U.K. | Japan | Australia | Canada | France |
| **Stocks** | | | | | | | | | | | | | | |
| U.S. | 1.00 | | | | | | | | | | | | | |
| Germany | 0.78 | 1.00 | | | | | | | | | | | | |
| U.K. | 0.83 | 0.78 | 1.00 | | | | | | | | | | | |
| Japan | 0.55 | 0.51 | 0.46 | 1.00 | | | | | | | | | | |
| Australia | 0.72 | 0.60 | 0.73 | 0.47 | 1.00 | | | | | | | | | |
| Canada | 0.80 | 0.75 | 0.77 | 0.47 | 0.66 | 1.00 | | | | | | | | |
| France | 0.75 | 0.90 | 0.82 | 0.51 | 0.56 | 0.74 | 1.00 | | | | | | | |
| **Bonds** | | | | | | | | | | | | | | |
| U.S. | 0.09 | 0.22 | 0.06 | 0.05 | −0.03 | 0.12 | 0.13 | 1.00 | | | | | | |
| Germany | −0.02 | 0.11 | −0.01 | −0.19 | −0.08 | 0.01 | 0.03 | 0.82 | 1.00 | | | | | |
| U.K. | 0.13 | 0.18 | 0.12 | −0.07 | 0.02 | 0.05 | 0.10 | 0.85 | 0.79 | 1.00 | | | | |
| Japan | 0.06 | 0.18 | 0.12 | −0.01 | −0.02 | 0.06 | 0.11 | 0.82 | 0.66 | 0.78 | 1.00 | | | |
| Australia | 0.05 | 0.19 | 0.06 | −0.01 | 0.04 | 0.16 | 0.10 | 0.92 | 0.81 | 0.77 | 0.77 | 1.00 | | |
| Canada | 0.02 | 0.12 | 0.01 | −0.03 | 0.01 | 0.11 | 0.04 | 0.89 | 0.85 | 0.71 | 0.67 | 0.95 | 1.00 | |
| France | −0.05 | 0.08 | −0.05 | −0.20 | −0.09 | 0.00 | 0.00 | 0.76 | 0.98 | 0.70 | 0.57 | 0.76 | 0.83 | 1.00 |

**Table 25.12   Correlation of U.S. Equity Returns with Country Equity Returns**

| | Sample Period (monthly excess returns in $U.S.) | |
| --- | --- | --- |
| | 1967–2001* | 1970–1989† |
| World | 0.95 | 0.86 |
| United Kingdom | 0.83 | 0.49 |
| Canada | 0.82 | 0.72 |
| Germany | 0.75 | 0.33 |
| Sweden | 0.73 | 0.38 |
| Netherlands | 0.71 | 0.56 |
| Australia | 0.71 | 0.47 |
| France | 0.70 | 0.42 |
| Denmark | 0.67 | 0.33 |
| Hong Kong | 0.67 | 0.29 |
| Spain | 0.65 | 0.25 |
| Switzerland | 0.65 | 0.49 |
| Norway | 0.63 | 0.44 |
| Japan | 0.58 | 0.27 |
| Italy | 0.55 | 0.22 |
| Austria | 0.46 | 0.12 |
| Belgium | 0.46 | 0.41 |

*Source: Datastream.
†Source: Campbell R. Harvey, "The World Price of Covariance Risk," *Journal of Finance,* March 1991.

**Figure 25.6 International diversification. Portfolio standard deviation as a percent of the average standard deviation of a one-stock portfolio**

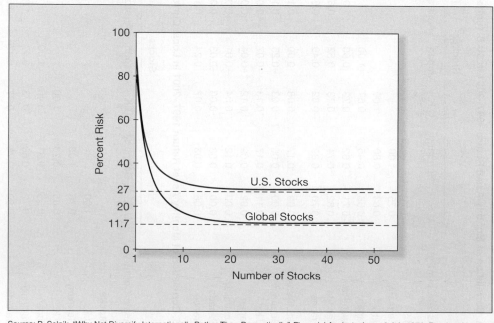

Source: B. Solnik, "Why Not Diversify Internationally Rather Than Domestically," *Financial Analysts Journal,* July 1976. Reprinted by permission.

# DANCING IN STEP

Individual stock markets are increasingly being driven by global rather than local factors. But why do national markets not have minds of their own? They did have once.

Traditionally, one way that investors sought to reduce risk was by diversifying overseas: when American shares slumped, the loss there would be offset by a gain in, say, European shares. That, at any rate, was the theory. In recent years, however, stock markets seem to have moved more closely in step with one another. The correlation between changes in American and European share prices has risen from 0.4 in the mid-1990s to 0.8 last year.

The health of a market's home economy may matter less than it used to for a number of reasons. First, the scrapping of controls on capital (combined with more efficient trading systems) has increased cross-border trading of shares, creating something closer to a global equity market. Second, it has become increasingly common for big companies to be listed on more than one market. Third, as a result of the wave of cross-border mergers and acquisitions, overseas profits account for a bigger slice of many companies' overall profits—high-tech firms are especially global in their reach. And finally, the Internet has made it easier for investors to get information on foreign firms. So firms in the same industry, but in different economies, are valued on a similar basis.

By breaking down movements in share prices into global effects, country-specific effects, and firm-specific effects, a new study by economists at the IMF tries to find out what percentage of a stock's performance is due to global rather than country factors. The model distinguishes between two kinds of global factors: the global business cycle and global-industry effects, which similarly influence firms in the same sector but in different countries.

The study finds that there has indeed been a big increase in the importance of global factors—of both kinds—in explaining movements in share prices since the mid-1990s.

across stocks, the greater the curvature of the efficient frontier and the greater the risk reduction for any desired *expected* return. So far, so good. But suppose we replace *expected* returns with *realized* average returns from a sample period to construct an efficient frontier; what is the possible use of this graph?

The ex post efficient frontier (derived from realized returns) describes the portfolio of only one investor—the clairvoyant who actually expected the precise averages of realized returns on all assets and estimated a covariance matrix that materialized, precisely, in the actual realizations of the sample period returns on all assets. Obviously, we are talking about a slim to empty set of investors. For all other, less than clairvoyant investors, such a frontier may have value only for purposes of performance evaluation.

In the world of volatile stocks, some stocks are bound to realize large, *unexpected* average returns. This will be reflected in ex post efficient frontiers of enormous "potential." They will, however, suggest exaggerated diversification benefits. Such (elusive) potential was enumerated in Chapter 24 on performance evaluation. It has no meaning as a tool to discuss the potential for future investments for real-life investors.

## Realistic Benefits from International Diversification

While recent realized returns can be highly misleading estimates of expected future returns, they are more useful for measuring prospective risk. There are two compelling reasons for this. First, market efficiency (or even near efficiency) implies that stock prices will be impossible to predict with any accuracy, but no such implication applies to risk measures. Second, it is a statistical fact that errors in estimates of standard deviation and correlation from realized data are of a lower order of magnitude than estimates of expected returns. For these reasons, using risk estimates from realized returns does not exaggerate as much the potential benefits from diversification.

**Figure 25.7
Ex post efficient
frontier of
country
portfolios,
1997–2001**

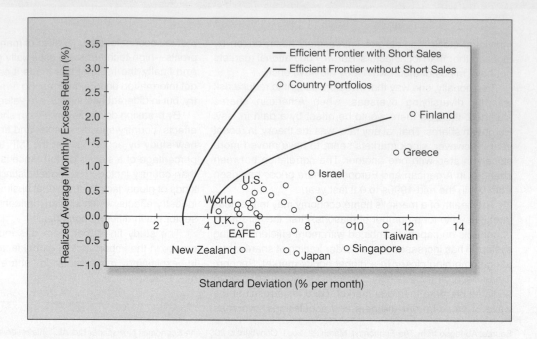

Figure 25.7 shows the efficient frontier using realized average monthly returns on the stock indexes of the 25 developed countries, with and without short sales. Even when the (ex post) efficient frontier is constrained to preclude short sales, it greatly exaggerates the benefits from diversification. Unfortunately, such misleading efficient frontiers are presented in many articles and texts on the benefits of diversification.

A more reasonable description of diversification is achievable only when we input reasonable equilibrium expected returns. Absent superior information, such expected returns are best based on appropriate risk measures of the assets. The capital asset pricing model (CAPM) suggests using the beta of the stock against the world portfolio. To generate expected excess returns (over the risk-free rate) for all assets, we specify the expected excess return on the world portfolio. We obtain the expected excess return on each asset by multiplying the beta of the asset by the world portfolio expected excess return. This procedure presupposes that the world portfolio will lie on the efficient frontier, at the point of tangency with the world capital market line. The curvature of the efficient frontier will not be affected by the estimate of the world portfolio excess return. A higher estimate will shift the curve upward. The capital market line will have a steeper slope.

We perform this procedure with risk measures estimated from actual returns and further impose the likely applicable constraint on short sales. We use the betas to compute the expected return on individual markets, assuming the expected excess return on the world portfolio is .6% per month. This is a larger excess return than the average realized over the period 1996–2001, but is in line with the average return over the previous 50 years. Varying this estimate would not qualitatively affect the results shown in Figure 25.8 (which is drawn on the same scale as Figure 25.7). The figure shows a realistic assessment that reveals modest but significant benefits from international diversification using only developed markets. Incorporating emerging markets would slightly increase these benefits.

**Figure 25.8
Efficient
frontier of
country portfolios
(world expected
excess return =
.6% per month)**

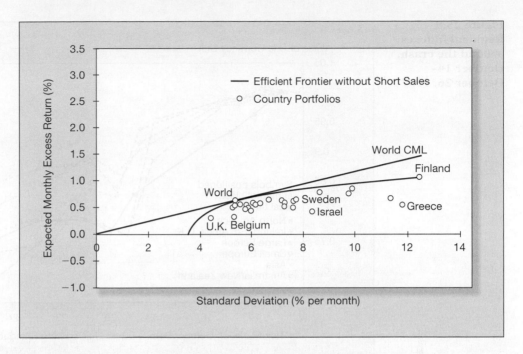

Are Benefits from
**International
Diversification
Preserved in
Bear Markets?**

Some studies[4] suggest that correlation in country portfolio returns increases during periods of turbulence in capital markets. If so, benefits from diversification would be lost exactly when they are needed the most. For example, a study by Roll[5] of the crash of October 1987 shows that all 23 country indexes studied declined over the crash period of October 12–26. This correlation is reflected in the movements of regional indexes depicted in Figure 25.9. Roll found that the beta of a country index on the world index (estimated prior to the crash) was the best predictor of that index's response to the October crash of the U.S. stock market. This suggests a common factor underlying the movement of stocks around the world. This model predicts that a macroeconomic shock would affect all countries and that diversification can only mitigate country-specific events. Our best guess is that the diversification benefits shown by the world CAPM model are realistic.

## 25.4    INTERNATIONAL INVESTING AND PERFORMANCE ATTRIBUTION

The benefits from international diversification may be modest for passive investors but for active managers international investing offers greater opportunities. International investing calls for specialization in additional fields of analysis: currency, country and worldwide industry, as well as a greater universe for stock selection.

---

[4] F. Longin and B. Solnik, "Is the Correlation in International Equity Returns Constant: 1960–1990?" *Journal of International Money and Finance* 14 (1995), pp. 3–26; and Eric Jacquier and Alan Marcus, "Asset Allocation Models and Market Volatility," *Financial Analysts Journal* 57 (March/April 2001), pp. 16–30.

[5] Richard Roll, "The International Crash of October 1987," *Financial Analysts Journal,* September/October 1988.

**Figure 25.9
Regional indexes
around the crash,
October 14–
October 26, 1987**

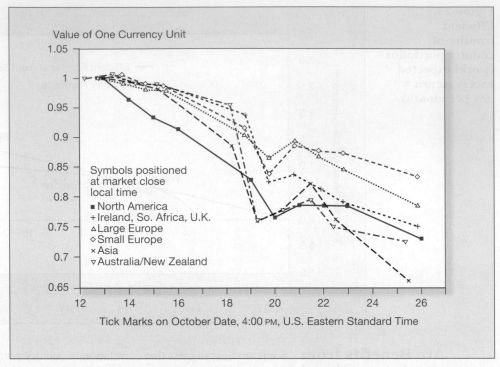

**Constructing a
Benchmark Portfolio
of Foreign Assets**

Active international investing, as well as passive, requires a benchmark portfolio (the bogey). One widely used index of non-U.S. stocks is the **European, Australian, Far East (EAFE) index** computed by Morgan Stanley Capital International. Additional indexes of world equity performance are published by Morgan Stanley Capital International Indices, Salomon Brothers, Credit Suisse First Boston, and Goldman Sachs. Portfolios designed to mirror or even replicate the country, currency, and company representation of these indexes would be the obvious generalization of the purely domestic passive equity strategy.

An issue that sometimes arises in the international context is the appropriateness of market-capitalization weighting schemes in the construction of international indexes. Capitalization weighting is far and away the most common approach. However, some argue that it might not be the best weighting scheme in an international context. This is in part because different countries have differing proportions of their corporate sector organized as publicly traded firms.

Table 25.13 shows 1996 and 2001 data for market capitalization weights versus GDP for countries in the EAFE index. As in Table 25.13, these data reveal substantial disparities between the relative sizes of market capitalization and GDP. Since market capitalization is a stock figure (the value of equity at one point in time), while GDP is a flow figure (production of goods and services during the entire year), we expect capitalization to be more volatile and the relative shares to be more variable over time. Some discrepancies are persistent, however. For example, the U.K.'s share of capitalization is about double its share of GDP, while Germany's share of capitalization is much less than its share of GDP. These disparities indicate that a greater proportion of economic activity is conducted by publicly traded firms in the U.K. than in Germany. Table 25.13 also illustrates the influence of stock market volatility on market-capitalization weighting schemes. For example, as its stock

## Table 25.13   Weighting Schemes for EAFE Countries

| | 2001 | | 1996 | |
| Country | % of EAFE Market Capitalization | % of EAFE GDP | % of EAFE Market Capitalization | of EAFE % GDP |
| --- | --- | --- | --- | --- |
| Japan | 25.8 | 31.0 | 43.5 | 31.5 |
| United Kingdom | 19.6 | 10.6 | 15.5 | 8.0 |
| Germany | 7.9 | 13.8 | 6.3 | 16.0 |
| France | 9.8 | 9.8 | 5.6 | 10.4 |
| Netherlands | 5.0 | 2.8 | 4.4 | 2.8 |
| Switzerland | 5.5 | 1.8 | 3.9 | 2.0 |
| Hong Kong | 4.7 | 1.2 | 3.8 | 1.0 |
| Australia | 3.2 | 2.7 | 2.8 | 2.7 |
| Italy | 5.0 | 8.1 | 2.7 | 8.3 |
| Taiwan | 1.7 | 2.1 | 2.0 | 1.9 |
| Spain | 2.9 | 4.3 | 1.9 | 4.1 |
| Sweden | 1.9 | 1.6 | 1.8 | 1.8 |
| Singapore | 1.0 | 0.6 | 1.7 | 0.6 |
| Belgium | 1.2 | 1.7 | 1.1 | 1.8 |
| Denmark | 0.8 | 1.2 | 0.6 | 1.2 |
| Finland | 1.4 | 0.9 | 0.5 | 0.9 |
| Norway | 0.6 | 1.2 | 0.4 | 1.1 |
| New Zealand | 0.2 | 0.4 | 0.4 | 0.4 |
| Ireland | 0.7 | 0.8 | 0.3 | 0.5 |
| Austria | 0.2 | 1.4 | 0.3 | 1.5 |
| Portugal | 0.4 | 0.8 | 0.3 | 0.8 |
| Greece | 0.5 | 0.9 | 0.2 | 0.8 |
| Luxemburg | 0.2 | 0.1 | 0.1 | 0.1 |

Source: Datastream.

market swooned in the 1990s, Japan's share of EAFE capitalization declined from 44%, more than its share of GDP in 1996 to 26%, below its share of GDP in 2001.

Some argue that it would be more appropriate to weight international indexes by GDP rather than market capitalization. The justification for this view is that an internationally diversified portfolio should purchase shares in proportion to the broad asset base of each country, and GDP might be a better measure of the importance of a country in the international economy than the value of its outstanding stocks. Others have even suggested weights proportional to the import share of various countries. The argument is that investors who wish to hedge the price of imported goods might choose to hold securities in foreign firms in proportion to the goods imported from those countries. The box on the next page considers the question of global asset allocation for investors seeking effective international diversification.

**Performance Attribution**   We can measure the contribution of each of these factors following a manner similar to the performance attribution techniques introduced in Chapter 24.

1. **Currency selection** measures the contribution to total portfolio performance attributable to exchange rate fluctuations relative to the investor's benchmark

# INTERNATIONAL INVESTING RAISES QUESTIONS

As Yogi Berra might say, the problem with international investing is that it's so darn foreign.

Currency swings? Hedging? International diversification? What's that?

Here are answers to five questions that I'm often asked:

- Foreign stocks account for some 60% of world stock market value, so shouldn't you have 60% of your stock market money overseas?

The main reason to invest abroad isn't to replicate the global market or to boost returns. Instead, "what we're trying to do by adding foreign stocks is to reduce volatility," explains Robert Ludwig, chief investment officer at money manager SEI Investments.

Foreign stocks don't move in sync with U.S. shares and, thus, they may provide offsetting gains when the U.S. market is falling. But to get the resulting risk reduction, you don't need anything like 60% of your money abroad.

- So, how much foreign exposure do you need to get decent diversification?

"Based on the volatility of foreign markets and the correlation between markets, we think an optimal portfolio is 70% in the U.S., 20% in developed foreign markets, and 10% in emerging markets," Mr. Ludwig says.

Even with a third of your stock market money in foreign issues, you may find that the risk-reduction benefits aren't all that reliable. Unfortunately, when U.S. stocks get really pounded, it seems foreign shares also tend to tumble.

- Can U.S. companies with global operations give you international diversification?

"When you look at these multinationals, the factor that drives their performance is their home market," says Mark Riepe, a vice president with Ibbotson Associates, a Chicago research firm.

How come? U.S. multinationals tend to be owned by U.S. investors, who will be swayed by the ups and downs of the U.S. market. In addition, Mr. Riepe notes that while multinationals may derive substantial profits and revenue abroad, most of their costs—especially labor costs—will be incurred in the U.S.

- Does international diversification come from the foreign stocks or the foreign currency?

"It comes from both in roughly equal pieces," Mr. Riepe says. "Those who choose to hedge their foreign currency raise the correlation with U.S. stocks, and so the diversification benefit won't be nearly as great."

Indeed, you may want to think twice before investing in a foreign-stock fund that frequently hedges its currency exposure in an effort to mute the impact of—and make money from—changes in foreign-exchange rates.

"The studies that we've done show that stock managers have hurt themselves more than they've helped themselves by actively managing currencies," Mr. Ludwig says.

- Should you divvy up your money among foreign countries depending on the size of each national stock market?

At issue is the nagging question of how much to put in Japan. If you replicated the market weightings of Morgan Stanley Capital International's Europe, Australasia and Far East index, you would currently have around a third of your overseas money in Japan.

That's the sort of weighting you find in international funds, which seek to track the performance of the EAFE or similar international indexes. Actively managed foreign-stock funds, by contrast, pay less attention to market weights and on average, these days have just 14% in Japan.

If your focus is risk reduction rather than performance, the index—and the funds that track it—are the clear winners. Japan performs quite unlike the U.S. market, so it provides good diversification for U.S. investors, says Tricia Rothschild, international editor at Morningstar Mutual Funds, a Chicago newsletter.

"But correlations aren't static," she adds. "There's always a problem with taking what happened over the past 20 years and projecting it out over the next 20 years."

currency, which we will take to be the U.S. dollar. We might use a benchmark like the EAFE index to compare a portfolio's currency selection for a particular period to a passive benchmark. EAFE currency selection would be computed as the weighted average of the currency appreciation of the currencies represented in the EAFE portfolio using as weights the fraction of the EAFE portfolio invested in each currency.

2. **Country selection** measures the contribution to performance attributable to investing in the better-performing stock markets of the world. It can be measured as the

## Table 25.14   Example of Performance Attribution: International

| | EAFE Weight | Return on Equity Index | Currency Appreciation $E_1/E_0 - 1$ | Manager's Weight | Manager's Return |
|---|---|---|---|---|---|
| Europe | 0.30 | 10% | 10% | 0.35 | 8% |
| Australia | 0.10 | 5 | −10 | 0.10 | 7 |
| Far East | 0.60 | 15 | 30 | 0.55 | 18 |

**Overall Performance (dollar return = return on index + currency appreciation)**

EAFE:      .30(10 + 10) + .10(5 − 10) + .60(15 + 30) = 32.5%

Manager:   .35(8 + 10) + .10(7 − 10) + .55(18 + 30) = 32.4%

Loss of .10% relative to EAFE

**Currency Selection**

EAFE:      (0.30 × 10%) + (0.10 × (−10%)) + (0.60 × 30%) = 20% appreciation

Manager:   (0.35 × 10%) + (0.10 × (−10%)) + (0.55 × 30%) = 19% appreciation

Loss of 1% relative to EAFE

**Country Selection**

EAFE:      (0.30 × 10%) + (0.10 × 5%) + (0.60 × 15%) = 12.5%

Manager:   (0.35 × 10%) + (0.10 × 5%) + (0.55 × 15%) = 12.25%

Loss of 0.25% relative to EAFE

**Stock Selection**

          (8% − 10%)0.35 + (7% − 5%)0.10 + (18% − 15%)0.55 = 1.15%

Contribution of 1.15% relative to EAFE

**Sum of Attributions (equal to overall performance)**

Currency (−1%) + country (−.25%) + selection (1.15%) = −.10%

---

weighted average of the equity *index* returns of each country using as weights the share of the manager's portfolio in each country. We use index returns to abstract from the effect of security selection within countries. To measure a manager's contribution relative to a passive strategy, we might compare country selection to the weighted average across countries of equity index returns using as weights the share of the EAFE portfolio in each country.

3. **Stock selection** ability may, as in Chapter 24, be measured as the weighted average of equity returns *in excess of the equity index* in each country. Here, we would use local currency returns and use as weights the investments in each country.

4. **Cash/bond selection** may be measured as the excess return derived from weighting bonds and bills differently from some benchmark weights.

Table 25.14 gives an example of how to measure the contribution of the decisions an international portfolio manager might make.

**CONCEPT CHECK☞ QUESTION 3**

Using the data in Table 25.14, compute the manager's country and currency selection if portfolio weights had been 40% in Europe, 20% in Australia, and 40% in the Far East.

## INTERNATIONAL PORTFOLIOS

This Excel model provides an efficient frontier analysis similar to that in Chapter 6. In Chapter 6 the frontier was based on individual securities, whereas this model examines the returns on international exchange traded funds and enables us to analyze the benefits of international diversification. Go to the Online Learning Center at **www.mhhe.com/bkm**.

| | A | B | C | D | E | F | G | H | I | J |
|---|---|---|---|---|---|---|---|---|---|---|
| 58 | | | Bordered Covariance Matrix for Target Return Portfolio | | | | | | | |
| 59 | | EWD | EWH | EWI | EWJ | EWL | EWP | EWW | SP 500 | |
| 60 | Weights | 0.00 | 0.00 | 0.08 | 0.38 | 0.02 | 0.00 | 0.00 | 0.52 | |
| 61 | 0.0000 | 0.00 | 0.00 | 0.00 | 0.00 | 0.00 | 0.00 | 0.00 | 0.00 | |
| 62 | 0.0000 | 0.00 | 0.00 | 0.00 | 0.00 | 0.00 | 0.00 | 0.00 | 0.00 | |
| 63 | 0.0826 | 0.00 | 0.00 | 4.63 | 3.21 | 0.55 | 0.00 | 0.00 | 7.69 | |
| 64 | 0.3805 | 0.00 | 0.00 | 3.21 | 98.41 | 1.82 | 0.00 | 0.00 | 53.79 | |
| 65 | 0.0171 | 0.00 | 0.00 | 0.55 | 1.82 | 0.14 | 0.00 | 0.00 | 2.09 | |
| 66 | 0.0000 | 0.00 | 0.00 | 0.00 | 0.00 | 0.00 | 0.00 | 0.00 | 0.00 | |
| 67 | 0.0000 | 0.00 | 0.00 | 0.00 | 0.00 | 0.00 | 0.00 | 0.00 | 0.00 | |
| 68 | 0.5198 | 0.00 | 0.00 | 7.69 | 53.79 | 2.09 | 0.00 | 0.00 | 79.90 | |
| 69 | 1.0000 | 0.00 | 0.00 | 16.07 | 157.23 | 4.59 | 0.00 | 0.00 | 143.47 | |
| 70 | | | | | | | | | | |
| 71 | Port Via | 321.36 | | | | | | | | |
| 72 | Port S.D. | 17.93 | | | | | | | | |
| 73 | Port Mean | 12.00 | | | | | | | | |
| 74 | | | | | | | | | | |
| 75 | | | | | | | | | | |
| 76 | | | | | Weights | | | | | |
| 77 | Mean | St. Dev | EWD | EWH | EWI | EWJ | EWL | EWP | EWW | SP 500 |
| 78 | 6 | 21.89 | 0.02 | 0.00 | 0.00 | 0.71 | 0.00 | 0.02 | 0.00 | 0.26 |
| 79 | 9 | 19.66 | 0.02 | 0.00 | 0.02 | 0.53 | 0.02 | 0.00 | 0.00 | 0.41 |
| 80 | 12 | 17.93 | 0.00 | 0.00 | 0.08 | 0.38 | 0.02 | 0.00 | 0.00 | 0.52 |
| 81 | 15 | 16.81 | 0.00 | 0.00 | 0.14 | 0.22 | 0.02 | 0.00 | 0.00 | 0.62 |
| 82 | 18 | 16.46 | 0.00 | 0.00 | 0.19 | 0.07 | 0.02 | 0.00 | 0.00 | 0.73 |
| 83 | 21 | 17.37 | 0.00 | 0.00 | 0.40 | 0.00 | 0.00 | 0.00 | 0.00 | 0.60 |
| 84 | 24 | 21.19 | 0.00 | 0.00 | 0.72 | 0.00 | 0.00 | 0.00 | 0.00 | 0.28 |
| 85 | 27 | 26.05 | 0.00 | 0.00 | 1.00 | 0.00 | 0.00 | 0.00 | 0.00 | 0.00 |
| 86 | | | | | | | | | | |
| 87 | | | | | | | | | | |

## SUMMARY

1. U.S. assets are only a part of the world portfolio. International capital markets offer important opportunities for portfolio diversification with enhanced risk–return characteristics.

2. Exchange rate risk imparts an extra source of uncertainty to investments denominated in foreign currencies. Much of that risk can be hedged in foreign exchange futures or forward markets, but a perfect hedge is not feasible unless the foreign currency rate of return is known.

3. Several world market indexes can form a basis for passive international investing. Active international management can be partitioned into currency selection, country selection, stock selection, and cash/bond selection.

## KEY TERMS

cash/bond selection
country selection
covered interest arbitrage
    relationship

currency selection
European, Australian,
    Far East (EAFE) index
exchange rate risk

interest rate parity
    relationship
political risk
stock selection

## WEBSITES

www.beginnersinvest.about.com/cs/globalinvesting
www.global-investor.com
www.numeraire.com

The sites above contain links to many facets of global investing. They also contain useful primers on international finance.

www.site-by-site.com

The Site-by-Site international portal and research center has extensive links to information on international investing.

www.adr.com
www.adrbny.com

Visit these sites for information on ADRs.

www.corporateinformation.com/memberhome.asp (research a country/region)
www.g7.utoronto.ca
www.imf.org
www.cm1.prusec.com/yardweb.nsf/Yardeni?readform

Obtain information about regions and economic issues at the above sites.

www.bloomberg.com/markets
www.oanda.com
www.cme.com/prd/fx
www.xe.com/ucc (Currency Converter)
www.x-rates.com

These sites provide information on foreign exchange.

www.census.gov/foreign-trade/www
www.ita.doc.gov/td/industry/otea
www.macalester.edu/research/economics/PAGE/HAVEMAN/Trade.Resources/
TradeData.html

Visit these sites to gather international trade and statistical data.

www.econ.pncbank.com/cra.htm
www.grai.com/links.htm
www.ambest.com/ratings/cr

These sites offer country risk analysis.

Visit us at www.mhhe.com/bkm

## PROBLEMS

1. You are a U.S. investor who purchased British securities for £2,000 one year ago when the British pound cost U.S.$1.50. What is your total return (based on U.S. dollars) if the value of the securities is now £2,400 and the pound is worth $1.75? No dividends or interest were paid during this period.
   a. 16.7%
   b. 20.0%
   c. 28.6%
   d. 40.0%

2. The correlation coefficient between the returns on a broad index of U.S. stocks and the returns on indexes of the stocks of other industrialized countries is mostly _____, and the correlation coefficient between the returns on various diversified portfolios of U.S. stocks is mostly _____.

   a. less than .8; greater than .8.
   b. greater than .8; less than .8.
   c. less than 0; greater than 0.
   d. greater than 0; less than 0.

3. An investor in the common stock of companies in a foreign country may wish to hedge against the _____ of the investor's home currency and can do so by _____ the foreign currency in the forward market.

   a. depreciation; selling.
   b. appreciation; purchasing.
   c. appreciation; selling.
   d. depreciation; purchasing.

4. Suppose a U.S. investor wishes to invest in a British firm currently selling for £40 per share. The investor has $10,000 to invest, and the current exchange rate is $2/£.

   a. How many shares can the investor purchase?
   b. Fill in the table below for rates of return after 1 year in each of the nine scenarios (three possible prices per share in pounds times three possible exchange rates).

| Price per Share (£) | Pound-Denominated Return (%) | Dollar-Denominated Return for Year-End Exchange Rate | | |
| --- | --- | --- | --- | --- |
| | | $1.80/£ | $2/£ | $2.20/£ |
| £35 | | | | |
| £40 | | | | |
| £45 | | | | |

   c. When is the dollar-denominated return equal to the pound-denominated return?

5. If each of the nine outcomes in problem 4 is equally likely, find the standard deviation of both the pound- and dollar-denominated rates of return.

6. Now suppose the investor in problem 4 also sells forward £5,000 at a forward exchange rate of $2.10/£.

   a. Recalculate the dollar-denominated returns for each scenario.
   b. What happens to the standard deviation of the dollar-denominated return? Compare it to both its old value and the standard deviation of the pound-denominated return.

7. Calculate the contribution to total performance from currency, country, and stock selection for the manager in the example below. All exchange rates are expressed as units of foreign currency that can be purchased with one U.S. dollar.

| | EAFE Weight | Return on Equity Index | $E_1/E_0$ | Manager's Weight | Manager's Return |
| --- | --- | --- | --- | --- | --- |
| Europe | 0.30 | 20% | 0.9 | 0.35 | 18% |
| Australia | 0.10 | 15 | 1.0 | 0.15 | 20 |
| Far East | 0.60 | 25 | 1.1 | 0.50 | 20 |

8. If the current exchange rate is $1.75/£, the 1-year forward exchange rate is $1.85/£, and the interest rate on British government bills is 8% per year, what risk-free dollar-denominated return can be locked in by investing in the British bills?

9. If you were to invest $10,000 in the British bills of problem 8, how would you lock in the dollar-denominated return?

10. John Irish, CFA, is an independent investment adviser who is assisting Alfred Darwin, the head of the Investment Committee of General Technology Corporation, to establish a new pension fund. Darwin asks Irish about international equities and whether the Investment Committee should consider them as an additional asset for the pension fund.

   *a.* Explain the rationale for including international equities in General's equity portfolio. Identify and describe three relevant considerations in formulating your answer.

   *b.* List three possible arguments against international equity investment and briefly discuss the significance of each.

   *c.* To illustrate several aspects of the performance of international securities over time, Irish shows Darwin the accompanying graph of investment results experienced by a U.S. pension fund in the recent past. Compare the performance of the U.S. dollar and non-U.S. dollar equity and fixed-income asset categories, and explain the significance of the result of the account performance index relative to the results of the four individual asset class indexes.

11. You are a U.S. investor considering purchase of one of the following securities. Assume that the currency risk of the Canadian government bond will be hedged, and the 6-month discount on Canadian dollar forward contracts is −.75% versus the U.S. dollar.

| Bond | Maturity | Coupon | Price |
| --- | --- | --- | --- |
| U.S. government | 6 months | 6.50% | 100.00 |
| Canadian government | 6 months | 7.50% | 100.00 |

Calculate the expected price change required in the Canadian government bond which would result in the two bonds having equal total returns in U.S. dollars over a 6-month horizon. Assume that the yield on the U.S. bond is expected to remain unchanged.

12. A global manager plans to invest $1 million in U.S. government cash equivalents for the next 90 days. However, she is also authorized to use non-U.S. government cash equivalents, as long as the currency risk is hedged to U.S. dollars using forward currency contracts.

 a. What rate of return will the manager earn if she invests in money market instruments in either Canada or Japan and hedges the dollar value of her investment? Use the data in the following tables.

 b. What must be the approximate value of the 90-day interest rate available on U.S. government securities?

| Interest Rates (APR) 90-Day Cash Equivalents | |
| --- | --- |
| Japanese government | 2.52% |
| Canadian government | 6.74% |

| Exchange Rates Dollars per Unit of Foreign Currency | | |
| --- | --- | --- |
| | Spot | 90-Day Forward |
| Japanese yen | .0119 | .0120 |
| Canadian dollar | .7284 | .7269 |

13. Suppose two all-equity-financed firms, ABC and XYZ, both have $100 million of equity outstanding. Each firm now issues $10 million of new stock and uses the proceeds to purchase the other's shares.

 a. What happens to the sum of the value of outstanding equity of the two firms?

 b. What happens to the value of the equity in these firms held by the noncorporate sector of the economy?

 c. Prepare the balance sheet for these two firms before and after the stock issues.

 d. If both of these firms were in the S&P 500, what would happen to their weights in the index?

14. After much research on the developing economy and capital markets of the country of Otunia, your firm, GAC, has decided to include an investment in the Otunia stock market in its Emerging Markets Commingled Fund. However, GAC has not yet decided whether to invest actively or by indexing. Your opinion on the active versus indexing decision has been solicited. The following is a summary of the research findings:

> Otunia's economy is fairly well diversified across agricultural and natural resources, manufacturing (both consumer and durable goods), and a growing finance sector. Transaction costs in securities markets are relatively large in Otunia because of high commissions and government "stamp taxes" on securities trades. Accounting standards and disclosure regulations are quite detailed, resulting in wide public availability of reliable information about companies' financial performance.
>
> Capital flows into and out of Otunia, and foreign ownership of Otunia securities is strictly regulated by an agency of the national government. The settlement procedures under these ownership rules often cause long delays in settling trades made by nonresidents. Senior finance officials in the government are working to deregulate capital flows and foreign ownership, but GAC's political consultant believes that isolationist sentiment may prevent much real progress in the short run.

 a. Briefly discuss aspects of the Otunia environment that favor investing actively, and aspects that favor indexing.

 b. Recommend whether GAC should invest in Otunia actively or by indexing. Justify your recommendation based on the factors identified in part (a).

**STANDARD &POOR'S**

Enter the Market Insight database at **www.mhhe.com/business/finance/edumarket insight** and link to Standard & Poor's main website by double clicking the *Standard & Poor's* logo in the upper left of the page. At the main page, top left, link to *Credit Rating Actions.* All recent credit rating actions are reported at this site for regions of the world, countries, and companies around the world. From the pull-down menu, select a country and review the recent rating changes. Want a credit rating for a specific country/company? Link to the *Credit Rating List,* then move through the pull-down menus.

**E-INVESTMENTS
International
Diversification**

Should U.S. investors hold foreign stocks? This question has been debated by investment advisers and investors alike. In theory, an investor should be able to reduce risk as long as the investments aren't perfectly correlated. In an article that was published by the Federal Reserve Bank of New York, Asani Sarkar and Kai Li investigated the benefits of international diversification. The article can be found on the bank's website at **www.newyorkfed.org**. Go to *Research,* then *Research Publications,* then *Staff Reports,* and find the report number 89 from 1999.

After reading this article, address the following questions:

What two measures did the authors use to examine the potential benefits of international diversification?

Compare the deletions of stock returns for G7 countries with emerging market countries. What should that imply about benefits of diversification? Were the benefits associated with diversification solely due to the ability to short sell? What is the potential impact of global market integration on diversification benefits?

How did the authors investigate the impact of global market integration?

**SOLUTIONS
TO CONCEPT
CHECKS**

1. $1 + r(\text{US}) = [1 + r_f(\text{UK})] \times (E_1/E_0)$

   *a.* $1 + r(\text{US}) = 1.1 \times 1.0 = 1.10$. Therefore, $r(\text{US}) = 10\%$.

   *b.* $1 + r(\text{US}) = 1.1 \times 1.1 = 1.21$. Therefore, $r(\text{US}) = 21\%$.

2. You must sell forward the number of pounds you will end up with at the end of the year. This value cannot be known with certainty, however, unless the rate of return of the pound-denominated investment is known.

   *a.* $10,000 \times 1.20 = 12,000$ pounds

   *b.* $10,000 \times 1.30 = 13,000$ pounds

3. *Country selection:*

$$(0.40 \times 10\%) + (0.20 \times 5\%) + (0.40 \times 15\%) = 11\%$$

This is a loss of 1.5% (11% versus 12.5%) relative to the EAFE passive benchmark.

*Currency selection:*

$$(0.40 \times 10\%) + (0.20 \times (-10\%)) + (0.40 \times 30\%) = 14\%$$

This is a loss of 6% (14% versus 20%) relative to the EAFE benchmark.

Visit us at www.mhhe.com/bkm

# THE PROCESS OF PORTFOLIO MANAGEMENT

Translating the aspirations and circumstances of diverse households into appropriate investment decisions is a daunting task. The task is equally difficult for institutions, most of which have many stakeholders and often are regulated by various authorities. The investment process is not easily reduced to a simple or mechanical algorithm.

While many principles of investments are quite general and apply to virtually all investors, some issues are peculiar to the specific investor. For example, tax bracket, age, risk tolerance, wealth, job prospects, and uncertainties make each investor's circumstances somewhat unique. In this chapter we focus on the process by which investors systematically review their particular objectives, constraints, and circumstances. Along the way, we survey some of the major classes of institutional investors and examine the special issues they must confront.

There is of course no unique "correct" investment process. However, some approaches are better than others, and it can be helpful to take one high-quality approach as a useful case study. For this reason, we will examine the systematic approach suggested by the Association for Investment Management and Research (AIMR). Among other things, the AIMR administers examinations to certify investment professionals as Chartered Financial Analysts. Therefore, the approach we outline is also one that a highly respected professional group endorses through the curriculum that it requires investment practitioners to master.

The basic framework involves dividing the investment process into four stages: specifying objectives, specifying constraints, formulating policy, and later monitoring and updating the portfolio as needed. We will treat each of these activities in turn. We start with a description of the major types of investors, both individual and institutional, as well as their special objectives. We turn next to the constraints or circumstances peculiar to each investor class, and we consider some of the investment policies that each can choose.

We will examine how the special circumstances of both individuals as well as institutions such as pension funds affect investment decisions. We also will see how the tax system can impart a substantial effect on investment decisions. In an Appendix, we present a spreadsheet model of the lifetime savings/investment decision that you can adapt to a wide variety of special circumstances as well as tax regimes.

## 26.1    MAKING INVESTMENT DECISIONS

The basic idea is to subdivide an investor's major steps (objectives, constraints, and policies) into concrete considerations of the various aspects, making the task of organization more tractable. The standard format appears in Table 26.1. In the next sections, we elaborate briefly (there is a lot more to be said than this text will allow) on the construction of the three parts of the investment process, along the lines of Table 26.1.

**Objectives**    Portfolio objectives center on the **risk–return trade-off** between the expected return the investors want (*return requirements* in the first column of Table 26.1) and how much risk they are willing to assume (*risk tolerance*). Investment managers must know the level of risk that can be tolerated in the pursuit of a higher expected rate of return. The nearby box is an illustration of a questionnaire designed to assess an investor's risk tolerance. Table 26.2 lists factors governing return requirements and risk attitudes for each of the seven major investor categories we will discuss.

### Table 26.1    Determination of Portfolio Policies

| Objectives | Constraints | Policies |
|---|---|---|
| Return requirements | Liquidity | Asset allocation |
| Risk tolerance | Horizon | Diversification |
| | Regulations | Risk positioning |
| | Taxes | Tax positioning |
| | Unique needs | Income generation |

# RISK TOLERANCE QUESTIONNAIRE

Here is an example of a short quiz used by financial institutions to help estimate risk tolerance.

| Question | 1 Point | 2 Points | 3 Points | 4 Points |
|---|---|---|---|---|
| 1. I plan on using the money I am investing: | Within 6 months. | Within the next 3 years. | Between 3 and 6 years. | No sooner than 7 years from now. |
| 2. My investments make up this share of assets (excluding home): | More than 75%. | 50% or more but less than 75%. | 25% or more but less than 50%. | Less than 25%. |
| 3. I expect my future income to: | Decrease. | Remain the same or grow slowly. | Grow faster than the rate of *inflation*. | Grow quickly. |
| 4. I have emergency savings: | No. | — | Yes, but less than I'd like to have. | Yes. |
| 5. I would risk this share in exchange for the same probability of doubling my money: | Zero. | 10%. | 25%. | 50%. |
| 6. I have invested in stocks and stock mutual funds: | — | Yes, but I was uneasy about it. | No, but I look forward to it. | Yes, and I was comfortable with it. |
| 7 My most important investment goal is to: | Preserve my original investment. | Receive some growth and provide income. | Grow faster than inflation but still provide some income. | Grow as fast as possible. Income is not important today. |

Add the number of points for all seven questions. Add one point if you choose the first answer, two if you choose the second answer, and so on. If you score between 25 and 28 points, consider yourself an *aggressive investor*. If you score between 20 and 24 points, your risk tolerance is above average. If you score between 15 and 19 points, consider yourself a *moderate investor*. This means you are willing to accept some risk in exchange for a potential higher rate of return. If you score fewer than 15 points, consider yourself a *conservative investor*. If you have fewer than 10 points, you may consider yourself a very conservative investor.

Source: Securities Industry Association, downloaded from **partners.financenter.com/businessweek/learn/guides/investbasic/invprofile.fcs**.

## Table 26.2    Matrix of Objectives

| Type of Investor | Return Requirement | Risk Tolerance |
|---|---|---|
| Individual and personal trusts | Life cycle (education, children, retirement) | Life cycle (younger are more risk tolerant) |
| Mutual funds | Variable | Variable |
| Pension funds | Assumed actuarial rate | Depends on proximity of payouts |
| Endowment funds | Determined by current income needs and need for asset growth to maintain real value | Generally conservative |
| Life insurance companies | Should exceed new money rate by sufficient margin to meet expenses and profit objectives; also actuarial rates important | Conservative |
| Non–life insurance companies | No minimum | Conservative |
| Banks | Interest spread | Variable |

**Individual Investors**   The basic factors affecting individual investor return requirements and risk tolerance are life-cycle stage and individual preferences. A middle-aged tenured professor will have a different set of needs and preferences than a retired widow, for example. We will have much more to say about individual investors later in this chapter.

**Personal Trusts**   **Personal trusts** are established when an individual confers legal title to property to another person or institution (the trustee) to manage that property for one or more beneficiaries. Beneficiaries customarily are divided into **income beneficiaries,** who receive the interest and dividend income from the trust during their lifetimes, and **remaindermen,** who receive the principal of the trust when the income beneficiary dies and the trust is dissolved. The trustee is usually a bank, a savings and loan association, a lawyer, or an investment professional. Investment of a trust is subject to trust laws, as well as "prudent investor" rules that limit the types of allowable trust investment to those that a prudent person would select.

Objectives for personal trusts normally are more limited in scope than those of the individual investor. Because of their fiduciary responsibility, personal trust managers typically are more risk averse than are individual investors. Certain asset classes such as options and futures contracts, for example, and strategies such as short-selling or buying on margin are ruled out.

**Mutual Funds**   Mutual funds are pools of investors' money. They invest in ways specified in their prospectuses and issue shares to investors entitling them to a pro rata portion of the income generated by the funds. The objectives of a mutual fund are spelled out in its prospectus. We discussed mutual funds in detail in Chapter 4.

**Pension Funds**   Pension fund objectives depend on the type of pension plan. There are two basic types: **defined contribution plans** and **defined benefit plans.** Defined contribution plans are in effect tax-deferred retirement savings accounts established by the firm in trust for its employees, with the employee bearing all the risk and receiving all the return from the plan's assets.

The largest pension funds, however, are defined benefit plans. In these plans the assets serve as collateral for the liabilities that the firm sponsoring the plan owes to plan beneficiaries. The liabilities are life annuities, earned during the employee's working years, that start at the plan participant's retirement. Thus it is the sponsoring firm's shareholders who bear the risk in a defined benefit pension plan. We discuss pension plans more fully later in this chapter.

**Endowment Funds**   **Endowment funds** are organizations chartered to use their money for specific nonprofit purposes. They are financed by gifts from one or more sponsors and are typically managed by educational, cultural, and charitable organizations or by independent foundations established solely to carry out the fund's specific purposes. Generally, the investment objectives of an endowment fund are to produce a steady flow of income subject to only a moderate degree of risk. Trustees of an endowment fund, however, can specify other objectives as dictated by the circumstances of the particular endowment fund.

**Life Insurance Companies**   Life insurance companies generally try to invest so as to hedge their liabilities, which are defined by the policies they write. Thus there are as many objectives as there are distinct types of policies. Until a decade or so ago there were only two types of life insurance policies available for individuals: whole-life and term.

A **whole-life insurance policy** combines a death benefit with a kind of savings plan that provides for a gradual buildup of cash value that the policyholder can withdraw at a later point in life, usually at age 65. **Term insurance,** on the other hand, provides death benefits only, with no buildup of cash value.

The interest rate that is embedded in the schedule of cash value accumulation promised under a whole-life policy is a fixed rate, and life insurance companies try to hedge this liability by investing in long-term bonds. Often the insured individual has the right to borrow at a prespecified fixed interest rate against the cash value of the policy.

During the inflationary years of the 1970s and early 1980s, when many older whole-life policies carried contractual borrowing rates as low as 4% or 5% per year, policyholders borrowed heavily against the cash value to invest in money market mutual funds paying double-digit yields. In response to these developments the insurance industry came up with two new policy types: **variable life** and **universal life.** Under a variable life policy the insured's premium buys a fixed death benefit plus a cash value that can be invested in a variety of mutual funds from which the policyholder can choose. With a universal life policy, policyholders can increase or reduce the premium or death benefit according to their needs. Furthermore, the interest rate on the cash value component changes with market interest rates. The great advantage of variable and universal life insurance policies is that earnings on the cash value are not taxed until the money is withdrawn.

**Non–Life Insurance Companies**   Non–life insurance companies such as property and casualty insurers have investable funds primarily because they pay claims *after* they collect policy premiums. Typically, they are conservative in their attitude toward risk. As with life insurers, non–life insurance companies can be either stock companies or mutual companies.

**Banks**   The defining characteristic of banks is that most of their investments are loans to businesses and consumers and most of their liabilities are accounts of depositors. As investors, the objective of banks is to try to match the risk of assets to liabilities while earning a profitable spread between the lending and borrowing rates.

## 26.2   CONSTRAINTS

Both individuals and institutional investors restrict their choice of investment assets. These restrictions arise from their specific circumstances. Identifying these restrictions/constraints will affect the choice of investment policy. Five common types of constraints are described below. Table 26.3 presents a matrix summarizing the main constraints in each category for each of the seven types of investors.

| Table 26.3   Matrix of Constraints | | | | |
| --- | --- | --- | --- | --- |
| **Type of Investor** | **Liquidity** | **Horizon** | **Regulations** | **Taxes** |
| Individuals and personal trusts | Variable | Life cycle | None | Variable |
| Mutual funds | High | Variable | Few | None |
| Pension funds | Young, low; mature, high | Long | ERISA | None |
| Endowment funds | Low | Long | Few | None |
| Life insurance companies | Low | Long | Complex | Yes |
| Non–life insurance companies | High | Short | Few | Yes |
| Banks | High | Short | Changing | Yes |

### Liquidity

**Liquidity** is the ease (and speed) with which an asset can be sold and still fetch a fair price. It is a relationship between the time dimension (how long will it take to dispose) and the price dimension (any discount from fair market price) of an investment asset.

When an actual concrete measure of liquidity is necessary, one thinks of the discount when an immediate sale is unavoidable. Cash and money market instruments such as Treasury bills and commercial paper, where the bid–asked spread is a fraction of 1%, are the most liquid assets, and real estate is among the least liquid. Office buildings and manufacturing structures can potentially experience a 50% liquidity discount.

Both individual and institutional investors must consider how likely they are to dispose of assets at short notice. From this likelihood, they establish the minimum level of liquid assets they want in the investment portfolio.

### Investment Horizon

This is the *planned* liquidation date of the investment or part of it. Examples of an individual **investment horizon** could be the time to fund a child's college education or the retirement date for a wage earner. For a university endowment, an investment horizon could relate to the time to fund a major campus construction project. Horizon needs to be considered when investors choose between assets of various maturities, such as bonds, which pay off at specified future dates. The nearby box discusses the interaction of investment horizon and investment risk.

### Regulations

Only professional and institutional investors are constrained by regulations. First and foremost is the **prudent investor rule.** That is, professional investors who manage other people's money have a fiduciary responsibility to restrict investment to assets that would have been approved by a prudent investor. The law is purposefully nonspecific. Every professional investor must stand ready to defend an investment policy in a court of law, and interpretation may differ according to the standards of the times.

Also, specific regulations apply to various institutional investors. For instance, U.S. mutual funds (institutions that pool individual investor money under professional management) may not hold more than 5% of the shares of any publicly traded corporation. This regulation keeps professional investors from getting involved in the actual management of corporations.

### Tax Considerations

Tax consequences are central to investment decisions. The performance of any investment strategy is measured by how much it yields after taxes. For household and institutional investors who face significant tax rates, tax sheltering and deferral of tax obligations may be pivotal in their investment strategy.

### Unique Needs

Virtually every investor faces special circumstances. Imagine husband-and-wife aeronautical engineers holding high-paying jobs in the same aerospace corporation. The entire human capital of that household is tied to a single player in a rather cyclical industry. This couple would need to hedge the risk of a deterioration of the economic well-being of the aerospace industry by investing in assets that will yield more if such deterioration materializes.

Similar issues would confront an executive on Wall Street who owns an apartment near work. Because the value of the home in that part of Manhattan probably depends on the vitality of the securities industry, the individual is doubly exposed to the vagaries of the stock

Conventional wisdom among investment professionals holds that the longer stock is held, the safer it is. For investors with long time horizons, such as young people saving for retirement, stocks are said to be a safe asset. The longer the time horizon the less likely is a shortfall—something that occurs if the value of a stock portfolio at the horizon date is less than what an investor would have received by investing in safe bonds, such as Treasury bonds, maturing on that same date. And history does suggest that the expected average compound return on stocks exceeds the risk-free rate of interest.

However, the probability of a shortfall is a flawed measure of risk because it ignores the severity of the financial loss should a shortfall occur. A measure that does account for both the likelihood and the severity of a potential shortfall is the price an investor would have to pay to insure against it. If stocks were indeed less risky in the long run, the cost of insuring against earning less than the risk-free rate of interest should decline as the length of the investment horizon increases. But reality is quite the opposite.

The structure of insurance against shortfall is effectively a put option with a maturity that is equal to the investment horizon and with a strike price that is set at the forward price of the underlying stock portfolio. The put price, representing the cost of insuring against a shortfall, increases as the investment horizon lengthens. This pattern is easily confirmed for maturities of up to three years by inspecting prices for exchange-traded puts on individual stocks and on broad stock-index portfolios. This is also true for proprietary pricing models that are used by investment and commercial banks to assess their own cost for longer-maturity puts that they sell over the counter.

What are the investment implications of this finding? What about the popular notion that young people should, because of their longer time horizon, put more money in stocks than the older investors?

Finance theory holds that there is no necessary relationship between an investor's age and the optimal proportion to invest in stocks. However, one important way of determining an investor's best asset allocation is the time and risk profile of his or her future labor income. The ratio of future labor income to other assets (such as retirement savings) is usually large when investors are young. It decreases as they approach retirement. If one's future labor income is relatively secure, it may be best to start out in the early years with a high proportion of an investment portfolio in stocks and reduce it over time as suggested by conventional wisdom. But, conventional wisdom may not apply to those who face substantial risk in their labor income—entrepreneurs or stock brokers, for example, whose income is highly sensitive to stock market risk. For such investors, their human capital already provides a large stock market exposure and the opposite policy may be best; that is, to start out with a relatively low fraction of the portfolio in stocks and increase it over time.

Source: Abridged from Zvi Bodie, "Long View Turns Out to Be Risky Business," *The Financial Times*, April 1, 2002. Copyright: The Financial Times Limited 1995–2002.

market. Because both job and home already depend on the fortunes of Wall Street, the purchase of a typical diversified stock portfolio would actually increase the exposure to the stock market.

These examples illustrate that the job is often the primary "investment" of an individual, and the unique risk profile that results from employment can play a big role in determining a suitable investment portfolio.

Other unique needs of individuals often center around their stage in the life cycle, as discussed below. Retirement, housing, and children's education constitute three major demands for funds, and investment policy will depend in part on the proximity of these expenditures.

Institutional investors also face unique needs. For example, pension funds will differ in their investment policy, depending on the average age of plan participants. Another example of a unique need for an institutional investor would be a university whose trustees allow the administration to use only cash income from the endowment fund. This constraint would translate into a preference for high-dividend-paying assets.

The box on the next page explores some of the issues that interact with an investor's particular situation. We turn next to an examination of the specific objectives and constraints of the major investor types.

# LOOKING TO LOWER YOUR RISK? JUST ADD MORE

If you're like a lot of investor these days, you're looking to make your portfolio "less risky."

The way to do that is by adding more risk, or at least more types of risk.

That strange twist—adding more to get less—is why risk is one of the hardest elements of investing to understand.

The first rule in risk is the hardest for many investors to accept: There is no such thing as a "risk-free investment."

Avoiding one form of risk means embracing another; the safest of investments generally come with the lowest returns, while the biggest potential gainers bring larger potential losses.

The primary risks in fund investing include the following.

**Market risk:** This is the big one, also known as principal risk, and it's the chance that downturn chews up your money.

**Purchasing power risk:** Sometimes called "inflation risk," this is the "risk of avoiding risk," and it's at the opposite end of the spectrum from market risk. In a nutshell, this is the possibility that you are too conservative and your money can't grow fast enough to keep pace with inflation.

**Interest-rate risk:** This is a key factor in the current environment of declining rates, where you face potential income declines when a bond or certificate of deposit matures and you need to reinvest the money.

Goosing returns using higher-yielding, longer-term securities creates the potential to get stuck losing ground to inflation if the rate trend changes again.

**Timing risk:** This is another highly individual factor, revolving around your personal time horizon. Simply put, the chance of stock mutual funds making money over the next 20 years is high; the prospects for the next 18 months are murky.

If you need money at a certain time, this risk must be factored into your asset allocation.

**Liquidity risk:** Another risk heightened by current tensions, it affects everything from junk bonds to foreign stocks. If world events were to alter the flow of money in credit markets or to close some foreign stock exchanges for an extended period, your holdings in those areas could be severely hurt.

**Political risk:** This is the prospect that government decisions will affect the value of your investments. Given the current environment, it is probably a factor in all forms of investing, whether you are looking at stocks or bonds.

**Societal risk:** Call this "world-event risk." It was evident when the first anthrax scares sent markets reeling briefly. Some businesses are more susceptible (airlines, for example), though virtually all types of investing have some concerns here.

Even after all of those risks, some investments face currency risk, credit risk, and more. Every type of risk deserves some consideration as you build your holdings.

Ultimately, by making sure that your portfolio addresses all types of risk—heavier on the ones you prefer and lighter on those that make you queasy—you ensure that no one type of risk can wipe you out.

That's something that a "less risky" portfolio may not be able to achieve.

Source: Abridged from Charles A. Jaffee's article of the same title, *Boston Sunday Globe,* October 21, 2001. BOSTON SUNDAY GLOBE ("GLOBE STAFF"/"CONTRIBUTING REPORTER" PRODUCED COPY ONLY) by CHARLES A. JAFFEE. Copyright 2001 by GLOBE NEWSPAPER CO (MA). Reproduced with permission of GLOBE NEWSPAPER CO (MA) in the format Textbook via Copyright Clearance Center.

## 26.3 ASSET ALLOCATION

Consideration of their objectives and constraints leads investors to a set of investment policies. The policies column in Table 26.1 lists the various dimensions of portfolio management policymaking—asset allocation, diversification, risk and tax positioning, and income generation. By far the most important part of policy determination is asset allocation, that is, deciding how much of the portfolio to invest in each major asset category.

We can view the process of asset allocation as consisting of the following steps:

1. Specify asset classes to be included in the portfolio. The major classes usually considered are the following:

    a. Money market instruments (usually called *cash*).
    b. Fixed-income securities (usually called *bonds*).
    c. Stocks.
    d. Real estate.
    e. Precious metals.
    f. Other.

| E-INVESTMENTS | Use the free Quicken Retirement Planner at **www.quicken.com/retirement/planner** to come up with a long-run asset allocation plan for yourself or for someone close to you. |
|---|---|
| **Asset Allocation Plans** | a. In the section entitled "Risk and Reward" choose the lowest target rate of return for which a recommended asset mix is provided. What asset mix corresponds to this rate of return? |
| | b. Now increase the expected rate of return and describe what happens to the asset mix. What asset class appears to be missing? |
| | c. If this asset class were added, how would your answers to (a) and (b) change? |

Institutional investors will rarely invest in more than the first four categories, whereas individual investors may include precious metals and other more exotic types of investments in their portfolios.

2. Specify capital market expectations. This step consists of using both historical data and economic analysis to determine your expectations of future rates of return over the relevant holding period on the assets to be considered for inclusion in the portfolio.

3. Derive the efficient portfolio frontier. This step consists of finding portfolios that achieve the maximum expected return for any given degree of risk.

4. Find the optimal asset mix. This step consists of selecting the efficient portfolio that best meets your risk and return objectives while satisfying the constraints you face.

## Policy Statements

Institutions such as pension plans and endowment funds are governed by boards that issue official statements of investment policy. These statements often provide information about the objectives and constraints of the investment fund. The following is an example of such a policy statement for a defined benefit pension plan.

> The plan should emphasize production of adequate levels of real return as its primary return objective, giving special attention to the inflation-related aspects of the plan. To the extent consistent with appropriate control of portfolio risk, investment action should seek to maintain or increase the surplus of plan assets relative to benefit liabilities over time. Five-year periods, updated annually, shall be employed in planning for investment decision making; the plan's actuary shall update the benefit liabilities breakdown by country every three years.
>
> The orientation of investment planning shall be long term in nature. In addition, minimal liquidity reserves shall be maintained so long as annual company funding contributions and investment income exceed annual benefit payments to retirees and the operating expenses of the plan. The plan's actuary shall update plan cash flow projections annually. Plan administration shall ensure compliance with all laws and regulations related to maintenance of the plan's tax-exempt status and with all requirements of the Employee Retirement Income Security Act (ERISA).

## Taxes and Asset Allocation

Until this point we have glossed over the issue of income taxes in discussing asset allocation. Of course, to the extent that you are a tax-exempt investor such as a pension fund, or if all of your investment portfolio is in a tax-sheltered account such as an individual retirement account (IRA), then taxes are irrelevant to your portfolio decisions.

But let us say that at least some of your investment income is subject to income taxes at the highest rate under current U.S. law. You are interested in the after-tax holding-period return (HPR) on your portfolio. At first glance it might appear to be a simple matter to figure out what the after-tax HPRs on stocks, bonds, and cash are if you know what they are before taxes. However, there are several complicating factors.

The first is the fact that you can choose between tax-exempt and taxable bonds. We discussed this issue in Chapter 2 and concluded there that you will choose to invest in tax-exempt bonds (i.e., municipal bonds) if your personal tax rate is such that the after-tax rate of interest on taxable bonds is less than the interest rate on "munis."

Because we are assuming that you are in the highest tax bracket, it is fair to assume that you will prefer to invest in munis for both the short maturities (cash) and the long maturities (bonds). As a practical matter, this means that cash for you will probably be a tax-exempt money market fund.

The second complication is not quite so easy to deal with. It arises from the fact that part of your HPR is in the form of a capital gain or loss. Under the current tax system you pay income taxes on a capital gain only if you *realize* it by selling the asset during the holding period. This applies to bonds as well as stocks, and it makes the after-tax HPR a function of whether the security will actually be sold at the end of the holding period. Sophisticated investors time the realization of their sales of securities to minimize their tax burden. This often calls for selling securities that are losing money at the end of the tax year and holding on to those that are making money.

Furthermore, because cash dividends on stocks are fully taxable and capital gains taxes can be deferred by not selling stocks that appreciate in value, the after-tax HPR on stocks will depend on the dividend payout policies of the corporations that issued the stock.

These tax complications make the process of portfolio selection for a taxable investor a lot harder than for the tax-exempt investor. There is a whole branch of the money management industry that deals with ways to defer or avoid paying taxes through special investment strategies. Unfortunately, many of these strategies conflict with the principles of efficient diversification.

We will discuss these and related issues in greater detail later in this chapter.

## 26.4    MANAGING PORTFOLIOS OF INDIVIDUAL INVESTORS

The overriding consideration in individual investor goal-setting is one's stage in the life cycle. Most young people start their adult lives with only one asset—their earning power. In this early stage of the life cycle an individual may not have much interest in investing in stocks and bonds. The needs for liquidity and preserving safety of principal dictate a conservative policy of putting savings in a bank or a money market fund. If and when a person gets married, the purchase of life and disability insurance will be required to protect the value of human capital.

When a married couple's labor income grows to the point at which insurance and housing needs are met, the couple may start to save for any children's college education and their own retirement, especially if the government provides tax incentives for retirement savings. Retirement savings typically constitute a family's first pool of investable funds. This is money that can be invested in stocks, bonds, and real estate (other than the primary home).

**Human Capital and Insurance**    The first significant investment decision for most individuals concerns education, building up their human capital. The major asset most people have during their early working years is the earning power that draws on their human capital. In these circumstances, the risk of illness or injury is far greater than the risk associated with financial wealth.

The most direct way of hedging human capital risk is to purchase insurance. Viewing the combination of your labor income and a disability insurance policy as a portfolio, the rate of return on this portfolio is less risky than the labor income by itself. Life insurance is a hedge against the complete loss of income as a result of death of any of the family's income earners.

### Investment in Residence

The first major economic asset many people acquire is their own house. Deciding to buy rather than rent a residence qualifies as an investment decision.

An important consideration in assessing the risk and return aspects of this investment is the value of a house as a hedge against two kinds of risk. The first kind is the risk of increases in rental rates. If you own a house, any increase in rental rates will increase the return on your investment.

The second kind of risk is that the particular house or apartment where you live may not always be available to you. By buying, you guarantee its availability.

### Saving for Retirement and the Assumption of Risk

People save and invest money to provide for future consumption and leave an estate. The primary aim of lifetime savings is to allow maintenance of the customary standard of living after retirement. As Figure 26.1 suggests, your retirement consumption depends on your life expectancy at that time. Life expectancy, when one makes it to retirement at age 65, approaches 85 years, so the average retiree needs to prepare a 20-year nest egg and sufficient savings to cover unexpected health-care costs. Investment income may also increase the welfare of one's heirs, favorite charity, or both.

The evidence in Table 26.4 supports the life-cycle view of investment behavior. Questionnaires suggest that attitudes shift away from risk tolerance and toward risk aversion as investors near retirement age. With age, individuals lose the potential to recover from a disastrous investment performance. When they are young, investors can respond to a loss by working harder and saving more of their income. But as retirement approaches, investors realize there will be less time to recover. Hence the shift to safe assets.

**Figure 26.1   Long life expectancy is a double-edged sword**

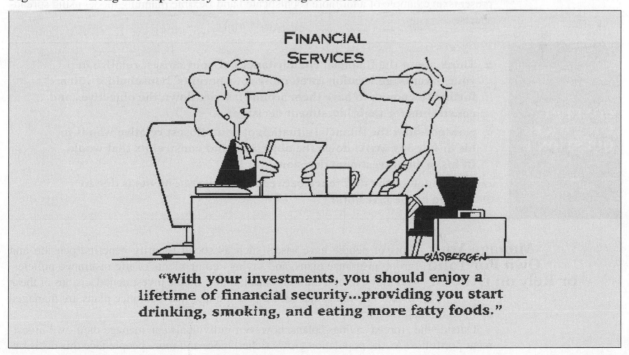

**Table 26.4   Amount of Risk Investors Said They Were Willing to Take (by Investor Age)**

|  | Under 35 | 35–54 | 55 and Over |
| --- | --- | --- | --- |
| No risk | 54% | 57% | 71% |
| A little risk | 30 | 30 | 21 |
| Some risk | 14 | 18 | 8 |
| A lot of risk | 2 | 1 | 1 |

Source: Market Facts, Inc., Chicago, IL.

**Retirement Planning Models**   In recent years, investment companies and financial advisory firms have created a variety of "user-friendly" interactive tools and models for retirement planning. Although they vary in detail, the essential structure behind most of them can be explained using The American Saving Education Council's "Ballpark Estimate" worksheet. The worksheet assumes you'll need 70% of current income, that you'll live to age 87, and you'll realize a constant real rate of return of 3% after inflation. For example, let's say Jane is a 35-year-old working woman with two children, earning $30,000 per year. Seventy percent of Jane's current annual income ($30,000) is $21,000. Jane would then subtract the income she expects to receive from Social Security ($12,000 in her case) from $21,000, equaling $9,000. This is how much Jane needs to make up for each retirement year. Jane expects to retire at age 65, so (using panel 3 of the worksheet) she multiplies $9,000 × 16.4 equaling $147,600. Jane has already saved $2,000 in her 401(k) plan. She plans to retire in 30 years so (from panel 4) she multiplies $2,000 × 2.4 equaling $4,800. She subtracts that from her total, making her projected total savings needed at retirement $142,800. Jane then multiplies $142,800 × .020 = $2,856 (panel 6). This is the amount Jane will need to save annually for her retirement. The appendix to this chapter presents an example of a far more sophisticated and flexible planning model using spreadsheets.

---

**CONCEPT CHECK☞ QUESTION 1**

*a.* **Think about the financial circumstances of your closest relative in your parents' generation (preferably your parents' household if you are fortunate enough to have them around). Write down the objectives and constraints for their investment decisions.**

*b.* **Now consider the financial situation of your closest relative who is in his or her 30s. Write down the objectives and constraints that would fit his or her investment decision.**

*c.* **How much of the difference between the two statements is due to the age of the investors?**

---

**Manage Your Own Portfolio or Rely on Others?**   Lots of people have assets such as social security benefits, pension and group insurance plans, and savings components of life insurance policies. Yet they exercise limited control, if any, on the investment decisions of these plans. The funds that secure pension and life insurance plans are managed by institutional investors.

Outside the "forced savings" plans, however, individuals can manage their own investment portfolios. As the population grows richer, more and more people face this decision.

## Sample of American Saving Education Council Worksheet

### BALLPARK E$TIMATE®

1. How much annual income will you want in retirement? (Figure 70% of your current annual income just to maintain your current standard of living. Really.)     **$ 21,000**

2. Subtract the income you expect to receive annually from:

   • Social Security

   If you make under $25,000, enter $8,000; between $25,000 – $40,000, enter $12,000; over $40,000, enter $14,500     **–$ 12,000**

   • Traditional Employer Pension—a plan that pays a set dollar amount for life, where the dollar amount depends on salary and years of service (in today's dollars)     –$ _____

   • Part-time income     –$ _____

   • Other     –$ _____

   **This is how much you need to make up for each retirement year**     **=$  9,000**

   Now you want a ballpark estimate of how much money you'll need in the bank the day you retire. So the accountants went to work and devised this simple formula. For the record, they figure you'll realize a constant real rate of return of 3% after inflation, you'll live to age 87, and you'll begin to receive income from Social Security at age 65.

3. To determine the amount you'll need to save, multiply the amount you need to make up by the factor below.     **$147.600**

   | Age you expect to retire: | | Your factor is: |
   |---|---|---|
   | | 55 | 21.0 |
   | | 60 | 18.9 |
   | | **65** | **16.4** |
   | | 70 | 13.6 |

4. If you expect to retire before age 65, multiply your Social Security benefit from line 2 by the factor below.     +$ _____

   | Age you expect to retire: | | Your factor is: |
   |---|---|---|
   | | 55 | 8.8 |
   | | 60 | 4.7 |

5. Multiply your savings to date by the factor below (include money accumulated in a 401(k), IRA, or similar retirement plan):     **–$  4,800**

   | If you want to retire in: | | Your factor is: |
   |---|---|---|
   | | 10 years | 1.3 |
   | | 15 years | 1.6 |
   | | 20 years | 1.8 |
   | | 25 years | 2.1 |
   | | **30 years** | **2.4** |
   | | 35 years | 2.8 |
   | | 40 years | 3.3 |

   **Total additional savings needed at retirement:**     **=$142,800**

6. To determine the ANNUAL amount you'll need to save, multiply the TOTAL amount by the factor below.     **$  2,856**

   | If you want to retire in : | | Your factor is: |
   |---|---|---|
   | | 10 yrs. | .085 |
   | | 15 yrs. | .052 |
   | | 20 yrs. | .036 |
   | | 25 yrs. | .027 |
   | | **30 yrs.** | **.020** |
   | | 35 yrs. | .016 |
   | | 40 yrs. | .013 |

This worksheet simplifies several retirement planning issues such as projected Social Security benefits and earnings assumptions on savings. It also reflects today's dollars; therefore you will need to re-calculate your retirement needs annually and as your salary and circumstances change. You may want to consider doing further analysis, either yourself using a more detailed worksheet or computer software or with the assistance of a financial professional.

Managing your own portfolio *appears* to be the lowest-cost solution. Conceptually, there is little difference between managing one's own investments and professional financial planning/investment management.

Against the fees and charges that financial planners and professional investment managers impose, you will want to offset the value of your time and energy expended on diligent portfolio management. People with a suitable background may even look at investment as recreation. Most of all, you must recognize the *potential* difference in investment results.

Besides the need to deliver better-performing investments, professional managers face two added difficulties. First, getting clients to communicate their objectives and constraints requires considerable skill. This is not a one-time task because objectives and constraints are forever changing. Second, the professional needs to articulate the financial plan and keep the client abreast of outcomes. Professional management of large portfolios is complicated further by the need to set up an efficient organization where decisions can be decentralized and information properly disseminated.

The task of life-cycle financial planning is a formidable one for most people. It is not surprising that a whole industry has sprung up to provide personal financial advice.

**Tax Sheltering**    In this section we explain three important tax sheltering options that can radically affect optimal asset allocation for individual investors. The first is the tax-deferral option, which arises from the fact that you do not have to pay tax on a capital gain until you choose to realize the gain. The second is tax-deferred retirement plans such as individual retirement accounts, and the third is tax-deferred annuities offered by life insurance companies. Not treated here at all is the possibility of investing in the tax-exempt instruments discussed in Chapter 2.

**The Tax-Deferral Option.**  A fundamental feature of the U.S. Internal Revenue Code is that tax on a capital gain on an asset is payable only when the asset is sold; this is its **tax-deferral option.** The investor therefore can control the timing of the tax payment. This conveys a benefit to stock investments.

To see this, compare IBM stock with an IBM bond. Suppose both offer an expected total return of 12%. The stock has a dividend yield of 4% and expected price appreciation of 8%, whereas the bond pays an interest rate of 12%. The bond investor must pay tax on the bond's interest in the year it is earned, whereas the stockholder pays tax only on the dividend and defers paying capital gains tax until the stock is sold.

Suppose one invests $1,000 for 5 years. Although in reality interest is taxed as ordinary income while capital gains and dividends are taxed at a rate of only 15% for most investors, to isolate the benefit of tax deferral, we will assume that all investment income is taxed at 15%. The bond will earn an after-tax return of 12% × (1 − .15) = 10.2%. The after-tax accumulation at the end of 5 years is

$$\$1,000 \times 1.102^5 = \$1,625.20$$

For the stock, the dividend yield after taxes is 4% × (1 − .15) = 3.4%. Because no taxes are paid on the 8% annual capital gain until Year 5, the before-tax accumulation will be

$$\$1,000 \times (1 + .034 + .08)^5 = 1,000(1.114)^5 = \$1,715.64$$

In Year 5, when the stock is sold, the (now-taxable) capital gain is

$$\$1,715.64 - \$1,000(1.034)^5 = 1,715.64 - 1,181.96 = \$533.68$$

Taxes due are $80.05, leaving $1,635.59, which is $10.39 more than the bond investment yields. Deferral of the capital gains tax allows the investment to compound at a faster rate until the tax is actually paid. Note that the more of one's total return that is in the form of price appreciation, the greater the value of the tax-deferral option.

**Tax-Deferred Retirement Plans.** Recent years have seen increased use of **tax-deferred retirement plans** in which investors can choose how to allocate assets. Such plans include IRAs, Keogh plans, and employer sponsored "tax-qualified" defined contribution plans. A feature they have in common is that contributions and earnings are not subject to federal income tax until the individual withdraws them as benefits.

Typically, an individual may have some investment in the form of such qualified retirement accounts and some in the form of ordinary taxable accounts. The basic investment principle that applies is to hold whatever bonds you want to hold in the retirement account while holding equities in the ordinary account. You maximize the tax advantage of the retirement account by holding it in the security that is the least tax advantaged.

To see this point, consider the following example. Suppose Eloise has $200,000 of wealth, $100,000 of it in a tax-qualified retirement account. She has decided to invest half of her wealth in bonds and half in stocks, so she allocates half of her retirement account and half of her nonretirement funds to each. She could reduce her tax bill with no change in before-tax returns simply by shifting her bonds into the retirement account and holding all her stocks outside the retirement account.

| **CONCEPT CHECK☞ QUESTION 2** | Suppose Eloise earns a 10% per year rate of interest on bonds and 15% per year on stocks, all in the form of price appreciation. In 5 years she will withdraw all her funds and spend them. By how much will she increase her final accumulation if she shifts all bonds into the retirement account and holds all stocks outside the retirement account? She is in a 28% tax bracket for ordinary income, and her capital gains income is taxed at 15%. |
|---|---|

**Deferred Annuities.** **Deferred annuities** are essentially tax-sheltered accounts offered by life insurance companies. They combine the same kind of deferral of taxes available on IRAs with the option of withdrawing one's funds in the form of a life annuity. Variable annuity contracts offer the additional advantage of mutual fund investing. One major difference between an IRA and a variable annuity contract is that whereas the amount one can contribute to an IRA is tax-deductible and extremely limited as to maximum amount, the amount one can contribute to a deferred annuity is unlimited, but not tax-deductible.

The defining characteristic of a life annuity is that its payments continue as long as the recipient is alive, although virtually all deferred annuity contracts have several withdrawal

| **E-INVESTMENTS Tax Deferral** | You will have several opportunities for tax-deferred savings/investing plans over your career. See the calculator example at **www.taxsavvyinvesting.com/wsp/wspDisplay.asp?DOCID=1344.**<br><br>The benefits of participating in these tax-deferred programs become very evident as your income and marginal tax bracket increase. How does tax deferral benefit the individual investor? What are the possible pitfalls? |
|---|---|

options, including a lump sum of cash paid out at any time. You need not worry about running out of money before you die. Like social security, therefore, life annuities offer longevity insurance and thus would seem to be an ideal asset for someone in the retirement years. Indeed, theory suggests that where there are no bequest motives, it would be optimal for people to invest heavily in actuarially fair life annuities.[1]

There are two types of life annuities, **fixed annuities** and **variable annuities.** A fixed annuity pays a fixed nominal sum of money per period (usually each month), whereas a variable annuity pays a periodic amount linked to the investment performance of some underlying portfolio.

In pricing annuities, insurance companies use **mortality tables** that show the probabilities that individuals of various ages will die within a year. These tables enable the insurer to compute with reasonable accuracy how many of a large number of people in a given age group will die in each future year. If it sells life annuities to a large group, the insurance company can estimate fairly accurately the amount of money it will have to pay in each future year to meet its obligations.

Variable annuities are structured so that the investment risk of the underlying asset portfolio is passed through to the recipient, much as shareholders bear the risk of a mutual fund. There are two stages in a variable annuity contract: an accumulation phase and a payout phase. During the *accumulation* phase, the investor contributes money periodically to one or more open-end mutual funds and accumulates shares. The second, or *payout*, stage usually starts at retirement, when the investor typically has several options, including the following:

1. Taking the market value of the shares in a lump sum payment.
2. Receiving a fixed annuity until death.
3. Receiving a variable amount of money each period that depends on the investment performance of the portfolio.

**Variable and Universal Life Insurance.** Variable life insurance is another tax-deferred investment vehicle offered by the life insurance industry. A variable life insurance policy combines life insurance with the tax-deferred annuities described earlier.

To invest in this product, you pay either a single premium or a series of premiums. In each case there is a stated death benefit, and the policyholder can allocate the money invested to several portfolios, which generally include a money market fund, a bond fund, and at least one common stock fund. The allocation can be changed at any time.

Variable life insurance policies offer a death benefit that is the greater of the stated face value or the market value of the investment base. In other words, the death benefit may rise with favorable investment performance, but it will not go below the guaranteed face value. Furthermore, the surviving beneficiary is not subject to income tax on the death benefit.

The policyholder can choose from a number of income options to convert the policy into a stream of income, either on surrender of the contract or as a partial withdrawal. In all cases income taxes are payable on the part of any distribution representing investment gains.

The insured can gain access to the investment without having to pay income tax by borrowing against the cash surrender value. Policy loans of up to 90% of the cash value are available at any time at a contractually specified interest rate.

---

[1] For an elaboration of this point see Laurence J. Kotlikoff and Avia Spivak, "The Family as an Incomplete Annuities Market," *Journal of Political Economy* 89 (April 1981).

A universal life insurance policy is similar to a variable life policy except that, instead of having a choice of portfolios to invest in, the policyholder earns a rate of interest that is set by the insurance company and changed periodically as market conditions change. The disadvantage of universal life insurance is that the company controls the rate of return to the policyholder, and, although companies may change the rate in response to competitive pressures, changes are not automatic. Different companies offer different rates, so it often pays to shop around for the best.

## 26.5    PENSION FUNDS

By far the most important institution in the retirement income system is the employer-sponsored pension plan. These plans vary in form and complexity, but they all share certain common elements in every country. In general, investment strategy depends on the type of plan.

Pension plans are defined by the terms specifying the "who," "when," and "how much," for both the plan benefits and the plan contributions used to pay for those benefits. The *pension fund* of the plan is the cumulation of assets created from contributions and the investment earnings on those contributions, less any payments of benefits from the fund. In the United States, contributions to the fund by either employer or employee are tax-deductible, and investment income of the fund is not taxed. Distributions from the fund, whether to the employer or the employee, are taxed as ordinary income. There are two "pure" types of pension plans: *defined contribution* and *defined benefit*.

**Defined Contribution Plans**    In a defined contribution plan, a formula specifies contributions but not benefit payments. Contribution rules usually are specified as a predetermined fraction of salary (e.g., the employer contributes 15% of the employee's annual wages to the plan), although that fraction need not be constant over the course of an employee's career. The pension fund consists of a set of individual investment accounts, one for each employee. Pension benefits are not specified, other than that at retirement the employee may apply that total accumulated value of contributions and earnings on those contributions to purchase an annuity. The employee often has some choice over both the level of contributions and the way the account is invested.

In principle, contributions could be invested in any security, although in practice most plans limit investment choices to bond, stock, and money market funds. The employee bears all the investment risk; the retirement account is, by definition, fully funded by the contributions, and the employer has no legal obligation beyond making its periodic contributions.

For defined contribution plans, investment policy is essentially the same as for a tax-qualified individual retirement account. Indeed, the main providers of investment products for these plans are the same institutions such as mutual funds and insurance companies that serve the general investment needs of individuals. Therefore, in a defined contribution plan much of the task of setting and achieving the income-replacement goal falls on the employee.

An employee is 45 years old. Her salary is $40,000 per year, and she has $100,000 accumulated in her self-directed defined contribution pension plan. Each year she contributes 5% of her salary to the plan, and her employer matches it with another 5%. She plans to retire at age 65. The plan offers a choice of two funds: a guaranteed return fund that pays a risk-free real interest rate of 3% per year and a stock index fund that has an expected real rate of return of 6% per year and a standard deviation of 20%. Her current asset mix in the plan is $50,000 in the guaranteed fund and $50,000 in the stock index fund. She plans to reinvest all investment earnings in each fund in that same fund and to allocate her annual contribution equally between the two funds. If her salary grows at the same rate as the cost of living, how much can she expect to have at retirement? How much can she be *sure* of having?

**Defined Benefit Plans**   In a defined benefit plan, a formula specifies benefits, but not the manner, including contributions, in which these benefits are funded. The benefit formula typically takes into account years of service for the employer and level of wages or salary (e.g., the employer pays the employee for life, beginning at age 65, a yearly amount equal to 1% of his final annual wage for each year of service). The employer (called the "plan sponsor") or an insurance company hired by the sponsor guarantees the benefits and thus absorbs the investment risk. The obligation of the plan sponsor to pay the promised benefits is like a long-term debt liability of the employer.

As measured both by number of plan participants and the value of total pension liabilities, the defined benefit form dominates in most countries around the world. This is so in the United States, although the trend since the mid-1970s is for sponsors to choose the defined contribution form when starting new plans. But the two plan types are not mutually exclusive. Many sponsors adopt defined benefit plans as their primary plan, in which participation is mandatory, and supplement them with voluntary defined contribution plans.

With defined benefit plans, there is an important distinction between the pension *plan* and the pension *fund*. The plan is the contractual arrangement setting out the rights and obligations of all parties; the fund is a separate pool of assets set aside to provide collateral for the promised benefits. In defined contribution plans, by definition, the value of the benefits equals that of the assets, so the plan is always fully funded. But in defined benefit plans, there is a continuum of possibilities. There may be no separate fund, in which case the plan is said to be unfunded. When there is a separate fund with assets worth less than the present value of the promised benefits, the plan is underfunded. And if the plan's assets have a market value that exceeds the present value of the plan's liabilities, it is said to be overfunded.

**Alternative Perspectives on Defined Benefit Pension Obligations**   As previously described, in a defined benefit plan, the pension benefit is determined by a formula that takes into account the employee's history of service and wages or salary. The plan sponsor provides this benefit regardless of the investment performance of the pension fund assets. The annuity promised to the employee is therefore the employer's liability. What is the nature of this liability?

There is a widespread belief that pension benefits in final-pay formula plans are protected against inflation at least up to the date of retirement. But this is a misperception. Unlike social security benefits, whose starting value is indexed to a general index of wages, pension benefits even in final-pay private-sector plans are "indexed" only to the extent that

(1) the employee continues to work for the same employer, (2) the employee's own wage or salary keeps pace with the general price index, and (3) the employer continues to maintain the same plan. Very few private corporations in the United States offer pension benefits that are automatically indexed for inflation; thus workers who change jobs wind up with lower pension benefits at retirement than otherwise identical workers who stay with the same employer, even if the employers have defined benefit plans with the same final-pay benefit formula. This is referred to as the *portability problem*.

Both the rule-making body of the accounting profession (the Financial Accounting Standards Board) and Congress have adopted the present value of the nominal benefits as the appropriate measure of a sponsor's pension liability. FASB Statement 87 specifies that the measure of corporate pension liabilities to be used on the corporate balance sheet in external reports is the accumulated benefit obligation (ABO)—that is, the present value of pension benefits owed to employees under the plan's benefit formula absent any salary projections and discounted at a nominal rate of interest. Similarly, in its Omnibus Budget Reconciliation Act (OBRA) of 1987, Congress defined the current liability as the measure of a corporation's pension liability and set limits on the amount of tax-qualified contributions a corporation could make as a proportion of the current liability. OBRA's definition of the current liability is essentially the same as FASB Statement 87's definition of the ABO.

The ABO is thus a key element in a pension fund's investment strategy. It affects a corporation's reported balance sheet liabilities; it also reflects economic reality.

Statement 87, however, recognizes an additional measure of a defined benefit plan's liability: the projected benefit obligation (PBO). The PBO is a measure of the sponsor's pension liability that includes projected increases in salary up to the expected age of retirement. Statement 87 requires corporations to use the PBO in computing pension expense reported in their income statements. This is perhaps useful for financial analysts, in that the amount may help them to derive an appropriate estimate of expected future labor costs for discounted cash flow valuation models of the firm as a going concern. The PBO is not, however, an appropriate measure of the benefits that the employer has explicitly guaranteed. The difference between the PBO and the ABO should not be treated as a liability of the firm, because these additional pension costs will be realized only if the employees continue to work in the future. If these future contingent labor costs are to be treated as a liability of the firm, then why not book the entire future wage bill as a liability? If this is done, then shouldn't one add as an asset the present value of future revenues generated by these labor activities? It is indeed difficult to see either the accounting or economic logic for using the PBO as a measure of pension liabilities.

| | |
|---|---|
| **CONCEPT CHECK ☞ QUESTION 4** | **An employee is 40 years old and has been working for the firm for 15 years. If normal retirement age is 65, the interest rate is 8%, and the employee's life expectancy is 80, what is the present value of the accrued pension benefit?** |

**Pension Investment Strategies**   The special tax status of pension funds creates the same incentive for both defined contribution and defined benefit plans to tilt their asset mix toward assets with the largest spread between pretax and after-tax rates of return. In a defined contribution plan, because the participant bears all the investment risk, the optimal asset mix also depends on the risk tolerance of the participant.

In defined benefit plans, optimal investment policy may be different because the sponsor absorbs the investment risk. If the sponsor has to share some of the upside potential of the pension assets with plan participants, there is an incentive to eliminate all investment risk by investing in securities that match the promised benefits. If, for example, the plan sponsor has to pay $100 per year for the next 5 years, it can provide this stream of benefit payments by buying a set of five zero-coupon bonds each with a face value of $100 and maturing sequentially. By so doing, the sponsor eliminates the risk of a shortfall. This is an example of **immunization** of the pension liability.

If a corporate pension fund has an ABO that exceeds the market value of its assets, FASB Statement 87 requires that the corporation recognize the unfunded liability on its balance sheet. If, however, the pension assets exceed the ABO, the corporation cannot include the surplus on its balance sheet. This asymmetric accounting treatment expresses a deeply held view about defined benefit pension funds. Representatives of organized labor, some politicians, and even a few pension professionals believe that the sponsoring corporation, as guarantor of the accumulated pension benefits, is liable for pension asset shortfalls but does not have a clear right to the entire surplus in case of pension overfunding.

If the pension fund is overfunded, then a 100% fixed-income portfolio is no longer required to minimize the cost of the corporate pension guarantee. Management can invest surplus pension assets in equities, provided it reduces the proportion so invested when the market value of pension assets comes close to the value of the ABO. Such an investment strategy, first introduced in Chapter 16, is known as *contingent immunization*.

**Investing in Equities.** If the only goal guiding corporate pension policy were shareholder wealth maximization, it is hard to understand why a financially sound pension sponsor would invest in equities at all. A policy of 100% bond investment would minimize the cost of guaranteeing the defined benefits.

In addition to the reasons given for a fully funded pension plan to invest only in fixed-income securities, there is a tax reason for doing so too. The tax advantage of a pension fund stems from the ability of the sponsor to earn the pretax interest rate on pension investments. To maximize the value of this tax shelter, it is necessary to invest entirely in assets offering the highest pretax interest rate. Because capital gains on stocks can be deferred and dividends are taxed at a lower rate than interest on bonds, corporate pension funds should invest entirely in taxable bonds and other fixed-income investments.

The nearby box discusses a British firm with just such an all-bond policy. Yet we know that in general pension funds invest from 40% to 60% of their portfolios in equity securities. Even a casual perusal of the practitioner literature suggests that they do so for a variety of reasons—some right and some wrong. There are three possible correct reasons.

The first is that corporate management views the pension plan as a trust for the employees and manages fund assets as if it were a defined contribution plan. It believes that a successful policy of investment in equities might allow it to pay extra benefits to employees and is therefore worth taking the risk.

The second possible correct reason is that management believes that through superior market timing and security selection it is possible to create value in excess of management fees and expenses. Many executives in nonfinancial corporations are used to creating value in excess of cost in their businesses. They assume that it can also be done in the area of portfolio management. Of course, if that is true, then one must ask why they do not do it on their corporate account rather than in the pension fund. That way they could have their tax shelter "cake" and eat it too. It is important to realize, however, that to accomplish this feat, the plan must beat the market, not merely match it.

Note that a very weak form of the efficient markets hypothesis would imply that management cannot create shareholder value simply by shifting the pension portfolio out of bonds and into stocks. Even when the entire pension surplus belongs to the shareholders, investing in stocks just moves the shareholders along the capital market line (the market trade-off between risk and return for passive investors) and does not create value. When the

# BOOTS INVESTS 100% IN BONDS

In magnificent defiance of the received wisdom, the Boots pension fund has sold all its equities and is now entirely invested in long-dated bonds, £2.3 billion of them. This matching of assets and liabilities is at odds with the behaviour of the vast majority of other UK pension funds. Boots' decision is sure to be controversial.

What makes Boots' action important to the rest of us is that its pension fund has a typical liability profile. While it is easy to grasp that the liabilities for pensioners can be hedged with bonds (and hence that equities are a gamble), what Boots has done explodes the myth that equities somehow hedge the liabilities for workers' pensions. These too are bond-like. Admittedly they stretch further into the future and have more of an inflation-linked component. It is self-evident that bond investment improves the security of members' pensions.

But what has never been clear is whether equity investment by a pension fund makes a jot of difference to the value of the business. Theorists contend that, from a shareholder's point of view, any investment that does not match each year's pension outgo is the same as trying to improve your household's finance by stopping your fire insurance. To be sure, your cashflow is better . . . that is, until your house burns down.

The Boots' trustees have set themselves a plain English objective: *"to ensure that the value of the fund's assets is always enough to pay all pensions, regardless of movements in financial markets."* Innocuous-sounding this may be, but few other trustees in the country aspire to such an objective. The costs of investing a pension fund are not small. Transaction costs, managers' fees and so on all add up. Boots reckons it has removed a whole layer, some £10 million a year. And operating a complex equity/bond portfolio soaks up company management time without, so the textbooks assert, adding a penny to shareholder value.

Boots' highly logical decision is a landmark event in UK pension fund investment. It confronts head-on the central challenge of investment—the management of risk. Boots has achieved a win/win: its employees' pensions are more secure, and its shareholders' risk has been reduced. And it has done this by focusing on what pension funds are there for—to provide pensions.

Source: John Shuttleworth, *Pensions*, Oct/Nov 2001, PricewaterhouseCoopers UK.

net cost of providing plan beneficiaries with shortfall risk insurance is taken into account, increasing the pension fund equity exposure reduces shareholder value unless the equity investment can put the firm above the capital market line. This implies that it makes sense for a pension fund to invest in equities only *if* it intends to pursue an active strategy of beating the market either through superior timing or security selection. A completely passive strategy will add no value to shareholders.

For an underfunded plan of a corporation in financial distress there is another possible reason for investing in stocks and other risky assets—federal pension insurance. Firms in financial distress have an incentive to invest pension fund money in the riskiest assets, just as troubled thrift institutions insured by the Federal Savings and Loan Insurance Corporation (FSLIC) in the 1980s had similar motivation with respect to their loan portfolios.

**Wrong Reasons to Invest in Equities.** The wrong reasons for a pension fund to invest in equities stem from interrelated fallacies. The first is the notion that stocks are not risky in the long run. This fallacy was discussed at length in Appendix C to Chapter 8. Another related fallacy is the notion that stocks are a hedge against inflation. The reasoning behind this fallacy is that stocks are an ownership claim over real physical capital. Real profits are either unaffected or enhanced when there is unanticipated inflation, so owners of real capital should not be hurt by it.

Let us assume that this proposition is true, and that the real rate of return on stocks is uncorrelated or slightly positively correlated with inflation. If stocks are to be a good hedge against inflation risk in the conventional sense, however, the nominal return on stocks has to be *highly* positively correlated with inflation. However, empirical studies show that stock returns have been negatively correlated with inflation in the past with a low $R^2$. Thus even in the best of circumstances, stocks can offer only a limited hedge against inflation risk.

## 26.6    FUTURE TRENDS IN PORTFOLIO MANAGEMENT

The last two decades of the 20th century saw enormous growth in the amount of money invested in mutual funds in the United States. The two major causes of this growth were the widespread introduction of tax-deferred retirement savings (401k) plans by employers and the dramatic rise in stock prices. But starting in the spring of 2000, a long decline in stock prices began.

What direction will portfolio management take in the future? While we do not have a crystal ball, we can make some predictions based on the theory of portfolio selection presented in earlier chapters of this text.[2] The websites of many financial service firms currently provide free interactive asset allocation models. In these models there are several asset classes—stocks, bonds, cash, and so forth—but none of them is risk-free. Our first prediction is that in the future, these interactive asset-allocation models will recognize that a new class of risk-free assets has come into existence—inflation-indexed bonds.

In 1998 the U.S. Treasury started issuing inflation-indexed savings bonds, called I-bonds. I-bonds have features that make them especially attractive to individual investors.[3] Among these features are the following:

- I-bonds are accrual-type bonds, so you receive all the interest and principal back when you redeem them.

- You pay income tax on I-bonds only when you redeem them.

- The Treasury guarantees a fixed schedule of inflation-adjusted redemption values on I-bonds, so that you always receive your principal plus accrued interest no matter when you cash them in.

- You pay no fees when buying or redeeming I-bonds at your local bank.

As individual investors become aware of the existence of I-bonds, they are sure to become a very popular investment vehicle, especially for the risk-averse investors seeking to avoid the risk of stocks.

Our second prediction is that there will be growth in "personal funds" as substitutes for mutual funds. The Internet has enabled firms to offer individual investors personalized funds that provide ease of use and broad diversification at a cost that is competitive with mutual funds.[4] Personal funds allow individuals to overcome some drawbacks of mutual funds, such as the following:

1. When you buy shares in a mutual fund you not only get a share of the fund's assets, you also get a share of the deferred tax liability on unrealized capital gains earned before you joined. Every time the fund manager realizes some of these gains by selling stock, you get hit with a tax bill on your share. Thus, you might get stuck paying taxes on "gains" that you never earned.

2. It's often hard to determine exactly what types of stocks a fund will invest in. Even when you know its past strategy, the fund manager can change direction. And managers come and go. If your fund manager leaves and you're stuck with an inferior replacement, you'll face taxes if you sell shares to invest elsewhere.

3. Fund holdings overlap. While you want diversification, you could wind up owning the same stocks in different mutual funds.

---

[2] This discussion is based on Zvi Bodie, "Life-Cycle Investing in Theory and Practice," *Financial Analysts Journal,* January/February 2003.

[3] The features of these bonds are explained at www.savingsbonds.gov/sav/sbifaq.htm.

[4] For example, visit www.netfolio.com, www.personalfund.com.

Personal funds can overcome these drawbacks without sacrificing the diversification benefits and ease of use that mutual funds provide.

A third prediction we feel confident in making is that the future will see many more "structured" investment products created by investment firms employing the technology of financial engineering.[5] Some of these already exist, such as products that offer a return tied to equity markets yet guarantee some minimum return. For example, Merrill Lynch offers a family of structured securities called "Market Index Target-Term Securities" (MITTS) tied to a variety of stock price indexes. At maturity the holder receives at least the principal amount. Such products have become common in both Europe and the United States.

## SUMMARY

1. When discussing the principles of portfolio management, it is useful to distinguish among seven classes of investors:

   a. Individual investors and personal trusts.
   b. Mutual funds.
   c. Pension funds.
   d. Endowment funds.
   e. Life insurance companies.
   f. Non–life insurance companies.
   g. Banks.

   In general, these groups have somewhat different investment objectives, constraints, and portfolio policies.

2. To some extent, most institutional investors seek to match the risk-and-return characteristics of their investment portfolios to the characteristics of their liabilities.

3. The process of asset allocation consists of the following steps:

   a. Specifying the asset classes to be included.
   b. Defining capital market expectations.
   c. Finding the efficient portfolio frontier.
   d. Determining the optimal mix.

4. People living on money-fixed incomes are vulnerable to inflation risk and may want to hedge against it. The effectiveness of an asset as an inflation hedge is related to its correlation with unanticipated inflation.

5. For investors who must pay taxes on their investment income, the process of asset allocation is complicated by the fact that they pay income taxes only on certain kinds of investment income. Interest income on munis is exempt from tax, and high-tax-bracket investors will prefer to hold them rather than short- and long-term taxable bonds. However, the really difficult part of the tax effect to deal with is the fact that capital gains are taxable only if realized through the sale of an asset during the holding period. Investment strategies designed to avoid taxes may contradict the principles of efficient diversification.

6. The life-cycle approach to the management of an individual's investment portfolio views the individual as passing through a series of stages, becoming more risk averse in later years. The rationale underlying this approach is that as we age, we use up our human capital and have less time remaining to recoup possible portfolio losses through increased labor supply.

7. People buy life and disability insurance during their prime earning years to hedge against the risk associated with loss of their human capital, that is, their future earning power.

---

[5] For example, see Zvi Bodie and Dwight B. Crane, "The Design and Production of New Retirement Saving Products," *Journal of Portfolio Management*, Winter 1999, pp. 77–82.

8. There are three ways to shelter investment income from federal income taxes besides investing in tax-exempt bonds. The first is by investing in assets whose returns take the form of appreciation in value, such as common stocks or real estate. As long as capital gains taxes are not paid until the asset is sold, the tax can be deferred indefinitely.

The second way of tax sheltering is through investing in tax-deferred retirement plans such as IRAs. The general investment rule is to hold the least tax-advantaged assets in the plan and the most tax-advantaged assets outside of it.

The third way of sheltering is to invest in the tax-advantaged products offered by the life insurance industry—tax-deferred annuities and variable and universal life insurance. They combine the flexibility of mutual fund investing with the tax advantages of tax deferral.

9. Pension plans are either defined contribution plans or defined benefit plans. Defined contribution plans are in effect retirement funds held in trust for the employee by the employer. The employees in such plans bear all the risk of the plan's assets and often have some choice in the allocation of those assets. Defined benefit plans give the employees a claim to a money-fixed annuity at retirement. The annuity level is determined by a formula that takes into account years of service and the employee's wage or salary history.

10. If the only goal guiding corporate pension policy were shareholder wealth maximization, it would be hard to understand why a financially sound pension sponsor would invest in equities at all. A policy of 100% bond investment would both maximize the tax advantage of funding the pension plan and minimize the costs of guaranteeing the defined benefits.

11. If sponsors viewed their pension liabilities as indexed for inflation, then the appropriate way for them to minimize the cost of providing benefit guarantees would be to hedge using securities whose returns are highly correlated with inflation. Common stocks would not be an appropriate hedge because they have a low correlation with inflation.

## KEY TERMS

| | | |
|---|---|---|
| risk–return trade-off | term insurance | tax-deferred retirement |
| personal trusts | variable life | plans |
| income beneficiaries | universal life | deferred annuities |
| remaindermen | liquidity | fixed annuities |
| defined contribution plans | investment horizon | variable annuities |
| defined benefit plans | prudent investor rule | mortality tables |
| endowment funds | tax-deferral option | immunization |
| whole-life insurance policy | | |

## WEBSITES

www.smartmoney.com/oneasset
www.asset-analysis.com
www.efficientfrontier.com
www.metlife.com/Applications/Corporate/WPS/CDA/PageGenerator/0,1674,P2599,00.html
cgi.money.cnn.com/tools/assetallocwizard/assetallocwizard.html
Visit these sites for information and models relating to asset allocation.

www.fee-only-advisor.com/book.cfm
Access the online book for issues related to individual investing, including discussions pertaining to portfolio allocation for individual investors.

**WEBSITES**

**Visit us at www.mhhe.com/bkm**

## PROBLEMS

CFA® PROBLEMS

1. Angus Walker, CFA, is reviewing the defined benefit pension plan of Acme Industries. Based in London, Acme has operations in North America, Japan, and several European countries. Next month, the retirement age for full benefits under the plan will be lowered from age 60 to age 55. The median age of Acme's workforce is 49 years. Walker is responsible for the pension plan's investment policy and strategic asset allocation decisions. The goals of the plan include achieving a minimum expected return of 8.4% with expected standard deviation no greater than 16.0%.

   Walker is evaluating the current asset allocation (Table 26A) and selected financial information for the company (Table 26B). There is an ongoing debate within Acme Industries about the pension plan's investment policy statement (IPS). Two investment policy statements under consideration are shown in Table 26C.

**Table 26A   Acme Pension Plan: Current Asset Allocation**

| | |
|---|---|
| International Equities (MSCI World, excluding U.K.) | 10% |
| U.K. bonds | 42 |
| U.K. small capitalization equities | 13 |
| U.K. large capitalization equities | 30 |
| Cash | 5 |

**Table 26B   Acme Industries Selected Financial Information (in millions)**

| | |
|---|---|
| Acme Industries total assets | £16,000 |
| Pension plan data: | |
| Plan assets | 6,040 |
| Plan liabilities | 9,850 |

**Table 26C   Investment Policy Statements**

|  | IPS X | IPS Y |
|---|---|---|
| **Return requirement** | Plan's objective is to outperform the relevant benchmark return by a substantial margin. | Plan's objective is to match the relevant benchmark return. |
| **Risk tolerance** | Plan has a high risk tolerance because of the long-term nature of the plan and its liabilities. | Plan has a low risk tolerance because of its limited ability to assume substantial risk. |
| **Time horizon** | Plan has a very long time horizon because of the plan's infinite life. | Plan has a shorter time horizon than in the past because of plan demographics. |
| **Liquidity** | Plan needs moderate level of liquidity to fund monthly benefit payments. | Plan has minimal liquidity needs. |

**Table 26D   Asset Allocations (in %)**

|  | Current | Graham | Michael |
|---|---|---|---|
| U.K. large capitalization equities | 30 | 20 | 40 |
| U.K. small capitalization equities | 13 | 8 | 20 |
| International equities (MSCI World ex-U.K.) | 10 | 10 | 18 |
| U.K. bonds | 42 | 52 | 17 |
| Cash | 5 | 10 | 5 |
| Total | 100 | 100 | 100 |
| Expected portfolio return (%) | 9.1 | 8.2 | 10.6 |
| Expected portfolio volatility (standard deviation in %) | 16.1 | 12.8 | 21.1 |

a. Determine, for each of the following components, whether IPS X or IPS Y has the appropriate language for the pension plan of Acme Industries. Justify each response with one reason.

　i. Return requirement

　ii. Risk tolerance

　iii. Time horizon

　iv. Liquidity

Note: Some components of IPS X may be appropriate, while other components of IPS Y may be appropriate.

b. To assist Walker, Acme has hired two pension consultants, Lucy Graham and Robert Michael. Graham believes that the pension fund must be invested to reflect a low risk tolerance, but Michael believes the pension fund must be invested to achieve the highest possible returns. The fund's current asset allocation and the allocations recommended by Graham and Michael are shown in Table 26D. Select which of the three asset allocations in Table 26D is most appropriate for Acme's pension plan. Explain how your selection meets each of the following objectives or constraints for the plan:

　i. Return requirement

　ii. Risk tolerance

　iii. Liquidity

2. Your client says, "With the unrealized gains in my portfolio, I have almost saved enough money for my daughter to go to college in 8 years, but educational costs keep going up." Based on this statement alone, which one of the following appears to be least important to your client's investment policy?

   a. Time horizon.
   b. Purchasing power risk.
   c. Liquidity.
   d. Taxes.

3. The aspect least likely to be included in the portfolio management process is

   a. Identifying an investor's objectives, constraints, and preferences.
   b. Organizing the management process itself.
   c. Implementing strategies regarding the choice of assets to be used.
   d. Monitoring market conditions, relative values, and investor circumstances.

4. Sam Short, CFA, has recently joined the investment management firm of Green, Spence, and Smith (GSS). For several years, GSS has worked for a broad array of clients, including employee benefit plans, wealthy individuals, and charitable organizations. Also, the firm expresses expertise in managing stocks, bonds, cash reserves, real estate, venture capital, and international securities. To date, the firm has not utilized a formal asset allocation process but instead has relied on the individual wishes of clients or the particular preferences of its portfolio managers. Short recommends to GSS management that a formal asset allocation process would be beneficial and emphasizes that a large part of a portfolio's ultimate return depends on asset allocation. He is asked to take his conviction an additional step by making a proposal to executive management.

   a. Recommend and justify an approach to asset allocation that could be used by GSS.
   b. Apply the approach to a middle-aged, wealthy individual characterized as a fairly conservative investor (sometimes referred to as a "guardian investor").

5. Jarvis University (JU) is a private, multiprogram U.S. university with a $2 billion endowment fund as of fiscal year-end May 31, 2002. With little government support, JU is heavily dependent on its endowment fund to support ongoing expenditures, especially because the university's enrollment growth and tuition revenue have not met expectations in recent years. The endowment fund must make a $126 million annual contribution, which is indexed to inflation to JU's general operating budget. The U.S. Consumer Price Index is expected to rise 2.5% annually and the U.S. higher education cost index is anticipated to rise 3% annually. The endowment has also budgeted $200 million due on January 31, 2003, representing the final payment for construction of a new main library.

   In a recent capital campaign, JU only met its fund-raising goal with the help of one very successful alumna, Valerie Bremner, who donated $400 million of Bertocchi Oil and Gas common stock at fiscal year-end May 31, 2002. Bertocchi Oil and Gas is a large-capitalization, publicly traded U.S. company. Bremner donated the stock on the condition that no more than 25% of the initial number of shares may be sold in any fiscal year. No substantial additional donations are expected in the future.

   Given the large contribution to and distributions from the endowment fund, the endowment fund's investment committee has decided to revise the fund's investment policy statement. The investment committee also recognizes that a revised asset allocation may be warranted. The asset allocation in place for the JU endowment fund as of May 31, 2002, is given in Table 26E.

| Table 26E    Jarvis University Endowment Fund Asset Allocation as of May 31, 2002 | | | | | |
|---|---|---|---|---|---|
| Asset | Current Allocation (millions) | Current Allocation Percentage | Current Yield | Expected Annual Return | Standard Deviation of Returns |
| U.S. money market bond fund | $    40 | 2% | 4.0% | 4.0% | 2.0% |
| Intermediate global bond fund | 60 | 3 | 5.0 | 5.0 | 9.0 |
| Global equity fund | 300 | 15 | 1.0 | 10.0 | 15.0 |
| Bertocchi Oil and Gas common stock | 400 | 20 | 0.1 | 15.0 | 25.0 |
| Direct real estate | 700 | 35 | 3.0 | 11.5 | 16.5 |
| Venture capital | 500 | 25 | 0.0 | 20.0 | 35.0 |
| TOTAL | $2,000 | 100% | | | |

a. Prepare the components of an appropriate investment policy statement for the Jarvis University endowment fund as of June 1, 2002, based only on the information given.

Note: Each component in your response must specifically address circumstances of the JU endowment fund.

b. Determine the most appropriate revised allocation percentage for each asset in Table 26E as of June 1, 2002. Justify each revised allocation percentage.

6. Susan Fairfax is president of Reston Industries, a U.S.-based company whose sales are entirely domestic and whose shares are listed on the New York Stock Exchange. The following are additional facts concerning her current situation:

Fairfax is single, aged 58. She has no immediate family, no debts, and does not own a residence. She is in excellent health and covered by Reston-paid health insurance that continues after her expected retirement at age 65.

Her base salary of $500,000/year, inflation-protected, is sufficient to support her present lifestyle but can no longer generate any excess for savings.

She has $2,000,000 of savings from prior years held in the form of short-term instruments.

Reston rewards key employees through a generous stock-bonus incentive plan but provides no pension plan and pays no dividend.

Fairfax's incentive plan participation has resulted in her ownership of Reston stock worth $10 million (current market value). The stock, received tax-free but subject to tax at a 35% rate (on entire proceeds) if sold, is expected to be held at least until her retirement.

Her present level of spending and the current annual inflation rate of 4% are expected to continue after her retirement.

Fairfax is taxed at 35% on all salary, investment income, and realized capital gains. Assume her composite tax rate will continue at this level indefinitely.

Fairfax's orientation is patient, careful, and conservative in all things. She has stated that an annual after-tax real total return of 3% would be completely acceptable to her if it was achieved in a context where an investment portfolio created from her accumulated savings was not subject to a decline of more than 10% in nominal terms in any given 12-month period. To obtain the benefits of professional assistance, she has approached two investment advisory firms—HH Counselors ("HH") and Coastal Advisors ("Coastal")—for recommendations on allocation of the investment portfolio to be created from her existing savings assets (the "Savings Portfolio") as well as for advice concerning investing in general.

**Table 26F    Susan Fairfax Proposed Asset Allocation, Prepared by Coastal Advisors**

| Asset Class | Proposed Allocation (%) | Current Yield (%) | Projected Total Return (%) |
|---|---|---|---|
| Cash equivalents | 15.0 | 4.5 | 4.5 |
| Corporate bonds | 10.0 | 7.5 | 7.5 |
| Municipal bonds | 10.0 | 5.5 | 5.5 |
| Large-cap U.S. stocks | 0.0 | 3.5 | 11.0 |
| Small-cap U.S. stocks | 0.0 | 2.5 | 13.0 |
| International stocks (EAFE) | 35.0 | 2.0 | 13.5 |
| Real estate investment trusts (REITs) | 25.0 | 9.0 | 12.0 |
| Venture capital | 5.0 | 0.0 | 20.0 |
| *TOTAL* | 100.0 | 4.9 | 10.7 |
| Inflation (CPI), projected | | | 4.0 |

a. Create and justify an investment policy statement for Fairfax based only on the information provided thus far. Be specific and complete in presenting objectives and constraints. (An asset allocation is not required in answering this question.)

b. Coastal has proposed the asset allocation shown in Table 26F for investment of Fairfax's $2 million of savings assets. Assume that only the current yield portion of projected total return (comprised of both investment income and realized capital gains) is taxable to Fairfax and that the municipal bond income is entirely tax-exempt.

Critique the Coastal proposal. Include in your answer three weaknesses in the Coastal proposal from the standpoint of the investment policy statement you created for her in (a).

c. HH Counselors has developed five alternative asset allocations (shown in Table 26G) for client portfolios. Answer the following questions based on Table 26G and the investment policy statement you created for Fairfax in (a).

 i. Determine which of the asset allocations in Table 26G meet or exceed Fairfax's stated return objective.

 ii. Determine the three asset allocations in Table 26G that meet Fairfax's risk tolerance criterion. Assume a 95% confidence interval is required, with 2 standard deviations serving as an approximation of that requirement.

d. Assume that the risk-free rate is 4.5%.

 i. Calculate the Sharpe ratio for Asset Allocation D.

 ii. Determine the two asset allocations in Table 26G having the best risk-adjusted returns, based only on the Sharpe ratio measure.

e. Recommend and justify the one asset allocation in Table 26G you believe would be the best model for Fairfax's savings portfolio.

7. John Franklin is a recent widower with some experience in investing for his own account. Following his wife's recent death and settlement of the estate, Mr. Franklin owns a controlling interest in a successful privately held manufacturing company in which Mrs. Franklin was formerly active, a recently completed warehouse property, the family residence, and his personal holdings of stocks and bonds. He has decided to retain the warehouse property as a diversifying investment but intends to sell the private company interest, giving half of the proceeds to a medical research foundation in memory of his deceased wife. Actual transfer of this gift is expected to take

## Table 26G   Alternative Asset Allocations, Prepared by HH Counselors

| Asset Class | Projected Total Return | Expected Standard Deviation | Asset Allocation A | Asset Allocation B | Asset Allocation C | Asset Allocation D | Asset Allocation E |
|---|---|---|---|---|---|---|---|
| Cash equivalents | 4.5% | 2.5% | 10% | 20% | 25% | 5% | 10% |
| Corporate bonds | 6.0 | 11.0 | 0 | 25 | 0 | 0 | 0 |
| Municipal bonds | 7.2 | 10.8 | 40 | 0 | 30 | 0 | 30 |
| Large-cap U.S. stocks | 13.0 | 17.0 | 20 | 15 | 35 | 25 | 5 |
| Small-cap U.S. stocks | 15.0 | 21.0 | 10 | 10 | 0 | 15 | 5 |
| International stocks (EAFE) | 15.0 | 21.0 | 10 | 10 | 0 | 15 | 10 |
| Real estate investment trusts (REITs) | 10.0 | 15.0 | 10 | 10 | 10 | 25 | 35 |
| Venture capital | 26.0 | 64.0 | 0 | 10 | 0 | 15 | 5 |
| TOTAL | | | 100 | 100 | 100 | 100 | 100 |
| **Summary Data** | | | | | | | |
| | | | Asset Allocation A | Asset Allocation B | Asset Allocation C | Asset Allocation D | Asset Allocation E |
| Projected total return | | | 9.9% | 11.0% | 8.8% | 14.4% | 10.3% |
| Projected after-tax total return | | | 7.4% | 7.2% | 6.5% | 9.4% | 7.4% |
| Expected standard deviation | | | 9.4% | 12.4% | 8.5% | 18.1% | 10.1% |
| Sharpe ratio | | | 0.574 | 0.524 | 0.506 | — | 0.574 |

place about 3 months from now. You have been engaged to assist him with the valuations, planning, and portfolio building required to structure his investment program appropriately.

Mr. Franklin has introduced you to the finance committee of the medical research foundation that is to receive his $45 million cash gift 3 months hence (and will eventually receive the assets of his estate). This gift will greatly increase the size of the foundation's endowment (from $10 million to $55 million) as well as enable it to make larger grants to researchers. The foundation's grant-making (spending) policy has been to pay out virtually all of its annual net investment income. As its investment approach has been very conservative, the endowment portfolio now consists almost entirely of fixed-income assets. The finance committee understands that these actions are causing the real value of foundation assets and the real value of future grants to decline due to the effects of inflation. Until now, the finance committee has believed that it had no alternative to these actions, given the large immediate cash needs of the research programs being funded and the small size of the foundation's capital base. The foundation's annual grants must at least equal 5% of its assets' market value to maintain its U.S. tax-exempt status, a requirement that is expected to continue indefinitely. No additional gifts or fund-raising activities are expected over the foreseeable future.

Given the change in circumstances that Mr. Franklin's gift will make, the finance committee wishes to develop new grant-making and investment policies. Annual spending must at least meet the level of 5% of market value that is required to maintain the foundation's tax-exempt status, but the committee is unsure about how much higher than 5% it can or should be. The committee wants to pay out as much

| Table 26H   Capital Markets Annualized Return Data | | |
|---|---|---|
| | **Historic Averages** | **Intermediate Term Consensus Forecast** |
| U.S. Treasury bills | 3.7% | 4.2% |
| Intermediate-term U.S. T-bonds | 5.2 | 5.8 |
| Long-term U.S. T-bonds | 4.8 | 7.7 |
| U.S. corporate bonds (AAA) | 5.5 | 8.8 |
| Non-U.S. bonds (AAA) | N/A | 8.4 |
| U.S. common stocks (all) | 10.3 | 9.0 |
| U.S. common stocks (small-cap) | 12.2 | 12.0 |
| Non-U.S. common stocks (all) | N/A | 10.1 |
| U.S. inflation | 3.1 | 3.5 |

as possible because of the critical nature of the research being funded; however, it understands that preserving the real value of the foundation's assets is equally important in order to preserve its future grant-making capabilities. You have been asked to assist the committee in developing appropriate policies.

a. Identify and briefly discuss the three key elements that should determine the foundation's grant-making (spending) policy.

b. Formulate and justify an investment policy statement for the foundation, taking into account the increased size of its assets arising from Mr. Franklin's gift. Your policy statement must encompass all relevant objectives, constraints, and the key elements identified in your answer to part (*a*).

c. Recommend and justify a long-term asset allocation that is consistent with the investment policy statement you created in part (*b*). Explain how your allocation's expected return meets the requirements of a feasible grant-making (spending) policy for the foundation. (Your allocation must sum to 100% and should use the economic/market data presented in Table 26H and your knowledge of historical asset-class characteristics.)

8. Your neighbor has heard that you successfully completed a course in investments and has come to seek your advice. She and her husband are both 50 years old. They just finished making their last payments for their condominium and their children's college education and are planning for retirement. What advice on investing their retirement savings would you give them? If they are very risk averse, what would you advise?

9. Claire Pierce, a vice president for Spencer Design, is a 42-year-old widow who is a resident of the United States. She has two children: a daughter, aged 21, and a son, aged 7. She has a $2,200,000 portfolio; half of the portfolio is invested in Spencer Design, a publicly traded common stock, which has a cost basis of $350,000. Despite a substantial drop in the value of her portfolio over the last 2 years, her long-term annual total returns have averaged 7% before tax. The recent drop in value has caused her great anxiety, and she believes that she could no longer tolerate an annual decline greater than 10%.

Pierce intends to retire in 20 years, and her goals, in order of priority, over the next 20 years are:

• Funding the cost of her daughter's upcoming final year of college, which has a present value of $18,000, and her son's future college costs, which have a present value of $91,000.

- Increasing the portfolio to a level that will fund her retirement living expenses, which she estimates to be $180,000 after tax for the first year of her retirement.
- Building her "dream house" in 5 years, the cost of which (including land) has a present value of $375,000.
- Giving, if possible, each of her children $1,000,000 when they reach age 40.

After subtracting the present value (before tax) of her children's education costs and her homebuilding costs, the present value of her portfolio is $1,509,000. With continued annual growth of 7% before tax, the portfolio's value will be approximately $3,928,000 at the end of 20 years.

Pierce's annual salary is $145,000, her annual living expenses are currently $100,000, and both are expected to increase at an inflation rate of 3% annually. Taxes on income and short-term capital gains (holding period 1 year or less) are substantially higher than taxes on long-term capital gains (holding period greater than 1 year). For planning purposes Pierce wants to assume that all returns are fully taxable and that her average tax rate on all income and gains is 30%. The inflation and tax rates are expected to remain constant. Currently, Pierce rents a townhouse, has no debt, and adamantly intends to remain debt-free. Spencer Design has no pension plan, but provides company-paid medical insurance for executives for life and for their children to age 25. After tax, Pierce's salary just covers her living expenses and therefore does not allow her to make further meaningful capital contributions to her portfolio.

Pierce has prepared the following investment policy statement:

---

**Claire Pierce's Investment Policy Statement**

The portfolio should be invested conservatively, as I want to protect its principal value. My salary covers my current living expenses, but the portfolio will need a moderate level of liquidity to cover the college expenses. My desire to give each of my children one million dollars when they reach age 40 requires the portfolio to have a long-term focus but allows for a low return objective in keeping with my low risk tolerance. Because of my tax circumstances, the portfolio should focus on securities that generate little or no taxable income.

---

a. Prepare the objectives portion of a new investment policy statement for Pierce. Indicate how each of your two objectives addresses a different weakness in Pierce's current investment policy statement.

b. Prepare the constraints portion of a new investment policy statement for Pierce. Indicate how each of your four constraints addresses a different weakness in Pierce's current investment policy statement.

Note: The legal and regulatory constraint is not applicable and should not be included among the constraints addressed in your response.

c. Pierce indicates that Spencer Design has a leading and growing market share, as the industry is quite fragmented. The company has shown steady fundamental growth trends, and Pierce intends to hold her Spencer Design stock, which is expected to return at least 9% annually before tax with a standard deviation of returns of 20%. Pierce has decided to invest the balance of her assets in one of the three alternative portfolios described in Table 26I. Recommend which one of the three alternative portfolios in Table 26I is most appropriate for the balance of Pierce's assets.

d. Pierce is considering three alternative portfolio managers for that portion of her equity portfolio that is not in Spencer Design stock. The average market return

## Table 26I  Claire Pierce's Alternative Portfolios for Balance of Assets

|  | Portfolio A | Portfolio B | Portfolio C | Expected Annual Return (before tax) | Standard Deviation of Returns |
|---|---|---|---|---|---|
| Money market | $   51,000 | $   51,000 | $  550,000 | 4.2% | 2.5% |
| Bonds | 491,000 | 792,000 | 330,000 | 6.4 | 7.8 |
| Equities | 558,000 | 257,000 | 220,000 | 10.8 | 17.8 |
| *TOTAL* | $1,100,000 | $1,100,000 | $1,100,000 | | |

## Table 26J  Claire Pierce's Alternative Portfolio Managers

| Manager | Description |
|---|---|
| F | Manager of a portfolio that is equally weighted among the stocks in the S&P 500 Index. Portfolio holdings are adjusted quarterly. |
| G | Manager of a market-weighted value index portfolio that consists of the half of the S&P 500 Index with the lowest price-to-book value ratios. Portfolio holdings are adjusted quarterly. |
| H | Manager of an actively managed large-capitalization portfolio with an average holding period of 7 years. |

and standard deviation characteristics and fees for each of the managers are expected to be very similar. The three managers are further described in Table 26J. Recommend which one of the three portfolio managers in Table 26J is most appropriate for Pierce's equity portfolio.

10. Claire Pierce, now 47 years old, has recently married a co-worker at Spencer Design. Pierce and her husband are buying their dream house at a total cost of $550,000 and have decided to make an immediate down payment of $300,000 and finance the remainder over 15 years. Pierce also indicates that her son has contracted a rare disease, requiring major surgery; the disease will prevent him from attending college. Although Pierce and her husband have medical insurance that will pay her son's ongoing medical expenses, her son's surgery will cost an additional $150,000 immediately. The cost of medical expenditures is expected to grow at a rate exceeding the general inflation rate for the foreseeable future. Pierce has decided to quit work to care for her son, whose remaining life expectancy is 40 years. She also insists on the need to provide care for her son when she and her husband are no longer capable of doing so. Pierce's parents died 1 year ago and her daughter is now financially independent. Pierce's husband intends to retire in 25 years.

Given these circumstances, the investment portfolio held by Pierce and her husband will need to provide an amount equal to $1,200,000 (present value) after tax to meet their living expenses until retirement. They also want their portfolio to grow enough to cover their living expenses at retirement, which they estimate to be $280,000 annually after tax. They believe a before-tax portfolio growth rate of approximately 8 to 10% annually will be needed to achieve this goal. Based on a retirement spending goal of $280,000, their corresponding effective post-retirement spending rate will be approximately 6 to 7% annually after tax.

Pierce summarizes her new financial information in Table 26K. She indicates that her portfolio and her husband's portfolio should be considered as one. She further states that her husband has taken well above-average risk in the past but he is now willing to leave the investment management decisions to her.

**Table 26K   Claire Pierce's New Financial Information**

| | Claire Pierce | Husband | Combined | Current Allocation Percentage of Combined Portfolio |
|---|---|---|---|---|
| Salary | $0 | $150,000 | $150,000 | — |
| Assets | | | | |
| Money market | $ 61,000 | $ 27,000 | $ 88,000 | 2.4% |
| Diversified bond fund | 1,129,000 | 0 | 1,129,000 | 30.5 |
| Equities | | | | |
| Large-capitalization equities | 385,000 | 0 | 385,000 | 10.4 |
| Emerging market equities | 0 | 407,000 | 407,000 | 11.0 |
| Spencer Design common stock | 1,325,000 | 122,000 | 1,447,000 | 39.1 |
| Undeveloped commercial land | 0 | 244,000 | 244,000 | 6.6 |
| Total portfolio | $2,900,000 | $800,000 | $3,700,000 | 100.0% |

a. Indicate how each component of Pierce's investment policy statement should change as a result of Pierce's new circumstances. Justify each of your responses with reasons based on Pierce's new circumstances.

b. Recommend whether the current allocation percentage (given in Table 26K) for each of the following assets should be decreased or increased as a result of Pierce's new circumstances. Justify each of your responses with one reason based on Pierce's new circumstances.

   i. Spencer Design common stock.
   ii. Money market.
   iii. Diversified bond fund.
   iv. Large-capitalization equities.
   v. Emerging market equities.
   vi. Undeveloped commercial land.

11. George More is a participant in a defined contribution pension plan that offers a fixed-income fund and a common stock fund as investment choices. He is 40 years old and has an accumulation of $100,000 in each of the funds. He currently contributes $1,500 per year to each. He plans to retire at age 65, and his life expectancy is age 80.

   a. Assuming a 3% per year real earnings rate for the fixed-income fund and 6% per year for common stocks, what will be George's expected accumulation in each account at age 65?

   b. What will be the expected real retirement annuity from each account, assuming these same real earnings rates?

   c. If George wanted a retirement annuity of $30,000 per year from the fixed-income fund, by how much would he have to increase his annual contributions?

12. What is the least-risky asset for each of the following investors?

   a. A person investing for her 3-year-old child's college tuition.

   b. A defined benefit pension fund with benefit obligations that have an average duration of 10 years. The benefits are not inflation-protected.

   c. A defined benefit pension fund with benefit obligations that have an average duration of 10 years. The benefits are inflation-protected.

13. The difference between a Roth IRA and a conventional IRA is that in a Roth IRA taxes are paid on the income that is contributed but the withdrawals at retirement are tax-free. In a conventional IRA, however, the contributions reduce your taxable

income, but the withdrawals at retirement are taxable. Try using the Excel spreadsheet introduced in the Appendix to answer these questions.

  *a.* Which of these two types provides higher after-tax benefits?

  *b.* Which provides better protection against tax rate uncertainty?

---

**E-INVESTMENTS**
**Personal**
**Diversification**

Go to **www.money.com/money/depts/retirement** and find the calculator for diversifying your portfolio. When you work in a given industry, other industries may be more effective in diversifying your overall economic well-being. This calculator shows good and bad choices for diversification for different employment industries.

Select the following industries and obtain the listing of the 10 best and 10 worst industries for diversification.

Oil and gas (drilling and equipment)

Homebuilding

Electronics (semiconductor)

Are the industries identified as best and worst considerably different for these three employment industries? Contrast the differences present in the categories for these industries.

---

**SOLUTIONS TO CONCEPT CHECKS**

1. Identify the elements that are life-cycle driven in the two schemes of objectives and constraints.

2. If Eloise keeps her present asset allocation, she will have the following amounts to spend after taxes 5 years from now:

*Tax-qualified account:*

| | |
|---|---|
| Bonds: $50,000(1.1)^5 \times .72$ | $= \$ 57,978.36$ |
| Stocks: $50,000(1.15)^5 \times .72$ | $= \$ 72,408.86$ |
| Subtotal | $\$130,387.22$ |

*Nonretirement account:*

| | |
|---|---|
| Bonds: $50,000[1 + (.10 \times .85)]^5$ | $= \$ 75,182.83$ |
| Stocks: $50,000(1.15)^5 - .15 \times [50,000(1.15)^5 - 50,000]$ | $= \$ 92,982.68$ |
| Subtotal | $\$168,165.51$ |
| Total | $\$298,552.73$ |

If Eloise shifts all of the bonds into the retirement account and all of the stock into the nonretirement account, she will have the following amounts to spend after taxes 5 years from now:

*Tax-qualified account:*

| | |
|---|---|
| Bonds: $100,000(1.1)^5 \times .72$ | $= \$115,956.72$ |

*Nonretirement account:*

| | |
|---|---|
| Stocks: $100,000(1.15)^5 - .15 \times [100,000(1.15)^5 - 100,000]$ | $= \$185,965.36$ |
| Total | $= \$301,922.08$ |

Her spending budget will increase by $3,369.35.

3. The contribution to each fund will be $2,000 per year (i.e., 5% of $40,000) in constant dollars. At retirement she will have in her guaranteed return fund:

$$\$50,000 \times 1.03^{20} + \$2,000 \times \text{Annuity factor}(3\%, 20 \text{ years}) = \$144,046$$

That is the amount she will have for *sure.*

**SOLUTIONS TO CONCEPT CHECKS** *(Concluded)*

In addition the expected future value of her stock account is:

$50,000 × 1.06$^{20}$ + $2,000 × Annuity factor(6%, 20 years) = $233,928

4. He has accrued an annuity of .01 × 15 × 15,000 = $2,250 per year for 15 years, starting in 25 years. The present value of this annuity is $2,812.13:

PV = 2,250 × Annuity factor(8%, 15) × PV factor(8%, 25) = 2,812.13

# APPENDIX: A SPREADSHEET MODEL FOR LONG-TERM INVESTING

## Saving for the Long Run

Our objective here is to quantify the essentials of savings/investment plans and adapt them to environments in which investors confront both inflation and taxes. As a first step in the process, we set up a spreadsheet for a simple retirement plan, ignoring for the moment saving for other objectives.

**A Hypothetical Household** Imagine you are now 30 years old and have already completed your formal education, accumulated some work experience, and settled down to plan the rest of your economic life. Your plan is to retire at age 65 with a remaining life expectancy of an additional 25 years. Later on, we will further assume that you have two small children and plan to finance their college education.

For starters, we assume you intend to obtain a (level) annuity for your 25-year retirement period. Suppose your gross income this year was $50,000, and you expect annual income to increase at a rate of 7% per year. In this section, we assume that you ignore the impact of inflation and taxes. You intend to steadily save 15% of income and invest in safe government bonds that will yield 6% over the entire period. Proceeds from your investments will be automatically reinvested at the same 6% until retirement. Upon retirement, your funds in the retirement account will be used to purchase a 25-year annuity (using the same 6% interest rate) to finance a steady consumption annuity. Let's examine the consequences of this framework.

**The Retirement Annuity** We can easily obtain your **retirement annuity** from Spreadsheet 26A.1, where we have hidden the lines for ages 32–34, 36–44, 46–54, and 56–64. You can obtain all the spreadsheets in this chapter from the Web page for the text available at the Online Learning Center: **www.mhhe.com/bkm**.

Let's first see how this spreadsheet was constructed. To view the formulas of all cells in an Excel spreadsheet, choose "Preferences" under the "Tools" menu, and select the box "Formulas" in the "View" tab. The formula view of Spreadsheet 26A.1 is also shown on the next page (numbers are user inputs).

Inputs in row 2 include: retirement years (cell A2 = 25); income growth (cell B2 = .07); age (column A); and income at age 30 (B4 = 50,000). Column B computes income in future years using the growth rate in cell B2; column C computes annual savings by applying the savings rate (cell C2) to income; and column E computes consumption as the difference between income and savings: column B − column C. Cumulative savings appear in column D. To obtain the value in D6, for example, multiply cell D5 by 1 plus the assumed rate of return in cell D2 (the ROR) and then add current savings from column C.

**Spreadsheet 26A.1   The savings plan**

| | A | B | C | D | E |
|---|---|---|---|---|---|
| 1 | Retirement Years | Income Growth | Savings Rate | ROR | |
| 2 | 25 | 0.07 | 0.15 | 0.06 | |
| 3 | Age | Income | Savings | Cumulative Savings | Consumption |
| 4 | 30 | 50,000 | 7,500 | 7,500 | 42,500 |
| 5 | 31 | 53,500 | 8,025 | 15,975 | 45,475 |
| 6 | 32 | 57,245 | 8,587 | 25,520 | 48,658 |
| 9 | 35 | 70,128 | 10,519 | 61,658 | 59,608 |
| 19 | 45 | 137,952 | 20,693 | 308,859 | 117,259 |
| 29 | 55 | 271,372 | 40,706 | 943,477 | 230,666 |
| 39 | 65 | 533,829 | 80,074 | 2,457,518 | 453,755 |
| 40 | Total | 7,445,673 | 1,116,851 | Retirement Annuity | 192,244 |

| | A | B | C | D | E |
|---|---|---|---|---|---|
| 1 | Retirement Years | Income Growth | Savings Rate | ROR | |
| 2 | 25 | 0.07 | 0.15 | 0.06 | |
| 3 | Age | Income | Savings | Cumulative Savings | Consumption |
| 4 | 30 | 50000 | =B4*$C$2 | =C4 | =B4-C4 |
| 5 | 31 | =B4*(1+$B$2) | =B5*$C$2 | =D4*(1+$D$2)+C5 | =B5-C5 |
| 39 | 65 | =B38*(1+$B$2) | =B39*$C$2 | =D38*(1+$D$2)+C39 | =B39-C39 |
| 40 | Total | =SUM(B4:B39) | =SUM(C4:C39) | Retirement Annuity | =PMT($D$2,$A$2,-$D$39,0,0) |

Finally, C40 shows the sum of dollars saved over the lifetime, and E40 converts cumulative savings (including interest) at age 65 to a 25-year annuity using the financial function PMT from Excel's function menu. Excel provides a function to solve for annuity levels given the values of the interest rate, the number of periods, the present value of the savings account, and the future value of the account: PMT(rate, nper, PV, FV).

We observe that your retirement fund will accumulate approximately $2.5 million (cell D39) by age 65. This hefty sum shows the power of compounding, since your contributions to the savings account were only $1.1 million (C40). This fund will yield an annuity of $192,244 per year (E40) for your 25-year retirement, which seems quite attractive, except that the standard of living you'll have to get accustomed to in your retirement years is much lower than your consumption at age 65 (E39). In fact, if you unhide the hidden lines, you'll see that upon retirement, you'll have to make do with what you used to consume at age 51. This may not worry you much since, with your children having flown the coop and the mortgage paid up, you may be able to maintain the luxury to which you recently became accustomed. But your projected well being is deceptive: get ready to account for inflation and taxes.

**CONCEPT CHECK ☞ QUESTION A.1**

If you project an ROR of only 5%, what savings rate would you need to maintain the same retirement annuity?

## Accounting for Inflation

Inflation puts a damper on your plans in two ways: First, it erodes the purchasing power of the cumulative dollars you have so far saved. Second, the *real* dollars you earn on your portfolio each year depend on the *real* interest rate, which is approximately equal to the nominal rate minus inflation. Since an appropriate savings plan must generate a decent *real* annuity, we must recast the entire plan in real dollars. We will assume your income still is forecast to grow at a 7% rate, but now you recognize that part of income growth is due to inflation, which is running at 3% per year.

**A Real Savings Plan**    To convert nominal dollars to real dollars we need to calculate the price level in future years relative to today's prices. The "deflator" (or relative price level) for a given year is that year's price level divided by today's. It equals the dollars needed at that future date which provide the same purchasing power as $1 today (at age 30). For an inflation rate of $i = 3\%$, the deflator for age 35 is $(1 + i)^5$, or in Excel notation, $(1 + i)^5 = 1.03^5 = 1.16$. By age 65, the deflator is 2.81. Thus, even with a moderate rate of inflation, nominal dollars will lose a lot of purchasing power over long horizons. We also can compute the *real* rate of return (rROR) from the nominal ROR of 6%: rROR $= (ROR - i)/(1 + i) = 3/1.03 = 2.91\%$.

Spreadsheet 26A.2, with the formula view below it, is the reworked Spreadsheet 26A.1 adjusted for inflation. In addition to the rate of inflation (cell C2) and the real rate of return (F2), the major addition to this sheet is the price level deflator (column C). Instead of nominal consumption, we present **real consumption** (column F), calculated by dividing nominal consumption (column B − column D) by the price deflator, column C.

The numbers have changed considerably. Gone is the luxurious retirement we anticipated earlier. At age 65 and beyond, with a real annuity of $49,668, you will have to revert to a standard of living equal to that you attained at age 34; this is less than a third of your real consumption in your last working year, at age 65. The reason is that the retirement fund of $2.5 million (E39) is worth only $873,631 in today's purchasing power (E39/C39). Such is the effect of inflation. If you wish to do better than this, you must save more.

In our initial plan (Spreadsheet 26A.1), we envisioned consuming a level, nominal annuity for the retirement years. This is an inappropriate goal once we account for inflation, since it would imply a declining standard of living starting at age 65. Its purchasing power at age 65 in terms of current dollars would be $64,542 (i.e., $181,362/2.81), and at age 90 only $30,792. (Check this!)

It is tempting to contemplate solving the problem of an inadequate retirement annuity by increasing the assumed rate of return on investments. However, this can only be accomplished by putting your savings at risk. Much of this text elaborates on how to do so

**Spreadsheet 26A.2    A real retirement plan**

| | A | B | C | D | E | F |
|---|---|---|---|---|---|---|
| 1 | Retirement Years | Income growth | Rate of Inflation | Savings rate | ROR | rROR |
| 2 | 25 | 0.07 | 0.03 | 0.15 | 0.06 | 0.0291 |
| 3 | Age | Income | Deflator | Saving | Cumulative Savings | rConsumption |
| 4 | 30 | 50,000 | 1.00 | 7,500 | 7,500 | 42,500 |
| 5 | 31 | 53,500 | 1.03 | 8,025 | 15,975 | 44,150 |
| 9 | 35 | 70,128 | 1.16 | 10,519 | 61,658 | 51,419 |
| 19 | 45 | 137,952 | 1.56 | 20,693 | 308,859 | 75,264 |
| 29 | 55 | 271,372 | 2.09 | 40,706 | 943,477 | 110,167 |
| 39 | 65 | 533,829 | 2.81 | 80,074 | 2,457,518 | 161,257 |
| 40 | Total | 7,445,673 | | 1,116,851 | Real Annuity | 49,668 |

| | A | B | C | D | E | F |
|---|---|---|---|---|---|---|
| 1 | Retirement Years | Income Growth | Rate of Inflation | Savings Rate | ROR | rROR |
| 2 | 25 | 0.07 | 0.03 | 0.15 | 0.06 | =(E2-C2)/(1+C2) |
| 3 | Age | Income | Deflator | Savings | Cumulative Savings | rConsumption |
| 4 | 30 | 50000 | 1 | =B4*$D$2 | =D4 | =(B4-D4)/C4 |
| 5 | 31 | =B4*(1+$B$2) | =C4*(1+$C$2) | =B5*$D$2 | =E4*(1+$E$2)+D5 | =(B5-D5)/C5 |
| 39 | 65 | =B38*(1+$B$2) | =C38*(1+$C$2) | =B39*$D$2 | =E38*(1+$E$2)+D39 | =(B39-D39)/C39 |
| 40 | Total | =SUM(B4:B39) | | =SUM(D4:D39) | Real Annuity | =PMT($F$2,$A$2,-$E$39/$C$39,0,0) |

efficiently; yet it also emphasizes that while taking on risk will give you an *expectation* for a better retirement, it implies as well a nonzero probability of doing a lot worse. At the age of 30, you should be able to tolerate some risk to the retirement annuity for the simple reason that if things go wrong, you can change course, increase your savings rate, and work harder. As you get older, this option progressively fades, and increasing risk becomes less of a viable option. If you do choose to increase risk, you can set a "safety-first target" (i.e., a minimum acceptable goal) for the retirement annuity and continuously monitor your risky portfolio. If the portfolio does poorly and approaches the safety-first target, you progressively shift into risk-free bonds—you may recognize this strategy as a version of dynamic hedging.

The difficulty with this strategy is twofold: First it requires monitoring, which is time-consuming and may be nerve-racking as well. Second, when decision time comes, it may be psychologically hard to withdraw. By shifting out of the risky portfolio if and when your portfolio is hammered, you give up any hope of recovery. This is hard to do and many investors fail the test. For these investors, therefore, the right approach is to stick with the safe, lower ROR and make the effort to balance standard of living before and after retirement. Avoiding sleepless nights is ample reward.

Therefore, the only variable we leave under your control in this spreadsheet is the rate of saving. To improve retirement lifestyle relative to the preretirement years, without jeopardizing its safety, you will have to reduce consumption during the saving years—there is no free lunch.

| CONCEPT CHECK☞ QUESTION A.2 | If you project a rate of inflation of 4%, what nominal ROR on investments would you need to maintain the same real retirement annuity as in Spreadsheet 26A.2? |
| --- | --- |

**An Alternative Savings Plan**   In Spreadsheet 26A.2, we saved a constant fraction of income. But since real income grows over time (nominal income grows at 7% while inflation is only 3%), we might consider deferring our savings toward future years when our real income is higher. By applying a higher savings rate to our future (higher) real income, we can afford to reduce the current savings rate. In Spreadsheet 26A.3, we use a base savings rate of 10% (lower than the savings rate in the previous spreadsheet), but we increase the savings target by 3% per year. Saving in each year $t$ therefore equals a fixed savings rate times annual income (column B), times $1.03^t$. By saving a larger fraction of income in later years, when real income is larger, you create a smoother profile of real consumption.

Spreadsheet 26A.3 shows that with an *initial* savings rate of 10%, compared with the unchanging 15% rate in the previous spreadsheet, you can achieve a retirement annuity of $59,918, larger than the $49,668 annuity in the previous plan.

Notice that real consumption in the early years is greater than with the previous plan. What you have done is to postpone saving until your income is much higher. At first blush, this plan is preferable: It allows for a more comfortable consumption of 90% of income at the outset, a consistent increase in standard of living during your earning years, all without significantly affecting the retirement annuity. But this program has one serious downside: By postponing the bulk of your savings to a later age, you come to depend on your health, longevity, and, more ominously (and without possibility of insurance), on a successful future career. Put differently, this plan achieves comfort by increasing risk, making this choice a matter of risk tolerance.

**Spreadsheet 26A.3    Saving from real income**

| | A | B | C | D | E | F |
|---|---|---|---|---|---|---|
| 1 | Retirement Years | Income Growth | Rate of Inflation | Savings Rate | ROR | rROR |
| 2 | 25 | 0.07 | 0.03 | 0.1 | 0.06 | 0.0291 |
| 3 | Age | Income | Deflator | Savings | Cumulative Savings | rConsumption |
| 4 | 30 | 50,000 | 1.00 | 5,000 | 5,000 | 45,000 |
| 5 | 31 | 53,500 | 1.03 | 5,511 | 10,811 | 46,592 |
| 9 | 35 | 70,128 | 1.16 | 8,130 | 44,351 | 53,480 |
| 19 | 45 | 137,952 | 1.56 | 21,492 | 260,927 | 74,751 |
| 29 | 55 | 271,372 | 2.09 | 56,819 | 947,114 | 102,471 |
| 39 | 65 | 533,829 | 2.81 | 150,212 | 2,964,669 | 136,331 |
| 40 | Total | 7,445,673 | | 1,572,466 | Real Annuity | 59,918 |

| | A | B | C | D | E | F |
|---|---|---|---|---|---|---|
| 1 | Retirement Years | Income Growth | Rate of Inflation | Savings Rate | ROR | rROR |
| 2 | 25 | 0.07 | 0.03 | 0.1 | 0.06 | =(E2-C2)/(1+C2) |
| 3 | Age | Income | Deflator | Savings | Cumulative Savings | rConsumption |
| 4 | 30 | 50000 | 1 | =B4*C4*$D$2 | =D4 | =(B4-D4)/C4 |
| 5 | 31 | =B4*(1+$B$2) | =C4*(1+$C$2) | =B5*C5*$D$2 | =E4*(1+$E$2)+D5 | =(B5-D5)/C5 |
| 39 | 65 | =B38*(1+$B$2) | =C38*(1+$C$2) | =B39*C39*$D$2 | =E38*(1+$E$2)+D39 | =(B39-D39)/C39 |
| 40 | Total | =SUM(B4:B39) | | =SUM(D4:D39) | Real Annuity | =PMT($F$2,$A$2,-$E$39/$C$39,0,0) |

| CONCEPT CHECK☞ QUESTION A.3 | Suppose you like the plan of tilting savings toward later years, but worry about the increased risk of postponing the bulk of your savings to later years. Is there anything you can do to mitigate the risk? |
|---|---|

## Accounting for Taxes

To initiate a discussion of taxes, let's assume that you are subject to a **flat tax** rate of 25% on taxable income less one exemption of $15,000. An important feature of this (and the existing) tax code is that the tax rate is levied on nominal income and applies as well to investment income. (This is the concept of double taxation—you pay taxes when you earn income and then you pay taxes again when your savings earn interest). Some relief from the effect of taxing nominal dollars both in this proposal and the current U.S. code is provided by raising the exemption, annually, by the rate of inflation. To adapt our spreadsheet to this simple tax code, we must add columns for taxes and after-tax income. The tax-adjusted plan is shown in Spreadsheet 26A.4. It adapts the savings plan of Spreadsheet 26A.2.

The top panel of the sheet deals with the earning years. Column D adjusts the exemption (D2) by the price level (column C). Column E applies the tax rate (cell E2) to taxable income (column B − column D). The savings rate (F2) is applied to after-tax income (column B − column E), allowing us to calculate cumulative savings (column G) and real consumption (column H). The formula view shows the detailed construction.

As you might have expected, real consumption is lower in the presence of taxes, as are savings and the retirement fund. The retirement fund provides for a real, before-tax annuity of only $37,882, compared with $49,668 absent taxes in Spreadsheet 26A.2.

The bottom panel of the sheet shows the further reduction in real consumption due to taxes paid during the retirement years. While you do not pay taxes on the cumulative savings in the retirement plan (you did that already as the savings accrued interest), you do pay

## Spreadsheet 26A.4   Saving with a simple tax code

| | A | B | C | D | E | F | G | H |
|---|---|---|---|---|---|---|---|---|
| 1 | Retirement Years | Income Growth | Rate of Inflation | Exemption Now | Tax Rate | Savings Rate | ROR | rROR |
| 2 | 25 | 0.07 | 0.03 | 15000 | 0.25 | 0.15 | 0.06 | 0.0291 |
| 3 | Age | Income | Deflator | Exemption | Taxes | Savings | Cumulative Savings | rConsumption |
| 4 | 30 | 50,000 | 1.00 | 15,000 | 8,750 | 6,188 | 6,188 | 35,063 |
| 5 | 31 | 53,500 | 1.03 | 15,450 | 9,605 | 6,584 | 13,143 | 36,224 |
| 9 | 35 | 70,128 | 1.16 | 17,389 | 13,775 | 8,453 | 50,188 | 41,319 |
| 19 | 45 | 137,952 | 1.56 | 23,370 | 31,892 | 15,909 | 245,334 | 57,864 |
| 29 | 55 | 271,372 | 2.09 | 31,407 | 69,943 | 30,214 | 733,467 | 81,773 |
| 39 | 65 | 533,829 | 2.81 | 42,208 | 148,611 | 57,783 | 1,874,346 | 116,365 |
| 40 | Total | | | | 1,884,163 | 834,226 | Real Annuity= | 37,882 |
| 41 | **RETIREMENT** | | | | | | | |
| 42 | Age | Nom Withdraw | Deflator | Exemption | Taxes | | Funds Left | rConsumption |
| 43 | 66 | 109,792 | 2.90 | 43,474 | 17,247 | | 1,877,014 | 31,931 |
| 47 | 70 | 123,572 | 3.26 | 48,931 | 15,743 | | 1,853,382 | 33,056 |
| 52 | 75 | 143,254 | 3.78 | 56,724 | 12,200 | | 1,721,015 | 34,656 |
| 57 | 80 | 166,071 | 4.38 | 65,759 | 6,047 | | 1,422,954 | 36,503 |
| 62 | 85 | 192,521 | 5.08 | 76,232 | 0 | | 883,895 | 37,882 |
| 67 | 90 | 223,185 | 5.89 | 88,374 | 0 | | 0 | 37,882 |
| 68 | Total | 4,002,944 | | | 203,199 | | | |

| | A | B | C | D | E | F | G | H |
|---|---|---|---|---|---|---|---|---|
| 1 | Retirement Years | Income Growth | Rate of Inflation | Exemption Now | Tax Rate | Savings Rate | ROR | rROR |
| 2 | 25 | 0.07 | 0.03 | 15000 | 0.25 | 0.15 | 0.06 | =(G2-C2)/(1+C2) |
| 3 | Age | Income | Deflator | Exemption | Taxes | Savings | Cumulative Savings | rConsumption |
| 4 | 30 | 50000 | 1 | =$D$2*C4 | =(B4-D4)*$E$2 | =(B4-E4)*$F$2 | =F4 | =(B4-E4-F4)/C4 |
| 5 | 31 | =B4*(1+$B$2) | =C4*(1+$C$2) | =$D$2*C5 | =(B5-D5+G4*$G$2)*$E$2 | =(B5-E5)*$F$2 | =G4*(1+$G$2)+F5 | =(B5-E5-F5)/C5 |
| 39 | 65 | =B38*(1+$B$2) | =C38*(1+$C$2) | =$D$2*C39 | =(B39-D39+G38*$G$2)*$E$2 | =(B39-E39)*$F$2 | =G38*(1+$G$2)+F39 | =(B39-E39-F39)/C39 |
| 40 | Total | | | | =SUM(E4:E39) | =SUM(F4:F39) | Real Annuity= | =PMT($H$2,$A$2,-$G$39/$C$39,0,0) |
| 41 | **RETIREMENT** | | | | | | | |
| 42 | Age | Nom Withdraw | Deflator | Exemption | Taxes | | Funds Left | rConsumption |
| 43 | 66 | =$H$40*C43 | =C39*(1+$C$2) | =$D$2*C43 | =MAX(0,(G39*$G$2-D43)*$E$2) | | =G39*(1+$G$2)-B43 | =(B43-E43)/C43 |
| 44 | 67 | =$H$40*C44 | =C43*(1+$C$2) | =$D$2*C44 | =MAX(0,(G43*$G$2-D44)*$F$2) | | =G43*(1+$G$2)-B44 | =(B44-E44)/C44 |
| 67 | 90 | =$H$40*C67 | =C66*(1+$C$2) | =$D$2*C67 | =MAX(0,(C66*$G$2-D67)*$E$2) | | =G66*(1+$G$2)-B67 | =(B67-E67)/C67 |
| 68 | Total | =SUM(B43:B67) | | | =SUM(E43:E67) | | | |

taxes on interest earned by the fund while you are drawing it down. These taxes are quite significant and further deplete the fund and its net-of-tax earning power. For this reason, your consumption annuity is lower in the early years when your fund has not yet been depleted and earns quite a bit.

In the end, despite a handsome income that grows at a real rate of almost 4%, an aggressive savings rate of 15%, a modest rate of inflation, and a modest tax, you will only be able to achieve a modest (but at least low-risk) real retirement income. This is a reality with which most people must struggle. Whether to sacrifice more of today's standard of living through an increased rate of saving, or take some risk in the form of saving a real annuity and/or invest in a risky portfolio with a higher expected return, is a question of preference and risk tolerance.

Of course, this model is just a beginning. Its description of the tax code is overly simplistic. You probably would want to add a progressive tax feature to the spreadsheet. You would want to add as well opportunities for tax sheltering (e.g., IRAs and 401k plans), Social Security, and large expenditures such as housing purchase and college education. But the model is highly adaptable and lays out a basic framework that can accommodate taxes, inflation, and a variety of institutional features such as tax-sheltered savings plans. We invite you to download the model from this text's website (**www.mhhe.com/bkm**) and adapt it to your needs.

**SOLUTIONS TO CONCEPT CHECKS**

A1. When ROR falls by 1% to 5%, the retirement annuity falls from $192,244 to $149,855 (i.e., by 22.45%). To restore this annuity, the savings rate must rise by 4.24 percentage points to 19.24%. With this savings rate, the entire loss of 1% in ROR falls on consumption during the earning years.

A2. Intuition suggests you need to keep the real rate (2.91%) constant, that is, increase the nominal rate to 7.03% (confirm this). However, this will not be sufficient because the nominal income growth of 7% has a lower real growth when inflation is higher. Result: You must increase the real ROR to compensate for a lower growth in real income, ending with a nominal rate of 7.67%.

A3. There are two components to the risk of relying on future income: disability/death and career failure/unemployment. You can insure the first component, but not the second.

# THE THEORY OF ACTIVE PORTFOLIO MANAGEMENT

Thus far we have alluded to active portfolio management in only three instances: the Markowitz methodology of generating the optimal risky portfolio (Chapter 8); security analysis that generates forecasts to use as inputs with the Markowitz procedure (Chapters 17 through 19); and fixed-income portfolio management (Chapter 16). These brief analyses are not adequate to guide investment managers in a comprehensive enterprise of active portfolio management.

You may also be wondering about the seeming contradiction between our equilibrium analysis in Part 3—in particular, the theory of efficient markets— and the real-world environment where profit-seeking investment managers use active management to exploit perceived market inefficiencies.

Despite the efficient market hypothesis, it is clear that markets cannot be perfectly efficient; hence there are reasons to believe that active management can have effective results, and we discuss these at the outset. Next we consider the objectives of active portfolio management. We analyze two forms of active management: market timing, which is based solely on macroeconomic factors; and security selection, which includes microeconomic forecasting. We show the use of multifactor models in active portfolio management, and we end with a discussion of the use of imperfect forecasts and the implementation of security analysis in industry.

# 27.1   THE LURE OF ACTIVE MANAGEMENT

How can a theory of active portfolio management be reconciled with the notion that markets are in equilibrium? You may want to look back at the analysis in Chapter 12, but we can interpret our conclusions as follows.

Market efficiency prevails when many investors are willing to depart from maximum diversification, or a passive strategy, by adding mispriced securities to their portfolios in the hope of realizing abnormal returns. The competition for such returns ensures that prices will be near their "fair" values. Most managers will not beat the passive strategy on a risk-adjusted basis. However, in the competition for rewards to investing, exceptional managers might beat the average forecasts built into market prices.

There is both economic logic and some empirical evidence to indicate that exceptional portfolio managers can beat the average forecast. Let us discuss economic logic first. We must assume that if no analyst can beat the passive strategy, investors will be smart enough to divert their funds from strategies entailing expensive analysis to less expensive passive strategies. In that case funds under active management will dry up, and prices will no longer reflect sophisticated forecasts. The consequent profit opportunities will lure back active managers who once again will become successful.[1] Of course, the critical assumption is that investors allocate management funds wisely. Direct evidence on that has yet to be produced.

As for empirical evidence, consider the following: (1) Some portfolio managers have produced streaks of abnormal returns that are hard to label as lucky outcomes; (2) the "noise" in realized rates is enough to prevent us from rejecting outright the hypothesis that some money managers have beaten the passive strategy by a statistically small, yet economically significant, margin; and (3) some anomalies in realized returns have been sufficiently persistent to suggest that portfolio managers who identified them in a timely fashion could have beaten the passive strategy over prolonged periods.

These conclusions persuade us that there is a role for a theory of active portfolio management. Active management has an inevitable lure even if investors agree that security markets are nearly efficient.

Suppose that capital markets are perfectly efficient, that an easily accessible market-index portfolio is available, and that this portfolio is for all practical purposes the efficient risky portfolio. Clearly, in this case security selection would be a futile endeavor. You would be better off with a passive strategy of allocating funds to a money market fund (the safe asset) and the market-index portfolio. Under these simplifying assumptions the optimal investment strategy seems to require no effort or know-how.

Such a conclusion, however, is too hasty. Recall that the proper allocation of investment funds to the risk-free and risky portfolios requires some analysis because $y$, the fraction to be invested in the risky market portfolio, $M$, is given by

$$y = \frac{E(r_M) - r_f}{.01A\sigma_M^2} \tag{27.1}$$

where $E(r_M) - r_f$ is the risk premium on $M$, $\sigma_M^2$ its variance, and $A$ is the investor's coefficient of risk aversion. Any rational allocation therefore requires an estimate of $\sigma_M$ and $E(r_M)$. Even a passive investor needs to do some forecasting, in other words.

Forecasting $E(r_M)$ and $\sigma_M$ is further complicated by the existence of security classes that are affected by different environmental factors. Long-term bond returns, for example, are

---

[1] This point is worked out fully in Sanford J. Grossman and Joseph E. Stiglitz, "On the Impossibility of Informationally Efficient Markets," *American Economic Review* 70 (June 1980).

driven largely by changes in the term structure of interest rates, whereas equity returns depend on changes in the broader economic environment, including macroeconomic factors beyond interest rates. Once our investor determines relevant forecasts for separate sorts of investments, she might as well use an optimization program to determine the proper mix for the portfolio. It is easy to see how the investor may be lured away from a purely passive strategy, and we have not even considered temptations such as international stock and bond portfolios or sector portfolios.

In fact, even the definition of a "purely passive strategy" is problematic, because simple strategies involving only the market-index portfolio and risk-free assets now seem to call for market analysis. For our purposes we define purely passive strategies as those that use only index funds *and* weight those funds by fixed proportions that do not vary in response to perceived market conditions. For example, a portfolio strategy that always places 60% in a stock market–index fund, 30% in a bond-index fund, and 10% in a money market fund is a purely passive strategy.

More important, the lure into active management may be extremely strong because the potential profit from active strategies is enormous. At the same time, competition among the multitude of active managers creates the force driving market prices to near efficiency levels. Although enormous profits may be increasingly difficult to earn, decent profits to the better analysts should be the rule rather than the exception. For prices to remain efficient to some degree, some analysts must be able to eke out a reasonable profit. Absence of profits would decimate the active investment management industry, eventually allowing prices to stray from informationally efficient levels. The theory of managing active portfolios is the concern of this chapter.

## 27.2   OBJECTIVES OF ACTIVE PORTFOLIOS

What does an investor expect from a professional portfolio manager, and how does this expectation affect the operation of the manager? If the client were risk neutral, that is, indifferent to risk, the answer would be straightforward. The investor would expect the portfolio manager to construct a portfolio with the highest possible expected rate of return. The portfolio manager follows this dictum and is judged by the realized average rate of return.

When the client is risk averse, the answer is more difficult. Without a normative theory of portfolio management, the manager would have to consult each client before making any portfolio decision in order to ascertain that reward (average return) is commensurate with risk. Massive and constant input would be needed from the client-investors, and the economic value of professional management would be questionable.

Fortunately, the theory of mean-variance efficient portfolio management allows us to separate the "product decision," which is how to construct a mean-variance efficient risky portfolio, and the "consumption decision," or the investor's allocation of funds between the efficient risky portfolio and the safe asset. We have seen that construction of the optimal risky portfolio is purely a technical problem, resulting in a single optimal risky portfolio appropriate for all investors. Investors will differ only in how they apportion investment to that risky portfolio and the safe asset.

Another feature of the mean-variance theory that affects portfolio management decisions is the criterion for choosing the optimal risky portfolio. In Chapter 8 we established that the optimal risky portfolio for any investor is the one that maximizes the reward-to-variability ratio, or the expected excess rate of return (over the risk-free rate) divided by the standard deviation. A manager who uses this Markowitz methodology to construct the optimal risky portfolio will satisfy all clients regardless of risk aversion. Clients, for their part, can evaluate managers using statistical methods to draw inferences from realized rates of return about prospective, or ex ante, reward-to-variability ratios.

William Sharpe's assessment of mutual fund performance[2] is the seminal work in the area of portfolio performance evaluation (see Chapter 24). The reward-to-variability ratio has come to be known as **Sharpe's measure:**

$$S = \frac{E(r_P) - r_f}{\sigma_P}$$

It is now a common criterion for tracking performance of professionally managed portfolios.

Briefly, mean-variance portfolio theory implies that the objective of professional portfolio managers is to maximize the (ex ante) Sharpe measure, which entails maximizing the slope of the CAL (capital allocation line). A "good" manager is one whose CAL is steeper than the CAL representing the passive strategy of holding a market-index portfolio. Clients can observe rates of return and compute the realized Sharpe measure (the ex post CAL) to evaluate the relative performance of their manager.

Ideally, clients would like to invest their funds with the most able manager, one who consistently obtains the highest Sharpe measure and presumably has real forecasting ability. This is true for all clients regardless of their degree of risk aversion. At the same time, each client must decide what fraction of investment funds to allocate to this manager, placing the remainder in a safe fund. If the manager's Sharpe measure is constant over time (and can be estimated by clients), the investor can compute the optimal fraction to be invested with the manager from equation 27.1, based on the portfolio long-term average return and variance. The remainder will be invested in a money market fund.

The manager's ex ante Sharpe measure from updated forecasts will be constantly varying. Clients would have liked to increase their allocation to the risky portfolio when the forecasts are optimistic, and vice versa. However, it would be impractical to constantly communicate updated forecasts to clients and for them to constantly revise their allocation between the risky portfolios and risk-free asset.

Allowing managers to shift funds between their optimal risky portfolio and a safe asset according to their forecasts alleviates the problem. Indeed, many stock funds allow the managers reasonable flexibility to do just that.

## 27.3   MARKET TIMING

Consider the results of the following two different investment strategies:

1. An investor who put $1,000 in 30-day commercial paper on January 1, 1927, and rolled over all proceeds into 30-day paper (or into 30-day T-bills after they were introduced) would have ended on December 31, 1978, fifty-two years later, with $3,600.
2. An investor who put $1,000 in the NYSE index on January 1, 1927, and reinvested all dividends in that portfolio would have ended on December 31, 1978, with $67,500.

Suppose we defined perfect **market timing** as the ability to tell (with certainty) at the beginning of each month whether the NYSE portfolio will outperform the 30-day paper portfolio. Accordingly, at the beginning of each month, the market timer shifts all funds into either cash equivalents (30-day paper) or equities (the NYSE portfolio), whichever is predicted to do better. Beginning with $1,000 on the same date, how would the perfect timer have ended up 52 years later?

---

[2] William F. Sharpe, "Mutual Fund Performance," *Journal of Business, Supplement on Security Prices* 39 (January 1966).

This is how Nobel Laureate Robert Merton began a seminar with finance professors 25 years ago. As he collected responses, the boldest guess was a few million dollars. The correct answer: $5.36 *billion*.[3]

These numbers highlight the power of compounding. This effect is particularly important because more and more of the funds under management represent retirement savings. The horizons of such investments may not be as long as 52 years but are measured in decades, making compounding a significant factor.

Another result that may seem surprising at first is the huge difference between the end-of-period value of the all-safe asset strategy ($3,600) and that of the all-equity strategy ($67,500). Why would anyone invest in safe assets given this historical record? If you have internalized the lessons of previous chapters, you know the reason: risk. The average rates of return and the standard deviations on the all-bills and all-equity strategies for this period are:

|  | Arithmetic Mean | Standard Deviation |
|---|---|---|
| Bills | 2.55 | 2.10 |
| Equities | 10.70 | 22.14 |

The significantly higher standard deviation of the rate of return on the equity portfolio is commensurate with its significantly higher average return.

Can we also view the rate-of-return premium on the perfect-timing fund as a risk premium? The answer must be "no," because the perfect timer never does worse than either bills or the market. The extra return is not compensation for the possibility of poor returns but is instead attributable to superior analysis. It is the value of superior information that is reflected in the tremendous end-of-period value of the portfolio.

The monthly rate-of-return statistics for the all-equity portfolio and the timing portfolio are:

| Per Month | All Equities (%) | Perfect Timer No Charge (%) | Perfect Timer Fair Charge (%) |
|---|---|---|---|
| Average rate of return | 0.85 | 2.58 | 0.55 |
| Average excess return over return on safe asset | 0.64 | 2.37 | 0.34 |
| Standard deviation | 5.89 | 3.82 | 3.55 |
| Highest return | 38.55 | 38.55 | 30.14 |
| Lowest return | −29.12 | 0.06 | −7.06 |
| Coefficient of skewness | 0.42 | 4.28 | 2.84 |

Ignore for the moment the fourth column ("Perfect Timer—Fair Charge"). The results of rows 1 and 2 are self-explanatory. The third row, standard deviation, requires some discussion. The standard deviation of the monthly rate of return earned by the perfect market timer was 3.82%, far greater than the volatility of T-bill returns over the same period. Does this imply that (perfect) timing is a riskier strategy than investing in bills? No. For this analysis standard deviation is a misleading measure of risk.

[3] This demonstration has been extended to recent data with similar results.

To see why, consider how you might choose between two hypothetical strategies: The first offers a sure rate of return of 5%; the second strategy offers an uncertain return that is given by 5% *plus* a random number that is zero with probability .5 and 5% with probability .5. The characteristics of each strategy are

|  | Strategy 1 (%) | Strategy 2 (%) |
|---|---|---|
| Expected return | 5 | 7.5 |
| Standard deviation | 0 | 2.5 |
| Highest return | 5 | 10.0 |
| Lowest return | 5 | 5.0 |

Clearly, Strategy 2 dominates Strategy 1 because its rate of return is *at least* equal to that of Strategy 1 and sometimes greater. No matter how risk averse you are, you will always prefer Strategy 2, despite its significant standard deviation. Compared to Strategy 1, Strategy 2 provides only "good surprises," so the standard deviation in this case cannot be a measure of risk.

These two strategies are analogous to the case of the perfect timer compared with an all-equity or all-bills strategy. In every period the perfect timer obtains at least as good a return, in some cases a better one. Therefore the timer's standard deviation is a misleading measure of risk compared to an all-equity or all-bills strategy.

Returning to the empirical results, you can see that the highest rate of return is identical for the all-equity and the timing strategies, whereas the lowest rate of return is positive for the perfect timer and disastrous for all the all-equity portfolio. Another reflection of this is seen in the coefficient of skewness, which measures the asymmetry of the distribution of returns. Because the equity portfolio is almost (but not exactly) normally distributed, its coefficient of skewness is very low at .42. In contrast, the perfect timing strategy effectively eliminates the negative tail of the distribution of portfolio returns (the part below the risk-free rate). Its returns are "skewed to the right," and its coefficient of skewness is therefore quite large, 4.28.

Now for the fourth column, "Perfect Timer—Fair Charge," which is perhaps the most interesting. Most assuredly, the perfect timer will charge clients for such a valuable service. (The perfect timer may have otherworldly predictive powers, but saintly benevolence is unlikely.)

Subtracting a fair fee (discussed later) from the monthly rate of return of the timer's portfolio gives us an average rate of return lower than that of the passive, all-equity strategy. However, because the fee is *constructed* to be fair, the two portfolios (the all-equity strategy and the market-timing-with-fee strategy) must be equally attractive after risk adjustment. In this case, again, the standard deviation of the market timing strategy (with fee) is of no help in adjusting for risk because the coefficient of skewness remains high, 2.84. In other words, mean-variance analysis is inadequate for valuing market timing. We need an alternative approach.

## Valuing Market Timing as an Option

The key to analyzing the pattern of returns to the perfect market timer is to recognize that perfect foresight is equivalent to holding a call option on the equity portfolio. The perfect timer invests 100% in either the safe asset or the equity portfolio, whichever will yield the higher return. This is shown in Figure 27.1. The rate of return is bounded from below by $r_f$.

To see the value of information as an option, suppose that the market index currently is at $S_0$ and that a call option on the index has an exercise price of $X = S_0(1 + r_f)$. If the market outperforms bills over the coming period, $S_T$ will exceed $X$, whereas it will be less than $X$ otherwise. Now look at the payoff to a portfolio consisting of this option and $S_0$ dollars invested in bills:

**Figure 27.1
Rate of return
of a perfect
market timer**

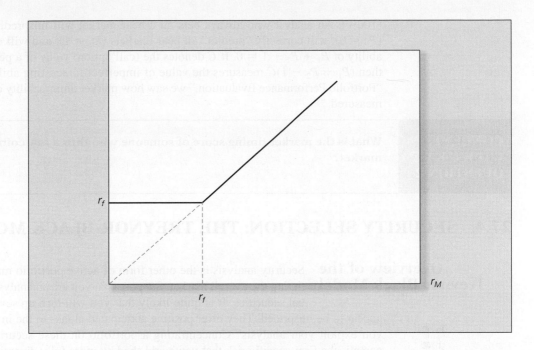

| | $S_T < X$ | $S_T \geq X$ |
|---|---|---|
| Bills | $S_0(1 + r_f)$ | $S_0(1 + r_f)$ |
| Option | $0$ | $S_T - X$ |
| Total | $S_0(1 + r_f)$ | $S_T$ |

The portfolio pays the risk-free return when the market is bearish (i.e., the market return is less than the risk-free rate), and it pays the market return when the market is bullish and beats bills. Such a portfolio is a perfect market timer. Consequently, we can measure the value of perfect ability as the value of the call option, because a call enables the investor to earn the market return only when it exceeds $r_f$. This insight lets Merton[4] value timing ability using the theory of option of valuation, and calculate the fair charge for it.

**The Value of
Imperfect Forecasting**    Unfortunately, managers are not perfect forecasters. It seems pretty obvious that if managers are right most of the time, they are doing very well. However, when we say "most of the time," we cannot mean merely the percentage of the time a manager is right. The weather forecaster in Tucson, Arizona, who *always* predicts no rain, may be right 90% of the time. But a high success rate for a "stopped-clock" strategy clearly is not evidence of forecasting ability.

Similarly, the appropriate measure of market forecasting ability is not the overall proportion of correct forecasts. If the market is up two days out of three and a forecaster always predicts market advance, the two-thirds success rate is not a measure of forecasting ability. We need to examine the proportion of bull markets ($r_M > r_f$) correctly forecast *and* the proportion of bear markets ($r_M < r_f$) correctly forecast.

If we call $P_1$ the proportion of the correct forecasts of bull markets and $P_2$ the proportion for bear markets, then $P_1 + P_2 - 1$ is the correct measure of timing ability. For example, a forecaster who always guesses correctly will have $P_1 = P_2 = 1$, and will show ability of 1

---

[4] Robert C. Merton, "On Market Timing and Investment Performance: An Equilibrium Theory of Value for Market Forecasts," *Journal of Business,* July 1981.

(100%). An analyst who always bets on a bear market will mispredict all bull markets ($P_1 = 0$), will correctly "predict" all bear markets ($P_2 = 1$), and will end up with timing ability of $P_1 + P_2 - 1 = 0$. If $C$ denotes the (call option) value of a perfect market timer, then $(P_1 + P_2 - 1)C$ measures the value of imperfect forecasting ability. In Chapter 24, "Portfolio Performance Evaluation," we saw how market timing ability can be detected and measured.

> **CONCEPT CHECK ☞ QUESTION 2**
>
> **What is the market timing score of someone who flips a fair coin to predict the market?**

## 27.4   SECURITY SELECTION: THE TREYNOR-BLACK MODEL

### Overview of the Treynor-Black Model

Security analysis is the other form of active portfolio management besides timing the overall market. Suppose that you are an analyst studying individual securities. It is quite likely that you will turn up several securities that appear to be mispriced. They offer positive anticipated alphas to the investor. But how do you exploit your analysis? Concentrating a portfolio on these securities entails a cost, namely, the firm-specific risk that you could shed by more fully diversifying. As an active manager you must strike a balance between aggressive exploitation of perceived security mispricing and diversification motives that dictate that a few stocks should not dominate the portfolio.

Treynor and Black[5] developed an optimizing model for portfolio managers who use security analysis. It represents a portfolio management theory that assumes security markets are *nearly* efficient. The essence of the model is this:

1. Security analysts in an active investment management organization can analyze in depth only a limited number of stocks out of the entire universe of securities. The securities not analyzed are assumed to be fairly priced.

2. For the purpose of efficient diversification, the market index portfolio is the baseline portfolio, which the model treats as the passive portfolio.

3. The macro forecasting unit of the investment management firm provides forecasts of the expected rate of return and variance of the passive (market-index) portfolio.

4. The objective of security analysis is to form an active portfolio of a necessarily limited number of securities. Perceived mispricing of the analyzed securities is what guides the composition of this active portfolio.

5. Analysts follow several steps to make up the active portfolio and evaluate its expected performance:
   a. Estimate the beta of each analyzed security and its residual risk. From the beta and macro forecast, $E(r_M) - r_f$, determine the *required* rate of return of the security.
   b. Given the degree of mispricing of each security, determine its expected return and expected *abnormal* return (alpha).
   c. The cost of less-than-full diversification comes from the nonsystematic risk of the mispriced stock, the variance of the stock's residual, $\sigma^2(e)$, which offsets the benefit (alpha) of specializing in an underpriced security.

---

[5] Jack Treynor and Fischer Black, "How to Use Security Analysis to Improve Portfolio Selection," *Journal of Business,* January 1973.

      *d.* Use the estimates for the values of alpha, beta, and $\sigma^2(e)$ to determine the optimal weight of each security in the active portfolio.

      *e.* Compute the alpha, beta, and $\sigma^2(e)$ of the active portfolio from the weights of the securities in the portfolio.

6. The macroeconomic forecasts for the passive index portfolio and the composite forecasts for the active portfolio are used to determine the optimal risky portfolio, which will be a combination of the passive and active portfolios.

Treynor and Black's model did not take the industry by storm. This is unfortunate for several reasons:

1. Just as even imperfect market timing ability has enormous value, security analysis of the sort Treynor and Black proposed has similar potential value.[6] Even with far from perfect security analysis, proper active management can add value.

2. The Treynor-Black model is conceptually easy to implement. Moreover, it is useful even when some of its simplifying assumptions are relaxed.

3. The model lends itself to use in decentralized organizations. This property is essential to efficiency in complex organizations.

## Portfolio Construction

Assuming that all securities are fairly priced, and using the index model as a guideline for the rate of return on fairly priced securities, the rate of return on the *i*th security is given by

$$r_i = r_f + \beta_i(r_M - r_f) + e_i \tag{27.2}$$

where $e_i$ is the zero mean, firm-specific disturbance.

Absent security analysis, Treynor and Black (TB) took equation 27.2 to represent the rate of return on all securities and assumed that the market portfolio, $M$, is the efficient portfolio. For simplicity, they also assumed that the nonsystematic components of returns, $e_i$, are independent across securities. As for market timing, TB assumed that the forecast for the **passive portfolio** already has been made, so that the expected return on the market index, $r_M$, as well as its variance, $\sigma_M^2$, has been assessed.

Now a portfolio manager unleashes a team of security analysts to investigate a subset of the universe of available securities. The objective is to form an active portfolio of positions in the analyzed securities to be mixed with the index portfolio. For each security, $k$, that is researched, we write the rate of return as

$$r_k = r_f + \beta_k(r_M - r_f) + e_k + \alpha_k \tag{27.3}$$

where $\alpha_k$ represents the extra expected return (called the *abnormal return*) attributable to any perceived mispricing of the security. Thus, for each security analyzed the research team estimates the parameters $\alpha_k$, $\beta_k$, and $\sigma^2(e_k)$. If all the $\alpha_k$ turn out to be zero, there would be no reason to depart from the passive strategy and the index portfolio $M$ would remain the manager's choice. However, this is a remote possibility. In general, there will be a significant number of nonzero alpha values, some positive and some negative.

One way to get an overview of the TB methodology is to examine what we should do with the active portfolio once we determine it. Suppose that the **active portfolio** $(A)$ has been constructed somehow and has the parameters $\alpha_A$, $\beta_A$, and $\sigma^2(e_A)$. Its total variance is the sum of its systematic variance, $\beta_A^2\sigma_M^2$, plus the nonsystematic variance, $\sigma^2(e_A)$. Its covariance with the market index portfolio, $M$, is

$$\text{Cov}(r_A, r_M) = \beta_A\sigma_M^2$$

---

[6] Alex Kane, Alan Marcus, and Robert Trippi, "The Valuation of Security Analysis," *Journal of Portfolio Management,* Spring 1999.

Figure 27.2 shows the optimization process with the active and passive portfolios. The dashed efficient frontier represents the universe of all securities assuming that they are all fairly priced, that is, that all alphas are zero. By definition, the market index, $M$, is on this efficient frontier and is tangent to the (dashed) capital market line (CML). In practice, the analysts do not need to know this frontier. They need only to observe the market-index portfolio and construct a portfolio resulting in a capital allocation line that lies above the CML. Given their perceived superior analysis, they will view the market-index portfolio as inefficient: The active portfolio, $A$, constructed from mispriced securities, must lie, by design, above the CML.

To locate the active portfolio $A$ in Figure 27.2, we need its expected return and standard deviation. The standard deviation is

$$\sigma_A = [\beta_A^2 \sigma_M^2 + \sigma^2(e_A)]^{1/2}$$

Because of the positive alpha value that is forecast for $A$, it may plot above the (dashed) CML with expected return

$$E(r_A) = \alpha_A + r_f + \beta_A[E(r_M) - r_f]$$

The optimal combination of the active portfolio, $A$, with the passive portfolio, $M$, is a simple application of the construction of optimal risky portfolios from two component assets that we first encountered in Chapter 8. Because the active portfolio is not perfectly correlated with the market-index portfolio, we need to account for their mutual correlation in the determination of the optimal allocation between the two portfolios. This is evident from the solid efficient frontier that passes through $M$ and $A$ in Figure 27.2. It supports the optimal capital allocation line (CAL) and identifies the optimal risky portfolio, $P$, which

**Figure 27.2**
**The optimization process with active and passive portfolios**

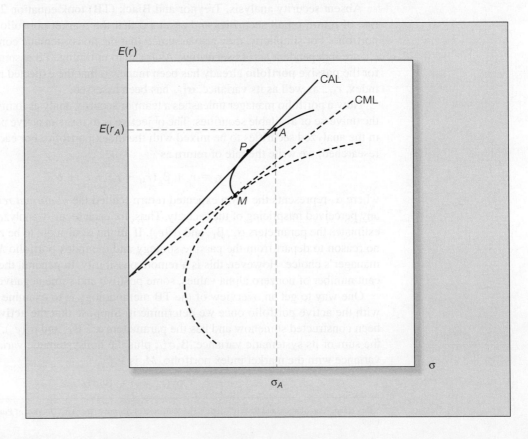

combines portfolios $A$ and $M$ and is the tangency point of the CAL to the efficient frontier. The active portfolio $A$ in this example is not the ultimate efficient portfolio, because we need to mix $A$ with the passive market portfolio to achieve optimal diversification.

Let us now outline the algebraic approach to this optimization problem. If we invest a proportion, $w$, in the active portfolio and $1 - w$ in the market index, the portfolio return will be

$$r_p(w) = wr_A + (1 - w)r_M$$

To find the weight, $w$, which provides the best (i.e., the steepest) CAL, we use equation 8.7 from Chapter 8, which describes the optimal risky portfolio composed of two risky assets (in this case, $A$ and $M$) when there is a risk-free asset:

$$w_A = \frac{[E(r_A) - r_f]\sigma_M^2 - [E(r_M) - r_f]\text{Cov}(r_A, r_M)}{[E(r_A) - r_f]\sigma_M^2 + [E(r_M) - r_f]\sigma_A^2 - [E(r_A) - r_f + E(r_M) - r_f]\text{Cov}(r_A, r_M)} \quad (8.7)$$

Now recall that

$$E(r_A) - r_f = \alpha_A + \beta_A R_M \qquad \text{where } R_M = E(r_M) - r_f$$
$$\text{Cov}(R_A, R_M) = \beta_A \sigma_M^2 \qquad \text{where } R_A = E(r_A) - r_f$$
$$\sigma_A^2 = \beta_A^2 \sigma_M^2 + \sigma^2(e_A)$$

$$[E(r_A) - r_f] + [E(r_M) - r_f] = (\alpha_A + \beta R_M) + R_M = \alpha_A + R_M(1 + \beta_A)$$

Substituting these expressions into equation 8.7, dividing both numerator and denominator by $\sigma_M^2$, and collecting terms yields the expression for the optimal weight in portfolio $A$, $w^*$,

$$w^* = \frac{\alpha_A}{\alpha_A(1 - \beta_A) + R_M \dfrac{\sigma^2(e_A)}{\sigma_M^2}} \quad (27.4)$$

Let's begin with the simple case where $\beta_A = 1$ and substitute into equation 27.4. Then the optimal weight, $w_0$, is

$$w_0 = \frac{\dfrac{\alpha_A}{R_M}}{\dfrac{\sigma^2(e_A)}{\sigma_M^2}} = \frac{\alpha_A/\sigma^2(e_A)}{R_M/\sigma_M^2} \quad (27.5)$$

Here is some intuition for this result. If the systematic risk of the active portfolio is average, that is, $\beta_A = 1$, then the optimal weight is the "relative advantage" of portfolio $A$ as measured by the ratio: alpha/[market excess return], divided by the "disadvantage" of $A$, that is, the ratio: [nonsystematic risk of $A$]/[market risk]. Some algebra applied to equation 27.4 reveals the relationship between $w_0$ and $w^*$:

$$w^* = \frac{w_0}{1 + (1 - \beta_A)w_0} \quad (27.6)$$

$w^*$ increases when $\beta_A$ increases because the greater the systematic risk, $\beta_A$, of the active portfolio, $A$, the smaller is the benefit from diversifying it with the index, $M$, and the more beneficial it is to take advantage of the mispriced securities. However, we expect the beta of the active portfolio to be in the neighborhood of 1.0 and the optimal weight, $w^*$, to be close to $w_0$.

What is the reward-to-variability ratio of the optimal risky portfolio once we find the best mix, $w^*$, of the active and passive index portfolios? It turns out that if we compute the square of Sharpe's measure of the risky portfolio, we can separate the contributions of the index and active portfolios as follows:

$$S_P^2 = S_M^2 + \frac{\alpha_A^2}{\sigma^2(e_A)} = \left[\frac{R_M}{\sigma_M}\right]^2 + \left[\frac{\alpha_A}{\sigma(e_A)}\right]^2 \tag{27.7}$$

This decomposition of the Sharpe measure of the optimal risky portfolio, which by the way is valid *only* for the optimal portfolio, tells us how to construct the active portfolio. Equation 27.7 shows that the highest Sharpe measure for the risky portfolio will be attained when we construct an active portfolio that maximizes the value of $\alpha_A/\sigma(e_A)$. The ratio of alpha to residual standard deviation of the active portfolio will be maximized when we choose a weight for the $k$th analyzed security as follows:

$$w_k = \frac{\alpha_k/\sigma^2(e_k)}{\sum_{i=1}^n \alpha_i/\sigma^2(e_i)} \tag{27.8}$$

This makes sense: The weight of a security in the active portfolio depends on the ratio of the degree of mispricing, $\alpha_k$, to the nonsystematic risk, $\sigma^2(e_k)$, of the security. The denominator, the sum of the ratio across securities, is a scale factor to guarantee that portfolio weights sum to one.

Note from equation 27.7 that the square of Sharpe's measure of the optimal risky portfolio is increased over the square of the Sharpe measure of the passive (market-index) portfolio by the amount

$$\left[\frac{\alpha_A}{\sigma(e_A)}\right]^2$$

The ratio of the degree of mispricing, $\alpha_A$, to the nonsystematic standard deviation, $\sigma(e_A)$, is therefore a natural performance measure of the active component of the risky portfolio. Sometimes this is called the **information ratio.**

We can calculate the contribution of a single security in the active portfolio to the portfolio's overall performance. When the active portfolio contains $n$ analyzed securities, the total improvement in the squared Sharpe measure equals the sum of the squared information ratios of the analyzed securities,

$$\left[\frac{\alpha_A}{\sigma(e_A)}\right]^2 = \sum_{i=1}^n \left[\frac{\alpha_i}{\sigma(e_i)}\right]^2 \tag{27.9}$$

The information ratio for each security, $\alpha_i/\sigma(e_i)$, is a measure of the contribution of that security to the performance of the active portfolio.

The best way to illustrate the Treynor-Black process is through an example that can be easily worked out in a spreadsheet. Suppose that the macroforecasting unit of Drex Portfolio Inc. (DPF) issues a forecast for a 15% market return. The forecast's standard error is 20%. The risk-free rate is 7%. The macro data can be summarized as follows:

$$R_M = E(r_M) - r_f = 8\%; \sigma_M = 20\%$$

| E-INVESTMENTS | |
|---|---|
| **Calculating the Information Ratio** | Go to **www.the401k.com**. Click through *Reference,* then *Focus on 401(k) Newsletter,* where you can choose the Second Quarter 2001 newsletter. This choice allows you to review the calculation of the information ratio. How can the portfolio manager take extra risk to "beat" the market indexes? What does the information ratio measure? |

At the same time the security analysis division submits to the portfolio manager the following forecast of annual returns for the three securities that it covers:

| Stock | $\alpha$ | $\beta$ | $\sigma(e)$ | $\alpha/\sigma(e)$ |
|-------|------|------|-------|----------|
| 1 | 7% | 1.6 | 45% | .1556 |
| 2 | −5 | 1.0 | 32 | −.1563 |
| 3 | 3 | 0.5 | 26 | .1154 |

Note that the alpha estimates appear reasonably moderate. The estimates of the residual standard deviations are correlated with the betas, just as they are in reality. The magnitudes also reflect typical values for NYSE stocks. Equations 27.9, 27.7, and the analyst input table allow a quick calculation of the DPF portfolio's Sharpe measure.

$$S_P = [(8/20)^2 + .1556^2 + .1563^2 + .1154^2]^{1/2} = \sqrt{.2220} = .4711$$

Compare the result with the Sharpe ratio for the market-index portfolio, which is only $8/20 = .40$. We now proceed to compute the composition and performance of the active portfolio.

First, let us construct the optimal active portfolio implied by the security analyst input list. To do so we compute the appraisal ratios as follows (remember to use decimal representations of returns in the formulas):

| Stock | $\alpha/\sigma^2(e)$ | | $\dfrac{\alpha_k}{\sigma^2(e_k)}\Big/\displaystyle\sum_{i=1}^{3}\dfrac{\alpha_i}{\sigma^2(e_i)}$ | |
|-------|------|------|------|------|
| 1 | $.07/.45^2 =$ | .3457 | .3457/.3012 = | 1.1477 |
| 2 | $-.05/.32^2 =$ | −.4883 | −.4883/.3012 = | −1.6212 |
| 3 | $.03/.26^2 =$ | .4438 | .4438/.3012 = | 1.4735 |
| Total | | .3012 | | 1.0000 |

The last column presents the optimal positions of each of the three securities in the active portfolio. Obviously, Stock 2, with a negative alpha, has a negative weight. The magnitudes of the individual positions in the active portfolio (e.g., 114.77% in Stock 1) seem quite extreme. However, this should not concern us because the active portfolio will later be mixed with the well-diversified market-index portfolio, resulting in much more moderate positions, as we shall see shortly.

The forecasts for the stocks, together with the proposed composition of the active portfolio, lead to the following parameter estimates for the active portfolio:

$$\alpha_A = 1.1477 \times .07 + (-1.6212) \times (-.05) + 1.4735 \times .03$$
$$= .2056 = 20.56\%$$
$$\beta_A = 1.1477 \times 1.6 + (-1.6212) \times 1.0 + 1.4735 \times .5 = .9519$$
$$\sigma(e_A) = [1.1477^2 \times .45^2 + (-1.6212)^2 \times .32^2 + 1.4735^2 \times .26^2]^{1/2}$$
$$= .8262 = 82.62\%$$
$$\sigma^2(e_A) = .8262^2 = .6826$$

Note that the negative weight (short position) on the negative alpha stock results in a positive contribution to the alpha of the active portfolio. Note also that because of the assumption that the stock residuals are uncorrelated, the active portfolio's residual variance is simply the weighted sum of the individual stock residual variances, with the squared portfolio proportions as weights.

The parameters of the active portfolio are now used to determine its proportion in the overall risky portfolio:

$$w_0 = \frac{\alpha_A/\sigma^2(e_A)}{R_M/\sigma_M^2} = \frac{.2056/.6826}{.08/.04} = .1506$$

$$w^* = \frac{w_0}{1 + (1 - \beta_A)w_0} = \frac{.1506}{1 + (1 - .9519) \times .1506} = .1495$$

Although the active portfolio's alpha is impressive (20.56%), its proportion in the overall risky portfolio, before adjustment for beta, is only 15.06%, because of its large nonsystematic standard deviation (82.62%). Such is the importance of diversification. As it happens, the beta of the active portfolio is almost 1.0, and hence the adjustment for beta (from $w_0$ to $w^*$) is small, from 15.06% to 14.95%. The direction of the change makes sense. If the beta of the active portfolio is low (less than 1.0), there is more potential gain from diversification, hence a smaller position in the active portfolio is called for. If the beta of the active portfolio were significantly greater than 1.0, a larger correction in the opposite direction would be called for.

The proportions of the individual stocks in the active portfolio, together with the proportion of the active portfolio in the overall risky portfolio, determine the proportions of each individual stock in the overall risky portfolio.

| Stock | Final Position | | |
|---|---|---|---|
| 1 | .1495 × 1.1477 | = | .1716 |
| 2 | .1495 × (−1.6212) | = | −.2424 |
| 3 | .1495 × 1.4735 | = | .2202 |
| Active portfolio | | | .1495 |
| Market portfolio | | | .8505 |
| | | | 1.0000 |

The parameters of the active portfolio and market-index portfolio are now used to forecast the performance of the optimal, overall risky portfolio. When optimized, a property of the risky portfolio is that its squared Sharpe measure exceeds that of the passive portfolio by the square of the active portfolio's information ratio:

$$S_P^2 = \left[\frac{R_M}{\sigma_M}\right]^2 + \left[\frac{\alpha_A}{\sigma(e_A)}\right]^2$$

$$= .16 + .0619 = .2219$$

and hence the Sharpe measure of the DPF portfolio is $\sqrt{.2219} = .4711$, compared with .40 for the passive portfolio.

Another measure of the gain from increasing the Sharpe measure is the $M^2$ statistic, as described in Chapter 24. $M^2$ is calculated by comparing the expected return of a portfolio on the capital allocation line supported by portfolio $P$, CAL($P$), with a standard deviation equal to that of the market index, to the expected return on the market index. In other words, we mix portfolio $P$ with the risk-free asset to obtain a new portfolio $P^*$ that has the same standard deviation as the market portfolio. Since both portfolios have equal risk, we can compare their expected returns. The $M^2$ statistic is the difference in expected returns. Portfolio $P^*$ can be obtained by investing a fraction $\sigma_M/\sigma_P$ in $P$ and a fraction $(1 - \sigma_M/\sigma_P)$ in the risk-free asset.

The risk premium on CAL($P^*$) with total risk $\sigma_M$ is given by (see Chapter 24)

$$R_{P^*} = E(r_{P^*}) - r_f = S_P\sigma_M = .4711 \times .20 = .0942, \text{ or } 9.42\% \qquad (27.10)$$

and

$$M^2 = [R_{P^*} - R_M] = 9.42 - 8 = 1.42\% \tag{27.11}$$

At first blush, an incremental expected return of 1.42% seems paltry compared with the alpha values submitted by the analyst. This seemingly modest improvement is the result of diversification motives: To mitigate the large risk of individual stocks (verify that the standard deviation of stock 1 is 55%) and maximize the portfolio Sharpe measure (which compares excess return to total volatility), we must diversify the active portfolio by mixing it with $M$. Note also that this improvement has been achieved with only three stocks, and with forecasts and portfolio rebalancing only once a year. Increasing the number of stocks and the frequency of forecasts can improve the results dramatically.

For example, suppose the analyst covers three more stocks that turn out to have alphas and risk levels identical to the first three. Use equation 27.9 to show that the squared appraisal ratio of the active portfolio will double. By using equation 27.7, it is easy to show that the new Sharpe measure will rise to .5327. Equation 27.11 then implies that $M^2$ rises to 2.65%, almost double the previous value. Increasing the frequency of forecasts and portfolio rebalancing will deploy the power of compounding to improve annual performance even more.

**CONCEPT**
**CHECK** ☞
**QUESTION 3**

*a.* **When short positions are prohibited, the manager simply discards stocks with negative alphas. Using the preceding example, what would be the composition of the active portfolio if short sales were disallowed? Find the cost of the short-sale restriction in terms of the decline in performance ($M^2$) of the new overall risky portfolio.**

*b.* **What is the contribution of security selection to portfolio performance if the macro forecast is adjusted upward, for example, to $R_M = 12\%$, and short sales are again allowed?**

# 27.5   MULTIFACTOR MODELS AND ACTIVE PORTFOLIO MANAGEMENT

Portfolio managers use various multifactor models of security returns. So far our analytical framework for active portfolio management seems to rest on the validity of the index model, that is, on a single-factor security model. Using a multifactor model will not affect the construction of the active portfolio because the entire TB analysis focuses on the residuals of the index model. If we were to replace the one-factor model with a multifactor model, we would continue to form the active portfolio by calculating each security's alpha relative to its fair return (given its betas on *all* factors), and again we would combine the active portfolio with the portfolio that would be formed in the absence of security analysis. The multifactor framework, however, does raise several new issues.

You saw in Chapter 10 how the index model simplifies the construction of the input list necessary for portfolio optimization programs. If

$$r_i - r_f = \alpha_i + \beta_i(r_M - r_f) + e_i$$

adequately describes the security market, then the variance of any asset is the sum of systematic and nonsystematic risk: $\sigma^2(r_i) = \beta_i^2 \sigma_M^2 + \sigma^2(e_i)$, and the covariance between any two assets is $\beta_i \beta_j \sigma_M^2$.

How do we generalize this rule to use in a multifactor model? To simplify, let us consider a two-factor world, and let us call the two factor portfolios $M$ and $H$. Then we generalize the index model to

$$r_i - r_f = \beta_{iM}(r_M - r_f) + \beta_{iH}(r_H - r_f) + \alpha_i + e_i$$
$$= R_\beta + \alpha_i + e_i \qquad (27.12)$$

$\beta_{iM}$ and $\beta_{iH}$ are the betas of the security relative to portfolios $M$ and $H$. Given the rates of return on the factor portfolios, $r_M$ and $r_H$, the fair excess rate of return over $r_f$ on a security is denoted $R_\beta$ and its expected abnormal return is $\alpha_i$.

How can we use equation 27.12 to form optimal portfolios? As before, investors wish to maximize the Sharpe measures of their portfolios. The factor structure of equation 27.12 can be used to generate the inputs for the Markowitz portfolio selection algorithm. The variance and covariance estimates are now more complex, however:

$$\sigma^2(r_i) = \beta_{iM}^2 \sigma_M^2 + \beta_{iH}^2 \sigma_H^2 + 2\beta_{iM}\beta_{iH}\text{Cov}(r_M, r_H) + \sigma^2(e_i)$$
$$\text{Cov}(r_i, r_j) = \beta_{iM}\beta_{jM}\sigma_M^2 + \beta_{iH}\beta_{jH}\sigma_H^2 + (\beta_{iM}\beta_{jH} + \beta_{jM}\beta_{iH})\text{Cov}(r_M, r_H)$$

Nevertheless, the informational economy of the factor model still is valuable, because we can estimate a covariance matrix for an $n$-security portfolio from

$n$ estimates of $\beta_{iM}$

$n$ estimates of $\beta_{iH}$

$n$ estimates of $\sigma^2(e_i)$

1 estimate of $\sigma_M^2$

1 estimate of $\sigma_H^2$

rather than $n(n + 1)/2$ separate variance and covariance estimates. Thus the factor structure continues to simplify portfolio construction data requirements.

The factor structure also suggests an efficient method to allocate research effort. Analysts can specialize in forecasting means and variances of different factor portfolios. Having established factor betas, they can form a covariance matrix to be used together with expected security returns generated by the CAPM or APT to construct an optimal passive risky portfolio. If active analysis of individual stocks also is attempted, the procedure of constructing the optimal active portfolio and its optimal combination with the passive portfolio is identical to that followed in the single-factor case.

In the case of the multifactor market even passive investors (meaning those who accept market prices as "fair") need to do a considerable amount of work. They need forecasts of the expected return and volatility of each factor return, *and* they need to determine the appropriate weights on each factor portfolio to maximize their expected utility. Such a process is straightforward in principle, but it quickly becomes computationally demanding.

## 27.6   IMPERFECT FORECASTS OF ALPHA VALUES AND THE USE OF THE TREYNOR-BLACK MODEL IN INDUSTRY

Suppose an analyst is assigned to a security and provides you with a forecast of $\alpha = 20\%$. It looks like a great opportunity! Using this forecast in the Treynor-Black algorithm, we'll end up tilting our portfolio heavily toward this security. Should we go out on a limb? Before doing so, any reasonable manager would ask: "How good is the analyst?" Unless the answer is a resounding "good," a reasonable manager would discount the forecast. We can quantify this notion.

Suppose we have a record of an analyst's past forecast of alpha, $\alpha^f$. Relying on the index model and obtaining reliable estimates of the stock beta, we can estimate the true alphas (after the fact) from the average realized excess returns on the security, $\overline{R}$, and the index, $\overline{R}_M$, that is,

$$\alpha = \overline{R} - \beta\overline{R}_M$$

To measure the forecasting accuracy of the analyst, we can estimate a regression of the forecasts on the realized alpha:

$$\alpha^f = a_0 + a_1\alpha + \varepsilon$$

The coefficients $a_0$ and $a_1$ reflect potential bias in the forecasts, which we will ignore for simplicity; that is, we will suppose $a_0 = 0$ and $a_1 = 1$. Because the forecast errors are uncorrelated with the true alpha, the variance of the forecast is

$$\sigma^2_{\alpha^f} = \sigma^2_\alpha + \sigma^2_\varepsilon$$

The quality of the forecasts can be measured by the squared correlation coefficient between the forecasts and realization, equivalently, the ratio of explained variance to total variance

$$\rho^2 = \frac{\sigma^2_\alpha}{\sigma^2_\alpha + \sigma^2_\varepsilon}$$

This equation shows us how to "discount" analysts' forecasts to reflect their precision. Knowing the quality of past forecasts, $\rho^2$, we "shrink" any new forecast, $\alpha^f$, to $\rho^2\alpha^f$, to minimize forecast error. This procedure is quite intuitive: If the analyst is perfect, that is, $\rho^2 = 1$, we take the forecast at face value. If analysts' forecasts have proven to be useless, with $\rho^2 = 0$, we ignore the forecast. The quality of the forecast gives us the precise shrinkage factor to use.

Suppose the analysts' forecasts of the alpha of the three stocks in our previous example are all of equal quality, $\rho^2 = .2$. Shrinking the forecasts of alpha by a factor of .2 and repeating the optimization process, we end up with a much smaller weight on the active portfolio (.03 instead of .15), a much smaller Sharpe measure (.4031 instead of .4711), and a much smaller $M^2$ (.06% instead of 1.42%).

The reduction in portfolio expected performance does not reflect an inferior procedure. Rather, accepting alpha forecasts without acknowledging and adjusting for their imprecision would be naïve. We must adjust our expectations to the quality of the forecasts.

In reality, we can expect the situation to be much worse. A forecast quality of .2, that is, a correlation coefficient between alpha forecasts and realizations of $\sqrt{.2} = .45$, is most likely unrealistic in nearly efficient markets. Moreover, we don't even know this quality, and its estimation introduces yet another potential error into the optimization process. Finally, the other parameters we use in the TB model—market expected return and variance, security betas and residual variances—are also estimated with errors. Thus, under realistic circumstances, we would be fortunate to obtain even the meager results we have just uncovered.

So, should we ditch the TB model? Before we do, let's make one more calculation. The "meager" Sharpe measure of .4031 squares to .1625, larger than the market's squared Sharpe measure of .16 by .0025. Suppose we cover 300 securities instead of three, that is, 100 sets identical to the one we analyzed. From equations 27.7 and 27.9 we know that the increment to the squared Sharpe measure will rise to $100 \times .0025 = .25$. The squared Sharpe measure of the risky portfolio will rise to $.16 + .25 = .41$, a Sharpe measure of .64, and an $M^2$ of 4.8%! Moreover, some of the estimation errors of the other parameters that plague us when we use three securities will offset one another and be diversified away with many more securities covered.[7]

What we see here is a demonstration of the value of security analysis we mentioned at the outset. In the final analysis, the value of the active management depends on forecast quality. The vast demand for active management suggests that this quality is not negligible. The optimal way to exploit analysts' forecasts is with the TB model.

## SUMMARY

1. A truly passive portfolio strategy entails holding the market-index portfolio and a money market fund. Determining the optimal allocation to the market portfolio requires an estimate of its expected return and variance, which in turn suggests delegating some analysis to professionals.

2. Active portfolio managers attempt to construct a risky portfolio that maximizes the reward-to-variability (Sharpe) ratio.

3. The value of perfect market timing ability is considerable. The rate of return to a perfect market timer will be uncertain. However, its risk characteristics are not measurable by standard measures of portfolio risk, because perfect timing dominates a passive strategy, providing "good" surprises only.

4. Perfect timing ability is equivalent to the possession of a call option on the market portfolio, whose value can be determined using option valuation techniques such as the Black-Scholes formula.

5. With imperfect timing, the value of a timer who attempts to forecast whether stocks will outperform bills is determined by the conditional probabilities of the true outcome given the forecasts: $P_1 + P_2 - 1$. Thus if the value of perfect timing is given by the option value, $C$, then imperfect timing has the value $(P_1 + P_2 - 1)C$.

6. The Treynor-Black security selection model envisions that a macroeconomic forecast for market performance is available and that security analysts estimate abnormal expected rates of return, $\alpha$, for various securities. Alpha is the expected rate of return on a security beyond that explained by its beta and the security market line.

7. In the Treynor-Black model the weight of each analyzed security is proportional to the ratio of its alpha to its nonsystematic risk, $\sigma^2(e)$.

8. Once the active portfolio is constructed, its alpha value, nonsystematic risk, and beta can be determined from the properties of the component securities. The optimal risky portfolio, $P$, is then constructed by holding a position in the active portfolio according to the ratio of $\alpha_A$ to $\sigma^2(e_A)$, divided by the analogous ratio for the market-index portfolio. Finally, this position is adjusted using the beta of the active portfolio.

9. When the overall risky portfolio is constructed using the optimal proportions of the active portfolio and passive portfolio, its performance, as measured by the square of Sharpe's measure, is improved (over that of the passive, market-index, portfolio) by the amount $[\alpha_A / \sigma(e_A)]^2$.

10. The contribution of each security to the overall improvement in the performance of the active portfolio is determined by its degree of mispricing and nonsystematic risk. The contribution of each security to portfolio performance equals $[\alpha_i / \sigma(e_i)]^2$, so that for the optimal risky portfolio,

$$S_P^2 = \left[\frac{E(r_M) - r_f}{\sigma_M}\right]^2 + \sum_{i=1}^{n} \left[\frac{\alpha_i}{\sigma(e_i)}\right]^2$$

[7] Empirical work along these lines can be found in: Alex Kane, Tae-Hwan Kim, and Halbert White, "The Power of Portfolio Optimization," UCSD Working Paper, July 2000.

11. Applying the Treynor-Black model to a multifactor framework is straightforward. The forecast of the market-index mean and standard deviation must be replaced with forecasts for an optimized passive portfolio based on a multifactor model. The proportions of the factor portfolios are calculated using the familiar efficient frontier algorithm. The active portfolio is constructed on the basis of residuals from the multifactor model.

12. Implementing the model with imperfect forecasts requires estimation of bias and precision of raw forecasts. The adjusted forecast is obtained by applying the estimated coefficients to the raw forecasts.

**KEY TERMS**

| | | |
|---|---|---|
| Sharpe's measure | passive portfolio | information ratio |
| market timing | active portfolio | |

**WEBSITES**

www.investorsoftware.net/InvestorPrimer/InvestmentPerformance.html
www.nysscpa.org/cpajournal/2001/0600/features/f064401.htm
Learn more about the Sharpe measure at these sites.

www.sniper.at
www.stockmarkettiming.com
The sites above give valuable market timing information.

www.financewise.com/public/edit/riskm/ewrm/ewrm-port-x.htm
www.financewise.com/public/edit/riskm/ewrm/ewrm-portfolio.htm
www.business.com/directory/financial_services/commercial_finance/treasury/
insurance_and_risk_management/sources_and_managing_risk/portfolio_
diversification
Visit these sites for further information on the Treynor-Black Model.

www.russell.com/AU/Institutional_Investors/Russell_Library/Investment_
Articles_and_Updates/Information_Ratios_Explained.asp
www.the401k.com/news/quarter11997/information_ratio.html
Visit these sites to gain a better understanding of the information ratio.

**PROBLEMS**

1. The 5-year history of annual rates of return in excess of the T-bill rate for two competing stock funds is

| The Bull Fund | The Unicorn Fund |
|---|---|
| −21.7% | −1.3% |
| 28.7 | 15.5 |
| 17.0 | 14.4 |
| 2.9 | −11.9 |
| 28.9 | 25.4 |

*a.* How would these funds compare in the eye of a risk-neutral potential client?

*b.* How would these funds compare by Sharpe's measure?

*c.* If a risk-averse investor (with a coefficient of risk aversion $A = 3$) had to choose one of these funds to mix with T-bills, which fund should he choose, and how much should be invested in that fund on the basis of available data?

2. Historical data suggest that the standard deviation of an all-equity strategy is about 5.5% per month. Suppose that the risk-free rate is now 1% per month and that market volatility is at its historical level. What would be a fair monthly fee to a perfect market timer, based on the Black-Scholes formula?

3. In scrutinizing the record of two market timers, a fund manager comes up with the following table:

| | |
|---|---|
| Number of months that $r_M > r_f$ | 135 |
| Correctly predicted by timer A | 78 |
| Correctly predicted by timer B | 86 |
| Number of months that $r_M < r_f$ | 92 |
| Correctly predicted by timer A | 57 |
| Correctly predicted by timer B | 50 |

a. What are the conditional probabilities, $P_1$ and $P_2$, and the total ability parameters for timers A and B?

b. Using the data of problem 2, what is a fair monthly fee for the two timers?

4. A portfolio manager summarizes the input from the macro and micro forecasters in the following table:

| Micro Forecasts | | | |
|---|---|---|---|
| Asset | Expected Return (%) | Beta | Residual Standard Deviation (%) |
| Stock A | 20 | 1.3 | 58 |
| Stock B | 18 | 1,8 | 71 |
| Stock C | 17 | 0.7 | 60 |
| Stock D | 12 | 1.0 | 55 |

| Macro Forecasts | | |
|---|---|---|
| Asset | Expected Return (%) | Standard Deviation (%) |
| T-bills | 8 | 0 |
| Passive equity portfolio | 16 | 23 |

a. Calculate expected excess returns, alpha values, and residual variances for these stocks.

b. Construct the optimal risky portfolio.

c. What is Sharpe's measure for the optimal portfolio and how much of it is contributed by the active portfolio? What is the $M^2$?

d. What should be the exact makeup of the complete portfolio for an investor with a coefficient of risk aversion of 2.8?

5. Recalculate problem 4 for a portfolio manager who is not allowed to short sell securities.

a. What is the cost of the restriction in terms of Sharpe's measure and $M^2$?

b. What is the utility loss to the investor ($A = 2.8$) given his new complete portfolio?

6. A portfolio management house approximates the return-generating process by a two-factor model and uses two factor portfolios to construct its passive portfolio. The input table that is constructed by the house analysts looks as follows:

| Micro Forecasts | | | |
| --- | --- | --- | --- |
| Asset | Expected Return (%) | Beta on M | Beta on H | Residual Standard Deviation (%) |
| Stock A | 20 | 1.2 | 1.8 | 58 |
| Stock B | 18 | 1.4 | 1.1 | 71 |
| Stock C | 17 | 0.5 | 1.5 | 60 |
| Stock D | 12 | 1.0 | 0.2 | 55 |

| Macro Forecasts | | |
| --- | --- | --- |
| Asset | Expected Return (%) | Standard Deviation (%) |
| T-bills | 8 | 0 |
| Factor M portfolio | 16 | 23 |
| Factor H portfolio | 10 | 18 |

The correlation coefficient between the two factor portfolios is .6.

   *a.* What is the optimal passive portfolio?

   *b.* By how much is the optimal passive portfolio superior to the single-factor passive portfolio, *M*, in terms of Sharpe's measure?

   *c.* Analyze the utility improvement to the *A* = 2.8 investor relative to holding portfolio *M* as the sole risky asset that arises from the expanded macro model of the portfolio manager.

7. Construct the optimal active and overall risky portfolio with the data of problem 6 with no restrictions on short sales.

   *a.* What is the Sharpe measure of the optimal risky portfolio and what is the contribution of the active portfolio?

   *b.* Analyze the utility value of the optimal risky portfolio for the *A* = 2.8 investor. Compare to that of problem 6.

8. Recalculate problem 7 with a short-sale restriction. Compare the results to those from problem 7.

9. Suppose that based on the analyst's past record, you estimate that the relationship between forecast and actual alpha is:

$$\text{Actual abnormal return} = .3 \times \text{Forecast of alpha}$$

Use the alphas from problem 4. How much is expected performance affected by recognizing the imprecision of alpha forecasts?

Go to **www.mhhe.com/business/finance/edumarketinsight**. At the Market Insight *Company* page, enter the stock ticker symbol BGEN for Biogen Inc. Link to *Charting By Prophet.* Your S&P Market Insight database provides a sophisticated stock performance charting service for each company in the database. Under the Tools pull-down menu, compare BGEN's recent performance with the S&P 500.

Visit us at www.mhhe.com/bkm

**SOLUTIONS TO CONCEPT CHECKS**

1. We show the answer for the annual compounded rate of return for each strategy and leave the monthly rate for you to compute.

Beginning-of-period fund:

$$F_0 = \$1,000$$

End-of-period fund for each strategy:

$$F_1 = \begin{cases} \$3,600 & \text{Strategy} = \text{Bill only} \\ \$67,500 & \text{Strategy} = \text{Market only} \\ \$5,360,000,000 & \text{Strategy} = \text{Perfect timing} \end{cases}$$

Number of periods: $N = 52$ years

Annual compounded rate:

$$[1 + r_A]^N = \frac{F_1}{F_0}$$

$$r_A = \left(\frac{F_1}{F_0}\right)^{1/N} - 1$$

$$r_A = \begin{cases} 2.49\% & \text{Strategy} = \text{Bills only} \\ 8.44\% & \text{Strategy} = \text{Market only} \\ 34.71\% & \text{Strategy} = \text{Perfect timing} \end{cases}$$

2. The timer will guess bear or bull markets completely randomly. One-half of all bull markets will be preceded by a correct forecast, and similarly for bear markets. Hence $P_1 + P_2 - 1 = \frac{1}{2} + \frac{1}{2} - 1 = 0$.

3. *a.* When short positions are prohibited, the analysis is identical except that negative-alpha stocks are dropped. In that case the sum of the ratios of alpha to residual variance for the remaining two stocks is .7895. This leads to the new composition of the active portfolio. If $x$ denotes new portfolio weights, then

$$x_1 = .3457/.7895 = .4379$$
$$x_2 = .4438/.7895 = .5621$$

The alpha, beta, and residual standard deviation of the active portfolio are now

$$\alpha_A = .4379 \times .07 + .5621 \times .03 = .0475$$
$$\beta_A = .4379 \times 1.6 + .5621 \times .5 = .9817$$
$$\sigma(e_A) = [.4379^2 \times .45^2 + .5621^2 \times .26^2]^{1/2} = .2453$$

The cost of the short sale restriction is already apparent. The alpha has shrunk from 20.56% to 4.75%, while the reduction in the residual standard deviation is more moderate, from 82.62% to 24.53%. In fact, a negative-alpha stock is potentially more attractive than a positive-alpha one: Since most stocks are positively correlated, the negative position that is required for the negative-alpha stock creates a better diversified active portfolio.

The optimal allocation of the new active portfolio is

$$w_0 = \frac{.0475/.6019}{.08/.04} = .3946$$

$$w^* = \frac{.3946}{1 + (1 - .9817) \times .3946} = .3918$$

Here, too, the beta correction is essentially irrelevant because the portfolio beta is so close to 1.0.

Finally, the performance of the overall risky portfolio is estimated at

$$S_P^2 = .16 + \left[\frac{.0475}{.2453}\right]^2 = .1975; \quad S_P = .44$$

It is clear that in this case we have lost about half of the original improvement in the Sharpe measure. Note, however, that this is an artifact of the limited coverage of the security analysis division. When more stocks are covered, then a good number of positive-alpha stocks will keep the residual risk of the active portfolio low. This is the key to extracting large gains from the active strategy.

We calculate the "Modigliani-square," or $M^2$ measure, as follows:

$$E(r_{P*}) = r_f + S_P \sigma_M = .07 + .44 \times .20 = .158, \text{ or } 15.8\%$$
$$M^2 = E(r_{P*}) - E(r_M) = 15.8\% - 15\% = 0.8\%$$

which is a bit less than half the $M^2$ value of the unconstrained portfolio.

b. When the forecast for the market-index portfolio is more optimistic, the position in the active portfolio will be smaller and the contribution of the active portfolio to the Sharpe measure of the risky portfolio also will be smaller. In the original example the allocation to the active portfolio would be

$$w_0 = \frac{.2056/.6826}{.12/.04} = .1004$$

$$w^* = \frac{.1004}{1 + (1 - .9519) \times .1004} = .0999$$

Although the Sharpe measure of the market is now better, the improvement derived from security analysis is smaller:

$$S_P^2 = \left(\frac{.12}{.20}\right)^2 + \left(\frac{.2056}{.8262}\right)^2 = .4219$$
$$S_P = .65; \qquad S_M = .60$$

**SOLUTIONS
TO CONCEPT
CHECKS**
*(Concluded)*

# APPENDICES

# QUANTITATIVE REVIEW

Students in management and investment courses typically come from a variety of backgrounds. Some, who have had strong quantitative training, may feel perfectly comfortable with formal mathematical presentation of material. Others, who have had less technical training, may easily be overwhelmed by mathematical formalism. Most students, however, will benefit from some coaching to make the study of investment easier and more efficient. If you had a good introductory quantitative methods course, and like the text that was used, you may want to refer to it whenever you feel in need of a refresher. If you feel uncomfortable with standard quantitative texts, this reference is for you. Our aim is to present the essential quantitative concepts and methods in a self-contained, nontechnical, and intuitive way. Our approach is structured in line with requirements for the CFA program. The material included is relevant to investment management by the ICFA, the Institute of Chartered Financial Analysts. We hope you find this appendix helpful. Use it to make your venture into investments more enjoyable.

# A.1  PROBABILITY DISTRIBUTIONS

Statisticians talk about "experiments," or "trials," and refer to possible outcomes as "events." In a roll of a die, for example, the "elementary events" are the numbers 1 through 6. Turning up one side represents the most disaggregate *mutually exclusive* outcome. Other events are *compound,* that is, they consist of more than one elementary event, such as the result "odd number" or "less than 4." In this case "odd" and "less than 4" are not mutually exclusive. Compound events can be mutually exclusive outcomes, however, such as "less than 4" and "equal to or greater than 4."

In decision making, "experiments" are circumstances in which you contemplate a decision that will affect the set of possible events (outcomes) and their likelihood (probabilities). Decision theory calls for you to identify optimal decisions under various sets of circumstances (experiments), which you may do by determining losses from departures from optimal decisions.

When the outcomes of a decision (experiment) can be quantified, that is, when a numerical value can be assigned to each elementary event, the decision outcome is called a *random variable.* In the context of investment decision making, the random variable (the payoff to the investment decision) is denominated either in dollars or as a percentage rate of return.

The set or list of all possible values of a random variable, *with* their associated probabilities, is called the *probability distribution* of the random variable. Values that are impossible for the random variable to take on are sometimes listed with probabilities of zero. All possible elementary events are assigned values and probabilities, and thus the probabilities have to sum to 1.0.

Sometimes the values of a random variable are *uncountable,* meaning that you cannot make a list of all possible values. For example, suppose you roll a ball on a line and report the distance it rolls before it comes to rest. Any distance is possible, and the precision of the report will depend on the need of the roller and/or the quality of the measuring device. Another uncountable random variable is one that describes the weight of a newborn baby. Any positive weight (with some upper bound) is possible.

We call uncountable probability distributions *continuous,* for the obvious reason that, at least within a range, the possible outcomes (those with positive probabilities) lie anywhere on a continuum of values. Because there is an infinite number of possible values for the random variable in any continuous distribution, such a probability distribution has to be described by a formula that relates the values of the random variable and their associated probabilities, instead of by a simple list of outcomes and probabilities. We discuss continuous distributions later in this section.

Even countable probability distributions can be complicated. For example, on the New York Stock Exchange stock prices are quoted in eighths. This means the price of a stock at some future date is a *countable* random variable. Probability distributions of countable random variables are called *discrete distributions.* Although a stock price cannot dip below zero, it has no upper bound. Therefore a stock price is a random variable that can take on infinitely many values, even though they are countable, and its discrete probability distribution will have to be given by a formula just like a continuous distribution.

There are random variables that are both discrete and finite. When the probability distribution of the relevant random variable is countable and finite, decision making is tractable and relatively easy to analyze. One example is the decision to call a coin toss "heads" or "tails," with a payoff of zero for guessing wrong and 1 for guessing right. The random variable of the decision to guess "heads" has a discrete, finite probability distribution. It can be written as

| Event | Value | Probability |
|-------|-------|-------------|
| Heads | 1 | .5 |
| Tails | 0 | .5 |

This type of analysis usually is referred to as *scenario analysis*. Because scenario analysis is relatively simple, it is used sometimes even when the actual random variable is infinite and uncountable. You can do this by specifying values and probabilities for a set of compound, yet exhaustive and mutually exclusive, events. Because it is simple and has important uses, we handle this case first.

Here is a problem from the 1988 CFA examination.

Mr. Arnold, an Investment Committee member, has confidence in the forecasting ability of the analysts in the firm's research department. However, he is concerned that analysts may not appreciate risk as an important investment consideration. This is especially true in an increasingly volatile investment environment. In addition, he is conservative and risk averse. He asks for your risk analysis for Anheuser-Busch stock.

1. Using Table A.1, calculate the following measures of dispersion of returns for Anheuser-Busch stock under each of the three outcomes displayed. Show calculations.

   *a.* Range.
   *b.* Variance: $\Sigma \Pr(i)[r_i - E(r)]^2$.
   *c.* Standard deviation.
   *d.* Coefficient of variation: $CV = \sigma/E(r)$.

2. Discuss the usefulness of each of the four measures listed in quantifying risk.

The examination questions require very specific answers. We use the questions as framework for exposition of scenario analysis.

Table A.1 specifies a three-scenario decision problem. The random variable is the rate of return on investing in Anheuser-Busch stock. However, the third column, which specifies the value of the random variable, does not say simply "Return"—it says "Expected Return." This tells us that the scenario description is a compound event consisting of many elementary events, as is almost always the case. We streamline or simplify reality in order to gain tractability.

Analysts who prepare input lists must decide on the number of scenarios with which to describe the entire probability distribution, as well as the rates of return to allocate to each one. This process calls for determining the probability of occurrence of each scenario, *and* the expected rate of return *within* (conditional on) each scenario, which governs the outcome of each scenario. Once you become familiar with scenario analysis, you will be able to build a simple scenario description from any probability distribution.

## Expected Returns

The expected value of a random variable is the answer to the question, What would be the average value of the variable if the "experiment" (the circumstances and the decision) were repeated infinitely? In the case of an investment decision, your answer is meant to describe the reward from making the decision.

### Table A.1    Anheuser-Busch Companies, Inc., Dispersion of Potential Returns

| Outcome | Probability | Expected Return* |
|---------|-------------|------------------|
| Number 1 | .20 | 20% |
| Number 2 | .50 | 30 |
| Number 3 | .30 | 50 |

*Assume for the moment that the expected return in each scenario will be realized with certainty. This is the way returns were expressed in the original question.

Note that the question is hypothetical and abstract. It is hypothetical because, practically, the exact circumstances of a decision (the "experiment") often cannot be repeated even once, much less infinitely. It is abstract because, even if the experiment were to be repeated many times (short of infinitely), the *average* rate of return may not be one of the possible outcomes. To demonstrate, suppose that the probability distribution of the rate of return on a proposed investment project is $+20\%$ or $-20\%$, with equal probabilities of .5. Intuition indicates that repeating this investment decision will get us ever closer to an average rate of return of zero. But a one-time investment cannot produce a rate of return of zero. Is the "expected" return still a useful concept when the proposed investment represents a one-time decision?

One argument for using expected return to measure the reward from making investment decisions is that, although a specific investment decision may be made only once, the decision maker will be making many (although different) investment decisions over time. Over time, then, the average rate of return will come close to the average of the expected values of all the individual decisions. Another reason for using the expected value is that admittedly we lack a better measure.[1]

The probabilities of the scenarios in Table A.1 predict the relative frequencies of the outcomes. If the current investment in Anheuser-Busch could be replicated many times, a 20% return would occur 20% of the time, a 30% return would occur 50% of the time, and 50% return would occur the remaining 30% of the time. This notion of probabilities and the definition of the expected return tells us how to calculate the expected return.[2]

$$E(r) = .20 \times .20 + .50 \times .30 + .30 \times .50 = .34 \text{ (or 34\%)}$$

Labeling each scenario $i = 1, 2, 3$, and using the summation sign, $\Sigma$, we can write the formula for the expected return:

$$E(r) = \Pr(1)r_1 + \Pr(2)r_2 + \Pr(3)r_3 \tag{A.1}$$

$$= \sum_{i=1}^{3} \Pr(i)r_i$$

The definition of the expectation in equation A.1 reveals two important properties of random variables. First, if you add a constant to a random variable, its expectation is also increased by the same constant. If, for example, the return in each scenario in Table A.1 were increased by 5%, the expectation would increase to 39%. Try this, using equation A.1. If a random variable is multiplied by a constant, its expectation will change by that same proportion. If you multiply the return in each scenario by 1.5, $E(r)$ would change to $1.5 \times .34 = .51$ (or 51%).

Second, the deviation of a random variable from its expected value is itself a random variable. Take any rate of return $r_1$ in Table A.1 and define its deviation from the expected value by

$$d_i = r_i - E(r)$$

What is the expected value of $d$? $E(d)$ is the expected deviation from the expected value, and by equation A.1 it is necessarily zero because

$$E(d) = \Sigma \Pr(i)d_i = \Sigma \Pr(i)[r_i - E(r)]$$
$$= \Sigma \Pr(i)r_i - E(r) \Sigma \Pr(i)$$
$$= E(r) - E(r) = 0$$

---

[1] Another case where we use a less-than-ideal measure is the case of yield to maturity on a bond. The YTM measures the rate of return from investing in a bond *if* it is held to maturity and *if* the coupons can be reinvested at the same yield to maturity over the life of the bond.

[2] We will consistently perform calculations in decimal fractions to avoid confusion.

# Measures of Dispersion

**The Range.** Assume for a moment that the expected return for each scenario in Table A.1 will be realized with certainty in the event that scenario occurs. Then the set of possible return outcomes is unambiguously 20%, 30%, and 50%. The *range* is the difference between the maximum and the minimum values of the random variable, 50% − 20% = 30% in this case. Range is clearly a crude measure of dispersion. Here it is particularly inappropriate because the scenario returns themselves are given as expected values, and therefore the true range is unknown. There is a variant of the range, the *interquartile range,* that we explain in the discussion of descriptive statistics.

**The Variance.** One interpretation of variance is that it measures the "expected surprises." Although that may sound like a contradiction in terms, it really is not. First, think of a surprise as a deviation from expectation. The surprise is not in the *fact* that expectation has not been realized, but rather in the *direction* and *magnitude* of the deviation.

The example in Table A.1 leads us to *expect* a rate of return of 34% from investing in Anheuser-Busch stock. A second look at the scenario returns, however, tells us that we should stand ready to be surprised because the probability of earning exactly 34% is zero. Being sure that our expectation will not be realized does not mean that we can be sure what the realization is going to be. The element of surprise lies in the direction and magnitude of the deviation of the actual return from expectation, and that is the relevant random variable for the measurement of uncertainty. Its probability distribution adds to our understanding of the nature of the uncertainty that we are facing.

We measure the reward by the expected return. Intuition suggests that we measure uncertainty by the expected *deviation* of the rate of return from expectation. We showed in the previous section, however, that the expected deviation from expectation must be zero. Positive deviations, when weighted by probabilities, are exactly offset by negative deviations. To get around this problem, we replace the random variable "deviation from expectations" (denoted earlier by $d$) with its square, which must be positive even if $d$ itself is negative.

We define the *variance,* our measure of surprise or dispersion, by the *expected squared deviation of the rate of return from its expectation.* With the Greek letter sigma square denoting variance, the formal definition is

$$\sigma^2(r) = E(d^2) = E[r_i - E(r)]^2 = \Sigma \Pr(i)[r_i - E(r)]^2 \qquad (A.2)$$

Squaring each deviation eliminates the sign, which eliminates the offsetting effects of positive and negative deviations.

In the case of Anheuser-Busch, the variance of the rate of return on the stock is

$$\sigma^2(r) = .2(.20 - .34)^2 + .5(.30 - .34)^2 + .3(.50 - .34)^2 = .0124$$

Remember that if you add a constant to a random variable, the variance does not change at all. This is because the expectation also changes by the same constant, and hence deviations from expectation remain unchanged. You can test this by using the data from Table A.1.

Multiplying the random variable by a constant, however, *will* change the variance. Suppose that each return is multiplied by the factor $k$. The new random variable, $kr$, has expectation of $E(kr) = kE(r)$. Therefore, the deviation of $kr$ from its expectation is

$$d(kr) = kr - E(kr) = kr - kE(r) = k[r - E(r)] = kd(r)$$

If each deviation is multiplied by $k$, the squared deviations are multiplied by the square of $k$:

$$\sigma^2(kr) = k^2\sigma^2(r)$$

To summarize, adding a constant to a random variable does not affect the variance. Multiplying a random variable by a constant, though, will cause the variance to be multiplied by the square of that constant.

**The Standard Deviation.** A closer look at the variance will reveal that its dimension is different from that of the expected return. Recall that we squared deviations from the expected return in order to make all values positive. This alters the *dimension* (units of measure) of the variance to "square percents." To transform the variance into terms of percentage return, we simply take the square root of the variance. This measure is the *standard deviation*. In the case of Anheuser-Busch's stock return, the standard deviation is

$$\sigma = (\sigma^2)^{1/2} = \sqrt{.0124} = .1114 \text{ (or } 11.14\%) \tag{A.3}$$

Note that you always need to calculate the variance first before you can get the standard deviation. The standard deviation conveys the same information as the variance but in a different form.

We know already that adding a constant to $r$ will not affect its variance, and it will not affect the standard deviation either. We also know that multiplying a random variable by a constant multiplies the variance by the square of that constant. From the definition of the standard deviation in equation A.3, it should be clear that multiplying a random variable by a constant will multiply the standard deviation by the (absolute value of this) constant. The absolute value is needed because the sign of the constant is lost through squaring the deviations in the computation of the variance. Formally,

$$\sigma(kr) = \text{Abs}(k)\sigma(r)$$

Try a transformation of your choice using the data in Table A.1.

**The Coefficient of Variation.** To evaluate the magnitude of dispersion of a random variable, it is useful to compare it to the expected value. The ratio of the standard deviation to the expectation is called the *coefficient of variation*. In the case of returns on Anheuser-Busch stock, it is

$$CV = \frac{\sigma}{E(r)} = \frac{.1114}{.3400} = .3285 \tag{A.4}$$

The standard deviation of the Anheuser-Busch return is about one-third of the expected return (reward). Whether this value for the coefficient of variation represents a big risk depends on what can be obtained with alternative investments.

The coefficient of variation is far from an ideal measure of dispersion. Suppose that a plausible expected value for a random variable is zero. In this case, regardless of the magnitude of the standard deviation, the coefficient of variation will be infinite. Clearly, this measure is not applicable in all cases. Generally, the analyst must choose a measure of dispersion that fits the particular decision at hand. In finance, the standard deviation is the measure of choice in most cases where overall risk is concerned. (For individual assets, the measure $\beta$, explained in the text, is the measure used.)

**Skewness**    So far, we have described the measures of dispersion as indicating the size of the average surprise, loosely speaking. The standard deviation is not exactly equal to the average surprise though, because squaring deviations and then taking the square root of the average square deviation results in greater weight (emphasis) placed on larger deviations. Other than that, it is simply a measure that tells us how big a deviation from expectation can be expected.

Most decision makers agree that the expected value and standard deviation of a random variable are the most important statistics. However, once we calculate them another question about risk (the nature of the random variable describing deviations from expectations) is pertinent: Are the larger deviations (surprises) more likely to be positive? Risk-averse decision makers worry about bad surprises, and the standard deviation does not distinguish good from bad ones. Most risk avoiders are believed to prefer random variables with likely *small negative surprises* and *less* likely *large positive surprises,* to the reverse, likely *small good surprises* and *less* likely *large bad surprises.* More than anything, risk is really defined by the possibility of disaster (large bad surprises).

One measure that distinguishes between the likelihood of large good-vs.-bad surprises is the "third moment." It builds on the behavior of deviations from the expectation, the random variable we have denoted by $d$. Denoting the *third moment* by $M_3$, we define it:

$$M_3 = E(d^3) = E[r_i - E(r)]^3 = \Sigma \Pr(i)[r_i - E(r)]^3 \qquad \text{(A.5)}$$

Cubing each value of $d$ (taking it to the third power) magnifies larger deviations more than smaller ones. Raising values to an odd power causes them to retain their sign. Recall that the sum of all deviations multiplied by their probabilities is zero because positive deviations weighted by their probabilities exactly offset the negative. When *cubed* deviations are multiplied by their probabilities and then added up, however, large deviations will dominate. The sign will tell us in this case whether *large positive* deviations dominate (positive $M_3$) or whether *large negative* deviations dominate (negative $M_3$).

Incidentally, it is obvious why this measure of skewness is call the third moment; it refers to cubing. Similarly, the variance is often referred to as the second moment because it requires squaring.

Returning to the investment decision described in Table A.1, with the expected value of 34%, the third moment is

$$M_3 = .2(.20 - .34)^3 + .5(.30 - .34)^3 + .3(.50 - .34)^3 = .000648$$

The sign of the third moment tells us that larger *positive* surprises dominate in this case. You might have guessed this by looking at the deviations from expectation and their probabilities; that is, the most likely event is a return of 30%, which makes for a small negative surprise. The other negative surprise (20% − 34% = −14%) is smaller in magnitude than the positive surprise (50% − 34% = 16%) *and* is also *less* likely (probability .20) relative to the positive surprise, 30% (probability .30). The difference appears small, however, and we do not know whether the third moment may be an important issue for the decision to invest in Anheuser-Busch.

It is difficult to judge the importance of the third moment, here .000648, without a benchmark. Following the same reasoning we applied to the standard deviation, we can take the *third root* of $M_3$ (which we denote $m_3$) and compare it to the standard deviation. This yields $m_3 = .0865 = 8.65\%$, which is not trivial compared with the standard deviation (11.14%).

## Another Example: Options on Anheuser-Busch Stock

Suppose that the current price of Anheuser-Busch stock is $30. A call option on the stock is selling for 60 cents, and a put is selling for $4. Both have an exercise price of $42 and maturity date to match the scenarios in Table A.1.

The call option allows you to buy the stock at the exercise price. You will choose to do so if the call ends up "in the money," that is, the stock price is above the exercise price. The profit in this case is the difference between the stock price and the exercise price, less cost of the call. Even if you exercise the call, your profit may still be negative if the cash flow from the exercise of the call does not cover the initial cost of the call. If the call ends up "out of the money," that is, the stock price is below the exercise price, you will let the call expire worthless and suffer a loss equal to the cost of the call.

The put option allows you to sell the stock at the exercise price. You will choose to do so if the put ends up "in the money," that is, the stock price is below the exercise price.

Your profit is then the difference between the exercise price and the stock price, less the initial cost of the put. Here again, if the cash flow is not sufficient to cover the cost of the put, the investment will show a loss. If the put ends up "out of the money," you again let it expire worthless, taking a loss equal to the initial cost of the put.

The scenario analysis of these alternative investments is described in Table A.2.

The expected rates of return on the call and put are

$$E(r_{call}) = .2(-1) + .5(-1) + .3(4) = .5 \text{ (or } 50\%)$$
$$E(r_{put}) = .2(.5) + .5(-.25) + .3(-1) = -.325 \text{ (or } -32.5\%)$$

The negative expected return on the put may be justified by the fact that it is a hedge asset, in this case an insurance policy against losses from holding Anheuser-Busch stock. The variance and standard deviation of the two investments are

$$\sigma^2_{call} = .2(-1 - .5)^2 + .5(-1 - .5)^2 + .3(4 - .5)^2 = 5.25$$
$$\sigma^2_{put} = .2[.5 - (-.325)]^2 + .5[-.25 - (-.325)]^2 + .3[-1 - (-.325)]^2 = .2756$$
$$\sigma_{call} = \sqrt{5.25} = 2.2913 \text{ (or } 229.13\%)$$
$$\sigma_{put} = \sqrt{.2756} = .525 \text{ (or } 52.5\%)$$

These are very large standard deviations. Comparing the standard deviation of the call's return to its expected value, we get the coefficient of variation:

$$CV_{call} = \frac{2.2913}{.5} = 4.5826$$

Refer back to the coefficient of variation for the stock itself, .3275, and it is clear that these instruments have high standard deviations. This is quite common for stock options. The negative expected return of the put illustrates again the problem in interpreting the magnitude of the "surprise" indicated by the coefficient of variation.

Moving to the third moments of the two probability distributions:

$$M_3(call) = .2(-1 - .5)^3 + .5(-1 - .5)^3 + .3(4 - .5)^3 = 10.5$$
$$M_3(put) = .2[.5 - (-.325)]^3 + .5[-.25 - (-.325)]^3 + .3[-1 - (-.325)]^3$$
$$= .02025$$

### Table A.2 Scenario Analysis for Investment in Options on Anheuser-Busch Stock

|  | Scenario 1 | Scenario 2 | Scenario 3 |
|---|---|---|---|
| Probability | .20 | .50 | .30 |
| **Event** | | | |
| 1. Return on stock | 20% | 30% | 50% |
| Stock price (initial price = $30) | $36.00 | $39.00 | $45.00 |
| 2. Cash flow from call (exercise price = $42) | 0 | 0 | $3.00 |
| Call profit (initial price = $.60) | −$.60 | −$.60 | $2.40 |
| Call rate of return | −100% | −100% | 400% |
| 3. Cash flow from put (exercise price = $42) | $6.00 | $3.00 | 0 |
| Put profit (initial price = $4) | $2.00 | −$1.00 | −$4.00 |
| Put rate of return | 50% | −25% | −100% |

Both instruments are positively skewed, which is typical of options and one part of their attractiveness. In this particular circumstance the call is more skewed than the put. To establish this fact, note the third root of the third moment:

$$m_3(\text{call}) = M_3(\text{call})^{1/3} = 2.1898 \text{ (or } 218.98\%)$$
$$m_3(\text{put}) = .02^{1/3} = .2725 \text{ (or } 27.25\%)$$

Compare these figures to the standard deviations, 229.13% for the call and 52.5% for the put, and you can see that a large part of the standard deviation of the option is driven by the possibility of large good surprises instead of by the more likely, yet smaller, bad surprises.[3]

So far we have described discrete probability distributions using scenario analysis. We shall come back to decision making in a scenario analysis framework in Section A.3 on multivariate statistics.

**Continuous Distributions: Normal and Lognormal Distributions**

When a compact scenario analysis is possible and acceptable, decisions may be quite simple. Often, however, so many relevant scenarios must be specified that scenario analysis is impossible for practical reasons. Even in the case of Anheuser-Busch, as we were careful to specify, the individual scenarios considered actually represented compound events.

When many possible values of rate of return have to be considered, we must use a formula that describes the probability distribution (relates values to probabilities). As we noted earlier, there are two types of probability distributions: discrete and continuous. Scenario analysis involves a discrete distribution. However, the two most useful distributions in investments, the normal and lognormal, are continuous. At the same time they are often used to approximate variables with distributions that are known to be discrete, such as stock prices. The probability distribution of future prices and returns is discrete—prices are quoted in eighths. Yet the industry norm is to approximate these distributions by the normal or lognormal distribution.

**Standard Normal Distribution.** The normal distribution, also known as Gaussian (after the mathematician Gauss) or bell-shaped, describes random variables with the following properties and is shown in Figure A.1:

- The expected value is the mode (the most frequent elementary event) and also the median (the middle value in the sense that half the elementary events are greater and half smaller). Note that the expected value, unlike the median or mode, requires weighting by probabilities to produce the concept of central value.

- The normal probability distribution is symmetric around the expected value. In other words, the likelihood of equal absolute-positive and negative deviations from expectation is equal. Larger deviations from the expected value are less likely than are smaller deviations. In fact, the essence of the normal distribution is that the probability of deviations decreases exponentially with the magnitude of the deviation (positive and negative alike).

- A normal distribution is identified completely by two parameters, the expected value and the standard deviation. The property of the normal distribution that

---

[3] Note that the expected return of the put is $-32.5\%$; hence the worst surprise is $-67.5\%$, and the best is $82.5\%$. The middle scenario is also a positive deviation of $7.5\%$ (with a high probability of .50). These two elements explain the positive skewness of the put.

**Figure A.1
Probabilities
under the
normal
density**

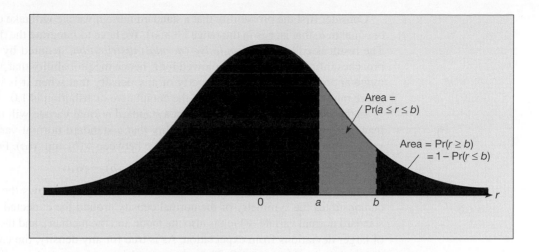

makes it most convenient for portfolio analysis is that any weighted sum or normally distributed random variables produce a random variable that also is normally distributed. This property is called *stability*. It is also true that if you add a constant to a "normal" random variable (meaning a random variable with a normal probability distribution) or multiply it by a constant, then the transformed random variable also will be normally distributed.

Suppose that $n$ is any random variable (not necessarily normal) with expectation $\mu$ and standard deviation $\sigma$. As we showed earlier, if you add a constant $c$ to $n$, the standard deviation is not affected at all, but the mean will change to $\mu + c$. If you multiply $n$ by a constant $b$, its mean and standard deviation will change by the same proportion to $b\mu$ and $b\sigma$. If $n$ is normal, the transformed variable also will be normal.

Stability, together with the property that a normal variable is completely characterized by its expectation and standard deviation, implies that if we know one normal probability distribution with a given expectation and standard deviation, we know them all.

Subtracting the expected value from each observation and then dividing by the standard deviation we obtain the *standard normal distribution,* which has an expectation of zero and both variance and standard deviation equal to 1.0. Formally, the relationship between the value of the standard normal random variable, $z$, and its probability, $f$, is given by

$$f(z) = \frac{1}{\sqrt{2\pi}} \exp\left(\frac{-z^2}{2}\right) \tag{A.6}$$

where "exp" is the quantity $e$ to the power of the expression in the parentheses. The quantity $e$ is an important number just like the well-known $\pi$, which also appears in the function. It is important enough to earn a place on the keyboard of your financial calculator, mostly because it is used also in continuous compounding.

Probability functions of continuous distributions are called *densities* and denoted by $f$, rather than by the "Pr" of scenario analysis. The reason is that the probability of any of the infinitely many possible values of $z$ is infinitesimally small. Density is a function that allows us to obtain the probability of a *range of values* by integrating it over a desired range. In other words, whenever we want the probability that a standard normal variate (a random variable) will fall in the range from $z = a$ to $z = b$, we have to add up the density values, $f(z)$, for all $z$s from $a$ to $b$. There are infinitely many $z$s in that range, regardless how close $a$ is to $b$. *Integration* is the mathematical operation that achieves this task.

Consider first the probability that a standard normal variate will take on a value less than or equal to $a$, that is, $z$ is in the range $[-\infty, a]$. We have to integrate the density from $\infty$ to $a$. The result is called the *cumulative (normal) distribution,* denoted by $N(a)$. When $a$ approaches infinity, any value is allowed for $z$; hence the probability that $z$ will end up in that range approaches 1.0. It is a property of any density that when it is integrated over the entire range of the random variable, the cumulative distribution is 1.0.

In the same way, the probability that a standard normal variate will take on a value less than or equal to $b$ is $N(b)$. The probability that a standard normal variate will take on a value in the range $[a, b]$ is just the difference between $N(b)$ and $N(a)$. Formally,

$$\Pr(a \le z \le b) = N(b) - N(a)$$

These concepts are illustrated in Figure A.1. The graph shows the normal density. It demonstrates the symmetry of the normal density around the expected value (zero for the standard normal variate, which is also the mode and the median), and the smaller likelihood of larger deviations from expectation. As is true for any density, the entire area under the density graph adds up to 1.0. The values $a$ and $b$ are chosen to be positive, so they are to the right of the expected value. The leftmost colored shaded area is the proportion of the area under the density for which the value of $z$ is less than or equal to $a$. Thus this area yields the cumulative distribution for $a$, the probability that $z$ will be smaller than or equal to $a$. The gray shaded area is the area under the density graph between $a$ and $b$. If we add that area to the cumulative distribution of $a$, we get the entire area up to $b$, that is, the probability that $z$ will be anywhere to the left of $b$. Thus the area between $a$ and $b$ has to be the probability that $z$ will fall between $a$ and $b$.

Applying the same logic, we find the probability that $z$ will take on a value greater than $b$. We know already that the probability that $z$ will be smaller than or equal to $b$ is $N(b)$. The compound events "smaller than or equal to $b$" and "greater than $b$" are mutually exclusive *and* "exhaustive," meaning that they include all possible outcomes. Thus their probabilities sum to 1.0, and the probability that $z$ is greater than $b$ is simply equal to one minus the probability that $z$ is less than or equal to $b$. Formally, $\Pr(z > b) = 1 - N(b)$.

Look again at Figure A.1. The area under the density graph between $b$ and infinity is just the difference between the entire area under the graph (equal to 1.0) and the area between minus infinity and $b$, that is, $N(b)$.

The normal density is sufficiently complex that its cumulative distribution, its integral, does not have an exact formulaic closed-form solution. It must be obtained by numerical (approximation) methods. These values are produced in tables that give the value $N(z)$ for any $z$, such as Table 21.2 of this text.

To illustrate, let us find the following probabilities for a standard normal variate:

$$\Pr(z \le -.36) = N(-.36) = \text{Probability that } z \text{ is less than or equal to } -.36$$
$$\Pr(z \le .94) = N(.94) = \text{Probability that } z \text{ is less than or equal to } .94$$
$$\Pr(-.36 \le z \le .94) = N(.94) - N(-.36) = \text{Probability that } z \text{ will be in the range } [-.36, .94]$$
$$\Pr(z > .94) = 1 - N(.94) = \text{Probability that } z \text{ is greater than } .94$$

Use Table 21.2 of the cumulative standard normal (sometimes called the area under the normal density) and Figure A.2. The table shows that

$$N(-.36) = .3594$$
$$N(.94) = .8264$$

In Figure A.2 the area under the graph between $-.36$ and $.94$ is the probability that $z$ will fall between $-.36$ and $.94$. Hence

$$\Pr(-.36 \le z \le .94) = N(.94) - N(-.36) = .8264 - .3594 = .4670$$

**Figure A.2
Probabilities
and the
cumulative
normal
distribution**

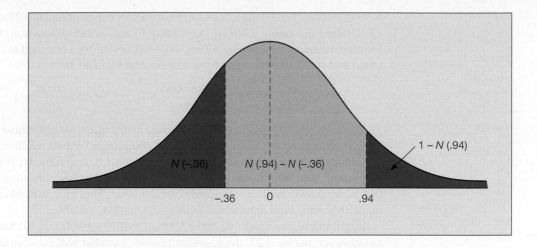

The probability that $z$ is greater than .94 is the area under the graph in Figure A.2, between .94 and infinity. Thus it is equal to the entire area (1.0) less the area from minus infinity to .94. Hence

$$\Pr(z > .94) = 1 - N(.94) = 1 - .8264 = .1736$$

Finally, one can ask, What is the value $a$ for which $z$ will be smaller than or equal to $a$ with probability $P$? The notation for the function that yields the desired value of $a$ is $\Phi(P)$, so that

$$\text{If } \Phi(P) = a, \text{ then } P = N(a) \tag{A.7}$$

For instance, suppose the question is, Which value has a cumulative density of .50? A glance at Figure A.2 reminds us that the area between minus infinity and zero (the expected value) is .5. Thus we can write

$$\Phi(.5) = 0, \text{ because } N(0) = .5$$

Similarly,

$$\Phi(.8264) = .94, \text{ because } N(.94) = .8264$$

and

$$\Phi(.3594) = -.36$$

For practice, confirm with Table 21.2 that $\Phi(.6554) = .40$, meaning that the value of $z$ with a cumulative distribution of .6554 is $z = .40$.

**Nonstandard Normal Distributions.** Suppose that the monthly rate of return on a stock is closely approximated by a normal distribution with a mean of .015 (1.5% per month), and standard deviation of .127 (12.7% per month). What is the probability that the rate of return will fall below zero in a given month? Recall that because the rate is a normal variate, its cumulative density has to be computed by numerical methods. The standard normal table can be used for any normal variate.

Any random variable, $x$, may be transformed into a new standardized variable, $x^*$, by the following rule:

$$x^* = \frac{x - E(x)}{\sigma(x)} \tag{A.8}$$

Note that all we have done to $x$ was (1) *subtract* its expectation and (2) *multiply* by one over its standard deviation, $1/[\sigma(x)]$. According to our earlier discussion, the effect of transforming a random variable by adding and multiplying by a constant is such that the expectation and standard deviation of the transformed variable are

$$E(x^*) = \frac{E(x) - E(x)}{\sigma(x)} = 0; \qquad \sigma(x^*) = \frac{\sigma(x)}{\sigma(x)} = 1 \qquad (A.9)$$

From the stability property of the normal distribution we also know that if $x$ is normal, so is $x^*$. A normal variate is characterized completely by two parameters: its expectation and standard deviation. For $x^*$, these are zero and 1.0, respectively. When we subtract the expectation and then divide a normal variate by its standard deviation, we standardize it; that is, we transform it to a standard normal variate. This trick is used extensively in working with normal (and approximately normal) random variables.

Returning to our stock, we have learned that if we subtract .015 and then divide the monthly returns by .127, the resultant random variable will be standard normal. We can now determine the probability that the rate of return will be zero or less in a given month. We know that

$$z = \frac{r - .015}{.127}$$

where $z$ is standard normal and $r$ the return on our stock. Thus if $r$ is zero, $z$ has to be

$$z(r = 0) = \frac{0 - .015}{.127} = -.1181$$

For $r$ to be zero, the corresponding standard normal has to be $-11.81\%$, a negative number. The event "$r$ will be zero or less" is identical to the event "$z$ will be $-.1181$ or less." Calculating the probability of the latter will solve our problem. That probability is simply $N(-.1181)$. Visit the standard normal table and find that

$$\Pr(r \leq 0) = N(-.1181) = .5 - .047 = .453$$

The answer makes sense. Recall that the expectation of $r$ is 1.5%. Thus, whereas the probability that $r$ will be 1.5% or less is .5, the probability that it will be *zero* or less has to be close, but somewhat lower.

**Confidence Intervals.** Given the large standard deviation of our stock, it is logical to be concerned about the likelihood of extreme values for the monthly rate of return. One way to quantify this concern is to ask: What is the interval (range) within which the stock return will fall in a given month, with a probability of .95? Such an interval is called the *95% confidence interval.*

Logic dictates that this interval be centered on the expected value, .015, because $r$ is a normal variate (has a normal distribution) which is symmetric around the expectation. Denote the desired interval by

$$[E(r) - a, E(r) + a] = [.015 - a, .015 + a]$$

which has a length of $2a$. The probability that $r$ will fall within this interval is described by the following expression:

$$\Pr(.015 - a \leq r \leq .015 + a) = .95$$

To find this probability, we start with a simpler problem, involving the *standard normal variate,* that is, a normal with expectation of zero and standard deviation of 1.0.

What is the 95% confidence interval for the standard normal variate, $z$? The variable will be centered on zero, so the expression is

$$\Pr(-a^* \leq z \leq a^*) = N(a^*) - N(-a^*) = .95$$

You might best understand the substitution of the difference of the appropriate cumulative distributions for the probability with the aid of Figure A.3. The probability of falling outside of the interval is $1 - .95 = .05$. By the symmetry of the normal distribution, $z$ will be equal to or less than $-a^*$ with probability of .025, and with probability .025, $z$ will be greater than $a^*$. Thus we solve for $a^*$ using

$$-a^* = \Phi(.025), \text{ which is equivalent to } N(-a^*) = .025$$

We can summarize the chain that we have pursued so far as follows. If we seek a $P = .95$ level confidence interval, we define $\alpha$ as the probability that $r$ will fall outside the confidence interval. Because of the symmetry, $\alpha$ will be split so that half of it is the probability of falling to the right of the confidence interval, while the other half is the probability of falling to the left of the confidence interval. Therefore, the relation between $\alpha$ and $P$ is

$$\alpha = 1 - P = .05; \qquad \frac{\alpha}{2} = \frac{1 - P}{2} = .025$$

We use $\alpha/2$ to indicate that the area that is excluded for $r$ is equally divided between the tails of the distributions. Each tail that is excluded for $r$ has an area of $\alpha/2$. The value $\alpha = 1 - P$ represents the entire value that is excluded for $r$.

To find $z = \Phi(\alpha/2)$, which is the lower boundary of the confidence interval for the standard normal variate, we have to locate the $z$ value for which the standard normal cumulative distribution is .025, finding $z = -1.96$. Thus we conclude that $-a^* = -1.96$ and $a^* = 1.96$. The confidence interval for $z$ is

$$[E(z) - \Phi(\alpha/2), E(z) + \Phi(\alpha/2)] = [-\Phi(.025), \Phi(.025)]$$
$$= [-1.96, .196]$$

**Figure A.3   Confidence intervals and the standard normal density**

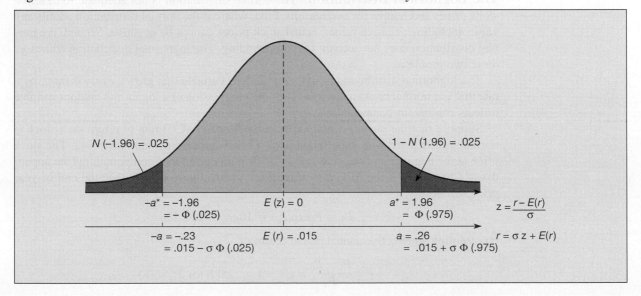

To get the interval boundaries for the nonstandard normal variate $r$, we transform the boundaries for $z$ by the usual relationship, $r = z\sigma(r) + E(r) = \Phi(\alpha/2)\sigma(r) + E(r)$. Note that all we are doing is setting the expectation at the center of the confidence interval and extending it by a number of standard deviations. The number of standard deviations is determined by the probability that we allow for falling outside the confidence interval ($\alpha$), or, equivalently, the probability of falling in it ($P$). Using minus and plus 1.96 for $z = \pm \Phi(\emptyset/.25)$, the distance on each side of the expectation is $\pm 1.96 \times .127 = .249$. Thus we obtain the confidence interval

$$[E(r) - \sigma(r)\Phi(\alpha/2), E(r) + \sigma(r)\Phi(\alpha/2)] = [E(r) - .249, E(r) + .249]$$
$$= [-.234, .264]$$

so that

$$P = 1 - \alpha = \Pr[E(r) - \sigma(r)\Phi(\alpha/2) \leq r \leq E(r) + \sigma(r)\Phi(\alpha/2)]$$

which, for our stock (with expectation .015 and standard deviation .127), amounts to

$$\Pr[-.234 \leq r \leq .264] = .95$$

Note that because of the large standard deviation of the rate of return on the stock, the 95% confidence interval is 49% wide.

To reiterate with a variation on this example, suppose we seek a 90% confidence interval for the annual rate of return on a portfolio, $r_p$, with a monthly expected return of 1.2% and standard deviation of 5.2%.

The solution is simply

$$\Pr\left[E(r) - \sigma(r) \Phi\left(\frac{1-P}{2}\right) \leq r_p \leq E(r) + \sigma(r) \Phi\left(\frac{1-P}{2}\right)\right]$$
$$= \Pr[(.012 - .052 \times 1.645) \leq r_p \leq (.012 + .052 \times 1.645)]$$
$$= \Pr[-.0735 \leq r_p \leq .0975] = .90$$

Because the portfolio is of low risk this time (and we require only a 90% rather than a 95% probability of falling within the interval), the 90% confidence interval is only 2.4% wide.

**The Lognormal Distribution.** The normal distribution is not adequate to describe stock prices and returns for two reasons. First, whereas the normal distribution admits any value, including negative values, actual stock prices cannot be negative. Second, the normal distribution does not account for compounding. The lognormal distribution addresses these two problems.

The lognormal distribution describes a random variable that grows, *every instant,* by a rate that is a normal random variable. Thus the progression of a lognormal random variable reflects continuous compounding.

Suppose that the *annual continuously compounded* (ACC) rate of return on a stock is normally distributed with expectation $\mu = .12$ and standard deviation $\sigma = .42$. The stock price at the beginning of the year is $P_0 = \$10$. With continuous compounding (see appendix to Chapter 5), if the ACC rate of return, $r_C$, turns out to be .23, then the end-of-year price will be

$$P_1 = P_0\exp(r_C) = 10e^{.23} = \$12.586$$

representing an effective annual rate of return of

$$r = \frac{P_1 - P_0}{P_0} = e^{r_C} - 1 = .2586 \text{ (or 25.86\%)}$$

This is the practical meaning of $r$, the annual rate on the stock, being lognormally distributed. Note that however negative the ACC rate of return ($r_C$) is, the price, $P_1$, cannot become negative.

Two properties of lognormally distributed financial assets are important: their expected return and the allowance for changes in measurement period.

***Expected Return of a Lognormally Distributed Asset.*** The expected annual rate of return of a lognormally distributed stock (as in our example) is

$$E(r) = \exp(\mu + \sigma^2/2) - 1 = \exp(.12 + .42^2/2) - 1 = e^{.2082} - 1$$
$$= .2315 \text{ (or } 23.15\%)$$

This is just a statistical property of the distribution. For this reason, a useful statistic is

$$\mu^* = \mu + \sigma^2/2 = .2082$$

When analysts refer to the expected ACC return on a lognormal asset, frequently they are really referring to $\mu^*$. Often the asset is said to have a normal distribution of the ACC return with expectation $\mu^*$ and standard deviation $\sigma$.

***Change of Frequency of Measured Returns.*** The lognormal distribution allows for easy change of the holding period of returns. Suppose that we want to calculate returns monthly instead of annually. We use the parameter $t$ to indicate the fraction of the year that is desired; in the case of monthly periods, $t = 1/12$. To transform the annual distribution to a $t$-period (monthly) distribution, it is necessary merely to multiply the expectation and variance of the ACC return by $t$ (in this case, 1/12).

The monthly continuously compounded return on the stock in our example has the expectation and standard deviation of

$$\mu(\text{monthly}) = .12/12 = .01 \text{ (1\% per month)}$$
$$\sigma(\text{monthly}) = .42/\sqrt{12} = .1212 \text{ (or 12.12\% per month)}$$
$$\mu^*(\text{monthly}) = .2082/12 = .01735 \text{ (or 1.735\% per month)}$$

Note that we divide variance by 12 when changing from annual to monthly frequency; the standard deviation therefore is divided by the square root of 12.

Similarly, we can convert a nonannual distribution to an annual distribution by following the same routine. For example, suppose that the weekly continuously compounded rate of return on a stock is normally distributed with $\mu^* = .003$ and $\sigma = .07$. Then the ACC return is distributed with

$$\mu^* = 52 \times .003 = .156 \text{ (or 15.6\% per year)}$$
$$\sigma = \sqrt{52} \times .07 = .5048 \text{ (or 50.48\% per year)}$$

In practice, to obtain normally distributed, continuously compounded returns, $R$, we take the log of 1.0 plus the raw returns:

$$R = \log(1 + r)$$

For short intervals, raw returns are small, and the continuously compounded returns, $R$, will be practically identical to the raw returns, $r$. The rule of thumb is that this conversion is not necessary for periods of 1 month or less. That is, approximating stock returns as normal will be accurate enough. For longer intervals, however, the transformation may be necessary.

## A.2 DESCRIPTIVE STATISTICS

Our analysis so far has been forward looking, or, as economists like to say, ex ante. We have been concerned with probabilities, expected values, and surprises. We made our analysis more tractable by assuming that decision outcomes are distributed according to relatively simple formulas and that we know the parameters of these distributions.

Investment managers must satisfy themselves that these assumptions are reasonable, which they do by constantly analyzing observations from relevant random variables that accumulate over time. Distribution of past rates of return on a stock is one element they need to know in order to make optimal decisions. True, the distribution of the rate of return itself changes over time. However, a sample that is not too old does yield information relevant to the next-period probability distribution and its parameters. In this section we explain descriptive statistics, or the organization and analysis of such historic samples.

### Histograms, Boxplots, and Time Series Plots

Table A.3 shows the annual excess returns (over the T-bill rate) for two major classes of assets, the S&P 500 index and a portfolio of long-term government bonds, for the period 1926 to 1993.

One way to understand the data is to present it graphically, commonly in a *histogram* or frequency distribution. Histograms of the 68 observations in Table A.3 are shown in Figure A.4. We construct a histogram according to the following principles:

- The range (of values) of the random variable is divided into a relatively small number of equal-sized intervals. The number of intervals that makes sense depends on the number of available observations. The data in Table A.3 provide 68 observations, and thus deciles (10 intervals) seem adequate.

- A rectangle is drawn over each interval. The height of the rectangle represents the frequency of observations for each interval.

- If the observations are concentrated in one part of the range, the range may be divided to unequal intervals. In that case the rectangles are scaled so that their *area* represents the frequency of the observations for each interval. (This is not the case in our samples, however.)

- If the sample is representative, the shape of the histogram will reveal the probability distribution of the random variable. Our total of 68 observations is not a large sample, but a look at the histogram does suggest that the returns may be reasonably approximated by a normal or lognormal distribution.

Another way to represent sample information graphically is by *boxplots*. Figure A.5 is an example that uses the same data as in Table A.3. Boxplots are most useful to show the dispersion of the sample distribution. A commonly used measure of dispersion is the *interquartile range*. Recall that the range, a crude measure of dispersion, is defined as the distance between the largest and smallest observations. By its nature, this measure is unreliable because it will be determined by the two most extreme outliers of the sample.

The interquartile range, a more satisfactory variant of the simple range, is defined as the difference between the lower and upper quartiles. Below the *lower* quartile lies 25% of the sample; similarly, above the *upper* quartile lies 25% of the sample. The interquartile range therefore is confined to the central 50% of the sample. The greater the dispersion of a sample, the greater the distance between these two values.

In the boxplot the horizontal broken line represents the median, the box the interquartile range, and the vertical lines extending from the box the range. The vertical lines representing the range often are restricted (if necessary) to extend only to 1.5 times the interquartile

## Table A.3   Excess Return (Risk Premiums) on Stocks and Long-Term Treasury Bonds (Maturity Premiums)

| Year | Equity Risk Premium | Maturity Premium | Year | Equity Risk Premium | Maturity Premium |
|------|---------------------|------------------|------|---------------------|------------------|
| 1926 | 8.35 | 4.50 | 1963 | 19.68 | −1.91 |
| 1927 | 34.37 | 5.81 | 1964 | 12.94 | −0.03 |
| 1928 | 40.37 | −3.14 | 1965 | 8.52 | −3.22 |
| 1929 | −13.17 | −1.33 | 1966 | −14.82 | −1.11 |
| 1930 | −27.31 | 2.25 | 1967 | 19.77 | −13.40 |
| 1931 | −44.41 | −6.38 | 1968 | 5.85 | −5.47 |
| 1932 | −9.15 | 15.88 | 1969 | −15.08 | −11.66 |
| 1933 | 53.69 | −0.38 | 1970 | −2.52 | 5.57 |
| 1934 | −1.60 | 9.86 | 1971 | 9.92 | 8.84 |
| 1935 | 47.50 | 4.81 | 1972 | 15.14 | 1.84 |
| 1936 | 33.74 | 7.33 | 1973 | −21.59 | −8.04 |
| 1937 | −35.34 | −0.08 | 1974 | −34.47 | −3.65 |
| 1938 | 31.14 | 5.55 | 1975 | 31.40 | 3.39 |
| 1939 | −0.43 | 5.92 | 1976 | 18.76 | 11.67 |
| 1940 | −9.78 | 6.09 | 1977 | −12.30 | −5.79 |
| 1941 | −11.65 | 0.87 | 1978 | −0.62 | −8.34 |
| 1942 | 20.07 | 2.95 | 1979 | 8.06 | −11.60 |
| 1943 | 25.55 | 1.73 | 1980 | 21.18 | −15.19 |
| 1944 | 19.42 | 2.48 | 1981 | −19.62 | −12.86 |
| 1945 | 36.11 | 10.40 | 1982 | 10.87 | 29.81 |
| 1946 | −8.42 | −0.45 | 1983 | 13.71 | −8.12 |
| 1947 | 5.21 | −3.13 | 1984 | −3.58 | 5.58 |
| 1948 | 4.69 | 2.59 | 1985 | 24.44 | 23.25 |
| 1949 | 17.69 | 5.35 | 1986 | 12.31 | 18.28 |
| 1950 | 30.51 | −1.14 | 1987 | −0.24 | −8.16 |
| 1951 | 22.53 | −5.43 | 1988 | 10.46 | 3.32 |
| 1952 | 16.71 | −0.50 | 1989 | 23.12 | 9.74 |
| 1953 | −2.81 | 1.81 | 1990 | −10.98 | −1.63 |
| 1954 | 51.76 | 6.33 | 1991 | 24.95 | 13.70 |
| 1955 | 29.99 | −2.87 | 1992 | 4.16 | 4.54 |
| 1956 | 4.10 | −8.05 | 1993 | 7.09 | 15.34 |
| 1957 | −13.92 | 4.31 | | | |
| 1958 | 41.82 | −7.64 | Average | 8.57 | 1.62 |
| 1959 | 9.01 | −5.21 | Standard deviation | 20.90 | 8.50 |
| 1960 | −3.13 | 11.12 | Minimum | −44.41 | −15.19 |
| 1961 | 24.76 | −1.16 | Maximum | 53.69 | 29.81 |
| 1962 | −11.46 | 4.16 | | | |

Source: Data from the Center for Research of Security Prices, University of Chicago.

range, so that the more extreme observations can be shown separately (by points) as outliers.

As a concept check, verify from Table A.3 that the points on the boxplot of Figure A.5 correspond to the following list on page 1025:

**Figure A.4
A. Histogram
of the equity
risk premium;
B. histogram
of the bond
maturity
premium.**

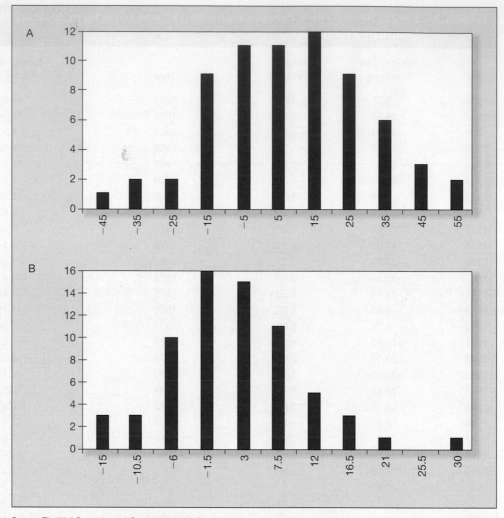

Source: *The Wall Street Journal,* October 15, 1997. Reprinted by permission of *The Wall Street Journal,* © 1997 Dow Jones & Company, Inc. All Rights Reserved Worldwide.

| | Equity Risk Premium | Bond Maturity Premium |
|---|---|---|
| Lowest extreme points | −44.41 | −15.19 |
| | −35.34 | −13.40 |
| | −34.47 | −12.86 |
| | −27.31 | −11.66 |
| | −21.59 | −11.60 |
| | −19.62 | −8.34 |
| | −15.08 | −8.16 |
| | −14.82 | −8.12 |
| | −13.92 | −8.05 |
| | −13.17 | −8.04 |
| | −12.30 | −7.64 |
| | | −6.38 |
| | | −5.79 |
| | | −5.47 |
| | | −5.43 |
| | | −5.21 |
| Lowest quartile | −4.79 | −3.33 |
| Median | 8.77 | 1.77 |
| Highest quartile | 22.68 | 5.64 |
| Highest extreme points | 29.99 | 8.84 |
| | 30.51 | 9.74 |
| | 31.14 | 9.86 |
| | 31.40 | 10.40 |
| | 33.74 | 11.12 |
| | 34.37 | 11.67 |
| | 36.11 | 13.70 |
| | 40.37 | 15.34 |
| | 41.82 | 15.88 |
| | 47.50 | 18.28 |
| | 51.76 | 23.25 |
| | 53.69 | 29.81 |
| Interquartile range | 27.47 | 8.97 |
| 1.5 times the interquartile range | 41.20 | 13.45 |
| From: | −11.84 | −4.95 |
| To: | 29.37 | 8.49 |

Finally, a third form of graphing is *time series plots,* which are used to convey the behavior of economic variables over time. Figure A.6 shows a time series plot of the excess returns on stocks and bonds from Table A.3. Even though the human eye is apt to see patterns in randomly generated time series, examining time series' evolution over a long period does yield some information. Sometimes, such examination can be as revealing as that provided by formal statistical analysis.

**Sample Statistics**  Suppose we can assume that the probability distribution of stock returns has not changed over the 68 years from 1926 to 1993. We wish to draw inferences about the probability distribution of stock returns from the sample of 68 observations of annual stock excess returns in Table A.3.

**Figure A.5
Boxplots of
annual equity
risk premium
and long-term
bond (maturity)
risk premium
(1926–1993)**

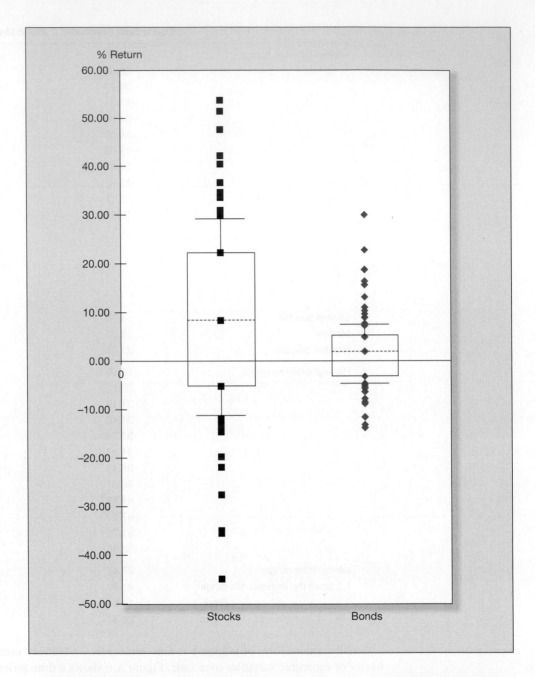

A central question is whether given observations represent independent observations from the underlying distribution. If they do, statistical analysis is quite straightforward. Our analysis assumes that this is indeed the case. Empiricism in financial markets tends to confirm this assumption in most cases.

**Estimating Expected Returns from the Sample Average.** The definition of expected returns suggests that the sample average be used as an estimate of the expected value. Indeed, one definition of the expected return is the average of a sample when the number of observations tends to infinity.

**Figure A.6  A. Equity risk premium, 1926–1993; B. bond maturity premium, 1926–1993.**

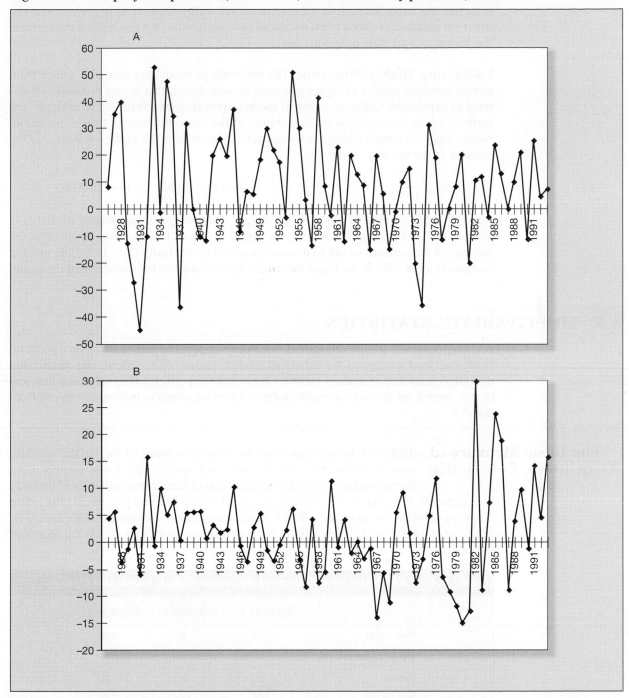

Denoting the sample returns in Table A.3 by $R_t$, $t = 1, \ldots, T = 68$, the estimate of the annual expected excess rate of return is

$$\bar{R} = \frac{1}{T} \Sigma R_t = 8.57\%$$

The bar over the $R$ is a common notation for an estimate of the expectation. Intuition suggests that the larger the sample, the greater the reliability of the sample average, and the larger the standard deviation of the measured random variable, the less reliable the average. We discuss this property more fully later.

**Estimating Higher Moments.** The principle of estimating expected values from sample averages applies to higher moments as well. Recall that higher moments are defined as expectations of some power of the deviation from expectation. For example, the variance (second moment) is the expectation of the squared deviation from expectation. Accordingly, the sample average of the squared deviation from the average will serve as the estimate of the variance, denoted by $s^2$:

$$s^2 = \frac{1}{T-1} \, \Sigma(R_t - \overline{R})^2 = \frac{1}{67} \, \Sigma(R_t - .0857)^2 = .04368 \qquad (s = 20.90\%)$$

where $\overline{R}$ is the estimate of the sample average. The average of the squared deviation is taken over $T - 1 = 67$ observations for a technical reason. If we were to divide by $T$, the estimate of the variance would be downward-biased by the factor $(T - 1)/T$. Here too, the estimate is more reliable the larger the sample and the smaller the true standard deviation.

## A.3 MULTIVARIATE STATISTICS

Building portfolios requires combining random variables. The rate of return on a portfolio is the weighted average of the individual returns. Hence understanding and quantifying the interdependence of random variables is essential to portfolio analysis. In the first part of this section we return to scenario analysis. Later we return to making inferences from samples.

**The Basic Measure of Association: Covariance** Table A.4 summarizes what we have developed so far for the scenario returns on Anheuser-Busch stock and options. We know already what happens when we add a constant to one of these return variables or multiply by a constant. But what if we combine any two of them? Suppose that we add the return on the stock to the return on the call. We create a new random variable that we denote by $r(s + c) = r(s) + r(c)$, where $r(s)$ is the return on the stock and $r(c)$ is the return on the call.

| Table A.4 | Probability Distribution of Anheuser-Busch Stock and Options | | |
|---|---|---|---|
| | **Scenario 1** | **Scenario 2** | **Scenario 3** |
| Probability | .20 | .50 | .30 |
| **Rates of Return (%)** | | | |
| Stock | 20 | 30 | 50 |
| Call option | −100 | −100 | 400 |
| Put option | 50 | −25 | −100 |
| | **E(r)** | **σ** | **σ²** |
| Stock | .340 | 0.1114 | 0.0124 |
| Call option | .500 | 2.2913 | 5.2500 |
| Put option | −.325 | 0.5250 | 0.2756 |

From the definition, the expected value of the combination variable is

$$E[r(s + c)] = \Sigma \Pr(i) r_i(s + c) \tag{A.10}$$

Substituting the definition of $r(s + c)$ into equation A.10 we have

$$\begin{aligned} E[r(s + c)] &= \Sigma \Pr(i)[r_i(s) + r_i(c)] = \Sigma \Pr(i) r_i(s) + \Sigma \Pr(i) r_i(c) \\ &= E[r(s)] + E[r(c)] \end{aligned} \tag{A.11}$$

In words, the expectation of the sum of two random variables is just the sum of the expectations of the component random variables. Can the same be true about the variance? The answer is "no," which is, perhaps, the most important fact in portfolio theory. The reason lies in the statistical association between the combined random variables.

As a first step, we introduce the *covariance,* the basic measure of association. Although the expressions that follow may look intimidating, they are merely squares of sums; that is, $(a + b)^2 = a^2 + b^2 + 2ab$, and $(a - b)^2 = a^2 + b^2 - 2ab$, where the $a$s and $b$s might stand for random variables, their expectations or their deviations from expectations. From the definition of the variance

$$\sigma_{s+c}^2 = E[r_{s+c} - E(r_{s+c})]^2 \tag{A.12}$$

To make equations A.12 through A.20 easier to read, we will identify the variables by subscripts $s$ and $c$ and drop the subscript $i$ for scenarios. Substitute the definition of $r(s + c)$ and its expectation into equation A.12:

$$\sigma_{s+c}^2 = E[r_s + r_c - E(r_s) - E(r_c)]^2 \tag{A.13}$$

Changing the order of variables within the brackets in equation A.13,

$$\sigma_{s+c}^2 = E[r_s - E(r_s) + r_c - E(r_c)]^2$$

Within the square brackets we have the sum of the deviations from expectations of the two variables, which we denote by $d$. Writing this out,

$$\sigma_{s+c}^2 = E[(d_s + d_c)^2] \tag{A.14}$$

Equation A.14 is the expectation of a complete square. Taking the square, we find

$$\sigma_{s+c}^2 = E(d_s^2 + d_c^2 + 2d_s d_c) \tag{A.15}$$

The term in parentheses in equation A.15 is the summation of three random variables. Because the expectation of a sum is the sum of the expectations, we can write equation A.15 as

$$\sigma_{s+c}^2 = E(d_s^2) + E(d_c^2) + 2E(d_s d_c) \tag{A.16}$$

In equation A.16 the first two terms on the right-hand side are the variance of the stock (the expectation of its squared deviation from expectation) plus the variance of the call. The third term is twice the expression that is the definition of the covariance discussed in equation A.17. (Note that the expectation is multiplied by 2 because expectation of twice a variable is twice the variable's expectation.)

In other words, the variance of a sum of random variables is the sum of the variances *plus* twice the covariance, which we denote by $\text{Cov}(r_s, r_c)$, or the covariance between the return on $s$ and the return on $c$. Specifically,

$$\text{Cov}(r_s, r_c) = E(d_s d_c) = E\{[r_s - E(r_s)][r_c - E(r_c)]\} \tag{A.17}$$

The sequence of the variables in the expression for the covariance is of no consequence. Because the order of multiplication makes no difference, the definition of the covariance in equation A.17 shows that it will not affect the covariance either.

We use the data in Table A.4 to set up the input table for the calculation of the covariance, as shown in Table A.5.

First, we analyze the covariance between the stock and the call. In Scenarios 1 and 2, both assets show *negative* deviations from expectation. This is an indication of *positive co-movement*. When these two negative deviations are multiplied, the product, which eventually contributes to the covariance between the returns, is positive. Multiplying deviations leads to positive covariance when the variables move in the same direction and negative covariance when they move in opposite directions. In Scenario 3 both assets show *positive* deviations, reinforcing the inference that the co-movement is positive. The magnitude of the products of the deviations, weighted by the probability of each scenario, when added up, results in a covariance that shows not only the direction of the co-movement (by its sign) but also the degree of the co-movement.

The covariance is a variance-like statistic. Whereas the variance shows the degree of the movement of a random variable about its expectation, the covariance shows the degree of the co-movement of two variables about their expectations. It is important for portfolio analysis that the covariance of a variable with itself is equal to its variance. You can see this by substituting the appropriate deviations in equation A.17; the result is the expectation of the variable's squared deviation from expectation.

The first three values in the last column of Table A.5 are the familiar variances of the three assets, the stock, the call, and the put. The last three are the covariances; two of them are negative. Examine the covariance between the stock and the put, for example. In the first two scenarios the stock realizes negative deviations, while the put realizes positive deviations. When we multiply such deviations, the sign becomes negative. The same happens in the third scenario, except that the stock realizes a positive deviation and the put a negative one. Again, the product is negative, adding to the inference of negative co-movement.

With other assets and scenarios the product of the deviations can be negative in some scenarios, positive in others. The *magnitude* of the products, when *weighted* by the probabilities, determines which co-movements dominate. However, whenever the sign of the products varies from scenario to scenario, the results will offset one another, contributing to a small, close-to-zero covariance. In such cases we may conclude that the returns have either a small, or no, average co-movement.

**Table A.5   Deviations, Squared Deviations, and Weighted Products of Deviations from Expectations of Anheuser-Busch Stock and Options**

|  | Scenario 1 | Scenario 2 | Scenario 3 | Probability-Weighted Sum |
|---|---|---|---|---|
| Probability | 0.20 | 0.50 | 0.30 |  |
| Deviation of stock | −0.14 | −0.04 | 0.16 |  |
| Squared deviation | 0.0196 | 0.0016 | 0.0256 | 0.0124 |
| Deviation of call | −1.50 | −1.50 | 3.50 |  |
| Squared deviation | 2.25 | 2.25 | 12.25 | 5.25 |
| Deviation of put | 0.825 | 0.75 | −0.675 |  |
| Squared deviation | 0.680625 | 0.005625 | 0.455635 | 0.275628 |
| Product of deviations ($d_s d_c$) | 0.21 | 0.06 | 0.56 | 0.24 |
| Product of deviations ($d_s d_p$) | −0.1155 | −0.003 | −0.108 | −0.057 |
| Product of deviations ($d_c d_p$) | −1.2375 | −0.1125 | −2.3625 | −1.0125 |

**Covariance between Transformed Variables.** Because the covariance is the expectation of the product of deviations from expectation of two variables, analyzing the effect of transformations on deviations from expectation will show the effect of the transformation on the covariance.

Suppose that we add a constant to one of the variables. We know already that the expectation of the variable increases by that constant, so deviations from expectation will remain unchanged. Just as adding a constant to a random variable does not affect its variance, it also will not affect its covariance with other variables.

Multiplying a random variable by a constant also multiplies its expectation, as well as its deviation from expectation. Therefore, the covariance with any other variable will also be multiplied by that constant. Using the definition of the covariance, check that this summation of the foregoing discussion is true:

$$\text{Cov}(a_1 + b_1 r_s, a_2 + b_2 r_c) = b_1 b_2 \text{Cov}(r_s, r_c) \tag{A.18}$$

The covariance allows us to calculate the variance of sums of random variables, and eventually the variance of portfolio returns.

## A Pure Measure of Association: The Correlation Coefficient

If we tell you that the covariance between the rates of return of the stock and the call is .24 (see Table A.5), what have you learned? Because the sign is positive, you know that the returns generally move in the same direction. However, the number .24 adds nothing to your knowledge of the closeness of co-movement of the stock and the call.

To obtain a measure of association that conveys the degree of intensity of the co-movement, we relate the covariance to the standard deviations of the two variables. Each standard deviation is the square root of the variance. Thus the product of the standard deviations has the dimensions of the variance that is also shared by the covariance. Therefore, we can define the correlation coefficient, denoted by $\rho$, as

$$\rho_{sc} = \frac{\text{Cov}(r_s, r_c)}{\sigma_s \sigma_c} \tag{A.19}$$

where the subscripts on r identify the two variables involved. Because the order of the variables in the expression of the covariance is of no consequence, equation A.19 shows that the order does not affect the correlation coefficient either.

We use the covariances in Table A.5 to show the *correlation matrix* for the three variables:

|       | Stock | Call | Put   |
|-------|-------|------|-------|
| Stock | 1.00  | 0.94 | -0.97 |
| Call  | 0.94  | 1.00 | -0.84 |
| Put   | -0.97 | -0.84| 1.00  |

The highest (in absolute value) correlation coefficient is between the stock and the put, $-.97$, although the absolute value of the covariance between them is the lowest by far. The reason is attributable to the effect of the standard deviations. The following properties of the correlation coefficient are important:

- Because the correlation coefficient, just as the covariance, measures only the degree of association, it tells us nothing about causality. The direction of causality has to come from theory and be supported by specialized tests.
- The correlation coefficient is determined completely by deviations from expectations, as are the components in equation A.19. We expect, therefore, that it

is not affected by adding constants to the associated random variables. However, the correlation coefficient is invariant also to multiplying the variables by constants. You can verify this property by referring to the effect of multiplication by a constant on the covariance and standard deviation.

- The correlation coefficient can vary from $-1.0$, perfect negative correlation, to $1.0$, perfect positive correlation. This can be seen by calculating the correlation coefficient of a variable with itself. You expect it to be $1.0$. Recalling that the covariance of a variable with itself is its own variance, you can verify this using equation A.19. The more ambitious can verify that the correlation between a variable and the negative of itself is equal to $-1.0$. First, find from equation A.17 that the covariance between a variable and its negative equals the negative of the variance. Then check equation A.19.

Because the correlation between $x$ and $y$ is the same as the correlation between $y$ and $x$, the *correlation matrix is symmetric about the diagonal*. The diagonal entries are all $1.0$ because they represent the correlations of returns with themselves. Therefore, it is customary to present only the lower triangle of the correlation matrix.

Reexamine equation A.19. You can invert it so that the covariance is presented in terms of the correlation coefficient and the standard deviations as in equation A.20:

$$\text{Cov}(r_s, r_c) = \rho_{sc} \sigma_s \sigma_c \qquad (A.20)$$

This formulation can be useful, because many think in terms of correlations rather than covariances.

**Estimating Correlation Coefficients from Sample Returns.** Assuming that a sample consists of independent observations, we assign equal weights to all observations and use simple averages to estimate expectations. When estimating variances and covariances, we get an average by dividing by the number of observations minus one.

Suppose that you are interested in estimating the correlation between stock and long-term default-free government bonds. Assume that the sample of 68 annual excess returns for the period 1926 to 1993 in Table A.3 is representative.

Using the definition for the correlation coefficient in equation A.19, you estimate the following statistics (using the subscripts $s$ for stocks, $b$ for bonds, and $t$ for time):

$$\overline{R}_s = \frac{1}{68} \sum_{i=1}^{68} R_{s,t} = .0857; \qquad \overline{R}_b = \frac{1}{68} \sum R_{b,t} = 0.162$$

$$\sigma_s = \left[ \frac{1}{67} \sum (R_{s,t} - \overline{R}_s)^2 \right]^{1/2} = .2090$$

$$\sigma_b = \left[ \frac{1}{67} \sum (R_{b,t} - \overline{R}_b)^2 \right]^{1/2} = .0850$$

$$\text{Cov}(R_s, R_b) = \frac{1}{67} \sum [(R_{s,t} - \overline{R}_s)(R_{b,t} - \overline{R}_b)] = .00314$$

$$\rho_{sb} = \frac{\text{Cov}(R_s, R_b)}{\sigma_s \sigma_b} = .17916$$

Here is one example of how problematic estimation can be. Recall that we predicate our use of the sample on the assumption that the probability distributions have not changed over the sample period. To see the problem with this assumption, suppose that we reestimate the correlation between stocks and bonds over a more recent period—for example, beginning in 1965, about the time of onset of government debt financing of both the war in Vietnam and the Great Society programs.

Repeating the previous calculations for the period 1965 to 1987, we find

$$\overline{R}_s = .0312; \qquad \overline{R}_b = -.00317$$
$$\sigma_s = .15565; \qquad \sigma_b = .11217$$
$$\mathrm{Cov}(R_s, R_b) = .0057; \qquad \rho_{sb} = .32647$$

A comparison of the two sets of numbers suggests that it is likely, but by no means certain, that the underlying probability distributions have changed. The variance in the rates of return and the size of the sample are why we cannot be sure. We shall return to the issue of testing the sample statistics shortly.

## Regression Analysis

We will use a problem from the CFA examination (Level I, 1986) to represent the degree of understanding of regression analysis that is required for the ground level. However, first let us develop some background.

In analyzing measures of association so far, we have ignored the question of causality, identifying simply *independent* and *dependent* variables. Suppose that theory (in its most basic form) tells us that all asset excess returns are driven by the same economic force whose movements are captured by a broad-based market index, such as excess return on the S&P 500 stock index.

Suppose further that our theory predicts a simple, linear relationship between the excess return of any asset and the market index. A linear relationship, one that can be described by a straight line, takes on this form:

$$R_{j,t} = a_j + b_j R_{M,t} + e_{j,t} \tag{A.21}$$

where the subscript $j$ represents any asset, $M$ represents the market index (the S&P 500), and $t$ represents variables that change over time. (In the following discussion we omit subscripts when possible.) On the left-hand side of equation A.21 is the dependent variable, the excess return on asset $j$. The right-hand side has two parts, the explained and unexplained (by the relationship) components of the dependent variable.

The explained component of $R_j$ is the $a + bR_M$ part. It is plotted in Figure A.7. The quantity $a$, also called the intercept, gives the value of $R_j$ when the *independent* variable is zero. This relationship assumes that it is a constant. The second term in the explained part of the return represents the driving force, $R_M$, times the sensitivity coefficient, $b$, that transmits movements in $R_M$ to movements in $R_j$. The term $b$ is also assumed to be constant. Figure A.7 shows that $b$ is the slope of the regression line.

The unexplained component of $R_j$ is represented by the *disturbance* term, $e_j$. The disturbance is assumed to be uncorrelated with the explanatory variable, $R_M$, and of zero expectation. Such a variable is also called a noise variable because it contributes to the variance but not to the expectation of the dependent variable, $R_j$.

A relationship such as that shown in equation A.21 applied to data, with coefficients estimated, is called a *regression equation*. A relationship including only one explanatory variable is called *simple regression*. The parameters $a$ and $b$ are called (simple) *regression coefficients*. Because every value of $R_j$ is explained by the regression, the expectation and variance of $R_j$ are also determined by it. Using the expectation of the expression in equation A.21, we get

$$E(R_j) = a + bE(R_M) \tag{A.22}$$

**Figure A.7
Simple regression
estimates and
residuals. The
intercept and
slope are chosen
so as to minimize
the sum of
the squared
deviations from
the regression
line.**

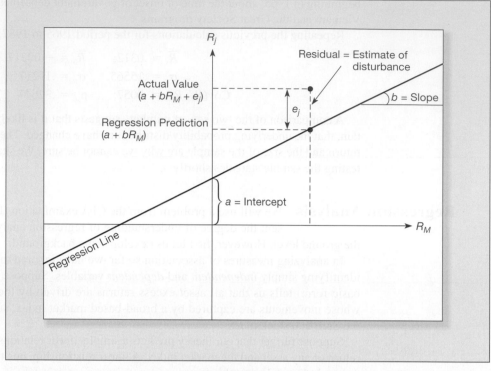

The constant $a$ has no effect on the variance of $R_j$. Because the variables $r_M$ and $e_j$ are uncorrelated, the variance of the sum, $bR_M + e$, is the sum of the variances. Accounting for the parameter $b$ multiplying $R_M$, the variance of $R_j$ will be

$$\sigma_j^2 = b^2\sigma_M^2 + \sigma_e^2 \tag{A.23}$$

Equation A.23 tells us that the contribution of the variance of $R_M$ to that of $R_j$ depends on the regression (slope) coefficient $b$. The term $(b\sigma_M)^2$ is called the *explained variance*. The variance of the disturbance makes up the *unexplained variance*.

The covariance between $R_j$ and $R_M$ is also given by the regression equation. Setting up the expression, we have

$$\begin{aligned} \text{Cov}(R_j, R_M) &= \text{Cov}(a + bR_M + e, R_M) \\ &= \text{Cov}(bR_M, R_M) = b\text{Cov}(R_M, R_M) = b\sigma_M^2 \end{aligned} \tag{A.24}$$

The intercept, $a$, is dropped because a constant added to a random variable does not affect the covariance with any other variable. The disturbance term, $e$, is dropped because it is, by assumption, uncorrelated with the market return.

Equation A.24 shows that the slope coefficient of the regression, $b$, is equal to

$$b = \frac{\text{Cov}(R_j, R_M)}{\sigma_M^2}$$

The slope thereby measures the co-movements of $j$ and $M$ as a fraction of the movement of the driving force, the explanatory variable $M$.

One way to measure the explanatory power of the regression is by the fraction of the variance of $R_j$ that it explains. This fraction is called the *coefficient of determination* and denoted by $\rho^2$.

$$\rho_{jM}^2 = \frac{b^2\sigma_M^2}{\sigma_j^2} = \frac{b^2\sigma_M^2}{b_M^2\sigma_M^2 + \sigma_e^2} \tag{A.25}$$

Note that the unexplained variance, $\sigma_e^2$, has to make up the difference between the coefficient of determination and 1.0. Therefore, another way to represent the coefficient of determination is by

$$\rho_{jM}^2 = 1 - \frac{\sigma_e^2}{\sigma_j^2}$$

Some algebra shows that the coefficient of determination is the square of the correlation coefficient. Finally, squaring the correlation coefficient tells us what proportion of the variance of the dependent variable is explained by the independent (the explanatory) variable.

Estimation of the regression coefficients $a$ and $b$ is based on minimizing the sum of the square deviation of the observations from the estimated regression line (see Figure A.7). Your calculator, as well as any spreadsheet program, can compute regression estimates. A past CFA examination included this question:

### Question.

Pension plan sponsors place a great deal of emphasis on universe rankings when evaluating money managers. In fact, it appears that sponsors assume implicitly that managers who rank in the top quartile of a representative sample of peer managers are more likely to generate superior relative performance in the future than managers who rank in the bottom quartile.

The validity of this assumption can be tested by regressing percentile rankings of managers in one period on their percentile rankings from the prior period.

1. Given that the implicit assumption of plan sponsors is true to the extent that there is perfect correlation in percentile rankings from one period to the next, list the numerical values you would expect to observe for the slope of the regression, and the $R$-squared of the regression.

2. Given that there is no correlation in percentile rankings from period to period, list the numerical values you would expect to observe for the intercept of the regression, the slope of the regression, and the $R$-squared of the regression.

3. Upon performing such a regression, you observe an intercept of .51, a slope of $-.05$, and an $R$-squared of .01. Based on this regression, state your best estimate of a manager's percentile ranking next period if his percentile ranking this period were .15.

4. Some pension plan sponsors have agreed that a good practice is to terminate managers who are in the top quartile and to hire those who are in the bottom quartile. State what those who advocate such a practice expect implicitly about the correlation and slope from a regression of the managers' subsequent ranking on their current ranking.

### Answer.

1. Intercept $= 0$
   Slope $= 1$
   $R$-squared $= 1$

2. Intercept $= .50$
   Slope $= 0.0$
   $R$-squared $= 0.0$

3. 50th percentile, derived as follows:
   $y = a + bx$
   $\quad = .51 - 0.05(.15)$
   $\quad = .51 - .0075$
   $\quad = .5025$

Given the very low *R*-squared, it would be difficult to estimate what the manager's rank would be.

4. Sponsors who advocate firing top-performance managers and hiring the poorest implicitly expect that both the correlation and slope would be significantly negative.

**Multiple Regression Analysis**    In many cases, theory suggests that a number of independent, explanatory variables drive a dependent variable. This concept becomes clear enough when demonstrated by a two-variable case. A real estate analyst offers the following regression equation to explain the return on a nationally diversified real estate portfolio:

$$RE_t = a + b_1 RE_{t-1} + b_2 NVR_t + e_t \qquad (A.26)$$

The dependent variable is the period *t* real estate portfolio, $RE_t$. The model specifies that the explained part of that return is driven by two independent variables. The first is the previous period return, $RE_{t-1}$, representing persistence of momentum. The second explanatory variable is the current national vacancy rate, $NVR_t$.

As in the simple regression, *a* is the intercept, representing the value that RE is expected to take when the explanatory variables are zero. The (slope) regression coefficients, $b_1$ and $b_2$, represent the *marginal* effect of the explanatory variables.

The coefficient of determination is defined exactly as before. The ratio of the variance of the disturbance, *e*, to the total variance of RE is 1.0 *minus* the coefficient of determination. The regression coefficients are estimated here, too, by finding coefficients that minimize the sum of squared deviations of the observations from the prediction of the regression.

# A.4    HYPOTHESIS TESTING

The central hypothesis of investment theory is that nondiversifiable (systematic) risk is rewarded by a higher *expected* return. But do the data support the theory? Consider the data on the excess return on stocks in Table A.3. The estimate of the expected excess return (the sample average) is 8.57%. This appears to be a hefty risk premium, but so is the risk—the estimate of the standard deviation for the same sample is 20.9%. Could it be that the positive average is just the luck of the draw? Hypothesis testing supplies probabilistic answers to such concerns.

The first step in hypothesis testing is to state the claim that is to be tested. This is called the *null hypothesis* (or simply the *null*), denoted by $H_0$. Against the null, an alternative claim (hypothesis) is stated, which is denoted by $H_1$. The objective of hypothesis testing is to decide whether to reject the null in favor of the alternative while identifying the probabilities of the possible errors in the determination.

A hypothesis is *specified* if it assigns a value to a variable. A claim that the risk premium on stocks is zero is one example of a specified hypothesis. Often, however, a hypothesis is general. A claim that the risk premium on stocks is not zero would be a completely general alternative against the specified hypothesis that the risk premium is zero. It amounts to "anything but the null." The alternative that the risk premium is *positive,* although not completely general, is still unspecified. Although it is sometimes desirable to test two unspecified hypotheses (e.g., the claim that the risk premium is zero or negative, against the claim that it is positive), unspecified hypotheses complicate the task of determining the probabilities of errors in judgment.

What are the possible errors? There are two, called Type I and Type II errors. Type I is the event that we will *reject* the null when it is *true*. The probability of Type I error is called the *significance level*. Type II is the event that we will *accept* the null when it is *false*.

Suppose we set a criterion for acceptance of $H_0$ that is so lax that we know for certain we will accept the null. In doing so we will drive the significance level to zero (which is good). If we will never reject the null, we will also never reject it when it is true. At the same time the probability of Type II error will become 1 (which is bad). If we will accept the null for certain, we must also do so when it is false.

The reverse is to set a criterion for acceptance of the null that is so stringent that we know for certain that we will reject it. This drives the probability of Type II error to zero (which is good). By never accepting the null, we avoid accepting it when it is false. Now, however, the significance level will go to 1 (which is bad). If we always reject the null, we will reject it even when it is true.

To compromise between the two evils, hypothesis testing fixes the significance level; that is, it limits the probability of Type I error. Then, subject to this present constraint, the ideal test will minimize the probability of Type II error. If we *avoid* Type II error (accepting the null when it is false) we actually *reject* the null when it is indeed *false*. The probability of doing so is one minus the probability of Type II error, which is called the *power of the test*. Minimizing the probability of Type II error maximizes the power of the test.

Testing the claim that stocks earn a risk premium, we set the hypotheses as

$$H_0:E(R) = 0 \quad \text{The expected excess return is zero}$$
$$H_1:E(R) > 0 \quad \text{The expected excess return is positive}$$

$H_1$ is an *unspecified alternative*. When a null is tested against a completely general alternative, it is called a *two-tailed test* because you may reject the null in favor of both greater or smaller values.

When both hypotheses are unspecified, the test is difficult because the calculation of the probabilities of Type I and II errors is complicated. Usually, at least one hypothesis is simple (specified) and set as the null. In that case it is relatively easy to calculate the significance level of the test. Calculating the power of the test that assumes the *unspecified* alternative is true remains complicated; often it is left unsolved.

As we will show, setting the hypothesis that we wish to reject, $E(R) = 0$ as the null (the "straw man"), makes it harder to accept the alternative that we favor, our theoretical bias, which is appropriate.

In testing $E(R) = 0$, suppose we fix the significance level at 5%. This means that we will reject the null (and accept that there is a positive premium) *only* when the data suggest that the probability the null is true is 5% or less. To do so, we must find a critical value, denoted $z_\alpha$ (or critical values in the case of two-tailed tests), that corresponds to $\alpha = .05$, which will create two regions, an acceptance region and a rejection region. Look at Figure A.8 as an illustration.

If the sample average is to the right of the critical value (in the rejection region), the null is rejected; otherwise, it is accepted. In the latter case it is too likely (i.e., the probability is greater than 5%) that the sample average is positive simply because of sampling error. If the sample average is greater than the critical value, we will reject the null in favor of the alternative. The probability that the positive value of the sample average results from sampling error is 5% or less.

If the alternative is one-sided (one-tailed), as in our case, the acceptance region covers the entire area from minus infinity to a positive value, above which lies 5% of the distribution (see Figure A.8). The critical value is $z_\alpha$ in Figure A.8. When the alternative is two-tailed, the area of 5% lies at both extremes of the distribution and is equally divided

**Figure A.8** **Under the null hypothesis, the sample average excess return should be distributed around zero. If the actual average exceeds $z_\alpha$, we conclude that the null hypothesis is false.**

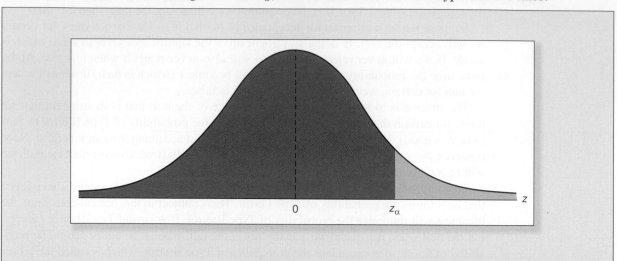

between them, 2.5% on each side. A two-tailed test is more stringent (it is harder to reject the null). In a one-tailed test the fact that our theory predicts the direction in which the average will deviate from the value under the null is weighted in favor of the alternative. The upshot is that for a significance level of 5%, with a one-tailed test, we use a confidence interval of $\alpha = .05$, instead of $\alpha/2 = .025$ as with a two-tailed test.

Hypothesis testing requires assessment of the probabilities of the test statistics, such as the sample average and variance. Therefore, it calls for some assumption about the probability distribution of the underlying variable. Such an assumption becomes an integral part of the null hypothesis, often an implicit one.

In this case we assume that the stock portfolio excess return is normally distributed. The distribution of the test statistic is derived from its mathematical definition and the assumption of the underlying distribution for the random variable. In our case the test statistic is the sample average.

The sample average is obtained by summing all observations ($T = 68$) and then multiplying by $1/T = 1/68$. Each observation is a random variable, drawn independently from the same underlying distribution, with an unknown expectation $\mu$, and standard deviation $\sigma$. The expectation of the sum of all observations is the sum of the $T$ expectations (all equal to $\mu$) divided by $T$, therefore equal to the population expectation. The result is 8.57%, which is equal to the true expectation *plus* sampling errors. Under the null hypothesis, the expectation is zero, and the entire 8.57% constitutes sampling error.

To calculate the variance of the sample average, recall that we assumed that all observations were independent, or uncorrelated. Hence the variance of the sum is the sum of the variances, that is, $T$ times the population variance. However, we also transform the sum, multiplying it by $1/T$; therefore, we have to divide the variance of the sum $T\sigma^2$ by $T^2$. We end up with the variance of the sample average as the population variance divided by $T$. The standard deviation of the sample average, which is called the *standard error*, is

$$\sigma(\text{average}) = \left(\frac{1}{T^2}\Sigma\sigma^2\right)^{1/2} = \left(\frac{1}{T^2}T\sigma^2\right)^{1/2} = \frac{\sigma}{\sqrt{T}} = \frac{.2090}{\sqrt{68}} = .0253 \qquad \text{(A.27)}$$

Our test statistic has a standard error of 2.53%. It makes sense that the larger the number of observations, the *smaller* the *standard error* of the estimate of the expectation.

However, note that it is the variance that goes down by the proportion $T = 68$. The standard error goes down by a much smaller proportion, $\sqrt{T} = 8.25$.

Now that we have the sample mean, 8.57%, its standard deviation, 2.53%, and know that the distribution under the null is normal, we are ready to perform the test. We want to determine whether 8.57% is significantly positive. We achieve this by standardizing our statistic, which means that we subtract from it its expected value under the null hypothesis and divide by its standard deviation. This standardized statistic can now be compared to $z$ values from the standard normal tables. We ask whether

$$\frac{\bar{R} - E(R)}{\sigma} > z_\alpha$$

We would be finished except for another caveat. The assumption of normality is all right in that the test statistic is a weighted sum of normals (according to our assumption about returns). Therefore, it is also normally distributed. However, the analysis also requires that we *know* the variance. Here we are using a sample variance that is only an *estimate* of the true variance.

The solution to this problem turns out to be quite simple. The normal distribution is replaced with *Student-t* (or *t*, for short) *distribution*. Like the normal, the *t* distribution is symmetric. It depends on degrees of freedom, that is, the number of observations less one. Thus, here we replace $z_\alpha$ with $t_{\alpha, T-1}$.

The test is then

$$\frac{\bar{R} - E(R)}{\sigma} > t_{\alpha, T-1}$$

When we substitute in sample results, the left-hand side is a standardized statistic and the right-hand side is a *t*-value derived from *t* tables for $\alpha = .05$ and $T - 1 = 68 - 1 = 67$. We ask whether the inequality holds. If it does, we *reject* the null hypothesis with a 5% significance level; if it does not, we *cannot reject* the null hypothesis. (In this example, $t_{.05, 67} = 1.67$.) Proceeding, we find that

$$\frac{.0857 - 0}{.0253} = 3.39 > 1.67$$

In our sample the inequality holds, and we reject the null hypothesis in favor of the alternative that the risk premium is positive.

A repeat of the test of this hypothesis for the 1965 to 1987 period may make a skeptic out of you. For that period the sample average is 3.12%, the sample standard deviation is 15.57%, and there are $23 - 1 = 22$ degrees of freedom. Does that give you second thoughts?

## The *t*-Test of Regression Coefficients

Suppose that we apply the simple regression model (equation A.21) to the relationship between the long-term government bond portfolio and the stock market index, using the sample in Table A.3. The estimation result (% per year) is

$$a = .9913, \qquad b = .0729, \qquad R\text{-squared} = .0321$$

We interpret these coefficients as follows. For periods when the excess return on the market index is zero, we expect the bonds to earn an excess return of 99.13 basis points. This is the role of the intercept. As for the slope, for each percentage return of the stock portfolio in any year, the bond portfolio is expected to earn, *additionally*, 7.29 basis points. With the average equity risk premium for the sample period of 8.57%, the sample average for bonds is $.9913 + (.0729 \times 8.57) = 1.62\%$. From the squared correlation coefficient you know that the variation in stocks explains 3.21% of the variation in bonds.

Can we rely on these statistics? One way to find out is to set up a hypothesis test, presented here for the regression coefficient $b$.

$H_0$: $b = 0$    The regression slope coefficient is zero, meaning that changes in the independent variable do not explain changes in the dependent variable

$H_1$: $b > 0$    The dependent variable is sensitive to changes in the independent variable (with a *positive* covariance)

Any decent regression software supplies the statistics to test this hypothesis. The regression customarily assumes that the dependent variable and the disturbance are normally distributed, with an unknown variance that is estimated from the sample. Thus the regression coefficient $b$ is normally distributed. Because once again the null is that $b = 0$, all we need is an estimate of the standard error of this statistic.

The estimated standard error of the regression coefficient is computed from the estimated standard deviation of the disturbance and the standard deviation of the explanatory variable. For the regression at hand, that estimate is $s(b) = .0493$. Just as in the previous exercise, the critical value of the test is

$$s(b)t_{\alpha, T-1}$$

Compare this value to the value of the estimated coefficient $b$. We will reject the null in favor of $b > 0$ if

$$b > s(b)t_{\alpha, T-1}$$

which, because the standard deviation $s(b)$ is positive, is equivalent to the following condition:

$$\frac{b}{s(b)} > t_{\alpha, T-1}$$

The $t$-test reports the ratio of the estimated coefficient to its estimated standard deviation. Armed with this *t-ratio,* the number of observations, $T$, and a table of the *Student-t* distribution, you can perform the test at the desired significance level.

The $t$-ratio for our example is $.0729/.0493 = 1.4787$. The $t$-table for 68 degrees of freedom shows we cannot reject the null at a significance level of 5%, for which the critical value is 1.67.

A question from a past CFA exam calls for understanding of regression analysis and hypothesis testing.

### Question.

An academic suggests to you that the returns on common stocks differ based on a company's market capitalization, its historical earnings growth, the stock's current yield, and whether or not the company's employees are unionized. You are skeptical that there are any attributes other than market exposure as measured by beta that explain differences in returns across a sample of securities.

Nonetheless, you decide to test whether or not these other attributes account for the differences in returns. You select the S&P 500 stocks as your sample, and regress their returns each month for the past five years against the company's market capitalization at the beginning of each month, the company's growth in earnings throughout the previous 12 months, the prior year's dividend divided by the stock price at the beginning of each month, and a dummy variable that has a value of 1 if employees are unionized and 0 if not.

1. The average $R$-squared from the regression is .15, and it varies very little from month to month. Discuss the significance of this result.

2. You note that all of the coefficients of the attributes have $t$-statistics greater than 2 in most of the months in which the regressions were run. Discuss the significance of these attributes in terms of explaining differences in common stock returns.

3. You observe in most of the regressions that the coefficient of the dummy variable is $-.14$ and the $t$-statistic is $-4.74$. Discuss the implication of the coefficient regarding the relationship between unionization and the return on a company's common stock.

### *Answer.*

1. Differences in the attributes' values together explain about 15% of the differences in return among the stocks in the S&P 500 index. The remaining unexplained differences in return may be attributable to omitted attributes, industry affiliations, or stock-specific factors. This information by itself is not sufficient to form any qualitative conclusions. The fact that $R$-squared varied little from month to month implies that the relationship is stable and the observed results are not sample specific.

2. Given a $t$-statistic greater than 2 in most of the months, one would regard the attribute coefficients as statistically significant. If the attribute coefficients were not significantly different from zero, one would expect $t$-statistics greater than 2 in fewer than 5% of the regressions for each attribute coefficient. Because the $t$-statistics are greater than 2 much more frequently, one should conclude that they are definitely significant in terms of explaining differences in stock returns.

3. Because the coefficient for the dummy variable representing unionization has persistently been negative and since it persistently has been statistically significant, one would conclude that disregarding all other factors, unionization lowers a company's common stock return. That is, everything else being equal, nonunionized companies will have higher returns than companies whose employees are unionized. Of course, one would want to test the model further to see if there are omitted variables or other problems that might account for this apparent relationship.

# REFERENCES TO CFA QUESTIONS

Each end-of-chapter CFA question is reprinted with permission from the Association for Investment Management and Research (AIMR), Charlottesville, VA. Following is a list of the CFA questions in the end-of-chapter material and the exams and study guides from which they were taken and updated.

**Chapter 2**
1–3.  1996 Level I CFA Study Guide, © 1996
13.  1994 Level I CFA Study Guide, © 1994
15.  1994 Level I CFA Study Guide, © 1994

**Chapter 3**
22.  1986 Level I CFA Study Guide, © 1986
23.  1986 Level I CFA Study Guide, © 1986
24.  1986 Level I CFA Study Guide, © 1986

**Chapter 5**
11.  1992 Level I CFA Study Guide, © 1992
12.  1992 Level I CFA Study Guide, © 1992
13–17.  1993 Level I CFA Study Guide, © 1993

**Chapter 6**
 7.  1991 Level I CFA Study Guide, © 1991
 8.  1991 Level I CFA Study Guide, © 1991
 9.  1991 Level I CFA Study Guide, © 1991

**Chapter 7**
18.  1991 Level I CFA Study Guide, © 1991
19.  1991 Level I CFA Study Guide, © 1991
20.  1993 Level I CFA Study Guide, © 1993
21.  1993 Level I CFA Study Guide, © 1993
22.  1993 Level I CFA Study Guide, © 1993
23.  1991 Level I CFA Study Guide, © 1991

**Chapter 8**
15–17.  1982 Level III CFA Study Guide, © 1982
21.  1993 Level I CFA Study Guide, © 1993
22.  1993 Level I CFA Study Guide, © 1993
23.  1992 Level I CFA Study Guide, © 1992
24.  1992 Level I CFA Study Guide, © 1992
25–27.  1994 Level I CFA Study Guide, © 1994
30.  2001 Level III CFA Study Guide, © 2001
31.  2001 Level II CFA Study Guide, © 2001

32.  2000 Level II CFA Study Guide, © 2000

**Chapter 9**
21.  1993 Level I CFA Study Guide, © 1993
22.  1993 Level I CFA Study Guide, © 1993
23.  1993 Level I CFA Study Guide, © 1993
24.  1992 Level I CFA Study Guide, © 1992
25.  1994 Level I CFA Study Guide, © 1994
26.  1993 Level I CFA Study Guide, © 1993
27.  1994 Level I CFA Study Guide, © 1994
28.  1994 Level I CFA Study Guide, © 1994
29.  2002 Level II CFA Study Guide, © 2002
31.  2000 Level II CFA Study Guide, © 2000

**Chapter 10**
14.  1982 Level I CFA Study Guide, © 1982
16.  1993 Level I CFA Study Guide, © 1993
17.  1993 Level I CFA Study Guide, © 1993
18.  1993 Level I CFA Study Guide, © 1993
19.  1994 Level I CFA Study Guide, © 1994

**Chapter 11**
 4.  2001 Level II CFA Study Guide, © 2001
13–19.  1991–1993 Level I CFA study guides

**Chapter 12**
 6.  1993 Level I CFA Study Guide, © 1993
 7.  1993 Level I CFA Study Guide, © 1993
 8.  1993 Level I CFA Study Guide, © 1993
 9.  1993 Level I CFA Study Guide, © 1993
10.  1993 Level I CFA Study Guide, © 1993
11.  1992 Level I CFA Study Guide, © 1992
12.  1992 Level I CFA Study Guide, © 1992
31.  1996 Level III CFA Study Guide, © 1996
32.  1996 Level III CFA Study Guide, © 1996
33.  1996 Level III CFA Study Guide, © 1996
34.  2000 Level III CFA Study Guide, © 2000
35.  2001 Level III CFA Study Guide, © 2001

## Chapter 13

12. 1993 Level I CFA Study Guide, © 1993
13. 1993 Level I CFA Study Guide, © 1993
14. 2002 Level II CFA Study Guide, © 2002

## Chapter 14

6. 1993 Level I CFA Study Guide, © 1993
7. 1994 Level I CFA Study Guide, © 1994
27. 1999 Level II CFA Study Guide, © 1999
29. 1992 Level II CFA Study Guide, © 1992
30. 1993 Level I CFA Study Guide, © 1993
31. 1992 Level I CFA Study Guide, © 1992

## Chapter 15

1. 1993 Level II CFA Study Guide, © 1993
2. 1993 Level I CFA Study Guide, © 1993
8. 1993 Level II CFA Study Guide, © 1993
10. 1994 Level I CFA Study Guide, © 1994
11. 1994 Level II CFA Study Guide, © 1994
15. 1999 Level II CFA Study Guide, © 1999
20. 1996 Level II CFA Study Guide, © 1996
25. 2000 Level II CFA Study Guide, © 2000

## Chapter 16

6. 1993 Level II CFA Study Guide, © 1993
8. 1992–1994 Level I CFA study guides
10. 1993 Level I CFA Study Guide, © 1993
12. 1993 Level I CFA Study Guide, © 1993
14. 1993 Level I CFA Study Guide, © 1993
19. 1996 Level III CFA Study Guide, © 1996
23. 1998 Level II CFA Study Guide, © 1998
24. From various Level I study guides
25. 1994 Level III CFA Study Guide, © 1994
29. 2000 Level III CFA Study Guide, © 2000
30. 2000 Level III CFA Study Guide, © 2000
31. 2000 Level II CFA Study Guide, © 2000
32. 2001 Level II CFA Study Guide, © 2001
33. 1992 Level II CFA Study Guide, © 1992

## Chapter 17

3. 1993 Level I CFA Study Guide, © 1993
4. 1993 Level I CFA Study Guide, © 1993
14. 1993 Level II CFA Study Guide, © 1993
15. 1993 Level II CFA Study Guide, © 1993
17. 1998 Level II CFA Study Guide, © 1998
19. 1995 Level I CFA Study Guide, © 1995
20. 1993 Level I CFA Study Guide, © 1993

## Chapter 18

1. 1998 Level II CFA Study Guide, © 1998
2. 1998 Level II CFA Study Guide, © 1998
5. 1995 Level II CFA Study Guide, © 1995
9. 2001 Level II CFA Study Guide, © 2001
10. 2001 Level II CFA Study Guide, © 2001
11. 2001 Level II CFA Study Guide, © 2001
13. 1996 Level III CFA Study Guide, © 1996
14. 2001 Level II CFA Study Guide, © 2001
15. 1998 Level II CFA Study Guide, © 1998
19. 1993 Level I CFA Study Guide, © 1993
21. 1993 Level I CFA Study Guide, © 1993
22. 1993 Level I CFA Study Guide, © 1993

## Chapter 19

1. 1998 Level II CFA Study Guide, © 1998
5. 1998 Level II CFA Study Guide, © 1998
6. 1999 Level II CFA Study Guide, © 1999
7. 1992 Level I CFA Study Guide, © 1992
8. 1994 Level I CFA Study Guide, © 1994
9. 1998 Level II CFA Study Guide, © 1998
10. 1992 Level I CFA Study Guide, © 1992
11. 1992 Level I CFA Study Guide, © 1992
12. 1992 Level I CFA Study Guide, © 1992
13. 1992 Level I CFA Study Guide, © 1992
14. 1998 Level I CFA Study Guide, © 1998
15. 1994 Level I CFA Study Guide, © 1994
16. 1992 Level I CFA Study Guide, © 1992
17. 1993 Level II CFA Study Guide, © 1993
18. 1993 Level II CFA Study Guide, © 1993
19. 1994 Level II CFA Study Guide, © 1994
20. 1990 Level II CFA Study Guide, © 1990

## Chapter 20

10. 2002 Level II CFA Study Guide, © 2002
14. 2000 Level II CFA Study Guide, © 2000
25. 2001 Level II CFA Study Guide, © 2001
26. 2002 Level II CFA Study Guide, © 2002
27. From various Level I study guides

## Chapter 21

23. 1998 Level II CFA Study Guide, © 1998
27. 1998 Level II CFA Study Guide, © 1998
30. 2000 Level II CFA Study Guide, © 2000
37. 1997 Level III CFA Study Guide, © 1997

## Chapter 22

12. 2000 Level II CFA Study Guide, © 2000
15. 1993 Level II CFA Study Guide, © 1993

17. 1986 Level III CFA Study Guide, © 1986
21. 2000 Level III CFA Study Guide, © 2000

**Chapter 23**

5. 2001 Level II CFA Study Guide, © 2001
10. 1995 Level III CFA Study Guide, © 1995
14. 1991 Level III CFA Study Guide, © 1991
15. 2003 Level II CFA Study Guide, © 2003
25. 1985 Level III CFA Study Guide, © 1985
26. 1996 Level II CFA Study Guide, © 1996

**Chapter 24**

12. 1995 Level III CFA Study Guide, © 1995
13. 1981 Level I CFA Study Guide, © 1981
14. 1986 Level II CFA Study Guide, © 1986
15–24. From various Level I CFA study guides
25. 2001 Level III CFA Study Guide, © 2001
26. 2000 Level III CFA Study Guide, © 2000
27. 2002 Level III CFA Study Guide, © 2002

**Chapter 25**

1–3. From various Level I CFA study guides
10. 1986 Level III CFA Study Guide, © 1986
11. 1991 Level II CFA Study Guide, © 1991
12. 1995 Level II CFA Study Guide, © 1995
14. 1998 Level II CFA Study Guide, © 1998

**Chapter 26**

1. 2001 Level III CFA Study Guide, © 2001
2. 1988 Level I CFA Study Guide, © 1988
3. 1988 Level I CFA Study Guide, © 1988
4. 1988 Level I CFA Study Guide, © 1988
5. 2002 Level III CFA Study Guide, © 2002
6. 1996 Level III CFA Study Guide, © 1996
7. 1993 Level III CFA Study Guide, © 1993
9. 2002 Level III CFA Study Guide, © 2002
10. 2002 Level III CFA Study Guide, © 2002

**Abnormal return.** Return on a stock beyond what would be predicted by market movements alone. Cumulative abnormal return (CAR) is the total abnormal return for the period surrounding an announcement or the release of information.

**Accounting earnings.** Earnings of a firm as reported on its income statement.

**Acid test ratio.** See quick ratio.

**Active management.** Attempts to achieve portfolio returns more than commensurate with risk, either by forecasting broad market trends or by identifying particular mispriced sectors of a market or securities in a market.

**Active portfolio.** In the context of the Treynor-Black model, the portfolio formed by mixing analyzed stocks of perceived nonzero alpha values. This portfolio is ultimately mixed with the passive market index portfolio.

**Adjustable-rate mortgage.** A mortgage whose interest rate varies according to some specified measure of the current market interest rate.

**Agency problem.** Conflicts of interest among stockholders, bondholders, and managers.

**Alpha.** The abnormal rate of return on a security in excess of what would be predicted by an equilibrium model like CAPM or APT.

**American depository receipts (ADRs).** Domestically traded securities representing claims to shares of foreign stocks.

**American option, European option.** An American option can be exercised before and up to its expiration date. Compare with a *European option*, which can be exercised only on the expiration date.

**Announcement date.** Date on which particular news concerning a given company is announced to the public. Used in *event studies*, which researchers use to evaluate the economic impact of events of interest.

**Anomalies.** Patterns of returns that seem to contradict the efficient market hypothesis.

**Appraisal ratio.** The signal-to-noise ratio of an analyst's forecasts. The ratio of alpha to residual standard deviation.

**Arbitrage.** A zero-risk, zero-net investment strategy that still generates profits.

**Arbitrage pricing theory.** An asset pricing theory that is derived from a factor model, using diversification and arbitrage arguments. The theory describes the relationship between expected returns on securities, given that there are no opportunities to create wealth through risk-free arbitrage investments.

**Asked price.** The price at which a dealer will sell a security.

**Asset allocation decision.** Choosing among broad asset classes such as stocks versus bonds.

**Asset turnover (ATO).** The annual sales generated by each dollar of assets (sales/assets).

**At the money.** When the exercise price and asset price of an option are equal.

**Auction market.** A market where all traders in a good meet at one place to buy or sell an asset. The NYSE is an example.

**Average collection period,** or **days' receivables.** The ratio of accounts receivable to sales, or the total amount of credit extended per dollar of daily sales (average AR/sales $\times$ 365).

**Balance sheet.** An accounting statement of a firm's financial position at a specified time.

**Bank discount yield.** An annualized interest rate assuming simple interest, a 360-day year, and using the face value of the security rather than purchase price to compute return per dollar invested.

**Banker's acceptance.** A money market asset consisting of an order to a bank by a customer to pay a sum of money at a future date.

**Basis.** The difference between the futures price and the spot price.

**Basis risk.** Risk attributable to uncertain movements in the spread between a futures price and a spot price.

**Benchmark error.** Use of an inappropriate proxy for the true market portfolio.

**Beta.** The measure of the systematic risk of a security. The tendency of a security's returns to respond to swings in the broad market.

**Bid–asked spread.** The difference between a dealer's bid and asked price.

**Bid price.** The price at which a dealer is willing to purchase a security.

**Binomial model.** An option valuation model predicated on the assumption that stock prices can move to only two values over any short time period.

**Black-Scholes formula.** An equation to value a call option that uses the stock price, the exercise price, the risk-free interest rate, the time to maturity, and the standard deviation of the stock return.

**Block house.** Brokerage firms that help to find potential buyers or sellers of large block trades.

**Block sale.** A transaction of more than 10,000 shares of stock.

**Block transactions.** Large transactions in which at least 10,000 shares of stock are bought or sold. Brokers or "block houses" often search directly for other large traders rather than bringing the trade to the stock exchange.

**Bogey.** The return an investment manager is compared to for performance evaluation.

**Bond.** A security issued by a borrower that obligates the issuer to make specified payments to the holder over a specific period. A *coupon bond* obligates the issuer to make interest payments called coupon payments over the life of the bond, then to repay the *face value* at maturity.

**Bond equivalent yield.** Bond yield calculated on an annual percentage rate method. Differs from effective annual yield.

**Bond indenture.** The contract between the issuer and the bondholder.

**Book-to-market effect.** The tendency for stocks of firms with high ratios of book-to-market value to generate abnormal returns.

**Book value.** An accounting measure describing the net worth of common equity according to a firm's balance sheet.

**Brokered market.** A market where an intermediary (a broker) offers search services to buyers and sellers.

**Budget deficit.** The amount by which government spending exceeds government revenues.

**Bull CD, bear CD.** A *bull CD* pays its holder a specified percentage of the increase in return on a specified market index while guaranteeing a minimum rate of return. A *bear CD* pays the holder a fraction of any fall in a given market index.

**Bullish, bearish.** Words used to describe investor attitudes. *Bullish* means optimistic; *bearish* means pessimistic. Also used in bull market and bear market.

**Bundling, unbundling.** A trend allowing creation of securities either by combining primitive and derivative securities into one composite hybrid or by separating returns on an asset into classes.

**Business cycle.** Repetitive cycles of recession and recovery.

**Calendar spread.** Buy one option, and write another with a different expiration date.

**Callable bond.** A bond that the issuer may repurchase at a given price in some specified period.

**Call option.** The right to buy an asset at a specified exercise price on or before a specified expiration date.

**Call protection.** An initial period during which a callable bond may not be called.

**Capital allocation decision.** Allocation of invested funds between risk-free assets versus the risky portfolio.

**Capital allocation line (CAL).** A graph showing all feasible risk–return combinations of a risky and risk-free asset.

**Capital gains.** The amount by which the sale price of a security exceeds the purchase price.

**Capital market line (CML).** A capital allocation line provided by the market index portfolio.

**Capital markets.** Includes longer-term, relatively riskier securities.

**Cash/bond selection.** Asset allocation in which the choice is between short-term cash equivalents and longer-term bonds.

**Cash delivery.** The provision of some futures contracts that requires not delivery of the underlying assets (as in agricultural futures) but settlement according to the cash value of the asset.

**Cash equivalents.** Short-term money-market securities.

**Cash flow matching.** A form of immunization, matching cash flows from a bond portfolio with an obligation.

**Certainty equivalent rate.** The certain return providing the same utility as a risky portfolio.

**Certificate of deposit.** A bank time deposit.

**Clearinghouse.** Established by exchanges to facilitate transfer of securities resulting from trades. For options and futures contracts, the clearinghouse may interpose itself as a middleman between two traders.

**Closed-end (mutual) fund.** A fund whose shares are traded through brokers at market prices; the fund will not redeem shares at their net asset value. The market price of the fund can differ from the net asset value.

**Collar.** An options strategy that brackets the value of a portfolio between two bounds.

**Collateral.** A specific asset pledged against possible default on a bond. *Mortgage bonds* are backed by claims on property. *Collateral trust bonds* are backed by claims on other securities. *Equipment obligation bonds* are backed by claims on equipment.

**Collateralized mortgage obligation (CMO).** A mortgage pass-through security that partitions cash flows from underlying mortgages into classes called *tranches* that receive principal payments according to stipulated rules.

**Commercial paper.** Short-term unsecured debt issued by large corporations.

**Commission broker.** A broker on the floor of the exchange who executes orders for other members.

**Common stock.** Equities, or equity securities, issued as ownership shares in a publicly held corporation. Shareholders have voting rights and may receive dividends based on their proportionate ownership.

**Comparison universe.** The collection of money managers of similar investment style used for assessing relative performance of a portfolio manager.

**Complete portfolio.** The entire portfolio, including risky and risk-free assets.

**Constant growth model.** A form of the dividend discount model that assumes dividends will grow at a constant rate.

**Contango theory.** Holds that the futures price must exceed the expected future spot price.

**Contingent claim.** Claim whose value is directly dependent on or is contingent on the value of some underlying assets.

**Contingent immunization.** A mixed passive-active strategy that immunizes a portfolio if necessary to guarantee a minimum acceptable return but otherwise allows active management.

**Convergence property.** The convergence of futures prices and spot prices at the maturity of the futures contract.

**Convertible bond.** A bond with an option allowing the bondholder to exchange the bond for a specified number of shares of common stock in the firm. A *conversion ratio* specifies the number of shares. The *market conversion price* is the current value of the shares for which the bond may be exchanged. The *conversion premium* is the excess of the bond's value over the conversion price.

**Convexity.** The curvature of the price-yield relationship of a bond.

**Corporate bonds.** Long-term debt issued by private corporations typically paying semiannual coupons and returning the face value of the bond at maturity.

**Correlation coefficient.** A statistic in which the covariance is scaled to a value between minus one (perfect negative correlation) and plus one (perfect positive correlation).

**Cost-of-carry relationship.** See spot-futures parity theorem.

**Country selection.** A type of active international management that measures the contribution to performance attributable to investing in the better-performing stock markets of the world.

**Coupon rate.** A bond's interest payments per dollar of par value.

**Covariance.** A measure of the degree to which returns on two risky assets move in tandem. A positive covariance means that asset returns move together. A negative covariance means they vary inversely.

**Covered call.** A combination of selling a call on a stock together with buying the stock.

**Covered interest arbitrage relationship.** See interest rate parity theorem.

**Credit enhancement.** Purchase of the financial guarantee of a large insurance company to raise funds.

**Credit risk.** Default risk.

**Cross hedge.** Hedging a position in one asset using futures on another commodity.

**Cross holdings.** One corporation holds shares in another firm.

**Cumulative abnormal return.** See abnormal return.

**Currency selection.** Asset allocation in which the investor chooses among investments denominated in different currencies.

**Current ratio.** A ratio representing the ability of the firm to pay off its current liabilities by liquidating current assets (current assets/current liabilities).

**Current yield.** A bond's annual coupon payment divided by its price. Differs from yield to maturity.

**Cyclical industries.** Industries with above average sensitivity to the state of the economy.

**Day order.** A buy order or a sell order expiring at the close of the trading day.

**Days' receivables.** See average collection period.

**Dealer market.** A market where traders specializing in particular commodities buy and sell assets for their own accounts. The OTC market is an example.

**Debenture or unsecured bond.** A bond not backed by specific collateral.

**Dedication strategy.** Refers to multiperiod cash flow matching.

**Default premium.** A differential in promised yield that compensates the investor for the risk inherent in purchasing a corporate bond that entails some risk of default.

**Defensive industries.** Industries with little sensitivity to the state of the economy.

**Deferred annuities.** Tax-advantaged life insurance product. Deferred annuities offer deferral of taxes with the option of withdrawing one's funds in the form of a life annuity.

**Defined benefit plans.** Pension plans in which retirement benefits are set according to a fixed formula.

**Defined contribution plans.** Pension plans in which the employer is committed to making contributions according to a fixed formula.

**Degree of operating leverage.**   Percentage change in profits for a 1% change in sales.

**Delta (of option).**   See hedge ratio.

**Delta neutral.**   The value of the portfolio is not affected by changes in the value of the asset on which the options are written.

**Demand shock.**   An event that affects the demand for goods and services in the economy.

**Derivative asset/contingent claim.**   Securities providing payoffs that depend on or are contingent on the values of other assets such as commodity prices, bond and stock prices, or market index values. Examples are futures and options.

**Derivative security.**   See primitive security.

**Detachable warrant.**   A warrant entitles the holder to buy a given number of shares of stock at a stipulated price. A detachable warrant is one that may be sold separately from the package it may have originally been issued with (usually a bond).

**Direct search market.**   Buyers and sellers seek each other directly and transact directly.

**Discount bonds.**   Bonds selling below par value.

**Discount function.**   The discounted value of $1 as a function of time until payment.

**Discretionary account.**   An account of a customer who gives a broker the authority to make buy and sell decisions on the customer's behalf.

**Diversifiable risk.**   Risk attributable to firm-specific risk, or nonmarket risk. *Nondiversifiable* risk refers to systematic or market risk.

**Diversification.**   Spreading a portfolio over many investments to avoid excessive exposure to any one source of risk.

**Dividend discount model (DDM).**   A formula stating that the intrinsic value of a firm is the present value of all expected future dividends.

**Dividend payout ratio.**   Percentage of earnings paid out as dividends.

**Dollar-weighted return.**   The internal rate of return on an investment.

**Doubling option.**   A sinking fund provision that may allow repurchase of twice the required number of bonds at the sinking fund call price.

**Dow theory.**   A technique that attempts to discern long- and short-term trends in stock market prices.

**Du Pont system.**   Decomposition of firm profitability measures into the underlying factors that determine such profitability.

**Dual funds.**   Funds in which income and capital shares on a portfolio of stocks are sold separately.

**Duration.**   A measure of the average life of a bond, defined as the weighted average of the times until each payment is made, with weights proportional to the present value of the payment.

**Dynamic hedging.**   Constant updating of hedge positions as market conditions change.

**EAFE index.**   The European, Australian, Far East index, computed by Morgan Stanley, is a widely used index of non-U.S. stocks.

**Earnings management.**   The practice of using flexibility in accounting rules to improve the apparent profitability of the firm.

**Earnings retention ratio.**   Plowback ratio.

**Earnings yield.**   The ratio of earnings to price, E/P.

**Economic earnings.**   The real flow of cash that a firm could pay out forever in the absence of any change in the firm's productive capacity.

**Economic value added (EVA).**   The spread between ROA and cost of capital multiplied by the capital invested in the firm. It measures the dollar value of the firm's return in excess of its opportunity cost.

**Effective annual yield.**   Annualized interest rate on a security computed using compound interest techniques.

**Effective duration.**   Percentage change in bond price per change in the level of market interest rates.

**Efficient diversification.**   The organizing principle of modern portfolio theory, which maintains that any risk-averse investor will search for the highest expected return for any level of portfolio risk.

**Efficient frontier.**   Graph representing a set of portfolios that maximize expected return at each level of portfolio risk.

**Efficient market hypothesis.**   The prices of securities fully reflect available information. Investors buying securities in an efficient market should expect to obtain an equilibrium rate of return. Weak-form EMH asserts that stock prices already reflect all information contained in the history of past prices. The semistrong-form hypothesis asserts that stock prices already reflect all publicly available information. The strong-form hypothesis asserts that stock prices reflect all relevant information including insider information.

**Elasticity (of an option).**   Percentage change in the value of an option accompanying a 1 percent change in the value of a stock.

**Electronic communication network (ECN).**   A computer-operated trading network offering an alternative to formal stock exchanges or dealer markets for trading securities.

**Endowment funds.**   Organizations chartered to invest money for specific purposes.

**Equivalent taxable yield.**   The pretax yield on a taxable bond providing an after-tax yield equal to the rate on a tax-exempt municipal bond.

**Eurodollars.**   Dollar-denominated deposits at foreign banks or foreign branches of American banks.

**European, Australian, Far East (EAFE) index.**   A widely used index of non-U.S. stocks computed by Morgan Stanley.

**European option.**   A European option can be exercised only on the expiration date. Compare with an American option, which can be exercised before, up to, and on its expiration date.

**Event study.**   Research methodology designed to measure the impact of an event of interest on stock returns.

**Excess return.**   Rate of return in excess of the risk-free rate.

**Exchange rate.**   Price of a unit of one country's currency in terms of another country's currency.

**Exchange rate risk.**   The uncertainty in asset returns due to movements in the exchange rates between the dollar and foreign currencies.

**Exchange-traded funds (ETFs).**   Offshoots of mutual funds that allow investors to trade portfolios of securities just as they do shares of stock.

**Exchanges.**   National or regional auction markets providing a facility for members to trade securities. A seat is a membership on an exchange.

**Exercise or strike price.**   Price set for calling (buying) an asset or putting (selling) an asset.

**Expectations hypothesis (of interest rates).**   Theory that forward interest rates are unbiased estimates of expected future interest rates.

**Expected return.**   The probability-weighted average of the possible outcomes.

**Expected return–beta relationship.**   Implication of the CAPM that security risk premiums (expected excess returns) will be proportional to beta.

**Face value.**   The maturity value of a bond.

**Factor beta.**   Sensitivity of security returns to changes in a systematic factor. Alternatively, factor loading; factor sensitivity.

**Factor loading.**   See factor beta.

**Factor model.**   A way of decomposing the factors that influence a security's rate of return into common and firm-specific influences.

**Factor portfolio.**   A well-diversified portfolio constructed to have a beta of 1.0 on one factor and a beta of zero on any other factor.

**Factor sensitivity.**   See factor beta.

**Fair game.**   An investment prospect that has a zero risk premium.

**Federal funds.**   Funds in a bank's reserve account.

**FIFO.**   The first-in first-out accounting method of inventory valuation.

**Filter rule.**   A rule for buying or selling stock according to recent price movements.

**Financial assets.**   Financial assets such as stocks and bonds are claims to the income generated by real assets or claims on income from the government.

**Financial engineering.**   The process of bundling and unbundling securities.

**Financial intermediary.**   An institution such as a bank, mutual fund, investment company, or insurance company that serves to connect the household and business sectors so households can invest and businesses can finance production.

**Firm-specific risk.**   See diversifiable risk.

**First-pass regression.**   A time series regression to estimate the betas of securities or portfolios.

**Fiscal policy.**   The use of government spending and taxing for the specific purpose of stabilizing the economy.

**Fixed annuities.**   Annuity contracts in which the insurance company pays a fixed dollar amount of money per period.

**Fixed-charge coverage ratio.**   Ratio of earnings to all fixed cash obligations, including lease payments and sinking fund payments.

**Fixed-income security.**   A security such as a bond that pays a specified cash flow over a specific period.

**Flight to quality.**   Describes the tendency of investors to require larger default premiums on investments under uncertain economic conditions.

**Floating-rate bond.**   A bond whose interest rate is reset periodically according to a specified market rate.

**Floor broker.**   A member of the exchange who can execute orders for commission brokers.

**Forced conversion.**   Use of a firm's call option on a callable convertible bond when the firm knows that bondholders will exercise their option to convert.

**Foreign exchange market.**   An informal network of banks and brokers that allows customers to enter forward contracts to purchase or sell currencies in the future at a rate of exchange agreed upon now.

**Foreign exchange swap.**   An agreement to exchange stipulated amounts of one currency for another at one or more future dates.

**Forward contract.**   An agreement calling for future delivery of an asset at an agreed-upon price. Also see futures contract.

**Forward interest rate.**   Rate of interest for a future period that would equate the total return of a long-term bond with that of a strategy of rolling over shorter-term bonds. The forward rate is inferred from the term structure.

**Fourth market.**   Direct trading in exchange-listed securities between one investor and another without the benefit of a broker.

**Fully diluted earnings per share.**   Earnings per share expressed as if all outstanding convertible securities and warrants have been exercised.

**Fundamental analysis.**   Research to predict stock value that focuses on such determinants as earnings and dividends prospects, expectations for future interest rates, and risk evaluation of the firm.

**Futures contract.**   Obliges traders to purchase or sell an asset at an agreed-upon price on a specified future date. The long position is held by the trader who commits to purchase. The short position is held by the trader who commits to sell. Futures differ from forward contracts in their standardization, exchange trading, margin requirements, and daily settling (marking to market).

**Futures option.**   The right to enter a specified futures contract at a futures price equal to the stipulated exercise price.

**Futures price.**   The price at which a futures trader commits to make or take delivery of the underlying asset.

**Geometric average.**   The $n$th root of the product of $n$ numbers. It is used to measure the compound rate of return over time.

**Globalization.**   Tendency toward a worldwide investment environment, and the integration of national capital markets.

**Gross domestic product (GDP).**   The market value of goods and services produced over time including the income of foreign corporations and foreign residents working in the United States, but excluding the income of U.S. residents and corporations overseas.

**Hedge fund.**   A private investment pool, open to institutional or wealthy investors, that is exempt from SEC regulation and can pursue more speculative policies than mutual funds.

**Hedge ratio (for an option).**   The number of stocks required to hedge against the price risk of holding one option. Also called the option's delta.

**Hedging.**   Investing in an asset to reduce the overall risk of a portfolio.

**Hedging demands.**   Demands for securities to hedge particular sources of consumption risk, beyond the usual mean-variance diversification motivation.

**Holding-period return.**   The rate of return over a given period.

**Homogenous expectations.**   The assumption that all investors use the same expected returns and covariance matrix of security returns as inputs in security analysis.

**Horizon analysis.**   Forecasting the realized compound yield over various holding periods or investment horizons.

**Illiquidity premium.**   Extra expected return as compensation for limited liquidity.

**Immunization.**   A strategy that matches durations of assets and liabilities so as to make net worth unaffected by interest rate movements.

**Implied volatility.**   The standard deviation of stock returns that is consistent with an option's market value.

**In the money.**   In the money describes an option whose exercise would produce profits. Out of the money describes an option where exercise would not be profitable.

**Income beneficiary.**   One who receives income from a trust.

**Income fund.**   A mutual fund providing for liberal current income from investments.

**Income statement.**   A financial statement showing a firm's revenues and expenses during a specified period.

**Indenture.**   The document defining the contract between the bond issuer and the bondholder.

**Index arbitrage.**   An investment strategy that exploits divergences between actual futures prices and their theoretically correct parity values to make a profit.

**Index fund.**   A mutual fund holding shares in proportion to their representation in a market index such as the S&P 500.

**Index model.**   A model of stock returns using a market index such as the S&P 500 to represent common or systematic risk factors.

**Index option.**   A call or put option based on a stock market index.

**Indifference curve.**   A curve connecting all portfolios with the same utility according to their means and standard deviations.

**Industry life cycle.**   Stages through which firms typically pass as they mature.

**Inflation.**   The rate at which the general level of prices for goods and services is rising.

**Information ratio.**   Ratio of alpha to the standard deviation of diversifiable risk.

**Initial public offering.**   Stock issued to the public for the first time by a formerly privately owned company.

**Input list.**   List of parameters such as expected returns, variances, and covariances necessary to determine the optimal risky portfolio.

**Inside information.** Nonpublic knowledge about a corporation possessed by corporate officers, major owners, or other individuals with privileged access to information about a firm.

**Insider trading.** Trading by officers, directors, major stockholders, or others who hold private inside information allowing them to benefit from buying or selling stock.

**Insurance principle.** The law of averages. The average outcome for many independent trials of an experiment will approach the expected value of the experiment.

**Interest coverage ratio,** or **times interest earned.** A financial leverage measure (EBIT divided by interest expense).

**Interest rate.** The number of dollars earned per dollar invested per period.

**Interest rate parity theorem.** The spot-futures exchange rate relationship that prevails in well-functioning markets.

**Interest rate swaps.** A method to manage interest rate risk where parties trade the cash flows corresponding to different securities without actually exchanging securities directly.

**Intermarket spread swap.** Switching from one segment of the bond market to another (from Treasuries to corporates, for example).

**Intrinsic value (of a firm).** The present value of a firm's expected future net cash flows discounted by the required rate of return.

**Intrinsic value of an option.** Stock price minus exercise price, or the profit that could be attained by immediate exercise of an in-the-money option.

**Investment bankers.** Firms specializing in the sale of new securities to the public, typically by underwriting the issue.

**Investment company.** Firm managing funds for investors. An investment company may manage several mutual funds.

**Investment-grade bond.** Bond rated BBB and above or Baa and above. Lower-rated bonds are classified as speculative-grade or junk bonds.

**Investment horizon.** Time horizon for purposes of investment decisions.

**Investment portfolio.** Set of securities chosen by an investor.

**Jensen's measure.** The alpha of an investment.

**Junk bond.** See speculative-grade bond.

**Law of one price.** The rule stipulating that equivalent securities or bundles of securities must sell at equal prices to preclude arbitrage opportunities.

**Leading economic indicators.** Economic series that tend to rise or fall in advance of the rest of the economy.

**Leakage.** Release of information to some persons before official public announcement.

**Leverage ratio.** Ratio of debt to total capitalization of a firm.

**LIFO.** The last-in first-out accounting method of valuing inventories.

**Limited liability.** The fact that shareholders have no personal liability to the creditors of the corporation in the event of bankruptcy.

**Limit order.** An order specifying a price at which an investor is willing to buy or sell a security.

**Liquidation value.** Net amount that could be realized by selling the assets of a firm after paying the debt.

**Liquidity.** Liquidity refers to the speed and ease with which an asset can be converted to cash.

**Liquidity preference theory.** Theory that the forward rate exceeds expected future interest rates.

**Liquidity premium.** Forward rate minus expected future short interest rate.

**Load fund.** A mutual fund with a sales commission, or load.

**London Interbank Offered Rate (LIBOR).** Rate that most creditworthy banks charge one another for large loans of Eurodollars in the London market.

**Long hedge.** Protecting the future cost of a purchase by taking a long futures position to protect against changes in the price of the asset.

**Macaulay's duration.** Effective maturity of bond, equal to weighted average of the times until each payment, with weights proportional to the present value of the payment.

**Maintenance,** or **variation, margin.** An established value below which a trader's margin cannot fall. Reaching the maintenance margin triggers a margin call.

**Margin.** Describes securities purchased with money borrowed from a broker. Current maximum margin is 50 percent.

**Market–book-value ratio.** Ratio of price per share to book value per share.

**Market capitalization rate.** The market-consensus estimate of the appropriate discount rate for a firm's cash flows.

**Market model.** Another version of the index model that breaks down return uncertainty into systematic and nonsystematic components.

**Market or systematic risk, firm-specific risk.** Market risk is risk attributable to common macroeconomic factors. Firm-specific risk reflects risk peculiar to an individual firm that is independent of market risk.

**Market order.** A buy or sell order to be executed immediately at current market prices.

**Market portfolio.** The portfolio for which each security is held in proportion to its market value.

**Market price of risk.** A measure of the extra return, or risk premium, that investors demand to bear risk. The reward-to-risk ratio of the market portfolio.

**Market segmentation or preferred habitat theory.** The theory that long- and short-maturity bonds are traded in essentially distinct or segmented markets and that prices in one market do not affect those in the other.

**Market timer.** An investor who speculates on broad market moves rather than on specific securities.

**Market timing.** Asset allocation in which the investment in the market is increased if one forecasts that the market will outperform T-bills.

**Market-value-weighted index.** An index of a group of securities computed by calculating a weighted average of the returns of each security in the index, with weights proportional to outstanding market value.

**Marking to market.** Describes the daily settlement of obligations on futures positions.

**Mean-variance analysis.** Evaluation of risky prospects based on the expected value and variance of possible outcomes.

**Mean-variance criterion.** The selection of portfolios based on the means and variances of their returns. The choice of the higher expected return portfolio for a given level of variance or the lower variance portfolio for a given expected return.

**Measurement error.** Errors in measuring an explanatory variable in a regression that leads to biases in estimated parameters.

**Membership or seat on an exchange.** A limited number of exchange positions that enable the holder to trade for the holder's own accounts and charge clients for the execution of trades for their accounts.

**Minimum-variance frontier.** Graph of the lowest possible portfolio variance that is attainable for a given portfolio expected return.

**Minimum-variance portfolio.** The portfolio of risky assets with lowest variance.

**Modern portfolio theory (MPT).** Principles underlying analysis and evaluation of rational portfolio choices based on risk–return trade-offs and efficient diversification.

**Modified duration.** Macaulay's duration divided by 1 + yield to maturity. Measures interest rate sensitivity of bond.

**Momentum effect.** The tendency of poorly performing stocks and well-performing stocks in one period to continue that abnormal performance in following periods.

**Monetary policy.** Actions taken by the Board of Governors of the Federal Reserve System to influence the money supply or interest rates.

**Money market.** Includes short-term, highly liquid, and relatively low-risk debt instruments.

**Mortality tables.** Tables of probability that individuals of various ages will die within a year.

**Mortgage-backed security.** Ownership claim in a pool of mortgages or an obligation that is secured by such a pool. Also called a *pass-through,* because payments are passed along from the mortgage originator to the purchaser of the mortgage-backed security.

**Multifactor CAPM.** Generalization of the basic CAPM that accounts for extra-market hedging demands.

**Multifactor models.** Model of security returns positing that returns respond to several systematic factors.

**Municipal bonds.** Tax-exempt bonds issued by state and local governments, generally to finance capital improvement projects. General obligation bonds are backed by the general taxing power of the issuer. Revenue bonds are backed by the proceeds from the project or agency they are issued to finance.

**Mutual fund.** A firm pooling and managing funds of investors.

**Mutual fund theorem.** A result associated with the CAPM, asserting that investors will choose to invest their entire risky portfolio in a market-index mutual fund.

**Naked option writing.** Writing an option without an offsetting stock position.

**Nasdaq.** The automated quotation system for the OTC market, showing current bid–asked prices for thousands of stocks.

**Neglected-firm effect.** That investments in stock of less well-known firms have generated abnormal returns.

**Net asset value (NAV).** The value of each share expressed as assets minus liabilities on a per-share basis.

**Nominal interest rate.** The interest rate in terms of nominal (not adjusted for purchasing power) dollars.

**Nondiversifiable risk.** See systematic risk.

**Nonsystematic risk.** Nonmarket or firm-specific risk factors that can be eliminated by diversification. Also called unique risk or diversifiable risk. Systematic risk refers to risk factors common to the entire economy.

**Normal backwardation theory.** Holds that the futures price will be bid down to a level below the expected spot price.

**Notional principal.** Principal amount used to calculate swap payments.

**On the run.** Recently issued bond, selling at or near par value.

**Open-end (mutual) fund.** A fund that issues or redeems its own shares at their net asset value (NAV).

**Open (good-till-canceled) order.** A buy or sell order remaining in force for up to 6 months unless canceled.

**Open interest.** The number of futures contracts outstanding.

**Optimal risky portfolio.** An investor's best combination of risky assets to be mixed with safe assets to form the complete portfolio.

**Option elasticity.** The percentage increase in an option's value given a 1% change in the value of the underlying security.

**Original issue discount bond.** A bond issued with a low coupon rate that sells at a discount from par value.

**Out of the money.** Out of the money describes an option where exercise would not be profitable. In the money describes an option where exercise would produce profits.

**Over-the-counter market.** An informal network of brokers and dealers who negotiate sales of securities (not a formal exchange).

**Par value.** The face value of the bond.

**Passive investment strategy.** See passive management.

**Passive management.** Buying a well-diversified portfolio to represent a broad-based market index without attempting to search out mispriced securities.

**Passive portfolio.** A market index portfolio.

**Passive strategy.** See passive management.

**Pass-through security.** Pools of loans (such as home mortgage loans) sold in one package. Owners of pass-throughs receive all principal and interest payments made by the borrowers.

**Peak.** The transition from the end of an expansion to the start of a contraction.

**P/E effect.** That portfolios of low P/E stocks have exhibited higher average risk-adjusted returns than high P/E stocks.

**Personal trust.** An interest in an asset held by a trustee for the benefit of another person.

**Plowback ratio.** The proportion of the firm's earnings that is reinvested in the business (and not paid out as dividends). The plowback ratio equals 1 minus the dividend payout ratio.

**Political risk.** Possibility of the expropriation of assets, changes in tax policy, restrictions on the exchange of foreign currency for domestic currency, or other changes in the business climate of a country.

**Portfolio insurance.** The practice of using options or dynamic hedge strategies to provide protection against investment losses while maintaining upside potential.

**Portfolio management.** Process of combining securities in a portfolio tailored to the investor's preferences and needs, monitoring that portfolio, and evaluating its performance.

**Portfolio opportunity set.** The expected return–standard deviation pairs of all portfolios that can be constructed from a given set of assets.

**Preferred habitat theory.** Holds that investors prefer specific maturity ranges but can be induced to switch if risk premiums are sufficient.

**Preferred stock.** Nonvoting shares in a corporation, paying a fixed or variable stream of dividends.

**Premium.** The purchase price of an option.

**Premium bonds.** Bonds selling above par value.

**Present value of growth opportunities (PVGO).** Net present value of a firm's future investments.

**Price value of a basis point.** The change in the value of a fixed-income asset resulting from a 1 basis point change in the asset's yield to maturity.

**Price-weighted average.** Weighted average with weights proportional to security prices rather than total capitalization.

**Price–earnings multiple.** See price–earnings ratio.

**Price–earnings ratio.** The ratio of a stock's price to its earnings per share. Also referred to as the P/E multiple.

**Primary market.** New issues of securities are offered to the public here.

**Primitive security, derivative security.** A *primitive security* is an instrument such as a stock or bond for which payments depend only on the financial status of its issuer. A *derivative security* is created from the set of primitive securities to yield returns that depend on factors beyond the characteristics of the issuer and that may be related to prices of other assets.

**Principal.** The outstanding balance on a loan.

**Private placement.** Primary offering in which shares are sold directly to a small group of institutional or wealthy investors.

**Profit margin.** See return on sales.

**Program trading.** Coordinated buy orders and sell orders of entire portfolios, usually with the aid of computers, often to achieve index arbitrage objectives.

**Prospectus.** A final and approved registration statement including the price at which the security issue is offered.

**Protective covenant.** A provision specifying requirements of collateral, sinking fund, dividend policy, etc., designed to protect the interests of bondholders.

**Protective put.** Purchase of stock combined with a put option that guarantees minimum proceeds equal to the put's exercise price.

**Proxy.** An instrument empowering an agent to vote in the name of the shareholder.

**Prudent investor rule.** An investment manager must act in accord with the actions of a hypothetical prudent investor.

**Pseudo-American call option value.** The maximum of the value derived by assuming that an option will be held until expiration and the value derived by assuming that the option will be exercised just before an ex-dividend date.

**Public offering, private placement.** A *public offering* consists of bonds sold in the primary market to the general public; a *private placement* is sold directly to a limited number of institutional investors.

**Pure yield curve.** Refers to the relationship between yield to maturity and time to maturity for zero-coupon bonds.

**Pure yield pickup swap.** Moving to higher yield bonds.

**Put bond.** A bond that the holder may choose either to exchange for par value at some date or to extend for a given number of years.

**Put-call parity theorem.** An equation representing the proper relationship between put and call prices. Violation of parity allows arbitrage opportunities.

**Put option.** The right to sell an asset at a specified exercise price on or before a specified expiration date.

**Quality of earnings.** The realism and conservatism of the earnings number and the extent to which we might expect the reported level of earnings to be sustained.

**Quick ratio.** A measure of liquidity similar to the current ratio except for exclusion of inventories (cash plus receivables divided by current liabilities).

**Random walk.** Describes the notion that stock price changes are random and unpredictable.

**Rate anticipation swap.** A switch made in response to forecasts of interest rates.

**Real assets, financial assets.** *Real assets* are land, buildings, and equipment that are used to produce goods and services. *Financial assets* are claims such as securities to the income generated by real assets.

**Real consumption.** Nominal consumption divided by the price deflator.

**Real interest rate.** The excess of the interest rate over the inflation rate. The growth rate of purchasing power derived from an investment.

**Realized compound yield.** Yield assuming that coupon payments are invested at the going market interest rate at the time of their receipt and rolled over until the bond matures.

**Rebalancing.** Realigning the proportions of assets in a portfolio as needed.

**Registered bond.** A bond whose issuer records ownership and interest payments. Differs from a bearer bond, which is traded without record of ownership and whose possession is its only evidence of ownership.

**Registered trader.** A member of the exchange who executes frequent trades for his or her own account.

**Registration statement.** Required to be filed with the SEC to describe the issue of a new security.

**Regression equation.** An equation that describes the average relationship between a dependent variable and a set of explanatory variables.

**REIT.** Real estate investment trust, which is similar to a closed-end mutual fund. REITs invest in real estate or loans secured by real estate and issue shares in such investments.

**Remainderman.** One who receives the principal of a trust when it is dissolved.

**Replacement cost.** Cost to replace a firm's assets. "Reproduction" cost.

**Repurchase agreements (repos).** Short-term, often overnight, sales of government securities with an agreement to repurchase the securities at a slightly higher price. A *reverse repo* is a purchase with an agreement to resell at a specified price on a future date.

**Residual claim.** Refers to the fact that shareholders are at the bottom of the list of claimants to assets of a corporation in the event of failure or bankruptcy.

**Residual income.** See economic value added (EVA).

**Residuals.** Parts of stock returns not explained by the explanatory variable (the market-index return). They measure the impact of firm-specific events during a particular period.

**Resistance level.** A price level above which it is supposedly difficult for a stock or stock index to rise.

**Retirement annuity.** Stream of cash flows available for consumption during one's retirement years.

**Return on assets (ROA).** A profitability ratio; earnings before interest and taxes divided by total assets.

**Return on equity (ROE).** An accounting ratio of net profits divided by equity.

**Return on sales (ROS), or profit margin.** The ratio of operating profits per dollar of sales (EBIT divided by sales).

**Reversal effect.** The tendency of poorly performing stocks and well-performing stocks in one period to experience reversals in following periods.

**Reversing trade.** Entering the opposite side of a currently held futures position to close out the position.

**Reward-to-variability ratio.** Ratio of a portfolio's risk premium to its standard deviation.

**Reward-to-volatility ratio.** Ratio of excess return to portfolio standard deviation.

**Riding the yield curve.** Buying long-term bonds in anticipation of capital gains as yields fall with the declining maturity of the bonds.

**Risk arbitrage.** Speculation on perceived mispriced securities, usually in connection with merger and acquisition targets.

**Risk-averse, risk-neutral, risk lover.** A *risk-averse* investor will consider risky portfolios only if they provide compensation for risk via a risk premium. A *risk-neutral* investor finds the level of risk irrelevant and considers only the expected return of risk prospects. A *risk lover* is willing to accept lower expected returns on prospects with higher amounts of risk.

**Risk-free asset.** An asset with a certain rate of return; often taken to be short-term T-bills.

**Risk-free rate.** The interest rate that can be earned with certainty.

**Risk lover.** See risk-averse.

**Risk-neutral.** See risk-averse.

**Risk premium.** An expected return in excess of that on risk-free securities. The premium provides compensation for the risk of an investment.

**Risk–return trade-off.** If an investor is willing to take on risk, there is the reward of higher expected returns.

**Risky asset.** An asset with an uncertain rate of return.

**Scatter diagram.** Plot of returns of one security versus returns of another security. Each point represents one pair of returns for a given holding period.

**Seasoned new issue.** Stock issued by companies that already have stock on the market.

**Secondary market.** Already existing securities are bought and sold on the exchanges or in the OTC market.

**Second-pass regression.** A cross-sectional regression of portfolio returns on betas. The estimated slope is the measurement of the reward for bearing systematic risk during the period.

**Sector rotation.** An investment strategy which entails shifting the portfolio into industry sectors that are forecast to outperform others based on macroeconomic forecasts.

**Securitization.** Pooling loans for various purposes into standardized securities backed by those loans, which can then be traded like any other security.

**Security analysis.** Determining correct value of a security in the marketplace.

**Security characteristic line.** A plot of the excess return on a security over the risk-free rate as a function of the excess return on the market.

**Security market line.** Graphical representation of the expected return–beta relationship of the CAPM.

**Security selection.** See security selection decision.

**Security selection decision.** Choosing the particular securities to include in a portfolio.

**Semistrong-form EMH.** See efficient market hypothesis.

**Separation property.** The property that portfolio choice can be separated into two independent tasks: (1) determination of the optimal risky portfolio, which is a purely technical problem, and (2) the personal choice of the best mix of the risky portfolio and the risk-free asset.

**Serial bond issue.** An issue of bonds with staggered maturity dates that spreads out the principal repayment burden over time.

**Sharpe's measure.** Reward-to-volatility ratio; ratio of portfolio excess return to standard deviation.

**Shelf registration.** Advance registration of securities with the SEC for sale up to 2 years following initial registration.

**Short interest rate.** A one-period interest rate.

**Short position or hedge.** Protecting the value of an asset held by taking a short position in a futures contract.

**Short sale.** The sale of shares not owned by the investor but borrowed through a broker and later repurchased to replace the loan. Profit is earned if the initial sale is at a higher price than the repurchase price.

**SIC codes.** Standard Industry Classification. These codes are assigned by the U.S. government for the purpose of grouping firms for statistical analysis.

**Simple prospect.** An investment opportunity where a certain initial wealth is placed at risk and only two outcomes are possible.

**Single-country funds.** Mutual funds that invest in securities of only one country.

**Single-factor model.** A model of security returns that acknowledges only one common factor. See factor model.

**Single index model.** A model of stock returns that decomposes influences on returns into a systematic factor, as measured by the return on a broad market index, and firm-specific factors.

**Sinking fund.** A procedure that allows for the repayment of principal at maturity by calling for the bond issuer to repurchase some proportion of the outstanding bonds either in the open market or at a special call price associated with the sinking fund provision.

**Skip-day settlement.** A convention for calculating yield that assumes a T-bill sale is not settled until 2 days after quotation of the T-bill price.

**Small-firm effect.** That investments in stocks of small firms appear to have earned abnormal returns.

**Soft dollars.** The value of research services that brokerage houses supply to investment managers "free of charge" in exchange for the investment managers' business.

**Specialist.** A trader who makes a market in the shares of one or more firms and who maintains a "fair and orderly market" by dealing personally in the stock.

**Speculation.** Undertaking a risky investment with the objective of earning a greater profit than an investment in a risk-free alternative (a risk premium).

**Speculative-grade bond.** Bond rated Ba or lower by Moody's, or BB or lower by Standard & Poor's, or an unrated bond.

**Spot-futures parity theorem,** or **cost-of-carry relationship.** Describes the theoretically correct relationship between spot and futures prices. Violation of the parity relationship gives rise to arbitrage opportunities.

**Spot rate.** The current interest rate appropriate for discounting a cash flow of some given maturity.

**Spread (futures).** Taking a long position in a futures contract of one maturity and a short position in a contract of different maturity, both on the same commodity.

**Spread (options).** A combination of two or more call options or put options on the same stock with differing exercise prices or times to expiration. A money spread refers to a spread with different exercise price; a time spread refers to differing expiration date.

**Squeeze.** The possibility that enough long positions hold their contracts to maturity that supplies of the commodity are not adequate to cover all contracts. A *short squeeze* describes the reverse: short positions threaten to deliver an expensive-to-store commodity.

**Standard deviation.** Square root of the variance.

**Statement of cash flows.** A financial statement showing a firm's cash receipts and cash payments during a specified period.

**Stock exchanges.** Secondary markets where already-issued securities are bought and sold by members.

**Stock selection.** An active portfolio management technique that focuses on advantageous selection of particular stocks rather than on broad asset allocation choices.

**Stock split.** Issue by a corporation of a given number of shares in exchange for the current number of shares held by stockholders. Splits may go in either direction, either increasing or decreasing the number of shares outstanding. A *reverse split* decreases the number outstanding.

**Stop-loss order.** A sell order to be executed if the price of the stock falls below a stipulated level.

**Straddle.** A combination of buying both a call and a put on the same asset, each with the same exercise price and expiration date. The purpose is to profit from expected volatility.

**Straight bond.** A bond with no option features such as callability or convertibility.

**Street name.** Describes securities held by a broker on behalf of a client but registered in the name of the firm.

**Strike price.** See exercise price.

**Strip, strap.** Variants of a straddle. A *strip* is two puts and one call on a stock; a *strap* is two calls and one put, both with the same exercise price and expiration date.

**Stripped of coupons.** Describes the practice of some investment banks that sell "synthetic" zero-coupon bonds by marketing the rights to a single payment backed by a coupon-paying Treasury bond.

**Strong-form EMH.** See efficient market hypothesis.

**Subordination clause.** A provision in a bond indenture that restricts the issuer's future borrowing by subordinating the new leaders' claims on the firm to those of the existing bond holders. Claims of *subordinated* or *junior* debtholders are not paid until the prior debt is paid.

**Substitution swap.** Exchange of one bond for a bond with similar attributes but more attractively priced.

**Supply shock.** An event that influences production capacity and costs in the economy.

**Support level.** A price level below which it is supposedly difficult for a stock or stock index to fall.

**Swaption.** An option on a swap.

**Systematic risk.** Risk factors common to the whole economy, nondiversifiable risk; also called market risk.

**Tax anticipation notes.** Short-term municipal debt to raise funds to pay for expenses before actual collection of taxes.

**Tax deferral option.** The feature of the U.S. Internal Revenue Code that the capital gains tax on an asset is payable only when the gain is realized by selling the asset.

**Tax-deferred retirement plans.** Employer-sponsored and other plans that allow contributions and earnings to be made and accumulate tax-free until they are paid out as benefits.

**Tax-timing option.** Describes the investor's ability to shift the realization of investment gains or losses and their tax implications from one period to another.

**Tax swap.** Swapping two similar bonds to receive a tax benefit.

**Technical analysis.** Research to identify mispriced securities that focuses on recurrent and predictable stock price patterns and on proxies for buy or sell pressure in the market.

**Tender offer.** An offer from an outside investor to shareholders of a company to purchase their shares at a stipulated price, usually substantially above the market price, so that the investor may amass enough shares to obtain control of the company.

**Term insurance.** Provides a death benefit only, no build-up of cash value.

**Term premiums.** Excess of the yields to maturity on long-term bonds over those of short-term bonds.

**Term structure of interest rates.** The pattern of interest rates appropriate for discounting cash flows of various maturities.

**Third market.** Trading of exchange-listed securities on the OTC market.

**Times interest earned.** Ratio of profits to interest expense.

**Time value (of an option).** The part of the value of an option that is due to its positive time to expiration. Not to be confused with present value or the time value of money.

**Time-weighted return.** An average of the period-by-period holding-period returns of an investment.

**Tobin's *q*.** Ratio of market value of the firm to replacement cost.

**Tracking portfolio.** A portfolio constructed to have returns with the highest possible correlation with a systematic risk factor.

**Tranche.** See collateralized mortgage obligation.

**Treasury bill.** Short-term, highly liquid government securities issued at a discount from the face value and returning the face amount at maturity.

**Treasury bond or note.** Debt obligations of the federal government that make semiannual coupon payments and are issued at or near par value.

**Treynor's measure.** Ratio of excess return to beta.

**Triple-witching hour.** The four times a year that the S&P 500 futures contract expires at the same time as the S&P 100 index option contract and option contracts on individual stocks.

**Trough.** The transition point between recession and recovery.

**Turnover.** The ratio of the trading activity of a portfolio to the assets of the portfolio.

**Unbundling.** See bundling.

**Underwriting, underwriting syndicate.** Underwriters (investment bankers) purchase securities from the issuing company and resell them. Usually a syndicate of investment bankers is organized behind a lead firm.

**Unemployment rate.** The ratio of the number of people classified as unemployed to the total labor force.

**Unique risk.** See diversifiable risk.

**Unit investment trust.** Money invested in a portfolio whose composition is fixed for the life of the fund. Shares in a unit trust are called redeemable trust certificates, and they are sold at a premium above net asset value.

**Universal life policy.** An insurance policy that allows for a varying death benefit and premium level over the term of the policy, with an interest rate on the cash value that changes with market interest rates.

**Uptick, or zero-plus tick.** A trade resulting in a positive change in a stock price, or a trade at a constant price following a preceding price increase.

**Utility.** The measure of the welfare or satisfaction of an investor.

**Utility value.** The welfare a given investor assigns to an investment with a particular return and risk.

**Variable annuities.** Annuity contracts in which the insurance company pays a periodic amount linked to the investment performance of an underlying portfolio.

**Variable life policy.** An insurance policy that provides a fixed death benefit plus a cash value that can be invested in a variety of funds from which the policyholder can choose.

**Variance.** A measure of the dispersion of a random variable. Equals the expected value of the squared deviation from the mean.

**Variation margin.** See maintenance margin.

**Volatility risk.** The risk in the value of options portfolios due to unpredictable changes in the volatility of the underlying asset.

**Warrant.** An option issued by the firm to purchase shares of the firm's stock.

**Weak-form EMH.** See efficient market hypothesis.

**Weekend effect.** The common recurrent negative average return from Friday to Monday in the stock market.

**Well-diversified portfolio.** A portfolio spread out over many securities in such a way that the weight in any security is close to zero.

**Whole-life insurance policy.** Provides a death benefit and a kind of savings plan that builds up cash value for possible future withdrawal.

**Workout period.** Realignment period of a temporary misaligned yield relationship.

**World investable wealth.** The part of world wealth that is traded and is therefore accessible to investors.

**Writing a call.** Selling a call option.

**Yield curve.** A graph of yield to maturity as a function of time to maturity.

**Yield to maturity.** A measure of the average rate of return that will be earned on a bond if held to maturity.

**Zero-beta portfolio.** The minimum-variance portfolio uncorrelated with a chosen efficient portfolio.

**Zero-coupon bond.** A bond paying no coupons that sells at a discount and provides payment of face value only at maturity.

**Zero-investment portfolio.** A portfolio of zero net value, established by buying and shorting component securities, usually in the context of an arbitrage strategy.

**12b–1 fees.** Annual fees charged by a mutual fund to pay for marketing and distribution costs.

## CHAPTER 16
### MANAGING BOND PORTFOLIOS

www.about.com
This site contains links to many facets of the fixed-income market. Enter "bonds" in the input box.

bonds.yahoo.com/calculator.html

bonds.yahoo.com
Yahoo has general information, a bond market glossary, and several bond calculators.

www.smartmoney.com/bonds
This site has several tools that apply to concepts covered in this chapter, among them a template for analyzing interest rate swaps and a portfolio allocation model that allows you to enter information concerning your expectations and risk aversion.

webster.directhit.com/Webster/search.aspx?qry=Bond+Duration

webster.directhit.com/Webster/search.aspx?qry=Bond+Portfolio+Ma nagement&meta=rs
Ask Jeeves about bond duration. This site provides helpful information and discussions about duration, and bond portfolio management.

www.investinginbonds.com/info/bondbasics/key.htm
Visit this site to review bond investment basics and strategies.

www.morganstanleyindividual.com/investmentproducts/bonds/strategies
Morgan Stanley offers bond portfolio strategies for personal investors.

## CHAPTER 17
### MACROECONOMIC AND INDUSTRY ANALYSIS

www.prudential.com/yardeni
This site, supported by Dr. Ed Yardeni of Prudential Financial, is a comprehensive site with complete analysis of economic indicators for both the U.S. and global economies.

www.federalreserve.gov/otherfrb.htm
The banks of the Federal Reserve System provide significant economic data for the domestic and international economy. Most of the regional banks also provide regional economic analysis for their regions. The above links to each of the regional banks.

www.federalreserve.gov/policy.htm
Review the minutes from recent Federal Open Market Committee meetings, upcoming meeting dates, and recent Beige Book economic analysis from around the United States.

www.economagic.com
Economagic offers current economic data and reports.

www.tcb-indicators.org
The Conference Board provides business cycles indicators.

online.wsj.com/public/us

www.smartmoney.com

www.barrons.com
Current news and analysis of the economy, industries, and individual companies are available with an online subscription to *The Wall Street Journal.* Subscribers gain access to *Barron's* and *Smart Money* as well. More limited information is available for free at the above sites.

*Visit these sites for general information on the economy.*

www.economics.about.com

www.investormap.com/data-econ.htm

moneycentral.msn.com/investor/research/profile.asp

www.bloomberg.com

## CHAPTER 18
### EQUITY VALUATION MODELS

*Go to the following sites for information on earnings announcements and other material announcements:*

www.fulldisclosure.com/highlight.asp?client=cb

www.earningswhispers.com

*These websites make it possible to listen in on conference calls related to earnings announcements:*

www.bestcalls.com

www.investorbroadcast.com

www.fool.com/community/resource/company_research.htm
You can research specific company information at this site.

*These websites provide stock screeners:*
moneycentral.msn.com/investor
See lower-left menu.

screen.yahoo.com/stocks.html

www.stocktables.com

## CHAPTER 19
### FINANCIAL STATEMENT ANALYSIS

www.sec.gov

www.cfonet.com

www.fei.org

www.aicpa.org/index.htm

*Visit the above sites for articles about financial accounting issues.*

www.nasdaq.com

moneycentral.msn.com/investor/home.asp

yahoo.marketguide.com

www.edgar-online.com

www.hoovers.com

www.freeedgar.com

www.smartmoney.com

www.executivelibrary.com/research.asp

*Financial Statement Data is available at the websites listed above. Enter the stock symbol and look for ratios.*

www.Edgarscan.pwcglobal.com/servlets/edgarscan
Examine financial ratios for time trend and cross-company comparisons. Compare a company's financials with an industry or a company of choice. Use EdgarScan and the Benchmarking Assistant.

Gozips.uakron.edu/~drd/cs4.html
Visit this site for general industry information.

Gozips.uakron.edu/~drd/cs5.html
This site offers stock performance updates and charting services.

## CHAPTER 20
### OPTIONS MARKETS: INTRODUCTION

www.amex.com
The American Stock Exchange has excellent general information on options. Link to *Options*, and then to *Education*.

www.cme.com
The Chicago Mercantile Exchange offers excellent information on options and futures. See the *Getting Started* and *Education* links.

www.nymex.com
This is the New York Mercantile Exchange website. Review the Reference links. (continued on next page)

www.options.about.com/money/options
The Options Industry Council site contains extensive educational material, including access to an Options Toolbox. The toolbox is an excellent source that allows you to simulate different options positions and examine the pricing on options.

*The two sites below have extensive links to many derivative-related websites:*

www.numa.com

www.phlx.com/educat/index.html

*The following are exchange sites:*

www.cme.com

www.amex.com

www.cboe.com

www.nasdaq.com

www.cbt.com

www.numa.com/ref/exchange.htm
This site offers links to options and futures exchanges around the world.

## CHAPTER 21
### OPTION VALUATION

stocks.about.com
From the home page, left margin, link to *Derivatives.*

biz.yahoo.com/opt

*The above sites have extensive links to many other sites. They include sections on education, exchanges, research, and quotes as well as extensive sources related to futures markets.*

www.optionscentral.com
The Options Industry Council site "options central" contains comprehensive educational material, including access to the freely available Options Toolbox. The toolbox allows you to simulate different options positions and examine option pricing.

*These sites contain extensive links to several derivatives-related websites:*

www.numa.com

www.phlx.com

*The following sites offer options analysis and calculators:*

www.optionstrategist.com

www.schaeffersresearch.com

www.fintools.com/calculators.html

www.optionsclearing.com
See *Education* link for three valuation models.

www.adamscapital.com/option_valuation3.html

## CHAPTER 22
### FUTURES MARKETS
*The sites listed below are a good place to start looking for websites related to futures and derivatives. They contain information on services as well as other links.*

www.stocks.about.com
Link to *Derivatives.*

www.numa.com

*Exchange sites:*
www.mgex.com
Minneapolis Grain Exchange
www.nybot.com
New York Board of Trade

www.nymex.com
New York Mercantile Exchange

www.cbot.com
Chicago Board of Trade

www.cme.com
Chicago Mercantile Exchange

www.kcbt.com
Kansas City Board of Trade

*Links to many exchanges:*
www.numa.com/ref/exchange.htm

www.cftc.gov/cftc/cftchome.htm
Commodity Futures Trading Commission

## CHAPTER 23
### FUTURES AND SWAPS: A CLOSER LOOK

www.numa.com
NumaWeb calls itself the Internet's home page for financial derivatives. The site has numerous links to other derivative-related sites. It also has a calendar to track release of economic statistics and contract expiration dates.

stocks.about.com
This site contains links and references to all types of futures and option contracts. Link to *Derivatives.*

www.adtrading.com
This applied derivatives site contains articles on current topics related to derivatives. It also has a calendar to track release of economic statistics and contract expiration dates.

www.isda.org
The International Swap and Derivatives Organization's web page contains some basic information on markets for swaps and provides limited educational links.

www.iafe.org
The International Association of Financial Engineers' web page contains some basic information on derivatives as well as an extensive list of additional sources.

www.cme.com/products/currency/index.cfm
This site lists the Chicago Mercantile Exchange currency contracts.

*The following sites contain information on futures, swaps and ot her derivative instruments. Many of the sites also contain general information on risk management.*

www.ino.com

www.riskinstitute.ch
See the *Glossary*

www.contingencyanalysis.com

www.finpipe.com/derivatives.htm

www.swapsmonitor.com/index.htm

www.erisks.com

## CHAPTER 24
### PORTFOLIO PERFORMANCE EVALUATION

www.morningstar.com

www.bloomberg.com

www.mutualfunds.about.com

www.fool.com/school/mutualfunds/performance/record.htm

www.thestreet.com/funds/deardagen/10087858.html

www.chicagotribune.com/business/investing/personalfinance/chi-021007qty-fund-graphic,0,3509228.graphic